P. L.

CHRIS
ENGL

Born in 1929, David L. Edwards was educated at the King's School, Canterbury, and after reading history at Oxford was elected a Fellow of All Souls College. He later taught in the Divinity Faculty at Cambridge, where he was Dean of King's College.

He is the author of many books, most recently *The Futures of Christianity* (1987), *Essentials: a Liberal-Evangelical Dialogue* with John Stott (1988) and *The Cathedrals of Britain* (1989), but has been chiefly occupied with his work as a priest of the Church of England. He was Editor of the SCM Press for eight years, Canon and Sub-Dean of Westminster Abbey for a similar period, and Dean of Norwich before returning to London as Provost of Southwark Cathedral from 1983. He has also served as the Speaker's Chaplain in the House of Commons and as Chairman of Christian Aid, and has been for many years a weekly contributor to the *Church Times*.

David L. Edwards

CHRISTIAN ENGLAND

Collins
FOUNT PAPERBACKS

. Durham Cathedral from the river Wear.

This book was first published as three volumes by
William Collins Sons & Co. Ltd, London
in 1981, 1983 and 1984, and subsequently by
Fount Paperbacks, London
in 1982, 1984 and 1985 respectively
This combined edition, with new Prefaces,
first published by Fount Paperbacks, London in 1989

Printed and bound in Great Britain by
William Collins Sons & Co. Ltd, Glasgow

Preface

This book tells the story of English Christianity from its origins to the First World War. It combines three volumes which were first published separately in 1981–84 and later reprinted as paperbacks. I always hoped that the story would be read as a whole, and now I can thank the readers whose encouraging interest in past editions has made the present publication possible. Despite the defects I wrote with as little bias as I could manage, with humble attention to the studies of the professional historians and literary critics but also with the ambition to show a non-academic public that these Christians were always human and often fascinating. Edward Gibbons declared: 'For the man who can raise himself above the prejudices of party and sect, the history of religion is the most interesting part of the history of the human spirit.' And it gives me special pleasure to know from the response to my efforts that a serious interest in the history of English religion exists far beyond the ranks of the regular churchgoers and far beyond this island's shores.

I have taken the opportunity to correct some errors, to update the references to the scholarly authorities and to add new Prefaces to Volumes Two and Three offering a few further reflections.

Almost all of the research and writing was done while I was Dean of Norwich, and I repeat my gratitude to my colleagues who allowed me the leisure, and to my secretary, now Mrs Jean Bean, who typed and retyped successive drafts. I also remain indebted to All Souls College, Oxford, and to King's College, Cambridge, for hospitality to a former Fellow, to the Cambridge University Library and to the London Library for many loans, and to Lady Collins and her successors in publishing for persistent encouragement. Nor can I ever forget how much I owe to the churches I have served in London and to my wife Sybil.

London 1988   D.L.E.

Volume One

TO THE REFORMATION

Contents

Part One

THE FIRST
ENGLAND

CHAPTER ONE

PRELUDE: ROMANS AND CELTS

An impression of the Roman church at Silchester.

ENGLAND BEFORE THE ENGLISH

The Anglo-Saxon tribesmen who started to occupy England less than four hundred years after the birth of Christ retained the values which had given some dignity to their lives on the coastal plains on the other side of the North Sea.

They believed in hard work on the land. Many of the fields, roads and villages of the English countryside were made by them, and there were also settlements by 'Saxons' in Gaul (now France) and across Germany. Theirs was 'the saga of man against the forest' – or the epic of the heavy plough against the

heavy soil.[1] In peace or war, they believed in loyalty. 'The
chiefs fight for victory, the companions for the chiefs', Tacitus
had observed about the first-century barbarians in the area
which the Romans called Germania; it was a tribute they
would have loved. Above all they believed in courage – in
that, rather than in success. Their ships were taken without
fear across seas or up rivers, and a fifth-century bishop
marvelled that the Saxons seemed to regard shipwreck as a
form of training; but for all their courage, they had no great
hopes of what lay at the end. They were very conscious that
the fields, roads and villages which they or their oxen made
would not be their personal memorials, since others would
soon live there and would not remember them. Even their
most heroic leaders were among the subjects of fate, whose
destiny lay in the darkness. Over all the Anglo-Saxon mind
hangs the shadow of failure – failure which can be redeemed
by the defiance of fate in work and in courage.

The most famous of Old English poems, *Beowulf*, opens
with a picture of the royal barge of old King Scyld, shining
with ice and all ready to sail. On it they place a cargo of
treasure, a mass of weapons and armour, a heap of jewels; a
golden standard is high overhead. Then they push the ship out
to sea and it disappears bearing the body of the king. Such
death-defying loyalty to the dead, even to the defeated dead,
was much praised and much practised by these Anglo-Saxons.
The two most famous lines in their poetry are spoken by a
warrior who is about to lay down his life when his lord ('the
man so dear') has already been killed. Byrthwold cries out
towards the end of the battle fought at Maldon in Essex one
August day in 991:

> Mind must be stronger, heart must be bolder,
> Courage must be greater, as our power grows less.

When these heroic values received the seed of the Christian

---

[1] H. R. Loyn, *Anglo-Saxon England and the Norman Conquest* (London,
1962), p.36. There is a fine chapter on 'The Making of the Landscape' in
P. H. Sawyer, *From Roman Britain to Norman England* (London,
1978).

religion, a fascinating society was the harvest. These people made *Englaland* – a word which came into general use in the century before the Norman conquest. Their England became a country more deeply Christian than most 'Christian' societies have managed to be; and its religion, now defying fate with faith, was a creed fit for heroes and their admirers. The Anglo-Saxons were loyal to the men and women who were now the enduring and conquering soldiers of Christ. As their surviving biographies or letters prove, within their Church the strongest link between leaders and led was often a loyalty of love. In their monasteries they read the lives and deaths of their heroic saints to each other, as in their banqueting halls a *scop* (minstrel) would sing of the lives and deaths of their fighting heroes. They worked heroically to cover England with stone crosses, timber churches and stone churches. These, at least, might escape the doom of death. One timber church (at Greenstead in Essex) and parts of more than three hundred stone churches are still standing, and there is evidence that there were once more than four hundred Anglo-Saxon churches in Kent alone. They filled these churches with the superb work of their craftsmen, although almost all such treasures were to be looted by Vikings or Normans. And their courage spread the faith they had adopted to Germany and to Scandinavia. Eventually English was virtually to replace Latin as the international language of Christianity, as English forms of the religion spread to continents far beyond the knowledge or imagination of these Anglo-Saxons.

But there is a very strange prelude to the story of Christian England. For centuries before the arrival of the Anglo-Saxon invaders the Christian Church had been present in the island, although the invaders seem to have made very little contact with it. The Britons who were now enslaved or kept as slaves did not communicate their religion to their new masters. Those who remained free in the west of the island became Welsh (the English word *wealas* meant 'foreigners') and produced great saints during these years. St David, for example, although of royal blood, was so austere that he forbade his monks to use oxen when they could draw their ploughs themselves. Under such leadership the Welsh accepted the gentle yoke of Christ with enthusiasm. But the forgiveness of those enemies who had stolen most of their island they evidently found too difficult. There is no record of a single Welshman becoming a missionary among the English.

Archaeology — particularly the investigation of buried pottery — has shown that the English arrived in successive waves from about 375. Sometimes they were invited as mercenaries by the Romans or the British. More often they arrived uninvited. These settlers — Angles, Saxons, Jutes, Frisians and others — mostly resumed the life they had lived on the mainland, despising the towns, villas and churches of Roman Britain. They had little of the humility which in Gaul led the invading barbarians to adopt the town life, language and religion of the Roman empire. Only occasionally, it seems, did they marvel at the higher civilization they now encountered.

A fragment of a poem is preserved in the library of Exeter Cathedral; it is usually called *The Ruin*. It is probably a description of the Roman spa, Aquae Sulis, which the English renamed Bath. At the time the poem was written this was a ghost town. The poet meditated on buildings which seemed the work of giants, completed a hundred generations ago and now being pulled down by fate. Tiles lay smashed on the ground and frost was eating the plaster. A wall stained red and grey with lichen had survived the rise and fall of kingdoms — but now was crumbling. Skilled master-masons had raised the city — and now were in the earth's hard embrace. This hall had been filled with cheerful noise in the days of pleasure before the massacre and the plague — but now the scene of banquets was becoming rubble. Heroes had been merry and proud here, flushed with wine, glittering in their armour or splashing in the hot springs — but now the city was bright no more.

In general, it seems, the Anglo-Saxons found the Roman towns and villas already decayed or abandoned, and had few sensitive feelings about the ruins or about the way of life they represented. In some cities — London or York, Canterbury or Winchester, Rochester or Lincoln, Gloucester or Chichester, Dorchester-on-Thames or Carlisle — there was some continuity of occupation. A life of St Cuthbert written some fifteen years later shows us the saint as a marvelling tourist in Carlisle in 685; he was taken round the city wall and saw the fountain 'wondrously built by the Romans'. But a different story is told by traces of squatters' fires on the mosaic floor of the great Ditchley Park villa or in the nave of the abandoned little church at Silchester. It seems that it did not usually occur to the Anglo-Saxons to make proper use of Roman buildings. The villas — country mansions spread over the south, where life for the gentry would not be as gracious again until the eighteenth century — held no attraction to the settlers. They made their peasants' huts, their farmers' more comfortable homes, and even their royal halls, of wood. When in 674 Benedict Biscop, fresh from one of his visits to Rome, built a stone church for his monks at Wearmouth, he could obtain the stones locally, for Hadrian's Wall, the fortified northern frontier of the Roman empire, was only three miles away. But he had to send to Gaul for men who understood how to mix mortar, lay stones and make glass, some of which still survives.

Where almost all the buildings were reduced to ruins, other forms of human self-expression did not survive even in fragments. The literature of Roman Britain, written on papyrus or in a few cases on parchment, was entirely rotted by damp or consumed by fire. Thousands of letters or memoranda must have been written every year, but not one has been found — unless the monk Gildas, writing on *The Ruin and Conquest of Britain* about 550, is quoting from a genuine letter of 446 when he gives us the futile plea of the British to the consul Aetius: 'the barbarians drive us into the sea, and the sea drives us back to the barbarians. The two kinds of death give us the choice of being drowned or slaughtered.'

How complete was the break with the Roman past may be seen in the naming of the days of the week in English. All the names but one (Saturn's day) honour Anglo-Saxon divinities. The day of the sun is followed by the day of the moon; the day of Tiu by the day of Woden (these were two gods of war); the day of Thor, the god of thunder, rain and fertility, by the day of Woden's wife, Frig. The chief Christian festival is still called in English by the name of the Anglo-Saxon spring goddess,

Eostre. In the long run the invaders settling in an island on the edge of the Roman world could not escape coming to terms with that world if they wished to trade and prosper; thus the English took names for the months from the Romans. But in day-to-day reality for many years, life in England owed very little to the centuries in which Rome had conquered the known world and had been conquered by the religion of Christ.

THE CHURCH IN BRITAIN

What, then, remains of the Christianity which was the religion of a minority in the Romans' Britannia?

There are some relics of temples of the old British tribal religion, which the Romans tolerated although they broke the power of the Druid priests and stopped their human sacrifices. One such temple, to the god Nodens, was built at Lydney in Gloucestershire on a considerable scale as late as the closing years of the fourth century. There are also many relics of unofficial cults such as Mithraism (supremely the soldier's creed) – and of the official Roman religion. A column has survived in Cirencester which the governor of that part of Britain re-erected to Jupiter during the fourth-century reaction against Christianity led by the emperor, Julian the Apostate. And other archaeological finds bring before our eyes relics of Christianity, a religion which for a time the Roman empire treated as it had treated the barbaric superstition of the Druids.

The most dramatic find (in the 1940s) has been the Mildenhall Treasure. This consists of silver goods which were buried, presumably in the 360s during the disturbances caused by the 'barbarian conspiracy' which brought invaders from west, north and east simultaneously. It is a mainly pagan collection, and as a work of art the great dish is the equal of any other Roman object now in the British Museum. The name of Eutherios, a highly placed minister under Julian, is scratched on the bottom of two of the pieces. The treasure includes three spoons marked with the Greek letters *Chi Rho* for Christ (not with a cross, still to Roman eyes the instrument of a low-born criminal's execution). Those spoons begin the story of Christian art in the island.

Less artistic but still impressive is the earliest known collection of Christian silver in the Roman empire, found at Water Newton in Huntingdonshire in 1975. It seems that it, too, was hidden in the fourth century, perhaps during a time of persecution. From many places in Roman Britain come spoons, rings, bowls, tombstones or lead tanks (presumably for baptisms) marked with Christian symbols. In Cirencester and Manchester there survive cryptograms scratched on plaster, containing A and O to represent the first and last letters of the Greek alphabet and PATER NOSTER, 'Our Father'. Thus Christ and his teaching were defiantly made public at a time when it was dangerous either to display his cross or to name him.

Traces of buildings which probably were small Christian churches have been found at Silchester (built about 360) and Caerwent, although no building known to have been used as a cathedral or major parish church has yet been discovered. Several Roman villas which have been excavated seem to have had Christian owners. The most remarkable evidence of this kind so far unearthed has been brought together in the British Museum. From Hinton St Mary in Somerset comes a large mosaic floor excavated in 1963 and including a portrait of a clean-shaven Christ with *Chi Rho* behind him. Beside him are two pomegranates symbolizing eternal life. In the same mosaic floor is a scene from pagan mythology (Bellephoron slaying the Chimaera) which seems to hint, like the pomegranates, at Christ's victory over death. From Lullingstone in Kent, where four rooms in a villa seem to have been set apart as a 'house church', comes a wall-painting of six well-dressed people, three at least of them *orantes*, worshippers who pray standing with outstretched arms. These may be portraits of the family that owned the villa. Three times *Chi Rho* is encircled with the laurel wreath of victory. Both the floor and the wall-painting seem to date from the middle, or second half, of the fourth century. Like many passages in the New Testament, they are reminders that during its early centuries the Church was based largely on Christian homes.

When we try to get at the life behind these scanty remains of Christianity in Roman Britain, we are in difficulties.

A story was preserved by Nennius when he compiled his *History of the Britons* in the first half of the ninth century. It was to the effect that a British king, Lucius, had accepted baptism from missionaries sent by the pope in 167. That is clearly a legend. But a book *Against the Jews* by Tertullian of Carthage (a rhetorical writer) boasts that 'parts of Britain inaccessible to the Romans were indeed conquered by Christ'. That was written about two hundred years after the birth of Christ. If the boast is accurate, it shows that the Church was then present in south-west Britain, an area not yet reached by the Roman conquest which had begun in AD 43. Presumably the religion had been carried there by traders across the Channel from a prosperous and heavily Romanized Gaul, but students of history are unable to say who was the first Christian whose feet walked on this land.

Much later legends told of the establishment of the monastery at Glastonbury in this dim period; even of the coming of Joseph of Arimathea with the Holy Grail, the cup used at the Last Supper – or with the Christ child himself in the hidden years about which the gospels are silent.

Archaeology establishes that Glastonbury was inhabited in the first century AD, and that there was in this period considerable traffic across the Channel. We also know that the British kept control of this area long after the south-east had fallen to the Saxons. When Ine, King of the West Saxons 688-722, arrived in Glastonbury as its conqueror, he found there a wooden church already revered as ancient and he gave extensive lands to its clergy. This church survived until it was burned down in 1184.

In Britain under Roman occupation, some Christians were executed during one or other of the persecutions of the third century. One of them, probably put to death in 208-9, became famous. The earliest reference to the 'blessed martyr Alban' comes in a biography of St Germanus, Bishop of Auxerre, written about 480 and describing a visit which the bishop had paid to Britain about thirty years before. The author, Constantius, told of how the visitor had added other relics of saints to the martyr's shrine, but he did not say where the shrine was. The earliest surviving statement that it was on the outskirts of Verulamium was provided by Gildas, more than three hundred years after the event. Gildas adds some stories which seem too tall about the miracles surrounding the martyrdom, but there may well be more substance in his report that Alban was a Roman soldier who had sheltered a Christian priest escaping from Gaul and who had been baptized by him. Bede's *Ecclesiastical History* tells us that a 'church of wonderful workmanship' was flourishing in the 720s on the site of the martyrdom. Some seventy years later Offa, King of the Mercians, founded St Alban's Abbey as penance for the murder of another king (St Ethelbert) in which he had been involved.

Gildas and Bede tell us also of the martyrdom of Aaron and Julius at Caerleon and of 'many more of both sexes in several places'. Aaron's name suggests that he was a converted Jew.

Two third-century writers, Origen and Hippolytus, vaguely mention Christianity in Britain, but the earliest clear evidence comes in the Acts of the Council of Arles in 314. The council was attended by five persons from Britain: Eborius Bishop of York, Restitutus Bishop of London, Adelfius Bishop of Lincoln (but this is not certain since the scribe wrote *Colonia Londinensium* instead of *Colonia Lindunensium*), a priest and a deacon. The fact that this party travelled to an official meeting is an indication that the bishops, priests and deacons of Britain already thought of themselves as officials in a fellowship spanning the Roman world. (And these Roman days were never to be completely forgotten: in the empire Britannia was a part known as a *diocesis*, and the Church was always to call the area of a bishop's jurisdiction a 'diocese'.) The council, which included thirty-three bishops, was held in August in a city not far from the French Mediterranean coast. All must have seemed warmth and peace, with the emperor himself summoning the Christian leaders and assuring them of his protection. Yet that council in August 314 met less than ten years after the abdication of the last of the emperors who persecuted the Church, Diocletian. Such had been the results of the conversion to Christianity (if that is not too strong a phrase) of the emperor Constantine. In a ceremony momentous for the Church and the world, in the Roman military headquarters on the site of the present York Minster, Constantine had been proclaimed Augustus or emperor by the troops on 25 July 306. He was then not much over twenty. His father, the emperor Constantius, had died in York earlier that day.

When the council summoned by Constantine to Nicaea in 325 had defined orthodox Christian belief, the British were among those listed by Athanasius as accepting its decrees. It is, however, probable that during the fourth century the Church in Britain remained a minority concentrated in the towns. In 359 three other British bishops who had travelled abroad to attend a church council accepted an offer by the imperial treasury to refund their expenses. Other British and Gaulish bishops present refused to do so – and a bishop from Gaul 'often' criticized the three. This we are told by Sulpicius Severus, a writer best known for his biography of St Martin of Tours. St Martin was a monk-bishop who insisted on living in poverty and it is possible that the three British bishops were monks like him, or missionaries in areas where the Church had few resources. At any rate, Sulpicius Severus tells us that he defended their attitude to the Welfare State.

Of the labours of these and other bishops in the conversion of Roman Britain, we know nothing. Only one bishop's name can be linked with any definite work. A manuscript survives in the library at Monte Cassino in Italy and is marked as being by a bishop called Fastidius. Apparently it is the book *On the Christian Life* which another fifth-century writer says Fastidius wrote to a certain Fatalis about 425, together with a book on how to be a widow. If so, it is the earliest recorded expression of simple themes which were to be repeated, generation after generation, in this island over fifteen centuries ahead. The reader is urged to practise modesty, contentment and good works; not to be sad, for Christ means 'anointed' and the Christian is anointed with the oil of gladness; not to turn the poor away, for the Christian must imitate Christ in all things. A prayer is added. It was attacked as being too confident that the hands being lifted up to heaven were clean. A more eminent scholar, Pelagius, had to issue a denial that he had composed it.

The controversy over this prayer was part of a doctrinal crisis. Pelagius, who had been born in Britain about 380, went abroad and became a well-known theologian, emphasizing the freedom and ability of man to co-operate with the grace of God. This teaching conflicted with the emphasis then being placed by St Augustine of Hippo on the complete sinfulness of man, who must rely totally on God's forgiveness and redeeming power. It is reported that Pelagius was horrified to hear in Rome a quotation of the famous prayer by St Augustine: 'Grant what thou commandest, and command what thou wilt'. The dispute intensified when, after the fall of Rome to the barbarians in 410, Pelagius went to live indiscreetly near Augustine in North Africa. It is believed that he died, having been excommunicated by the pope, in Palestine (an early example of theologians who have appealed over the heads of the bishops to the teacher of Galilee). But the cheerful liberalism of Pelagius soon reached his native Britain. The contemporary chronicler Prosper says that it was spread by Agricola, a bishop's son. It was well received, on a scale sufficient to alarm orthodox churchmen.

Bishop Germanus was summoned from Auxerre in Gaul, and was accompanied by a neighbour and fellow-bishop, Lupus of Troyes. It was during this visit in 429 that they visited St Alban's shrine, but their main purpose was to preach against the liberal heresy of Pelagius — which they did, 'not only in churches but also at crossroads and in fields and lanes', and not only in sermons but also in debates. The Pelagians are said to have been 'distinguished by their riches, resplendent in their dress, and surrounded by an adoring crowd'; but the visitors soon won over the crowd. We seem to see a British Church with a considerable following among both the sophisticated and the simple, and with enough peace of mind to be tempted to take a benevolent view of human nature.

When he records these theological disputes, Constantius the biographer of Germanus adds that the bishop was (with Lupus) invited to join an expedition against the Picts and the

Saxons who had invaded the north. Before his ordination the bishop had been a *dux* or military commander. Constantius claims that Germanus now used the approach of Lent to instruct a great part of the British army, which was duly baptized. On Easter Day the soldiers paraded still wet with the baptismal water. They then set up the Easter acclamation *Alleluia*, and the enemy promptly fled. Whatever we make of this story, it is by no means impossible that the visiting bishop gave his hosts military as well as theological guidance. The bishops of Gaul were expected to defend every aspect of a Christian civilization. We begin to see the Church taking on many strange tasks because it had received the legacy of the Roman empire.

Constantius also claims that Germanus and another bishop were asked back for a second visit fourteen years later, but this time concentrated on the area later called Wessex. They were so successful in their second mission that Constantius believed that when he was writing about his hero in 480 the British were entirely free of the Pelagian heresy.

Despite the '*Alleluia* victory' they were not at all secure from a military or economic point of view. And from across the North Sea poured in thousands of barbarians, finding the coast which had come to be known as the 'Saxon shore' no barrier. In 383 Magnus Maximus, a Christian general in the Roman army who had been born in Spain and had married a British girl (Helena), led his troops from Britain to the mainland, declaring himself emperor. From that date the Roman military presence in Britain was inadequate, although some troops remained for some years and two of their commanders are known. The general Stilico was a giant of a man, the son of a barbarian cavalry officer. Another general, having taken the ambitious name Constantine, led his troops out of Britain in 407 in order to take his chance in the politics of the empire. A contemporary historian, Orosius, says that this adventurer summoned his son Constans, who had been a Christian monk, to join him.

No Roman coins later than 407 have been found in Britain. In theory the island remained part of the empire; about 425 an official document, the *Notitia Dignitatum*, assigned to

Britain an army of six thousand under the command of a 'count'. But in 410 the emperor Honorius recognized that he was cut off from this island on the edge of the world by the great barbarian invasion of Gaul and Italy. When appealed to, he therefore formally instructed the British *civitates* (cities with their surrounding regions) that they must look to their own defence. In the terms of Roman law it was the grant of permission to civilians to use arms. In practice it meant that the British *civitates* became petty kingdoms, each depending on its chief's energy. The most powerful of these rulers appears in the history of Nennius as Vortigern or 'overlord'. He invited Saxon mercenaries to settle in the island, recognizing that despite the emperor's words the British were not able to defend themselves against the barbarians from the north or against their own tendency to civil war. The Britons, needing a strength greater than their own, had summoned the English.

THE AGE OF ARTHUR

We now enter an age where historians can find few lights to guide them. The history of Christianity is particularly obscure. It is always possible that archaeology will be more illuminating, but on the basis of discovery and reflection up to 1980 it would seem that Romano-British Christianity was a minority religion, in striking contrast with the popularity of the Church in Gaul, Italy or North Africa. Surveying the evidence to the end of the fourth century, W. H. C. Frend writes of 'two main zones of Christian activity. The first comprises the Romanized and urbanized south and south-east from the Wash to Exeter, the second from York north-west to include Carlisle and the Cumbrian coast, the military zone, especially the western end of it'. Entering the fifth century, he finds that the scanty evidence points to 'a Church which, though rich in personalities and ideas, lacked the popular support that ensured its survival elsewhere in the West . . . Generally, as the Roman towns and villas were abandoned, only sites of special holiness continued as centres of Christianity'.[2]

So the little candle of the Romano-British Church seems scarcely to flicker in the barbaric darkness. We do not know more than a handful of these Christians even by name. We do not know their thoughts, and we do not know much about the objects they used daily. Unlike the pagan invaders of their island, they did not bury goods which their dead could use in an after-life. What we do know is depressing. The trinkets which have survived from the Britain of this period are of poor quality; the homesteads which have been excavated were evidently built with defence rather than enjoyment in mind; and the only really impressive objects dug up by the archaeologists are bronze hanging bowls found in Anglo-Saxon graves, almost certainly looted from British churches or homes. The descent from the level of civilization reached in Roman towns and villas could scarcely be sadder.

There is, however, other evidence. A great scholar points out that it was 'in this period of freedom between the Roman and Saxon Occupations that the ideals and literature took shape which still characterize the Celtic peoples wherever the Celtic languages are spoken'.[3] And these ideals and literature were largely shaped by Christianity. The Celtic peoples adopted the faith, often with great zest. Although Roman influences weakened as the empire faded into history and the Continent seemed more remote, the Celts did not reject the Latin language or the pre-eminence of the Bishop of Rome or any other reminder of the fact that the Christian faith had been carried to them through the Roman empire. Because Britain had belonged to the Romans, some of them could read and write (as the early Anglo-Saxons could not, apart from 'runic' letters crudely carved on wood, bone or stone). It is therefore entirely right to speak about Celtic *civilization*, using a word which is itself derived from Latin. But it was a civilization almost completely different from life in Roman Britain;

---

[2] W. H. C. Frend, *'Ecclesia Britannica:* Prelude or Dead End?' in *Journal of Ecclesiastical History* (Cambridge, 1979), pp.129-144.

[3] N. K. Chadwick, *Celtic Britain* (London, 1964), p.34.

and the most striking difference was the centrality of a fervent Christian faith.

Theirs was a faith spread by monks. The Celtic literature was preserved in monasteries like any other literature in Western Europe at the time, but this guardianship of culture was only one part of the monk's significance in Celtic religion.

Again and again when we explore this new kind of Christianity we find communities of monks setting the pace spiritually. They were the custodians of the Bible, acknowledging its holiness by taking it literally and obeying it wholeheartedly; even the food regulations in the Old Testament were received as the law of God. The Bible was also venerated by being copied and decorated (or 'illuminated') with the best art of the time – all that now remains to prove the intensity of this Celtic monastic devotion. The monks maintained a strenuous round of corporate and private prayer, worshipping their holy and demanding God in the little huts as well as in the simple chapels that together made up their monasteries. From the Celtic word *ciric*, referring to the holy burial ground in such a monastery, descended the later word 'church'. From this base they went out to evangelize and to minister to converts, staying close to the people in their standard of living although their morality was, no doubt, high above the common level. We shall watch Irish monks playing a crucial role in the conversion of England. So far as we know, the monks of Roman Britain had not been nearly so prominent in the maintenance and spread of Christianity. But their successors were a new breed. In this dark age of which we know so little the monks emerged as the Church's vastly influential elite.

It is also significant that the monks of Celtic Christianity ministered not to a town but to an area of the countryside. The Celtic peoples were organized in tribes. These tribes seem to have been of mixed racial origins. What united them was not an army and an administration with urban centres, as in the Roman civilization, but a strong common culture based on their shared faith. When their monks told them about the tribes of Ancient Israel making a covenant with their God and their neighbours, these tribesmen must have recognized their spiritual ancestors. Somehow the British Christians, after the withdrawal of the Roman legions, had changed Christianity into this powerful new shape, monastic and tribal – a mutation as difficult as that which had changed the Church from being one Jewish sect among many, daily expecting the end of the world, into being the guardian and rebuilder of a civilization which spoke Greek or Latin around the Mediterranean. Christianity would survive many empires and cultures because it had in it this extraordinary capacity to adapt; and while adapting, to inspire.

We can recover only hints of the creative process. There are small signs to be found in regions which neither Romans nor Saxons were able – or, perhaps, willing – to conquer. Latin names under Christian symbols appear on tombstones in Wales or Cornwall, or are Celticized to appear in the family trees of Welsh chieftans. The red dragon of Wales is a version of the *draco* or standard carried before Roman soldiers on the march, and some six hundred words in the Welsh language are derived from Latin. The ruins of a Celtic monastery amid the spectacular scenery of Tintagel on the north Cornish coast were associated by later legends with King Arthur, but are in fact the foundations of a monastery built before 500, the oldest known monastery in the British Isles. The Welsh were for long scorned by the civilized (a word based on the Latin *civis*, a citizen) as mere countrymen, *pagani*, the word from which 'Powys' descended. Their numbers seem to have been enlarged by emigration from Ireland when Roman rule was over. But it did not take long for them to become Christians. How this happened is the subject of legends interspersed with a few saints' names preserved in the dedication of ancient churches or villages. In the south there was, for example, St Illtyd, who is believed to have been an active Christian from about 475 to about 535, the founder of a famous monastery, probably in the modern Llantwit Major but possibly on Caldey Island.

Illtyd is said to have been born in Brittany (or Armorica, 'the land by the sea'). The evidence about British links with Brittany and Normandy in the fifth century is far from complete, but it is enough to suggest a substantial migration of the British beginning in the middle of the century. Many saints' names and place names preserved by the Bretons and Normans are close to Welsh names, and the Breton language is so close to Cornish that it is related that, when both languages were in everyday use, the fishermen could understand each other when they met in their little boats in the middle of the narrow sea. The biography of St Paul Aurelian gives a vivid picture of its hero arriving in a Roman town then inhabited only by animals. He was, however, accompanied by other refugees who shared his own noble birth and by 'sufficient slaves'; and before long the Roman town bore his own name.

We may suspect that story as a flourish in a ninth-century book about a fifth-century saint. More useful as evidence is the fact that Sidonius, a bishop in Gaul, corresponded with the leader of the first group of British settlers, Riothamus; these settlers seem to have been invited over as mercenaries to fight the invading Visigoths. In 461 the name of a British bishop, *Mansuetus episcopus Britannorum*, appears among the bishops attending a small council in Tours. Since it seems unlikely that Mansuetus would have crossed the Channel for a minor occasion in such troubled times, the probability is that he was ministering to the settlers in New Britain. It is also probable that in the end the colony became substantial. Whether invited to fight as mercenaries, or lured by the prospect of empty lands, or encouraged to leave the old country by Irish or English invasions, gradually the Britons over the Channel grew in numbers. It has been claimed that 'we can envisage a migration attaining five, if not six, figures — perhaps, over three centuries, up to a quarter- or half-million people (the population of England and Wales in late Roman times could have been of the order of two to three million)'.[4] Here, we may say, was Britain's first transatlantic colony, complete with colonial churches.

There was also a mission to the north — to the Picts. These lived in what is now Scotland and were allies, not subjects, of Rome. ('Picts' comes from the Roman soldier's sneer: 'painted

---

[4] Charles Thomas, *Britain and Ireland in Early Christian Times* (London, 1971), p.69.

men!') But they were only a short sea journey away up the west
coast, and it seems that some of the Romanized British made
that journey and took their Church with them. According to
Bede, the first bishop to live among the Picts was 'Nynia, a
most venerable and holy man, of the nation of the Britons,
who had been instructed properly in the faith and the
mysteries of the truth at Rome'.

This refers, it seems, to a time shortly before 450, but it
represents a tradition handed on by Bishop Pecthelm to Bede
for inclusion in his *Ecclesiastical History* almost three hundred
years later. Pecthelm had become bishop of the area when the
English had conquered it. Bede added that there still existed
in his day a 'stately church in which rest the bodies of Nynia
and many other saints'. Dedicated to St Martin of Tours, this
church was usually called *Candida Casa* or White House, from
the limewashed plaster covering its stones. Modern scholars
are cautious about some of the details of this tradition. It is,
for example, difficult to believe that St Ninian (as his name
would be remembered) was trained in far-off Rome. He may
well have been trained by St Martin, or at any rate influenced
by his holiness, but if he dedicated his church to this recently
dead saint it was an unusual gesture. In 1949 walls more than
three foot thick and of a great age were excavated in a
cemetery in the area of Whithorn Cathedral. They belonged
to a small oratory of stones bedded in clay, still showing a few
traces of whitened plaster. Nearby was found a tombstone
erected probably in the fifth century commemorating one
Latinus and his unnamed daughter aged four, under the
words *Te Dominum Laudamus*, 'We praise thee, O Lord'.
Not far away on the coast is St Ninian's Cave, with many Latin
crosses carved on the rock face. And in Kirkmadrine on the
next peninsula is an inscription on a tombstone: 'here lie the
holy and eminent *sacerdotes* Ides, Viventius and Mavorius'.
Sacerdotes probably meant 'bishops'. Evidently at the time of
the plantation of the British Church in Brittany, some success
had also come to this British mission to the north.

There are many traces in Welsh literature of the British
kingdom of Rheged, based on Carlisle, celebrated for its king
Urien, holding its own until the middle of the seventh century.

But no trace of its church life, said to have been strong, has been recovered in the ground. We are left with the thought that 'if, as we learn from Bede, the churches in this area were not built of stone, it is in no way surprising that neither the structures nor any documents which they have contained should have survived'.[5]

Fortunately, simple stone churches and lesser objects survive in Ireland and Wales, and our knowledge has been enriched by the art of photography from the air. When aerial surveys were first published in the 1960s they revealed the sites of many monasteries long buried in fields but just discernible in the late evening sunshine.[6] And we know that the most dramatic mission of the British Church in the fifth century reached Ireland.

The Irish were then generally called *Scotti* (what is now Scotland was partly colonized from Ireland). There is evidence of a concern for them as well as for the Britons in Auxerre, which under the saintly bishop Germanus was a centre of Christian life in Gaul. A deacon called Palladius seems to have belonged to the Church in Auxerre, although he may have been an official in Rome itself. He was the man who persuaded Pope Celestine to send Germanus on the anti-Pelagian mission to Britain. He was subsequently, in 431, himself sent by the pope as a bishop to 'the *Scotti* who believe in Christ' (in the words of the contemporary chronicler, Prosper). Nothing is known about the length or success of his mission, but it seems probable that it was cut short by death. It is the first recorded instance of missionary activity by the papacy.

The main apostle of the Irish, Patrick, was not only far more prominent in folk-memory and legend, but was also the author of two documents which have survived. One is a short autobiography or *Confessio* written 'before I die'. The other is a letter rebuking a British king, Coroticus, for a raid on the

---

[5] N. K. Chadwick, *The British Heroic Age* (Cardiff, 1976), p.123.

[6] See L. Laing, *The Archaeology of Late Celtic Britain and Ireland, c.400-1200* (London, 1975), and his more popular *Celtic Britain* (London, 1979).

Irish which had resulted in the death of some of Patrick's converts or their enslavement for sale to the Picts. Coroticus, a
nominal Christian, was firmly excommunicated until he had
made a full restitution.

From these sober documents in strong but rough Latin, the
outline of the true life of Patrick (in Latin, Patricius) emerges.
He was the son of a Roman British deacon, Calpurnius, and
the grandson of a priest, Potitus. He grew up in a village
called Bannavern; where this was we do not know. When
nearly sixteen he was captured by raiders and taken as a slave
to Ireland. After six years of misery minding his master's
cattle, he escaped and returned to his family, only to receive a
vision bidding him return to Ireland as an evangelist. In this
dream he received a letter asking him to 'come again and walk
among us'. He was made a bishop for the Irish about 425. He
seems to have walked over much of northern and central
Ireland; to have made his headquarters in Armagh where one
of the kings had his fort; and to have planted the Church
extensively before his death about 460. Tradition says he
founded dioceses with himself as archbishop, but no other
bishop in Ireland is mentioned in his *Confessio*.[7]

When the Irish Church emerges into the light of history, we
find that the bishops were not the rulers of the Church in a
definite area but were monks of exceptional holiness whose
functions were to ordain priests and to bless oils for the sick;
the leadership was exercised by the nobly born abbot of the
monastery belonging to the tribe. The period during which
this system emerged has been buried in obscurity, however.
Although the 'Breastplate of St Patrick' has been popular as a
hymn ever since its translation into English in the nineteenth
century, the earliest version known belongs to a time three
centuries after Patrick's death. What we can find in it – or in
the hymn 'Be thou my vision, O Lord of my heart' – is the
atmosphere of this obscure period. Here was a faith deeply
personal but also securely orthodox, accepting battle against
the magic of paganism, creating a Celtic Christianity full of

---

[7] See R. P. C. Hanson, *St Patrick: His Origins and Career* (Oxford, 1968).

confidence in its Lord and in itself.

This missionary expansion of British Christianity, taking the Church into the Celtic realms of Wales, Brittany, Scotland and Ireland cannot be pursued in a book about England.[8] But the story hints at the missionary energy of the British Church. Obviously the missionaries who planted the Church in the Celtic fringe of Britain were thoroughly enthusiastic, and therefore not entirely typical. But it is illuminating to notice what criticisms were made of the British bishops by some of these enthusiasts. Both the missionary Patrick and the monk Gildas suggest that the British bishops were admired for their learning and social graces although inadequate as spiritual leaders. This indicates a Church which had not only fathered some radically critical sons but had also become established, with deep roots in society.

Some evidence that this Church still had a few links with the rest of the international Christian community is provided by an incident which took place in or about 475. The Roman town of Avitacum was shortly to fall to the Visigoths in their march across Gaul. A letter from Sidonius Apollinaris, who had a villa there, congratulates Faustus, a Briton who had become Abbot of Lérins and Bishop of Riez, on the authorship of a theological book brought to Avitacum by a travelling British monk, Bishop Riochatus.

The surviving evidence also suggests that, with an improvement in their morale, the Britons were able to make a military rally against the invaders tormenting them – and against their own Saxon mercenaries, previously thought indispensable, who had revolted. Gildas, writing towards the middle of the next century, alludes to a series of fifth-century victories gained under the leadership of Ambrosius Aurelianus. This rally culminated about 500 in a victory at Badon Hill (often identified with the hill fort called Badbury Rings near Wimborne in Dorset, but possibly another of the five Badburys in England). And when he edited his history some three hundred

---

[8] See M. Dillon and N. K. Chadwick, *The Celtic Realms* (revised, Dublin, 1972).

years later, Nennius named the victor of Badon Hill: Artorius. This is 'King Arthur', whose chivalry was one of the most popular themes in the entertainment of medieval Europe.

Arthur's name is not given by Gildas who is thought to have been a contemporary. But Gildas certainly writes after a generation of peace (apart from civil wars); the whole point of his book is to warn the Britons that because they do not deserve it this peace is about to come to an end. It is therefore reasonably certain that about the year 500 there were leaders of Britain's defence who were more effective than the petty kings who had found themselves in charge after the with-drawal of the Roman army — and also more effective than the five Welsh and Cornish tyrants whom Gildas denounced. Did one of these leaders have the Roman name Artorius?

A Welsh poem, *Y Gododdin*, which was probably written about 600, praises one hero who glutted the black ravens with the bodies of his enemies 'although he was not Arthur'. This reference may have been added later, but it does not stand quite alone. At least four, perhaps five, people called Arthur are known to have been born in Celtic parts of Britain during the late sixth and early seventh centuries, although the name is previously unknown in Britain apart from the single case of a Roman officer of the second century.

There is a somewhat more substantial collection of Arthur-ian references in a manuscript now in the British Museum (Harley 3859). This seems to have been copied out early in the twelfth century from material originally put together in the monastery at St Davids in Wales during the second half of the tenth century. Part of this material is a record of events added to dates of Easter (the so-called *Annales Cambriae*). The last event probably occurred in 957. For the year 518 is recorded: 'The battle of Badon in which Arthur carried the cross of our Lord Jesus Christ on his shoulders for three days and three nights and the Britons were the victors'. For the year 539 is recorded: 'The *gueith* (Welsh for battle) of Camlann in which Arthur and Medraut perished and there was plague in Britain and Ireland'. Also in this manuscript there is material usually dated in the first half of the ninth century and referred to as a *History of the Britons* by Nennius. This informs us that

'Arthur fought against them in those days with the kings of the Britons, but he himself was leader of the battles (*dux bellorum*).' Twelve victories are named, ending with Badon, where '960 men fell in one day from one charge by Arthur, and no one overthrew them but Arthur alone'. The location of the sites named has been much disputed, but it seems that his campaigns took this *dux bellorum* from Scotland to Cornwall. Obviously he is envisaged as a cavalry commander. It is thought that this passage is based on an old Welsh battle-song.

Many have debated the problems involved in assessing the historical value of these references to Arthur and in the attempt to link them with archaeology. For example, in Somerset the hill-top fort at Cadbury was excavated in the 1960s and fortifications of the sixth (or late fifth) century enclosing about eighteen acres with a perimeter of about twelve hundred yards were revealed. Within these ramparts were found remains of a timber hall, sixty-three by thirty-four feet. Already in 1532 the antiquary John Leland was of the opinion that this was the site of Arthur's court, Camelot (although that name was invented by Crétien of Troyes in the twelfth century), but it may be more scientific to confine ourselves to the conclusion that here was a major fort used defensively, presumably by the British against the Saxons. While the debate continues all that can be said here is that it seems possible for reasonable people to believe that a British general called Arthur was successful during the conflicts of the sixth century.[9]

The international fame of Arthur is shown by a carving on the north doorway of Modena Cathedral in Italy, executed before 1120. It depicts an armed and mounted knight labelled 'Artus de Bretania' attacking one 'Burmaltus'. In the background is a castle containing a woman, Winlogee (the Breton name for Guinevere). In England, however, the legend was given its first big boost by the fervent Welsh bishop and story-teller, Geoffrey of Monmouth, who put it into Latin in the 1130s. In his *History of the Kings of Britain* he based Arthur

---

[9] A scholarly summary of the 'small kernel of Arthurian fact' is found in Leslie Alcock, *Arthur's Britain* (London, 1973), pp.1-88.

on the Roman and Welsh town of Caerleon-on-Usk and had
him conquer much of Western Europe before being betrayed
at home by Mordred and Guanhumara (Guinevere). This
great hero's chief counsellor was the magician Merlin and
when mortally wounded he was carried away to the Island of
Avalon.

The legend of the betrayed conqueror was picked up by the
wandering minstrels, the troubadours, who sang it into the
hearts of royal and noble households in France. Fresh scope
was provided by the growing interest in Arthur's knights, said
to feast with him at a round table to show their equality.
These poets with an aristocratic market developed, for instance, the tale of the tragic love of Sir Tristan (a Cornishman
who died in Brittany) for Iseult (an Irish princess). The story
of Arthur and his knights, ever more richly embroidered,
proved worthy of the genius of Goltfried of Strasbourg and
Chrétien of Troyes: and now the climax was the discovery of
the Holy Grail used at the Last Supper. A young knight called
either Perceval or Gawain was led to this treasure by the Fisher
King – for the story was lush with mythology and symbolism.
The Frenchman Wace's *Roman de Brut* was translated into
English and expanded by the Worcestershire priest Layamon
between 1189 and 1199 – it was Arthur's first appearance in
English literature. More prosaically, in 1191 the monks of
Glastonbury, then needing to attract the tourists because they
needed cash to rebuild their monastery, discovered the grave
and with it a financial resurrection. Beneath the coffin a
leaden cross was inscribed: 'Here lies entombed the renowned
King Arthur with Guinevere his second wife in the Island of
Avalon'.

In the fourteenth century a warrior-king, Edward III,
attempted to cast the glamour of chivalry and piety over his
favourite fellow-soldiers, then embarked on another European
adventure, by modelling the Order of the Garter on Arthur's
knights; and at Windsor they feasted at a round table. In the
fifteenth century in order to while away his imprisonment Sir
Thomas Malory had the idea of combining the romances
about Arthur, his court and his death, to form the first
English novel that can be called a major work of art. William

Caxton edited and printed his book in 1485, advertising: 'herein may be seen noble chivalry, courtesy, humanity, friendliness, hardihood, love, friendship, cowardice, murder, hate, virtue and sin'. Malory's book, although denounced by the Elizabethan schoolmaster Roger Ascham as 'open slaughter and bold bawdry', did much to form the layman's idea of the gentleman in the Tudor Age when medieval knights were no more. Shakespeare laughed at Arthurian legends but could think of no more fitting end for Falstaff than 'he's in Arthur's bosom, if ever man went to Arthur's bosom'. Drawing on Malory as well as on his own genius for the celebration of nostalgia, Alfred Tennyson moved the Victorians with his twelve poems about the stately court of the 'once and future king'. Hugely successful novels prove that the spell is still strong in the twentieth century. When John Kennedy's White House was nicknamed 'Camelot' almost everyone knew what was meant.[10]

Coleridge said that it was by the legends of Arthur that his imagination was 'habituated to the Vast'. In real history, however, Arthur's Britain was doomed. Gradually the British were cut off from a Christian Europe which itself was being swallowed into the darkness of an age ravaged by barbarians. The isolation of the British was not complete, it seems; archaeologists studying tombstones surviving in Wales from this period have found in them some evidence of continuing contact with changing fashions in Gaul. But evidence suggesting the confusion of the times is found in the date of Easter. This has always been a problem, as is shown to this day by the celebration of different Easters in the church of the Holy Sepulchre in Jerusalem. The council of Arles in 314 found it necessary to discuss it, and was able to agree that the pope should solve the problem. Owing to its origins in a Jewish community, Easter has been calculated by the date of a full moon, while the ordinary year for Romans Celts and Saxons alike had its calendar determined by the sun. To add to the compli-

---

[10] See *Arthurian Literature in the Middle Ages*, ed. R. S. Loomis (Oxford, 1959), and for a summary of the whole tradition Elizabeth Jenkins, *The Mystery of King Arthur* (London, 1975).

cation, the Church decided that Easter must fall on a Sunday; it was to be the first Sunday after the full moon on or after the spring equinox. But when, in the solar calendar, was that? In 444 Pope Leo the Great decided that the method of dating Easter should be changed; one motive was to avoid the coincidence of Good Friday with a Roman sports day. The Church in Britain accepted this change, and the Church remaining in Britain's Celtic parts later defended it with great obstinacy. But in 457 a new way of fixing the date of Easter, worked out by Victorius of Acquitane, was adopted by the Roman church. This calendar was gradually adopted in Gaul (the bishops there agreed on it in 541) but not in Britain; the island was spritually cut off from Europe.

Sixth-century Britain seemed so remote from the Byzantine world of the civilized East that Procopius in far-off Caesarea believed that after death the souls of men were ferried from Gaul to this fog-bound island inhabited by the British with *Angiloi* (Angles) and *Frissones* (Frisians). And archaeology has made a comment on the primitive nature of any other trade still being conducted. So far as we know, Arthur's Britain used no coinage after 430.

Gildas (about 550) could denounce it as a society not fit to survive, as the Ancient Israelites had been denounced by their own prophets in the time of the Assyrian and Babylonian invasions. To this indignant critic the Old Testament was 'a mirror reflecting our own life'. He gives an impression that in Wales and what else was left of Post-Roman Britain Church and State were equally corrupt. Vortipor, tyrant of the Demetians in south-west Wales, was 'from top to bottom' stained with murders and adulteries. This may seem to be merely the rhetoric of a moralizing monk who too easily assumed the mantle of a prophet. But in Carmarthen Museum is preserved a tombstone reading MEMORIA VOTEPORIGIS PRO-TICTORIS. It is a rough stone; the lettering is crude and the spelling is worse. It is hard to believe that the ruler thus commemorated was fully worthy of the title *protector*, derived from the bodyguard of a Roman emperor – or of the cross on the stone. It would seem that Arthur, if he had ever existed, had left degenerate heirs. Yet that is not all that can be said about British or Celtic Christianity in the age of Gildas. For Gildas himself clearly made a large impact on his time. A modern scholar has gone so far as to claim that when Gildas had written his great protest 'within ten years monasticism had become a mass movement, in South Wales, Ireland and northern Gaul. Its extensive literature reveres Gildas as its founding father, named more often than any other individual'.[11]

THE ENGLISH CONQUEST

Until the middle of the sixth century the Germanic peoples settling in England were, it seems, confined to Kent, Sussex and southern Hampshire; to Essex, East Anglia, Lindsey and the East Riding of Yorkshire; and inland to the upper Thames region and to the area between what were long after to become the university cities of Oxford and Cambridge. But the fragmentary evidence suggests that the main British force was weakened by a plague which swept through Europe in 549, and then overwhelmed by another revolt or invasion (or both) about 570. Thus the disasters which the Jeremiah-like Gildas had prophesied came to pass. However, the whole land did not move immediately into the firm control of the English. Much of it was moor, forest or fen with few or no inhabitants. Felix's *Life* of the hermit Guthlac, written about 740, pictures him alone at Crowland in the desolate fens near the Wash; he lived in a long grave, presumably dating from Roman times, which robbers had conveniently dug open. Even in the cultivated parts of the island, not all the fields immediately fell to the new rulers. As we have noted, the area around Glastonbury was not colonized by the West Saxons until the 710s and 720s. Guthlac, before he became a hermit, had been a soldier, and Felix tells us that even in his solitude the hermit was troubled by dreams of attacks by the Britons – for in the

---

[11] John Morris, introducing *Gildas: The Ruin of Britain and Other Works*, ed. M. Winterbottom (London, 1978).

700s it was still the case that 'the Britons, the implacable enemies of the Saxon race, were troubling the English with their attacks'.

Victories in these times must have been somewhat like the naval victories which the English were to win in the centuries ahead, defeating those enemies who had appeared but not necessarily leading to the immediate colonization of a whole territory. And we have now to notice some exceptions to the general rule that there was little real contact between the conquerors and the conquered. While it is probable that many of the British fled to the west and became the Welsh, those who stayed were not all slaughtered. A few personal names seem to be evidence of intermarriage between the triumphant Anglo-Saxons and the remaining Britons. These include the famous names of Cerdic who was regarded as the founder of the royal house of Wessex, Caedwalla, King of the West Saxons 685-8, and the poet Caedmon. It is known that the Northumbrian king Oswiu married a princess of the British kingdom of Rheged (and, when she died, an Irish princess). Cumberland retained its British name, as the land of the Cymry. The country north of the Humber seems to have had few English settlers in the early years, and the names of both the Anglo-Saxon kingdoms into which it was divided, Deira and Bernicia, were British. Even Kent, which the English colonized much more thickly, remained the land of the Cantii. Numerous slaves are found in Anglo-Saxon laws; for example, the *wealhs* of Wessex.

So it is likely that the Christian faith was still kept or remembered not only in Wales or Cornwall or Wessex which remained independent, but also inside England, in the huts of many slaves as well as in a few centres of special holiness such as St Alban's shrine at Verulamium. But it is also possible that many clung to gods and goddesses of pre-Roman paganism; perhaps the Christian landowners of the 'age of Arthur' had failed or neglected to convert their slaves or tenants. It is possible, too, that many who had been converted now tamely abandoned their Christian faith, or kept quiet about it until new Christian missionaries came. Sir Keith Feiling pictured the sad end in the emptying Roman city of Silchester: 'one day

the Christian priest serving its small Christian church, finding
no flock left to minister to, put out the light on the altar for
the last time'.[12] All that we know is that Christianity was not
handed on by the British to the English on any large scale –
any more than their language was. Only six villages are known
to have been called Eccles by the English, although fourteen
other place-names include the word. It is a little indication
that a British church (in Welsh, *egles*) was seldom a prominent feature in the landscape. And it is reckoned that not
more than sixteen nouns in the language spoken by enslaved
Britons entered the Anglo-Saxon language.

This failure to impress the conquering English is all the
more striking in the light of subsequent history. When in their
turn the English became the victims of invasion, the invading
Danes were soon converted to their enemies' religion. Even the
conquering Normans did not ultimately succeed in imposing
the French language on the country. But it is clear that in the
fifth and sixth centuries there was an extraordinary depth in
the hatred between the Anglo-Saxon invaders and their
victims, creating the gap over which no religion or language
could travel. Still in the seventh century, according to St
Aldhelm, the Welsh clergy refused to greet any Englishman
unless he wished to take refuge among them – and had first
done forty days' penance for being English.

We cannot tell fully what caused this total failure to forgive
the atrocities which no doubt both sides perpetrated. But
R. P. C. Hanson has commented that the work of Gildas
suggests that there was already a spiritual failure in the British
Church before the invaders' triumph became complete – a
failure in tragic contrast with earlier missionary achievements.
He writes: 'Patrick does not hesitate to excommunicate a
British tyrant who has conducted a cruel massacre, and it
seems clear that he expects his instructions for both boycott
and excommunication to be obeyed. One gathers from Gildas
that, though the Church of his day has plenty of atrocities to
witness, it cannot do more than deplore and denounce their
perpetrators. The British Church of Patrick's day converts

---

[12] Keith Feiling, *A History of England* (London, 1950), p.18.

savage barbarians; the British Church of Gildas's day merely
abuses them. Gildas shows quite a wide acquaintance with
theology, rhetoric and learning, but in his day they appear to
be in danger of degenerating into verbosity and pedantry.
Patrick certainly has very little learning and no rhetoric
whatever, but he is aware of his deficiency and honest about
it, and succeeds in a surprising way in compensating for his
lack of these things. Gildas writes much about God's wrath
and punishment, Patrick constantly harps upon God's loving
care'.[13]

So the heirs of Arthur may have been less than chivalrous.
The English were, however, also less gentlemanly on arrival
than they later liked to admit. And the poison stayed in the
system. Bede may well be reckoned the most truly educated
and attractive man to be found anywhere in his day. But when
he was drawing his *Ecclesiastical History* to a close in 731, he
still could not find it in him to forgive 'the Britons, who would
not pass to the English a knowledge of the Christian faith'.
Although he accepted a fellow-Englishman's story of the
British Ninian's mission to the Picts, he ignored the British
Patrick's more important mission to Ireland. And his narrative shows an Englishman's bitter hatred of the Welsh. He
seems never to have pondered the reason why, clinging to a
Christian tradition already ancient, the Welsh would not
accept the authority of intruders.

Bede tells the story of how 'the warlike King of the English,
Ethelfrid, made a very great slaughter of that perfidious
nation'. This was in a battle near Chester about 615. The
pagan king observed that the monks of Bangor Iscoed and
other Welsh priests had come to watch the battle and to pray
for victory to 'their God'. He therefore commanded that they
were to be attacked first, and 'about twelve hundred' were cut
down. 'Thus', Bede gloats, 'was fulfilled the prophecy of the
holy Bishop Augustine that those perfidious men should be
punished by temporal death because they had despised the
offer of eternal salvation'. It is an astonishing verdict on a tradition which had built and maintained the Christian Church

[13] R. P. C. Hanson, *St Patrick*, p.199.

in Roman or Celtic Britain across almost four hundred difficult years.

All that the Romanized Britons handed over to the English was the land itself. But what a legacy it was! Gildas lets us glimpse the island for which men fought savagely. 'Virtually on the edge of the world . . . it is protected on all sides by a vast ring of sea, almost impossible to cross . . . but it has the benefit of . . . two splendid rivers, the Thames and the Severn, up which luxuries from overseas used to be brought by ship. It is ornamented with twenty-eight cities and many castles, and well equipped with fortifications. . . . Like a bride arrayed in her jewels, the island is decorated with wide plains and agreeably placed hills, excellent for vigorous farming, and with mountains specially suitable for the pasture of cattle. Flowers of many colours make them a delightful picture. To water it the island has sparkling fountains . . . and clear rivers that glide with a gentle murmur. . . .'

CHAPTER TWO

THE CONVERSION
OF ENGLAND

· Saxon Church at Brixworth · Northamptonshire ·

WHY KINGS WERE BAPTIZED

A modern historian has made a fair comment. 'The question
is sometimes put why the Anglo-Saxons were converted to
Christianity so quickly. The truth is that they were not converted at all quickly. In spite of there being good political and
cultural reasons for the conversion of kings to Christianity,
in spite of an extraordinary galaxy of able and saintly
missionaries, it took nearly ninety years to convert just the
kings and the greater part of their aristocracy, not to speak of
the countryside which was a question of centuries. In the

course of that near-ninety years hardly a court was converted which did not suffer at least one subsequent relapse into paganism before being reconverted. The old religious instincts died hard.'[1]

The correctness of that judgement is confirmed by the evidence that church councils, bishops and preachers had to do battle against pagan magic long after the official conversion of the people. In 786 the first legates (ambassadors) to visit England from papal Rome commented on the survival of pagan practices. Some twenty years later Alcuin in a letter to Etherhard, Archbishop of York, pointed out that some of the people were carrying magic amulets and 'taking to the hills where they worship, not with prayer, but in drunkenness'. The hill of Harrow overlooking London was one such scene of pagan worship; *hearh* means 'holy place'. Inevitably the monks to whom we owe most of our knowledge of Anglo-Saxon history did not wish to record many details of a heathen religion, but the *Life* of St Wilfrid told how, when he and his companions were shipwrecked on the coast of Sussex, a pagan priest stood on top of the cliff shouting curses at them. Bede included in his *De Temporum Ratione* an account of the pagan English year (which began on 25 December) and in one of his stories about the miracles of St Cuthbert gives us a glimpse of a 'large multitude' of peasants standing on the shore at the mouth of the river Tyne. They were jeering at some monks whose little boats were being swept out to sea by the fierce wind. Cuthbert rebuked them, only to hear these further insults: 'Nobody shall pray for them! May God save none of them! For they have robbed us of the old religion and nobody knows how to cope with all these changes!'

The toughness of paganism at a higher social level is illustrated by Bede's mention of the fact that the East Anglian aristocrats killed their king, Sigbert, 'because he was too ready to forgive his enemies'. It is also significant that the Saxons who stayed behind on the mainland were the last of the west German tribes to be converted. They killed the two English

[1] Henry May-Harting, *The Coming of Christianity to Anglo-Saxon England* (London, 1972), p.29.

missionaries, the brothers Black Hewald and White Hewald, sent to preach to them at the end of the seventh century, and their eighth-century conversion was completed only at the point of the sword. We may well ask: what factors eventually made for the success of the new message of Christian humility among the proud, determined and conservative Anglo-Saxons?,

Their society always depended on the unquestioning willingness of most people to work and fight for their lords, specially for their kings. No new religion could make an impact on such a society except with the good will of the kings, and it is not surprising that Christianity spread from the top downwards.[2] The question, therefore, is what first attracted the kings. And the answer seems to lie in the example of Gaul across the Channel. Its now prosperous invaders had become Christians.

An incident was related in the clumsy Latin *Life of St Gregory* by an anonymous monk of Whitby between 704 and 714 (the first book known to have been written by an Englishman). It was an incident which thoroughly deserved the fame it has enjoyed since Bede included it in his *Ecclesiastical History* fifteen or twenty years after that first telling. One day in Rome the future pope, Gregory, noticed some fair-skinned, blond and generally good-looking young men. Asking to what people they belonged, he was told 'the Angles'; and he commented that they looked more like angels. He was further told that they came from the kingdom of Deira (the modern Yorkshire) and made a further pun about *Dei ira*, the wrath of God from which he wished to save them. The incident is revealing because it shows that slaves were being sold from England to traders in Gaul, presumably by the kings who had captured them during fights between the rival Anglo-Saxon war-bands. And whatever Gregory may or may not have said on that day in Rome, there survives a letter of his dated September 595. As pope he ordered his agent in Gaul to

---

[2] See W. A. Chaney, *The Cult of Kingship in Anglo-Saxon England* (Manchester, 1970), and J. M. Wallace-Hadrill, *Early Germanic Kingship in England and on the Continent* (Oxford, 1971).

buy Englishmen between seventeen and eighteen years of age for training in monasteries. We may conclude that the trade between England and Gaul, including the slave-trade, produced a more general interest in England on the Continent – and, to match this, an interest in Christianity among the English.

Ethelbert, King of Kent, ruled the part of England most involved in the European common market. A fifth-century glass factory has been excavated in Faversham; it had been equipped by some of the Franks who had conquered Gaul. Other archaeological sites confirm how extensive the international trade was. A part of this connection with the Continent was Ethelbert's marriage before he became King of Kent with Bertha, daughter of Charibert, the Christian king reigning in Paris. The queen was accompanied by her chaplain, Bishop Liudhard, and attended services conducted by him in the small Roman church a little to the east of Canterbury dedicated to St Martin. The failure of Bertha and Liudhard to convert Ethelbert may have been due to their own laziness; a letter from Pope Gregory rebuked the queen. But Liudhard may not have lived long in England; certainly he disappears from the story. And the king, for all his wish to link Canterbury with Paris, seems to have been intensely suspicious lest the acceptance of the Franks' religion as well as a Frankish princess should involve submission to them politically.

He was also suspicious of Christianity as a magic different from the magic of his own people. Bede tells us that when in 597 Augustine landed in Kent as the envoy of Pope Gregory, Ethelbert insisted on hearing him in the open air. But the missionary probably had a special reason to overcome his own great nervousness, for the pope's correspondence hints clearly that Augustine landed only when Gregory had been assured of Ethelbert's welcome.[3] And it is clear that when he had been baptized the king expressed his respect for the new priests handsomely. In his laws anyone stealing his bishop's property was compelled to make restitution elevenfold. For the king's

---

[3] Margaret Deansley has given us a portrait of this first English archbishop in *Augustine of Canterbury* (London, 1964).

own property, ninefold was enough. What is not so clear is
how deep Ethelbert's conversion went. His second wife and his
eldest son were both pagans.[4]

It was, it seems, easier for a king to accept a missionary
from far-distant Rome because no risk seemed to be involved
of political submission. As the monks in black chanted their
Latin prayers on English soil around a silver cross and a
painted image of Jesus (according to Bede), probably no one
foresaw the full extent to which future popes would revive the
worldly claims of the Caesars. But perhaps Augustine and his
fellow-monks did even then have some beginnings of an insight into the future of the bishopric of Rome. They came
from St Andrew's monastery which Gregory had founded in
his own former mansion on the Coelian Hill, when he had
turned to the monastic life from his work as the secular
'prefect' of Rome. Monks belonging to the Italian tradition
regulated by the great St Benedict (who was born in or about
480) have seldom been missionaries. But these monks knew
how imperious was the will of a pope who took an interest in
an island on the edge of the world which Rome had ruled.
When they had turned back from their perilous journey to
England, they had been sent forward by Gregory the Great
himself, exercising authority over them and their fears without
hesitation.

More than eight hundred of this creative pope's letters are
preserved in Rome. Some thirty concern the mission to
England. They show that despite the suspicions of later
historians Gregory had no long-term plans to establish papal
supremacy by taking a personal initiative in missions beginning with Augustine's; on the contrary, as he struggled to
pacify and convert the Lombard invaders in Italy, he expected
the end of the world to come soon. (So, for that matter, did

---

[4] The evidence that Kent under Ethelbert remained largely pagan is
assembled in Appendix I to H. G. Richardson and G. O. Sayles, *Law
and Legislation from Aethelberht to Magna Carta* (Edinburgh, 1966). A
summary of 'The archaeology of Anglo-Saxon England in the pagan
period' has been provided by Catherine Hills in *Anglo-Saxon England*,
ed. Peter Clemoes (Cambridge, 1979), pp.297-327.

every one of those Anglo-Saxon Christians who have left us their thoughts on the subject.) But standing as he believed he did in a brief period between the end of the empire and the end of the world, his mind was also full of memories of Roman rule. He knew that the chief Roman cities in Britain had been London the commercial centre and York the military headquarters. Accordingly he ordered that the chief bishops were to be established in London and York, each having under him twelve dioceses.

It was a new kind of Roman colonization, and in July 598 Gregory wrote from Rome to Eulogius, Patriarch of Alexandria, gleeful about the baptism on Christmas Day of some ten thousand of the English. They were a people 'placed in a corner of the world and until this time worshipping sticks and stones'. The number of such baptisms reported from Augustine's years based on Canterbury may well reflect the presence in the area of many who had links, at least in their family traditions, with the British Church. But the decisive factor was the willingness in Kent to draw closer to the Continent. This is made clear by Bede's narrative, which was based on the traditions of Canterbury communicated to him by Abbot Albinus and on letters of Pope Gregory brought to Jarrow from Rome by Nothelm, a London priest employed by Albinus to help Bede.[5] And the next steps in the spread of Christianity were connected just as clearly with Anglo-Saxon high politics.

Redwald, King of the East Angles, was persuaded by Ethelbert to accept baptism; but Bede tells us that on his return home Redwald was told by his wife to forget his conversion, except to the extent of placing a Christian altar alongside the pagan one in his private temple. Almost cer-

---

[5] These letters seem to be largely, but not completely, genuine. The most interesting among them, the so-called *Responsiones*, are not found in Gregory's own register of correspondence and contain at least one clear anachronism, but may well be substantially Gregorian. See P. Meyvaert's study in *England before the Norman Conquest*, ed. P. Clemoes and K. Hughes (Cambridge, 1971), pp.15-34. Jeffrey Richards, *Consul of God* (London, 1980), is the latest English tribute to Pope Gregory.

tainly this acceptance and rejection of Ethelbert's Christianity corresponded with Redwald's acceptance and rejection of Ethelbert's overlordship. And probably a memorial of his semi-Christian attitude survives in the treasure buried with a ship at Sutton Hoo, near Rendlesham in Suffolk where the East Anglian kings had a residence. The treasure, discovered in 1939, is now in the British Museum.

It is not certain that the burial did honour Redwald, who died about 625, but the evidence all seems to be compatible with this identification. Some of the highly skilled goldsmiths and jewellers who made this treasure may have been English, but others were Swedish. There is also evidence supplied by coins and other objects of trade with Gaul and, through Gaul, with Byzantium the capital of the eastern empire. A large dish bears the mark of Anastasius, emperor 491-518. It was a burial in the old pagan style, full of the equipment which the warrior-king would need on his voyage into eternity (there was even a lyre for his music); but perhaps most impressive of all is the presence of a couple of silver spoons in the Byzantine style. One is inscribed SAULOS, the other PAULOS. They link the owner of this treasure with the baptism of Saul of Tarsus, who became Paul the Apostle to the Gentiles. And it is possible that the king did not entirely lapse from the faith into which he had been baptized. No definite traces of a human body have ever been found in this magnificent pagan tomb. It has been asked: did the king receive a Christian burial quietly elsewhere?[6]

Redwald took over from Ethelbert as overlord of the Southern English, and was in his turn eclipsed by the victories of Edwin, the king of the Angles to the north of the Humber. The site of Edwin's simple palace at Yeavering, including a grandstand for semi-democratic assemblies, was excavated in the 1950s; but we should not think that Edwin lacked authority. His power over the Scots resulted in the naming of Edwin's Borough, still preserving his name as Edinburgh.

Edwin married Ethelberga, a daughter of King Ethelbert,

---

[6] See *The Sutton Hoo Ship Burial*, ed. R. L. S. Bruce-Mitford, vol. i (London, 1975).

and accepted Bishop Paulinus (an Italian sent by Pope Gregory to England in 601) in his court as her chaplain. Various pressures were brought on him to embrace his queen's faith, including a letter from Pope Boniface reproduced by Bede, but what seems to have been decisive was the memory of the time he had spent as an exile at Redwald's court. He had then been in fear of his life, but had met a stranger who had promised him safety and had laid his hand on his head in blessing. (Bede tells this story — and has the generosity to add that the refugee had been delivered from death by the insistence of Redwald's pagan queen that in honour a king must protect his guests.) Now, years later at Edwin's own court, Paulinus revealed that he had been the stranger. Together this powerful ruler and his friend the bishop won thousands of converts. It was to be remembered as a golden age. Bede claims that a mother with a new-born babe could have walked 'throughout the island, from sea to sea, without receiving any harm'; and that brass dishes were placed by fountains near the highways for the convenience of travellers — were placed there, and remained there. He had talked with a monk who recalled a conversation with an old man who had been baptized in the Trent at noon-day, with a crowd of other converts. This old man even remembered what St Paulinus looked like: 'tall of stature, a little stooping, with black hair, a thin face, a slender and hooked nose, his whole appearance both venerable and majestic'.

This fruitful alliance of Church and State lasted for no more than six years (627-633). It collapsed when Edwin was overthrown and killed by another alliance — between his fellow-Christian, King Caedwallon the Briton, and his fellow-Englishman, the pagan King Penda of the Mercians (meaning Borderers) in the Midlands. Paulinus had to flee with Queen Ethelberga to the south, where he was given a fresh sphere as Bishop of Rochester. Only James the Deacon carried on as a Christian missionary in the north, in his solitariness advertising what the withdrawal of royal patronage meant to the new religion.

So politics and economics played their parts in the adoption of Christianity by three successive Anglo-Saxon overlords; and

significant evidence about the alliance of Church and State
was included in Bede's *Ecclesiastical History*. Indeed, the
History seems to have been modelled on the work of Bishop
Eusebius – the historian who had celebrated the effects of the
conversion of the emperor Constantine in far-off Caesarea
(where Pilate had once had his headquarters) back in the
fourth century. Bede knew the work of Eusebius through
Rufinus, who had translated and completed the Greek book.

If we had fuller evidence about missions which Bede barely
mentions, we should probably find similar reasons for the
support given by other kings to other missionaries. Sigbert,
King of the East Angles, who had become a Christian while an
exile in Gaul, welcomed Felix, a bishop from Burgundy – and
in seventeen years Felix managed to plant the Church in the
area where Paulinus had failed. He died about 650. Cynegils,
King of the West Saxons, had the Northumbrian king,
Oswald, as his sponsor when baptized. This baptism was the
prelude to effective work by Birinus, a missionary bishop
consecrated in Milan, who established a primitive cathedral
in Dorchester-on-Thames and also founded a church in
Winchester before his death (also about 650). How much depended on a king's liking for a particular bishop is shown by
the fact that the next king of the West Saxons, Cenwalla, got
rid of two bishops whom he disliked – Agilbert (a Frank) and
Wine (who is reckoned as the first Bishop of Winchester).

Peada, the future king of the Mercians, was baptized when
he married the daughter of another Northumbrian king,
Oswiu; and he arranged for the conversion of the Midlands to
begin even during the lifetime of his pagan father, Penda.
Four priests were sent by King Oswiu to begin this mission in
653. Two were brothers. One of these, St Chad, later (in 669)
became the first Bishop of the Mercians, building his
people's unity by holiness and tirelessly preaching until his death
in 672. The other, St Cedd, did not stay long in the Midlands
but evidently this was not due to any lack of missionary zeal.
In 654 he was recalled to become Bishop of the East Saxons.
The churches he founded during his subsequent work included the monastery at Lastingham, quietly remote on the
Yorkshire moors.

The nave of the church which Cedd built in his own diocese at Bradwell-on-Sea, using Roman bricks from the nearby fort of Othona, is used for worship to this day. It is a simple building, but one which sums up this whole first age in Christian England's story: an age when kings and their peoples were baptized because the Christian Church was given prestige by the civilization of Gaul and Rome. To become a Christian meant to cease to be a barbarian.

LINDISFARNE OR ROME?

Chad and Cedd had, however, been trained not in any of the centres where men felt close to the prosperity of Gaul and to the religion of Rome, but on the holy island of Lindisfarne in the North Sea – a centre of the mission commonly called Celtic or Irish. We must now consider this very impressive mission as a possible rival to a distinctly Roman form of Catholicism as the religion of England.

Bede's *Ecclesiastical History* was the work of a man who was very much a Roman Catholic; indeed, it was to be translated in 1565 by Thomas Stapleton, an exiled Roman Catholic priest, to prove the claim that the Roman Catholic mission to Elizabethan England was identical with the mission on which St Gregory had sent St Augustine. But one of Bede's charms is that his imagination has been caught by the holiness of men who did not look, as he looked, towards Rome. He quotes someone who listened to Fursey, an Irish saint who lived in voluntary self-exile among the East Angles in the 630s. This informant remembered the saint describing a vision of fire – and sweating although it was winter.

Bede also tells how Augustine did not rise from his chair when the British bishops came to meet him. In contrast, when he became a bishop Chad had to be pushed on to a horse. Missionaries trained at Lindisfarne had previously refused to use horses despite the length of their preaching tours; they knew that horses separated them from the people they might meet on the way. Bede shows us how Augustine was so ignorant of lay life that he had to seek instructions from Pope Gregory on an amazing variety of sexual and other problems. In contrast, the missionary saints who looked to Lindisfarne, despite their preference for the continuous prayer-life of a hermit, identified themselves with the world of the poor. Bede, it seems, could not help loving them more than Augustine, who had to be rebuked by Pope Gregory for the sin of pride. He knew that these men whose hearts had been fired by an Irish sanctity had spread fire among simple people, who judged missionaries by how they lived.

The early history of the Celtic Church from which their inspiration came is not well mapped. (How much of the early history of the English Church would we have known if Bede's *History*, the fruit of his old age, had perished?) What is known shows that, in its isolation from the rest of the Christian world, the strongly tribal society of the Irish had retained or developed a number of customs which now made them look peculiar in the eyes of Rome; yet they retained the energy of the unsophisticated, the uncorrupt. Two passions had grown strong in them. One was for the learning to be found in Christian books. They could see and touch and even in some cases read those books, to them the thrilling embodiment of the world beyond their shores. The other Celtic passion was for 'pilgrimage for the love of God'. By this they meant the heroic self-discipline of one who exiled himself from the land of his birth and his heart. Perhaps there was in this potent emotion a more worldly love of adventure, even a touch of tourism. With whatever motives, Irish monks were to be found as far east as Kiev in Russia, as far west as Iceland; and the story was to grow that St Brendan's leather boat reached an earthly paradise, North America.

All these characteristics of the Irish missionary movement come out in the story of St Columba. He was a prince who had become a monk but had still got involved in a battle with a rival tribe, it is said over the possession of a manuscript. Ashamed (or perhaps exiled) after this bloodletting, Columba led his monks to settle on the very beautiful island of Iona, and made at least one expedition to the nearby, and almost equally beautiful, country of the Picts. He died on Iona in

597, eight days after the baptism of Ethelbert in Canterbury.

Iona became linked with the story of England because a young Northumbrian prince, Oswald, became a Christian while in exile among the Irish monks on Iona. Returning home, Oswald drove back the British and was acknowledged king in 633. Once in power, he asked the monks of Iona for a missionary. The first man to be sent soon retreated to his base, complaining that the English were too uncouth. Oswald and the Northumbrians were then sent a saint: Aidan. And Aidan was humble enough to win love. Bede tells the story of how the king gave an exceptionally fine horse to Aidan – who passed the gift on to a beggar. A spiritual force stronger than Gregorian Rome's imperialism as represented by Augustine had come to woo and to captivate the English.

The heart of the Christian mission lies for Bede, it seems, not in Augustine's Canterbury but on Aidan's island of Lindisfarne. He dedicated his great *History* to King Coelwulf, who was soon to begin twenty-seven years as a monk on Lindisfarne. There, within sight of Bamburgh, the Bernician royal castle on the rocky coast, St Aidan established a monastery in 635. The huts of this monastery, made of wood and thatch, were so lowly that no archaeologist has found traces of them beneath the tough grass and the salt winds. It was England's Iona.

Aidan, for whom King Oswald was content to act as interpreter, was a great saint – but not the greatest to be associated with this holy island. St Cuthbert, an English monk who moved with his abbot from Melrose to Lindisfarne in 664, found the island too crowded for his liking, and in 676 withdrew to pray alone on one of the nearby Farne Islands. He would, Bede tells us, pray all night in the cold sea, but once had his feet warmed by two seals on the sand, to the amazement of a monk who was spying on him. (To this day Britain's largest colony of grey seals is found here.) Reluctantly he agreed to be consecrated bishop in 685 but loved to return to this place of prayer. And he loved to fast, so that in his weakness the vision of God might grow strong. Shortly before his death in 687 he was cut off on his island by a great storm, when too ill to move. He has as his food five onions. When the alarmed monks eventually reached him, it was his gentle boast that four of the onions were untouched.

When his skeleton was disinterred in 1827 it was found that this austerly uncomplaining man had been riddled with tuberculosis and tormented by ulcers. But he had been buried with some eloquent, although small, treasures: a cross for his breast made with all the skill of the pagan jeweller, a large ivory comb, a portable altar. Incorporated into the cross was a shell which had come from the Indian Ocean. In death the English shepherd-boy had become a prince of the Church, a king in the marvellous new realm of Christian holiness.[7]

The courage of saints such as Aidan and Cuthbert, moving out so simply to God and to the people, may be contrasted with an incident which took place in Canterbury in or about 616. Mellitus, Bishop of London, had been forced out of his diocese by the pagan reaction under Ethelbert's son Eadbald. During his retreat to Canterbury he had been joined by Justus, Bishop of Rochester, who was similarly discouraged. They had urged Laurentius, Augustine's successor at Canterbury, to join them in flight. They had already crossed the Channel to the safety of Gaul, leaving Laurentius to say his prayers in church during what he believed would be his last night in England. During the night, however, the despondent archbishop had a dream about St Peter, who rebuked his cowardice. So he stayed put; King Eadbald was amazed and converted by his new courage; and Mellitus and Justus were recalled. We cannot imagine those true saints, Aidan and Cuthbert, needing any such reminder about their duty.

But for all the attractiveness of the humble and holy men associated with Lindisfarne, they lacked something: authority to teach a creed, to organize an institution, to command. When the English Church was united, the union came around the authority of St Peter and his successors in the Bishopric of Rome. That union lasted for almost exactly nine hundred years and when it had perished in the sudden storm of the Reformation its restoration seemed a cause still worthy of the dedication of many English martyrdoms.

---

[7] See *The Relics of St Cuthbert*, ed. C. F. Battiscombe (Oxford, 1958).

The unification was made possible by the decision at the small English synod meeting at Whitby in 664 to accept the latest papal way of dating Easter as a symbol of Christian Rome's general authority. It may seem that the decision might easily have gone in favour of the Celtic or Irish Church with its own Easter; but the defenders of the outmoded Celtic date in the synod at Whitby had little real hope of success. The king (Oswiu) who presided over the synod was married to a queen (King Edwin's daughter, Eanfled) who, having been brought up in Kent, already observed the Catholic Easter. Over most of Ireland at this time the latest Catholic date had already been accepted; the northern Irishmen who clung obstinately to a separate date (on Iona itself, until 716) were not typical of the Irish as a whole. The authority of Rome in this matter was almost bound to prevail, in England as in Ireland. A reference was made by King Oswiu ('smiling a little,' says Bede) to the danger of offending St Peter when one knew that one would have to appear oneself at the gates of heaven, but the practical point was the need to accept the verdict of the living pope for the sake of unity. The best of the English missionaries trained by the Irish seem to have been ready enough to bow to this verdict. Chad and Cedd conformed. So did Tuda the new Northumbrian bishop (a Southern Irishman) and Eata the new abbot of Lindisfarne (an Englishman trained by St Aidan), although Bishop Colman, who had spoken against the Roman date at Whitby, felt obliged to resign and to return to Iona after his defeat. For all the attractiveness of the Lindisfarne tradition, the prestige of Rome proved unanswerable.

In England the unification of the Church around the authority of the papacy was dominated by the contrasting personalities of two great churchmen, both of them highly authoritarian: St Wilfrid and St Theodore.

Wilfrid was an Englishman who travelled to Rome when not yet twenty, and was always fascinated by it. With youthful eloquence in the debates at Whitby he urged the claims of Rome as the claims of Peter the prince of the apostles. He was appointed to be bishop of the Northumbrians with his cathedral in York, but felt it necessary to go to Gaul in order to secure an appropriately valid and splendid consecration.

Twelve bishops conveyed the grace of the apostles to him, and he was carried into the sanctuary on a golden chair – perhaps more like an emperor than an apostle. In his absence King Oswiu grew impatient and appointed the more modest and agreeable Chad as his successor, but on his return Wilfrid raged, and Chad was packed off to become the first Bishop of Lichfield.

During disputes about the extent of his jurisdiction and income as bishop of Northumbrians, the far from humble Wilfrid twice returned to Rome in order to argue his case. In the course of those disputes, when exiled from his own northern territory, he found himself among the Middle Saxons, the still wholly pagan South Saxons and even the pagan and terrifying Frisians on the German coast; and in every case he immediately began work as a missionary, for he was a bishop of the Universal Church. But his chief delight was to build, decorate, equip and secure estates for his magnificent churches at Hexham and Ripon, with everything in the Roman style, for monks living according to the rule of St Benedict. The crypts of his churches remain. In York he restored the little cathedral built by Paulinus. As he lay dying, aged seventy-five, he had his treasures brought to his bed and divided them up so that these monasteries and his other followers could 'buy friends' for themselves when he was gone. He was a proud, although devout, prelate (a bishop for forty-five years) who although he died in 710 belonged in spirit to the high Middle Ages. We know of him through a biography written by his admiring disciple, Eddius Stephanus.[8] Plainly he embarrassed Bede.

Theodore had a less dramatic but more steadily creative personality. Born in St Paul's own city of Tarsus, he had spent most of his life as a scholarly monk in the East but had moved to teach in Rome. When the Englishman Wighard, seeking consecration as Archbishop of Canterbury, had died of the plague in Rome, and when two other Roman monks had declined invitations to replace him, Pope Vitalian turned to Theodore, then aged sixty-six. Next year (668) the old man set

---

[8] It was edited and translated by Bertram Colgrave (Cambridge, 1927).

out for England – and during twelve years achieved a work of organization more remarkable than the achievement of any Archbishop of Canterbury before or since. With his fellow-monk Hadrian who accompanied him from Rome he presided over a school at Canterbury. A teacher with English pupils was like a boar surrounded by hounds, it was said, but so effective was the teaching that Bede assures us that some of the men emerging from this Canterbury school were fluent equally in their native language, in Latin and in Greek. The tireless old archbishop summoned the first general council of the whole English Church to meet at Hertford in 672 and planned annual councils although the difficulties of travel were so great that this optimistic plan had to be abandoned. He founded dioceses, issued laws ('canons') to regulate church life, deposed unsatisfactory bishops, and handed down the appropriate judgements on the moral problems of the lesser members of his flock in his *Poenitentiale*. For example, he decreed that if a man could not buy back a wife who had been violently taken into slavery he was free to marry again after five years.

Although little visible evidence of Theodore's achievement has survived the centuries, we can still enter its atmosphere by visiting the parish church at Brixworth in Northamptonshire. Built about 680, it looks like a fortress outside. Inside it resembles a *basilica*, a Roman hall for the administration of justice; and the bricks of which it is made are Roman. The whole building speaks of the restoration of Roman rule to this island, although the new empire needed no legions. It is not surprising that although Wilfrid was one of the thorns in St Theodore's elderly flesh the two men were reconciled before death, for ultimately they both claimed authority not as English potentates but as ambassadors of Rome.

What drew the Anglo-Saxons to Rome was, no doubt, in part a worldly lure. In 747 an English missionary who was always suspicious of the worldliness of the eternal city (St Boniface) complained that there was scarcely a city on the road to Rome without its Englishwoman who had come as a pilgrim and remained as an adulteress or prostitute. But there was also a strong religious motive to inspire the long and

dangerous journey. Two kings of the West Saxons in succession – the young Caedwalla, exhausted after fighting his
way to the throne, and Ine the mature law-giver – died as
pilgrims in Rome. King Alfred's father, Ethelwulf, left estates
in Wessex in order that there would always be plenty of oil in
the lamps of the churches of Peter and Paul in Rome on Easter
Eve. Gradually the pilgrims became so numerous that a *schola
Saxonum* was established in the English quarter of the city,
with an English church (now Santo Spirito in Sassia). Towards
the end this tradition was clouded by the intrusion of an
Englishman, Stigand, into the archbishopric of Canterbury in
place of the Norman, Robert of Jumièges, whom the pope
continued to regard as the legitimate archbishop; and this was
one of the reasons why Duke William's Normans conquered
under the blessing of a papal banner. But it is revealing that
the English showed themselves to be nervous about Stigand's
right to function as archbishop. To the end they were loyal to
the distant pope, proud of being a small part of the greater
Christian world under Rome, conscious in particular of what
they owed to Pope Gregory. England was more regular than
any other country in sending a tax to Rome (Peter's Pence); so
regular that popes began to claim that it proved England's
acknowledgement of a duty to pay tribute.

A wide world began to be opened to the English by their
conversion to the religion taught in Rome.

In the 660s an Englishwoman – beautiful, devout and determined – was regent in the kingdom of the Franks. Balthild
had been a slave girl bought for household duties in the
palace, but had attracted the notice of King Clovis II, who
had married her. When Clovis died and their son was not old
enough to rule, she assumed control of the government until
the turbulent barons persuaded her to retire to the monastery
of Chelles near Paris, one of a number which she had founded
while queen.

In the 670s a young westcountryman, Aldhelm, was studying the culture of the day in Canterbury under Archbishop
Theodore and Abbot Hadrian. He wrote an excited letter to
the Bishop of Winchester, proudly apologizing for not being
able to spend Christmas with the old man; he was too pre-

occupied with his books, which included a Roman law book as
well as arithmetic, music, versification, astronomy and every
aspect of ecclesiastical learning. Aldhelm went on to become a
great scholar, Abbot of Malmesbury, Bishop of Sherborne
and, after his death in 709, a saint. We have a hundred or so
riddles by him in Latin. He wrote a Latin which was too
elaborate to be elegant, but it was modelled on the work of
Irish scholars (his first teacher had been an Irishman,
Maelduib) – and was far more fluent than the barbaric Latin
being written in Italy at this time. He gloated over these rich,
strange words, watching them glow and flash like one of the
Anglo-Saxon warriors turning over captured treasure. King
Alfred reckoned St Aldhelm the best of all the Old English
poets, although no poem of his in his native language has
survived.

In the 680s a Frankish (or, as we can begin to say, French)
bishop named Arculf was caught in a storm at sea and
wrecked on Britain's western coast. He found his way to the
monastery on the island of Iona and told his story to its abbot,
Adamnan. He had been to see the holy places in Palestine.
Adamnan wrote it down and took his book with him on a visit
to the Northumbrian court. Eventually the book reached Bede
and the gist of it was incorporated into his *History*. There the
material seems irrelevant – but Bede evidently thought it
exciting that such a book had been written in his own lifetime,
when the Muslims, as he knew, were sweeping through Spain
into Gaul. He delighted to think of any English connection
with Jerusalem and Galilee.

In the 720s a young Englishman from Wessex, Willibald,
was a pilgrim in Rome. Leaving his brother Wynbald there,
he decided to visit even holier places, although these were now
under a firm Muslim occupation. Working his way through
Sicily, Asia Minor and Cyprus, he saw the scenes of the earthly
life of the Saviour and then returned to Rome after two years
in Constantinople. He spent ten years in the monastery which
St Benedict had founded at Monte Cassino, but in 740 was
ordered by the pope to join his brother and sister in the
English mission to what is now Germany. There St Willibald
laboured until his death in 786; he was the first Bishop of

Eichstatt. He told his story to an English nun who wrote a book about it – the first English travel book.

SONGS OF ENGLAND'S CONVERSION

So English Christians could now explore a European and Mediterranean world. But the spiritual world of the Bible excited their imaginations still more, with results which survive in fragments of craftsmanship and of poetry.

The oldest surviving book written in England (but covered with red leather made from the skin of an African goat) is a copy of St John's gospel, now a treasure of Stonyhurst College. The writing suggests that it was created by Bede's fellow-monks in Northumbria; just possibly, it was Bede's own copy of his favourite gospel. St Augustine had received in Canterbury an Italian copy of the four gospels still preserved at Corpus Christi College, Cambridge, and now the English were competing. St Wilfrid gave to his church at Ripon a book of the gospels (now lost) which, we are told, was written in golden letters on purple-tinted parchment and guarded in a jewelled, golden case.

The finest of the religious poems of the Anglo-Saxons is *The Dream of the Rood*. It seems to have been written well before 750. Passages from it were carved on the high red sandstone cross still standing at Ruthwell near Dumfries, and a single copy of the full poem has been preserved in the cathedral library at Vercelli in Italy. The poet presents a dream about the cross (which, as we have seen, even the Christians among the Romans had for long avoided in art). He has seen the cross golden, jewelled, suffused with light and adored by angels. But he has also dreamed about its history. He has heard it speak to him. The cross remembers the time when it was cut down and set on a hill. It remembers, too, the time when the Lord of mankind, 'the young hero, God Almighty', mounted it with eager zeal. That warrior was pierced with nails, reviled by his enemies, killed and covered with darkness, leaving the tree blood-drenched, heart-broken.

> All creation wept,
> Bewailed the King's death. Christ was on the cross.

The cross remembers, too, watching Christ being taken down, 'tired after the great agony', and buried in a sepulchre of bright stone while a dirge was sung. Then the cross itself was cut down and buried. But now the young warrior who died as a true hero is risen, the cross is greatly honoured as the tree of triumph, and the poet, remembering his dead friends who now 'live with the High Father', prays that the cross may soon carry him to heaven 'where the Lord's host is seated at the feast'.

Here an anonymous Old English poet's imaginative genius has interpreted the biblical stories in terms already familiar to the Anglo-Saxons – cutting down the trees of the forest; listening to nature (was it only the wind that spoke among the trees?); gold, jewels and the feast as the rewards of the battle; the victory gained by the warrior's courage and endurance; the permanent honour won by accepting a lonely defeat without flinching. Such were some of the themes of a much longer poem, *Beowulf*, an epic which seems to have been composed at about the same time as *The Dream of the Rood*.

Beowulf is a pagan poem in many senses: Christ is never mentioned, there is no statement of any explicitly Christian theme, the hero is a noble pagan and he is never criticized. In a leisurely way the poem includes, or alludes to, many subsidiary stories which presumably were part of the pagan folklore which the Anglo-Saxons brought with them. But the poet who has shaped this material is a Christian, as is shown by allusions to the Creation, Cain and Abel, the Flood and the Judgement, and by a few denunciations of reliance on heathen gods; not all these passages are likely to be later Christian interpolations in the poem, although some may be. Presumably he was a minstrel at an eighth-century court, perhaps the Mercian court of the great King Offa whose ancestors get a brief mention.

He wrote to entertain warriors after dinner in some royal

hall very like the one where some of the action of his poem takes place. That means that efforts which have been made to interpret his work as an elaborate allegory designed to put across Christian teachings are probably far-fetched. Although this was not an art intended primarily to appeal to monks, some of the more worldly-minded monks, and the young noblemen they were educating, would have enjoyed it. In the 790s Alcuin found it necessary to rebuke the monks of Lindisfarne for their love of the heroes of Germanic pagan mythology: 'what has Ingeld to do with Christ?' Only one ancient copy of *Beowulf* has survived (with scorch marks from a fire in 1731); and in the same manuscript is found a Bible-based poem celebrating the courage of Judith who killed an Assyrian general after a drunken feast — which suggests that this copy may have been treasured in some monastery, anyway the most likely place for the survival of any literature.

Beowulf tells of Grendel, a demon who inhabited wild moors and fens but also attacked the banqueting hall of Hrothgar, King of the Danes. Beowulf, a young prince of the Geats (in the country now Sweden), seizes at the opportunity for adventure and glory. After a voyage — described with gusto — Beowulf arrives at Hrothgar's hall, Heorot, and after a great fight mortally wounds the demon. A feast with lavish gifts follows, but then Grendel's mother returns to avenge her son. Undeterred, Beowulf pursues the older demon. 'It is better for a man to avenge his friend than to mourn him long', he reminds King Hrothgar. 'We must all expect an end to life in this world; let him who can win fame before death, for that is a dead man's best memorial'. And Beowulf does win fresh fame, tracking Grendel's mother to the lake where she lives and eventually killing her after an underwater contest. Rewarded with another feast and further gifts, and with a long moral exhortation by old Hrothgar, he returns to his own people and becomes their king for half a century of prosperity.

In his old age Beowulf undertakes his last battle, with a dragon who guards a buried hoard of treasure. Determined to win more fame and gold, or else to accept the common lot of death, he fights and kills the dragon; but he is deserted by all his followers (apart from one Swede, Prince Wiglaf) and mortally wounded. He lives long enough to rejoice over the treasure, and after his death and cremation all of it is buried with his ashes amid many laments.

So 'they buried the gold and left that princely treasure to the keeping of earth, where it yet remains, as useless to men as it was before'. Beowulf is remembered as 'the gentlest and most gracious of men, the kindest to his people, the most eager for fame' – but the final impression left by the epic is of a funeral. The fame is tragic. At the end Beowulf's people, the Geats, know that they are now doomed to be conquered by the Swedes. There are many other mentions of feuds and deaths, and we are reminded that even the great hall of Heorot is soon to be burned down by enemies. The demons and the dragons symbolizing evil are conquered, but the heroes are also mortals, under the impartially ruthless sovereignty of fate. *Beowulf* is an entertainment for a feast, and it is the celebration of heroes. But it is also, in the words of J. R. R. Tolkien, an elegy about 'man at war with the hostile world and his inevitable overthrow in time'. It is a poem about a doomed pagan world, and therefore to its own Christian author it is the revival in a new and happier world of the tragedy of the heathen, the sadness of 'an ancient dirge'.[9]

Such was the world rescued from the devils of the darkness by the 'young hero, God Almighty' who fights in *The Dream of the Rood*.

Celebration of the biblical light in the darkness became (and remained for many centuries) the chief theme of the English poets. An early passage in *Beowulf* tells of a harp player in Heorot singing of the creation. God made the world a shining plain; he established the sun and the moon to light its inhabitants; he decked the earth with leaves and branches; he gave life to all that moves. And Bede attributes the same theme to Caedmon, the first Englishman to compose religious poems.

---

[9] J. R. R. Tolkien, 'Beowulf: the Monsters and the Critics', in *Proceedings of the British Academy* (London, 1936), pp.245-295. M. E. Goldsmith, *The Mode and Meaning of Beowulf* (London, 1970), also emphasizes the Christian content.

In the 670s Caedmon was a lay brother attached to St
Hilda's monastery on the hill by the sea at Whitby. The story
goes that one night he was asleep in the stable where he looked
after the horses. He had escaped a feast because he had been
once more embarrassed when the harp was passed round with
the invitation to sing. But in his dream he heard a voice:
'Caedmon, sing some song to me'. 'I cannot sing'. 'But you
shall sing!' 'What shall I sing?' 'Sing the beginning of the creation!' Caedmon's hymn has been preserved. Its nine-line
tribute to the 'Father of glory' who 'made the beginning of
every wonder' is not remarkable except for one thing. This
illiterate herdsman had memorized not only the beginning of
the Bible but also the secular songs he had heard in the hall;
and he had fused the two. 'What Caedmon did was – so far as
we know, for the first time – to apply the whole technical
apparatus of that Germanic heroic poetry which the Anglo-
Saxons had brought with them from their continental homelands to a specifically Christian version of the story of
Creation'.[10]

Later poems in this tradition are more sophisticated. There
are only four whose authorship is known. These are by Cynewulf, a scholarly churchman who probably worked in Mercia
and who added his name asking for his readers' prayers about
750. One of these poems, *Elene*, tells the story of the discovery
of the cross by St Helen, the mother of the emperor Constantine; this alleged event, together with the subsequent distribution of innumerable pieces of the 'true' cross, encouraged
devotion of the kind that gave birth to *The Dream of the
Rood*. But Cynewulf knew his public; probably he belonged to
it himself. Writing within a tradition of fighting and seafaring, he gave the English glowing accounts of Constantine's
legendary battle against the Huns and of his mother's long
voyage to the Holy Land. When he adapted a Latin legend to
form his *Juliana*, what interested him most was the opportunity to celebrate the saint's heroism in her conflicts with the
devil. Another of his poems, on *The Fates of the Apostles*,

---

[10] C. L. Wrenn, *A Study of Old English Literature* (London, 1967),
p.102.

presents the Twelve as the Lord's companions who were glad
to fight his battles and to lay down their lives for him.
Cynewulf's *The Ascension of Christ*, based on a sermon by
Pope Gregory the Great, is also full of images that would
delight an Anglo-Saxon audience, presenting Christ's ascension into the sky as a sea-voyage into heaven.

Another long poem that has survived, *Andreas*, tells of the
loyalty of two of the apostles to each other. Braving a storm at
sea, cold and hunger, imprisonment and torture, Andrew
rescues Matthew from death among the cannibals. Other
Anglo-Saxon Christian poetry puts Lucifer (Satan) at the head
of his war-band in rebellion against his true overlord, God,
and pictures the Exodus as a voyage through a storm at sea.

All this presentation of the Christian message draws on the
tradition of Germanic heroic paganism, to which Tacitus
refers when he mentions that some of the barbarians would
sing poems about the descent of their kings from their
gods. Anglo-Saxon Christian poetry, celebrating holiness as
heroism, demonstrates how wise Pope Gregory was in 601 to
cancel his initial instruction to Augustine that all pagan
temples were to be destroyed. His second order, that the
temples were to be converted to Christian use and pagan
festivals turned into Christian feasts, was more typical of the
whole successful strategy to reclothe the Christian message in
Anglo-Saxon dress. The Gospel was accepted because it was
thoroughly interpreted in terms with which the English could
feel at home.

Inevitably the Gospel became dangerously English, for the
pagan culture influenced Christians even while they used it for
their own purposes; they knew that it was a great deal more
than the worship of 'sticks and stones', despite the distant Pope
Gregory's ignorant boast in 598. Missionaries spreading
Christianity through Asia and Africa in the nineteenth and
twentieth centuries became very nervous about any mixture
of the Christian and the heathen; it seemed to them 'syncretism' – a betrayal of the Gospel. In Anglo-Saxon England
there certainly was syncretism. A compromise between the
Gospel and paganism is shown in, for example, the Franks
casket in the British Museum. This is a box made of whale

bone, carved with Christian images such as the Adoration of the Magi but also with scenes of Roman history and pagan mythology. Many of the Christian leaders of Anglo-Saxon England would have condemned such a compromise. But because it treated many pagan traditions tenderly, the Christian mission seemed less of a threat to the Anglo-Saxons than its greatest enthusiasts would have made it. If a Christian poet wrote *Beowulf*, that helps to explain why no missionary in Anglo-Saxon England had to be remembered as a martyr.

BEDE AMONG THE SAINTS

When Bede completed his *Ecclesiastical History of the English People* in 731, he could tell of many saints. Despite all the political and economic influences in the Christianization of this society, the heart of the conversion of the English people was personal religion; for despite all the attractions of contacts with Gaul and Rome, of the sea-links with Iona and Jerusalem, the most fascinating allurement offered by the new religion was the hope of heaven. We gather from Bede's stories, and from other sources, that between 610 and 830 about thirty English kings or queens became monks or nuns. They were seeking a kingdom beyond the empire of death.

Bede's best known story is a little drama of this psychological reality behind the conversion of the English. In the debate about the preaching of Paulinus before King Edwin in his hall, the chief of the pagan priests, Coifi, said that the old religion had not brought him adequate rewards; 'there are many who receive greater favours from you'. Coifi proved that he was a man of exceptional energy when he rode from the royal hall on the king's stallion (a thing no priest had ever done) and set fire to the temple which he had served. But 'another of the king's chief men' spoke about the old religion at a deeper level. Man's life on earth was, he said, like the swift flight of a sparrow through the hall, from door to door, leaving and returning to the dark winter outside. 'So this life of man appears for a short space, but of what went before, or what is to follow, we are utterly ignorant'. The Christian message appealed because it seemed to provide information about this matter.

The women's response is specially striking. In pagan Anglo-Saxon society women were not always treated as insignificant; the stories about Redwald's formidable queen show that. But there is no suggestion that any escape was possible for women whose ambition was other than handing round the goblets and the gifts to the heroes (as Queen Wealhtheow did in *Beowulf*). The way in which the new religion, with its offer of heaven, captured the devotion of outstanding women, and made them intrepid heroines, is shown in the record of the Anglo-Saxon abbesses. Many of these were of noble, if not royal, birth. Some of them ruled monasteries including monks. This tradition of the 'double monastery', which deeply shocked later reformers, was taken over from the flourishing monastic life of Gaul, and since it provided 'orphanage, boarding-school, old people's home, hotel and, not least, avenue of occupation for meddlesome women', it has been reckoned 'the greatest single blessing bestowed by Christianity' on seventh-century England.[11]

St Etheldreda, for example, was the natural daughter of a Christian king of the East Angles. While a girl she must have set her heart on the life of a nun, for although she married twice (the second time to King Egfrid of the Northumbrians), she steadfastly refused to consummate either union. In the end she was allowed to found a double monastery at Ely amid the desolate fens. She was encouraged by Wilfrid in this spiritual ambition; that did not endear him to her husband. She ruled Ely as abbess, noted for her austerities, until her death in 679. And the next year saw the death of another famous saint and abbess of royal birth, Hilda. She had ruled Hartlepool and Streaoneshalh (as Whitby was called before the Danes came). The latter monastery, where Caedmon worked, has been excavated. It consisted of many small houses and cells within enclosing walls. Little signs of gracious living in this

---

[11] Joan Nicholson, concluding '*Feminae glorosiae:* Women in the Age of Bede', in *Medieval Women*, ed. D. Baker (Oxford, 1978), pp.15-29.

seaside monastery came to light during the excavation: spindles and pens, many coins and fine specimens of imported pottery, even nail-cleaners and ear-picks.

But the most impressive saint coming to meet us from Bede's *History* is, readers tend to feel, Bede himself.

He was a genuine scholar, endlessly collecting the best knowledge of his day. This is shown not only by the *History* where at the beginning Bede listed his sources, but also by his earlier books in which he expounded grammar, rhetoric, science, chronology, martyrology and above all the Holy Scriptures. Day after day and far into the night, he pondered the meaning of books. He once wrote that the words of the Bible had three meanings. There was the *literal* meaning, which was like cooking on the griddle. The more advanced *allegorical* meaning was like using the frying pan; and finally there was the *mystical* meaning, like cooking in the oven. His raw material consisted of the books which Benedict Biscop had brought back from six journeys to Rome, together with many more recent additions to a library which modern scholars have catalogued on the basis of references in his own works. The only surviving book known for certain to have belonged to this collection is a copy of the Acts of the Apostles in Oxford. In Florence is a copy of the complete Bible which Bede's beloved abbot, Coelfrid, took with him as a present for the pope when in his old age he determined to go on pilgrimage to Rome. It is said that manufacture of this one Bible must have consumed the skins of more than 1,500 calves. But the best monument to Bede's scholarship lies in the custom of dating events from the year believed to have seen the birth of Christ. This *Anno Domini* method was invented by a sixth-century Roman monk, Dionysius Exiguus. Bede adopted it and popularized it; his *History* is the first major work to use it. A memorial of the older method of dating is preserved in the dedication stone of St Paul's church in Jarrow, where he worshipped. Inscribed partly in Latin and partly in Old English letters, the stone records that the building was dedicated on 'the ninth of the Kalends of May in the fifteenth year of King Ecgfrith and the fourth year of Colfrith, abbot'. This refers to 23 April 685.

Bede's literary work was, of course, not purely academic. It was part and parcel of his work as a monk, celebrating the grace of the God whose praises he sang several times a day, looking back to a golden age of holiness and evangelism. How his mind was working not long after the completion of his *History* comes out in his long letter of 734 to his former pupil, Egbert, now Bishop of York.

This was a letter full of pride in the 'innumerable blameless people of chaste conduct, boys and girls, young men and maidens, old men and women' to be found in the Northumbrian Church. But Bede was not complacent. Egbert must study scripture devoutly and make sure that the people could repeat at least the Lord's Prayer and the Apostles' Creed, in English if not in Latin. He must ordain more priests, for some of the outlying villages and hamlets have not seen a bishop for years although they all have to pay their dues. He must try to get more bishops consecrated – for did not St Gregory himself plan for an Archbishop of York with twelve bishops under him? (Egbert was in fact made archbishop shortly after Bede wrote.) And he must stop laymen from founding spurious monasteries in order to get their lands exempt from taxation; the defences of the kingdom are in danger. Right into his sixties, when he wrote his *History* and this letter, Bede was a concerned and active churchman, with a policy for the future.

The modern reader has to summon patience when Bede seems to be wasting words on miracle-stories while denying us information which we should greatly have preferred. But he was a man of his time, fundamentalist in his approach to the Bible, credulous in his zest for the collection of tales of the supernatural. And his time was a period of universal belief in the supernatural. Pagans expected gifts from the gods in exchange for the gifts which men offered to them – as did the priest Coifi in Bede's own story. The ambassadors of Christianity could offer no less. They, too, had to produce victory in battle, good crops, many children, deliverance from disease and death; or at least to produce the necessary impression. Exactly what happened (if anything did) to give rise to the miracle stories, is a question which perhaps no man is now wise enough to answer – but some of the holy men of the day may well have exercised the psychic powers as all around them would have expected. Far more remarkable is the fact that Bede supplies us with so much down-to-earth evidence about the foundation of the English Church. Incidentally it was the birth of England as a unit; although he was a monk not a traveller and there were large areas from which he had received little information (Wessex, for example), Bede was interested in the whole country. He passionately believed in its religious unity. Peculiar Irish customs about dating Easter, or about the fashion in shaving a monk's head, must, he insisted, not be allowed to disrupt the unity. Long before they had any political unity other than the temporary dominance of an overlord (*Bretwalda*), the English people as seen by Bede had this unity in their faith and their Church: and in this perspective, his zeal for Catholic uniformity is understood to be more than trivial.

Bede wrote in order to build up Christian England. Probably the chief audience which he had in mind was monks in other monasteries, when his *History* would be read out at refectory meals, but his theme was the English people. And he lets us see that under God English men and women had created their unity by the holiness they had in common. For that, it seems, was the miracle that interested Bede most. In his history of the abbots of the monastery where he had lived since the age of seven, there was no story of the supernatural. No conversation with angels marked his last hours on the eve of Ascension Day 735, as related by the monk Cuthbert. Instead we are told of his talk with his pupils. 'Learn quickly,' he begged them, 'for I do not know how long I shall live'. We are told of his dictation to one boy in particular, Wilbert, who took down a translation of St John's gospel into English. He completed that work; then in his little cell he sang his last *Gloria* ('Glory be to the Father and to the Son and to the Holy Spirit'). 'All who saw the death of our father Bede used to say that they had never seen any other man end his days with such great devotion and peace of mind.' The sparrow had escaped from the hall, to find light.

His translation of St John is now lost. Most of the church which he loved at Jarrow was finally demolished in 1783.

What were believed to be his bones were, however, taken to Durham Cathedral and have been honoured there since the eleventh century, not far from St Cuthbert's own last resting place. And another treasure rescued when the Vikings devastated Northumbria is the visual equivalent of Bede's *History*.

In the British Museum one of the most spectacular 'illuminated' manuscripts is painted delicately in blue, red, green, yellow and purple. Some of the decoration is abstract, particularly when the initials are adorned or whole pages (the 'carpet' pages) are filled with labyrinthine patterns. But we find also stylized representations of birds such as cormorants and of animals including dogs. Echoes of Irish art are to be found here, but clearly much of this is native Anglo-Saxon art, not unlike the Sutton Hoo treasure. And we find four lifelike portraits of men – the four evangelists of the New Testament. This is the book of the Lindisfarne gospels, written in a lovely Latin script and using a text derived from a church in Naples, with an accompanying lectionary suggesting readings for use in worship. A note records that the writing (presumably also the decoration) was done by Eadfrith who became Bishop of Lindisfarne in 698, and that the book was bound by his successor, Ethelwald.

Copied in a windowless hut close to the cold, often tempestuous, wind and the incessant surge of the North Sea, these gospels are high art, fully the equal of any achievement elsewhere in seventh-century Europe. Working only a hundred years after Augustine's fearful journey to Kent, little more than sixty years after Aidan had crossed the sea from Iona to test whether high courage might not do something among the uncouth, heathen tribesmen, Bishop Eadfrith has creamed the culture of the Christian world. Models originating in Iona or Naples or the courts of the Anglo-Saxon warrior-kings have been brought together to make the beauty of holiness and to adorn a saint's grave in Bede's England.

CHAPTER THREE

THE ANGLO-SAXON ACHIEVEMENT

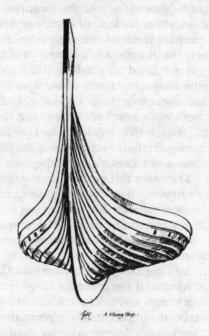

Gill · A Viking Ship ·

A TERROR-STRICKEN WORLD

The Anglo-Saxons seem to have found life hard and sad on the whole. Their numbers were probably never more than a million and a half. The analysis of their graves has suggested that eighty per cent were dead by the age of forty. Many of their bones give evidence of torturing arthritis, and the excavation of their homes has indicated that most of the peasants and slaves lived in perpetually damp huts, with the floor dug out of the earth. Their quickest way to riches lay in looting, after massacring, other Anglo-Saxons. Their poets celebrated their successful kings as men who had brought treasure back for distribution among their own followers. But the reality must have been sordid.

Aelfric's Colloquy is a conversation-piece written to show the correct use of Latin by a Dorset schoolmaster at the end of the tenth century; an English translation accompanies it. It affords a few glimpses of the life of the people. A ploughman is made to speak about his work, beginning at daybreak when he drives the oxen to the field: 'For fear of my lord, there is no winter so severe that I dare hide at home.' He has to plough a full acre or more every day, accompanied only by a lad who goads the oxen and is 'hoarse because of the cold and the shouting'. The shepherd then explains that from the early morning he has to stand over the sheep 'with dogs, lest wolves devour them' – but he adds: 'I am loyal to my lord'. The fisherman confesses that he prefers catching eels, pike, minnows, turbot and trout to any whale-hunt 'because of my timid spirit'. The other trades represented are those of the huntsman, the fowler, the shoemaker, the salter (salt was the indispensable preservative), the baker, the cook, the blacksmith and the merchant. Here is a fairly complex society, but for those who are neither lords nor monks most of life is drudgery, close to the earth. Even the merchant, doomed to buy and sell, does not consider his travels fun.

Anglo-Saxon poetry (of which some 30,000 lines survive) not only celebrates heroes who merrily distribute the loot in the banqueting halls. It often conveys the sense that daily life is a test of endurance, as uncomfortable as the sharp battle. In one poem a wife complains about her joyless lodging and finds no cheer in thinking about her even more desolate husband, who has been exiled for a crime. In another, a wife is miserable because she is separated from her lover, and her husband's embraces give her 'some joy' but are essentially hateful. In a more encouraging poem, the minstrel Deor who has lost his position at court is consoled – by recalling stories he has himself sung of heroes who endured. One lament preserved in Exeter Cathedral's library (*The Wanderer*) is by an exile, weary and friendless. He dreams of the feasts he enjoyed when at home with his lord – and wakes up to see only the yellow waves, the sea birds, snow, hail and frost. Another lament also found at Exeter (*The Seafarer*) is by a professional sailor. He has been condemned to earn his living on the cold and stormy sea; but he knows that what condemned him was his own impatience with the land. The spring, with the wild flowers returning to woods and fields, makes a man restless; then his heart becomes 'eager to depart on his journey, far upon the waves of the sea'. And even while he writes, 'the mind's desire is urging my spirit to the voyage, that I should seek the far-distant land of strange peoples'.

It is significant that the later Anglo-Saxons, whose ancestors had once taken to the sea with such gusto, appreciated and therefore preserved this poem which seems to expect all its hearers to regard seafaring as one more disaster. They no longer loved the sea; it has, indeed, been suggested that the author of *The Seafarer* may have regarded life on the cruel sea as a pilgrim's exile, undertaken with religious motives in order to purge the self. The Anglo-Saxons certainly never expected fresh pirates to follow their own ancestors' example in seeking a 'land of strange peoples' across the North Sea. On the contrary, they placed some of their most venerable monasteries — Lindisfarne, Wearmouth, Jarrow, Whitby and others — on the coast. There they left them unguarded. Yet it was their fate to incur the full fury of the onslaught of the Vikings — first Norwegians, then Danes, then invaders from the Viking kingdom of Dublin. A disaster greater than any anticipated in their poetry overwhelmed them.

An explosion of energy threw Scandinavians all over the west during the three and a half centuries, 750-1100. Norwegians went to the Orkneys, the Shetlands, the Hebrides, the other Western Isles, the east coast of Ireland, Iceland, Greenland and Vinland (Newfoundland). Swedes crossed the Baltic Sea. Danes poured into England, Normandy and the region of the Loire. The Vikings even penetrated the Mediterranean and ravaged the Riviera.

The explosion was all the more frightening because it was not entirely due to simple land-hunger. This was certainly a major factor in the case of the Norwegians, but had the Danes been interested only in land they would presumably have cleared some of the forests in nearby Sweden. The Vikings were thugs whose chance had come now that the empire of Charlemagne had destroyed the once mighty Frisian fleet and had then promptly decayed as Charlemagne's successors proved that they were not his true heirs. The North Sea and the world now lay open, and men who had been exiled for crimes, younger sons, the disappointed or the inordinately ambitious, seized their opportunity. Vikings were trained to massacre and to plunder, and that they did like machines. And their ships – long enough to hold rowers who supplemented the sail, strong enough to cross the oceans, light enough to carry, shallow enough to use beaches as landing places and islets in estuaries as winter strongholds – still arouse the respect of later generations. The example preserved in the museum at Oslo is frightening in comparison with the far simpler rowing boat excavated from the peat bog at Nydam in Schleswig, the area from which the Angles had crossed the sea to England.

The impact of this Viking terror did as much as the Moslem armies from the south to frustrate the hope that dawned for Europe, including England, when Charlemagne was crowned Emperor in Rome on Christmas Day 800. The wonder is that in England so much of the Christian civilization survived – and expanded.

It survived because it was now the higher civilization, embodying the more powerful religion. But it might never have expanded. It might have survived in aloof, self-conscious isolation from the barbarians, as Welsh Christianity had survived when the English had first come to England. The earliest stone towers in English churches are found near the east coasts; evidently they were built as lookouts and refuges during the Viking raids. People took their families and their few treasures there – and their faith. In Anglo-Saxon literature we come across more than a few hints that withdrawal was a spiritual temptation for these battered believers. The poem about *The Wanderer* ended: 'All security remains for us in the Father of heaven.' Its companion-piece, *The Seafarer*, ended: 'Let us think where we have a home and how we may get there.' Such an emphasis on taking refuge in eternity could easily have become merely defensive and escapist, the high watchtower. But the temptation was resisted. The English Christians – or enough of them to count – were outgoing evangelists. They took the Gospel back to Germany. Their educated understanding of the implications of that Gospel lay at the heart of the civilizing mission of the empire of Charlemagne. And finally, the Anglo-Saxons led by King Alfred took the Gospel to the Vikings who had inflicted terrible loss and suffering on them. They quietly converted the Danes who had seized half England, and then they sent some of their best sons over the North Sea to build the Church in Scandinavia. The heroic endurance which was the chief quality they admired in men or women found its noblest expression in this expansion of the Church among cruel barbarians; in these beginnings of the English Christian mission which was one day to reach America, Africa, Asia and the islands of the Pacific.

No Bede arose to celebrate the achievement. Had Alfred lived longer, perhaps he would have been the man to write a comprehensive sequel to Bede's *History*; or at least he might have got it written at his court. He almost certainly commissioned the translation of Bede's work into English, but many of the best known stories about the late Anglo-Saxon period were written down long after the coming of the Normans: Alfred himself and the cakes, King 'Canute' and the waves, Lady Godiva's naked ride through Coventry. Much that would now make these Anglo-Saxons vividly alive for us was lost for ever under the Normans, when English books got thrown out of the libraries and English memories got forgotten in the harshness of life after the island's conquest. And the surviving anecdotes or chronicles were never pulled together, as Bede would have done. In the absence of an Anglo-Saxon history of it all, the modern student has to make his own attempt to tell an astonishing story.

THE CONVERSION OF GERMANY

The English missionary movement on the continent could look back on Wilfrid's winter among the Frisians (678-9) as the beginning of it all — but that was not a true beginning, for Wilfrid was essentially a Northumbrian prince bishop delayed on his journey to Rome, without the slightest intention of ending his days among heathen foreigners on the German coast. The real founder of the movement, St Willibrord, was a monk at Ripon under Wilfrid; he had been placed there while very young by his father, who spent his later years in a hermitage near the mouth of the Humber. When Wilfrid fell from ecclesiastical power in 678, the young monk retreated to Ireland. There he absorbed not only more learning but also a stronger desire for 'pilgrimage for the love of God'. This desire, perhaps combining the austere self-discipline of a voluntary exile with a touch of the more human curiosity about travel, had already changed Europe. Led by St Columbanus (about 590) many Irish monks had crossed over to the Continent to wander or to found new houses of prayer and study. Their influence had reached out through the kingdom of the Franks to penetrate many Germanic tribes, although the obstinately heathen Frisians and Saxons remained impervious to the Irish charm.

The idea of 'pilgrimage for the love of God' was in the air. In Ireland Willibrord met another Englishman, Bishop Egbert, who, when his life was preserved during a plague, had in gratitude made a vow of perpetual 'pilgrimage' or exile. Egbert had converted the monks of Iona to the Roman customs including the dating of Easter and had wanted to continue Wilfrid's work among the Frisians. Deterred from going himself (Bede says, by a storm accompanied by a dream), he had sent one Wicbert who had returned after two fruitless years. Now Egbert enthusiastically entrusted the Frisian mission to Willibrord and eleven companions.

The twelve were further encouraged by the protection of the Frankish ruler, Pippin, and by the blessing of the pope. Willibrord succeeded in his missionary work wherever (and for so long as) Frankish supremacy in the area could support it, and in 695 he was made the first Archbishop of Utrecht, taking the Roman name of Clemens. He was over eighty when he died in 739. Unfortunately he remains a shadowy figure to us. His correspondence perished, as did much of his achievement; the separate Frisian archbishopric did not survive. His first biographer was his kinsman Alcuin, writing half a century after his death when many legends were already surrounding the memory of him. A splendid copy of the gospels, presumably brought over from England by him, is preserved in the monastery which he founded at Echternach.

Far more is known about Wynfrid who was renamed Boniface when he, too, was made an archbishop in Rome. His biography was written by Willibald whom we have already met as an English traveller and bishop. Wynfrid was from Devon; he was educated in the monastery at Exeter, having been born (according to tradition) in Crediton. Made Abbot of Nursling near Southampton, he felt impelled to exile himself from his country, which he never saw again when he had sailed from London in 718, not yet forty years old. Willibrord tried to persuade him to become his assistant and successor in Utrecht, but the ex-abbot's probing travels and ambitions were now larger. He was determined to conquer wide German territories for Christ and, when Irish or other missionaries had got there first, to order all things in obedience to the papacy. He, too, was glad to accept the protection of the rulers of the Franks; but Christian Rome, which those rulers ignored for most of the time, was his real authority. He paid more than one visit to Rome to seek a clear commission and later wrote to it frequently for detailed instructions. When he was made a bishop and an archbishop in Rome, he did not hesitate to take oaths of obedience virtually the same as those taken by Italian bishops. It is not too much to say that these two Englishmen renamed Clemens and Boniface repaid the papacy for its past gift of the Gospel to England by this eighth-century gift of a spiritual empire over the Netherlands, the Franks and the Germans. 'The whole character of western Christendom had been transformed,' writes a modern historian of the papacy. 'It was an extraordinary accession to the papacy's sphere of authority, an immense increase in the number of those who looked to Rome as the source of true religion. . . .'[1]

---

[1] Geoffrey Barraclough, *The Medieval Papacy* (London, 1968), p.50.

Boniface was promoted to his archbishopric a few months from the day when the Arabs were defeated at Poitiers. As he fought with other weapons against the heathen beyond the Rhine, he knew that he was the representative of Roman civilization as well as of Roman Catholicism. Bishop Daniel of Winchester once wrote to encourage him. 'If the heathen gods are all-powerful . . . how is it that they spare us Christians who are turning almost the whole earth away from their worship? . . . We Christians possess lands rich in oil and wine and abounding in other resources, but the gods have left to the pagans lands stiff with cold. . . .' It was in keeping with this mission in the defence and enlargement of Christendom that Boniface once asked some English nuns to make a copy of the letters of St Peter in gold, to impress the simple folk to whom he had to preach. And it was in keeping with the Roman genius for organization that he regarded his key work as the establishment in the years 739-741 of eight German dioceses and a German synod (church council), followed by five years and five reforming synods to bring the discipline of the Frankish church up to Roman standards.

The decrees of the German synod were dated from the Incarnation. It was the first such public use of the method of dating popularized among the English by Bede. It was no coincidence that in surviving letters Boniface asked for copies of books by Bede – or that he asked Nothelm, the priest who had gone to the archives in Rome on Bede's behalf and was now Archbishop of Canterbury, for 'a copy of the letter containing, it is said, the questions of Augustine, first prelate and preacher of the English, and the replies of the sainted pope Gregory . . . for the registrars say that it is not to be found in the archives of the Roman church'. 'I beg also', he added, 'that you will let me know in what year of the Incarnation the first missionaries sent by St Gregory to the English people arrived'.

Boniface was joined by many recruits from England who became bishops, abbots, monks and nuns in Germany, and his correspondence shows that he set himself to maintain close links between the mother country and the German mission by frequent prayers, letters and small gifts (manuscripts, a cloak, incense, pepper, hunting falcons for a King of Kent, two small casks of wine for an Archbishop of York 'in token of our mutual affection, to use it for a merry day with the brethren'). The practical interest taken in this mission all over England both demonstrated and advanced the unity of the English. A Bishop of Leicester among the Middle Angles wrote to Boniface assuring him of prayers for the conversion of the Saxons, 'for they are our people'. When the great man had died, the Archbishop of Canterbury wrote to Boniface's successor, a West Saxon named Lull, rendering thanks to God 'that the English people were found worthy to send out this gifted student of heavenly learning, this noble soldier of Christ, with many pupils well taught and trained, to far-off spiritual conflicts'. Lull's own letters include a request for the complete works of Bede, sending in return a silk robe to cover Bede's relics.

Another incident shows the courage of such missionaries. There survives a letter written to King Ethelbald of Mercia by Boniface and six other bishops of English birth now on the Continent. The letter compliments the king on his good works: almsgiving, the repression of robbery, the defence of the poor, the maintenance of peace. But it boldly continues: 'we have learned from many sources that you have never taken to yourself a lawful wife.' So far from being chaste as befits a bachelor, the king has been promiscuous – and 'these atrocious crimes are committed in convents with holy nuns, with virgins consecrated to God'. He is told that even the heathen in Saxony punish women severely for adultery. How much more should an English Christian king be rebuked for these sins! The letter burns with patriotism as well as with moral indignation. Boniface wrote a covering letter to Herefrid, the unfortunate priest who was to read out the rebuke, addressing an illiterate king who was then the most powerful man in England. 'The well-doing and fair fame of our race are our joy and delight', he wrote, 'but their sins and their evil repute fill us with grief and sorrow'.

We are not told what were the king's immediate reactions to this letter. But it is probable that only the intervention of Boniface secured the holding of the very important Synod of

Clofeshoh in 746, at which King Ethelbald was present. (Clofeshoh was probably a royal manor, but where is not known.) This council of the English Church agreed on new regulations similar to the reforms which Boniface was securing in this period for the Church in the territories controlled by the Franks. Bishops were to see that the houses of monks and nuns remained devout, studious and quiet (did the king blush?). They were also to visit all parish churches once a year, insisting that priests should be able to understand the Latin of the services and to explain them to the laity. Most of these churches would be fairly large monasteries or 'minsters', but some of the minsters no longer held monks and with some reluctance the bishops agreed to visit them too, acknowledging their secularized status. And the council recognized the growing number of small churches to which a priest would be appointed by the lord of the manor and 'instituted' by the bishop. Three years later King Ethelbald issued a charter in which he freed all the churches from taxation apart from the duty to repair bridges and fortresses. The English parish system was coming to birth.

Above all, England was moved by the story of the martyrdom of St Boniface. It seems likely that his biographer (Willibald) was right to say that he was killed because the books he was carrying about were thought to be treasure. On the whole the Germanic pagans treated Christian missionaries with nothing worse than suspicion and insults. But it was spiritually impressive that the Archbishop of Mainz, so far from being content with the work which had come to him as an ecclesiastical organizer and reformer throughout Germany and France, chose when more than seventy years old to take up again missionary work among the Frisians to the north-east of the Zuider Zee. They were, he knew, dangerous; a letter has been preserved in which he begged the Frankish ruler to take care of his English and other fellow-missionaries when he was gone. Thousands of the Frisians were baptized, but on 5 June 755, when he was about administer confirmation, Boniface was killed together with his companions whom he had told to be 'heroic in the Lord' (according to his biographer). His body was taken by boat first to Utrecht and then, rowed for a month up the Rhine, to his cathedral at Mainz; it was a ship-burial to eclipse Sutton Hoo and *Beowulf*. Finally he was buried in the great monastery he had founded at Fulda; the book he was reading, damaged by a sword-blow, is still shown.[2]

THE EDUCATION OF EUROPE

During Boniface's lifetime, and for quarter of a century after it, Alcuin lived quietly in York. He was first a brilliant pupil, then a teacher, in the school attached to York Minster (which was splendidly rebuilt in this period); a deacon, never a priest. His greatest enthusiasm was the minster's library, which he proudly catalogued in one of his many poems, *On the Saints of York*. In 782 he was on his way back to York from Rome, where he had been to ask the pope for the *pallium* (the sign of an archbishop's dignity) for his close friend, Albert. In Parma he met Charlemagne, the ruler of the Franks. That great man asked him to become his adviser on religious and educational matters, teaching in the palace school at Aachen. Fourteen years later he invited him to take over St Martin's old monastery at Tours. There he could use the profits of vast estates as abbot and as the creator of a school and library.

It was the largest educational opportunity ever offered to an Englishman, for it gave him the leading position in the whole revival of religion and learning as Charlemagne struggled to recreate the empire and civilization of Rome. Alcuin was always the schoolmaster, and very much the agent of Charlemagne; his own nickname was 'Flaccus' after the Roman poet Horace, but Charlemagne was 'David', the hero-king. In his own sphere, however, he possessed something of Boniface's organizing genius. He organized the copying out of manuscripts, a rescue-operation for literature; and the Carolingian miniscule handwriting used in them was the an-

---

[2] *The Letters of St Boniface* were edited and translated by E. Emerton (New York, 1940), and J. C. Sladden wrote a biography of *Boniface of Devon* (Exeter, 1980).

cestor of the type adopted many centuries later by the printers of Europe. He revised the Latin text of the Bible, often corrupted by the carelessness of copyists. And he secured uniformity in the services of the Church; the prayer for purity which still begins the Holy Communion service is there because of his influence, as is the recitation of the Nicene Creed during that service. Alcuin was the first to keep All Saints' Day in France.

Many of his letters survive.[3] Like Boniface's they are tenderly affectionate towards his companions in the Continental work and towards those he had left behind in England. One modern scholar's assessment of him is that he was 'in every respect a collector. He amassed huge quantities of information on all manner of subjects. He collected riches; he collected friends; and, especially during the last years of his life, he collected intercessors in all countries to pray for the salvation of his soul'.[4] But that verdict is needlessly cold. It is better to leave him with the epitaph he wrote for his grave: 'My name was Alchuine, and wisdom was always dear to me'.

ALFRED THE CHRISTIAN KING

On 8 June 793 Vikings from Norway sacked the island of Lindisfarne. 'It is nearly 350 years since we and our fathers inhabited this most lovely land', wrote Alcuin. 'It was not thought that such an invasion from the sea was possible. The church of St Cuthbert is spattered with the blood of the priests of God, stripped of all its furnishings, exposed to the plundering of pagans – a place more sacred than any other in Britain.' And the only solution of the Viking problem that seemed possible to Alcuin was moral rearmament. 'Consider the luxurious dress, hairstyles and general behaviour of leaders

---

[3] See *Alcuin of York*, ed. Stephen Allott (York, 1974).

[4] Heinrich Fichtenau, *The Carolingian Empire* (Oxford, 1957), p.95. A far more friendly portrait is to be found in E. S. Duckett, *Alcuin, Friend of Charlemagne* (New York, 1951).

and people', he urged King Ethelred. 'See how you have desired to imitate the pagan way of cutting hair and beards'. In other letters he quoted the warnings of Gildas to the British two centuries before.

In the following year Norwegian Vikings plundered Bede's old monastery and school at Jarrow, whether or not it had paid sufficient attention to Alcuin's advice: 'Look at the treasures of your library, the beauty of your churches, the excellence of your buildings, the order of the religious life. . . . The boys should learn to assist the worship of the heavenly king, not to dig out the earths of foxes or to course hares. . . . Liven sleepy minds by the example of Bede. Sit with your teachers, open your books, study the text, grasp its sense. . . .'

The English had to learn harder lessons about warfare than Alcuin could ever teach. Fortunately for them, they were taught by a man who combined something of Alcuin's love of learning with a mastery of his own military trade: Alfred the Great, King of the West Saxons 871-890.

Alfred is remembered as the father of the English navy, for he commanded the building of a fleet and trained the Saxons to resume their old courage and skill as sailors. He could equally be remembered as the father of the English army, for instead of resting content with the old militia (*fyrd*) which had tended to melt away at harvest time, he imposed a more systematic conscription (and taxation) and arranged for half this larger army to be on duty at one time. Or he could be remembered as the father of the English town, for he instructed as many of the English as possible to gather in a *burh* – Hastings, for example, or Chichester or Southampton or Oxford or Exeter – and fortify it.

Or Alfred could be remembered as the father of the English nation; it is certainly significant that the adjective *Englisc* came into regular use in his time. In the evolution of the national monarchy the fact that he was the only English king remaining in arms was decisive. In the days of Boniface and Alcuin the greatest English power had been in the Midlands. Offa, King of the Mercians 757-796, had dared to quarrel with Charlemagne and had persuaded the pope to make his own Bishop of Lichfield an archbishop. He had styled himself

'King of the English' and even 'emperor', ruling between the
Thames and the Humber, constructing a great dyke against
the Welsh (which largely survives), and minting a gold coinage
which Arab traders would recognize as being like theirs. But
in the ninth century the leadership had passed to Egbert, King
of the West Saxons, a strong man who had the wisdom to be
guided in policy by St Swithin (Bishop of Winchester
852-862). Finally the Mercian kingdom, like the Northumbrian, had fallen victim to the Danish and other raiders and
settlers. At Easter 878 even Wessex seemed to depend on the
Danes' mercy, which was non-existent. Alfred controlled only
the Isle of Athelney. But he fought on; and eight years later,
he rode into London. In the words of the *Anglo-Saxon
Chronicle* (the history, in various local editions, which was
itself a new expression of nationhood): 'all the English people
submitted to Alfred except those who were under the power of
the Danes'. And when Alfred issued laws to this people – on
the whole conservative laws, although there were new provisions for the protection of the weak and for limiting the
bloodfeud – he prefaced them by reciting the Ten Commandments.

Here, however, we can remember Alfred chiefly as the
father of English prose and as the godfather of a religious
revival. Fortunately we possess a *Life* by Asser, a Welsh priest
persuaded by him to spend half the year at the court of
Wessex. It is the first biography of an English layman, naive
and unfinished, artistically inferior to Einhard's biography of
Charlemagne which was presumably one of its models. But the
book also imitated the biographies of saints; and whereas
Einhard had been a layman writing about an emperor, now
'the churchman's patronizing when writing of a layman . . .
comes through the story'.[5] Alfred, we are informed, when he
learned to read late in life resembled the penitent thief. The

---

[5] Beryl Smalley, *Historians in the Middle Ages* (London, 1974), p.71.
Asser's Life of King Alfred, edited by W. H. Stevenson, has been
republished with an essay by Dorothy Whitelock (Oxford, 1959). N. P.
Brooks stressed the greatness of Alfred's achievement in *Transactions of
the Royal Historical Society* (London, 1979), pp.1-20.

priest's strange failure to understand Alfred's truly heroic and Christian achievement may help to account for the fact that the king was never canonized as a saint. Alfred's was the manly religion encapsulated in the proverb attributed to him:

> If thou hast a woe, tell it not to the weakling.
> Tell it to the bow in thy saddle, and ride singing forth.

Asser tells us that Alfred had a notebook by him day and night. He would copy into it extracts from other books which specially helped or comforted him, 'flowers gathered from all sorts of masters'. And he also kept by him a book of psalms; William of Malmesbury records a tradition that he was working to produce a complete Psalter in English when he died.

Charlemagne could not write; he kept tablets with letters on them beneath his pillow, hoping that something would seep through. Alfred, in contrast, astonished his contemporaries by being a studious prince and king. There is a story that as a young boy he admired the pictures in a book of English poetry. His mother promised that he would have the book once he could recite it by heart, and it was not long before he claimed his prize. He learned Latin while a king, although he claimed that when he came to the throne there were very few priests able to translate it into English ('and I cannot remember a single one south of the Thames'). He had to fight against decay within the English Church, therefore, as well as against the Danes; possibly one reason for this decay was that so many of the English Church's most active sons had become missionaries abroad. And despite the pressures of war and administration, literary work was for him an essential part of a Christian king's duties, as was the encouragement of craftsmen. He wrote, as he fought, for Christendom.

He translated into English Pope Gregory's book of advice on *Pastoral Care* and had copies sent to his bishops. The lovely Alfred Jewel found at Athelney in 1693 and now in Oxford may have been part of the encouraging bookmarker which we know accompanied this gift. The king also translated the *Consolation of Philosophy* written by a sixth-century Christian statesman, Boethius, in prison before his execution with the *Soliloquies* of St Augustine of Hippo. Alfred declared that this work was like cutting enough timber to make a mere cottage; it was for others to cut more according to their own needs. Boethius and Augustine had already been favourites with Alcuin, and were to have an immense influence on the Middle Ages throughout western Europe, but being a king introducing the English to unknown treasures, Alfred was not too nervous to edit and adapt them boldly. And to remind his fellow-countrymen of the world to which they belonged, he sponsored an English version of the *Universal History* of Orosius, adding an account of voyages related to him by two travellers who happened to be at his court, Ohthere and Wulfstan.

No doubt this busy king who had only just learned Latin had expert assistance in such books, but they all bore the stamp of his personality. And although the *Anglo-Saxon Chronicle* was not his work directly, it must have been due to an impetus coming from him that during his reign it expanded from brief notes to a narrative which is the earliest example of continuous, original prose in English.

After a decisive battle at Edington and more than a week of private talk, Alfred persuaded Guthrum, the general of the Danish army which had almost crushed the life out of Wessex, to accept baptism and to settle with his followers in England in peace. At this momentous baptism, at Aller near Athelney in 878, Alfred stood godfather to Guthrum, who took the English name of Athelstan. The Danish army moved into East Anglia, the East Midlands and Essex; and by a treaty with Alfred in 886 this 'Danelaw' was accepted as a peaceful kingdom with a firm frontier. This legitimized a very considerable area of conquest for the Danes. But the treaty provided for the equality of English and Danes, class by class, in the *wergild* (the payment due after a killing). It was a charter for the pirates' orderly settlement. This process is still commemorated in the English language, where not only the word 'sail' but also the word 'law' has Scandinavian origins.

THE CONVERSION OF SCANDINAVIA

The English word 'cross' is also Scandinavian in origin. It memorializes the fact that the Danes in England gradually followed Guthrum's path into Christianity; one, Oda, became Archbishop of Canterbury in 941. The story of the conversion is now lost, but a modern scholar refers to this as 'the fundamental fact concerning the religious life of the ninth century . . . : that Christianity was so deeply rooted in the countryside that within a few years the pagan conquerors had been converted to Christianity through the force of their English neighbours' practice and precept, without benefit of missionary activities from those parts of England which remained unconquered, and despite the fact that the bastions of organized religion in their own areas had been destroyed'.[6]

We have evidence of the new settlers' original paganism in some sculptures and some place names. If we need any reminder that the English must have been terrified of these heathen murderers, we have a letter written by Pope Formosus in the 890s telling the English bishops that he has considered excommunicating them because he has received no reports of attempts to convert the Danes. We also have some evidence in art to mark the impact of Irish evangelism among the Vikings. At Kirk Andrea on the Isle of Man a cross has the Vikings' high god (Odin, the equivalent of the Saxons' Woden) on one side with Christ on the other. But there are very few traces left in art of the reception of the message of Christ the new 'white' god; one such is a cross at Gosforth depicting the Christian Saviour in the style of the Vikings' Baldur.

We have, it seems, no evidence at all of the conversations between the English and the settlers in which the Christian religion was expounded and accepted. The main evidence provided by archaeology is negative: few Danish pagan burial grounds have been found. Such scraps of evidence as survive

---

[6] D. J. V. Fisher, *The Anglo-Saxon Age* (London, 1973), p.155.

suggest that the early Danish settlers 'adopted Christianity eagerly and early and that heathenism had ceased to be a powerful force among them by about 900 or at least by the end of the reign of Edward the Elder (899-924)'.[7] But we are left to wonder how Danes felt when they joined in the veneration of the tomb of St Edmund the Martyr, the last native King of the East Angles, killed while resisting the Danes in 872. The greatest of the Danish kings, Cnut, made the monastery built where St Edmund was buried richer than any other landowner in Suffolk.

In the end, not only the Danish settlers but also the Scandinavians remaining in their homelands were baptized. In Denmark itself the first missionary was the monk Anskar from Picardy, brought there by Harold Gormsson, the king who had been baptized while on a visit to a Frankish ruler, Louis the Pious. Anskar subsequently visited Sweden and became the first Archbishop of Bremen, but when this 'Apostle of the North' died in 865 the Scandinavians had returned to their old religion. The real progress of Christianity in Denmark seems to have begun more than a century later, and to have been greatly influenced by the conversion of the Danelaw in England. In 965 the Danish king, Harold Bluetooth, became a Christian. He was the father of Sweyn and the grandfather of Cnut, and an inscription still survives in Jelling in Denmark: 'King Harold had this monument made in memory of his father, Gorm, and his mother Thyri. Harold won all Denmark and Norway and made the Danes Christian'.

Paganism was still more obstinate in Norway than in Denmark, although the two kings Haakon and Olav Trygavason, who were both made Christians in England, endeavoured to persuade their fellow-countrymen to follow them – and Olav, who was killed in 1030, was remembered as a saint because he had thousands baptized more or less forcibly. The Christianization of Sweden was a slow process in the eleventh and twelfth centuries, and much of it was the work of English

---

[7] F. T. Wainwright, *Scandinavian England* (London, 1975), p.282. See also G. F. Jensen, 'The Vikings in England: A Review' in *Anglo-Saxon England*, ed. Peter Clemoes (Cambridge, 1975), pp.181-206.

missionaries. In any analysis of that process, almost as worthy of honour as Alfred himself are kings who were generals and statesmen: his son Edward the Elder and his grandson Athelstan.

What, we may ask, would a Christian priest teach an ex-Viking who asked for baptism? The official answer was given in 796 by Alcuin to Charlemagne, citing the authority of St Augustine of Hippo. 'A man must be taught first about the immortality of the soul, the future life, rewards for good and evil and both kinds of eternity. Then he must be told the particular sins for which he must suffer eternal punishment with Satan and the good deeds for which he may enjoy ever-lasting glory with Christ. The belief in the Holy Trinity must be carefully taught. The advent of the Son of God, our Lord Jesus Christ, into the world to save mankind must be expounded, with the mystery of his passion, the truth of his resurrection and ascension to heaven, and his coming to judge all nations'.

But such an outline of the official catechism scarcely explains what would have drawn the heathen Saxon or Dane in the first place. Part of the paganism of the Vikings was the myth, preserved in the great Norse Sagas of Iceland, that one day the heroic dead would be summoned by the gods from their feasting in Valhalla. The help of these warriors would be needed against the evil snake that was encircling all the earth. And that last fight would fail. Then would come the 'twilight of the gods' as chaos reigned. But in fact the Christian saviour conquered the Vikings' gods; and two scholars who have studied the story of the Vikings have asked themselves why the Christian Gospel was eventually believed as news of victory. These historians answer that the Scandinavians accepted Christianity for much the same reasons as the Anglo-Saxons. It promised prosperity in this life, and claimed to lighten the darkness surrounding it. Here was the unexpected treasure that the Viking voyages had brought home. But they add: 'perhaps in time Christianity's most conspicuous gift to the north was to add a dimension of pity to the lives of a hard people, brought up to admire and condemn but not to sympathize'.[8]

REBUILDING THE ENGLISH CHURCH

The hidden process of this conversion of ex-Vikings in England must have been helped greatly by the power, prestige and piety of Alfred's successors in the Christian monarchy of Wessex. The bones of these great kings are still treasured with his own in the mortuary chests of Winchester Cathedral: his son Edward the Elder and his grandson Athelstan.

Edward's generalship was matched by that of his sister Ethelfled, Lady of Mercia. Their joint campaign of 917-918 reconquered the Midlands and East Anglia, and before the end of Edward's reign every Danish colony south of the Humber had been annexed to Wessex. Under Athelstan English power reached out to subdue Northumbria, where Viking raiders from Ireland had established a kingdom based on York. Athelstan also conquered the British in Cornwall and made the Welsh princes his vassals. Since he was also acknowledged as King of Mercia, his boast that he was 'King of All Britain' was largely justified. It is possible to find a reason for these English kings' triumph in the fact that the Danes in England, or the Vikings from Ireland, did not develop a strong political unity of their own once the first fury of their conquest had abated. But the praise which the kings received personally was, it seems, well earned. That praise found its most lasting expression in the poem (incorporated in the Anglo-Saxon Chronicle) on the battle of Brunanburh, fought and won in 937 against a combined army of Vikings, Celtic British and Scots:

> Athelstan the King, lord of men,
> Giver of gold to warriors, and his brother too,
> Edmund the prince, won lasting glory. . . .

---

[8] Peter Foote and David Wilson, *The Viking Achievement* (London, 1970), p.416. For Scandinavian paganism, see E. O. G. Turville-Petre, *Myth and Religion of the North* (London, 1964), and two books by James Graham-Campbell, *The Vikings* with Dafydd Kidd and *The Viking World* with magnificent illustrations (both London, 1980).

In this celebration of heroic warriors the language is deliberately archaic; one in every seven of the phrases has been found in earlier poems which have also survived. But the effect is still strong:

> The king and the prince went back to their country,
> The land of Wessex, triumphing in war.
> They left behind them corpses to be food
> For the black-coated raven, with its horny beak,
> And for the eagle, white-backed and dark-breasted,
> The greedy war-hawk and that grey wild beast,
> The wolf. . . .

The Christian character of Alfred's kingdom came out more attractively in the work made possible by peace. Plegmund, an able Mercian priest who was appointed Archbishop of Canterbury in 890, led a reorganization of the now flourishing Church, creating five new dioceses (Ramsbury, Wells, Crediton, Selsey and Dorchester-on-Thames). Later, bishops were appointed to minister to the Cornish (based on St Germans) and in East Anglia (based on North Elmham). This last development was one of the fruits of the peace in the years between 955 and 980. The laws then issued in the name of King Edgar summed up the whole Anglo-Saxon conception of Christian justice; as did the supreme symbolic ceremony, the coronation of Edgar at Bath on Whit Sunday 973. The sacred character of English kingship was made clear in the oath which developed for use at coronations, whether or not these precise words were used in 973 – an oath to assure true peace to the Church of God; to 'forbid robbery and all unrighteous deeds'; and to exercise 'justice and mercy in the decision of all cases', so as to win God's mercy.

During King Edgar's peace the central figure in English religious life was St Dunstan, who presided at the coronation. He was trained for high politics as a young nobleman at Athelstan's court, and never hesitated to advise or to contradict kings. While still only a young man he had to drag one of them, Eadwig 'the Fair', back to a banquet with his lords when he had just gone to amuse himself with the ladies. Dunstan was exiled when one of the ladies involved in this in-

cident became queen. But when his ally Edgar (Eadwig's
brother) came to power and he became Archbishop of Canterbury, he showed where his heart lay – not in politics but in the
Church. At a time when the papacy itself was in eclipse (it did
not really revive until 1046), Dunstan was the ablest and most
purposeful archbishop England had known since the death of
Theodore in 690.

His purpose was the reconstruction of the Church, and his
main strategy was the revival of the monasteries. Most of the
earlier English monasteries had been destroyed by the Danes,
and those that were left were not fully under the rule of
St Benedict, which on the Continent had now become the
criterion of a strictly religious life. King Alfred's patronage of
monks and nuns had been premature. Dunstan himself was
not impetuous; to the end of his life, the monks of Canterbury
Cathedral were not strictly Benedictine, leaving that to their
neighbour and rival, St Augustine's Abbey. Nor was he a
puritan bigot; he was skilled in metalwork, painting (a drawing of himself kneeling before Christ survives), music and
organ-building. But he owed his first education to Irish monks
who were maintaining some Christian life at Glastonbury near
the village of his birth and boyhood, and while a young
nobleman he took a monk's vows. He then made his mark over
fifteen years as the pioneering abbot of Glastonbury, more
than bringing back past glories. His chief interest while archbishop was, it seems, the establishment of other Benedictine
monasteries surrounded by other great estates. Monks had
converted England to Christianity. Monks would now rescue it
from the morally ruinous effects of the Danish invasions. It has
been estimated that as a result of the enthusiasm of Dunstan
and his associates, between 960 and 1060 there grew to be
about sixty religious houses for men and women, owning
about a sixth of the land south of the Humber and the Mersey.
'The servant of God, Dunstan', as his first biographer put it,
'shone as the first abbot of the English nation'.

Dunstan's closest collaborator was Oswald, a man of Danish
descent who was both Archbishop of York and Bishop of
Worcester (the Vikings had done so much damage in the
north that the two dioceses could support only one bishop). A

third name is linked with theirs: Ethelwold, Abbot of Abingdon (where he educated King Edgar) and Bishop of Winchester. He was much more of a fanatic.

A book of bishop's blessings (a 'Benedictional') was copied and adorned for Ethelwold in Winchester between 971 and 984. Richly decorative frames surrounded the text and some exquisite miniatures. The English art of painting was in full vigour. But Ethelwold was not content to bestow blessings. Reaching into the Danelaw, his was the iron will that restored the monasteries at Ely, Peterborough and Thorney as strict and prosperous houses. On the first Saturday in Lent 964 he stormed into Winchester Cathedral and told the clergy to become Benedictine monks or to leave at once. The king's lay representative stood at the door with a drawn sword. When the clergy had gone, monks were introduced from Abingdon. That decisive day in Winchester established a peculiarly English institution, the cathedral which was also a Benedictine monastery. It also indicated where the leaders of the nation's religious life were to come from; in the last century of Anglo-Saxon England, three quarters of the bishops were monks. A clear rule of life for the monks and nuns was drawn up by Ethelwold in the *Regularis Concordia* (Monastic Agreement), published at Winchester in an Easter council under the king.[9]

Two authors among the other leaders in this revival of the Church are also remembered, partly because their writing brought Anglo-Saxon or 'Old English' prose to its classic best. One was Aelfric, a product of Ethelwold's reformed school at Winchester, who while a monk at Cerne Abbas in Dorset and at Eynsham in Oxfordshire devoted himself to the production of English Christian literature. He wrote lives of the saints; he translated the first seven books of the Old Testament and expounded other scriptures; he supplied parish priests with sermons and bishops with letters which would invigorate their clergy; he even compiled the first Latin grammar in English.

Another author rich in rhetoric but much more urgently masterful was Wulfstan, Bishop of London, promoted to hold the sees of York and Worcester together in 1002. In the first

---

[9] Translated and edited by Thomas Symons (London, 1953). Douglas Dales has provided a biography of *Dunstan, Saint and Statesman* (London 1988).

book of English political theory (*The Institutes of Polity*),
Wulfstan held up the ideal of the Anglo-Saxon state in which
the king ('Christ's substitute') exercised the eight essential
virtues – truthfulness, patience, generosity, wisdom after
taking counsel, favour to the righteous, moderation in taxes,
equity in judgements. Supporting the king were the three
classes: those who prayed, those who worked and those who
fought. And Wulfstan had the courage to say when the ideal
was not reached. In a famous sermon of 1014 he denounced
the collapse of morality in the state he knew, deliberately
repeating the warnings which Gildas had delivered when the
Anglo-Saxons came and which Alcuin had revived in the days
of the first Viking raids. It was probably the most outspoken
sermon ever preached by an English archbishop; in its own
way as ruthless as the army of Sweyn Forkbeard, then terrorizing England.[10]

FROM EDGAR TO HAROLD

The quality of the English kings declined disastrously after the
murder of St Dunstan's ally Edgar at the age of thirty-two in
975. (And Edgar was no saint: he married a nun.) King
Edgar's eldest son, Edward, was murdered at Corfe Castle in
Dorset and the guilt lay with his younger son, Ethelred – who,
although ruthless enough in gaining the crown, turned out to
be 'the Unready': the nickname means 'No Counsel'. Ethelred
has been very notorious to historians, as he was to his subjects.
Endlessly the English leaders, with no policy of concerted and
sustained resistance, paid out Danegeld to buy off trouble
from the Danes. Endlessly trouble came – for example, the
murder in 1012 of an Archbishop of Canterbury, St Alphege
(more properly Aelfeah), by the Danes during a drunken feast
at Greenwich when he had refused to allow a ransom to be
raised for his release. Sir Frank Stenton has summed up the

---

[10] See M. McC. Gatch, *Preaching and Theology in England: Aelfric and
Wulfstan* (Toronto, 1957).

impression left by a chronicle of the early eleventh century (written by a monk at Abingdon, this was the first detailed, contemporary history of England to take up the tradition of Bede). It is the impression of 'an ancient and rich society, helpless before a derisive enemy because its leaders were incapable of government'.[11]

The ineptitude of Ethelred and his chief ministers coincided with a new development in the art of war. Instead of picking up horses in England as had been the habit of earlier Vikings, the Danish army now landed cavalry, which was already trained and equipped; and probably not even Alfred, Edward or Athelstan would have been able to resist that fury. Ethelred's son, Edmund Ironside, was a far better general than his father and although he failed to secure the rest of the country he forced Sweyn Forkbeard's son Cnut to acknowledge him as King of Wessex. Then, worn out by the war, he died in 1016; and all the English acknowledged the immensely able Cnut as their king. Their acceptance was eased by the fact that he had become a Christian.

Sweyn had come to accept Christianity in Denmark, but never more than half-heartedly; Cnut, although ruthlessly brutal towards rebels actual or potential, was in his own estimation a model of piety. He took pride in being a friend of bishops. He used the Danish fleet to destroy pirates and then sent it back to Denmark. He then used England as a base from which to secure the throne of Denmark and to conquer Norway for a time. He issued to the English a law code which began with a long reminder of their religious duties; and almost all the laws appear to have been based on those of Edgar and other Anglo-Saxon lawmakers. Here as in other matters he seems to have been advised by Archbishop Wulfstan – who thus by his own statesmanship averted some of the doom he had predicted to his stunned congregation in York Minster in 1014. Cnut gave lands to reward the Danes,

---

[11] F. M. Stenton, *Anglo-Saxon England* (Oxford, 1947), p.388. The third edition of this masterly survey (1971) includes some revisions. See also his essays *Preparatory to Anglo-Saxon England*, ed. D. M. Stenton (Oxford, 1970).

particularly their chief men the 'earls', for keeping the peace in England, but the two most prominent earls to be found in the country after his reorganization were both Englishmen: Godwine of Wessex and Leofric of Mercia. Eleven years after being accepted as king of the English, Cnut travelled to Rome in order to attend the coronation of Conrad, the Holy Roman Emperor. He sent back to England a proud report of his favourable reception by 'the princes of all the peoples'. He boasted, too, of his success in obtaining concessions to ease the journeys of future English pilgrims to Rome. To that extent, therefore, the Alfred tradition prevailed even in the day of the Danish supremacy.

This could have been the beginning of a Scandinavian empire centred on an England which was increasingly prosperous; an empire proud of its laws and its churches. But when Cnut's life was cut short at the age of forty in 1035 (he was buried where his treasure was, at Winchester), he left no strong successor. None of his children reached middle age. The fascinating possibility which had been opening up was over. Eventually Edward, son of Ethelred, was elected king in 1042 and reigned until the end of 1065. He shared Cnut's piety – to the extent that in his last years he concentrated on the building of Westminster Abbey next to his main residence, and is known to history as 'the Confessor'. He was by no means as monkish as he was later made out to have been by monks; his was the piety of a king capable of worldly action. His 'greatest and only significant failure', writes one modern historian, 'was his failure to generate an heir'.[12] But he did not possess Cnut's outstanding ability. During his reign Earl Godwine of Wessex and his son Harold were not really subject to his rule, and his attempted coup against them in 1051-52 only consolidated their power. Any heir of King Edward would have to fight Earl Harold.

Part of the strength of these Earls of Wessex lay in their ability to speak for their fellow-Englishmen against the Normans who surrounded the king. Edward's mother was

[12] D. J. V. Fisher, *The Anglo-Saxon Age*, p.348. See Frank Barlow, *Edward the Confessor* (London, 1970).

Emma, the sister of Richard, Duke of Normandy; she had been married into the English royal family as a token of the Normans' response to a plea for help against the Danes. When Elthred her first husband had died, this adjustable lady had been married again to a Dane, Cnut. Edward, however, had been brought up in Normandy until invited back to England by Cnut's son Hartha Cnut at the age of twenty-five. Inevitably his ideas and his favourites were now Norman. Reflecting this, Westminster Abbey was built in the style of the churches attached to royal or ducal palaces in France. Inevitably, too, he was no friend to the overmighty Earl Godwine. His own elder brother Alfred had been captured by Earl Godwine's men and handed over by them to the Danes, who had blinded him and allowed him to die in misery. Although Edward was married to Earl Godwine's daughter, not surprisingly the marriage was cold and childless.

When King Edward died a week after the consecration of his fashionable and therefore French abbey, the Normans felt that their hour had come. Duke William immediately began preparations to conquer a country which he claimed — almost certainly with truth — Edward had definitely promised him. Himself descended from Norsemen, William was to take up the task snatched by a murderer from the great King Cnut thirty years before.

THE NORMAN CONQUEST

While in France Earl Harold had already sworn loyalty to William (in 1064). He was, however, elected and consecrated king in Westminster on the very day of King Edward's burial. He reigned for nine months. An able man, he might have founded a strong new Anglo-Saxon dynasty had the fortunes of war been different; but the dice were loaded against him. His own brother Tostig, who had been the rapacious Earl of Northumbria until the Northumbrians had rebelled against his rule, now became his enemy, allying with the Scots and the Norwegians in a brutal attempt to seize the throne. At first their campaign was successful. Near York the troops of the northern English earls, Edwin and Morcar, were cut down. But on Monday, 25 September 1066 King Harold himself met the invaders in battle at Stamford Bridge. It was the last battle between the English and the Vikings from east or north. These invaders had darkened two and a half centuries; but Stamford Bridge saw a complete victory for Harold and for England. Tostig and the Norwegian king were killed. Only a remnant of their routed army survived to sail home. Unfortunately, however, these were not the only adventurers willing to try their luck against the questionable new English king. To the south lived hard men sprung from the Vikings of a previous generation: the Normans.

The expeditionary force assembled by Duke William's promises of wealth seems to have numbered some six thousand. It embarked two days after the battle in the north and found an undefended landing place at Pevensey on the south coast. During the next few weeks Harold gave another impressive display of kingship and generalship, settling the affairs of the north and marching some 250 miles into Sussex. There he waited for his own troops to recover and to be joined by the main English militia from the southern shires (the *fyrd*), which would have greatly outnumbered the Normans. But he was not joined by the northern earls and the southern *fyrd* was slow to assemble. Perhaps there was treachery; perhaps not. He trusted too much in his defensive position, a hill which seemed to block the road to London. On Saturday 14 October he was attacked by the Normans, who were forced to gamble.

At an early stage in the battle Duke William had to exercise all his personal courage to rally his left flank. But as the day wore on his mounted knights were able to dislodge the English infantry by pretending to flee and, when the English pursued them on foot, turning for a massacre. It was a manoeuvre so risky that only trained and disciplined soldiers could have brought it off. To the end the English fought courageously, but by nightfall their king, his brothers and the flower of their army lay dead. Even then there might have been another more successful battle against the Normans when the main English army at last assembled – if only the English had possessed another leader.

As it was, William conquered because he now had no real rival. In order to show his determination and particularly in order to alarm London, he devastated the countryside. It was not long before the city opened its gates. Terrified bishops were assembled to officiate at his coronation in Westminster Abbey on Christmas Day, although the traditional acclamation was misunderstood by nervous soldiers as the start of a riot.

The country's great churches were almost all either burned down (in accidents which were not inconvenient) or else brazenly pulled down to make way for Norman work. In Canterbury a fire happened; in Winchester the old cathedral was demolished when the largest church in Europe, a cathedral with a nave five hundred feet long, had been built in 1079-93 on the orders of the Conqueror's two cousins, Walkelin bishop of the diocese and his brother Simon, prior of the monastery. One of the Conqueror's own chaplains, William of Poitiers, left on record an indiscreet boast about the quantity and quality of the treasures sent from England to adorn churches in Normandy and Rome. This loot must have included a large amount of the *opus Anglicanum*, the needlework for which English women were famous throughout Europe. A few fine specimens remained in Durham, hidden in St Cuthbert's coffin where they had been placed by the great King Athelstan in 934; and when the Norman conquest was commemorated in a tapestry exhibited in his cathedral by Odo Bishop of Bayeux, he ordered English needlewomen to do the work. Such work still suggests something about the quality of the civilization which perished with King Harold on the hill near Hastings that October evening in 1066. Fortunately, too, some books remained in English monasteries. Some of them have preserved to our own day the excellence of the art honouring the Bible in the period of the 'Winchester School' – the period which in secular life had been the sordid time of Ethelred and Danegeld. There is nothing degenerate about these books, with their calmly beautiful colours and the excitement of their free-flowing line drawings. Nor is there anything second-rate about the small quantity of sculptures, ivory carvings and metalwork which has also survived the Normans' pillaging, some of it in museums far from England.

The people of the Anglo-Saxon Church did not escape the consequences of 1066. Some of the elite could escape abroad. English exiles took up service in Constantinople, to defend the still-surviving eastern empire of Rome. Agatha, daughter of King Harold, married the King of the Russians. But at home revolts against the Normans, such as that led by Hereward the Wake in the Fens with the monastery of Ely as its base, proved futile. English bishops and abbots found themselves gradually replaced by Normans. English parish priests found that they had to accept the authority of new, and probably much harsher, lords. And the English Christian laity disappeared into an underworld.

It is rather surprising how much pride was still taken in the English heritage under the Norman regime. The Anglo-Saxon Chronicles were still compiled in at least three monasteries (the chronicler at Peterborough wrote in Old English until 1154), and books such as those of Bede in Latin, or Alfred or Aelfric in English, continued to be copied. A little group of monks mainly English (but including a few Frenchmen such as the ex-knight, Reinfrid) reoccupied Bede's old monastery at Jarrow in the 1070s. A Norman monk-bishop then summoned them to found a monastery around the shrine of St Cuthbert in Durham Cathedral; and they took what they believed were Bede's bones with them. The latest datable Old English poem to have survived, written about 1105, praised Durham, where 'God's servant lies and waits for Judgement'. And two historians, monks with English mothers, contemporaries who died during the 1140s, both set themselves the task of doing for their own time what Bede had done for his. Orderic of St Evroul wrote an *Ecclesiastical History* of the Normans in the setting of Christendom, and William of Malmesbury wrote on *Deeds of the Kings* and *Deeds of the Bishops* in England. But they were not true successors of Bede. Their histories were far more untidy, because they lacked his simplifying vision of the emergence of a Christian people. Orderic knew that the Normans had done much for monks, and as half a Norman himself he was proud enough of their victories, but he had no illusions about their turbulence and harshness. William, who had met many of the leading men of the day, exercised tact in describing them. But he had a sharp eye for their selfishness. In their own ways, Orderic and William paid their tributes to the side defeated in 1066, to their mothers' memories.

However, only the Church preserved the public use of English. Parish priests — or at least the good shepherds among them — would expound the gospels in the language which the natives spoke at home. But the language of public worship and of formal business in the Church was Latin and the lay elite spoke French. It has been reckoned that by the middle of the twelfth century 'it appeared very possible that French and not English would be the language of England'.[13] Even when English revived and flourished as the 'Middle English' of the fourteenth and fifteenth centuries, it preserved for ever traces of the colonial period — the time when the enslaved natives had looked after the *sheep* and their French-speaking masters sitting around the fire in the hall had eaten the *mutton*; when the English had been responsible for the *cows* or the *pigs* and the Normans had enjoyed the *beef* and the *pork*.

In what remained of the eleventh century, it cannot have been easy for anyone to echo in English the creed to be found in King Alfred's translation of Boethius: 'I hold, as do all Christian men, that it is God's providence that rules, and not fate.'

---

[13] R. W. Chambers, *On the Continuity of English Prose from Alfred to More and His School* (Oxford, 1932), p.lxxxix.

PART ONE: FURTHER READING
(in addition to the books in the footnotes)

1 Prelude: Romans and Celts

BARLEY, M. W., and HANSON, R. P. C. (ed.), *Christianity in Britain, 300-700*, Leicester, 1968.

CHADWICK, N. K., *The Age of the Saints in the Early Celtic Church*, Oxford, 1963.

COLLINGWOOD, R. G., and RICHMOND, I. A., *The Archaeology of Roman Britain*, revised, London, 1969.

FRERE, S., *Britannia*, London, 1969.

HARDINGE, L., *The Celtic Church in Britain*, London, 1972.

LIVERSIDGE, J., *Britain in the Roman Empire*, London, 1968.

SALWAY, P., *Roman Britain*, Oxford, 1981.

THOMAS, C., *Christianity in Roman Britain to AD 500*, London, 1981.

2 The Conversion of the English

BLAIR, P. H., *The World of Bede* (virtually a commentary on the *History*), London, 1970.
Northumbria in the Days of Bede, London, 1977.

BONNER, G. (ed.), *Famulus Christi: Essays in Commemoration of the Thirteenth Centenary of the Birth of the Venerable Bede*, London, 1976.

COLGRAVE, B., and MYNORS, R. A. B. (ed.), *Bede's Ecclesiastical History of the English People*, Oxford, 1969.

DUCKETT, E. S., *Anglo-Saxon Saints and Scholars*, New York, 1947.

GIRVAN, R., and BRUCE-MITFORD, R., *Beowulf and the Seventh Century*, London 1971.

WEBB, J. F., *Lives of the Saints* (translated in Penguin Classics), London, 1965.

3 The Anglo-Saxon Achievement

BARLOW, F., *The English Church 1000-1066*, revised, London 1978.

DUCKETT, E. S., *St Dunstan of Canterbury*, London, 1955.

FISHER, E. R., *The Greater Anglo-Saxon Churches*, London, 1962.

LEVISON, W., *England and the Continent in the Eighth Century*, Oxford, 1946.

LOYN, H. R., *The Vikings in Britain*, London, 1977.

PARSONS, D. (ed.), *Tenth Century Studies*, London, 1975.

RICE, D. T., *English Art 871-1100*, Oxford, 1952.

ROBINSON, J. A., *The Times of St Dunstan*, Oxford, 1923.

SAWYER, P. H., *The Age of the Vikings*, revised, London, 1971.

WALLACH, L., *Alcuin and Charlemagne*, Ithaca, N.Y., 1959.

General

BROOKS, R., *The Early History of the Church of Canterbury*, Leicester, 1984.

CAMPBELL, J., JOHN, E., and WORMALD, P., *The Anglo Saxons*, London, 1981.

DEANSLEY, M., *The Pre-Conquest Church in England*, revised, London, 1963.

Sidelights on the Anglo-Saxon Church, London, 1962.

GATCH, M. McC., *Loyalties and Traditions: Man and His World in Old English Literature*, New York, 1971.

GODFREY, J., *The Church in Anglo-Saxon England*, Cambridge, 1962.

KENDRICK, F. D., *Anglo-Saxon Art to AD 900*, London, 1938.

Late Saxon and Viking Art, London, 1949.

KENNEDY, C. W., *Early English Christian Poetry*, London, 1952.

SWANTON, M. (ed.), *Anglo-Saxon Prose*, London, 1975.

TAYLOR, H. M. and J., *Anglo-Saxon Architecture*, 2 vols, Cambridge, 1965.

WHITELOCK, D. (ed.), *English Historical Documents, c.500-1042*, London, 1955.

WILSON, D., *The Anglo-Saxons* (mainly archaeological), revised, London, 1971.

Part Two

THE MIDDLE
AGES

CHAPTER FOUR

FREEDOM UNDER THE KING

Canterbury Cathedral . Choir and High Altar .

THE CONQUEROR'S CHURCH

The main interest in the next period, 1066-1215, is political. Anglo-Saxon England had been ruined by its political failures, more fundamentally than by its military defeats. It was the work of William the Conqueror to impose order on the country, although it was the no less essential work of other men coming after him to impose law on the king. And the Church knew that both in the establishment of law and in the winning of freedom its own welfare was at stake.

A chant called *Royal Praises* has survived. Its use under

William I probably began at his coronation, and there is evidence about its frequent use under Henry III two centuries later. The clerks who sang it first solemnly saluted their monarch, enthroned in state: 'To the most serene William, the great and peacegiving king, crowned by God, life and victory!' They continued to sing of Christ's victory, in such a way as to suggest that the king's was not very different. And the fervent royalism expressed in this chant was defended by an anonymous priest in Rouen, making a contribution to political theory about 1100. This priest believed, of course, that the king's beliefs and morals ought to be blameless; but the king was sacred, his right to rule was given directly by God, all his priests were his subjects, and the pope had no power to intervene.[1]

For most of the time, the bishops of medieval England were enthusiastic advocates and agents of the king who had been 'crowned by God'. The explanation is not merely that almost all of them owed their appointments to him. The service of England's Christian monarchy was held to be a sacred duty not only by time-servers but also by some bishops whose spiritual integrity matched their intellectual power. This tradition reached back deep into Anglo-Saxon England, but at the head of the line after the Norman Conquest stood the Conqueror's archbishop, Lanfranc.

Although William did not want an immediate change at Canterbury, eventually Stigand had to go. A worldly man, he had been given the archbishopric by Earl Godwine while retaining his income as Bishop of Winchester, and his appointment had never been recognized in Rome. He made room for Lanfranc, who was archbishop for almost twenty years from 1070. During the king's many absences from England this austere and able monk shared political responsibility with two Norman bishops who had come over in 1066: Odo of Bayeux the king's half-brother and Geoffrey de Mowbray, Bishop of Coutances. He was, however, more in the king's confidence than they could ever be – a status recognized

---

[1] See G. H. Williams, *The Norman Anonymous of 1100* (Cambridge, Mass., 1951).

by his position as the richest landowner in England after the king. They were essentially Norman aristocrats, rewarded for their support of William first by rich bishoprics in Normandy and then by large estates in England. But they were always liable to turn traitor; on suspicion of this, Bishop Odo was imprisoned in 1082. Lanfranc, on the other hand, was a monk through and through, a man whose loyalty to William had become a matter of firm religious principle. When Norman earls rebelled against William in 1075, it was he who called out the English militia and assured his absent king that there was no cause for alarm.

An Italian, he practised as a lawyer in Pavia and then crossed the Alps to earn his living as a schoolmaster in Avranches in Normandy. He was drawn to the life of a monk at Bec, only eight years after the foundation of that monastery by Herluin. The community he joined was still so poor that he was persuaded to make some money for it by taking in pupils – and was still so disorganized that he was persuaded to administer it as prior. Duke William joined the circle of his admirers. The story told of their first real encounter throws light on the characters of the two men. William's marriage with Matilda was condemned by the strictest churchmen because they were too closely related. Lanfranc accordingly opposed it and was banished from Normandy for the offence. Meeting his duke, he asked for a better horse so that he might ride more quickly into exile. William's interest was stirred by the brave joke, it is said; the two men became friends and after many talks Lanfranc was sent to persuade the pope to issue a dispensation for the marriage. The pope consented if William would found two monasteries, and of one of these – St Stephen's, Caen – Lanfranc became the first abbot.

Much of what he wrote has been lost, but from his years at Bec and Caen there survive a number of books. These show his great talents as a master of grammar and argument; as a commentator on the psalms, St Paul's letters and the Latin Fathers of the Church; and as one who defended the transformation of the bread and wine into the Body and Blood of Christ (the doctrine later defined as 'transubstantiation') against another Norman teacher, Berengar. Berengar had used the newly developed skill in reasoned debate ('dialectic') in order to insist that Christ's own phrase 'this is my body' demonstrated that 'this' remained bread. In the eyes of those of his contemporaries who interested themselves in such matters Lanfranc had been even more rational, as well as much more orthodox, in his counter-argument, insisting that the 'bread' was now bread only in appearance; its essence was the body of Christ. Such was the renowned teacher who in his late fifties, when he had already refused the archbishopric of Rouen in Normandy, was persuaded by the Conqueror to set the English Church in order.

Some of his reorganization while Archbishop of Canterbury proved abortive. He attempted to make himself ecclesiastically supreme throughout England, Wales, Scotland, Ireland and the northern isles. He quoted Bede's history and impressive charters forged by the Canterbury monks (we need not suppose that he knew they were forgeries). His successor persisted in the attempt, but it had to be abandoned – with the result that throughout the Middle Ages (indeed, until the twentieth century) only a papal 'legate', who need not be the Archbishop of Canterbury, could unite the clergy of the provinces of Canterbury and York into a single council to consider the welfare of the English Church. Lanfranc also failed in an effort to insist that in future all the parish priests of England should have the sex-lives of monks. Even he did not insist that the clergy should put away the wives or the other women to be found established in most of the parsonages, and the evidence suggests that the practice of clerical marriage or concubinage remained common long after his day. Illustrations in medieval manuscripts show many priests in gaily coloured gowns – in green, yellow or scarlet; the sombre black does not seem to have become standard until the fifteenth century, by when clerical marriage was unknown. But in many other spheres where he sought order, order was established by the Conqueror's archbishop.

Lanfranc introduced from the Continent the new ecclesiastical or 'canon' law; in his day it was not as elaborate as it later became, but at least he consigned Anglo-Saxon church law into oblivion. In the library of Trinity College, Cambridge, is preserved a law book of Decretals brought over by Lanfranc from the library at Bec: it is a missionary lawyer's Bible, the key to the whole difference between this systematic, long-lasting, reform and the revival over which King Edgar and Archbishop Dunstan had presided. In Anglo-Saxon England there had been no neat separation of church courts from the ordinary courts of the state. From the national *witenagemot* downwards, one court would handle all matters – secular, ecclesiastical or moral. Now (in 1072) ecclesiastical and moral questions were withdrawn from the ordinary courts and a separate system of church courts was set up, presided over by bishops and archdeacons or their deputies. Thus were sown the seeds of future conflict between Church and State.

Lanfranc took a special interest in reshaping the English monasteries on the best Continental models, and compiled his *Monastic Constitutions* in order to arrange the monk's life in minute detail. The monasteries thus reformed included Canterbury Cathedral, which was rebuilt after a fire.[2] Church councils were held to regulate church life outside the monasteries. When he was free to do so the king presided, but Lanfranc's was the master mind in details. Each diocese was now to have clear boundaries, with a centre of population as its own centre. The vast, disordered Anglo-Saxon dioceses of Selsey, Sherborne, Wells, Lichfield, Dorchester and Elmham were given new centres in Chichester, Salisbury, Bath, Chester, Lincoln and Thetford (later Norwich) with new bishops to rule them. It was the logical completion of the policy begun under Edward the Confessor, when the diocese of Crediton had been given a new centre in Exeter.

While the English Church was being reformed in these and other ways, claims that only the papacy could order the life of the Church in accordance with the mind of Christ were resisted. In Rome it was hoped that William would be in a weak position because of what he owed to papal support of his claim in 1066 – and because of the personal power of the new pope, formerly Archdeacon Hildebrand, before whom the

[2] *The Monastic Constitutions of Lanfranc* have been translated and edited by David Knowles (London, 1951).

emperor Henry IV humbled himself in the snow at Canossa. But William had no intention of yielding to the demand for allegiance which reached distant England from the pope. 'I never promised it', the king replied in 1080, 'nor do I find that my predecessors ever paid it to yours'. The king exercised a veto over the recognition of any pope, over the reception of papal letters or envoys in England, and over punishment by the Church of the leading aristocrats, the king's tenants-in-chief; and he advised Lanfranc to ignore repeated requests to come to Rome for instructions. And Gregory VII, normally both inflexible and passionate, accepted the rebuff. One reason was his fear that William might recognize a rival claimant to the papacy. But he also had to acknowledge the effectiveness of the reforms being carried out by Lanfranc in alliance with his invincible king.[3]

Four other bishops and twenty-two abbots came over from Norman monasteries to work in England under the Conqueror. Given the conditions of the time, the Normanization of church leadership was inevitable. Bishops and abbots could not be financed except by the grant of estates which in almost all cases now carried with them the obligation to provide a stated number of knights for the king's army – the essence of 'feudalism'. They had to be men on whose loyalty the king could rely. Accordingly William took care not to reproduce in England the pattern which existed in Normandy, where many of the bishops were recruited from a small circle of aristocratic families. As bishops, he preferred monks or his own chaplains. However, among the imported Norman bishops only one, Herfast, who was sent to East Anglia, was discreditable: Lanfranc had to tell him to switch his attention from dice to the study of the Bible. And among the Englishmen left undisturbed until their deaths were two saints: Ethelwig, Abbot of Evesham, and Wulfstan, Bishop of Worcester. St Wulfstan was a monk, elected bishop by his brethren in 1062. His continuance as bishop, surrounded by Englishmen, until 1095 is explained partly by the strong support he gave to William I against rebellious barons and to William II against the Welsh.

---

[3] See Margaret Gibson, *Lanfranc of Bec* (Oxford, 1978).

But his *Life*, written by the monk Coleman as the last echo of Anglo-Saxon ecclesiastical history, makes it clear that a man so holy (yet not stupid) would never have collaborated with his country's new colonial rulers had he not believed that this acceptance of fact was in the interests of the English Church. Wulfstan was not ashamed to be the colleague of Lanfranc.

A twentieth-century authority judged that this Italian lawyer played a greater part in organizing the Church in England than any other Archbishop of Canterbury between Theodore of Tarsus in the seventh century and Thomas Cranmer in the sixteenth. But, he added, when praising Lanfranc it would be unjust to ignore the Conqueror himself – 'a ruler resolved of set purpose to raise the whole level of ecclesiastical discipline in his dominions'.[4]

A bastard (his mother was said to be a tanner's daughter in Falaise), William became Duke of Normandy while a little boy. He developed into a great man in the hardest of schools: fourteen years of almost continuous war against the other descendants of pirates who now constituted the aristocracy of Normandy. Almost all the guardians of his boyhood were murdered during those terrible years. The man who survived was fiercely determined, but cunning enough not to be impatient; outstanding in his age as a general but also as a diplomat; ruthless and illiterate, but sharing to the full the Norman aristocracy's admiration for monks, the cavalry of God. Such qualities won some tributes from the English. When he died in 1087, 'things both good and bad' were written in one of the Anglo-Saxon Chronicles. Although a brutal and grasping oppressor, the Conqueror was also 'very wise . . . and stronger than any predecessor of his had been'.

SEEKING A CHRISTIAN KING

The Conqueror's tragedy was that he had no power to make his sons men like him. The eldest, Robert, whom he intended

---

[4] David Knowles, *The Monastic Order in England* (Cambridge, 1940), pp.93, 143.

to be Duke of Normandy, when aroused could be as ferocious as his father – but was so lacking in military skill and in general intelligence that he could not hold the duchy down. He spent the last twenty-seven years of his life in prison. For some of this time he was in Cardiff castle, and a Welsh poem containing the line 'Woe to him that is not old enough to die' is attributed to him. He lived until the age of eighty, and his wooden effigy is still to be seen in Gloucester Cathedral.

William the Ruddy or Rufus did fulfil his father's intention that he should be King of the English and was a strong soldier, but it was typical of him that he sold vacant bishoprics for cash, incurring all the Church's condemnation of 'simony' and not gaining bishops with moral authority over the clergy. When Lanfranc died he kept the archbishopric of Canterbury vacant, preferring to transfer its revenues to his exchequer rather than to secure its support for his throne. It seems that he resented the years when, at his father's command, he had been Lanfranc's pupil in Canterbury. It was also typical of his lack of discretion that when in 1093 he did allow an appointment (he was terror-stricken because he thought he was dying), the appointment was an error, politically speaking. He nominated for Canterbury a theologian without a trace of Lanfranc's interest in politics and without any of his willingness to co-operate with worldly men.

The archbishop was Anselm, who had spent thirty-three years as a monk at Bec. He had been generally expected to follow Lanfranc ever since the latter's death in 1089, but that did not make the appointment sensible – or, it seems, genuinely attractive to him. Gradually Anselm, without being willing to renounce any of the bishops' wealth, adopted an extreme position. He held that no bishop should express obedience by doing homage to a mere king – whereas Lanfranc had never hesitated to support a king's right to sentence a bishop such as Odo of Bayeux (or the far more religiously minded William of St Calais, Bishop of Durham) for disloyalty. An archbishop so lacking in a taste for practical affairs would probably not have acquired a reputation so immense as Anselm's, had there not been the dramatic contrast between him and his king. William Rufus scandalized a brutal

age by flaunting his contempt for religion, his greed for money
and his homosexual practices. 'By the holy face of Lucca!' he
once swore to the meek and saintly Gandulf, Bishop of
Rochester. 'I shall not repay God with good for the evil he has
done me!' Against him was pitted St Anselm, to whose
character we shall return.

The Conqueror's third son, Henry, outwitted his brothers,
defeating and imprisoning Robert and almost certainly inspir-
ing the murder of William Rufus while they were both hunting in the New Forest one August afternoon in 1100. He did
much to secure order and justice in his dominions, and after
his death people looked back on his reign as a golden age. His
merits or promises as a king were such that the saintly Anselm
helped to establish him by turning a blind eye to the probability of conspiracy to murder, by accepting his hasty coronation by the Bishop of London, and by marrying him to a
descendant of the old English dynasty, Princess Matilda of
Scotland. But Henry lacked his father's strength of character,
and modern historians incline to the view that his chief interest in the extension of royal justice in England lay in its
profitability to finance the wars in France. The prosperity of
the English Church in his reign (one sign of which was the
creation of the diocese of Ely in 1109) does not seem to have
been due to his initiative. The author of a modern study concludes that 'it is peculiarly difficult to construct an account
around the personality of Henry. The king is an elusive
character with a marked capacity for concealing his motives
and emotions'.[5]

The Conqueror's sons, although so unattractive, were
served by able churchmen. Ranulf Flambard, Bishop of
Durham, was the chief minister of William Rufus. Clearly he
was not fit to be a Christian bishop, but he deserves some
credit for his agile industry in running the country – and for
the architecture he commissioned at all three of the churches
with which he was connected: St Martin's church in Dover,
Christchurch in Hampshire and the nave of Durham
Cathedral. Although Flambard fell from power on Henry I's

---

[5] Martin Brett, *The English Church under Henry I* (Oxford, 1975), p.3.

accession and had to escape to his native Normandy, it says something for his cheerfully secular energy that he was able to make first himself, then his brother and then his son Bishop of Lisieux, before dying (after a peaceful and apparently penitent old age) in the recovered possession of his Durham bishopric. A characteristic glimpse of him at the height of his power comes in the story of how once he attempted to seduce his mistress's niece, Theodora. Saying she would first close the door, she escaped through it instead – and, having beaten off another man's arduous attempt to marry her legally, lived to become a famous recluse and prioress, Christina of Markyate.[6]

Far more respectable – although he, too, openly acknowledged that the law of priestly celibacy was not for him – was Henry I's chief minister, Roger, Bishop of Salisbury. One chronicler says that the king first came across him in Normandy and was delighted by the rapidity with which he could say Mass; but this bishop's serious merit was that he wasted no time as an administrator. As 'justiciar' he was, it seems, the true architect of almost everything that men later praised about the reign of Henry I. The Anglo-Norman state disintegrated into civil war on the king's death; his only legitimate son had been drowned when the *White Ship* met a storm in the Channel and its crew, like their passengers, were drunk. But Bishop Roger remained steadily at the helm of such law and order as survived. He was also a faithful family man. His wife's name was Matilda; his son Roger was chancellor of the kingdom, another son (or nephew) worked in the exchequer, his nephew Nigel (Bishop of Ely) was treasurer, and another nephew, Alexander Bishop of Lincoln, was prominent at court. Although for some unknown reason they were known by the surname Poore, this family had great wealth and influence and deserved them, for they were 'the real moulders of the highly organized royal household administration and the financial machine, which even all the disturbances of Stephen's unquiet reign could not destroy'.[7]

---

[6] For Flambard see R. W. Southern in *Medieval Humanism and Other Studies* (Oxford, 1970), pp.182-205. C. H. Talbot edited the *Life of Christina of Markyate* (Oxford, 1959).

The Poore family supported the claim of Stephen of Blois to the throne on the death of Henry I, presumably because they distrusted the capacity of Henry's daughter Matilda. She was an ill-tempered and foolish woman who remembered too often that she was an emperor's widow. But Stephen did not have an unarguable claim: his mother Adela was the Conqueror's daughter. Nor, as it turned out, did he have much of a character to argue for him. When he moved against the Poores, with his eyes on the castles and treasures which they had taken care to amass, he lost the Church's support.

One of those alienated from King Stephen (partly by his treatment of the Poores) was his brother, Henry of Blois, the immensely rich Abbot of Glastonbury and Bishop of Winchester. More gifted than Stephen, this royal monk was elected Archbishop of Canterbury, only to find that at Stephen's request the pope refused to allow the move or 'translation' from Winchester. As a consolation he was appointed papal legate, thus taking precedence over Canterbury; and he tried to get Winchester made into an archbishopric. For eight years no subject in the kingdom was more powerful. His enthusiasm for art is shown by his commissioning of the Winchester Bible, the giant among twelfth-century English manuscripts, enriched by the art of at least six masters. His affection for the English past is shown by his ordering the removal of the mortuary chests containing the bones of the West Saxon kings from Hyde Abbey to his own cathedral (where they have remained). He was an enlightened patron of architecture and a connoisseur of antiques. While on a visit to Rome, he once amazed the crowd by going to the market place to buy ancient statues. When his brother gradually lost control of the country and finally died, Henry of Blois found it wisest to spend a period reorganizing the finances of the famous monastery of Cluny in France, where he had been trained as a young man. Under Henry II he returned to Winchester to perform the role of an elder

---

[7] H. A. Cronne, *The Reign of Stephen* (London, 1970), p.219. E. J. Kealey has provided a biography of *Roger of Salisbury, Viceroy of England* (Berkeley, Cal., 1972).

statesman together with the less expected duties of a conscientious diocesan bishop. 'For all the adventures and intrigues
and extravagances and ambitions of his middle life', writes a
modern scholar with a personal tendency to austerity, 'Henry
had always remained not only blameless in his private life but
also unsoured, uncoarsened, unhardened and undefiled'.[8] He
is best remembered as the founder of the Hospital of St Cross
in Winchester, the greatest of all medieval almshouses for the
poor.

The archbishop elected when Henry of Blois was disappointed was Theobald, who like Anselm had been Abbot of
Bec.[9] He regarded a stable monarchy as essential to the good
order of the Church. Becoming convinced (as was the pope)
that such a monarchy would never be established under
Stephen or his son Eustace, he arranged the treaty by which
Stephen accepted the succession of the Empress Matilda's son,
Henry II. He collaborated with the new king until his own
death in 1161. His household at Canterbury became a centre
of ecclesiastical law and administration. It trained four future
archbishops and six future bishops, and as was natural some of
these took part in the government of the country. It was
Theobald who recommended the most brilliant member of his
staff, Thomas Becket, Archdeacon of Canterbury, formerly
clerk to the sheriffs of London, to serve King Henry as his
chancellor in 1155. He once summed up his approach in a
letter to Henry: 'When the members of the Church are united
in loyalty and love, when princes show due reverence to priests
and priests render faithful service to princes, then do kingdoms enjoy that true peace and tranquility which must always
be the goal of our desire'.[10]

The theory of the Christian monarchy encapsulated in that
sentence was worked out at length in a treatise on politics and
morality.

At the turn of the 1150s and 1160s, a period while Thomas

[8] David Knowles, *The Episcopal Colleagues of Thomas Becket* (Cambridge, 1951), p.36.
[9] See A. Saltman, *Theobald, Archbishop of Canterbury* (London, 1956).
[10] W. L. Warren, *Henry II* (London, 1973), p.422.

Becket was superintending the siege of Toulouse in France, Archbishop Theobald's learned secretary, John of Salisbury, dedicated and sent to him a new book. It was his *Policraticus*, or 'Statesman's Manual'. Like many another medieval treatise, it compared the State with a man's body. Of course the priests constituted the soul of this body. But the peasants were its feet, the soldiers its hands, the judges its eyes – and the king was its head. Although the king received his authority from God through the clergy (whose own authority was higher), it was he who supplied the brain-power which kept the whole body functioning harmoniously. Under such leadership, the peaceful progress of a society inspired by the Christian culture of Paris and Chartres (which was what John of Salisbury really cared about) would be secure.[11]

THE CHURCH UNDER HENRY II

After Theobald's death in 1161, Henry II chose Thomas Becket as Archbishop of Canterbury. We shall later make an attempt to understand the sense in which this extraordinary man was a saint. Here we ask only why he was the central figure in a heated controversy about Church and State.

The king was astonished when his friend became critical of him only a few months after his promotion, and had the two men remained close it is hard to see that England would have been less Christian. If Becket had stayed on as Chancellor of England as was the king's intention, the new archbishop would not have been called upon to administer any policy hostile to the vital interests of the Church. Or if Gilbert Foliot, Bishop of Hereford, had become Archbishop of Canterbury instead of Bishop of London on Theobald's death (as, it seems, both he and the monks at Canterbury hoped), the Church would not have suffered. Foliot was no courtier. His life as an austere abbot at Gloucester, and as a bishop active in his diocese,

---

[11] See *The World of John of Salisbury*, ed. M. Wilks (Oxford, 1984).

proved that he belonged fully to the movement for greater discipline and holiness in the Church under the pope's inspiration. His dislike of Becket cannot be put down to mere jealousy. He sincerely despised his archbishop. To him Becket was a fool, whose quarrel with the king involved no question of faith or morals.[12]

Naturally the matter would not have been expressed like that in Rome. To papal Rome in the Middle Ages, the increase of its power at the expense of kings was always a question of faith and morals. But it is significant that the pope did not make the exiled Becket a cardinal or a member of his own court. It was not until Becket had been out of England for six years that Pope Alexander III threatened Henry II with the penalties of excommunication and interdict. These penalties were to bring King John to his knees; and the threat of them now made Henry II swallow his pride, so that he allowed Becket to go home. The pope's patience during the previous six years is remarkable. More curiously still, neither interdict nor excommunication followed the archbishop's murder. It seems that the pope was not entirely convinced about the martyr. His letters show irritation at Becket's independence, indiscretion and obstinacy.

The famous quarrel between the king and the archbishop became so bitter because of personal factors. These included Henry's deep resentment that his former friend, on whom he had loaded honours and whom he had taken into his close confidence, had picked one quarrel after another with him. Another factor, as the drama moved towards its finale, was the archbishop's determination to get killed. John of Salisbury was a loyal secretary to Thomas Becket as he had been loyal to old Theobald, but it is clear that he was puzzled. Here he was dealing with a man fundamentally different from the ecclesiastical politicians whom he so shrewdly portrayed in his *History of the Pontiffs*. Becket, as John learned, was a man driven by no common, earthly ambition; yet he had none of Theobald's quiet acceptance of monastic discipline in con-

---

[12] See *Gilbert Foliot and His Letters*, ed. A. Morey and C. N. L. Brooke (Cambridge, 1965).

fidence of the heavenly reward. In the end John had to abandon his strange master to his chosen destiny, saying: 'no one here wants to die for the sake of dying except you'.

Admittedly Henry was being provocative when, having twice extracted from Becket promises to obey the ancient customs of the realm, he had these customs drawn up in a formal code (the Constitutions of Clarendon, 1164) – and demanded that the archbishop should publicly accept them. Becket refused to endorse the Constitutions by formally sealing them and soon made it very clear that he repented on his former assent. Although at the beginning of the controversy his fellow-bishops were more consistent than he was in refusing to accept the 'customs', they later became very alarmed at the dangers in the crisis and ineffectively tried to heal the breach. The bishops' confusion is, however, not entirely surprising. Their stand against the Constitutions of Clarendon corresponded with the generally accepted teaching in the Church of the day, now that the Church's canon law had been codified much more clearly than in Lanfranc's or Anselm's time (thanks largely to the work of the monk Gratian).[13] On the other hand, almost all the customs included in these Constitutions of 1164 had been the practice in England before the Church had taken advantage of the anarchy of Stephen's reign. And they continued to be the general practice in France, for example. On the question of appeals to the papal court, what Henry II wanted was to be asked for his consent first; and that had certainly been the demand of William the Conqueror. On the question of clerics who were criminals (a question created by the Conqueror's insistence that 'spiritual persons' should be dealt with by the bishops), what he wanted was that they should be tried by an ecclesiastical court, degraded from holy orders if found guilty, and handed over to a royal official for punishment.

---

[13] The theological background has been studied by Beryl Smalley in *The Becket Controversy and the Schools* (Oxford, 1973), and the legal background by L. C. Gabel in *Benefit of Clergy in the Later Middle Ages* (Northampton, Mass., 1929) and Henry Mayr-Harting in *Journal of Ecclesiastical History* (London, 1965), pp.39-53.

When the drama was over — when Henry had been scourged in public at the martyr's tomb in Canterbury and poor Bishop Foliot had had to undergo his worst ordeal by reading out the royal declaration of penitence — it was found that the working of English law had changed less than men expected.

The only major concessions on the king's side were two. First, appeals to Rome were to be allowed as a last resort in ecclesiastical controversies. Second, a cleric convicted of a crime in a church court would not be punished by the secular authority. But neither of these concessions, not even thè second which was humiliating, necessarily spelt disaster to the State. The king had to come to terms with the pope's growing authority; even the Constitutions of Clarendon had envisaged *some* appeals to Rome. Henry could now gain from a deal with the papacy, as was to be demonstrated in the bargain struck by his son, John. And clerical criminals could still be condemned in the king's court, and suffer the confiscation of their goods there and then, before being allowed to escape to the bishop's court by pleading 'benefit of clergy'. In the bishop's court the old-fashioned method of 'compurgation' was used; twelve neighbours of substance had to be gathered to swear to the innocence of the accused cleric. Most of the accused were then released, but if they were so guilty as to be notorious they could be imprisoned for life in the bishop's prison. Should they be released by the bishop, or escape, they could be outlawed and forced to flee the country. The over-riding practical need, we may conclude, was to have justice which actually worked. The papacy's legal processes, which had hitherto been subject to many delays and confusions, were now becoming far more efficient and it was inevitable that they should appeal to some of the English in some situations. But the English Church on its own was not in much of a position to act as policeman or judge. This was tacitly acknowledged when the Church abandoned the claim that it alone was competent to try and punish murderers of priests or other offenders against their dignity. The claim was made ridiculous by a fine piece of irony: Becket's own murderers were never properly punished.

In one of his fits of rage Henry cried out that he wanted to be rid of this priest. Four knights immediately hurried to Canterbury from the king's Christmas court near Bayeux. But all this was not because of a dispute over the competence of rival courts. What finally stung the king to fury, and what the knights shouted about in Canterbury Cathedral, was Becket's refusal to accept the ceremony of crowning the king's eldest son. This coronation was important to Henry II; it was intended both to bind the 'young king' to him and to strengthen his chance of succeeding to the throne in peace – two hopes which history was to mock. It had occurred in Becket's absence. A long record of defending the rights and privileges of his office with a complete obstinacy now came to a climax. Having just staged what had seemed to be his final reconciliation with Henry, the archbishop, back in Canterbury, excommunicated the bishops who had taken part in the honour paid to the 'young king'. They were not to enter any church or to be befriended by any Christian. It was this act directed against bishops that led to the end. The king exploded in anger and the four knights rode into Canterbury on the afternoon of 29 December 1170. They subsequently claimed that it had been their intention to carry out an arrest which the king had ordered, until the emotion of the moment got the better of them. This may well have been the truth; in the twelfth century one did not lightly murder an archbishop in his cathedral, or expect a king to approve. It seems that to the end Becket could not be grasped or placed by his contemporaries. They were dealing with problems of law and politics. As he went to his martyr's death, he was dealing with – what?

After that drama quieter actors were needed. The next Archbishop of Canterbury was a placid monk, Roger of Dover, who specialized in ecclesiastical law but was determined to stay at peace with his king. The next Bishop of Winchester after Henry of Blois was Richard of Ilchester, a civil servant specializing in financial problems. The king had commended him to the monks of Winchester with the well-remembered words: 'I order you to hold a free election, but forbid you to elect anyone but Richard my clerk'.[14] Arch-

---

[14] C. Duggan has studied his career in *Transactions of the Royal Historical Society* (London, 1966), pp.1-21.

bishop Roger gave no trouble and Richard of Ilchester gladly remained in the king's service while a bishop.

Henry's closest friend among the bishops was, however, St Hugh of Avalon. At his special request this true saint became in 1180 prior of the exceptionally austere new monastery (a Charterhouse) founded by the king at Witham and then, in 1186, Bishop of Lincoln. The king loved Hugh so obviously that the baseless rumour spread that he was his father, but the *Life* written by Adam, the bishop's chaplain during the last three years of his life, reveals the truth. There was a rare combination of strengths in him; and it aroused respect in king and monk, priest and people, alike. Self-discipline was united with self-confidence (he was a Burgundian nobleman's son); and the intellectual equipment of a scholar (although he was no author) was assisted by a ready sense of humour. He once had a previously sulky king in fits of laughter by a brief, sharp joke based on William the Conqueror's descent from the tanner in Falaise. And all the time the desire for a silent union with God was compatible with efficiency in the pastoral care of a diocese and in the business of the royal court.[15]

Such bishops supported their king in principle, although in St Hugh's case at any rate they did not lack the courage to disagree when they thought it necessary. In a more tactful way they were what Becket's murderers claimed to be, roaring out as they left Canterbury Cathedral that December evening: *réaux, réaux* ('king's men, king's men'). And it is possible to see why the king commanded such allegiance; why good men were his men.

He was the founder of the Plantagenet or Angevin dynasty in England, so named because his mother had married Geoffrey Plantagenet, court of Anjou. When he inherited the English throne at the age of twenty-one in 1154, he was already Duke of Normandy and lord of rich lands to the south in France; and he had married Eleanor of Acquitaine, who had brought with her still richer lands further to the south. At the court of this famous and extremely independent-minded

---

[15] *The Life of St Hugh of Lincoln* was edited by D. L. Douie and H. Farmer in 2 vols. (London, 1961-62). There is a modern biography by D. H. Farmer (London, 1985).

lady the civilization of love, as sung by the troubadours, reached its height of glamour, chivalry and courtesy; of unreality. A man of astounding energy and capacity for business, Henry did not go in for glamour. He was determined to defend his own rights, and to see justice done to others, in any place brought to his attention between Scotland and Spain. And even that did not satisfy him. He was encouraged to conquer Ireland by Pope Hadrian IV – Nicholas Breakspear, the son of a minor official of St Albans Abbey and the only Englishman ever to sit on the papal throne. The king landed there in 1171, the beginning of England's tragic involvement in the neighbouring island. Such a ruler made and enforced law by his own exertions, although in England he relied a great deal on his great justiciar, Ranulf de Glanvill. Himself too restless to concentrate on church services or to remain in any one spot for long, Henry seems to have had a real admiration for genuinely devout monks or hermits and made many gifts to them. When Gilbert of Sempringham, the Lincolnshire country priest who had started the only religious 'order' ever to have a medieval Englishman as its founder, arrived at Henry's court on business, the king forestalled him. He hurried to his lodgings, to receive the saint's blessing.[16]

With his grey eyes, freckled face and uncertain temper, with his indifference to comfort or pomp despite his wealth and power, with the positive delight he took in an unkempt appearance, Henry fascinated his generation by his personality as much as by the extent of the lands he ruled. And the clergy had special reasons to be interested in him. His conception of justice guaranteed massive privileges for the Church and the Becket controversy never touched them. The clergy administered their vast and steadily growing possessions with almost no interference from the king's officers. If bishops and abbots were usually appointed after consulting the king, no one thought the royal interest in these great landowners unreasonable. From laymen the clergy collected tithes (tenths of crops), mortuaries (normally a dead man's best beast or

[16] Rose Graham, *St Gilbert of Sempringham and the Gilbertines* (London, 1901), p.19.

gown), oblations (financial contributions four times a year), and fees. They punished, often by fines, laymen accused of fornication, adultery, incest, usury, defamation, perjury, blasphemy or heresy. Ecclesiastical courts decided all the many legal problems connected with contracts, marriages or wills. It is reasonable to suppose that this position of rich privilege mattered to the clergy far more than did the question of how to punish clerics convicted of serious crimes; and that the legal question did not involve many priests who were murderers. From the days of Edward I to the days of Henry VIII the bishops' records show that the clerics or 'clerks' whom Becket saved from the gallows were almost all men in minor orders: parish clerks, readers, acolytes and the like, many of them earning their livings like laymen. Even schoolboys were given the tonsure that brought them within the privileged clerical caste. It was widely believed that laymen ought to escape secular justice even if they were not in such minor orders, provided only that they could read a little Latin; Psalm 51:1 was regarded as the 'neck verse'.

So we can see the reason why modern students of the controversy of the 1160s find it difficult to believe that the Christian Church's vital interests were at stake when Henry II was resisted to the death by his former friend and agent, Thomas Becket.

THE GREAT CHARTER

Henry II's sons, however, proved as unworthy of the throne as did the Conqueror's. Geoffrey, his son by his mistress Rosamund Clifford, was made Bishop of Lincoln at the age of fourteen, Chancellor of England and finally Archbishop of York, despite his protest that he preferred dogs to priests. The legitimate son called by King Henry's own name and crowned at his wish (despite Becket) lived long enough to break his father's heart before dying prematurely. The next son and fellow-rebel, Richard, was while King of the English interested only in his crusade, courageous but futile. To him the country

was a source of income and chroniclers reported his remark
that he would sell London if he could find a buyer.

During King Richard's absence the administration of
England was entrusted to Hugh de Puiset, Bishop of Durham,
and William Longchamp, Bishop of Ely – the former a handsome and acceptable aristocrat, the latter a civil servant of
humble birth who was said to look like an ape and to be so
overbearing that he was forced to leave the country.[17]

On his return in 1193 Richard found time to secure the
appointment of his principal assistant during the crusade,
Herbert Walter, as Archbishop of Canterbury. A nephew of
Henry II's justiciar Ranulf de Glanvill, and himself highly
trained as a lawyer and administrator, the new archbishop
served Richard with great efficiency as justiciar for five years.
He made enemies by his financial demands on behalf of the
absent king, and his own monks at Canterbury protested to
Rome against his absorption in secular affairs, with the result
that he fell from political power. But early in the next reign he
was back in power as chancellor for six years, conducting the
administration of King John. Hubert Walter was to Richard
and John all that Henry II had hoped for from Thomas
Becket.[18]

King John was never popular in his lifetime, and has joined
the rogues' gallery in many assessments of his reign from his
own century to this. He is reputed to have been utterly incompetent because during his reign (in 1204) the duchy of
Normandy was conquered by the French king; yet the link
across the Channel made in 1066 had always been fragile and
the so-called 'Angevin empire' of Henry II had been nothing
more than a federation, united by a dominating personality.
John is known to have been cruel and rapacious and his
murder of Prince Arthur outraged his informed contemporaries; yet the records of his reign show him dispensing
much justice and some charity. He did not look like a Christian king (he was physically undersized) or behave like one (he

---

[17] See G. V. Scammell, *Hugh de Puiset, Bishop of Durham* (Cambridge, 1956).

[18] There are two recent studies of *Hubert Walter*, by C. R. Cheney (London, 1967) and C. R. Young (Durham, N.C., 1968).

talked with his cronies during services); yet he founded a monastery at Beaulieu in Hampshire. He offended the barons as much because he was no soldier as because he was no gentleman, and fell foul of the Church not because of some unspeakable sin but because of a dispute over the archbishopric of Canterbury.

On Hubert Walter's death in 1205 the king's candidate for Canterbury was his secretary, the Bishop of Norwich, but the monks of the cathedral monastery (with whom lay the formal right to elect) hurriedly chose one of their own number. The situation was sufficiently unclear to allow a formidable pope, Innocent III, to appoint Cardinal Stephen Langton, with whom he had formed a close friendship while they were both teaching at the University of Paris. Langton was not accepted by the king and had to spend six years waiting for his revenues or for admission to England. The enraged pope now placed the kingdom under an 'interdict' and excommunicated the king. The excommunication meant that no Christian was supposed to have anything to do with John: since most of his civil servants were bishops or priests, it was an effective blow. Only one bishop remained in England, at Winchester. The interdict of 1208 decreed that no services were to be held in the parish churches. The Mass was allowed in monasteries – but only behind closed doors. Infants could not be baptized except at home or in the church porch; the dead could not be buried in consecrated ground; the living could not receive Holy Communion except when at the point of death; church bells were silent. King John retaliated by plundering the Church, but when the pope threatened to authorize the French king to take over England a shrewd deal was made. Near Dover on 15 May 1212 John resigned the kingdoms of England and Ireland to the papacy, and received them back in return for homage and an annual tribute, together with the promise of a restitution of the money seized from the Church in the royal counter-attack.

On that day the submission of England to Rome which William the Conqueror had avoided was achieved – and it remained the formal position for more than a century. However, the most important immediate result of John's humiliation was that Pope Innocent was now put firmly on his side in his struggles with the barons and the French; and the pope's agents received new orders. Chief among those agents in England was the Archbishop of Canterbury.

When he had taken up his revenues and responsibilities in the settlement of 1212, the archbishop had to cope with a complicated situation. He later became famous as a leader of the barons who extracted concessions from John. The king made a temporary peace in the meadow called Runnymede on the banks of the Thames on 15 June 1215: it was the great charter, Magna Carta. Langton, indeed, is reputed to have been not only the midwife of the charter but its father; for, according to more than one chronicler of the time and to many subsequent historians, he began the idea of a great new charter by reading Henry I's coronation charter to the barons assembled in St Paul's Cathedral. Actually, the evidence is less clear cut. There can be no doubt that Langton had the intellectual equipment to influence the course of events in 1215 and that he shared the ideas from which the great charter drew its strength, but evidence that Langton produced Henry I's charter, or was always on the side of the barons against King John, is unsatisfactory. The archbishop was always prominent; Innocent III noted (with pain) that the opposition to John dated from Langton's arrival in England. But the king was never able to pin a charge of treason on him, and on the whole 'the evidence presents him as a mediator and a moderator, rather than an originator'.[19]

Stephen Langton was a mediator because he had to serve his pope and his king, as well as his fellow-barons and his conscience. And he experienced a mediator's usual lack of thanks. He was suspended from his archbishopric, and forced into another exile, by Innocent III when he delayed excommunicating the enemies of the pope's new royal protégé. He had to wait for the election of another pope before he could resume his work in England.

Thus even when the king was the notorious John, there was solid substance in the idea of the Christian monarchy of England. It should not come as a surprise when we find

---

[19] J. C. Holt, *Magna Carta* (Cambridge, 1965), p.188.

Cardinal Langton in the next reign protecting the interests of
the young king, Henry III, against the barons; at one crisis, in
1224, he ordered the bishops to take over the most important
royal castles from the barons, as trustees for the king. Nor,
indeed, should we be amazed when we find him assuring a
London congregation in 1213 that 'because you are layfolk it is
your business to believe that your prelates are men who do all
things discreetly and with wisdom'.[20] Langton was never a
democrat. He was not sent to England in order to encourage
democracy. His mission was to carry out the policy of Pope
Innocent III.

Innocent, a Roman nobleman autocratic by temperament,
was the first pope to use the title 'Vicar of Christ' (the title that
Archbishop Wulfstan two hundred years before had applied
to the King of the English), and he was the first pope to insist
that he alone in his 'plenitude of power' had the right to
authorize the veneration of a saint; to appoint to ecclesiastical
posts throughout Christendom by 'provision'; to be the universal pastor. Of course such a pope was determined to say who
should be the next Archbishop of Canterbury; he was also
determined to decide who should be the next Patriarch of
Constantinople or the next Holy Roman Emperor. What interested him was not Magna Carta but the reforming programme of the Fourth Lateran Council, held in Rome in the
same year, 1215. This was the council that defined the Faith
.(against the new Albigensian heretics in France) and the Mass
(developing Lanfranc's teaching into the full doctrine of the
'transubstantiation' of bread and wine into Christ's body and
blood). The council insisted that the archbishops should hold
provincial synods every year; that the bishops should teach
regularly and reform morals; that the parish priests should
reside in their parishes, with a reasonable income and security; that the laity should be married only in church and the
clergy not at all; and, most important, that at least once a year
every lay person in Christendom should confess his or her sins
to the parish priest and receive absolution and communion. It
was a programme not of one nation's democracy but of a

[20] C. R. Cheney, *From Becket to Langton* (Manchester, 1956), p.155.

whole Christian civilization's discipline. The great pope identified with it wanted King John to support it more than he wanted anything else in England.[21]

THE CHURCH AGAINST TYRANNY

In strange company with a pope whom he regarded as a foreign enemy of 'this England', William Shakespeare cared nothing for Magna Carta; his *King John* did not mention it. Why, then, has history taken the great charter so seriously? Why has it seen King John's momentary agreement with the barons as the climax to which all events after the Norman Conquest lead? Why has the Church been praised for fighting for more than its own freedom? It was the first clause in Magna Carta, as in Henry I's coronation charter, that the English Church 'may be free and enjoy its liberties and rights unimpaired'. But why has the document thus introduced – a document full of liberties for barons, of rights already defined in feudal custom – been venerated as the English-speaking world's first charter of liberty, putting that world in debt to the English Church?

Part of the answer to these questions is the truth that the Church was the only body in England strong enough to prevent the monarchy which the Conqueror had founded from becoming a tyranny.

As we have seen, in every reign bishops and other churchmen worked hard and prayed hard as servants of the Christian monarchy. It was typical that the *Dialogus de Scaccario*, the handbook which for many years set the pattern for the working of the king's exchequer (and the efficiency of the English exchequer was the wonder and envy of all other kings), was compiled by a Bishop of London, Richard Fitz Nigel. But Thomas Becket was by no means the only servant of the king to put his loyalty to the Church above all other earthly loyalties. On innumerable occasions bishops who owed their

---

[21] See C. R. Cheney, *Pope Innocent III and England* (Stuttgart, 1976).

promotion to a king were found pursuing the Church's objectives rather than his, and even before they were rewarded with high ecclesiastical office civil servants who were clerics must always have had in mind this possible future tension in their loyalties. When a man had become a bishop a show of independence might incur the royal wrath – but not total disaster. A rebellious lay baron could be defeated, imprisoned or executed by a king. But a bishop was more of a problem. Men felt uneasy at the idea of roughing him up – was he not the priest who could 'make God' in the Mass, the tribe's chief magician? It was also out of the question for the king to risk permanently alienating the whole body of the clergy on whom he depended from his coronation onwards. In that generally illiterate age, only the clergy could propagate the sacred status of an anointed king – and only they could organize his household, gather his taxes, add up his accounts, issue his orders and conduct his diplomacy. Besides, all the kings from William the Conqueror to John (William Rufus alone excepted) seem to have been orthodox believers, convinced that the clergy held the keys to heaven or hell and that before death the God known best to them bestowed or withheld victory and wealth. The moral power of the clergy in the Middle Ages was displayed when in 1070 the pope's legate persuaded the Norman bishops to impose penances on all who had shed blood in the invasion of England. Those who had fought without pay for King William had to perform a year's penance for each life taken. Mercenaries had to do the same penance for taking part in the expedition as for homicide. So those who had conquered with the Conqueror still had to kneel before a mysteriously higher power.

Had the power of the clergy not checked the monarch's power, the course of English history might have been very different. For the monarchy fastened on England by the Norman Conquest was a tyranny in the making.

Admittedly William needed the support of other aristocrats from France to conquer England, to hold it down, and to defend his realm against external foes or internal traitors. Throughout his life he knew very little peace, and all his hopes depended on the fighting capacity of some five thousand trained troops which his English tenants-in-chief were obliged to provide at his demand. But he was determined to reduce this dependence on others to the minimum. He built on the old position of the monarchy in England, already the best administered country in eleventh-century Europe, in order to develop Europe's most united state. He inherited in England a taxation system (developed out of the need to buy off the Vikings with Danegeld) and a coinage superior to anything in Normandy. He maintained the administrative structure of shires divided into 'hundreds' (or in some regions into areas called 'weapon-takes'); and royal letters or 'writs' were for many years still sent to them in Old English. And he made one dramatic innovation.

He was the anointed king and claimed to inherit through his coronation any mystique or administrative support which had gathered around Edward the Confessor's throne. But he had not succeeded to the kingdom in peace, despite Edward the Confessor's probable wishes; he was the Conqueror. As such he claimed that the entire country was his to hold or to grant to his favourites in return for their promises. He had a power of which no Anglo-Saxon king (and no Duke of Normandy) had ever dreamed. To keep the aristocracy in personal touch with him, he turned the Anglo-Saxon *witenagemot* into a Great Council which brought the great lords to his court at least every Christmas, Easter and Whitsun. In 1086 he assembled at Salisbury all the chief landowners of England, whether or not they were directly his own tenants, and made them all do homage to him, making it clear that no loyalty owed to any other lord should be allowed to conflict with their duty to their king. During the same year the king caused Domesday Book to be compiled. The most detailed survey of any kingdom to be made in the Middle Ages, its purpose was to record the estates held by the king's chief tenants, county by county, comparing the position in 1086 with that on 'the day when King Edward was alive and dead'. Given time, it could have become the basis of a taxation far more grinding than anything achieved by William Rufus or John. Given successors of his own ability, William could have founded an absolute monarchy.

That the Great Council of the king turned out to be the

ancestor of a democratic Parliament, that some of the barons combined against the king for purposes larger than their self-enrichment, and that England learned that the king's will was not the highest law in every sphere – all this was due to the moral leadership provided by churchmen more than to any other personal influence. We know the balance of power in 1086 exactly.[22] Domesday Book showed an England of which about twenty per cent was owned directly by the king and his family. More than half was held from him by tenants-in-chief, the aristocracy, of whom only about five per cent were native English. The remaining quarter was owned by the Church. These figures matter because they show that the Church could hold the balance in politics, if strong personalities were at its head; that bishops could one day help barons to impose law on the king, as they had already helped the king to impose order on the country.

To appreciate what was involved, we need to go back over the story we have told, to get at the secrets of the fame of two celebrated archbishops, St Anselm and St Thomas.

ANSELM

Anselm was born in Italy like Lanfranc, but belonged to a noble family. His father was given up to a secular way of life (although he became a monk on his deathbed) and quarrelled with his sensitive son. The boy loved his mother and her death plunged him into such continuing unhappiness that he left home.

In his wandering Anselm came to Bec – and to Lanfranc, who became his second father. For a time he hesitated about staying at Bec, fearing that Lanfranc would become too domineering; he had not come to be bullied by a second father. But his genius was different from Lanfranc's. He was no organizer, except of thoughts; no teacher, except of

---

[22] It is well summed up by R. V. Lennard, *Rural England 1086-1135* (Oxford, 1959), pp.25-30. See Michael Wood, *Domesday* (London, 1987).

friends. Where he excelled was in friendship with his fellow-monks. Through this, he had the ability to attract them into the spiritual progress he was himself making. While Abbot of Bec he was a firm but kind father of the family, and a spiritual teacher in many conversations; in the verdict of Dom David Knowles, 'perhaps the nearest approach to the ideal abbot that the Benedictine centuries ever saw'.[23] He wrote prayers which are still moving to read. He was a devotional and theological pioneer in the cult of the Virgin Mary, the heavenly mother. And in the realm of pure theology he continued to teach as he had done in conversations with his monks, for he developed a method which seemed to many contemporaries (including Lanfranc) to be too adventurous to be worthy of theology's grandeur. He would not quote authorities from the history of the Church. He would not even quote Holy Scripture itself at any length. Among friends, like a father talking at the supper table, he would rely on the warmed heart, the converted mind, to go straight to God. The courage and the energy with which he abandoned the reliance on earlier, written authorities had some precedent in the thought of Lanfranc's theological enemy Berengar of Tours, but no one could dismiss Anselm as they dismissed Berengar. Within orthodox Christian thought he made a new beginning, to which is rightly applied the adjective: revolutionary.[24]

His supreme achievement, establishing him as the first great theologian of medieval Europe, was the writing of three short books, two dating from 1077-78. In the *Monologion* he meditated on the reality of the Creator. The existence of good things required the existence of the highest good. The existence of anything required the existence of the Supreme Being. But having completed these arguments, he continued to be preoccupied. Surely there must be a simpler argument which would confirm by reasoning what was already held by

---

[23] David Knowles, *The Evolution of Medieval Thought* (revised, London, 1970), p.99.

[24] See G. R. Evans, *Anselm and Talking about God* (Oxford, 1978), with *A Companion to the Study of St Anselm*, ed. J. Hopkins (Minneapolis, Minn., 1972).

Christian faith? (For him faith came first; his was the method of *fides quaerens intellectum*, faith seeking understanding, or *credo ut intelligam*, 'I believe in order that I may understand'). At length, one night during Matins in the monastery, the argument came to him. Only a fool said there was no God: so Psalm 14:1 declared. But even the fool knew what the word 'God' meant. It meant a reality greater than any other reality which could be conceived. But to conceive of 'God' as existing only in the mind meant to conceive of a reality inferior to the 'God' who existed not only in the mind but also in fact; so that the 'God' in whom the atheist did not believe was not the real God whom Christians worshipped. The man who had a fully adequate understanding of 'God' must believe in God's full existence.

Anselm wrote the *Proslogion* in order to work out the argument that flashed into his head while his brethren sang the service that night. In Anselm's time Lanfranc, when the book was submitted to him, was distressed that it made so little use of the Scriptures or the Fathers; and in the eighteenth century the philosopher Kant demolished its logic. Its intellectual clarity, power and independence are, however, amazing when one remembers that Anselm knew the Greek philosophers only through their Christian interpreters or translators (Plato through Augustine, Aristotle through Boethius) – yet did not fall very far below their level. Whether or not the argument was faulty (and it is an extraordinarily difficult argument either to understand or to disprove in a hurry), it was the perfect reflection of the way in which Anselm's mind worked. For him, the path to religious faith began in goodness. The road ascended to God through the wisdom which, being raised above the everyday world, saw clearly what the philosophers called the 'universals'. These 'universals' were the unities of classes of things, the patterns deeper than the variety on the surface of things. And the chief of the 'universals' was God. Yet God was utterly unique, for he alone satisfied the heart's longing to worship. When another Norman monk wrote a reply to the *Proslogion*, pointing out that one could conceive of the large island of Atlantis lying out in the western seas without necessarily believing that it was really there, Anselm calmly replied: to think about Atlantis was not the same thing as thinking about God. He was so sure of the reality of God, so sure that he and his friends were day by day and night by night not addressing a void, that he never could understand the atheistic 'fool'. His task was to think not whether, but why, the Christian's faith in God was true.

This was the mind that had to endure contact with the mind of William Rufus – and watch the royal body enjoying itself. This was the mystic who had to sit listening to arguments about the law of feudalism at the king's court. Protesting against his appointment to Canterbury, he said that would be like yoking an old sheep to an untamed bull. The yoke did not leave the sheep spiritually undamaged, as we can see from the sad record of Anselm's conscientious absorption in defending the complete rights of his archbishopric. He was not exempt from the general medieval obsession with the rights of an office – 'rights' which others might describe as privilege or pride. Courage he never lacked, nor the freedom to exercise it; he once wrote that man's freedom lay in his ability to maintain uprightness of will. But out of a sense of duty he became bogged down in controversies very different from the level where his spirit was at home. From Bec he had sent out a stream of loving letters to other monks, guiding them in the spiritual life; he rightly felt those letters to be edifying, and collected them for publication. But the last letter which he wrote before dying was to suspend the Archbishop of York from the exercise of his office until he should have acknowledged the supremacy of Canterbury (York's relative status was unclear until a papal decision of 1119). It was an attitude which fell short of the highest holiness.

Anselm was not on morally unassailable ground even in the cause for which he defied both William Rufus and Henry I. As if the life of the Christian Church had been at stake, he objected to the ceremonies in which the king would hand a new bishop his ring and staff ('crozier') and the bishop would, in return, put his hands between the king's, as a sign of feudal homage.

In tones of profound conviction Anselm repeated the argu-ment he had heard in Rome, that a priest's hands which 'created' Christ afresh out of the bread and wine in the Mass should not be polluted by being placed between the blood-stained hands of a soldier-king. Yet before the decrees of the Council of Claremont and the pope settled the matter for him, he had himself consecrated bishops who had received their rings and staffs from the hands of William Rufus; he had received his own ring and staff from the royal hands, although he later protested that he had been physically forced to undergo this indignity and the details of what took place in William's sick room are obscure. In the end, although as a result of the controversy this ceremony of 'investiture' was abandoned, there was no change in the ceremony of homage to the king before a man who had been elected as bishop or abbot was allowed to assume office – as was inevitable when the bishop or abbot was a major landowner in a feudal state. And the king continued to have the decisive word in the choice of almost all the bishops.

So Anselm's years as archbishop were a prolonged martyr-dom. Secular business made him weary or ill; his mind, he said, was seized by 'a horror such as an infant might feel when face to face with some terrible ghost'. He hated life at the court of William Rufus, the cruel, cynical and blaspheming lout who pawed other men in his drink. What endured from the wreck of those years was a book which he began to write in Canterbury and which he completed when exiled to an Italian mountain village in 1098: *Cur Deus Homo*.

To this little masterpiece three other short books were attached. An earlier essay entered the depths of the mystery of the Trinity, and there were two later treatises, one exploring the depths of sin and the answer to it through the Lord's birth from a virgin, another exploring man's free will and God's foreknowledge. Normally Anselm did not write for the common man. How could someone 'whose mind is so dark that it cannot distinguish between his own horse and its colour', he once asked, understand God who is three persons in One? How could a man whose very conception was due to his parents' sin of lust understand the All-Holy? But *Cur Deus Homo* was a book for its time – and for subsequent ages.

Why had God become man? Simply, because it was necessary. God was lord over all his creation, as the king was lord over England. His 'honour' had been offended by man's sin, as a king's honour would be offended by a baron's rebellion; and in heaven as on earth, discipline must be upheld. But while a baron might offer 'satisfaction' to an offended king, the offering required to satisfy God's honour must be greater than the whole of the creation. If God's honour remained unsatisfied, then man's soul must be left to the devils as a hare is left to a yelping pack of hounds. (Anselm once explained this to his companions while a hare was taking shelter under his horse.) And the offering needed to save man could be provided only by God becoming man and sacrificing himself. This was the understanding of Christ's cross in terms of feudalism that came to Anselm as he sat, alternately bored and revolted, at the feudal court of the Conqueror's son.

Anselm's secretary and biographer, the Canterbury monk Eadmer, told the story that Pope Urban II greeted him as 'one who is almost our equal, being as it were pope and patriarch of another world'. Whether or not that compliment was ever actually paid, Eadmer saw that another world than the world of William Rufus or Henry I had been brought into view by the life and thought of his master. It was the world of an invisible kingdom, the kingdom of spiritual reality; a world where what decided issues was what a pope, not a king, thought. It was a world dominated by the cross of Christ — only, this cross was no longer seen as in *The Dream of the Rood*. Here was no longer an object to be contemplated in the vision of devout ecstasy; here was a necessity in reasoning, the reasoning of the law court. The cross was not the place where Christ did battle against evil, for evil was not now thought strong enough to offer battle; it was the place where God's own justice was satisfied by God's own action in God's own way. Anselm dwelt in a world high above the devils and devil-possessed men whose hands were bloody.

The new ideals did not make for smooth co-operation between the higher clergy and the crown — as Eadmer found when he had to put his principles into practice as Bishop of St Andrews, discovering that the King of the Scots was no more amenable than the King of the English. But Eadmer — himself an Englishman, the country's best historian since Bede, a patriot who delighted to honour the Anglo-Saxon saints – was able to see that under the brutal sons of the Conqueror an Archbishop of Canterbury had made an alternative to their monarchy not only possible but also imperishably public.

After Anselm, the Church under the papacy would now always be, at least potentially, a rival to the crown in medieval England. In the nineteenth century an Anglican scholar who was no uncritical admirer of the papacy wrote that Anselm had a vision of 'a throne of judgement, different in its origin and authority from all earthly thrones; a common father and guide of Christians whom all acknowledged, and who was clothed with prerogatives which all believed to come from above; a law of high purpose and scope, embodying the greatest principles of justice and purity, and aiming, on the widest scale, at the elevation and improvement of society; an administration of this law, which regarded not persons and was not afraid of the face of man, and told the truth to ambitious emperors and adulterous kings and queens'.[25]

He died shortly before Easter 1109. He had told Eadmer to destroy the biography he was writing. Fortunately for us, the obedient monk did so only after making a copy of it. Together with his *History of Recent Events in England*, Eadmer's *Life* is the main source of our knowledge of St Anselm, the only theological genius ever to be burdened by the duties of the archbishopric of Canterbury.[26]

THOMAS BECKET

Called to Canterbury in 1162, Thomas Becket was acutely aware of the example set by Anselm. He tried to persuade the pope formally to declare his predecessor a saint (a step not

[25] R. W. Church, *St Anselm* (London, 1870), p.267.
[26] The *Life* has been translated by R. W. Southern (London, 1963) and the *History* by Geoffrey Bosanquet (London, 1964). See also R. W. Southern, *St Anselm and His Biographer* (Cambridge, 1963).

taken until the fifteenth century). Just before dying he invoked the name of Alphege, the archbishop murdered by the Danes – whose memory, which Lanfranc had tried to suppress, had been restored by Anselm. And it seems that this heritage of the saints of Canterbury who had resisted oppressors was the crucial factor in the transformation of Becket's life when he had accepted election as archbishop. Previously he had not even been ordained as a priest; instead, during his eight brilliant years as the king's chancellor he had lived the life of a polished gentleman, except that he had preserved his piety and chastity. When made a priest and a bishop, he instantly signalled his sense of entering a new heritage by ordering that the day when he became a bishop should be perpetually observed as Trinity Sunday. He resigned the chancellorship and devoted himself to prayer and good works. During a visit to the pope he also resigned his great new ecclesiastical office, so that he could receive it back from hands holier than any king's. Little time passed before he was appearing in public not only as the lavish dispenser of charity but also as the inflexible defender of the Church's rights, expecting and even stimulating persecution by a tyrant, until the moment came when he walked into the king's council at Northampton clutching his tall archbishop's cross.

It seems that Henry never understood what had changed Thomas. Although in many moods he demanded nothing less than the traitor's ruin, the last talk which the king ever had with his former friend was still dominated by his hurt bewilderment at the betrayal. He then seems to have expressed a whimsical hope that somehow the old relationship could be restored. When the news of Becket's death was brought to him he stayed for three days in his room, fasting, weeping or in a stupor. Enemies such as Bishop Foliot put Becket's change in 1162 down to simple hypocrisy – or at least they made this accusation when most exasperated. But the real secret seems to be that Becket was determined to be as magnificently the hero-archbishop as he had been the hero-chancellor, even if the new role involved austerity, conflict, exile and death. He would not yield an inch of the estates of the archbishopric, not an inch of its legal position, not an inch of the glory bequeathed by its saints. He had only to stand firm, whatever the cost, and he would be vindicated by the applause of God and God's saints. This was an attitude far subtler and more courageous than play-acting to secure the world's cheers. One of his large staff who became one of his many biographers, Herbert of Bosham, put his finger on it: 'He was generous far beyond the demands of his high office, expansive to all, magnificent to all and beyond all, great of heart, great in height, and great in display'.

During his lifetime Thomas Becket was no saint. John of Salisbury urged him to devote his exile to the study of the psalms and of theology; but Becket, having quietened his conscience and inflamed his emotions by abasements before his God in prayer, arose from prayer to study ecclesiastical law and to argue like a lawyer. When he studied the Bible, the passages he noticed most were those when prophets or priests denounced the kings of Ancient Israel; or when Christ or St Stephen suffered persecution. He was no doubt sincere in frequently regretting his former worldliness and in constantly bemoaning his present unworthiness, but he lacked the self-forgetful love as well as the self-transcending joy of the saints. Even his most dramatic scenes – his brave inflexibility at Northampton, his last minutes in Canterbury – had to be spoiled by unsaintly remarks to his enemies, insults which betrayed how unregenerate was his temper. But he had such a respect for the saints' examples that he acted like one when he could. His heart had been so touched by the Church's spiritual glory that he was content to adorn this glory in death, even if unable to do so in life. His death could not completely vindicate his cause in politics or law; that was impossible while the English Church remained part of a country ruled by a Christian monarch. But his dealings with death did vindicate his personal reputation – and, with that, the reputation of the Church among the common folk. His posthumous career must make us remember St Paul's boast: 'dying, and behold we live'.

As early as 1173 he was formally canonized as a saint. Thus the papacy gave to him in his tomb the unqualified support which it had denied him during his conflicts. Not much longer was needed for him to become a hero in the folk religion of England. It was as if a popular referendum said an over-whelming 'yes' to Thomas Becket, the civil servant turned prelate, the churchman who had demanded that murderers should not be hanged if they were clerics, the ecclesiastical grandee who had insisted that the Archbishop of York should be punished for placing a crown on the head of the king's eldest son. People were enthusiastic about the 'holy, blissful martyr' for many reasons. He was a miracle-worker in his tomb; the doctor of the obscure, the penniless and the hopeless. Riding to his shrine through Kent made a pleasant trip. The offerings at his shrine could reconstruct and enrich Canterbury Cathedral when most of the building in which he had died, the building which had stood as a monument to Lanfranc, had been destroyed by fire. The fact that he had withstood the most powerful king of his time, an Angevin (and did not St Bernard say of the Angevins: 'from the Devil they came and to the Devil they will return'?), captured the imaginations of many of the English. So the rumour spread that he had himself been an Englishman, although in real life both his parents were solid Norman colonists. But we have also to ask why the fame of St Thomas of Canterbury spread so quickly and lasted so long throughout Christendom, from Norway to the Holy Land; and the best answer is that his story showed that the heroic days of the Catholic Church were not over. The thrill had not entirely gone from the rich, proud in-stitution. There was still dew at noon.

It is clear from the abundant records about his death that what impressed his household and the surrounding monastery was Becket's combination of two spiritually magnificent gestures in his farewell performance. Dying without physical resistance – even if he had exchanged a few insults with the knights – he deliberately identified himself with all the univer-sal Church's martyrs and with the crucified Christ. And when he was dead, a vermin-infested hair shirt was found beneath his official robes. So Thomas Becket proved himself to be more than Anselm's worthy successor in the struggle to impose law as the Church understood it on the king. Gladly sacrificing his life in that struggle, he joined the class of St Cuthbert in

Durham, St Edward in Westminster, and the martyrs of England such as St Edmund and St Alban. In his tomb he reigned, a prince of Christendom.[27]

ENGLAND IN CHRISTENDOM

Stephen Langton was one of the innumerable Englishmen devoted to the Martyr of Canterbury, during whose lifetime he had been born in Lincolnshire. While waiting for admission to King John's England Langton chose to live in the Cistercian monastery at Pontigny, where Becket had spent his exile. In July 1220, when his troubles were over, he was the preacher at a splendid ceremony in the rebuilt cathedral at Canterbury. King Henry III (then aged thirteen) was present, as were many bishops and other lords. They had assembled to honour the removal or 'translation' of the martyr's body from his first tomb to his new shrine, soon to become the most expensively decorated grave in the world. This ceremony, with the lavish hospitality around it, bankrupted Langton but ensured a rich future for St Thomas.

Far less evidence has survived about Langton's character than about Anselm's or Becket's; the biography written by Matthew Paris has disappeared. But modern scholars can study a considerable number of the lectures or sermons which he delivered during his twenty years at the University of Paris as student or teacher. They show a fine mind at work, although a mind without Anselm's gift for philosophy or Becket's for drama. Langton was a first-class scholar, one of the pioneers in the medieval study of the Old Testament. His division of the Bible into chapters was used when later Bibles were being copied out in Paris or elsewhere, and was in the end taken over when printing began; thus every copy of the Bible became a memorial to Langton. He also wrote commentaries on the Bible and these books had immense influence on

---

[27] The best recent biographies of *Thomas Becket* are by David Knowles (London, 1970) and Frank Barlow (London, 1986).

the thirteenth century. Through the Paris years he expounded
the work of Israel's prophets, before he was unexpectedly
challenged to become a prophet himself.[28]

Almost certainly from Langton's pen in Paris came the
Golden Sequence. In a modern English translation of the
famous hymn, this prayer to the Holy Spirit arises from
Christendom in the early Middle Ages:

> Heal our wounds; our strength renew;
> On our dryness pour thy dew;
>   Wash the stains of guilt away;
> Bend the stubborn heart and will;
> Melt the frozen, warm the chill;
>   Guide the steps that go astray.

The finest element in the Norman achievement was the fact
that they compelled England to join this civilization which had
now given birth to the University of Paris. The nation hewed
out by William the Conqueror, his companions and his successors, became a place where moral leadership could be given
by Christians of the stature of Lanfranc, Anselm and
Langton – men whose minds had been formed in France. In
this England the Church for which Becket died could, for all
its faults, do something to protect the life to which the *Golden
Sequence* referred. This taking of England into the Christendom of Europe can be compared with the results of other
amazing conquests made by the Normans: in Sicily or
southern Italy, in north Africa or the area around the biblical
city of Antioch in Syria. Everywhere they pulled their subjects
into the mainstream of the European tradition; into what
Charles Homer Haskins, in his pioneering book of 1927,
taught students to call *The Renaissance of the Twelfth
Century*.

The Norman adventures in the Mediterranean were Viking
raids on the grandest possible scale. Their leaders – Robert
Guiscard who started his Italian career as a brigand in 1047,
or his brother Count Roger of Sicily, or his son Bohemund,

---

[28] There has been no biography since F. M. Powicke, *Stephen Langton* (Oxford,
1928). R. W. Southern has supplied a biography of *St Anselm* (Oxford, 1986).

Prince of Antioch – were morally and intellectually primitive while being ruthlessly efficient fighters. A characteristic Norman exploit was the sack of Rome in 1084, 173 years after the baptism of the Norwegian pirate chief Rollo before he was allowed to settle in Normandy. But the strange fact is that Rollo and the other Scandinavian settlers in the north of France, like the Danes who settled in the east of England, adopted the Christian Church – if not the Christian morality – with zest. Perhaps they were anxious to appear, although not to be, civilized; or perhaps their motive was a never satisfied religious or superstitious hunger. William the Conqueror's father, Duke Robert, surprised his contemporaries by abandoning the power struggle in Normandy to go crusading. He died during the crusade, leaving his little bastard son to begin a lifetime of battles. In the conquest of Sicily as in Duke William's conquest of England, the Normans fought under the blessing of the papacy, and they liked to be reminded by their minstrels of the heroism of Charlemagne's knights riding against the Saracens. They were devoted to St Michael, the archangel with the sword. Their piracy was now christened as a crusade.

They remained in many ways barbarous; yet they became patrons of religion and learning. In Sicily the court of Roger the Great, king 1130-54, was a cosmopolitan centre, rendering priceless services to Christian Europe by welcoming the culture of the Arabs including medicine and philosophy. It was a traffic – the word comes from the Arabic – in intellectual as well as material wealth. Adelard of Bath, who spent much of his life as a civil servant under Henry I, acquired in the Norman kingdom of Sicily most of the knowledge which enabled him to be a bravely creative figure in scientific humanism among his fellow-countrymen when he returned to England. In Sicily the feudal government, fastened on a country previously turbulent and backward, enabled an Arab-Norman civilization to flourish.

A similar verdict would be valid about England. When the Anglo-Norman kingdom was established by the slaughter of the Anglo-Saxon aristocracy, by the devastation of the north and by all the rough 'justice' which brought a Norman baron's tenants and serfs to heel, it appeared that the glory of England was over. 'To the ordinary Englishman who had lived from the accession of King Edward to the death of King William', Sir Frank Stenton wrote, 'the Conquest must have seemed an unqualified disaster'.[29] Yet without the impact of the Normans, wrote another distinguished historian, 'true medieval society is unimaginable'.[30] From the soil which the conquerors trod down there grew a civilization richly English, richly European, richly Christian.

[29] F. M. Stenton, *Anglo-Saxon England*, p.677.
[30] J. M. Wallace-Hadrill, *The Barbarian West* (London, 1946), p.146.

CHAPTER FIVE

THE AGE OF FAITH

· Westminster Abbey · Choir and High Altar ·

WHY THEY BUILT CHURCHES

England's cathedrals and other churches surviving from the Middle Ages have often been described as the products of the people's faith. It is a description which needs some qualification.

Medieval church-building was a more sophisticated, even commercial, business than some legends have suggested. Although the peasants of a manor might be compelled by their consciences or their lords to lend a hand when their parish church was being built or rebuilt, or to provide their carts to take stone or timber to a cathedral, much evidence

survives of payments for labour and materials at the normal
rates. Although a monastery's sacrist or 'warden of the works'
would control a fabric fund and its disbursements, monks did
not as a rule build their churches with their own hands. Before
the Cistercian monks became (for a time) frequent exceptions
to this rule, one Norman abbot, Hugh of Selby, was talked
about as a very rare exception; in his enthusiasm for church
building he wore a labourer's smock. People contributed –
mainly through offerings at the shrines in the cathedral (hence
the importance of inheriting, or developing, a saint's shrine),
or through subscriptions in exchange for indulgences (promises of a reduction of time spent suffering in purgatory after
death), or through legacies (trusting to be remembered when
in purgatory). But the bishops and the monasteries also paid
for building projects out of their own great wealth as landowners. And despite all this income, finance remained a problem. That is shown by the patience which bishops or monks
often had to exercise before their projects reached completion.
The history of almost any great church shows that it was built
by stages.

The actual building was under the control of a master
mason, a man who knew stone because he had himself been a
stonemason but who was now a highly skilled professional.
Such an expert was well equipped (and well paid) to negotiate
with clients, to prepare designs reflecting current fashions, to
provide materials including vast quantities of stone and
timber, and to manage a large gang of masons and other
craftsmen. These master masons were not anonymous. It was
only accidental that not many of them were well remembered.
It has been possible for modern scholars to recover many of
their names, which deserve fame more than do most of the
architects of later generations. And stonemasons often went
from job to job in a region in order to secure a lifetime's
employment, and sometimes left marks on the stone to show
it. This was one of the most mobile trades in the Middle Ages,
and one of the most carefully organized.[1]

---

[1] See L. F. Salzman, *Building in England down to 1540* (revised, Oxford,
1967), and John Harvey, *Medieval Craftsmen* (London, 1975).

So a little knowledge corrects the talk about medieval churches being built by the people's faith. Deeper reflection, however, shows the substantial truth in such talk. The churches were in reality the factories of the industry to which medieval England attached the greatest importance; the chief public buildings of a period which was in truth the Age of Faith, or at least the Age of Acquiescence.

The work was done with a thoroughness and speed which must suggest popular enthusiasm. No doubt there was a welcome to this provision of employment because the money might easily have been wasted on wars, knights' tournaments or rich men's feasts, but there was also a positive approval of this particular expenditure. A contemporary poem on the building of Salisbury Cathedral paid tribute to the 'workmen's faith' along with the 'king's virtue' and the 'bishop's devotion'. We also know that the canons of the cathedral agreed to contribute a quarter of their incomes for seven years. Much other evidence reminds us that in this age church-building was popular. The wealth of the estates owned by the bishops or the monasteries itself testified to this: as was often said, the land had been given in exchange for the promise of prayers. The wealth was the monastery's or the aristocracy's investment in the hope of eternal happiness according to the Church's doctrine. When objections were occasionally raised to the passion which so many kings, bishops and abbots exhibited for building, it was because an over-elaborate church might distract the worshippers from the purer type of prayer, or because an over-luxurious monastery might destroy the monastic ideal, not because the building would impoverish the people.

The fundamental truth was that a new medieval church was the creation of a whole society and therefore that society's pride. Resentful workmen could not have carved those smiles on angels' faces. A society seething with rebellion would not have made that foliage to adorn the capital of a column: on the pillars of the chapter house at Southwell Minister, the leaves of oak, hawthorn, hop, vine and ivy are as alive today as in a summer of the 1290s. The women of thirteenth-century England were famous (as those of the eleventh-century had been) for their embroidery of ecclesiastical vestments, the *opus Anglicanum* of which only fragments survive. Pope Innocent IV wrote in 1246 that the excellence of this embroidery, which he coveted for Rome, made England seem to him a 'garden of delights, an inexhaustible well'. The men who created so much beauty out of stone must have approached their work in a similar spirit. We have no reason to doubt that in the huts that surrounded a great medieval church as it was being built there existed a faith about the universe and its divine Architect, although words were not what the builders used to express that faith. It cannot be claimed that thirteenth century England was thoroughly Christian. The statistics of murder in this period would prevent such a sentimental assessment. But a great church could raise to heaven the faith of a society where daily life was often nasty and short. As André Malraux was to sum it up, 'the cathedral is the expression of man's gratitude to God: it presents to him creation turned Christian'.[2]

There were protests about Henry III's expenditure on Westminster Abbey because it was financed out of taxes, then regarded as disasters to be justified only by emergencies. But the building itself was admired as a house fit for kings and for the King of Kings. When the new abbey was consecrated on 13 October 1269, with the solemn removal or 'translation' of the bones of St Edward the Confessor to his sumptuous shrine, no one of whom we have record lamented that it would have been cheaper to repair the Confessor's own church instead of pulling it down. At one stage some eight hundred men were directly engaged on the site, in addition to all the others who quarried the stone, felled the timber, collected the jewels and rich cloth, poured out their skill on the metalwork, the mosaics and the tiles, lent money for wages or administered the special fund established by the king for the work which absorbed him over twenty-four years.

The building of Westminster Abbey was, indeed, the

---

[2] Marcel Aubert, *High Gothic Art* (London, 1964), p.58. Contrast J. B. Given, *Society and Homicide in Thirteenth-Century England* (Stanford, Cal., 1977).

climax and main justification of this reign. Henry was not a master of men. Over his tomb close to the Confessor's shrine, the first bronze effigy to be seen in England was made by William Torel in the 1290s; the face is gentle and worried. Constantly the political history of the reign shows the simplicity of his mind. He asserted himself, only to be surprised by the opposition of his barons and to be unable to hold his own. This opposition to him should not be thought of as parliamentary. The barons knew that 'in the end they depended upon the king, just as the king depended on them', Sir Maurice Powicke commented. 'They had asked for power they did not really want. As Simon de Montfort bitterly remarked, they turned tail, as Englishmen always did.' The basic problem at this stage was, it seems, the king's personality; he was 'not a big enough man to win the confidence of his barons, and so to give himself that they gave themselves to him'.[3] So politically Henry III was not a success. But he was self-giving, and therefore highly effective, as a patron of the Church and of art. His devotion was as simple as his politics. In the University of Paris and in centres of theology in Italy his contemporary, St Thomas Aquinas (who died in 1274), was in this period constructing an intellectual edifice of dazzling courage and authority, a great system which would combine the orthodoxy of the Bible and the Church with the philosophy of Aristotle; but when St Louis, King of France, asked Henry why he did not hear more sermons, he replied that he preferred the Mass (he attended at least three Masses every day whenever possible), since it was better to see his friend than to hear him spoken about. The king was charitable, with a large, systematic and personal generosity recorded in his accounts; but high in what he did for his divine friend was the creation of beauty.

Much of Henry's reign was consumed by conflicts over money and power, since he became king at the age of nine and inherited from his father John an aristocracy insistent on the charters which protected them against the crown; but in the creation of his own great church at Westminster he had his

---

[3] F. M. Powicke, *The Thirteenth Century* (revised, Oxford, 1962), p.72.

best opportunity to show what money and power under his control could achieve. Another feature of the reign was the bitter rivalry between the English barons and the French civil servants such as Peter des Roches (Bishop of Winchester) and his nephew or son Peter des Rievaux; but in the building of Westminster Abbey there was international co-operation. The king caused the latest French fashions to be copied by Henry 'de Reyns' (was this Reims in France?) and by the masons under him in enduring stone, to general admiration. Sir Maurice Powicke judged that this abbey, the tallest church yet raised in England, was 'the most strenuous and concentrated, as it was also the most gracious, expression of a rich artistic life; and this life, fanned into intensity by the king, was in its turn the outcome of a social activity which engaged the interests of thousands of people, and meant more to them than all the political and ecclesiastical issues of the day . . . Henry had a passion for metal and jewel work, for vestments and sacred vessels curiously wrought and adorned with gems, for pictures and sculpture. He knew what he wanted, he could describe it in detail, was lavish in expenditure upon it, and exacting in the performance of it. If he had concentrated his mind upon affairs of state as successfully as he did upon works of art, he might have been the greatest of our kings, though possibly not the most beneficent.'[4]

The fact that the rebuilding of Westminster Abbey evoked enthusiasm is surely significant. Here was no pyramid built by brutalized slaves for a tyrant. What, then, was the society that created the king's own abbey and the bishops' cathedrals?

PARISHES AND MONASTERIES

It is not easy to recover the history of the parishes, but we know that many parish churches received additions or other improvements in the thirteenth century. In part this was a

---

[4] F. M. Powicke, *King Henry III and the Lord Edward* (Oxford, 1947), pp.572-3.

reflection of the general rise in agricultural prosperity and the trebling of the population in the period 1050-1300 — the period in which the surnames arose which were to show future generations that their ancestors had been butchers, carpenters, clerks, cooks, masons, millers, potters, shepherds, skinners, tailors, tanners, thatchers or tylers.

'England', Graham Hutton has written, 'had been covered with new churches, big and small, mainly between 1150 and 1250, after which it was largely a matter of pulling down and rebuilding them. . . . The magnitude of both the Church's and its parishioners' offerings, converted into stone and furniture and fittings of all kinds, was colossal. Parish churches shot up almost cheek-by-jowl in town and city parishes — over a hundred in London with barely 40,000 in-habitants before 1348, over twenty-five in big towns like Norwich or York with only eight thousand to ten thousand people. As better trade, communications and agriculture brought villages nearer to each other, churches grew bigger and more imposing. Hoskins has calculated that in tiny Rutland alone there were over fifty medieval churches, one to every two hundred and fifty souls, though each capable of holding many more. Such emulation in building, out of a low standard of life, cannot have been due solely to pride, even pride in local achievement. The desire to glorify God in an age of deep belief, and in an era of short and uncertain human lives, is apparent on all sides in these new and imposing parish churches; for their naves were the people's first and only communal buildings'.[5]

There was a growing emphasis on preaching. Large churches in the towns began to be built for the Franciscan or Dominican friars whom we are about to meet and the naves of parish churches were made more spacious so that a parish priest or a visiting friar could be heard clearly — although there were as yet few pulpits from which to speak or pews or chairs on which to sit. At the same time small chapels or

---

[5] Graham Hutton, *English Parish Churches* (London, 1976), p.68. The reference is to W. G. Hoskins, *The Making of the English Landscape* (London, 1955).

'chantries' began to be set aside and staffed with their own priests (endowed with rents from property) where Mass could be sung or said until the end of time for the souls of the founder, his family and his friends. So a well-to-do merchant could now secure the services which in the previous age a baron had secured by endowing a monastery.

A network of parishes over the whole land now brought every man, woman or child in a population around 2,250,000 into the personal responsibility of a priest. More than eight thousand parishes were registered in a survey of 1291, the *Taxatio Papae Nicholai*, and later evidence adds about 1,500 more. Some of the parishes, specially in the north, were still very large, but it has been estimated that the average included some three hundred souls in the country and about two hundred in the towns. Some 23,000 priests, assisted by perhaps ten thousand clerics in the minor orders, staffed these parishes, in addition to perhaps 25,000 monks, nuns, friars and hermits. Inevitably the evidence has been lost which would enable us to do justice to the missionary and pastoral work involved in the creation and maintenance of this far-reaching system. Most of what we know of the spiritual life and work of the priests is derived from the little books of instruction compiled for them by the most pastorally minded bishops. But it is reasonable to guess that the thirteenth century saw the development of an unprecedented intimacy between priest and people, based on the new insistence on an annual confession before Easter. This confession was no hurried affair. The priest was urged to examine his parishioner in detail about the orthodoxy of his beliefs as well as about his keeping of the moral commandments. There is also evidence that the Holy Communion was now being celebrated much more frequently. The ideal was a daily Mass, supplemented by the lesser services or 'offices' said together by the parish priest and the clergy who assisted him and who were usually called chaplains. Thus, in theory at any rate, each parish church would be a little monastery.

It has been estimated that when Henry III came to throne in 1217 there were about 180 large monasteries in England, with about five hundred smaller communities, owning between them perhaps a fifth of the country's total wealth. The

monastic population, little over a thousand in 1066, was probably about 12,500 in 1217 and about 17,500 in 1340.[6] About a
quarter of the parish churches were 'appropriated' to the
monasteries. It meant that the 'tithe' (tenth) payable to the
'rector' or 'parson' on the agricultural produce of the parish
belonged to the monks although they were obliged to appoint
and pay a 'vicar' (substitute) or chaplain to undertake the
pastoral care of the parish. A major effort was made by the
bishops in the thirteenth century to improve the financial position, security and housing of these vicars; and it did not help
that the richest monasteries were exempt from the local
bishop's jurisdiction and subject only to their own abbots and
the pope. A relic of that unsatisfactory arrangement remains
to this day in medieval churches where the nave, used and
paid for by the laity of the parish, is grander than the chancel,
occupied by the clergy and paid for by the rector. Evidently
the parish church was regarded as a source of income for the
monastery, not the monastery as a source of help for the parish
church.

The bishops were not the only people to look at the monks
critically. Already in the reign of Henry II the Welsh
eloquence of an embittered Archdeacon of Oxford, Gerald,
had begun a flourishing literary tradition of attacks on the
monks' practices, although their ideals remained sacred.
When economically active, the monks were condemned for
avarice; when inactive, for idleness. When their estates provided knights to serve the king, this was regarded as worldly;
when they did not, the loss to the country was lamented. The
resentment overflowed from such grumbles into legislation. In
1259 the statute of *Mortmain* enacted that no further land was
to be given into the 'dead hand' of a monastery. No doubt
much of the criticism is unfair, and the chief effect of the
statute was that in future the king was needed to grant licences
for the further endowment of monasteries. The statistics of
monastic growth spoke louder than the critics. But the

---

[6] D. Knowles and R. N. Hadcock, *Medieval Religious Houses: England
and Wales* (revised, Cambridge, 1971), provided an annotated list.
However, all medieval statistics are uncertain.

monasteries of the thirteenth century produced no spiritual
teacher able to stand comparison with the more worldly genius
of Matthew Paris, the lively and widely travelled journalist
and cartoonist who followed Roger of Wendover as the
chronicler of St Albans Abbey in 1235. The best known abbot
from the beginning of this century is Samson of Bury St
Edmunds, because his life was written by his chaplain, Jocelin
of Brakelond (and written up with gusto by Thomas Carlyle in
Past and Present, 1843). And Samson, although he ruled his
monks and managed his estates masterfully over almost thirty
years from 1182, was no spiritual giant. Jocelin noticed that
his master was happier outside than inside the monastery.
Others have noticed about Jocelin – and about his brethren as
they stand revealed in his artless chronicle – 'the deep essential
self-satisfaction and sense of superiority, broken only at the
surface by the ripples of domestic quarrel or external litigation'.[7]

In his history of *The Religious Orders of England* in the
thirteenth century (1948), Dom David Knowles told of much
steady discipline, of growing efficiency, of reforms to lift unsatisfactory monasteries to the level of the others; his final
impression was of a 'state of equilibrium'. But he observed
that the monasteries no longer resembled a tree 'white as a
bride with April blossom'. He entitled only one of his chapters
with the name of a leading monk – and that man was Henry of
Eastry, elected prior of the cathedral monastery of Christ
Church, Canterbury, in 1285. Henry was a devout monk but
chiefly a superb businessman who before his death in 1331 had
developed the previously insolvent monastery's estates to a
level of productivity never matched before or after. It was a
major contribution to the improvement of agriculture (together with the growth of the towns the most prominent
feature of the economic history of the time), but we may doubt
whether under such leadership Canterbury Cathedral would
have been the centre of popular religious enthusiasm, had it
not been for the archbishops buried in it, notably St Thomas.

---

[7] G. G. Coulton, *Five Centuries of Religion*, vol. ii (Cambridge, 1927),
p.46.

Fortunately, however, the spiritual life of England no longer depended entirely on the parish priests or the old-fashioned Benedictine monks. So far the story of English Christianity had been very largely the story of heroes and their influence. Kings made the decisions nationally; more locally, landowners built and endowed monasteries and parish churches. Saints were princes in the life of the spirit, celebrated for their heroism as Beowulf and other lay heroes had been celebrated; more locally, church life was governed by bishops, abbots and the more forceful type of priest. Thomas Becket was, at least in his own eyes, one such hero. But now, as the pilgrims began to crowd into Canterbury and to seek the other saints' shrines, the people entered the story of English Christianity; for 'the great flood of devotional fervour which overwhelmed Western Europe in the late twelfth and early thirteenth centuries had as one of its springs the refusal of the laity, the Latinless, the illiterate, to be excluded from the apostolic life of the Church.'[8]

Although those who worked with their hands found their greatest opportunity in building or adorning their churches, or in the practical duties of lay officials such as churchwardens who administered the affairs of the parishes, we do know of some who gave themselves to prayer. In the twelfth century we meet, for example, St Godric – a Norfolk pedlar, sailor and merchant, who in his voyages came to know and love the holy island of Lindisfarne; who went on pilgrimages to see Rome and the Holy Land for himself; who went to school with the children of Durham in order to be able to read the psalms; and who finally settled in his own hermitage at Finchale. A contemporary wrote a biography of him, describing his extraordinarily long white beard, his skin roughened by a sailor's

---

[8] Edmund Colledge in *Pre-Reformation English Spirituality*, ed. James Walsh (London, 1966), p.29.

life, his knees hardened by a hermit's. And women could enter
this life of the spirit freely. To help three noblewomen who
chose a disciplined, corporate life of prayer in seclusion, a
beautiful treatise was written in the English of the West
Midlands around 1200 – the 'Anchoresses' Rule' or *Ancren
Riwle*. With a lively use of proverbs, anecdotes and everyday
illustrations to adorn its great theme, this anonymous masterpiece summoned them to spiritual adventure, not to the mere
keeping of a rule.

The most popular spiritual movement of the twelfth century
was more highly organized: the Cistercian Order, so named
from its mother house at Cîteaux in Burgundy.

These 'White Monks' set themselves to live according to a
rule more austere than the rule of the ordinary Benedictine
'Black Monks'. In the sixth century both St Gregory the Great
and his ambassador St Augustine of Canterbury had been
moulded by the monastic tradition which went back to St
Benedict (480-550 approximately). In the eighth century the
learned holiness of this Benedictine tradition had come to
another climax in Bede and his brethren. In the tenth century
the adoption of St Benedict's rule in English cathedrals and
monasteries had been a decisive step in the recovery of
discipline and moral order after the fury of the Vikings. But St
Benedict himself had no intention of imposing exceptional
poverty or fasting or any other form of heroism. His one aim
was the recitation of the services of the 'Divine Office', the
opus Dei, in a stable community. The spirit of the worship
would spread into the common life with its ordered round of
manual or intellectual work (*laborare est orare*: 'to work is to
pray'). As a matter of course the monks would provide
hospitality, charity and education, but that would be incidental to the worship and the common life. Since St Benedict's
day many of the monasteries of his order had become the
chief buildings in cities or towns, maintained by troops of
servants and owning more estates than most of the neighbouring barons, each a prosperous little kingdom under its abbot's
rule. They had been endowed lavishly by landowners anxious
that after death their souls, and their families', should be
assured of prayers. But all the time the Benedictine Order

included some men who desired to escape further from the world's distractions, to sacrifice themselves more fully in order to save their own souls.

The movement for greater strictness within this great Benedictine tradition gained a centre when the abbey of Cîteaux in Burgundy was founded by some monks of Molesme in 1098. Among them was a Dorset man, St Stephen Harding, who subsequently became abbot. The movement gained a genius as its spokesman when, twenty years later, a group of young noblemen entered Cîteaux as novices; for the leader of this group was St Bernard. Bidden by Stephen Harding to found a new monastery in 1115, he established a house at Clairvaux and became its abbot. He was a spiritual pioneer who happened to be also a writer and an organizer with a capacity to mould the mind of a generation. His writings spread his mysticism; he based the soul's communion with God firmly on an exact knowledge of the Bible, on loyalty to the Church, and on a passionately personal devotion to Christ and his Mother, addressed in human terms more intimately than had been thought right for many centuries. Bernard's organizing power was soon used in the wider affairs of the Church. He upheld Pope Innocent II against rivals, was rewarded with many privileges for the Cistercian Order, and lived to see a Cistercian monk as pope (Eugenius III). This pope made another Cistercian, Henry Murdac, Archbishop of York as part of the rapid extension of the movement throughout Christendom.

The Cistercians always kept their monasteries linked as a family by an annual visit to be paid by each abbot to the mother house from which his own had derived. They built their houses right away from the towns, abandoning any attempt to run a school or a welfare centre, abandoning also the ownership of estates which were obliged to produce knights for the king's service, refusing to get entangled in the profits or responsibilities of parish churches, building their own churches with plain architecture and no painting on the walls. They dispensed with servants; instead they worked in the fields themselves and an essential role was given to the *conversi*, illiterate lay brothers who did the work on the buildings, in the fields and among the sheep. In their austere routine of life meat was as rare as heat. In their churches there was little colour but much intensity of prayer.

The first such house in England was founded very quietly in Surrey, but the movement attracted notice when White Monks went north in 1132. In York their austerity stirred the consciences of some of the monks of a very rich house, St Mary's Abbey, who left to found the abbey of Fountains, then in a remote spot. In this they were encouraged by Thurstan, who as Archbishop of York 1119-40 was a creative leader of church life in the north. Before long the York pilgrims into the wilderness raised a church of which the massively simple nave still survives, although it is now roofless. The Dean of York was among the early recruits at Fountains.[9] Soon there were many hundreds, and other Cistercian houses were built in Yorkshire, among them one at Rievaulx, in the valley of the Rye. One of the first recruits there was Ailred, who fell under Bernard's influence while they were together in Rome in 1141, and who became his English equivalent.

The descendant of a long line of married priests who had staffed St Wilfrid's church at Hexham, Ailred moved away from this comfortable heritage. First he used his education and his charm to work at the court of King David of Scotland, whose son had been sent to school at Hexham. As the king's steward he was at the centre of the whole process by which David (the son of Malcolm who had overthrown Macbeth and married St Margaret of Scotland) brought his country into the European world of Roman Catholicism and feudalism. Doubtless Ailred could have become a bishop, but he grew dissatisfied. While on a mission to the Archbishop of York he came across the new Cistercian experiment (about 1133), and throwing himself into it became its abbot in 1147. He was the warmly affectionate and spiritually encouraging father of the whole community as it struggled to grow in disciplined sanctity. His writings, and his biography by his pupil Walter

---

[9] A biography of *Thurstan* has been provided by Donald Nicholl (York, 1964), and a study of the drama in 1132 by Denis Bethell in *Journal of Ecclesiastical History* (Cambridge, 1966), pp.11-27.

Daniel, celebrate an achievement of Christian friendship – a royal court composed of mostly illiterate Cistercians in the valley of the Rye. In Ailred's leadership we can see Cicero's famous treatise on friendship quoted and practised but subordinated to the overwhelming inspiration of the New Testament. The affection which he offered drew many hearts despite his stern motto 'be still, be silent, endure'. Walter Daniel called him 'friendship's child, for his whole occupation was to love and to be loved'.

The use of many hands to make virgin soil productive corresponded with the economic reality of the time, an age of expanding food-supply and population; but inevitably the success of the Cistercians meant that they did not for long continue in the idyllic innocence which appears in everything written by, or about, Ailred. In Italy a disillusioned Cistercian monk, Joachim of Fiore, attracted much attention before his death in 1202 by prophecies that a decadent Church was about to be replaced by an 'Age of the Spirit'. It has, indeed, been suggested that not even the White Monks of Rievaulx were the totally consecrated band of brothers of whom Ailred liked to write.

Pioneering agriculture rapidly brought wealth to these men who had fled from the towns and the feudal system. The Cistercian Order became a major force in the international wool trade, and its self-discipline meant that some of its members (Ailred among them) were entrusted with affairs of state. Baldwin, the abbot of the Cistercian house at Ford in Devon, attracted the notice of Henry II and found himself first Bishop of Worcester and then, in 1184, Archbishop of Canterbury. He was a holy man and a scholar in the tradition of Lanfranc and Anselm, writing on the sacrament of the altar and on the commendation of the Christian faith. But this White Monk was involved in a bitter dispute with the Black Monks of his own cathedral, whose luxury he denounced; and involved, too, in King Richard's crusade, the reality of which broke his heart.

Other great movements arose now that the normal Black Monks no longer satisfied the spiritual ambitions of the age. There were, for example, about thirty-seven houses of the austere Carmelite Friars, originating in a union of hermits under St Berthold on Mount Carmel in the Holy Land. There were the Black (or Augustinian or Austin) Canons, brother-hoods of priests living under a semi-monastic rule of life attributed to St Augustine of Hippo but also undertaking some pastoral work in the parishes; by the end there were some three hundred such houses in medieval England, mostly small and poor. There were the White Canons, companies of austere preachers and parish priests who derived their ideals from the work of St Norbert in the valley of Prémontré; their official title was Premonstratensian Canons. In England they had some thirty houses, as did the White (or Augustinian) Friars, originating in a union of Italian hermits in 1244. But the real successors to the Black Monks as spiritual pioneers were about 180 houses of the Grey and Black Friars, as the Franciscans and Dominicans were called. Their ideal was to combine the austerity of the Cistercians and Carmelites with an involvement in the life of the people going much deeper than the Black or White Canons. For a time, these friars (brothers) seemed to be bringing back Christianity's earliest and purest days – or inaugurating at long last the Age of the Spirit of which Abbot Joachim had dreamed.

THE FRIARS

A great and shrewd pope, Innocent III, gave the Franciscan Order his blessing in 1210. At that stage the order was still in real life which it always remained in the mind of St Francis: a mainly lay fellowship, going to the extremes of a pure love of God and humanity, totally identified with the poor, delighted when it was thought foolish. Its ideals seemed completely dif-ferent from those of the Dominican Order, given papal ap-proval six years later; for the Dominicans were the Order of Preachers, attempting a reasoned defence of orthodoxy, naturally attached to the universities. Within a short period, however, before any of the friars reached England, the little brothers of St Francis had gravitated to the universities just like St Dominic's scholarly preachers.

This move is not so inexplicable as it may seem. The universities which emerged in the twelfth and thirteenth centuries were a phenomenon of the Age of Faith. They were chiefly intended to provide a general education for the clergy; theology was the 'queen of sciences' in the higher studies; and where the speciality was law or medicine that training, too, was Christian in its whole atmosphere. Yet like the friars, the universities were free and easy in comparison with earlier medieval institutions, subject neither to the discipline of a monastery nor to the supervision of a bishop. One of the reasons why universities emerged in Oxford and Cambridge was that in neither place was there a bishop. And the scholars were prepared to pay the price of this independence amid a feudal society. Most medieval scholars were always poor. They were often, as a consolation, also young; undergraduates were of an age which we should expect to find still at school. Such centres, full of unattached young men, bursting with idealism and eagerness, seemed to offer both the best sources of recruitment for the new Christian work and also the best means of training recruits. So the move to the universities is understandable. Whether or not we applaud all its consequences depends on what we make of St Francis and his extraordinary intention.

Francesco Bernadone was a charming Italian, the son of a merchant, in his youth the leader of the merry-makers in the beautiful and prosperous town of Assisi, to the end of his days a great lover and poet of humanity and of nature (whereas the founder of the Dominicans was a Spanish puritan, born of an ancient family, a scholar from boyhood). The conversion of Francis of Assisi was brought about by the direct challenge of the simplest sayings in the gospels, and it led immediately to kissing a leper. What shocked Francis was the gap between the Church of Jesus and the poor; his answer was to lead into the world an army of men as devoted to Lady Poverty as the troubadours were devoted to their mistresses (whereas Dominic found his vocation preaching against the Albigensian heretics in the south of France when the Cistercians had failed – and he organized his order to concentrate on pure doctrine, purity of life being only one of the proofs of orthodoxy). Francis appealed to romantics. He invented the Christmas crib with live animals, and was said to have preached to birds. He attracted teenagers; St Clare was only seventeen when she founded the Second Order of Franciscans. He also appealed to the mature; he won the heart of Dominic when the two saints met in Rome in 1216. He attracted and fascinated because he was supremely the 'mirror of Christ'. Before his death in 1226 the chief sign of distinction which he had received was the fruit of his identification with his Master: the stigmata, the marks of crucifixion on his own body. His last testament was a plea that no Franciscan should ever get involved in the ownership of property or in ecclesiastical politics – a plea which, after bitter controversies, the 'Spirituals' who followed his instructions failed to get established as the test of Franciscan life. The authorities declared him a saint and his successor, Brother Elias, built a very costly shrine for his body, adorned by the best art of the time.

One of the closest companions of St Francis was William the Englishman (and another Englishman, Laurence, was one of St Dominic's earliest recruits). The Franciscans first landed in England on 10 September 1224, two days before Francis received the stigmata. Their story was still fresh when it was told by Brother Thomas of Eccleston in his chronicle written in 1258-9. There were nine of them, including only one priest. Some of them were in Oxford by the end of October. That winter their joyful patience amid poverty began to win fresh converts to their way; it was noticed that their bare feet left blood on the ice as they walked on their errands of mercy. The rapid expansion of their numbers (there were 1,242 Franciscans in England by 1255) meant that Christian love was being taken into the poorer parts of the developing towns – into homes which the monks had deliberately abandoned and which most parish priests did not, it seems, visit with enough pastoral zeal. And Christian love was being made more lovable; there survives a 'Love-song of Friar Thomas of Hales', written before 1272, in which a Franciscan urges a frankly romantic love of Christ on a girl who has joined the order. But a major reason for the expansion of the English Franciscans was their appeal to Oxford men; and gradually their university links brought their aims closer to those of the Dominicans – who had landed in England three years previously and, after receiving Cardinal Langton's blessing at Canterbury, had gone straight to Oxford.

Under an Englishman, Haymo of Faversham, the international leader or Minister General of the Franciscans 1240-44, it became clear that priests, not laymen, would be dominant in the order. Under St Bonaventure, Minister-General 1257-74, himself the 'Seraphic Doctor' of Dante's *Paradiso* and the creator of a systematic theology based on the teaching of St Augustine of Hippo, it became clear that the emphasis would be upon a disciplined life within stone-built convents, with a rigorous intellectual training for all who could profit by it. The glories of the Franciscan Order came to be scholars. One such was Alexander of Hales, the Englishman who shaped the mind of Bonaventure by his lectures in Paris – and the first Christian to employ all the works of Aristotle in his exposition of the Faith. St Clare lived in seclusion for more than forty years, sleeping on the floor of her cell, eating very little, praying almost without a pause, never wasting time on a book; but now Grey Friars were to be found intellectually intoxicated in lecture halls and libraries. Franciscan missionaries took the Gospel to the slums of Europe and to the world of Islam, to China and Mongolia; but for some the most alluring country came to be the realms of the intellect, approached through the lecture halls of Paris and Oxford, and that was not the vision of St Francis. Brother Giles was a saint, the intimate friend and companion of Francis, who would go into ecstasies when the children of Perugia cried 'Paradiso!' (naturally the children would often raise the cry, to see what happened). And Brother Giles once let slip his own cry: 'Paris, Paris, why did you destroy the Order of St Francis?'

OXFORD AND GROSSETESTE

Oxford became a centre of study under circumstances which remain obscure despite all the researches of its grateful sons. It contained monasteries but in an age when men were losing their confidence that the monasteries could educate enough teachers and leaders for the Church, Oxford could offer more than a gathering of monks. The flourishing town was accessible from London, the Midlands, the west and the south. Early in the twelfth century scholars are known to have given instruction there; Robert Pullen, later a cardinal, did in 1133. When English students were recalled from Paris during the Becket dispute in 1167 they concentrated on Oxford, particularly on the church of St Mary-the-Virgin. In the 1180s we find a boastful Welshman reading aloud a book about Ireland 'before a great audience at Oxford, where of all places in England the clergy are most strong and pre-eminent in learning'.[10] By 1209 the students were sufficiently numerous to make an impact in their first fight against the townsmen. The chronicle of Matthew Paris claims that some three thousand masters and scholars left Oxford until the university was granted a fresh security by the papal legate in 1214, under its own chancellor to be appointed by the Bishop of Lincoln.

One of the early lecturers in logic at Oxford, Edmund Rich of Abingdon, was eminent in holiness as well as philosophy. There was a story of how as a boy of about twelve, walking alone in the fields, he had had a vision of Jesus as a boy walking beside him, Certainly the records indicate that in his maturity he was a man of great moral force to whom all parties instinctively turned during the political crises of the 1230s. After a spell as one of the canons of the old cathedral at Salisbury (when it was his custom to spend half the year in a

---

[10] *The Autobiography of Giraldus Cambrensis*, ed. H. E. Butler (London, 1937), p.97.
J. I. Catto edited the first volume of *A History of the University of Oxford* (Oxford, 1984).

monastery), he was made by successive popes first Archbishop of Canterbury and then a saint. Dying on his way to a council in Rome, he was buried among the Cistercians of Pontigny where Becket and Langton had taken refuge.[11] But St Edmund was not the greatest of the founders of Oxford's fame.

Born about 1168 in a Suffolk home with no wealth, Robert Grosseteste somehow acquired an education, was ordained, and spent most of the years 1200-35 teaching in the university at Oxford. He was never an adventurous theologian; never an Anselm. Like his contemporary Langton he relied on the Bible. The morning should be given to the Bible; his other authorities — principally St Augustine of Hippo and the newly discovered works of Aristotle — could wait until the afternoon. In the exposition of such authorities he developed a massive learning. More unusual, however, was his scientific bent. He had a mathematical ability to match the far-off Arabs through whose skill the West was now learning to be numerate. As often happens with mathematicians, his love and understanding of music also went deep. He investigated many scientific problems — the reform of the calendar around the more accurate dating of Easter (he shared this interest as well as a love of the Bible with Bede), the composition of the rainbow or the stars, the whole scientific method of induction and experiment. He was particularly fascinated by light, which he regarded as a very subtle substance, analysing how it reached the human eye but also delighting to write or preach about the light of the soul. He was able to get others to share his intellectual enthusiasm, becoming the university's first chancellor and stamping on it his own emphasis on science. He has been assessed as 'the first great English scientist and philosopher of science. At a time when guidance was essential, he provided England's young university with a creative understanding of science that made it for a time the leading scientific centre in Christendom and enabled it to contribute to the modern world something entirely new'.[12]

---

[11] See C. H. Laurence, *St Edmund of Abingdon* (Oxford, 1960).

[12] A. C. Crombie in *Robert Grosseteste: Scholar and Bishop*, ed. D. A. Callus (Oxford, 1955), p.115.

But Grosseteste had one still stronger interest: the reform of the Church in the service of God and the people. When the Franciscans opened a lecture hall in Oxford, they invited the university's leading scholar to preside over it; and he accepted. Eventually he bequeathed his own books to these beloved friars. About five years later (in 1235), at an age when university teachers of later generations felt ripe for a pensioned retirement, he accepted election as Bishop of Lincoln, then the most populous diocese in the country, stretching from the Humber to the Thames. He made a point of taking Franciscans and Dominicans with him. He exercised a tireless and fearless rule over eighteen years, and no Englishman did more to follow up Cardinal Langton in enforcing the reforming programme of the Lateran Council of 1215. When resisting what he thought was wrong, he was quite willing to defy the saintly Archbishop of Canterbury or the king. When the pope attempted to intrude a nephew into a canonry of Lincoln, Grosseteste (who normally held an exalted view of the papacy as the sun of the Church, all other bishops being mere moon or stars) replied: 'as an obedient son I disobey, I contradict, I rebel.'

One of the bishop's friends was Simon de Montfort, Earl of Leicester, later to be over-praised because the enlargement of the 'parliament' (consultation) of the Great Council of the realm under his influence was thought to make him the founder of parliamentary democracy. Himself a hard man and no saint, the earl discussed Christian ideals with the bishop and their mutual friend, Adam Marsh the Franciscan leader at Oxford. He entrusted him with the education of his sons and even lent him his cook.[13] But Grosseteste was no politician. He disapproved of bishops serving as civil servants or judges, and was no more of a democrat than was Montfort himself.

His passion was to insist on the highest standards of religious discipline throughout his diocese. In his poem *Le Chasteau d'Amour* he made an elaborate comparison between Christ's

---

[13] M. W. Labarge, *Simon de Montfort* (London, 1962), pp.74-79.

Church, love's fortress, with a castle of that feudal age; and he defended it. In a single year he deposed seven abbots and four priors from their slack rule of monasteries. When the Dean of Lincoln resisted the bishop's attempt to reform the cathedral, he found himself first forbidden to enter the great church and then removed from office; and Grosseteste successfully fought the cathedral clergy's appeal to Rome. Appearing as an old man before the pope and his fellow-bishops, he declared what the work of a pastor meant to him. It must include 'the truthful teaching of the living truth, the awe-inspiring condemnation of vice and the severe punishment of it when necessary. It consists also in feeding the hungry, giving drink to the thirsty, covering the naked, receiving guests, visiting the sick and those in prison especially those who belong to the parish. . . . By the doing of these things is the people to be taught the holy duties of the active life'. And he did his utmost to make sure that every priest appointed to a church anywhere in his diocese understood these duties.

Not content with this activity, while Bishop of Lincoln Grosseteste strengthened his previous knowledge of Greek enough to devote his leisure to the work of a translator. A small library of important works in Greek was made available to Latin-readers by him or by other translators in his employment. It was his recreation. It is remarkable that a churchman so venerated by the people, the contemporary of St Edmund and spiritually his equal, was never formally canonized as a saint; and that no biography was written of him before a worthless poem of 1503. But it is not surprising, in an age when popes made saints and monks wrote biographies.

SCIENCE AND DEMOCRACY

The contrast is great between 'St Robert of Lincoln' – as Grosseteste was often called, despite the lack of official recognition – and Roger Bacon.

Bacon was a genius but spent most of his old age under suspicion and (according to tradition) under confinement, having alienated or alarmed the Church of his day by the quarrelsome freedom with which he expressed independent views on contemporary topics and personalities. He greatly admired Grossesteste, although there is no evidence that he was his pupil. Born about 1215, he devoted himself to the study of the Bible, of Greek and Hebrew (he compiled dictionaries), of Aristotle and of science, partly in Oxford but mainly in Paris. Gradually he developed an eager ambition to explore the world around him. Why should he not do for his own day what Aristotle had done for his? He would rely on experience and experiment, confident that all true knowledge, ancient or modern, would be found to confirm God's timeless revelation of himself in the scriptures. For metaphysical theologians such as his contemporary St Thomas Aquinas, he had only contempt.

He did not have the philosophical ability to construct a system of ideas to rival the new system of Aquinas. Nor was his thought fully scientific as future generations were to define science. He was always having a dialogue in his mind with Aristotle, the 'master of those who know'. He was fascinated by astrology's teaching about the influence of the stars on the destinies of men; and by alchemy's attempt to turn baser metals into gold. He was sure that Antichrist was about to appear, heralding the end of the world. One of the reasons why he urged Christians to be scientists was that the Antichrist would be one. Yet at an uncanny number of points he urged the importance of experiments which, when pursued after his time, were to shape the modern world. It may be the case that he invented the telescope, the microscope and the thermometer. He argued for the possibility of cranes, of self-propelling boats, of submarines, of flying machines, of a continent across the Atlantic, of many other marvels.

This miraculously gifted inventor had a magnificent trust in the intellect, arguing that irrationality was the essence of barbarism. He longed for the English ('who are, and have been, distinguished more than all others for their learning') should be the architects of a thoroughly reasonable civilization based on science as well as faith. And his great opportunity came when in 1265 Pope Clement IV, a scholarly Frenchman, asked him to outline an intellectual programme for the Church. Bacon told the pope that he had already spent a vast sum on 'secret books, different kinds of experiments, the acquisition of languages, instruments, tables and other things'; and with a frantic haste he attempted to survey all knowledge and to suggest all desirable reforms for the pope's benefit. Unfortunately Clement IV died in 1268 without making any response of which we have evidence.[14]

In about his fortieth year, at approximately the same time as Grosseteste's move to be Bishop of Lincoln, Bacon became a Franciscan. Exactly why he joined the friars we do not know; he was devout, but his main motive may have been to secure backing for his researches. Among the friars he would have found more than a few with intellectual interests similar to his own, as well as others shocked by his boldness. Having been for many years under suspicion and perhaps in prison, he was eventually released to write and to die in peace (in 1292). His last work was a *Compendium of Theology*.

Thus the Franciscans unexpectedly contributed to the growth of the English universities – a word which must be in the plural, since in 1209 a large number of masters and students migrated from Oxford to Cambridge after their dispute with the townsmen, and some stayed behind. The Franciscans arrived in Cambridge in 1225, a year before the first known appointment of a chancellor in the university.

The Dominicans also contributed to the growth of the universities, but it will be more interesting to glance at what they did for parliamentary democracy. In contrast with the monks who had all been placed under the benevolent despotism of abbots, the Dominicans were given by their founder a constitution which gave elected friars, gathered in chapters, the decisive say in the affairs of the order. There is evidence that Black Friars accustomed to this measure of democracy encouraged the clergy in general to demand to be consulted about taxation by pope or king: 'proctors' or elected represen-

---

[14] See S. C. Easton, *Roger Bacon and the Search for a Universal Science* (Oxford, 1952), and for the background Alexander Murray, *Reason and Society in the Middle Ages* (Oxford, 1978).

tatives of the clergy were summoned in 1256 and 1269 in accordance with the maxim that 'what touches all must be approved by all'. The Dominicans also influenced the barons and townsmen who because of their abilities wanted to secure their services; and this influence helped to popularize the idea that the king himself must consult the 'faithful men of the realm' in regular parliaments before he levied taxes.[15]

So the contributions made to the life of England by the vitality of the friars and the scholars were extremely diverse; out of their poverty they made many rich. A record of the table-talk of Robert Grosseteste gives it some unity, however. 'The Bishop said to Brother Peter that places standing over water are not healthy, unless on a lofty site. He said, moreover, that it pleased him greatly when he saw the sleeves of the Brethren patched. And he said that pure pepper was better than ginger in a sauce. He said also that he rejoiced when he saw that his scholars did not care about his lectures, so long as he had prepared them carefully, because an occasion of vainglorying was thus taken from him, and he lost nothing of his merit'.[16] Thus the great bishop, taking his ease at table, casually assembled amateur science and holy poverty, the joys of the palate and of the mind.

THE BISHOPS

Robert Grosseteste and St Edmund of Abingdon, although outstanding, did not stand in isolation among the bishops of thirteenth century England. A typical figure showing the greater strictness of the new age was Richard Poore. He was bishop and builder of Salisbury Cathedral, a much admired pastor and administrator. He faithfully carried out the

---

[15] See M. V. Clarke, *Medieval Representation and Consent* (London, 1936), and G. L. Haskins, *The Growth of English Representative Government* (Oxford, 1948).
[16] *The Coming of the Friars Minor*, ed. E. G. Salter (London, 1926), p.114.

Church's official policy of regarding the presence of a wife or concubine in a rectory or vicarage as a major sin; this campaign, generalled by the inflexible Anselm in the 1100s, had been led to a more or less total victory by Pope Calixtus II at the council of Reims in 1123. Yet Richard Poore was an illegitimate son of Henry II's clerk who became Bishop of Winchester, Richard of Ilchester. His brother Herbert had been Bishop of Salisbury before him. He may also have been descended from Roger Poore, whom we have already met as Bishop of Salisbury and as the father or uncle of men eminent in Church and State in King Stephen's reign. Times were changing.

Bishops in the Middle Ages were not, on the whole, expected to make their mark as pastors or preachers. Diocesan bishops were not even regarded chiefly as dispensers of sacraments: they were primarily judges, reformers of abuses, enablers of legal transactions. A bishop did not go round making himself popular. He expected people to come to the manor house where he was staying at the time and there petition for whatever favour they wanted. He employed a considerable staff of expert clerks, a vicar-general to take charge of the administration, specially during his absence from the diocese, and a 'suffragan' bishop (often a friar) to carry out ecclesiastical duties such as confirmations for which he had no time. This meant that the official life of the diocese could function smoothly while he was himself far away performing his other duties as a counsellor to the king and perhaps also as a hardworking head of the civil service. Yet a surprising number of thirteenth-century bishops were admired as men of God.

One reason was that they had a clear reforming programme to apply to their dioceses – the decrees of the Lateran Council of 1215 supplemented by the legislation accepted by church councils assembling under two able and forceful legates from Rome, Cardinal Otto (1237) and Ottobuono Fiesci who was in England 1265-8. And they were active. One modern authority has written that 'on the whole bishops of that period were men of ability and principle, and long vacancies and absences from the diocese were probably rarer than in the troubled

twelfth century or in the last two centuries before the Reformation. . . . The impression of painstaking fulfilment of duty
grows upon the reader as he passes through one register after
another.'[17] Another scholar has said about these bishops that
'as leaders, administrators, visitors, builders, and patrons of
learning and the arts, they have never been excelled'.[18]

For almost twenty years two friars held the archbishopric of
Canterbury (which for almost thirty years, 1240-69, had been
in the hands of an Italian, Boniface of Savoy, appointed
because he was the queen's uncle). Robert Kilwardby, the
Dominican provincial prior, made a conscientious archbishop
between his appointment in 1273 and his removal to Italy as a
cardinal five years later – a move which stressed that no archbishop, however English, was now much more than an agent
of the pope. His successor at Canterbury, John Pecham, had
been the leader of the English Franciscans and an equally eminent scholar. In the world of theology both he and Kilwardby
did their utmost to resist the influence of their contemporary,
St Thomas Aquinas, on the ground that he was an innovator.
What had been good enough for Stephen Langton, appealing
to the plain Bible and not troubling to digest the metaphysics
of Aristotle, was good enough for these stalwart English conservatives. But as archbishop until 1292, Pecham was an
unresting reformer. Administration must be up-to-date, while
doctrine was changeless.

Since he regarded himself as a judge of abuses in church life
throughout the province of Canterbury including Wales, he
managed to hold disciplinary 'visitations' in all the dioceses
and to sweep through many monasteries, tightening up their
rule of life or reorganizing their finances. He fought particularly against pluralism, the system (or non-system) which
had allowed a single priest to be nominally the rector of many
parishes, paying only part of the income to the priest who
did the pastoral work. Bogo de Clare, a son of an Earl of
Gloucester and a notorious pluralist, was one of the wealthiest

---

[17] David Knowles, *The Religious Orders in England*, vol. i (Cambridge, 1948), p.111.

[18] F. M. Powicke, *The Thirteenth Century*, p.485.

men in the kingdom. His household accounts show that in a year he was content to spend more on ginger to spice his dinners than on paying a vicar to serve one of his parishes. The other bishops, too, were expected to condemn pluralism, but had often taken advantage of it on the way up. As an ex-friar, Pecham could hit out.

As the chief officer in England of the Catholic Church whose pope had appointed him to Canterbury after rejecting the king's candidate, this fierce archbishop conducted another campaign to defend and enlarge the independence of the Church's courts. Fresh copies of Magna Carta were ordered to be posted.up in all the cathedrals each Easter. Although his puritanism did not make him popular, neither his energy nor his integrity could be doubted. His most lasting monument was an outline of doctrine and morals issued in 1281 in order to guide parish priests. The mysteries were now made clear and numbered. Neatly listing and expounding the fourteen articles of faith, the ten commandments, the seven deadly sins, the seven principal virtues, the seven works of mercy, the seven sacraments and the three persons of the Trinity, this document was a constantly consulted authority in English parish life up to the end of the Middle Ages. An edition was printed at Oxford as late as 1520.[19]

Another former chancellor of Oxford who devoted himself to the care of a diocese – in his case, Chichester 1245-53 – was St Richard of Wych (Droitwich). He had known poverty as a boy; it is related that he and the fellow-student with whom he shared a room were so poor that they had only one gown (the equivalent of the modern coat) between them. In it, one of them at a time would go out to a lecture. Richard did not forget the lessons of poverty when he had been taken into the household of St Edmund of Abingdon and launched on an ecclesiastical career. This scholar who had specialized in canon law has been remembered chiefly by his humility while a bishop (he was a vegetarian and he walked through Sussex on foot), and by his prayer that he might see Jesus more clearly, love him more dearly and follow him more nearly.

---

[19] See D. L. Douie, *Archbishop Pecham* (Oxford, 1952).

One of the bishops who resisted Pecham's attempt to exercise jurisdiction over all the dioceses was Thomas Cantilupe, Bishop of Hereford. But he did not resist in order to cover up intellectual sloth or moral evil. He, too, had been chancellor at Oxford – and Chancellor of England during the year when Simon de Montfort and his fellow-barons were the virtual rulers of the country (1265). Pecham excommunicated Cantilupe, who was, however, such a model of holiness that after his death in 1282 his tomb became a centre of faith in miracles and he was canonized as a saint. His uncle Walter Cantilupe, Bishop of Worcester 1236-66, had been a local pastor and national figure of much the same quality in the previous generation, the friend of Robert Grosseteste and of Simon de Montfort.

Finally we can look at the strange story of St William of York, the thirteenth century's attempt to draw from the conflicts of the previous century a martyr who could be the northern equivalent of St Thomas of Canterbury.

William had been a nobleman for whom an ecclesiastical income was necessary; his father was the illegitimate son of the Count of Blois, his mother the illegitimate daughter of King Stephen. As Treasurer of York Minster he seems to have been amiable but no more. His royal grandfather secured his election as Archbishop of York in 1140, but he was accused by Bernard, Ailred and other Cistercians of having bought the appointment (simony) and of unchastity. In reply his irritated rich friends sacked Fountains Abbey. In 1147 he was deposed by the Cistercian pope in favour of Henry Murdac, Abbot of Fountains. This sordid tale now begins to reflect some of the idealism which was to shine in the next century. William withdrew to Winchester, where he lived a quiet and austere life until Henry Murdac had died and there was a new pope. In 1154 he returned to York as archbishop, only to die a month later (an archdeacon was accused of administering poison). Once dead, he was venerated as a saint so ardently that his official canonization followed in 1227.

Whatever his real character may have been, the fact that a cult flourished around St William's shrine demonstrates the eagerness of the thirteenth century to honour a bishop who could be regarded as a saint in the great church where he had been enthroned. And under Walter de Gray, Archbishop of York for forty years from 1215, the cult helped to finance the construction of the majestic transepts of York Minster. They still stand, with their climax in the Five Sisters Window, still filled with more than a hundred thousand jewel-like pieces of thirteenth-century glass.

THE CATHEDRALS

The nineteen cathedrals of medieval England were the mother churches of large numbers of parishes. Although parishioners did not attend 'diocesan services' of the modern type, their obligations to their cathedrals were brought home by the custom of bringing financial offerings on Mothering Sunday (in mid-Lent) and Whit Sunday. At all times of the year people would be found in these busy churches, praying before the saints' shrines or the altars which often contained holy relics, and unless the cathedral was also a monastery its nave was available to local people for many everyday purposes; the atmosphere in the nave of St Paul's in London, for example, was decidedly secular. The place of the cathedral in the loyalties of the people is shown by the facts that people from all over the diocese could be expected both to contribute to building projects and to leave money in their wills for the fabric.

In these limited but important senses the medieval cathedral was the people's church even if it was also a church providing incomes for many canons (Lincoln had fifty-eight) or monks. The cathedrals at Canterbury, Rochester, Winchester, Worcester, Norwich, Ely and Durham were Benedictine monasteries. Bath and Coventry were also cathedral monasteries but they shared their status in the diocese with 'secular' Wells and Lichfield; and significantly, in these two dioceses during the thirteenth century the 'secular' churches came decisively to the fore as the main cathedrals. The cathedral might be less splendid than the greatest monastic

churches, Westminster or Glastonbury, St Albans or Bury St
Edmunds. It might be rivalled by the large 'collegiate
churches' in the towns, such as Beverley, Southwell and Ripon
in the diocese of York. But it was still significant just because it
was the cathedral, where the bishop's throne (*cathedra*) was.
In remote Carlisle the fairly small and poor church staffed by
Augustinian canons became a cathedral in 1133; and over a
century and a half from 1245, its choir was rebuilt to fit this
dignity.

English ecclesiastical architecture, to be seen on a sumptuous scale in these cathedrals as in the great abbeys, was
marked by three styles between 1050 and 1350. The nineteenth century named these styles: Romanesque or Norman,
Early English, and Decorated or Geometric Gothic. Each style
had its origins in France.

The Norman conquerors were used to the idea of the grand
church. St Hugh of Cluny, who ruled his abbey for sixty years
and was one of the Benedictine Order's greatest reformers,
taught that a very large church demonstrated, or at least
encouraged, a very large piety. The abbey at Cluny set the
standard by being the largest church in Christendom, with a
constant round of magnificent worship. The Normans
brought their own trained masons to England; when they
could, they used the limestone quarried near Caen in their
homeland. Already before the conquest Edward the Confessor's abbey had given a revolutionary indication of what was
to come; it was over three hundred feet long, whereas the
cathedral of East Anglia, then at North Elmham, was smaller
by two-thirds. Now the conquerors set out to adorn England
with churches which would rise to the ideal taught at Cluny
and exemplified at Westminster.

The Romanesque style had originated in Lombardy around
800. The semi-circular arches, often echoed in the arcading
on the walls, were inspired not only by practical considerations
but also by the aqueducts and other remains of the Roman
civilization in Europe. As we can still see, when St Albans
Abbey was magnificently rebuilt by the Normans many
thousands of Roman bricks were used from the ruins of nearby
Verulamium. Battle Abbey, built where the decision of 1066

had been reached, introduced into England the French fashion of a passage or ambulatory around the main altar of a great church – a feature still preserved in the Norman cathedral at Norwich and in Tewkesbury Abbey. Other features which the Norman builders developed in England were not so prominent in France: the large crypt beneath the church to provide more chapels, the long nave to accommodate crowds or to make processions impressive, the high lantern tower (which often collapsed). Knowing what they wanted, they also knew that they wanted it quickly and everywhere. William of Malmesbury wrote of Lanfranc's new Canterbury Cathedral that its speed was as admirable as its beauty. Almost all the monasteries were rebuilt on a grand scale as soon as the new Norman abbot felt that he had got the monks under his control and the neighbouring landowners on his side. Only in Exeter and Lichfield was the old cathedral kept – and there, only for the time being.

The Normans came to their triumph in Durham Cathedral. It was begun by Bishop William of St Calais, one of William the Conqueror's clerks, who had temporarily fallen foul of the king in 1088 for failing to provide enough knights to fight rebels. But now in 1093 after a period of exile the bishop was in favour again; and to celebrate he began this building, splendidly sited above the river Wear. It was completed when there was no bishop in the 1130s, thanks to the enthusiasm of the monks whose church it had become. The ribbed stone vaulting was an architectural and technical miracle; the cheaper but less fireproof alternative, a painted wooden ceiling, can still be seen in the twelfth-century nave and transepts at Peterborough. At Durham, however, the chief miracle was the order of the whole building. The massive pillars and arches were relieved by some geometric ornamentation, and the very thick walls were made slightly less severe by two galleries, the tribune and the clerestory; but any decoration was subordinated to the vast building's structured lines. Any sculpture of the human figure would be inconceivable here (although the human figure is represented, with great dignity, in the sixteen 'illuminated' manuscripts which are still to be found in the cathedral's library, surviving from a larger gift by

Bishop William). This cathedral has often been called a castle
of God, defending the Norman colony in England against the
Scots to the north and any rebels to the south, but it might
equally be called a campaign in stone, with every detail subordinated to a strict command. Here was not the ultimate advance in design and ornamentation of which the Romanesque
style was capable; to find that, we must look at the two rich
towers of Exeter Cathedral (about 1150), or the five-aisled
Galilee which that proud prelate, Hugh de Puiset, added at
the very dramatic west end of Durham (about 1180). These
works — or the Durham Castle which Bishop de Puiset rebuilt
as a setting for his feudal splendour — were so much more
elaborate that their period within the Romanesque style is
called 'transitional'. But as a proud affirmation of the
Normans' faith in themselves and their God, Durham
Cathedral is supreme.

The new style which came to be called 'Early English' by
proud patriots originated to the south-east of Normandy, in
the fertile Île de France which was at last being given peace
under the immediate control of pious kings. The royal abbey
of St Denis, consecrated in 1144, advertised the new style and
the cathedral of Notre Dame in Paris, begun in 1163, still
displays it in its full energy, while the cathedrals of Chartres
and Reims, built in the first half of the thirteenth century, are
probably its greatest glories. The style consisted essentially of a
combination of the pointed arch and the vault ribbed with
thin webs of cut stone, engineering developments which made
possible a whole new architecture of variety and adventure;
the great window, partitioned by tracery, to make the church
radiant with light and joyously colourful with the stories of the
Bible or the saints, glowing in the glass; and the 'flying but-
tress' outside to support the weight of stone vault as the ambition grew to raise this thin shell of stone and glass higher and
higher. Nothing was at rest. On the other hand, nothing was
dull or sad. The building itself was a drama, no less than was
the worship which it sheltered and inspired.

The first major use of this style in England seems to have
been in Malmesbury Abbey, but its most public impact came
when the choir of Canterbury Cathedral was rebuilt after the

fire of 1174. It is clear from the account of the building by the monk Gervase — the first architectural history to have survived in England — that in Canterbury men were aware (and, to begin with, surprised) that they were importing a revolution from France.

The master mason of the new work was William from Sens, where a new Gothic cathedral had just been completed. When he fell from scaffolding, his work was carried on by William the Englishman, with whose activity 'English Gothic architecture begins'.[20] The intention was to eclipse the memory of the choir which had been largely destroyed, although that choir had been a marvel when consecrated in 1130. ('Nothing like it could be seen in England', wrote William of Malmesbury, 'either for the light of its glass windows, the gleaming of its marble pavements, or the many coloured paintings which led to the wondering eyes to the panelled ceiling above'.) Only two chapels of that choir were left standing, with the crypt below adorned by fabulous or grotesque figures carved on the capitals of its columns (a reminder that cathedral-building was not all solemn). On these foundations the new choir arose. Pointed arches intermingled with rounded, the details were chiselled not cut with an axe, and the vault was of stone not wood. The windows were gradually filled with stained glass showing biblical scenes and the miracles of St Thomas in rich colours (mostly blue and red). Impressive steps led up to the chapel built to glorify the saint's magnificent shrine, and the whole effect was of soaring joy, with decoration richer than any known in France added by the use of marble from Purbeck in Dorset. The pilgrims coming to the new shrine of St Thomas marvelled and told the tale.

The Gothic style spread, although few of the Canterbury details were copied. It was to be seen in Chichester and Glastonbury where the great churches had to be rebuilt after fire; in the complete rebuilding of Wells Cathedral between 1175 and 1260; in the new Cistercian abbeys among which the ruins of Roche in Yorkshire are the best. In Lincoln in 1192, when an earthquake had shaken the hill on which his ca-

---

[20] Paul Frankl, *Gothic Architecture* (London, 1962), p.49.

thedral stood, St Hugh laid the first stone in what proved to be the very lengthy rebuilding of the great church. The brilliantly inventive Geoffrey de Noiers was his architect and gave him asymetrical vaulting, crockets growing senselessly out of pillars and staggered double arcading in the aisles – experiments which were not repeated. Further building was done at Lincoln under Bishop Grosseteste.

Gradually the Gothic style developed in daring and grace. The excitement of it proved so infectious that Bishop Richard Poore determined to have nothing less than a complete new cathedral. He abandoned the cathedral which stood next to the castle on the windy hill at Old Sarum, although that great church had been consecrated by St Osmund and enlarged as recently as the 1130s. In 1220 was begun the creation of Salisbury Cathedral on a new level site by the river Avon a couple of miles to the south. The design is attributed to Elias, one of the canons. The whole of the cathedral which we see preserves that design apart from the central tower and spire which were added (by a Wiltshire master mason, Richard Farleigh) in the middle of the next century. Apart from that, Salisbury Cathedral took only thirty-eight years to build; however, it cost as much as 42,000 marks, at a time when bishops seem to have regarded five marks a year as an adequate stipend for a priest in a parish. Undeterred by this expense, the builders added a great cloister and chapter house, unnecessary because Salisbury Cathedral was not a monastery; and when he was moved from Salisbury to be Bishop of Durham, Richard Poore planned the splendid new east end of the cathedral there – the 'chapel of the nine altars'.

The designers now felt able to give the churches more and more of the decoration which people wanted – in the stonework and the tracery of the windows as well as in the rich colouring of the painter's work added so often to the limewashed interiors. They also felt confident enough of their buttresses to reduce their walls still more drastically in favour of their windows. The new 'decorated' phase of the Gothic style was summed up for the French by the Sainte Chapelle built in Paris by Louis, king and saint – and for the English by Westminster Abbey, which Henry III raised in holy competition with his French brother-in-law. The great windows of the royal abbey's transepts and of its octagonal chapter house encouraged others to similar feats: the rose window surmounting the seven lancet windows above the high altar of St Paul's Cathedral in London, or the east window under which they reburied St Hugh at Lincoln in 1280. The wonderfully carved walls of yellow stone in the Angel Choir around the great bishop's tomb were scarcely less radiant than the glass.

Westminster Abbey was thus as challenging for architects from 1250 onwards as Canterbury Cathedral had been a century before. The king's own work was followed up by the glorious rebuilding of Exeter Cathedral to a single 'decorated' design over a hundred years from 1275, to give only one example; but 'during the early decades of the fourteenth century about every great church in England was added to or partly rebuilt in this richly ornamented style. . . . Many of the larger parish churches were rebuilt with arcades and windows of curvilinear tracery. . . . Almost all the ports and upland towns that were growing rich from the export of wool built or refashioned their churches in the new style. . . . All were decorated with the same profuse wealth of carving. . . .'[21] A special trend of the period was the building of Lady Chapels, to express the growing devotion to the Virgin Mary; the most splendid was at Ely.

Westminster Abbey did not, however, yet include a complete new nave or west front; even Henry III's tax-fed purse was not bottomless. At Westminster the nave was not finished until 1502 and the north front, then the main entrance, was modelled after the cathedral at Amiens. Breathtakingly long and elaborate west fronts, suggesting the walls of the heavenly Jerusalem, reached England elsewhere. At Peterborough a unique west front exhibited three soaring arches. At Lincoln an immensely impressive stone screen spread to right and left of the great doors admitting into the nave the people of this diocese which stretched south to the Thames. At Wells under Bishop Jocelin (1206-1244) the west front was enriched by an

---

[21] Arthur Bryant, *The Age of Chivalry* (London, 1963), p.252, with a list of some of the churches.

unrivalled series of more than three hundred and fifty life-sized statues, leading up to the resurrection of the dead, rows of angels and apostles, and Christ in majesty. Some of these statues were of biblical figures, but others portrayed the kings and saints of England, before as well as after the Conquest. This generous selection illustrated the movement, often to be seen in the thirteenth century, to honour the heroes and heroines of the Anglo-Saxon Church; England was becoming one proud nation. Lavishly painted, these statues which now look weather-beaten and venerable were then popular art. But they were probably also great art. Undismayed by the ravages of time, a modern expert is convinced that 'their faces shine with physical beauty, keen intelligence and humane benevolence not to be found again until the time of the High Renaissance'.[22]

---

[22] Peter Brieger, *English Art, 1216-1307* (Oxford, 1956), p.272.

CHAPTER SIX

REBELS AND PILGRIMS

· The Medieval Parish Church · Chipping Camden ·

THE AGE OF CHIVALRY?

The long reign of Henry III (1216-72) can be summed up with a reasonable amount of accuracy as the Age of Faith. The next period, to the end of the fourteenth century, was more complicated.

Superficially much of it makes a tale of victory and prosperity – the Age of Chivalry. It was a period when England was ruled by two military heroes, Edward I (1272-1307) and Edward III (1327-77). The feats performed under the latter were celebrated in the famous chronicle of the French priest,

Jean de Froissart, and in the still more famously patriotic Shakespearean tribute to this 'dear, dear land' which was 'this earth of majesty, this seat of Mars'. And matching the success of the English armies in Wales and France was the strength of the English Church. In 1323 Pope John XXII declared it heresy to assert that Christ and his apostles had not owned property. It was not a heresy that tempted English churchmen. In 1380 the Commons assembled in Parliament claimed that the clergy owned a third of the nation's wealth (therefore they should pay a third of the taxes). But this Age of Chivalry was also an age of rebellion. This 'land of such dear souls' witnessed the deposition and murder of two kings (Edward II in 1327 and Richard II at the end of the century) and the beheading of an Archbishop of Canterbury in the course of the Peasants' Revolt of 1381. It also saw the beginnings of a rebellion against the spiritual authority of the bishops. Mystics went on pilgrimage into a country of the soul far beyond the official routine of the Church. The leading theologian of the 1370s openly attacked the papacy.

More typical Englishmen relished stories which mocked the hypocrisy of monks and friars. Between the 1300s and the 1370s, it has been estimated, the number of monks, friars and nuns in England almost halved, falling to some eight thousand. This tendency was not due entirely to the Black Death and other plagues, although disease was an obvious enemy.

Bishops were among Edward I's most loyal servants. Robert Burnell, who had been in his employment while he was still the Lord Edward, became the mainstay of his kingdom as his chancellor for sixteen years, and the king twice nominated him for Canterbury, although each time the pope was able to insist on another man. To Burnell, who became Bishop of Bath and Wells, should be given most of the credit for the law and order long remembered as glories of a reign when the king's peace was embodied in famous statutes and shown also in the freedom which the king enjoyed to conquer Wales and Scotland. After Burnell's death his place at the right hand of Edward I was taken by another bishop, Walter Langton. So we may correctly picture this king enthroned in Westminster Abbey's coronation chair (made in 1296) and attended by loyal churchmen. However, the baronial opposition which gathered against the ageing king, and forced him to undergo the humiliation of 'confirming the charters' in 1297, had an archbishop as its leader: Robert of Winchelsea, a distinguished scholar of Paris and Oxford, elected by the monks of Canterbury in 1294. His main quarrel with Edward I was over the taxation of the clergy for the wars. Here he had to defend the refusal of Pope Boniface VIII (proclaimed in *Clericis Laicos*) to recognize any king's right to tax the clergy without papal consent — except in emergencies, as even Boniface had to add a year later. During this crisis the enraged king outlawed all the English clergy and the archbishop went into exile; but Edward I made no further attempt to tax the clergy directly.

Thus even in Edward I's time the unity of Church and State was not totally serene. However, the warrior-king was at heart a thoroughly orthodox churchman, like his father. Among the many indications of this we may notice the fact that he found time in his busy reign to visit the shrine of Our Lady at Walsingham in Norfolk (founded in the 1130s, and patronized by Henry III) ten times. The character of his son and heir was very different.

Attempting to gain the Church's favour at the beginning of his reign, Edward II recalled Archbishop Robert from exile. The king wanted to be left in peace for his favourite amusements — swimming, racing, metalwork, farmwork and dining with his men-friends. But the recall was one of his many blunders. The archbishop was no more inclined to compromise under Edward II than he had been under his more formidable father. The disputes began again and were not to end until the death in 1327 of a king who would have been far happier as a country gentleman.

Since that death had to be enveloped in the piety of the Age of Chivalry — in the incense which covered the stench — Edward II was buried close to the high altar of the great abbey at Gloucester. Abbot Thokey co-operated with the government when it planned an elaborate funeral and one of the most lovely of all canopied medieval tombs. His successor, John of Wigmore, was a skilled sculptor and embroiderer and with both hands he seized the opportunity for a new architecture now presented by the people's offerings. The dark Romanesque choir which they had inherited at Gloucester was out of keeping with the spirit of the age, which loved light. It was the age when Adam of Walsingham the monastery's sacrist and William Hurley the master-carpenter built at Ely the octagonal lantern-tower (the only Gothic dome in Europe) to catch all the light over the Fens, the great sunrises and sunsets. In keeping with this desire to see the sun even while at prayer, the old Gloucester choir was partly demolished and partly modernized. Light now flooded into the choir where Edward II lay in splendour; and although most of the glass in the immense east window was white, some of it was to be filled with the heraldry of local knights who fought chivalrously for Edward III in France. But more unusual was the stonework. Slender columns now rose without interruption from the floor to the vault. Stone screens masked clumsier Norman work to add to the effect of simple elegance, elegance fit for a king.

The decoration at Gloucester was not so rich as could be seen elsewhere in fourteenth-century England; and the arches were not so pointed. If we want to see how the merchants of Bristol rejoiced in their wealth as they offered it to their God, we can look at their church of St Mary Redcliffe: at the exotic carving around the main entrance door suggesting Spanish, Arab or even Indian trade, or at the dazzling geometry of the vaults high above ('lierne' vaulting, so called because most of the ribs were not needed functionally). The new work at Gloucester seemed to be hinting that such a display of wealth was vulgar. No decoration could be as beautiful as clean lines; no sharpness of an arch as uplifting as the unity of this simple, all-embracing design. The 'Perpendicular' architecture preferred by the monks of Gloucester relied for its impact on its total composition and perfect proportions. 'For the first time', as an expert has commented, 'a rectangle of panelling is seen as the unit for the composition of a wall, whether the panel be left empty or filled with stone or with glass'.[1] And it was prob-

---

[1] Joan Evans, *English Art, 1307-1461* (Oxford, 1949), p.68.

ably no coincidence that the monks had connections with the
royal household, since earlier work seems to have been done in
the same style in the now vanished St Stephen's Chapel in the
palace at Westminster (and in the chapter house of old St
Paul's Cathedral). The simplicity of this Perpendicular style
was in the course of its development to contain its own rich
sophistication (a splendid example is the 'fan' vaulting of the
cloisters at Gloucester); but always there was this ruling unity.
Perpendicular was the only major style in architecture to be
developed in England and to be almost entirely confined to
the English. It is far more beautiful, the English will always
think, than its less disciplined Continental contemporary,
'flamboyant' Gothic.

In 1395 Richard II sent to the pope a book about the
miracles wrought at the tomb of Edward II, petitioning for his
royal predecessor to be canonized as a saint. But the true story
of Edward's death belongs to a world infinitely more sordid
than the Perpendicular architecture at Gloucester. After completely alienating the aristocracy by his support of his arrogant
and very greedy favourites, the Despensers, the king was forced
to abdicate by the threat, conveyed harshly by a bishop, that
he would be deposed and his children disinherited if he refused.[2] At Berkeley castle he was murdered on the orders of his
queen, Isabella, and her lover, Roger Mortimer, Earl of
March, who was at that time the uncrowned king. The story
spread that death had been caused by an iron poker inserted
into the ex-king, a reminder that one of his offences against
the aristocrats' code had been his homosexuality. And
although Roger Mortimer was soon hanged, the aristocracy
never expressed regret that Edward had been forced to
abdicate. Even Walter Reynolds, who had been the king's
treasurer and chancellor and had been rewarded by him with
the archbishopric of Canterbury, tried to mediate between
him and his enemies. In the final crisis he became their

---

[2] The bishop was Adam Orleton. See R. M. Haines, *The Church and Politics in
Fourteenth Century England* (Cambridge, 1978); Natalie Fryde, *The Tyranny and Fall
of Edward II* (Cambridge, 1979); Jeffrey Denton, *Robert Winchelsey and the Crown*
(Cambridge, 1980); J. R. Wright, *The Church and the English Crown, 1305-1334*
(Toronto, 1980); M. Buck, *Politics, Finance and the Church in the Reign of Edward II*
(Cambridge, 1983).

mouthpiece in attacking a tyrant. Celebrating the accession of a new king, the archbishop discoursed on a text with a great future before it: 'the voice of the people is the voice of God.'

EDWARD III AND HIS BISHOPS

Edward III's reign saw no repetition of that dramatic crack in the unity of England under the Christian monarchy. It was, indeed, the period when the 'Age of Chivalry' may be held to have flourished (always remembering that when that phrase came into use in the Victorian Age 'chivalry' was thought to be inferior to the higher virtues of the 'Age of Heroism' now vanished). During most of the reign Church and State seemed happily interlocked.

A working arrangement was reached between the English monarchy and the papacy on the key question of who was to appoint the Church's leadership. After 1344 it was recognized in practically all cases that the pope had the right to appoint or 'provide' bishops for the seventeen English dioceses. At the same time, however, it became normal for the king to produce his own candidate and for the pope to 'provide' him; thus the only losers were the monks or canons of the cathedral, who had enjoyed the right of 'free' election of their bishop on at least some occasions in the previous century. In 1345, when some of his cardinals complained that the king's candidate was too flippant to be a bishop, Pope Clement VI declared that if the King of England asked for an ass to be made a bishop he would grant his request. Not all popes were so complacent; they might make difficulties about 'illiterate' favourites of the king. But on the whole this arrangement between pope and king worked smoothly.[3] In the 1440s Thomas Gascoigne, a fiercely critical chancellor of Oxford University, was to complain that 'there are three things today that make a bishop in

---

[3] Peter Heath in *Church and Realm (1272-1461)* (London, 1988) provided a narrative of the tensions between king, pope, clergy, gentry and people through a turbulent period, based on the latest research. But he also stressed the unity of medieval society, so that the change from *Praemunire* to Protestantism was a 'revolution' (p.357).

England: the will of the king, the will of the pope or the court of Rome, and the money paid in large quantities to that court'. One factor was that the popes inherited from the days when John had surrendered to Innocent III the tradition of being the patron, or at any rate the ally, of the King of England. Not for nothing did the first two words that have survived in the handwriting of an English king refer to this relationship. *Pater sancte* ('holy father') was written on a confidential letter to the pope from Edward III when he was eighteen, in the hope that in future the recipient would recognize the king's writing.

In 1351-53 Parliament passed two statutes which later became famous: *Provisors* and *Praemunire*. On the fact of them, these statutes prohibited papal appointments to English ecclesiastical posts, or appeals away from the royal judges in disputes over ecclesiastical appointments. The prohibitions were strengthened when the statutes were revised in the 1390s. The effect of these statutes was not to stop all further appointments by the pope, but they did strengthen the hands of the king or the local authority if either wished to frustrate a particular appointment. Fewer foreigners occupied English ecclesiastical posts – and the fact that any did so continued to be the subject of loudly patriotic protests in Parliament and elsewhere. Parishes to which laymen appointed priests were seldom involved in papal 'provisions'. In the cathedrals and in the growing number of well-endowed 'collegiate' churches, however, canons were often appointed by the pope. In 1398 it was agreed that one out of every three such vacancies should be filled by 'provisions'. One reason why this system was tolerated was that it provided for the promotion of graduates without powerful patrons; Pope Clement VI – again parodying the system – promised parishes to all poor clerics who would claim them from him within two months of his coronation. The main losers were the bishops, who for the rest of the Middle Ages had curiously little influence on the careers of their clergy.[4]

The role which the papacy could now play in the lives of the

[4] See Geoffrey Barraclough, *Papal Provisions* (Oxford, 1935).

abler clergy was illustrated in the careers of two monks who were contemporaries in Norwich Cathedral Priory and at Gloucester College, Oxford. In earlier days they would have spent quiet lives in their beautiful monastery. As it was, both were sent to represent their Benedictine order at the papal court. As a result Thomas Brunton (or Brinton) was 'provided' in 1366 to the bishopric of Rochester, and from this base became the fourteenth century's outstanding preacher in England; more than a hundred of his sermons survive.[5] He was outspoken against the rich if these were oppressive or the poor if these were rebellious; against the clergy if these were slack or the laity if these were anticlerical. Preferring an international stage, Adam Easton remained at the papal court as one of the twenty (or so) cardinals who at that stage constituted the international Church's government. He was prolific in his scholarly answers to contemporary attacks on the privileges of popes and priests. He learned Hebrew in order to deal with appeals to the Old Testament.

For most of the reign of Edward III, the government machine was run by churchmen. The most prominent were both humbly born but became Bishops of Winchester – now one of the most lucrative posts in the whole medieval Church, worth more than £3,000 a year at a time when a ploughman earned less than £3. William of Edington, who was the king's treasurer or chancellor 1344-63, devoted himself not only to financing the war in France but also to increasing the beauty of his cathedral.

William of Wykeham, Edington's pupil in the civil service and successor at Winchester, was a leading minister, 1363-71. His administration coincided with the recovery of the French and he was deprived of his political office – and for a short time of his ecclessiastical income also. At the height of his prosperity he held a dozen eccleiastical posts in addition to his golden bishopric. But he, too, was a faithful Bishop of Winchester according to his own lights, dedicating much of his wealth to the foundation of a great school (Winchester

---

[5] *The Sermons of Thomas Brinton, Bishop of Rochester*, were edited by M. A. Davlin in 2 vols. (London, 1954).

College) and a monumental Oxford college (New College); and under his direction the Winchester nave was modernized in the new Perpendicular style. William of Wynford was his master mason in all three great works. Not for nothing had William of Wykeham made his first mark in the civil service as a manager of building projects for Edward III.[6] The last political act to which Edward III gave his assent was the restoration of his estates to his former minister. It was rumoured by the cynical that Bishop William had bribed the dying king's lively mistress. But on most occasions common sense inspired a king to keep on good terms with his bishops – as we can learn from the earlier story of Edward III's relations with John of Stratford.

Stratford was chancellor for most of the 1330s and Archbishop of Canterbury from 1333. In 1340 he was dismissed from his secular office; the king blamed him for the lack of funds for the war. His response was to preach in Canterbury Cathedral on the anniversary of Becket's martyrdom, invoking also memories of Stephen Langton and Magna Carta. He then excommunicated all who should infringe the liberties of the Church (pointedly excepting the royal family) and led the opposition to the king in the next parliament so alarmingly that he had to be restored to prominence on the king's council. The incident, with its display of ecclesiastical muscle, helps to show why a chapel in honour of St Thomas of Canterbury was endowed by this archbishop in the parish church of Stratford-on-Avon.[7]

THE FATE OF RICHARD II

The grim castle of Pontefract was one of the centres of power for Earls and Dukes of Lancaster. It was also the scene of the cult of Earl Thomas, executed here after the collapse of his rebellion against Edward II in 1322.

---

[6] See W. G. Hayter, *William of Wykeham* (London, 1970).
[7] See R. M. Haines, *Archbishop John Stratford* (Toronto, 1986).

Amid sentimentality about his death on Edward II's personal orders, people forgot that Thomas, the richest man in England after the king, had been in reality no more than an overmighty lout. Although the earl called himself 'King Arthur' in his letters, he had never let chivalry restrain his passions; he had been happy enough to gloat over the severed head of the royal favourite, Piers Gaveston, when that wretch had been dragged to his death from an Oxfordshire rectory. A modern biographer writes of Thomas: 'unscrupulous, violent and avaricious, he was not a man to convince others that he could either lead or govern'.[8] People remembered only that he had defended the charters against the king; that he had been the friend of an archbishop, Robert of Winchelsea, whose memory was already being linked with Becket's. When he had suffered 'martyrdom' outside Pontefract castle, the cult of Thomas of Lancaster as the champion of Church and people grew to the extent that Edward III had to place guards around the castle to deter pilgrims. This cult became one of the many traditions reminding aristocrats, particularly aristocrats who were bishops, that opposition to a king could be sacred.

William Courtenay, for instance, did not flinch when one evening after dinner in 1385 Richard II drew his sword on him and had to be restrained from using it. Courtenay, an earl's brother, was Edward I's great-grandson. He had been a bishop since the age of twenty-eight. As Archbishop of Canterbury 1381-96 he proved himself able and wise. Such a man could look down on an ill-tempered king even while he knelt before him. And Thomas Arundel, another earl's brother, whom the monks elected to follow Courtenay at Canterbury, was almost as impregnably aristocratic. He has been a bishop since the age of twenty. His appointments as chancellor in 1386 and Archbishop of York in 1388 were intended to conciliate the nobility. His removal from the former office signalized Richard's attempt at personal rule in 1389; his return to it two years later showed the failure of that attempt; and his banishment in 1397, when his brother was beheaded, inaugurated the final period of Richard's tyranny. Arundel

[8] J. R. Maddicott, *Thomas of Lancaster* (Oxford, 1970), p.319.

shared his exile with his cousin, Henry Bolingbroke – and shared Bolingbroke's indignation when Richard deprived him of his inheritance as Duke of Lancaster. When Henry triumphed over Richard, it was Arundel who placed him on the vacant throne, becoming his chief counsellor. Only one bishop (Carlisle) publicly denounced the usurper and privately plotted to restore Richard.

In the nave of Westminster Abbey – rebuilt in this period, but modestly in keeping with the design of the rest of the church under Henry III – can be seen a portrait of Richard II. It is the earliest surviving portrait of an English monarch. It was painted about 1390, although it has been clumsily restored since then. It shows the king with the regalia used at his coronation in 1377: the crown, the sceptre of justice, the orb displaying the cross over the globe. (The beautifully decorated *Liber Regalis*, coming from the same period and still in the library of Westminster Abbey, gives us the whole coronation service.) Under a cloak of ermine is a tunic very beautifully embroidered in gold. The king's stare is meant to be imperious. At this stare in real life, we are told, courtiers had to bend the knee. Not far away, in Westminster Hall, we can still see the walls which the king's master mason Henry Yevele (an architectural genius) adapted from the Normans' work and the immense hammer-beam roof, with thirteen arched trusses of oak and decorative angels, built under the direction of Hugh Herland the king's carpenter in 1393-1400. This hall was to be the scene of the monarch's principal feasts.

Up Whitehall, in the National Gallery, is the most exquisite painting surviving from the English Middle Ages: the Wilton Diptych (an altar-piece with two panels). The history of this diptych is mysterious until it appears in the collection of Charles I, but it seems to be one of the signs of the king's increasing obsession with his isolated dignity after the death of his queen, Anne of Bohemia, in 1394, closely followed by the death of their only son. He not only ordered the total destruction of the palace at Sheen which had been their favourite home, but also prepared his own tomb in Westminster Abbey in 1395 where he could lie alongside Anne. Like the Westminster portrait, the Wilton Diptych probably recalls the king's coronation; it shows Richard as a boy of about the appropriate age, ten. The king is being introduced into the court of heaven by three saints – St Edmund the Martyr and St Edward the Confessor who preceded him as English monarchs and his own patron, St John the Baptist, who has put a hand on his shoulder. In front of the young king is the Christ child with his mother; Christ is about to give him a standard. Attractive angels stand around, crowned with white roses, wearing above their hearts the king's badge, the white hart, together with a collar characteristic of the French court from which Richard's second queen, Isabella, came in 1396. Almost certainly this diptych was painted to adorn the king's own portable altar. Morning by morning he would draw strength from it as he received communion from his chaplain.

The colours on the diptych are delightful, suggesting that the banquets to be held in Westminster Hall would be a feast for eye as well as for palate. We cannot be surprised that Richard, who ordered the first English cookery book to be compiled, was also the first Englishman known to have used a handkerchief. But in November 1399 he was taken to spend the winter in Pontefract castle, and early in February 1400 his corpse was publicly exhibited. The new king's council had ordered that the body should be shown, whether living or dead; with that broad hint, no death warrant was needed. The body showed no sign of violence. Nor did the skeleton when it was examined in the Victorian Age. Almost certainly Richard of Bordeaux, the Black Prince's son, the splendid grandson of the splendid Edward III, had been starved to death, having been left through the winter cold and alone. The fate of this prince haunted many imaginations, until in 1595 Shakespeare made the tragedy of *Richard II* – including, however, a fight in the dungeon at the end – the summit of his dramatic achievement to that date. The summit was higher than the level reached a few years previously in Christopher Marlowe's *Edward II*; because while Marlowe had satisfied the appetite of a Tudor audience for a mixture of splendour and brutality, Shakespeare touched the heart with pity for the fallen king on whose own horse (Barbary) Bolingbroke rode 'in London streets, that coronation day'.

The chronicler Adam of Usk claimed that he heard Richard cry out after his deposition: 'My God! A wonderful land is this, and a fickle! Which hath exiled, slain, destroyed or ruined so many kings, rulers and great men, and is ever tainted and toileth with strife and variance and envy!' And if we look at the economic problems beneath the tensions between the king and the nobility, we find the tremors of an earthquake.

One problem was that the two warrior-kings, Edward I and III, overstrained the resources of the kingdom. Their conquests left impressive memorials behind them – Caernarvon and the other castles built by Edward I in a Wales which stayed conquered; or the tomb of Edward the Black Prince, Edward III's much acclaimed son and general, beside the shrine of St Thomas of Canterbury; or the Order of the Garter based on Windsor Castle for the leading knights in the conquest of France. But the conquests had to be financed and defended. Both in Scotland and in France this ultimately proved impossible, and the aggression which was the dark side of the Age of Chivalry (of course, a side which the chivalrous claimed not to exist) brought retribution on king and people.

At the age of sixty-eight, deep in debt, Edward I had to begin one more campaign against the Scots; he died during it, and at Bannockburn in 1314 the army he had bequeathed to his son was slaughtered. Edward III raised cash for his wars in France by loans or taxes from the wool trade, with disastrous consequences for that trade. By the 1370s, when he was senile and under the control of his mistress Alice Perrers (who robbed his corpse), almost all his conquests had melted away. The average Englishman seems to have blamed the king's ministers – hence the fall of William of Wykeham in 1371, when there was a cry from the generals and their fellow-laymen that no more bishops should be given the chief offices of state. But the real limitation on English military power was that the money ran out. The French had only to avoid major battles and victory would be theirs. In the long run it was not enough to be aggressive or to develop the longbow, the technological secret of the famous English victories at Crécy and Poitiers. One of Richard II's more sensible policies was to secure peace with France, which meant that he was solvent.

Quite apart from the difficulties in taxation, the French wars bequeathed serious problems for the future. The easiest way in which Edward III could field an army far larger than anything envisaged by the Normans was to let his generals recruit their own men by pay and by promises of ransoms or plunder. This encouraged the system which has been called 'bastard feudalism'. The successful magnate now had an army of 'retainers' who looked to him for pay and patronage. During a war they could be absorbed in France. In time of peace 'bastard feudalism' was a recipe for civil war – and locally in England the peace was now beginning to be kept by unpaid 'justices of the peace' under the influence of the local magnates, instead of by the royal justices of previous centuries.

The economic activity of England had been expanding steadily and in 1341 had supported the first gold coinage. But overpopulation had become a menace; famines had resulted from bad weather in 1314-17. Now, at the middle of the fourteenth century, the economy was very badly damaged by the Black Death, although the conclusion that one third of the population perished does not command complete acceptance among scholars.

New and deadly forms of plague – bubonic plague spread by rats, and pneumonic plague spread by person-to-person contagion – reached England in August 1348 and had caused great devastation by the end of the following year. There were other severe outbreaks in 1361, 1369 and 1379. The hundreds of thousands who died in 1349 included two Archbishops of Canterbury (Thomas Bradwardine, a mathematician and theologian of distinction, had entered into the archbishopric in the previous week), William Ramsey the greatest architect of the age, Richard Rolle the great mystic, William of Ockham the great philosopher (although he was in exile in Munich), the abbot and forty-eight monks at St Albans and the abbot and twenty-six monks at Westminster (about half these communities). People who were less well-nourished and who lived less hygienically suffered even more terribly, not only in the overcrowded towns but also deep in the countryside where fields and whole villages were abandoned because of the depopulation. In six dioceses of which we have knowledge, over forty per cent of the new parish priests appointed in 1348-9 replaced dead men.

Since agriculture and most trades depended so heavily on manual labour, it was extremely difficult to repair the ravages inflicted by the Black Death. Many modern experts believe that the economic effects of the disaster were still being felt two hundred years after 1348; and that the fascination with death, so characteristic of the later Middle Ages, was born of this plague. The Church, too, suffered very greatly from the loss of manpower. This was one of the reasons that led the Cistercian monks to abandon the system of getting their agricultural work done by lay brothers. The crisis inspired William of Wykeham to found a school and a college to train priests. On the other hand, some parts of the country escaped relatively lightly, and the nation's dependence on the labour-intensive production of raw materials (wool, hides, grain and coal) for export was anyway decreasing as manufacturing (for example, of cloth) increased; the Wife of Bath in *The Canterbury Tales* was a prosperous clothier. Moreover, the surviving peasants were in a position to demand higher wages, although at the same time the decreased demand for land also meant that tenants could force landlords to accept lower rents.

The landowners naturally fought back with all the power at their command. They did their utmost to enforce the old obligations to give manual labour to the lord of the manor, without charge where these obligations of serfs or 'villeins' had survived the growth of an economy based on rents and wages. The Statute of Labourers (1351) prohibited wages above the pre-plague rates, the movement of workmen or servants until their contracts had been fulfilled, the increase of prices on goods sold directly by their makers, and the charging of more than 'reasonable' prices on foodstuffs. Popular resentment built up over thirty years, but it is not surprising that the governing class was on the whole complacent. The social system was generally accepted as having been ordained by God and as being impregnable. England was still a land of villages, and it was assumed that any discontent would remain local. And employers and purchasers were willing to bend the laws if they needed labour or goods and were prepared to pay new prices for them: so inflation, at least in the prices of manufactured goods, could not be prevented. But the government had grown discredited during the senility of Edward III – and was now leaderless during the minority of Richard II, since the jealousies of the aristocracy ruled out the appointment of a regent. The only thought was how to replenish the exchequer. A poll tax of a shilling a head was decreed as an emergency measure. It created a worse emergency as the poor found themselves and their families counted and made to pay no less than the rich.

Trouble over the collection of the tax broke out first in Essex and then in Kent, probably because the landowners in the south-east of England had been slower than those elsewhere to recognize the new facts of life for the poor. The Kentishmen elected Wat Tyler (an ex-soldier) as their leader and released a priest, John Ball, from the archbishop's prison in Canterbury. On Wednesday, 12 June 1381 rebels from the two counties were encamped outside the city of London and John Ball preached to them with a radical message of equality, quoting the contemporary catchphrase:

Whan Adam dalf and Eve span,
Who was thanne a gentilman?

On the next day they entered the city and burned down some of its most luxurious houses. The governing class was now in total disarray. It was saved only by the personal courage of King Richard, a boy not yet fifteen. On the Friday he left the Tower of London to parley with the rebels from Essex in the fields at Mile End. For some reason which has never been explained, the Tower was left feebly guarded and its drawbridge was not raised. Presumably the king hoped that the ministers he had left behind would now escape, as his mother did; but the chancellor who was also Archbishop of

Canterbury, Simon Sudbury, and the treasurer of the kingdom, Sir Robert Hales, were found and executed by the mob. A little boy, Henry Bolingbroke, who was to be Richard's successor, was rescued by a faithful servant — and, it has been suggested, never forgave Richard for leaving him to his fate. The king meanwhile pacified the rebels in the fields by promises: serfs would be released from bondage, wages would be unfrozen, traitors would be punished.

On the Saturday, after a visit to Westminster Abbey to make his confession and receive communion (while there he witnessed a lynching), Richard faced the rebels from Kent at Smithfield. Wat Tyler, still suspicious, argued with him, until the Mayor of London, losing his temper, struck down a man so impertinent. The boy-king who was the Black Prince's son retained an almost incredible presence of mind, shouting orders to the enraged mob. His words came to be reported as: 'Sirs, will you shoot your king? I am your captain, follow me'. And they followed — only to find themselves surrounded by troops summoned by the mayor. Once again Richard kept his head, insisting that the peasants should disperse peacefully with a promise of pardon. We cannot wonder that in later years he was under the illusion that political problems needed only dramatic action by him; that he had only to exert his will for the nobility to fall into line behind him; that he could even get away with the gamble of depriving Henry Bolingbroke of his inheritance as Duke of Lancaster — his last, fatal error.

Outside London there were some almost equally dramatic and revealing scenes in 1381. In St Albans the abbot, the great Thomas de la Mare, whose rule over half a century after the Black Death took the monastery to the height of its wealth and prestige, was forced to seal a charter setting free all the serfs on his estates. In Bury St Edmunds rebels beheaded the prior, the monk who controlled the monastery's estates and the chief justice of the kingdom who lived nearby. In both places the townsmen demanded more freedom from the monks who had previously controlled civic life in detail, while in Cambridge the documents setting out the university's privileges were burned amid derision in the market square. Other rebels plundered the city of Norwich and terrified Norfolk until the bishop's cavalry surrounded them and hanged their leader. Among the rebels there seems to have been some talk about a 'Great Society' but their real unity was only a hatred of the bishops, monks and scholars along with the rest of the rich – a hatred fanned by the egalitarian preaching of John Ball and (surviving sermons show) of many another village priest or poor friar, the Communists of their day.

When the rising died down all the concessions made under threat of violence were withdrawn. But in a broader perspective it cannot be said that the Peasants' Revolt was a total failure. The shock seems to have encouraged a process which might have been inevitable anyway as being in the landowners' interests: the substitution of tenants or employees for serfs, and the rise of wages to their economic level (they doubled in the period 1346-96). And there was not to be another poll tax for over a century.

THE CHURCH OF PIERS PLOWMAN

Those few violent days in June 1381 make us wonder what was going on in the fourteenth century at the levels of society beneath the kings, bishops and other aristocrats who commissioned art and architecture and who attracted the attention of the chroniclers. About any previous period we should have had to admit ignorance. But the illustrations in the Luttrell Psalter suddenly enable us to see the everyday life of the countryside in the 1330s: and some fascinating literature has survived to give us glimpses of the thinking and religion of the English people.

There were devotional books to guide English-reading Christians. The earliest to have survived is *Handlyng Synne*, based on an older book in French in 1303. Its author was Robert Mannyng, who wrote it to help his fellow-priests in Lincolnshire and then turned his hand to a history of England in more than 25,000 rhyming lines. Many sermons by English-speaking preachers have also been preserved. These preachers belonged to a tradition as vigorous and creative then as preaching was to be in the seventeenth century. They de-nounced the selfishness of the rich and offered salvation to the poor. They found mysterious or exciting symbolism in the familiar Bible stories. They told homely stories and repeated popular proverbs. Individually such preachers could not stand comparison with the poets or great writers, but they had far more influence.

The most popular poets were the authors of lyrics, for the medieval English were well-known as a people who enjoyed singing. Some of these lyrics had secular words. One of the most popular lyrics was already a hundred years old in the fourteenth century:

> Summer is icumen in
> Lhude sing! cucu.

But the natural association of spring, joy and love had already led to many love poems addressed in English to Christ and his mother, particularly together at Bethlehem or Calvary. These were fresh, simple and direct in comparison with the more carefully theological Latin hymns of the Church – although they often kept in touch with that source by brief snatches of Latin. And the music of the lyrics which remained secular could be used for religious words; this was a speciality of the Franciscan preachers, conceived of by St Francis himself as *joculatores Dei*, 'God's minstrels'. The largest surviving collec-tion of medieval English lyrics (the British Museum manu-script Harley 2253, compiled before 1315) mixes the themes of the preacher and the minstrel. Some of the music, secular or religious, would be dance music; the *carole* (a French word) was any song to which men and women could dance in a ring holding hands, for example during the festivities after Christmas. The twelfth-century chronicler Thomas of Ely quotes one *carole* 'to this day sung publicly in dances'. He claims that it dated back to the time of a Danish king who had heard the monks singing across the waters of the Fens:

> Merie sungen the muneches binnen Ely
> Tha Cnut ching reu ther by.
> 'Roweth, cnites, noer the land,
> And here we thes muneches saeng'.

So, as the fourteenth century sang and danced its way into an ever more joyful and intimate devotion, the miracle of simple grace that has become such a popular twentieth-century carol began to be possible, in praise of the Virgin Mother:

I sing of a maiden
That is makeles (matchless):
King of alle kinges
To here son she ches (chose).

He cam al so stille
There his moder was,
As dew in Aprille
That falleth on the grass . . .

The manuscript in which this poem was found also contains ballads, carols and Latin verse; perhaps it was the song book of a travelling minstrel. Earlier lyrics have been found containing some of the same words; even this matchless lyric sprang out of the life of the people. Fourteenth-century piety was, however, less escapist than such lyrics might suggest. It was expressed also in plays presenting biblical scenes to the people in English.

These developed out of the simpler drama which had for some time been part of the celebration of Christmas or Easter in some of the great churches (in Latin). The shepherds or Magi had come to do homage to the Christ child; the women had come weeping to Christ's empty tomb. Twelfth-century statutes of Lichfield Cathedral provide for such liturgical drama. There is a reference to 'holy dramas' representing the sufferings of martyrs being performed in London in a biography of Thomas Becket by his contemporary, William Fitzstephen. We know that clergy presented biblical plays. In 1244 Bishop Grosseteste ordered his archdeacons to put a stop to it, but the practice continued; at Christmas 1378 the minor clergy of St Paul's Cathedral presented scenes from the Old Testament. Now in the fourteenth century the laymen incorporated in craft-guilds in several towns such as Chester, York, Lincoln and Norwich took the drama out of the churches on to wagons called 'pageants' which were pulled round the streets. The clergy were, it seems, still suspicious – but the laity had lifted drama out of the moral and artistic degeneration of the public stage since Roman times. Each guild would play a separate scene. Although probably the original authors were scholars, it is clear that each scene could be adapted by local talent. The plays presented episodes in the story of man's salvation from the Fall of the Angels to the Last Judgement, but above all from the story of Christ. They were often performed at Whitsun or on the feast of Corpus Christi in the early summer; probably the combination of scenes to form a whole play on this feast was first copied from the Continent 'about the end of the first quarter of the fourteenth century at some place probably in the north of England'.[9]

At least one of these dramatists – the unknown author of the Towneley Shepherds' Play – was a major comic poet, but the most important Christian poetry about the life of the age was a poetry of protest.

Some Latin poems about fourteenth-century life survive, the most substantial being John Gower's *Vox Clamantis* which denounced rebellious peasants and greedy merchants alike, and could be dedicated to Richard II in the first edition and to Henry IV in the second. Gower also wrote in English. But a greater English poet worked many of the preachers' themes into images as vivid as those of the lyrics, in unrhymed alliterative verse. He was William Langland, and his poem – surviving in three texts showing how he revised and lengthened it again and again, from the 1360s to the 1390s – was *Piers Plowman*. Doggedly conservative while also being radical in its attacks on the new rich, and profoundly Catholic despite its many protests, it is 'the most thoroughly English of all our religious poems'.[10]

The name of the hero was traditional. One of the letters connected with the rising of 1381 that has survived to suggest a well-prepared conspiracy seems to use this name as a code-word for the rebellion itself: 'John Sheep, priest of Col-

[9] Hardin Craig, *English Religious Drama of the Middle Ages* (Oxford, 1955), p.133.

[10] R. W. Chambers, *Man's Unconquerable Mind* (London, 1939), p.90.

chester . . . greeteth well John Nameless and John the Miller,
and John Carter, and biddeth them that they . . . stand
together in God's name, and biddeth Piers Plowman go to his
work, and chastise well Hob the robber. . . .' William
Langland, however, was no advocate of armed rebellion. He
dreamed of a saintly pope, of a pure Church, of a penitent
commonwealth, of the great barn called Unity; of 'brethren of
one blood: alike beggars and earls'. Justice was to be established by the appeal of the conscience, not by force; and love
was always greater than justice. He was not afraid, any more
than the popular preachers were, any more than John Gower
was, to handle these non-violently revolutionary themes. What
defeated him was not the novelty of his essential vision but the
novelty of his attempt to turn it into a long English poem; and
the novelty of the questions that occurred to him on the way.
He felt a vocation to do in England what Dante had done in
Italy, although his questioning was more thorough and his
genius less majestic than Dante's. His success was enough to
win a public large for his time. More than fifty medieval
manuscripts of *Piers Plowman* have survived, suggesting that
the poem was read in many devout middle-class homes and
that sections of it were recited to a wider audience. Sir Adrian
Fortescue copied it all out by hand in the 1530s, and the
demand for it justified a printed edition in 1550. Its popularity may well have influenced the number of wall-paintings
surviving in churches and representing Christ as a ploughman.

To this poem he dedicated his life, as a few autobiographical references make clear. Tall and thin, he was nicknamed
'Long Will' and sometimes thought to be crazed. Born in the
1330s, in an Oxfordshire where his kind of poetry was
flourishing as a popular art, he spent much of his life in
London, living with 'Kitte my wyf and Calote my douhter' in a
cottage on Cornhill. He could not be a priest – first because
his patron died and then because, being honest, he was
officially married – but he tried to earn a living by singing
services in commemoration of the dead. At times he thought
that the praise of honest manual labour in his poem indicated
how he, too, ought to live; but he was sustained by a sense of a
vocation to be a poet. He presents himself as a dreamer, often

rebuked for his stupidity, often learning from his experience.

He divides his poem into two parts: *Vision* and *Life*. In his vision he sees the 'field full of folk' while asleep one warm morning in May among the Malvern Hills.

Some of the folk are ploughing and sowing, with no time for pleasure, producing the food which others will waste. Theirs is the common lot of poverty, cold and hunger. But most of the folk are greedy for worldly gain. The dreamer hears labourers singing bawdy songs over their shoddy work; cooks offering hot pies, and innkeepers bawling out their advertisements; Lady Mede (Money) having a grand Westminster wedding to Falsehood. Some of the folk are wandering through the countryside – tramps living by their wits, pilgrims full of lying talk, friars and pardoners deluding the people, parish priests on their way to London, pleading that since the plague their parishes have become too poor to live in. A hundred men are seen in silk gowns, making speeches. There are lawyers, as useless as the priests. Sickened by this world where everything is for sale including the law, the dreamer meets Holy Church and asks 'how I may save my soul'. Her answer is that he must find Truth, who is also Love. Piers the ploughman then appears and leads the search. He reaches Truth and is offered a pardon for sin. But when it is read out to him, this document turns out to be only the promise which is sternly moral: that those who have done well will go into eternal life and the others into eternal punishment. Knowing that this is no pardon at all, he tears it up – and quarrels with the priest who defends it. The sins of those who do *not* do well have to be forgiven as sparks from London chimneys are extinguished in the Thames. The Gospel must be about the divine compassion, which must be yet greater than the dreamer's.

The section of the poem is complex, even turgid, as the solitary poet wrestles with the mysteries of his religion. How is faith related to reason, morality to theology? Heartless learning, he sees, is as evil as covetousness. But the poem is clarified as it describes three types of a truly Christian life: Do Well, Do Bet (Better) and Do Best.

'Do Well' is the life of patient poverty, of active goodness, open to any layman or hard-working pastor: 'to see much and suffer more'. We are then shown the life of 'Do Bet' – a life in which perfect love is first contemplated and then practised, a life to be found in the best priests although not only in them. To this section belongs the famous picture of Christ dressed in the armour of Piers (for Piers is the mankind whose nature Christ took), going to joust against the Devil and Death. The conquest of hell is vividly imagined. The dreamer wakes to find that the bells are ringing on Easter morning. He calls his wife and daughter to come with him to church.

After this climax we are given a much shorter dream about 'Do Best', the mixed life of contemplation and activity characteristic of the ideal bishop. Piers is now seen as St Peter, and for him Grace builds a barn big enough to hold Christendom (and beyond Christendom, the dreamer has seen, there are Saracens who 'pray and have perfect faith in one God who is holy and mighty, and they ask for his grace'). But unlike Dante, Langland does not attempt a description of Paradise. The poem does not offer easy answers; even its end is inconclusive. Antichrist is seen coming and waging war, and Conscience who also comes to do battle doubts his own power. So Conscience sets out on one more pilgrimage, to find the perfect pope.

William Langland has rejected or ignored many of the claims of the institutional Church which he knows too well. But he does not reject any of its doctrines about God or the meaning of life. He praises true hermits and true priests. He tells us that the monk's cloister is a place for books and happiness. The revolution in which he takes part comes first by imagining the orthodox doctrines in powerfully human terms, and then by applying them without compromise to the realities of a corrupt society. So in effect he builds his own church: the poem itself. The reader of *Piers Plowman* can still explore 'the nave for the people, the choir for the clergy, yet like so many churches in the Middle Ages so crowded with tombs, rood-screens, chantries and side-altars that the total effect is a most curious blending of order and confusion.'[11]

---

[11] H. W. Wells, 'The Construction of Piers Plowman', in *Middle English Survey*, ed. E. Vasta (Notre Dame, Ind., 1975), p.168.

THE *GAWAIN* POET

An essentially similar approach is made in four poems which may all be the work of another fourteenth-century poet, more secure in his status and in the mastery of his art. His name is not known (Langland's own name is known to us only because of a scribbled note on one copy of his poem). These poems, like Langland's, are in unrhymed alliterative verse, but in the English of a district far from London: the north-west Midlands. They have survived in a single manuscript.

The longest is *Sir Gawain and the Green Knight*. On its surface it is a colourful, sometimes humorous, romance about King Arthur's knights; a poem which takes a glowing delight in aristocratic pastimes such as hunting. It seems to belong to a world entirely different from the London streets which we tread in *Piers Plowman*. But just as in Anglo-Saxon times an aristocratic entertainment such as *Beowulf* could be seen, on deeper analysis, to be a Christian poet's attempt to make his privileged listeners think out what constituted true moral or spiritual heroism, so this story told by the *Gawain*-poet was full of matters which could both attract and instruct the nobility or gentry.

King Arthur's court at its New Year festivities is startled by the appearance of the Green Knight, a figure who comes out of Celtic mythology, a vegetation-god who is now the symbol of life. The Green Knight asks that his head should be cut off and in return promises to execute his executioner: life is like that. But the Green Knight is able to ride away cheerfully, carrying the head which Sir Gawain has agreed to sever: life is like that, too. So a fearful Sir Gawain has to follow, to the Green Chapel where the second half of the bargain is to be kept. On his way he comes across a castle and the generous host offers Christmastide hospitality while he himself goes out hunting; this is the Green Knight in disguise. Sir Gawain, being no adulterer, resists the blandishments of his hostess in her lord's absence, apart from a few kisses; chivalry triumphs.

But he does accept one small gift, a girdle, without informing his host; he is not perfect. Eventually he reaches the uncanny Green Chapel, to find that the blows of the Green Knight do him no damage, except that his neck is grazed once. He must be punished to that extent because he accepted the girdle. He then returns to tell his story over dinner at Arthur's Round Table. It is a complex story on which modern literary critics, who have a strong appetite for the study of symbolism and a thirst for disputations with each other, have feasted.

We can understand more readily the Christian messages of the other three poems found in the same manuscript. *Patience* interprets the Old Testament story of Job, while *Purity* links together a dozen books of the Bible in a poet's sermon. The *Pearl* begins with the poet's loss of a pearl in the grass of a garden in August. His grief, it turns out, is really for his daughter, dead before her second birthday. But while he is asleep in his misery beside her grave in that garden he sees her in the garden of Paradise ('then saw I there my little queen'); and he talks with her. She rebukes his stubborn earthiness but when he tries to join her across the stream of death, he wakes up – to find that 'all is well with me in this dungeon of grief'. He has been to his own Green Chapel.

This poet is far less of a preacher than Langland; thus it is possible for a modern commentator on his work to reckon that he did not have any profound interest in morality or salvation, 'except insofar as they could provide a framework for the imaginative exploration of situations and feelings'.[12] But such caution is excessive. 'The pure and constant values of heaven', observes another scholar, 'are contrasted in all four poems with the tarnished standards of earth. . . . The poet consistently sees society as corrupt; even the civilization of Arthur, that golden, chivalric court in its "first age", is essentially cowardly and frivolous. . . . And the *Gawain*-poet is unyielding on this point: to accept God's appointed mission is to bring upon oneself the scorn and fury of the world. . . . Only a handful of heroes can hope for the mercy of God and for salvation in the orthodox Christian way, through the merits of Christ.

---

[12] W. A. Davenport, *The Art of the Gawain-Poet* (London, 1978), p.220.

Thus the father of the pearl-maiden and Gawain have in the end attained a measure of wisdom, though they are overcome by a sense of their own unworthiness and by a perception of the evil of the world in which they live'.[13]

SPIRITUAL WRITERS

During a brief lull from his duties as a statesman and general, Henry, first Duke of Lancaster, wrote down an elaborate self-examination. This was in 1354; he was to die of the plague seven years later. The duke compares himself with a sick man who needs the medicine which only Christ's atonement can provide. Like a poet he thinks in pictures and naturally we are interested in the picturesque details of his confession, revealing the home-life of an aristocrat — but there can be no doubt that his repentance was genuine. He accuses himself of exploiting the poor and of avoiding their stench. He is ashamed that he has so loved his bed, wines and sauces, the smells of flowers, fruit and women. He has taken too much pride in the strength of his arms and in the rings on his fingers. He has danced too vigorously, hoping it would lead to kisses or more. He has loved the lusty kisses of low-born women more than the restrained greetings of the aristocracy. He has bred sins as he has bred salmon. Now he needs Christ's sweat of agony as a sick man needs a broth; or Christ's mother's tears as a sick man needs to be refreshed by rosewater. Christ's body is compared with the pips of a pomegranate, then a special delicacy for the rich sick; and his blood with a hot bath, then an experience almost equally rare. Duke Henry says that he needs a priest to dig for his sins as a huntsman with a rod digs a fox out, and perhaps the manuscript that has survived was written on his chaplain's advice. But he also says that his own conscience is the terrier to sniff for the sins, and he leaves the impression that if the need arose he could sin-hunt without clerical assistance.[14]

---

[13] Charles Moorman, *The Works of the Gawain-Poet* (Jackson, Miss., 1977), pp.46-7.

This self-critical duke wrote in French but his was, it seems, the kind of household that would have enjoyed a recital of *Sir Gawain and the Green Knight*. It was a sign of the retreat of the French language in England when he apologized for his imperfect fluency '*pur ceo jeo sui englais*'. One of Richard II's courtiers, Sir John Clanvowe, became (so far as we know) the first English layman after King Alfred to write a devotional book in English, on *The Two Ways* to death and to life. And his book was part of a widespread movement to make devotion more personal. This was the age of the great mystics among the German Dominicans, Eckhart, Tauler and Suso, and of Ruysbroeck in Flanders. In Rome itself a hermit was elected pope (Celestine V in 1294 – though he abdicated after a few weeks). Far up in the north of England, one man withdrew from his comfortable life as a monk in Durham Cathedral, then at the height of its wealth and prestige about the middle of the fourteenth century. He prayed on the Farne Islands where St Cuthbert had prayed; and he wrote what he learned. He once thought he saw Christ with a smile saying: 'Love and you will be saved.'

More prolific as an author both in Latin and in English, both in verse and prose, was another hermit, Richard Rolle – and more is known about him because after his death in 1349 the Cistercian nuns of Hampole near Doncaster, whose spiritual guide he had been, collected evidence in the hope that he would be officially recognized as a saint.[15] Rolle was a Yorkshire man who when aged nineteen, in the 1320s, refused to return to the arid studies of Oxford. Instead he got his sister to give him two frocks and his father's rain-hood, which he cut up to make a hermit's dress. His sister ran away shouting 'My brother is mad!' However, the local squire, whose sons had known him at Oxford, gave him shelter. Thus Richard was able to fulfil the vocation which he later cel-

---

[14] *Le Livre de Sentz Medicines* by Duke Henry was edited by E. J. Arnold (Oxford, 1940) and a biography of *The King's Lieutenant* was written by Kenneth Fowler (London, 1969).

[15] See F. M. Comper, *The Life and Lyrics of Richard Rolle* (London, 1928).

ebrated in poems and almost thirty prose pieces. He wrote
with enthusiasm about the psalms (which he translated into
English) and other parts of the Bible, but his most famous
work was his *Incendium Amoris* (*The Fire of Love*) of 1343.

It began encouragingly: 'I cannot tell you how surprised I
was the first time I felt my heart begin to warm'. He recalled
that even as an adolescent he had 'ardently longed for the
pleasures of heaven more than for the delights of physical
love'. He wrote about worldly women in cruel terms, but
about prayer in the frank language of ecstasy. One day in his
hermitage he had felt an 'unusually pleasant heat' while at
prayer; one evening before supper, while reciting psalms, he
had heard heaven's song. Such pleasures had become regular
for him; and he could now promise these and greater joys to
all contemplatives who abandoned the world for the love of
God. In comparison with what he had found in this prolonged
love affair with God, he saw little merit and no attraction in
any life in the world — although he admitted that men 'unable
to persevere quietly in interior longing' might make suitable
bishops.

Such enthusiasm, warmly advertising the delights of private
prayer without too much mention of church services, was
welcomed widely, as is shown by the number of surviving
manuscripts. It is interesting today as proof that the experiences known as 'Pentecostal' or 'charismatic' were not
unknown in the Middle Ages. Rolle was, however, suspected
of over-enthusiasm by maturer experts. This is shown by the
existence of two other books, which seem to have been written
partly as replies to him although each is a spiritual classic in its
own right.

The Cloud of Unknowing was written in English by an
anonymous priest, probably in the East Midlands, who was
also the author of at least four tracts with two translations of
mystical theology. He wrote *The Cloud*, he tells us, for a
friend aged twenty-four and for others 'really and wholly
determined to follow Christ perfectly'. He had nothing to offer
those merely attracted by promises of supernatural warmth
and celestial song. He wrote to stress that the contemplative
life was work ('a full great travail') and that most of the work

was God's; that memory, and even thought, must be forgotten in the 'naked intent' to love the 'unmade' God; that a 'cloud of unknowing' must be acknowledged to exist between man and his Maker; that God is No-thing, No-where; but that this cloud hiding God could be pierced by 'a sharp dart of longing love'. 'He may well be loved, but not thought. By love he may be gotten and holden, but by thought never.'[16]

The longest and most authoritative of these treatises on the hidden life of prayer comes from a canon of the small Augustinian house of Thurgaton in Nottinghamshire, Walter Hilton, who died in 1396. He had been both a doctor of theology at the University of Paris and a hermit. He wrote *The Ladder of Perfection* for a young woman who had 'forsaken the world, turning to our Lord'. She must not prize warm feelings or angelic music; 'however delightful these things may be, they are less valuable than the practice of virtue and the knowledge and love of God'. Probably because she could not understand Latin, she is told that 'you cannot very well make use of reading the scriptures'. Instead she is urged to ascend the 'degrees of contemplation' by discipline in prayer, by meditation about Jesus, by the practice of humility and charity – although neither humility nor charity is to be extended to heretics. It is all sober counsel, by a man who by climbing this long ladder himself has become very holy, very wise and rather cautious. No other English guide to mysticism has had such influence; many editions have been printed since 1494.[17]

More courageously original are *Revelations of Divine Love*, the first book to have been written in English by a woman. Some comparisons can be made between it and the teachings of two other women of the fourteenth century, the Swedish St Bridget and St Catherine of Siena, but in each case what we see is a woman teaching with authority as an advanced mystic. The anonymous author of this extraordinary English book was

---

[16] Quotations are from the translations of *The Fire of Love* and *The Cloud of Unknowing* by Clifton Wolters in the Penguin Classics (London, 1971-72).

[17] See *The Scale of Perfection*, ed. Gerald Sitwell (London, 1953).

a recluse or 'anchoress'; her cell adjoined St Julian's church in Norwich. She is therefore known as Dame or Mother Julian.

The book was based on 'showings' which came to this 'simple creature that could no letter' in her thirtieth year, 1373. After a week's sickness, she was believed to be dying. As she gazed on the crucifix held before her by her parish priest, she thought she saw Christ bleed and heard him speak. Fifteen 'showings' lasted from four to nine o'clock on the morning of 8 May, and one more came on the night of the 9th. She seems to have made a record not long afterwards; one precious copy of this document has survived. But for most of the rest of her life she pondered the meaning of those few hours, and the longer edition of her book was not completed before 1394. If she really was illiterate in 1373 she must have learned to read and write. Rightly or wrongly many echoes from other mystics – even from theologians – have been found in her own book, which shows every sign of having been written with care. Her genius was original, but not so original as to be isolated; her message was based on a direct spiritual intuition, but shaped and reshaped with a craftsman's care, as Langland shaped *Piers Plowman*.

In the very first 'showing' she saw 'a little thing, the quantity of an hazel-nut, in the palm of my hand; and it was as round as a ball. I looked thereupon with my eye of understanding and thought: *What may this be? And it was answered me generally thus: It is all that is made. . . . It lasteth, and ever shall, for that God loveth it.* And so All-thing hath the Being by the love of God'. She gradually learned to look more deeply into that mystery of God's creative goodness. It is a mystery, needing to be revealed; yet God 'will be seen and he will be sought, he will be abided and he will be trusted. . . . For he full gracious and homely'. Christ's suffering reveals the graciousness of God; Julian dares to picture Christ as a workman in grubby clothes and even to say that 'the deep wisdom of the Trinity is our Mother'. Her thought is much more solidly Trinitarian than is most of the other piety of the period; she really does give equal glory to Father, Son and Holy Spirit. It is not that she neglects the Son, however. She hears Christ speak. 'If thou art pleased, I am pleased: it is a joy, a bliss, an endless satisfying to me that ever suffered I passion for thee; and if I might suffer more I would suffer more.' At the end of her book she only understands more profoundly, through her deeper understanding of Christ's cross, what was there in her early vision – the vision of the universe as small as a hazel-nut in God's hand. 'I was answered in ghostly understanding', she tells us, 'saying thus: *Would'st thou learn thy Lord's meaning in this thing? Learn it well: Love was his meaning. Who shewed it thee? Love. What shewed he thee? Love. Wherefore shewed it he? For love. Hold thee therein and thou shalt learn and know more in the same. But thou shalt never know nor learn therein other thing without end.'*

Her whole heart is given to this courteous, chivalrous Christ. 'Our Lord Jesus oftentimes said: *I it am, I it am: I it am that is highest, I it am that thou lovest, I it am that thou enjoyest, I it am that thou servest, I it am that thou longest for, I it am that thou desirest, I it am that thou meanest, I it am that is all.'* But she boldly adds that any act of love is part of Christ: 'and then I saw that each kind compassion that man hath on his even-Christians with charity, it is Christ in him'. She thinks the presence of Christ strong even in the sinner, for she has a charitable view of human nature: 'in every soul that shall be saved is a godly will that never assented to sin, nor ever shall.' And Christ prays with the sinner all the time: 'I am the Ground of thy beseeching. First it is my will that thou have it; and after, I make thee to will it; and after, I make thee to beseech it.'

Although she, too, is a recluse she has none of Rolle's contempt for mankind. She loves the people in the street outside her cell. 'The charity of God maketh in us such a unity that, when it is truly seen, no man can part himself from other.' And she is far more interested in the unchanging reality of God. 'I saw soothfastly (truly) that our Lord was never wroth, nor ever shall be. For he is God: good, life, truth, love, peace. . . .' And so hers is not the worship of a God hidden in a cloud, to be approached up a long ladder. 'God is nearer to us than our own soul: for he is the Ground in whom our soul standeth.' We begin to see in this extraordinary book the significance of the light that floods Perpendicular churches, for here is a religion of light: 'Our faith is our light in our night: which light is God, our endless day.' And here, affirmed during years of plague in a city which was for a time occupied by the rebellious peasants of 1381 before their tragedy, is an optimistic faith: 'And all shall be well, and all shall be well, and all manner of thing shall be well.'[18]

A THEOLOGICAL REVOLUTION

Contemporary with this woman mystic who saw Christ as clearly as anyone has ever seen him in England was the first Englishman to become a major heretic.

John Wyclif was born about 1330, a Yorkshireman. Up to 1378 his life was that of an Oxford theologian: the long training, the share in academic controversies, the search for sources of income so that the life of study and disputation might be maintained. In the Middle Ages unless a scholar was also a monk or a friar maintained at the university by his order this search took the form of a hunt for rich rectories and canonries in cathedrals, since there was no salary for a university lecturer as such. Wyclif was not unsuccessful as an absentee pluralist. For brief periods he was also the head of two small Oxford colleges (Balliol and Canterbury). He was a distinguished don who in an earlier age might have ended up a bishop like Robert Grosseteste or Stephen Langton; his favourite English philosopher was Grosseteste, and he was the first Englishman to lecture on the whole Bible since Langton. But in fact his employment outside Oxford was as a propagandist employed by the laymen who had been at the top in politics since the fall of Bishop William of Wykeham – most conspicuously John of Gaunt, Edward III's second son. Even that was no radical

---

[18] Quotations are from *Revelations of Divine Love*, ed. Grace Warrack (London, 1901). It was this edition that rescued this mystic from obsurity. For a commentary, see *Julian of Norwich: Showings*, ed. E. Colledge and J. Walsh (London, 1979). Grace Jantzen provided the best study of *Julian of Norwich* (London, 1987).

departure from the Oxford tradition. Previous Oxford theologians had spoken out against the wealth of monks and friars;
for example, Richard Fitzralph had done so sensationally in
the 1350s. It is true that there had not been such an open
attack on the bishops' wealth or the pope's power before
Wyclif's zest for controversy stirred up the 1370s; Fitzralph
had himself been an Irish archbishop, and he had hoped that
the pope might reform the friars. But we may be sure that
plenty of anticlerical tongues had wagged in Oxford.

Wyclif's last appearance before parliament as a government
spokesman, in October 1378, was to defend other government
agents who had caused a scandal by killing a prisoner who had
taken refuge in Westminster Abbey. But by now he was being
taken by his own arguments into territory even more scandalous to the medieval mind. If all authority or 'lordship'
depended on 'grace' or the will of God (as Archbishop Fitzralph had himself argued), was it not possible to draw more
daring conclusions? Might not the only material support to
which the clergy were entitled be the offerings of their
parishioners year by year? Might not the confiscation of the
rest of the Church's wealth be in accordance with God's will –
and save the laity from all further taxes? And if a rich bishop
such as William of Wykeham might be deprived of 'lordship',
might not a worldly pope be deposed?

During 1378 Wyclif had to appear before William
Courtenay, then Bishop of London, to defend himself against
complaints made to the pope that he was a heretic, but
escaped with a formal reproof. His escape was a reminder that
the moral authority of a pope among the English was not now
what it had been. In the 1350s King John's homage to the pope
was formally revoked by Parliament. The act symbolized a
new resentment – with new reasons. From 1309 to 1377 the
popes lived in Avignon, in the south of France. They lived in
expensive luxury (although respectably). They were the
victims of an ever-growing absorption in everyday legal
business; petitioners who got what they wanted out of them
were pleased, those who did not were resentful, and no one
thought them semi-divine priest-kings, dwelling in a spiritual
world high above criticism. Above all, they lived in Avignon.

It was beautiful, it was free of riots and plagues – but it was not Rome. This period of self-imposed exile, the 'Babylonish Captivity', created what was virtually a French papacy at a time when the French were the enemies of the English. And now in 1378 the prestige of the papacy, but not its financial appetite, was further weakened when some of the cardinals, mostly French, elected Clement VII to reside in Avignon as a rival to Urban VI in Rome, whom the English continued to recognize. The Great Schism, a scandal which was to last until 1417, had begun. These were years when it was not easy to venerate popes.

In Oxford Wyclif continued to lecture – on the Bible; on the Church; on the papacy; on the Eucharist. The delivery of the last course of lectures brought about his condemnation by a narrow majority on a committee of fellow-theologians at Oxford – a condemnation which he defied by an openly heretical *Confession* in May 1381. His chief offence was to deny that the 'substance' of bread or wine could be annihilated when the priest said the Mass. This philosophical point was of wider interest when a public figure, such as he had become, opened up a subject which had been thought closed in Lanfranc's time three centuries before. Might he not be casting doubt on the whole idea of the Mass as a miraculous new sacrifice by the priest which secured the forgiveness of sinners living and dead? The laity of England had given the monasteries and parish churches countless tithes and endowments precisely in order that thousands upon thousands of Masses should be offered every day. Wyclif's controversial view was even more noteworthy in the year when society was shaken by the peasants' revolt. Whatever its theological merit, it was a tactical mistake. Next year he was forbidden by council in London to teach in his university or to preach. He retired to his rectory at Lutterworth in Leicestershire, though he did not cease to write belligerent pamphlets, and died on the last day of 1384.

He was a great simplifier – in this, resembling Dame Julian of Norwich. But he claimed no visions. What he taught was, he argued, what had always been the essence of Christianity. He proclaimed the Church of the 'elect', those who had been predestined by God to be saved through true belief; the Bible, interpreted literally, as God's saving word to true believers; Christ, truly man as well as God, the brother as well as the saviour of true believers. These were not in themselves strange ideas. All who followed the doctrine of St Augustine of Hippo emphasized predestination; this had been the special emphasis of Archbishop Thomas Bradwardine. All who objected to the over-rich allegorizing which was hiding the simple message of the Bible shared Wyclif's belief that the Bible was a history of real people and of their plain teachings; this had been the special belief of the Franciscans. All who rejoiced in the divine humanity of Christ – as so many of the carols did, as Dame Julian did after the 'showings' of the divine love in her experience – shared Wyclif's insistence that Christianity was about Christ. But what was unprecedented was the defiance with which he appealed to the Bible over the heads of popes and prelates and defended his convictions when they had been condemned by ecclesiastical authority; a defiance 'increasingly dominated by his obsession with the Church's betrayal of Christ'.[19]

In his retirement at Lutterworth, he was protected by the political authority of his aristocratic patrons. But he was undeterred in pursuing a path which ultimately alienated all patrons from his followers. Determined to make available to those who read no Latin the one visible authority to which he still appealed in religion, he inspired the translation of the whole Bible from Latin into English, a task never before undertaken. At least, that is what enemies and friends agreed after his death – but the actual making of the 'Wyclif Bible' is lost in obscurity. It seems that the work was begun by Nicholas of Hereford, Wyclif's most outspoken supporter at Oxford, while still at the university before 1380 (when he conceived the

---

[19] See Gordon Leff, 'John Wyclif: The Path to Dissent', in *Proceedings of the British Academy* (London, 1966), pp.143-180. For the background, see the studies of Gordon Leff in *Bradwardine and the Pelagians* (Cambridge, 1957), *Richard Fitzralph* (Manchester, 1963) and *Heresy in the Later Middle Ages* (2 vols., Manchester, 1967); and J. A. Robson, *Wyclif and the Oxford Schools* (Cambridge, 1961).

crazy idea of converting the pope, and was lucky to escape from the papal prison). John Purvey, Wyclif's secretary at Lutterworth, seems to have taken the lead in completing the work after his master's death. What part, if any, was played by Wyclif himself is not known. The first translation was woodenly literal but was soon radically revised and improved, to become the parent of all the versions which were to shape the faith and language of the English.[20]

We understand more of Wyclif if we compare him with William of Ockham, who had fascinated Oxford half a century before.

Wyclif was no disciple of Ockham's; he preferred to base his mature philosophy on the work of John Duns the Scot who had studied and taught at Oxford at the turn of the thirteenth and fourteenth centuries. (John Duns was the man who most un-fairly gave rise to the word 'dunce' at a time when all medieval philosophy was despised, but in fact he was a deep and subtle thinker.) In philosopy Ockham was a brilliant radical. He charged into the debate about 'universals' (for example, man-kind) in relation to individuals (for example, a man). Early in the twelfth century Adelard of Bath, despite all that he did to bring in Arab science from the West, had also taught em-phatically that 'universals' were ideas in the mind of God, ideas which the human mind could abstract out of its intuition of individual things; while Anselm of Canterbury, as we have already seen, had regarded an understanding of the reality of 'universals' as any intelligent man's first step along to the road to understanding belief in God. But now William of Ockham, a young Franciscan lecturing at Oxford in the early 1320s, denied that 'universals' could be known in this way. To him, they were mere signs attached by the mind of groupings of in-dividuals; 'no universal exists in any way at all outside the knower's mind'. In the study of the individual lay wisdom.

This Oxford radical urged his startled contemporaries to desist from exploring what was theoretically possible in meta-physics and to concentrate on what could be known through

---

[20] See Margaret Deansley, *The Lollard Bible* (Cambridge, 1920), and S. L. Fristedt, *The Wyclif Bible*, 3 vols. (Stockholm, 1953-73).

experience (or, he added, inferred from the highly individual God's self-revelation). By implication he was calling men away from speculative controversies – on these he wielded 'Occam's razor' – back to the more scientific path explored by Robert Grosseteste and Roger Bacon. He was also calling men to faith; but it seemed to be faith of a new quality. He did not deny that theology could be a science based on what God had chosen to make known. What he did deny was that truths of religion such as the existence of God or the soul could be proved by reason alone; they were matters of faith. Nor could ethics be derived from what was known to be natural. A Christian's behaviour was a response to the revealed commandments of God – a matter of the individual's will, accepting God's will which might have been very different. What mattered decisively was not therefore the calm operation of reason, but an act by the will, which could not act except in trust, in faith. Faith was a leap.

His radicalism alarmed conservatives at Oxford, who in 1324 forced William to defend himself on charges of heresy at the papal court in Avignon. There the whole luxurious atmosphere so shocked the young Franciscan that he joined himself to the party of the 'Spirituals' who within his own order were resisting Pope John XXII. Eventually he fled to join the emperor Ludwig, the papacy's chief enemy, and for twenty years deployed his logical powers in the imperial political service – where he was the colleague of an even more outspoken antipapal writer, Marsilius of Padua.

William of Ockham wielded a great influence on the history of European philosophy (where his denials were developed into the system called Nominalism, from the teaching that 'universals' were mere names). He had much less influence on the history of English religion. He was not an innovating theologian; he was interested in improving the logic by which a man could accept the unchanging Faith. A mystery such as transubstantiation in the Mass he simply accepted (or so he declared) by an act of will. And until entangled in other controversies after leaving England, he was never involved in politics. He kept his radicalism within limits – within limits which Wyclif broke. In the end he was only the forerunner of a

theological revolution, just as Wyclif was only the forerunner
of Protestantism.[21]

GEOFFREY CHAUCER'S PILGRIMAGE

It is indeed tempting to regard Wyclif as the most significant
figure in fourteenth-century England. Much of this complicated century's story — political and social disturbances, protests against the corruption of the Church, quests for a deeper
personal religion — can be told so that his brave heresy sums it
up, and we can begin to talk about 'the decline' of the Middle
Ages in Church and State. Such an interpretation would, however, not do justice to the fourteenth-century facts.

One fact was that the Christian monarchy suffered no disastrous loss of power. More significant in the long run than the
drama of the depositions and deaths of Edward II and
Richard II when they had fallen foul of the nobility was the
fact that Henry IV retained most of Richard's civil servants
and most of Richard's political policy (Richard's behaviour in
the last two years, when driven almost mad by his wife Anne's
death and by the executions of his best friends, being scarcely
a policy). The monarchy carried on. And so did the Church.

Bishop Thomas Brunton freely attacked idle parish priests;
he once complained that some clergy were entrusted with the
care of a thousand souls who would not have been given the
care of a thousand apples. But he knew he could say such
things — to attentive congregations. More significant than the
protests against the worldliness of the monks and friars was the
fact that at the end of the century people were still begging for
their prayers, still making many gifts to them, still joining
their ranks. The numbers of monks and friars seem to have
stopped falling around 1375 and (although they never returned to their thirteenth-century level) to have begun climb-

---

[21] See P. Boehner, *Ockham: Philosophical Writings* (London, 1957), and
A. S. McGrade, *The Political Thought of William of Ockham* (Cambridge, 1974).

ing to a level which fell again only during the sixteenth century. The rate of increase appears to have been higher than
the growth of the population as a whole. And more significant
than any appearance of heresy was the continuing strength of
orthodox English piety. The rebels of 1381 wanted to deliver
the Church from feudalism, just as they wanted to deliver the
king from traitors; that was all. And if the peasants accepted
the Church's doctrine, so did the well-to-do. During the fourteenth century England's parish churches were adorned by
more than a hundred thousand monumental brasses, of which
some four thousand have survived to the present day. During
this century three great towers surmounted by spires crowned
Lincoln Cathedral; these were the skyscrapers of the still
faithful Middle Ages. Above all, the exceptionally devout and
articulate, from Duke Henry of Lancaster to Dame Julian of
Norwich, were pilgrims rather than rebels.

The key interpreter of the age was, it seems clear, not John
Wyclif but Geoffrey Chaucer, not the rebel but the observer
who was in the end happy to conform.

Chaucer's attitude can easily be misunderstood because it
was a part of his sophistication to keep himself out of trouble
and even out of his poetry. Unlike his Wife of Bath, he accepted 'auctoritee'. The first record about him is the expenditure of seven shillings in London on 4 April 1357 on behalf
of Countess Elizabeth, whose page he was; smart shoes, red
and black breeches and a short cloak were bought for him. He
received his last payment from the king's exchequer on 5 June
1400, having been in the service of the royal family or the
government for almost the whole of the intervening period.
His wife's sister was the mistress, and then the third wife, of a
king's son, John of Gaunt; and his grandson married the
Countess of Suffolk. He wrote a poem exhorting Richard II to
combine courage with justice, but he was not so closely identified with Richard that he lost his head when the king's
enemies were in power (as did his fellow-poet, Thomas Usk).
Like his friend John Gower he accepted Henry IV's patronage
happily enough. He was in London for the Peasants' Revolt of
1381 but his only reference to it is humorous, in his comic
masterpiece, the *Nun's Priest's Tale*. In his poems he appears

either as a wooden-headed dreamer who needs to have his own
visions explained to him or the 'Chaucer' on the Canterbury
road who contributes a ludicrous parody of Arthurian
romances (*Sir Thopas*) and, when interrupted by the host,
continues with the long, edifying but dull 'tale of Melibee and
Dame Prudence' in prose translated from the French. Yet the
real Chaucer obviously enjoyed the skill with which he told
bawdy stories through the mouths of other pilgrims. It is
therefore possible to misunderstand his attitude as being
morally and religiously neutral. As one scholar has said: 'For
all his intelligence and piety he has no spiritual vision. He
never seems angry, and rarely condemns. He is no zealous
reformer; he has neither the faith nor the optimism for that;
he has too subtle a mind, is too convinced of the badness of the
world. He maintains a well-bred, courtly, imperturbable front
which nothing can shock'.[22]

But in the last analysis this unshockability is not unlike the
compassion of the Creator in whom Chaucer believed – for
John Dryden spoke truly when he said that Chaucer's toleration of humanity was the provision of 'God's plenty'.
'Dryden's metaphor is so apt', writes Trevor Whittock,
'because the abundance of humanity constantly reminds us of
the Creator; and while each pilgrim will differently conceive
Him and the reasons for his own journey, this pilgrimage is
still a common one'.[23] The climax of the *Canterbury Tales* was
the *Parson's Tale*, a straightforward treatise on the seven
deadly sins with a call to penitence, compiled on the basis of
three works in French.

Chaucer took his own leave with an epilogue giving thanks
for 'our Lord Jhesu Christ, of whom procedeth al wit and al
goodnesse' and asking for the reader's prayers. He made
'retracciouns' of his worldly books including 'the tales of
Caunterbury thilke that sownen into (make for) synne' with
'many a song and many a leccherous lay'. One of the books he
thus retracted was 'the book of Troilus', but *Troilus and
Criseyde* itself ended with a picture of its tragic hero now in

---

[22] D. S. Brewer, *Chaucer* (London, 1953), p.137.
[23] *A Reading of the Canterbury Tales* (Cambridge, 1968), p.52.

heaven looking down at 'this litel spot of earth' and laughing at those who mourned his death. Then Chaucer had addressed his audience, presumably at the amorous court of Richard II in the early 1380s:

> O yonge fresshe folkes, he or she,
> In which that love up groweth with your age,
> Repeyreth hom (return home) from worldly vanyte. . . .

When he felt that his own end was near, he rented a house in the shadow of Westminster Abbey, where he was buried in the transept which subsequently became the Poets' Corner. So much for his hatred of monks! But perhaps the most persuasive evidence of his genuine piety was supplied when he was at the height of his powers. His poetry is thoroughly medieval, which means that its background cannot be understood without some knowledge of theology and church art.[24] Above all, his poetry — for all his complete and glad acceptance of life — shows 'the acceptance of full moral responsibilities; it involves very sensitive and sure ethical discriminations and judgements'.[25] And these are the moral verdicts of a Christian who prays. 'In his many prayers, especially to the Virgin, Chaucer blends a joyful lyricism with splendour of thought and of diction, as he does nowhere else. Humility and exaltation, simplicity and magnificence, go hand in hand'.[26]

His attitude to human frailty was as profoundly Christian as Dame Julian's. Many will reckon that it was far more Christian than John Wyclif's bitterly uncharitable tirades, perhaps also more Christian than William Langland's puritanism (Langland noticed only that pilgrims told lies to each other). Chaucer was, of course, not a theologian; he earned his living as a courtier, soldier, diplomat, controller of customs in London and the king's clerk of works. Nor was he a mystic; in the year that Dame Julian saw Christ bleed on the crucifix in Norwich he had his own life-turning experience in

---

[24] This was stressed, probably over-stressed, in D. W. Robertson's *Preface to Chaucer* (Princeton, N.J., 1962).

[25] John Speirs, *Chaucer the Maker* (London, 1951), p.204.

[26] D. S. Brewer, *op. cit.*, p.151.

Florence, where during a brief visit he began his familiarity
with the new literature of Dante, Boccaccio and Petrarch. But
when he set himself to reproduce Boccaccio in English, he did
it without the Italian's contempt for human nature. In his
Troilus and Criseyde, which was derived from Boccaccio, both
the overwhelmed lover and the pretty young widow who for a
time is faithful to him are portrayed with understanding and
respect. So far from being lewd, they have to be pushed into
bed together by Criseyde's lecherous uncle Pandarus (in Boccaccio, a mere go-between) with the plea that it is raining. So
far from being contemptibly fickle, Criseyde is allowed to
show us why life and love must go on; she needs someone else
to live with and to love during the prolonged absence of
Troilus. Troilus is a suitable mouthpiece for philosophy which
Chaucer has derived from Boethius:

> Love, that of erthe and se hath governaunce,
> Love, that his hestes (hosts) hath in hevenes hye. . . .
> Love, that knetteth (knits) lawe of compaignie,
> And couples doth in virtu for to dwelle. . . .

Chaucer wrote this long poem, which has often been called
the first English novel, using leisure from his supervision of the
collection of customs in London. He had already tried his
hand at a number of poems which show his ambition to do in
English what several poets had already done in France (most
notably those whose work he translated in his *Romaunt of the
Rose*). His own earlier poems were all in praise of love – to him
an inexhaustible theme, mostly amusing, sometimes serious,
sometimes sad. It was about love, and only by implication
about the poet's trade, that he wrote 'the lyf so short, the craft
so long to lerne'. The poems have a set pattern: the reading of
a book, the sleep, the dream, the supernatural interpreter of
the dream as a celebration of love. And they have a style: as
aristocratic as *Sir Gawain and the Green Knight* but twice as
elegant because now freed from the prison-house of alliter-
ation inherited from the Anglo-Saxons. In his *Boke of the
Duchess* he mourns for Blanche, John of Gaunt's first wife,
dead in her early twenties. It is all conventional, but even here
she is alive:

I saw hir daunce so comlily,
Carole and singe so swetely,
Laugh and pleye so womanly,
And loke so debonairly.

The *Parlement of Fowles* (probably written to celebrate the bretrothal of Richard II to Anne of Bohemia) is the most attractive work of that early period. It develops a tradition which had made a brief appearance in English under Henry II with the writing of *The Owl and the Nightingale*; there the two birds debate their rival merits and agree to submit to the judgement of 'Master Nicholas of Guildford' (probably the author). In Chaucer's mind there could be no question about the superiority of the nightingale. He was a troubadour of sweet lovers in the spring, singing as they sang in sunnier France; but he would sing in English. In 1363 English was used for the first time in the chancellor's speech opening Parliament. Chaucer would use it for a debate about humanity's most attractive theme.[27]

It seems, however, that when he moved from the city of London out to Greenwich in 1386 he resolved to write 'som comedye' about English life – and about life slightly lower in the social scale. He abandoned his collection of tales called the *Legend of Good Women* because his imagination had been fired by a more mixed group. His *Canterbury Tales* could not be about the peasants; Geoffrey Chaucer (a London wine merchant's son) did not know them. But it was about a splendid variety of middle class types – 'sondry folke, by adventure yfalle in felaweshipe'. As he watched the pilgrims to Canterbury passing near his Greenwich home, an idea caught fire in the poet's mind: the idea of the human richness of Christian England.[28]

We are struck by the number of rogues on this pilgrimage, particularly rogues in the full-time service of the Church. Prioress Eglentyne (Sweet Briar), the monk and the friar have

[27] See C. S. Lewis, *The Allegory of Love* (Oxford, 1936), and C. Muscatine, *Chaucer and the French Tradition* (Berkeley, Cal., 1957).

[28] See D. R. Howard, *The Idea of the Canterbury Tales* (Berkeley, Cal., 1976).

all forgotten the austere ideals of their orders. The nun is a coy, delicately living, sentimental spinster, devoted to 'smale houndes', compassionate to mice; the monk a country gentleman dressed up to look like a monk (more expensively than most laymen could afford), the bell on his bridle as loud as any chapel bell. The friar 'knew the tavernes wel in every toun' — and the women. The lesser officials of the Church, the 'summoner' to the archdeacon's court and the 'pardoner' peddling ecclesiastical indulgences and fake relics, more directly trade on people's credulity. They are almost totally repulsive; 'of his visage children were aferd'. But we should also notice the saints. There is the knight who embodies the ideals of the Age of Chivalry — true, perfect and a gentleman:

> He was a verray parfit gentil knyght.

There is the 'clerk of Oxenford' who would prefer 'at his beddes heed twenty books, clad in black or red' to a rich wardrobe. There is the 'poure persoun of a toun' who preached Christ's message 'but first he folwed it hymselve'. And there is the parson's brother the ploughman, a hero to Chaucer in common with Langland:

> Lyvynge in pees and parfit charitee,
> God loved he best with al his hoole herte.

Although medieval readers are likely to have admired the preaching, no doubt the main attraction of the *Canterbury Tales* has always lain in the tales told by the sinners — by those who would say with the Wife of Bath that Christ's message was not for them:

> He spak to them that wolde live parfitly;
> And lordlinges, by your leve, that am not I.

After the courtly tragedy of fighting over a girl in Ancient Greece told by the knight, we are all ears for the ribald anecdotes of village life exchanged (with insults) by the miller and the reve. These are some of the tales of which the dying Chaucer repented; but as soon as we meet the rich old Oxford carpenter's wife, eighteen-year-old Alisoun, we know that we are going to like her while we laugh at the bedroom farce

which results from her being 'wylde and yong'. Even more do
we relish that great lover of life, the Wife of Bath, although
she has worn down five husbands.

For Chaucer the world is no monastery. The world lives by
the interplay of the sexes and by the making of money, and the
shipman is not the only pilgrim of whom this is true:

> Of nyce conscience took he no keep.

And this is more than a chuckling matter, for Chaucer has
noticed much more than the look on the Wife of Bath as she
inspects the parish clerk's legs in the procession behind her
fourth husband's bier. He knows, as the merchant's tale
demonstrates, what is the horror of old Januarie's loveless
marriage. He knows – and gives us the pardoner's tale in order
to make sure we know – what moral degradation results from
avarice. And we have no reason to suppose that he had a
basically flippant attitude towards the public violence of his
time. On the contrary, his poem called *The Former Age* shows
his seriously conservative values:

> For in oure dayes nis (nothing) but covetyse,
> Doublenesse, and treasoun, and envye,
> Poyson, mansalughtre, and mordre in sondry wyse.

But he is not one to condemn those who share his own flesh
and blood. He does not write off the young squire who is 'as
fressh as is the month of May' merely because the boy is at
present 'a lovyere and a lusty bacheler'. He expects the boy to
marry – how many of these tales are about marriage! – and to
end up as a knight like his father; or at least like the pot-
bellied, red-faced franklin whose tale is about married bliss.

Even the pardoner's sins of hyprocrisy and deceit – which
(in accordance with the Christian tradition) Chaucer regards
as much worse than any lust of the flesh – do not finally put a
man outside the common pilgrimage. The host insults the
pardoner after the nauseating smugness of his tale (offered as
a 'moral' tale 'though myself be a ful vicious man'), but is persuaded by the knight to kiss him as a sign of peace. When the
pardoner is pardoned it may be the most Christian moment of
the fourteenth century. And so they ride on, until the sun

begins to set and the parson is persuaded to preach his sermon – for, as the host declares,

Thou shouldest knytte up wel a greet mateere.

Chaucer never described the arrival at the shrine – or the return journey, although in the prologue he had the host, Harry Bailey, ordain that each of the pilgrims is to tell two tales on the journey back as well as two on the road to Canterbury. He no doubt visited Canterbury, where in the 1390s the master mason Henry Yevele (his colleague at the court of Richard II) was building that forest of stone, the Perpendicular nave of the cathedral: 'the supreme triumph of English architecture, which is to say, of English art.'[29] But the 'greet mateere' for Chaucer was the *journey* of people; he never aspired to be a Dante, majestically eloquent about destinations. His ambition was so to describe these people's journey that the English language (which he knew to be changing rapidly in his time, as several passages of his poetry show explicitly) would make another great advance. That is why, when presenting him in a twentieth-century book, it is surely right to quote his words without modernization; it is a tribute to what he did for English. 'Chaucer', writes Ian Robinson, 'recognized the different powers of English and brought them together. He did not, as used occasionally to be thought, himself compose the English language; but he did make it, with the help of his contemporaries and his readers, the language of a great literature'. English was to be no longer the less-than-French dialect of a region, or the less-than-Latin language of sermons and private devotions. Specially in the London or court dialect which Chaucer used, it was to be the language of a great people. We owe to the *Canterbury Tales* an 'extraordinary feat of genius': the 'seeing England whole' which is also 'the creation of a national literature'.[30]

That was the advance which Chaucer most desired. He did, however, also notice that these people were on a pilgrimage.

---

[29] John Harvey, *English Cathedrals*, p.98.

[30] Ian Robinson, *Chaucer and the English Tradition* (Cambridge, 1972), pp.283-4.

He did not attribute a deeply religious motive to most of them, but he knew what such a motive might be. When his mood in contemplating the world was 'her is non hoom, her nis but wildernesse', he embodied the spirit of a sincere pilgrim's progress in his short *balade* called *Truth*:

> Forth, pilgrim, forth! Forth, beste, out of thy stal!
> Know thy contree, look up, thank God of al;
> Hold the heye (high) way, and lat thy gost (spirit) thee lede;
> And trouthe thee shal delivere, it is no drede (dread).

CHAPTER SEVEN

THE SUDDEN STORM

St. George's Chapel and the Castle at Windsor.

A SECURE CHURCH

Right up to the 1530s the Church of popes and monks, the Mass and the pilgrimage, the cathedral and the hermitage, seemed eternal in England.

In telling the history of the so-called 'decline' of the Middle Ages it is possible to put all the emphasis on the protests, taking them as preparations for Protestantism. Almost any noise can be interpreted as a rumble of the coming storm. In 1427 Pope Martin V rebuked Cardinal Henry Beaufort for the arrest of a papal tax gatherer. In 1528 Simon Fish, a London

barrister who had fled to Antwerp after daring to take the
leading part in an anticlerical play, wrote a much discussed
pamphlet. It was entitled *A Supplication for Beggars*, and
Henry VIII is said to have kept it 'in his bosom' for several
days. Fish urged that the time had come to end papal taxation
once and for all; to end a situation in which the English clergy,
one-four-hundredth of the population, owned a third of the
land. He wrote, as he acted, with gusto. From the century between these incidents in 1427 and 1528, many complaints
could be gathered. Englishmen protested against papal taxation, for that took good money out of England; against papal
appointments of foreigners to lucrative posts in the English
Church; against priests who drew incomes from parishes
where they did not reside; against the exemption of the clergy
from the ordinary courts; against abuses which laymen experienced in the ecclesiastical courts; against the far too frequent use of the penalty of excommunication (a penalty which
was an ecclesiastical court's only weapon when, for example,
one of the parties in a dispute about a will failed to appear in
court). These were complaints which the House of Commons
took up when it met in November 1529, and so began the
'Reformation Parliament'.

Sometimes the complaints were bitter. Among the grumbles
about the tithes due to the parish priests a particular resentment accompanied the custom by which a priest claimed a
'mortuary' or one of the possessions of a dead man in lieu of
unpaid tithes. The notorious case of Richard Hunne, found
hanging in the Bishop of London's prison in 1514 and subsequently burned by the Church as a suicidal heretic, had
begun with a quarrel over a mortuary. This merchant tailor
had refused to give the local rector the cloth under which his
dead baby son had been carried to church.[1] And all the time
there was, no doubt, resentment among the laity at the wealth
of many ecclesiastics, who had secured to themselves possessions a great deal larger than that cloth from an infant's
funeral.

But while there were all these protests at abuses, the system

---

[1] See A. Ogle, *The Tragedy of the Lollards Tower* (Oxford, 1949).

itself seemed secure, any storm remote. Among the literate, piety was still supreme; of the 349 titles of books printed between 1468 and 1530 and now in the British Library, 176 are religious. Among the people (who remained mostly illiterate), the Robin Hood of the late medieval Midlands ballads was admired for his daring as he extracted money out of fat abbots — but even this fearless anticlerical had to have his own fat chaplain, Friar Tuck. English piety at these different social levels was much boasted about by a nation as patriotic as it was orthodox. In 1427 Pope Martin's letter was addressed to one of the wealthiest men in that world, a bishop of royal blood who was also Chancellor of England. The pope's complaint was not that the ill-treatment of his representative proved that the English were determined to ruin the Church but that the incident had occurred in a land 'which considers itself better than all other Christian nations in devotion, faith and the worship of God'.[2]

A century later England was still the same, content to live and think within the sound of church bells. Even in London, whose citizens were often ready to believe the worst of the clergy, many pious gifts to the Church were still being made.[3] A recent study of the diocese of Lincoln concludes that 'few Tudor parishioners were as anticlerical as Simon Fish' — because according to these parishioners' complaints to bishops or archdeacon, 'the rectors, vicars or curates who served them seem to have exhibited few of the enormities described by Simon Fish'.[4] Certainly the clergy were not as a class provocatively rich; the average net stipend of a vicar in Lincoln diocese in 1526 was under £7. Another study of local church life concludes that in Essex — a county much influenced by the lingering effects of the Lollardy started by John Wyclif, burdened by monasteries which seemed second-rate and

----

[2] *The English Church and the Papacy in the Middle Ages*, ed. C. H. Lawrence (London, 1965), p.235.

[3] See J. A. F. Thomson, 'Piety and Charity in Late Medieval London', *Journal of Ecclesiastical History* (Cambridge, 1964), pp.178-195.

[4] Margaret Bowker, *Secular Clergy in the Diocese of Lincoln, 1495-1520* (Cambridge, 1968), p.180.

futile, and soon to be sympathetic with the new excitements of
the German Protestantism of Martin Luther – traditional
piety flourished mightily in the parishes early in the sixteenth
century. 'Many people were passionately devoted to religion.
The parish church provided not only for the religious but also
for the social life of the people, and was bound up with the
day-to-day administration of the local community's life.'[5] For
the more remote and conservative areas such as Lancashire,
the Durham region or Cornwall, the detailed evidence to the
same effect is still stronger. England was overwhelmingly
Catholic.[6]

The only tax which the laity had to pay to Rome was Peter's
Pence, amounting to a mere £200 a year. The clergy were indeed taxed by the papacy. The 'tenth' which they had to pay
was the pioneer of the modern income tax. Bishops had to pay
'annates' equivalent to their first year's revenue. But since they
professed that the papacy was essential to the Church, the
clergy could not well argue that Rome had no financial
needs – and anyway, they were not beggared. The annual
total of all the taxes they sent to Rome came to under
£5,000 – only about £1,000 more than the income of the
Bishop of Winchester and some £30,000 less than the
estimated income of Cardinal Thomas Wolsey. The clergy
could afford to produce a large sum when in 1500 Pope
Alexander VI called for one more crusade – and a much
larger sum (over £100,000) when, just over thirty years later,
Henry VIII threatened them with the penalties in the statute
of *Praemunire* because they had received the pope's legate
(Wolsey) without licence from the Crown. The real question
was not about clerical taxation. It was whether, taxed or un-
taxed, some of the clergy were too rich. To that question the
powerful laity of England in the 1530s returned a decisive

[5] J. E. Oxley, *The Reformation in Essex to the Death of Mary* (Manchester, 1965), p.1.
[6] See Christopher Haigh, *Reformation and Resistance in Tudor
Lancashire* (Cambridge, 1975); for Durham M. E. James, *Family,
Lineage and Civil Society* (Oxford, 1974); A. L. Rowse, *Tudor Cornwall*
(revised, London, 1969).

yes – although this was not an answer which helped the lay 'beggars' on whose behalf Simon Fish had claimed to be writing. However, if some of the late medieval clergy prospered excessively, most of the late medieval laity were themselves neither paupers nor basically hostile to the clergy. As the Act of 1532 which threatened the pope with loss of his revenue from England declared, both the king and the people liked to think of themselves as good Catholics. They claimed to be 'as obedient, devout, catholic and humble children of God and Holy Church as any people be within any realm christened'. Basically it was because of this general acceptance of the Catholic religion that the income of the Church, surveyed in the incomplete *Valor Ecclesiasticus* of 1535, came to £320,180. Probably the complete figure was not far short of £400,000, at a time when a labourer's average annual income seems to have been about two and a half pounds.

THE LOLLARDS

The fate of the Lollards after John Wyclif's stirring protests shows both the power and the popularity of Catholicism in late medieval England. More than seventy Lollards were burned at the stake in public under the statutes of 1401 and 1414. Floggings were far more frequent; these and public penance were the normal punishments for first offenders. Such penalties must have alarmed anyone tempted to heresy who was not already terrified by the thought of the everlasting punishment widely believed to await all heretics. The persecution was particularly effective in frightening off people such as university theologians or Members of Parliament, who in the fourteenth century had been prominent supporters of Wyclif. As late as 1395 a group of knights had put their names to 'Twelve Conclusions', a Lollard manifesto. As late as 1411 Archbishop Arundel had aroused fierce opposition in Oxford when he clumsily tried to stamp out the Wyclif tradition there. But ten years later Oxford had almost forgotten its loyalty to its dead teacher and the Lollards (the word was Dutch and meant 'babblers') had gone underground. Wyclif's own secretary, John Purvey, and his Bible translator, Nicholas of Hereford, recanted. Another of his most prominent Oxford associates, Philip Repton, ended up as Bishop of Lincoln. Such leadership as the Lollards possessed was almost all uneducated; a hunted sect, they produced no system to rival either the organization or the theology of the Catholic Church. In these circumstances the courageous persistence of humble folk in their religious convictions despite the prestige and power of their persecutors is, surely, both surprising and moving.

However, modern scholars who have investigated the fragmentary records that remain conclude that one of the chief problems of the Lollards right through the fifteenth century was their unpopularity. The public seems to have been genuinely shocked by their perversity and not at all distressed by their deaths. The explanation seems to be not only that heretics might be flogged or burned but also that heretics were thought to be antisocial. Fuel for the fire of anti-Lollard panic was provided when the movement's greatest lay leader, Sir John Oldcastle (Lord Cobham), formerly a friend of the king's, was foolish enough to lead a rebellion in 1414. There were various other outbreaks, bringing back memories of the Peasants' Revolt of 1381; but like Oldcastle's crazy attempt to enter London armed one January evening, they were easily suppressed. Another conspiracy was discovered in 1431.

In August 1407 William Thorpe was brought to trial before Archbishop Arundel in Saltwood Castle. His account of the trial, no doubt edited in his own favour, survives. It contains an interesting tribute to John Wyclif. Thorpe remembered how 'he was holden of full many men the greatest clerk that they knew then living' and the archbishop admitted that he was 'a great clerk and many men held him a perfect liver'. The conversation rambled. At one stage Arundel was defending pilgrimages and the use of music during them. 'When one of them that goeth barefoot striketh his toe upon a stone and hurteth him sore and maketh him bleed, it is well done that he or his fellow begin then a song or else take out a bagpipe.' At various points this aristocratic archbishop showed that he was human, and it is possible that in the end Thorpe escaped with his life. But Arundel's sometimes patronizing, often irritated, contempt for the Lollards expressed fifteenth-century public opinion. 'Ye presume that the Lord hath chosen you only for to preach as faithful disciples and special followers of Christ.' It did not take much for such bafflement to harden into persecution.[7]

The tragedy was that this bitter atmosphere, where revolution was pitted against reaction, made reform virtually impossible. K. B. McFarlane has pointed out that in the previous age there were many signs pointing to reform. 'The chief characteristic of English religious life in the fourteenth century is the growth of moral fervour among the laity. It was inspired and whipped up by the sermons and discourses of mendicants and other poor preachers and it infected the clergy also, but its strength was derived from its success among laymen. . . . The contemporary spirit in religion was puritan, biblical, evangelical, anarchic, anti-sacerdotal, hostile to the established order in the Church. Hence there was widespread sympathy with at least the moral content of the Lollard teaching.'[8] The doctrinal content of Lollardy was of course more difficult for a conservative (or indifferent) public to swallow, but the emphasis on the simplicity and transcendence of God, the opening of the Bible to the laity and the insistence on biblical preaching were positive proposals to which the Church might have listened to its own great advantage. But because reform became branded as heretical and treasonable, the Church made none of the adjustments which might have been expected in the earlier stages of Wyclif's career. No Bible in the language of the people was authorized in England until 1537. Equivalent translations were allowed and widely used on the Continent, and Archbishop Arundel promised that

---

[7] *Fifteenth Century Prose and Verse*, ed. A. W. Pollard (London, 1903), pp.97-174. See also J. A. F. Thomson, *The Later Lollards, 1414-1520* (Oxford, 1965); A. G. Dickens, *Lollards and Protestants in the Diocese of York, 1509-1558* (Oxford, 1959); Claire Cross, *Church and People 1450-1660* (London, 1976), pp.9-52.

[8] K. B. McFarlane, *Lancastrian Kings and Lollard Knights* (Oxford, 1972), pp.224-5. See also Margaret Aston, *Lollards and Reformers* (London, 1984).

something would be done for the English. But nothing was done. No spiritual or theological renewal based on lay knowledge of the Bible was accepted. Renewal was not going to be accepted on any other intellectual basis, either. This was shown by the fate of Reginald Pecock.

This very able and eloquent Welshman formed the ambition to refute the Lollard heresies. He would do so, however, not by the exercise of ecclesiastical power, not even by an appeal to the Fathers of the Church or to texts of Holy Scripture, but – as Anselm had done in his day – by reasoned theology, by what he called the 'doom of reason'. Believing that these issues were of concern to all, he wrote mainly in English, not Latin, although his choice of language meant that he had to invent many new words to translate the Latin technical terms. His theology would take an honest account of difficulties in the orthodox positions. He admitted, for example, that Moses had been the editor rather than the sole author of the books attributed to him; that the apostles had not written the Apostles' Creed; that the Roman emperor Constantine had not given the papacy its vast estates in Italy. He expounded mysteries such as Christ's descent into hell after his crucifixion in such a way as to suggest that they were mysterious. He summed up his own doctrine in a 'new English creed', which has not survived.

To this self-imposed duty of authorship, with all the necessary study, he gave the best of his life. He was financed from a variety of sources – as a Fellow of Oriel College, Oxford; as a rector in Gloucestershire; in the mastership of a small college in London recently founded by a rich merchant, Richard Whittington of nursery rhyme fame. He continued to write books while Bishop first of St Asaph and then of Chichester. But his literary labours won him no reward. There were complaints that he neglected preaching and pastoral work – complaints which he unwisely answered by arguing in public that a bishop was not obliged to be a preacher. There was alarm because he wrote in English. Had he confined himself to Latin he might have been given the considerable liberty which scholars still enjoyed for their speculations, but by working in a language which the ordinary man might understand he exposed himself to the charge of unsettling the people's faith with intellectual doubts. Yet the man in the medieval street certainly could not have understood these books, had he ever come across them in handwritten copies. They were far too closely argued, and far too heavily packed with technical terms, to appeal to the laity whose ignorance of theology was happy and whose devotional reading presupposed a religion of the heart not of the mind. The radical courage of these books, the seriousness and toughness of their argumentation, might have appealed to middle-class Lollards — only, Pecock happened to be a bishop of a Church which in this period was burning heretics, and his writing was intended to help the burners rather than the burned. He was very energetically supplying theology to a market which did not exist; and which would have greatly disturbed his fellow-bishops by its existence, had it existed.

He might have been dismissed as a scholar who lacked the common touch. But his character was more controversial than that. He was an arrogant man ('this peacock', said his critics); perhaps he had to be, to risk so many experiments. The habitual tone of self-praise to be found in his books, and presumably also in his conversation, probably did as much as any sentence in his voluminous writings to bring about a sensation in 1457. He was tried for heresy by a court under the Archbishop of Canterbury — the only English bishop to be subjected to this ordeal in the Middle Ages. He apologized and retracted. His opinions, he said, had always been tentative and subject to the teaching of the Church, although the essential charge against him was that he had denied or ignored 'the auctorite and determinacioun of our Mudder Holie Church'. He thus saved himself from the stake and Pope Calixtus III ordered his restitution to Chichester. On that pope's death he was, however, forced to resign and was confined to a cell in a monastery without books or writing materials. There he soon died (in 1461), perhaps of boredom.[9]

Knowing how the sudden storm that was to break in the

---

[9] See V. H. H. Green, *Bishop Reginald Pecock* (Cambridge, 1945, and C. W. Brockwell, *Bishop Reginald Pecock and the Lancastrian Church* (Lewiston, N.Y., 1985).

1530s was to damage many things which poor Bishop Pecock, his judges and even the Lollards themselves all held sacred, we read the religious history of the fifteenth century as a tragedy – the tragedy of a wasted opportunity, in a Catholic Church hastening to catastrophe. However, that was not how things looked at the time.

A POPULAR RELIGION

Late medieval England knew a real, although patchy, prosperity. Although some of the traditional cities – York or Lincoln, Norwich or Winchester – were by now decaying, and the 'enclosures' of agricultural land to make pastures for sheep began to reduce rural employment substantially from the 1480s, it has been estimated that the wages of a builder's labourer had more purchasing power in the fifteenth century than they were to have again until the 1860s.[10] Although the population seems to have been inadequate to the economy for much of the fifteenth century (this helped to keep wages high, but more than one foreign tourist noticed the vast stretches of uncultivated land), the evidence suggests that after 1475 it began increasing – and that unemployment did not become a major problem until about 1525. In 1497 the Venetian ambassador sent home a report on the English economy. It seemed to him the richest country in Europe. He had noticed silver tankards in the inns (although admittedly without English wine to put into them) and fifty-two goldsmiths' shops in one street in London. The people, he said, were well-fed and well-dressed. With 'incredible courtesy' they kept their hats off while talking with each other, although they did not make public the 'very violent' sexual passions which they were believed to enjoy in private. They were fiercely proud of

---

[10] See R. B. Dobson, 'Urban Decline in Late Medieval England', in *Transactions of the Royal Historical Society* (London, 1977), pp.1-22. But a summary of recent research into prices and wages is provided by C. S. L. Davies, *Peace, Print and Protestantism* (London, 1976), pp.334-8.

England and if they saw a handsome foreigner would say, 'he looks like an Englishman'.[11]

The Catholic Church, triumphant over heresy, prospered with the bulk of the people. The Italian visitor just quoted was under the impression that the English attended Mass daily. That was not widely true, but a comprehensive modern survey of the clergy's life and work during the 'decline' of the Middle Ages concluded that 'the Church in England continued to pursue its old paths, an unchangeable and apparently impregnable institution, mechanical no doubt in its processes, restrained from beneficial innovations by the prevailing spirit of legalism, but presenting a calm and unruffled front to the political chaos and social change'.[12] A more recent study presents a similar picture of thousands of complacent clergy.[13]

The trouble was that most of the priests were not fully professional, for no one thought it necessary to train them for preaching or pastoral work. They were, on the whole, not unspiritual (so far as we know); but they did not produce any English equivalent to St Thomas a Kempis, whose *Imitation of Christ* was beginning to cross over from the Continent into a few English hearts. They were, on the whole, not completely illiterate, and the number of graduates was steadily increasing; but the evidence surviving suggests that not many of them owned Bibles, presumably because not many of them were thoroughly at home in Latin. Many of them were to accept all the religious revolutions of the sixteenth century – much to the disgust of later Roman Catholics and Protestants. When the storm broke in the 1530s only one bishop (John Fisher) did not bend; and the most effective role in the theological defence of the Church was left to a layman, Sir Thomas More. More had once written that the clergy on his dream-island, Utopia, were elected by the citizens, were married if they so wished, and could be women. The Utopian priests were 'of exceeding holiness and therefore very few'.

---

[11] J. R. Lander, *The War of the Roses* (London, 1965), pp.310-313.

[12] A. H. Thompson, *The English Clergy and their Organization in the Later Middle Ages* (Oxford, 1947), p.6.

[13] Peter Heath, *The English Parish Clergy on the Eve of the Reformation* (London, 1969). Barrie Dobson collected essays on the *The Church, Politics and Patronage in the Fifteenth Century* (Gloucester, 1984).

If we want to penetrate the spiritual life of this conservatively Christian England, we do not turn to its leaders or to its theologians. We have to go instead to its music, to its drama and to the churches themselves.

During the fifteenth century the most lovely poems in English were not the verbose efforts of the official poets who were, at least in their own eyes, Chaucer's successors. The best poems were the carols — no longer, it seems, usually danced but now sung by a soloist and chorus polyphonically, to tunes which for the most part seem to have been specially composed. About five hundred fifteenth-century lyrics of this sort have survived, with about a hundred and thirty musical settings.[14] We catch the reverent wonder at the heart of orthodoxy:

> A God and yet a man?
>> A mayde and yet a mother?
> Witt wonders what witt can
>> Conceave this or the other.
>
> A god, and can he die?
>> A dead man, can he live?
> What witt can well replie?
>> What reason reason give?

We are swept into the festivity:

> Nowell, nowell, nowell, nowell.
> Who is there that singeth so,
>> Nowell, nowell, nowell?
> I am here Sire Christesmasse.
> Wellcome, my Lord, Sir Christemasse,
> Wellcome to us all, both more and less.
>> Come near, nowell.

We are moved by the tenderness:

> Lullay, myn lykyng, my dere sone,
>> my swetyng,
> Lullay my dere herte, my owen
>> dere derlyng.

---

[14] See *Religious Lyrics of the Fifteenth Century*, ed. Carleton Brown (Oxford, 1939).

And we are thrilled by the optimism:

> Now is wele and all thing aright
> And Christ is come as a trew knight
>   For our broder is king of might. . . .

Music appears to have been the art in which the English most excelled. In Latin church music John Dunstable, for example, became a composer of European stature while musician to an English general, the Duke of Bedford. This was the period when organs became widely used in parishes and when the professional choirs of the great churches rose to unprecedented standards under musicians of the calibre of Robert Fairfax, organist of St Alban's Abbey and a composer used by Henry VIII. The world of church music which was to be enriched in the Elizabethan age by the genius of Tye, Tallis and Byrd was already singing.

In drama, the performances of the biblical plays developed – too far for some puritan tastes, so that the 'morality' plays such as the famous *Everyman* (itself a translation from the Dutch) were introduced, putting the ethical sermon on the stage. The earliest to have survived, *The Castle of Perseverance* written about 1425, put Man in a castle besieged by the personified vices. The clergy seem to have thought such scenes safer than popular interpretations of the Bible, but here, too, dramatists and actors could be lively. At the end of the fifteenth century a priest, Henry Medwall, who had already written a morality play (*Nature*), wrote England's first secular drama, telling of the loves of Lucres and her maid. Probably it was Christmas entertainment for the household of the Archbishop of Canterbury. From personified vices or virtues to real girls turned out to be no long step, but the road was also short if taken in the opposite direction; a non-ecclesiastical play could still be highly moral. Even in the sceptical Christopher Marlowe's *Doctor Faustus*, completed in the spring of 1589, may be heard many echoes of the spiritual drama of Everyman on his road to death and judgement a century before. The first English historical drama, John Bale's *King Johan*, was written by a Protestant (born in 1495) who also produced three plays on biblical themes and a morality play. In *King Johan* – where King John is praised as a Christian hero fighting popery – characters appear such as Sedition and Civil Order. Such was the tradition behind Shakespeare's history plays, which are always strongly moral in their plots and constitute the most memorable expression of Protestant England's sense of continuity with the English Middle Ages.

To this day, if we use our eyes in English churches we see proof of how assured and popular the Catholic Church looked as the Reformation drew near. 'In the fifteenth century,' a modern authority writes, 'hardly a parish but did something to its own church, whether by popular effort or through private enterprise of landowner or merchant. Those parts of the country which maintained a relatively high level of prosperity, particularly in Somerset and East Anglia, lavished money on fine builders' work and enrichment of every sort. . . . The screenwork, the paintings and statues, the benches – commonly in use for the first time – the stalls, the roof carvings, exist in incredible variety to tell the tale. The level of handicraft very seldom dropped below excellence: sturdy construction allied to high finish has seldom been maintained for so long on such a high plane.'[15]

Churches in the Perpendicular style such as St Mary's, Warwick (with its superb chapel memorializing the Beauchamp earls), or the churches of Chipping Campden, Fairford and Northleach in the Cotswolds, and Long Melford, Lavenham and Cavendish in East Anglia, or the chancel of Holy Trinity, Stratford-upon-Avon, where Shakespeare was to be buried, still stand and still delight. Largely paid for out of the profits of the wool and cloth trades, they are the most conspicuous achievements of a wider movement which solidly testifies to the vitality of religion in the late medieval parishes. England was, of course, already covered with churches – with too many, for during the fifteenth century many churches in abandoned villages, or in towns which had never fully recovered from the Black Death's ravages, were in ruins. The existing wealth of ecclesiastical architecture at the time is

---

[15] John Harvey, *The Perpendicular Style* (London, 1978), p.160.

suggested vividly by the notebook of a retired businessman, the first of England's enthusiastic amateur antiquarians, who between 1478 and his death in 1485 rode all over England, picking up bits of history, turning over libraries (although he had only one good eye), measuring innumerable churches by his own elderly paces.[16] But in thousands of parish churches there was new work showing the character of the English Middle Ages in their so-called 'decline' – the towers, often magnificent; the belfries, so impressive to the ear; the capacious porches where contracts were solemnized and weddings begun; the little rooms above the porches, where often boys were taught; the roofs (specially East Anglia's angel-roofs or the 'wagon' ceilings of the west country) which exhibited the carpenter's skill in an age when even rich men's houses were still being made mainly of wood; the foliage, beasts or people carved on the 'finials' at the ends of the newly introduced benches; the charming and often humorous misericords under the seats in the choir stalls; the elaborate font-covers and rood-screens; the chapels maintained competitively by rival gilds of tradesmen; the large naves, paid for by the people of the parish and used for the preaching they relished; the rood-lofts where the musicians would gather with their instruments; the many wall paintings and banners; the portrayal of prominent parishioners with a considerable naturalism on brasses, on alabaster effigies and in the picture-windows (where the invention of 'silver stain' helped the portraiture and added to the general atmosphere of a golden glory); the chantries where the really rich could be remembered by name (it seems that there were about three thousand of these endowed in parish churches or cathedrals); the great windows letting in the daylight from an England which seemed stable in its religious and social order despite the minor disorders on which historians, looking round for troublesome incidents, have concentrated too gloomily.

If we ask what inspired these men and women to lavish such wealth on their parish churches – or on the colleges of chantry priests, the hospitals and the schools which were other impor-

---

[16] See *William Worcestre: Itineraries*, ed. J. H. Harvey (Oxford, 1969).

tant foundations of this period — we can in many cases turn to their wills, reinforced by other surviving evidence of their attitudes. We find that they hoped to enter eternal bliss through the prayers of those on earth whose good will they had secured by their benefactions. In the letters of the fifteenth-century Paston family in Norfolk we meet a grasping and ruthless clan, but one which always takes it for granted that money spent on funerals and Masses is well spent. It has been truly said that 'almost all forms of medieval philanthropy had the purchase of prayers as their ultimate goal'.[17]

THE UNIVERSITIES

In 1429 the intellectual battle against heresy still seemed paramount in Oxford. Richard Fleming, Bishop of Lincoln, in that year founded Lincoln College for graduates prepared to equip themselves for this fight by the study of orthodox theology. In the previous year he had what were supposed to be John Wyclif's bones dug up and burned, and the ashes cast into a nearby river. But when Henry Chichele, Archbishop of Canterbury, founded All Souls College in Oxford nine years later, a slightly more worldly note could be struck. Although most of the forty fellows were to pursue theological studies, sixteen were to be lawyers. The doctrinal crisis had passed and in the mind of an eminently effective administrator the needs of administration on the basis of law could be given priority.

Not long after these contrasting foundations the nearby Divinity School was rebuilt; and in the 1480s Thomas Kemp, Bishop of London, paid for an appropriately elaborate vault, of an intricate pattern, under which the theological lecturers

---

[17] J. T. Rosenthal, *The Purchase of Paradise: Gift Giving and the Aristocracy, 1307-1485* (London, 1972), p.10. See also the two volumes by W. K. Jordan surveying the period 1480-1660: *The Charities of London* and *Philanthropy in England* (London, 1959-61). H. S. Bennett included a revealing chapter on religion in his *The Pastons and their England* (Cambridge, 1922).

and their students might discuss further and further refinements of orthodoxy. Although the nature of God's foreknowledge of human affairs was one of the favourite topics in the fifteenth-century university, those who lectured in that hall had not the slightest inkling of a Protestant future. Over this vault was housed Duke Humphrey's Library given in the 1440s, the nucleus of what was to grow into the assembly of the English-speaking world's learning in the Bodleian Library. Outside the city walls Magdalen College was founded by William of Waynflete, Bishop of Winchester, and built in the period 1474-1509. Between the chapel and the river lay, on one side, a cloister so impressive as to suggest that the college was going to be a monastery; on the other side a great tower, to house the bells which would summon the scholars to their devotions. Emphasizing that the aristocracy would find themselves at home in such surroundings, the founder expressly provided for the admission of twenty sons of *nobiles* who were to pay fees.

In the sixteenth century the foundation of colleges continued at Oxford. One college was deliberately conservative – Brasenose, endowed in 1508 by William Smythe, Bishop of Lincoln and a hammer of heretics, together with a devout merchant, Sir Richard Sutton. Parallel with this was the foundation of St John's College at Cambridge by Henry VII's mother Lady Margaret Beaufort, who had already virtually refounded Christ's College; these, too, were intended to be bastions of orthodoxy. Two other new Oxford colleges, however, brought the new learning of the time – Greek not Trojan, as the Oxford wits had it – into the education of men intending to be priests. Richard Foxe, Bishop of Winchester and formerly Henry VII's and Henry VIII's most trusted agent, founded Corpus Christi College in 1515, urging the study not of the medieval theologians but of the Greek and Latin classics, the Bible and the Fathers.

Ten years later Thomas Wolsey founded Cardinal College. He was influenced by the example of the founder of Magdalen College; as student, fellow, bursar and master of the grammar school he had spent all the years from 1482 to 1505 at Magdalen. But now Cardinal Wolsey was master of England

and determined that his college should eclipse all others. To
endow it he secured from Rome the suppression of almost
thirty small and decayed religious houses including St Frides-
wide's, whose fine church became its chapel (and is now
Oxford Cathedral). To supply its students, this butcher's son
founded a school in his native Ipswich larger than the colleges
at Eton and Winchester. To staff it, he attracted the brightest
teachers of the day, full of the new learning and the new
hopes – and of the alarmingly new theology, as it turned out.
Nothing but Latin or Greek was to be spoken within these
walls. Under a dean and sub-dean Cardinal College was to
house a hundred canons, with lecturers, 'censors', treasurers,
stewards, domestics and a lavish chapel staff. The best musician of the day, John Taverner, was hired to take charge of
the organ and the choir. The college was to train two hundred
men at a time to be priests (not monks) – with more emphasis
on law than on theology. 'Tom Quad' still preserves the
founder's name and the dining hall is still emblazoned with his
arms, although it is also still evident that the cloister he
planned for it was never completed. In 1546 Cardinal College
became the royal foundation of Christ Church, on a reduced
but still substantial scale.

Thus the medieval system by which undergraduates were
housed without much supervision in small 'halls' or private
residences, and were free to attend lectures or not as they
wished, was slowly being replaced by a system of colleges and
tutors. A touch of luxury was reaching an Oxford which still
kept most of the atmosphere of a market-town:

Towery city and branchy between towers;
Cuckoo-echoing, bell-swarmèd, lark-charmèd,
  rook-racked, river-rounded;
The dapple-eared lily below thee. . . .[18]

---

[18] Gerard Manley Hopkins, 'Dun Scotus's Oxford' (1879).

THE GREAT CHURCHES

The evidence from the monasteries is more debatable. The monastic population of England seems to have risen during the fifteenth century from about 9,500 to some twelve thousand, and in many houses this was clearly a time of secure prosperity.[19] In the next century numbers fell since many more opportunities in lay life were being opened. However, the investigations of twentieth-century scholars would not support any idea of a dramatic decay in these religious houses. On the contrary, the evidence suggests that in most of them the routine of life was kept up with no great anxiety. The main problems of the smaller houses were financial rather than religious or moral. In the greater houses the very prosperity created moral problems but their inmates seem to have been too traditionally minded to be greatly worried and in some of the favoured monasteries new building demonstrated a proud assurance in the Tudor Age. Bath Abbey was being rebuilt magnificently during the 1530s. Much of the sixteenth-century work in the monasteries was to improve the comforts of the domestic quarters, but at Sherborne, for example, or Peterborough, new fan vaulting adorned the monastic church. The king himself founded a complete new abbey as late as 1536, at Bisham; and in that year the Act of Parliament suppressing the smaller monasteries spoke of 'divers great and solemn monasteries wherein (thanks be to God) religion is right well kept and observed'.

The richest of the monasteries was Glastonbury. According to a government inquiry (the *Valor Ecclesiasticus*) in 1535 its net income was £3,311, almost a thousand pounds more than the next richest, Westminster Abbey and Canterbury Cathedral. In August 1534 its new organist contracted to serve Abbot Whiting and his successors for life (and on the basis of

---

[19] See, for example, R. B. Dobson, *Durham Cathedral Priory 1400-1450* (Cambridge, 1973).

that agreement was still drawing an annuity in 1568). During the next four years eight new monks joined the great abbey, whose accounts for 1538-39 survive. 'In them we can see the machinery of the abbey moving slowly onwards like the hands of a great clock. The enormous quantities of foodstuffs come in; the ditches and watercourses are cleansed of weeds and slime, the nettles round the chapel of St Michael on the Tor are scythed down, the abbey church is stripped of ivy, the candelabra are cleaned up, the girls' gild at St John's church receives a midsummer gift of beer; the plumber and porter between them, at considerable expense, veil the great rood in Lent. Who could know that it was for the last time? That what they and their forebears had done for centuries was never to be done again, that before the summer's foliage had withered the heart's beat of that vast body was to cease, that the weeds and nettles and ivy were to resume their kingdom, and that a silence was to fall?'[20]

Specially dramatic is the line of royal chapels raised in splendour during a period when, as we look back, we know that the medieval Church was doomed by action to be taken by the monarchy itself.

In 1441 King Henry VI, then still a teenager, having just founded at Eton a college for seventy 'poor and needy' boys and a large chapel staff, planned King's College at Cambridge. By 1445 he had decided that it should have seventy scholars. Dominating this college, which was to be recruited entirely from Eton, was a perpetual reminder of the combined authority of the monarchy and the orthodox faith: a very large chapel of which the king laid the foundation stone in 1446. His master mason was Reginald Ely. Work was interrupted when Henry was deposed in 1461, begun again when Edward IV was at peace fifteen years later, interrupted again when Richard III was killed in battle, and completed between 1508 and 1515, largely at the expense of Henry VII. The great fan

---

[20] David Knowles, *The Religious Orders in England*, vol. iii (Cambridge, 1959), pp. 348-9. See also R. W. Dunning, 'Revival at Glastonbury, 1530-39', in *Renaissance and Renewal in Christian History*, ed. D. Baker (Oxford, 1977), pp. 213-222.

vault was designed by the master mason John Wastell, but
fortunately the plan to gild and paint it was never carried out.
This was the chapel that moved William Wordsworth in 1820:

> Give all thou canst; high Heaven rejects the lore
> Of nicely-calculated less or more;
> So deemed the man who fashioned for the sense
> These lofty pillars, spread that branching roof
> Self-poised, and scooped into ten thousand cells,
> Where light and shade repose, where music dwells. . . .

By 1531 twenty-five vast windows in the chapel had been
glazed with coloured glass mainly linking Old and New Testament scenes, the work of artists from the Low Countries. A
Renaissance oak screen displayed the initials H and A tied with
love-knots: it was the honeymoon period of Henry VIII and
Anne Boleyn. No less splendid choir stalls housed the scholars
as they meekly knelt to hear Mass. The rest of Henry VI's
design, which was to have included a cloister and bell tower,
was never completed; and there can be no doubt that Henry
VI would not have approved of the chapel itself as completed
by Henry VIII, its walls spattered with the royal insignia. A
detailed document drawn up in 1448 included instructions
that the architecture was to be 'clean and substantial' but not
'curious' or 'busy'.

The Yorkist king who overthrew Henry VI halted the work
at Cambridge and for a time closed down the school at Eton,
where the nave of the chapel was never built. He decided to
leave behind a very different chapel. In Windsor Castle
Edward IV caused St George's Chapel to be entirely rebuilt,
with Henry Janys as his master mason. Here was to be no band
of scholars; the chapel was to the shrine of the king's favourites
(and foreign guests) in the charmed circle of the revived Order
of the Garter, modelled on the Order of the Golden Fleece at
the much envied court of the dukes of Burgundy. And in
Windsor, in a church to be visited between feasts, there was to
be no restraint; the architecture was to take the Perpendicular
style forward in luxury, and all the fittings were to be
appropriately rich and royal. It was to be a setting fit for the
fifty knights' stalls carved in 1478-85 around the high altar,

beside which was to be found the king's own resting place. Although the elaborate instructions for a tomb in Edward IV's will were never carried out, the ironwork surrounding his grave, forged under the supervision of the Cornish John Tresilian, is the finest iron surviving from the English Middle Ages. The work at Windsor stopped not long after the king's death, to be resumed when in 1503 a Knight of the Garter, Sir Reginald Bray who had been Henry VII's chief financial agent, bequeathed a great legacy to pay for most of its completion.

In the same year a princely abbot, John Islip, laid the foundation stone of the new Lady Chapel in Westminster Abbey. It was to be built even more sumptuously, although on a smaller scale, than the chapel at Windsor. The will of Henry VII provided all the money necessary for three purposes. The king wished to honour the Virgin Mary. He wished also to erect a shrine in which Henry VI's body could be placed when it had been brought from Windsor on the completion of his official canonization as a saint (then awaited). And he wished to build a mausoleum for himself and his descendants.

This will was a classic document of the Middle Ages, combining an obviously sincere belief in the Catholic Church's doctrines about life after death with an equally sincere belief that money mattered. Ten thousand Masses were to be said for the repose of the king's soul within a month of his death; the priests were to be paid sixpence a Mass, double the standard rate. Nineteen great churches were placed under contract to remember him perpetually. Silver pyxes to hold the Body of Christ for adoration were to be placed at his expense in all parish churches which did not already possess one. A new pilgrims' road was to be built from Windsor to Canterbury. But the commemoration was to have its undying centre in Westminster, where three extra priests were to join the royal abbey in order to serve the perfectly equipped altars of the new Lady Chapel. Peter Torrigiano came from Renaissance Florence to spend six years making a tomb in bronze, marble and copper gilt for Henry VII and his queen in the centre of the chapel, and to begin a still larger tomb for Henry VIII (never completed). Statues of more than a hundred saints looked down from the walls. The vaulting of the chapel, with fans centred on pendants, was more intricately elaborate than the vault at King's College and was probably designed by William Vertue, who made the vault at Windsor and built Bath Abbey in the same period. The glass was as fine as that at King's, and some of the same glaziers worked at it; it was to be destroyed by seventeenth-century Puritans. The whole building surrounded the king's body, brought here one May morning in 1509, with a traditional sanctity. The criticism that it was extravagant had probably never entered the mind of Henry VII. His whole purpose had been to stay on the throne of England. Now he was resolved to purchase the kingdom of heaven.

Thus the great chapels at Cambridge, Windsor and Westminster testified to the piety of Lancastrian, Yorkist and Tudor kings. But the closing period of the Middle Ages also erected a monument showing how the higher clergy could still flourish with the support of kings.

The great central tower of Canterbury Cathedral ('Bell Harry Tower') was raised during the 1490s, using about half a million bricks although it was encased in stone. Although the number of pilgrims to Canterbury had now declined, the cathedral monastery and its archbishop could still rely on great possessions and on royal patronage. There were now reminders of this at either end of the nave – in the stone Screen of the Six Kings and in the west window which portrayed twenty-one kings, from Cnut to Henry VI. In the north transept Edward IV and his large family looked down from another magnificent window to the scene of Becket's martyrdom. The new tower was commissioned by a mighty archbishop, Cardinal John Morton, Henry VII's chancellor. His enthusiasm for the work was matched by the prior of the monastery, William Sellinge. Sellinge had brought back from Italy a store of Greek and Latin manuscripts – but, so far as we know, little trace on his mind of the turbulence of this period when in Florence the passionately reforming friar, Savonarola, was executed for dramatic attacks on the papacy. At Canterbury John Wastell was master-mason for Cardinal Morton and Prior Sellinge: his fan vault at the base of his tower, above the six kings on their screen, was as perfect as his contemporary miracle in King's College Chapel. The tower was surmounted by a steeple and a large gilt angel.

Bell Harry Tower was not the last great work in medieval Canterbury. It is true that Canterbury's archbishop was eclipsed when the Archbishop of York, Thomas Wolsey, who was also Bishop of Durham (later of Winchester), became the king's first minister, the pope's legate and a cardinal, but there seemed no reason to believe that the English Crown had broken off its historic alliance with the Canterbury of Augustine, Dunstan and Lanfranc. John Morton, Philip Deane and William Warham had all been archbishops enjoying Henry VII's complete confidence and often employed by him in affairs of state. Why should men not expect Wolsey to contribute to the Canterbury tradition one day, if the papacy eluded his grasp? And why should his successors not continue to unite the English Church and State? The future seemed sunny. An imposing new gatehouse was ready when Henry VIII, accompanied by the Emperor Charles V and Cardinal Wolsey, rode through it to worship in Canterbury Cathedral on Whit Sunday 1520.

HENRY IV AND HENRY V

When we try to meet the people who came to parish churches or universities, monasteries or cathedrals during the 'decline' of the Middle Ages, naturally the evidence is less dramatic because it was not an age of many outstanding personalities. But the story of the kings in this period enables us to see not only the outline of the story of England but also something of the place of religion in it; to see not only why national unity was thought to be of paramount importance in Tudor England but also why obedience to the king as he maintained that unity was thought to be a religious duty.

Providing one of the rare glimpses we have into Henry IV's character, his contemporary John Capgrave tells us that the king was interested in casuistry, the science of Christian ethics;

that he delighted to dispute hypothetical moral questions with scholars at his court. Unfortunately for his peace of mind, moral problems did not remain merely hypothetical for Henry IV. Speaking in 1399 'in the name of Fadir, Son and Holy Gost' (as was solemnly recorded) he pretended that his claim to the throne was based on his royal descent; in fact, as everyone knew, it was based on a successful rebellion, and he lived to be penitent although not to make restitution. Beginning barely four months after this charade, others rebelled against him – most alarmingly, the great Percy family in the north, whose support had been indispensable during the usurpation. Combined with this threat was a rebellion in Wales led by the formidable Owen Glendower. Another conspiracy led to the execution in 1405 of Richard Scrope, Archbishop of York, although the Chief Justice resigned rather than take any part in a bishop's beheading.

It seems clear that after these rebellions which brought home to him the nature of his own, and which brought out in him a hot temper which he had not displayed in 1399, Henry IV's health collapsed. Although in his youth he had been a greatly admired soldier (he had gone on a 'crusade' with the Teutonic Knights), for months at a time he was now bedridden. The symptoms of various illnesses, so far as we can recover them, point to a neurosis. His will, dictated in 1409, began 'I Henry, sinful wretch . . .' and looked back on 'the lyffe I have mispendyd'. A modern scholar writes: 'Henry had always been a devout man, a conventionally devout man perhaps, but by contemporary standards (and they were high) above the average in punctilious devotion, a pilgrim as well as a soldier, and one who had earned widespread commendation abroad for his regularity at Mass and almsgiving. There can be little doubt that he ought to offer amends by abandoning his usurped throne, but he knew also that his sons would wish him to retain it for his dynasty and that there was therefore no release for him that way. His eldest son's obvious impatience to succeed him roused all his old tenacity and so, racked by sickness and remorse, he clung to his royal power until his death on 20 May 1413.'[21]

Henry IV died in the Jerusalem Chamber of Westminster

Abbey; then aged forty-seven, he had had a stroke while visiting the shrine of St Edward the Confessor. His heir was soon talking about his past sins and future hopes with a recluse who lived elsewhere in the abbey. There and then, at the age of twenty-five, Henry V decided to put away his boon companions, to live chastely, to be a model son of the Church. He had only nine more years to live and he never became the crusading knight of the still powerful ideal. But he made the Lancastrian dynasty undeniably respectable.

He got rid of Archbishop Arundel as chancellor because the archbishop had been too closely identified with the usurpation, and installed instead Edward III's grandson, his own uncle and tutor, Bishop Henry Beaufort. He pardoned the families of those implicated in rebellions against his father. He brought the body of Richard II to lie in Westminster Abbey near his Queen Anne and St Edward, and ordered his own tomb nearby (his father was buried beneath an unflattering alabaster effigy in Canterbury). He became the hero of his subjects, partly because he was the first medieval English king to prefer speaking and writing in English. In particular he was the hero of the clergy. Some music has survived composed by the king for the services of his chapel, which he attended with constant devotion; and his accounts show his personal interest in the members of the choir and other church musicians.[22] While briefly back in England from the war, in May 1421, he summoned all the abbots to the Chapter House of Westminster Abbey and told them roundly that his ancestors had endowed their monasteries in order to secure their prayers, and he expected them to back up the army by disciplined intercessions supported by austerity. And even the abbots seem to have been stirred by such an appeal from a great military hero. His father had felt too insecure on his own throne to be able to afford to claim anyone else's; thus the chief battles of Henry IV's reign, apart from the expeditions to

---

[21] K. B. McFarlane, *Lancastrian Kings and Lollard Knights*, p.104. A similar verdict was reached by J. L. Kirby, *Henry IV of England* (London, 1970).

[22] But the 'roy Henry' of the music in the Old Hall manuscript may be Henry IV.

Scotland and Wales and the repression of English revolts, had been verbal, with Crown and Commons negotiating taxes in exchange for satisfactory replies to petitions. Now Henry V felt able to play a more heroic role; he conquered much of France, no doubt deceiving himself about the justice of his cause as his father had done when overthrowing Richard II. He did not survive long enough to find any cause for repentance. While he lived he basked in the patriotic enthusiasm which Shakespeare's *Henry V* was to recapture – the enthusiasm which lives for us also in the triumphant song:

> Oure kinge went forth to Normandy
> With grace and might of chivalry.
> Ther God for him wrought mervelusly:
> Wherfore Englande may call and cry,
> *Deo gracias.*

His methods of warfare were not confined to the grace of chivalry. 'He was a hero,' as Hazlitt wrote, regretting that such a man had appealed to Shakespeare, ' – that is, he was ready to sacrifice his own life for the pleasure of destroying thousands of other lives.' What Henry V ordered to be done in France brought about the macabre popularity of the horrifying Dance of Death (first as an actual dance, then in paintings). No doubt he justified the ruthlessness with which he starved out Rouen – with refugees in their thousands dying of hunger and cold in the ditch between the city walls and the English besiegers – by the argument that the city, although it did not acknowledge this, was in rebellion against him as the rightful King of France. But, as a modern biographer notes, 'even by the brutal standards of his own day there are deeds in the record which besmirch his name. . . . The crucifying of the gunners of Louviers, the hanging of the hostages at Montereau, the execution of the trumpeter after the siege of Meaux, and the fate of the unknown soldier who had insulted him from the walls of Rouen were unworthy of any great general in any age'.[23] An admiring chaplain who accompanied the invasion of France recorded, among many other signs of

---

[23] H. F. Hutchinson, *Henry V* (London, 1967), p.222.

the king's piety, the fact that as he moved through the many celebrations after his victories he showed no delight. To this priest it was proof that Henry V, waging war solely for the sake of justice since France was rightfully his, ascribed his triumphs solely to God. With greater scepticism about kings' motives we may think that what was being revealed was a cold inhumanity morally inferior to the alleged warm excesses of Henry's youth – and his youth may not have been as boisterous as the chroniclers and Shakespeare depicted, since the records show that he spent much of it fighting against the Welsh or presiding at council meetings.

The invasion of France was on the whole a disaster for the English as well as for the French, although by 1420 Henry was acknowledged as regent by about half the French population, married to a daughter of the French king, and promised the throne for himself and his heirs.

The disaster was not only that as Queen of England Katherine gave birth to a son afflicted with the strange nervous disease of the French dynasty. The real tragedy was that the victory of Agincourt in 1415 deceived the English, particularly the aristocracy, into thinking that the fruits of war – or of civil war if foreign adventures were lacking – would be greater than the fruits of peace. The peace policy of Richard II, which had brought real prosperity as well as much beauty to Chaucer's England as it recovered from the scourge of the Black Death, was now abandoned with glee, but it would have been happier for England in the long run had Henry V been compelled in 1415 to conclude a treaty with the French providing only for mutual recognition and trade. Already his capture of Harfleur had been won only after the loss of thousands of English lives by dysentery and fever, and his march to Calais after that siege has been aptly called 'the most foolhardy and reckless adventure that ever an unreasoning pietist devised'.[24] At Agincourt his army of less than six thousand was outnumbered by six to one and would have lost the day had not the French generals insisted on throwing their chances away. They clumsily exposed their cavalry to the

---

[24] J. H. Wylie, *Henry V*, vol. ii (Cambridge, 1919), p.76.

English archers and failed to exert discipline as the chaos mounted. How narrow an escape it had been for Henry V and his 'happy few' is shown by their nervousness which added a grim epilogue to their victory. They butchered their prisoners towards the end of the battle, apart from a few aristocrats whose ransoms would go to the king; the arrival of further French forces had been reported mistakenly.

In Henry's later campaigning the essential picture did not change. Beyond doubt he was a courageous and tireless worker and a first-class general with eyes for finance, diplomacy, supply and public relations at home and abroad as well as for a battle or a siege; but the main causes of his success were the imbecility of the French king, the ineptitude of the French court, the readiness of many of the French to accept a conqueror, and the major error made by those who still resisted when they murdered John the Fearless, Duke of Burgundy. That murder made sure of Burgundian co-operation with the English for the time being, and Henry's only real hope of keeping two kingdoms in his hands and those of his descendants lay in this alliance to hold down France. But the alliance, although strengthened by England's link with Burgundian Flanders through the wool and cloth trades, was fragile. All the largest factors of economics, geography and language were against it.

At the time, the English invasion of France seemed to many on the Continent a nuisance because it interfered with the serious business of ending the scandal of the existence of more than one pope. The English delegation to the Council of Constance managed to get itself recognized as a 'nation' equal with the Germans, French, Italians and Spaniards; but more relevant to the work of the council was the tension between the English and the French. The hatred between the two nations proved so disturbing that the Holy Roman Emperor, Sigismund, came to England on a futile peace mission. In the end Martin V emerged as pope of a united Christendom. He was not able to secure the repeal of the anti-papal English statutes of *Provisors* and *Praemunire*; Archbishop Chichele wept as he pleaded for the pope, but the English realities remained unchanged. Nor was the new pope able to secure the acceptance

of Henry Beaufort as his legate in England with wide powers;
when Beaufort indiscreetly accepted appointment as a
cardinal without the king's permission, he had to avert his
royal nephew's wrath by a massive gift to the war finances. But
on his side, Henry V had too many distractions to be able to
achieve a permanently satisfactory settlement of the Church
while he was in a strong bargaining position. Had his mind not
been on the war, his diplomacy might have taken advantage of
a creative moment which was not to recur during the rest of
the Middle Ages: an opportunity in the 1410s for a new deal
between the pope, the council and the nations, perhaps
eventually leading to a Catholic Reformation. Probably the
hope of a 'conciliar' Church where the spiritual initiative
could come from pastorally minded bishops advised by
theologians, instead of from Italian popes immersed in the
politics and art of the Renaissance, was always illusory; but as
a 'might have been' it is interesting. Much may have been lost
because this highly effective king, who always insisted that
every major initiative must remain in his hands, saw it as his
chief Christian duty to conquer France.[25]

Whatever may have been the morality or wisdom of the
war which won such glory for Henry V, he certainly was a
'pietist'. Eminent churchmen felt able to support him wholeheartedly – and were promoted for their support. His first
chancellor, Cardinal Beaufort of Winchester, who had added
to the wealth of the see by much shrewd business in the wool
trade and other fields, was the principal source of loans to
finance the war. When the archbishopric of Canterbury was
vacant the king secured the appointment of Henry Chichele, a
quietly able lawyer, a diplomat and administrator. He also
used his father's secretary, Thomas Langley, now a cardinal
and Bishop of Durham, in many central affairs as his
chancellor, as well as in the maintenance of peace in the
north. John Kemp, who soon became Bishop of London, was
Chancellor of Normandy in the period when it was intended to

---

[25] See E. F. Jacob, *Essays in the Conciliar Epoch* (revised, Manchester,
1953).

turn it into an English colony.[26]

The best memorial of his reign was the foundation of two religious houses of strict life. His father had undertaken this work of piety when officially exonerated by the pope for the execution of Archbishop Scrope, but nothing had been done. Henry V founded two communities in 1415 before setting out for Harfleur and Agincourt, near the reconstructed palace of Sheen. One was a Charterhouse for forty Carthusian monks, and was called the House of Jesus of Bethlehem. The other was for monks, nuns and lay brothers living under an abbess according to the rule drawn up by St Bridget of Sweden; it was known as the Abbey of Mount Syon. In a hundred years of steady and strict devotion these two houses heard each other's bells ringing across the Thames. It was perhaps in reliance on such deeds that when Henry V lay dying (probably of dysentery) in the castle of Vincennes in August 1422, he shouted to the demon he thought he saw: 'Thou liest, thou liest! My portion is with the Lord Jesus Christ!'

A SAINT ON THE THRONE

Henry V died before he could see his son — and more mercifully never saw that son's future. He left Henry VI to be brought up by the old Duke of Exeter, and trusted that he would inherit two kingdoms — England over which Humphrey, Duke of Gloucester, was to be protector, and France, which meanwhile was to have John, Duke of Bedford, as its regent. It is recorded that at the age of three and a half the boy-king managed to walk from the west door to the choir of St Paul's

---

[26] There is no modern biography of Beaufort or Kemp, but there are studies of *Archbishop Henry Chichele* by E. F. Jacob (London, 1967) and *Thomas Langley and the Bishopric of Durham* by R. L. Storey (London, 1961). G. L. Harriss, 'Cardinal Beaufort — Patriot or Usurer?' in *Transactions of the Royal Historical Society* (London, 1970), concludes that the cardinal neither obtained interest on his loans — nor made them, or any other political moves, except in his own long-term self-interest.

Cathedral, with an approving Parliament around him. But he
did not march on to complete the conquest of France or to
rebuild the walls of Jerusalem – which is said to have been the
deathbed wish of his father. Instead, the reign of Henry VI
witnessed the recovery of French morale. Partly this was
thanks to the peasant-girl Jeanne d'Arc who so dramatically
inspired the French to relieve Orleans and to crown their own
king – and whom the English cruelly and futilely burned as a
witch and a heretic.

The turning point came in 1435, when the Burgundians
deserted their English alliance. Some of the English still
believed that greater and greater ruthlessness would bring the
French back into subjection; a memorandum survives in
which one particularly mercy-scorning and profit-making
general, Sir John Fastolf (the name that seems to have suggested 'Falstaff' to Shakespeare), argues this case for scorching
the earth. But shrewder statesmen such as Cardinal Beaufort
and William de la Pole, Duke of Suffolk, saw clearly that the
problem was now how to extricate England from Henry V's
wildly expensive gamble. Certainly the young Henry VI,
although crowned in Paris in 1431 as a counterblast to the coronation inspired by Jeanne, never showed any ambition to
become a general himself. Instead he grew up to be more holy
than most priests or monks. While he never renounced the
claim to France, he never enforced it – or any other claim.
Indeed, his only policy in the period when his reign amounted
to personal rule, 1445-50, was 'peace at any price in the
French war.'[27]

One of the mysteries surrounding Henry VI is how this
character, so opposite to the military virtues of his father and
grandfather, developed. We know that his upbringing was entrusted to a devout nobleman, the Earl of Warwick, but this is
not enough to account for his virtual pacifism. Perhaps the
decisive influence was that of the priest Thomas Netter, his
tutor until he was ten. His meekness, his mercifulness, his
reckless generosity to his friends and to the poor, his in-

---

[27] B. P. Wolffe in *Fifteenth-century England*, ed. S. B. Chrimes, C. D.
Ross and R. A. Griffiths (Manchester, 1972), p.38.

difference to luxury, his support of scholars (he would tip the
boys of his college at Eton when he met them), the exceptional
purity of his morals (he warned the Eton boys never to go near
his own court), and the monk-like strictness of his devotions:
all these traits are reported as running through all the stages of
his life — his boyhood, the troubled years when his minority
had ended (at the age of sixteen), his five years' imprisonment.
When he noticed the exposed bosoms of some girls brought in
to dance at a Christmas feast, he observed: 'Fy, fy, for shame!
Forsothe ye be to blame!' When he found the men bathing in
the warm waters at Bath totally naked, he left immediately in
indignation. And when he was wounded in the neck, he commented: 'Forsothe and forsothe ye do fouly to smyte a kynge
enoynted so.' At a time when every annointed king was expected to dress splendidly, he preferred a long gown like a
merchant and boots like a farmer. The principal feasts of the
year he would mark by adding a hair shirt next to his skin.
Sundays he devoted entirely to religion; and on a weekday he
would be irritated when he was trying to read a religious book
and a duke knocked on the door wanting to talk politics.

John Blacman, a Carthusian monk who was for a time his
spiritual director, wrote a 'Compilation of the Meekness and
Good Life of King Henry VI' containing those anecdotes. Such
a character impressed contemporaries up to a point. The
religion of the age was illustrated when in the year of his foundation of his college at Cambridge Henry VI was believed to
be the subject of magical arts. The wife of Humphrey, Duke of
Gloucester, was accused of making a wax image of the king
and melting it down. Her two accomplices were executed —
one by being hanged, drawn and quartered, the other by
being burned — and the duchess was condemned to walk barefoot around London for three days, accompanied by the
mayor, sheriffs and others, before being imprisoned for life.
An age so sure about witchcraft was sensitive of the sacred
aura surrounding the 'enoynted' king. But it did expect a king
to rule, with the co-operation of an aristocracy which he could
dominate by force of character. This came out when the Duke
of Gloucester, who had exerted much influence with much irresponsibility, was himself arrested and charged with treason.

It seems that the shock brought about a fatal heart attack. In a country basically so royalist, a strong king could have done much to impose his will on affairs and if he had been devout as well that would have been to his advantage. But Henry VI did not rule – except when aroused by his wife, Margaret of Anjou. Queen at the age of fifteen, this proud and passionate Frenchwoman already possessed a personality much stronger than her husband's. She was encouraged to exert her personality (if she needed any encouragement) by observing what happened to the king's favourites who were blamed for the loss of France. Adam Moleyns, Bishop of Chichester and a leading civil servant, was murdered when he went to pay the seamen at Portsmouth; William Ayscough, Bishop of Salisbury, who had heard the king's confessions and officiated at his wedding, was killed in his own diocese; and after an attempted flight the Duke of Suffolk's headless body was thrown on the beach at Dover. In Kent a rebellion was led by a certain Jack Cade, protesting that the king's council had sanctioned misgovernment and should be renewed under the Duke of York.

With France apart from Calais gone, for any ruler of England the 1450s would have been a testing time. The glamour which had surrounded Edward III, Henry V and their generals had now come to nothing. The vast investment of blood and treasure in the conquest of France had yielded a nil return. Yet the possibility of growing rich by trade, manufacturing or agricultural improvements was largely hidden from the English aristocracy, still educated in the outdated myths of Norman feudalism and Arthurian chivalry, still living mainly off rents. Some landlords were efficient in estate management (notably Cardinal Beaufort), but the evidence of declining rents is widespread. The huge and scattered estates of the Earls of Lancaster, for example, halved in profitability, 1400-75. Industrialization on anything like the scale to be seen in Flanders seemed inconceivable in England, when the most obvious way to make a profit was to export wool or unfinished cloth to Flanders (as Beaufort had done). Trading was not for aristocrats; anyway, what with German competition and the general violence of the times, English exports slumped in the period 1425-80. Therefore to ambitious but unbusinesslike Percies, Nevilles and other aristocrats or would-be nobility, the way ahead seemed to lie through the extension of local power and its profits. A great landlord could 'maintain' his tenants, hired retainers or other dependents so as to form a private army which could terrorize a neighbour-hood – and go unchecked, for the local administration of justice could itself be controlled. Although it is inaccurate to speak of the nobility as being anxious to rebel (one factor being the highly alarming penalties for treason), this was a situation where influence over a neighbourhood counted for everything and the national interest or the king's justice for very little. Characteristic of popular attitudes in the fifteenth century were the Robin Hood ballads, which projected back into the past a situation where an honest man must expect nothing from the law, where the king is far-off although good and the sheriff is a local gangster. Characteristic of more aristocratic fantasies were the Arthurian legends which Sir Thomas Malory tells us he compiled while in prison. Although attempts have been made to find an imprisoned Malory who would be more at home at Arthur's round table, and one such has been located in Yorkshire, most scholars remain fairly sure that Sir Thomas was a Warwickshire man convicted of crimes such as cattle-thieving and rape.[28]

In this national crisis Henry was fatally incompetent. He could not provide the 'good and sad' government for which the House of Commons (in a petition typical of its attitude throughout this century) had asked in 1429. A more or less complete programme for the 'governance of England' and for the defence of the laws was drawn up in books by Sir John Fortescue, who served the king as Chief Justice from 1442 until exiled in his cause in 1471. Based on the co-operation of King,

---

[28] See J. R. Lander, *Conflict and Stability in Fifteenth Century England* (London, 1969), and J. G. Bellamy, *Crime and Public Order in England in the Later Middle Ages* (London, 1973). The ballads, first mentioned in *Piers Plowman*, have been studied in R. B. Dobson and J. Taylor, *Rymes of Robyn Hood* (London, 1976). For Malory or the Malories see William Matthews, *The Ill-Framed Knight* (Berkeley, Cal., 1966), and A. B. Ferguson, *The Indian Summer of English Chivalry* (Durham, N.C., 1960).

Council, Parliament and aristocracy, the programme remained locked in books because the indispensable king lacked the political will. Indeed, his personality added to the political problems. A basic cause of the disorders which wrecked the rest of his reign was, in the judgement of a modern authority, the fact that he managed to make rebellion seem respectable 'because the nobility was unable to rescue the kingdom from Henry's inanity by any other means'.[29]

At the beginning of the disastrous 1450s Henry briefly bestirred himself to discipline Richard, Duke of York, who was now expecting the succession to the throne – and to beget a son, Edward. However, by the time this prince was born the king was not able to recognize him. In the summer of 1453 his mind gave way; for eighteen months he was unable to move or to respond to those around him. One of the many letters surviving from this period as a chronicle of a Norfolk family, the Pastons (a family as grasping and as turbulent as any in England), shows us the king at Windsor. He is being presented with his son and heir. 'The kyng yave no maner answere. . . . Alle their labour was in veyne, for they departed thens without any answere or countenaunce savyng only that ones he looked on the Prince and caste downe his eyene ayen, without any more.'

Eventually the king more or less recovered, although there was at least one relapse. Politically speaking the recovery was a pity, since it removed the competent and extremely rich Duke of York from power and made the Yorkists' forceful response inevitable.

Queen Margaret and her ally, Edmund Beaufort, Duke of Somerset, now resumed control and the Yorkists replied by open rebellion, their strongest man being the Duke of York's nephew, Richard Neville, Earl of Warwick. During a battle in the streets of St Albans, almost in the shadow of the great abbey, the Yorkists killed Somerset and captured the king. It

---

[29] K. B. McFarlane, 'The Wars of the Roses', in *Proceedings of the British Academy* (1964), pp.87-119. This judgement was developed further in the same author's lectures on *The Nobility of Later Medieval England* (Oxford, 1973).

was not long before Queen Margaret took her revenge, but the banishment of her enemies brought no lasting peace. In 1460 she had to escape with her son into Wales when the Yorkists returned in triumph, again capturing the king. This time Richard of York claimed the throne for himself, but under pressure from Warwick and others temporarily accepted the status of Prince of Wales and Protector, with the right of succession after Henry's death. To this arrangement Henry consented; but to say that his wife did not would be to put her response mildly. Queen Margaret stirred up a counterattack in the north which was temporarily successful. At the battle of Wakefield Richard of York was defeated and killed; his head was set up over the south gate of York decorated by a paper crown. It was then the turn of the Yorkists to counterattack under the leadership of their new duke (Edward) and the now unappeasable Warwick. After a slaughter of Lancastrians at Towton near York amid a snowstorm on Palm Sunday 1461, Margaret was forced to flee, with King Henry in tow; and amid the acclamations of his soldiers and of the London citizens (but no Parliament was involved) Edward IV was enthroned as the rightful king 'by descent', the entire House of Lancaster being dismissed as usurpers. After many wanderings and half-hearted attempts to arrange one more Lancastrian rally, Henry was captured and brought to the Tower of London.

That this was not the end of Henry VI was due to developments which add to the impression that the top of public life in England had gone mad. Edward IV, fancying himself for a time as another Henry V, revived the claim to the throne of France and the alliance with Burgundy. In England he so conducted himself as to alienate the people and (what mattered more) the king-maker, Warwick. Louis XI of France promptly arranged for a reconciliation between Warwick and Queen Margaret and equipped an invasion in their names. Henry VI was cleaned up and brought out of the Tower. In a dazed condition he then resumed his troubled reign for another six months. This period was ended by the return of Edward IV, the battle of Barnet, the killing of Warwick, the battle of Tewkesbury, the killing of Henry VI's son Prince Edward, and the imprisonment of the tigress-like Queen Margaret, who was eventually ransomed by the French.

On 21 May 1471 King Edward rode into London and that same night King Henry, who was now back in the Tower, died. We have no reason to doubt that he was put to death. His body — bleeding in its open coffin, or so the report went — was taken to Chertsey Abbey but reburied in 1481 in St George's Chapel, Windsor, where his tomb became the centre of devotions and healings.[30] John Blacman quotes his Latin prayer which may be translated: 'O Lord Jesu Christ, who didst create me, redeem me, and foreordain me unto that which now I am; thou knowest what thou wilt do with me; deal with me according to thy most compassionate will.' The prayer became famous. In his will Henry VII said that he had used it from his childhood.

THE YORKIST KINGS

The story of the 'Wars of the Roses' (a name given by Sir Walter Scott) has been told here — although only in outline — because of the traumatic effect which these disturbances had upon English public opinion. The actual damage done to the population or the economy does not seem to have been widespread. But great damage was done by the fact that the English nobility had been without a leader since the death of Henry V. For a time there was a cult of Henry VI as a martyred saint; but it is significant that when Henry VII had failed to persuade the papacy to proceed to an official canonization, Henry VIII, although still a devout Catholic prince, did not pursue the matter. As the nation knew, the supreme lesson of Henry VI's so-called 'reign' was that a king was of no earthly use unless he could act like a king. For a king, to be a 'good lord' was more important than being a good man.

---

[30] *Miracles of King Henry VI*, ed. R. A. Knox and S. Leslie (Cambridge, 1923), shows the cult of a saint getting into full swing.

Churchmen aware of political realities were not blind to this. Given the chance, they would have been the king's supporters and servants in strong government; in Sir John Fortescue's ideal for the Lancastrian monarchy, as set out in his *Governance of England*, half the king's council was to consist of bishops (four) and lesser clergy (twelve). As it was, churchmen in politics toiled away with some frustration. Henry Chichele – a merchant's son, an industrious and highly professional product of Winchester College and New College, Oxford, and Archbishop of Canterbury 1414-43 – recalled in 1433 that in the previous eleven years he had missed only thirty-three of the almost daily meetings of the king's council. Middle-class bishops such as Chichele, who liked order in administration as much as they liked beauty in architecture, kept the king's government functioning during Henry VI's minority. They had their rewards, of course: on one January morning in 1426 the king's council, consisting of six bishops and three secular peers, decided who should be the next Archbishop of York and the next Bishops of Lincoln, Ely, Norwich, London, Chichester and Worcester. But they had their problems in this period when the mightiest laymen, Bedford and Gloucester, were consumed by jealousy and the semi-royal Cardinal Beaufort was busy enriching himself and his nephews. One day in January 1427 Archbishop Chichele was spokesman for the rest of the council in asking the Duke of Bedford whether he sincerely agreed that the council, not he, had the ultimate authority; and the next day John Kemp, now Chancellor of England as well as Archbishop of York, put the same awkward question to the Duke of Gloucester, who happened to be ill in bed.

However, these men who ran England kept their thoughts about the king – and about royal dukes – well away from the official documents which alone have survived. What did Thomas Bekynton, who became his secretary in 1437, make of Henry VI? We do not know; if we had known, we should not have found him as Bishop of Bath and Wells, 1443-66.[31] We may guess that, as he grew up, the officials had to recognize

---

[31] See Arnold Judd, *The Life of Thomas Bekynton* (Chichester, 1961).

that Henry VI was never going to be a king in the full medieval sense; that he was, as one detached observer (Pope Pius II) put it, 'a man more timorous than a woman, utterly devoid of wit or spirit, who left everything in his wife's hands'. Yet right up to the Yorkist coup, the leading churchmen considered themselves bound to Henry VI their hero's son and their own anointed king. And so did most of the nobility. As J. L. Lander points out, 'in view of Henry VI's peculiar combination of weakness and wilfulness, which very adversely affected their own interests, it is surprising how many of the aristocracy remained loyal to him for so long'.[32] What became clear during this reign was that whoever supplied strong government would earn the gratitude and prayers of a people which still expressed its gratitude most characteristically in its prayers; of a people which showed its own capacity most effectively in building and adorning its churches.

Edward IV, who for a time seemed the answer to England's prayers, did not share the profound personal religion of his predecessor on the throne or of his own mother (Duchess Cecily) and sister (Margaret, Duchess of Burgundy). When he became king at the age of nineteen the contrast between him and the bookish, sickly and shabby Henry VI must have seemed total.

Edward was tall (almost six and a half feet), handsome, charming, fashionable, clever, hard-working; a master of the art of being a king. His self-confidence was such that he thought he could afford to anger the mighty Warwick and the rest of the nobility by secretly marrying an impoverished Lancastrian widow, Elizabeth Woodville, simply because he had fallen in love with her; she is said to have been one of the few women who at first resisted his advances. When he suspected Warwick's brother George Neville, Archbishop of York and for seven years Chancellor of England, of plotting against him, he had him sent to prison in Calais. The experience so shook the princely archbishop that he died before he was forty-five. The king's own brother, George Duke of Clarence, was put to death as a traitor. Edward was a man of action, all

---

[32] J. R. Lander, *Crown and Nobility, 1450-1509* (London, 1976), p.55.

that Henry VI could never be. He was also strenuous to maintain order and to enforce the law — and shrewd enough to limit his expenditure so as to avoid direct taxation which would have been unpopular. He made a profitable peace with France when he saw that war was likely to get nowhere, and set realistic limits to his subsequent intrigues in diplomacy. He took a large share in the peacetime wool and cloth trade and levied customs on his fellow-merchants. He applied up-to-date methods to the management of the Crown's own estates and extracted forced loans or 'benevolences' from his fellow-landlords. Tightening up the central administration which he directed personally, and refraining from the feckless grants to which Henry VI had been prone, he was, it seems, the first English king since Henry II to die solvent.

He had only one major problem. He was mortal. In his early forties his lechery and gluttony seem to have caught up with him; he grew overweight and suddenly, in April 1483, died while on a fishing trip. He had been almost completely a man of the world; yet he had been happy to incur vast expenditure on St George's Chapel, Windsor, for being a successful man of the world in the last quarter of the fifteenth century still meant being a son of the Church. His deathbed was devout. During his life he arranged for members of the strictest group of the Franciscans, the 'Observants', to be brought over from the Continent to a new friary close to one of his palaces, at Greenwich. And when he boasted that he had three concubines, 'one the merriest, another the wiliest, harlot in the realm', he added that the third was among all harlots the holiest.

In Tudor history-writing (a tradition which descended from Sir Thomas More and the papal tax-collector, Polydore Vergil, through Edward Hall to William Shakespeare), Edward IV was a good king in comparison with his brother, Richard III. Richard was portrayed as a monster, physically as well as morally repulsive. The reality was, however, a more subtle tragedy, rather like *Macbeth*: the tragedy of a man fit to be a king but not born to be one.

At the time of his coronation, Richard seemed, no less than Edward, the answer to the widespread longing for strong

government. The ceremony—the best attended and most
sumptuous coronation of the English Middle Ages—had this
very serious content. During his brother's reign Richard, then
Duke of Gloucester, had been in charge of the north and of
the wars against the Scots. He had shown loyalty to the king,
political capacity and a sense of justice. During his short reign
he seems to have continued his brother's essential policy, including at least a show of piety, to which he added abhorrence
of his brother's morals and favourites. Had he lived, his act in
causing the body of Henry VI to be reburied near his brother's
grave at Windsor—the saint near the sinner—might have led
to a more ambitious programme of religious patronage. Anyway, there appeared to be no real alternative to Richard in the
eyes of most of the bishops and nobles attending the coronation. Edward IV's eldest son, whom Richard had seized, was
just thirteen years of age. By medieval standards that was not
particularly young, but the prince had been under the control
of his mother and her rapacious family; and neither the
nobility nor the people had ever taken to that family. It could
well be argued—and Richard did argue—that the richly experienced royal duke who had been named 'protector' of the
realm in the late king's will was forced to seize the throne in
order to protect himself and his country from the Woodvilles.

The other claimant to the throne, Henry Tudor, Earl of
Richmond, had been a penniless exile since 1469. For almost
all this time he depended on the favour of the Duke of
Brittany—and, when that failed, he threw himself on the
French king's mercy. He had not yet acquired any experience
of war or administration; he had been brought up in Wales,
and had spent only a few weeks in England; and his right to
the crown of England was obscure. The Tudor connection
with the crown had begun when Owen Tudor, a Welsh adventurer, for a time butler to the Bishop of Bangor, had secured
employment at the English court and made an improbable
marriage with Katherine, the lonely widow of Henry V; and
when the ever-generous Henry VI had made their son
Edmund Earl of Richmond. Edmund had, moreover, been
allowed to marry Margaret Beaufort, who could trace her
descent from John of Gaunt's mistress—although when the

Beauforts had been legitimated they had also been barred from the throne. Henry Tudor was an ambitious young Welshman who made the most of these royal drops in his blood, and who now strengthened his royal connections by contracting to marry Elizabeth the eldest daughter of Edward IV; but he certainly did not seem the inevitable King of England. At the beginning of 1484 Elizabeth who was to have been his bride went to live at Richard's court – and there were rumours that Richard was about to marry her. For these reasons we can have some slight sympathy with those bishops who accepted the story put about by one of their own number (Bath and Wells) that Richard was his brother's true heir since Edward V was illegitimate. The claim, not in itself improbable, was that Edward IV had already betrothed himself to another at the time of his marriage.

What destroyed Richard III was the opposite of the carnal self-indulgence that had brought his brother to a premature grave. It was the totality of his dedication to power. The queen fled to sanctuary in Westminster Abbey before coming to terms with him, but he had Lord Hastings and Earl Rivers, two of Edward IV's leading friends and servants, executed without the formality of a trial. There is no good reason to doubt that he gave the orders which led to the murders of Edward V and his brother Richard, the 'Princes in the Tower', who were seen no more after the summer of 1483.[33] Such ruthlessness had many precedents in the history of medieval

---

[33] The princes' skeletons were almost certainly those that were discovered in 1674, examined in 1933, and reburied in Westminster Abbey. People were most unlikely to kill an ex-king without making sure of the present king's wishes. P. M. Kendall, *Richard the Third* (London, 1955), tried to incriminate Buckingham who was Constable of the Tower, but Richard himself never shifted the blame in this way. In 1502 it was put about that Sir James Tyrell had confessed to carrying out the execution, before being executed himself on another charge. However, Richard's guilt cannot be regarded as proved. Sir Thomas More's vivid narrative was written some thirty years after 1483. Henry VII never directly charged Richard. See Alison Hanham, *Richard III and His Early Historians* (Oxford, 1975), and Elizabeth Jenkins, *The Princes in the Tower* (London, 1978).

England, as it was to have many sequels under the Tudors. But it enabled Tudor propaganda to depict Richard as the dragon (complete with a hunchback – one of the imaginative touches), and Henry Tudor as the knight in shining armour.

The decisive moment did not occur, however, until 22 August 1485, at Bosworth in Leicestershire. Already one revolt against Richard, led by his former accomplice the Duke of Buckingham, had failed. Now Thomas Lord Stanley arrived with a Lancastrian force and it was not clear whether he would join his king. He had been steward of Richard's household and Richard held his son as a hostage, but since 1473 he had been the third husband of Henry's formidable mother. Henry had only about five thousand troops, mostly raised in Wales. Richard's army was larger and his own courage was great. Seeing Henry, he led his household guards in a direct attack; he staked all. At this moment the Stanley forces were thrown into the battle against him; the Earl of Northumberland whom he had ordered to guard his flank stood by cynically; and he was cut down crying 'Treason!' That evening his naked corpse, with a halter round the neck, was carried to burial by the Franciscans in Leicester. Dead at the age of thirty-two, he was the last of the Plantagenet kings.

HENRY VII

The new king was crowned by Thomas Bourgchier, Archbishop of Canterbury, who in his own person symbolized the continuity of the national life through the fifteenth century despite the changing and unsatisfactory kings. Bourgchier was born about 1412, the son of a knight who had fought at Agincourt and of the immensely rich Anne Plantagenet. He began accumulating ecclesiastical offices before he went to Oxford as an undergraduate, and was made Bishop of Worcester when not yet twenty-five. As a member of the king's council he was rewarded with richer sees: first Ely and then, in 1454, Canterbury. After a year as chancellor of the realm he quarrelled with Queen Margaret and therefore lost that secular post; but he remained archbishop and enjoyed the satisfaction of crowning Edward IV. Throughout that reign he flourished, becoming a cardinal. But in his seventies things went wrong. Intending to crown Edward V, he persuaded the boy king's mother to release his brother from sanctuary in Westminster Abbey, only to find the coronation cancelled and both boys murdered. However, he unheroically proceeded to anoint and crown Richard III, as he was now performing the same office for the man for whose sake Richard had been killed. It is not altogether surprising that before his death in 1486 the old man quietly retired, without resigning the archbishopric.

His successor was John Morton, another man who served more than one master in his time. At one stage this talented lawyer was a servant of Henry VI, to the point of sharing Queen Margaret's exile; then he entered the service of Edward IV and rose in it, becoming Bishop of Ely. His practical ability was shown in his supervision of the making of a great 'cut' or drain from Wisbech to Ely, transforming much of the agriculture of his marshy diocese. Richard III, presumably feeling that the bishop had been too close to his brother, was hostile; the alarmed bishop fled into exile, while keeping his communications with the centre of politics open. He was able to warn the future Henry VII that the Duke of Brittany was about to hand him over to Richard – with the results that Henry fled in disguise to the French king and always felt that Morton had saved his life. Besides, Morton was undeniably a shrewd man capable of great toil in the new king's service. No less a judge than Sir Thomas More, who as a lad waited on him at table and listened to his conversation, has left a portrait of him in *Utopia*: 'of a mean stature. . . . In his face did shine such an amiable reverence, as was pleasant to behold. . . . In the law he had profound knowledge, in wit he was incomparable, and in memory wonderful excellent.' In 1483 Morton became the king's chancellor and Archbishop of Canterbury, and he occupied both positions until his death in 1500. He was also made a cardinal – a sign of the complete harmony in which Henry VII lived with the popes of the time, whose concentration on Renaissance politics was similar to his own. The king began the practice of appointing an Italian as

Bishop of Worcester, as a reward for services in Rome.[34]

If the ecclesiastical history of Henry's reign is almost a total blank, the political history contains some omens to indicate the future. On the surface it was largely a continuation of Yorkist policy; Henry's marriage with Edward IV's daughter was symbolic, as was the invention of a Lancastrian red rose in order that it might be married with the existing Yorkist white rose to produce the Tudor red-and-white. Henry's interest in finance, so detailed that it shocked many of those around him, was only a heightening of the interest taken by Edward IV. On the surface the reign had touches of comedy — as in the stories of the two imposters Lambert Simnel (an Oxford tradesman's son) and Perkin Warbeck (a Fleming), who claimed to be sons of the Duke of Clarence and King Edward respectively. But toughness was necessary because the situation was not comic. The rebellions around Simnel and Warbeck were supported by many, abroad and at home (including the Stanley who had saved Henry's life at Bosworth); and in 1497 other rebels were allowed to march all the way from Cornwall to London — a fact which mattered far more to the king than did John Cabot's discovery of 'New Found Land' in a voyage from Bristol in the same year. It was indeed fortunate for Henry VII that Richard III's only son and his queen had both died. Had there been a plausible Yorkist candidate at liberty, Henry's own fate might well have resembled Richard's. As it was, he kept the crown placed on his head by Thomas Bourgchier, although to do so needed all his statecraft — including his ability to derive his revenue from non-parliamentary sources.

After the death in 1502 of his fifteen-year-old son Arthur, whom he had married off to the Spanish princess Catherine of Aragon as part of his diplomacy, all the king's hopes had centred on his second son, Henry. In 1509 he left to this son a quiet country, a prosperous economy and a full treasury. He also bequeathed the conviction that a king must govern sternly if he was to survive. In Roper's *Life of Sir Thomas More* there is a story which, whether true or not, is not false to the

---

[34] Christopher Harper-Bill studied Morton's Primacy in *Journal of Ecclesiastical History* (Cambridge, 1978), pp.1-21.

atmosphere of the reign now closed. Richard Foxe, Bishop of Winchester, invited the young More to join him in the king's service. He had himself become Henry's secretary before Bosworth, and had been so busy ever since that although Bishop first of Bath and Wells and then of Durham, he had never seen those cathedrals. Now in 1504 he held glittering prizes before the young man's eyes. But Richard Whitford, then Foxe's chaplain but soon to become a monk, took More aside to warn him of the moral danger. 'For my lord, my master', he said, 'to serve the king's turn, will not stick to agree to his father's death.'

THOMAS WOLSEY

Another story is told of Thomas More and the new king, Henry VIII, whose service he had entered. The two men once walked up and down More's garden in Chelsea for an hour, deep in talk, the king's arm around his friend's neck. When congratulated later on this mark of royal favour, More observed that if his head could win the king a castle in France it would be taken off his shoulders. The story hints at the dazzling attractiveness of the young Henry – athlete, musician, inexhaustible in revelry but also well educated, able to talk with More as an intellectual equal. It also suggests his wilfulness, which had, no doubt, been increased by his father's policy of keeping him in strict seclusion, away from any young man who might have acted as his equal. Henry's accession was marked by the imprisonment, and later by the execution, of his father's chief fund-raisers, Edmund Dudley and Richard Empson. His would be the popularity not only of punishing such agents of his father's policy, but also of buying a reputation the opposite of his father's miserliness. A king of this temperament, not eighteen when he came to the throne, needed glory but needed someone to organize it for him.

The glory was to be the conquest of France, fully blessed by the pope. The minister was to be Thomas Wolsey, a member of the king's council and his chief secretary from 1509, Archbishop of York from 1513, the king's chief minister from 1514, chancellor from 1515 – an administrator of prodigious industry and decisiveness, all the more hungry for power, money and display because until he became a chaplain to the aged Archbishop Deane at Canterbury in 1501 at the age of thirty he had had a stage no bigger than the Oxford college where he was bursar and schoolmaster. The king's servant whom Wolsey had first served and then displaced, Richard Foxe, retreated to his work as the bishop of a diocese ('to do some satisfaction', as he confessed, 'for eighteen years' negligence'). William Warham, Archbishop of Canterbury, also went into semi-retirement, timidly resentful of his fellow-archbishop's pre-eminence in Church and State.

Wolsey was showered with favours from a somewhat reluctant Rome at the king's request. He was made a cardinal and given the extraordinary position of *legatus a latere* (in 1518, extended for his life in 1524). This meant that he exercised most of the papacy's legal functions and rights of appointment in relation to the English Church; no resident Englishman had ever before wielded such ecclesiastical power. His opportunity to reform the Church – the reason given by the papacy for this power – was, however, wasted apart from minor affairs. He never visited his diocese of York until he had fallen from political power. Since he also drew the revenues of Durham or Winchester, and administered other dioceses which were either vacant or occupied by Italians, the cardinal's mockery of a bishop's proper work was blatant. He accepted election as Abbot of St Albans (the monks had yielded to the king's pressure) merely in order to add one more income to his amazing wealth. His illegitimate son, Thomas Wynter, was loaded with ecclesiastical offices. Being a cardinal seemed to be for him essentially an occasion for pomp glorifying his person – pomp which survives for us in the biography written after his fall by the still loyal George Cavendish, the assistant or 'usher' who arranged much of the display. The cardinal's own energy, with an eye for a thousand details, was devoted most wholeheartedly to building palaces for himself: York Place in Westminster (later the palace of Whitehall) was next to the royal court, and Hampton Court was also on the

Thames but healthily in the country. Such a man appeared to his resentful fellow-bishops to be really interested only in the profits of ecclesiastical jurisdiction, not in righting abuses; and when he lectured monks or friars he succeeded merely in giving reform a bad name. This wasted opportunity was, it seems, on his conscience when he remarked to Sir William Kingston shortly before his death in November 1530: 'If I had served God as deligently as I have done the king, he would not have given me over in my grey hairs.'

Wolsey did not serve the king by supervising any radically new programme in domestic politics. The extension of the legal activity of the king's council into a regular court called after the 'star chamber' in which it met to hear complaints of violence was his main achievement, but high-sounding proclamations about meeting economic problems seem to have produced little effective action. One reason was his unwillingness to face the House of Commons; during the fourteen years of his ascendancy only one Parliament was summoned. All this was in contrast with the approach to be made by Thomas Cromwell, who became his chief assistant (Cromwell was used, for example, in the suppression of decayed monasteries in order to endow the college at Oxford and the school at Ipswich with a minimum of expense to their founder). Cromwell, when national power came to him, pursued a systematic policy of radical reform in Church and State – and rose to his position as Henry's chief minister by his ability to manage, or at least to understand, the House of Commons. Wolsey's capacious mind no doubt included some ideals about the enforcement of justice against 'overmighty' men; but he had too much petty business on hand to be the creator of the new England. The most important effect of his administration of Church and State was to show Henry VIII what power over both institutions could be held by the king's man – and to raise the question: why should not the king's man be the king? The most widespread reputation which Wolsey left behind was that of a tyrant, acting as if he had been begotten by a king instead of by a butcher. Dying on his way south to the Tower of London, the shattered cardinal was buried in Leicester, like Richard III. It took the mature, compassionate genius of

Shakespeare (in *Henry VIII*, the last play in which he had a major share) to see that Wolsey, like Richard III, had talents greater than those of any rightful king; so that both men, as they fall in defeat, worthily arouse our admiration.[35]

THE BREAK WITH ROME

The tragedy of the 1520s was that this superbly able minister and his king were fascinated chiefly by the chance of winning a European reputation in foreign affairs, and principally by the old dream of the conquest of France. Finding the revival of the Hundred Years' War no easy matter despite large expenditure, Wolsey organized instead the glory of spectacular, but temporary, peacemaking. The Treaty of London in 1518 and the Field of Cloth of Gold two years later provided what turned out to be the last great public pageants of the European Middle Ages. And in search of further European glory, Henry VIII put his name to a book in 1521: a *Defence of the Seven Sacraments* against the new German heretic, Martin Luther. A delighted pope, Leo X, took the occasion to pay him the compliment for which he had been angling: the royal defender of the Catholic faith and his successors were to be known for ever as *Fidei Defensores*. The title still appears on the coins of the United Kingdom.

The irony of this 'Defender of the Faith' title, however, is that within four years of its award Henry had taken the path which eventually led to his break with Rome. He had ceased to sleep with his queen (seven years his senior) and had fallen in love with Anne Boleyn, an eighteen-year-old brunette at court. Her elder sister, Mary, had already been his mistress. Anne, seeing how easily Henry had discarded Mary, refused to yield to him until she was sure of becoming his wife; and such surprising obstinacy made Henry all the more resolved to have

---

[35] Because in the end Wolsey mattered so little to England, no scholar has yet felt stimulated to replace A. F. Pollard's *Wolsey* (London, 1929). But see Charles Ferguson, *Naked to Mine Enemies* (London, 1958).

his marriage with Catherine declared no marriage at all. What was needed, then called a divorce, would nowadays be a decree of nullity. And since the pope would not agree, out of Henry's resolve to marry Anne arose the abolition of the jurisdiction of the papacy in England.

Historians as well as innumerable dramatists and film-makers have reckoned Henry's psychology to have been a major factor in this crisis. The prince whom all had applauded in 1509 had grown into a handsome monster, an egotist whose assurance that his will (for the moment) was the will of God was equalled only by his cruelty in destroying any whose existence stood in his way. It is very difficult for us to see his conduct in the 1520s in any more favourable light when we have noted how heartless his behaviour became when the constraints of medieval convention were finally abandoned and the mature man was free to reveal himself. Dressed all in yellow, he celebrated Catherine's death (from cancer) in January 1536 with a Mass of thanksgiving and a banquet — and four months later had Anne Boleyn executed, betrothing himself the next day to Jane Seymour. Nor is it possible to take with complete seriousness those who advised Henry in matters of conscience. Thomas Cranmer, the Cambridge theologian and chaplain to the Boleyns who was made Archbishop of Canterbury in 1533 in order that he might annul the marriage with Catherine, six years later declared the marriage with Anne null, in order to add to her griefs before her execution. The ground alleged was, it seems, that Henry had already enjoyed a sexual relationship with his bride's sister.

There were, however, complications. However repulsive may have been the behaviour of Henry VIII and of his clerical toadies, almost all historians believe that Henry and churchmen such as Cranmer were convinced of the righteousness of their case. It is at least certain that Henry did not take one way out of his dilemma; although his reign was to be soaked in the blood of men and women executed as traitors, he did not arrange for his first wife's death. It is also clear that the king and his assistants could produce substantial arguments both in ethics and in politics.

Catherine of Aragon's marriage with Henry had taken place

in the 'observant' Franciscans' church at Greenwich in June
1509. It had been validated in the eyes of ecclesiastical lawyers
by a papal dispensation from the obstacle arising from the fact
of her previous marriage with Arthur, Prince of Wales.
Although one passage in the Old Testament (Deuteronomy
25:5) commanded an Israelite to marry his brother's widow in
order to raise children, there were other laws from another
period in Ancient Israel's history (Leviticus 18:16, 20:21)
which prohibited the practice. Accordingly this papal dispensation had been thought necessary, and had been obtained in
1503, before Henry and Catherine were betrothed. It could
now be argued that the pope had been mistaken to set aside a
moral command in the law of Moses. (Indeed, during the
delay between betrothal and marriage, in 1505, Henry had
sworn before Bishop Foxe that he had not consented to the
betrothal and would never ratify it by marriage; presumably
this secret oath had been part of his father's devious
diplomacy.) Pursuing this line, it was in the 1520s possible for
Cardinal Wolsey to be confident that he could arrange
matters – and for an academic body as orthodox as the University of Paris to agree with the English universities that
Catherine had not been free to marry Henry. It is true that
Catherine consistently denied that her marriage with Arthur
had been consummated, but because her Spanish advisers
were anxious to get her married to Henry while retaining the
small financial advantages of being Arthur's widow, she made
the fatal mistake of agreeing not to have her virginity recorded
in a papal document at the time of the dispensation of 1503.
Indeed, because the papacy had not then noted this all-
important fact about Catherine's first marriage the dispensation for her second could be held to be invalid; a point
which the sharp-witted Wolsey saw, but which later got
obscured. More relevant than his bride's virginity to Henry's
conscience was the succession of miscarriages and mishaps
(five infants failed to survive) which had been the tragedy of
their marriage. Only one child, and that a sickly girl (Mary),
had been spared to live; and Henry did not find it impossible
to persuade himself that this was a sign of the wrath of God on
incest. Leviticus 20:21 decreed the punishment of childlessness

on a man who had taken his brother's wife. Or it did so in the Latin version known to Henry; the translation of the New English Bible (1970) reads simply: 'they shall be proscribed.'[36]

When we turn to the political aspects of the problem, we enter a less shadowy world. It was not unknown for decrees of nullity to be granted by the papacy to royal and noble petitioners. In 1491 Louis XII of France had arranged one in order to marry Anne the heiress of Brittany (his brother's widow). In 1527-28 the existing marriages both of Henry's sister (Queen Margaret of Scotland) and of his future brother-in-law (the Duke of Suffolk) were annulled. Over many years signs came from Rome, holding out hopes of a similar concession to the English king. It seems probable that Pope Clement VII would have made the concession, had Catherine not been exceptionally obstinate in sticking to her marriage and had she not been the aunt of the emperor Charles V — whose troops, having crushed the French, sacked Rome in 1527 and thereafter held the pope a virtual prisoner. It is even possible that Charles V would have withdrawn his objections had he been persuaded that Henry VIII would be a reliable and effective ally in the struggle against France for the control of Italy. As it was, however, during tortuous negotiations leading to a great variety of schemes and experiments (at one stage Henry proposed that he might be licensed to commit bigamy), it slowly became clear that the emperor was adamant. It followed that the pope, although he was always eager to evade and to procrastinate, and although privately he urged Henry to go ahead and marry leaving others to sort out the legalities, was not going to oblige with a formal pronouncement.

To Henry's mind this attitude in Rome was a political disaster as well as a personal affront. He needed an heir — and one whose title could not be questioned. He could not be sure that his daughter would live to inherit the throne or that, if she did, she would escape the fates of Edward II, Richard II

---

[36] The best short treatment of the legal problems is to be found in J. J. Scarisbrick, *Henry VIII* (London, 1968), Chapter 7. The negotiations were studied by G. de C. Parmiter, *The King's Great Matter* (London, 1967).

and Edward V. The anarchy in England in the time of the last reigning queen, Matilda, was not a good precedent. Like his father Henry was conscious of the fragility of the Tudor claim to the thone; England's leading nobleman, the Duke of Buckingham, was executed in 1521 for this reason. Henry was also afraid that whoever married Mary might be the effective ruler of England, and that such a man might have to be a foreigner – a fear which was by no means groundless, as the unpopularity of Mary's marriage with Philip of Spain showed in the 1550s. Before his legitimate son Edward was born (and survived infancy) in 1537, Henry even nursed the hope that his bastard, Henry Fitzroy, might be acknowledged as king one day. Accordingly the boy was made Duke of Richmond, Lord Admiral and Lord Lieutenant in Ireland, with precedence over Mary. But he died in 1536.

Henry's campaign to marry Anne began in the middle of 1525. It did not end until their secret wedding in January 1533; the previous month she had become pregnant, presumably consenting at long last because she was by now absolutely sure of Henry's determination and their joint hopes had been briefly raised by the promise of French support at Rome. The delay of seven years is to be explained partly by Henry's extraordinary character. Although he was always devoted to his pleasures he was also a political realist; in his heart he must have known that his heir would have to be legitimate. Although always ruthless he was also always self-righteous, so that he wished still to be in a position to play the preacher when his matrimonial problems had been settled. Although he was often impatient, he kept hoping that this cause, so obviously wise and right, would prevail in Rome, resulting in a boy's birth which would be honourable and majestic in the eyes of the world. Although he was morally indignant when frustrated, he could be diverted from his anger by the almost endless round of sport and feasts in which he indulged; and although he was on occasion brutally decisive he was reluctant to do routine work, with the result that much was left to his ministers. Wolsey tried method after method, delay after delay, in order to avert a fatal conflict between his position as the king's chief minister and his position as the Englishman to whom the pope had delegated most of his powers. When Wolsey fell in 1529, he was replaced by a group of aristocrats with little to contribute to policy-formation. Sir Thomas More, who made no secret of his disapproval of the king's matrimonial plans, acted as chancellor. Although Edward Foxe (later Bishop of Hereford) was a radical close to the king, it was not until 1533 that Henry had as chief minister a man who could suggest and superintend a creatively radical policy, in the person of Thomas Cromwell.

The fundamental cause of the delay, however, was the enormity of the step necessary if the papacy were to be ignored in the 'great matter' of the king's marriage. Until this problem arose the English monarchy and the papacy seemed to be allied for ever, in the control of the Church as well as in European diplomacy. Not many Englishmen went to Rome; Cardinal Wolsey never did, although when the papacy was vacant there was some thought that he might sacrifice his many English incomes in order to accept it. But those few who spent five weeks or so on the journey to Rome were not often morally outraged at the end of it. A typical Englishman was Christopher Bainbridge, Wolsey's predecessor as Archbishop of York, who had fitted into Renaissance Rome, its splendours and its wars, very happily as Henry's ambassador and a resident cardinal.[37] In England the unity of Christendom under the pope had been damaged by the Lollards and by the parliamentary statutes, *Provisors* and *Praemunire*, and had not been articulated in any very definite way by theologians. But it had been for many centuries a theme of religion – and the theme was still there. The only man of unblemished integrity and theological stature among Henry's bishops, John Fisher of Rochester, wrote no fewer than seven learned and acute books in his support of Queen Catherine and of the papacy. Even old William Warham at Canterbury (a Fellow of New College, Oxford, a lawyer and a diplomat, who found himself made Bishop of London in 1501 and Archbishop two years later) once went through a short period when he

---

[37] See D. S. Chambers, *Cardinal Bainbridge in the Court of Rome, 1509-14* (Oxford, 1965).

recalled Becket's example, before adding his silence to his clergy's. Thomas Cranmer, chosen archbishop by the king on Warham's convenient death, still used the seal of his predecessors at Canterbury: a representation of Thomas Becket.

In order to break this traditional acceptance of the papacy, a large array of arguments had to be assembled. The chronicles of England as well as the archives in Rome were quarries for Henry's agents. The ghost of King Arthur, whose conquests were believed to have reached Rome, was invoked in order to justify the claim that Britain had always been an 'empire'. The submission of King John to Pope Innocent had to be interpreted as a brief surrender to foreign aggression – and it had to be stressed that the fourteenth-century anti-papal statutes of *Praemunire* cancelled out any other precedents. This assembly of authorities was an important task for those now serving the king. But it also seems clear that their supreme task was stiffening their king's courage to break with Rome – until the January night in 1547 when Archbishop Cranmer, summoned to his master's deathbed, found him already speechless; whereupon Henry, 'holding him with his hand, did wring his hand in his as hard as he could'.

Not even a politician as clever as Thomas Cromwell, or a theologian as loyal and as conveniently learned as Thomas Cranmer, could give Henry all the support needed for the essential step. To secure this, Henry summoned the 'Reformation Parliament' which enacted nothing less than a revolution during its seven sessions from November 1529 to July 1536 – exalting the Crown over the Church as it had never been exalted before, but also exalting itself as the sovereign 'King in Parliament'.[38]

The anticlericalism voiced in the House of Commons was now used to frighten the clergy into buying Henry's good will and into acceptance of the king's claim to be 'protector and only supreme head of the English Church' – although in a motion moved by Bishop John Fisher the clergy in the Convocation of Canterbury added 'as far as the law of Christ allows' and in the smaller Convocation of York Cuthbert Tunstall,

---

[38] See S. E. Lehmberg, *The Reformation Parliament* (Cambridge, 1970).

Bishop of Durham, added a protest even to this qualified title. In 1532 a 'supplication' came from the Commons against the workings of the ecclesiastical courts (and against tithes too, although this was soon forgotten). It, too, was used as a stick to beat the priests. On 15 May a cowed and small meeting of the Convocation of the clergy of the Canterbury province submitted to the Crown for fear of the Commons. In future no convocation was to be summoned without a royal writ, no 'canon' law was to be enacted in future without the royal assent, and the existing laws of the Church were to be revised without reference to Rome by a committee appointed by the king. In August William Warham, who had presided over this surrender, found a merciful release through death.

Thus was the way prepared for the decisive moves of 1533 — the appointment of Cranmer to Canterbury (with the pope's feeble consent); the Act to 'restrain' or forbid appeals to Rome; the declaration by the subservient Convocation of Canterbury that Henry's marriage with Catherine was invalid; Cranmer's formal judgement to the same effect; Anne's sumptuous coronation; Henry's excommunication by Rome. Only one matter could not be controlled by the king: Anne's child was a girl.

In the next year the Act of Succession provided for an oath to be taken throughout the kingdom acknowledging the new marriage and its offspring. Other Acts accompanied it. All payments to, and legal business in, Rome were forbidden, and it was no longer heresy to deny the pope's primacy. The king alone was to appoint bishops and was to receive a tenth of all clerical incomes. The earlier submission of the clergy to the king as their 'Supreme Head' was turned into English law without any reference to the saving clause about the 'law of Christ'. It was made treason even to speak (let alone act) against the king as a 'heretic, schismatic, tyrant, infidel, or usurper of the crown'. The Preamble to the Statute of Appeals in 1533 declared that, on the contrary, 'by divers sundry old authentic histories and chronicles it is manifestly declared . . . that this realm of England is an empire . . . governed by one supreme head and king . . . unto whom a body politic, compact of all sorts and degrees of people, divided in terms and by

names of spirituality and temporality, be bounded and owe to
bear next to God a natural and humble obedience . . .'

Those who regard this break with Rome in 1533-34 as
deeply tragic have understandably been among those who
have stressed that the treason laws under Henry VIII constituted a reign of terror. Yet the comparison with Hitler or
Stalin should not be pressed too far. Henry had no large police
force and no standing army; on the contrary, weapons were
widely distributed in the homes of the people. The executions
of traitors in his reign, however frightening or sickening,
stopped far short of a massacre. The truth seems to be that
what he did was generally accepted; or at least, that enough
people who disagreed with what he did were terrified of the
disorder that would result from disobeying the consecrated
king. The effective terror was that exercised in their own
minds by this prospect. To later generations the 'natural and
humble obedience' of sixteenth-century Englishmen – who
customarily protested their loyalty immediately before they
were executed as traitors – has been a loyalty beyond comprehension, an abasement before monarchs who with the exception of the first Elizabeth did not deserve such flattery. But we
must understand this emotion if we are to understand the best,
as well as the average, of the period. A horror of rebellion was
an emotion felt deeply by the mind that created the Church of
England's Book of Common Prayer and by William Shakespeare. At any rate, in 1534 almost all the clergy of England
signed, or otherwise accepted, a declaration that the Bishop of
Rome had no greater jurisdiction in the realm of England
than any other foreign bishop – which meant: none at all.
Reproducing the signatures of sixty-six bishops, abbots or
other dignitaries to one such document, a modern Roman
Catholic history of the English Reformation gives this caption
to the picture: 'The Fort is Betrayed.'[39] And the fort which the
clergy surrendered was not defended heroically by the laity.

One explanation is that it was possible to accept an argument which Henry VIII put forward when it suited him (for
example, in a letter to Cuthbert Tunstall, Bishop of Durham):

---

[39] Philip Hughes, *The Reformation in England*, vol. i (London, 1950).

to make the king supreme over 'the Church' or 'the spirituality'
meant no more than acknowledging power over the clergy
which he already had clearly over the laity. Another factor is
that even after all this legislation many refused to believe that
the break with Rome could be final; and that is another explanation of the willingness to surrender. Lorenzo Campeggio
was the cardinal who had been sent to England in the course
of the long farce of examining Henry's petition to the pope.
When Catherine had died and Anne had been executed in
1536, Campeggio once again prepared to visit England in
order to reconcile Henry to the Church – and to recover his
own bishopric of Salisbury. The pope and the emperor both
hailed the two women's deaths as providential. Within
England many who took the new oath may have done so in the
belief that within a short time the king and the pope wuld
once more reach agreement. And once the oath had been
taken, it was hard to develop a conscientious scruple which
would destroy one's chances of remaining a prosperous citizen,
or the pastor of a parish, or a bishop. Tunstall, for example,
who had already been Bishop of London from 1522 to 1530,
retained the ample revenues and performed the useful duties
of the bishopric of Durham from 1530 to 1552, and lost them
then only because the Duke of Northumberland coveted the
estates. He recovered the bishopric in 1554, for another five
years, until finally conscience drove him to refuse to accept the
supremacy of Elizabeth, in his eighty-fifth year.[40] No doubt
the fear of being branded – more literally, of being hanged
and, while still half-alive, disembowelled – as a traitor influenced the secret struggles of many consciences; but we have
to account for the ease with which so many assented in public
to acts which their consciences must often have rejected or
questioned. It seems reasonable to suppose that they told
themselves that their assent would be temporary.

However, any optimists who believed that the *status quo*
would soon be restored misjudged Henry. Even now that the
immediate cause of his break with Rome had been removed,
he liked being the English Church's 'Supreme Head'; it suited

---

[40] See Charles Sturge, *Cuthbert Tunstall* (London, 1938).

his consummate vanity. As teacher of his people he issued Ten Articles of Faith, mainly conservative but in places agreeing with the new Lutheran theology and defending only three, not seven, sacraments (Baptism, the Mass and Penance). And having tasted blood when he asserted this legal and theological supremacy, Henry now began to move against the English Church's fattest and softest piece of flesh: the monasteries.

In 1534 there were very few convinced Protestants in England, but when the monastic estates had been distributed to the laity the king was only one in a large number of influential Englishmen with a vested interest in opposing any idea of a return to the religion of the Middle Ages. When in the 1550s Henry's daughter Mary — a fanatical Catholic as a result of the humiliating injustice done to her mother and herself — was on the throne and determined to restore the old religion, the one piece of wisdom agreed on by almost all her advisors, and even accepted by herself, was not to touch the gentry's possession of the lands which had belonged to the monasteries. Cardinal Pole was not allowed into the country to reconcile England to Rome until he had very reluctantly accepted this condition. If the clergy's cowardice betrayed the fort, the laity's greed took the fort over; for many hundreds of religious houses now provided either a nucleus for a gentleman's handsome manor house or building materials for humbler men. The betrayed castle became the Englishman's home.

THE END OF THE MONASTERIES

When in 1537 Roger Aske was a prisoner in the Tower of London, condemned for treason with no hope of life, he wrote for Thomas Cromwell and his agents a statement of his cause. 'The abbeys in the north parts', he affirmed, 'gave great alms to poor men and laudably served God.' But now he saw only desolation: 'the blessed consecration of the sacrament now not used, the ornaments and relics of the Church irrevently used, the tombs and sepulchres of honourable and noble men pulled down and sold, none hospitality now in those places kept. . . .

Also the abbeys were one of the beauties of this realm to all
men and strangers passing through the same. . . .' And in
1593, clothing Roger Aske's nostalgia in local detail, a former
lay official looked back at the life of the cathedral monastery
in Durham. He could recall from his boyhood exactly what the
routine had been and what had been the ornaments of the
great church, now desolate for him. He wished to write it all
down before he, too, died.[41]

Yet what is most surprising about the end of the 825
religious houses in England and Wales is not how much, but
how little, opposition it aroused. The monasteries were not
occupied by armed force; they surrendered to the king. Only
the comparatively recent foundations of the London Carthusians, the Bridgettines and the 'observant' Franciscans refused
to take the 1534 oath to the king or put up anything like a
united front against the secular aggression; in almost all the
houses, the superiors were able to obtain the consent of the inmates to the oath and later to the surrender. Many tens of
thousands of laymen were intimately involved in the fortunes
of these houses as the descendants of their founders, as their
tenants or neighbours, as lodgers or employees, or simply as
tradesmen; and most of those so involved seem to have kept
silent apart from petitioning for their share in the loot.

The explanation cannot be that there were precedents for
the destruction which began in 1536. The nearest precedents
were three. The Knights Templar had been an order both
military and religious until suppressed by Pope Clement V in
1312 (with greater brutality than Henry VIII ever had to show
towards the monks); but almost all their lands had been
transferred to the Order of St John of Jerusalem. The 'alien
priories' (small houses controlled by Norman and other
foreign monasteries) had been suppressed by kings from
Edward I to Henry V; but almost all their estates had been
used for the endowment of chapels, colleges, schools and the
Carthusian monastery at Sheen. Wolsey had secured the
transfer of the incomes of some small and decayed religious

---

[41] David Knowles, *The Religious Orders in England*, vol. iii (Cambridge,
1959), pp.129-137, 328.

houses to his colleges in Oxford and Ipswich; but the austere and orthodox Bishop Fisher had done the same for education in Cambridge. The destruction of the English and Welsh religious houses was a sudden and major revolution not only in economics but also in politics and religion.

The explanation of the quietness of this revolution cannot be that these houses were notorious for their moral or financial disorder. Historians have the advantage of being able to study the records of the 'visitations' by the bishops or the bishops' officials. These documents record in detail some scandals and much slackness, but the picture as a whole is certainly not one of gross immorality. The least viable houses were, it is obvious, the smallest, and even historians who lament the destruction of the greater houses with all their treasures in the spiritual life and in art agree that it would have been sensible to effect a radical reduction in the numbers of houses. But the surviving accounts do not suggest that there was widespread dishonesty or insolvency. We can also read the reports of the coarse Richard Layton and the other commissioners who were hurriedly sent in 1535 to extract evidence of corruption, to announce an austere future and to invite desertions from the monastic vows. But not even these reports persuade historians that the monastic system as a whole was seriously beyond reform.

What is clear is that by 1535 in most monasteries the old fire was burning low. The services in church, and no doubt also the prayers in private, were maintained as they had been for centuries and as they seemed certain to be for centuries to come; but in return the monks, nuns and friars expected a life as comfortable as that of the nearby gentry, apart from marriage. There was little sense of flight from the world in order to gain eternal salvation. The religious houses no longer harboured many who wished to climb the ladder of spiritual perfection or to devote themselves to scholarship and education. They were no longer unique as places where the dead could be prayed for; chantries existed for this purpose in many parish churches. They no longer contributed much to the administration, agriculture or trade of the kingdom; laymen such as Thomas More, or priests as secular-minded as Thomas

Wolsey, or the landowners whom Wolsey had tried to discipline, or the merchants who were growing into substantial
capitalists (specially in London), had taken away all these
roles in which monks had for long been conspicuous. They no
longer copied out manuscripts; the printers had taken over.

Yet while the fire burned low, the immense rewards which
had come to the monasteries for their past political and
economic contributions continued. That was shown to the
government by the mouth-watering financial statistics of the
Valor Ecclesiasticus, gathered in 1535. Indeed, wealth — its
advantages as well as its worries — had choked the growth of
that spiritual harvest which, far more than any secular contribution, had been the passionate concern of every one of the
founders of these religious orders. It was assumed, and rightly,
that the monks, nuns and friars would not continue to offer to
God ordered prayer and fervent charity as consecrated communities once their lavish buildings and endowments had
been surrendered. A return to the simplicity of the origins of
monasticism — to the poverty of the Irish monks recorded by
Bede, for example — would have been extremely difficult and
was never contemplated. It is also revealing how few of those
who had been monks before 1540 wished to resume the life
when that became possible, although difficult, in 1555 under
the Catholic Queen Mary. Had these religious orders retained
more of their original ideals they would have been respected
more deeply both by the laity and by themselves, and might
have been defended so vigorously that they would have been
allowed to keep some of their property by a king whose own
anxiety to seem respectable had just been laboriously
demonstrated.

Another reason why the monasteries closed quietly was that
the move against them, like the break with Rome, was made
little by little, so that not until towards the end was any
religious radicalism undeniable.

In 1533 there was a rumble of the coming storm when
John Leland was commissioned to investigate the monastic
libraries — a task which enabled him to save countless volumes
as the storm broke, although much of the medieval legacy was
then lost for ever, in literature as in art. In 1536 an Act was

passed to provide for the dissolution of religious houses whose lands did not yield more than £200 a year. Although the previous year's visitation had yielded no proof that all such houses were undisciplined, the suppression of about two hundred small communities could be presented as a rationalization acceptable to all reformers, and the government propaganda machine managed by Thomas Cromwell was busy manufacturing or encouraging talk of the good purposes to which the revenues would be put. Education and charity were stressed, but the defence and administration of the realm without taxes also seemed a charitable purpose, and a 'Court of Augmentations of the King's Revenue' was established with regional officers to receive the surrendered buildings and estates. The inmates of the suppressed houses were given the choice of moving to the surviving monasteries or becoming parish priests.

Even this limited measure contributed to the rebellion known as the Pilgrimage of Grace. This broke out in Lincolnshire and Yorkshire in the autumn of 1536. It spread into Lancashire and elsewhere, but by March it was over. Essentially it seems to have been a rebellion organized by conservative gentry who vainly hoped for intervention by the emperor Charles V, but like the Peasants' Revolt of 1381 this one was fed by many local grievances against landlords; and as in 1381 this 'pilgrimage' was encouraged by priests who preached religious idealism to the excited people. In some places — particularly in Lancashire and in the mind of Robert Aske the most eloquent rebel — the suppression of the smaller religious houses was a particular grievance in a general reaction against social and religious change. And since abbots and monks were involved in such treason, this provided firm ground for the assault on the remaining religious houses.

During the period 1537-40 there was frantic activity in these houses. Many tried to buy good will by paying for licences of exemption from the existing Parliamentary Act, by bribing the royal officials, or by pensioning strong laymen in the neighbourhood. Many decided that the time had come to secure employment or pensions for themselves (the average after tax was £6 a year for an ex-monk, but there was more generous provision for superiors). But the storm raged on. In 1538 Richard Ingworth, formerly the provincial prior of the Dominicans but now Bishop of Dover, 'visited' all the friars and within little more than twelve months had obtained the surrender of the great majority. In the same year the chief pilgrims' shrines were demolished; wagonloads of treasure came to the king from the shrine of St Thomas of Canterbury. In 1539 a new Act of Parliament gave security both to the king and to almost all lay tenants or purchasers of monastic lands which had been surrendered, thus encouraging a fresh wave of surrenders into the hands of commissioners sent to sweep through the country. Where there was unwillingness to surrender, impatient methods were used towards the end. Abbot Whiting of Glastonbury was hanged – it was claimed, for concealing some of the treasures of his church. Similar fates, for alleged treason, overtook the heads of other rich Benedictine houses at Reading and Colchester before Christmas 1539. When Evesham Abbey was suppressed on 30 January 1540, the monks in the choir were not allowed to complete the psalm they were singing at Evensong. In March of that year the cathedral monasteries at Canterbury and Rochester, which had been obstinate, were dissolved; and Waltham Abbey was the last to surrender.

The Order of St John of Jerusalem was dissolved by another Act later in 1540. Apart from a few conventual hospitals (mopped up in 1545), no religious house was now left. Between eight and nine thousand monks, nuns and friars, with an unknown number of lay servants, had to find new homes.

The surrender of the larger houses was accompanied by more talk about colleges, schools, hospitals and the pastoral care of the people. Eventually the eight cathedrals which had been staffed by monks or canons were, with Westminster Abbey, entrusted to Deans and Chapters. Six new dioceses were created with cathedrals' and bishops' incomes derived from the former monasteries: Westminster (until 1550), Gloucester, Bristol, Oxford, Peterborough and Chester. At Canterbury Cranmer dreamed of a substantial college in the cathedral, but what happened was the endowment of a grammar school – as in ten other cathedral cities. Fortunately

Cranmer was able to secure that the King's Scholars at Canterbury as elsewhere should be 'poor' boys, while others argued that such a good education ought to be reserved for the sons of the gentry. Ten 'Regius' professorships were endowed by the king at Oxford and Cambridge along with his great foundations of Christ Church, Oxford (the former Cardinal College), and Trinity College, Cambridge. All this was excellent but it was less than the dream, and the expenditure which was authorized for other edifying purposes accounted for only a small part of the wealth which passed through the Court of Augmentations.

More of the profit from the religious houses was devoted to the fortification of the coasts against threatened invasion and still more to the other current needs of the government. The fall of the efficient Cromwell in 1540 increased both those needs and the appetites of buyers. Before the death of Henry VIII over half of the former monastic estates had been granted away or (and this was far more usual) sold off – normally at a price twenty times the annual rent which the land would fetch on the open market. In 1540 Henry was trying to persuade James V of Scotland that if he, too, would end the 'untruth and beastly living of those monks', then he, too, would be able to 'live like a king'.[42] But in real life what Henry's government needed was cash – and taking it from the sale of monastic lands was far more popular than asking Parliament for taxation. Still greater was the need of those who governed England during the minority of Henry's son; the Court of Augmentations had to finance the Duke of Somerset's wars in Scotland and France. By the accession of Elizabeth I, over three-quarters of these vast estates had gone. Much of the land was resold fairly quickly, and most of it ended up in small or medium-sized holdings. This was, of course, a decisive shift of power in English society – away from the Church, not to the Crown but to the gentry.

In the 1530s the Crown's own lands were worth less than a third of the net income of the monasteries according to the

---

[42] This splendid example of royal self-congratulation is printed in *The Letters of Henry VIII*, ed. M. St. C. Byrne (London, 1936), pp.288-9.

Valor Ecclesiasticus (£131,361). Had the Crown kept the monasteries' estates and exploited them, its ultimate dependence on the gentry represented in Parliament would have been far less and the whole course of English history might have been different. But there is no evidence that this was ever a serious intention. Nor does it seem probable that the authorities were ever really determined to pursue the much-advertised vision of a massive new endowment for education and other forms of charity.[43]

SPIRITUAL UNDERCURRENTS

One of the arguments used to encourage the surrender of the monasteries was that English kings had endowed many of them. The monks were merely handing back to Henry VIII what was rightfully his own. Innumerable other signs were given that Henry wished to minimize any impression that the break with Rome meant any break with the religion accepted by King Ethelbert from St Augustine and defended in the British 'empire' (the Tudors loved the word) by King Arthur. Up to the death of Henry VIII it is fair to describe the English Reformation as an essentially political and economic change, dictated by two needs which were scarcely theological — the need felt by the king to beget a legitimate male heir, and the need felt by the gentry to get hold of the monastic lands. The religion of the bulk of the people remained Catholic. This continuity was shown by the rapturous welcome to a Catholic princess, Mary, when she inherited the throne in 1553 — and further illustrated by the Duke of Northumberland, who had tried to stop Mary but who now returned to the Catholic faith before being executed for treason. Probably Protestants were still in the minority in the 1570s and 1580s under Elizabeth I.

---

[43] In addition to the masterly volume by David Knowles quoted on p.296, see *Letters to Cromwell and Others on the Suppression of the Monasteries* edited by G. H. Cook (London, 1965), and Joyce Youings, *The Dissolution of the Monasteries* (London, 1971).

But the denial of the authority of the pope and the drastic reduction in the authority and wealth of the clergy made, or at least uncovered, a vacuum which was in the end largely filled by the most vigorous variety of contemporary Christianity: Protestantism.

Late medieval Catholicism, for all its popularity, was a standing invitation to reform. In the fifteenth century and again in 1512-17, great Councils of the Church said so; and in Spain something was actually done. In the early sixteenth century, 'everyone wanted reform, or professed to want reform' – although 'when churchmen spoke of reformation, they were almost always thinking of administrative, legal or moral reformation; hardly ever of doctrinal reformation'.[44]

We have already seen some of the administrative and legal changes which in England the laity desired and achieved. But we ought also to notice that popular piety often spoke in a new way about the aspiration or hunger or suffering of the troubled individual; late medieval loyalty to the doctrine of the Catholic Church had this element of tension in it. The most popular devotions of the fifteenth century centred on the suffering of the incarnate Christ (this was the time when the devotion of 'the stations of the cross' developed); and on the humble purity of the mother of Christ (this was the century in which it became customary to recite the *Angelus* and rosary prayers in honour of Our Lady). Above all there was the emphasis on the power of the sacrifice of Christ, and of the intercession of his mother, to free the souls of the living and the dead from the pains of purgatory. Running through such devotions there was an individualism which had not been nearly so widespread in previous ages. The devotion was paid to the human Christ and Mary, remembering the dead by name, and it was stressed what ordinary people could do for their own salvation and that of their families and friends by the recital of prayers and by hiring priests to offer many Masses. Even the 'primers' or prayer books which were now being printed in abundance never suggested that the laity should corporately follow the priest's Latin words (often

---

[44] Owen Chadwick, *The Reformation* (London, 1964), pp.12-13.

spoken softly) in the liturgy of the Mass; prayers in English were given for them to say privately although they were all in church. Laymen did not receive communion together except on a few occasions in the year when they were 'houselled' or given the consecrated bread, the wine always being kept for the priest alone.

All this made for a powerful religion, powerful because it was popular. For the time being, enough individuals found their spiritual food within the inherited system after these relatively minor developments. Modern talk suggesting that 'the Church anticipated in discipline the Soviet-Nazi theory of Totalitarianism'[45] does not take account of the fact that to the end, despite the Inquisition abroad and the persecution of the Lollards in England, the medieval Church had no police. And the dismissal of medieval religion as 'magic' does not take account of the fact that the Church fought many popular superstitions. The great time for magic was when the Catholic Church had been brought low.[46] But after the religious changes of the sixteenth century – changes which transformed Catholicism in addition to creating Protestantism – it was possible to look back and see that the power of the Gospel as God's gracious answer to human needs and aspirations, producing assurance and joy in the believer, had previously been deficient.

Professor A. G. Dickens, who has examined countless printed and unprinted records of popular and conventional religion in late medieval England, has stressed these characteristics: 'its effort to attain salvation through devout observances, its fantastic emphasis on saints, relics and pilgrimages, its tendency to allow the personality and teaching of Jesus to recede from the focus of the picture. That the connection of such writings with the Christianity of the Gospel is rather tenuous could be demonstrated with almost mathematical precision'. And although it was a popular religion, fear was very prominent. Devotional manuals and people's wills,

---

[45] G. G. Coulton, *Medieval Panorama* (Cambridge, 1938), p.458.

[46] See Keith Thomas, *Religion and the Decline of Magic* (revised, Harmondsworth, Middx., 1971).

the echoes we have of popular preaching and the more elevated defence put up for Catholicism by, for example, Sir Thomas More – all this evidence points to 'a dogmatic and detailed emphasis upon the horrors of purgatory and the meens whereby sinners could mitigate them. . . . Medieval men were faced by quite terrifying views of punishment in the life to come; it was small wonder that they felt more comfortable with the saints than with God, or that they came to regard the Blessed Virgin as a merciful mediatrix for ever seeking to placate the divine wrath of the Son as Judge'.[47]

Professor Dickens is also one of the modern scholars, of various religious persuasions, who make the point that not enough pastoral work was being done to commend this faith to any of the English who may have had secret hesitations over it. The pope seemed to be an Italian politician, not a spiritual leader. The bishops had for long been in most cases ecclesiastical lawyers and civil servants rather than preachers or pastors, and this tendency was stronger in England than in most of the rest of late medieval Europe. There were plenty of clergy, but far too many of them were chantry priests whose duty was to pray for the souls of the dead, not to be pastors of the living; and astonishingly little was done throughout the Middle Ages to train parish priests, to encourage their pastoral work, or to take pastoral care of them in their own problems and griefs. It was not until 1555, under Queen Mary, that a council of the Catholic Church in England set up seminaries to train priests. And the use of parish churches to swell the incomes of often distant monasteries cannot have added to an Englishman's sense that his own priest was his pastor and friend. For all its popularity, late medieval religion was becoming vulnerable as Catholicism in England had not been since the conversion of the invading Danes.

It is, of course, impossible to know how many individuals were dissatisfied amid all the evident success of late medieval religion. Very few people wrote anything that gives a real clue. Few Englishmen read anything at all; Thomas More guessed

---

[47] A. G. Dickens, *The English Reformation* (revised, London, 1967), pp.17-20.

that only four out of every ten of his contemporaries could read English, Stephen Gardiner guessed only one out of every hundred. What we do know is that a few academic radicals, unusually sensitive and intellectual, were for a time attracted by the possibility that the philosophy of Plato might help to turn late medieval Catholicism into the 'philosophy of Christ'.

Such Christian Platonists did not realize how far Platonism was from the religion of Jesus or St Paul, but one explanation of this failure was the tradition that Dionysius, St Paul's leading convert in Athens, had as a Christian written a Platonic book. In 1455 an Italian scholar, Lorenzo Valla, exposed the falsity of this tradition, and about 1501 an Oxford scholar, William Grocyn, brought Valla's arguments to England; but even then the appeal of Plato to devout Catholics was great. Thomas More's *Utopia* was, in a sense, an adaptation of Plato's *Republic*. This appeal was not only a reaction against the philosophical authority of Aristotle in the medieval universities, or an excitement that more Latin translations of Plato and the Platonists were becoming widely known. Because Plato had written about a republic, he helped a few in the late Middle Ages to explore in their minds the possibility of a society wider than the Church they knew, a society where reason rather than dogma and precedent decided issues and where wise men rather than bishops trained as lawyers governed. Because Plato had written about love, he now helped some who were dissatisfied both by the selfish materialism of everyday life and by the Church's traditional contempt for the world. Christian Platonists began to suggest (with greater or less caution) that nature's deepest instincts would, if trusted, lead to God, because there was in every man's soul a spark of divinity descended from God. And because Plato had written about God's eternity and beauty, about God as most desirable rather than most terrible, he now fed some souls starved by the normal diet in late medieval religion.

A churchman influenced by Platonism was John Colet, Dean of St Paul's in London, 1505-19. When he died, only one work of his had been published: a sermon to the clergy of Canterbury Convocation in 1511, pleading for moral reform.

'Truly ye are gathered often times together,' he declared, 'but, by your favour to speak the truth, yet I see not what fruit cometh of your assembling, namely to the Church.' Some of his own papers, and tributes paid to him by others, have, however, enabled modern scholars to study more of his life and thought.

In 1492 he went from Oxford to Italy for four years, studying both in Rome and in Florence, then the centre of interest in Plato. On his return to his university he delivered public lectures on the Bible. Notes of what he said on Genesis, Romans and 1 Corinthians have survived, showing that he had moved from the elaborate medieval method of analysing the possible (or impossible) meanings of a scriptural text, back to the simple meaning of a teacher – Moses (as he thought) or Paul – who belonged to history. In Colet's exposition this simple meaning of the Bible often turned out to be close to Plato, but the method was one which was to have very different results in different hands.

While Dean of St Paul's, Colet continued to expound St Paul's thought and found many listeners. Although the canons of his cathedral claimed that he treated them like monks, and his bishop suspected him of heresy, he charmed his fellow-Londoners by many edifying conversations over simple meals. His father had twice been Lord Mayor of London, and when the dean was left a fortune he devoted it to the foundation of St Paul's School. He chose William Lily as its head because he could teach Greek and was generally progressive, and he entrusted its management to the married laymen of the Mercers' Company. His sermon rebuking the clergy assembled in the Convocation of Canterbury in 1511 was bold and unpopular, but another incident is reported from Good Friday two years later. This much admired and beloved dean was summoned to preach before the king at Greenwich, and preached a pacifist sermon. Unfortunately Henry was just about to send his fleet, anchored nearby, to what he hoped would be the conquest of France. After the sermon, having been summoned by his monarch, the preacher so explained himself that Henry called for wine, exclaiming 'this is the doctor for me!' Two years later Colet had a still more difficult task. He preached at the great

service in Westminster Abbey when Cardinal Wolsey's red hat
was received from Rome. His theme was a call to humility,
holiness and devotion to pastoral work. These virtues, so uncharacteristic of the cardinal, were necessary in the leaders of
Christ's Church.[48]

THE REFORMATION

A man similarly charming (at least to other men), although a
far greater scholar and more prolific author, was Desiderius
Erasmus.

When this Dutchman visited Oxford in 1499, he was probably about thirty years old and beginning to shake off the
disadvantages of his illegitimate birth and a spell in a
monastery for which he had no vocation. He had been invited
to England by a young nobleman to whom he had acted as
tutor, but had gravitated to the university (it was the year
when Vasco da Gama sailed back from India). While in
Oxford the visitor made friends with Colet, who urged him to
lecture on the Bible, as he did. Firmly but politely Erasmus
replied that he must first gain a complete mastery of Greek,
which Colet had never attained. By the time of his next
appearance in England, in 1505, he had conquered this
language (his India); so he was able to present Archbishop
Warham with a Latin version of a Greek play by Euripides,
and to work with Thomas More on translation of the satires of
Lucian.

Four years later he was back again, hoping for effective
patronage from Warham, staying with More, writing a prayer
and a summary of Christianity for Colet's new school, before
going on to spend thirty months in a tower-study overlooking
the town and river at Queens' College, Cambridge. While
there he was absorbed in editing Greek and Latin classics and
the letters of St Jerome – and in grumbles about the small

[48] See Leland Miles, *John Colet and the Platonic Tradition* (London,
1962), and Sears Jayne, *John Colet and Marsilio Ficino* (Oxford, 1963).

audiences at his lectures on Greek, about the climate and about the beer. But it was in Cambridge that he resolved to do for his time what St Jerome's Latin version (the 'Vulgate') had done for Christendom since the end of the fourth century. He began a fresh translation of the New Testament into classical Latin direct from the Greek, and when he returned to the Continent where he belonged he knew the need which scholars now had for a printed Greek New Testament based on the manuscripts. Both works, in Latin and Greek, appeared in Basel in 1516 and aroused a storm of protest by conservatives convinced that the Vulgate had alone been given authority by the Holy Spirit and the Catholic Church. Together with much other writing which taught the message of the Bible as he understood it, these publications put Erasmus at the head of the reforming liberals of Europe. Both the emperor, Charles V, and the pope, Leo X, pledged support.

But on the eve of All Saints' Day 1517 a far more obscure theologian, Martin Luther, nailed his ninety-five 'theses' (arguments inviting disputation) to the door of the church in the little town of Wittenberg in Saxony. Their most dramatic feature was an attack on the granting of 'indulgences' (remissions from periods in purgatory) in return for a confession of sins and a gift to papal funds. The attack had a double significance. Within Germany it could be used as a theological blessing on the desire of princes to throw off the authority of an Italian pope, to bring local churchmen to heel and to loot church lands; in England Henry VIII and his supporters bestowed their own blessing on such actions without the aid of any major theologian. But in the Christian world as a whole, Luther's attack of 1517 announced the total dissatisfaction of a religious genius with late medieval piety. As a student of theology he had failed to find food for his mind. As a monk he had failed to find peace for his conscience. As a pilgrim to Rome he had been dismayed. As a professor he had not even tried to fit the Old Testament or the letters of St Paul into the categories of Platonism, as Colet had cautiously done in Oxford. Pursuing the 'theology of the cross' which had already been developed in later medieval German mysticism (and by Dame Julian in England), he had broken through to the in-

sight that a Christian was declared righteous before God not
because of his devotions or works or merits but because of
God's own righteousness revealed upon Christ's cross – the
righteousness in which that Christian must put his entire trust.
By 1513 in his own style (which was very German, often coarse
and almost always still in dialogue with the academic theology
and popular religion of the Middle Ages), Luther had rediscovered the Gospel of God's grace. This he now taught in lectures on the psalms, in lectures on *Romans*, and in declarations to all who would listen.

In a short history of Christian England there is no need to
retell the story of Protestant Europe, a separate entity once
Luther had been condemned by the pope in 1520 and by the
emperor in 1521. Nor is there any need to recount the history
of the Counter-Reformation, the profoundly renewed Catholicism which gradually arose in response. Nor need we survey
in full the tragedy that had overwhelmed the hopes of
academic radicalism and liberal reform by the death of
Erasmus in 1536. What is vital here may be said briefly.

Erasmus was very reluctant to get involved in controversy
with Luther, whose freedom as a theologian he defended.
Even more was he reluctant to risk being identified with the
peasants' revolt and the extremist religious movements which
erupted in Germany once Luther had broken the spell cast by
the authority of the medieval Church. When he did tackle
Luther after many entreaties from fellow-Catholics, it was on
the subject of the dignity of man. Luther, he declared in a
famous pamphlet of 1524, had underestimated both the
freedom and the power of the human will to respond to God's
grace. Luther replied vitriocally, asserting the helplessness of
sinful man as St Augustine had asserted it against the British
heretic Pelagius more than eleven hundred years previously.
But the real conflict between the two men in religion was not
completely covered by this controversy. The real contrast
between Luther and Erasmus – as between Augustine and
Pelagius – was that the former, despite his pessimism, was the
prophet, with the stronger will to mould the Christian world's
religion since he had a stronger experience of the mastering
and dynamic will of God. Like Pelagius, Erasmus appealed to

his fellow-men to be as reasonable, as self-controlled and as helpful as he was. To such a man, Christ was the great example – and when Erasmus grew serious or at any rate sentimental (towards the end of *The Praise of Folly*, for example, or when he was writing to educate the young) it was the gentleness of Christ that he most stressed. Like Augustine, Luther spoke alongside men and women who were swayed by their passions and depressed by guilt and the sense of total futility; and so he spoke to them. To a Luther, surrounded and invaded by coarse evil, Christ was the hero and the saviour, bringing near the God who previously had been far-off and hostile. Salvation by Christ alone, and 'justification' by faith in him alone, offered the one key needed to the Bible – and to the knowledge and love of God. Luther complained that Erasmus spoke about God in an ice-cold way. God to him was 'a glowing furnace full of love'.

The contrast between liberal reform and Protestant reformation helps us to understand what happened when a religious vacuum had been created in England by the policy of Henry VIII (who disgusted both Erasmus and Luther). The gap was not filled by the kind of reform of which John Colet would have approved. It was filled by a religion which often damaged or destroyed what the academic radicals and liberal reformers held dear: peace, internationalism, the calm consideration of the Bible, the constructive improvement of institutions, the charitable appeal to people's own ideals, pastoral love.

The new version of Christianity, Protestantism, was so named from the protest of the minority against the majority of German princes gathered at Speyer in 1529; but in some nations, including England, it was destined to become the religion of the majority. It had power; it exerted a fascination in people's hearts, and wielded an influence over their lives, not often to be seen in liberal Catholicism. It seemed to be the living voice of the Bible and the vital truth about God and man in their eternity-deciding relationship. And so it seemed to be the answer to the problem which Thomas Linacre, physician to Henry VIII and founder of the Royal College of Surgeons, a devout Catholic and a good scholar, is said to have put to himself when, towards the end of his life, he read the gospels in Greek for the first time. It is reported that on so doing he exclaimed: 'Either this is not the Gospel or we are not Christians.'[49]

ENGLAND'S FIRST PROTESTANTS

The new theology attracted a little group of Cambridge men who gathered in an inn which although officially called the White Horse (it stood next to King's College) was nicknamed 'Little Germany'.

Among the many who observed this group with suspicion was Thomas Cranmer, the son of a Nottinghamshire squire who had in 1503 entered Jesus College, Cambridge (founded six years before in a former nunnery). With uncharacteristic bravado Cranmer had married soon after becoming a Master of Arts, sacrificing his hopes of a life as a priest, but after less than a year this first wife and their infant child had died and he had resumed his advanced studies in theology. Now in the 1520s he studied the Bible and the theologians all the more intensively, pen in hand, trying to decide what to make of Luther's challenge. This in itself showed a rare independence and caution; on the other hand, he was not in any other way distinguished. During a residence in Cambridge of more than twenty-five years he wrote no book and held no important office.

The turning-point of Cranmer's life came at a supper party on an August evening in 1529. The other guests at the table were two of the king's leading officials, Stephen Gardiner and Edward Foxe. Cranmer suggested that they should seek the opinion of theologians about the king's matrimonial prob-

---

[49] The best introductions are R. H. Bainton, *Erasmus of Christendom* (London, 1969); George Faludy, *Erasmus of Rotterdam* (London, 1970); James Atkinson, *Martin Luther and the Birth of Protestantism* (London, 1968); Gerhard Ebeling, *Luther: An Introduction to His Thought* (London, 1970).

lems. The suggestion was not novel. What was novel was the thought emerging as the evening wore on that Cranmer himself might write a theological book advocating the king's cause. He did so, satisfactorily, and was sent to repeat his arguments in papal Rome and in Italian universities. The book was written in the London house of Anne Boleyn's father; and when the time came for Henry to appoint a new Archbishop of Canterbury in January 1533, the Boleyn family successfully urged the recall of Thomas Cranmer, then on an embassy to the emperor. It was therefore as Archbishop of Canterbury that Cranmer further pursued his studies of the theology of the Continental Reformation, in the intervals of attending to the dangers of politics such as the fate of Anne Boleyn (whose final confession he heard in prison, with what effects on his own conscience we do not know). It seems clear that he gradually became convinced of the validity of almost the whole of the Lutheran case, but that his instincts were all for caution and above all for the need to retain his king's benevolence. Such instincts were not inappropriate; without Henry's favour he would almost certainly have been executed during the reaction against Protestantism in the 1540s. He did not really come into his own until Henry was dead – perhaps not until he himself had been burned by Queen Mary in 1556, leaving behind him the memory of the Protestant martyr whose great theological learning and mastery of English had been deployed in his editorship of the Book of Common Prayer, beginning with the English Litany of 1545. Perhaps his experience of moral surrender under Henry VIII had been necessary for the expressions of penitence in that Prayer Book to be so eloquent.[50]

Other Cambridge men were more quickly courageous.[51]

One of them, Thomas Bilney, had been absorbed in legal and theological studies until he got hold of the translation of the New Testament by Erasmus; he would afterwards explain that he had been interested in its Latin. He had found in it the

---

[50] See Jasper Ridley, *Thomas Cranmer* (Oxford, 1962).
[51] See W. Clebsch, *England's Earliest Protestants, 1520-1535* (New Haven, N.J., 1964).

sentence about Christ Jesus coming into the world to save sinners, and it had converted him to seriousness in practising and preaching a Gospel based entirely on this New Testament, with this as the key text. He threw himself into the service of the poorest, becoming in John Foxe's words 'laborious and painful to the desperates; a preacher to the prisoners and comfortless; a great doer in Cambridge'. The change in him had led to charges of heresy, although he was no Lutheran; and he had recanted. But he could find no peace of mind when he resumed his academic life. One evening he told his colleagues in Trinity Hall that he must 'go up to Jerusalem' as a simple Bible-preacher, saving the sinners of his native county, Norfolk. He was soon in trouble with the Bishop of Norwich and in 1531 was burned. One of those who watched him die was Matthew Parker, then a boy but to become Archbishop of Canterbury under Elizabeth I.

Another future bishop deeply impressed by Bilney's holiness was a Cambridge colleague, Hugh Latimer, who had been stiff in a conservative Catholicism. Bilney reached him by making his confession to him as a priest, and years later Latimer was still extolling 'little Bilney, that blessed martyr of God'. Bilney's example strengthened Latimer to preach as a Protestant and to die as a martyr (in 1555).

Another martyr, urged by William Tyndale to 'remember Bilney', was John Frith, a product of Henry VI's two colleges at Eton and Cambridge. Because of his brilliant promise he was recruited by Wolsey for the staff of Cardinal College but, being suspected of Lutheran leanings, found himself imprisoned in its fish cellar. Others died there, but Frith escaped to become a Protestant propagandist, living in poverty, moving obscurely among the people. When arrested as a vagrant, he escaped again by talking Latin and Greek with the local schoolmaster. Imprisoned in the Tower of London, he still pamphleteered against Sir Thomas More in controversy about purgatory and the Mass, the manuscripts being smuggled for printing in Antwerp. He was burned for heresy in 1533 at the age of thirty, alongside a tailor's apprentice. His writings suggest that had he lived he would have become an intellectual, as well as a moral, leader of the English Reformation.

When Cardinal Wolsey presided at a great burning of Lutheran books one day in February 1526 an Augustinian friar, Robert Barnes, threw a faggot on the bonfire. He was attempting to satisfy the authorities, for in the little Cambridge church of St Edward on Christmas Eve he had preached a sermon against the worldliness of churchmen – a discourse which was not unnaturally interpreted as an attack on the cardinal; hence his penitence that February morning. But now the printing press was making Protestantism more than a matter of moral indignation which was soon overwhelmed by the authority of the Church. The printers made Luther's Gospel a 'safe stronghold' (as his own most famous hymn proclaimed God to be), and in 1526 another event took place, more decisive than the book-burning. In exile, William Tyndale completed the printing of his English translation of the New Testament. While living in London Barnes got hold of it, absorbed it and sold copies of it to others. Inspired by it, he eventually fled from England and became a Lutheran. He often had supper with Luther, who teased him as 'St Robert'. In 1535 he returned to England under the protection of the king, who was at that time trying to make allies in Germany. Thomas Cromwell employed him and even arranged an interview at which he tried to explain the Reformation to Henry VIII. But Henry never fully trusted him; he persisted in preaching the religion he had learned from Tyndale's New Testament and from the Lutheran lectures in Wittenberg; and in 1540, two days after Cromwell's own execution, he was burned with two other Protestants. At the stake he protested that he did not know for what heresies he had been condemned. He died, he said, a completely orthodox Christian.

William Tyndale, who had changed Barnes' life, was a man whose vocation it was to translate the Bible. As a student at Oxford and Cambridge he was disgusted by the conservatism of the theologians nicknamed the 'Trojans' but equipped himself with a knowledge of Greek. While chaplain to a Gloucestershire squire he was fired by the ambition to produce a New Testament for the English. He once shouted at a conservative with whom he had been arguing: 'If God spare my life, ere many years I will cause a boy that driveth the plough

to know more of Scripture than thou dost.' He sought the
patronage of the Bishop of London, but was snubbed. No
doubt the bishop – Cuthbert Tunstall, who had been cautiously encouraging to Erasmus – feared that he was now dealing with another Lollard, but actually Tyndale had little
admiration for the Lollard Bible; he disliked the Latinity still
to be found in the fourteenth-century English and wanted his
own version, based on the Greek as edited by Erasmus, to be
direct and dramatic, to reach that sixteenth-century plough-
boy.

　Eventually Tyndale escaped to Luther's Wittenberg. He
closely studied Luther's German translation of 1522 and when
his own New Testament appeared it included prefaces often
based on Luther's. That in itself was a fatal defect in the eyes
of Thomas More, who was also indignant about particular
translations. Words which More (soaked as he was in the Latin
Vulgate) would have translated as church, priest, confess and
do penance appeared in this new New Testament as congregation, senior, acknowledge and repent. Whatever might be
thought of such innovations in an English New Testament, at
least tribute might have been paid to the staggering intellectual and physical courage of Tyndale's undertaking. The
printing of the first edition of 1525 in Cologne (of which only
one fragment survives) was interrupted by a raid on the
printers, so that Tyndale had to resume work with a fresh
printer in Worms (producing an edition of three thousand of
which two copies remain). It is surely to his credit that,
although the authorities did their utmost to silence him, to
stop his book reaching England and to punish its readers, and
although he was in such a hurry, he achieved one of the most
influential feats of the mind in English history by his translation. It is usually reckoned that the 1611 Authorized (or
King James) Version of the English Bible did more than any
other book to shape the mind of the English-speaking world,
and that at least three-quarters of it was based on Tyndale. He
twice revised his New Testament translation (1534-35) as he
pondered the meaning of the original Greek – but not in ways
which pleased his Catholic critics.

　He also set out to translate the Old Testament, and completed it as far as 2 Chronicles. The first five books were published with provocative notes in Antwerp in 1530. He had immense handicaps in this task. He had to spend two years learning Hebrew (a language with which he fell in love, saying that 'the Hebrew tongue agreeth a thousand times more with the English than with the Latin') and then lost all his notes and money in a shipwreck. He was also distracted from his vocation by further controversy, against his fellow-exile George Joye as well as against the Catholic Thomas More. In one book, of 1528, he delighted Henry VIII by urging *The Obedience of a Christian Man*, only to infuriate him by denouncing his second marriage. His Old Testament work was incomplete when on the orders of the emperor he was burned as a heretic at Vilvorde near Brussels in 1536. But a letter he wrote to the prison governor asking for a Hebrew Bible, dictionary and grammar has survived and he looked forward to the day when his Bible would be finished and made the basis of an official English Bible. That was the meaning of his last prayer as given in John Foxe's *Book of Martyrs* (1563): 'Lord, open thou the King of England's eyes'.[52]

Within a year his prayer was granted. This was not surprising; seven years before, Henry had characteristically promised his people an English Bible when they started behaving well enough to deserve it. When Tyndale died an English version of the whole Bible had just been printed, probably in Zurich, and hopefully dedicated to the king. It was the work of Miles Coverdale, a Yorkshireman and formerly an Augustinian friar in Cambridge (and secretary to Robert Barnes). More recently Coverdale had assisted Tyndale himself, in a shared exile. Those parts of the Bible which Tyndale had not covered in published work were, however, based largely on the Latin, although helped by Luther's German. Coverdale had a good ear for music in the English language. One proof of this is that his translation of the psalms was incorporated into the first Book of Common Prayer in 1549 and (despite its frequent departures from the meaning of the Hebrew) remained in successive English prayer books until the twentieth century,

---

[52] See C. H. Williams, *William Tyndale* (London, 1969).

deeply loved. But he lacked Tyndale's mastery of Hebrew and Greek, and scholars close to Henry VIII such as Thomas Cranmer deplored this amateurishness. Less scholarly critics mocked the passage which claimed that Adam and Eve had used fig-leaves to make themselves trousers or 'breeches'. The English Bible which the king licensed for distribution in 1537 was therefore based largely on Tyndale's work; Coverdale's was used only for the books which Tyndale had not reached. This Bible was edited by John Rogers, a London parish priest who had become chaplain to the English merchants of Antwerp and who had obtained his friend Tyndale's unpublished manuscripts. The book was printed in Antwerp and was named 'Matthew's Bible' so as to conceal the identity of the editor. Rogers did not, however, deny himself the pleasure of including anti-Catholic comments. He was to become the first of the Protestant martyrs burned under Queen Mary.

Coverdale remained active, revising Matthew's Bible to become the Great Bible of 1539, splendidly printed in Paris and London and free of controversial comments. Later editions of this Great Bible, in 1540 and 1541, were 'overseen' by two conservative bishops (Tunstall and Heath) at the king's request; and 'one book of the whole Bible of the largest volume in English' was ordered to be available in every cathedral and parish church, where crowds of people gathered to hear readings from a book so long denied them. So the Holy Bible at last enjoyed Henry VIII's patronage. Thomas Cromwell was Coverdale's own patron in England, and after that minister's execution he worked quietly in Denmark and Bavaria. When Protestantism recovered the ascendancy he was called home to be Bishop of Exeter and, after a further exile on the restoration of Catholicism, enjoyed great popularity as a preacher under Elizabeth I.[53]

In his book of 1528 Tyndale had urged obedience to a Christian king – a theme frequent in English Christianity ever since King Ethelbert's baptism by St Augustine, but given a

---

[53] See J. F. Mozley, *William Tyndale* (London, 1937) and *Coverdale and His Bibles* (London, 1953), and S. L. Greenslade in *Cambridge History of the Bible*, vol. ii (Cambridge, 1963), pp.141-174.

new power. The need, he argued, was to end a situation in which 'emperors and kings are nothing nowadays but even hangmen unto the pope and bishops to kill whosoever they condemn without any more ado'. He claimed that, so far from preaching the overthrow of the government and the social order, those who wanted Christianity to be reformed on the basis of the plain, literal meaning of the Bible would be found to be the most loyal subjects of the king, rendering to Caesar the things that were Caesar's. Particularly would their enthusiasm overflow if Henry VIII gave the Bible to the people in the people's language. And the English Protestant who, more than any other, fulfilled Tyndale's prophecy was Thomas Cromwell.

Cromwell's early life is obscure, as is his personal religion; but somehow he developed the determination to construct under Henry VIII a commonwealth which would be biblical in its religion and rational in its government. Not only were the riches of the monasteries and the powers of the clergy over the laity to be ended in a revolution. Many other legacies of the Middle Ages were to be reformed away similarly – the often slack administration of the central offices of state and of the crown lands; the remaining separation of Wales from the English pattern of local government; the resistance of the men who controlled Ireland to orders from London; the 'liberties' and 'sanctuaries' which had meant that the king's justice did not run even throughout his English kingdom; the uncertainties about land ownership which had been the pretexts for much litigation and violence in the heyday of 'bastard' feudalism. Every birth in England was to be registered in the parents' parish church (this was one of the reforms which Cromwell was able to effect permanently), and until the registration of the burial that life was to be lived in peaceful work according to the commands of God and the king. The king's council was to be as benevolently active as was possible, fixing food prices, resisting any further conversion of arable land to sheep farming, encouraging exports. There was even a scheme which Cromwell accepted, but did not live to enact, for a ministry to organize employment (a Council to avoid Vagabonds), financed by an income tax. Parliament was to be an occasion not so much for the representation of local grievances as for the union of the people in the service of God as interpreted by the king.

Like his own master and teacher Wolsey, Cromwell rose to the top by sheer ability and capacity for work, and like Wolsey he was while in power the recipient of innumerable petitions for his favour (which, again like Wolsey, he liked to grant when possible). But unlike Wolsey he indulged in no personal pomp. All that was left to his royal master. His chosen instruments were words, quietly spoken in council, carefully written to his many agents, drafted and redrafted to make Acts of Parliament — words which would reshape a nation by a Reformation both religious and political.

Born about 1485, the son of a clothier in Putney who also kept an ale house, Cromwell later said that he had been a 'ruffian' in his youth. He is believed to have sought either adventure or escape from the English authorities as a mercenary soldier in Italy, but ended up as a minor merchant in Venice, Antwerp and London. He acquired some legal knowledge and built up a practice as an attorney for London merchants, but his main work in the 1520s was as Cardinal Wolsey's chief assistant, particularly in the suppression of small religious houses: a useful rehearsal for the larger drama of the 1530s. On Wolsey's fall he remained surprisingly loyal when all others fled; he cleared up his former master's affairs and did what he could to defend his interests with the king and the parliament. The king noticed Cromwell's ability more than this lingering loyalty, and had included him in his own council by the end of 1530. Once there, this former 'ruffian' was able to outstrip not only the Dukes of Norfolk and Suffolk, but also Sir Thomas More with his troublesome conscience, as well as Stephen Gardiner — a man about twelve years his junior who could well have been expected to be his political senior.

Gardiner was, like Cromwell, the son of a clothier, but his father was far more prosperous. In his youth he had mixed a salad for Erasmus while on a visit to Paris and had become a student and teacher of both civil and ecclesiastical law at Cambridge before entering Wolsey's service. He had gone to Rome to try to browbeat Pope Clement into compliance with the king's wish to get rid of Queen Catherine, and had been rewarded with the post of principal secretary to the king. The year 1531 found him Bishop of Winchester. Yet he had not been made Archbishop of Canterbury and was now politically eclipsed by Cromwell. The reason was not that Gardiner was opposed to the claim of Henry to be 'on earth supreme head of the Church of England'. In 1533 he wrote a book, *De Vera Obedientia*, to defend this title. But although Gardiner came to the same conclusion as Tyndale, it was from a very different starting point: the tradition of senior bishops serving the crown, a tradition going back to the Normans and even to the Anglo-Saxons. Although obedient, he had shown himself to be too medieval a figure, too much inclined to minimize what 'Supreme Head' might mean, too much the defender of the clergy.[54]

Radically new measures required a radically new minister – and a layman. In January 1535, therefore, Cromwell, who had already been responsible for the secular administration over a couple of years, was designated as the king's 'vicegerent in spirituals'. As Henry's deputy, his was now a legal power over the Church greater than the power which Wolsey had enjoyed as the pope's legate; and his authority symbolized the triumph of the laity by including doctrine in its scope. Letters poured out of Cromwell's office with instructions for archbishops, bishops and preachers – and with orders to sheriffs and justices of the peace to keep an eye on the clergy.

In the end religion – plus Stephen Gardiner's rivalry – was Thomas Cromwell's undoing. Jane Seymour's death in 1537 (having given birth to the future Edward VI) freed the king to marry a Continental princess. The way seemed open to making the dynasty as well as the nation thoroughly Protestant. Anne, sister of the Protestant Duke of Cleves in Germany, was selected as Henry's next bride. The way also seemed open to such despotism as was possible for a king with no large civil service, no standing army and now no real prospect of a revenue which would enable him to dispense with

---

[54] See S. E. Muller, *Stephen Gardiner and the Tudor Reaction* (London, 1926).

Parliament. There were executions of great Catholic aristocrats in England – a Percy and a Courtenay – suspected of
treason, and Parliament agreed that in future royal proclamations were to be obeyed as though they were Acts of Parliament. But Cromwell's policy to make the king and kingdom of
England Protestant now ran up against two problems: the
king's never-slumbering sexuality and his reawakened conscience as a Catholic.

Henry took an instant dislike to Anne of Cleves. Although
he went through with the marriage, he claimed that he found
himself with the new problem of being physically unable to
consummate it. Within a few days of the wedding he was
demanding another divorce. Not long before this disaster he
had already expressed the feeling that enough was enough by
way of religious reform. In June 1539 the Act of Six Articles
passed Parliament and was never repealed during the rest of
the reign. It had been agreed upon by the king and conservatives such as (among the laity) the Duke of Norfolk and
(among the clergy) Stephen Gardiner. It provided for the
burning of any heretic who denied the miracle of 'transubstantiation' in the Mass, and for the punishment of any who
asserted the necessity of giving the wine as well as the bread to
the laity. It ordered the laity still to confess their sins to priests,
and priests to remain unmarried or be hanged. Hugh Latimer
signalled the setback for Protestantism by resigning the
bishopric of Worcester.

In public Cromwell – like Cranmer, who sent his secret
wife, Margaret, away to Germany – took the blow as a loyal
subject. Privately he intrigued through a difficult winter. The
spring brought him an honour, the earldom of Essex. In May
the conservative but timid Bishop of Chichester was taken to
the Tower of London, to be examined for possible complicity
in a treasonable plot. All seemed set for another purge of the
Catholics. But the king, who had not authorized the bishop's
arrest, was now approached by the Duke of Norfolk and
Bishop Gardiner and told very different stories. Thomas
Cromwell, they argued persuasively, was himself a traitor –
and a heretic also. He was arrested in the council chamber
and the duke tore the Garter star from his neck. Parliament

(including Cranmer in the House of Lords) obligingly sentenced both him and his theological favourite, Robert Barnes, to death at the king's pleasure; and having been spared long enough to provide sordid details which could be used in divorcing Anne of Cleves, he was executed on 28 July. He was the victim of the terror which he had wielded against the enemies of the Reformation. But his fall also reflected that terror's inadequacy. He had been unable to kill off Catholicism (just as those now temporarily triumphant were to be unable to kill off Protestantism). He died, he said, 'in the Catholic faith of the Holy Church'. He would have shown more of his customary attention to detail if he had acknowledged that he died the victim of the Catholic faith's continuing hold on the hearts of the English.[55]

But because England was still so largely Catholic even in 1540, it would be wrong to end this story with the personal dramas of Protestants. We shall learn more about England in this age of the sudden storm if we look at three people whose piety, although lay, was definitely Catholic — Margery Kempe, William Caxton and Thomas More.

MARGERY KEMPE

Margery Kempe's autobiography was unknown until 1936 apart from the publication of eight pages by the printer Wynkin de Worde in 1501. When the manuscript came to light it turned out to be an early copy of what she had begun to dictate to a priest in 1436. She had had an earlier

[55] The best introductions are A. G. Dickens, *Thomas Cromwell and the English Reformation* (London, 1959), and B. W. Beckingsale, *Thomas Cromwell* (London, 1978). G. R. Elton has supplied more detailed studies in his trilogy: *The Tudor Revolution in Government* (Cambridge, 1953): *Policy and Police: The Enforcement of the Reformation in the Age of Thomas Cromwell* (Cambridge, 1972); *Reform and Renewal: Thomas Cromwell and the Common Weal* (Cambridge, 1973).

draft — compiled by a man who, she complained, could not write English — read back to her.[56]

She was very frank about her nervous breakdown after the birth of her first child in her twentieth year; the failure of her attempts to run a brewery and a horse-mill in order to pay for her extravagant tastes as a young married woman; her sensuality (she had fourteen children) which turned into a fixed refusal of sexual relations with her husband or anyone else (she was 'ever afraid of being ravished'). When she had to nurse her incontinent husband for several sordid years before he died, she was sure she deserved it after all the carnal delights of their marriage. She told of her journeys to learn more of religion — to Rome, Jerusalem and Compostella in Spain. More locally, she went to Norwich; there she talked with Mother Julian, who told her that 'the Holy Ghost moveth ne'er a thing against charity, for if he did he would be contrary to his own self for he is all charity'. She was herself not all charity; she sturdily spoke her mind. When the Archbishop of York, scenting heresy in her independence, told her 'I hear it said that thou art a right wicked woman', she replied: 'I also hear it said that ye are a wicked man.' When the Archbishop of Canterbury (Arundel) had kept her waiting among his servants she rebuked him for employing men who swore so much. She talked with him about his soul and hers in the garden of Lambeth Palace until the stars came out. When the monks tried to silence her as she wept 'nearly all day' in Canterbury Cathedral itself, she argued back. She was still indignant when she rejoined her husband who had retreated to their lodgings. She was a constant worshipper in her parish church of St Margaret in King's (then Bishop's) Lynn. She obtained special permission to receive the Holy Communion each Sunday. Although her parish priests cannot have welcomed her outbursts of tears when she saw a crucifix or heard a sermon about the Lord's sufferings, they were perhaps encouraged when she received a vision telling St Margaret's not to give in to pressure from its daughter-church (the chapel of St Nicholas) for the right to baptize infants and receive the fees.

[56] *The Book of Margery Kempe*, ed. W. Butler-Bowdon (London, 1936).

She was delighted when she came across a priest willing to read to her, over eight years, from the Bible and from mystics such as Rolle and Hilton. Her own book shows how carefully she listened and remembered – but, also, that she attached more significance to her frequent 'dalliance' with Christ and his mother.

The first of these conversations began typically: 'Jesus, of what shall I think?' The reply was: 'Daughter, think of my mother. . . .' She did not need to travel from Lynn to Bethlehem to be close to that family; and from her 'dalliance' with it in her prayers a homely religion grew strong. She prayed for her neighbours and gave them advice and practical help, with unceasing energy. She loved to see 'the Precious Sacrament borne about the town with lights and reverence, the people kneeling' – but would set up a different kind of cry if in the street she saw a child or horse being beaten. In her book we meet not only her invincible personality but also her conventional faith. Cross-examined at Leicester about her attitude to the Mass, she gave an outline of lay orthodoxy: 'Sirs, I believe in the Sacrament of the Altar on this wise; that whatever man hath taken the order of priesthood, be he ever so vicious a man in his living, if he say duly those words over the bread, that Our Lord Jesus Christ said when he made his Maundy among his disciples, where he sat at the Supper, I believe that it is his very flesh and his blood, and no material bread; and never may it be unsaid, be it once said.' She triumphed against many accusations that she was a Lollard, and we may suspect that she enjoyed winning the debates with men as well as the privilege of suffering with Christ. The Archbishop of York's steward once pompously rebuked her: 'Holy folk should not laugh.' 'Sir', she retorted, 'I have great cause to laugh, for the more shame I suffer, and despite, the merrier I may be in our Lord Jesus Christ'.

For all her 'nerves' and flamboyant eccentricity Margery Kempe did, it seems, win through to some of the happiness of the saints. We are told by her scribe that 'by process of time, her mind and her thought were so joined to God that she never forgot him, but continually had mind of him and beheld him in all creatures'. That does not sound like hysteria. And she won this vision of God by using what the medieval Church offered, despite all her defiance of bourgeois conventions. Her religion was based on her own parish church, she loved the Mass, she believed in it, she poured out her soul to priests, she delighted in pilgrimages, the Church's heaven came to be more real and more attractive to her than her own husband and children.

WILLIAM CAXTON

No development was more important than printing in the destruction of the faith accepted by Margery Kempe and millions like her. Printing was what enabled Martin Luther to bombard his enemies rapidly and effectively. Printed books spread Luther's doctrines through the English ports such as Lynn, as almost two centuries earlier the ships' rats had spread the Black Death — and one great difference between the new age and the age of Wyclif was that now the Church found it futile to excommunicate a heretic whose thoughts had been printed. The burning of books, even the burning of their authors, could not destroy whole editions; suppressing them by buying them up (which was the gentle Warham's policy when he had to act as Archbishop of Canterbury) merely financed new editions; and police vigilance in the ports, backed up by very severe penalties for those caught with forbidden books, could not keep England completely free of the pestilential literature. Yet William Caxton who brought printing to England seems to have accepted the faith of the medieval Church as thoroughly as Margery Kempe herself. When the churchwardens of St Margaret's, Westminster, paid for the use of four torches and the tolling of the bell at his burial in 1491 they were honouring a fellow-parishioner who had been regular at worship and who had given some of the many devotional books printed at his press for sale to help church funds.

Caxton tells us something of his own life in his history of Troy. (This was the first book he translated and the first he

printed, in Bruges in 1475; it had been commissioned by
Margaret, Duchess of Burgundy and sister of Edward IV, no
doubt because it was believed that Britain had been founded
by a refugee from Troy, one Brutus.) He had been brought up
in Kent but had 'continued by the space of thirty years for the
most part in the countries of Brabant, Flanders, Holland and
Flanders'. He had been a businessman engaged in the export
of English cloth and of anything else that would sell and had
risen to be 'governor' of the English merchants at Bruges. It
was when he lost that well-paid official post in 1471, and had
to set up on his own, that he saw the potential in printing – an
art which had been invented in the 1430s and then developed
by the genius of Johann Gutenberg of Mainz. Caxton learned
printing in Cologne and, having gained confidence, set up a
press and a shop in Westminster in 1476.

His shop backed on the monks' chapter house in Westminster Abbey and confronted the door into the great church
used by those whose work lay in the royal palace and the law
courts. No site could have been more convenient for his
purposes. He printed and published (and when necessary
translated) books to entertain courtiers and other laymen. His
Canterbury Tales and his *Morte d'Arthur* were only the
biggest volumes in a stream of publications which appealed to
memories of the Age of Chivalry and to other aristocratic (or
would-be-aristocratic) tastes. The contents of these books were
old-fashioned because that was what his lay patrons wanted.
One of the first books which he printed in England was a collection of the sayings of the ancient philosophers translated by
the queen's brother, Lord Rivers. But his religious publications were equally old-fashioned, because that was what
the Church encouraged. The first document which he printed
in England was an 'indulgence' from the pope to those who
contributed to a projected crusade; and his biggest book in the
religious field – 600,000 words of it, which he translated from
Latin and French while Richard III was king and while
Edward IV's widow was hiding in sanctuary in the abbey a few
yards away – was a collection of saints' lives for reading in
church or privately, the *Golden Legend* ('legend' meaning
simply 'reading').

He remained a businessman who knew his market, but his enthusiasm, shown in the prefaces he wrote for many of the books he issued, is such as to prevent us supposing that his kind of publishing went against the grain. It is probable that the manual labour of printing was something he only supervised; but the chivalrous and clerical culture of his time fired him with the willingness to undergo the ill-paid labours of a translator.[57]

THOMAS MORE

When Caxton died, Thomas More was aged thirteen – a page in the household of the Archbishop of Canterbury, Cardinal Morton. His adult life can be recounted as the uncomplicated story of a martyr for the Catholic Church in England; and no storyteller's art is needed to make it moving.[58] Even people who neither share his faith nor understand it readily admire the cool courage he showed at his trial and execution in 1535 'in and for the faith of the Holy Catholic Church'. He was 'the king's good servant but God's first' – those words of his on the scaffold rang through his Europe and have echoed clearly into a world with few of the landmarks he knew. He died on 6 July, the eve of the feast of the 'translation' of the body of St Thomas of Canterbury to his final shrine. When taunted at his trial that his refusal to accept Henry VIII as 'Supreme Head' of the English Church had put him in a minority against the bishops, the king's council and Parliament itself, he appealed to the Catholic consensus of a thousand years. In Westminster Hall, the scene of so much that had happened in the Middle Ages, he told his successor as chancellor: 'If I should speak of those that are already dead, of whom many be now holy saints

---

[57] See G. D. Painter, *William Caxton* (London, 1976).

[58] But tribute should be paid to the art as well as to the scholarship of R. W. Chambers, *Thomas More* (London, 1935), a biography which has this theme. See also a Roman Catholic writer's tribute to St Thomas: E. E. Reynolds, *The Field is Won* (London, 1968).

in heaven, I am very sure that it is the greater part of them that, all the while they lived, thought in this case the way that I think now; and therefore am I not bounden, my Lord, to conform my conscience to the council of one realm against the General Council of Christendom. For of the foresaid holy bishops I have, for every bishop of yours, above one hundred; and for one council or Parliament of yours (God knoweth what manner of one), I have all the councils made these thousand years. And for this one kingdom, I have all other Christian realms.'

Somehow More found time to be a prolific controversialist in defence of the faith of the Catholic Church.[59] He stated (and no one denied) that he had edited the material which various 'makers' had assembled so that Henry VIII could win honour for his book against Luther. He replied to Simon Fish's anticlerical pamphlet with a *Supplication of Souls* urging the claims of the dead in purgatory to have their souls remembered by the pious. He wrote other, far larger, more scurrilous and more dreary books against Luther, Tyndale and the other heretics who had wickedly disturbed the peace of Christendom; he was specially licensed to read their works by Cuthbert Turnstall, then Bishop of London, in 1528. In these replies he was the lawyer appealing to a jury – playing to the gallery with homely humour, blackening his opponents' reputations, twisting their arguments so that they made nonsense, defending his own side whether or not it was fully defensible. While chancellor he prided himself on being the enemy of heretics as well as of murderers and thieves; he said so on the epitaph which he wrote when he expected to be buried in Chelsea Old Church. And being the enemy of heretics meant, in some cases, doing all that a lay judge could do to make sure they were burned. This frantic activity resulted from his indignation against the Protestantism of the 1520s, but his personal religion was not a late development. As a young man he had made his home for 'three years or more' among the strict Carthusian monks, wondering all the time whether or not it

---

[59] See R. Pineas, *Thomas More and Tudor Polemics* (Bloomington, Ind., 1968).

was his vocation to be a priest. In the end he had decided that he did not have a vocation to remain unmarried, although his family lived a semi-monastic life as they grew up. He was a model Catholic layman, attending Mass daily, singing in his parish church's choir (even while Lord Chancellor), using a block of wood as a pillow, wearing a hair shirt.

Yet More's martyrdom was of a kind different from the other executions of those who refused to swear the oath about the royal supremacy in 1535.

John Fisher died as an old, weary and sick bishop, who was probably not sorry when the pope's defiant gesture in making him a cardinal precipitated his death. It was said that he looked like a skeleton when he went to his execution. He had heard the confessions of Henry VII and had preached at his funeral. He had taught the faith of the Church for so many years during and since the days when he had dominated Cambridge that he had no mind to dissimulate when the loathsome Solicitor-General, Richard Rich, came to his prison. Rich claimed that the king had sent him to ask him as a priest about the theological and ethical correctness of the new title; and with his reply 'that the king was not, nor could be, by the Law of God, Supreme Head on earth of the Church of England' Fisher signed – and knew that he was signing – his own death warrant.[60] More, in contrast, was far more subtle in refusing to incriminate himself. When at his trial Rich reported a roughly similar conversation which he had had with him, More accused his accuser of perjury and tore his character into ribbons. Richard Rich had tried to trick the cleverest lawyer of the day.

Thomas More was with his daughter, the beloved 'Meg', as they watched the priors of three Carthusian monasteries being dragged in their habits on wattle hurdles to excrutiatingly painful deaths. He told her to note that they were as cheerful as bridegrooms, because they were being taken to heaven. He had, he added, been so worldly that he did not deserve the same reward. And in a sense what he said was true. The three priors, John Houghton, Robert Lawrence and Augustine

---

[60] See E. Surtz, *The Works and Days of John Fisher* (London, 1967).

Webster, were contemplative monks with simple convictions, remote from the world's intrigues, pure in their silence and austerity.[61] So were the other Carthusian monks who were chained to posts and left to starve to death in the Tower of London while More was a prisoner there. The only human kindness they experienced as they died was shown by More's adopted daughter Margaret Giggs, who, disguised as a milk-maid, made some courageous visits to put meat into their mouths and to wash the filth off their bodies.

More's life, when he had decided not to join the Carthusians, took him far from their great simplicity of faith and life. He freely acknowledged that for much of his life he had thought the pope's authority to be of human origin, 'for the more quietness of the ecclesiastical body'. He knew perfectly well how unspiritual the popes of his time were, and had urged King Henry to tone down his praise of the papacy in his book against Luther. He once confessed that he had not seriously studied the papacy's theological claims until 1524; but after his one youthful fling as a Member of Parliament opposing Henry VII in 1504, he knew all the arguments for obeying the king – and accepted almost all of them. He had been Henry VIII's courtier from 1517 to 1532, often discussing the classics or the stars or theology or politics with his master; frequently summoned to the royal supper table for light conversation; entrusted with many important missions. Indeed, he accepted the great post of chancellor from Henry at a time when he knew that the king was resolved to marry again and would not be able to keep for ever his promise not to involve him in this 'great matter'. He kept that post through two and a half years, and revealed that he had many sleepless nights before at last deciding to defy his king at one point. There was, it is clear, a long, secret battle in his conscience before he was able to tell William Roper, as they rowed him from his home in Chelsea to the crucial examination in Lambeth Palace about his attitude to the royal supremacy: 'I thank our Lord, the field is won.'

---

[61] See David and Gervase Matthew, *The Reformation and the Contemplative Life* (London, 1934).

What makes Thomas More worthy to stand at the end of the line of the saints of England up to the Reformation is that he was acutely aware of the defects left in Church and State after the Christian centuries. He was not a simple martyr.

He was always the friend of Erasmus and was for many years his most reliable supporter. It was in his house that, returning bitterly disillusioned from the Rome of Pope Julius II in the summer of 1509, Erasmus wrote *Moriae Encomium*, 'the Praise of Folly', with all its satire on monks and theologians; and it was he who wrote to warn Erasmus that a copy of *Julius Exclusus*, the more severe lampoon on the worldly pope, had been found in the scholar's own handwriting. His own first book was an admiring translation of a short *Life* of the Florentine nobleman, Pico della Mirandola, whose beliefs had been more Platonist than Catholic. He did not write much in his twenties or thirties, despite his intimate association with scholars such as Grocyn, Linacre and Lily who were bringing to England a love of Greek literature in its original language; but this silence as an author was due to his busy involvement in legal and other work in the City of London. It is clear from the records that he was a lawyer thoroughly trusted by the city merchants, as his father was before him.

It is also clear from his *Utopia*, which he began to write in 1515 in the intervals of negotiations on behalf of the City of London with the merchants of Flanders, that he nursed radical thoughts. He had no respect for rich abbies; although there were 'gorgeous' churches and monks in Utopia, the monks there had no wealth. Nor did he have any respect for money-making landlords; in Utopia there was no private property. No money was used within the country, gold being thought suitable to make chains. Nostalgia for the Age of Chivalry — the widespread emotion which had brought fame to Malory and profit to Caxton — More treated with con-temptuous silence. He did not even have much respect left for the grasping colleagues with whom he had worked; in Utopia there were no lawyers and very few merchants, because such men were not needed by the Utopians as they moved about their prosperous family farms or spacious cities in uniforms of undyed cloth like Franciscan friars' habits. Added later, the first book of *Utopia* showed what were the ideals with which More now entered the king's service after many heart-searchings. It was written around an indignant picture of the miseries of the English poor. Although he had accepted the role of a subordinate to Wolsey he hated the cardinal's arrogant magnificence as much as he hated the wars he launched, and when he replaced Wolsey as chancellor he openly expressed that hatred to Parliament. Compliments to the cardinal are also on record from the period of Wolsey's power. They were no doubt a courtier's flattery, justified in More's conscience only by the thought of the justice over which the cardinal presided and by the wish to get more actively involved in that justice. A philosopher entering the service of a king whom he still trusted, More aspired to bring justice to the English poor – and wealth to their country by peaceful industry and trade.

When he wrote *Utopia*, he wanted to hold up a mirror to a nation 'where they speak still of the commonwealth, but every man procureth his own private gain'. So he had to use discretion. That was why the book took the form of a conversation with a Portuguese explorer in a garden at Antwerp, remained in Latin until 1551, and was presented as an entertainment almost in the same class as Amerigo Vespucci's recent account of his transatlantic discoveries. The ambiguity of the dialogue, the appeal in Latin to scholars only (More declared that it would be better to burn the book than to translate it), and the flippancy ('many things be in the Utopian weal public, which in our cities I may rather wish for than hope after') – all these devices provided a protective smokescreen which was effective then and has been effective since. C. S. Lewis wrote: 'All seem to be agreed that it is a great book, but hardly any two agree as to its real significance; we approach it through a cloud of contradictory eulogies. . . . If it were intended as a serious treatise it would be very confused indeed.'[62] Lewis reckoned *Utopia* 'a holiday work, a spontaneous overflow of intellectual high spirits'; but it is also

---

[62] C. S. Lewis, *English Literature in the Sixteenth Century* (Oxford, 1954), pp.167-9.

possible, and more convincing, to regard More's intention as fundamentally serious, the overflow of his ideals now that he was for a few months released from the daily pressure of law and business in London.[63]

He did not judge the social evils of his time by the traditional teaching of the medieval Church. In the imaginary island which he created to be a contrast with Tudor England there were no guilds of tradesmen or merchants any more than there were orders of knighthood, although such groups had been among the medieval Church's chief instruments in regulating society. Only the monarchy and the family were left standing (but the prince could be deposed for tyranny). Most of the inhabitants of the island were not even Christians. What regulated Utopia was reason — specially the reasoning that 'there is a certain godly power unknown, everlasting, incomprehensible, inexplicable, far above the capacity and reach of man's wit'. In Utopia this led to practices, such as euthanasia and divorce, of which More no doubt disapproved as a good Catholic; whether as a Catholic he would have felt obliged to condemn the strict family planning practised in Utopia is more difficult to say. But his serious purpose, amid a certain amount of not always serious provocation, was to stimulate Christians into thinking out what was reasonable, not what was traditional, for Christendom. And when he appealed to 'reason' More had in mind the Sermon on the Mount, not the cynicism of power politics as expounded in Italy by his contemporary, Niccolo Machiavelli.

More did not keep the ideals expressed or implied in *Utopia* untarnished. As Speaker of the House of Commons in Wolsey's Parliament of 1523 he found himself pleading for taxes. His treatment of heretics while chancellor did not completely accord with the Utopians' hatred of violence in religious disputes — although even in Utopia there was no toleration for those who denied the existence of God or the immortality of the soul, while the punishment for a moral offence such as

---

[63] See R. Ames. *Citizen Thomas More and His Utopia* (Princeton, N.J., 1949), and J. H. Hexter. *The Vision of Politics on the Eve of the Reformation* (London, 1973).

adultery was first enslavement (there were many slaves) and, after a second offence, death. But during his imprisonment in the Tower of London he wrote short books, letters and prayers; and in them compromise was forgotten and the violence of the polemical style he had used against the Protestants dropped away.

He wrote a *Dialogue of Comfort against Tribulation*, again diplomatically distancing the scene from England; this time two Hungarian Christians were strengthening themselves from the Bible against 'the terror of shameful and painful death' at the hands of the Turks. He wrote in Latin an exposition of Christ's passion in the medieval style, halted when his writing materials were taken away from him. He then wrote letters to his family with charcoal from his fire: letters as tender and as noble as can be found in the literature of true heroism. By constant meditation on Christ's agony in Gethsemane and sufferings on Calvary, he made his soul ready for the end which was (he said several times) the entry into being 'merry in heaven'. He was, as he knew, now in a realm purer than religious controversy. When a group of rich clergymen had offered him a large sum after his resignation as chancellor as a reward for his anti-Protestant books, he had refused the money, declaring that people would be better off reading books such as Hilton's *Ladder of Perfection* or the more recent *Imitation of Christ*. But unexpectedly this lawyer and courtier, this friend of Erasmus and author of *Utopia*, was high on the ladder of Christlike perfection while preparing to mount the scaffold as a martyr for that in which he really believed.

More's prison writings, and above all his conduct at his trial and execution, may therefore be said to be the climax of the story of Christian England to the Reformation. And he has been remembered – by those who have revered him as a Catholic martyr; by those who have more highly valued his *Utopia*; by those who have been impressed most by the fact that the head which conceived *Utopia* was placed voluntarily on the executioner's block for the sake of an ideal not in *Utopia*. He was respected as a courageous Christian gentleman even at the height of Protestant patriotism. Three pages almost certainly in Shakespeare's handwriting form part of a sympathetic play, *Sir Thomas More*. As translated into English by Ralph Robinson in 1551, More wrote that the Utopians 'suppose the dead to be present among them when they talk of them, though to the dull and feeble eyesight of mortal men they be invisible. . . . Therefore they go more courageously to their business . . .'[64]

---

[64] J. J. Scarisbrick, *The Reformation and the English People* (Oxford, 1984), summed up many local studies magisterially. Endorsing the thesis there expounded, Christopher Haigh, *The English Reformation Revised* (Cambridge, 1987), collected essays by himself and other scholars which tended to stress the continuity of the Catholic religion through the sudden storm of the Reformation. In contrast with Margaret Bowker's analysis of a conservative bishop's steady work in *The Henrician Reformation: the Diocese of Lincoln under John Longland, 1521-47* (Cambridge, 1981), David Starkey studied the devastation of the medieval Church resulting from the ups and downs of factions at court in *The Reign of Henry VIII* (London, 1985). Against this background J. A. Guy has re-examined *The Public Career of Sir Thomas More* (Brighton, 1980), and Richard Marius has supplied a new biography of *Thomas More* (New York, 1984).

PART TWO: FURTHER READING
(in addition to the books in the footnotes)

4. Freedom under the King

BARLOW, F., *The English Church, 1066-1154*, London, 1979.

BROOKE, Z. N., *The English Church and the Papacy from the Conquest to the Reign of John*, London, 1968.

CANTOR, N. F., *Church, Kingship and Lay Investiture in England, 1089-1135*, Princeton, N.J., 1958.

DOUGLAS, C., *William the Conqueror*, London, 1964.
The Norman Achievement, 1050-1100, London, 1969.
The Norman Fate, 1100-1154, London, 1976.

LE PATOUREL, J., *The Norman Empire*, Oxford, 1976.

POOLE, A. L., *From Domesday Book to Magna Carta*, Oxford, 1951.

SOUTHERN, R. W., *The Making of the Middle Ages*, London, 1953.

WARREN, W. L., *King John*, London, 1961.

5 The Age of Faith

BATSFORD, H., and FRY, C., *The Cathedrals of England* (architectural), revised, London, 1960.

BOASE, T. S. R., *English Art, 1100-1216*, Oxford, 1953.

BRENTANO, R., *Two Churches: England and Italy in the Thirteenth Century*, Princeton, N.J., 1968.

BROOKE, R. B. *The Coming of the Friars*, London, 1975.

CLAPHAM, A. W., *English Romanesque Architecture after the Conquest*, Oxford, 1934.

COLVIN, H. M., *The White Canons in England*, Oxford, 1951.

CLANCHY, M. T., *England and its Rulers 1066-1272*, (London, 1983).

EDWARDS, K., *The English Secular Cathedrals in the Middle Ages* (their life), Manchester, 1949.

GIBBS, M., and LANG, J., *Bishops and Reform, 1215-72*, Oxford, 1935.

HILL, B., *English Cistercian Monasteries and their Patrons in the Twelfth Century*, Urbana, Ill., 1968.

HINNESBUSCH, W. A., *The Early English Friars Preachers*, Rome, 1951.

MOORMAN, J. R. H., *Church Life in England in the Thirteenth Century*, Cambridge, 1945.

A History of the Franciscan Order, Oxford, 1968.

MORRIS, R., *Cathedrals and Abbeys of England and Wales*, London, 1979.

ROTH, F., *The English Austin Friars*, 2 vols., New York, 1961-66.

SOUTHERN, R. W., *Western Society and the Church in the Middle Ages*, London, 1970.

WOOD, S., *English Monasteries and their Patrons in the Thirteenth Century*, Oxford, 1955.

WOOD-LEGH, K. L., *Perpetual Chantries in Britain*, Cambridge, 1965.

6 Rebels and Pilgrims

BENNET, H. S., *Chaucer and the Fifteenth Century*, Oxford, 1947.

BROWN, C. (ed.), *Religious Lyrics of the Fourteenth Century*, revised, Oxford, 1952.

HILTON, R., *Bond Men Made Free: Medieval Peasant Movements and the English Uprising of 1381*, London, 1973.

HUSSEY, S. S., *Chaucer: An Introduction*, London, 1971.

KEEN, M. H., *England in the Later Middle Ages*, London, 1973.

KNOWLES, D., *The English Mystical Tradition*, London 1961.

LAWLOR, J., *Piers Plowman: An Essay in Criticism,*, London, 1962.

McFARLANE, K. B., *John Wyclif and the Beginnings of English Nonconformity*, London, 1952.

McKISACK, M., *The Fourteenth Century*, Oxford, 1959.

MATTHEW, G., *The Court of Richard II*, London, 1968.

OWST, G. R., *Literature and Pulpit in Medieval England*, revised, Cambridge, 1961.

PANTIN, W. A., *The English Church in the Fourteenth Century*, Cambridge, 1955.

PEARSALL, D., *Piers Plowman by William Langland*, London, 1979.

SALTER, E., *Piers Plowman: An Introduction*, Oxford, 1969.

SISAM, K. (Ed.), *Fourteenth Century Verse and Prose*, Oxford, 1921.

TRISTRAM, E. W., *English Wall Painting of the Fourteenth Century*, London, 1955.

VASTA, E. (ed.), *Interpretations of Piers Plowman*, Notre Dame, Ind., 1968.

WOOD-LEGH, K. L., *Church Life in England under Edward III*, Cambridge, 1934.

ZIEGLER, P., *The Black Death*, London, 1969.

7 The Sudden Storm

ASTON, M. E., *Thomas Arundel*, Oxford, 1967.

BENNET, H. S., *English Books and Readers, 1475-1557*, Cambridge, 1952.

BLECH, J. W., *Preaching in England in the Late Fifteenth and Sixteenth Centuries*, Oxford, 1964.

CHRIMES, S. B., *Henry VII*, London, 1972.

DU BOULAY, F. R. H., *An Age of Ambition: English Society in the Later Middle Ages*, London, 1970.

ELTON, G. R., *Reform and Reformation: England, 1509-58*, London, 1977.

HAIGH, C., *The Last Days of the Lancashire Monasteries and the Pilgrimage of Grace*, Manchester, 1964.

HOSKINS, W. G., *The Age of Plunder: King Henry's England, 1500-47*, London, 1976.

JACOB, E. F., *The Fifteenth Century*, revised, Oxford, 1969.

MACKIE, J. D., *The Earlier Tudors, 1485-1558*, Oxford, 1952.

McCONICA, J. K., *English Humanists and Reformation Politics*, Oxford, 1965.

PORTER, H. C., *Reformation and Reaction in Tudor Cambridge*, Cambridge, 1958.

ROSS, C., *Edward IV*, London, 1974.

RUPP, E. G., *Studies in the Making of the English Protestant Tradition*, Cambridge, 1947.

SMITH, L. B., *Tudor Prelates and Politics*, Princeton, N.J., 1953.

STOREY, R. L., *Diocesan Administration in Fifteenth Century England*, York, 1959.

General

BETJEMAN, J. (ed.), *Collins Guide to English Parish Churches*, London, 1958.

BLAKE, N. F. (ed.), *Middle English Religious Prose*, London, 1972.

BUTLER, L. H., and WILSON, C. G., *Medieval Monasteries of England*, London, 1979.

DAVIES, R. T. (ed.), *Medieval English Lyrics*, London, 1963.

DICKINSON, J. C., *The Later Middle Ages*, London, 1979.

FINUCARE, R., *Miracles and Pilgrims*, London, 1977.

GRAY, D., *Themes and Images in the Medieval English Religious Lyric*, London, 1972.

HARRISON, F. L., *Music in Medieval Britain*, London, 1958.

KNOWLES, D., *The Religious Orders in England*, 3 vols., Cambridge, 1948-59.

LAURENCE, C. H. (ed.), *The English Church and the Papacy in the Middle Ages*, London, 1965.

MYERS, A. R. (ed.), *English Historical Documents, 1327-1485*, London, 1969.

ORME, N., *English Schools in the Middle Ages*, London, 1973.

POSTAN, M. M., *The Medieval Economy and Society*, London, 1972.

REYNOLDS, S., *English Medieval Towns*, Oxford, 1977.

RICKERT, M., *Painting in Britain: The Middle Ages*, London, 1964.

RODES, R. E., *Ecclesiastical Administration in Medieval England*, Notre Dame, Ind., 1977.

STONE, B., *Medieval English Verse* (translated in Penguin Classics), London, 1971.

SUMPTION, J., *Pilgrimage: An Image of Medieval Religion*, London, 1974.

ULLMANN, W., *A Short History of the Papacy in the Middle Ages*, revised, London, 1974.

WEBB, G., *Architecture in Britain: The Middle Ages*, London, 1956.

WOODFORDE, C., *English Stained and Painted Glass*, Oxford, 1954.

WOOLF, R., *The English Religious Lyric in the Middle Ages*, Oxford, 1968.

The English Mystery Plays, London, 1972.

Outline of Events

c. 200	'Parts of Britain conquered by Christ' (Tertullian)
c. 208	Martyrdom of St Alban
306	Constantine proclaimed emperor in York
314	British bishops at Council of Arles
c. 375	Anglo-Saxon settlements begun
410	Honorius tells Britons to defend themselves
c. 425	St Patrick made bishop for Ireland
429	St Germanus in controversy against Pelagians
c. 450	St Ninian's mission to Picts
461	Bishop Mansuetus at Council of Tours – from Brittany?
c. 500	Celtic monastery founded in Tintagel
c. 518	Arthur's victory at Badon Hill?
c. 550	Gildas writes on *Ruin and Conquest of Britain*
c. 570	Anglo-Saxon victory
597	St Augustine preaches in Kent; St Columba dies on Iona
627	St Paulinus baptizes King Edwin
c. 635	St Aidan preaches in Northumbria; St Felix in East Anglia
c. 650	Missions to West Saxons and Mercians
664	Synod of Whitby accepts Catholic Easter
668	St Theodore Archbishop of Canterbury
c. 675	St Etheldreda at Ely; St Hilda and Caedmon at Whitby
687	St Cuthbert's death
c. 695	*Lindisfarne Gospels*
710	St Wilfrid's death; West Saxons reach Glastonbury
731	Bede completes *Ecclesiastical History of English People*
c. 750	*Dream of the Rood; Beowulf*; Cynewulf's poetry
775	Martyrdom of St Boniface
782	Alcuin begins work for Charlemagne
793	Vikings sack Lindisfarne
878	King Alfred at baptism of Guthrum the Dane

937	King Athelstan's victory at Brunanburh
937	King Edgar's coronation at Bath by St Dunstan
1012	Martyrdom of St Alphege
1014	Wulfstan's sermon in York
1035	Death of King Cnut
1065	Death of St Edward the Confessor
1066	William the Conqueror's victory near Hastings
1070	Lanfranc Archbishop of Canterbury
1093	St Anselm Archbishop of Canterbury; Durham Cathedral begun
1147	St Ailred Abbot of Rievaulx
1170	Martyrdom of Archbishop (St) Thomas Becket
1174	Fire leads to rebuilding of Canterbury Cathedral
1186	St Hugh of Avalon Bishop of Lincoln
1214	Oxford University chartered
1215	*Magna Carta*; Lateran Council's reforms
1220	Salisbury Cathedral begun
1221	Dominicans reach England
1224	Franciscans reach England
1235	Robert Grosseteste Bishop of Lincoln
c. 1240	West front of Wells Cathedral
c. 1260	Five Sisters window in York Minster
1269	Westminster Abbey rebuilt by Henry III
c. 1280	Angel Choir of Lincoln Cathedral
1292	Death of Roger Bacon
1327	Death of Edward II leads to Perpendicular choir at Gloucester
1343	Richard Rolle completes *The Fire of Love*
1348	Black Death reaches England
1351	Statute of *Provisors*, followed by *Praemunire*
1363	William of Wykeham Edward III's chief minister
1373	'Showings' to Dame Julian of Norwich
c. 1375	*Gawain* poet at work
1377	Coronation of Richard II
1381	Peasants' Revolt
1384	Death of John Wyclif
1386	Geoffrey Chaucer begins *Canterbury Tales*
c. 1390	William Langland completes *Piers Plowman*
1401	Statute for burning Lollards

1415 Henry V's victory at Agincourt
1441 Henry VI founds King's College, Cambridge
1461 Death of Bishop Reginald Pecock
1483 Edward IV buried in St George's Chapel, Windsor
1485 Henry VII's victory at Bosworth; Caxton's edition
      of Malory
1514 Thomas Wolsey Henry VIII's chief minister
1525 William Tyndale's New Testament in English
1531 Martyrdom of Thomas Bilney
1533 Thomas Cranmer Archbishop of Canterbury
1534 Henry VIII legally Supreme Head of Church
1535 Martyrdom of Sir (St) Thomas More
1536 Suppression of monasteries begins
1537 Matthew's Bible in English authorized
1540 Execution of Thomas Cromwell

INDEX

Volume Two

FROM THE REFORMATION TO THE EIGHTEENTH CENTURY

Contents

Preface: From Medieval to Early Modern

In the sixteenth century Protestants and Roman Catholics all adhered to the Christian religion although in England governments bearing those names persecuted 'traitors' or 'heretics' in conflicts which were a mixture of religion and politics. In the next century Anglicans and Nonconformists also supported or tolerated persecutions of each other, and engaged in disputes which came to a climax in civil war, but they were all Christians. This volume makes these points. They may seem boringly obvious points but they need making, not only in the service of truth – always the historian's supreme duty – but also in the hope that the quarrels between Christians in the past may be thoroughly buried. Because it encourages not propaganda but mutual respect and forgiveness, true history works for a less poisoned future, where the movement which is already so strongly making for Christian reconciliation and reunion may be assisted by memories which are healed because comprehensive. My own attitude is that in none of these little systems which once divided Christian England was Jesus of Nazareth pinned down or exactly mirrored; yet in none of them was the spirit of Christ absent.

The Preface to the first edition of this volume, in 1983, quoted these lines from T. S. Eliot's *Little Gidding*:

> We cannot revive old factions
> We cannot restore old policies
> Or follow an antique drum.
> These men, and those who opposed them
> And those whom they opposed
> Accept the constitution of silence
> And are folded in a single party.
> Whatever we inherit from the fortunate
> We have taken from the defeated . . .
> We die with the dying:

> See, they depart, and we go with them.
> We are born with the dead:
> See, they return, and bring us with them.

The controversies of the centuries are so important in the history of England, and are still so problematic for all who care about English-speaking religion, that I remain sure that it was worthwhile to write a non-academic book which I claimed (perhaps pretentiously) to be 'the first ecumenical history of English Christianity'. Many reviewers and readers have encouraged me. But some further studies and reflections, and comments which I have received from those more expert than I am in particular fields, have made me regret that I did not sufficiently stress some truths which would strengthen my theme.

Research into the evidence which survives in local archives and in obscure printed sources is gradually building a picture of 'popular religion' in this period. The picture is often different in atmosphere from any collection of portraits of monarchs, statesmen, poets, bishops, theologians, martyrs and saints, because it shows us ordinary people with passions, worries and unreflective habits very like our own. Here are many thousands of clergymen like Vicar Aleyn of Bray in Berkshire, who on being taunted about his submission to every change in religion from the reign of Henry VIII to that of Elizabeth I is reported (by Thomas Fuller in the next century) to have replied: 'Not so, for I have always kept my principle, which is this, to live and die the Vicar of Bray.' That is a famous anecdote. Somewhat more scientific evidence about the sixteenth century has been summed up: 'the impression derived from churchwardens' accounts is that altars, roods and lofts, statues and holy-water stoups and so on were taken down in Edward's reign, put back in Mary's and taken down again after Elizabeth's accession without great drama or disorder.' And in the seventeenth century the monarchy itself was taken down and put back with limited participation by the people.[1]

When lay folk did take sides in the religious controversies of the time they stayed out of trouble as far as they could and concentrated not on a close examination of the rival theologies but on matters

---

[1] J. J. Scarisbrick, *The Reformation and the English People* (Oxford, 1984), p. 89.

more prominent in real life. Their questions, as we occasionally
overhear them, are who now owns the land of the monasteries or has
influence as the local squire or magistrate; whether one likes the
present appearance of the parish church or the looks of those who
never go near it; what one has to pay to the local parson or say to
one's spouse or parents; why one eats fish on Fridays (or does not)
or is proud to be able to read the Bible (or is not); where one
happened to be born or to be listening when a faith was being taught
attractively. Here is a people which is on the whole conservative
and not only insular but also village-minded. It is a people which on
the whole, during most of the sixteenth century, feels that the
Catholic Church, with the priest at Mass, probably represents
serious Christianity now as in the previous thousand years (whether
or not one is devout oneself). It is a people which on the whole,
during most of the seventeenth century, feels that (whether or not
one is deeply Protestant) the Pope and Catholic foreigners generally
are a threat to a nation which is beginning to prosper proudly. And
it is a people which, when the religious storms have blown
themselves out during the eighteenth century, on the whole settles
down into the unenthusiastic acceptance of a religion 'by law
established', with tolerated minorities practising a religion of much
the same tone. The substance of this religion is not charismatic or
mystical but moral, whether or not one is very moral oneself. It is a
religion of reasonableness, honesty, duty and respectability. It is not
aloof from the world; it echoes Sir Toby's famous question, 'Dost
thou think, because thou art virtuous, there shall be no more cakes
and ale?' The refusal of most people to run risks in order to restore
Catholicism, the speed of the downfall of the Puritans and the
security of the Established Church in the eighteenth century
(despite the worldliness of many of its clergy as well as its laity)
suggests that Sir Toby spoke for the country. Probably the most
unpopular aspect of the medieval Church had been the system of
'bawdy' courts where the bishops' officials could examine and
excommunicate those who defamed their neighbours or were
friendly with them to the point of fornication. For much of this later
period much evidence suggests that the bishops were expected to
enforce morality through these courst and that the lay magistrates
were expected to reinforce their efforts – but their summons and
sentences could be ignored more safely than in the Middle Ages. To

a large extent the bishops acting as moral censors suffered the same fate as the Puritans who were their enemies.

Religion no doubt meant different things to different people – from the saints of the rival schools of spirituality through a wide spectrum of knowledge and interest to the sinners more or less happily succumbing to various temptations – but it was probably often valued chiefly because it was believed to provide some explanations of life's mysteries and some assurances among life's dangers. Accepting this estimate of religion, an investigator of social history has written: 'Amid this bewildering chaos of evidence and questions it seems clear that one tenable conclusion is that for most people Christianity meant much the same in 1760 as it had two centuries before, certainly as far as its social contents were concerned.'[2] And a large part of the English people clung to beliefs which only bordered on religion as defined officially. Daily life was thought to be controlled by the Devil, or by lesser evil spirits, or by curses of enemies, or by the stars, or by Fortune, but some protection could be secured by the recital of prayers or spells addressed to the consecrated Bread, or to the local statue of the Virgin Mary, to the tomb of a saint or to the pre-Christian spirits who in an emergency could be placated or enrolled by witches or 'cunning' men. Gradually in the centuries covered by this volume this underworld which at its brightest was fairyland – Max Weber's 'enchanted garden' – lost its hold on the emotions. Scientific medicine and agriculture seemed more reliable. England moved from the time when such 'magic' or 'superstition' was condemned by the clergy (but in practice associated with many of the rites of the Church) through the time when it was condemned by the educated (although even in such circles its appeal could linger on) to the time when most people laughed at old wives' tales. There was a crisis when magic was repugnant to Bible-based Protestantism and could no longer flourish as a half-hidden part of the folk religion half-baptised by popular Catholicism, but was still able to fascinate many simple people. That was the crisis when odd women called witches were hunted cruelly. But the public crisis passed, leaving

---

[2] J. A. Sharp, *Early Modern England: A Social History 1550–1760* (London, 1987), p. 253. Alan Macfarlane, *Marriage and Love in England 1300–1840* (Oxford, 1986), is the best of many recent studies in 'population history'.

magic to return to the usually hidden underworld of superstition. In 1736 witchcraft ceased to be recognized as a crime.

Those who wish to defend one may protest, in my view rightly, that this picture of the unheroic religion of the English people under the Tudors, Stuarts and Hanoverians was on view in the 1983 edition of this volume, although without the vivid detail which is possible for the industrious historian of one locality or one small period. But I can see now that I ought to have emphasized more than I did that among those English people who did take Christianity seriously and even heroically – a category far wider than the public figures and the writers – the transition from medieval to early modern had certain characteristics not confined to Protestant or Roman Catholic, Anglican or Nonconformist. I believe that these common characteristics do something to explain both the intensification of religious feeling in this period and its increasing separation from the main spirit of the community.

One of the changes is from community mindedness – the collective religion of the village, the tribe, the nation or (as in the case of medieval Europe) the continent – to personal commitment. Individualism had been growing towards the end of the Middle Ages, but this was a new phenomenon. The noble courage of the Protestant and Catholic martyrs under Mary I and Elizabeth I, with which this volume opens, is a pointer to a change from the general acquiescence in the religious revolution imposed by governments under Henry VIII and Edward VI. Although few people had any wish to be martyred, the possibility grew that the individual might choose to defy the local authority and eventually the Crown, pleading the rights and compulsion of the conscience. When priests trained abroad made the Mass available (although often rarely and with great difficulty) in many (not all) parts of the country, there was a sense in which every serious English Christian had to make a personal decision which could be costly for or against the 'old religion' – and now Catholicism was itself transformed by the Counter-Reformation with all its development of the interior life, the 'garden of the soul', by spiritual exercises. And when Protestantism reacted against the threat of this renewed Catholicism by urging the further reformation of the National Church, there was a sense in which every serious English Christian had to make a personal decision for or against Puritanism – a movement which demanded from every individual conversion, Bible study, private prayer and consistent holiness. We are in the presence of a painfully new tension in loyalties when we watch Roman Catholics being told to renounce their allegiance to Elizabeth I, or Puritans being told that it is a holy work to cut off the head of Charles I, or bishops of the Church of England being told to break their oaths of allegiance to James II, all for religious reasons. There are striking contrasts between the timidity of the Roman Catholic bishops in the 1530s and their courage in the 1550s, and between the conformity of the parish clergy at the accession of Elizabeth I and the decision of a fifth of them to lose their livings rather than to accept the Act of Uniformity under Charles II: we see men daring not to conform. Even in less strenuous times the nation remained fractured, and every serious English Christian had to decide whether or not to be Nonconformist, whether Catholic or Protestant. In all of this we see a new England – new in comparison with the unity of earlier ages. Anglo-Saxon or English protest against Norman or Angevin domination had mainly taken the form of pilgrimages to the shrines within great Catholic churches, and later on although there had been grumbles about the power and wealth of churchmen the Catholic priesthood had been well recruited, the Catholic churches had been ever more lavishly decorated and endowed, spirituality had blossomed on the tree of orthodoxy and the Catholic faith had been thought impregnable against Lollard or other heresy. Now we witness the triumph of the idea of personal commitment after a choice.

Another change is often described as the triumph of the laity. It should not be exaggerated. There had been much lay initiative in the Middle Ages, ranging from the power which many kings had often exercised in appointment and taxation to the patronage of rich individuals or fraternities which had made possible the building and embellishment of the parish churches. And after the Reformation there was much clerical initiative; in church Catholics still exalted the priest and Protestants could not answer the preacher. But it is also true that between 1530 and 1560 the clergy's role in England was reduced drastically. The medieval clergy had been regarded as mediators between heaven and hell, as the custodians of the relics of the saints who had brought heaven near, as the makers of the body and blood of Christ in the Mass, as priests of God with the power to absolve the laity's sins (after an annual private confession made compulsory in 1215), as men with the power to free souls from Purgatory with their prayers, as educators of the young and as the source from which the civil service was recruited. The overthrow of these rulers of the mind of England was achieved and maintained because Henry VIII's determination to curtail their power and prestige, and to confiscate most of their endowments, appealed to most of the aristocracy and gentry, whether or not these were militantly anticlerical. Even under Mary I, when heretics were being burned at the behest of bishops, almost no monasteries were refounded because the monastic estates remained in lay ownership. In the next century the Anglican clergy recovered some of their political and economic position, but at the cost of the violent Puritan backlash and not with the final result of a return to anything like the medieval status of the priestly caste. The Puritan preacher in the end became the congregation's employee. Almost the same change occurred in the Roman Catholic community, where priests were few and either persecuted or kept in obscurity.

When lay Christians chose a version of Christianity in personal commitment, it was different from any medieval version.

Medieval religion had involved people's emotions mainly through participation in (or attendance at) ceremonies in church conducted by the clergy. Obviously, devout Christians prayed their own prayers; in Volume One some evidence was summarized which makes that a feeble understatement. And obviously, morality was preached and to some extent practised; the seven deadly sins were widely thought to be sinful. But in the Middle Ages the emphasis was on the drama of the Church. This was enacted supremely in the miraculous Mass but was also dramatic in seasonal processions and touched human lives at many turning points through baptisms, exorcisms, blessings, weddings, and requiems, the 'rites of passage' to which modern anthropologists and sociologists pay great attention. When lay people endorsed the clergy's worship, the usual means was a semi-sacramental act: they built or beautified churches, chapels or chantries, they lit candles, they crossed themselves, they went on pilgrimages to other churches. The cathedral or parish church was also the centre of much of their social lives, from the solemn meeting of the merchants' guild to the 'church ale' held in the churchyard to raise funds. And specially on All

Souls Day it was believed that those whose bodies were buried
around the church had not passed beyond the range of its prayers.
Something of this tradition remained in Elizabethan and later
England, but on the whole in this period the emphasis shifted to the
spiritual pilgrimage of the individual who could be alone and to the
scenes of this pilgrim's progress outside the church building which
on a weekday might be locked or deserted. There was a new
intensity of concern about the Christian family (strengthened for
Protestants by the marriage of the clergy) and the Christian
business (strengthened by the end of the medieval prestige of the
monk and by the end of the medieval prohibition of usury). Now
Christians knew that they had to make their own moral decisions
about their conduct and they believed that it was on these choices
of theirs that they would be judged. The clergy were now praised
not if they prayed for the dead but if they educated the young to earn
their livings decently; not if they supervised the construction and
repair of churches but if they administered charities. The loyalty of
the Roman Catholic or High Church Anglican to the priest did not
mean a return to medieval attitudes; on the contrary, frequent
confession and communion, urged as the ideal although not always
provided or accepted, were the equipment of the new style of lay
pilgrimage through the world.

   Medieval religion had been based on images rather than words.
(Therefore my Volume One had to be illustrated, and I am grateful
for the line drawings by George Murray which are small reminders
to the reader of the wealth to be looked at.) Obviously an elaborate
theological structure could be raised on the foundation of the
Church's life, and sermons could form an exciting part of that life,
but most people in the Middle Ages were illiterate and their love
was given not to the very expensive books but to things that could
be seen and touched. No age of Christian art has even approached
the creativity of the periods which in England are so curiously called
'Norman' and 'Gothic', and the splendour is all the more
astounding when we remember that the population was always
under three millions. It is one of the great tragedies of English
history that the rebellion against medieval religion had to involve
the destruction of so much of this beauty, now preached against as
'idolatry' or simply regarded as a target for loutish vandalism. But
there was a compensation, for this part of the story of English

religion is a prolonged celebration of the power of the translated and printed Bible over the hearts and minds of the anonymous as well as the famous. The Ten Commandments were written up over the holy table in church, replacing images over the altar, which was now often made less prominent than the Bible-preaching pulpit. The power of the Scriptures was unleashed in the Roman Catholic community as well as among those Christians who would affirm with William Chillingworth: 'The Bible, the Bible only I say, is the religion of Protestants.' It was through personal encounter with the Bible, more than through anything seen in church, that the serious English Christian was now meeting not only a pageant of unforgettable characters and incidents but also the unutterable mystery, salvation and demand of the All-holy. The many who could not read were now at a disadvantage, but even they could hear th Bible read at length in church, preached about in sermons which were more frequent and systematic than in the Middle Ages, and discussed in tavern and home, while the metrical psalms loved by the Puritans were beginning the translation of the Bible into hymns. Hymns were to sustain the piety of Dissent in dark ages and to capture the audiences of the Wesleys.

Although England in the middle of the eighteenth century was still a Christian country in many ways, these changes may be interpreted as the forerunners of secularization, the process which will form the background of Volume Three. And just as there is an underworld of magic to be glimpsed beneath official religion in this period, so there is an ill-documented world in which people are busy only with the pressures and temptations of secular life. In villages not everyone has Catholic or Puritan reasons for staying away when the church bell rings. Already in the cities there are dissolute gentry and unchurched slums. These elements and pockets of secularization have many causes. But some generalizations may be submitted. One that cannot be questioned (for Dean Swift's savage irony spoke for a multitude) is that the murderous disputes of the religious enthusiasts gravely discredited all their creeds and encouraged uncertainty about Christianity itself. Other suggestions seem true but may be debatable. When religion ceases to be an aspect of the life of a whole society and become a matter of personal choice, it may be about to become the privilege of the few who feel that they are predestined to be saved. Or it may be about to become a hobby which seems not merely optional but also unfashionable and remote from reality as socially perceived. When the clergy are deprived of power and wealth they may eventually be deprived of all respect either because they add nothing of value to what the Holy Spirit teaches the individual or because they are seen as the ambassadors of a supernatural country which does not exist. When ceremonies in church are no longer at the centre of religion, it may be felt in the long run that religion has no strong centre at all; that family and business and the pleasure of life in Vanity Fair are everything. When traditional images have lost their power to symbolize eternal truths the religious imagination may be starved, and when the impact of biblical words has lost its freshness, churchgoing may appeal only to a bookish minority which either accepts every word in the Scriptures as the Word of God or else has the perhaps rare skill and patience to attempt to discern the Word amid the words. Ultimately the godless world, which to Shakespeare seems thinkable in *King Lear,* appears inescapable to the majority, partly because of these new styles of religion which are richly creative for the minority which is intensely religious.

Those who are dismayed by the secularization and uglification of modern society have often been inclined to hark back to the Middle Ages. That was the spirit of the 'Gothic revival' which swept Western Europe, including England, amid the factories of the nineteenth century. Only in our own time has the Latin of the Mass been largely abandoned by Roman Catholics. But two things are certain. One is that the Middle Ages cannot be brought back. Another is that those who are Christians in a post-Reformation style can produce many lives and some thoughts which deserve our admiration, whether or not we share their passionate beliefs.[3]

D.L.E.

---

[3] John Bossy surveyed *Christianity in the West 1400-1700* (Oxford, 1985) with this perspective. Jean Delumeau, *Catholicism between Luther and Voltaire* (in English, 1978), was also suggestive. But E. Le Roy Ladurie's *Montaillou* (in English, London 1978), a portrait of a remote Pyrenean village resulting from examinations by the Inquisition, was a reminder of the rarity of solid evidence about religious attitudes outside the ranks of the educated. The nearest English equivalent is mentioned in this book, p.492 note. The essays on *Parish, Church and People* edited by Susan Wright (London, 1988) are an example of how local light can be thrown on national themes.

Part One

CHRISTIANS UNDER THE TUDORS

CHAPTER ONE

PRELUDE: THE FAITH AND THE TRAGEDY

TWO ARMIES OF MARTYRS

Almost three hundred English men and women were executed as Protestants in the reign of Mary I (1553–58). The first to die was John Rogers, one of the translators of the English Bible, who was executed by burning at Smithfield in London on 4 February 1555. When his widow went to clear his few belongings out of his prison cell, she found his account of his examination before some of Queen Mary's leading councillors. According to this document, there had been an argument about the authority of the Bible. 'Thou canst prove nothing by Scripture', John Rogers had been assured. 'The Scripture is dead; it must have a lively exposition.' The man thus prepared to patronize the Bible was Stephen Gardiner, Lord Chancellor of England and Bishop of Winchester, a priest-lawyer eminent in public affairs almost continuously since his days as Cardinal Wolsey's secretary. He was the lord of four palaces and of a regiment of servants; and he was presiding over this trial in the church which later became Southwark Cathedral, next to his London palace. 'No,' John Rogers had replied, 'the Scripture is alive. . . .' 'Thou wilt not burn in that gear when it cometh to the purpose,' Sir Richard Southwell had sneered. But John Rogers had recorded the conversation – or his version of it – because he had rightly been sure that his faith that the Bible was alive would be stronger than the pains of his death.

As part of a series of misjudgements which showed how little idea Queen Mary's government had of how to win a propaganda war, the preachers whom they were about to turn into martyrs were often allowed to write long letters to each other

and to the nation at large. They were even allowed to exhort
the public at some length while chained to the stake as the
faggots were being lit. And many of the executions were
bungled. The wood used was often green; the rushes were often
soggy; the gunpowder provided as a touch of charity often
failed to ignite; there were no gags to stop either 'last words' or
equally moving screams of pain. Never in English history did
preachers occupy more influential pulpits. 'Good people,' said
Rowland Taylor to his parishioners at Hadley in Suffolk, 'I
have taught you nothing but God's holy word, and those
lessons that I have taken out of God's holy book I have come
hither to seal with my blood.' And this intellectually gifted
man, who had qualified to practise as a barrister, kissed the
stake to which he was being tied for his final ordeal.

Another Protestant preacher, John Bradford, who had
toured his home county, Lancashire, trying to win the people's
hearts from Catholicism, delivered his most telling sermon as
he was being burned to death. To a young man, John Leaf, an
apprentice candlemaker, who was suffering with him, he cried
out: 'Be of good comfort, brother, for we shall have a merry
supper with the Lord this night!'

In February 1555 Bishop John Hooper was executed near
his own cathedral in Gloucester. His life had produced a
mixture of reactions in his contemporaries. He had never
settled to enjoy the beauties of the cathedral and the countryside. The diocese had been alarmed by his zeal as an inspector
of the parishes, insisting on the new Protestant worship,
inquiring fiercely into the morals of the laity, testing the clergy
on their knowledge of the Bible – with results which he went
round quoting in righteous indignation. He had disturbed the
peace. His fellow bishops had been irritated by the obstinacy
with which he refused to wear the old Catholic vestments or to
come to terms with the old Catholic sentiments. But the last
impression which he made, as he burned for almost three-
quarters of an hour, left an image more powerful than the
complaints. His martyr's agony accompanied by a sinner's
penitence was to provide the most horrific passage in John
Foxe's history of the Protestant martyrs. 'When he was black in
the mouth, and his tongue swollen that he could not speak, yet

his lips went till they were shrunk to the gums; and he did knock his breast with his hands until one of his arms fell off, and then knocked still with the other, what time the fat, water and blood dropped out at his fingers' ends, until by renewing of the fire his strength was gone and his hand did cleave fast in knocking to the iron upon his breast. So immediately bowing forwards, he yielded up his spirit.'

In October 1555, in Oxford, a white-bearded and infirm bishop, Hugh Latimer, who had been Bishop of Worcester under Henry VIII and a mighty preacher under Edward VI, was similarly exhorting his own fellow sufferer, Nicholas Ridley, who had been Bishop of London: 'Be of good comfort, Master Ridley, and play the man. We shall this day light such a candle by God's grace in England as I trust shall never be put out.' And Ridley did 'play the man' although in private notes to one another in prison both bishops had confessed to torturing fears, 'so fearful that I would creep into a mousehole'.

One of those who watched these bishops suffer (and Ridley was still alive and screaming when his legs had been burned away) was Thomas Cranmer, the scholar who had been summoned into the story by Henry VIII's decision to make him Archbishop of Canterbury because of his convenient views on the royal divorce. Eventually in March 1556 Cranmer was also burned to death in Oxford. Fear had made him unable to stand upright under the intellectual and physical pressures. He wrote out both Catholic and Protestant versions of a final speech, although he kept the Protestant version hidden in his clothes, in an agony of indecision. For a time, in recantations of increasing thoroughness, he abandoned his Protestantism as heretical; then, in disgust at the cruelty of those still resolved to burn him, he dramatically withdrew these recantations; then he confessed, when questioned as he ran to the stake, that he would have accepted the Pope had the Papists spared his life. But after all these symptoms of the confusion of a scholar under temptations and tortures, his final appeal was to the authority of 'every word and sentence taught by our Saviour Jesus Christ, his apostles and prophets in the Old and New Testament'. There his conscience came to rest, and he held steadily in the flames the hand which had signed the recantations of his Bible-based Protestant convictions. His last words were St Stephen's: 'I see heaven open and Jesus on the right hand of God.'

Many laymen were more simply courageous; six Protestants, being burned together at Colchester, clapped their hands as the flames mounted. About fifty-five women suffered the same fate. Joan Waste of Derby had been blind all her twenty-two years, but had drawn her own conclusions from the New Testament – read to her by John Hurst, who had nothing else to do since he was in prison for debt. She was now burned. Cecily Ormes, the wife of a cloth-weaver, recited a woman's song from the English Bible as she was being burned in Norwich: 'My soul doth magnify the Lord.'[1]

But these Protestants who were ready to die for what they believed about the Bible did not form the only army of martyrs to be seen in Tudor England.

More than eight hundred young Englishmen left home in order to train abroad as priests in the mission which sought to revive the Roman Catholic Church in Elizabeth's England.[2] More than a hundred of them were executed on their return, beginning with St Cuthbert Mayne at Launceston in Cornwall in 1577. Already, before this heroic acceptance of danger and death in the English mission, a small but remarkable number of priests had left Oxford, Cambridge and other comfortable posts for exile, even while the majority of Catholics were conforming to the Elizabethan establishment. One of these self-exiled scholars, Thomas Stapleton, had produced books to encourage a new pride in the Catholic past. From his pen had come the first English translation of Bede's *Ecclesiastical History of the English People*, telling the story of the conversion of the Anglo-Saxons; *The Fortress of the Faith*, a book showing that

---

    [1] A modern edition of the classic account (abbreviated) is *Foxe's Book of Martyrs*, ed. G. A. Williamson (London, 1965), and a modern study is D. M. Loades, *The Oxford Martyrs* (London, 1970).
    [2] See M. R. O'Connell, *Thomas Stapleton and the Counter-Reformation in England* (New Haven, Conn., 1964). H. O. Evennett, *The Spirit of the Counter-Reformation* (Cambridge, 1968), and A. D. Wright, *The Counter-Reformation in Europe* (London, 1981), are the best summaries.

Protestants needed to be converted back to the old religion; and a book praising the three martyred Thomases – St Thomas the apostle, St Thomas of Canterbury, and St Thomas More. The Catholic past had become a call to martyrdom.

'In condemning us,' said one Jesuit, Edmund Campion, to his judges before they sentenced him to death in 1581, 'you condemn all your own ancestors – all the ancient priests, bishops and kings – and that was once the glory of England, the island of saints and the most devoted child of the See of Peter. For what have we taught . . . that they did not uniformly teach?' He had been a Fellow of St John's College, Oxford, and had performed brilliantly in debates before the Queen during her state visit to the university fifteen years before; the de-lighted Queen had promised him her patronage. Now he had been tortured on the rack so severely that in his clumsiness 'he likened himself to an elephant'.

When he was led out to his doom it was noticed that he had no nails left. During the execution he was 'quartered'. This meant that the hangman was paid to cut him down while he was still alive, drag his bowels out while he watched, and cut his body up. Sometimes the victim was allowed to die before this final punishment for treason was inflicted; sometimes the crowd insisted on such mercy. In Campion's case a drop of blood fell from the butchery on the head of a young law student, Henry Walpole. It made him join the Jesuits – and the martyrs. Campion and Walpole were among the forty English martyrs canonized as saints in Rome in 1970.

When the hangman held up the bleeding quarters of Father Mumford Scott, 'some noticed that his knees were hardened as horn by much prayer'. A notorious Protestant sadist, Richard Topcliffe, specialized in torturing priests, and often used for this purpose his own house which was near to Westminster Abbey. When he applied this treatment to a delicate poet, St Robert Southwell, who was a Jesuit, he is said to have done so with the jeer: 'Yes, you are Christ's fellow!' At his trial Southwell said that he had been tortured ten times, 'each one worse than death'.

Laymen also showed great courage. Some were sufficiently influential, or cunning, to escape the severest penalties, but it

must have required great courage for a squire who had been
devoted to farming and sport, his family and his neighbourhood, perhaps as a Justice of the Peace, to refuse the oath
acknowledging the Queen's ecclesiastical supremacy, and pay
the heavy fines resulting from such a refusal towards the end of
her reign. When in 1580 the Queen offered the ablest lawyer of
the day, Edmund Plowden, the Lord Chancellorship, he replied that he found no reason to swerve from the Catholic faith
in which they had both been brought up. Some less prominent
lay people paid with their lives for any outspoken loyalty to
Catholicism, although most escaped with a fine or a threat. We
read of a farmer who, making his last journey up the ladder to
the hangman's rope in Winchester, blessed his ten children
with the prayer that their deaths would be no worse than his. St
Margaret Clitherow, the wife of a prosperous and Protestant
butcher in York, harboured Catholic priests and was arrested.
In order to avoid the necessity of friends, neighbours and her
own children giving evidence against her, she refused to plead
and was therefore crushed to death. And the humble could be
bold when they still had a chance to escape. John Rigby, a
servant sent to explain that his master's daughter was too ill to
appear in court, was interrogated about his own religion and,
knowing that the confession might mean his death (as it did),
replied that he was a Catholic. Robert Colton, a simple boy of
Wisbech, when examined by the Archbishop of Canterbury
and other formidable elders at Lambeth Palace, replied: 'I
hear say that England hath been a Catholic Christian country
a thousand years afore this queen's reign and her father's. If
that were the old highway to heaven, then why should I forsake
it? I have no goods to leave. I pray you give me leave to save my
soul.'

Under Queen Elizabeth I about three hundred of the Eng-
lish sacrificed their lives in order to save their souls as Roman
Catholics. And the example of their courage inspired their
Church, then and for centuries to come. Before going to his
brave death Edmund Campion is reported to have told the
Lord Chief Justice: 'We knew that we were not lords of our own
lives. To be condemned . . . is both gladness and glory to us.
God lives: posterity will live: their judgement is not so liable to

corruption as that of those who are now going to sentence us to death.'[3]

ONE FAITH?

Such was the witness given by two armies of martyrs, Protestant and Catholic, to the fact that England during the second half of the sixteenth century was a country where religious belief was widespread and mattered intensely. For almost a thousand years it had been Christian England, a people not entirely holy or moral but taking pride in its saints and monasteries, a scene of honour for the clergy and of genuine devotion among many of the laity. Although there had been some rebels there had been more pilgrims and many more conformists right up to the sudden storm of the Reformation in the 1530s. That storm had, however, resulted in a spectacle which remains, in Sir Maurice Powicke's words, 'one of the most mysterious things in our history'.[4] For after all the centuries when England had belonged to Catholic Christendom, there had been little intensity in the opposition to the religious or pseudo-religious innovations decreed under King Henry VIII.

It was not that Protestantism soon became popular; for years the new creed remained repulsive or virtually unknown to the conservative people inhabiting most of rural England, and even in the towns and in the more sophisticated south-east passionate Protestants often complained that they were treated as madmen. But when the monasteries and convents were invited to surrender to the agents of Henry VIII, surprisingly little resistance was offered; the northern rebellion known as the Pilgrimage of Grace was suppressed quite easily. Even when the ministers of Edward VI suppressed the whole vast

---

[3] Philip Caraman provided an anthology of vivid passages in *The Other Face: Catholic Life under Elizabeth I* (London, 1960). David Farmer included many of the forty martyrs in *The Oxford Dictionary of Saints* (1978), with bibliographies.

[4] F. M. Powicke, *The Reformation in England* (London, 1941), p. 7.

cult of prayers for the dead, and stripped the parish churches of
beauty which had been accumulating for many centuries, the
revolution met with little open defiance. As fresh orders came
from the King's council, radically contradicting previous
orders and tearing up the traditions of many centuries, the
majority of the English spoke only in order to mutter a medley
of old and new prayers. They lay low, their ambitions being to
escape hunger and relax in the timeless rites of the family and
the village. The bishops usually compromised – for example,
Stephen Gardiner, who was to condemn Protestants to death
under Mary I, wrote a book defending the claims of Henry
VIII over the Church. Only St John Fisher, a theologian who
had been given the poorest English bishopric (Rochester), and
St Thomas More, a layman who had in his time been something of a liberal and something of a courtier, produced
intelligent defences of Catholicism. It certainly is mysterious
that so many were acquiescent during such devastating
changes.

Then came another very curious development. England
became a country which produced and admired martyrs.
Naturally the pain of martyrdom was embraced only by a few,
and the piety was not universal. There are many hints in the
surviving evidence that not everyone went to church – and that
not every churchgoer opened his heart to what came in through
his ears. Still, after the middle of this century the revival of
religious intensity was on a scale inconceivable during the
humiliating decline of medieval Catholicism. Catholic or Protestant or merely national, English Christianity was now bursting with life – and ready to defy death, or at least to applaud
heroes.

If we judge the situation solely by the known sales of books,
we have to conclude that to Shakespeare's contemporaries the
most interesting subject was religion. *A Pensive Man's Practice* by
one layman, John Norden, went through more than forty
editions between 1584 and 1627. And preaching mattered.
Educated Elizabethan laymen developed such a taste for
theology that the time was coming when the House of Commons would often spend a whole day in St Margaret's church
across the street in Westminster, in order to fast, to pray and to

hear immense sermons on the state of the nation. For the illiterate or semi-literate mass of the population, words spoken in the pulpit possessed an interest now hard to imagine as possible. Under Henry VIII and his three crowned children, London crowds would gather Sunday by Sunday to listen to the preacher shouting at 'Paul's Cross'. The open-air pulpit outside St Paul's Cathedral, it was the storm-centre of religious controversy. We have to guess what it felt like to live in a village where the pulpit was the only place where news from far off London could be given authoritatively, where arguments and stories illustrating them could be launched to stimulate mind and imagination, and where all life could be judged according to the values which the community at least pretended to respect. Innumerable examples have survived of women who would analyse what the preacher had said for the instruction of their children and servants; of men who would discuss sermons when they met to drink.[5]

The literature of the time often hints that scepticism developed among some of the educated. Christopher Marlowe was an 'atheist' to many of those who watched his meteoric illumination of the possibilities of the Elizabethan theatre, and somewhat later Sir Walter Ralegh, that all-round Elizabethan, was rumoured to preside over a school of atheism. But the 'atheism' was certainly not of the kind familiar in the nineteenth and twentieth centuries. It was more an individualism which failed to pay respect to the dogmas and ethics declared in the pulpits and the schoolrooms; an exuberant, Renaissance pride in life defying the conventions, not a twentieth-century humanism defying a meaningless universe. Marlowe's plays showed an imagination still deeply excited by the old Christian images of worldliness, ambition and damnation. Ralegh's *History of the World* was set within an acceptance

---

[5] Glimpses of the power of the pulpit are given in books such as J. W. Blench, *Preaching in England in the Late Fifteenth and Sixteenth Centuries* (Oxford, 1964); Millar Maclure, *The Paul's Cross Sermons 1534–1642* (Toronto, 1958); J. F. Wilson, *Pulpit in Parliament* (Princeton, N.J., 1969); *In God's Name: Examples of Preaching in England, 1534–1662*, ed. John Chandos (London, 1971); *The English Sermon 1550–1650*, ed. Martin Seymour-Smith (London, 1976).

of the Old Testament chronology and he wrote a devotional, if finally half-sceptical, poem 'but two hours before his death' in 1618:

> Even such is Time, which takes in trust
> Our youth, our joys, and all we have,
> And pays us but with age and dust;
> Who in the dark and silent grave,
> When we have wandered all our ways,
> Shuts up the story of our days:
> And from which earth, and grave, and dust,
> The Lord shall raise me up, I trust.

He began his last speech, near the executioner, by saying that he was going to meet God within the quarter-hour. In the next generation Ralegh became a hero to Puritans; Oliver Cromwell, for example, loved his *History*.

The power of religion in England from about 1550 to about 1660 is agreed by all modern scholars. It is, however, controversial to claim that Catholicism and Protestantism were essentially one religion, making for the modern student a single field of study. In this period the most sacred rite of the medieval Church, the Mass, was commonly denounced by Protestants as superstitious, blasphemous and idolatrous. This was because it was believed that Roman Catholics were ensnared by this rite into the power of wicked priests, who demanded money for the magic of each Mass. It was also believed that Roman Catholics thought that what the priest did in the Mass was a fresh killing of Christ, for the bread had been changed physically into his body. It was believed that with their talk about the 'Sacrifice of the Mass' they denied the uniqueness of Christ's atoning death (his 'full, perfect and sufficient sacrifice, oblation and satisfaction for the sins of the whole world'), and that they worshipped the bread instead of worshipping the true, invisible Father through the one, living, eternal Christ. Roman Catholics, on the other hand, believed that the 'Lord's Supper' celebrated by Protestants (usually with no great frequency) was intended to be no more than a pathetic memorial to an absent, very distant, Saviour. It did not convey God's grace as did the blessed sacrament in Christ's true

Church. It did not plead to the father as did Calvary's propitia-
tory sacrifice, which was sacramentally re-enacted morning by
morning in the Mass, timeless in its Latin mystery and majesty. And Roman Catholics often alleged that Protestants –
whether they remembered their Saviour or forgot him – based
their religion solely on their emotions, so that they ended up by
being far more interested in themselves, in their ambitions and
chaotically conflicting opinions, than in the Gospel entrusted
to the One, Holy, Catholic and Apostolic Church along with
the sacraments.

Behind the dispute about the Mass or the Lord's Supper
there was, or there seemed to be, a dispute about the very
meaning of reconciliation with God. As late as 1963 a distinguished Roman Catholic historian still found it necessary to
assure his readers that this division was absolutely fundamental. He referred to 'the abyss that must forever separate the
two religions that differ in their accounts of what reconciliation
with God means, the one building upon a belief that grace is a
reality in the soul, the other upon the belief that grace is no
more than acceptability in God's sight'.[6]

Many similar assessments of the magnitude of the 'abyss'
separating Catholic from Protestant could be quoted from the
Protestant side. Indignant theologians often alleged that
Roman Catholics held that man was acceptable in God's sight
because of his 'works', chiefly works of piety as ordered by the
Church. They also claimed that to Roman Catholics 'faith'
meant not a personal, reasoned trust in the Saviour but merely
believing what the Church teaches. Such credulity seemed a
faith fit for dumb beasts – as was often said. 'Wherein then do
we disagree?' asked Richard Hooker about the Church of
England's attitude to official Roman Catholic teaching as
defined by the Council of Trent. 'We disagree about the nature
of the very essence of the medicine whereby Christ cureth our
disease.' Many Protestants have been sure that the Bishop of
Rome, so far from being the universal pastor and teacher, the
representative of Christ on earth, was the great tempter and

---

[6] Philip Hughes, *The Reformation in England*, Vol. 2 (revised, London, 1963), p. 79.
Hans Küng's reconciling work on *Justification* appeared in English in 1964.

corrupter, the Antichrist predicted in the last book of the Bible.

'The 'abyss' then seemed deep and wide. Indeed, it is still sometimes convenient to refer to the 'old religion' and the 'new religion', for Roman Catholicism and Protestantism have often been so called. This book is, however, written in the conviction that the talk about the gap between old and new 'religions' as an unbridgeable 'abyss' has been wrong. Since essentially there was one religion, here is the one story of English Christianity. What united these English Christians was far more significant than what separated them, although they sometimes tortured, burned or hanged each other because of their religious opinions or because of the political loyalties inextricably mixed with those opinions. Both the Catholic Mass and the Protestant Lord's Supper were, after all, attempts to do what Jesus had commanded should be done as the memorial of his self-sacrifice, making the bread mean his body and the wine mean his blood and the memory mean his life to the believing community. And both the Catholic and Protestant doctrines of 'grace' were attempts to express in broken human words the common Christian experiences – being changed deeply by the intervention of God in the soul, but still needing to trust in God's mercy as declared through Christ; living gratefully a good life, but still needing to say that no merits of one's own can finally earn the right to heaven. On both sides of the alleged 'abyss' the faith of a Christian was to be seen. It was a trust in Christ known through the Bible and the Church, a trust which resulted in the Christian 'works' of love, joy, peace, patience, kindness, goodness, fidelity, gentleness and self-control. The courage of all the martyrs was the same. So, at its heart, was their Christianity. It inspired their living and dying. If it did not inspire them to enough charity, the blame should not be placed on the gospels which define Christianity.

In 1541 eminent Catholic and Protestant theologians met at Regensburg and reached agreement on the doctrine of grace: the Christian is 'justified' by faith in God through Christ, but the faith must be made effective in love. The agreement was soon repudiated on both sides, and a hundred years later was remembered only by a few scholars. Clearly it was a mere paper agreement, unrelated to the psychological, economic and political realities which moulded societies in the days of the Reformation and Counter-Reformation. The religion which it described was divided at levels deeper than the reconciling formula – and the divisions were going to remain deep century after century. Nowhere were these divisions to go deeper than in England, the country where Parliament and the Pope acknowledged different sovereigns over long periods, and where the Roman Catholic community which had been in a position to burn Protestants was reduced by Protestant vengeance to the life or half-life of a small group, full of dilemmas and fears as well as an obstinate loyalty, on the margins of society. The examples of the martyrs were cited again and again in order to light fresh fires of bigotry and to disembowel any living hope of reconciliation. It was the central tragedy of these centuries that so much religious energy was wasted because religious labels got attached to conflicting social movements, royalist or rebellious, affluent or angry, conservative or innovating. An island people which was to have the energy to govern a quarter of mankind, to begin the modern age's industrial revolutions, and to create a more enduring empire in literature, was for many years absorbed in conflicts between Christians. Thus the development of a spiritually splendid Christian civilization was crippled by the poison of a hatred which contradicted the central teachings of the gospels, and we have only a few gestures of charity or lines of poetry as memorable symbols to show us the Christian England that might have been.

But in this book we shall not be entirely preoccupied by the disputes. We shall attempt to look beneath the divisions and to glimpse the unity of a religion as it wells up into the lives of English Christians. We shall try to catch them at prayer; listen to them singing; see their hearts breaking or lifting; find out what was the holiness they sought; go with them across the Atlantic, or into Catholic houses as exiles in Europe, or into dreams of the open road while in an English prison. We shall study some of their poetry. We shall watch the Bible coming alive to them and promising a merry supper, or we shall watch them turning back to the Catholic Church as the old highway

to heaven. We shall accompany them on the journeys of
Christian discipleship; on old pilgrimages made new by personal conviction, suffering and delight.

CHAPTER TWO

THE PROTESTANT REVOLUTION

THE DEATH OF HENRY VIII

On the night of 28 January 1547, in the palace in Whitehall which he had taken from Cardinal Wolsey, King Henry VIII lay dying. He had ruled England for not much less than forty years. Those around him had been frightened to warn him that the end was very near, and because of the delay in sending for a priest he had grown speechless before the arrival of the Archbishop of Canterbury, Thomas Cranmer.

When the Archbishop came, the King grasped his hand and refused to release it. Cranmer charitably understood this to be the last sign of the great monarch's trust in his Saviour. At any rate, Henry had many reasons to be grateful to an archbishop who had been so unfailingly helpful over his matrimonial problems. As the King and Cranmer held hands and death advanced, in the long gallery outside the chamber Edward Seymour, Earl of Hertford, was impatiently pacing up and down. Seymour, by birth merely a knight's son, had become the brother of Henry's third queen. That had given him his chance to display abilities which no other soldier of his day could match. He reckoned himself fully competent to discharge the office of 'Protector of the Realm' now that his nephew Edward, not ten years old, was to be king.

The obstacle was that the dying king had been empowered by an Act of Parliament to arrange the succession by will, and the latest edition of King Henry's will had made no provision for any Protector. Everything was to be decided in the young king's name by a council of twelve executors and when Edward came of age (at eighteen) he was to be fully entitled to cancel any decision reached during his minority. However, Seymour knew that he could overcome that obstacle. He had in his pocket the key to the safe in which this will was kept. More important, he had beside him that night Sir William Paget, the leading secretary of state. Seymour and Paget had made a deal. They had agreed that the one was to be the Protector, and the other the chief councillor, and that until the king's council had been persuaded by Paget to accept this arrangement the death was to be kept secret.

At three o'clock in the morning, therefore, when Henry was safely dead, Seymour rode into a freezing night. He was hurrying to inform King Edward of his accession to the throne and to take him into custody. The only hitch in the plot was that he accidentally rode off with the key to the safe, thus delaying by a short period Paget's ability to perform his part of the bargain. But on the Monday Seymour was back in London with King Edward – and was acknowledged by the council as Protector of the Realm. He soon began governing by proclamations rather than by Acts of Parliament, and reduced the authority of the Privy Council to its lowest level in the century. Paget felt cheated. And so, gradually, did England.

One of the reasons why Seymour was impatient during the uncertainty surrounding King Henry's dying was patriotism. As a general he had been ashamed of the military and financial disasters of the last years of the reign. Determined that Mary Queen of Scots should marry Edward VI, he was now to crush the Scots in the battle of Pinkie and to build a network of garrisoned forts in the vain hope of holding the conquered country in subjection. (With a wit rarely given to peoples so treated, the Scots called this 'the rough wooing'.) He had, too, a soldier's contempt for civilians whose acquisitive philosophy was too loudmouthed. He wanted things done decently; he was to advocate justice for the poor. But this soldier did not forget to make justice for himself his highest priority while he was Protector of the Realm and Duke of Somerset. Even a mere secretary could accumulate a fortune in such times – as did the wide-awake Protector's wide-awake secretary, Sir Thomas Thynne, who built the great house at Longleat. 'Somerset's own behaviour towards the property of the Church', writes a modern scholar, 'appears essentially acquisitive: it is difficult

even to dignify it with the title of a policy.'[1] Somerset House
was to rise palatially beside the Thames, replacing three
bishops' London houses and incorporating stones taken from
the cloister of St Paul's Cathedral and from a number of parish
churches. In the county of Somerset and in Wiltshire a vast
estate was to be accumulated, incorporating manors taken
from the Crown or the Church.

Thomas Cranmer was also bound to be prominent in the
reign which was beginning on that winter's night in 1547.
Right up to the moment when he finally lost consciousness, the
old king had treated his archbishop as his personal friend, to be
sheltered from any accusation. But even a king so obsessed
with himself cannot have been without a suspicion that his
friend had indeed become a Protestant – exactly as his enemies
alleged.

In 1544, looking for divine assistance in the war with France
and Scotland, Henry had commanded Cranmer to provide an
English litany (prayers sung in procession). Weaving together
material from medieval and Lutheran sources, the Archbishop
had produced a litany of great dignity, apart from a prayer for
deliverance 'from the tyranny of the Bishop of Rome and all his
detestable enormities'. Since then he had been interested
chiefly in the prospect of creating other services for an English
Prayer Book. He had studied, consulted, pondered and experimented. A turning point had been conversation with
Nicholas Ridley, then a parish priest in Kent, in 1546. Ridley
had been studying a ninth-century treatise *Of the Body and Blood
of the Lord*, by Ratramn. This independently-minded French
monk had insisted that Christ's presence in the Holy Communion was spiritual, thus offering an alternative to the more
physical doctrine of 'transubstantiation' which later became
orthodoxy. Cranmer was to recall in 1555 that 'Dr Ridley did
confer with me, and by sundry persuasions and authorities of
doctors drew me quite from my opinion'.

---

[1] Felicity Heal, *Of Prelates and Princes* (Cambridge, 1980), p. 137. This is a
detailed study of the economic and social position of the Tudor episcopate.
Sentimental pictures of Somerset as 'the good duke' have been corrected by M. L.
Bush, *The Government Policy of Somerset* (London, 1975), and D. E. Hoak, *The King's
Council in the Reign of Edward VI* (Cambridge, 1976).

The drafting of an English *Order of the Communion* had begun (with the king's permission) in August 1547. When it appeared, it was likely to reflect the theology of Ridley and Ratramn, if not the Protestantism of the great contemporary Continentals such as Luther and Calvin. Or at least it was unlikely that Cranmer would merely translate into English the Latin Mass which his king still loved. When on his deathbed Henry clutched his Archbishop's hand, he was no longer clutching conventional Catholicism. In his will he had commended his soul to the Virgin and the saints, and ordered Masses to be said for his soul's repose 'while the world shall endure'. But the hand which he clutched was to be thrust into the flames in Cranmer's last grand gesture as a Protestant martyr, not ten years later. And that hand had already begun to write an English Prayer Book.[2]

The tyrant who now lay dying had been determined not to damage his own conservative conscience, or his prospects of alliances with continental powers, by permitting Protestant heresies to be uttered openly in his realm. Under the Act for Abolishing Diversity in Opinions in 1539, it had been made a criminal offence, punishable by burning, for anyone to voice any denial of the old creed or any contempt for the old Mass. This penalty had been inflicted on a woman, Anne Askewe, in July 1546. In his harangue delivered to the House of Lords on Christmas Eve 1546 the King had warmed to his role as defender of the Catholic faith, and a too familiar treatment of the Bible by Protestants had fallen under his special displeasure. But Henry had not consistently acted in a way which would make sure of a Catholic future for the country. He had refused to include the leader of the Catholic-minded bishops, Stephen Gardiner, in the council which (as he hoped) was to govern England, explaining: 'I myself could use him, and rule him to all manner of purposes, as seemed good to me; but so shall you never do.' While the King lay dying the leading

---

[2] The standard biography is Jasper Ridley, *Thomas Cranmer* (Oxford, 1962). An earlier study, C. H. Smyth, *Cranmer and the Reformation under Edward VI*, is still valuable (reprinted London, 1973). For his thought see G. W. Bromiley, *Thomas Cranmer, Theologian* (London, 1956), and *The Works of Thomas Cranmer*, ed. G. E. Duffield (Appleford, Berks., 1964).

Catholic-minded nobleman, the old Duke of Norfolk, was in the Tower of London awaiting execution for treason. The Duke's heir, the Earl of Surrey, an arrogant young man (and a minor poet) who had been guilty of a plot to seize Prince Edward, had already been beheaded. Equally significant had been Henry's choice of a devout Protestant, Catherine Parr, who was the author of two devotional books, as the last of his six wives. Charmed by her beauty and tact, he had frustrated a plot of Bishop Gardiner to get her executed for heresy and treason. And he had entrusted the education of his heir to scholars who made no secret of their own leanings towards Protestantism. The future king's mind was being shaped by Richard Cox, the headmaster of Eton, and John Cheke, lecturer in Greek at Cambridge. Effectively, Henry VIII's legacy to England was far less clear than was the personal Catholicism reflected in his will.

Although he uttered no word to this effect that has survived, the dying king must have known that a scheme for equal councillors wielding an interim authority was doomed from the start. The country – as he of all men was aware – needed government, not a regency to be administered by a committee. He did not trouble to include in his will any provision for the appointment of new councillors to replace any who died. He must have known that a strong man would rise to the top before the new king could take over – and was likely to be, in appearance at any rate, a Protestant. But it seems that Henry had ceased to care. Grossly fat, tormented by the pain of an ulcerous leg, the tyrant who had always been so ruthlessly selfish was not interested in a future he could not control.[3]

THE PROTESTANT WIND

When Henry VIII's massive corpse had been buried in St George's Chapel, Windsor, it was inevitable that England should be swept by a Protestant wind. It was also inevitable

---

[3] The best biography is J. J. Scarisbrick, *Henry VIII* (London, 1968).

that those who achieved the overthrow of Catholicism would
not fail to secure their own enrichment. It has been estimated
that in the course of the reign of Edward VI Crown lands with a
capital value (twenty years' rent) exceeding £400,000 were
granted away, mostly to members of his council or senior
government officials, and lands which were to yield much more
than the £320,000 paid for them were sold off by the Crown.
Most of these lands (almost a thousand manors) had come to
the Crown from the suppression of the monasteries and the
endowed 'chantries'. The real value of these money sums is
indicated by the probability that between half and three-
quarters of the parish priests lived on less than £10 a year. It
was a massive transfer of power over England.[4]

The new authorities allowed the obstinately Catholic Princess Mary to make the solemn celebration of the Mass the
central event in the life of her well-provided household. It was
typical of their general reluctance to interfere with the private
thoughts of the people or with the private practices of the
gentry. They burned no one, repealing Henry's heresy laws
and relaxing the laws about treason. But the main effect of the
new atmosphere was to liberate Protestant propaganda, particularly in London, and this assisted Protector Somerset and
his associates in their determination to transform the appearance and the public activities of the churches. For all their
willingness to tolerate private Catholicism, they saw very
clearly that the public position of the medieval Church must be
destroyed completely. Otherwise they could not be sure of
retaining the pleasant houses which they were making for
themselves out of the Church's ruins.

Homilies were ordered to be read in every church, advocating mildly Protestant doctrines but waxing most eloquent on
the duty of obedience. 'Where there is no right order,' the
clergy were to warn the people, 'there reigneth all abuse, carnal
liberty, enormity, sin and Babylonical confusion' and 'no man
shall sleep in his house or bed unkilled.' These substitutes for
sermons were the work of Cranmer. Injunctions were issued

---

[4] These were the estimates of W. K. Jordan, *Edward VI: The Young King* (London,
1968), pp. 103–34.

commanding every parish church to possess the whole Bible in English and a copy of the *Paraphrases of the New Testament* by Erasmus. A pulpit must be provided for preaching and no more than two candles must be lit on the altar. Parliament passed an act establishing Communion for the people in both 'kinds' (bread and wine). Commissioners were sent out to see that these orders were obeyed, and Bishop Gardiner was confined in a fairly comfortable prison for refusing to assist in their enforcement; at last his conscience as a Catholic had prevailed over his loyalty as a civil servant. Bishop Bonner of London, who at first tried to resist, was frightened into silence. Lest the Church's leaders should nurse independent ideas in the future, Parliament made it clear that bishops were not elected by the Church but were to be appointed by the King's Letters Patent, which could be withdrawn.

Next the Protestant pressure was directed against the chantries, which were abolished by Act of Parliament in 1547. Chantries had been a prominent feature of late medieval religion. Thousands of benefactors had provided for Mass to be said for the repose of their own souls and for those of their families; as we have seen, Henry VIII had done so himself. Special altars, sometimes very elaborate, had added to the beauty of cathedrals or parish churches, and some great collegiate churches had been founded on this basis. The priests serving these altars had not normally been involved in the pastoral work of a parish, but had assisted the parish priest in services and had sometimes been willing (or required) to teach boys or assist the poor. The main motive in the multiplication of the chantries had, however, reflected a genuine acceptance of the teaching of the medieval Church that time spent amid the cleansing pains of Purgatory after death could be shortened by the prayers of those still on earth, particularly by the repetition of the 'sacrifice of the Mass'. To many medieval businessmen, it seemed the greatest bargain going.

Now all this lavish investment in heaven was swept away as useless. More than 2,500 chantry priests were either persuaded to serve in the parishes, or else pensioned. Endowments worth, it has been reckoned, about £500,000 in capital value (twenty years' rent) came under the control of the Court of Augmen-

tations of the King's Revenue. This was about a quarter of the
wealth of the old monasteries. Most of these lands ended up in
the hands of laymen, and one estimate is that only about
£80,000-worth was left in the Crown's possession in 1553.
Probably in the end the causes of education and charity gained
by the transfer of wealth. England was to owe much to the
immediate foundation (more accurately, the reorganization) of
schools and hospitals, in many cases bearing King Edward's
name, and many of the laymen now enriched felt moved to
make their own gifts in due course. But the suppression of the
chantries was undeniably a major change in English religion.
Only a few years before 1547 it would have been resented
bitterly as an act robbing ancestors, parents or dead children of
all hope of Paradise. It is a measure of the rapid collapse of
the old belief in Purgatory that there was now so little disturbance.[5]

Gradually the Protestant wind of change increased in force.
In February 1548 the council ordered the removal of all
'images' from the churches and chapels of the whole realm. It
was an order which caused some churchwardens to hide the
'idols' away in the hope of better times; the old Catholic fittings
were to be found, for example, concealed in the great church at
Ripon in Yorkshire in 1567. The parish churches now at last
began to look more consistently Protestant, with the paintings
of the saints on the walls whitewashed over, the statues of the
Virgin Mary and the saints near the altars removed, the great
roods in the naves dismantled, the crucifixes smashed.
Although we have very little evidence as to what the average
man thought about it all, probably 'the scar left on the edifice of
worship was in a true sense also a scar on the faith of many
thousands of humble and unlettered men'.[6]

A little later the council abolished the use of candles at
Candlemas, ashes on Ash Wednesday, palms on Palm Sunday,

[5] See W. K. Jordan, *Edward VI: The Threshold of Power* (London, 1970), pp.
181–239, and Alan Kreider, *English Chantries: The Road to Dissolution* (Cambridge,
Mass., 1979).

[6] W. K. Jordan, *Edward VI: The Young King*, p. 184. See also J. Phillips, *The
Reformation of Images: The Destruction of Art in England, 1535–1660* (Berkeley, Cal.,
1973).

'creeping to the cross' on Good Friday, holy bread and holy water. By September the excitement with which reformers urged on their followers, provoking conservative reactions, had grown alarmingly intense and all preaching had to be prohibited temporarily. But the authorities had no hesitation in encouraging the more learned type of Protestantism by importing theologians who, they believed, would direct the wind of change in the proper direction.

It was a bad time for the Reformation on the continent; the Catholic emperor's troops had won a resounding victory at Mühlberg. Some forty Protestant theologians arrived in England to take up ecclesiastical or university posts. Melancthon, the leading Lutheran after Luther's own death in 1546, refused to make the journey, but he sent many letters of advice in response to Cranmer's flattery – as did the Swiss reformers, Jean Calvin in Geneva and Heinrich Bullinger in Zürich. The renowned preacher of Strasburg, Martin Bucer, chose England as his place of exile, to become Regius Professor of Divinity at Cambridge. The equivalent chair at Oxford was filled by an Italian ex-monk, Pietro Martire Vermigli (Peter Martyr). In the universities scholars of this calibre could fire off lectures and sermons in Latin with some effect, although in Oxford – always the more conservative of the two universities – people in the streets shouted obscene insults at the new professor's wife. Many less distinguished refugees crossed the English Channel to become students or tradesmen. They formed a large congregation in London – the first congregation to be left free to worship in a thoroughly Protestant way, disregarding English laws and bishops. They were sustained by the sermons of John à Lasco, who also instructed the Archbishop during a long stay as his guest in Lambeth Palace; he had been a Polish nobleman and a Hungarian bishop. Thus stimulated, Cranmer dreamed of a wholly reformed Church of England as the very heart of a successful Protestant response to the Catholic revival; and of a Council of London to unite European Protestantism theologically. But Protestant unity was a doomed hope, which the reformers on the continent had already abandoned.

In March 1548, a new *Order of the Communion* was set forth by royal proclamation, inserting English devotions in the Latin Mass; these included the subsequently famous 'prayer of humble access'. The pamphlet was, however, a temporary measure. That autumn Cranmer placed drafts for a new Prayer Book before conferences of bishops and theologians held in Chertsey Abbey and Windsor Castle. The clergy in their Canterbury and York Convocations were almost certainly not consulted; some doubt on this matter arises because the King, in a letter to Princess Mary, claimed that they had been and the records of the Convocation of Canterbury were later destroyed by fire. When the final draft was annexed to an Act of Uniformity, the main debate took place in the House of Lords.

There Cranmer made a number of speeches showing that his mind was still in some confusion, but Nicholas Ridley, Bishop of Rochester since 1547, more lucidly defended the Communion service in the proposed book. On the key question, he was clear that 'bread is made by the Holy Ghost holy and remaineth bread still'. Just as 'a burning coal is more than a coal for there is fire in it', so Christ's divinity was present in the bread – but it was also present 'everywhere', while Christ's manhood was 'ever in heaven'. This doctrine, revived by the Protestant Reformers, was held to have been the teaching of the New Testament and of the Fathers of the Church until Lanfranc, Archbishop of Canterbury under William the Conqueror, had begun to work out the medieval doctrine of transubstantiation, defined by the Lateran Council of 1215. The medieval doctrine was now explicitly denied by Ridley's declaration that 'the natural substance of bread remaineth as it was before'. Against this battering Nicholas Heath, Bishop of Worcester, could only reassert what 'the people commonly called the Church' had come to believe: that in the Mass the bread became 'the body that was wounded with the spear and gushed out blood'.

Seven other bishops eventually voted with Heath, along with two lay peers, but the majority in the Lords was sufficient for the proposals, endorsed by a much larger majority in the Commons, to become law and to be enforced from Whit Sunday 1549. Clergy who refused to use it were threatened with the loss of their benefices, even with life imprisonment.

This first Book of Common Prayer was well suited to its position in an Act of Uniformity. The new aim was that 'now from henceforth all the whole Realm shall have but one use' in place of the diversity of medieval practice. Cranmer adapted much material – for example, the superb weekly 'collects' – from the Sarum Use which had become customary in Salisbury Cathedral and had already been adopted in many other churches. He was determined to replace rivals such as the 'uses' of Bangor, Hereford, Lincoln and York. Another aim was simplicity. Here Cranmer drew on the proposals of Cardinal Quinones, the reforming general of the Franciscans, who in 1535 had planned the abolition of two-thirds of the Saints' Days, but the main influence came from the many Protestants who had encouraged him to 'put away ... our excessive multitude of ceremonies'. The ceremonies abandoned included 'unction' (anointing with holy oil) at Confirmation. The backbone of the new book was the Bible – the whole Old Testament read chapter by chapter once a year, the whole New Testament read three times a year, and the whole Psalter recited once a month, always using Coverdale's magnificent English. In place of the eight services of the medieval daily 'office' only two services were to be said daily – Mattins and Evensong, each with two biblical lessons. But as the debate in the Lords showed, the flashpoint was 'the Supper of the Lord and the Holy Communion, commonly called the Mass'.

This service had so obviously been influenced by theological essays or actual services published for use in those parts of Germany which had accepted the Reformation, for example the *Consultation* drawn up by Bucer and Melancthon for Hermann von Wied, Archbishop of Cologne, in 1542. The central prayer of the Mass in the Sarum Use survived to such an extent that the English Protestant extremist John Hooper announced that he could not receive communion if it was used. To add to the worries of Protestants, Bishop Gardiner, now imprisoned in the Tower of London, announced that he could use the book. Indeed, all the bishops except Day of Chichester gave it their approval.

However, many people suspected – and rightly – that

Cranmer's mind had already moved beyond the ambiguity of the official book to an understanding of the service which was essentially the same as that held by continental Protestants such as Bucer or Bullinger. It seemed only a matter of time before a further revision would more completely destroy the Mass of the Catholic centuries. Meanwhile this new service was entirely in English – itself a revolution after almost a thousand years of Latin. John Merbecke, a Protestant clergyman on the musical staff of St George's Chapel, Windsor, hurriedly supplied the government's printer with simple plainsong-style music to go with the new words. And on closer examination, the service was seen to be new in character. No longer was there a mention of the priest's offering of the Mass as a sacrifice on behalf of the living and the dead; no longer would he lift up to God the miraculously changed bread and wine amid the people's adoration. The whole emphasis was now on the communion of the people, receiving 'these holy mysteries as a pledge of his love and a continual remembrance of the same . . . for us to feed upon spiritually' (as it was put in an 'exhortation' introduced into the 1548–49 services). The atmosphere was to be austerely biblical. Although the scriptural readings in this Communion service were mostly retained from the Middle Ages, at Morning and Evening Prayer the 'lessons' made very few concessions to the calendar, the supreme purpose being to read the Bible through whatever the season. To Catholic-minded Englishmen, it was ominous.

The year 1549 saw another change in the appearance of the Church. Although fast days were kept (for the sake of 'the men using the trade of living by fishing in the sea', it was explained), sexual abstinence was no longer required of the clergy; all laws prohibiting the marriage of priests were ended. Here was one more blow at the old idea of the priest as a mystery-man. The parson using the new Prayer Book was not expected to mumble Latin at the altar, to 'make God' out of the bread in the Mass, to live without a woman. Instead of the Virgin in the church, there was to be a wife in the vicarage. Many parishioners must have been deeply shocked.

In the summer of 1549 a rebellion broke out in Cornwall and Devon, fanned by priests. Already, two years before, an archdeacon come to inspect the destruction of Catholic images had been murdered. The rebels now demanded the restoration of the Latin Mass and of King Henry's heresy laws; the restriction of the people's communion to Easter, and then only in the bread; the endowment of two large monasteries in each county; the return of Cardinal Reginald Pole to the country with a seat on the King's council; the withdrawal of the English Bible; and the abolition of the Prayer Book. It was alleged that the new service in English was 'like a Christmas game'. The Cornishmen claimed they did not understand English, laying themselves open to Cranmer's scornful inquiry: did they understand Latin? The rebellion spread and besieged Exeter with plans for a march on London. Its repression was a bloody business.

Sir William Paget warned Protector Somerset of the danger in which his government now stood. He had made himself unpopular among the men who administered the State by his haughtiness (only exceeded by his wife's), and his religious policy had not endeared him to the people. As Paget bravely reminded him, 'the use of the old religion is forbidden by a law and the use of the new is not yet printed in the stomachs of eleven of the twelve parts in the realm'. However, the equally conservative north remained quiet, presumably still recovering from its rebellion against Henry VIII in 1536–37. It does not seem likely that reactions to his religious policy would have severely damaged Protector Somerset, had they not coincided with risings by men made desperate by economic change.

It was an age of inflation. The main cause seems to have been the pressure of the expanding population, which appears to have doubled during the sixteenth century in England. Another cause was the expansion of the money supply: silver flowed into Europe from the Spanish mines in South America, while the rapid development of banking and other features of capitalism made it easier for those who were credit-worthy to get credit. Still another cause was the improvement of industrial technology and of agriculture, making it easier for the efficient or the fortunate to prosper and spend, while labourers found it increasingly difficult to afford food or fuel.

Such changes were making the rich richer and the poor poorer; and their symbol was the 'enclosure' of common lands, long regarded as the property of the people of the village, to provide pasture for a landowner's sheep. Most of the profits to be made out of the production of wool, for making the undyed cloth which was England's principal export, had been made before 1550, and most of the enclosures had taken place before 1500 – but it was only now, when speech was rather more free, that men dared to complain openly about the greed of the rich. The denunciation of social justice became a theme of the Protestant preachers who modelled themselves on the prophets of Israel. The most noted attack on the rich was delivered by Bishop Hugh Latimer in his sermon 'Of the Plough' at Paul's Cross in London on New Year's Day 1548. But it was not only preachers who complained. A group of lay intellectuals, the heirs of the 'Commonwealth men' who had gathered round Thomas Cromwell under Henry VIII, emerged with proposals which were the first example in English history of the imperfect science of economics being applied to the impossible art of government.[7]

Discontent became explosive. The government needed to pay for its disastrous wars, but was not willing to levy large taxes or to halt the grant or sale of Crown lands to its own members or their friends; so it issued coins containing smaller and smaller amounts of gold or silver. This debasement of the coinage began in 1544 and sank to further depths in 1547 and 1549. It shook confidence everywhere and pushed up the rate of inflation.

Protector Somerset did not know what to do. He rebuked the rich; he issued proclamations against enclosures; he opened up the royal deer park at Hampton Court; he sent a commission to investigate grievances in the Midlands; he imposed a tax on sheep. By these measures he brought little help to the poor. But he alarmed his fellow landowners. Already his prestige had suffered through the half-mad jealousy and arrogance of his brother Thomas, who had married Henry VIII's widow

---

[7] See Julian Cornwall, *The Revolt of the Peasantry in 1549* (London, 1977), and G. R. Elton, *Reform and Reformation: England 1509–58* (London, 1977), pp. 310–27.

Catherine Parr and seen her die. He had then attempted to capture the heart of the fifteen-year-old Princess Elizabeth and to persuade the King to end the protectorate. Thomas Seymour had been executed (without trial) as a traitor, but the incident had not been forgotten by the equally ruthless men who now saw Edward Seymour as a traitor to his class. And the Protector was in no position to appeal to the people over the heads of his fellow aristocrats; his own record as a landowner by no means accorded with the later legend of 'the good duke'.

A month after the Cornish rebellion against the Prayer Book, 'Kett's rebellion' broke out in Norfolk and Suffolk. These were the richest agricultural counties, the most populous and the most Protestant. Led by a man of the middle class, Robert Kett, the rebellion symbolically dismantled enclosures of common lands, effectively unnerved the gentry, and attracted about ten thousand angry people, mostly poor, to a camp overlooking Norwich. From there demands were issued, combining many grievances about rents and the grazing of rich men's sheep at the expense of peasant rights with a few requests for Protestant clergymen who would be effective preachers and pastors. One of the clergymen who came to preach under the 'Oak of Reformation' in the rebels' camp was the future Archbishop of Canterbury, Matthew Parker, and the new Prayer Book was used daily. But Parker, while enjoying this uncharacteristic adventure, seems to have taken care to warn his congregation against the sin of rebellion; and eventually, at the end of August, professional and largely German troops arrived, commanded by John Dudley, Earl of Warwick since 1547. The mercenaries butchered Kett's men, who had mistakenly supposed that the government would respond sympathetically. Totally ruthless, the Earl of Warwick was the hero of the hour with the gentry and the merchants. By October he was able to strike against the politically isolated, militarily powerless and personally unpopular Duke of Somerset. Archbishop Cranmer added his own blow. Although he had been passionately indignant against the lower-born rebels in the summer, Cranmer was now shrewd enough to see that his political ally's days of power were over, whatever the legal situation might be; and he deserted him. He presided over the council which sent Somerset to prison in the Tower of London. In the confusion there was a brief and foolish revival of the conservatives' hopes; the Mass was said again in some Oxford college chapels. Then England found itself entering a period when the junta headed by Warwick would help itself to the fruits of political victory and would stir up a fiercer storm of Protestant change.

THE PROTESTANT STORM

Because England could not afford a foreign policy Boulogne was sold off to the French, leaving only Calais as the last remnant of Henry V's empire. The government also abandoned the gestures in favour of social justice – gestures which, however futile their effect may have been, had encouraged popular resentment against landlords. There was now to be a stern discipline and the poor were to accept their lot. It has been reckoned that the price of food for a labourer's family, which had increased by half during the 1540s (after increasing by half over the period 1510–40), doubled during the 1550s. At the same time the new government began to lay the foundations of an economic recovery which would benefit the rich by restoring the value of the gold and silver in the coins; the debasement of the currency had proved too disastrous. And those who had supplanted Protector Somerset proceeded to complete the downfall of the medieval Church, the field where the richest pickings lay.

There was still no thought of religious liberty for all. An independently-minded housewife, Joan Boucher, was burned in 1550. She was heretical on the subject of the Incarnation, denying that Christ had taken the flesh of the Virgin Mary. She taunted her judges for burning her 'for a piece of flesh', reminding them that under Henry VIII they had burned Anne Askew 'for a piece of bread' although they had themselves now come to abandon the belief that in the Mass the bread was changed substantially. At the same time, in order to demonstrate further the orthodoxy of England's new rulers, a

German surgeon living in London was burned for denying the divinity of Christ.

Archbishop Cranmer approved of these burnings. He also adopted a disciplinarian's attitude when John Hooper was appointed Bishop of Gloucester but refused to wear the medieval vestments. Cranmer had him bullied and even imprisoned, to make him yield the point before he could be consecrated as a bishop. The Archbishop knew how important it was for the official English Reformation to be seen to be theologically respectable and properly dressed. He was now, however, able to make sure that the transfer of wealth to the gentry from the Church was morally respectable.

Although his dislike of the naked greed of the men now in power became obvious, so did his unwillingness even to contemplate heading a move against them. He almost entirely ceased to attend council meetings – although he successfully resisted an attempt to deprive the see of Canterbury of its surviving wealth by protesting at the prospect of 'stark beggary'.

After the formal deprivation of the imprisoned Gardiner and Turnstall, the bishoprics of Winchester and Durham were reduced to the level of a stipend thought proper by laymen who believed that they were themselves better able to resist, or at least to enjoy, wealth's temptations. There were not many clergymen as conscientious as the Dean of Durham who refused an offer of an extra £1,000 a year with promotion as Bishop of Durham, because he would not agree that two-thirds of the bishop's traditional income was to be handed over to the Crown. The new Bishop of Winchester was John Ponet, aged thirty-six. He had married a butcher's wife during her husband's lifetime, but had then divorced her and married again; and he was more obliging than the Dean of Durham over financial arrangements with the government. John Hooper, Bishop of Gloucester, was persuaded to add the work of the Bishop of Worcester to his own, thus releasing more estates for hungry laymen. Thomas Thirlby, Bishop of Westminster, was moved to Norwich, and his little diocese, created in 1540, was suppressed altogether. It seemed probable that soon all the bishops would be placed on stipends of a suitable modesty.

At the head of the invasion of the bishops' estates was John Dudley, Earl of Warwick. For many years he had been quietly rebuilding the family fortune which had seemed lost for ever when his father, Henry VII's financial agent, had been executed to appease the people in 1510. He still moved with some caution. The fallen Protector was released from prison and John Dudley's eldest son was married to one of his daughters. But when Somerset could not resist an attempt to recover his political position, he was condemned for felony (although the Lords refused to declare him guilty of treason) and 'had his head cut off upon Tower Hill between eight and nine in the morning'. So King Edward coldly recorded in his diary. The Earl of Warwick took trouble to win the young king's admiration, was elevated to the dukedom of Northumberland, and devoted himself to the acquisition of land, particularly in the north.

With the triumphant new duke as its president, the council ordered the completion of the removal from the parish churches of all the painted statues, silver plates, rich vestments and other accessories of Catholic worship. 'Idols' were to be destroyed ruthlessly, although an exception was made 'for a monument of any king, prince or nobleman or other dead person which hath not been commonly reputed or taken for a saint'. Commissioners were sent out to ensure that these temptations to superstition were sent to London for sale by the government. Enterprising churchwardens had everywhere either secreted their treasures or sold them off and applied the money to church repairs; perhaps two-thirds of the goods had disappeared in this way before the government issued its decree. But another reason for the quiet reception of the order may well have been that people saw that it was useless complaining to these noblemen, who were in no danger of being taken for saints by posterity.

Under Northumberland the council did what it could to encourage those who might fill the religious vacuum created by the old Church's fall. The new Protestantism did not have nearly enough propagandists; it seems that only about a hundred clergymen in the whole country could be trusted enough by the bishops to be licensed as preachers. But some of

the preachers sponsored by the government were veritable
apostles of the new religion. Bernard Gilpin toured Northumberland, preferring the worst weather because then his
hearers would not be distracted by their agricultural work.
Hugh Latimer preached to king and people a vision of Church
and State purified and glorified. And the Protestants were now
able to enforce their convictions; for example, in 1550 Nicholas
Ridley began to exert his reforming authority as Bishop of
London after Edmund Bonner's deprivation.[8]

Cranmer, despite his unhappiness about the Duke of Northumberland's predatory regime, seized the opportunity to produce ecclesiastical reforms. He had been nursing ideas for
some time. Through the turbulent summer of 1549 he was
working on a new 'ordinal' or book of ordination services,
which after revision was authorized by the council in March
1550. Key passages – the 'exhortation' and 'examination' in
the Ordering of Priests – had been drafted by Martin Bucer.
The 'minor orders' from subdeacon downwards were abolished. Although the Catholic orders of bishop, priest and
deacon were retained from the Middle Ages (to the indignation
of Bishop Hooper), the atmosphere of the new services was
decidedly Protestant (to the indignation of the remaining
bishops of a Catholic mind). The whole emphasis was on
preaching and pastoral work, not on the priest's power to offer
the 'sacrifice of the Mass'; and to drive the point home it was
now ordered that the medieval stone altars in the parish
churches should be replaced systematically by wooden tables.
New bishops were no longer to be consecrated with the medieval ceremonies, putting on a mitre, a ring and gloves. In 1552
further changes were made. New bishops were no longer to be
given the pastoral staff, and new priests were no longer to be
given the vessels (the paten and chalice) of the Mass – although
St Thomas Aquinas had taught that this formed the essential
'matter' of the sacrament of ordination, and in 1439 a pope had
endorsed that teaching. What new priests of the Church of
England did receive, from 1550 onwards, was a Bible.

[8] See Jasper Ridley, *Nicholas Ridley* (London, 1951), and A. G. Chester, *Hugh Latimer, Apostle to the English* (Philadelphia, Pa., 1954).

In July 1550 Cranmer published his only substantial exercise in theological theory: *A Defence of the True and Catholic Doctrine of the Sacrament of the Body and Blood of Christ*. It was attacked, as a denial of Catholic doctrine, in a lengthy book which Stephen Gardiner wrote that summer in a prison cell in the Tower of London – an attack to which the council replied by depriving the author both of his bishopric and of his writing materials. Since Gardiner somehow gathered materials with which to engage in a further literary controversy with the Archbishop, a more effective step was taken when the council encouraged Cranmer to edit a new and more Protestant version of the Book of Common Prayer. Writing from Geneva, Jean Calvin urged the Archbishop to make haste; 'to speak plainly, I fear that so many autumns wasted in procrastination may be followed by an eternal winter'. The lines on which revision was to proceed were laid down by Martin Bucer, who published detailed *Censura* or criticisms of the 1549 book shortly before his death. From Oxford Peter Martyr wrote in with other suggestions, most of which were accepted by the bishops.[9]

The new Prayer Book was authorized by Parliament in an Act of Uniformity passed just before Easter 1552, prescribing its use in the parish churches and imprisonment for any of the laity who absented themselves; at the third offence, imprisonment was to be for life. (In 1549 only the clergy refusing to use the new service had been punished.) It did not completely meet all Protestant demands. This was to be shown by Jean Calvin's cool judgement in January 1555 that the book of 1552 was satisfactory in the main but contained 'bearable follies'. However, in England in 1552 conservatives were horrified to see how extensive were the changes which had been made to satisfy the Protestant spokesmen.

In the Holy Communion service the revisers had altered every phrase which in 1549 had allowed men such as Gardiner to say that the doctrine of Christ's 'real presence' was taught. The old title, 'the Mass', was no longer given even as an alternative, and the old vestments were no longer to be worn.

---

[9] C. L. R. A. Hopf studied *Martin Bucer and the English Reformation* (Oxford, 1946).

At the last moment, when the book had already been passed by
the bishops and Parliament and printed, the council on its own
authority ordered the insertion of a 'rubric' or note which
explained that the retention of the custom of kneeling at this
service did not imply the recognition of any 'real and essential
presence there being of Christ's natural flesh and blood'. This
order by the council was made because the king had been
impressed by a vehement sermon against idolatry preached by
John Knox; and it greatly annoyed Cranmer. But the denial of
medieval teaching was not out of keeping with Cranmer's own
stately prayer that 'we, receiving these thy creatures of bread
and wine . . . may be partakers of his most blessed body and
blood' – not, as in the 1549 book, that the bread and the wine
'may be unto us the body and blood'. The heart of the new
service was reached when the priest delivered the bread to the
communicant, saying: 'Take and eat this in remembrance that
Christ died for thee, and feed on him in thy heart by faith, with
thanksgiving.'

Elsewhere the changes in the Prayer Book were almost
equally distressing to conservatives. Familiar customs such as
the 'exorcism' or expulsion of devils at Baptism and the
'signing with the cross' at Confirmation were swept away. The
sick could no longer have the Body and Blood of Christ
'reserved' for them to receive privately, and when believed to
be dying they could no longer be anointed with holy oil. The
revised funeral service abolished prayers which implied any
belief that the condition of the dead might be affected by the
intercessions of the living. And the medieval vestments, which
Cranmer had so recently defended against Hooper, were also
abandoned. Ridley looked thoroughly Protestant when, in St
Paul's Cathedral on 1 November 1552, he used the new Prayer
Book for the first time.[10]

Early that year, in order to expound more fully the Protestantism behind the new Prayer Book, the council ordered

---

[10] The best survey of Cranmer's liturgical work is to be found in G. J. Cuming, *A
History of Anglican Liturgy* (London, 1969). See also C. W. Dugmore, *The Mass and the
English Reformers* (London, 1958), and Peter Brooks, *Thomas Cranmer's Doctrine of the
Eucharist* (London, 1965).

Cranmer to produce a set of short 'articles' of belief which it
proceeded to revise. Cranmer had a draft ready because for
some time he had been in the habit of asking certain questions
of preachers he was being asked to license, and he had been
discussing the possible contents of a new statement of doctrine
with fellow bishops while concentrating on the revision of
worship. Eventually Forty-two Articles were authorized by a
royal mandate in June 1552, requiring all clergy, all schoolmasters, and all members of the universities on taking their
degrees to subscribe to them. The Articles were never submitted to any gathering of the clergy, although they were issued
with the false claim that they had been 'agreed on by the
Bishops and other learned and godly men, at a Synod holden in
London'. Cranmer protested at this contemptuous display of
lay power by the telling of a lie. His protests were disregarded.

The Articles allied the Church of England with Lutherans
and Calvinists on the continent, although some of their
phraseology was more gentle than were some other documents
of the Reformation, and they did not seek to establish an
English position about problems disputed between the Reformation's sons. The definition of the Church was all that Luther
had fought for: 'the visible Church of Christ is a congregation
of faithful men, in the which the pure Word of God is preached
and the Sacraments be duly administered according to Christ's
ordinance in all those things that of necessity are requisite to
the same.' The word 'bishop' did not occur in that definition,
although the next sentence did refer to the Bishops of Rome:
'the Church of Rome hath erred, not only in their living and
manner of ceremonies, but also in matters of faith.' And
predestination was defined in accordance with Calvin's
teaching. 'Predestination to life', the article affirmed, 'is the
everlasting purpose of God, whereby (before the foundations of
the world were laid) he hath constantly decreed by his counsel
secret to us, to deliver from curse and damnation those whom
he hath chosen in Christ out of mankind, and to bring them by
Christ to everlasting salvation, as vessels made to honour.'
This doctrine was said to be 'full of sweet, pleasant, and
unspeakable comfort to godly persons', but other articles made
it clear that those *not* included in the number 'chosen in Christ

out of mankind' would never be saved. It was futile to trust in 'the merit of our own works or deservings'. A man would not be saved because of diligence 'to frame his life according to the light of Nature'.

This statement of doctrine, clearly the work of a committee, has been searched for ambiguities which might permit a Catholic interpretation; in the seventeenth century Francis Davenport, and in the nineteenth J. H. Newman, exercised their ingenuity in order to make out a case. But when read dispassionately against its historical background, the document is seen as an almost total rejection of the medieval system of the Pope's supremacy, the infallible General Council, the sacrifice of the Mass, and so forth. Catholic doctrines taught by Henry VIII to his obedient people were now 'a fond thing verily invented and grounded upon no warrant of Scripture, but rather repugnant to the Word of God'. No fewer than eighteen of the articles attacked the Protestant extreme of Anabaptism, however. It is clear that one important motive of those who published such a document in the 1550s was to assert the orthodoxy of the Church of England against the expanding left wing of the Reformation as well as against medieval Catholicism.

Cranmer knew perfectly well that Luther and Calvin had inspired legislation as well as new worship and theology, and it was his intention to accompany the doctrinal summary with a new code of 'canons' or ecclesiastical law – a project authorized by Parliament as long ago as 1533. Here, too, he had been brooding and drafting for some time, and was ready when the project was entrusted to a commission of thirty-two by Parliament in 1550. Peter Martyr was again a chief adviser. A fairly comprehensive document, the *Reformatio Legum Ecclesiasticarum*, was completed.

As was fitting while the memory of Henry VIII was green, the proposed code displayed a liberal attitude towards the dissolution of marriage. Adultery, desertion or ill-treatment could justify a divorce, and the innocent party might remarry. The proposed code also reflected the new practice of continental Protestantism by requiring an annual synod in every diocese, where representatives of the laity as well as of the clergy were to consult with the bishop. Another proposal was that the bishop should be more personally involved in the administration of discipline, instead of delegating such duties to the archdeacons and legal officials in the practice inherited from the Middle Ages. As the eager activities of Bishops Ridley and Hooper were showing at this time, the effect would be to transform the bishop's role. But here again, a main motive was to discipline the extremism of the radicals. Englishmen taking advantage of the confusion of the times to propagate new heresies, or to indulge in old vices, were to be brought before the reconstituted ecclesiastical courts, and solemnly excommunicated. An excommunicated person, the new articles reminded the people, 'ought to be taken of the whole multitude of the faithful, as an Heathen and Publican, until he be openly reconciled by penance.' Hardened heretics were to be handed over to the secular authorities for punishment, presumably death. Adulterers were to be imprisoned for life.

It was, no doubt, the prospect of restoring power to the clergy on this scale that made the council under Northumberland's leadership abandon the project of a revision of church law. The code was not published until in 1571 John Foxe brought it out unofficially, and Thomas Norton, a Puritan MP, led an abortive move to get it made official. Even then, no action was taken. Shakespeare's contemporaries had no wish to see all adulterers imprisoned for life.

THE CRISIS OF 1553

The fate of the proposed revision of church law confirmed Archbishop Cranmer's dislike of the Duke of Northumberland and his accomplices, and a more outspoken theologian, John Knox, told Northumberland to his face that he was a 'dissembler'. It does not, however, seem that any of the Protestants had any idea about how close they were to a Catholic reaction. It was generally expected that King Edward would enjoy a long life, marry and beget an heir who would be educated as a Protestant. The King, himself an increasingly well-informed and sincere Protestant, argued heatedly when attempting to dissuade his sister Mary from her insistence on attending Mass. With his piety, his white skin and his reddish hair, he looked unworldly – but he was no bookworm. He was keenly interested in sport, politics and administration. And he was imperious. During 1552 he began issuing orders which implied that he would soon become as much of a dictator as his father had been. Had he lived to the same age as his father, his reign would have lasted until 1593.

After the Christmas festivities in 1552, however, the King fell ill. At first there was no great alarm. His sister Mary visited him and they exchanged small talk. Northumberland continued to keep her informed of her brother's condition, although gradually the rumour spread that he had poisoned the King. To the doctors it became clear that the King had the disease now known as pulmonary tuberculosis – and that it would be fatal, although he was only sixteen years of age.

The danger to Protestantism was frightening. Henry VIII's will had provided for the succession of the Catholic Mary if Edward died childless. The King had himself made plans to exclude both his sisters. Mary's exclusion was to be expected because she would undo all his work, but he also excluded Elizabeth, presumably because, as an unmarried woman of twenty years and uncertain opinions, she was too unreliable. The one legal argument which he could use was that Acts of Parliament, never repealed despite Henry's will, had made both Mary and Elizabeth bastards. Perhaps intending to secure Parliamentary approval, he had prepared a 'device for the succession' in which he bequeathed the Crown first 'to the Lady Jane's heirs male'. This referred to Lady Jane Grey, the eldest daughter of Frances, Duchess of Suffolk, a daughter of Henry VIII's younger sister Mary. King Henry in his own will had paid no attention to the claim of the royal Stuarts of Scotland through descent from his elder sister, Margaret, so that King Edward had this precedent for setting aside Mary, Queen of Scots, who was a Catholic. Now, when his own death seemed near, he persuaded the Duchess of Suffolk to renounce her rights and made a simple alteration in this handwritten 'device', so that it read: 'to the Lady Jane and her heirs male'.

Lady Jane was aged sixteen, a cultured and sweet-tempered young lady, and the wife of the Duke of Northumberland's son, the Earl of Guildford. In June the King – encouraged but, it seems, not forced by Northumberland – exerted all his remaining authority to get the judges and the council to endorse his 'device' in her favour. They all knew that if the scheme miscarried it would be treason against Mary; their lives were at stake. Some of them, Cranmer included, had enough courage to protest at the change in King Henry's will. An unrepealed statute had made it treason to contravene that will and had laid it down that, unless that will were to decree otherwise, the Crown should go to the Lady Mary if Edward died without issue. But Edward insisted on his way, and it seemed treason to disobey while he was the living king. On 6 July 1553 he died.

The preparations for the reign of Queen Jane were then put into effect. Behind the plot was an army of three thousand and all the hope of a Protestant England. But the troops sent from London under Lord Robert Dudley to secure Mary found that she had been warned and had escaped. From that moment all was lost. While she remained at freedom increasing numbers rallied to her stronghold in Suffolk, Framlingham Castle. The sailors ordered to guard the East Anglian coast mutinied in her favour, and even Bishop Hooper went about urging submission to her because she was the legitimate successor. In London the councillors, for the most part sheltering in the Tower, were in mental turmoil. Collectively they had to uphold the queen they had proclaimed; individually they were preparing to abandon Jane to her fate. Sir William Petre, for example, was happy to serve as a highly efficient secretary of state through all the changes between 1544 and 1557.

To counter this instinctive royalism, Northumberland needed to display very great determination, energy and skill. Instead he went through the drama as if in a daze. For some months he had been telling his few intimate friends that he was ill, tired and depressed; and now he seemed to be more conscious of the divisions and hesitations among his fellow councillors than of the need to capture Mary at any price. On 20 July, pathetically attempting to imitate the enthusiasm of similar scenes in London the previous day, he threw his cap in the air in the market place at Cambridge and proclaimed Mary queen. Almost exactly a month later, he was executed as a traitor.

On the day before his death he took part in a Mass in the chapel of the Tower of London, explaining to the congregation: 'Truly, I profess here before you all that I have received the sacrament according to the true Catholic faith; and the plague that is upon the realm and upon us now is that we have erred from the faith these sixteen years.' It may have been an attempt to move the heart of Queen Mary. Later that day he wrote to the Earl of Arundel, a potential mediator: 'O good my lord, remember how sweet life is, and how bitter the contrary.' But both his treason and his failure had been so complete that it is difficult to believe that he seriously expected to be spared; he had himself not spared the Duke of Somerset, who in his turn had not spared his own brother. He must have known that the game was up. The probable explanation of his return to the faith of his boyhood is that as death became inescapable he thought Protestantism poor equipment for it.

Many of his fellow countrymen shared his willingness to abandon the 'new religion' at this stage. England – or enough of England to be decisive – evidently felt that a return to the religion 'which hath continued throughout all Christendom since Christ' (as Northumberland said on the scaffold) was either right in itself or, at the least, an acceptable price to pay for political and social stability under King Henry's daughter. The reign of Edward VI had been a time when preachers such as Hugh Latimer had heralded the reign of righteousness and truth. But out of the range of the preacher's visionary rhetoric, every-day life had seemed less edifying. With the churches stripped, their comforting customs prohibited, and the poor experiencing the beggary which even the bishops feared, Protestantism seemed to have done nothing but damage and 'the sordid competition of all classes for a share in ecclesiastical spoils impugned the credit both of the government and of the religious principles which the government was claiming to promote'.[11]

---

[11] A. G. Dickens, *The English Reformation* (revised London, 1967), p. 298. B. L. Beer's *Northumberland* (Kent, Ohio, 1973) added a few touches to the narrative in *Edward VI: The Threshold of Power* by another American scholar, W. K. Jordan.

CHAPTER THREE

THE CATHOLIC REACTION

QUEEN MARY'S CHURCH

Mary's reign began very hopefully, and her finest hour was in those weeks in the summer of 1553 when, at the age of thirty-seven, she gained the throne of England by courageously insisting that she had inherited it and was fully worthy of it.[1] Her strongest supporters, the agents of the emperor Charles V, had urged her to accept Queen Jane, but she knew herself and her people better. She had been admirably brave in clinging to her rights and to her religion in the reigns of her father and brother. Under Henry she had been paraded in situations designed to emphasize her inferiority to Anne Boleyn's child. Under Edward she had been bullied in repeated attempts to make her abandon the Mass which had become her chief comfort. People knew she had at length submitted to her father after Anne Boleyn's execution, accepting his supremacy over the Church in England and the unlawfulness of his marriage with her now dead mother, Catherine of Aragon; they understood that this concession had made it possible for him to appoint her as his heir should Edward die childless. But they did not hold it against her. It was almost universally believed that a daughter owed obedience to a father and a subject to a sovereign.

Now that she was herself the sovereign, she often played the role convincingly. She was interested in administration and worked long hours at it. On many occasions she knew how to dress majestically, how to behave graciously, how to make a stirring speech; we should not always see her in the light of her tragic end. She was in a number of ways her father's daughter,

---

[1] D. M. Loades, *The Reign of Mary Tudor* (London, 1979), is the best study.

and many of those who supported her against Queen Jane
trusted that she would revive her father's religious policy.
Until December 1554 she did exercise a supremacy over the
Church while securing the repeal of the Protestant legislation
passed in her brother's reign. Her coronation titles included
'Supreme Head of the Church'; a secret dispensation arrived
from Rome permitting this for the time being. On later documents the ambiguous style 'etc.' was preferred, but still she
exercised the supremacy. She deprived about eight hundred
clergymen of their livings on the grounds that they were
married and that she had decided that the Church's medieval
law was to be revived, although at this time the marriage of
priests was still perfectly legal by Act of Parliament. In March
1554 she deprived seven bishops of their sees and nominated
seven new ones for election by their cathedral chapters (having
secretly and illegally made sure of approval from Rome). Had
she simply put the religious clock back to her father's time, and
had she married an Englishman as proof of this patriotic
Catholicism, she would probably have continued to please her
people well enough – and she would have recovered much of
the happiness which she had known as a little girl adored by
her sometimes sentimental father.

There were, however, already signs when she became queen
that she was in conscience firmly persuaded that a Catholic
ought to obey the Pope in religion; that her mother, defended
by the Pope, had been entirely in the right. There were also
signs that the strains in her life since her father had put her
mother away had inflicted deep psychological damage on her.

In July 1550 she had nearly agreed to escape from England
on a ship sent over by her cousin and constant patron, the
emperor Charles V. When the Emperor's agents had reached
her house she had dithered at the last moment, refusing to go
with them but repeating: 'What is to become of me?' Had she
fled abroad then, there can be little doubt that Parliament
would have felt free to overturn King Henry's will and exclude
her from the succession. In the event she had decided to remain
– and thus to be available for the present reversal of her
fortunes, which she attributed to the direct intervention of
God. But her behaviour while queen showed that in deepest

reality her heart had left England with its prejudices far
behind. She soon disclosed her determination to marry the
Emperor's son, Philip of Spain. She had been lonely for too
long. There had been only talk of marriage for her (her first
betrothal had been at the age of two, to the Dauphin of
France); she had not known what it was to be happy – or so she
said. She was pathetically thrilled to be a bride. And after all
the years during which she had relied so entirely on the
Emperor for advice and protection, she was delighted to be
marrying his son. She was marrying, moreover, a prince of
the proudly Catholic country from which her mother had
come.

The mere prospect of this Spanish match ended Mary's
honeymoon with her people. One of the leaders of a nationalist
conspiracy in January 1554 was Edward Courtenay, a Catholic aristocrat with some Plantagenet blood. He had hoped to
marry the Queen himself. Another was Lady Jane Grey's
father, the Duke of Suffolk. A future queen, Elizabeth, almost
certainly knew of the plot and would have taken advantage of it
had it succeeded. The most forceful rebel was Sir Thomas
Wyatt, a gentleman of Kent, who led an attack on London in
February. After a fortnight of uncertainty, the attack failed –
one important factor being the steadfast courage of Queen
Mary, who earlier had spoken direct to the Commons, silenc-
ing their objections to the marriage on which she had set her
heart. But inevitably the rebellion was punished, and the
executions began to create the image of 'Bloody Mary'.

In the early stages of her reign she had been so little thirsty
for the blood of Protestants that in the period 1553–55 some
eight hundred of them were allowed to leave England for
safety.[2] The exodus had included Peter Martyr from Oxford,
Bishop Ponet of Winchester, and John Knox, who under
Edward VI refused the bishopric of Rochester as being too
Papistical an office. There seems little doubt that Mary's
government would have been relieved had the most famous
Protestant leaders, Cranmer, Latimer, Hooper and Rogers,
also taken the opportunity to escape. Cranmer, for example,

---

[2] C. H. Garrett studied *The Marian Exiles* (Cambridge, 1938).

had not been imprisoned until two months after Mary's accession. He had provoked the action by an attack on the Mass as a device of Satan. Even then he had been given time to send his wife and children abroad and to have a last talk with Peter Martyr, urging him to flee. Mary had been so merciful to the conspiracy to prevent her succession that she had spared the life of Queen Jane and had taken a third of Queen Jane's council into her own; thus Sir William Paget was still a leading minister. But now in the spring of 1554, Lady Jane Grey, her husband and her father were executed like Wyatt and many others. Courtenay was exiled. Elizabeth, after a brief imprisonment, was released, having given a promise of good behaviour. For the rest of the reign the Protestant princess lay low, attending the Mass and refusing to have anything further to do with the minor protests or plots which were to punctuate her sister's reign.

Mary's marriage on 25 July 1554 in Winchester Cathedral was conducted by Bishop Gardiner, who had already officiated at the coronation. Although he had at first favoured marriage with Courtenay, Gardiner had come to accept the advantages of a firm alliance with the House of Hapsburg, clinging to the provision in the marriage treaty that Spaniards should not hold office in England. Within a year of the marriage he had written a secret memorandum for Philip, advising him how to handle the English so as to allay their suspicions but end up by ruling them. It was a document inspired by the famous book of advice to a Borgia prince by Machiavelli.[3]

Mary's long-frustrated pleasure in married life was so obvious that before long her doctors were assuring her that she was pregnant. Public rejoicings and prayers were ordered. Letters were prepared announcing the birth of the next King of England, who by the marriage treaty was to rule the Low Countries as well, with the prospect of succession to the whole Spanish empire if Philip's son by a previous marriage left no heir. Every possible domestic preparation was made in the palace at Hampton Court, and the Queen's confinement

---

[3] *A Machiavellian Treatise by Stephen Gardiner* was edited by P. S. Donaldson (Cambridge, 1975).

became the topic of a nation's talk. But the pregnancy was imaginary; modern medical opinion is that it was the result of an ovarian dropsy which caused abdominal swelling. In the end even a heartbroken Queen came to admit that there would be no child. Her private prayer book survives; the prayer before childbirth is stained with tears.

The prolonged farce angered Philip. He was eleven years Mary's junior, and was now as bored as he was embarrassed by his time among the English, whose language he could not speak. The ambitions recommended by the cynical Bishop of Winchester did not seem worth the time of a prince of Spain. In reality, since Gardiner had failed in his efforts to have Elizabeth executed, or at least excluded from the succession, the only alternative to the recognition of her as the next queen of England would be a Spanish coup. Such a move was utterly inconceivable as a piece of practical politics; so that the Bishop's Machiavellian memorandum was not so realistic, after all. Queen Mary's failure to produce a child had made her whole reign futile, and Philip was in no mood to waste more time on it. In August 1555 he cut his losses. He left England in order to attend to his responsibilities in the Netherlands – and to the young, beautiful and cheerful women to be found there. He returned for three months in the summer of 1557, solely in order to secure a declaration of war against the French and the Pope (who had excommunicated him). After that he never saw his wife again.

Plunged deeper into melancholy by the slowly apprehended truths that she was barren and that her husband had deserted her, the Queen found some consolation in the frequent comparisons made between her and Mary the mother of the Lord. Her portraits show the increasing marks on her of a sense of mission deepening into mania. She had been preserved through so many dangers in order that she might undertake a great work for God and his true Church, and she had been denied so many worldly pleasures in order that she might concentrate on her religious duties. Her white and haggard face reflected her physical, and perhaps also her mental, illness. Her staring eyes were those of a woman who could scarcely sleep but would often sob her heart out in private; and her lips became those of a publicly inflexible fanatic.

Until his death in November 1555, her Lord Chancellor was Stephen Gardiner, who thus in his old age, after five years in prison, enjoyed the power which had evaded him under his master Henry VIII. He was impatient for the full restoration of their estates to bishops, monasteries and chantries. When this was refused, he insisted more successfully on the full enforcement of the late medieval heresy laws against obstinate heretics whose wills clashed with his. The cruelty was not out of character, for it seems fair to say that Gardiner 'spoilt his abilities by ruthless arrogance, unvarying deviousness, and a relentless hatred for men who disagreed with him . . . Among the power-hungry politicians of the age he stood out as the one man who played the game invariably for keeps: none of his opponents escaped a violent death'.[4] Protestants being tried by him delighted to embarrass him by quoting his defence of Henry VIII's supremacy over the Church, particularly in his treatise *De Vera Obedientia* which was reprinted by those now in exile. Protestants also reprinted the commendation once given to that anti-papal book by Edmund Bonner, now restored as Bishop of London and very active against heretics.

Gardiner, who knew that he was hated, sometimes expressed sorrow for his violent temper but often hotly denied the charge of cruelty. He could not claim to have been completely consistent; and no doubt Queen Mary was among those who remembered how he had eloquently supported her father against her mother. His nicknames included 'Wily Winchester' and 'Doctor Doubleface'. But two consistent themes had indeed run through his life ever since his birth in the fifteenth century. He had kept the Catholic faith taught to him as a boy; he had remained faithful to that even under Edward VI. And he had served the Crown. For as long as he could under Edward VI, although he had obviously hated the Protestants in power, this highly skilled lawyer had defended himself by arguing that he was only waiting for the new king to come of age, and that until then King Henry's will was sacred. It has proved possible to write a modern biography of Wily Winches-

[4] G. R. Elton, *Reform and Reformation*, p. 394.

ter around the belief that 'after attaining eminence he became the devoted servitor of Church and Commonwealth'.[5]

The central figure in the full restoration of Catholicism was a prelate far less worldly than Gardiner. Cardinal Reginald Pole landed at Dover as the papal legate (ambassador) on 20 November 1554, and ten days later presided at a highly emotional ceremony reconciling England to the papacy. He had been appointed legate fifteen months before, but the Emperor had held him up in his journey since he had made no secret of his opposition to the Spanish marriage, and the English had been not at all impatient to receive him. Parliament wished to make absolutely sure that no question of the forcible restoration of church lands would arise.

Pole, unlike Gardiner, was a true aristocrat. His mother, Margaret Countess of Salisbury, had been the daughter of the Duke of Clarence, Edward IV's brother. He was also a man of deep prayer and wide culture. His time in Oxford had caused Sir Thomas More to declare him 'no less conspicuous for his virtue than for his learning'. He had gone to Italy for further study in 1521, and had returned there in 1530, since the service of Henry VIII implied in the offer of the Archbishopric of York on Cardinal Wolsey's fall was too distasteful.

He had been made a cardinal and appointed to high office in the papal states. When in 1536 Pope Paul III intended to make changes in the Vatican, Pole had been one of the reformers drawing up the programme. When the Council of Trent met to undertake reform in the winter of 1545–46, he had been one of the three cardinals presiding. When the cardinals were electing a new pope in the winter of 1549–50, he had been the Emperor's candidate and had come within one vote of the majority needed. But he had shown a cautious sympathy with moderates such as Cardinal Contarini (a fellow aristocrat), who saw the need to reform a corrupt Church. These moderates had been converted to a personal, Christ-centred religion themselves and, while loyally Catholic, did not condemn Lutheranism as totally heretical. The arrival of the French cardinals had cost Pole the papacy, but he may also have been thought too

---

[5] J. A. Muller, *Stephen Gardiner and the Tudor Reaction* (London, 1926), p. 301.

much the aloof English aristocrat, still a deacon not a priest. It was typical of him that he withdrew from the Council of Trent with the plea that his health had broken down under the strain. His heart had never been in the politics surrounding the papacy, and he was now glad to be recalled to an England he had not seen for almost a quarter of a century. It was a curious consequence of his response to his new vocation as a pastor among his fellow countrymen that he was at last willing to be ordained a priest – two days before his consecration as Archbishop of Canterbury, in March 1556.

During Pole's time in England, however, the former Cardinal Caraffa became Pope Paul IV. The new pope, a very stupid man, had two hatreds: for the Spaniards who had conquered his native Naples, and for reformers who for all he knew might be heretics. Both hatreds were satisfied by the insults now delivered to Philip of Spain's wife and to Pole, who was stripped of his title as papal legate to England. The title was then given to a Franciscan friar who, like the Pope, was in his eighties and totally conservative. As a member of a reforming circle under suspicion among the now triumphant guardians of ultra-orthodoxy, Pole was summoned to Rome to answer accusations of heresy before the tribunal of the Inquisition. With the support of his queen he refused to travel, and was saved from further humiliation by the long illness which led to his death. Such was the reward of his loyalty to the papacy.[6]

Why, then, was Pole described by his successor at Canterbury as the 'cannibal' of the English Church? Why did he always refuse to meet his predecessor? – thus showing considerably less courtesy than Cranmer had shown to Bishop Gardiner when at the height of his power. Why did this scholar who had risked the accusation of heresy in order to do theological justice to the Lutherans fail to take the Protestantism of his fellow countrymen seriously? And why did this spiritually-minded aristocrat who was too fastidious to be much involved in the gruesome business of burning heretics (in his own

---

[6] William Shenk, *Reginald Pole, Cardinal of England* (London, 1950), has been supplemented by David Fenlon, *Heresy and Obedience in Tridentine Italy: Cardinal Pole and the Counter-Reformation* (Cambridge, 1972).

diocese he left it to the Bishop of Dover) nevertheless allow so much energy to be diverted to that policy, so that a modern scholar can truly say that 'the Marian Church was far more concerned with the few who defied it than with the many who ignored it'?[7]

One explanation is that the Cardinal had a cosmopolitan aristocrat's contempt for the lowborn and half-educated Protestant extremists who supplied many of the victims of the purge over which he presided. Archbishop Cranmer's own attitude had not been very different. But another motive seems to have dominated the Cardinal's heart in this matter. He passionately despised Cranmer and the other bishops who had done Henry VIII's bidding. He despised them because to him Henry was not a monarch to be judged by normal standards; he was a monster. Pole had abandoned his habitual caution and good manners to say as much in the only big book he ever produced – *De Unitate Ecclesiae*, written in 1536 immediately after the shock of the executions of More and Fisher. His loathing had deepened when, pursuing revenge, Henry had executed not only the Cardinal's brother and a cousin but also his old and saintly mother. On Pole's side also, mercy had become impossible.

The desire to discredit Henry's archbishop seems to have been the reason why Cranmer was now tormented. He was held in prison, sometimes in harsh conditions, all the time from his arrest in September 1553 to his execution in March 1556. Although he had been sentenced to be hanged as a traitor, he was kept for burning as a heretic. But first his will must be broken. His mind must be confused by the arguments of theologians robust in health and with access to books; the enormity of his present offence of defying King Henry's daughter must be brought home to trouble his conscience; the prospect of great physical pain must be allowed to torture this timid scholar's imagination; and the hope of obtaining his sovereign's mercy must be sustained long enough to make him grovel. Even when at the height of his physical and intellectual powers Cranmer had turned for instruction to Henry VIII or

---

[7] D. M. Loades, *The Oxford Martyrs*, p. 148.

Nicholas Ridley, Martin Bucer or Peter Martyr; now, provided with instructors who had the power of life or death over him, he would be made to confess the error of his ways. But after all these humiliations he would still not be allowed to live, because his life of service to Henry VIII had been unforgivable. Pole's policy was to make Cranmer repent – but still perish in agony.

Pole also possessed a returned exile's belief that nothing of importance had happened in his absence. When he first spoke to Parliament about his sacred mission, he promised that 'all matters that be past' would be 'cast into the sea of forgetfulness'. That was received as a tactful hint that the lay owners of the lands of the monasteries, the chantries and the bishops were safe, and that all the clergy ordained or promoted since the beginning of the schism would be secure in their offices. But Pole's aloofness also implied a very arrogant dismissal of all the religious effects of Cranmer's work and of the whole influence of the English Bibles and the English Prayer Books. This mistake led to a fatally inadequate response to the religious challenge of the 1550s.

The two and a half years during which Pole was both papal legate and Archbishop of Canterbury were too short to leave behind more than a fragmentary impression of what was the potential in the reconstruction of the Catholic Church. In some ways the Cardinal was wisely cautious. On Christmas Eve 1554 he made a present to the owners of church lands by explicitly leaving the question of their ownership to their consciences. He also seems to have involved himself in politics as little as he could; and he rejected repeated offers of assistance from the newly-founded Jesuit Order, preferring to rely on loyal Englishmen.

In some other ways Pole was wisely creative. In November 1555 he summoned the bishops and clergy of the Convocations of Canterbury and York to a national synod in London, and his opening address blamed the evils of recent years on the slackness of priests. In response decrees were passed dealing with the most prominent abuses in the late medieval system. Pastors must reside among their flocks, must live frugally, must be chaste and charitable, must preach systematically, and must be trained in new seminaries to be created. An

English translation of the New Testament was to be authorized, together with an official catechism to be used in teaching.
Having laid this foundation for the long overdue renewal of the
Catholic system, Pole sent commissioners to inspect the dioceses and to reform the universities.

The main problem which these inspectors faced was the
shortage of priests – or of priests willing to live as unmarried
men. It was ominous that two Spanish friars, de Soto and de
Garcina, who made themselves obnoxious at Cranmer's trial
and execution, had to be appointed as professors of Divinity
and Hebrew at Oxford. The new bishops chosen by Pole, or by
Stephen Gardiner before his arrival, were, however, chosen
well – as was to be seen when they all remained faithful to the
old religion in the next reign. Bishops were encouraged to give
a lead to the parish clergy, who were also to be heartened by an
improvement in their stipends; the Queen promised to renounce the 'first fruits' and 'tenths' which since Henry VIII's
time had gone as taxes to the Crown. Pole also gave his blessing
to the restoration of religious houses, hoping that these would
be only the first fruits of a wide recovery of the monastic life.
Amid appropriate celebrations the Benedictines returned to
Westminster Abbey, the Dominicans to Smithfield, the Franciscans to Greenwich, the Carthusians to Sheen.[8]

Pole was, however, outstanding neither as a spiritual leader
nor as an administrator. He has been criticized fairly for
concentrating too much on the legalities when the real problem
was the irreversible decline of medieval religion, shown by the
fact that of about 1,500 former monks, nuns or friars still alive
in England in the 1550s barely a hundred volunteered to staff
the restored religious houses. What England needed, if its
Catholicism was ever to be secure again, was a radical renewal
in religion. We may speculate that had Catholicism been
destined to remain established in England, Pole would have
been remembered as a transitional figure, making way for an
archbishop more typical of the ardent, energetic Catholicism of

---

[8] See David Knowles, *The Religious Orders in England*, Vol. 3 (Cambridge, 1959),
pp. 421–43, and R. H. Pogson on 'Revival and Reform in Mary Tudor's Church'
in *The English Reformation Revised*, ed. C. Haigh (Cambridge, 1987), pp. 139–56.

the Counter-Reformation. But all his schemes were doomed. So was his queen; and so was he.

Both Mary and he were ailing anyway, but their disappointments seem to have crushed any will to survive. One sign of their slackening grip was that they left five sees vacant for Elizabeth to fill, making it far easier for the changes in religion accompanying her accession to be given the prestige of legality. Queen Mary's melancholy intensified when the war with France, into which England had been dragged by Philip, resulted in the loss of the last remnant of the medieval English empire, Calais. The Cardinal's gloom deepened when the Pope, who was now his enemy, made it clear that his standing in Rome was completely lost. Both the Queen and the Cardinal were also aware that the burning of heretics had succeeded neither in attracting nor in terrorizing the English. Since January 1556 it had no longer been the practice to offer royal pardons to heretics at the stake if they would recant before the fire was lit, because of the eloquent contempt with which the offer had almost always been received. The Queen knew that she was hated by her people, and the Cardinal was not under the illusion that he was loved.

In one last cruel deception, Mary's doctors did not contradict her wild hope that the latest swelling showed that she was after all about to give birth to an heir. In fact the swollen stomach was a symptom of a dropsy which proved fatal. As the dropsy grew worse, the popular turning to Elizabeth grew more open. It was already clear that her half-sister had triumphed simply by surviving. Mary could only send her, with some jewels, a note expressing hope that she would always remain loyal to the Catholic faith.

Early in the morning of 17 November 1558, having heard a last Mass in her bedroom in her palace in Westminster, Mary died. Her will provided that her mother's body was to be brought to Westminster Abbey, to lie beside her own; in fact, Mary was to share a grave there with the triumphant Elizabeth. The news of the Queen's death was taken across the river to Cardinal Pole as he lay mortally ill in Lambeth Palace. It brought on his own last agonies.

JOHN FOXE AND THE PROTESTANT VICTORY

> God knows it is not force nor might,
>   nor war nor warlike band,
> Nor shield and spear, nor dint of sword,
>   that must convert the land.
> It is the blood by martyrs shed,
>   it is that noble train,
> That fight with word and not with sword,
>   and Christ their captain.

St Henry Walpole, the author of that poem on the execution of the Jesuit, St Edmund Campion, was willing to become a martyr himself; and his courage will impress those untouched by his verse. Hundreds of Englishmen who accepted death under Elizabeth I, in what they considered to be the defence of the Catholic faith, testified as eloquently as brave men could to the innermost reality of their religion. Of course such a religion survived Queen Mary and Cardinal Pole. It did not depend on a queen's wish to be reconciled to a pope and it could not be discredited by a pope's hostility to a cardinal – or by any other error among all the tragedies of Queen Mary's reign. The spiritual splendours of an English Catholicism loyal to Rome went back to the arrival of St Augustine in Canterbury in the sixth century and were to be increased by a great record of 'blood by martyrs shed' in the sixteenth century. We cannot be at all surprised that the bulk of the English people was slow to embrace any alternative to this faith; nor is it amazing that a remnant of the English people has always remained faithful to it. Yet it is a fact of history that the ancient glories of Roman Catholicism were in the end eclipsed in the minds of most Englishmen by the moral victory of Protestantism. And we have to ask why the new form of Christianity – an innovation which had seemed an intolerable novelty under Henry VIII, and which had been disgraced by the conduct of many who had called themselves Protestants when briefly flourishing in the reign of Edward VI – was in the end to convert the land.

It is not enough to reply that Mary was succeeded by a Protestant. As we are about to see, Elizabeth's personal position and the history of her reign were both far more complicated than that. She had to compromise. She could never have imposed a thoroughgoing Protestantism on a persistently Catholic people. For now the religious issue was becoming more important than the monarchy itself, in the eyes of some at any rate. Under Mary Protestant leaders slowly began to move away from the simple belief that the legitimate sovereign always deserved support and obedience – the belief that had been of such advantage to Mary in 1553. In exile John Ponet published *A Short Treatise of Politic Power*; it was the first book in English to say openly that a tyrant should be disobeyed, even killed, and to leave the judgement about who was a tyrant to the individual's conscience. Thus loyalty to the conscience was beginning to count for more than loyalty to the Crown, and in Elizabeth's own reign many Englishmen were to show by their lives and deaths that by the ultimate test their supreme loyalty was not to her. Such evidence demonstrates that the answer to the question 'Why did Protestantism gradually prevail?' is not to be found entirely in the personal Protestantism of an allegedly despotic Elizabeth.

The true answer can be glimpsed in the work of John Foxe. He never attained – or sought – any office in the Church higher than a canonry in Salisbury Cathedral. He wrote a big book, known familiarly as his 'Book of Martyrs'. Its full title was *Acts and Monuments of these latter and perilous days, touching matters of the Church, wherein are comprehended and described the great persecutions and horrible troubles, that have been brought and practised by the Romish prelates, specially in this Realm of England and Scotland, from the year of our Lord a thousand, unto the time now present.*

Born in 1517, Foxe became a Fellow of Magdalen College, Oxford where to the dismay of his colleagues he underwent a serious conversion and emerged a Protestant. He eventually had to leave Oxford – and England, for in 1554 he was allowed to go into exile and to earn a meagre living as a proof-reader with a printer in Switzerland. He was not the stuff of which martyrs were made, but already before he escaped from the Catholic reaction he had begun to collect materials for his book about martyrs. Some of his researches were published in Latin soon after his escape and they made known to Europe the story of the Lollards, the English heretics who had already suffered under Catholic prelates long before Martin Luther's more famous protest. A second Latin volume followed in 1559, but by now Foxe's ambition was clearer. It was to tell the story of Luther and his fellow Protestants to England, with a comprehensiveness which no previous English author had attempted. Above all, his ambition was to tell the world the story of the Englishmen who had accepted death when he had himself sought safety.

His whole life was to be given to this mission. He was not interested in ecclesiastical promotion; he disliked wearing the surplice which the Queen now ordered, but above all he disliked taking time off from his literary labours. He ruined his health by his obsession, despite his family's pleas – although he found time to befriend the poor and the troubled, as the crowd at his funeral was to show. And his insistence on writing won for him countless readers. The first English edition of his great work appeared in 1563, and an expanded edition in two volumes followed in 1570. Until his death at the age of seventy he continued to revise the work, inserting corrections or additions supplied by many correspondents. In 1571 it was ordered that every cathedral, and the dining room of every cathedral canon or superior clergyman, should possess a copy.

Foxe was convinced that the Pope was the Antichrist prophesied in the Revelation of St John the Divine. The sufferings of the medieval Lollards and of the Protestants had been the sufferings of the saints, also prophesied; Satan had been let loose for a time. Now the hour of the full vindication of the saints was drawing near, and the triumph of Queen Elizabeth was a pledge of the total victory of Christ. Meanwhile the Protestant martyrs deserved to be celebrated as the Catholic saints had been. To help this, a 'Kalendar' giving the days on which they could be remembered was added to the 1563 edition (although so ridiculed that it was later withdrawn). Protestantism was the dawning of light amid the darkness of an evil world – a world so dark that even that light could be obscured by Protestants who were unworthy. Foxe was embarrassed by Henry VIII, and openly critical of the greed shown by Protestants under Edward VI; the guilt, he maintained, had been purged only in the martyrs' flames. He

deplored Protestant cruelties. He was not even willing to
applaud the Elizabethan government's execution of Papists as
traitors. He begged for Edmund Campion's life to be spared.
He acknowledged no duty to defend the most extreme Protestants; in his index some executions were referred to as the
deaths of 'Anabaptists justly condemned'. But even in relation
to these extremists who were in the wrong he favoured mercy,
and in the early years of Elizabeth's reign he loved to boast that
'her sword is a virgin, spotted and polluted with no drop of
blood'. In 1575 'Father Foxe' (for that was the affectionate
nickname which all used) was so sickened by the order to burn
some Anabaptists that he petitioned the Queen: 'I befriend the
lives of men since I myself am a man. . . . Would that I might
be able to help the very beasts!' The very long sermon which he
delivered at Paul's Cross on Good Friday 1570 fully showed
that his plea was for mercy because he passionately awaited the
imminent second coming of the one Judge, who had been
crucified by the Church and State of his day.

The theology of Foxe was one which many Protestants
shared, and as passages from his book were read or read out, or
as the many woodcuts illustrating it were pondered, the theology came alive. Here – collected with an industry which was
almost a martyrdom in itself – were documents which added to
the authentic atmosphere. And here was a narrative so dramatic that it may have taught a lesson or two to the young
William Shakespeare. Foxe treasured the conversations of the
martyrs as they went through the torments to their heavenly
reward; and when the evidence supplied to him failed, he was
not afraid to supply remarks considered appropriate.

The result in the popular mind was to associate Catholicism
with cruelty. Already under Queen Mary the suffering of the
Protestants had aroused far more sympathy than had surrounded the earlier burnings of Lollards; especially towards
the end of the persecution, when it had clearly failed, local officials had to be bullied by the council in London to detect heretics and to be present at their deaths, and the spectators dared
to make some demonstrations of admiration and good will.
But there is no evidence that the popular reaction against the
burnings had been so strong that it would have brought down

the government by itself. Mary's heart was broken by the loss of Philip and of Calais far more than by worry about what her subjects might be feeling. One factor was that, despite what some later historians may have imagined, England had never been filled with the stench of burning human flesh. The burnings took place mainly in the south-east, the area most influenced by continental Protestantism. No heretics at all were burned in the dioceses of Durham, Carlisle, York, Hereford and Worcester; only one each in the dioceses of Chester and Exeter; only two each in the dioceses of Lincoln and Peterborough. The effective, nationwide revulsion against the persecution seems to have come in the next reign, and supremely after the publication of Foxe's book. Roman Catholic attempts to discredit him show how devastating his propaganda was – but they were feeble and mostly in Latin.

In the sixteenth century (and later) the power of religious prejudice was such that the mere suffering of men and women would not have moved many hearts by itself. After all, the martyrs themselves did not disapprove of the death penalty for heresy. In November 1538 Cranmer, for example, associated himself with Henry VIII in condemning John Lambert to be burned for denying the real presence of Christ in the consecrated bread at the Mass. Two others who were also to be burned as Protestants, Robert Barnes and John Taylor, are known to have supported that decision at the time. But Foxe was a propagandist of rare power – and Queen Mary's government had supplied him with rare material.

It could be said that bishops such as Hooper, Latimer, Ridley and Cranmer, accepted martyrdom as a hazard of their profession, and had chosen it rather than exile. But the lay men and women who were reported to be heretics, and who then refused to save their lives by professing the Catholic faith, came out of obscurity. Some of them, when questioned about how many sacraments there were in the Catholic faith, replied that they could not remember the number – without immediately laying themselves open to the charge of being liars. Yet they were plainly not Anabaptists or other cranks. They were simple men and women who belonged to England. They died with a courage which moved their fellow laity. Cruelty against them seemed more abominable than any execution of a bishop or nobleman. In the 1580s Sir William Cecil was still using as an unanswerable debating point the story of the pregnant woman who had been burned; when she had given birth, the baby had been thrown into the fire to perish with her.

These 'great persecutions', as Foxe's title showed, had been practised against simple English folk by 'the Romish prelates'. 'Romish'! In that one category Philip of Spain and Cardinal Pole could be included despite their troubles with Rome, and the adjective summoned up all the contempt of patriotic Englishmen. And 'prelates'! In that one category Stephen Gardiner and his associates could be placed together with the bishops who had burned the Lollards, and the noun aroused all the anticlerical feelings of the age. These 'Romish prelates' had persecuted the saints since 'the year of our Lord a thousand', yet in 'the time now present' their power was crumbling away and the Reformation of the Church was moving on to the final coming of the Church's Lord. In its enlarged edition of 1570 Foxe's history stretched back to the earliest days of Christianity and to the conversion of the Roman empire through the agency of the emperor Constantine (a king born in Britain, Foxe emphasized), before reaching John Wyclif and the Lollards in Book IV and the 'dreadful and bloody regiment' of Queen Mary on page 1,567. Thus the misdeeds of the 'Romish prelates' were set by John Foxe in the context of a total interpretation of history.

Protestants willing to take part in the overthrow of the 'Romish prelates' could now tell themselves that their cause was not mere greed or heresy. It was the cause of martyrs, including English men and women as lay as they were themselves. It was the cause of God. Their time, bloody and messy as it might seem, was giving birth to the Lord Christ's glorious new age.[9]

---

[9] See J. F. Mozley, *John Foxe and His Book* (London, 1940); William Haller, *Foxe's Book of Martyrs and the Elect Nation* (London, 1963); and V. N. Elsen, *John Foxe and the Elizabethan Church* (Berkeley, Cal., 1973). The background was studied by Helen C. White, *Tudor Books of Saints and Martyrs* (Madison, Wisc., 1963). For the widespread belief that the final battle between Christ and Antichrist was imminent, see Paul Christianson, *Reformers and Babylon* (Toronto, 1978), and K. R. Firth, *The Apocalyptic Tradition in Reformation Britain* (Oxford, 1979).

CHAPTER FOUR

THE ELIZABETHAN CHURCH

THE QUEEN'S RELIGION

At the age of twenty-five, on 17 November 1558, Elizabeth knelt and recited Psalm 118 in Latin on being informed that she was Queen of England and must go to the Tower of London to prepare for her coronation. Although the psalm was a celebration of escape, she had suffered in ways which would have left many people emotionally crippled; somewhat similar experiences had deeply damaged her sister. On Palm Sunday 1554 Elizabeth had been taken to the Tower and accused of complicity in Wyatt's rebellion. She had been kept in prison for two months, and no one would have been amazed had she met a traitor's death. A copy of her letter to Mary refusing to come to court at the time of Wyatt's rebellion (because, she claimed, of ill-health) had been intercepted in the French ambassador's mail to his masters. It was not unreasonable to suspect that Elizabeth had supplied it.

In her brother's reign she had also been in peril. Thomas Seymour, Protector Somerset's over-ambitious brother, had flirted and romped with her. The incident had set tongues wagging and his head rolling after execution as a traitor. And in her father's reign, twenty-four hours before her mother's execution, the Archbishop of Canterbury had declared her a bastard. Although that archbishop had now been burned as a heretic, she always remained a whore's child in the eyes of Catholic Europe except when princes were seeking her as an ally or as a wife. Queen Mary had often pointed out the physical likeness between Elizabeth and the court musician Mark Smeaton, believed to have been one of Anne Boleyn's lovers.

All Christians were then agreed that no woman could become a priest. Some now argued with passion that no woman could be a monarch; for example, John Knox in his *First Blast of the Trumpet against the Monstrous Regiment of Women*, published in Geneva shortly before Elizabeth's accession. The exclusion of women from power was – or was said to be – the law of God. The practical difficulty of having a woman on the throne had been amply demonstrated by the disaster of Queen Matilda who had fled the country in 1148 and by the total disaster of Queen Mary. Elizabeth's probable successor was Mary Stuart, Queen of Scots, until she was executed in 1587. It was clear that Mary, although beautiful (which Elizabeth was not), was destitute of common sense, unable to rule either men or her own emotions. And it was not always clear that Elizabeth was going to be vastly more successful. Had she died in 1562 (as she nearly did, of smallpox), she would have bequeathed a chaos almost as great as the shambles she had inherited from her sister. In 1562 she named Robert Dudley Protector of the Realm in the event of her death; he was the son of the Duke of Northumerland who had been executed in 1553, and in power he would probably have been no better than his father. So slender was the thread on which depended England's peace and prosperity under this mortal queen.

But England and the world discovered that Elizabeth was one of the ablest politicians, crowned or uncrowned, in all history. Pope Sixtus V openly admired her and wished that Catholic monarchs possessed her spirit. In England the festivals of her birthday and accession replaced the medieval spectacles of the Church; it was government propaganda, of course, but it was not only that. She earned her reputation the hard way. Her experience of being accused of treason seemed only to have strengthened her will to be a survivor. The incident when she had been compromised by a teenager's flirtation had left her determined never to let her heart rule her head; and the weakness of her position as a woman alleged to be illegitimate had made her all the more resolved not only to get the better of bishops but to display to her people the 'heart of a king and of a king of England too'. Her sister's experience had not encouraged her to saddle herself with a husband, and the idea that she was the Virgin Queen, married to her people, seems to have been more than a poetic fancy.

Since her death the glory of the Elizabethan age has continued to be acknowledged by England and the world. It was the moment when the English governing class and their assistants such as Shakespeare multiplied their assets by the exploitation of agriculture, industry and trade, launched their naval and imperial conquests, and created the most splendid literature seen in the world since the glories of Greece and Rome. This reign was also a time when the common people suffered much; the profits went to those to whom much had already been given. But the only rebellion to reach London was led by Elizabeth's ex-favourite, the Earl of Essex; and it lasted one day.

Only a part of the explanation of the Elizabethan phenomenon lies in the extraordinary ability and industry of William Cecil (Lord Burghley from 1571), for forty years the Queen's principal minister. He had already held high office in the service both of Somerset and of Northumberland under Edward VI, and had led the councillors in their submission to Queen Mary in 1553. Although he was a discreet Protestant (and his wife was one emphatically), he had been allowed to live in peace under Mary as the squire of Wimbledon. He believed in the continuity and efficiency of government. His eye for the practical possibility matched Elizabeth's – as did his taste for moderation, except when treason or hostility to England's ruler was clear. In pursuit of this agreed policy he sometimes argued with success against some mood of Elizabeth's but he never doubted for one moment who governed England.[1] In order to show that he was not indispensable, she persisted in favouring his rival Robert Dudley (created Earl of Leicester in 1564), whom he disliked and distrusted. She refused to see him, or to receive letters from him, for four months after the execution of Mary Queen of Scots; with royal or feminine logic she blamed the deed on him. His work was carried on into the next reign by his son Robert – but for five years the Queen refused to consent to any formal appointment

---

[1] A recent study is B. W. Beckinsale, *Burghley, Tudor Statesman* (London, 1967).

of Robert Cecil to the secretaryship. She owed more to the Cecils than she acknowledged, but it was her age.[2]

One of the least expected successes of the Elizabethan age was the Church 'established' by the Act of Uniformity to which the Queen gave her assent on 8 May 1559. The Church of England has seldom been described as glorious, for it has always been the result of a compromise between Catholic and Protestant, conservative and radical; and so it was under Elizabeth I. The arrangements made for it by the Queen in Parliament in 1559 were generally expected to have a short life; 'no one really wanted the Prayer Book'.[3] In the event, however, the Queen insisted on treating the 1559 settlement as sacred, because every subsequent House of Commons in her reign would have lessened the compromise by a more Protestant emphasis unacceptable to her – and although the Elizabethan settlement was to be overthrown in the Puritan revolution of the next century, back it was to come. In the twentieth century, during the reign of Elizabeth II, the Church of England was still 'established'.

Elizabeth I took the title 'Supreme Governor of the Church'. She did not claim to be 'Supreme Head', as her father and brother had done. Even Thomas Cranmer had acknowledged that the title 'Supreme Head of the Church' most fitly belonged to Christ. Now, when it suited them, Elizabeth and her ministers could pretend that nothing was involved in the new title beyond every Christian monarch's duty to make sure that pure religion was being practised in the realm in accordance with the teachings of the Bible and the bishops. In 1569 a 'Declaration of the Queen's Proceedings' was issued in an attempt to reassure Catholics at the time of the conservative rebellion in the north. A copy survives corrected in the Queen's own hand. The declaration stressed that she had never claimed

---

[2] Introductions include Paul Johnson, *Elizabeth I: A Study in Power and Intellect* (London, 1974), and the four volumes by A. L. Rowse: *The England of Elizabeth: The Structure of Society, The Expansion of Elizabethan England, The Elizabethan Renaissance: The Life of Society* and *The Elizabethan Renaissance: The Cultural Achievement* (London, 1950–72). Wallace MacCaffrey summed up modern studies of the politics in *The Shaping of the Elizabethan Regime, 1558–72*, and *Queen Elizabeth and the Making of Policy, 1572–88* (Princeton, N.J., 1969–81).

[3] G. J. Cuming, *A History of Anglican Liturgy*, p. 131.

any right 'to define, decide or determine any article or point of the Christian faith and religion, or to change any ancient ceremony of the Church from the form before received and observed by the Catholic and Apostolic Church'. Her ecclesiastical title was defended on the ground that 'we are by God's grace the sovereign prince and queen next under God, and all the people in our realm are immediately born subjects to us and to our crown and to none else'. She was Supreme Governor of the Church as of every other English institution, but in the Church this simply involved seeing 'the laws of God and man to be duly observed' and providing that 'the Church may be governed and taught by archbishops, bishops and ministers' – duties which 'we think properly due to all Christian monarchs'.

The reality was, however, different. In 1559 the Acts of Supremacy and Uniformity were passed in defiance of solidly hostile votes by the bishops in the House of Lords, and in the knowledge that the clergy when meeting in the Convocation of Canterbury earlier in the year had shown themselves obstinately loyal to the old religion. Until the end of 1559 the Queen was unable to find bishops prepared to carry out her policy, so that she or her council governed the Church in a straightforward manner, issuing detailed injunctions to guide the clergy. When bishops were secured, they were nominated by her; Deans and Chapters elected them, but had these clergy of the cathedrals refused to do their duty they would have been outlawed, as the law made unambiguously plain. And the bishops were ordered about by her. If she sheltered behind them (as she did when convenient), it was because she had no wish to be involved in ecclesiastical controversies, not because she doubted her God-given powers. When an Archbishop of Canterbury refused to obey her, she had him placed under house arrest; and the two next archbishops were promoted because they were eager to be the Crown's agents in a campaign against those who wanted to move forward from 1559.

Clergymen had to do what she wanted, like her other subjects. When Alexander Nowell, Dean of St Paul's, was preaching in her presence on Ash Wednesday and was becoming controversial, she screamed at him: 'Leave that alone! To your text, Mr Dean! To your text! Leave that; we have heard enough of that! To your subject!' But if clergymen obeyed her they were safe, and laymen who criticized them were told firmly to leave religion to those who understood it. In 1571 she berated those MPs who had shown themselves so 'audacious, arrogant and presumptuous' as to meddle with religion and bring in ecclesiastical legislation without the prior approval of the bishops and clergy. Eighteen years later she informed the Commons that she was 'most fully and firmly settled in her conscience, by the word of God, that the estate and government of the Church of England, as it now standeth in this Reformation, may justly be compared to any church which hath been established in any Christian kingdom since the apostles' times'.[4]

It has often been assumed that her motivation in securing and defending the 1559 settlement was purely (or impurely) political, and it seems true to say that she always put first her duty to survive on the throne. But it is not necessary to deny the sincerity of her belief that her survival was a duty. All the Tudors had the knack of identifying their interests with God's and the people's. Moreover, it can be argued that she was the truest Christian in a family which always made a parade of its piety. Her attitude towards others, although usually shrewd and sometimes shrewish, was more deeply charitable than that of any other Tudor. Perhaps that reflected credit on her tutor, Roger Ascham. Although a Protestant clergyman and a learned scholar, he was far from being a fanatic; he wrote the standard book on archery, and was a great hunter (and a compulsive gambler). Although she consented to very severe punishments for real or alleged treason, it is impossible to think of her as an implacable persecutor like her sister, who executed hundreds never accused of treason. There is no reason to doubt that her agonies of mind when she had to order the death of the Duke of Norfolk or Mary Queen of Scots were genuine, although politically she had no choice. In Henry VIII's reign

---

[4] Relevant documents were collected by Claire Cross in *The Royal Supremacy in the Elizabethan Church* (London, 1969). Carl S. Mayer studied *Elizabeth I and the Religious Settlement of 1559* (St Louis, Mo., 1960) and N. L. Jones, *Faith by Statute* (London, 1982).

of thirty-eight years, eighty-one heretics were burned; in Elizabeth's reign, three years longer, five.

She not only mentioned her dependence on God in public speeches (all monarchs did that); she also prayed in private and attended Morning Prayer daily. As a young woman she translated a religious poem by Queen Margaret of Navarre (*The Mirror of the Sinful Soul*) which, we are told, 'initiated a new species of English religious literature of mystical transcendence and spiritual fervour'.[5] She also translated Queen Catherine Parr's book of prayers into Latin, French and Italian. She caused a *Book of Prayers* for her household's use to be published in 1560; and she left behind her a book, only three by two inches in size, containing prayers handwritten about 1575.

Such prayers could be dismissed as literary exercises, and there is no certainty that she actually did write the most famous little poem attributed to her:

> Christ was the Word that spake it;
> He took the Bread and brake it:
> And what the Word did make it,
> That I believe, and take it.

It does not seem to have been attributed to Elizabeth before 1643, and it appeared in the 1635 edition of John Donne's poems. We do, however, possess a report of what she said to Parliament on 29 March 1585. She referred to one of her characteristics which became obscured in the legend about her – her habit of daily study. 'I suppose few, that be no professors, have read more. . . . And yet, amidst my many volumes, I hope God's book hath not been my seldomnest lectures.' She rebuked both the conservatism of the 'Romanists' and the 'new-fangledness' of others: 'I see many overbold with God almighty, making too many subtle scannings of his blessed will, as lawyers with human testaments.' And without stooping to give precise biblical references, she declared about her rejection of both the Catholic and the Protestant extremes: 'I mean to guide them both by God's holy true rule.'

---

[5] J. B. Collins, *Christian Mysticism in the Elizabethan Age* (Baltimore, Md., 1940), p. 87.

During her long, last illness Elizabeth refused to discuss politics. She was unwilling even to name her successor. When speechless, 'she took great delight in hearing prayers, and would often at the name of Jesus lift up her hands and eyes to heaven'. She died gripping Archbishop Whitgift's hand, although Bishop Goodman of Gloucester was to remember that while healthy she had been an independent Christian. 'Queen Elizabeth', he recalled, 'was wont to say she had rather speak to God herself, than to hear another speaking of God; she seldom heard sermons, but only in Lent.'[6]

THE ESTABLISHED CHURCH

In the Church which Elizabeth governed, bishops were appointed in order to execute her policies. They were not primarily hoping to be loved; and they did not all devote much time in order to administer Confirmation in the villages where most of the people lived. They were involved in politics almost to the same extent as the statesman-bishops of the Middle Ages (although only two of them were ever admitted to the Privy Council). The basic difference was that they were now expected to live and work in their own dioceses, busying themselves with local, not national, administration, treated by the council like paid magistrates useful in the management of ecclesiastical matters, sometimes also entrusted with a wider role if this was convenient. For example, they collected taxes from the clergy.[7] It was, however, a crucial defect in their

---

[6] Her piety was studied by J. P. Hedges, *The Nature of the Lion* (London, 1962). The scholarly circle to which she belonged was explored by Winthrop S. Hudson, *The Cambridge Connection and the Elizabethan Settlement of 1559* (Durham, N.C., 1980).

[7] See Ralph Houlbrooke, 'The Protestant Episcopate 1547–1603: The Pastoral Contribution', in *Church and Society in England: Henry VIII to James I*, ed. F. Heal and R. O'Day (London, 1977), pp. 78–98. This volume contains other valuable essays drawing together recent studies of local church life. Other material is in *Princes and Paupers in the English Church*, with the same editors (Leicester, 1981). Felicity Heal investigated the finances of the Elizabethan bishops in *Of Prelates and Princes*, pp. 202–327. Patrick Collinson investigated their work and much else in *The Religion of Protestants: The Church in English Society, 1559–1625* (Oxford, 1982).

position that no real attempt was made to help the bishops by reforming the church courts – a modernization which could not have been undertaken except by command of the Queen. It was her policy to use, but to curb, the power of her bishops.[8]

It is therefore possible to see the history of the Elizabethan Church of England as a series of attempts by the bishops to discipline, at the command of the Queen, all those who retained Christian convictions, whether Catholic or Protestant. It is also possible to pour scorn on the failures of these unromantic bishops to achieve even the limited objectives entrusted to them by the Queen's council. They were men without the prestige of aristocratic birth, so important in that intensely class-conscious society. (For a time the two archbishops, at Canterbury and York, were men who had been born and brought up in the same parish of St Bees on the Cumbrian coast, Edmund Grindal being a farmer's son although Edwin Sandys was a gentleman's.) Bishops were criticized if they seemed to be wealthy, and the Queen's lay favourites hastened to relieve them of their estates. At the same time they were criticized if they did not entertain the leading laity with a noble hospitality. They often felt themselves obliged to provide for their families, but when they did so they were condemned for robbing the Church. Most of these bishops, with little previous experience of parish life or of diocesan administration, possessed limited personal talents to apply to their formidable and uncertain tasks, and with administrative and legal machinery unchanged since the Middle Ages they issued orders and excommunications which the laity and even the clergy often treated with derision.

The Elizabethan Bishops of Chichester, for example, were a poor lot. The only outstanding man among them was Richard Curteys, appointed in 1570. An ardent preacher with Calvinist convictions, he was determined to hasten the progress of the Reformation in the parishes of a rural and conservative diocese. But he involved himself in unedifying disputes with many of his clergy and made the supreme mistake of summoning

---

[8] Ralph Houlbrooke studied *Church Courts and the People during the English Reformation* (Oxford, 1979).

most of the gentry of Sussex to his cathedral, where he harangued them. He seemed so troublesome that in 1578 the Privy Council suspended him from his duties. No successor was appointed until 1585, when the choice fell on an obscure clergyman aged seventy-eight who did very little in his eleven years as bishop. And the next Bishop of Chichester lived mainly in London.

The main problem of the clergy serving in Sussex under such dismally bad leadership was poverty. Although it is very difficult to be precise about money values in a period when most rectors or vicars were paid mainly in kind (in tithes), the fees being relatively unimportant, we are told that only four parishes in the whole diocese yielded an income above £30 a year, that assistant curates often had to make do on £5 a year, and that many of the clergy carried on other trades in order to support their families. Inevitably many thousands of their parishioners remained rooted in the old religion and accepted guidance from the gentry or nobility who supported priests faithful to it. At Battle Abbey, for example, an aristocratic widow who had taken over the old monastic buildings ran a well-attended chapel complete with choir and pulpit. When headway was made against this conservatism – and the evidence suggests that some headway was made in the 1580s and 1590s – this seems to have been thanks largely to the energy of the Puritan preachers. But these preachers were suspected by the authorities of Church and State, and in 1605 Archbishop Bancroft silenced and deprived the foremost ten Sussex Puritans.[9]

The history of the Elizabethan diocese of Chichester is not the Church of England at its most impressive. But two facts deserve to be remembered. The first is negative: there was no violent conflict. Not many miles of sea separated Sussex from a France which was undergoing the misery of civil war as Catholics and Protestants battled for control, yet the equivalent in Sussex of the dreadful French massacre of 1572 was the scandal over the indiscretions of Bishop Curteys. And the

[9] R. B. Manning examined *Religion and Society in Elizabethan Sussex* (Leicester, 1969).

second fact which should be weighed is that the Church of England did function as the National Church in local reality.

Probably not all the inhabitants of any town or village could be found in church at service time. Those who were 'Romanists' or 'Recusants' out of loyalty to the old religion absented themselves. The really poor do not seem to have been expected to attend, and the really careless could be found at home or in the ale house, although the churchwardens were supposed to fine them twelve pence for each Sunday's absence. But all the evidence suggests that the great majority of England's parish priests remained at their posts under Elizabeth as they had done, however the storms of religious change blew, under her father, brother and sister. There certainly was a shortage of clergy at the beginning of the reign; in 1559 fewer than half of the parishes in the diocese of Canterbury had a resident clergyman, and the experiment of using lay readers or 'lectors' to take the services had to be attempted. But mass ordinations of new priests dealt with that emergency and it is clear that, whoever the priest was, he was needed. For the parish church remained the centre of social life, under the Tudors as in the Middle Ages.

It had no rival. Its bell summoned one and all. The Sunday assembly for Morning Prayer was the time to catch up with the news and gossip and perhaps also to absorb some edification. After service there would be sports in the churchyard. Christenings, weddings and funerals were the turning points in private lives; and the whole community's year was given its pattern by the festivities of Christmastide after the preparation of Advent, the drama of Easter following Lent, the May Day dancing to greet the spring in the churchyard, the 'church ale' at Whitsuntide in the churchyard or if wet in the church, the autumn harvest festivities which often returned to the churchyard for more merriment, the autumnal remembrances of All Saints and All Souls (although the authorities battled against the 'superstition' of prayers for the dead). The provision made by the Book of Common Prayer for Mattins and Evensong, or Morning and Evening Prayer, to be said daily in every parish church seldom seems to have been put into effect; but if the parish priest was conscientious he would say the litany in church every Wednesday and Friday morning, interceding for all in trouble.

The allocation of pews in the church was a matter of great interest and often of contention, since it marked a family's social status. The humiliation of sinners was also a matter of interest, and took place in church. Fornicators and adulterers were supposed to do penance in a white sheet before all the congregation during Morning Prayer on three successive Sundays, after the sentence by the court of the archdeacon or the bishop. (A month before his death William Shakespeare was relieved to learn that his son-in-law, Thomas Quinney, who had fathered a bastard, was to be spared this public humiliation and allowed to do penance in the bishop's chapel.) The whole congregation could meet to discuss parish affairs, although in many parishes, especially in towns, this touch of democracy was being replaced by a committee of the leading parishioners known as the 'vestry'. The unpaid churchwardens, elected for the year at Easter, were responsible not only for the maintenance of the church, churchyard and any 'church house', but also for a great variety of other business – the relief of the poor, the punishment of rogues and the upkeep of almshouses, roads, bridges and ponds, either by themselves or in collaboration with other officials. The schoolmaster, licensed by the bishop, often taught in the church; the trainbands (militia) kept their weapons there: the local magistrates often administered justice there. It might have many, many other uses, being in effect the village hall. And everyone, except suicides, was buried in the church or churchyard.[10]

In every parish church the Prayer Book of 1559 was used Sunday by Sunday. Morning Prayer and Litany formed the chief service, with Evening Prayer early in the afternoon, and Holy Communion perhaps once a month (but in many country parishes neither Evening Prayer nor Holy Communion would

[10] See A. Tindall Hart, *The Country Clergy in Elizabethan and Stuart Times* (London, 1958), and *The Man in the Pew, 1558–1660* (London, 1966). Many glimpses of parish life were provided by J. S. Purvis, *Tudor Parish Documents of the Diocese of York* (Cambridge, 1948), and W. K. Jordan, *The Charities of Rural England, 1480–1660* (London, 1961). See also R. L. Greaves, *Society and Religion in Elizabethan England* (Minnesota, 1981).

be held so often). By being used, the Prayer Book's beauty slowly found its way into the affections of the people – and the clergy. It was a sign of the times that towards the end of Elizabeth's reign the pressures brought to bear by bishops and archdeacons were resulting in a higher standard of maintenance in the church buildings. The demoralizing effects of the many orders to destroy superstitious images seem to have been largely overcome, and on Sundays parishioners saw a more or less decent substitute for the vanished glories of the Middle Ages. In innumerable parishes the church was repaired, often with the aid of a 'church rate', a tax levied by the churchwardens on all householders. It was often whitewashed, adorned with scriptural texts, strewn with straw or rushes to make kneeling easier, and given one new touch of colour – the royal arms. As in the Middle Ages, the chancel might well be in a worse state of repair than the nave, for the chancel was the responsibility of the 'rector' or 'parson' (the two terms were interchangeable, lesser clergy being called the 'vicar' or 'curate'). But bishops and archdeacons, when they conducted their 'visitations' in the medieval style, often made complaints designed to secure action from the rector. There was often a similar problem about the repair of the rectory, parsonage or vicarage, for which the clergyman was personally responsible.

Although Elizabethan England saw no great church building – were not its richest men's huge country houses the new cathedrals of the cult of Mammon? – these changes in the medieval parish church made it a suitable little theatre for the performance of the Prayer Book services.

Most of the services were not accompanied by sermons. A special licence was needed before a clergyman was allowed to expound the Bible's message in his own words, and over many areas for many years such licences were few. Many of the licensed preachers when they did arrive were enthusiastic Puritans, hostile to the remnants of Popery in the Prayer Book. But the bishops persisted in hoping that 'godly preachers' would persuade the people to love and use the authorized services. The steady hope of the Queen and her council (particularly of William Cecil, who was Chancellor of Cambridge University) was that the universities would persuade enough young men of the merits of the religious establishment, so that they would become preachers. And slowly such hopes were to a considerable extent fulfilled. The Church of England became an institution in which graduates were content to be employed. It was a quiet but major change. At the beginning of Elizabeth's reign the medieval pattern was still taken for granted and few graduates were to be found serving parishes. 'The non-resident clergy were university-educated, and socially, geographically and economically quite mobile: the parochial clergy were of local origin and modest education, and had little prospect of further preferment. . . . Yet the post-Reformation Church was committed to the task of reforming its clergy and finding well-educated and vocationally suitable men to fill its parishes, even down to the poorest rectories and vicarages, many of which were currently standing vacant.'[11] And this ideal was translated into practice to a surprising extent.

The official religion of Elizabethan England was enforced by the Justices of the Peace (unpaid magistrates) alongside the bishops and archdeacons. Probably many of the laity conformed because no alternative seemed open; and they were often bored stiff as they sat in churches which were cold and smelly (from the dead), listening to a parson droning on with the stereotyped worship ordered in an Act of Parliament, hearing homilies and other official hand-outs read from the pulpit. Men and women sat separately, and the atmosphere must have been rather like a school's. The churchwardens preserved discipline, reporting cases of brawling to their own superiors. Since the day of popular hymns had not yet come, the only opportunity to sing together was provided by the *Book of Psalms* in metre by Sternhold, Hopkins and others (1560) and by its Puritan rivals. No one could call the Elizabethan Church entertaining. But it made a people which had been Catholic for many centuries vociferously Protestant.

---

[11] Rosemary O'Day, *The English Clergy: The Emergence and Consolidation of a Profession 1558–1642* (Leicester, 1979), p. 6. M. H. Curtis studied this change from another angle in *Oxford and Cambridge in Transition 1558–1642* (Oxford, 1959). See also C. M. Dent, *Protestant Reformers in Elizabethan Oxford* (Oxford, 1983).

ELIZABETH'S FIRST ARCHBISHOP

Matthew Parker, whom Elizabeth chose as her first Archbishop of Canterbury, was consecrated a bishop by four others – William Barlow, Bishop of St David's under Henry VIII; John Hodgkin, who had been Suffragan Bishop of Bedford in the same reign; John Scory, Bishop of Chichester under Edward VI; and Miles Coverdale, Bishop of Exeter 1551–55. They used a service which had been authorized by Parliament along with the Prayer Book of 1552. By an oversight no 'ordinal' (book of ordination services) had been authorized in the 1559 Act of Uniformity, but the Crown claimed the power to supply this defect. The ceremony took place in the chapel of Lambeth Palace, early on the morning of 17 December 1559.

Anglicans have claimed that this was a valid consecration – an important claim, since Archbishop Parker was to consecrate other bishops and was thus to embody the Anglican assertion of continuity with the Catholic Church of the Middle Ages. The Roman Catholic authorities have not agreed with that claim – and the invalidity of the proceedings that December morning was one of the reasons given by Pope Leo XIII in 1897 for declaring Anglican ordinations 'absolutely null and utterly void'. It is not our duty to enter such controversies, but we may observe that not one of the bishops serving in Queen Mary's reign was willing to lend a hand in making Matthew Parker Archbishop of Canterbury, despite the government's many blandishments or threats; and the Pope was never consulted. It was an affair very different from the consecration of Cardinal Pole to be Archbishop of Canterbury. It was also very different from the consecration of Thomas Cranmer in St Stephen's chapel in the palace of Westminster in March 1535 – a ceremony performed by the Bishops of Lincoln, Exeter and St Asaph according to the Catholic rites on the basis of letters or 'bulls' issued in Rome by the Pope.

By choosing Matthew Parker for Canterbury and arranging at least a superficial continuity between him and his predecessors, Elizabeth's government demonstrated that its policy was to be Protestantism without disruption. Protestantism there had to be, but the government had to avoid giving needless offence to Catholics and quietly dropped Archbishop Cranmer's opinion that the Crown could simply appoint a bishop. The Queen wanted to reign in peace. And as her archbishop she had chosen a man of peace.

Parker was fifty-five when chosen. Most of his life had been spent in places of piety and study. He had been Dean of Stoke-by-Clare (a college suppressed in 1548), then Dean of Lincoln and Master of Corpus Christi College, Cambridge. Under Queen Mary he had been deprived of his posts but allowed to live in what he called 'delightful literary leisure'. He retired to his native Norfolk and spent the time turning the psalms into doggerel verse and writing a book – not published until 1567 – which preached what he practised: marriage for the clergy. The fact that he was so firmly married (after an engagement of seven years) might have been expected to damn him in Elizabeth's eyes, and his relationship with her never seems to have been close, although he had come into contact with her back in the 1530s during a brief spell as chaplain to her mother. It is unlikely that he was seriously attracted by the worldly side of the archbishopric. The Queen expected him to live in state like a nobleman and he did so; but he was at heart a scholarly and domestic gentleman. Whether or not the Queen actually insulted Mrs Parker quite so crudely as gossip maintained, the gossip showed the risks he was running.[12] In 1559 he found one excuse after another why he could not leave the university, and when the excuses ran out he did not answer letters. In 1535 Cranmer had also been slow to accept Canterbury (he rightly insisted on this at his trial), but had already allowed himself to become involved in the political service of Henry VIII. Parker's preference for the quiet of a study and a home in Cambridge probably went deeper.

The Queen's ministers persisted in urging him to accept the order, and there is no evidence that anyone else was ever in mind for Canterbury, although rumours circulated. The ex-

---

[12] The Queen was reported to have taken her leave after a feast thus: 'And you, *Madam* I may not call you, and *Mistress* I am ashamed to call you, so I know not what to call you, but yet I do thank you.' This anecdote was first printed in 1607.

planation seems to be that, although a careful administrator, Parker had no awkward theories of his own other than his conviction that any Protestant, lay or ordained, was entitled to be married. He was not a reformer likely to give trouble to a Tudor. Queen Mary let him live. Queen Elizabeth knew that he would never do more than complain in private. The test of this came when in a moment of temperament during 1561, she ordered the exclusion of clergymen's wives from cathedrals and colleges. Parker wrote to William Cecil that he was 'in horror to hear such words'. In order to carry out the Queen's policy while shielding her reputation he had been content to incur 'foul reports' from her Catholic or Protestant enemies, and now he was rewarded with this decree, which had left him 'neither joy of house, land or name'. But, confining his protest to this letter, he stayed put – as did the wives, for Elizabeth occasionally knew better than to insist on her way.

On other questions the Supreme Governor was, however, inflexible, and this meant that poor Parker had to issue and enforce his *Advertisements* of 1565 telling the clergy what clothes to wear. Being a sixteenth-century woman, the Queen knew that how a clergyman looked showed his position in society and in religion. Parker would probably have been indifferent to such details if left to himself, and was aggrieved when the Queen refused to acknowledge her personal responsibility for her orders, leaving him to bear all the Puritans' counter-attacks and 'foul reports'. He wore a worried look and a drooping moustache, as his portraits show – but of course he was prepared also to wear the clothes which his sovereign had commanded. He told others to obey the Queen because the vice that most angered him was disobedience. Both Catholic and Protestant dissenters 'have one mark to shoot at', he once reminded Cecil, 'plain disobedience; some of simplicity, some of wiliness and stubbornness'. When he had sacrificed the scholarly quiet of Cambridge in order to serve the Church of England at the Queen's command, he saw no reason why Puritans or Romanists should refuse to abandon their prefer-ences in the trivialities of church life once the Queen had made her wishes plain. He was deeply persuaded that God's blessing rested on England under Elizabeth. 'Where Almighty God is so much English as he is,' he once asked Cecil, 'should we not requite his mercy with some earnesty to prefer his honour and true religion?'

This scholarly archbishop's gentle goodness – which he called his 'cowardice' when feeling depressed – did something to commend the Queen's policy. She rebuked him for being too mild with those who wished to obey the Bible and the Bible only. He showed where his own heart lay by supervising a new translation of the Bible (the Bishops' Bible of 1568, revised in 1572), with 'no bitter notes upon any text'. But he was also gracious to the Catholic bishops surviving from the previous reign and left by the government half-imprisoned in his house; and he must have pleased many conservatives by his labours as patron and as editor in the printing of the works of medieval chroniclers, and by his supervision of a history of all the Archbishops of Canterbury. A short life of himself, the seventieth archbishop, was prepared for publication after his death. He took a special pride in the privileges of the great church of Canterbury but asserted that Christianity had flourished long before the landing of the first archbishop, who had suffered the handicap of being sent from Rome. Joseph of Arimathea had headed the missionary band sent from France by the apostle Philip in A.D. 63, and the Christian King Lucius had in the first Christian century exercised a supremacy over the Church not unlike Elizabeth's. Honouring another king, in 1574 he had Asser's *Life of Alfred* printed in type specially made to represent the original Anglo-Saxon.

He died the next year. He left a rich collection of ancient manuscripts and printed books to Corpus Christi College, Cambridge, where he had been happiest. With characteristic caution, he invited the master of another Cambridge college (Caius) to inspect the collection each year; if six manuscripts were missing, he was to be entitled to take the whole of the rest of the library with him to his own college. The Cambridge treasure, rescued from the dispersal of the monastic libraries and from many other sources, was priceless evidence about Christian England's heritage, now preserved – at least in part – through the storm of the Reformation. One item was a splendid

copy of the gospels sent from Rome to St Augustine, Canterbury's first archbishop.[13]

JEWEL AND HOOKER

John Jewel had a stronger appetite for controversy than
Matthew Parker could ever develop. His learning was as great
as Parker's, and it lay in fields immediately useful to the
government.

While an Oxford don in the 1540s, he wrote an *Oratio contra
Rhetoricum*. An academic piece, it attacked rhetoric with all the
skill of a scholar steeped in Latin literature, especially the
oratory of Cicero. It was natural that in the crucial early days
of Elizabethan England a scholar so eloquent found himself
talking incessantly. He was a Protestant spokesman at the
theological disputation held to advertise the new queen's
intentions in Westminster Abbey in March 1559. Four months
later he was nominated Bishop of Salisbury, to serve on a royal
commission to enforce the new settlement in the western
counties, destroying altars, statues, paintings and the other
symbols of Catholicism. In November he was back in London,
preaching with high drama at Paul's Cross. This became
famous as his 'Challenge Sermon'. Only 'if any learned man of
all our adversaries, or if all the learned men that be alive, be
able to bring any one sufficient sentence out of any old Catholic
doctor or father, or out of any old General Council, or out of the
Holy Scriptures of God, or any one example of the primitive
Church whereby it may be clearly and plainly proved, that
there was any private Mass in the whole world at that time, for
the space of six hundred years after Christ', would Jewel
subscribe to the doctrine taught by the Pope. Similarly he
challenged Roman Catholic teachings about the Pope being
the universal head of the Church; about the bread and wine of
the sacrament being 'really, substantially' Christ's body and
blood; about the frequent restrictions of communion to the

---

[13] See V. J. K. Brook, *A Life of Archbishop Parker* (Oxford, 1962).

priest alone and the invariable denial of the cup to the laity; about the 'worship' of images in churches; about the refusal to allow lay people to read the Bible in their own language. All these doctrines or practices were, he claimed, innovations like the practice of the private Mass.

In 1561, at Cecil's request, he wrote a letter in Latin defending the government from the rumour that England was in chaos because of the government's religious innovations. This letter was sent over to be printed in Paris without naming any author; Cecil wished to conceal the fact that the author was a highly placed official of the Church being defended. Next year, again at Cecil's request, the ever-ready bishop completed a longer *Apologia*, again in Latin because it was directed to the educated public of Europe. The whole purpose was to make the Elizabethan settlement of English religion theologically respectable in a Christendom where John Calvin still lived (until 1564), and where the chief event was the re-assembly of the reforming Council of Trent without Protestant participation (in 1562).

Jewel's *Apologia* aroused the admiration of leading Protestants and the contempt of learned Catholics. Within England translations were quickly prepared (the best being volunteered by a scholarly Protestant otherwise known to history as the mother of Sir Francis Bacon), but conservatives were by no means silenced. What can perhaps be agreed upon now is the fact that Jewel was no mean debater. In order to divert attention from the confusion in England resulting from the latest of the religious revolutions of the 1550s, he dwelt positively upon the clergy's united obedience to the queen and negatively on the variety to be found within the Catholic tradition (for example, in the multiplicity of the orders of monks, nuns, friars and canons). In order to justify the supremacy of the queen over the Church of England, he cited the role played by Christian emperors and kings from Constantine onwards. He stressed, too, the damage done by the alternative: the claim of the Bishops of Rome to universal jurisdiction. He minimized the New Testament passages referring to St Peter and the passages in the Church's Fathers referring to the popes of Rome, and made a more successful attempt to show that neither Christ nor the apostles nor any other of the undivided Church's acknowledged teachers had ever expressed any approval in advance of the claims of the medieval papacy. That was his negative achievement: a debater's achievement. Positively, he advocated the equality of bishops in the Catholic Church, with only a vague primacy of honour granted to archbishops such as the pope.

The confident tone of Bishop Jewel as the official apologist for the Elizabethan Church of England is interesting since in the previous reign he had behaved far more timidly. In Oxford he had functioned as a minor official during the trials of Ridley and Cranmer. Frightened by their fates, he had signed 'articles' of the Roman Catholic faith – seizing the pen and trying to make a joke of it: 'What, have you a mind to see how well I can write?' Only when warned that he was himself about to be arrested for heresy, and no doubt burned like Ridley and Cranmer, had he escaped to Germany, confessing his cowardice to the English Protestants already in exile. This unhappy incident had been recalled when as Bishop of Salisbury he had deprived Thomas Harding of a canonry in Salisbury Cathedral. The two men had gone to the same grammar school (at Barnstaple in Devon) and had been contemporaries at Oxford. But Harding had become a Protestant after graduating – and had urged Jewel to remain boldly faithful to the Protestant cause. Later Harding had returned to the Catholic fold, but his contempt for Jewel's cowardice had no doubt remained. We cannot wonder that having been expelled from Salisbury Cathedral, the now steadfastly Catholic Thomas Harding devoted a part of his exile to writing very rudely about Bishop John Jewel.

We need not accept Harding's estimate of his former friend, however. A different estimate suggests itself when we read Jewel on the Bible: 'Here is to be seen the triumph of God, the Lord of lords and the King of kings: how he hath made the name of his Son triumph over principalities and powers, and over the whole world. Here is a paradise full of delights; no tongue is able to speak of them, they are so many; no heart is able to conceive them, they be so great. Here is a shop, wherein is set out the wisdom and knowledge, the power, the judge-

ments, and mercies of God. Which way soever we look, we see
the works of his hands; his works of creation, and preservation
of all things; his works of severe justice upon the wicked, and of
gracious redemption to the believer. If we desire pleasant
music or excellent harmony, it speaketh unto us the words of
the Father . . .'[14]

Jewel, we may conclude, became a deeply convinced Protestant. But we know also that while officially defending the
Elizabethan Church he came near to resignation because he
did not regard the 1559 settlement as Protestant enough; and
in his official defence, he avoided the deep questions. Was the
settlement of 1559 to be only the beginning of a much more
radical transformation of the English Church, as Jewel and
those who with him had gone into exile from Queen Mary's
England certainly wished? If so, was there any prospect of
maintaining national unity or of restoring it? How should the
new despotism which England had found necessary (or at least
acceptable) be reconciled with a medieval tradition where the
powers of monarchs, although substantial and essential, had
been only one element in the complex feudal system? How
could the position of the English Crown be reconciled with the
international traditions both of Catholicism and of Protestantism? And what precisely was the status of the Church of
England's bishops? How could bishops govern the Catholic
Church when many fervent Protestants disliked the very name
of 'bishop', and when the Queen insisted on instructing them
in their duties? How could an international council of bishops
be held if it had to be summoned by monarchs who were often
at war with each other? If social conditions had changed
during the sixteenth century, could it not be agreed that they
had changed from age to age previously – and if so, was it
possible to agree on standards by which the legitimacy of
religious developments could be judged? Was the papacy
allowed to evolve as England had evolved? Could the Church

---

[14] Quoted in P. E. Hughes, *The Theology of the English Reformers* (London, 1965), p.
43. See W. M. Southgate, *John Jewel and the Problem of Doctrinal Authority* (Cambridge,
Mass., 1962), and J. E. Booty, *John Jewel as Apologist of the Church of England* (London,
1963).

evolve, or did the New Testament provide a perpetually authoritative pattern? Granted that the pattern laid down for England in 1559 could not be found in the New Testament, was it still right to enforce it?

Jewel died when he was not yet fifty, but he had defined the lines on which the spokesmen of the Church of England were to defend themselves from Roman Catholic claims over more than a hundred years. In 1610 Archbishop Bancroft ordered that a copy of 'Jewel's Apology' should be placed in every parish church in England.

Richard Hooker took up this defence of the Church of England but conducted it at a higher level and directed it mainly against Protestant objections. He was in an intimately personal sense Jewel's successor, for Jewel undertook to be his patron when he was a boy doing well at the grammar school at Exeter, and secured for him a place at his old college in Oxford. For sixteen years Hooker remained in this college; among other tasks he taught logic (basically Aristotle's) and Hebrew. Then he was appointed to the key pulpit among London's lawyers, as Master of the Temple – although he had the embarrassment that the defeated candidate for the post, Walter Travers, stayed on as assistant or 'Reader' and preached every Sunday afternoon to a larger congregation, contradicting what had been said in the morning. Travers was a Puritan and the controversy with him, however irritating, stimulated the Oxford scholar into beginning his masterpiece, *Of the Laws of Ecclesiastical Polity*. He accepted appointments to two country parishes – one near Salisbury, the other near Canterbury – in order to concentrate on what he had come to see as his life's work. The first four parts or 'books', having been submitted to Archbishop Whitgift and to the all-seeing Lord Burghley, were published in 1593, followed by a fifth four years later. This fifth book, by far the longest and most controversial, was a detailed defence of the customs of the Church of England, dedicated to Whitgift.

Hooker died in 1600, like Jewel not yet fifty years of age and like him worn out; as his biographer Isaak Walton put it, 'it is thought he hastened his own death by giving life to his books'. But writing in 1664 Walton also quoted what Pope Clement

VIII was reported to have said, when Thomas Stapleton had
read Hooker's first book to him: 'There is no learning that this
man hath not searched into: nothing so hard for his understanding. . . . His books will get reverence by age; for there is in
them such seeds of eternity, that if the rest be like this, they
shall last till the last fire shall consume all learning.'

The difficulties which Hooker faced were those which Jewel
had evaded. They were reflected in the delays which postponed
the publication of the remaining three parts of his great work,
left by him almost complete. The sixth and eighth books were
first printed in 1648, and the seventh followed in 1662. Both in
the seventeenth century and later there were speculations that
other hands had tampered with the manuscript to suit their
own wishes. It has aroused suspicion that the seventh book,
praising the power of bishops with far more enthusiasm than
can be found in Hooker's earlier writings, was given to the
world by Bishop John Gauden, at a time when bishops had just
been restored along with Charles II and when this particular
bishop was claiming his rewards (first the bishopric of Exeter,
then that of Worcester) for having compiled or forged *Eikon
Basilike*, the book of prayers attributed to the martyred king,
Charles I. Those modern scholars who accept these posthumously published books as authentic (at least in the main)
still point out that the problems tackled in them were not small.
Was the 'right of kings' divine, or did it ultimately derive from
the people under God? Had Members of Parliament the right
to change the religious legislation of 1559? Had bishops the
right to govern the Church – a right derived not from the
Church or from any earthly monarch but from Christ himself?
It seems understandable if, after wrestling with such conun-
drums and trying to keep intact his loyalty to a queen determined to govern MPs and bishops alike, Hooker felt exhausted
before a premature death.

Some of the character of his *magnum opus* was shaped by his
work as a university teacher. He appealed repeatedly to the
authority in philosophy of Aristotle, 'the most judicious philosopher whose eye scarce anything did escape which was to be
found in the bosom of nature'. He also appealed to the Old
Testament, where kings clearly ruled priests. So his specialist

knowledge of logic and Hebrew encouraged him to argue that
it was reasonable for Elizabeth I to be Supreme Governor of
the Church of England – and for the English to obey orders
issued by her authority in ecclesiastical affairs. But his mind
had to range far beyond his Oxford preoccupations, for now he
had to defend such a position against the whole tendency of the
Reformation since Jean Calvin's triumphant return to Geneva
in 1541: the tendency to rely on the New Testament as the only
real authority for Christians. He had to argue that what was at
stake in the detailed controversies between the Elizabethan
government and the Calvinist extremists was nothing less than
the question of whether or not the Christians' God blessed the
creative progress of human reasoning and the peaceful ordering of human society. He was an advocate of civilization.

He approached the controversies of the time about matters
such as clergymen's robes through a leisurely exposition of the
Eternal Law, the Celestial Law (for angels and other invisible
spirits), the Law of Reason which guides the conscience, the
laws commanded by the Scriptures and the laws decreed by the
nations to order human affairs where the Scriptures had not
spoken decisively.

This last category of law – 'positive' or 'municipal' law – is,
Hooker grants, alterable, to suit changing circumstances. It
also needs to be sanctioned by the agreement of the whole
people to live under a form of government, which need not be a
monarchy. But 'without order there is no living in public
society'. So there can be no right for the individual to prefer his
private judgement to the law of the State within the government's proper sphere; even when the government trespassed
beyond its power sphere, and the subject feels morally obliged
to offer a passive resistance, there can be no right to rebel. And
here Hooker came to the crux of the matter. Calvinists such as
his rival Walter Travers had, he argued, no right to defy the
orders of Queen Elizabeth and her ministers in ecclesiastical
affairs. The matters in dispute (clergymen's robes, for example) had not been regulated by the Scriptures. Therefore in
a Christian country such matters properly belonged to the
sphere of the government.

Hooker rejected the Protestant tradition which pitted

Church against State as 'two kingdoms'. He preferred to compare Church and State with two sides of a triangle. The Church ought always, everywhere, to be working for a day when its membership would be identical with the State's; and that day had long ago arrived in England, where 'there is not any man a member of the commonwealth, which is not also of the Church of England'. And any government ought to be working for the 'good life' of its subjects, as Aristotle had said; God had not ordained kings 'to fat up men like hogs'. And for Hooker, the Protestant tradition which confined the Church to the straitjacket of the New Testament was wrong. The Church had been perfectly right to develop (on this, Hooker was clearer than Jewel); to bring into its worship the glories of the world such as architecture and music; to endow the clergy with tithes or with a bishop's wealth, and to give some of them high authority; to elaborate a theology based on reason as well as on the Scriptures.

The immediate influence of such argumentation should not be exaggerated. Twelve hundred copies of the 1593 edition were printed and were not sold out until 1606. The old-fashioned reliance on Aristotle and the Church Fathers limited Hooker's appeal even among the intellectuals. The first words of his Preface show his sombre mood. 'Though for no other cause, yet for this; that posterity may know we have not loosely through silence permitted things to pass away as in a dream, there shall be for men's information extant thus much concerning the present state of the Church of God established among us, and their careful endeavour which would have upheld the same.' And the first words of his first book were similar, showing that he knew that he was unlikely to be popular, whereas 'he that goeth about to persuade a multitude, that they are not so well governed as they ought to be, shall never want attentive and favourable hearers'. The same sharp tone marks his comments surviving in the margin of a copy of an anonymous pamphlet attempting to reply to him (*A Christian Letter of Certain English Protestants*, 1599). His real influence came in the seventeenth century, and it lay among those Anglicans who wanted reassurance that the Elizabethan settlement which they had inherited was defensible spiritually and intellectually as well as politically. Thus James I, according to Walton, 'never did mention him but with the epithet of the learned, or judicious, or reverend, or venerable Mr Hooker'; and Charles I recommended a study of Hooker to his scholarly daughter, Elizabeth. His learning and holiness helped this continuing prestige. His opinions may not have been always to the liking of James or Charles; in private papers which have survived he clearly denied the divine right of kings. But they knew he was a theologian in the great tradition. And later Anglicans have found very congenial Hooker's balance of the claims of Scripture, tradition and reason in an atmosphere of quiet legality and piety.

'Of law', wrote Hooker when he lifted his eyes above the controversies of his age, 'there can be no less acknowledged, than that her seat is the bosom of God, her voice the harmony of the world, all things in heaven and earth do her homage, the very least as feeling her care, and the greatest as not exempted from her power, but angels and men and creatures of what condition so ever, though each in different sort and manner, yet all with uniform consent, admiring her as the mother of their peace and joy.' And Izaak Walton could record that, as he lay dying in his rectory in Kent, Richard Hooker 'was meditating the number and nature of angels, and their blessed obedience and order, without which peace could not be in heaven; and oh that it might be so on earth!'[15]

BYRD AND SPENSER

The Queen gave her direct patronage to two laymen whose genius was profoundly religious but whose convictions were very different. William Byrd's greatest music was a lament for the tragedy overwhelming an England which had been part of

---

[15] Recent studies include J. S. Marshall, *Hooker and the Anglican Tradition* (Sewanee, Tenn., 1963); *Studies in Richard Hooker*, ed. W. Speed Hill (Cleveland, Ohio, 1972); R. K. Faulkner, *Richard Hooker and the Politics of a Christian England* (Berkeley, Cal, 1981).

Catholic Christendom; yet he enjoyed the Queen's favour. So did Edmund Spenser, whose poetry celebrated the new day of imperial Protestantism. Together, Byrd and Spenser enable us to glimpse what it meant to the souls of men that the Elizabethan Church claimed to be in some sense Catholic while being predominantly Protestant.

William Byrd was the pupil and intimate friend of Thomas Tallis, whose personal religion is difficult to penetrate. Tallis was organist of Waltham Abbey in Essex in the 1530s. After the abbey's suppression he continued to compose settings for the old words of worship, but became a Gentleman of the Chapel Royal in 1540. He retained the favour of successive monarchs until his death in 1585, and set the new Prayer Book to music which is still being used daily in Anglican cathedrals in the twentieth century. He was buried in the Chapel Royal at Greenwich, and the form of his will suggests that he died an Anglican.

Of Byrd's religion we know more. Having become organist of Lincoln Cathedral when barely twenty years old, he joined the staff of the Chapel Royal in 1570 and was always favoured by the Queen. She granted him and Tallis jointly the monopoly of music-printing for twenty-one years – a grant which was profitable in a country so devoted to music-making. They collaborated in a collection of sacred songs dedicated to her in 1575. But from the 1580s onwards Byrd's name appeared on many lists of Recusants known to be loyal to Rome, although he seems to have been excused the normal fines. This conversion – or was it an unbroken loyalty to Rome? – had a profound influence on him. He still provided fine music to accompany the Prayer Book services in the Chapel Royal, but from 1593 onwards his main home was in the Essex village of Stondon Massey. During thirty years of quiet there, he poured his genius into volumes of sacred songs often Catholic in their sources, into a hundred Latin motets to accompany the Mass (his *Gradualia*, issued in 1605–07), and into three Latin Masses for three, four and five voices. Much of this music was dedicated to peers of known Papist convictions. It belonged clearly to the renewal of Catholicism in the Counter-Reformation. The Council of Trent had forbidden the use of music for the

Mass which was based on every-day songs or which was irreverently florid. In his dedication of the *Gradualia* Byrd said that the music had suggested itself while he was meditating on the texts; so he was composing restrained religious music just as the council had desired. He was doing in England what his equal in polyphonic composition, Palestrina, was doing in Rome itself. Deliberately he refrained from the repetition of secular or religious music already in stock; the composition must be free, personal, his own worship. And he refused to spin out the words of the Mass as an excuse for elaborate musical passages showing his talents or the choir's; the music must serve the sacred words.

When we hear the lamentations of Jeremiah over the desolation of Jerusalem set to this music, we can, however, hear something more than the exposition of the text. We can hear a Catholic Englishman's nostalgia for the glories of the devastated shrines of his own nation. And when Byrd pours out splendid praise for Easter or All Saints, he implies a tribute to the enduring faith of his suffering fellow Catholics. For all the austere intensity of his devotion, he is self-revealing.

Yet Elizabeth's Chapel Royal had room for this musician who was in love with God and with the Catholic past. In 1586 he was a guest in the same house as two newly arrived Jesuit priests, William Weston and Robert Southwell. Probably they sang a Mass together. Weston proudly noted in his journal that Byrd had 'sacrificed everything' for his religion, but that was not accurate. Elizabeth did not require many sacrifices from men such as William Byrd who, while genuinely feeling religious nostalgia, were willing to accept her political authority. She also protected Thomas Morley, another distinguished composer who was on the staff of her Chapel Royal, and Sebastian Westcote, the organist of St Paul's Cathedral. Like Byrd, they both openly adhered to the old religion. Their music-making was a sound which echoed her policy of tolerating peaceful conservatives.[16]

---

[16] See Edmund Fellowes, *William Byrd* (revised, Oxford, 1948), and Peter Le Huray, *Music and the Reformation in England, 1549-1660* (London, 1967), pp. 227-46. Joseph Kerman has studied *The Masses and Motets of William Byrd* (London, 1981).

The son of a modest home in London, born probably in 1552, Edmund Spenser was given his chance by the new Merchant Taylors' School. He was a student in a Cambridge dominated by the debate about Calvinism and its consequences. Accepting the prevailing Protestantism, he was determined to become a great poet. After a brief spell as the Bishop of Rochester's secretary he made his name by his *Shepherd's Calendar* (1579). It was undeniably a clever poem, but a young man's. Most dangerously, it was too clever in its allusions to the triangular relationship between the Earl of Leicester (who had become his chief patron), his countess and his queen. It was also indiscreet in his praise of a good shepherd called 'Agrin', since Archbishop Grindal was at that moment in disgrace with the Queen. Nor was the oblique reference to Grindal solemn enough to flatter an elderly archbishop. Spenser used the Greek legend about an eagle dropping an oyster on the white head of old Aeschylus in the belief that it was a piece of chalk. This may have seemed a learned and witty reference, but Grindal no doubt remembered that according to the legend the eagle's mistake had caused the death of Aeschylus. The clever young poet was rewarded by an appointment as secretary to the Lord Deputy in distant (and not at all witty) Ireland.

England's colonial war against the Irish could scarcely have been more degrading, but Spenser gained a large estate and leisure; he grew to love the countryside as much as he disliked and feared the natives. His leisure was devoted to a great poem, *The Faerie Queene*, and in 1590 he visited the court in order to present the Queen with the first half. Elizabeth encouraged him with a handsome pension and he went back to Ireland to complete this project and other writing. He also made a second marriage; his love for Elizabeth Boyle produced some marvellous sonnets. But his home at Kilcolman in Munster was wrecked in the rebellion of 1598 and, returning with official letters to the court in Westminster, he died, shattered. He was buried in Westminster Abbey near the grave of Geoffrey Chaucer, whose work in the creation of English as a poet's language he had pondered, imitated and taken to 'glory' (a key word for him).

His masterpiece has been variously judged. C. S. Lewis, who loved it, though it 'perhaps the most difficult poem in English'. He found special difficulty in getting at its author's religion. In the end he concluded that 'the religion that underlies the form of the poet's imagination is simply the worship of the "glad Creator" '. He quoted Spenser's own confession in his *View of the Present State of Ireland*: 'Little have I to say of religion. . . . Myself have not been much conversant in that calling'.[17] Lewis regarded Spenser's poetry as essentially a celebration of created life – its orderliness, its bounty. And it is obviously true that Spenser was by profession a civil servant not a theologian, and by vocation a sensuous poet rather than an original philosopher. His cold-blooded view of Ireland was that the English conquest needed to be completed with determination, and his view of poetry was that it was an incantation in elaborately ceremonious and pictorial – although also learned – language, which lured the reader able to understand it into an enchanted dream very different from the realities of Ireland. His religion encouraged both this colonialism (since the English were extending Christian civilization) and this escapism (since heroic poetry was an adornment of the civilization being propagated among 'savages' with sword and fire). But surely we have no need to doubt that there was a layman's Protestantism at the centre of Spenser's attempt 'to fashion a gentleman or noble person in virtuous and gentle discipline'. In another modern critic's judgement, *The Faerie Queene* is 'above all a Christian work, founded upon an unquestioning acceptance of the primary relation of creature to Creator, and of the need of men to live in the light of, and by the help of, God's grace. Book I, the most openly Christian and doctrinal, a sort of Pilgrim's Progress through the fallen world of error, doubt, sin, temptation and evil, the book about the achieving of truth and holiness, is the crucial book . . . the most successful, the most unified and the most perfect in its structure and in the relationship in it of structure to purpose and message.'[18]

The Christian pilgrim in this Book I is the Red Cross Knight

[17] C. S. Lewis, *Spenser's Images of Life* (Cambridge, 1967), p. 140.
[18] Peter Bayley, *Edmund Spenser: Prince of Poets* (London, 1971), p. 124.

('Saint George of merry England'). He comes to grief except when guided by a fair lady, Una, who represents Truth. He is healed of his sins by personified virtues in the House of Holiness, given baptism in the well of life, and strengthened by Communion as he receives balm from the tree of life. Such passages correspond with the explicitly Christian (if unoriginal) content of Spenser's hymns *To Heavenly Love* and *To Heavenly Beauty*. To doubt that here a Protestant stated his own ideals for the future of England is like doubting that a nostalgic Catholic let his heart's beat be heard in William Byrd's Latin church music.

'*The Faerie Queene*', concludes the author of an elaborate study of its many allegories, 'is a book of religious inspiration and moral instruction, comparable in its purpose with the Revelation of St John and the *Divine Comedy* of Dante' – and partly indebted to those inexhaustible sources.[19] As such it had a great impact on the élite which was able to read it, so that it helped to create a new type of English gentleman, as well-read as he was well-born, as courtly as he was brave, as Protestant as he was patriotic. Surely Spenser, no less than Byrd, should be remembered if we think that the Church which Elizabeth governed had no soul.[20]

SHAKESPEARE'S RELIGION

Coleridge wrote of 'the greatest genius that perhaps human nature has yet produced, our *myriad-minded* Shakespeare'. There has been widespread agreement with such an assessment – and few would doubt that Shakespeare had a personal religion. But there has been less agreement about what his religion was.[21] It has been claimed that at heart he was a

---

[19] J. E. Hankins, *Source and Meaning in Spenser's Allegory* (Oxford, 1971), p. 298.
[20] Fritz Caspari studied the emergence of the new ideal in *Humanism and the Social Order in Tudor England* (Chicago, Ill., 1954).
[21] The facts were set out by Samuel Schoenbaum in *William Shakespeare: A Compact Documentary Life* (Oxford, 1977), and the gossip and speculations by the same cool scholar in *Shakespeare's Lives* (Oxford, 1970). Introductions to the work include M. C. Bradbrook, *Shakespeare: The Poet in His World* (London, 1978). Kenneth Muir surveyed *The Sources of Shakespeare's Plays* (London, 1977).

Roman Catholic.[22] Simon Hunt, one of the five schoolmasters in charge of the boy's education, may have been the Simon Hunt who became a Jesuit in 1578. Another of his teachers, John Cottom, left Stratford-upon-Avon in 1581 to become a firm Recusant in his native Lancashire, and had a brother who was a priest executed along with Edmund Campion. No doubt a number of the Shakespeares' neighbours were also of the old religion, and it has been suggested that the boy's own father was. We know that John Shakespeare was prominent in the commercial and public life of Stratford until 1576. He rose to the position of bailiff, the equivalent of mayor, and as such must have taken the oath acknowledging the Queen's supremacy over the Church. But he ceased to attend council meetings, and for a period also the parish church. When Campion and his fellow Jesuit Persons were in the neighbourhood in 1580 they distributed copies of a Catholic profession of faith compiled by St Charles Borromeo in Milan, and it is said that a copy was found in 1757 in the tiles of the roof of the house in Henley Street where William Shakespeare was born. And more than half a century after William Shakespeare's death, Richard Davies, the rector of a nearby village, made a short note: 'He died a Papist.'

However, by far the most probable explanation of John Shakespeare's withdrawal from public life is the reason given by the justices of the peace for his absence from church in 1592: 'for fear of process of debt'. We know that he had good cause to be afraid of some 'process' being started by irate creditors if he appeared on public occasions; he sold off pieces of land and was let off contributions to the relief of the poor. He was never fined or reported as a Recusant. The copy of the Catholic statement which he is said to have endorsed (but no signature of his has survived) has disappeared. The scholar Edmond Malone, who saw it, was in the end convinced that it could not be genuine. And even if John Shakespeare did for a time find consolation in the old religion, it does not follow that his son copied him – or copied his Roman Catholic schoolmasters. When in 1585 William Shakespeare abandoned Stratford, it was not to train

---

[22] As by Peter Milward, *Shakespeare's Religious Background* (London, 1973).

as a priest: he left his father to house his wife Anne and their three young children, and he went (perhaps not directly) to learn and earn in London.

The evidence that in his maturity he was a conforming member of the Church of England is strong. His name is absent from all known lists of Recusants – unlike his friend and rival, Ben Jonson – and instead he appears in contexts which show that he was acceptable to the clergy. For example, in 1614 the Stratford corporation supplied him with a quart of sack and a quart of claret to help him entertain a visiting preacher. Perhaps he thought of his guest as Costard thought of the curate in *Love's Labour's Lost*: 'a foolish mild man, an honest man, look you, but soon dashed . . . a marvellous good neighbour, faith, and a very good bowler.' Far more important as evidence are the many echoes in the plays of the church services which he began attending when John Bretchgirdle baptized him on 26 April 1564. A. L. Rowse has summed up the evidence of the plays. 'Of all Shakespeare's "sources" the Bible and the Prayer Book come first and are the most constant. Altogether there were definite allusions to forty-two books of the Bible, including the Apocrypha . . . Phrases from Morning and Evening Prayer are constantly echoed . . . There are similar phrases and echoes from all the services, from Baptism and Holy Matrimony – references to which are numerous – the Commination service and the Churching of Women. He had attended them all many times . . . He was an orthodox, conforming member of the Church into which he had been baptized, in which he was brought up and married, in which his children were reared and in whose arms he at length was buried . . . Above all, it was the psalms, Sunday by Sunday at Morning and Evening Prayer, that made a life-long impression on him . . . It is impossible to exaggerate the importance of this grounding in childhood.'[23]

Shakespeare made his will on 25 March 1616, 'in perfect health and memory, God be praised'. It had the regular

---

[23] A. L. Rowse, *William Shakespeare* (London, 1963), pp. 41–7, is based on Richmond Noble's full study of *Shakespeare's Biblical Knowledge and Use of the Book of Common Prayer* (London, 1935).

Protestant introduction (ignoring the Virgin and the saints): 'I commend my soul into the hands of God my Creator, hoping and assuredly believing through the only merits of Jesus Christ my Saviour to be made partaker of life everlasting.' He asked to be buried in his parish church, and when he had died on 23 April, St George's Day, all that was mortal of him was put beneath a gravestone. This stone was inscribed with a curious message to the sexton who would normally have felt free to get rid of old bones:

> Good friend, for Jesu's sake forbear
> To dig the dust enclosed here . . .

But of course neither of these formal farewell utterances is conclusive evidence of a man's personal religion. It is possible to work through the plays collecting rather more eloquent passages which may testify to an acceptance of the conventional religion of his time. Thus we can take note of Isabella's creed in *Measure for Measure*:

> Why, all the souls that were were forfeit once
> And he that might the vantage best have took
> Found out the remedy.

But it is also possible to go through the plays collecting passages which suggest that Shakespeare's philosophy was the 'mixed and muddled scepticism of the Renaissance'.[24] Or we may suppose that the final 'message' of the plays is Macbeth's:

> Life's but a walking shadow: a poor player,
> That struts and frets his hour upon the stage
> And then is heard no more: it is a tale
> Told by an idiot, full of sound and fury,
> Signifying nothing.

The truth, however, seems to be that the plays express many philosophies, for their author was a dramatist not a philosopher. 'The play's the thing' – as he proved by neglecting to prepare his own plays for the printer.[25]

---

[24] T. S. Eliot, *Selected Essays* (London, 1932), p. 117.
[25] J. W. Leaver summed up the scholarly debate on 'Shakespeare and the Ideas of His Time' in *Shakespeare Survey 29* (Cambridge, 1976), pp. 79–91.

In the first scene of *Hamlet,* when the ghost has just disappeared, Marcellus agrees with Horatio that 'it faded on the crowing of the cock'. Then he reminds him of what 'some say' – that in the season

> Wherein our Saviour's birth is celebrated,
> The bird of dawning singeth all night long:
> And then, they say, no spirit can walk abroad . . .

Horatio replies:

> So have I heard and do in part believe it.

And almost all students of the plays would agree that while the dramatist often uses medieval superstitions still popular in his time, that does not disclose what he himself wholly believes.

This reserved attitude did not result from some quirk in this particular dramatist's temperament. Nor was it produced by some moral failure on his part. 'He sacrifices virtue to convenience', wrote Samuel Johnson, 'and is so much more careful to please than to instruct, that he seems to write without any moral purpose.' But it was taken for granted in Shakespeare's time that the drama of the London stage was not intended to instruct the public in Christian theology or morals. Direct instruction had been given by the old medieval drama under the Church's sponsorship, and such 'miracle' and 'morality' plays were still sometimes performed in Elizabethan England. But Shakespeare never used the Bible as the source of a whole play, as he used Hall's or Holinshed's chronicles of England or North's *Plutarch* for the Roman plays. He provided no play to mark an event in the life of the Church; the nearest he came to that was when he provided entertainments for the royal family which coincided with Christian festivals. Although many moral axioms are spoken by the characters he put on the stage, he did not write in order to commend the Church's moral teaching. His drama was Renaissance drama, directly modelled on Latin classics rather than on medieval Christian examples, investigating human rather than divine mysteries. When Francis Meres, a young clergyman, was praising his work in 1598, he called him 'honey-tongued' like Ovid, and

'most excellent' for comedies like Plautus and for tragedies like
Seneca. The London stage in Shakespeare's day was not so
offensive to the godly as it later became (so that the Puritans
closed it down entirely in 1642) – but it was already the last
place in the world where anyone expected to hear the Church's
creed expounded directly.[26]

To find Shakespeare's religion, if by that we mean his view of
ultimate reality, it is not enough to notice the belief or disbelief
expressed in a few lines in a play. We have to look at the whole
pattern of his work.

He made his name by *Henry VI* and *Richard III*, by light
comedies, and by revising a spectacular tragedy by Thomas
Kyd. The only serious theme which emerges from his early
plays – and which runs right through his work to the end – is
the majesty and responsibility of kingship. Curiously enough
the only manuscript which has survived in his handwriting,
127 lines of an early play about Sir Thomas More, puts into
More's mouth this conventional Tudor sentiment:

> For to the king God hath his office lent
> Of dread, of justice, power and command . . .

But the main impression left by this apprentice's work is of
exuberant, if superficial, facility. By 1592 Robert Greene, a
bitterly envious author near death, was attacking the upstart
dramatist's conceit.

However, in 1592 tragedy came very near in real life. The
plague closed down the London theatres and claimed many
Londoners. Next year Christopher Marlowe, a dramatist
whose achievement had until then been far greater than
Shakespeare's, was killed in a tavern brawl; later Shakespeare
was to salute him as the 'dead shepherd'. Had Shakespeare
died in the plague, no commanding height would have been
occupied by his name in the history of England. But from these
plague years come the sonnets, almost certainly written to be
read in private by his patron, Henry Wriothesley, Earl of

---

[26] See R. M. Frye, *Shakespeare and Christian Doctrine* (Princeton, N.J., 1963),
qualified by some of the essays collected in G. Wilson Knight's *Shakespeare and
Religion* (London, 1967).

Southampton, to whom two longer poems were dedicated when published in 1593-4. The sonnets record an inner turmoil. A young poet is gripped by all the existential questions which afflict any exceptionally insecure, sensitive and articulate youth: the remorseless passing of time, the frailty of beauty, the nearness of failure and death, the 'expense of spirit' which he deplores even while he yields to his sexual appetite. The fascinating but humiliating centre of his life is his infatuation with the mistress whom he has to share with his patron. 'Love's not Time's fool' is for such a man still a question. In the end no Christian answers are propounded, although Sonnet 108 casually mentions that the poet says his prayers daily.

After the plague, the eight golden years 1594-1601 saw Shakespeare at work with stupendous energy and originality. He purchased a shareholding in his company, the Lord Chamberlain's Men, presumably with Southampton's help, and that was the making of his fortune. For this company he wrote more and greater history plays, including *King John*, on the surface a routine 'No Popery' play but including the Bastard's profound realism; *Richard II*, which brought Henry Bolingbroke, a man of affairs, to take the country over from an incompetent ruler, but introduced deep musings by the doomed Richard; and *Henry V*, allowing the common soldiers to speak for themselves before they die. There was *Henry IV*, combining history with the more-than-man-sized creation of a comic hero, Falstaff; and *Julius Caesar*, combining history with the near-achievement of a tragic hero, Brutus. There was *The Merchant of Venice*, piercing the character of the Jew: 'If you prick us, do we not bleed?' There was *Romeo and Juliet*, turning someone else's dreary poem into ecstasy. And there was *Twelfth Night*, a celebration of the freedom, vigour and wit of women as well as their beauty – in an age so far from feminism that these parts had to be acted by boys. It seems to have been written in eight days for performance before the Queen in the great hall of Whitehall Palace on 6 January 1601. 'The play is done,' sang Robert Armin playing Feste, alone on the stage at the end,

> And we'll strive to please you every day.

But after that not even Shakespeare could produce more plays which would 'please'. He could not take the comedy of love further than he had done in *Twelfth Night*.

So he achieved the diagnosis of the human agony in the great tragedies. We naturally ask what in his life inspired the change of mood, but there is almost no evidence. The situation behind the sonnets is fairly clear; but we lack the key to unlock the tragedies.

In 1599 *Henry V* had included a reference to Essex's departure for Ireland, with Southampton in the expeditionary force which, it was hoped, would win another Agincourt. It was the mess that Essex made of this campaign (including the promotion of Southampton in defiance of the Queen) that set in motion the train of events leading to his crazy insurrection in February 1601. The rebellion led to Essex being executed and Southampton being imprisoned until the Queen's death. Shakespeare was himself implicated, however remotely. Shortly before their act of folly a number of Essex's supporters put on a performance of *Richard II*, and the point about Richard's deposition was not lost on Elizabeth. 'I am Richard II, know ye not that?' she remarked to William Lambarde when he was showing her some archives. The performance of this play was investigated at Essex's trial. Was this, then, the catastrophe for which we are looking? The sonnets had protested an unalterable love for Southampton. It can be assumed that Shakespeare was to some extent always loyal to his former patron; he was conspicuously not among the poets who paid tributes to the Queen immediately after her death, and in *Hamlet* the pompous old bore Polonius, whose death occurs so unceremoniously, seems to be a skit on the recently dead Lord Burghley, whom the Essex-Southampton circle always regarded as an enemy. It has been suggested that *The Phoenix and the Turtle*, published not long after the collapse of the rebellion in 1601, is a lament for Essex and his friends: 'truth and beauty buried be'. It is also possible that the career of Essex – impetuous but inconsistent, glamorous but in the end almost mad – contributed to the character of Hamlet. But it is unlikely that the poet, now famous and well-off, was profoundly dejected by the follies and fates of aristocrats. It seems more probable that he disapproved of their rebellion – as he certainly condemned rebellion in principle. The publication of the sonnets suggests that by 1609 (at the latest) any emotional relationship there may have been with Southampton belonged to the past, but there is no evidence, and little probability, that the Earl had ever admitted John Shakespeare's son to a truly intimate friendship.

Was there a sufficient disaster in the poet's private life? Had he written *King Lear* immediately after the death of his only son, Hamnet, in 1596, we might have had our answer. But he did not; and we are left to find the innocence of Hamnet reflected in young Arthur in *King John*, a play probably written that winter. Instead of collapsing, William Shakespeare secured recognition as a gentleman from the heralds and bought the grandest house in Stratford. Although Hamnet's twin Judith seems to have caused him anxiety – she was not married until she was thirty-one, and then unsatisfactorily – he was consoled by his eldest child, Susanna, who married a scholarly doctor. The tragedies include eloquent expressions of loneliness, and are full of disgust at sex; although such moods were already present in the sonnets, common sense suggests that their increase had something to do with his unsatisfactory marriage with an illiterate woman eight years older than he was. But there was no final breach between him and Anne. It is probable that he had provided for her handsomely before making his will, since had he not done so the law would have compelled him to leave his widow one third of his property – more than the 'second best bed' specially mentioned (perhaps for sentimental reasons) in that much-discussed document. In brief, we have no evidence of a dramatic catastrophe in his private life to account for the mood of the great tragedies of the 1600s.

It has accordingly been suggested that the main driving force behind the tragedies was the ambition to excel in that field, reckoned the chief challenge to any dramatist, when he was at the height of his powers and prosperity.[27] Yet it seems

---

[27] This was the argument of the 1934 lecture by C. J. Sisson on 'The Mythical Sorrows of Shakespeare' reprinted in *Studies in Shakespeare*, ed. Peter Alexander (Oxford, 1964), pp. 9–32.

worth repeating the chief themes of the plays, not in order to attempt any addition to the piles of literary criticism under which this mountain range of genius has been covered but solely in order that we may remember that the work done in this mysterious period had a unity.

Hamlet was an already familiar plot, handled in a play now lost by Thomas Kyd or one of his imitators; but into the simple plot of a delay in taking revenge Shakespeare poured poetry and genius when he got to work in 1600–01 (we know the date because of a number of contemporary references). Indeed, he permanently expanded the self-consciousness of the educated Englishman. It was an achievement which can be appreciated by comparing it with the crude contemporary psychology of 'humours'. The hero of *Hamlet* is an inexhaustibly ambiguous anti-hero. Driven forward by a traditional sense of duty and by courage (however fitful), capable of ruthlessness, he is a man like a god, the beauty of the world, the paragon of animals; yet he is also too clever to be guided by tradition, a man paralysed by self-analysis, sickened by a cynical weariness with existence, terrified of death, the quintessence of dust. By his own complexity which holds him back from the decisive action, he brings disaster to many – including the woman he loves, and himself. His life's achievement is simply to show what he is.

After *Hamlet* Shakespeare, it seems, tried to turn back to histories and comedies. But *Troilus and Cressida* could not be another celebration of love (as in Chaucer's poem of the same title) or of heroism (as in Chapman's 1598 translation of Homer's *Iliad*, dedicated to Essex). Around the unfaithfulness of Cressida is shown a chaos of sordid lust and pointless conflicts. As Thersites exclaims: 'lechery, lechery; still wars and lechery; nothing else holds fashion: a burning devil take them!' That verdict would be a valid comment on most of the characters in *All's Well that Ends Well* and *Measure for Measure*. Both plays became 'problem plays' – for the 'bed-tricks', the ensnaring of Bertram and the exposure of Angelo in a sex-mad world, were not truly comic themes. It was clear that the next masterpiece had to be a more straightforward tragedy. And it came. On All Saints' Day 1604 the royal court saw *Othello*, the first of three tragedies which were studies in pride.

Othello's killing of Desdemona is brought about by the sheer evil of Iago's suggestions to her husband. But the subtler tragedy concerns what is killed within Othello (whereas the Italian novel from which the plot came showed no interest at all in Othello's character). His nobility is killed by his pride. His pride is the reason why Iago can inflame his jealousy; his pride makes him his wife's implacable judge; and even when Emilia in her own dying speech has so terribly condemned him, his farewell speech is full of pride turned into self-pity.

Timon of Athens seems to have been a tragedy abandoned by its author while still in draft. It was not acted in his lifetime. The most obvious theme is the ingratitude of Timon's friends, but the subtler plot is that Timon has looked to his friends only for the confirmation of his pride. That flaw is what in the end makes him a hater of mankind; he lives like a beast and dies mysteriously alone by the salt sea. Another of the tragedies, *Coriolanus*, did receive performances – and it, too, was a study in the bitter fruits of pride. The Roman people's pride makes them ungrateful to Coriolanus, while his own pride makes him turn against his city. But neither the despairing Athenian nor the coldly arrogant Roman general has ever really fascinated an audience. What happens to a hater of men does not much affect men.

By their failures these two sequels to *Othello* show that not even this genius could be a genius always, able to grip an audience's profound attention and sympathy. But two trans-cendent plays were acted at court in 1606 – in the summer, when the King of Denmark was on a state visit, *Macbeth*; on the day after Christmas, *King Lear*.

At its simplest *Macbeth* was an entertainment provided by the company called the King's Men and written by a dramatist who had walked in scarlet to the coronation of King James I. It was a comment on the gunpowder plot of Guy Fawkes and others in the previous year. It condemned the murder of Duncan, and featured Banquo who was an ancestor of James; and it condemned witches, for whose reality James had argued in a book. But beneath this surface can be found layer upon layer of meditation about the corruption of a well-rewarded hero by an ungrateful and pitiless ambition incarnate in his wife, leading him into treachery, solitude, darkness and hell. Is it a total corruption? Here is the deepest fascination of *Macbeth*: the audience is brought to pity this 'dead butcher and his fiend-like queen'.

On its surface *Lear*, like *Macbeth*, shows that it is wrong to be disloyal to a king. But because Shakespeare added so much to the plot about the ungrateful daughters (taken from someone else's *King Leir*), he was able to present the whole world of human evil. It is evil to be proud – and Lear is himself full of flattered self-will. Then pride breeds misery. But the escape from evil begins when Lear, instead of pitying himself as Timon always does, pities other people. In *Hamlet*, *Othello* and *Macbeth* there had been many Christian images, and above all there had been the affirmation of the control of life by the divine justice and providence, but the Britain of *Lear* was pre-Christian. In the earlier tragedies some relief had been added at the end by the reaffirmation of the life of Athens or Rome, Denmark or Scotland, but *Lear* showed how trivial any political hope would be in comparison with the pitiable fate of man, the 'poor, bare fork'd animal' stretched out 'upon the rack of this tough world'.

'Who is it that can tell me who I am?' asks Lear in the first act. The human condition is now seen through godless eyes:

> Thou know'st the first time that we smell the air
> We wawl and cry. I will preach to thee: mark . . .
> When we are born, we cry that we are come
> To this great stage of fools.

Or if there are gods, they are evil:

> As flies to wanton boys, are we to the gods;
> They kill us for their sport.

Where human life begins is the place of corruption:

> But to the girdle do the gods inherit,
> Beneath is all the fiends';
> There's hell, there's darkness, there's the sulphurous pit,
> Burning, scalding, stench, consumption.

Only one morality can be expected after such a start:

> Humanity must perforce prey on itself
> Like monsters of the deep.

And only one end is to be expected:

> Men must endure
> Their going hence, even as their coming hither.

And it is the supreme tribute to *Lear* that, although it has perhaps the most improbable of all Shakespeare's plots, we feel for a time that here is the truth about life:

> The weight of this sad time we must obey,
> Speak what we feel, not what we ought to say.

How obsessive in all this work of the 1600s, despite the great variety of the plots taken from so many sources, is the theme that pride corrupts and causes ingratitude and treachery, and how profoundly sour is the attitude to sex! It is difficult to believe that this insistent message about arrogance and lust – a message coming from a distance far beyond the convention of tragic drama that pride comes before a fall, a message which had to be voiced even when Shakespeare was trying to write a comedy – was produced solely by a dramatist's professional skill. It seems more likely that at some date some event or events which we shall never know about worked on, and almost broke, his heart and mind. This need not have been at the time when the tragedies were written: emotional shock can be delayed in its effects. It is also possible, it seems, that the tragedies brought relief and healing to their own author – as to many other sad people. He saw the condition of the rest of humanity more fully than had been possible for him at the time of his self-absorbed, self-pitying sonnets. And some medicine for his own hurt was found in his compassion for fellow creatures. Lear's eyes were opened when he saw the 'poor naked wretches' on the heath in the storm. Are we to believe that he who was about to create Ophelia was not moved when a young woman was found drowned in a stream near Stratford shortly before Christmas 1579? Her name was Katherine Hamlett. Or that he who was about to create Cordelia as King

Lear's one loving daughter was not moved when the youngest daughter of old Sir Brian Annesley resisted her sisters' attempt to get him declared insane? Her name was Cordell.

After the great tragedies we enter the final period, when Shakespeare's output gives some signals of exhaustion. His death on what is believed to have been his fifty-second birthday (although the date of his birth is uncertain) seems to have come when the play of his life was felt to be over. But before the end came, his work showed his peace.

It is possible to argue that the new happiness was, like the previous dark period, solely a response to the demands of the theatre. Plays were now most profitable if written for performance by candlelight, either at court or indoors in private theatres such as the Blackfriars, used by Shakespeare's company from 1609 onwards. Plays should therefore be accompanied by stately music and dancing which would be snobbish reminders of more expensive dramatic entertainments, the 'masques' which King James and Queen Anne loved; and with a general message that all was well with the world, they should be aimed at an audience able to afford the Blackfriars seats. A sophisticated specimen of this style was *The Two Noble Kinsmen*, a play of 1613 mainly by John Fletcher, with some scenes by the old master. But again we should look at the unity of the serious work in this period and ask whether it shows anything of Shakespeare's heart.

The key figure is now a girl, lost and restored – but with that girl is recovered a whole world previously abandoned in disgust. This girl is 'all fire and air', as Cleopatra hopes to be – but the fire is less smoky, the air purer, than in that supreme tale of the mid-life crisis, *Anthony and Cleopatra* (which may have been written as early as the year of *Macbeth* and *Lear*). In the three acts which Shakespeare seems to have contributed to *Pericles, Prince of Tyre*, Marina ends her father's despairing grief. In *Cymbeline* Imogen's loving loveliness as she comes to her marriage with Posthumus is at the heart of the final mood of peace. In *The Winter's Tale* Perdita is restored to her father along with his wife, Hermione. In *The Tempest* Miranda's marriage is the centre-piece of the general reconciliation and deliverance on the magic island.

It is possible that this enchanting girl emerged in Shakespeare's mind out of his sources; but it does not seem very likely. Behind the girl did he see his daughter Susanna, the 'good Mistress Hall' described on her tombstone of 1649 as being 'wise unto salvation'? Or was it some other woman who consoled him for his less than fulfilling marriage, or some transfiguration of many women in the memory? Or was he deeply reconciled to his wife? We do not know. But it can be said that 'what is here asserted, under the guise of the play's poetic symbolism, is nothing less than a concept of spiritual resurrection . . . a re-integrated and regenerated humanity.'[28] For it seems clear – not so much from anything anyone says in a play as from the unity of the themes of this final period – that the dramatist had himself come to share Hermione's creed:

> If powers divine
> Behold our human actions, as they do,
> I doubt not then but increase shall make
> False accusation blush, and tyranny
> Tremble at patience.

The healing which is celebrated in this final period is partly the slow work of nature. Many passages in *The Tempest* say or sing that. The flowers of an English summer, the sheep-shearing feast, the jokes of countrymen – all these fill the sixteen-year gap at the centre of *The Winter's Tale*. But *Lear* is by itself sufficient to show the ugly face of nature, so that if the questions of the tragedies are to receive answers bringing peace, there must be a supernatural reality which is benevolent.

Caliban, whose previous remarks have shown that he takes a definitely unromantic view of nature, exits with:

> I'll be wise hereafter,
> And seek for grace.

At another turning point Miranda, confronting a gang of villains, declares:

---

[28] Derek Traversi, *Shakespeare: The Last Phase* (London, 1954), p. 40. See also Frances Yates, *Shakespeare's Last Plays: A New Approach* (London, 1975).

> O wonder!
> How many goodly creatures are there here!
> How beauteous mankind is! O brave new world
> That has such people in't!

Her father sensibly comments, ' 'Tis new *to thee*'. The cruel and cowardly old world has been transformed in a woman's mind by the action of what at the end of *Macbeth* is called 'the grace of Grace'; by what Ferdinand now proceeds to call 'immortal Providence'; by the gods whom Gonzalo thanks,

> For it is you that have chalk'd the way
> Which brought us hither.

And Prospero in his epilogue pulls the play together:

> And my ending is despair,
> Unless I be reliev'd by prayer,
> Which pierces so that it assaults
> Mercy itself and frees all faults.
> As you from crimes would pardon'd be
> Let your indulgence set me free.

None of these plays names the Christians' God, and although some critics have loved to spot the 'Christ figure' in them, actually the redeemer is a girl assisted by magic. It may therefore seem sentimental to suggest that the end of Shakespeare's spiritual journey brought an acceptance of the Christians' God in a spirit of forgiveness fully Christian and accompanied by the assurance of the 'brave new world' of Easter. Certainly any such suggestion ought to acknowledge that on the stage for which Shakespeare wrote any preaching was expected to be very oblique. But even in the 'problem plays', where apparently the spirit of comedy was entirely poisoned by cynicism, the themes of innocence, forgiveness and reconciliation had been heard and there had been glimpses of the restoration of order in society (as in nature), so that it is inaccurate to say that these poems show that Shakespeare then 'believed in nothing'. Not for nothing did the very title of *Measure for Measure* come from the Sermon on the Mount. And already in the tragedies there was power in good as well as in evil. This is, after all, what one would expect. As has often been pointed out, the origins lie in the Ancient Greek rites of purification, for the least that happens in true tragedy is that the audience is first taken out of its own concerns by a new terror and is then purified by the new emotion of pity. But something else often happens in tragedy, if through its medium the good is distinguished more sharply than before from the evil – even if good and evil mix, as mix they must, in the vulnerable hero. At the end, the good is seen to possess a power mysteriously present in those apparently damned – and secure beyond the worst than can happen. Tragedy, while impossible if the triumph of the good seems assured, is equally impossible if the triumph of the good is also impossible.

A cautious scholar has accordingly observed that 'there is a sense in which *King Lear* can be regarded as a Christian play. We are asked to imagine a world in which there is no knowledge of Christian teaching, in which there is a savage struggle for survival, in which men like ravenous fishes feed on one another; and we are driven to realize that man needs neither wealth, nor power, but patience, fortitude, love and mutual forgiveness.'[29] At the beginning of the twentieth century – a century when *Lear* has often seemed contemporary – one of the greatest of all commentators on Shakespeare pointed out that at the end Lear's sight is 'so purged with scalding tears that it sees at last how power and place and all things in the world are vanity except love'.[30]

Before Cordelia dies, Lear says it himself:

> We two alone will sing like birds i' th' cage:
> When thou dost ask me blessing, I'll kneel down
> And ask of thee forgiveness: so we'll live,
> And pray, and sing, and tell old tales, and laugh
> At gilded butterflies: and hear (poor rogues)
> Talk of court news, and we'll talk with them too,

---

[29] Kenneth Muir, *Shakespeare's Tragic Sequence* (London, 1972), p. 139. See also W. R. Elton, *King Lear and the Gods* (San Marino, Cal., 1960), and Ivor Morris, *Shakespeare's God: The Role of Religion in the Tragedies* (London, 1972).

[30] A. C. Bradley, *Shakespearean Tragedy* (revised, London, 1905), p. 285. John Bayley, *Shakespeare and Tragedy* (London, 1981), avoided Bradley's moralism but could not entirely dissent from this conclusion.

> Who loses, and who wins; who's in, who's out;
> And take upon's the mystery of things,
> As if we were God's spies: and we'll wear out
> In a wall'd prison, packs and sects of great ones,
> That ebb and flow by th' moon . . .
> Upon such sacrifices, my Cordelia,
> The gods themselves throw incense.

In *Lear* the contradiction of faith in God by the facts of life seems to be so severe that Christianity is not going to be 'what we feel'. The birth of the hope of a resurrection 'which does redeem all sorrows' is aborted. With Cordelia's dead body in his arms, Lear knows that this answer is given to Albany's prayer for her, 'The gods defend her':

> Never, never, never, never, never!

But an explicitly Christian mood fills every corner of the last play which Shakespeare wrote – with, it seems, some assistance from John Fletcher.

Like *The Tempest*, *Henry VIII* is a ceremonious play; because a gun was fired during a performance in June 1613 (possibly the first performance), the Globe was burned down. The characters cannot be reconciled – Tudor history was too well known for that. But they can be brought together in Shakespeare's glorifying mind. The London mob is infinitely more genial than the mob in *Coriolanus*. The pure woman in this play is Queen Catherine, long-suffering and morally triumphant in her meekness as she looks forward to death. Clergymen are seen in a kinder light than surrounds them in any other play. Even the proud Wolsey becomes human and moving in his repentance. Cranmer is portrayed as a humble Christian, but at the baptism of the future Queen Elizabeth he is filled with the spirit of prophecy: 'heaven now bids me . . .' Shakespeare had in 1608 watched his only granddaughter being baptized Elizabeth, and he was now writing at a time when the nation was rejoicing over the Protestant marriage of Princess Elizabeth. At the close of his life the greatest of all the Elizabethans – and of all the English – added his tribute to his dead queen:

She shall be lov'd and fear'd; her own shall bless her;
Her foes shake like a field of beaten corn . . .
God shall be truly known; and those about her
From her shall read the perfect ways of honour,
And by those claim their greatness, not by blood.

CHAPTER FIVE

DEFIANT CHRISTIANS

THE CATHOLIC
RECUSANTS

The story of the Recusants who refused to attend their parish churches under Elizabeth I out of loyalty to the old religion of Pope and Mass constitutes a tragedy to which perhaps only the genius we have been studying could do justice. Roger Dibdale, a priest executed in 1586, had been at school with William Shakespeare. There is, however, no evidence that Shakespeare was specially interested in the subject. His plays show a fascination with national monarchy, not with the papacy; with England, not with the Catholic Church. It appears that he took the conventional view that a Recusant was, at least potentially, a mere traitor to his sovereign; that inside the cloak of piety was the dagger of a Macbeth. Whatever may have been his share in the writing of *Sir Thomas More*, the play showed no interest in the religious issue behind the death of that martyr. And there seems to be a contemptuous reference to the Jesuit missionaries who were martyrs under Elizabeth in Sonnet 124:

> . . . the fools of time,
> Which die for goodness, who have lived for crime.

But the Roman Catholic community in Shakespeare's England contributed its share of heroes to the national heritage.[1] William Allen, for instance, who was made a cardinal in 1587 and appointed Archbishop of Malines shortly before his death, had as much ability and dedication as most Archbishops of

---

[1] Recent studies were summed up by Adrian Morey, *The Catholic Subjects of Elizabeth I* (London, 1978), and Peter Holmes, *Resistance and Compromise* (Cambridge, 1982).

Canterbury. Brought up in Lancashire, he taught in Oxford until 1563, for the last four years privately. After five wandering years during which he was ordained a Catholic priest in Malines, he settled down as the head of a new college in the new university at Douai in Flanders. There he pioneered the training of English priests: astonishingly, no one had ever attempted this systematically before 1568. By this step, taken on his own initiative, he made it possible for the Catholic laity of England to be served by a new generation of priests faithful to the religion taught in Rome.

At first he seems to have intended merely a training in devotion and theology for men who would be ready to answer the call when Catholicism was officially re-established, but before long he realized that the urgent need was for missionaries who would work as well as wait. Beginning in 1574, Allen sent to England not mere propaganda but men to live and to die. His finances were never far from disaster; he relied first on a Spanish subsidy and, when anti-English feelings among the citizens of Douai forced him to move his college to Rheims (1578–93), on a grant from the Duke of Guise. His human material was often unsatisfactory, as callow youths came over from England with confused religious opinions. By a regime of devout austerity and excellent teaching (he had Oxford and Cambridge professors on his staff) he made them into priests. Most were trained for a mission of constant discomfort and tension, riding from house to house with a one-in-two chance of arrest and a one-in-seven chance of execution, braving a certainty which to many a Tudor Englishman was probably as worrying as the risk of a painful death: official condemnation and popular execration as traitors. Before long Allen's extraordinary seminary was so attractive that it became too small, and eager recruits had to be sent for training elsewhere.

He accompanied his teaching by a stream of publications. Some of these books his former pupils could recommend to simple inquirers; others they could rely on as answers to their highly placed enemies. Before he died in 1594 his last message to the priests whom he had trained was a final warning that Catholics were on no account to be allowed to worship with Protestants. But, he added, those who did so 'for mere fear or saving their family, wife and children from ruin' were to be treated with 'great compassion and mercifulness'. It was an instruction typical of his combination of courageous idealism with humane friendliness. He boasted that his college, for all its strictness, did not need written rules.

After Allen's death the oversight of the English mission was mainly in the hands of Robert Persons (or Parsons), who had already been his ally in the foundation of colleges for the overflow of students. This successor's task was the harder since the hopes with which the older man had pioneered had not been fulfilled. Just before Persons died in 1610 John Donne bitterly attacked his influence in *Pseudo-Martyr*, a 400-page onslaught, followed by a satire in learned Latin translated as *Ignatius his Conclave*. (The conclave addressed by the founder of the Jesuits takes place in hell, and includes a proposal to send these missionaries on a mission to the moon.) Donne's own family had 'endured and suffered in their persons and fortunes', as many others had done, at the call of this man who fascinated some, repelled others and baffled most. In his preface to *Pseudo-Martyr*, Donne recalled how impressed he had once been 'by Persons, who by nature had a power and superiority over my will'.

At every stage of his adult life Persons made enemies, Catholic as well as Protestant. Some claimed that because he was a Somerset blacksmith's son he could not get on with his colleagues while he was a Fellow of Balliol College, Oxford. Whatever may have been the truth there, he committed himself to Roman Catholicism in the 1570s and became a Jesuit. The Society of Jesus had been founded by St Ignatius Loyola and given its constitution by the Pope in 1540; as the spearhead of the Counter-Reformation it was at the Pope's disposal in Rome itself, or in India or China or across the Atlantic or on the spiritual battlefields of the struggle for Europe. Persons was always disappointed that there were not enough recruits to form an English 'province' in the Jesuit order (that was not to come until 1623), but he gradually took over control of the English College in Rome, founded 1576–79, becoming rector in 1587. Disappointed also by the laxity which he observed in Rome and by the general lack of heroism which he discovered among English Catholics during his return to the country in 1580–81, he put his hopes in a new generation. In 1582 he persuaded the Duke of Guise to found the school for boys which, when moved to St Omer and placed under the control of the Jesuits, became the pioneer of Roman Catholic education for the English.[2]

Persons was sensitive to the human cost of the English mission; the walls of the chapel in the English College at Rome were painted with scenes showing priests being tortured and executed. But his answer was to go on dreaming. Among his unpublished papers was a *Memorial for the Reformation of England*, envisaging the future: a Council of Reformation was to appoint bishops and parish priests of good character and to remove those who proved disappointing. Church lands were to be recovered and seminaries, schools and hospitals financed out of them. England was to be given a third archbishopric (at Bristol) and a third university (at Durham). Meanwhile another answer to the realities awaiting the Jesuits in Elizabethan England was to set Persons' hopes on diplomatic intrigue and military force. He knew how to gain the ear of Philip of Spain and how to delude him into believing that Elizabeth could be overthrown with ease. Like Allen, Persons was a prolific writer. He was more prolific than wise, but one of his books, *The Christian Exercise appertaining to Resolution* (1584), became a best-seller and, in a censored version edited by a Puritan named Bunny, was used by many Protestants who shared his conviction that being a Christian meant being uncomfortable. In the next century a greater Puritan, Richard Baxter, used to say that his soul had been awakened by reading an old, torn copy of 'Bunny's *Resolution*' when a boy of fifteen.[3]

Persons wrote the first biography of St Edmund Campion and always kept on his person a portion of the rope which had

---

[2] See A. C. F. Beales, *Education under Penalty* (London, 1963).

[3] There is a memoir in *Letters and Memorials of Father Robert Persons*, Vol. 1, ed. L. Hicks (London, 1942), and see Bernard Basset in *The English Jesuits* (London, 1967), pp. 55–96. Martin Haile wrote about Allen as *An Elizabethan Cardinal* (London, 1914). T. H. Clancy studied *Papist Pamphleteers: The Allen-Persons Party and the Political Thought of the Counter-Reformation in England* (Chicago, Ill., 1964).

bound Campion to the scaffold. This famous Jesuit martyr made his way on foot to Rome in 1573, leaving behind a career of the highest promise at Oxford. He was happy teaching in the Jesuit college at Prague until sent on the order's first mission to England, in 1580 with Persons as leader. His existing reputation, his eloquence and his gift for friendship all contributed greatly to the mission's impact in stirring up the ardour of priests surviving from Queen Mary's time and in reaching families who were to send many sons to serve the mission in later years. Perhaps what made the biggest impression was his courage, for despite his disguise this gifted young man was convinced that he was going to this death. 'I cannot long escape the hands of the heretics,' he reported to the distant general of the Jesuit order, 'the enemies have so many eyes, so many tongues, so many scouts and crafts. I am in apparel very ridiculous; I often change it and my name also. I read letters sometimes myself that in the first front tell news that Campion is taken, which, noised in every place where I come, so filleth my ears with the sound thereof that fear itself hath taken away all fear.' With a strange fatalism he wrote an open letter to the Privy Council; when published from a secret press at Stonor Park, it became known as his 'brag'. He challenged not only the councillors but also the theologians of the universities to debate. He sounded confident, but he knew that he was going to a cruel death. Although 'racked with your torments . . . we have made a league – all the Jesuits of the world, whose succession and multitude must over-reach all the practices of England – cheerfully to carry the cross you shall lay upon us.' The death he had expected he met bravely during 1581.[4]

The priests who followed Campion in the English mission were a varied lot of men. Some were far more cunning; for example, Richard Holtby, 'a little man with a reddish beard' who was the leading priest in the north. Between his return to his native Yorkshire in 1591 and his peaceful death in 1640,

---

[4] Evelyn Waugh wrote a short study of *Edmund Campion* (London, 1935), relying largely on the biography by Richard Simpson (1867). E. E. Reynolds, *Campion and Parsons* (London, 1980), was better researched.

this Jesuit was never once arrested. Others were the opposite of cautious; for example, Thurstan Hunt, who organized the many Recusants of Lancashire. He was arrested in 1600 while attempting to rescue a fellow priest from captivity, and during his own imprisonment he wrote to the Queen to accuse the Bishop of Chester of wishing to see the Earl of Essex crowned king.

Naturally we know most of the men who, like Campion, could be eloquent on paper. Many hearts, particularly young men's hearts, must have been touched by the gallant courage of the Jesuit missioners of the 1590s in the Midlands and the south, John Gerard and William Weston; they were imprisoned but not executed. Both men were able journalists, and almost four hundred years later it is difficult to read their autobiographies with an unthrilled or unmoved heart. Scarcely less remarkable is the story of Henry Garnet. A shrewd and prudent man, he succeeded Weston as the superior of the Jesuits within England in 1586. He remained at this very difficult and dangerous post of leadership for twenty years. If he lacked the glamour of Persons, Campion, Gerard and Weston, he may be said to have achieved more solidly pastoral work. But in 1606 he was arrested and tortured. Already deeply depressed by his duty of attending many public executions of his fellow Jesuits, he seems to have broken down under twenty-two 'examinations' before his trial. One factor was his own confusion of mind once he had become vaguely aware of the gunpowder plot against James I and Parliament. 'I was very much distempered and could never sleep quietly afterwards, but sometimes prayed to God that it should not take effect', he told his judges. Later he cried passionately but uselessly: 'I would to God I had never known of the powder treason!'

After twenty years of discretion, Henry Garnet had been caught up in the treasonable and murderous plots of laymen who were great fools. And all that he could now do, in their defence and his own, was to equivocate – thus earning for himself a place in *Macbeth*. 'An equivocator . . . who committed treason enough for God's sake, yet could not equivocate to heaven', sneers the Porter in Act II. But he died with dignity

and his nephew, St Thomas Garnet, now banished, had the
courage to return next year to England and to death.[5]

One of the Jesuits, St Robert Southwell, wrote English
poetry of enduring quality during the six years while he was a
hunted mission priest (1586–92). During the three years which
he spent in solitary confinement, undergoing torture and
awaiting execution, he was not allowed writing materials.
When his prayer book or 'breviary' was recovered, its only clue
to this poet's mind was a row of pricks under the name of Jesus.

Of course we admire priests who undertook a mission where
the penalties were so terrible. Lord Mountjoy, who was to
conquer Ireland for Elizabeth, exclaimed when he had just
witnessed the execution of Robert Southwell: 'I cannot answer
for his religion, but I wish to God that my soul may be with his.'
Seeking an explanation of their heroism, we notice that many
of them fell under the influence of Allen or Persons, and above
all under the psychological pressure of the month spent in the
first experience of the *Spiritual Exercises* of St Ignatius Loyola at
an impressionable age. Robert Southwell, for example, was
sent from his father's manor house in Norfolk to be trained at
Douai in 1576 when about fifteen years old. Evidence survives
that the young man had to battle with ardent natural longings
before he became the complete Jesuit. But he entered the order
at the age of seventeen, and was sent to Rome. There he
became so fluent in Italian that he had to relearn English
before he could return on his doomed mission. Above all, he
became thoroughly practised in the *Spiritual Exercises* and in the
rest of the discipline of the Counter-Reformation. Hour by
hour in Rome, he learned to meditate in the manner which was
later to shape his poems. Memory, understanding and will
were all made to concentrate on one point, preferably a point in
the life of Christ but possibly another point in Catholic doctrine. All one's attention was, like sunlight, concentrated until

---

[5] Philip Caraman, a Jesuit author with many gifts, translated and edited the
autobiographies of *John Gerard* and *William Weston*, and also wrote about *Henry Garnet*
(London, 1951–57). Modern histories of *The Jesuits* have been provided by David
Mitchell and Hugh Aveling (London, 1980–81); Aveling's is better. Henry More's
history published in Latin in 1660 was edited by Francis Edwards as *The English
Jesuits* (London, 1981).

the point burst into flames. Here was a discipline which was to be of great significance for English poetry as well as for English prayer.[6]

Another potent source of inspiration was opened up when among Englishmen who still accepted the Pope's authority the Bible began to be given the place which had been denied to it throughout the Middle Ages. The first English version of the Bible ever to receive a Roman Catholic blessing was compiled abroad, for use in the training of priests for the English mission. It was printed at Rheims in 1582 (the New Testament only) and at Douai in 1609–10 (including the Old Testament). It was mainly the work of Gregory Martin. Starved of funds, based on the Latin Vulgate version not on the Hebrew or Greek, inventing half-Latin words in order to avoid English which the Protestants had taken over, prefaced by a feeble attempt to defend the previous refusal to give the laity a Bible they could understand, it had many defects which Protestants delighted to point out. But it did what it was meant to do. It aroused devotion; it inspired martyrdom.

POPES, POLITICS AND TREASON

Why did Englishmen of that spiritual quality have to live in the shadow of the executioner's scaffold?

In 1570 the involvement of Roman Catholicism in Elizabethan politics came to a head when a layman, John Felton, fastened to the gates of the Bishop of London's palace a 'bull' from Pope Pius V excommunicating and deposing the Queen. He had obtained a copy through an Italian banker living in London, Roberto Ridolfi. Felton was promptly arrested and executed, but his was not the only life lost through this bull, known from its first Latin words as *Regnans in excelsis*.

An outright declaration of war against the Elizabethan

---

[6] See Louis Martz, *The Poetry of Meditation* (New Haven, Conn., 1954); Christopher Devlin, *The Life of Robert Southwell, Poet and Martyr* (London, 1956); Joseph D. Scallon, *The Poetry of Robert Southwell, S. J.* (Salzburg, 1975).

government, *Regnans in excelsis* went so far as to say that the Queen had claimed to be 'Supreme Head' of the Church and that the papacy had never recognized her right to her throne – two claims which were historically inaccurate. Although there was no explicit command to rebel, or invitation to foreign powers to invade, much was implied by the bull's excommunication of all who obeyed the Queen's 'orders, mandates and laws'. Much was implied, too, by the encouragement given by papal diplomats to potential invaders. It was a document more controversial than any subsequent political move by a pope. Within fifteen years of its publication Pope Gregory XIII had felt obliged to explain that no Catholic need rebel against Elizabeth, 'things being as they are', and an eminent English Jesuit, Cardinal Robert Bellarmine, had publicly emphasized that a pope's power to depose a wicked prince was not effective unless the people concurred, thus beginning the retreat from the 'plenitude of power' claimed by the medieval papacy. Indeed, while the bull has never been explicitly disowned in Rome, in practice popes and their agents have been so far from continuing to act in the spirit of 1570 that they have laid themselves open to the charge of failing to denounce wicked rulers out of fear of doing damage to Roman Catholic interests narrowly interpreted. It is one of the many paradoxes in the history of papal Rome that the authority which declared war against Elizabeth I never excommunicated Adolf Hitler.

Regnans in excelsis created an intolerable strain in the conscience of any Englishman who wished to be at the same time a Catholic and a patriot. But it should be seen against its background. Ridolfi had been instrumental in arranging an engagement to marry between the leading English aristocrat of conservative inclinations, the Duke of Norfolk, and Mary, Queen of Scots, who had a clearer right than anyone else to inherit the throne from the still unmarried Elizabeth. In 1569 the atmosphere of conspiracy had exploded in the rebellion of the two northern earls, Northumberland and Westmorland, many of whose supporters had been poor and innocently devout Catholics. The rebellion had failed. The evidence suggests that the not very intelligent aristocrats leading it had set it off prematurely and without realistic objectives. The Earl of

Leicester, who had been involved on the periphery, had betrayed the plot to Cecil, the Duke of Norfolk had been imprisoned, and a summons to London had made the earls panic. Most of the Catholic gentry in the north had either supported the government or held aloof. But without waiting for the news of the rebels' fate to reach him, Pope Pius determined to relieve those who attempted to overthrow the Protestant government from any fear of having committed a sin. His chief motive was not political. Although in *Regnans in excelsis* he claimed to be 'ruler over all peoples and kingdoms', he was in practice an austerely living, very hardworking, Dominican friar, nicknamed 'Brother Woodenshoes' at the time and later canonized as a saint. He had been Grand Inquisitor and was interested chiefly in questions of belief and conscience. He made no effort to bring his bull to the English government's attention, beyond asking for it to be displayed in ports where English seamen would notice it. He neither consulted, nor officially informed, the Catholic monarchs who would have been expected to pay for any invasion of England in treasure and blood.

These monarchs were not pleased. Philip of Spain disapproved of the indiscretion of the Roman Pope even more than he had disapproved of the indiscretion of the English rebels. He had been interested in England chiefly as an ally against France, and he had shared the hope of the first of the Counter-Reformation Pope, Pius IV (1559–65), that some arrangement could be reached with the formidable Elizabeth. At the beginning of her reign there had even been some talk that he might marry her. Another Catholic monarch, the emperor Maximilian, openly begged the Pope to withdraw the bull, and in 1572–73 both Spain and France agreed not to press the claims of Mary, Queen of Scots to the throne of England. It was only gradually – and largely because English soldiers and sailors made themselves such a nuisance fighting Spaniards in the Netherlands and at sea – that Philip felt sufficiently provoked to take advantage of the papal condemnation of Elizabeth and to begin 'the enterprise of England' with its climax in the Armada of 1588.

St Pius V was not much aware of the likely political consequences of his bull in 1570. But he was aware of one need – the need to act dramatically if the Counter-Reformation was to influence England, for during the 1560s the government's fairly lenient policy had been bringing about a slow weakening of the old ties. Those who at least occasionally attended their parish churches while adhering to the old religion in their hearts were known as 'Church Papists', and although they had effectively deterred the Queen from making the Church of England militantly Protestant it had been anyone's guess how long they or their families would remain 'Papists' in any real sense. For this reason the conformity of the 'Church Papists' had been formally condemned by committees of theologians in Rome and at the Council of Trent in 1562, and by Pius V in 1566. An unknown number of priests who had served under Mary had by now become chaplains to the gentry, or had simply retired or gone underground, and these had enabled an unknown number of laity to hear Mass from time to time, but such a ministry had not amounted to a fully alternative Church – or to a permanent arrangement. Lady Magdalen, Viscountess Montague, a widow who had once been a maid of honour at the court of Queen Mary, in her country house continuously kept the most rigorous devotional diet of that period right up to her death in 1608; she housed three chaplains, and hearing three Masses a day was only a part of her nun-like routine.[7] But she was quite exceptional. A modern study of the laity as a whole up to 1573 is reasonably called 'The Dormant Years'.[8] So a resurrection was essential; and this Pope Pius knew.

However, when we have done all that we can to understand the motivation behind *Regnans in excelsis*, we may still conclude that it was a mistake. Without this papal interference the resurrection of Roman Catholicism in England would have been easier and larger.

A simple indignation that the Pope had invited Englishmen to commit treason was now the theme of government propaganda. It was also the theme of the Act of 1571 which made it treason for anyone to bring a papal bull into the country or to

---

[7] See *An Elizabethan Recusant House*, ed. A. C. Southern (London, 1950).
[8] W. R. Trimble, *The Catholic Laity in Elizabethan England* (Cambridge, Mass., 1964), pp. 8–68.

reconcile anyone to Rome on the basis of such a bull. Ten years later another Act of Parliament made a traitor's death the penalty for withdrawing the Queen's subjects from their 'natural obedience' – and made a year's imprisonment with a large fine the penalty for attendance at Mass.

A pamphlet distributed by William Cecil in 1583 defended the 'execution of justice' – meaning the executions of priests which began in 1577.[9] And when brave men persisted in obeying the Pope rather than the Queen, 'justice' was made still more severe. In 1585 it was made treason to be, or to assist, a seminary-trained priest in England. In 1593 'popish recusants' were forbidden to move more than five miles from their homes. The fines for refusal to attend the parish church became a fearsome deterrent: £20 a month, laid down in the 1581 Act, was a fine which only the richest could bear, although in practice its imposition was selective and spasmodic. Usually the real threat was that a Recusant might be imprisoned and all his property confiscated for inability to pay the fine, leaving his family to starve.

The ruthlessness which the Elizabethan government now displayed surprised Elizabeth herself. The new policy of terror, sending about three hundred Roman Catholics to their deaths, was in striking contrast with the mildness of the treatment meted out during the 1560s to priests and bishops who retained their religion from Queen Mary's reign. Fewer than two hundred parish priests had been deprived of their livings. Not one bishop had been executed. Even that much-hated persecutor, Edmund Bonner, had not met anything like the death he had inflicted on Protestants. Nicholas Heath, Archbishop of York and Lord Chancellor, had served on the Queen's council until January 1559 but had then bravely attacked her claim to supremacy over the Church in the House of Lords, which had meant a period in the Tower of London. In the end Heath had been allowed to retire with dignity to his estate in Surrey, where he died in 1579. John Feckenham, the Dean of St Paul's

---

[9] R. M. Kingdom edited William Cecil's *The Execution of Justice in England*, with William Allen's reply *A True, Sincere and Modest Defence of English Catholics* (Ithaca, N.Y., 1965).

who had volunteered to serve under Mary as the last Abbot of Westminster, lived until 1584 and although he was imprisoned because of his loyalty to the old religion the conditions of his imprisonment were not harsh.

The stern new policy of the 1570s also differed from the treatment of the laity in the 1560s. Although an Act of 1563 had made it a very serious crime (punishable by the total confiscation of property on the first offence and by death on the second) to refuse to take the oath acknowledging the Queen's supremacy over the Church, the enforcement of that law had not been pursued vigorously.

It is at least possible to believe that if from 1570 onwards the priests had confined themselves to the advocacy of the very powerful and attractive religion of the Counter-Reformation, without getting entangled in politics, the government would not have inflicted savage penalties on them and their converts. In his 1583 pamphlet Cecil felt obliged to make the idiotic claim that the warders 'whose office it is to handle the rack' were 'specially charged to use it in as charitable a manner as such a thing might be'. It is tempting to speculate about the influence that might have been secured by a generation of priests trained in the newly confident theology of the Counter-Reformation, inspired to minister to laity who found no food for their souls in the new-fangled Protestantism, openly supported by the many old-fashioned gentlemen who still retained great influence and patronage in the countryside, on good terms with the many old-fashioned clergy who had accepted posts in the Church of England, led by chief pastors who were allowed to stay alive, and in general treated no worse by the government than were the extreme Protestants who would have been their rivals.[10]

As it was, the seminary-trained priests sent into England from 1574 onwards had to labour under the most fearful of handicaps and paid horrific penalties for their devotion to the

---

[10] An impression of the strength of the Roman Catholic case may be gained from A. C. Southern, *Elizabethan Recusant Prose* (London, 1950); and the strength of the religious, rather than political, support was shown by Arnold Pritchard, *Catholic Loyalism in Elizabethan England* (London, 1979).

papacy which had issued *Regnans in excelsis*. The courage of the martyrs alleged to be traitors attracted some, but the resurrection of Roman Catholicism would probably have been far stronger had it not been identified with treason. At any rate, that was the conviction of an exceptionally well-informed and thoughtful observer: William Gifford, an Englishman who went into exile and became Archbishop of Rheims. He passionately believed that the whole policy of Pius V, William Allen and Robert Persons had been a tragic mistake.

The difficulties were familiar to Allen and Persons, as is shown by their surviving private correspondence if not by their morale-raising publications. But their awareness of the difficulties in converting their fellow countrymen one by one only led them deeper into the support of actions designed to make England Catholic by another act of state such as the succession of Queen Mary in 1553. Deeds such as the murder of the Dutch Protestant leader, William, Prince of Orange, in 1584 gave them no qualms – although in England it brought about an atmosphere of hysteria and an immense 'association' to defend the Queen. Pope Pius V encouraged the plot of Roberto Ridolfi for the restoration of Catholicism by the seizure of Elizabeth – the plot which cost the Duke of Norfolk his life. Pope Gregory XIII encouraged other plots to murder Elizabeth and ordered a *Te Deum* to be sung in thanksgiving when French Protestants were massacred. Why, then, should Allen or Persons hesitate? They were enthusiastic about the papally blessed rising in Ireland in 1579–80 and the Duke of Guise's abortive plots of 1581–83. Had Spanish troops landed off the Armada in 1588 they would have distributed a pamphlet against the Queen written by Persons in virulently personal terms – and, in the event, published by a gleeful Cecil. Had those troops occupied England, the Pope would have become the country's feudal overlord, as in the days of King John – an arrangement insisted on by Sixtus V in return for his cash. Had England been conquered then or later, Allen and Persons would have fully shared the delight of other Englishmen who indulged in exiles' dreams.[11]

---

[11] See A. H. Loomis, *The Spanish Elizabethans* (New York, 1963).

Men on the rack before execution, or facing financial ruin for themselves and their families, had to be rather more careful in their thoughts about the morality of treason. Many times Englishmen loyal to the Pope were being examined by authorities who had been unable to prove any treasonable act. (Jesuits, for example, were under strict orders not to talk about politics while in England.) They were then asked what they would do if the Pope were to send over an army to bring the kingdom back to its Catholic allegiance. They often tried evasion. Edmund Campion (who was to be executed under a medieval statute against traitors) replied that the question could be debated in the universities but did not concern him; his last words were a prayer for 'your queen and my queen'. John Gerard would say only that he would act as a true Catholic and a true subject. Others refused to answer at all. But privately Gerard confessed that a straightforward answer must be disloyal to the Pope or the Queen, and thus damage soul or body. It was called the 'bloody question', and Sir Francis Walsingham would sometimes attend the examination of priests in order to give himself the pleasure of asking it.

Naturally many hoped that a question so terrible would somehow go away. In 1585 four rich gentlemen of the old school and the old religion – Sir Thomas Tresham, Lord Vaux, Sir William Catesbury and Sir John Arundell – petitioned the Queen to the effect that while a gentleman's chaplain would feel in conscience bound to advise against attendance at the parish church a gentleman should be allowed to vouch for his own patriotic loyalty and that of his chaplain. But the Recusant from Sussex who managed to present this petition to the Queen in her garden at Greenwich died in prison, and his brother was executed. Sir Thomas Tresham, the leading petitioner and the leading landowner in Northamptonshire, was a man so sincerely patriotic that he begged to be allowed to enlist in the armed forces at the time of Armada, when almost seventy; 'an ancient and true servant unto her majesty', as the Queen's council itself was willing to declare in 1598. But he spent most of the years 1581–96 in prison, and when he died in 1605 was deep in debt because the fines had been a drain even on his finances.

Some criticism of the papacy surfaced even among Roman Catholic priests in England. Towards the end of Elizabeth's reign arrested priests who did not seem particularly dangerous were sent to concentration camps in Wisbech and Framlingham castles in East Anglia. Their imprisonment was not harsh. When William Weston arrived in 1594 and attempted to impose his idea of discipline, particularly disapproving of morris dancing and a hobbyhorse at Christmas, dissension arose. Similar quarrels rent the English College in Rome before the Jesuit triumph there. But the most scandalous controversy surrounded *A Conference about the Next Succession to the Crown of England*, a book of 1594 inspired by Persons. This discussed who should be the Catholic successor to Elizabeth, making it clear that the decision lay with Parliament guided by the Pope; and the clear implication was that Philip II's daughter Isabella was best suited. A publication so foolish brought to a head the dissatisfaction of many English Catholics with the Jesuits. In 1598 a group of priests begged Rome for the appointment of an English bishop. Instead the Pope appointed an 'archpriest', George Blackwell, who allied himself with the Jesuits. In response the anti-Jesuit opposition went to surprising lengths both in appealing to the Pope and in allying itself with the government; and Elizabeth's most able bishop, Richard Bancroft, much enjoyed himself stirring up the public controversy between Papists. Behind the clash of personalities and the pamphlet war lay the serious question, whether it was spiritually essential for faithful Catholics to expose themselves and their families to such punishments by a complete refusal to have anything to do with the Church of England, and by a complete acceptance of the Jesuit advocacy of the papacy's political claims.

Early in 1603, shortly before the Queen's death, thirteen priests put their names to a 'protestation' which sought to reassure both sides about the loyalties of patriotic Catholics. 'As we are most ready to spend our blood in the defence of her majesty and our country,' they declared, 'so we will rather lose our lives than infringe the lawful authority of Christ's Catholic Church.' But two of those who signed this protestation were

soon to be executed for refusing the oath of allegiance required
by the Queen's successor.

Naturally it is impossible for historians to be sure how
effective the English mission was on the basis laid down in
Regnans in excelsis. The contemporary literature about the
mission, although prolific, is ambiguous. Most of it was written
in order to edify and encourage fellow Catholics. It had a tale to
tell of the gratitude of thousands who rejoiced to be able once
again to receive the absolution of their sins and the sacrament
of the Body of Christ from a Catholic priest risking his life to
save their souls. But the same literature shows that the Catholics whom these priests served included not a few who were
willing to betray them. It seems to have been rare for a priest to
land without the government being tipped off both by its spies
abroad and by informers at home, and many arrests were made
in the midst of congregations to which only known Catholics
would have been admitted.

By 1600 there seem to have been only about three hundred
Roman Catholic priests in the country, including a dozen or so
Jesuits. This contrasted with the figure of about ten thousand
clergy of the Church of England. The returns made by the
Anglican parish priests to their bishops in 1603 reported a total
of 8,590 Recusants, and a modern authority reckons that even
including Roman Catholics who were children under the age of
sixteen, those who had avoided being reported, and those who
escaped any penalty by attending their parish churches, the
whole Roman Catholic community in the country was under
forty thousand, as compared with an Anglican communicant
population of two and a half millions.[12] The records of fines by
the government for Recusancy in the period 1593–1600 contain
only about five thousand names, most of them in Yorkshire,
Lancashire and Cheshire. Cheshire was often said to be riddled
with Popery, yet examination of the surviving records leads to
the surprising conclusion that 'in the whole of the reign of
Elizabeth I only 302 Recusants can be identified with any
certainty' – in a population around 64,000. An attempt at a

---

[12] John Bossy, *The English Catholic Community 1570–1850* (London, 1976), pp.
191–3.

thorough census of Recusants in Yorkshire in 1604 produced 3,500 in a population of more than three hundred thousand. In Lancashire the proportion of actual Recusants (not necessarily reported to the authorities) was far greater, since in that isolated county Protestantism had never really taken root outside the Manchester and Blackburn areas. It would have been extremely difficult for a Bishop of Chester or an Earl of Derby to enforce the religious laws, even with more activity than was displayed. William Cecil kept a map of Lancashire in his office, but could not solve the problem. It was typical that of the eight hundred Recusants 'presented' at the assizes of 1592, only eleven appear to have been forced to pay fines. At the assizes in 1630 almost 3,500 were reported, out of a population of about a hundred thousand. Outside Lancashire the statistics, although obviously always incomplete, suggest that the average Englishman with Catholic leanings was not prepared to accept the cause of the papacy as defined in and after 1570 and thus to defy Elizabeth's determined government.[13]

'The history of Elizabethan Catholicism', it has been said, 'is a progress from inertia to inertia in three generations.'[14] As its Roman Catholic author has acknowledged, that epigram was too gloomy; but another Roman Catholic historian has written accurately that when the century ended English Catholics were 'only too well aware that their community was disorderly, devoid of central authority, sharply divided, and an object of mockery to both Roman officials and English Protestant administrators.'[15]

---

[13] See K. R. Wark, *Elizabethan Recusancy in Cheshire* (Manchester, 1971); Hugh Aveling, *Northern Catholics: The Catholic Recusants of the North Riding of Yorkshire* (London, 1966); Christopher Haigh, *Reformation and Resistance in Tudor Lancashire* (Cambridge, 1975).

[14] See John Bossy, 'The Character of Elizabethan Catholicism' in *The Crisis in Europe, 1560–1660,* ed. T. Aston (London, 1965), pp. 223–46.

[15] Hugh Aveling, *The Handle and the Axe: The Catholic Recusants in England from Reformation to Emancipation* (London, 1976), pp. 71–2. See also Peter Holmes, *Resistance and Compromise: The Political Thought of the Elizabethan Catholics* (Cambridge, 1982).

THE DEMANDS OF THE PURITANS

The Protestant critics of the Elizabethan establishment were called 'Precisians' or 'Puritans'.[16] The latter word, coming into use in the 1560s, had the future before it. Indeed, Puritanism came to wield so great an influence in America as well as in England that historians have been eager to debate the question: who should be called a Puritan in these early, formative years? It has been tempting to define this 'ism' as a system in contrast with Anglicanism.[17] However, the Elizabethans did not often think in terms of theological systems. Of course the systematic theology of Jean Calvin was vastly influential.[18] But if the Elizabethan Puritans were Calvinists so was their archenemy, Archbishop Whitgift. No rigid party line was taken by those who wanted further progress in the English Reformation, and they were not all radicals in rebellion against the Establishment. Many clergymen and laymen who were prominent and comfortable in the universities, among rich merchants, in the great houses of the countryside or at court, were Puritans.[19] 'The common factor', writes a scholar who has supplied a useful analysis of the many modern definitions of Puritanism, 'is not so much a "Puritan spirit" as a dislike of the *status quo*. There was considerable agreement about what ought to be swept away but much less agreement about what to put in its place.'[20] All that can be done by historians aware of the confusion of the very lively debate is to make a list of changes desired by many of those who with varying degrees of

---

[16] The standard modern study is Patrick Collinson, *The Elizabethan Puritan Movement* (London, 1967), and documents have been collected by H. C. Porter in *Puritanism in Tudor England* (London, 1970).

[17] As in J. F. H. New, *Anglican and Puritan: The Basis of Their Opposition, 1558–1640* (London, 1964).

[18] The best study of the man is now T. H. L. Parker, *John Calvin* (London, 1975), and a recent study of his theological influence in England is R. T. Kendall, *Calvin and English Calvinism to 1649* (Oxford, 1980).

[19] This was demonstrated by C. K. and K. George, *The Protestant Mind of the English Reformation* (Princeton, N.J., 1961), and Peter Lake, *Moderate Puritans and the Elizabethan Church* (Cambridge, 1982).

[20] Patrick McGrath, *Papists and Puritans under Elizabeth I* (London, 1967), p. 46. See also Basil Hall's essay on 'Puritanism: The Problem of Definition' in *Studies in Church History*, Vol. 2, ed. G. J. Cuming (London, 1965), pp. 283–96.

moderation wanted what Milton was to call the 'reforming of Reformation itself'.[21]

Many Puritans objected to conventional features of the Baptism service. They were uneasy when the priest used the sign of the cross on the infant's forehead; it reminded them of the tricks of a pagan magician. They also disliked the custom by which godparents were chosen more for social than for theological reasons, while the natural parents were not featured. (In the Middle Ages infants had almost always been baptized when their mothers were still confined to bed.) They wanted the emphasis to be more clearly on the parents' faith as justifying the practice of infant baptism (if it could be justified: 'Anabaptists' thought not) – although with the parents could be associated godparents who were themselves godly Christians. Finally they objected to midwives and other women baptizing privately infants thought to be in danger of death. This custom seemed to ignore the fact that the infant had already been predestined by God to heaven or hell, without waiting for baptism.

Such objections to the Prayer Book's arrangements for Baptism already implied the whole 'reforming of Reformation'. For Puritans, religion should be based not on human wishes but on God's agreement with those on whom his favour rested (his 'covenant of grace'); not on social conventions but on personal faith; not on superstitious customs but on the Holy Bible. The Church was understood not as the whole baptized English people but as the gathering around the Bible of the 'elect' – those elected by God – who might be few. A Prayer Book suitable for such a Church ought to be based entirely on the Bible, more particularly on the Bible read with Calvinist eyes, not on Cranmer's eclectic gathering of treasures from all the centuries. To show what was needed a *Book of the Form of Common Prayers* was published in the mid-1580s, based on Calvin's work in Geneva thirty years before. The Bible was understood not as literature from which the Church selected passages at its own discretion, but as God's own self-revelation

---

[21] There are 630 entries in *Religious Controversies of the Elizabethan Age*, ed. Peter Milward (London, 1977), a survey of printed sources.

to his people, completely authoritative. Incidentally, the Bible
did not include the books known as the Apocrypha; these books
were rejected by the Jewish rabbis in their first century but
were used in Roman Catholic and Eastern Orthodox services.
Puritans had their own preferred version of the Bible, and it
was not the Bishops' Bible sponsored by Archbishop Parker in
1565. It was the Geneva Bible completed in 1560 by a group of
exiles led by William Whittingham – a translation scholarly in
its rendering of the Hebrew and Greek, adorned with many
prefaces and notes, clear in its printing (in Roman type – the
only Roman thing about it), sized compactly and sold inexpen-
sively. Less than a month after Parker's death in 1575 a licence
was issued for the printing of the Geneva Bible in England, and
its popularity can be illustrated from Shakespeare's plays.
Although he was no Puritan (he quoted from the Apocrypha),
his plays show that he took to using the Geneva Bible in the
mid-1590s.

Other demands applied the Puritan insistence on a Bible-
based Church to successive stages of the Christian life. It was
not thought necessary that a bishop should confirm a child
before admission to Holy Communion; the one essential qualification for communicating was personal faith. The service was
regarded as 'the Lord's Supper' where the faithful should sit
around a table (not a stone altar). The service was not a
sacrifice offered to God by a priest; it was a reminder to the
whole congregation of Christ's all-sufficient sacrifice on Calvary. Kneeling to receive the sacrament was rejected because it
was thought to suggest the worship of the bread and wine. So,
too, the wearing of medieval vestments (the white surplice or
the coloured chasuble or cope), the lighting of candles, the
veneration of crucifixes and respect for the images of saints
were all thought to imply the acceptance of medieval priestcraft and superstition; and the rejection of these practices was
passionate. Standing for the creed, bowing to the altar or at the
name of Jesus, even taking one's hat off because one was a man
in church – all these medieval customs smacked of idolatry.
The same austerity extended to weddings and burials. It
seemed unnecessary, or worse, for a bride to have a ring put on
her finger and for her to be blessed by a priest; marriage was a

contract not a sacrament, and the vital moment was the betrothal. And when a body was buried 'in sure and certain hope of the resurrection to eternal life', Puritans protested that the prospect of heaven for the mass of mankind was far from sure.

Similarly there seemed no need to celebrate Christmas, which was not dated in the Bible. About forty other 'feasts' on weekdays interrupted work. Almost as much damage to an economy which depended on hard labour might be inflicted by about a hundred 'fasts' in the Church's traditional calendar. On the other hand, the strict observance of Sunday could be derived from the biblical laws about the Sabbath and could be additionally justified as providing a much needed regular rest-day for those who obeyed the biblical commandment to toil. And there seemed no need to perpetuate the customs by which the medieval Church had given special responsibilities to laymen in the provision of music. Puritans tended to dislike skilled choirs, bell-ringing and organ-playing. The music they welcomed was congregational psalm-singing, with the psalms newly translated and rhymed and often sung to popular ballad tunes. That was music which the faithful could offer without expert leadership.[22]

There was a place for leaders in a Protestant Church, but it was a place very different from the priesthood of the Middle Ages. A minister – who might perhaps be called a 'priest' although the word 'presbyter' was certainly less misleading – was useful to his fellow Christians if he was expert in the Bible and able to expound it. Preaching was not therefore of secondary importance to taking services or visiting parishioners or conducting administration, as priests and their inspecting bishops had assumed for centuries. On the contrary, public and continual preaching of God's word was 'the ordinary mean and instrument of the salvation of mankind'. So Archbishop Grindal, in many ways a Puritan, once informed the Queen – whose own view was that three or four preachers in a county,

---

[22] The social implications of the Puritan demands were explored by Christopher Hill, *Society and Puritanism in Pre-Revolutionary England* (London, 1964).

all that had existed in her father's time or in the early years of her own reign, were quite enough.[23]

All Protestants agreed in principle that it was essential to support a preaching ministry, but here, too, Puritans tended to disapprove of arrangements inherited from the Middle Ages. One problem was that the 'tithes', which in theory guaranteed a tenth of the produce to the pastor of the parish, had sometimes been commuted for cash which with inflation declined in real value. With many forms of production and trade – sheep-farming, market-gardening, clothes-making, mining, shop-keeping in general – a cash settlement in lieu of tithes was almost inevitable, and offered endless scope for disagreement about what was fair. Another problem was that the 'great tithes' or 'rector's tithes' – a tenth of the corn, hay and wood – could be separated from the 'small tithes'. In perhaps a third of the parishes they had belonged to monasteries in the 1520s, leaving a small income to the vicar or chaplain who did the work. Now with the monasteries gone, these 'great tithes' had often descended to laymen; Shakespeare bought the right to tithes in Stratford. Or they might have been granted to bishops by the Crown in exchange for estates. It seems that of about 9,250 'livings' (churches with incomes attached to them), by 1603 about 3,850 were parishes where the rector's share of the tithes had been 'impropriated' to laymen. Richard Hooker estimated that the Church lost £126,000 a year in this way at a time when vicars could be expected to live on £10 or less a year. Yet another problem was that the incomes of many parishes could not sustain resident clergymen, or at least not clergymen with a graduate's sense of what an adequate income was. During the 1580s Archbishop Whitgift guessed that half the 'livings' in England were worth less than £10 a year, and that of some 8,800 parishes (the figure was an underestimate) 'there are not six hundred sufficient for learned men.'

Puritan preachers tended to regard all these arrangements as abuses. It was, however, not easy to suggest solutions. Many Puritan parishioners shared the general reluctance to pay tithes, let alone increase them. Some Puritan gentlemen re-

---

[23] See A. F. Herr, *The Elizabethan Sermon* (Philadelphia, Penn., 1940).

tained or bought up the 'great' tithes with the plea that it gave
them the right to appoint a godly vicar. And some Puritan
graduate preachers were not above collecting 'pluralities' –
incomes derived from more than one parish.[24]

Puritans did not feel committed to the maintenance of the
medieval system by which the Church was governed by
bishops. It was a matter of convenience; episcopacy (government by bishops) might be desirable in one place or period and
not in another. In the early years of Elizabeth's reign some
clergymen who would later have been classified as Puritans
became bishops, and the system seems to have been generally
accepted in the hope that the bishops would be reformers –
although it was ominous that some highly honoured Protestants refused to accept prominent posts in the restored system,
among them being Bishop Miles Coverdale and John Foxe.
Later, particularly when bishops were seen as disciplinarians
hired by the government against Puritans, criticism of the
system hardened.

Overlarge dioceses were a target of criticism. Church courts,
little changed since medieval days and staffed by laymen who
tended to be anti-Puritan, were particularly condemned.
There was indignation about the fact that because of the
frustration of Cranmer's efforts the 'canon' law of the Church
had never been revised. It was also thought to be scandalous
that the penalty of excommunication, described so solemnly in
the New Testament, was often imposed for relatively minor
offences against the Church's antiquated laws and courts, and
was so little regarded that many of the excommunicated never
troubled to have the penalty revoked. Discipline seemed to
Puritans to be an essential mark of a healthy Church. One way
of securing it was to appoint some of the faithful laymen of the
parish to be 'elders' with authority for 'spiritual rule'. Another
solution was to gather the faithful preachers in an area for
mutual correction and edification, in what came to be known
as a 'conference', 'classis' or 'presbytery'. Over these local
meetings could arise provincial and national 'synods' to decide

---

[24] See Christopher Hill, *Economic Problems of the Church from Archbishop Whitgift to
the Long Parliament* (Oxford, 1956) and E. J. Evans, *Contentious Tithe* (London, 1976).

the larger questions, and the bishops could safely disappear.
The whole system of Church courts should, however, be controlled by a clear and up-to-date 'Book of Discipline'. A key
text was Matthew 18:17: 'tell the church'. Sins and doubts
were to be reported to bodies equipped and eager to deal with
them – to bodies with a clear authority to excommunicate
sinners, however arrogant. Most shocking of all Puritan beliefs
in the eyes of the authorities was the conviction that even a
monarch was subject to this spiritual discipline exercised by
God's elect.

Preferring to regard all preachers as equal in status, Puritans
tended to dislike the surviving pomp of bishops – or any other
reminder that the bishops of the Church of England were
continuous with the bishops of the Middle Ages. But they had
to face the fact that not all clergy were equally faithful. Since
many rectors, vicars or curates were unable or unwilling to
preach as Puritans wished, and were obliged to comply with
the bishop's regulations, lay Puritans increasingly gave their
loyalty and their money to 'lecturers' or other unbeneficed
clergy. These lecturers could be appointed by those who paid
them and they could preach acceptably in the parish churches,
if necessary outside the normal times for services.[25] The only
alternative to letting off steam through this safety-valve
seemed to be the explosion of 'Separatism' – separating oneself
entirely from the Church of England. But in Tudor times this
remedy appealed to only a few. The hope of the rest was
that, given time, the Church would be reformed in accordance with demands which seemed so clearly in keeping with
the Scriptures and with the conscience of the educated
public.

Many of these demands of the Puritans were trifles, as they
were often reminded by their critics. That was one of the
factors delaying a confrontation or separation. But matters of
dress, or fashions in furniture, or styles of music, or ways of
enjoying holidays, or methods of supervision have often been
flashpoints in quarrels between Christians; and there was a

---

[25] See P. S. Seaver, *The Puritan Lectureships: The Politics of Religious Dissent 1560–
1640* (Stanford, Cal., 1970). John Morgan, *Godly Learning* (Cambridge, 1986),
showed that this was part of the generally positive attitude of the Puritans to
education and scholarship as then understood.

basic controversy here. Puritans wanted the Church of England not only to *be* a Reformed Church but also to look
thoroughly like one. It should be seen to be a sister church of
those Calvinists who were at the time offering heroic battle
against the revival of Popery on the Continent – fighting
against great odds in the Netherlands, or being massacred in
France. To be Reformed seemed to those who were so the clear
consequence of obedience to the Bible; and Puritans claimed to
subscribe not to any theological movement but simply to the
Bible.

Throughout Elizabeth's reign the majority of the House of
Commons wanted – or could be led by the more articulate
MPs to want – 'further Reformation' along these lines. The
same was true of the majority of the Privy Council. When the
Catholic theologians who had had their time under Queen
Mary had fled or come to terms, Oxford and Cambridge heard
very little except lectures of which Puritans approved. The
educated clergy who were licensed as preachers by the bishops
seem almost all to have been thorough-going Protestants,
although they chose to obey the bishops rather than the
Puritan extremists over trivial matters such as dress. In 1563
when the Convocation of Canterbury debated six Puritan
proposals (for example, that kneeling at the Holy Communion
should be voluntary), the motion in favour of them failed by
only one vote (59–58) when proxies had been called. That
gathering of the clergy did adopt the Thirty-Nine Articles of
Religion, based on the Forty-Two Articles of 1553 and therefore embodying many phrases dear to Lutherans or Calvinists
on the continent while preserving a certain caution. Article 29,
'Of the Wicked which eat not the Body of Christ', was so firmly
Protestant that the articles were published by the government
without it. In 1563 the Convocation added, for use in popular
instruction, a catechism reflecting the Calvinism of the Dean of
St Paul's who drafted it (Alexander Nowell). Eventually in
1571 the Thirty-Nine Articles, with Article 29 restored, received Parliamentary ratification. Undeterred by the government's caution, Puritans went on hoping for official support for
their cause, and the next year two brilliantly eloquent and
aggressive propagandists in their early twenties, John Field

and Thomas Wilcox, issued an *Admonition to Parliament* urging
MPs to hasten the day of radical reform.[26]

Many Puritans were convinced that the government's resistance to 'further Reformation' was unprincipled. The Queen
irritated them by her unwillingness to identify herself wholly
with the Reformation even when the Pope's claim to depose her
had shown beyond dispute that she was at war with Roman
Catholicism. Puritans were of course very reluctant to seem to
be traitors like the Papists; when John Stubbe issued a tract
warning the Queen against marrying a Papist (*The Discovery of
a Gaping Gulf*) and had the hand responsible cut off, he waved
his hat with the other, shouting: 'God save the Queen!' Yet
their impatience sometimes boiled over, and turned into indignation when the Queen appeared to be persecuting them
because of their obedience to God. Her only motive seemed to
be a cowardice inspired by worldliness.

THE QUEEN
AGAINST THE PURITANS

On three dramatic occasions we can hear Puritans speaking
their minds about Queen Elizabeth I.

On 20 June 1567 seven Protestant Londoners accused of
absenting themselves from their parish churches were examined by the Bishop of London (Grindal), the Lord Mayor
and others. When they objected to the uniform which the
Queen commanded for the clergy, the Lord Mayor told them
to think of it as being like the wearing of civic robes in local
government: how else could an alderman be recognized? 'The
Queen hath not established these garments and things for
any holiness' sake or religion, but only for a civil order and
comeliness.' Even the theologians admitted that the clothes
were comparatively unimportant, 'indifferent'. But these defenders of the Queen's policy were rebuked by John Smith:

---

[26] The Convocation of 1563 was put in its historical context by W. P. Haugaard,
Elizabeth and the English Reformation (Cambridge, 1968).

'How can you prove that indifferent, which is abominable?'
While the Protestant laymen quoted biblical texts at them, the
official theologians fell back on the authority of the Queen to
end an argument which was getting out of hand. 'Have we not
a godly prince? Answer, is she evil?' So Bishop Grindal demanded; and Thomas Bowland bravely replied, 'No: but the
servants of God are persecuted under her.'

On 25 February 1570 a famous Puritan preacher and writer
who was then chaplain at the Tower of London preached a
long sermon before the Queen. Edward Dering took Elizabeth
through the Bible, pointing out what godly princes had done
for the pure worship of God. The tour ended with plain
speaking about the Church of England. 'I would lead you first
to your benefices.' Then he mentioned all the charges there
could be on the income of a parish priest before it reached the
priest. 'Look after this upon your patrons. And lo, some are
selling their benefices, some farming them, some keep them for
their children, some give them to boys, some to servingmen, a
very few seek after learned pastors. And yet you shall see more
abominations than these. Look upon your ministry, and there
are some of one occupation, some of another . . . some ruffians,
some hawkers and hunters, some dicers and carders, some
blind guides and cannot see, some dumb dogs and will not
bark. And yet a thousand more iniquities have now covered the
priesthood. And yet you, in the meanwhile that all these
whoredoms are committed, you at whose hands God will
require it, you sit still and are careless.'

On 8 February 1576 Peter Wentworth, who represented
Tregoney in Cornwall, dared to attack the Queen in the House
of Commons, beginning his carefully written speech: 'Sweet
indeed is the name of liberty.' Resisting Puritan pressures, the
Queen had told the previous Parliament not to touch Bills
about religion unless these had first been 'considered or liked'
by the clergy. Wentworth protested: 'It was as much as to say:
Sirs, ye shall not deal in God's causes . . . God, even the great
and mighty God, whose name is the Lord of Hosts, great in
counsel and infinite in thought, and who is the only good
director of all hearts, was the last session shut out of doors.'
Wentworth was sent to the Tower of London for this brave

outburst. Although soon released, he was to die there in 1597 at the age of seventy-three, having given further offence.[27]

Why, then, did Elizabeth – so often admired for her statesmanship, so proud to 'count the glory of my crown, that I have reigned with your loves' – pursue a policy which alienated so many of the clerical and lay leaders of the Church she was pledged to protect? And why did she so divide the Protestant forces when the Papists were doing their utmost to dethrone her?

It is probable that the best clue to an answer is neither ecclesiastical nor theological. Despite outbursts against married clergymen and their wives, Elizabeth had no ambition to teach Christian doctrine. Although she admired her father, unlike her brother and sister she did not inherit his taste for the personal supervision of theology; and unlike her successor James I she did not enjoy discussing the subject. She dismissed arguments about doctrine as 'a dream of fools or enthusiasts', the speculations of theologians as 'ropes of sand or sea-slime leading to the moon'. Nor did Elizabeth have any appetite for ecclesiastical administration. Even her imperious father had for a time been glad to delegate the supervision of church life to Thomas Cromwell, and her opinionated sister had developed 'Commissioners Ecclesiastical' to attend to the details of the restoration of Catholicism. Elizabeth went further in the delegation of her powers as Supreme Governor. She allowed her Ecclesiastical Commissioners' powers and staff to develop mightily, so that they became known as the 'High Commission'. The commission for the province of Canterbury became a very important tribunal; Archbishop Whitgift once said that without it ecclesiastical law would have been a 'carcass without a soul'. It attracted business away from the old courts of the archbishops and bishops because it was prompt and efficient; and unlike the old church courts it could punish by fines and imprisonment. Common lawyers often objected to the High Commission's methods, since suspects could be put on oath to answer questions truthfully without being warned about the

---

[27] These explosions are recorded in *Elizabethan Puritanism*, documents edited by L. J. Trinterud (New York, 1971).

questions or confronted by their accusers or defended by a lawyer or presumed innocent until judged guilty by a jury. This '*ex officio* oath' seemed disgracefully un-English. Suspects judged guilty by those who had questioned them found it virtually impossible to appeal elsewhere. Nevertheless the Queen raised no objection, because while being unwilling to give her personal attention to such trifles she needed a machine so formidable against those who opposed her central policy.[28]

This central policy was conservative, partly because in her view the Puritan demands constituted a political danger. John Knox himself admitted that his relations with Elizabeth had been ruined by his attack on the 'monstrous regiment of women', and although he found his sphere in Scotland when the Queen had forbidden him to enter her kingdom, it is probable that his rejection of the idea of a woman as sovereign on biblical grounds was thought by her to be typical of his co-religionists. Certainly she was often ready to believe the worst about the loyalty of her Puritan subjects. A record survives of a conversation in 1585 when she attacked a group of bishops for failing to discipline ministers who 'preach what they list . . . to the breach of unity'. Such men, she said, were 'curious and busy fellows' whose preaching 'tendeth only to popularity'.

However, she must have known, right from the time of her triumphant entry into London as queen, that the Protestants were not a real threat to her throne. They supported her because they had no alternative monarch to nominate and a republic was inconceivable. These preachers, however irritating they might be, were not likely to become traitors in a time when only Elizabeth's life stood between them and a Catholic reaction under Mary, Queen of Scots. It therefore seems clear that the decisive factor in the Queen's ecclesiastical conservatism was her knowledge that to capitulate to all the Protestant demands would be to alienate the mass of her subjects. She was determined to woo Catholic-minded Englishmen into loyalty,

---

[28] See R. G. Usher, *The Rise and Fall of the High Commission* (revised, Oxford, 1968).

just as she was prepared to flirt with Catholic princes for political purposes; and it maddened her when Puritans nearly frustrated her.

She knew that the Catholicism of a thousand years could not be eradicated overnight. In 1564 the government ordered the bishops to assess the degree of support which the Justices of the Peace would give to its religious policy, for on them law and order in the countryside depended. The bishops reported that although 431 were favourable 157 JPs were hostile, and 264 indifferent or neutral: a reliable majority of ten at a time when for five years the national government had clearly favoured Protestantism. In 1561 Professor Nicholas Sander of Oxford assured Cardinal Morone that among the ordinary people the Protestants were a tiny majority: 'not so many as one in a hundred of the English is infected'. Whatever may have been the accuracy of such assessments, it is significant that as late as 1571 the Queen vetoed a proposal by Parliament that everyone should be required to receive communion in the Church of England at least once a year. She saw the need to adjust the National Church over which she was Supreme Governor to this reality of the nation's conservatism. She did not want to persecute Catholic-minded Englishmen until this was made to seem politically essential by a pope's claim to depose her. If, as Sir Francis Bacon observed, the Queen did not wish to 'make windows into men's hearts and secret thoughts', one reason was that she knew she would find there a religion still more conservative than her own. And she did not want to repel Catholic-minded Englishmen from attending their parish churches by making those churches too obviously Protestant. In this caution she was more realistic than was her indispensable William Cecil, or Sir Francis Walsingham (despite the invaluable efficiency of his work against plotting Papists). She knew better than her great aristocratic friends, the brothers who were Earls of Leicester and Warwick, and Francis Russell, Earl of Bedford. All these men thought it safe to be known as patrons of the Puritans. The Queen did not.

Her continuing and mounting indignation against the Puritans in the 1590s requires another explanation, for a fierce patriotism surrounded the defeat of the Spanish Armada of 1588 and its successors in 1596 and 1597. The English government could at last feel more relaxed about the possibility of a rebellion in which foreign invaders could have allied themselves with native religious conservatism to bring about a regime acceptable to the Pope; yet the war against the Jesuits and the 'seminary priests' went on relentlessly and, on the whole, successfully. It may well seem that in the 1590s Elizabeth could have afforded to make concessions to the Puritans without anxiety about the Church of England being made to look dangerously Protestant. Instead, she chose to accept the theory that the Puritans had joined the Papists as conspirators threatening the government.

The explanation seems to be that she was an old woman, irritated by her critics; resentful of their obstinate defiance as perhaps only a Tudor monarch could be; determined to use the new strength of her position to teach them the consequences of disobedience; and anyway too old and too bored to begin a period of religious reconstruction. And she had reason to think that public opinion was with her as she gave way to her prejudices. Ordinary Englishmen disliked the Puritans as killjoys and it is probable that Malvolio in *Twelfth Night* was understood as a caricature. Towards the end of her reign even the House of Commons, while still firmly Protestant, had lost heart for the defence of these too-earnest clergymen against the Queen's bishops. Elizabeth was by now a living legend, the Gloriana on whose behalf God had blown his winds against the fleets of Spain; and not many men were eager to incur her majestic rebukes or less majestic tantrums. But there was another factor operating in the 1590s. Precisely by making sure that the Puritans would see the bishops as their enemies, the Queen had made it certain that they would dream of a Presbyterian system without any bishops – and precisely by treating the Puritans always as her own enemies, Elizabeth had done all that she could to tempt them to treason. This she must have known and it must have made her very uneasy, although there is no real evidence that any Puritans yielded to the temptation. Sir John Neale has described this as 'the strangest paradox of her reign': 'Her Puritan fanatics had no more obstinate opponent; she, in turn, had no more devoted worshippers'.[29]

THE CAMPAIGN AGAINST
THE PURITANS

Detailed investigation of Elizabeth's first Parliament, meeting in January 1559, has shown how strong was the Protestant element in it, as in all its successors.[30] Some of the most influential men in the Commons were just back from exile; others had been dominated by Protestant-minded grandees such as Francis Russell, Earl of Bedford; around all shone the glow cast on Protestantism by the recent martyrdoms. Possibly the Queen would have been content at this early stage to secure Parliamentary recognition of her succession to the throne and of her supremacy over the Church. She had no wish to alienate Catholics, who were strong in the House of Lords. But she also knew that if she was to secure the loyalty she needed, she had to please Protestants. Accordingly the Parliamentary session was prolonged beyond Easter, and when the Act of Uniformity was forced through the Lords it reimposed the Prayer Book of 1552, not the more Catholic version of 1549.

All that the Queen and other conservatives could secure lay in the insistence that it must be an English, not a continental, book, and in four comparatively minor changes to the 1552 book. It was agreed to omit from the Litany a prayer for deliverance from 'the tyranny of the Bishop of Rome and all his detestable enormities'. The 'black rubric' which had been added by the council in 1552 was now abandoned and an additional phrase at the moment of communion was brought back from 1549; these two changes encouraged those who believed that Christ really was present, that the Body and Blood of Christ really were given, in the sacrament. And a new

---

[29] *Essays in Elizabethan History* (London, 1958), p. 124.
[30] Sir John Neale wrote the classic study of *Elizabeth I and her Parliaments* (2 vols., London, 1953–59). But more recent research has questioned his version of events in 1559; see, e.g., D. M. Loades, *The Reign of Mary Tudor*, p. 462.

order was made that the clergy should wear again the vestments which had been worn 'in the second year of the reign of King Edward VI' (1547–48) at least until the Queen issued 'further orders'. This suggested that the coloured copes and chasubles, as well as the white surplices, would become normal – a development which, however, did not occur until the nineteenth century.

However, although not all the details of the 1559 settlement were to her liking, and although it was widely believed that this settlement was only a temporary compromise, the Queen clung obstinately to it throughout her reign – with the result that, despite a few further modifications during the seventeenth century, essentially the 1559 book remained the standard of worship in the Church of England until the 1920s. The only modifications which the Queen allowed were all in a Catholic direction. During the 1560s a Latin Prayer Book was published for use in cathedrals and colleges containing various Catholic features, and a calendar restoring the main Saints' Days was added to the English Prayer Book. In the 'Vestiarian controversy' of the 1560s the Queen took a calculated risk in insisting that all the clergy, including Protestant theologians who were fighting the strong Catholicism of Oxford, should wear surplices as tokens of their obedience to her. Archbishop Parker was driven by her to issue strict *Advertisements* or regulations to this effect. Had the Oxford Protestants resisted in the spirit of the martyrs under Mary, Elizabeth would surely have been in deep trouble in the propaganda war. The two most prominently unsurpliced Protestants were Laurence Humphrey, President of Magdalen College, and Thomas Sampson, Dean of Christ Church. They were disciplined – but the gamble paid off, for they gave no trouble. Humphrey conformed and ended up as Dean of Gloucester; and Sampson, although he never wore a surplice, accepted a canonry at St Paul's Cathedral.

The Queen, however, did not really get on with clergymen. She could not flirt with them, she seldom troubled to charm them, and even the bishops who owed their positions to her favour were probably not much attached to her person while she plundered their estates and handed down brutal instructions. And she had few clergymen from whom to choose bishops to her taste.

It was ominous for her that when James Pilkington had refused the bishopric of Winchester on the terms she offered he still had to be made Bishop of Durham, owing to a shortage of other plausible candidates. He once expressed his unenthusiastic attitude towards the Supreme Governor: 'We are under authority and can innovate nothing without the Queen; nor can we alter the laws; the only thing left for our choice is, whether we will bear these things, or break the peace of the Church.' The Queen had to employ the learned John Jewel, Bishop of Salisbury, as her chief religious propagandist although he was contemplating resignation in 1560, after his first year in office, since he did not share her own liking for surplices and for the rest of what he called the 'scenic apparatus of divine worship'.

She had to authorize the appointment of the strongly Protestant Edmund Grindal to the key diocese of London (where he naturally failed to discipline the Puritans as she wished) before moving him to York (where he was more at home attempting to discipline the many Papists after the failure of their 1569 revolt) and finally to Canterbury (on William Cecil's strong recommendation). 'We who are now bishops,' Grindal once explained to the Swiss theological critic Bullinger, 'on our first return, and before we entered our ministry, contended long and earnestly for the removal of those things that have occasioned the present dispute; but as we were unable to prevail, either with the Queen or with Parliament, we judged it best, after a consultation on the subject, not to desert our churches for the sake of a few ceremonies, and those not unlawful in themselves, especially since the pure doctrine of the Gospel remained in all its integrity and freedom.'

That was not exactly enthusiasm for the Church of England as by law established; and the poor personal quality of two of Grindal's successors in London also showed how difficult it was for the government to find bishops both acceptable and reliable. John Aylmer was a hot-tempered and bitter man, soured by fourteen years as Archdeacon of London. Richard Fletcher, formerly the Queen's handsome favourite at court,

was suspended soon after his appointment to London because he suddenly married a widow – and the youth and uncertain morals of his bride caused additional scandal. He was restored to office but died next year while 'taking tobacco in his chair'. He is best remembered as the father of John Fletcher, Shakespeare's collaborator.

Edwin Sandys, appointed successively to Worcester, London and York, was another bishop whose character did little to commend the government to Puritans. His temper was as hot as Aylmer's, quarrels surrounded him, and he enriched his family at the Church's expense. A great story went round that he had been discovered in bed with an innkeeper's wife. Although he may well have been the victim of a plot, he foolishly tried to silence his accusers with money. He was, however, something of a Puritan at heart, stating in his will made in 1588 that although he accepted 'certain rites and ceremonies' as having been 'by political constitution authorized among us', he hoped that they would be 'disused little by little'. All Grindal's successors at York were definite Protestants until Richard Neile in 1632. The attitude of Matthew Hutton, the gentle scholar who was archbishop 1595–1606, showed how out of sympathy with the Queen such men were. 'The Puritans, whose fantastical zeal I mislike,' he once wrote, 'though they differ in ceremonies and accidents, yet they agree with us in the substance of religion.'[31]

This very strong current of opinion in favour of Puritan principles was brought to a head in December 1576 when Edmund Grindal, who had been Archbishop of Canterbury for about a year, was ordered by the Queen to suppress 'prophesyings' – the name given to informal gatherings of preachers for study and discussion of the Bible. Elizabeth feared treason, but Grindal (who had consulted his fellow bishops) defended the right of patriotic preachers to educate themselves for their pulpit work. He therefore refused to obey and offered his resignation. For good measure, he asked the Queen to leave church business to the bishops and even went

[31] Quoted in R. A. Marchant, *The Puritans and the Church Courts in the Diocese of York 1560–1642* (London, 1960), p. 23.

so far as to write: 'Remember, Madam, that you are a mortal creature.'

It was one of the bravest letters in the history of England. Its author was a man whose boyhood had been passed among the Lakes and whose young manhood was spent as a disciple of the martyr Ridley. While in exile under Queen Mary he had gathered reports about the Protestant martyrs and had shared them with John Foxe. A modern historian prejudiced against him wrote about this letter: 'his weakness of character flew to obstinacy'.[32] But so far from being weak or obstinate, Grindal had won the respect of many churchmen by his behaviour as a bishop since 1559, and great expectations surrounded his move to Canterbury. Nor had he disappointed his admirers by his first moves. Knowing how unsatisfactory was the administration of ecclesiastical law, he waded into reform. He sacrificed what might have been a great Primacy by his defiance of the Queen, for her fury was intense. She wanted Grindal to be deprived of his office, but since he refused to go quietly Elizabeth had to be restrained; her advisers dreaded the scandal. He never again performed the administrative functions of an archbishop, except in a few cases where the Queen's ministers gave him specific orders. He was kept under house arrest in Lambeth Palace. He went blind and, broken in spirit and health, died in 1583 while arrangements were at last in hand for his resignation.[33]

In Grindal's successor, John Whitgift, the Queen had a man after her own heart. He had driven Professor Thomas Cartwright from Cambridge when that provocative theologian had caused a sensation in the spring of 1570 by lecturing on the Acts of the Apostles. Cartwright had declared that the Church of England ought to be reformed so that it was more like the Church to be found in those Acts and in the continental centres of Protestantism; bishops, he had urged, should have purely spiritual functions, not jurisdictions. In response Whitgift,

[32] This misjudgement by W. H. Frere is to be found in *A Dictionary of English Church History*, ed. S. L. Ollard (revised, London, 1948), p. 261.
[33] Patrick Collinson's biography of *Archbishop Grindal* (London, 1980), not only brought this forgotten hero back to life but also illuminated his times.

who was then Master of Trinity College, had secured new statutes for the university from the Queen, greatly strengthening the authority of the heads of the colleges. Cartwright had been forced to live abroad, so as to taste the paradise about which he had lectured. And when radical young Puritans had published their *Admonition to Parliament* in 1572, Whitgift's scholarship and eloquence had been valuable to those in charge of Church and State. He had replied at length to their manifesto – only to have Cartwright leaping heavily to their defence with a *Second Admonition*.[34]

All that distinguished service against troublesome Puritans the Queen, no doubt, remembered gratefully. The Puritans remembered other things. Whitgift first came into contact with national politics in 1565 – when he identified himself with the Puritans. He then signed a letter to Cecil begging him to protect those in Cambridge whose consciences forbade them to wear surplices. Puritans also noted that thirty years later Whitgift was still in agreement with resident Cambridge theologians about the foundations of Calvinist orthodoxy, to be upheld in all the university's teaching. He issued the 'Lambeth Articles' to this effect – only to be compelled by the Queen to say that they were unofficial. When as Archbishop of Canterbury Whitgift enforced the Queen's policy against the Puritans, including the insistence on surplices, he seemed a mere time-server. And the records certainly suggest that Whitgift had in a sense been bought. He enjoyed several other sources of income, including the Deanery of Lincoln, while Master of Trinity College, and when he became a bishop he was given financial advantages which the Queen did not allow to any of his colleagues. The records also show that while he was at Cambridge the teacher with the most influence over him was Alexander Perne, the Master of Peterhouse, who had persuaded his own conscience to conform to the ecclesiastical policies of no fewer than four Tudor monarchs. Whitgift was the Queen's man, her 'little black husband' as she called him; and the Puritans, for all their own loyalty to her, were con-

---

[34] See D. J. McGinn, *The Admonition Controversy* (New Brunswick, N.J., 1949).

vinced that this was the only reason why he resisted their Bible-based demands.[35]

He received the full backing of the Queen and her council for most of his time as archbishop. For example, when in the Parliament of 1587 a Bill was produced to substitute the Geneva service book for the Book of Common Prayer it was confiscated, with dire threats to its sponsor. However, when Whitgift marked his arrival as Archbishop of Canterbury in 1583 by insisting that all the clergy of the Church of England should swear their acceptance of three 'articles' representing the policy of his royal mistress, he had to bow to protests which were shared by many on the Queen's council. One of those articles was virtually non-controversial among Protestants at that time: it acknowledged the royal supremacy over the Church. But the other articles insisted not only that the Thirty-Nine Articles (which contained some points which some Puritans disputed) were 'agreeable' to the Word of God but also that the Book of Common Prayer contained 'nothing contrary' to the Word of God (precisely the claim that many rejected). Eventually Whitgift had to agree that the new oath was to be demanded only of men who were being ordained or admitted into new benefices as rectors, vicars or cathedral clergy.

When as a member of the Ecclesiastical Commission he probed too deeply into the opinions of Puritans being examined, William Cecil protested: 'I think the Inquisitors of Spain use not so many questions to comprehend and trap their preys.' The most influential Elizabethan official was here appealing to the Queen's own principle that windows were not to be opened into men's souls, to check her campaign against the Puritans. The Parliaments meeting in 1584 and 1585 were far less polite as members fulminated against the persecution of godly preachers. And the new archbishop, although he defended himself at length, had to moderate his enthusiasm.[36] In

---

[35] For a far more sympathetic assessment see V. J. K. Brook, *John Whitgift and the English Church* (London, 1957).

[36] The correspondence between Burghley and Whitgift is printed in Claire Cross, *The Royal Supremacy and the Elizabethan Church*, pp. 199–205.

1585 his old enemy, Thomas Cartwright, returned to England under the protection of Cecil and of the Earl of Leicester, who appointed him master of the hospital he controlled in Warwick. And another sign of the vitality of Puritanism during these years was the foundation in 1587 of Emmanuel College, Cambridge, by the Chancellor of the Exchequer, Sir Walter Mildmay, in order to train Protestant preachers under a strict discipline.

In the 1590s the campaign against the Puritans continued, however. The great men who had protected them – Bedford, Leicester, Walsingham, William Cecil – died. Robert Cecil took over much of the administration, but the main influence over the Queen was exercised by Sir Christopher Hatton, the Lord Chancellor, who led the flattering cult of the 'Virgin Queen'. Hatton had none of William Cecil's sympathy with Puritan ideals. On the contrary, he encouraged one of his chaplains to concentrate his abundant energies on a systematic campaign against the Puritans. His name was Richard Bancroft.

In 1587 this able canon of Westminster Abbey was appointed to the High Commission and became its driving power. Strangely gifted as a detective, he tracked down the secret printing press which in 1588–89 had been pouring out anti-establishment pamphlets written violently and very readably by one 'Martin Marprelate' – but even he could not prove who 'Marprelate' really was.[37] Himself also gifted as a propagandist, he launched a savage personal attack on the Puritan leaders in a Paul's Cross sermon which immediately became famous in 1589. Having gathered a mass of evidence and shaped it to his own purposes, he claimed that the Puritans were occupying politically *Dangerous Positions* – the short title of a widely circulated pamphlet written by him in 1593. In 1597 this detective and pamphleteer was given the key position of Bishop of London, and he used it to intensify his crusade.[38]

---

[37] D. J. McGinn argued for John Penry in *John Penry and the Marprelate Controversy* (New Brunswick, N.J., 1966), and Leland Carlson for Job Throkmorton in *Martin Marprelate, Gentleman* (San Marino, Cal., 1981).

[38] See S. B. Babbage, *Puritanism and Richard Bancroft* (London, 1962).

Bancroft met no one among the Puritans to match him, for in 1588 their ablest organizer and journalist, John Field, died. With his base in London Field had been in effect General Secretary to the Puritan movement, keeping groups in touch with each other, maintaining morale but all the time seeing that the movement kept within the law. The committee which advised him had included Laurence Thomson, secretary to Sir Francis Walsingham; thus the committee had been able to keep in touch with the activities of the Queen's council itself. Field's death was a double disaster since letters found in his study were now quoted (perhaps out of context) to prove that what he had been holding together was a treasonable conspiracy. Thomas Cartwright and eight other prominent leaders were arrested in 1590 and brought before two courts, the High Commission and the Star Chamber. For a time their case looked bad, particularly when fanatics, one proclaiming himself the Messiah, announced that they would deliver them from prison. But in the end they were delivered by the lawyers. The Attorney General advised William Cecil that their conduct had not been illegal, and since they threatened to appeal to the Queen's council they were eventually released. For the rest of his life Cartwright kept out of trouble, although he never abandoned his convictions. He spent seven years on the island of Guernsey, which although an English possession was far from any bishop. Returning home to Warwick as an invalid, he died soon after the queen who had over the years frustrated him.[39]

Another Puritan leader in decline was Richard Hooker's rival Walter Travers, although his *Book of Discipline*, written in Latin in Geneva, remained the classic statement of the Presbyterian proposals for church government after its translation into English by Cartwright. For a time he was in the household of William Cecil as tutor to his son Robert, and it was thanks to Cecil's influence that he preached every Sunday afternoon to the lawyers of the Temple. But his refusal to be ordained by a bishop cost him the Mastership there and eventually he agreed

---

[39] See A. F. Scott Peason, *Thomas Cartwright and Elizabethan Puritanism* (Cambridge, 1928).

to leave the English scene, becoming the first Provost of Trinity College, Dublin.[40]

With giants such as Field, Cartwright and Travers out of the way, the smaller fry among the Puritans could be patronized witheringly or punished savagely. Whitgift, summoning some clergymen from Sussex, subjected them to a fireside chat in Lambeth and assured them that they were but 'boys' in comparison with 'us'. 'You are not called to rule in this Church of England,' he reminded them. More terrible treatment was meted out to three other clergymen: Henry Barrow, John Greenwood and John Penry were all hanged in 1593. In the same year an 'Act to Retain the Queen's Subjects in Obedience' was passed as part of a campaign to terrify Puritans as well as Papists. Under such pressures, the high spirits which had marked the 'Martin Marprelate' pamphlets disappeared, and the brave few who did form 'Separatist' congregations saw little future for their ideals in England. In 1582 Robert Browne, aptly nicknamed 'Troublechurch Browne', had escaped from Norwich to the Netherlands, to publish there his *Treatise of Reformation without Tarrying for Any* and to work it out in the shape of a pure congregation. But the congregation had split up in personal quarrels and he had crept back to England – to become the rector of a country parish until his death in 1633 (although he then died in Northampton gaol, for he had again attracted attention as a troublemaker). It is not surprising that Browne's name was now popularly used with contempt. 'Policy I hate,' declared Sir Andrew Aguecheek in *Twelfth Night*: 'I had as lief be a Brownist as a politician.'

A more substantial history followed the acceptance by Francis Johnson of a call to become pastor of Puritan 'Separatists' in London in 1592; a permanent congregation gathered around his preaching and his administration of Baptism and Lord's Supper. They used no set forms of prayer; John Greenwood informed the bishop examining him that even to repeat the Lord's Prayer was 'superstitious babbling'. But Johnson's congregation proved permanent only because it migrated first to Amsterdam and then to the new colony of Virginia. And it

---

[40] See S. J. Knox, *Walter Travers, Paragon of Elizabethan Puritanism* (London, 1962).

did not remain united; it split in Amsterdam on the issue of whether authority was to lie in the whole congregation or (as Johnson wanted) in the minister and a small group of elders. Another controversy was stirred up among the exiles in Amsterdam when an over-enthusiastic Cambridge theologian, John Smyth, argued that the minister must translate the lessons from the Hebrew or the Greek extempore, since no printed version in England was sufficiently inspired. Smyth baptized himself in order to show not only how futile had been his own earlier baptism as an infant, but also how difficult it was to find another minister worthy to perform this role. Eventually, however, before his premature death, he resolved to 'put an end to all controversies and questions about the outward Church and ceremonies with all men'; he would 'spend my time in the main matters wherein consisteth salvation'. Such were some of the problems surrounding the obscure Elizabethan birth of the Free Church tradition which was eventually to include many millions of Christians throughout the English-speaking world.[41]

Meanwhile in the Established Church few young graduates felt tempted to leave for the wilderness along with Browne, Johnson or Smyth – and although many of the clergy were Puritans at heart a new generation grew up who were to be the founders of the more definitely High Church movement, attaching much importance to the bishop's sacred functions. A modern student of this period has argued that the 'scornful condemnation of the late Elizabethan Church as a position born of compromise, timorously defended, and maintained only because the political exigencies admitted no deeper commitment, cannot stand in the face of the piety, learning and loyalty that flowered in the first generation of men whose religious experience was wholly within the life of Elizabethan Anglicanism. Bilson, Field, Mason, Hall, Morton, Montague, Overall, Andrewes, Laud – here is a numbering of the stars in the firmament of the early Stuart Church. Yet all came to manhood in the days of Whitgift's defence of the establishment against the Puritan challenge. The light that they shed over the

---

[41] See B. R. White, *The English Separatist Tradition* (Oxford, 1971).

first years of the seventeenth century was a brilliance reflected from the Elizabethan sunset'.[42]

It was by now the generally agreed Puritan policy to await the Queen's death and her replacement by a more 'godly' successor from a securely Protestant Scotland. When James VI eventually did ride south as King James I of England, he was greeted by carefully organized Puritan petitions, and showed that he was impressed by calling a conference at Hampton Court to discuss grievances. It is difficult to be sure exactly what took place there. William Barlow, Bishop of Lincoln, compiled the official report of the proceedings in answer to Puritan claims of victory, but his report, too, was full of bias. The most probable interpretation of the evidence suggests that John Rainolds, a much respected scholar who had been Dean of Lincoln and before that Richard Hooker's tutor at Oxford, was virtually the only Puritan who spoke up in the conversation.

As voiced by Rainolds, the requests were moderate – in contrast with the far-reaching plots which had been attributed to the Puritans by Richard Bancroft. He seems to have asked that the Church of England should no longer insist on the use of the sign of the cross in Baptism, on a child needing to be confirmed by a bishop before receiving the Holy Communion, on kneeling at the Communion, and on the wearing of the surplice at Morning and Evening Prayer. The Apocrypha should no longer be read as part of the Bible, and the form of 'subscription' to the Prayer Book and the Articles by clergymen should be changed. That was scarcely a revolution. But this scholar's moderation made little impression on a sarcastic king; Whitgift and Bancroft, who had been alarmed lest James should regard the constitution of the Church of England as a debating topic, need not have worried. The sound of men voicing theological opinions not his own was bound to madden James. Although when he had slept and recovered his temper the new king did make conciliatory promises, the only positive result of the conference was an agreement to collaborate on minor changes in the Prayer Book and on a new English version of the Bible.

---

[42] P. M. Dawley, *John Whitgift and the Reformation* (London, 1955), p. 193.

Basically, it seems, James accepted Elizabeth's own mistaken belief that some or many of the English Puritans were intent on the destruction of the monarchy, so that it was fortunate that when they appeared at Hampton Court they seemed to be, after all, only a small and contemptible group of troublemakers, who could quite easily be browbeaten. In a letter of 1590, written in anger when Penry and other preachers had fled to Scotland, the great Queen had warned him: 'Here is risen, both in your realm and mine, a sect of perilous consequence, such as would have no kings but a presbytery.' His own famous explosion at the end of a tiring day of arguments with Rainolds at Hampton Court in January was: 'Then Jack and Tom and Will and Dick shall meet, and at their pleasure censure me and my council and all our proceedings . . . Dr Rainolds, till you find that I grow lazy, let that alone . . . No bishop, no king . . . I will make them conform themselves or I will harry them out of this land or else do worse.'[43]

A HOLLOW VICTORY

In the short run, therefore, the Queen triumphed in her anti-Puritan campaign. And her triumph has often been applauded by those who would say with Sir Andrew Aguecheek that a Puritan deserved to be beaten 'like a dog'. ('Thy exquisite reason, dear knight?' asks Sir Toby Belch, to whom Sir Andrew replies: 'I have no exquisite reason for it, but I have reason good enough.') A relatively restrained modern scholar has recorded his impression that 'the foundations of Puritanism lay in hatred; in hatred of the natural world, hatred of its social institutions and hatred of human nature. Puritans insisted on the complete depravity of man and refused to place any confidence whatever in his rational and in his natural faculties. And yet, automatically, this desire of self-abasement

---

[43] M. H. Curtis reconstructed 'The Hampton Court Conference and its Aftermath' in *History* (London, 1961), pp. 1–6, with an emphasis which may exaggerate the King's disagreements with the bishops.

generated, as it was being indulged in, its very opposite: an arrogant pride. The Puritan who felt that he was one of the elect could indeed ride roughshod over all cautious objections and doubts, for he knew with certainty what the divine truth was. . . . This outlook naturally foreshadowed one of the most rigid systems of moralism human experience has ever known. The Puritan would condemn any pursuit of pleasure that was not orientated towards the super-natural.'[44] If all this is true, then the wise man of Elizabeth's reign was not John Field, the Puritans' General Secretary, but his son Nathan – who became a chorister in the Chapel Royal, an actor and a great lover of other men's wives.

But it seems reasonable to conclude that in the long run the damage which English Christianity sustained through Elizabeth's triumph was substantial. Considerable numbers of parish priests (how many we do not know) were forced to resign because they refused to promise to wear the surplice and to obey the other anti-Puritan regulations. Those who remained felt that their Protestant queen and their own bishops were deeply prejudiced against them despite all their piety and patriotism. Their discouragement must have been a real loss to the Church's pastoral effectiveness.

One example will be sufficient. Richard Greenham was a Puritan scholar of Cambridge who in 1570 became rector of Dry Drayton, a village not far away. Without seeking fame he became famous for the austerity of his life, his devotion to his parishioners and the vigour and frequency of his sermons. Students from Cambridge, and visitors from far and wide, sought him out and learned holiness and much else from him. But in 1588 Greenham left the parish, disappointed; he had, he said, converted only one family in almost twenty years. After that, he relied on the support of Puritan laymen in London. The Church of England under Elizabeth I was not so rich in manpower that it could neglect such a preacher and pastor with impunity. It may be observed that Greenham was not actually deprived of his parish. This was because he avoided controversy whenever he could – and because his bishop was

---

[44] Peter Munz, *The Place of Hooker in the History of Thought*, pp. 37–8.

Richard Cox. This veteran Bishop of Ely, who in younger days as a Headmaster of Eton had acquired a disciplinarian's fame, was indignant when Puritan defiance seemed to show a basic lack of patriotism (in exile under Mary, he had been indignant when the worship offered in Frankfurt was insufficiently patriotic). But he was not going to end work such as Greenham's because of a missing surplice (he had not been prepared to fight for surplices in Frankfurt). Nor was he himself prepared to obey the Queen in all things. He refused to minister in her chapel while it contained a crucifix; he refused to transfer the Bishop of Ely's house in London to Sir Christopher Hatton; and he refused to consider her prejudices when at the age of seventy he wanted to marry a widow. Richard Greenham wrote a letter to Cox in which he pleaded that his only interest lay 'in preaching Christ crucified unto myself and country people'; and the bishop was impressed.

For more than seventeen years after Cox's death the diocese of Ely was left without a bishop while the income went to the Crown. The see of Oxford was left vacant from 1559 to 1604, apart from inglorious bishops who briefly occupied it in the years 1567–68 and 1589–92. It was widely agreed that Elizabeth's enthusiasm for moving bishops from diocese to diocese was not unconnected with the custom which brought the 'first fruits' (more or less the first year's income in the new post) to the Crown. In contrast with this official plunder of the Church, the Puritans loved the Church to the point of self-sacrifice. Thomas Cartwright so loved his work for the Church that from student days he spent only five hours a night in bed. The clergy of this persuasion devoted themselves to frequent preaching, a duty understood to involve a close study of the Bible before expounding it at length, as well as much earnest private discussion of its message with parishioners and with neighbouring clergy. Out of their own purses Puritan laymen supported a 'shadow church' on a considerable scale in order to provide lecturers or assistant curates who would discharge a preacher's duty, thus interpreted, when the priest who received the parish's tithes was (at least to Puritan ears) 'dumb'.

It is unfair to see Puritanism through the eyes of its enemies – eyes always quick to spot any tendency to treason. Fortunately the minute book of the *classis* (conference) of about twenty Puritan clergymen in the Dedham district of Essex between 1582 and 1589 has been preserved. It does not record long discussions about the national government in Church or State, and we need not suppose that such discussions took place secretly. The whole emphasis is local and moral; there are ministers urging each other to do their duty as they see it. In fact they exercise over each other the kind of oversight which would in the Victorian Age and later come from an active bishop or archdeacon, and the earnest self-examination of these Christian ministers may fairly be said to be filling a vacuum left by the lack of leadership from the Church's official hierarchy.[45]

There have also been careful studies of how the Puritans actually worshipped or wished to worship. One scholar has explained how it came to be that the Puritans complained about the shortness as well as about the impersonal formality of an official Prayer Book service; their own worship combined a reverence for the Scriptures with a relevance to the conditions of the worshippers, and they often enjoyed it greatly. It was 'characterized by purity, simplicity and spirituality. It attempted to recreate the Pentecostal fervour and expectation of the Apostolic Church. Where it failed, it was only because spiritual earnestness could not be maintained on such a high plane of worship.'[46] And there have been studies of what the Puritans actually taught or wished to teach.[47] These studies have shown that the idea that they invented a 'Protestant ethic' which encouraged the competitive ruthlessness of capitalism has little historical foundation. It is true that many successful businessmen found their personal religion through the Puritan preachers. Repeating the commonplaces of Christian morality, these preachers promised God's blessing on the virtues of

---

[45] See *The Presbyterian Movement in the Reign of Queen Elizabeth as illustrated by the Minute Book . . .*, ed. R. G. Usher (London, 1905).

[46] Horton Davis, *The Worship of the English Puritans* (London, 1948), p. 259. This scholar developed the theme against a wide background in *Worship and Theology in England: From Cranmer to Hooker, 1534–1603* (Princeton, N.J., 1970).

[47] For example, E. G. Irvonwy Morgan, *The Godly Preachers of the Elizabethan Church* (London, 1965).

thrift, sobriety, chastity and industry; and they added a new Protestant emphasis on the dignity of a man's work or 'calling' in the world. But it is not true that a radically new social morality is found in Puritan sermons and books. Almost everything a Puritan preacher said about society in his day would have been said by the preaching friars in a medieval town.

Equally false is the idea that it was the habit of Puritan preachers to dwell gloomily on the doctrine of 'double predestination', which taught that God had from eternity predestined one fixed number (small) to heaven and another (much larger) number to the everlasting torments of hell. The eternal context of man's brief mortal life was always in the background of Puritan thinking, and the account of eternity given in the Calvinist tradition impressed the Puritans deeply because it seemed to be based on the Bible. But 'Calvinism' was understood differently by different Calvinists, and after an attempt to impose theological uniformity English theologians were in practice allowed a certain degree of freedom. When in the mid-1590s Professor Peter Baro, a refugee from France, and William Barrett, a young college chaplain, introduced liberal doctrines into Cambridge they were forced to resign; for they taught that Christ had died in order to make possible the salvation of all men, not merely of the predestined few. Their teaching shocked orthodox Calvinists because it gave some place to the freedom of the human will and to the importance of 'works' in salvation (and in fact young Barrett went abroad to become a Roman Catholic layman). That, however, did not prevent Baro's leading English disciple, John Overall, from being elected a professor in Cambridge and then moving to London as Dean of St Paul's.

It was generally agreed that the mysteries debated by such liberals with the strict Calvinists in the universities should be handled delicately, if at all, in the parishes. These were 'deep points'. The plain message to the parishes was that those who responded to the preaching were destined for the joys of salvation. In fact, Puritan preaching as it reached the parishes was virtually indistinguishable from a repetition of the New Testament – stern but not grim in its morality, awestruck but not despairing in its estimate of man's condition under the justice of God. When Puritans were exceptionally holy, their holiness seems to have been basically like the holiness of the saints in any age of Christianity. They condemned themselves rather than others, and they prayed for strength to love and serve God and neighbour. One of the leading Puritan theologians of the Elizabethan age was William Whitaker, Master of St John's College, Cambridge. His most important book was a *Disputation of Holy Scripture*, advocating the authority of the Bible against the Jesuit, Cardinal Bellarmine. Two of his sons became missionaries, expounding the Bible in Virginia during the years 1611–24. Such lives showed the main thrust of Elizabethan Puritanism.[48]

William Perkins became a Fellow of Christ's College, Cambridge, in 1584 and died in 1602. He was the author of a wide range of books of 'practical divinity' based on the Bible, such as expositions of the Lord's Prayer and the Apostles' Creed or a *Treatise of Vocations* which encouraged laymen to think of their jobs as God-given. His first 'rule' was that 'every person of every degree, state, sex, or condition, without exception, must have some particular and personal calling to walk in'; and although 'every man must judge that particular calling in which God hath placed him to be the best of all callings for him', yet 'a particular calling must give place to the general calling of a Christian when they cannot both stand together'. In England his reputation became such that between 1608 and 1635 his collected works, totalling over 2,500 pages, reached eight printings. His influence crossed the Atlantic with the Puritan emigrants. A modern scholar has said: 'Anyone who reads the writings of early New Englanders learns that Perkins was indeed a towering figure in Puritan eyes. Nor were English and American divines alone in their veneration for him. His works were translated into many languages and circulated in all Reformed communities; he was one of the outstanding pulpit orators of the day, and the seventeenth century, Catho-

---

[48] See Gordon Wakefield, *Puritan Devotion* (London, 1957). The thoughts of two clergymen are revealed in *Two Elizabethan Puritan Diaries*, ed. M. M. Knappen (Chicago, 1933), and those of a lady in Yorkshire who combined the lives of a housewife and a hermit in *The Diary of Lady Margaret Holtby*, ed. D. M. Meads (London, 1930).

lics as well as Protestant, ranked him with Calvin.'[49]

Perkins was the opposite of vague in his fundamental beliefs; his *Golden Chain* of 1591 brought together the teachings of Jean Calvin and of continental Calvinists such as Theodore Beza. He made, in fact, a rigid chain of the predestination theories – but this was not the main message which he entrusted to the young men sent from the university to preach to the English people. The main message was the Gospel as given in the New Testament long before Calvin. Sensitive readers of his systematic theology might be appalled by the thought that if they were not among the 'elect' predestined to heaven they were 'reprobates' given a temporary 'taste' of faith or morality only to be plunged with the accursed into hell, since 'God hath determined to reject certain men unto eternal destruction and misery and that to the praise of his justice'. But his main purpose was positive and pastoral. It was that preachers should assure believers that they were saved and ought to give thanks by good lives. He propounded 'a form of reasoning or practical syllogism':

> Everyone that believes is the child of God:
> But I do believe:
> Therefore I am the child of God.

He once wrote down 'the Order and Sum of the sacred and only method of Preaching':

1. To read the text distinctly out of the canonical Scriptures.

2. To give the sense and understanding of it, being read, by the Scripture itself.

3. To collect a few and profitable points of doctrine out of the natural sense.

4. To apply (if he have the gift) the doctrines rightly collected, to the life and manners of men in a simple and plain speech.[50]

---

[49] Perry Miller, *Errand into the Wilderness* (Cambridge, Mass., 1956), p. 57. See *The Work of William Perkins*, ed. Ian Breward (Abingdon, Berks., 1970), and the study of his thought in R. T. Kendall, *Calvin and English Calvinism to 1649*.

[50] Quoted in H. C. Porter, *Reformation and Reaction in Tudor Cambridge* (Cambridge, 1958), p. 225. See also his chapter on 'The Theology of William Perkins'.

What the Puritans wanted most was to revive religion. With all their limitations (they had no appreciation of visual beauty, or of poetry outside the Bible, or of Shakespeare's 'cakes and ale'), they argued boldly and persistently for the reformation of life in obedience to the New Testament and for the completion of the renewal of the medieval Church by a scriptural holiness. M. M. Knappen, a great authority, reckoned that of the quarter of Elizabeth's subjects who held firm opinions on religious questions, more than half were Puritans, because that was the most powerful brand of Christian idealism.[51] It was an Elizabethan tragedy that this noble contribution was branded as treason, creating agonies of conscience for laymen who wished to combine piety with patriotism, and thrusting sincere and brave religious leaders out into the wilderness. Church and State alike were impoverished when Puritan preachers were given an official treatment scarcely less hostile than the total rejection of the Roman Catholic missionaries. The identification of Roman Catholicism with treason was the error of popes, we may conclude; but the alienation of the Puritans was the error of the Queen.[52]

Puritanism, it is true, could not be stamped out. But despite the high and influential quality of many of the clergy and laity who adhered to it, it was not officially encouraged to enrich the quiet work of the Church of England in normal villages and towns. Nor, despite the high culture of some individual Puritans, was this movement allowed to become an integral part of the stupendous flowering of civilization in Elizabethan and Stuart England. Instead, the Puritan movement against which Elizabeth I had campaigned found other outlets. It encouraged the slow birth of an English-speaking republic on the other side of the Atlantic. In seventeenth-century England, it inspired events which ended in a violently destructive revolution.

---

[51] See M. M. Knappen, *Tudor Puritanism: A Chapter in the History of Idealism* (Chicago, Ill., 1939).

[52] The roughly similar dilemmas of the two groups in opposition were analysed by Elliot Rose in *Cases of Conscience: Alternatives Open to Recusants and Puritans under Elizabeth I and James I* (Cambridge, 1974).

Part Two

A WAR BETWEEN BELIEVERS

CHAPTER SIX

THE STUART CHURCH

JAMES I

Both James I and Charles I were believing members of the Church of England – the father a learned theologian, the son a martyr in some sense. And the deep interest which they both took in religion was typical of an age when the energies of Englishmen were expressed more creatively in religion than in any other sphere. The Stuarts ruled a country which was in the main authentically and enthusiastically religious. It was, however, less influenced by the New Testament in the matter of Christians loving each other, and no small part of the blame for a situation which led to civil war must rest on the two kings who made all-embracing claims to be responsible for their people's welfare. Through laziness in the father, and through blindness followed by obstinacy in the son, the kings failed to take the Puritan element in English Christianity with the seriousness which it deserved.[1]

A modern biographer has remarked that James 'took the Church of England to his heart in a long rapturous embrace that lasted for the rest of his life'.[2] The bishops of the Established Church, well schooled by Elizabeth, were submissive to a monarch – and James had been one since his coronation soon after his first birthday. The leading bishops, Whitgift and

---

[1] A useful collection of illustrative extracts is *Politics, Religion and Literature in the Seventeenth Century*, ed. William Lamont and Sybil Oldfield (London, 1975). Introductions to the politics include J. P. Kenyon, *Stuart England* (London, 1978), and Barry Coward, *The Stuart Age* (London, 1980).

[2] D. Harris Willson, *King James VI and I* (London, 1956), p. 197. Caroline Bingham, *James I of England* (London, 1981), is another good biography. Peter Milward, *The Religious Controversies of the Jacobean Age* (London, 1978), is a survey of the printed sources.

Bancroft, assured him that the old queen had been perfectly right to link the Puritans with those Presbyterian preachers who had bored him, and tried to dominate him, ever since John Knox had preached his coronation sermon. One of the many delights in becoming king of the far richer kingdom to the south was deliverance from those sermons, and James had not the least intention of suffering under English pulpits.

Now he would do the teaching. In an exhortation to his eldest son Henry written in 1598 (*Basilikon Doron*), he had mocked 'the preposterous humility of the proud Puritans, claiming to their parity and crying "We are all but vile worms", and yet who will judge and give law to their king but will be judged nor controlled by none.' James boasted about the lessons he taught to the Puritans at the Hampton Court conference of 1604: 'I peppered them soundly.' He preferred to have bishops not because they were princes of the Church but because they were deferential to his own mastery of 'kingcraft'. They would, he trusted, make others share their sense of his importance; that was why he had created three bishops for Scotland in 1610. He also liked bishops because most of them were learned in theology, where he was no less expert. He had himself been thoroughly trained as a scholar by his tutor George Buchanan, and he kept up bookish habits throughout his life. Nothing pleased him more than to have a bishop or potential bishop standing beside his chair while he dined, serving up quotations from the Bible and the Fathers which supported the royal doctrines. In this enjoyment of the company of leading clergymen, he was unlike Elizabeth. He was also unlike her in his respect for their interests. James warmly approved of a law of 1604 which forbade the bishops to alienate the estates of their sees. They were not even to transfer them to the Crown. The King wanted his bishops to enjoy their rights and to feel at ease, as he did.

He rightly expected his grateful bishops not to blench at his conceit, which was monumental ('If you will consider the attributes of God,' he informed Parliament in 1610, 'you shall see how they agree in the person of a king'); or at his table manners, which were disgusting; or at his homosexuality, which became blatant; or at the extravagant and often inebriated disorder of his court; or at his passion for hunting, which meant that his attention to politics was intermittent. These fellow theologians would surely either applaud or not notice. He also expected them to share his rejection of interference by the popes.

In theory he was willing to acknowledge some primacy in the religious position of the Bishop of Rome, but in practice Roman Catholicism meant to him the religion of his mother and of those who wished to assassinate him. His mother had arranged for his father's murder and had been nothing but a nuisance to him before her execution (which he secretly approved). He took the identification of Roman Catholicism with terrorism seriously; his clothes were specially padded and he hated to see a drawn sword. While King of England he wrote – or at any rate claimed the authorship of – four books defending the God-given rights of kings against the political pretensions of mere popes; and he hurt his Roman Catholic subjects more directly by approving the execution of seventeen of them. He had imbibed to the full the Calvinism of his education, and to prove his orthodoxy he had Edward Wightman, a draper who had denied the divinity of Christ, burned in 1612 – the last Englishman to suffer death for heresy. He personally briefed the English delegates sent to the international reaffirmation of Calvinist orthodoxy at the synod of Dort (Dordrecht) in 1618. He had previously given strict instructions to his ambassador to curtail the posthumous influence of Professor Jacob Harmensz of Leyden. The professor was to be important in English history because his Latinized name Arminius was given to an international movement, Arminianism.[3]

What the King really liked was the Calvinism of a bishop such as James Montague of Winchester (the editor of his collected works), or Toby Matthew of York, or Vaughan of London, or Davenant of Salisbury. It was the kind of Calvinism that taught that, among all God's elect, a king was particularly chosen for the blessings of the God who was not

---

[3] See Carl Bangs, *Arminius* (Nashville, Tenn., 1974); R. T. Kendall, *Calvin and English Calvinism to 1649*, pp. 141–64; *Reform and Reformation*, ed. Derek Baker (Oxford, 1979), pp. 195–243.

decisively interested in morality. In religion James (the 'British Solomon') was the nation's schoolmaster, but not usually a censorious one. He genially promoted a few bishops who were at least crypto-Arminians, such as Richard Neile of Durham. His teaching about witchcraft showed his general approach. In Scotland he had been fascinated by the subject and had written a treatise on *Demonology*, but in England he found that educated men laughed and he grew bored.[4] Almost forty years of plot and counter-plot in Scotland had made him thankful to be alive, so that his general attitude was 'live and let live' (excluding the deer). His motto was 'Blessed are the peacemakers', and he once wrote: 'I did ever hold persecution as one of the infallible notes of a false church.'

His relaxed attitude extended to family affairs and to foreign affairs, between which there was a good deal of overlap. He had married a Danish princess when he had needed an ally back in 1589, but he allowed her to find her own peace in the Roman Catholic faith while he comforted himself with the affections of handsome young men. Although he was delighted when his beautiful daughter Elizabeth married the Elector Palatine, a firm Protestant, and so became the 'queen of hearts', he was determined to establish and strengthen peace with Catholic Spain, consummating it if possible by a marriage alliance for his son. This meant that he did not share the enthusiasm of many of his subjects, including MPs, for intervention on the Protestant side when the Thirty Years' War started. The war began in earnest with the Catholic victories over his son-in-law, temporarily King of Bohemia, in 1619–20, but English Protestant passions were not allowed to lead to sustained action. To the indignation of the Puritans, the much-loved Elizabeth was left in exile and poverty in The Hague. Her royal father sent much sympathy – but little else.

At home the King's love of peace – and also of himself as the maker of peace – gave rise to the episode of the *Declaration of Sports*. This was ordered to be read in all churches in 1618, and was a treatise approving healthy exercise on a Sunday after-

---

[4] See Christina Larner in *The Reign of James VI and I*, ed. A. G. R. Smith (London, 1975), pp. 74–90.

noon. This royal defence of football, wrestling, archery, morris dances, Maypoles, Whitsun ales and so forth had several advantages in the eyes of the British Solomon. It pleased his people by his gracious patronage of their recreations; it kept them out of the alehouses where they might grumble about his government; it exercised them as potential soldiers available for any wars into which he might be forced; and it asserted his authority over those Puritans who preferred the people to spend Sunday afternoon reading the Bible, a book not always sound in its attitude to monarchs. But when he found that many of the clergy and some of the bishops strongly objected to his declaration, he withdrew it and so restored theological peace.

His permanent religious achievement was his sponsorship of the Authorized or King James Version of the Bible, published in 1611.

At the Hampton Court conference he agreed both with Puritan criticisms of the inaccuracies of the Bishops' Bible, and with the bishops' attack on the controversial notes and new words (such as *congregation* instead of the old *church*) in the Geneva Bible. Having thus made peace with all his fellow scholars, he announced a project which was to be the chief glory of his reign. There was to be a translation on which all could agree. No time was lost in appointing fifty-four translators to compare the Bishops' Bible and the rival English versions with the original Hebrew and Greek. These translators included some Puritan scholars, among them John Rainolds who had taken the lead at Hampton Court. Guided by 'rules' given to them in the King's name, they worked in six companies, at Oxford, Cambridge and Westminster, with a central committee and two final revisers (Bishops Bilson and Miles Smith). They had all the scholarship of the age at their command – and, fortunately for their self-confidence, did not realize how defective were the New Testament manuscripts on which their translation was based, or how incomplete was their mastery of Hebrew. Enough of the work of the early English translators, Tyndale and Coverdale, survived to give the 1611 version its tone of an already old-fashioned majesty, but the result went far beyond the light revision of the Bishops' Bible which was the original plan.

The acceptance of the new Bible took time. For many years even bishops as scholarly, and as deferential to royal opinions, as Lancelot Andrewes and William Laud continued to use the familiar Geneva Bible when preaching. Wisely, the King did not force the issue. The Bible which became famous as the 'Authorized Version' was in fact never authorized in any exclusive sense. Such a step might have aroused opposition for which the King had no taste. The way chosen was more effective: the King's Printer published the new version in a large (folio) edition suitable for use in churches, and no earlier translation was reprinted in that size. Read in churches with less and less competition, the new Bible gradually made its way into people's loyalties by the force of its language and by the quality of its scholarship with its multi-layered authorship. The language was not everyday; there was no equivalent here of Shakespeare's comic crowd scenes. Indeed, it was some-times not clear; St Paul's theology as translated here can never have been entirely and immediately plain to all churchgoers. But the biblical themes of grace and glory were presented with a dignity worthy of the great declamations in Shakespearean drama and the stories were told with a powerful simplicity. Popular appreciation of the achievement meant that the excite-ment with which the first English versions had been received was renewed and prolonged, and the effects did not begin to fade out of the consciousness of the English-speaking peoples until the twentieth century. The dedication to the king of this 'King James Version' (the American term) was well deserved – although its fulsomeness was in contrast with the restraint of the Bible when speaking about God.[5]

That was a major contribution to the religion of the English, but historians have asked: could there have been more?

The new translation of the Bible might have been accom-panied by a new settlement of the Church. It would surely not have been impossible for a king equipped to understand the issues involved to insist that the Church of England should be more fully reformed, or at least made more welcoming to

---

[5] See David Daiches, *The King James Version of the English Bible* (Chicago, Ill., 1941), and T. R. Henn, *The Bible as Literature* (London, 1970).

reformers. Even the dispute with Rome would have been made less destructive had there been a systematic attempt to win the loyalty of Roman Catholics who were willing to be loyal (like James's own wife). But this self-advertising king was no statesman. Robert Cecil, his chief minister until 1612, was treated like a useful dog and nicknamed 'the Beagle'. Archbishop Bancroft who served alongside him was, like Cecil, a highly competent administrator – and he had a policy, to build up the Church of England efficiently but narrowly. James, however, failed to appoint a successor to Bancroft who would continue that policy. The truth was that James, for all his pride in his mastery of 'kingcraft', had learned that trade in a country where the bureaucracy was primitive in comparison with that of England. He had grown accustomed to purchasing the support of potential troublemakers by titles and pensions, and he had never seen any need to appoint ministers capable of forming and executing a longterm policy. Survival had been his purpose, and bribery had been his method. His failures to appoint bishops who would make an impression as the agents of a coherent and farsighted policy only illustrated his general approach to 'kingcraft'. He appointed bishops to whom he took a fancy, or who were recommended to him by laymen whom he wished to please.[6]

A modern scholar has sadly commented on the results. 'The story of the first decade of James I's reign, Cecil's decade,' writes Professor Joel Hurstfield, 'is in Church as in State the story of solutions glimpsed and opportunities missed. No one in that brief interval of promise had sufficient of either the will or the power to solve the problems which for half a century had pressed for a solution: namely to broaden the Church sufficiently to meet the reasonable demands of the moderate Puritans and to broaden the state sufficiently to meet the reasonable demands of the moderate Catholics.'[7]

---

[6] Two instructive essays are by H. R. Trevor-Roper in his *Historical Essays* (London, 1957), pp. 139–45, and by Arthur P. Kautz in *Early Stuart Studies*, ed. H. S. Reinmuth (Minneapolis, Minn., 1970), pp. 152–79. But Patrick Collinson has sympathetically portrayed the Jacobean Church in his *The Religion of Protestants*.

[7] Joel Hurstfield, *Freedom, Corruption and Government* (London, 1973), p. 101.

CHARLES I

Although Charles I – whose reign began in 1625 – resembled his father in his attachment to the Church of England and its bishops, he did not favour orthodox Calvinists. His taste for Arminians needs some explaining, since the new king, essentially an aesthete, had none of his father's academic interest in theology.

Theologically Arminianism was defined by the 'Remonstrance' published by the Dutch supporters of the provocative Professor Harmensz in 1610, the year after his death. It maintained five points – that God has decreed the salvation of all who believe in Christ, that Christ died 'for all' but that only believers enjoy forgiveness of sins, that man must be regenerated by the Holy Spirit, that grace is 'not irresistible', and that perseverance is granted through 'the assistance of the grace of the Holy Spirit'. This creed aroused a very fierce controversy, for at each of these points the emphasis seemed to be on the possibility that any man might actively respond to the love of God declared in Christ's death, his will only being assisted by the Holy Spirit if he was willing to receive such assistance – and there was not a corresponding emphasis on the decree that some were eternally elect and others eternally damned whatever their own merits.

Summing up the orthodox reaction, the Synod of Dordrecht (Dort) proclaimed the five points of Calvinism, popularly recalled by the acrostic TULIP – total depravity, unconditional election, limited atonement (Christ died for the elect only), irresistible grace (saving the elect), the perseverance of the elect (only) until they safely reach heaven. Thus in orthodox Calvinism the sovereignty of God was reasserted against man's free will. In its practical consequences Arminianism had not originally been royalist; it had been the religion of self-confident businessmen critical of Prince Maurice and that had been the main reason why James I had been so much against it. John Milton, who was to argue that it had been right to execute King Charles, was an Arminian. But Arminianism appealed to Charles in his optimism at the beginning of his reign. It seemed a fit religion for a happy kingdom at peace (whereas in the Netherlands the narrow, angry, creed of orthodox Calvinism was still needed as a fighting creed against Spain). Above all, it appealed because of what William Laud and other churchmen who won influence over the new king told him. To them, Arminianism offered a suitable inspiration for a working partnership of kings and priests against Puritan troublemakers. To believe in free will as a theological theory meant to accept the King's will in practice. That was why, as George Morley (a future Bishop of Winchester) quipped, the answer to 'What do the Arminians hold?' was that they held all the best bishoprics and deaneries in the kingdom.[8]

Such importance had been attached to Charles's adherence to the Church of England that his Roman Catholic mother had not been allowed to bring him up. Like his father he had therefore starved of affection in his childhood; in his falsetto voice with a Scots accent, he always stammered badly. Like his father he had formed his first intimate, life-giving, friendship with a man. For James the liberator of the emotions had been Esmé Stuart, Duke of Lennox, in the 1580s; for 'Baby Charles' (as his father always called him) it was George Villiers, Duke of Buckingham, his beloved 'Steenie', in the 1620s. Both dukes flattered their royal friends with talk of the absolute powers of the Spanish and French monarchies. But Charles was never infatuated physically by any man; on the contrary, it would appear that he had for long avoided starting a friendship with Buckingham because he had disapproved of his own father's intimate relationship with him. After the shock of the murder of Buckingham in 1628 he never again gave his full friendship to any man, or did much to win any man's love; at court or in prison, he treated all men as his servants. Instead he fell fully in love with Henrietta Maria, his French Catholic queen whom he had married for political reasons four years before.

Together these two little people (the King was only five and a half feet tall and his Queen came up to his shoulder) were at the centre of the England of the 1630s.[9] Children were born

---

[8] In the 1630s Arminianism began to be tolerated even in the Netherlands. See A. W. Harrison, *Arminianism* (London, 1936), and Douglas Nobbs, *Theocracy and Toleration* (Cambridge, 1938).

[9] The best biographies are Pauline Gregg, *Charles I* (London, 1981), and Elizabeth Hamilton, *Henrietta Maria* (London, 1976).

from 1629 onwards, and the court which revolved around their exemplary family life was thoroughly respectable but also full of polite amusements. The courtiers were still supplied with food and drink on a sumptuous scale, but there was none of the gross vulgarity which James had enjoyed. Nor were theological disputations to be heard; Charles disliked arguments of any sort. Instead there was heavy and discriminating expenditure on art of the highest quality. Contemplating the silent beauty of a painting, a king could find reassurance. He could also find it in rituals. Stately acts of worship, masques and banquets became the court's routine, and something of their spirit seems to be perpetually in the air of the chapel of St James's Palace, the Banqueting House in Whitehall and the Queen's House in Greenwich – the surviving masterpieces which Inigo Jones achieved in his service of Stuart magnificence. Never has the English monarchy shown better taste.

Seldom has it been so cut off from the people. Its sophisticated luxury contrasted with the real poverty of many of the English, particularly many in London – but the court did not even appeal to those who might have been its allies because they, too, were privileged. The nobility and gentry (the bishops, too) were discouraged from attendance at court unless they had definite business there, and the King and Queen did not tour round other great people's houses. Queen Elizabeth had known how to capture the heart of a casually met visitor with a joke; but now King Charles passed through his courtiers, smiling distantly. His very love of beauty alienated him from his subjects, since there were so few English artists whom he could employ. Tensions arose both because of his acceptance of his wife's French Catholic priests (despite early explosions and later grumbles) – and because of his own Anglican piety. He was religious in a style very different from the Puritanism which animated large and growing numbers of his subjects. His father, for all his glaring faults, seems to have been more genuinely popular. James had often been adroit at handling individuals. He had thoroughly sympathized with other people's sexual and financial appetites, had been amused to see his guests' rich clothes covered with cream puddings, and had been delighted when ladies of the court, acting in masques, had rolled about drunk. Were they not all humanly depraved together? Yet the Puritan preachers had consoled themselves with the belief that their strange monarch was, like them, a Calvinist theologian. The coldly correct Charles was far more isolated. It is revealing that he refused to bow to the storm which burst when he reissued his father's *Declaration of Sports*. What was at stake for him was not that people should enjoy themselves, but that he should be obeyed. Until he was dead he was not widely loved.

This isolation of the King from ordinary men's feelings encouraged many in the country to suspect that Popery, or something close to it, flourished at court, but those with some inside knowledge knew that the King was satisfied with the Arminian version of Protestantism. It was a sign of things to come that the Duke of Buckingham, when he chaired a public debate on the topic of predestination at York House in February 1626, showed that his own (not very profound) opinions were Arminian. In the very first year of his reign Charles, with Buckingham's encouragement, sheltered an Arminian clergyman, Richard Montague, when the Commons had committed him to prison as the author of provocative (and, it was alleged, Papist) pamphlets. Three years later Montague was made Bishop of Chichester; the news of Buckingham's murder reached the bishops when they were assembled for this consecration. The King tried to dampen the controversy by reissuing the Thirty-Nine Articles with a declaration insisting on their 'literal and grammatical sense'. It was the royal will that disputes about predestination going beyond the Articles were to be 'shut up in God's promises'. But orthodox Calvinists were not going to be shut up, for they were convinced that Arminianism was not merely a heresy within Protestantism. A more dramatic conviction was voiced when the Commons debated religion in January 1629. Francis Rous, a bold Cornish MP, then announced: 'An Arminian is the spawn of a Papist.' When Parliament at last met again, in 1640, John Pym had high on the list of grievances 'innovations in religion'.[10]

---

[10] The course of this theological revolution was charted by Nicholas Tyacke in *Anti-Calvinists: The Rise of English Arminianism* (Oxford, 1987).

The civil war broke out after a chain of events which began with the King's attempt to impose on Scotland the Church of England's standards of beauty and order as these were interpreted by the Arminian clergy. His father had also nursed the ambition to unite his two kingdoms of England and Scotland religiously, but had been too shrewd – or too lazy – to do much about it. James had imposed bishops on the Scots in 1610, but these had been little more than chairmen of the ministers' presbyteries and they had not been ordained priests before being consecrated bishops. Seeking more power for these agents of his, James had visited Scotland in 1617, but he had taken no effective steps to impose his wishes when the Scots, virtually as one man, rejected them. Charles had already received warning of the Protestant nationalism of his northern subjects by the criticisms they had offered loudly when he had staged a pompous coronation in Edinburgh in 1633 and had appointed bishops to high political office, but he was undeterred. Encouraged by Laud and by these Scottish bishops, he conceived the totally unrealistic policy of imposing on the Church of Scotland (without consulting its General Assembly) a Prayer Book almost identical with the Book of Common Prayer of the Church of England. This was the work of Scotsmen and it used the word 'presbyter' not 'priest', but was in some other details less Protestant. The Communion service represented a partial return to the 1549 Prayer Book.[11]

Riots in Edinburgh rapidly led to the signing of a National Covenant to resist the bishops and their Papistical book to the death, and so Charles had the 'First Bishops' War' on his hands. Without the authority of Parliament to raise taxes, he could not equip an effective expeditionary force. Instead he made the situation worse by soliciting gifts from those who wished to be reckoned his friends, and by sending north a civilian army of militiamen. This army promptly made a truce with the Scots. The foolish Prayer Book was withdrawn, but Charles was unwilling to accept the further humiliation of making a final settlement with the lay-dominated assembly of

---

[11] Gordon Donaldson studied *The Making of the Scottish Prayer Book of 1637* (Edinburgh, 1954).

the Church of Scotland, abandoning his bishops as well as his Prayer Book.

At length a rich and blunt Yorkshireman, Thomas Wentworth, was called home from his seven years as the brutally effective administrator of Ireland and created Earl of Strafford and Lieutenant-General. His advice was taken. An army must be raised against the rebellious Scots; therefore taxes must be raised; therefore, after eleven years without one, a parliament must be summoned. It met on 17 April 1640.[12]

To see why the House of Commons – now at last given its opportunity – was bound to want to reform the Church, we must look at some English bishops.

FOUR BISHOPS

In Richard Bancroft James had inherited one of the ablest administrators in the whole history of the Church of England, and one who had proved his energy and skill as the right-hand man of Archbishop Whitgift in the campaign against the Elizabethan Puritans. It seemed inevitable that he should be appointed Archbishop of Canterbury as Whitgift's successor in December 1604.

Shortly before that appointment a new set of ecclesiastical laws or canons had been passed by the clergy in the Convocation of Canterbury and ordered by the King to be 'diligently observed . . . by all our loving subjects.' The key canon was 36, repeating the insistence of Whitgift in 1583 that all clergy should solemnly swear that the Prayer Book contained nothing contrary to the Word of God in the Bible. But there were 141 of these canons, codifying Tudor and earlier regulations; and in a series of visitations of his own diocese and many others, Bancroft embarked on a strenuous campaign to enforce them. Recruiting and encouraging competent lawyers and other

---

[12] Dame Veronica Wedgwood told the story of these years brilliantly in her *The King's Peace, 1637–41* (London, 1955), although some of her judgements have been revised in later scholarship.

staff, he proved that this medieval weapon of the visitation could still be wielded to good effect as various kinds of sinners or nonconformists were punished or rebuked – and as a check was made of their subsequent behaviour. And for the first time since the 1530s there was insistence on keeping proper records both in the ecclesiastical courts and in the parish churches.

Bancroft had the wisdom to advise that clergy who would conform to the Prayer Book in practice, but who could not swallow Canon 36, should be left alone. In the end, out of some ten thousand clergy only about ninety were deprived of their parishes for their open refusal to conform – and about a fifth of these seem to have been reinstated on promising obedience.[13]

One reason why most of the clergy were co-operative was that it was widely known that Bancroft had set his heart on raising their incomes. It was the Archbishop's old-fashioned ideal that a resident pastor should receive a full tenth of all the produce of his parish. Under his impetus the High Commission at the centre, and the revived diocesan courts at the circumference, began a long process of rescinding various arrangements which had in effect reduced the Elizabethan clergy to the economic status of servants. Payments customary in the Middle Ages, such as tithes on mining operations, had been waived; the agricultural tithes had been commuted for cash which fell in value; many tithes had been alienated to laymen. All these battles were fought again under Bancroft. At the same time adjacent parishes, individually too small to support a clergyman, were merged. There were still many 'pluralities', but these cases where one man was incumbent of more than one parish were at least to be licensed formally by the bishops. The glebe (the priest's own land) was exempt from tax, to help the poorer clergy. More frequent preaching by the clergy after training and licensing was encouraged. In the House of Lords in 1610 Bancroft even put forward a scheme for a national fund to buy out all the lay rectors' rights in the parishes, and to restore all the tithes to the clergy who did the

---

[13] This was the conclusion of S. B. Babbage, *Puritanism and Richard Bancroft*, pp. 217–19. R. G. Usher, *The Reconstruction of the English Church* (2 vols, New York, 1910), is still useful.

work. It was all part of a detailed plan to restore the clergy's tithes as literally one tenth of the national product.[14]

Many laymen naturally took fright at the prospect of the bishops recovering their disciplinary powers and clergymen recovering their economic status. There were protests in Parliament at any idea that canons such as those of 1604, agreed to only by the clergy, could be imposed on the laity. Spurred on by Sir Edward Coke who was Chief Justice until abruptly dismissed by the King in 1616, the judges attacked the right of the ecclesiastical courts, particularly the High Commission, to function with this new vigour. Defending towns and industries from taxation by the Church, they also declared that the clergy had no right to tithes 'of such things whereof the gain comes by the labour of man', except where a custom to the contrary could be proved. James was pleased to arbitrate between the enraged judges and the ecclesiastical lawyers, but characteristically did little more than to declare a truce. Despite hopes which had been raised both by the Puritans at the Hampton Court conference and by the Puritans' arch-enemy Bancroft, the parish clergy were left with no hope of any major improvement in their financial position. The complacent view of most of the laity was, it seems, that reform was desirable but impossible.

Bancroft's theology was considerably less energetic than his administration. He seems to have been a mild Calvinist. Although he was always talking about discipline, he had no religious vision of the Church with which to compete against the vision of the Puritan preachers. He also lacked an ideology with which to fight against the gentry whose vision was of an England where laymen prospered. An ecclesiastic who did have such a religious vision was Lancelot Andrewes, widely regarded – and, it was reported, recommended by the bishops to the King – as the natural successor to Bancroft at Canterbury in 1610.

Andrewes was the most admired preacher of his age, summoned to edify King James year after year on the great festivals of the Church. His learning and sanctity expressed themselves

---

[14] See Christopher Hill, *Economic Problems of the Church*, pp. 246–7.

not only in the pulpit but also in private; his notebook of
devotions and intercessions, *Preces Privatae*, has been treasured
by discerning Anglicans ever since its publication in 1648, long
after his death. He is said to have mastered fifteen modern and
six ancient languages, and his skill as a translator is preserved
in the Old Testament of the 1611 version. He seemed destined
to make the Church of England the spiritual leader of Europe –
as those who wished to flatter James often claimed it already
was. He was also an efficient administrator. From the Deanery
of Westminster he was promoted to be a bishop, first of
Chichester and then of Ely.

James, however, did not offer him Canterbury on Bancroft's
death, moving him instead to Winchester in 1618. The reason,
it seems, was that the high churchmanship of Andrewes
worried the laity, including the King. In his own chapel the
Bishop used candles and incense. What if this meant that he
hankered after a return to the medieval status of the clergy? It
seemed alarming that he had refused to be made a bishop
under Elizabeth because he was unwilling to drive a financial
bargain. While he claimed that he was no Arminian heretic, he
also refused to repeat the great Calvinist slogans. James did not
make him leader of the English delegation to the Calvinists'
Synod of Dort – or Archbishop of Canterbury.

We should not make a martyr out of Andrewes. He was one
of those who in 1613 voted at the King's behest in favour of the
divorce of Frances Howard (on the ground that her husband
was impotent towards her – but not towards other women) in
order that she might be free to marry the King's favourite
Robert Carr (later made Earl of Somerset). When in attendance on the Privy Council or in the House of Lords, he often
kept silence. Secretly he recorded his penitence in the tear-
stained notebook of *Preces Privatae*, and he prayed: 'Deliver me
from making gods of kings.' Yet in the pulpit his prose was 'not
inferior to that of any sermons in the language, unless it be
some of Newman's', in the judgement of T. S. Eliot.[15]

---

[15] See T. S. Eliot, *For Lancelot Andrewes* (London, 1928); Maurice F. Reidy, *Bishop
Lancelot Andrewes, Jacobean Court Preacher* (Chicago, Ill., 1955); Paul A. Welsby,
Lancelot Andrewes (London, 1958).

The man preferred for Canterbury in 1610 was far less complex. George Abbot was an Oxford theologian who combined moderate Calvinism with a firm belief in the royal supremacy – exactly the mixture that the King most relished.

He had made his mark in 1608 when he had accompanied the Earl of Dunbar, as his chaplain, on a mission from King James to seek to persuade the General Assembly of the Church of Scotland of the merits of government by bishops. The Scots had remained suspicious of bishops, but the King had been grateful to his emissaries for their efforts. Abbot therefore found himself being enthroned as Bishop of Lichfield and Coventry in December 1609, and as Bishop of London in February 1610. A year later his appointment as Archbishop of Canterbury was announced, when he had nearly given up hope because of the death of the Earl of Dunbar. According to his secretary George Calvert, the King gave Abbot a revealing explanation: 'It is neither the respect of his learning, his wisdom, nor his sincerity (although he is well persuaded that there is none of them wanting in him) that hath made him prefer him before the rest of his fellows, but merely the recommendation of his faithful servant Dunbar that is dead, whose suit [plea] on behalf of the bishop he cannot forget, nor will not suffer [allow] to lose his intention.' To add to his favour, the King made George Abbot's brother Robert (theologically his twin) Bishop of Salisbury.

Abbot was far less interested than Bancroft in ecclesiastical administration, and his appointment made sure that there would no longer be a firm hand on the helm. He did not set eyes on Canterbury Cathedral until he had been archbishop for four years. But surprisingly, he retained something of a Calvinist conscience. In the Howard divorce case of 1613, when Andrewes did what he was told, Abbot braved the wrath of the King; he kept on repeating that he was meant to be a judge, that he must abide by the law laid down in the Bible. He kept the archbishopric, but his relationship with the King was far cooler than before.

It was while relaxing after consecrating the new chapel of Bramshill House near Reading in July 1621 that Abbot met disaster. To his horror he found that a clumsy shot from his

cross-bow had killed a deerkeeper. Characteristically the King
reassured him about the accident and a royal commission
absolved him from guilt. The incident, however, made the
Archbishop a 'man of blood' and two rising churchmen, John
Williams and William Laud, then awaiting consecration as
bishops, refused to be touched by hands so stained. The reason
which Lancelot Andrewes gave for leniency to Abbot was
unheroic: 'Brethren, be not too busy to condemn any for
Uncanonicals according to the strictness thereof, lest we render ourselves in the same condition.'

For the rest of his life the homicide discredited the
Archbishop. His advocacy of war to help the Protestants in
Germany, and of an end to the plans for a marriage treaty with
Spain, irritated the old King without making him a hero to the
Puritans. After the death of James Abbot angered the new
King by refusing to license the printing of an adulatory sermon
by a Northampton clergyman, one Robert Sibthorpe. 'Where
the word of the King is, there is power,' the preacher had
declared, 'and who may say to him, "What doest thou?" ' King
Charles certainly felt able to ask that question of Archbishop
Abbot, who was suspended from his duties for a year. Even
when he had been restored, there was no power in his words.
Everyone knew that the King was merely waiting for the death
of the morose old Calvinist – who had killed a man – in order to
make William Laud archbishop.[16]

Had Abbot resigned or been deprived immediately after the
homicide, John Williams might have been promoted to Canterbury. As he smugly wrote to the Duke of Buckingham at that
juncture, 'His Majesty hath promised me one of the best places
in this Church.' The fear of that appointment may have
reconciled Andrewes to the prospect of Abbot being restored to
his functions as archbishop, since Andrewes was one of the
many Englishmen who disapproved of Williams as a Welsh
rogue.

When John Williams lay dying in 1650, he wished that he
could be 'assured that by my preaching I had converted one
soul to God.' But he still looked back proudly over his career: 'I

---

[16] See Paul A. Welsby, *George Abbot: The Unwanted Archbishop* (London, 1962).

have passed through many places of honour and trust both in Church and State, more than any of my order in England the seventy years before.' After a spell as secretary to the Lord Chancellor, he had attracted the favour of King James. He was a handsome bachelor, a brilliant conversationalist, a man for peace and pleasure. When the Deanery of Westminster fell vacant in 1620, he seemed thoroughly suitable. More surprisingly, he also seemed suitable for an additional job when next year Francis Bacon was dismissed for corruption from the post of Lord Chancellor or 'Lord Keeper of the Great Seal'. To be sure, Williams was not a lawyer – but he was, he declared, eager to study the law, and the not-too-legal-sounding title of 'Lord Keeper' could be used. To be sure, he was not yet a bishop – but he could be made Bishop of Lincoln, and promptly was so made, without resigning as Dean of Westminster. With Abbot in disgrace, it was Bishop Williams who talked devoutly in Latin with the dying King James, who closed the eyes of his corpse, and who preached a funeral sermon never surpassed in the records of flattery. But his basic cynicism about the Church is to be seen in the advice he had given to James when his son-in-law, Frederick, had been driven out by the conquering Catholics. He had not advocated military aid or the admission of ordinary refugees from the Palatinate or Bohemia, but he had acknowledged that provision had to be made for Frederick's two sons, Prince Rupert and Prince Maurice. He had proposed that they should be placed in the bishoprics of Durham and Winchester. A sermon of his survives as an exercise in the interpretation of the passage in the gospels where it is pointed out that those who wear soft clothing live in kings' houses (whereas St John the Baptist lived in the desert). John Williams approved of this factual observation and felt no hesitation in wearing soft clothing; the rebuke delivered in the Bible, he explained, was directed at those who wore richer dress than was appropriate to their station in life.

On the death of his royal patron Bishop Williams could not hope to retain power. He had already shocked the new King by his worldliness, and he soon caused fresh displeasure by making an attempt to mediate between Charles and the House of Commons. Deprived of his high political office, he retired to live as Bishop of Lincoln. He still lived in a high style, rebuilding the bishop's palace at Buckden, educating noblemen's sons as his pages, keeping open house to visiting peers and occasionally going south to his Westminster Deanery (always to be ordered back to his diocese by the implacable King). Eventually in 1637 the indignation at the King's court exploded. Williams was condemned on trumped-up charges, deprived of almost all his wealth, and imprisoned in the Tower.

Four years later a frightened Charles, at last acknowledging his abilities, made him Archbishop of York. Had Williams been put in charge of affairs in the 1630s, his very lack of principle would presumably have helped to prevent a head-on confrontation between the King and the Puritans. He was a consistent compromiser. After Strafford's trial he advised the King to sacrifice his fallen servant to the executioner's axe, and during the civil war he advised him to make terms with Parliament – exactly the advice he had tendered at the beginning of the reign. He retired to North Wales for the duration of the war. At first he organized the area's defence in the King's interest, but later he accepted and assisted the Parliamentary victory, so that the Royalists despised him as a turncoat.

What really interested him was, it seems, prosperity – his own but also other people's, spending the money on supporting education as well as food and drink, houses and gardens. As a motive it was not magnificent, but it may have been in the nation's interests as well as his own that he had the shrewdness to see that Puritanism had to be humoured if the nation's wealth was to be preserved and increased. Although personally the opposite of every ideal which the Puritans held, he knew the strength of their creed. That was why he urged and practised compromise, and why when he had lived to see England and Wales torn apart by civil war he died in despair.[17]

---

[17] B. D. Roberts provided a sympathetic biography called *Mitre and Musket* (London, 1938).

WILLIAM LAUD

William Laud was the tenth child born in a modest home which was also a small clothing factory, in Reading. All through his life he knew that men made jokes behind his back about his lowly origins, and it gave him an inferiority complex. But he knew that he had greatness in him – and that others did not. He once came out with the devastating truth about King Charles: 'a mild and gracious prince who knew not how to be, or be made, great.'

Although he became a competent scholar at Oxford, his only substantial publication was his *Conference with Fisher the Jesuit*, designed to impress the Duke of Buckingham's mother with the Church of England's claims. To him, administration was sacred. His real contribution to Oxford was made as chancellor of the university from 1629; he was a great organizer of other men's studies, a great censor of other men's conduct, dress and haircuts. He loved to dwell on the God-given powers of kings and bishops, who together must govern Church and State. 'The King is the sun. He draws some vapours, some support, some supply, from us.' Similarly, a bishop is the successor of the apostles, deriving his authority from Christ himself. A bishop's power, Laud said at his trial, is exercised only with the King's permission; but the power itself is 'by divine apostolical right and unalterable'.

Laud was obviously a man born to be a bishop. But how was he to become one? Men did not like him. He was too inhuman, with none of the Welsh gusto for life which John Williams displayed. With a tendency to correct all those around him went a tendency to lose his temper. 'A little red-faced man' was how one socially superior enemy described him. He had to find a patron, and the necessity was such that as chaplain to the Earl of Devon he officiated at the Earl's marriage with Lady Rich, who had been divorced for adultery with him. He thus sacrificed his conscience to his ambition – although he always kept the day of the wedding, St Stephen's Day, as a fast. Later he attached himself to Buckingham, and still displayed a high ambition; as he recorded in his journal during 1625, 'In my sleep it seemed to me that the Duke of Buckingham got into my

bed, where he showed me much love'. It was a dream, however, and in reality he received relatively minor promotion –
Dean of Gloucester, Bishop of St David's, Bishop of Bath and
Wells. King James analysed his character acutely: 'He hath a
restless spirit and cannot see when matters are well, but loves
to toss and change and bring things to a pitch of reformation
floating in his own brain.' In his worried dreams he saw his
rival John Williams, nine years his junior, outstripping him.
That is one key to the character of William Laud: a man with
an itch to govern and reform other people, he was not able to be
a martinet with sufficient scope until he was made Bishop of
London at the age of fifty-five – and even then he had to wait
another five years for Canterbury on Abbot's death. He had
grown impatient.

Another key is his high Anglican churchmanship. Those
who believed that this amounted to an inner conviction of the
truth of Roman Catholicism did not begin to understand his
psychology. When in August 1633 he was given to understand
that he might hope to be a cardinal if he became a Roman
Catholic, he replied that 'somewhat dwelt within me, which
would not suffer [allow] that, till Rome were other than it is.'
His Catholicism was purely English. It was a reaction against a
long experience of the general acceptance of disorder in English churches. When in Gloucester Cathedral he had moved
the Communion table to the east end and put a rail around it,
his bishop had sworn never to set foot in the cathedral again.
During the trial of one of his opponents who accused him of
superstition (William Prynne), Laud flashed out: ' 'Tis superstition nowadays for any man to come with more reverence into
a church than a tinker and his bitch come into an ale-house.'
He had grown embittered by the contempt in which most men
held his own clerical profession. It was a contempt which, he
had to admit, often seemed to be justified. Several of the
bishops appointed by James I showed little evidence of theological or spiritual interests: the convivial poet, Corbett, for
example. One of the richest deans, Newton of Durham, was not
ordained and never saw his cathedral. But Laud hated all this
sordid confusion. Against it, his task was to wield his commission from the King and a bishop's Christ-given authority.

When at last he was appointed Archbishop of Canterbury in 1633, he wrote to Strafford: 'They which have gotten so much power in and over the Church will not let go their hold.' For a moment he was dismayed by the size of the task. But in alliance with a king far more reliable than James he showed himself determined to continue and complete Richard Bancroft's efficient, if narrow, policies. He, too, codified the Church's law, although to enact new canons he had to wait until 1640 (when the clergy could be summoned to meet in Convocation alongside Parliament). He imitated Bancroft's example of devotion to discipline and kept up pressure on other bishops to imitate him. He made full use of Bancroft's instrument, the High Commission, and above all of the older court of Star Chamber, to impose fines and other penalties on those who resisted. From his king he received stronger support than Bancroft had enjoyed; in 1638 Charles plainly told the judges to attempt no interference in the working of the ecclesiastical courts without the Archbishop's licence. Laud pursued Bancroft's policy of attempting to extract proper incomes for the clergy out of the laity, meanwhile defying any squire who attempted to cheat his parson. He secured the suppression of a group of London Puritans (the 'Feoffees for Impropriations') who were found to be buying up the rector's tithes in parishes and using them for the benefit of their favoured ministers; and he did his utmost to end the Puritan patronage of 'lecturers' in the parishes by insisting on the rights of bishops. No man was to be ordained merely to be a lecturer, and no existing clergyman was to become or remain one without the bishop's licence.

Such a reassertion of a bishop's authority caused widespread alarm among Puritans who under George Abbot had forgotten what it felt like to be harried. No more than Bancroft did Laud suspend large numbers of clergy from their duties because of their nonconformity; there were fewer than a hundred such cases in the whole of England during his time as archbishop. Nor was Laud exceptionally savage in voting for the physical mutilation of the authorities' boldest critics. Although we are shocked that he could record complacently in his diary the whipping, ear-cropping, nose-slitting and ten-year imprisonment of a fellow theologian, Dr Alexander Leighton, who had written a book against the bishops, it is fair to remember that the Puritans were to show themselves stern censors and executioners when in power.

Laud, despite his enemies' propaganda, did not admire tyranny. Indeed, he once told Lord Saye and Sele that 'my very soul abominates' Calvinism – 'for it makes God, the God of all mercy, to be the most fierce and unreasonable tyrant in the world.' However, he certainly made many enemies. The clamour of the 1640s for the removal of the bishops and their whole system, 'root and branch', showed how deeply the Puritans had become alarmed by the activities of this meddlesome archbishop and of fellow Arminians such as Richard Neile (successively at Lincoln, Durham, Winchester and York) or Matthew Wren (who followed Francis White, also an Arminian, both at Norwich and at Ely). As early as 1625 Laud had drawn up a list of the prominent clergy for the Duke of Buckingham, branding his enemies 'P' for Puritan and his friends 'O' for 'Orthodox' – as if Calvinism had not been the Church of England's orthodoxy ever since Elizabeth's day. Now many preachers were afraid that 'true religion' would soon be banished from Laud's church.

Their alarm was shared by many gentlemen (including some MPs who were to take the King's side in the civil war). They feared that the claims of the clergy for more tithes, if supported by the King, might at length lead to some action being taken at the expense of the laity – a prospect which everyone thought had been banished for ever at the time of the Reformation. There seemed to be a threat to many lay possessions in the movement of opinion expressed by one Norfolk squire, Sir Henry Spelman, who on religious grounds publicly attacked the possession of tithes by laymen – and who was compiling an unpublishable book showing the fates of laymen who had taken over the ownership of lands rightly belonging to the monasteries. It seemed ominous that Laud sided against the gentry, in favour of the common people, in several local disputes brought before one of the royal courts or commissions on which he sat. He thought it the noblest part of the work of the King's council to defend the people against the 'private ends' of rich men; and when he was taken from Lambeth

Palace to prison in March 1641, after his impeachment by the Commons for high treason, his diary recorded his pride that 'hundreds of my poor neighbours stood there and prayed for my safety.' Thus he encouraged the gentry to fear that Church and King were lining up against them.[18]

As his power and ambition increased, Laud sent many agents to hold visitations on his behalf – even in Lincoln Cathedral, despite legal action by Bishop Williams. He took almost as keen an interest in the ecclesiastical affairs of the province of York, of Scotland and of Ireland, as in his own province of Canterbury. He made what efforts he could to curb the religious deviations of the English settlers in the Netherlands or America. And especially after the Earl of Portland's death in 1635, Laud's influence also penetrated many political affairs; he once claimed that 'a bishop may preach the Gospel more publicly and to far greater edification in a court of judicature, or at a council-table, where great men are met together to draw things to an issue, than many preachers . . .' He used this pulpit. More than anyone else he seems to have inspired the flow of detailed orders to magistrates about the relief of the poor and other local duties. The climax of his influence came in 1636, when at his suggestion the King appointed Bishop Juxon of London as Lord Treasurer. The clear implication was that only a clergyman would be sufficiently honest. 'No churchman had it since Henry VIII's time,' Laud wrote in his diary. 'I pray God to bless him to carry it so that the Church may have honour and the King and the State contentment by it. And now if the Church will not hold up themselves under God, I can do no more.'

All these activities, wise or foolish, sprang not only out of personal ambition but also out of a genuine love of the Church of England. While he was Bishop of London Laud achieved the restoration of St Paul's Cathedral, where the spire had been destroyed by lightning in 1561 and where the fabric had been visibly decaying for centuries; and to the repaired Gothic cathedral was added a giant classical portico by Inigo Jones, the gift of the King. While Archbishop of Canterbury Laud led

---

[18] See Christopher Hill, *Economic Problems of the Church*, pp. 245–447.

a campaign to get the surplice worn decently as the clerical uniform; to get the holy table fenced off and reverenced as a sacred altar; to get men's heads bowed humbly at the name of Jesus. When he was brought to trial in 1644 after three years in prison, he defended his record with such dignity and acuteness that the impeachment for treason had to be dropped and a simple Bill of Attainder introduced. When he was about to be executed in January 1645, he repeated the essence of his self-defence: 'I was born and baptized in the bosom of the Church of England established by law. In that profession I have lived; and in that I come now to die.' At greater leisure he had held up his proud vision of his Church during his learned argument with the Jesuit Fisher in 1622. 'To believe the Scripture and the Creeds, to believe these in the sense of the ancient primitive Church, to receive the four great General Councils, to believe all points of doctrine generally received as fundamental in the Church of Christ, is a faith in which to live and die cannot but give salvation.' Basically this pride in the Church of England was what was puzzling about William Laud. It would have been puzzling and alarming to many, even if he had taken more trouble to conciliate those who disliked his autocratic manner.

'We begin to live here in the Church Triumphant', wrote James Howell in 1635. Next summer the King visited Oxford, partly to see the newly completed Canterbury Quadrangle in St John's College where Laud had been President. If Laud had been capable of enjoyment, he would have enjoyed this festivity at the peak of his power. As it was, he confided to his diary his pleasure that after the feast which he had provided for the court only two spoons had disappeared.[19]

What judgement is fair on these bishops?

In Bancroft and Laud the Church of England possessed administrators who worked tirelessly for its welfare, narrowly conceived; yet their policy was not in the Church's long-term interests. They were so proudly allied with the monarchy, and

---

[19] See H. R. Trevor-Roper, *Archbishop Laud* (with a new Preface, London, 1962), and E. C. E. Bourne's case for the defence, *The Anglicanism of William Laud* (London, 1947). Charles Carlton, *Archbishop William Laud* (London, 1987), is balanced. Margaret Steig studied the diocese of Bath and Wells as *Laud's Laboratory* (London, 1982).

so provocatively full of the sense of a bishop's power, as to arouse hatred. Their activism, their insistence on uniformity, increased the likelihood that both kings and bishops would be pulled down by the vengeance of the Puritans whom they had alienated. The pity was that among the bishops only Bancroft and Laud were major figures who combined firm ambitions for the Church along with the royal favour. In Lancelot Andrewes the Church of England possessed a theologian greater in intellectual and spiritual stature than any of the archbishops – but he was incapable of working out a policy, for he depended on the corrupting James.

None of these bishops can by himself explain why the Church of England now commanded the devotion of its members to an extent not seen under Elizabeth I. To learn why, we must turn to three great poets.

JOHN DONNE

John Donne, Dean of St Paul's, wept while he preached in memory of Magdalen, Lady Danvers, one Sunday in 1627. She had been his friend for more than twenty years and by her first marriage was the mother of his fellow poet, George Herbert. That sermon's themes were to remain at the centre of all that he said until he preached the morbidly magnificent 'Death's Duel' shortly before his own death. He spoke of her devout life: she had said Morning and Evening Prayer daily with her family; and of her death-bed, 'as quiet as her grave'; and of her lovely body: 'that body which now, whilst I speak, is mouldering and crumbling into less and less dust, and so hath some motion, though no life'; and of her resurrection: 'that body at last shall have her last expectation satisfied, and dwell bodily, with that Righteousness, in these new Heavens and new Earth, for ever, and ever, and ever, and infinite, and super-infinite evers.'

Death is the theme which always makes Donne the preacher live. For much of the time, a twentieth-century reader can study his sermons without finding them powerful. Many of these words are Latin; clearly the Vulgate Bible in Latin is the version which has formed the preacher's mind. The theology or morality being conveyed, although with touches of Calvinism as in its insistence on God's choice of the elect, often seems to be essentially medieval, and behind the Middle Ages lie the Fathers such as Augustine or Tertullian, here imitated both in substance and in style. His friend Henry King, later Bishop of Chichester, recalled how Donne 'three days before his death delivered into my hands those excellent sermons of his now made public . . . together with which (as his best legacy) he gave me all his sermon-notes, and his other papers, containing an extract of near fifteen hundred authors.' In those discourses – so arduously prepared by a week's work, learned by heart so as to be delivered not read, and polished up further for the printer – the biblical text was expounded in a tradition which had been thought appropriate when addressing well-educated Englishmen over a thousand years.

Inevitably a modern public has altered in its expectations of a sermon and in its powers of endurance, but Donne's sermons still come alive when they approach death, 'the most inglorious and contemptible vilification, the most deadly and peremptory nullification of man, that we can consider.' He kept his hearers awake by images as alarming as the plague which often surrounded them in London. 'The Holy Ghost', he maintained, 'is an eloquent author, a vehement and an abundant author, but yet not luxuriant'; and that was his own style as he tolled the bell for those who, like himself, were about to die. 'All our life is but a going out to the place of execution, to death', he once pointed out. 'Now was there ever any man seen to sleep in the cart . . .?'

It is strange that Donne's style should have been called 'metaphysical'. Samuel Johnson popularized the description in the eighteenth century, but it surely ought to have been abandoned by later critics who have been, on the whole, more enthusiastic. Intellectual Donne always was. He despised the escapism of previous English poets (such as Spenser) into the ordered prettiness of a dream world. He always preferred to stimulate thought by hinting at the logic in some extraordinary association of images drawn from daily life (he wrote a poem about the flea crawling on his mistress). As has been observed, in true metaphysical poetry 'the intellectual parallel, or the recondite image, expresses awareness of a world in which the separate and apparently unrelated parts strangely echo one another.'[20] And Donne as he made these associations was often 'witty', pouring out paradoxes which combine the colloquial with the florid, the familiar with the audacious, the passionate with the learned. In his solemn 'Hymn to God the Father', set to music and often sung as an anthem in St Paul's Cathedral in his presence, he met his God with a pun ('thou hast done'). But he was never 'metaphysical' in the sense of being superior to physical reality. The great Samuel Johnson (who believed that genuine 'intercourse between God and the human soul' could not be the material of poetry) was completely wrong to say of the 'metaphysical poets' that 'to show their learning was their whole endeavour'. Answering the charge that he was always simply an egotist, Dame Helen Gardner has rightly claimed that 'the feeling that the subject is greater than the treatment, and the poem more important than the poet, goes well with the religious sense of the importance of the given'; and answering the charge that he was too intellectual, T. S. Eliot made his famous observation that 'a thought to Donne was an experience; it modified his sensibility.'[21]

In Donne's poetry, as in all 'metaphysical' poetry, three essential paradoxes are always present – the poet is acutely self-conscious, yet the poem does matter more; the poet is witty, yet never remote from important reality (Donne wrote of 'the feeling brain and the naked thinking heart'); the tone is conversational, but the imagery is unconventional because a strenuous effort is being made to experience and to communicate a new revelation of reality. It is, indeed, clear that Donne felt that writing poetry was like making love. He believed in love's disclosure of eternity:

> Love, all alike, no season knows, nor clime,
> Nor hours, days, months, which are the rags of time.

---

[20] Joan Bennett, *Five Metaphysical Poets* (Cambridge, 1964), p. 76.
[21] Helen Gardner, *Religion and Literature* (London, 1971), p. 193; T. S. Eliot, *Selected Essays*, pp. 281–91.

But love must take flesh:

> Love's mysteries in souls do grow,
> But yet the body is his book.

For such a man, although he wrote much about souls, complete
joy could never be disembodied. The actual body which the
worms have eaten, leaving behind only dust, must be raised.
When he prepares for his own death, he compares with
map-makers the doctors poring over his body; for his present
body, which may soon die, is only a feeble representation of the
body he will discover when he has died ('A Hymn to God, my
God, in my Sickness'). So this preacher of the resurrection can
celebrate the final glory of a woman's body with a rapture no
less physical than the ecstasy of Jack Donne the erotic poet:

> Licence my roving hands and let them go,
> Before, behind, between, above, below . . .
> To teach thee, I am naked first; why then,
> What need'st thou have more covering than a man?

A vividly imagined resurrection, triumphing over a vividly
imagined death 'for super-infinite evers' is what awakens us;
and we ask what life had given the preacher such a Gospel.

John Donne (1572–1631) was an Elizabethan man-about-
town who became a preacher only in his forties. Through his
mother he was descended from a leading Recusant family. Sir
Thomas More was his great-grand-uncle, and, when John was
only two years old, a grand-uncle had been hanged as a priest.
Two of his uncles, both Oxford scholars of great promise, had
passed their lives as exiled Jesuits. He had been unable to take
a degree because it would have meant taking the oath about the
Queen and the Church. His brother Henry had died of fever in
prison when he was twenty-four; he had been sheltering a
priest. John Donne had all that motivation to master intellectually the whole field in dispute, with results to be seen in his
anti-Jesuit book of 1610, *Pseudo-Martyr*. At the end of the book
he recalled how 'I have been ever kept awake in a meditation of
martyrdom, by being derived from such a stock and race.' His
intensely visual imagination always did belong to the same
world as the *Spiritual Exercises* of the Jesuits, where the pains of

hell and the pleasures of heaven were to be savoured sensually.

The passion with which he turned to experiments with women, and to experiments in verse celebrating his conquests, was keenly felt. Being (as he put it) 'love's martyr' was for him an alternative to the life and death of a Recusant. It was a worldly path; had he been obeying the morality instilled into him as a boy he would have remained a Roman Catholic. Love for him did not mean sighs about a lack of communication with the beloved, as had almost always been the posture of previous poets of love. It meant sex. But he still used his brain. Even when propelled into a girl's bed by simple lust he remained the self-conscious intellectual: his love poetry never portrays the girl but always examines his own experience. And a part of his brain, the part surviving from his boyhood, told him that all this was emptiness. During the very years when he could sincerely write 'I can love both fair and brown', he was seriously struggling to see what was at the top of the mountain obscured by the clouds of religious controversy:

> On a huge hill
> Cragged and steep, Truth stands, and he that will
> Reach her about must, and about must go.

And sexual intercourse could itself be thought about in religious terms:

> We die and rise the same, and prove
> Mysterious by this love.

In the end, he explored sex most fully through a marriage contracted in defiance of the conventions. He sailed as a gentleman-adventurer with Essex and Ralegh in their expeditions of 1596–97 during the war against Spain, and with this proof of his patriotic manliness entered the service of the Lord Keeper, Sir Thomas Egerton. By then he must have conformed to the Church of England. He seemed all set for a rich career when he fell in love with a niece of the wife of Sir Thomas, and married her secretly although she was still a minor. Sir Thomas dismissed him, and thirteen years of poverty followed. Letters and poems survive which show how unheroically he could fawn in his efforts to obtain employment. A book on suicide (not published until 1644) is other evidence of his depression, increased by much illness; 'Whensoever any affliction assails me methinks I have the keys of my prison in mine own hand and no remedy presents itself so soon to my heart as mine own sword.'

These years were, however, not wasted. His suffering gave him a sympathy lacking in the egotistical poems of his youth. His marriage with Ann was an education in fidelity and gave him many consolations: 'We had not one another at so cheap a rate that we should ever be weary of one another,' he reminded her after thirteen years of marriage. It may be said that she converted him to true love, in contrast with the cynicism of some of the early love-poems too closely modelled on the morals as well as the poetry of Romans such as Ovid. And *The Divine Poems* show that this deepening love of a faithful woman helped him to grow in the love of God. J. B. Leishman rightly draws attention to 'a continuous progress in seriousness, and even in devotional religiousness, co-existing, in a manner that many modern readers may find baffling and even, at times, disconcerting, with an unregenerate wit and worldliness and willingness to flatter the great'.[22]

In the damp study of a cottage at Mitcham, surrounded by squalling children, he became one of the most learned theologians of his age. He considered death itself in a learned way: the book on suicide was as scholarly as *Pseudo-Martyr*. When as early as 1607 he was urged by a friend who had just become Dean of Gloucester to become a priest in the Church of England, he refused because he felt unworthy. He knew that his reputation was as the author of poems which were pornographic by the standards of the day: 'some irregularities of my life have been so visible to some men . . .' But in 1612 he wrote to the King's favourite, the Earl of Somerset: 'I have resolved to make my profession divinity.' Three years later he finally was ordained, because he was persuaded by James I; he said so on the epitaph which he composed for his own grave. The King had steadily refused to place him as a civil servant; instead he had made promises about prospects in the Church. As Donne

---

[22] J. B. Leishman, *The Monarch of Wit* (London, 1951), p. 268.

was later to preach: 'When I asked perchance a stone, he gave
me bread; when I asked perchance a scorpion, he gave me a fish.'

When in the pulpit he denounced sins he knew what he was
talking about, and most members of the congregation knew
that he knew. When he preached at court he addressed men
who relished – or knew of – the witty gusto of his love poems,
passed from hand to hand in manuscript. When he addressed
the lawyers of Lincoln's Inn, as he did almost every week in the
period 1616–21, he spoke to men some of whom had enjoyed
the 1590s with him. 'Forgive me my crying sins, and my
whispering sins,' he once pleaded in the pulpit, 'sins of uncharitable hate, and sins of unchaste love.' He valued
preaching because it enabled him to communicate the Gospel
of forgiveness to others. 'What a coronation is our taking of
orders,' he said, 'and what an inthronization is the coming up
into a pulpit, where God invests his servants with his ordinance
. . . *woe be unto thee if thou do not preach*, and then enables him to
preach peace, mercy, consolation, to the whole congregation!'
But his prayer was all the more infectious for being still frankly
a penitent's, even an amateur's, prayer: 'a memory of yesterday's pleasures, a fear of tomorrow's dangers, a straw under
my knee, a noise in mine ear, a light in mine eye, an anything, a
nothing, a fancy, a Chimera in my brain, troubles my prayer.'
His faith was all the more touching because, as he confessed in
his 'Hymn to God the Father' (written when he had nearly died
of fever),

> I have a sin of fear, that when I have spun
> My last thread, I shall perish on the shore.

He knew how to preach to fellow sinners from the brink of
eternity, from the presence of the holy and immortal God; 'all
knowledge that begins not and ends not with his glory is but a
giddy, but a vertiginous circle, but an elaborate and exquisite
ignorance.' But the sense of sinful egotism, of sensual frailty, of
guilt (in, for example, the *Devotions* which he wrote during a
convalescence) went so deep that he knew that for himself the
coming of God into a human life must be as physical as sex:

> Batter my heart, three-person'd God; for you
> As yet but knock, breathe, shine and seek to mend;

> That I may rise, and stand, o'erthrow me, and bend
> Your force, to break, blow, burn and make me new . . .
> Take me to you, imprison me, for I
> Except you enthrall me, never shall be free,
> Nor ever chaste, except you ravish me.

What finally turned his mind to God was, it seems, not his ordination in 1615 but the death of his wife two years later. He grieved so intensely that he seemed 'crucified'. She was aged thirty-three and she died of exhaustion, a week after giving birth to her twelfth child, still-born. He drew the conclusion not that it had been wrong to inflict so many pregnancies on her but that it was always foolish to hope that any earthly happiness could be more than fleeting. Her death was the price he had to pay for the granting of his prayer:

> I turn my back to thee, but to receive
> Corrections, till thy mercies bid thee leave.
> O think me worth thine anger, punish me,
> Burn off my rusts, and my deformity,
> Restore thine image, so much, by thy grace,
> That thou may'st know me, and I'll turn my face.

It was only when he had fully turned his face to God after burying Ann that he saw the true pattern of his previous life. He was never totally ashamed of that life; he kept a portrait of himself as a melancholy young lover in his Deanery and bequeathed it to a friend in his will. For his whole life, he now saw, had been God's wooing of him. His days had not been destitute of achievement – and, as he once declaimed, 'to have something to do, to do it, and then to rejoice in having done it, to embrace a calling, to perform the duties of that calling, to joy and rest in the peaceful testimony of having done so; this is Christianly done, Christ did it; angelically done, angels do it; godly done, God does it.' But his real achievement had been to gain his convictions about the 'providence and goodness' of God and the resurrection to come. So he assured a friend shortly before his death, adding: 'I am therefore full of inexpressible joy and shall die in peace.'

All that discovery had to be made before John Donne could stand in the pulpit of St Paul's Cathedral on the evening of

Christmas Day 1624 and speak about a monarch more bounti-
ful than James VI of Scotland and I of England. 'If some king
of the earth have so large an extent of dominion, in north and
south, as that he hath winter and summer together in his
dominions, so large an extent east and west as that he hath day
and night together in his dominions, much more hath God
joined mercy and judgement together. He brought light of
darkness, not out of a lesser light; he can bring thy summer out
of winter though thou have no spring. Though in the ways of
fortune, or understanding, or conscience, thou have been
benighted till now, wintered and frozen, clouded and eclipsed,
damped and benumbed, smothered and stupefied till now,
now God comes to thee, not as in the dawning of the day, not as
in the bud of spring, but as the sun at noon to illustrate all
shadows, as the sheaves in harvest to fill all penuries. All
occasions invite his mercies, and all times are his seasons.'[23]

GEORGE HERBERT

Donne sent a copy of his personal seal with a poem to George
Herbert; and the other poet, then twenty years his junior,
repaid the compliment with three Latin epigrams. It is, however, clear that Herbert's own poetry was deeply indebted to
Donne and that their friendship went far deeper than this, their
only recorded exchange. We know that they were fellow guests
in a Chelsea house in 1625, when George Herbert was staying
with his mother and John Donne was escaping from the
plague.

In many ways Herbert resembled Donne. He remembered
his ambition for an active life:

---

[23] R. C. Bald assembled the facts in *John Donne : A Life* (Oxford, 1970). *John Donne: Essays in Celebration*, ed. A. J. Smith (London, 1972), and John Carey, *John Donne: Life, Mind and Art* (London, 1981), are the best of the voluminous criticism, although Professor Carey fails to prove his case that Donne's preaching was 'resolute self-deception'.

> Whereas my birth and spirit rather took
>   The way that takes the town,
> Thou didst betray me to a ling'ring book,
>   And wrap me in a gown.

'The Pearl' recalls at greater length the lures of the ways of
learning, honour and pleasure; and like Donne, Herbert could
use his learning to flatter King James. The two men's hesitations over a priest's life were also similar:

> Now I am here, what thou wilt do with me
> None of my books will show.

And in the end Herbert used the same 'witty' style in devotion
to the Christ of Easter:

> Awake, my lute, and struggle for thy part
>   With all thy art:
> The cross taught all wood to resound his name
>   Who bore the same;
> His stretched sinews taught all strings what key
> Is best to celebrate this most high day.

But Herbert's life and poetry were far more than imitations of
Donne. His mother was not a Recusant but a rich and accomplished lady, Donne's patron. Whereas Cambridge took much
persuading to award Donne an honorary doctorate despite the
King's command, that university delighted to honour George
Herbert, who was so outstanding in his classical scholarship
that he was appointed to lecture on the classics and to compose
official letters and addresses as Public Orator. In contrast with
Donne's notoriety as a poet of profligacy, Herbert from an
early age accepted his devout mother's guidance. He sent two
sonnets to her avowing his dedication to sacred poetry while he
was an undergraduate; as early as 1618 he described theology
as 'the platform of my future life'; and he made a respectable
match for Jane, the daughter of a proud Wiltshire family, when
he was aged thirty-six. In the second half of the 1620s Herbert
ceased to live in Cambridge, and, like Donne before 1615,
nursed hopes of employment in the service of the State; but
being so well connected, he did not need to stoop to Donne's
level by begging for favour or money. In 1624 he was a Member

of Parliament. The decisive question of Donne's life concerned the nature of love, and when he married he did not hesitate to throw away ambition for love. In contrast, the struggle for Herbert was against ambition, and it was the slow conquest of ambition that was the making of him as a saint and as a poet. He became famous because he renounced fame.

It shows the difference between the two men that Herbert was eventually willing to embrace the life of a country parson – whereas Donne, while drawing the incomes of rectories in Kent and Bedfordshire, went on living in or near London with no qualms of conscience. Once Herbert had made his great decision he adopted a preaching style much simpler than Donne's, without any allusion to the learning of his Cambridge years (or so we are told – no sermons by him have survived). He became every inch the priest, the mediator between God and the parish, the devoted pastor who reminded his people of man's calling to be 'the world's high priest'.

With the difference in the characters and the sermons of the two men went a difference as poets. It is not that Herbert was really as spontaneous as he can appear. A manuscript discovered in 1874 shows his poetry growing and being revised, the process almost certainly beginning well before his ordination. The real difference in the two men's art was that Herbert was a natural believer, while Donne was a natural sceptic. It is because Herbert has the supreme capacity to articulate faith that the editor of an anthology such as *The New Oxford Book of Christian Verse* (1981) finds himself testing poems by this question: 'Does it deserve to appear between the same covers as Herbert's "The Collar" or his "Church-monuments"?'

In Herbert's poems of struggle the lament is not for the loss of faith but for the temporary loss of religious emotion due to worldliness:

> But as I rav'd and grew more fierce and wild
>   At every word,
> Methoughts I heard one calling, *Child!*
> And I replied, *My Lord*.

The acceptance of 'my Lord' is ultimately inevitable because his invitation was understood long ago. Herbert's life was in the poem given the place of honour at the end of *The Temple*:

> Love made me welcome; yet my soul drew back,
>   Guilty of dust and sin.
> But quick-ey'd Love, observing me grow slack
>   From my first entrance in,
> Drew near to me, sweetly questioning
>   If I lack'd anything . . .

With all Herbert's delight in beauty went a religious hunger which nothing in this world could satisfy:

> Sweet spring, full of sweet days and roses,
> A box where sweets compacted lie;
> My music shows ye have your closes,
>   And all must die.
>
> Only a sweet and virtuous soul,
> Like season'd timber, never gives;
> But though the whole world turn to coal,
>   Then chiefly lives.

The joy found in his life and celebrated in his poems finds a very clear centre in the person of Christ, as in his long poem 'The Sacrifice'. It was his habit to speak of 'Jesus my Master'. And this joy provides the 'elixir' which redeems the most obscure drudgery:

> Who sweeps a room as for thy laws
>   Makes that and th' action fine.

It makes the Church 'shout' with psalms and makes the poet forget any 'tempests' so effectively that we do not know exactly why he waited until 1630 before becoming a priest:

> And now in age I bud again,
> After so many deaths I live and write;
>   I once more smell the dew and rain,
> And relish versing: O, my only Light,
>   It cannot be
>   That I am he
> On whom thy tempests fell all night.

Herbert was a parish priest for less than three years. He did not live in poverty; his will showed that he employed six domestic servants and two assistant curates. But before his death in 1633 he found time to add to, and revise, *The Temple*; to repair his church and rectory; to educate three orphaned nieces in his home; to overcome various illnesses; and to befriend his three hundred parishioners. His energy also led him to write notes about the duties of a country parson, it seems mainly in order to bring into focus his meditations about his duties. This little book published in 1652 as *A Priest to the Temple*. 'A pastor,' it began, 'is the deputy of Christ for the reducing of man to the obedience of God'; indeed, 'the country parson is in God's stead to his parish.' 'The country parson is exceeding exact in his life, being holy . . .'; indeed, 'the country parson's library is a holy life.' But the pastor must commend his authority by a holiness which country folk can understand, 'because country people live hardly, and therefore as feeling their own sweat.' So the priest needs temperance, prayerfulness, humility, hospitality and courtesy. And his charity must be practical: 'the country parson desires to be all to his parish, not only a pastor but a lawyer also, and a physician.' It was a revolutionary vision of the work of a country priest – work which all through English history had not been thought fit for a gentleman. The little book was, as he said, only 'a mark to aim at'; but it encouraged many others to have the same aim.

In real life Herbert was by no means the Laudian portrayed by Izaak Walton when he published a short *Life* of him in 1670. His patron was Laud's rival, John Williams, and he never fell out with his own brother Edward (Lord Herbert of Cherbury), who was definitely unorthodox in his religious thought. When examining *The Temple*, the Vice-Chancellor of Cambridge was startled to find how enthusiastic about the Puritan migration to America Herbert had remained despite his disappointment over the first colony in Virginia:

> Religion stands on tip-toe in our land,
> Ready to pass to the American strand.

But Herbert was certainly as devoted to the Church of England as ever Laud was. To him it was 'the mean' between the 'painted shrines' of Rome and the disorder of Protestantism:

> But, dearest Mother, what those miss,
> The mean, thy praise and glory is,
>   And long may be.

> Blessed be God, whose love it was
> To double-moat thee with his grace,
>   And none but thee.

In two of his most famous poems, he recorded what he felt when at worship in the Church of England:

> Church-bells beyond the stars heard, the soul's blood,
> The land of spices; something understood.
>
> Come, my Way, my Truth, my Life . . .
> Come, my Light, my Feast, my Strength . . .
> Come, my Joy, my Love, my Heart. . . .[24]

One of his closest friends, Nicholas Ferrar, had George Herbert's poems prepared for publication in his manor house at Little Gidding near Cambridge. Ferrar was disappointed over the Virginian colony, in which he had invested heavily. At Little Gidding a mixed community of men and women, his family and friends, lived somewhat like a monastery (the 'Arminian nunnery' was how it was denounced in a Puritan pamphlet) – reciting the whole Psalter once a day in hourly services to which different groups came, praying also through the night, practising crafts, visiting the sick and the poor. Ferrar died in 1637 and the community was dissolved in 1646. It was a curious experiment. Ferrar was a deacon not a priest, so that the Eucharist was never at the centre of this community's life; and it was too dependent on his wealth. But Little Gidding had brought the monastic ideal back to the Church of England, just as George Herbert's own experiment at Bremerton had brought back the highest idealism of the parish priest.[25]

---

[24] Studies include Rosemond Tuve, *A Reading of George Herbert* (London, 1952); Margaret Bottrall, *George Herbert* (London, 1954); Joseph H. Summers, *George Herbert: His Religion and His Art* (London, 1954); Helen Verdler, *The Poetry of George Herbert* (Cambridge, Mass., 1975); Amy M. Charles, *A Life of George Herbert* (Ithaca, N.Y., 1977); Kenneth Mason, *George Herbert, Priest and Poet* (Oxford, 1980).

[25] See A. L. Maycock, *Nicholas Ferrar of Little Gidding* (London, 1938); *The Ferrar Papers*, ed. B. Blackstone (Cambridge, 1938); *Conversations at Little Gidding*, ed. A. M. Williams (Cambridge, 1970).

HENRY VAUGHAN

Henry Vaughan paid George Herbert the tribute of very close imitation – in technique, in images, in direct quotations, even in his titles. In his Preface to the second part of *Silex Scintillans*, dated 1654, he paid him another tribute by writing about the stream of 'idle or sensual' poems produced by worldly 'wits' and adding this: 'the first that with any effectual success attempted a diversion of this foul and overflowing stream was the blessed man, Mr George Herbert, whose holy life and verse gained many pious converts (of whom I am the least).'

What Vaughan seems to mean is that Herbert's poetry helped him to see that his own direct apprehension of God in the beauty of nature could be connected with traditional Christianity. He was not always orthodox; he was influenced by the seventeenth-century revival of interest in the ancient 'Hermetic' books with their occult lore. Fascinated by the promise of the transformation of matter through alchemy, and by the prospect of the deification of man through the knowledge of God, both he and his twin brother Thomas (a clergyman) wrote or translated books in this esoteric tradition. But he also developed the ability to be conventionally devout like Herbert. His mysticism was in the end not 'nature-mysticism', meaning pantheism; it was the discovery of the Church's God. Indeed, the great poetry about nature arose simultaneously with the experience of a conversion to a full Christian faith – and died down as the excitement of the religious conversion faded. Vaughan seems to have found a quiet happiness by work as a translator 'in his sickness and retirement' and by practising as a country doctor, but his poetic silence from the enlarged *Silex Scintillans* in 1655 to his death in 1695 was broken only by one not very impressive book, in 1678.

We know very little for certain about the decisive years of his life, but in 1673 he told John Aubrey that his ambitions as a student of law in London had been 'wholly frustrated' by the 'sudden eruption' of the civil war. It seems that his health was damaged by his service in the Royalist army. He saw friends killed and their cause defeated, and about 1645 he crept back to the very lovely and remote valley of the Usk in Breconshire where he had been a boy and where his father was still a small landowner. There, in 1646–47, he prepared two volumes of inferior verse, feebly imitating Donne. In 1648 he was grief-stricken by a brother's death.

All this heartbreak was his making as a great poet. It caused him to cry when not yet thirty years of age:

> They are all gone into the world of light!
>   And I alone sit ling'ring here . . .
> I see them walking in an air of glory,
>   Whose light doth trample on my days:
> My days, which are at best but dull and hoary,
>   Mere glimmering and decays . . .
>
> Dear, beauteous death! the Jewel of the Just,
>   Shining nowhere, but in the dark . . .

But as the 1640s turned into the 1650s he gained the sense that the dead were, after all, alive and near:

> But these all night,
> Like candles, shed
> Their beams and light
> Us into bed.
> They are – indeed – our pillar fires
>   Seen as we go;
> They are that City's shining spires
>   We travel to.

Above all, he gained the sense that God was alive and near. The return of spring in the familiar valley brought back memories of the blessedness of childhood, but also hinted at a future with 'bright shoots of everlastingness'. In his 'Regeneration' he was another young Moses, awestruck by the burning bush:

> The unthrift sun shot vital gold,
>   A thousand pieces;
> And heaven its azure did unfold
>   Chequer'd with snowy fleeces;
> The air was all in spice,
>   And every bush
> A garland wore; thus fed my eyes,
>   But all the ear lay hush.

After all his misery he had found the God worshipped by nature:

O joys! infinite sweetness! with what flowers,
And shoots of glory, my soul breaks, and buds! . . .
     The rising winds,
     And falling springs,
     Birds, beasts, all things
Adore him in their kinds.
     Thus all is hurl'd
In sacred hymns and order, the great chime
And symphony of nature. Prayer is
     The world in tune . . .

This is the God in whom is 'a deep but dazzling darkness', the God who is great beyond all human imagination:

I saw Eternity the other night,
Like a great Ring of pure and endless light,
     And calm, as it was bright;
And round beneath it, Time, in hours, days, years,
     Driven by the spheres,
Like a vast shadow moved; in which the world
And all her train were hurl'd . . .

But this God is also the God of the Bible, the God of the Church, the God who saves men who need salvation, the God who in the poem just quoted offers another ring, the bridegroom's ring for his bride. He is the God who comes in Christ:

He is thy gracious friend
     And (O my soul awake!)
Did in pure love descend
     To die here for thy sake.
If thou canst get but thither,
     There grows the flower of peace,
The rose that cannot wither,
     Thy fortress, and thy ease.
Leave then thy foolish ranges;
     For none can thee secure,
But One who never changes,
     Thy God, thy life, thy cure.[26]

[26] Studies include E. C. Pettet, *Of Paradise and Light* (Cambridge, 1960); R. A. Durr, *On the Mystical Poetry of Henry Vaughan* (Cambridge, Mass., 1962); F. E. Hutchinson, *Henry Vaughan: A Life and Interpretation* (revised, Oxford, 1971).

CHAPTER SEVEN

THE COUNTER-REFORMATION

TWO ENGLISHMEN AND ROME

Many Englishmen could not feel that the Church of England was a fully satisfactory home for the new vitality of Christian faith and dedication in the first half of the seventeenth century. The Church depended too obviously on the personal whims of the Stuart kings, as in the previous half-century it had depended on the personality of Elizabeth I. That, as we have seen, was the fatal defect in the teaching and the work of its ablest bishops. The Established Church did not attract enough idealists to match the heroism of Recusants and Puritans. Even Donne and Herbert were slow to respond. It did not offer a clear creed or a strong discipline, despite royal proclamations ordering strict adherence to the Prayer Book and the 'literal' acceptance of the Thirty-Nine Articles. While its leaders disagreed quietly or openly about the precise mixture of Catholicism and Calvinism that might be held by theologians, its laity often went their own ways. It was a sign of lay laxity that in the middle of the 1650s Henry Vaughan married his deceased wife's sister, contrary to the Church's rules. In an age of ardent faith the Church of England often seemed out of place. It gave a dismaying impression of being a ramshackle department of the State, riddled with abuses, incoherent in its spiritual life, unable to command men's deepest loyalties despite the Laudian rally and the raptures of Donne, Herbert and Vaughan.

Two lives help to show the appeal of the Roman Catholic Counter-Reformation.

When made Bishop of Gloucester at the age of forty-three, Godfrey Goodman hoped for promotion to a wealthier see and when such a see presented itself in the shape of Hereford in 1633 he was so confident that he had secured it that he packed his furniture – only to have to unpack. To his friends he now 'showed his discontentment'. In 1636 he got in touch with Panzani the papal agent to the royal court, who reported to Rome: 'The Bishop of Gloucester . . . says the Divine Office according to the Roman Breviary and reads the Martyrology daily . . . He wanted to have an Italian priest in his house, who would be prepared to live with him *incognito* . . .' But the authorities in Rome were cautious, since Goodman was not willing to abandon his bishopric. To a friend at this time he said that 'the religion of England is more remiss than that of Rome, but Catholic it is'. He refused to subscribe to Laud's new canons, presumably because they included an attack on the 'gross superstition of Popery', but his temporary imprisonment for this offence did not save him from being impeached for treason together with the other bishops. He spent much of 1642 in the Tower near Laud's cell – although they never spoke. On his release he fled, like John Williams, back to his native Wales. The manuscript of the *Church History* which was to have been his *magnum opus* was destroyed in the pillaging of his home. At length he grew intolerably bored and in 1652 removed himself to a house in the churchyard of St Margaret's, Westminster, where he was to be buried. Although he had been forced to sell most of his books 'to buy bread', before his death in 1656 he was able to write, and to get published, a defence of Christian orthodoxy.

The confusion of his life was not completely cleared up by his will. He could not make a simple announcement that he died a Roman Catholic. He declared instead that he died, as he had lived, believing 'all the doctrine of God's Holy Catholic and Apostolic Church, whereof I do acknowledge the Church of Rome to be the Mother Church; and I do verily believe that no other Church hath any salvation in it, but only so far as it concurs with the faith of the Church of Rome.'[1]

It is in a few poems of Richard Crashaw that we can see most vividly what the Counter-Reformation had to contribute to the spiritual life of England. This poet was the son of a London clergyman who was a strong Puritan, and it was presumably in

---

[1] Geoffrey Soden provided a biography of *Godfrey Goodman* (London, 1953).

his father's collection of Papist books that the boy came across the religion to which he was to yield his allegiance. For long the young man was satisfied, or at least made do, with the Church of England's version of Catholicism. The two Cambridge colleges where he was a scholar (Pembroke) and a fellow (Peterhouse) were centres of Laudian or Anglo-Catholic piety and learning. In his time two famous high churchmen, Matthew Wren and John Cosin, occupied the post of Master of Peterhouse and busied themselves with Catholicizing the worship and appearance of the college chapel. Crashaw was given charge of Little St Mary's, the parish church adjacent to the college, and in that beautiful shrine would meditate and write poems. Some of these poems were tributes to George Herbert and the Little Gidding community.

So he might have lived out his days. But in 1643, when he was just over thirty years old, Cromwell's troops sacked those Cambridge colleges which they regarded as nurseries of Popish superstition. The priest-poet was convinced that he would never live to see the pleasantness of Anglican devotion restored. He resigned his posts in Cambridge and accepted the Roman Catholic faith which his previous teaching and poetry had only approached. He fled abroad and published his largest collection of poems, *Steps to the Temple* (a deliberate echo of Herbert), partly in order to attract a patron; he was destitute. For a time he was at the exiled Queen's court in Paris, and for a time in attendance on a cardinal in Rome. Finally he was granted a modest position as one of the priests who looked after the pilgrims to the Holy House at Loreto (which was believed to be the Virgin's home, transported by angels from Nazareth). And there after a few months he died, in 1649.

His most original poems show a joyful, even intoxicated, surrender to the spirit of the Counter-Reformation and to all the imagery most characteristic of Baroque architecture and painting. In them as in a Jesuit church in Rome, we are pounded by the restless vigour of the new hunger for faith and holiness, a hunger felt with all the senses; the insistence that because they are so intensely human even saints can sin again and again and be forgiven (two favourite figures are St Peter and St Mary Magdalen); the conviction that penitent saints can be penetrated and deeply ravished by the divine love (the comparison between prayer and sex is very frequent and very elaborate); the praise of heroic commitment and energy in devotion, preaching and charity; the proud delight both in the growing triumph of the one true Church and in the assured glories of heaven. It is a religion of weeping, longing, suffering and fighting. 'Is she a flaming fountain or a weeping fire?' Crashaw asks at one point, and his poetry is full of floods, flames, wounds and swords – until it ends in the blinding splendour of a supernatural light.

Contemplating a picture of St Teresa being pierced by the dart of God's love, Crashaw is excited into an ecstasy in his address to the saint:

> O thou undaunted daughter of desires!
> By all thy dower of lights and fires;
> By all the eagle in thee, all the dove;
> By all thy lives and deaths of love;
> By thy large draughts of intellectual day,
> And by thy thirsts of love more large than they;
> By all thy brim-fill'd bowls of fierce desire,
> By thy last morning's draught of liquid fire;
> By the full kingdom of that final kiss
> That seized thy parting soul, and seal'd thee His . . .

And the contemplation of the Nativity arouses a similar, although quieter, passion of wonder:

> Welcome, all wonders in one sight!
>   Eternity shut in a span.
> Summer in winter. Day in night.
>   Heaven in earth, and God in man.
> Great little one! whose all-embracing birth
>   Lifts earth to heaven, stoops heav'n to earth.
>
> To thee, meek majesty! soft King
>   Of simple graces and sweet loves,
> Each of us his lamb will bring,
>   Each his pair of silver doves
> Till burnt at last in fire of thy fair eyes,
>   Our selves become our own best sacrifice.[2]

---

[2] Studies of *Richard Crashaw* include those by Austin Warren and R. C. Wallerstein (London, 1957–59).

AFTER THE
GUNPOWDER PLOT

We have now to ask a prosaic question. Unlike Goodman or
Crashaw, most Englishmen could not read books about the
great Catholic tradition which had been vibrantly renewed in
the Counter-Reformation. For them, what were the chances of
discovering and inhabiting this old but new world of the spirit?

At first the death of Elizabeth held out hope to the Recusants. James I wanted, and obtained, peace with Spain. His
queen, Anne, had become a Roman Catholic in Scotland
during the 1590s and although she was no Crashaw heroine,
she gave hints; she always refused to communicate with the
Church of England. In 1603 old Sigebert Buckley, formerly a
monk of Westminster Abbey, marked the new mood by renewing his religious vows – thus putting himself in a position (or so
he claimed) to transmit all the rights of the Benedictines of
medieval England to the monks of a new generation. In May
1603 the new mood of leniency began to benefit the laity, whose
Recusancy fines were no longer collected, and in the same
mood the King restored the earldom of Arundel to young
Philip Howard, who had been brought up a strict Recusant,
and created another of the Howards Earl of Northampton. In
Rome Pope Clement nursed hopes of the King's conversion.

But the mood did not last. During the next winter the
government, irritated that the Recusants had not rallied more
decisively in gratitude, began enforcing the Elizabethan
statutes again. The desperate reply of some Recusants, led by
Robert Catesby, was the famous gunpowder plot. Some of
them had been involved in Essex's rebellion against Elizabeth
and their folly was demonstrated anew when one of them
warned his brother-in-law (Lord Mounteagle) to stay away
from the formal opening of Parliament on 5 November 1605.
During the night of 4–5 November Guy Fawkes, a soldier of
fortune from Yorkshire, was found with thirty-six barrels of
gunpowder in a cellar beneath the House of Lords.

No gesture by Recusant hotheads could have been better
calculated to alienate the King, who was always terrified of
assassination (particularly murder by gunpowder, which had

killed his father). And no move could have done more to discredit Roman Catholicism in the country at large. Jesuits had been half-heartedly aware of the plot and now paid the price, but it was equally convenient that no aristocrat was even remotely involved apart from the Earl of Northumberland, who was sent to the Tower. Had Fawkes let off his gunpowder, he and the other conspirators would still have found it extremely difficult to produce a monarchy and government to their liking. In the event, all that exploded was public opinion, thrilled by the drama and furious at an attempt which had nearly plunged the country into chaos. When in 1610 the news arrived of the murder of the King of France by a Catholic fanatic, there was a further outburst of English Protestant anger – and of shame among the English Recusants. It was this news from France that finally made Ben Jonson renounce his Roman Catholicism. Year by year Guy Fawkes and his plot were commemorated up and down England by processions, bonfires and anti-Papist oratory; an official service of thanksgiving for the nation's deliverance was authorized for use in churches until 1859. Indeed, the propaganda victory which the plotters handed on a plate to the goverment was so immense that the suggestion has been made that the government must have inspired the whole plot from first to last. No evidence has been produced to prove this interpretation, which seems improbable. It is more likely that some time before the arrest of Guy Fawkes the plot had been betrayed to the government by informers; there were many of these in the ranks of the Recusants (Ben Jonson was one of them). It seems just possible that the warning to Mounteagle was intended by a conspirator as a signal to others that they had been betrayed, although Guy Fawkes was left to his fate.[3]

After this disaster hope eventually revived – but in a way dangerous to any long-term popular revival of Roman Catholicism. For the hope that Recusants would be tolerated was now bound up with the expectation that the government would be forced to make concessions at home in the interests of its policy

---

[3] See Joel Hurstfield's reconstruction in *Early Stuart Studies*, ed. H. S. Reinmuth, pp. 95–121, and B. N. De Luna, *Jonson's Romish Plot* (Oxford, 1967).

of peace with the Catholic powers; and most Englishmen condemned that appeasing policy as unpatriotic. The Recusants who stood to gain by it were distrusted all the more.

In 1612 Henry, Prince of Wales, who had been popularly regarded as a young Elizabethan hero, died unmarried. Six years later Sir Walter Ralegh was executed to appease Spain. For thirteen years from 1613 the King hoped to see his next son and heir, Charles, married to a princess from Spain. For ten years from 1618 the chief minister was the Duke of Buckingham, whose wife, mother and two brothers were all known to be Roman Catholics (although the wife publicly conformed to Anglicanism). This period was ended by the Spaniards' refusal to release their princess and by the murder of Buckingham, but Protestant hostility was further inflamed when Charles did marry a French princess. Bowing to public opinion, the government reneged on the secret clause in the marriage treaty which promised toleration to the English Recusants. The permission to Henrietta Maria to import her own priests who were to officiate in her own chapels could not be withdrawn, however, and Puritans grew frantic when they thought of the Englishmen exposed to the moral danger of the Mass at court. During the first unhappy period of his marriage Charles fully shared his subjects' prejudices.

Although Charles I never deviated from the Church which had crowned and anointed him, there certainly were strong Roman Catholic influences at his court. In the mid-1630s they received a focus in the two papal agents, Gregorio Panzani and George Conn, with whom Bishop Goodman was in touch. Some aristocratic ladies were openly converted, and some prominent ministers – Portland, the Lord Treasurer, for example, or Cottington, the Chancellor of the Exchequer, or Sir Francis Windebank, the joint Secretary of State – were Roman Catholics at heart while not willing to suffer as Recusants. By 1640 almost a quarter of the House of Lords adhered to the old religion. But it was especially among men eminent in the arts that the Counter-Reformation made its appeal. The aesthetic activity which gave immortal beauty to the court of Charles I was steeped in the Catholic culture of Flanders or Italy. This connection was symbolized by the knighthoods conferred on

Rubens and his pupil, Van Dyck, painters who lavished their genius on the royal family, but the biggest *coup* came early: the purchase of the very rich art collection of the Dukes of Mantua. The dominant architect and masque-designer, Inigo Jones, was a Roman Catholic, as was the leading dramatist, James Shirley. John Bull was so indiscreet that he had to leave the Chapel Royal to become the organist of Antwerp Cathedral. As we observe the extent of this invasion by the colour, the elegance and the passionate prayer of the Counter-Reformation then so vigorous in Europe, we cannot wonder that many Puritans were alarmed.[4]

In the country as opposed to the court in this period, the position of the Recusants is hard to determine accurately. A Roman Catholic historian was surely right to suggest that probably 'the most contented and peaceful period which the harassed Catholics were to enjoy between the outbreak of the Elizabethan repression and the last years of the eighteenth century was that space of a generation lasting from the middle of the reign of James I to the outbreak of the civil war in 1642.'[5] And certainly there survive from these years moving examples of the faithfulness of English men and women to the Catholic Church despite all the penalties and temptations.[6] Although he had abandoned them, and had denounced their leaders, John Donne knew these Papists. 'Men and brethren,' he told his congregation in St Paul's in 1629, 'I am a Papist, that is, I will fast and pray as much as any Papist, and enable myself for the service of God as seriously, as sedulously, as laboriously, as any Papist.'

However, despite such heroism it seems probable that in England as a whole the Roman Catholic Church – defined as the community of those who habitually resorted to priests for baptism, confession and the Mass – was not large. An historian who has examined the records with detailed care estimates this community's strength at forty thousand in 1603 and no more than sixty thousand in 1641–42, when there was intense

---

[4] See Gordon Albion, *Charles I and the Court of Rome* (London, 1935).
[5] David Mathew, *Catholicism in England* (revised, London, 1948), p. 77.
[6] Philip Caraman edited an anthology of extracts called *The Years of Siege* (London, 1966).

activity to make a count of Recusants. An earlier historian thought that the number of two hundred thousand in 1641 was well-established and half a million possible. Another earlier estimate was 'about 320,000 to 360,000'.[7] The lowest estimate is probably the most accurate, although the higher figures suggest why there were so many Puritan fears, voiced loudly in the Parliaments of 1625–29, that Papists were everywhere. One indication of the failure of the community to grow on the ground was that priests quite often found themselves condemned either to unemployment or penury. In the 1630s the Jesuits reported to Rome that their priests in England, between a hundred and 180 in number, were each averaging between four and five converts a year. It was not very encouraging.

The Roman Catholic community's growth was so limited because the government's policy was cleverly designed to prevent that growth. There was a combination of severity with indulgence. Under James I and Charles I gentlemen who had priests to stay as guests or permanent lodgers were seldom penalized for it. The number of executions dropped (1607–10, eight; 1611–18, nine; 1619–25, none). In the fifteen years before the recall of Parliament in 1640, not a single Roman Catholic was executed apart from a priest, Edward Arrowsmith, and a labourer, Richard Herst, who suffered in Lancaster before the King's pardon could reach them. Thus the glamour of martyrdom ceased to surround the English mission. On the contrary, there were many temptations to laymen with Catholic hearts but worldly ambitions to conform to the religious establishment. An Earl of Arundel led the way. Such men knew that a compromise would be rewarded by cash in a period when great houses built by the most fortunate, and manor houses rebuilt spaciously by many others, told the tale: local influence still helped the accumulation and legal defence of estates, and influence at court was still the golden key to many lucrative offices and privileges out of which land could be bought, houses raised and families founded.

---

[7] John Bossy, *The English Catholic Community 1570–1850*, pp. 186–8; Bryan Magee, *The English Recusants* (London, 1938), pp. 94–112; M. J. Havran, *The Catholics in Caroline England* (Stanford, Cal., 1962), p. 83.

The evidence suggests that among the gentry the number of compromising 'Church Papists' was considerably larger than the number who stayed at home and, in relative poverty, obeyed the advice of the priests that Catholics must never worship with Protestants. It also seems that many of the Church Papists became as licentious or corrupt as their friends or competitors, so that they were further disinclined to confess their sins to a priest. And even if a gentleman did not go as far as this, he could still obtain exemption from the Recusancy fines at the price of behaviour which would be good in the government's eyes. In the end almost every Roman Catholic in England had to compromise – for the churches or churchyards controlled by the Anglican clergy were the only legal places for burial. The coffin of a Recusant squire would be brought into church silently and the parson would, if co-operative, read the Prayer Book service when the mourners had left. Corpses of lesser status, brought to the churchyard, might not escape greater insults.

But the government's policy was in some ways severe. Recusants wishing to clear their names of treachery had to take the 1606 Oath of Allegiance, renouncing not only the political claims of the papacy but also (in the opinion of many priests) all respect for the Pope. The first half of the oath denied a pope's right to depose a king or 'to authorize any foreign prince to invade or annoy him', and corresponded with many a patriotic Catholic's conscience. But the second half was deliberately offensive, abhorring the doctrine that kings deposed by popes may be 'deposed or murdered' by their subjects as not only 'damnable' but also 'impious and heretical'. The oath was intended to divide Roman Catholics, and it did. George Blackwell, the archpriest of the English mission, took the oath and was promptly deposed. The Pope denounced it and faithful Recusant laity accepted his ruling, however reluctantly. For more than a decade controversy about the Pope and the oath raged; Robert Persons and the great Cardinal Bellarmine wrote on one side, James I, Bishop Lancelot Andrewes and John Donne on the other. And executions of priests continued until 1616, when they were abandoned for the sake of reconciliation with Spain. Recusancy fines remained in theory very severe and could be imposed particularly on people whose economic position was middling, so that they were rich enough to pay without being so rich that they had bought exemptions from the officials.

The most devastating consequence of the government's patronizing attitude – not often making a martyr, but never recognizing the right of Roman Catholics to live in public as patriotic Englishmen – was that the community was demoralized by the absence of known and accepted leadership. The Tudor state had succeeded in deposing, exiling or executing all who traditionally would have been the Catholic authorities. No Englishman exercised the normal jurisdiction of a bishop of the Counter-Reformation until William Bishop in 1623. The arrival of a more formidable bishop, Richard Smith, in 1625, was part of the government's brief agreement to tolerate Henrietta Maria's fellow Catholics. His position was that of 'vicar apostolic' representing Rome and this position was more authoritative than that of the 'archpriests' of earlier years in the English mission, but he was so tactless in asserting a bishop's authority after this long gap that six years later Rome reminded him of where the power was meant to lie by a large curtailment of his jurisdiction. In anger Smith fled to France but refused to resign as England's Catholic bishop; he did not die until 1655. He left behind him a 'chapter' of priests whose authority was denied in Rome. Since no bishop was there to unite them, the Jesuits, the 'religious' and the 'secular' priests conducted bitter arguments in public. When the ecclesiastical leadership was so confused, the real authority was wielded by the nobleman or gentleman in whose house a priest was living – and among whose tenants or dependent neighbours could be found any congregation. It is not surprising that not much teaching or originality or spiritual dignity came from priests who were in effect chaplains liable to dismissal by the squire at a moment's notice. Nor is it surprising that the effect of evangelism was limited when the deployment of the clergy was decided by the availability of a gentleman's house to serve as a base.

A CATHOLIC HOLINESS

Had the Roman Catholic community in England been free to live its own life under its natural leaders, its history would presumably have been both more prosperous and more edifying. What might have been can be seen in an amazing fact: no fewer than five thousand English men or women entered religious houses on the continent during the first forty years of the seventeenth century. For example, the English Franciscan order was revived in a small convent in Douai in 1617. The contrast was very great with the mood of the sixteenth century, where specially in England this religious life had seemed finally overthrown and discredited; writing about 1580, the Recusant poet Robert Southwell had noted that in England, Germany and elsewhere the names of 'monk' and 'scoundrel' had the same meaning for most people. We might have expected English religion to have been changed on a large scale as a result of this large-scale renewal of monastic idealism. Instead, we find that the revival produced only fragmentary teaching, doomed to result either in neglect or in controversy. The English harvest of the Counter-Reformation was disappointing in quality.

The spiritual writer of this period most used by later Roman Catholics was Augustine (born David) Baker. The story of his early life can be pieced together from the autobiographical passages included in a commentary on a medieval treatise on prayer (Walter Hilton's *Cloud of Unknowing*) which he wrote in 1629. It is the story of a young Welsh lawyer who embraced the Roman Catholic faith as a result of his own studies accompanied by his own prayers. He was one of the first recruits made when the Benedictine order was revived in England under James I. Sent to Italy for training as a monk, his prayers became arid, his heart became homesick and he returned home. Back in England he tried again and became a priest. But he was, as he recalled, only a 'tepid' priest, who supported himself by resuming the work of a lawyer in London. It was in 1620 that he finally committed himself to the concentration on lonely mortification and mystical prayer (sometimes for eleven hours in a day) which lasted until his death in 1641. At first he was chaplain to a Recusant family in Devon; then, at last beginning the Benedictine community life, he spent nine years as spiritual director to the new little community of English nuns in Cambrai. Finally he was transferred to a convent in Douai for five years. But by now his health was feeble and his constant stress on mortification had become melancholy; and once again he was unbearably homesick. In 1683 he returned to London, to die of the plague. He left behind many writings about the spiritual life, and a selection from these (itself some five hundred pages long) was published by a disciple, Serenus Cressy, in 1657 under the title *Sancta Sophia*. This book did something to secure for him the audience he had never found before his death.[8]

Another Benedictine monk, John Barnes, was more interested in the age around him. He attempted to build a theological bridge between Catholicism and Protestantism, but was thought to be mad and taken to a Roman prison. The most creative theologian among the English Roman Catholics of this (or the next) century was Thomas White. Not for nothing was he the contemporary of the French genius, René Descartes. As interested in experimental science as in experimental prayer, he saw the need of the Counter-Reformation to modernize its theology to match its devotion. He wrote some forty books, but as 'Blacklaw' and under other pseudonyms. None of them had much effect. Like Augustine Baker after 1638, he found himself leading an independent gentleman's life – and like John Barnes he was thought to be mad by most of his co-religionists if they were aware of his existence. He spent thirty years exiled in Holland, returning to London to die in obscurity in 1676.

Another spiritual writer produced by the English Catholic community in this period, and one with a greater influence in the short term (although today he is largely forgotten), was Benet of Canfield. His *Rule of Perfection*, printed in eight languages from 1610 onwards, expounded a spirituality typical

---

[8] *Memorials of Father Baker* were edited by R. H. Connolly and J. McCann (London, 1933). Critical assessments include those by David Knowles, *The English Mystical Tradition* (London, 1961), pp. 178–87, and David Lunn, *The English Benedictines* (London, 1980), pp. 197–219.

of the Counter-Reformation. The one essential point is the
total surrender of the will to God, in conformity with the
crucified Christ. To do 'from the sole motive of pleasing God all
that one is aware that God desires, commands, counsels and
inspires' – that is perfection, and the Christian is called to
it, first through active obedience, then through the superior
contemplative life.

This teaching had such influence that it has aroused criticism from two very different viewpoints. In 1689 the *Rule of
Perfection* was put on the Roman index of books prohibited to
Catholics, two years after the papal condemnation of 'quietism'. Quietism was a tendency found in French spiritual
writers and alleged to exaggerate the extent to which the
perfect soul should be quietly passive. The danger seen in
Rome was that Catholics might be encouraged to disregard
intellectual and moral activity in accordance with the
Church's down-to-earth dogmas. In 1941 Aldous Huxley published a very different criticism. He pointed out that Benet's
most famous disciple was another Capuchin (Franciscan)
friar, Père Joseph, whose *Introduction to the Spiritual Life* was full
of his influence. This barefoot follower of St Francis, noted for
the austerity of his life and the many ecstasies of his prayers,
was the ruthless adviser and assistant of Cardinal Richelieu in
persecuting the French Protestants, in crushing all others
thought to oppose the French monarch, and in stirring up the
Thirty Years War (in alliance with the Swedes, who were
Protestants). Huxley enquired whether the mysticism taught
by Benet to Joseph was itself to blame, and developed a
criticism made at the time by Augustine Baker: that Benet
insisted that meditation on Christ's cross must be continued
even when the soul was becoming perfect, instead of the
abandonment of all images. Huxley suggested that Benet's
encouragement of thought about suffering instead of calm and
complete 'absorption in the ultimate reality' may have encouraged Père Joseph to inflict suffering both on himself and on
other people, believing that this was the will of God.[9]

[9] See R. A. Knox on Quietism in *Enthusiasm* (Oxford, 1950), pp. 231–355, and
Aldous Huxley, *Grey Eminence: A Study in Religion and Politics* (London, 1941).

A more generous verdict would say that Benet's teaching about the contemplation and imitation of Christ was in a great tradition and should not be blamed for the cruelties of contemporary politicians, but that something was lost because this powerful teacher never did a spell of pastoral work in his own country. Benet, by birth William Fitch, abandoned England soon after his conversion to Roman Catholicism while a dissolute student of law in 1585. His *Rule of Perfection* seems to have been completed before his thirtieth birthday in 1592, during his training in the Franciscan order in France and Italy. It was a book full of the ardour of a young convert who was very conscious of the glories of French Catholicism and of the price he had paid for his own surrender to the will of God. Sent on a mission to England in 1599, he was soon arrested and in 1602 expelled back to France, having written another book, *The Christian Knight*, during his captivity. These two books showed a splendid and astonishing maturity in the ways of contemplative prayer, and an impressive ability to summon fellow Catholics to heroism, but they did not have a great deal to say to, or about, those who had little wish to become perfect Christian knights. This was mainly because the author had given up mixing with such people; from his conversion to his death (in 1610) he lived among the élite. Had Benet lived and listened more among his own people, he could surely have been expected to develop a more compassionate understanding of the ordinary man or woman. Here, in his élitism, was the fatal defect in his teaching. It was, we may judge, the simple blindness of Père Joseph to the people's suffering, not the Christ-centredness of his advanced mysticism, that betrayed this near-saint into doing work which most ordinary people would reckon demonic.[10]

The leading Englishwoman devoted to the old religion in this period was Mary Ward, who had the bold plan of founding an Institute of the Blessed Virgin Mary for women, modelled

---

[10] Henri Bremond, *A Literary History of Religious Thought in France*, Vol. 2 (English translation, London, 1930), pp. 112–44, offered a rather puzzled discussion of the spirituality of the two friars, Benet and Joseph. The only full study is Optat de Veghel, *Benoit de Canfield* (Rome, 1949).

on the Jesuit order. After some years with the Poor Clares (the women Franciscans) she established her own little community with a school for girls at Omer in Flanders in 1609. But her further idea that women should move about the world in pastoral and teaching work horrified the ecclesiastical authorities when she went to Rome to seek approval for it in 1629. Her experiment was suppressed and she herself was imprisoned. She eventually managed to found modified communities of her Institute in Rome itself, and London and Yorkshire in the period 1639–42, but such was the suspicion with which she was still surrounded, right up to her death in 1645, that this highly promising order barely survived. Its rules did not receive papal approval until 1703. It seems fair to say that with Mary Ward's vision the post-1570 Roman Catholic community in England 'had been offered the opportunity of a second wind, which could have carried its phase of primitive expansion on through the seventeenth century. In rejecting it, it registered its determination to play safe, and missed the boat for a couple of generations'.[11]

All these were independently-minded radicals, impatient for holiness, who would have been a trial to any pastor charged with the care of them, but in this they were typical of a much wider English enthusiasm for religion in this period. Their particular tragedy was that they never found an adequate base for their ideals, so that their energies burned out on alien soil or in futile controversy. Most of their fellow countrymen regarded such 'Papists' as eccentrics who for wicked or inexplicable reasons had chosen to be identified with traitors such as Guy Fawkes. The pity of it all, the loss of English religion, can be felt when we reflect that the seventeenth century included 'a second Protestant Reformation, and a second Catholic Counter-Reformation, both more vigorous and more passionate than their sixteenth-century counterparts.'[12] Yet England's Counter-Reformation did not create a new world of spirituality to match the world of the Puritans.

---

[11] John Bossy, *op.cit.*, p. 282. Margaret Oliver provided a biography of *Mary Ward* (London, 1960).

[12] Hugh Aveling, *The Handle and the Axe*, p. 75.

CHAPTER EIGHT

THE PURITAN EXPLOSION

ENTERING A NEW WORLD

The passionate energy of many Englishmen refused to accept conformity under the control of England's bishops – or poverty under the pressure of England's over-population. They had to find freedom abroad.

It is reckoned that over twenty thousand Englishmen went to live on the continent in the years 1620–40. As we have seen, many were Recusants who found the Counter-Reformation in full force in their places of refuge. But there were also thousands of militant Protestants who chose to live in the Netherlands. There conditions would not be too disappointing if they could find jobs and form a little community around a favourite preacher. Some, however, could not adjust themselves to the Netherlands. There was a shortage of suitable employment. Life in a Dutch town, although acceptably Protestant, could also be disturbingly sophisticated and, by the standards of the English countryside, dissolute. These refugees, patriots even in exile, were alarmed by the thought that their children would probably be absorbed into the Dutch population. They longed for a country where a man might feed his family by his own honest labour on the land or in a village, and where he might obey the 'ordinances of God' – all the time speaking English. The major outlet for Protestants wishing to emigrate therefore became America.

The perils were obvious. The little ships crossing the Atlantic were tossed by storms and ravaged by diseases, and the usually miserable voyage took a minimum of five weeks. The 'Indians' might be cruelly hostile to the intruders; clearing the land of trees and stones was backbreaking work; starvation was the penalty if crops could not be grown in time; and should

these perils be survived, epidemics swept through the primitive
settlements in the wilderness. But there were attractions. John
Donne had heard the Elizabethan talk about the harvest of the
sea off Newfoundland, and speculation about other riches, and
so had found a new metaphor for sex:

> O my America! my New-found-land,
> My Kingdom, safeliest when with one man manned . . .

In 1609 he applied in vain for the secretaryship of the new
colony of Virginia. (Had he sailed for America then, his ship
would have been shipwrecked on the Bermudas – the adventure which gave Shakespeare material for *The Tempest*.)

In 1622 Dean Donne became a member of the council of the
Virginia Company and delivered the sermon before the company's annual feast. The evening was designed to advertise the
company, and that year the Dean had to use all his eloquence
'to keep the wheel in due motion' after the meagre returns on
the investment to date, and after the 'flood of blood' when the
colonists had been massacred by the Indians. He told his
congregation not to be disheartened by the losses but to
concentrate on the evangelism of the Indians: 'You shall have
much this island, which is but as the suburbs of the old world, a
bridge, a gallery to the new; to join all to that world that shall
never grow old, the kingdom of heaven.'

This colony with which John Donne was thus identified was
not dominated by men wishing to escape from the Church of
England. A clergyman, Robert Hunt, arrived with the first
colonists who founded Virginia in 1607. One of their earliest
acts was to fell trees to make rough walls and benches for a
church, with an old sail as the roof. More than two-thirds of
that congregation died of famine and disease during the first
year and it often seemed as if the little settlement in Chesapeake Bay was doomed, as earlier tiny colonies on the American coast sponsored by Sir Humphrey Gilbert and Sir Walter
Ralegh had been in the 1580s. But for the sake of morale among
the settlers Thomas Dale, who arrived as governor in 1611,
insisted that everyone should attend Morning and Evening
Prayer daily, and the same emphasis on the struggling colony's
religious dimension ran through the propaganda put out in

support of Virginia – for example, in the books and maps of Captain John Smith, the adventurer who gave New England its name.

There was a period when it seemed that it would be easy to make the Indians friendly and Christian. Pocahontas, the daughter of the local chief – a girl who (the story went) had earlier saved John Smith's life – was instructed in the faith of the Church of England by a Puritan chaplain, Alexander Whitaker. She was baptized Rebecca, married to an Englishman, and paraded at the court of James I before her rapid death. But on Good Friday 1622 Indians massacred some three hundred of the white men, not without provocation. Despite John Donne's eloquence in London that November, the missionary idealism of the colony went up in smoke – like the tobacco which had become its chief worldly asset; and the Dean's sermon proved to be the last in the series extolling the company as a missionary society. One result of this weakening in religious motivation was to expose the company further to the attacks of those who thought they could manage its affairs better than Sir Edwin Sandys and his associates (who included Shakespeare's patron, the Earl of Southampton). George Herbert's stepfather and Nicholas Ferrar his closest friend took the lead in trying to persuade the House of Commons to come to the rescue, but James I forbade discussion. Eventually, in July 1624, the company's charter was revoked.[1]

The colony in Virginia survived as a cluster of tobacco plantations under the direct control of the government. But more powerful motives were needed if there was to be colonization on a larger scale – and in practice that meant that Puritan motives were needed.[2] It is in the story of the Puritans in New England that we find the main fulfilment of the vision of the English-speaking world, as set out in the prophecy of Samuel Daniel:

---

[1] See Louis B. Wright, *Religion and Empire: The Alliance between Religion and Commerce in English Expansion, 1558–1625* (Chapel Hill, N.C., 1943).

[2] Two books by American scholars are illuminating: Wallace Notestein, *The English People on the Eve of Colonization, 1603–30* (New York, 1954), and Carl Brindenbaugh, *Vexed and Troubled Englishmen, 1590–1642* (New York, 1968).

And who in time knows whither we may vent
The treasure of our tongue, to what strange shores
This gain of our best glory shall be sent,
T' inrich unknowing nations with our stores,
What worlds in th' yet unformed Occident
May come refin'd with th' accents that are ours?

Puritan motives were shared by most of the 'Pilgrim Fathers' —
the passengers, a little over a hundred in number, who landed
from the *Mayflower* on the rocky coast of Massachusetts Bay in
November 1620. It had been agreed with a suspicious government (and with their backers, led by Thomas Western, a
London merchant) that they should settle in Virginia; it seems
to have been due to a navigational error that they ended up
hundreds of miles to the north. Anyway the need to establish a
'civil body politic' from scratch when there was some talk of
mutiny forced these Pilgrim Fathers to make a solemn 'compact' on the *Mayflower* before they landed; and the need to base
this 'compact' on religion (for no other basis seemed conceivable to seventeenth-century Englishmen) emphasized the religious origins of their adventure.

Those origins lay in a meeting for Puritan worship in
Scrooby, an obscure village just off the Great North Road,
about halfway between London and Scotland. The preacher to
this little congregation was John Robinson, who encouraged it
to emigrate with him to Leyden in the Netherlands. He might
have undertaken the further move to America, but the majority
of the congregation had persuaded him to stay in Leyden with
them. In his farewell to those leaving he had urged them to
accept other pastors, since 'the Lord hath more truth and light
yet to break forth out of his holy Word'. According to notes
made of this sermon (no full manuscript has survived), he also
looked forward to a further Reformation beyond the achievements of Luther and Calvin, as well as beyond the practices of
the Church of England. It is, however, clear that those who
joined the *Mayflower* had no intention of embarking on theological adventures. Although the group from Leyden made up
only a third of the Pilgrim Fathers (thirty-five, with sixty-six
'strangers'), it was successful in imposing the ideology they
had learned. When half of the pilgrims had survived the winter

and had gathered in a harvest, their thanksgiving feast was accompanied by prayer in the established Puritan style. However, for the most part they did not, it seems, regard themselves as being for ever separated from the Church of England, since they trusted that the biblical basis of their purer understanding of the Church would soon be acknowledged by the authorities at home. As Francis Higginson put it when he led a little company joining them: 'We will not say ... "Farewell, Babylon!" "Farewell, Rome!" but we will say, "Farewell, dear England! Farewell, the Church of God in England, and the Christian friends there! We do not go to New England as separatists from the Church of England; though we cannot but separate from the corruptions in it; but we go to practise the positive part of church reformation, and propagate the Gospel in America!" '

East Anglian Puritans dominated the New England Company, which received a grant of territory and sent three hundred colonists with two clergymen to Salem in Massachusetts in 1628–29. In 1630 they were joined by a larger party, led by John Winthrop, an able lawyer. By birth and by his own nature Winthrop was a leader of men; before sailing for the new world, he had been lord of the manor at Groton and a Justice of the Peace. But his legal career in London seemed to be blocked – as he could not help thinking, because he was a Puritan. His motives become clear in the paper which he drew up listing 'reasons for justifying the undertakers of the intended plantation in New England'.

The first two reasons were religious – to spread the Gospel (and incidentally 'to raise a bulwark against the kingdom of Anti-Christ which the Jesuits labour to rear up in these parts'), and to provide 'tabernacles and food' in the wilderness to which the true Church could flee from the 'desolation' and 'general calamity' of Protestantism in Europe. Winthrop then recited the economic woes of England amid the depressions of 1619–24 and 1629–31 caused by over-population and inflation. 'This land grows weary of its inhabitants, so as man who is the most precious of all creatures is here more vile and base than the earth we tread upon, and of less price than a horse or a sheep ... Many men spending as much labour and cost to

recover or keep sometimes an acre or two of land as would procure them many hundred as good or better in another country
. . . No man's estate will suffice to keep sail with his equals.'
It is clear from Winthrop's tone that he expected the response
to come not from the really poor but from farmers and tradesmen
who, to speak in a secular style, wanted to better themselves.

The same memorandum supplied three convenient answers
to the objection that 'we have no warrant to enter upon that
land which hath been so long possessed by others'. 'If we leave
them sufficient for their use, we may lawfully take the rest'; 'we
shall come in with the good leave of the natives'; 'God hath
consumed the natives with a great plague in those parts so
there be few inhabitants left.' The only real objection to the
adventure was seen to be that 'it is attended with many and
great difficulties'. But to that Winthrop gave the robust
answer: 'So is every good action.' This was the leader who,
preaching to his fellow passengers on the *Arabella* in mid-
Atlantic in the spring of 1630 declared: 'We shall be as a city
upon a hill, the eyes of all people are upon us.'[3]

THE HOLY EXPERIMENT OF NEW ENGLAND

New England's preachers preached a strong Gospel in their
wooden churches erected on soil never before touched by
man's implements.[4] The theology which supported their message can be seen in one of their favourite textbooks, *The Marrow
of Sacred Divinity*. Its author was William Ames, a Cambridge
theologian who because of his Puritan convictions had become
a refugee in the Netherlands. Ames accompanied his exposition of his faith by a major work on moral problems, which
became almost equally authoritative in New England, and
shortly before he died he was making plans to cross the Atlantic.[5]

---

[3] *The Puritan Tradition in America*, ed. A. T. Vaughan (New York, 1972), pp. 26–35.
Another valuable collection of documents is *The Puritans*, ed. Perry Miller and F. H.
Johnson (New York, 1963). See also Edmund S. Morgan, *The Puritan Dilemma: The
Story of John Winthrop* (Boston, Mass., 1958).

[4] See David D. Hall, *The Faithful Shepherd: A History of the New England Ministry in
the Seventeenth Century* (Chapel Hill, N.C., 1972).

[5] See K. L. Sprunger, *The Learned Dr William Ames* (Urbana, Ill., 1972).

Such Puritan doctrine has been called a 'federal' theology because, within an orthodox Calvinist framework, its stress was on the 'federal' covenant or agreement between the Creator and the believer. It taught that the God who granted this covenant to the elect was reasonable and reliable; that he had made his character well known in a clear revelation; and that he summoned the believer to study his revelation and to reason clearly about it and about the world which it illuminated. Nothing about the Puritans in New England is more impressive than the speed with which they established a college: Harvard College, founded in Cambridge, Massachusetts, by the appropriation of half the infant colony's taxes as early as 1636. The college was necessary in order to make these Puritans' sons reasonable, reliable and sound preachers of the Gospel. Its official theology was Calvinism as defined in *The Marrow*, to be studied every Saturday morning. To these New Englanders a college was almost as indispensable as was the congregation itself – defined by Ames as 'a society of believers joined together in a special bond for the continual exercise of the communion of saints among themselves'; as Christians covenanting with each other on the basis of God's covenant with them.

A few 'Praying Indians' were allowed to graduate at Harvard College. Their presence was a reminder that a professed purpose of the migration to New England was missionary; the cry of the Macedonians to St Paul, 'Come over and help us', appeared on the official seal of Massachusetts. As late as 1646, disturbed because very little missionary work had yet been achieved, John Eliot preached the first Puritan sermon in a Red Indian language. Three years later the first English missionary society was formed to support his work. In 1662 he brought out the whole of the Bible in the Algonquian language, an astonishing feat of translation; it was the first Bible to be printed in North America. The rationale of this missionary work, in Calvinist eyes, was that it was unsafe to assume that the heathen did not include any of God's elect who would be saved for ever by responding with faith on hearing the Gospel. But on the whole, the function of the American Indians was to provide land, willingly or unwillingly, for those on whom

God's covenanted favour rested, like the Canaanites whose role in Old Testament theology was modest.[6]

Some Christian villages were formed for these 'Praying Indians'; the first, for Mohicans, was granted land in 1651. But the 'holy experiment' pursued in the Puritan settlers' own towns and villages became incomparably more important than any missionary work among America's original inhabitants, for the hope was always that the success of this experiment would teach the whole of Christendom what true Christianity was. The experiment needed to be thoroughly and conspicuously holy and, although this may seem paradoxical in view of the Calvinist insistence on the faith of the elect, New England's emphasis on law was very pronounced. The rationale was that without obedience to God's law the saints could not prove their gratitude for their election – and the sinners would be even more thoroughly damned than they were already. The ideal society, as conceived by these Puritans, was one which was strictly regulated by magistrates enforcing the Ten Commandments and their consequences as interpreted by the best preachers. The stress on keeping the divine law in a holy life was so strong among the Puritans of New England that at times it almost abandoned the insistence in Calvinist orthodoxy on God's freedom to choose to favour the wicked. A modern historian observes that a typical New England preacher 'comes perilously close to the greatest danger that covenant theology creates: failing to maintain the distinction between works and grace.'[7] In view of the alarm raised by the Puritans about Arminianism in England, this development in America is curious.

When John Winthrop's little fleet took the largest party of Puritans yet seen in the new world to Massachusetts Bay in 1630, the most precious item in the cargo was this company's

---

[6] See A. T. Vaughan, *New England Frontier: Puritans and Indians, 1620–1675* (Boston, Mass., 1965), and Francis Jennings, *The Invasion of America* (Chapel Hill, N.C., 1975). C. W. Kellaway studied the history of the earliest missionary society in *The New England Company* (London, 1961).

[7] Everett Emerson, *Puritanism in America 1620–1750* (Boston, Mass., 1977), p. 59. Larzer Ziff, *Puritanism in America* (New York, 1973), also supplements Perry Miller's classic study of *The New England Mind* (2 vols, Cambridge, Mass., 1939–53).

royal charter. Although Charles I had not intended his covenant with a group of Puritans to be excessively gracious, his
clerks had omitted to specify that the charter declaring his
grace should be kept safely for possible revision in London.
The charter was also unexpectedly and accidentally gracious
in that it allowed those crossing the Atlantic to purchase so
many shares in the venture that by law they effectively controlled it. As had never been the case in Virginia, their 'holy
experiment' was their own.

These legal circumstances meant that strong-minded magistrates in the new colony could order its affairs in accordance
with the exhortations of strong-minded preachers. The Pilgrim
Fathers in the Plymouth area were, it is true, somewhat
suspicious of the clergymen (other than John Robinson, whom
they had left behind in the Netherlands). Their early services
in America were taken by an 'elder', William Brewster, and
even when professional preachers arrived power was kept
firmly in the hands of laymen such as William Bradford, the
governor of Plymouth for almost thirty years. In the larger
Massachusetts Bay colony the preachers were never magistrates themselves. But the preachers often gave the magistrates
direct advice from the pulpit, most publicly in the annual
'election sermon'. Preachers as spiritually powerful as John
Cotton or Thomas Hooker (both of whom arrived in 1633
with established reputations) had therefore great political
influence.[8] And when a primitive electoral system was established in 1631, it was decided that only those who had been
co-opted as church members, taking the Lord's Supper once a
month and walking in the way of righteousness, were to have
votes.

Some twenty thousand men and women were willing to
leave England during the 1630s to join a colony so constituted,
and they could not be stopped by the Lords Commissioners
for Plantations, a body set up by the King in 1632 with
Archbishop Laud in the chair. There was a sense in which they

---

[8] There are studies of *John Cotton* by Larzer Ziff (Princeton, N.J., 1962) and
Everett Emerson (New York, 1965), and of *Thomas Hooker* by George Williams
(Cambridge, Mass., 1975) and Frank Shuffelton (Princeton, N.J., 1977).

joined a monastery, like many of the Recusants fleeing in these years to the continent. John Cotton, writing about 1637, reported a procedure for the admission of new church members which would not have brought discredit to a monastery. First candidates were asked questions such as these. 'How it pleased God to work in them to bring them home to Christ? Whether the law had convinced them of sin? How the Lord had won them to deny themselves and their own righteousness and to rely on the righteousness of Christ?' The account which candidates gave of themselves had to be supported both by a public confession, of perhaps fifteen minutes, and by recommendations from existing members. Only then were candidates allowed to 'enter a holy covenant with God and with them', being assured in return that 'we likewise will walk towards you in all brotherly love and holy watchfulness'.

When the numbers of full church members who had been willing to undergo this procedure became too small an element in the colony to be plausible as its electorate, it was decided that men who were respectable Christians but not able or willing to pass all the tests for church membership could be given the vote, making use of the concept of the 'half-way covenant'. But the religious purity of the little commonwealth between the wilderness and the ocean was still thought by its leadership to be the main justification for its existence. Towards the end of his long governorship John Bradford grew weary and somewhat disillusioned with the Plymouth settlement, and ceased to record its history in order to find time to learn Hebrew, but in his history he had already summed up the lesson which he rightly believed would be drawn from the pioneering days. 'May and ought not the children of these fathers rightly say, "Our fathers were Englishmen which came over this great ocean, and were ready to perish in the wilderness, but they cried unto the Lord, and he heard their voice and looked upon their adversity"?'[9] The new Israel, rescued from all the perils of this exodus to America, had a duty to build the city of God in the wilderness – a very clear duty, although they

---

[9] The best edition is William Bradford, *Of Plymouth Plantation*, ed. S. E. Morison (New York, 1952).

knew that they were sinners. 'Sir,' someone said to Thomas
Hooker, the dying pastor, in 1647, 'you are going to receive the
reward of all your labours.' Hooker had built up, and dominated, the new settlement at Hartford in Connecticut. But he now
replied: 'Brother, I am going to receive mercy.' When Edward
Johnson came to write his *History of New England* (1654),
however, his theme was expressed in his sub-title: *The Wonder-
working Providence of Zion's Saviour in America*. Their experience
while labouring to establish a Christian civilization in the wilderness across an ocean had confirmed their belief in miracles.

Early in the eighteenth century spokesmen for the orthodox
Puritanism of New England still looked back and around with
pride. Despite all the sins to be expected from human nature,
the 'holy experiment' had been blessed. In his immense work
entitled *Magnalia Christi Americana* (1702), Cotton Mather had
no hesitation in announcing that a new chapter in church
history had been opened by men such as his grandfather, John
Cotton: 'I write the wonders of the Christian religion,' he
proclaimed, 'flying from the depravations of Europe to the
American strand.' Frequently the preachers compared the
colonists with the Ancient Israelites who had cried to the Lord
in the wilderness, had been given a good land, had been guilty
of backsliding, but had returned to the Lord, at least partially
and temporarily.

In 1646–48 a synod summoned to define Massachusetts
orthodoxy stated its doctrine in keeping with the Westminster
Confession recently drawn up by English Calvinist divines,
and its discipline on the basis of the covenant freely entered
into by church members but supported by the 'helpful' magistrates. At the same time as the construction of this 'Cambridge
Platform' dealing with church life, 'Laws and Liberties'
codified and developed the colony's earlier legislation with a
theological introduction and a strong peppering of biblical
references. Although in practice the laws of Massachusetts
were based more on English common law than on the Old
Testament, death was the penalty for idolatry, blasphemy or
adultery. A son 'of sixteen years of age which will not obey the
voice of his father or the voice of his mother' was to be put to
death in accordance with Exodus 21:17. A man drunk was

fined ten shillings; a man smoking in public one shilling. In 1639 a Boston shopkeeper narrowly escaped excommunication and was subjected to a heavy fine because he had overcharged his customers. In his sermon on the occasion John Cotton explicitly denounced the suggestion 'that a man might sell as dear as he can and buy as cheap as he can'. It was to such conditions that preachers looked back nostalgically in days when the colony had grown more worldly, when Puritans had become Yankees. Increase Mather asked in 1679: 'Where was there ever a place so like unto new Jerusalem as New England hath been?'[10]

THE BIRTH OF RELIGIOUS TOLERATION

Taking leave of the Pilgrim Fathers, John Robinson had prophesied that 'new light' would come to the Puritans in America. He would have been astonished had he known that later generations would praise the pilgrims who became settlers chiefly for their discovery of the idea of religious toleration. It was a slow discovery for, as we have often observed, Puritanism was not naturally tolerant. At first when the problem of religious diversity arose, the solution seemed to be to begin a new settlement where the rebellious form of Christianity could become the official religion. Then the American adventure became a more courageous recognition that the white light of the Christian Gospel was made up of many colours.

Even in Massachusetts, a colony planned to be uniform, there were independent spirits. Thomas Hooker was a preacher whose bent was more mystical than legal; one of his books was entitled *The Soul's Possession of Christ* (1638). He was given permission to lead a fresh exodus, to found the colony of Connecticut; and in Connecticut although the elected governor was to be 'always a member of some approved congregation', those electing him need not always be full church members themselves. Another preacher, Roger Williams, had

---

[10] See D. B. Rutman, *Winthrop's Boston: Portrait of a Puritan Town, 1630–49* (Chapel Hill, N.C., 1965).

252 *The Puritan Explosion*

been in a series of disputes with the Massachusetts authorities since landing in 1631. In January 1636 he was warned by Governor Winthrop that he was about to be shipped back to England. Instead he stumbled out of Salem into a snowstorm, was sheltered by some Indians, and went on to found a settlement at Providence. This eventually grew into the colony of Rhode Island, the first American colony to base itself permanently upon 'soul liberty', the guaranteed toleration of all Christians. As early as 1637 Mrs Anne Hutchinson, with her husband and her eleven children, was banished from Massachusetts for claiming direct 'revelations' from God. These revelations supported her enthusiasm for her interpretation of the message of her favourite preacher, John Cotton; what John Cotton really thought about his embarrassing admirer is not so clear. She found a temporary refuge on Rhode Island before moving on to more pioneering (and to death in one of the Indians' periodic massacres of the Dutch colonists to the north of Manhattan). Many others found freedom in Rhode Island, including Baptists, as the old 'Anabaptists' who denied the validity of infant baptism were coming to be called; and the colony received a royal charter on this broad basis in 1663. Thus gradually within a new colony it was admitted that dissenters who claimed 'soul liberty' did not need to found yet another new colony.[11]

Roger Williams had been trained at Cambridge as a Calvinist of impeccable orthodoxy, and he never abandoned that central belief. He was not a democrat; he was a Calvinist, a theocrat. But he had two revolutionary ideas. The first was that an English king had no right to dispose of the lands of the Indians to English colonists. The second was that the magistrates had no right to use worldly weapons to enforce laws about religion; for example, they had no right to punish any who broke the Sabbath calm of Sunday. Such malefactors ought to be left to the punishment of their own consciences. To Williams, Christ was not a pillar of the Puritan establishment, or of any other form of Christendom; he was a 'beggar's brat laid in a manger and a gallow's bird'. To follow Christ meant

---

[11] See Emery Battis, *Saints and Sectaries* (Chapel Hill, N.C., 1962).

the way of the cross – as Williams had himself felt when he had given up his legal career (where he had enjoyed the direct patronage of the formidable Sir Edward Coke) to become a minister of Christ, and when he had then given up a career in the Church of England in order to minister in the American wilderness.

Williams was no slack liberal. Those who took that narrow way must be thoroughly converted before taking it; one of his pamphlets was entitled *Christenings Make Not Christians*. Thus the Christian Church must be radically different from any political society; God's people and Caesar's must be separate. John Winthrop (who retained much bemused good will towards this amazing radical) understood him as teaching that a man should not pray with his wife unless he could be sure that she had been converted. It was essentially because those who followed Christ truly must be free and few that Williams rejected indignantly any suggestion that men might be compelled to conform outwardly in matters of religion. He returned to England in 1643 in order to urge his policy of toleration on Parliament, writing a long pamphlet which in its very title called 'persecution for cause of conscience' a 'bloody' teaching – only to have the book burned by the common hangman. Back in New England a pamphlet from John Cotton asserted that the so-called 'bloody' doctrine was in fact fully Christian; it had been 'washed in the blood of the lamb'.

In the course of his life (and he was about eighty years old when he died) Williams grew sceptical about the merits even of Christian organizations, however small. Although he often talked with Indians about Christ – 'God was pleased to give me a painful, patient spirit to lodge with them in their filthy, smoky holes' – he never tried to form an Indian congregation. He became a small landowner and opened a trading post, although he did not sell alcohol or guns to his beloved Indians as rival traders did; instead, he wrote the first book in English explaining the 'language of America'. He took a full part in the young life of the colony, even if it meant bearing arms against the Indians when to his great sorrow they turned against the settlers in 1675–76 ('King Philip's war') and burned his house and papers, reducing him to poverty. Much of his energy went into theological controversy against a new sect, the Quakers, but he never consented to any persecution of them. He made no attempt to build up a congregation of his fellow whites around his preaching, as men such as John Cotton – once his neighbour when they were both Church of England clergymen in Lincolnshire – had done so successfully. To follow Christ must mean to be a seeker, to the end. In the year before his death in 1683 he wrote to the governor of Massachusetts: 'Eternity (O eternity!) is our business.'[12]

This separation of Church and State was to save the life of American Christianity when the religious enthusiasm of the first days in New England was becoming a burden to the majority of the colonists – and when the diversity of the religious foundations of the various colonies was becoming a problem along the long path to co-operation and union. Even in Massachusetts when a new royal charter was issued in 1691 the religious qualification for voting disappeared. In the Connecticut valley churches, Samuel Stobbard was teaching that Christians should be admitted to the Lord's Supper even if they had not been able to convince the existing church members that they had been soundly converted. The profession of Christian faith and a good life were all that was required; 'all professors walking blamelessly are visible saints'. In 1700 this clergyman actually published such liberal notions. A year earlier, a church had been founded in Boston itself where admission to Baptism and Communion was left to the discretion of the minister, not to the votes of the congregation.

Meanwhile another experiment showed how wide was to be the liberty offered by America. Sir George Calvert renounced high office under James I in order to become a Roman Catholic in 1624. He was compensated by an Irish peerage as Lord Baltimore – and, under Charles I, by the grant of a huge tract of land around Chesapeake Bay to the north of Virginia. Both Baltimore and his royal master dreamed of solving the problem

---

[12] Recent studies include Edmund S. Morgan, *Roger Williams: The Church and the State* (New York, 1967); John Garrett, *Roger Williams, Witness beyond Christendom* (New York, 1970); W. Clark Gilpin, *The Millenarian Piety of Roger Williams* (Chicago, Ill., 1979).

of the Recusants by persuading them to migrate. On his death his son Cecil modified the project in order to make it pay, and in the hope that it would be more acceptable to New England's Puritans: it was to include Anglicans, although Roman Catholic and other Trinitarian Christians were to be free to practise their religion privately. In 1634 a boat carrying two Jesuit priests (as 'gentlemen adventurers') and sixteen Roman Catholic families, along with some two hundred other people, arrived in the fertile upper reaches of Chesapeake Bay to begin the new colony, Maryland – so named after Queen Henrietta Maria. The 'Act of Toleration' adopted in 1649 (at Baltimore's insistence after various internal conflicts) was the Christian world's most formal affirmation to that date of the principle of religious liberty. However, even then offences such as the denial of the divinity of Christ remained punishable by death, and gradually the Anglican influence in Maryland so prevailed that in 1702 the Church of England was established.[13]

That is why Rhode Island, although slightly younger than Maryland, is honoured as the first colony to make permanent an experiment which against all expectations became possible as Christianity entered the new world across the Atlantic: the clear separation of Church and State within a society still fundamentally Christian.

THE ENGLISH PURITANS

The influence of Puritanism ran underground while Charles I and Archbishop Laud governed England, but that did not stop the influence being powerful. The force that created New England could not be impotent in the colonists' home country.

We can see it in the career of John Preston – or rather, in his refusal to embrace a career if it meant any disloyalty to his main vocation, which was to be a pastor and preacher. The son of a Northamptonshire farmer, Preston won honours at Cam-

---

[13] T. O. Hanley examined *Their Rights and Liberties: The Beginnings of Religious and Political Freedom in Maryland* (Westminster, Md., 1959).

bridge; a memory survives of him reading St Thomas Aquinas 'as the barber cut his hair, and when any fell upon the place he read, he would not lay down his book but blow it off'. He specialized in the philosophy of Aristotle and studied medicine. Then the direction of his life was changed by a sermon by John Cotton; for the rest of that life, he stayed every summer in Cotton's vicarage. In Cambridge he became a winning teacher and trainer of young Puritans and Master of Emmanuel College. He was also summoned to succeed John Donne as the preacher to the lawyers of Lincoln's Inn. As he moved between Cambridge and London, many future MPs came under his influence as he had come under John Cotton's.

In 1621 he was given the key post of chaplain to the most powerful young man in the kingdom, Prince Charles, under the patronage of the reigning favourite, the Duke of Buckingham. When the old king died, Preston was the third man in the carriage which bore Charles and Buckingham away to being their joint ascendancy; and when John Williams was dismissed as Lord Keeper, Buckingham offered to obtain the post for him. Preston consulted his friends and rejected the offer. When not long afterwards the King and the Duke came out in favour of Arminianism, Preston broke with them. His closest friend was William Fiennes, Lord Saye and Sele – a man who was to exercise great influence among Puritan MPs in the 1640s. Preston would presumably have had a rather similar influence, had he not died of consumption a month after Buckingham's murder. He was little more than forty years old and had burned himself out.[14]

For many movements, such a leader's unwillingness to assume political office, his later breach with the king and the king's favourite, and his premature death, would all have been disasters. English Puritanism, however, had learned by the time of Preston's death not to depend on royal favour or on any one man's leadership. Its lay leaders were deprived of a national platform by the decision of the King to govern without

[14] See Irvonwy Morgan, *Prince Charles's Puritan Chaplain* (London, 1957); and Christopher Hill, *Puritanism and Revolution* (London, 1958), pp. 239–74.

Parliament, and its clerical leaders were deprived of prestigious offices. But that did not alter the attractiveness of Puritanism.

The sons of the gentry were taking themselves with a new seriousness. That was shown by their ambitions in the House of Commons and their wish to be educated at the universities or at the 'inns of court' where lawyers were trained. It was also shown by the earnest conviction of many of them that life was about something more important than careers, properties, families and sports. To such men Puritanism held out an invitation. Many older men rich in piety were rich in worldly possessions. Several Puritan earls revealed themselves fully in the 1640s – most notably Bedford, whose central influence was cut short by death, Warwick, who commanded the navy on Parliament's behalf, his son-in-law Manchester, the Major General of the army of the Eastern Association in East Anglia, and Essex, the Lord General of the Parliamentary army. The frequent meetings of the backers of the Massachusetts Bay Company, or the supporters of the shorter-lived Providence Island colony in the Caribbean, saw English as well as transatlantic affairs discussed by Puritan gentlemen.

Although the Puritans' favourite preachers were not now bishops, deans or professors, and were harassed by Archbishop Laud, they could still be heard – and read, for Laud's censorship did very little to stop the flood of edifying books by the best-known Puritan preachers, all linked with John Preston and with each other. A man such as John Dod, although silenced by James I after a nineteen-year ministry in one parish, was rescued by a Puritan squire who gave him another parish, in Northamptonshire (where John Preston was buried). Many thousands of readers delighted to find Dod's incisive and often witty preaching on the printed page, and he probably exercised as much influence as any bishop before his death in 1645 at the age of ninety. We have noticed that John Preston was converted by John Cotton; but the preacher who converted John Cotton, Richard Sibbes, was as influential as Preston (his intimate friend) among Cambridge students and London lawyers. Preston's leading disciple, Thomas Goodwin, was another prince of the Puritan pulpit. Goodwin could look back to his conversion, through a sermon at a funeral on the afternoon of Monday, 2 October 1620. Exiled under Laud, he never ceased to be influential and lived to become a leading theologian at Oxford.

Clergymen such as these were morally the leaders of their profession; and it was a profession that was full of men dissatisfied with the existing system and alienated from the official leadership. In this period when religion fascinated almost all thinking men, and when the universities were pouring out more graduates than ever before, the number of posts within the official Church able to support graduate preachers in the style they expected was limited, almost to the extent already seen under Elizabeth. This does not seem to have been a time of widespread poverty in the rectories. With rising prices of corn, rectors entitled to a tenth of the parish's harvest could do well. But many graduates with a good opinion of themselves failed to find patrons to appoint them to rectories. Some 3,800 vicars often found that because the 'great' tithes of corn were the property of a rector or (more likely) a layman, their own families must suffer. A lectureship in a town church might well be more attractive, and there the appointment was usually made by Puritan laymen.[15]

The decisive factor in the spread of Puritanism was, however, not any preacher's financial discontent. It was the transforming effect which a Puritan in the pulpit or in conversation could have on an individual who could be brought to believe that from eternity God had predestined him to heaven. Thomas Hooker, who wrote several books analysing the process of conversion, summed up 'the soul's preparation for Christ': 'to believe is the hardest thing that a man is put to under heaven.' But the effect of belief, once that light had dawned, was a readiness to receive a glorious salvation, and with salvation the gift of the Holy Spirit, producing all the harvest of a godly life. Although a preacher could be an invaluable guide in that life, the decisions had all to be taken by the individual, as he or she read the Scriptures with the aid of

---

[15] These were the conclusions drawn by Rosemary O'Day in *The English Clergy: The Emergence and Consolidation of a Profession, 1558–1642*.

the Spirit. Conversion with these results formed the theme of innumerable sermons preached at funerals and subsequently printed, and of many autobiographies.[16]

The great emphasis on the converted layman's experience explains why Puritanism was able to flourish in places where there was no dominant layman and no distinguished preacher of this persuasion. If need be, all that was really needed was a Christian believer, able to take family prayers in the approved style and to exhort his neighbours.[17] Probably it did Puritan gentlemen – and clergymen – no real harm that their exclusion from the seats of power in the 1630s threw them back on Bible study, prayer and private morality. The vast majority never crossed the Atlantic, but many seem to have become pilgrims in spirit.[18]

When they won their political victory in England, they inaugurated a new age. That age was called 'the Puritan revolution' by S. R. Gardiner, the historian whose many-volumed narrative of it (begun in 1863, continued by Sir Charles Firth and brought to completion by another disciple in 1955) has never been surpassed for richness of detail. In twentieth-century historical work the name has gone out of fashion, and that is understandable. The word 'revolution' – borrowed from astronomy and indicating a cyclical, not linear, pattern in events – was very seldom applied to English events at the time. It was a French historian, Guizot, who compared the 1640s with the French Revolution in a book of 1826. A century and a half later, few historians were eager to repeat the comparison. And if it was a revolution, was it Puritan? John Pym, speaking in the Parliament of 1621, rejected 'that odious and factious name of Puritans'. Almost twenty years later another MP, Sir Benjamin Rudyard, was still fuming about the

---

[16] The same theme ran through Geoffrey Nuttall, *The Holy Spirit in Puritan Faith and Experience* (Oxford, 1946); Gordon Wakefield, *Puritan Devotion* (London, 1957); Owen Watkins, *The Puritan Experience* (London, 1972).

[17] This was brought out by R. C. Richardson, *Puritanism in North-west England* (Manchester, 1972).

[18] Classic studies are by William Haller: *The Rise of Puritanism* (New York, 1938) and *Liberty and Reformation in the Puritan Revolution* (New York, 1955). Recent studies include Christopher Hill, *Society and Puritanism in Pre-Revolutionary England* (London, 1964), and Perez Zagorin, *The Court and the Country* (London, 1969).

imprecise nickname. 'Whosoever squares his actions by any
rule, divine or human, is a Puritan. Whosoever would be
governed by the King's laws, he is a Puritan.' So we need to
remember that the men going to Parliament in 1640 had no
idea of launching a revolution and little sense of belonging to a
single, cohesive Puritan movement. However, it remains true
that the train of events begun in 1640 became revolutionary. It
is also true that this result would have been impossible without
the energy and self-confidence given to Englishmen by the kind
of Protestantism that came to be classified as Puritanism. And
these truths deserve careful analysis because this civil war was
such a traumatic crisis in English history.

In our own materialistic age it has naturally been difficult for
historians to believe that any brand of the Christian religion
could once have wielded compelling authority. It has been
suggested instead that the key factor was the economic rise of
the gentry, determined to sweep away the outdated feudal
monarchy and aristocracy – an interpretation which fits in well
with the Marxist analysis of the long, unhappy prelude to the
rise of the proletariat. The counter-suggestion has been made
that in that age of inflation many of the 'mere' gentry were not
rising but falling, so that they looked with envy and hatred on
the few who were favoured by the Court with profitable offices,
grants of monopolies in certain trades or other support. Savage
controversies about the gentry's rise or fall have raged in
academic journals.[19]

Such debates between scholars were not a complete waste of
time. They acknowledged the truth that great movements in
society do not get started solely by speeches in Parliament or by
sermons in the pulpit, so that religion, like politics, must be
studied in its proper context, the total life of a society. Recent
controversies have also stimulated much useful research into
the financial affairs of hundreds of men who occupied leading
positions in the civil war, and into the life of the counties far
from London. But continuing research has shown how mis-

---

[19] See the extracts collected by Laurence Stone in *Social Change and Revolution in
England* (London, 1965), with R. K. Richardson, *The Debate on the English Revolution*
(London, 1977).

leading it can be to categorize the men who were to divide in 1642, and how much caution should be exercised when gener-alizing about economic trends in the 1630s. It seems to be generally true that the seventeenth century brought to the fortunate a growing profitability, in towns and countryside alike. But those who successfully exploited their estates, or other capital, had to be unusually efficient, resolute or lucky. Gentlemen who started with the same advantage as the fortun-ate declined because they could not compete, and one historian has ventured the opinion that the majority of the gentry 'may just have endured'.

Some generalizations about changing trends affecting the gentry and the merchants are obviously true: the monarchy could no longer obtain enough revenue to rule without par-liamentary taxation; the peerage could no longer exert a military discipline over vast districts in alliance with the Crown; some or many landowners and merchants who were to be able to influence Parliament had felt seriously frustrated or threatened by the policies of the Stuart kings; towns rather than rural areas, the more developed south and east rather than the relatively backward north and west, tended to side with Parliament when war came. But it does not follow that being a 'mere' gentleman or a 'mere' merchant without in-fluence at Court compelled one into rebellion in order to rescue one's economic interests. Lord Digby spoke in the Commons in 1641 about 'the liberty, the property of the subject fun-damentally subverted' – but ended up an ardent Royalist. Many impoverished gentlemen declared for the King. The enthusiastic supporters of Parliament included some who had held profitable offices from the King. Among them was John Pym, the first great organizer of the Parliamentary war effort. John Hutchinson, who commanded the garrison of Notting-ham in the Parliamentary interest, had attempted to buy an office of profit in the court of Star Chamber as late as 1649.[20] The supporters of Parliament included many landowners who had been doing well during the eleven years of 'tyranny'.

---

[20] His widow Lucy wrote a classic biography: *Memoirs of the Life of Colonel Hutchinson*, ed. James Sutherland (Oxford, 1973).

Research into the private affairs of MPs has found little
difference in the prosperity of the estates of those who took the
one side or the other. Research into their elections has shown
that if the election was contested (which was unusual) the
issues tended to be local not national. The merchants of
London were divided; when the King was feasted by the Lord
Mayor in November 1641 his position seemed secure, and it
needed drastic change in the composition of the Common
Council during the next month to make the City of London
Milton's 'mansion house of liberty'. In the counties, there were
many attempts to make neutral zones and there was much
reluctance to serve outside the county. And as the horror of
civil war engulfed the homes of the gentlemen of England, it
was not unknown for father and son, or for brothers, to take
different sides. Sir Edmund Verney, the King's standard-
bearer, was wretched to learn that his eldest son, Ralph, had
sided with Parliament; and John Milton's brother Christopher
was a Royalist.[21]

It seems, then, that among men with possessions, economic
grievances or ambitions were often less decisive than were
convictions about how England ought to be governed, and in
particular about how religion ought to be established in a
Christian country. This cannot be a surprise to anyone who
reflects how terrible a step it was for English gentlemen to
renew the medieval civil wars. The convictions of reasoning
men who thought this step necessary were often clothed in
religious terminology, and since this was an age of flourishing
religious faith, we are under no obligation to regard either side
as hypocritical.

On the Royalist side the convictions were no less real for not
being sanctimoniously eloquent. (Sir Jacob Astley's prayer
before the battle at Edgehill has become famous: 'Lord, thou

---

[21] Studies which have built up this picture include D. Brunton and D. H.
Pennington, *Members of the Long Parliament* (London, 1953), supplemented by M. F.
Keeler, *The Long Parliament 1640–41: A Biographical Study* (Philadelphia, Pa., 1954);
G. E. Aylmer, *The King's Servants* (London, 1961); Valerie Pearl, *London and the
Outbreak of the Puritan Revolution* (Oxford, 1961), supplemented by Robert Ashton,
The City and the Court 1603–43 (London, 1979); David Underdown, *Pride's Purge*
(London, 1971); J. S. Morrill, *The Revolt of the Provinces* (London, 1976).

knowest how busy I must be this day. If I forget thee, do not thou forget me . . . March on, boys!') The convictions of James I about the divine right of kings were now made more glamorous because the King was a fastidiously clean-living son of the Church of England (if almost more futile, since the King lacked his father's low cunning). According to Royalist beliefs at their extreme, a king was anointed in order to rule and it was the simple duty of his subjects to obey him. On the scaffold, a few minutes before his execution, Charles I declared that the people's freedom 'consists in having of government'. He did not mean 'having share in government, that is nothing pertaining to them'; 'a subject and a sovereign are clean different things.'

There was, however, a subtler form of Royalism, expressed by moderate Royalists such as Edward Hyde (later Earl of Clarendon) and in some moods or for some purposes by the King himself. At his trial Charles was surprisingly eloquent. He argued that most Englishmen were on his side, because they accepted his anointing by God to be their king as the best guarantee of the continuation of the mixture of laws and liberties which they had inherited from their ancestors. He was defending the achievements of many generations in the life of a generally happy and prosperous people. After this flagrant rebellion against England's monarchy which had been continuous since Anglo-Saxon days, no doubt many other ancient institutions would suffer a similar fate. So, claimed the King, 'it is not my case alone, it is the freedom and the liberty of the people of England' – against 'power without law'. He was 'the Martyr of the People'. And such appeals to conservative instincts touched the hearts of many thousands, drawn from all ranks of society, who were willing to sacrifice savings and lives for the King in the civil war.[22]

In opposition to the Royalist creed or creeds, Puritan religion gave rise to an ideology which appealed in somewhat the same way as a later revolutionary movement such as Marxism. It was a religion based on the Bible as squarely as Communism was to be based on the teachings of Marx, Lenin, Stalin or

[22] Dame Veronica Wedgwood has told the story of *The Trial of Charles I* (London, 1964.

Mao. Those who argued about politics on this basis constantly employed scriptural texts applauding the overthrow of wicked kings or wicked priests or wicked rich men and hailing the birth of a new age of righteousness. It was the conviction of those who in the end took Parliament's side that a new age could indeed dawn for England, and should dawn, because England deserved better than to be governed by kings such as Charles Stuart, ministers such as Buckingham or Strafford, and bishops such as Laud. An elected Parliament was morally entitled to decide through taxation what was to be the scope of the government's activity and through legislation what was to be the direction of the government's policy in vital matters such as religion.

As yet there was no thought of total freedom for all, but there certainly was the conviction that many Englishmen had definite 'liberties', political and religious, which had been flouted – and that Parliament had the power and the duty to assert these rights. The driving force behind this conviction can be discerned even in Ben Jonson's presentation of Zeal-of-the-Land Busy in *Bartholomew Fair* (1614). It was a pride in England fostered by a faith in England's proper religion, the religion of the Bible, the religion which promised the coming of the kingdom of God. The Bible announced the great dignity of men and women after salvation by Christ; and Puritans were sure that they, together with many of their fellow Englishmen, had been saved, becoming 'God's people', deserving God's kingdom. Meanwhile the 'saints' chosen by God must pray, watch and struggle for the great day; the imagery of spiritual warfare was constantly used. In 1643 Stephen Marshall, the preacher who was called 'the trumpet', reminded other Englishmen of the promise in the Revelation of St John the Divine that Christ and his saints would reign for a thousand years. It was the promise of the millennium, and 'we have the whole army of Protestant interpreters agreeing on the general scope and meaning of it'.[23]

---

[23] See William Shenk, *The Concern for Social Justice in the Puritan Revolution* (London, 1948), and Michael Walzer, *The Revolution of the Saints* (London, 1966). Much can be learned from W. P. Holden, *Anti-Puritan Satire, 1572–1642* (New Haven, Conn., 1954). H. R. Trevor-Roper's essays on *Catholics, Anglicans and Puritans* (London, 1987) are worthwhile.

But the saints of Puritan England were for the most part patient in awaiting the fulfilment of the divine promises, and were not agreed as to what form it should take in the government of the country when power was in their hands. This was because the visionary and dynamic utopianism of the Puritan sermon was almost always accompanied among the Puritan gentry by a conservative social philosophy. The promised kingdom would be revealed in God's time. It was not for mortal men to insist on knowing its date or its form. They must do their duty in the circumstances appointed by God – which for practical purposes meant, in their allotted place in the social order. So St Paul had taught: converted slaves must still accept slavery.[24]

Elizabethan and Stuart government propagandists often compared Puritanism with Popery because it was alleged to preach disobedience, but in fact English Puritanism never produced a preacher able either to depose a monarch or to ignite resistance by his claim to have the power of deposition. Being based so solidly on the Bible, Puritans always had to reckon with the very texts to which the Royalists appealed – texts urging obedience to kings, reverence for apostles and elders, the general acceptance of one's lot in life. Jean Calvin had himself given great weight to those texts and had been extremely reluctant to countenance any disorder. As much as Richard Hooker was that Puritan pundit, William Perkins, sure that in general 'orderly comeliness is part of the goodness of a thing' and that in particular 'as a king by his laws brings his people in order, and keeps them in subjection, so Christ by his word, and the preaching of it, as it were by a mighty army, draws his elect into his kingdom, and fashions them all to all holy obedience.' As we have just seen, Calvinism exported to America had erected a regime which was in many ways repressive in its insistence on 'holy obedience'. In England the

[24] The character of Puritanism as a search for spiritual liberty was well brought out by John S. Coolidge, *The Pauline Renaissance in England: Puritanism and the Bible* (Oxford, 1970). J. Sears McGee, *The Godly Man in Stuart England* (New Haven, Conn., 1976), similarly moved away from analysis in terms of Marxism, while stressing the Puritan dynamism in contrast with the official Church's constant plea for peace and charity.

very discipline on which the Puritan prided himself – discipline in private prayer and public worship, in chastity and sobriety, in honest toil – was extended to disciplined obedience to 'the magistrate', the 'powers that be' ordained by God as part of his stern response to the Fall of Adam. William Perkins, when he had boldly declared that when 'Christ is all' there is 'neither father nor mother, neither master, mistress, maid nor servant, nor husband nor wife, nor lord, nor subject, nor inferior', would always go on to remind his fellow Elizabethans that social distinctions had not yet been eliminated. This warning was endlessly repeated by Puritan preachers under the Stuarts. The Puritan movement included peers, rich aldermen in the cities and many gentlemen who controlled the countryside as deputy lieutenants, sheriffs or Justices of the Peace. In their eyes, Puritanism was an eminently respectable religion.

The case of William Prynne is fairly typical. A lawyer gifted both with moral courage and the power of invective, he wrote the best known warning against the doctrines of Laudians (*Anti-Arminianism*, 1629) and had his ears cropped on the orders of Laud and other judges for later, very outspoken, attacks on the bishops and on the Queen's participation in allegedly lewd plays. But he was so disillusioned by the moral disorder caused by the civil war that he moved in revulsion to oppose Cromwell vociferously, and to take part in Royalist plots. Before he died in 1669 he made a future Archbishop of Canterbury (Tillotson) his literary executor. The sincere concern of this unattractively abusive and long-winded lawyer was the moral purification of himself and his contemporaries.[25]

Opposition to the policies of Laud, Strafford and the others who had been the King's ministers in the 1630s was morally possible – indeed, imperative – for Puritan MPs; but as events unfolded they showed that the Puritans in Parliament had no agreed alternative programme. Did they want to keep bishops divested of power as in the primitive Church, or to give power to presbyteries of preachers as in Scotland, or to allow each congregation to be independent as in Massachusetts? Puritans

---

[25] W. M. Lamont studied *Marginal Prynne* (London, 1963). The ambiguity of *The Christian Polity of John Calvin* was brought out in Harro Höpfl's study (Cambridge, 1982).

were not agreed in an ecclesiastical policy, any more than they were agreed on what kind of constitutional, limited, monarchy they wanted. This was because the only political conviction that united them was the conviction of an opposition – and of a mostly conservative one. The Petition of Right presented by the Commons to an indignant king in 1628 had behind it the legal conservatism with which Sir Edward Coke had defied King James. In the 1640s there was again much talk about Magna Carta and about an English freedom older than the 'Norman yoke'. The extension of the tax of 'ship money' to inland shires in time of peace was an innovation in 1634, although upheld by a majority of the judges when a very rich gentleman, John Hampden, refused to pay it. Behind Hampden were rich men who had already refused to pay and had been let off – and even after the judgement against Hampden the sheriffs told to collect ship money often found themselves unable to enforce the order. Almost as much indignation was caused by the enforcement of outmoded payments to the king under feudal laws. In the 1630s these, too, seemed to be an innovation, to be resisted. But the opposition's loudest complaint was about innovations in religion, in particular about the Arminian theological revolution which seemed to be changing the face of the Church of England. The defence of the Protestant establishment was a cause which bestowed a halo on the not very heroic figure of a gentleman who refused to pay ship money or a feudal fee.

The opposition to the King's ministers in Parliament was, it is clear, a split within the English governing class – a split which most gentlemen did not wish to see become a revolution. Of the 493 members elected to the 'Long Parliament' in the autumn of 1640, fewer than a hundred seem to have expressed 'Court' rather than 'Country' views in the early stages. But it did not follow that the House of Commons was full of ardent revolutionaries. Those who managed the business of the House often complained that members were absent, indulging in the amusements of London or in their more interesting duties at home; and among members who did attend to the business, there was no unanimity. In November 1641 the Grand Remonstrance setting out the grievances of the Commons passed by

only eleven votes (159 to 148). More than fifty MPs served in
the King's army, and more than a hundred others in the
assembly which he summoned to Oxford in 1644–45. The
House of Commons remaining in Westminster included about
the same number. In 1645–46 244 new members were elected,
all pledged to support the 'Parliamentary' cause, but another
decisive vote on the last day of 1646 found 105 voting for the
prohibition of all preaching by laymen, 57 against. No fewer
than 231 MPs had to be excluded by the soldiers in 'Pride's
Purge' in December 1648 before the King's execution could be
secured; of the remaining MPs, some 250 in all, only about
sixty sat regularly because they were prepared to co-operate
with the army. Less than half of that sixty finally approved of
the King's execution.

The picture emerging from modern research seems, therefore, to support the older picture of the opposition to the
ministers of King Charles as a conservative affair given a
limited amount of courage by Puritanism.[26] But this split
within the governing class was not the only kind of hostility
which confronted the King's ministers. There was another
kind of Puritanism, or at least of Protestantism, and it was far
more revolutionary.

London was the centre of this extremist movement. Naturally, London preachers tended to be the most eloquent and the
most excited. And already in politically quieter days London
had witnessed a minor religious revolution: the permanent
establishment of congregations which were defiantly separate
from the Church of England.

There were three dozen of these 'separatist' churches in
existence by 1646. The earliest was a group around a Nottinghamshire squire, Thomas Helwys, who had gone into exile
rather than conform – and who in 1612 dared to return to

---

[26] Recent studies include Robert Ashton, *The English Civil War: Conservatism and
Revolution, 1603–49* (London, 1978); Anthony Fletcher, *The Outbreak of the English
Civil War* (London, 1981); and the 1973 volume of 'revisionist' essays: *The Origins
of the Civil War*, ed. Conrad Russell. Some of the theoretical background was
sketched by W. M. Lamont, *Godly Rule: Politics and Religion 1603–60* (London, 1969),
and David Little, *Religion, Order and Law: A Study in Pre-Revolutionary England*
(Oxford, 1970).

England. He also dared to publish a pamphlet dedicated to the King and pleading that 'the King is a mortal man and not God: therefore hath no power over the immortal souls of his subjects, to make laws and ordinances for them, and to set spiritual laws over them.' This plea for religious liberty (the first of its kind in English) landed him in prison. Another group was founded when a few laymen in a house in Southwark joined hands in a ring with a clergyman, Henry Jacob, who had dared to return from exile in 1616. They all believed that only adult baptism was valid, but these early Baptists were not Calvinists, for they rejected the doctrine that Christ had died only to save the 'elect'. Their creed was to become known as the 'General Baptist' position. But during the 1630s 'Particular Baptist' congregations were formed. These not only confined baptism to adults but also confined salvation to the elect. The first pastor of such a congregation was John Spilsbury, a cobbler by trade. Radicalism in religion began to include the belief that a congregation could get along without paying for a full-time pastor. And such radicalism in religion might encourage radicalism in politics.[27]

Whether or not preachers fanned its revolutionary spirit, by 1640 a large element in the London mob was spoiling for a fight with the authorities. It often staged demonstrations, beginning with one to welcome William Prynne on his release from prison. For months on end the mob did all it could to intimidate the Parliament sitting in Westminster. The howls of the angry people were probably decisive in making Lords and Commons press for the execution of Strafford and the imprisonment of Laud. Cries of 'Justice! Justice! Justice!' drowned hesitations. At various later turning-points in the plot the Parliamentary stage at Westminster was invaded by the mob. Cries for 'Bread!' often mingled with 'Justice!' – for the mob was a ragged army which the hunger and fear of so many in the countryside had brought together in London. 'The population of London and its suburbs may have numbered as many as 450,000 at this time', we are told. 'It . . . was by very

---

[27] These London separatist churches were studied by Murray Tolmie, *The Triumph of the Saints* (Cambridge, 1977).

far [the] largest urban area, no other town in the country having more than 25,000 inhabitants. London contained the most massive concentration of poor people in the whole kingdom, and a very high proportion of its population consisted of recent immigrants from the provinces. Crowded together in the slums, they shed many of the traditions of deference into which they had been born in their villages . . . London had grown too fast for its machinery of government, with the forces of repression at its disposal, to be able very easily to control its population and maintain order; but it had not grown too quickly for rumours and ideas to spread quickly over the whole area.'[28]

The most readily believed of these rumours was the tale that the King's ministers were about to bring in a large army of murdering Papists – from Ireland, from France, from Spain, from heaven knew where. The fear of a return of Popery was the most conspicuous feature of the Grand Remonstrance, and we cannot wonder, for the Pope was often being preached about as Antichrist. The accusation that he had plotted to introduce an army from Ireland was what destroyed Strafford. Laud's Arminian theology was probably not much understood by the London mob; but the rumour was that the bishops were friends of the Papists, allies of Antichrist. Fifteen thousand signatures were collected for the petition from London to Parliament in December 1640 calling for the abolition of the whole system of bishops, 'root and branch'. The mob had made the Papists the scapegoats for its own unhappiness and insecurity, and therefore it was out to get the bishops.[29]

The time-absorbing concentration of Londoners on the political excitements of 1640–42 increased the difficulties of production and trade – particularly in the cloth industry, which was depressed anyway. It was not long before the common people of lesser towns began to set up their own cries for justice and bread, and to voice their own fears that some-

---

[28] Brian Manning, *The English People and the English Revolution, 1640–49* (London, 1976), p. 71.
[29] The popular hatred which lumped Roman Catholics and Church of England bishops together has been studied by Christopher Hill in *Antichrist in Seventeenth-century England* (London, 1971).

how the Papists were to blame. Thousands of signatures were collected for petitions to Parliament demanding that something should be done – a concerted movement without precedent in English history. At the same time ominous riots occurred in some rural areas. The pressure of overpopulation which had influenced thousands of the most adventurous to start farming the virgin soil of North America also meant that the untilled land of England became more important. Many obscure country folk had supported themselves from the 'waste' lands (for example, from the reeds and the fowls of the Fens) and were hostile to the 'improvement' of these lands (for example, the drainage of the Fens) since it meant that in future they would have to pay rents. At the same time inflation meant that ambitious landlords were raising their rents and reducing the perquisites of their labourers – and all this in an age when the prices of staple foodstuffs steadily mounted. The evidence suggests that the 1630s had been years of misery for many thousands of obscure English families. Inevitably many peasants began rejoicing when stories reached them that the King, the lords and the gentlemen were at each other's throats in London. Hearing that Bishop John Williams was unlikely to reappear in his great house at Buckden, local women drove their cows into the newly extended park and, when a magistrate rebuked them, 'only answered him with contemptuous words'. Elsewhere violence as well as insults expressed the pent-up indignation of the peasantry. Puritanism, which had been basically a religion of gentlemen and merchants who admired preachers, was involved in one (and, it seems, only one) way. It was easy to cry that the landlords were open or concealed Papists – the very cry which some of these landlords in Parliament were setting up against the bishops.

There was no organized peasants' revolt, because there was no national leadership and no common cry apart from the hysterical fear of Popery. But the demonstrations in London and the riots in the countryside were like the first drops in a new storm. Alarm about disorder seems to have been an important factor in moving considerable numbers of the propertied, including MPs, to view the King's cause with much more sympathy. But Parliament needed soldiers to fight for it, was prepared to pay them, and drew them largely from the ranks of those who had suffered in the recent economic changes; and then revolution came nearer. In the army those soldiers might hear Puritan chaplains telling them that their strengths were greater, and their lives more precious, than those of the Royalist gentlemen, the Lord's enemies, whom they had to fight to the death. Some of the low-born soldiers might be made officers, so great were the necessities of war. As Oliver Cromwell wrote to the Suffolk county committee in 1643: 'I had rather have a plain russet-coated captain that knows what he fights for, and loves what he knows, than that which you call a gentleman and is nothing else.'

As the war fought with Puritan slogans proceeded, it became what the noblemen and gentlemen meeting in Parliament had never intended: a revolution.

A WAR BECOMES A REVOLUTION

In the 'Short Parliament' which met in April 1640 the attitudes which were to bring a foolish king to his execution were all displayed.[30] Although he claimed such great powers for anointed kings, he did not take the trouble to work out, or present, a coherent policy. Instead he got the Lord Keeper to ask for taxes and was surprised when the House of Commons, organized by John Pym, insisted on the redress of grievances before it would vote a supply of taxes. In reply he turned for help to the House of Lords and then, alleging that some MPs were in league with the rebellious Scots, abruptly dismissed Parliament.

Such actions were characteristic. Charles always relied on his counsellors – among whom the most disastrous (because the most ignorant) was his French queen – but he liked to play one counsellor off against another. In that way he hoped to show who was master. He did not pursue a consistent policy in

---

[30] The best narrative of the civil war remains C. V. Wedgwood, *The King's War 1641–47* (London, 1958). The best analysis is Ivan Roots, *The Great Rebellion, 1642–60* (London, 1966).

dealing with opposition because it was hard for him to believe in his heart that the opposition could exist. When he made gestures of co-operation with the gentry (in 1640 he offered to abandon the collection of ship money in exchange for some approved system of revenue raising), he did not make his gestures large enough. Charles never allowed a strong moderate party to form around him, although such a party could have controlled the Commons at any date before December 1648. On the other hand, he was always too much of a patriot to obtain the large subsidies from France or Spain which alone could have enabled him to finance his court, army and civil service without needing the good will of the Commons. He was never even able to make up his mind between France or Spain. All that he did in this field was to write letters, ineffectively asking for help and damaging his reputation when the letters became known in England. At almost every juncture he intrigued amateurishly, hoping to divide his enemies (as in his plea to the peers in 1640) but often succeeding only in alienating them all still further. Then his anger that a king should have to stoop to such devices would flare up and he would take hasty action intended to end the problem once and for all; action which usually misfired. In his own eyes and in the eyes of his followers, the King behaved almost always as a Christian gentleman. The one major error which Charles admitted was a moral error: he allowed himself to be released by Strafford from his own oath that his minister should not suffer in life or estate. Charles came to believe that, because of this sin, God had allowed him to be defeated by traitors and brought to execution. Otherwise the King's tone was one of injured innocence. Yet his enemies came to regard him as a 'man of blood' whose own blood should be shed, because the succession of futile tricks by which he attempted to divide and rule his subjects had cost those subjects dear and needed to be brought to an end by the axe.

For long Archbishop Laud and his supporters seem to have been blind to the danger to the Church of England in its reliance on a king who was such an inept politician. In the spring of 1640 this, too, was demonstrated. The Convocation of the clergy continued to sit after the dissolution of Parliament, in defiance of constitutional precedent. It voted the King a small sum of money, infuriating the dispersed MPs without substantially helping the King. And it accepted from Laud and the clergy a new set of canons, further alienating the Puritans. These canons ordered that bearing arms against a king 'on any pretext whatsoever' should always be held sinful, and that a sermon in praise of the divine right of kings should be preached in every church once a quarter. Another imposed on the clergy an oath of loyalty to the government of the Church by 'archbishops, bishops, archdeacons, deans, *et cetera*'. Many Puritans chose to believe that *et cetera* might include the Pope, although the oath went on to reject 'the usurpations and superstitions of the See of Rome'.

Twelve peers presented a petition for another parliament, but what made the summons of the 'Long Parliament' inevitable in November 1640 was another invasion by the Scots, who had to be bought off. This parliament lasted for so long because it insisted on the King's consent to an Act providing that it should never be dissolved without its own consent. In its initial stages Parliament was so largely united because its policy was conservative: to punish Strafford and Laud for their innovations and to prevent their repetition. Even when Strafford's impeachment for 'endeavouring to subvert the fundamental laws' had to be abandoned in response to his brilliant self-defence, the Act of Attainder which finally brought him to the block was supported by a majority in the Commons so large, and by a majority in the Lords so surprising, that the King added his own consent. Then a rapid series of measures demolished the apparatus on which Strafford and Laud had relied. A parliament must meet for at least fifty days every three years. Non-parliamentary taxes and the grants of commercial monopolies to royal favourites were declared illegal. The courts of Star Chamber and High Commission were abolished.

It seems perfectly possible that the King could now have established a moderate administration in England supported by bishops with strictly limited powers, had he been so determined. In the summer of 1641 he visited Scotland, set up a government consisting of his former enemies, and had the satisfaction of seeing the Scottish army in England disbanded. But he took no major steps to secure the loyalty of prominent English moderates; and in May 1641 he lost by death from smallpox an aristocrat much admired by Puritans, the Earl of Bedford, who given a chance would have become a reforming Lord Treasurer with his associate, John Pym, as Chancellor of the Exchequer.

A fresh crisis arose in October 1641, when the Irish Catholics seized the opportunity to rebel – for the Commons, having reason to distrust the King, insisted on control of the expeditionary force for which they were prepared to pay. Another result of the Irish rebellion was to enflame the anti-Papist emotions of the London mob; the fire seems to have been fanned by John Pym. That December the London apprentices occupied themselves by preventing the bishops from taking their seats in the House of Lords, shouting 'No bishops!' and 'No Popish lords!' At the suggestion of John Williams (now the Church's leading figure, with Laud in prison), the bishops replied by claiming that the proceedings of the Lords in their absence were invalid – a reply which greatly embarrassed those in Parliament who had been struggling for the survival of the bishops, their revenues and their remaining political powers. A dozen bishops were promptly impeached and sent off to the Tower. Their permanent exclusion from Parliament became inevitable when the King failed to carry off a counter-*coup*, the arrest of his five leading enemies in the Commons on charges of subverting the 'fundamental laws'.

The whole future of the bishops, and of much else, now depended on the outcome of the propaganda war which opened at the beginning of 1642. The King left the capital and moved around the country, having enlisted Edward Hyde as his chief propagandist and having agreed to Hyde's moderate constitutionalism as the line to be taken. The Commons – increasingly under the dominance of John Pym, who had escaped arrest – did not believe that the King seriously intended concessions. They strengthened their hold on the unpaid militia or 'trained bands' in London and the counties, and made sure of the navy. They appealed to their supporters to gather horses and arms, and thus encouraged the King to take

the advice of the militants who gathered round him to compete
with the moderates. On 22 August 1642 he raised his standard
at Nottingham. Soon afterwards he issued a manifesto to his
supporters: 'You shall meet with no enemies but traitors, most
of them Brownists, Anabaptists and Atheists; such who desire
to destroy both Church and State . . .'

Although both sides had appealed to arms in the belief that
the issue would be settled in a matter of months, none of the
early battles in the civil war decided much. For a few weeks it
seemed possible that the Royalists would simply march into
London – but London defended itself, and then sent its men to
relieve a city under a more prolonged siege, Gloucester. The
first decisive move was the Solemn League and Covenant
entered into by Parliament with the Scots in St Margaret's
church, Westminster, a year after the war's outbreak. Parliament, led by Pym, bought this military support by a promise to
establish a new system of church government, uniform in all
three kingdoms of England, Scotland and Ireland, 'according
to the Word of God and the example of the best reformed
Churches'. This treaty was decisive because the prospect of an
army from the north stiffened Parliament's supporters in the
field to resist the Royalist forces who had previously seemed
likely to prevail – and because the price paid showed the
political determination of the Parliamentary leadership. Pym
was willing to run the risk of relying on the Scots, rather than
run the risk of relying on the King; and when he died of cancer
in December 1643 he was succeeded in the leadership not by
more moderate but more extreme men. Oliver St John the
lawyer who was an implacable prosecutor, Harry Vane who
had returned from New England with a stern mission, Oliver
Cromwell the soldier – such men were resolved to win the war
against the King whatever instruments they had to use. On the
Royalist side one of the leading moderates, Lord Falkland,
died on the battlefield of Newbury, and the King's ear was
increasingly filled with the advice of professional soldiers such
as his nephew Prince Rupert, promising a military solution to
his problems.

Parliament's abolition of the jurisdiction of bishops and
archdeacons, and of cathedral deans and chapters, came in

January 1643. It was a step which had to be taken in order to satisfy both the consciences and the pockets of those now fighting for Parliament. Estates of bishops and cathedrals, sold off during the 1640s to those favoured by Parliament, raised over a million pounds, mostly spent on the war.

Recommendations about the positive reform of the Church were entrusted to a conference of 121 theologians, with thirty lay assessors, by an ordinance issued by Parliament in June 1643. As a gesture four bishops were included together with five doctors of divinity prepared to defend them; but this group made practically no contribution. The initiative was taken and held by Calvinist Presbyterians who talked the same theological language as the Scots, together with some 'Independents' who talked the same language as the English soldiers. This 'Westminster Assembly' met that summer in Westminster Abbey, moving when the autumn came to the Jerusalem Chamber where a fireplace offered some comfort. We may take a brief holiday from the civil war by considering the outcome. The main contribution which the conference made to the history of the Christian world was contained in its statement of Calvinist doctrine, the Westminster Confession, intended to provide a theological basis for agreement between the English and the Scots. Completed before the end of 1646, this document was approved by the General Assembly of the Church of Scotland in 1647 and by the English Parliament the following year. It was followed by two documents intended for the instruction of the laity – the Longer and Shorter Catechisms, largely drafted by the vicar of Boston in Lincolnshire, Anthony Tuckney. These, too, were officially adopted in Scotland and England. By the time that Tuckney died in 1670 he had seen his work rejected by government and theologians alike in England; yet Scotland remained faithful to it, the Westminster Confession continued to be a 'standard of faith' among all orthodox Presbyterians, and the Shorter Catechism was to teach many generations of the children of Presbyterian and other parents. The position adopted in response to the disputes caused by Arminianism was an affirmation of God's predestinating decree to save a 'certain and definite' number of angels and men 'without any foresight of faith or good works, or perseverance in either of them'. When some acknowledgement of 'second causes' in an individual's salvation was added in the teaching given by this Westminster Assembly, it was less emphatic. But the main lesson which was to be remembered by the young, from the Shorter Catechism of 1647, was the definition of the 'chief end of man': 'to glorify God and to enjoy him for ever'.[31]

Meanwhile the civil war in England was not enjoyable. Whether the Scots were going to prevail with their insistence on a Presbyterian church government, or Independents such as John Milton were going to persuade the English that 'new presbyter' would be little better than 'old priest', what was clear after the treaty with the Scots was that the Elizabethan settlement of English religion was at an end. And it was beginning to seem possible that the whole Elizabethan order of society might be among the victims of an increasingly bitter war. In August 1643 a crowd of women with white ribbons in their hats demonstrated outside the House of Commons, crying 'Peace!' The only result was that one of them was killed, along with two men looking on, as the demonstration was violently dispersed.

In 1644 the Scots arrived and, combining with Oliver Cromwell's troops from East Anglia, defeated Prince Rupert on Marston Moor on 2 July. To turn that victory into the complete defeat of the King, it now seemed essential to signalize the end of the old religious order by executing old William Laud on 2 January 1645. In the same month a new *Directory of Public Worship* compiled by the Puritan divines of the Westminster Assembly was substituted for the old Book of Common Prayer as the national standard intended to be observed in the parishes. Although this directory permitted a considerable variety, a rigid discipline marked the reorganization of the

---

[31] Narratives were compiled by B. B. Warfield, *The Westminster Assembly and its Work* (London, 1931), and S. W. Carruthers, *The Everyday Work of the Westminster Assembly* (Philadelphia, Pa., 1943). R. T. Kendall, *Calvin and English Calvinism to 1649*, pp. 185–208, concluded that there was 'complete fundamental harmony' in theology, although he disagreed with Warfield over the extent of the influence of Calvin. He argued that the Westminster divines owed more to Beza or to his English exponent, William Perkins, as modified by Ames.

military forces on which Parliament depended. This decisive period of retraining saw the birth of the 'New Model Army' which was to bring victory. The final move in the reorganization was to exclude the three earls, Essex, Manchester and Warwick, from command. Cromwell had moved the 'Self-Denying Ordinance' which compelled peers or MPs to resign their commissions, but since the House of Lords insisted on an amendment which made re-appointment possible, and since he seemed indispensable, he ended up as Lieutenant-General; Sir Thomas Fairfax, a professional soldier, remained his superior.

The great military fact of 1645 was the triumph of the New Model Army. Deploying superior numbers and discipline, and sending in its cavalry under Cromwell, it routed the Royalists at Naseby near Leicester. Not long afterwards Prince Rupert surrendered Bristol, to his royal uncle's fury. The King's only hope now lay in enlisting in his cause an army from outside England. His previous intrigues with this motive, documented in papers captured at Naseby, hardened opinion against him when printed as *The King's Cabinet Opened*; but he clung to the hope. At the end of April 1646 he slipped out of Oxford (which had been his wartime headquarters) and at Southwell gave himself up to the surprised Scots. He was counting on their instinctive loyalty to their sovereign. He was also counting on their suspicion of the New Model Army.

Most of the remaining members of the House of Commons shared the King's hope of a rally of the conservative forces. Oliver Cromwell had accused the Earl of Manchester of not really wanting to see the King defeated, but the Earl had replied with accusations far more damaging in the eyes of most MPs. Cromwell was alleged to have said that he wanted 'to live to see never a nobleman in England' and that he was ready to fight for religious liberty even if it meant drawing his sword against the Scots. Now after Naseby Cromwell sent the Speaker of the House of Commons a letter which did something to bear out the Earl's accusations. 'Honest men served you faithfully in this action,' he wrote. 'Sir, they are trusty. I beseech you in the name of God not to discourage them . . . He that ventures his life for the liberty of his country, I wish he trust God for the liberty of his conscience, and you for the liberty he fights for.'

When the Commons printed the letter they suppressed that last sentence, but it was a fact that the soldiers of the New Model Army, although recruited to be defenders of the Presbyterian MPs and the allies of the Presbyterian Scots, had not been subjected to any theological test. 'The State in choosing men,' Cromwell had declared, 'takes no notice of their opinions.' In practice the soldiers held a wide variety of opinions and were disturbingly willing to demand liberty for them. A fortnight after the battle of Marston Moor the attack on religious persecution had been launched in the book by Roger Williams, but that plea from an eccentric New England preacher had led to an outcry among the respectable; of course Christian England must be uniform – on a Presbyterian, if not an Anglican, basis. After the New Model Army's triumph at Naseby, John Lilburne's pamphlet claiming religious liberty as *England's Birthright* could not be howled down so readily. Even in the House of Commons some MPs who were elders in Presbyterian churches were now tending to vote with Independents such as Cromwell because they feared the tyranny of a Presbyterian Church established on a national scale. The majority of MPs had no wish to see any preacher's tyranny; in March 1646 they agreed to the establishment of presbyteries all over England, but only after insisting that anyone excommunicated would have the right to appeal to a parliamentary committee. Even less, however, did they wish to see Cromwell's soldiers dictating terms which seemed likely to destroy the whole stability of Church and State. A book of 1646 by Thomas Edwards catalogued the heresies which seemed to be poisoning and destroying the very life of Christian England. It was a long catalogue, and it was called *Gangraena*. MPs were among those who read it with horror.[32]

While the gentlemen in Parliament nursed these fears of anarchy, the people in the country seem to have been domin-

[32] See George Yule, *The Independents in the English Civil War* (Cambridge, 1958), and J. R. McCormack, *Revolutionary Politics in the Long Parliament* (Cambridge, Mass., 1973).

ated by the simple desire to see the conflict ended, the armies disbanded, trade restored and taxation lowered. The small armies which had fought the civil war had not done a great deal of physical damage, but they certainly had interrupted both commerce and agriculture. And to sustain the war, Parliament had taxed the country far more heavily than any Stuart king had ever attempted. The new excise duty on beer or tobacco was particularly unpopular. It seemed the right time for the settlement with the King which Parliament had always claimed to be seeking; and it was reasonable to calculate that an agreement could be reached by taking two steps – the King making an alliance with the Scots, and Parliament preferring this alliance to the greater risks of radical government by soldiers and religious leadership by heretics.

The essential preliminary was, however, that the King should accept the support of the Scots on their terms, even if it meant accepting Presbyterianism for the time being. When he made himself their prisoner, the Scots naturally thought that this was his intention. From France his queen urged him to abandon the Anglican bishops; to her they were not true Catholic bishops – and he could, of course, always go back on the gesture once he had regained power. Day after day, Presbyterians argued with the King by speech or writing, attempting to persuade him to sign the covenant against Popery and prelacy. He persistently refused. Instead of making this tactical alliance with his gaolers, he attempted to negotiate once again with Parliament; but here, too, he refused to yield on the vital point of abdicating control of the armed forces for twenty years. He told Henrietta Maria that they must not 'stir one jot' from the authority to which their son was heir – and that of the two possible concessions, the renunciation of the bishops would be the more dangerous to the monarchy, 'for people are governed by pulpits more than the sword'. His cause, he later added, was 'the cause of every king in Christendom'. Eventually the Scots preferred to reach an agreement with Parliament, which at least had money to pay them off, rather than with the bewilderingly obstinate king. Charles was therefore entrusted to the mercies of his English subjects.

EXECUTING A KING

The King had virtually signed his own death warrant when he refused to abandon the bishops in order to purchase the support of the Scots, at a time when he could continue to rely reasonably on the support of the moderates who still constituted the majority in Parliament. That is his best claim to the title of martyr. And perhaps subconsciously he now began a journey towards martyrdom – as that very different martyr, Thomas Becket, had done when laying down his life against a king almost six hundred years before. But just as the future St Thomas of Canterbury had complicated his later reputation by arrogant, perverse and argumentative behaviour almost till the moment when he had allowed the knights to strike him down in his own cathedral, so the future King Charles the Martyr now conducted himself in a way that was less than saintly. He plotted almost until the day when he gave his flawless last performance in the icy sunshine on the scaffold outside the Banqueting House in Whitehall. Indeed, the King probably did believe that, being endowed by God with the authority and wisdom monopolized by kings, he could divide his enemies and appeal to the still loyal hearts of his people. More than once he made the request to be allowed back to London. If only he could return to the capital where he had been crowned and anointed, surely he would return to an invincible popularity. In fact he was brought back to die – but even during his trial the emotion dominant in him was indignant, incredulous surprise that the judges appointed by what was left of the House of Commons actually were sentencing a king to death.

As spring turned into summer in 1647 he was kept in custody by Parliament at Holdenby House in Northamptonshire. He watched with pleasure the tensions growing between the MPs and the soldiers. Parliament blundered badly by refusing (at first) to pay the soldiers' arrears of pay and to assure them of pardon for any offences during the war. 'Agitators' were chosen to get something done about the soldiers' demands. One of the things they did was to send Cornet Joyce to take the King to Hampton Court; when Charles asked him for his commission, this junior officer simply pointed to the troops behind him. But the King still did not feel doomed, for as confusion mounted the army was seen to be split not only from Parliament but also within itself.

Fairfax, Cromwell and most of the other senior officers – the 'grandees' as they were called – were at this stage prepared to reach a compromise. Cromwell kept repeating that they must have a king; 'no men could enjoy their lives and estates quietly without the king had his rights.' On one occasion he even called Charles 'the uprightest and most conscientious man of his three kingdoms'. When Cromwell had changed his mind and had brought Charles to trial, Fairfax's wife was to shout in the King's defence. 'Not half the people,' she protested, wanted the trial. But in that summer of 1647 many of the rank and file of the army had no such tender feelings about the monarchy. They knew only that a new age was dawning. The King had been defeated and a thrilling opportunity had arrived to pull down others who had denied 'the people's just rights and liberties'. A declaration of the army, claiming those rights, boasted: 'We were not a mere mercenary army . . . but called forth and conjured by the several declarations of Parliament . . . against all particular parties or interests whatsoever.' And now, as the agitator of Fairfax's own regiment blurted out, there was 'no visible authority in the kingdom but the power and force of the sword'.

That summer the Levellers put about many radical ideas, although they were divided. Some wanted no more than the sovereignty of Parliament – a Parliament to be elected by all adult males who were not servants, alms-takers or Royalists (which would have excluded two-thirds of Englishmen). Others wanted one man, one vote (excluding only supporters of the King) leading to a radical redistribution of wealth, with communes to take over the agriculture from the feudal manors and the privately owned farms. On two points all Levellers were agreed. The King must be stripped of all his powers. The clergy must be stripped of the security of their right to tithes.[33]

---

[33] Recent studies include H. N. Brailsford, *The Levellers and the English Revolution* (London, 1961); C. B. Macpherson, *The Political Theory of Possessive Individualism* (Oxford, 1962), chapter 3; G. E. Aylmer, *The Levellers in the English Revolution* (London, 1975).

The army slowly marched on London and, once there, was in a position to impose its will. But in the autumn of 1647 it was very uncertain what its will was. The parish church of Putney was the scene of long debates as soldiers, all appealing to divine guidance and quoting rival texts of Scripture, stumbled towards formulating the political theories of Right and Left in response to the 'Agreement of the People' drawn up by the Levellers. Cromwell played an uncertain role for much of the time throughout these months of intoxicating confusion. He tended to back his fellow soldiers against his fellow MPs and had no wish to see Presbyterianism enforced, but he also expressed horror at the suggestion that men who had 'no interest but the interest of breathing' might have votes. In the Putney debates, he pleaded for compromise and unity. Colonel Thomas Rainborough displayed and urged more courage; not for nothing was he the brother-in-law of Governor Winthrop of Massachusetts. 'I do think the poorest man in England is not at all bound in a strict sense to that government that he hath not had a voice to put himself under.' And he boasted: 'When I leap I shall take so much of God with me, and so much of just and right with me, as I shall jump sure.'[34]

In the end it was Cromwell who jumped decisively. He persuaded the confused debaters in the Putney church that the agitators ought to return to the regiments. The reason given was that the agitators would then be better able to gather the soldiers' opinions in preparation for a fuller debate, but in fact a different policy towards the Levellers was becoming clear in Cromwell's mind. 'Break them,' he told his fellow officers, 'or they will break you.' When some of the troops demonstrated by sticking the slogan 'England's Freedom, Soldiers' Rights' in their hats, the General cut down the mutiny with his own sword.

Charles also attempted to jump, but once again he tried to be too clever, jumping in too many directions. For some time he seemed to be moving towards the worried generals and the

---

[34] See A. S. P. Woodhouse, *Puritanism and Liberty, Being the Army Debates 1647–49* (London, 1938); Leo F. Solt, *Saints in Arms: Puritanism and Democracy in Cromwell's Army* (Stanford, Cal., 1959); A. L. Morton, *Freedom in Arms* (London, 1975).

moderate MPs. He escaped from the soldiers' custody in Hampton Court (almost certainly with Cromwell's connivance) and took refuge in the Isle of Wight (which was commanded by Cromwell's cousin). From the greater security of Carisbrooke Castle he made – or seemed to make – handsome offers to the English moderates: he would renounce the control of the armed forces for his lifetime and the bishops for an experimental period of three years. But he dangled similar baits before the Scots, and refused his assent when MPs translated his bargaining offers into actual bills. His double-dealing was now apparent, and in January 1648 the Commons voted to hold no more negotiations with him. All now depended on what the Scots would do to support the Royalists, and in the spring and summer of 1648 a second civil war flared up.

It turned out that the King had jumped into the fire. The second civil war was widespread but short-lived. The decisive action was Cromwell's defeat of the invaders from Scotland at Preston. Even now the pressures for a settlement were such that many MPs were soon again trying to come to terms with the King (and again refusing to settle the arrears of the soldiers' pay); and a few of the army officers, including Fairfax the General, still shared the hope of a compromise. But other officers encouraged Colonel Pride, who was in command of the troops guarding Parliament, to exclude most of the MPs as traitors to 'the cause'. Pride's Purge, on 6 December, was accepted by Cromwell, although he had not initiated it. The officers now controlling the 'Rump Parliament' were increasingly dominated by Cromwell's personality – and determined, as Cromwell now was, to end the King's plots once and for all, before they cost more English lives. On the first day of January 1649 the Commons set up a special court to try Charles Stuart for treason in making war against Parliament and the kingdom. The refusal by the Lords to participate in an act so lacking in precedent was swept aside. Pushed by events which he called 'providences', Cromwell was jumping into a republic.

In the long run Cromwell was not wise to arrange for the King's execution, because the monarchy still occupied a unique place in the feelings, if not in the reasonings, of most Englishmen – and the dignity of the King as the end approached was the peak moment in the 'kingcraft' of the Stuart dynasty. The condemned man made sure that his famous last injunction to Bishop Juxon, 'Remember!', would be obeyed. The last words which he heard on 30 January 1649, from the executioner, were 'Your Majesty'. A great deep groan went up from the crowd when they saw his head severed. It is not much of an exaggeration to say that a shudder went through all Europe as the news spread. A book of prayers and meditations compiled by a clergyman, almost certainly John Gauden, was attributed to Charles and provided an edifying portrait of 'his Sacred Majesty in his Sufferings and Solitude'. Despite its Greek title *Eikon Basilike* (which was probably given in order to confuse the censors), it was a rapid and steady best-seller. In the long run, therefore, the King's execution added invaluably to the mystique of the monarchy. Again a comparison may be made with Thomas Becket's martyrdom – which did more for the Church than his life had ever done.

LEVELLERS AND RANTERS

In the practical politics of 1649 the Royalist cause seemed to be buried along with the King's corpse, taken to lie in a vault beside Henry VIII in St George's Chapel, Windsor, as snow fell. The reason why Charles had had to wait four hours in the Banqueting House before his execution was that it had suddenly been remembered that it was necessary for the Rump Parliament to pass an act forbidding the proclamation of a new king; but the precaution was probably not necessary, for the dead king's heir was a powerless, poverty-stricken exile. At home Royalists, stunned by the regicide, had to pay large fines or see their estates confiscated. Crown lands and church lands were sold off, and the triumphant officers enjoyed the financial fruits of victory. The House of Lords was formally abolished in March, and the monarchy followed two months later. In theory, all the sovereignty now resided in the House of Commons. In practice, however, the average sitting consisted of some eighty MPs, looking nervously over their shoulders to see what the army was thinking.

Further excited by this removal of old landmarks, the Levellers poured proposals into the soldiers' ears and pamphlets into the public debate. When a young trooper was shot for disobedience, his London funeral became a great demonstration in their favour, with their sea-green colours everywhere. A wider mutiny broke out in the army. This shocked Cromwell into resolute action again. He and Fairfax kept the loyalty of their own regiments and of enough other soldiers to end the disturbance, and when some of the mutineers fled he surprised them at Burford on Sunday 13 May. He killed some, imprisoned the rest in a church, and then publicly shot the ringleaders. A grateful Oxford University – so recently the Royalist headquarters – awarded the generals honorary doctorates and the City of London gave them a banquet.

Cromwell knew, however, that the struggle was not yet over, for Leveller propaganda could not be stopped by a few bullets or banquets. The distress of the people was too real; 1649 was a year when bad harvests, high taxation and the general dislocation caused by the war had reduced many English families to the misery which welcomes revolutionary talk. In London 'Honest John' Lilburne made himself conspicuous both as a radical pamphleteer against 'England's new chains' and as a prisoner in the Tower, and a jury failed to agree with the furious MPs that he was guilty of treason.[35] Still more dramatically, the 'True Levellers' set up a commune on St George's Hill near Kingston-upon-Thames. Because they began to cultivate the ground in a way that was supposed to encourage Communism all over England, they were nicknamed 'the Diggers'. Although the experiment collapsed, what was not so quickly forgotten was the eloquence of its leader, Gerrard Winstanley, pleading that once private property was abolished Christ would rise in his 'sons and daughters', the free English.[36]

[35] See Pauline Gregg, *Free-born John: A Biography of John Lilburne* (London, 1961).
[36] See *The Law of Freedom and Other Writings by Gerrard Winstanley*, ed. Christopher Hill (London, 1973), and T. Wilson Hayes, *Winstanley the Digger* (Cambridge, Mass., 1979).

In many parts of England in this revolutionary year 1649 there was an outburst of crude democracy in free speech and free behaviour. Back in 1646 *Gangraena* by Thomas Edwards had catalogued 199 heresies. Now there were more. The most vociferous of the radicals were known as 'the Ranters' – publicly deriding all the sacred conventions of Church and State, praising the people's wisdom along with the people's pleasures of sex, beer and tobacco, demanding the people's liberation, questioning the existence of God along with the privileges of the gentry. A typical incident occurred in the churchyard of Walton-upon-Thames. A soldier announced to the congregation, as it left after the Sunday afternoon service, that the Sabbath, the tithes, the ministers and the magistrates had all been abolished. He then produced a Bible, 'Here is a book you have in great veneration . . . but I must tell you, it is abolished. It containeth beggarly elements, milk for babes. But now Christ is in glory amongst us.' And taking the candle from his lantern, he set fire to the Bible. Parliament reacted by a Blasphemy Act, imposing a lifelong exile for a second offence.[37]

Alarmed by such extremists, the men in power were unwilling to disturb the social order further by destroying all the structure of the parishes or all the security of the clergy. Tithes were therefore still collected to support lay rectors or ordained ministers, and gentlemen who had not been branded as Royalists continued to be lay rectors or patrons of the parishes, appointing the ministers. The ecclesiastical rights of 'delinquent' gentry were taken over by county committees and those of the Crown reverted to individual congregations. In practice clergymen with a wide variety of opinions, including Anglican opinions or non-Calvinist Protestant opinions, were left free to preach. The only national authority was a committee of ministers and laymen given power to eject unsuitable ministers and schoolmasters. There was no General Assembly supervising the religion of England on the model provided by the General Assembly of the Church of Scotland, and the *Directory of Worship* which Parliament had accepted in 1645 had left much

---

[37] The best study is A. L. Morton, *The World of the Ranters* (London, 1970).

freedom in the hands of parish ministers. In brief, the tidy Presbyterian system which had been the aim of the majority when Parliament had made its Solemn League and Covenant with the Scots in 1643 did not exist in England six years later. Although the bishops had been reduced to obscurity and poverty, although the Westminster Assembly of divines had been able to reach a complete theological agreement about orthodox Calvinism, it had not proved possible to establish a Calvinist system of church government with a uniformity which would have satisfied Calvin's logical mind. Discipline remained less conspicuous than variety. England remained a land of compromises, with many remnants of the old order of squire and parson surviving alongside the radical ideas of the revolutionary movements.

OLIVER CROMWELL

At the head of the victorious English army was Oliver Cromwell. Even while surrounded by his troops or immersed in the affairs of the State he was essentially a solitary man, especially after the death of his friend, fellow soldier and son-in-law, Henry Ireton, in 1651.[38] Although the Royalists naturally accused him of consistent, ruthless and unlimited ambition, it would be fairer to call him an opportunist, responding to emergencies. A remark which he is said to have made to the French ambassador in July 1647 seems to have been honest in its mixture of uncertainty and a willingness to accept promotion: 'None rises so high as he who knows not wither he is going.'

The Royalists also associated him personally with the vandalism despoiling church buildings, and in the twentieth

---

[38] Biographies include Robert S. Paul, *The Lord Protector: Religion and Politics in the Life of Oliver Cromwell* (London, 1955), and Antonia Fraser, *Cromwell Our Chief of Men* (London, 1973). Maurice Ashley, *Oliver Cromwell and His World* (London, 1972), is splendidly illustrated. Assessments were collected as *Cromwell: A Profile*, ed. Ivan Roots (London, 1973).

century it is still being said about many a church that
'Cromwell stabled his horses here'. It is true that no evidence
suggests that Anglican doctrine or worship ever appealed to
him. On the other hand, he was no vandal – and no Presbyterian. Nor does he seem to have been completely an Independent, believing as a matter of theological principle in the
independence of each local congregation. So far as we know he
never formally joined a local congregation. He was thoroughly
a layman. His respect for preaching was far from being unlimited; he secured the right of a national committee controlled
by him to supervise all 'public preachers'. There is no evidence
that he habitually consulted any clergyman about what to do
while a farmer, while a soldier or while Lord Protector.[39]
Throughout his life his religious views seem to have been very
much his own. He wrestled for himself with the Scriptures and
with the evidence of events. In political success, above all in
military victory (he was never defeated), he found evidence of
God's approval and grew ecstatic. A letter to his daughter
Bridget in 1646 expressed some sympathy with the new sect of
the Seekers, but showed that he was too conscious of his own
vocation to success to join that group. 'To be a seeker is to be of
the best sect next to a finder, and such a one shall every faithful,
humble seeker be at the end.'

Born in 1599, he was in many ways an Elizabethan; his
mother, wife and favourite daughter were all called Elizabeth,
and when in power he was enthusiastic about the 'Western
Design' to fight Spain for the riches of America. He belonged to
the backbone of Elizabethan England, the class that had
provided the magistrates; he found several cousins sitting
alongside him in the Parliament of 1628. Most of the fairly
modest (and fluctuating) wealth of his family was based on
lands which were or which had been church lands, his biggest
asset at the end of the 1630s being the right to farm estates left
to Ely Cathedral. Basically he owed such education as he had
to Huntingdon Grammar School and its Puritan schoolmaster,
Thomas Beard, author of *The Theatre of God's Judgements*, a little
book about 'the admirable judgements of God upon the trans-

---

[39] See Geoffrey Nuttall in *The Puritan Spirit* (London, 1967), pp. 130–40.

gressors of his commandments'. Apart from this schooling, we know only of one year at Cambridge, possibly followed by some time studying law. He was not at all a glamorous figure; a Royalist MP has left a description of him aged forty-one, dressed in an ill-fitting plain cloth suit with specks of blood on his neck-band. The only clue from his early years that his personality was exceptional is provided by evidence that he underwent a nervous breakdown and a profound spiritual conversion at the end of the 1620s; there survives a note by a distinguished London physician whom he consulted, to the effect that he was 'extremely melancholy'. But with the life-long tendency to melancholia and self-doubt when inactive went a rare, almost manic, determination to act once his mind had cleared. Reports of the 1630s prove that he could be impetuous in his interventions in local politics. They also suggest that he seriously considered selling up and going to New England. He whispered to his neighbour in the Commons that had the Grand Remonstrance passed he certainly would have emigrated in 1641. And so there came the day in January 1644 when, having lived for some years in a house close by Ely Cathedral, brooding over his sins and the people's, he suddenly arrived in the cathedral and furiously drove out its surprised congregation.

His reputation became the reputation of a brilliant General. It remains mysterious just how, when already in his forties, he learned and communicated outstanding skills as a trainer and commander of the cavalry, the pikemen and the musketeers that conquered their King – although it is true that most of the officers on the King's side shared his own lack of previous military experience. What is clear is that the key was discipline, made possible by appealing to a morale inspired by religion. On the Royalist side Prince Rupert's cavalry scattered after a charge; their instinct was to plunder. On the Parliamentary side Cromwell's cavalry remained under orders, for their General had learned the lesson of the first, indecisive battle at Edgehill. Talking over the battle with his cousin John Hampden, Cromwell wondered how the 'base and mean fellows' on their side could ever 'encounter gentlemen that have honour and courage and resolution in them'. The

answer came to him: 'You must get men of spirit.' He meant
the Puritan spirit. The regiment which he raised for the
Eastern Association in 1643 surprised contemporaries by the
punishments which the soldiers accepted for drunkenness and
swearing, but the whole point was that the soldiers knew why
this discipline was necessary. Only men who were not the
traditional soldiery, brutal and licentious, could have the
self-respect required to remain disciplined in defeat or victory.

As the war proceeded Cromwell increasingly regarded it as a
crusade. 'Religion was not the thing at first contested for,' he
reflected, 'but God brought it to that issue at last . . . and at last
proved that which was most dear to us.' And he seemed to
become more and more flexible in his attitude to the religion in
which his men believed, on the one condition that it would
make them crusaders. At an early stage he had invited an
eminently respectable clergyman, Richard Baxter, to be chaplain to his own regiment of 'Ironsides'. Baxter had refused, and
when visiting the New Model Army after its victory at Naseby
had been horrified by developments. Most of the soldiers
seemed 'honest, sober, orthodox men', but about a twentieth
were 'proud, self-conceited, hot-headed Sectaries' – and it was
the minority that Cromwell seemed to favour, since by its 'heat
and activity' it was 'the soul of the army'. Baxter heard with
great alarm declarations 'sometimes for State Democracy and
sometimes for Church Democracy': the one seemed as bad as
the other. Now time would have to tell whether the majority of
soldiers would insist on democracy or would support a conservative regime headed by the General who had emerged
because, as he frequently claimed, God's hand was mysteriously on him.

A sense of being a man of destiny, God's avenging instrument, was strong in Cromwell as he led the various moves
needed in 1649–51 to crush attempts to put Charles II on his
father's throne. First he commanded the army in Ireland
through a campaign disgraced by atrocities which have never
been forgotten. Then, disregarding the resignation of Fairfax
who refused to take an oath of loyalty to the republic, he turned
against Charles and the Scots. Charles had made the firm

alliance which his father had rejected by signing the covenant against bishops, but the concession was now in vain. Cromwell, after making his famous plea to the Scots, 'in the bowels of Christ', to think it possible that they might be mistaken, defeated them at Dunbar and occupied Edinburgh – showing more mercy than in Ireland, since the Scots were not Papists. When an unenthusiastic Charles kept some Scottish supporters and accompanied an army of them in a hopeless march south, the war-weary English failed to rise and Cromwell caught up with the outnumbered invaders. Another famous victory at Worcester (on 3 September 1651) was received with widespread thanksgiving as the 'crowning mercy'. All that the shattered Royalists could do was to organize Charles's romantic escape back into exile.

Cromwell's army had shouted 'The Lord of Hosts!' at Dunbar. It now looked for its reward – and for a reward more solid than a demobilization which would leave power in the hands of the Rump Parliament. Cromwell, too, wondered what the future held for him, at a time when Milton was hailing him in a sonnet as 'our chief of men'. One autumn evening in 1652 he had a conversation with Bulstrode Whitelocke, strolling in St James's Park in Westminster. Cromwell was thinking aloud and groping his way forward as he often did until the moment came when God's providence called him into a display of military strength; and Whitelocke later recalled their talk – perhaps not with a perfect memory, for he wrote it down when Cromwell was dead and in disgrace and he was surviving as a shrewd, conservative lawyer.[40] According to this account, the General observed that MPs were 'engrossing all places of honour and profit to themselves and their friends' and so providing 'ground for people to open their mouths against them'. Yet they had been 'acknowledged the supreme power'. What was the solution? Cromwell knew that most of the English preferred a government 'with something of monarchical in it'. So 'what if a man should take it upon him to be king?'

---

[40] Whitelocke was portrayed by Ruth Spalding as *The Improbable Puritan* (London, 1975).

Whitelocke dismissed the daydream of King Oliver – 'the remedy would be worse than the disease' – and proposed instead that he should make an arrangement with the defeated but legitimate Charles II, 'to secure yourself and your friends and their fortunes'. Instead, on 20 April 1653, Cromwell acted with far less cynicism. He dismissed the Rump Parliament and dissolved the council which in its name had governed, or failed to govern, the country; and he set about establishing a Cromwellian regime in its place.

A nominated assembly was summoned: Cromwell's fear of free elections told its own tale. Nicknamed the 'Barebones Parliament' (after a member, Praise-God Barbone), it embarked on a comprehensive programme to reform the law, the revenues and other aspects of the nation's life. However, it showed itself to be almost equally divided on a crucial question. The radicals kept voicing the Levellers' demand for the abolition of tithes – a step which would have made the small farmers richer and the ministers entirely dependent on their congregations. The conservatives drew back, and not only because many laymen were still receiving tithes. Rather than accept the prospect of anarchy in religion and of financial loss to the gentry, these conservatives handed their power back to Cromwell; presumably they had been assured in advance that the offer would not be rejected. The maintenance of tithes had become a symbol of the need to maintain law and order in Church and State.

Before the end of 1653 the General had been installed as Lord Protector. The first written constitution in English history (the 'Instrument of Government') gave him great powers provided that he pursued a policy approved of by the Council of State, in effect a military junta. A minor role – mainly one of confirming the ordinances to be issued by this council – was allotted to a single-chamber parliament, to be elected once every three years by the propertied rather than by the people as a whole. Those who had acted against Parliament at any time since January 1641 were to be denied votes. From a strictly parliamentary point of view, this was a considerable anticlimax after the rhetoric of Pym and many others in the early 1640s.

On the basis of an army of thirty thousand men rather than any paper constitution, Cromwell governed a Commonwealth uniting England, Wales, Scotland and Ireland. He and his fellow officers pursued an aggressive foreign policy with some success – the first rulers of England to do so since the death of Henry V. The fleet commanded by Robert Blake distinguished itself and Jamaica was occupied. Thus the naval and imperial themes which were to dominate English history were announced and consecrated by anti-Spanish Protestantism (except that it was also necessary to fight a trading war against the Dutch). At home the regime kept the people quiet by treason laws which threatened the death penalty for anyone denying the supreme authority of the Lord Protector and the Parliament. There was a police and spy system, considerably the most efficient ever to be seen in England, with the country divided into eleven areas under major-generals. Equally relevant to Cromwell's success, however, was a general policy of non-interference with those who stayed quiet.

The ineffectiveness of the Royalist conspiracies supplied the most important commentary on this regime. Only minor problems were caused by minor indiscretions. Some of the less intelligent major-generals tried to enforce Puritan morals. Nationwide, there were the even more foolish official prohibitions of church weddings and the Christmas festivities – orders which were widely defied. The main problem was that stability depended on control by the army and, within the army, on control by a general with Cromwell's prestige.

Anglicans and Roman Catholics were lumped together in a way that would have amazed the Elizabethans, and their treatment showed the same combination of firmness with tolerance. The use of the Prayer Book was forbidden in 1655, the year of the main Royalist insurrection, but this stern measure was soon accompanied by a reassurance: 'His Highness doth declare that towards such of the said persons as have ... given ... a real testimony of their godliness and good affection to the present government, so much tenderness shall be used as may consist with the safety and good of the nation.' In other words, it was hinted that except when Royalists were troublemakers Cromwell would connive at the use of the

Prayer Book. And there is much evidence that Anglican
services were held discreetly up and down the country, especially baptisms, weddings and funerals. John Evelyn's diary
shows both that this Anglican gentleman regularly attended
the non-Anglican services in his parish church, and that he
could always find Prayer Book services to attend in London
when he so wished. Although marriage before a civil magistrate had been made compulsory in 1653, the Lord Protector's
own daughter Mary was married (to Lord Fauconberg) in the
chapel of Hampton Court according to the old service. James
Ussher, the moderate who had been Archbishop of Armagh
and a saintly scholar respected by all, received a Prayer Book
funeral in Westminster Abbey.[41]

In relation to Roman Catholics the old legislation remained
in force, and under it a priest aged seventy was executed in
1654. The law was toughened in 1657, under the excitement of
the war with Spain. But the local enforcement of fines for
recusancy was even more patchy than it had been under
Elizabeth or Charles I. Cromwell was content to leave it so; the
French ambassador was one of the many who were reminded
that the Lord Protector opposed all persecution of those who
remained quiet in politics. Indeed, in 1655 Cromwell went so
far as to arrange for the return of some Jews to London, ending
the prohibition imposed in 1290.

Presbyterians, Independents and Baptists all ministered in
the old parishes and were sustained by the old tithes; 'though a
man be of any of those three judgements,' said Cromwell, 'if he
have the root of the matter in him he may be admitted.' An
attempt was made to tackle the perennial problem of the
poverty of the clergy remaining in the parishes by supporting
the lower-paid ministers out of some of the lands which had
once belonged to the bishops and the cathedrals. Many priests
who had been ordained by bishops, and who had never
inwardly acquired the Puritan 'root of the matter', were also
allowed to carry on their work. They 'lay low', as one vicar put
it. Many used the new fashions in worship on Sundays while
sticking to the old services for baptisms, weddings and funer-

---

[41] R. Buick Knox studied *James Ussher, Archbishop of Armagh* (Cardiff, 1967).

als. Although this was a period when many congregations discovered with considerable excitement and joy that they were at last free and able to be the Christian Church in the style advocated by the Puritans, in more than two-thirds of England's parishes there was no change of minister under the Commonwealth.[42]

Among the preachers who flourished under this regime were men who were by any standards Christians completely dedicated to their ministry.[43] In 1654 two ordinances made the control of other preachers stricter. The task of examining candidates for the parish pulpits was now entrusted to a strong national committee of ministers and laymen – the 'Triers' or 'Commissioners for the Approbation of Public Preachers'. Unfortunately most of the records of their work were lost when they were suppressed, but a candid critic, Richard Baxter, paid them a compliment. 'To give them their due,' he later wrote, 'they did abundance of good to the Church. They saved many a congregation from ignorant, ungodly, drunken teachers.' In each county a local committee handled the task of ejecting unsatisfactory ministers. Like the national committee which had been functioning before 1654, these 'Ejectors' could be ruthless. Many ugly stories were told of violence used when evicting clergy and their families for loyalty to the Prayer Book, although in theory if they went quietly they were promised a fifth of the next incumbent's income. It has been estimated that between 1643 and 1660 about seven hundred and fifty posts of dignity in the old Church of England (from bishoprics to minor canonries in the cathedrals) were suppressed, that some eight hundred Anglicans were expelled from the universities, and that almost 2,500 parishes were 'sequestered' because their incumbents were 'delinquents'. Beyond doubt there was suffering, but there were many factors which complicated the

---

[42] See Geoffrey Nuttall, *Visible Saints: the Congregational Way 1640–1660* (Oxford, 1957). On the patchy establishment of the Presbyterian system in the country, nothing has yet replaced W. A. Shaw, *A History of the English Church during the Civil Wars and under the Commonwealth* (2 vols, London, 1900).

[43] Examples may be found in two biographies: R. P. Stearns, *The Strenuous Puritan: Hugh Peter* (Urbana, Ill., 1954), and V. de Sola Pinto, *Peter Sterry* (Cambridge, 1934).

picture – two or more of the superior posts had often been held by one man; some of those ejected later made their peace with the regime and were given fresh posts; and some who suffered had been unsatisfactory as pastors.[44]

In their triumph the Puritans were, of course, determined to show that the looseness of the organization of the National Church did not extend to any laxity in upholding orthodox Christianity against any who might take advantage of the disturbed times. When an ex-soldier, James Nayler, caused a scandal by re-enacting Christ's entry into Jerusalem by a ride into Bristol, the Commons debated and condemned the blasphemy. Cromwell protested against the savage punishment (which was not authorized under the Instrument of Government), but he was powerless to stop it; and he was not able to do more than express a private sympathy with the Quakers, a popular anti-clerical movement in which Nayler was a leading figure. More than once he allowed their remaining leader, George Fox, to hold earnest conversation with him. His dislike of religious persecution – 'I had rather that Mahometanism were permitted among us than that one of God's children should be persecuted' – remained from the convictions with which the New Model Army had been prepared to fight King and Parliament alike.

Little else of the idealism remained. He assured a Quaker, John Rogers, that tithes to support the clergy were not anti-Christian – only to be rebuked: 'You were once of another mind'. And it was true that he had changed. As he told his first Parliament, 'a nobleman, a gentleman, a yeoman: that is a good interest of the nation and a great one. The magistracy of the nation, was it not almost trampled underfoot, under despite and contempt by men of Levelling principles?' Now under the Lord Protector the traditional social system was protected; and if tithes had to be kept for this reason, Cromwell would pay the price. Looking back over his life, he once said: 'I did out of necessity undertake that business, not so much out of

---

[44] John Walker's *Attempt towards Recovering an Account of the Numbers and Sufferings of the Clergy of the Church of England* was published in 1714 and corrected by A. G. Matthews, *Walker Revised* (Oxford, 1948).

a hope of doing any good, as out of a desire to prevent mischief and evil.' That was more than a passing mood of depression. As one of the best of his modern biographers has put it, after 1653 'he was a tired, disillusioned old man, still confident that he enjoyed a special relationship with God, but with few positive ideas left, on the defensive. He no longer hoped to realize the rule of God's people in England: he saw himself as a constable whose task was to prevent Englishmen from flying at one another's throats. He was forced back upon the support of an army purged of radicals, an army which in the last resort had to be paid by taxes collected from the propertied class, the natural rulers of the countryside. The Revolution was over.'[45]

---

[45] Christopher Hill, *God's Englishman* (London, 1970), p. 143. The ferment of radical ideas during the English revolution was surveyed by Christopher Hill, *The World Turned Upside Down* (London, 1972).

CHAPTER NINE

THE PURITAN LEGACY

THE DEATH OF
CROMWELLIAN ENGLAND

While Oliver Cromwell lived, his system of government in
Church and State seemed secure. Many shared Cromwell's
own opinion that all that the exiled Charles Stuart cared for
was 'a shoulder of mutton and a whore'. In comparison, the
Lord Protector was a giant among men – and he could control
the army. The chief interest lay in the question whether
Cromwell would, or would not, accept the title of king. The
crown was urged on him by many MPs who wanted that
additional return to legality. In the end he refused, deterred
chiefly by the opposition within the army. Colonel Pride, who
had once purged the old Commons, organized an officers'
petition against any idea of a new king. But the Lord Protector
did accept a new constitution which gave him more power over
the council – and a second installation, a ceremony which came
close to a coronation. He created a second chamber in Parliament, and urged the Commons to be less niggardly in voting
taxes; he maintained a dignified court and his friends became
known as the 'Court' party. It was in many ways like the old
times of the Stuarts.

What the Lord Protector could not produce was an able son
– and in that, too, he resembled several crowned kings of
England. He quarrelled with John Lambert, who had become
his closest military and political associate but had been one of
the leaders of the opposition to the crowning. Lambert's
dismissal left no successor more obvious than Richard Cromwell, a diffident young man nicknamed 'Tumbledown Dick',
whose sole claim was being the oldest son. That showed the
fatal weakness in the whole regime of a semi-monarchy which

in reality depended on one general's hold on the army. Although the Royalists seemed to be in complete disarray, probably many Englishmen knew in their hearts that the legitmate monarchy's restoration was inevitable. This thought may well have been deep in the minds first of the soldiers, and then of Cromwell himself, when they acknowledged the impossibility of taking over the throne as Henry IV had taken it over from Richard II or Henry VII from Richard III.

The Lord Protector died on 3 September 1658. Towards the end of his great life he had grown manifestly exhausted although not yet sixty years old, and it was a sign of his exhaustion that he took no sensible action about his succession. To assume that his oldest son would inherit his position, as he seems to have done although there was no clear arrangement, was as unrealistic as Henry VIII's will had been back in 1547. England remained a republic and therefore in some sense a democracy; yet it was invited to accept as its Lord Protector, with powers greater than those of Charles I, a man who lacked the sacred mystique of hereditary kingship and whose own abilities were not impressive. In 1658 as in 1547, what England needed was government.

Trying to assert his authority over the generals, the new Lord Protector appealed to the soldiers – who refused to rescue him. A similar refusal came from Puritan ministers such as John Owen, who had once been among Oliver Cromwell's favourites and a preacher of sermons to Parliament announcing that God was doing great things through the triumphs of the godly.[1] Idealistic pamphleteers such as Richard Baxter and John Milton announced that the time had come to establish a government based on wisdom, but some force seemed necessary since disruptive ideals were also being voiced in this open debate. Revolutionary visionaries such as the Fifth Monarchy Men who had emerged back in 1652 as the heirs of the Levellers prophesied that the 'fifth monarchy' of the seventh chapter of the Book of Daniel was about to come to pass in England, bringing in the rule of King Jesus and the

---

[1] A biography of Owen has been provided by Peter Toon, *God's Statesman* (Exeter, Devon, 1971).

saints. Private property would be among the institutions destroyed as the world was made new.[2]

After the dissolution of the pathetic new Lord Protector's
even more pathetic Parliament it seemed possible that the
army might reimpose its rule, brushing aside the idealists and
revolutionaries. The trouble was that after all the changes
since 1640 the officers were left with no very clear idea as to
what they wanted. Two of the generals (Harrison and Overton) were Fifth Monarchy men. Others who had done well for
themselves seem to have begun reckoning with the rewards
that might accompany the inevitability of a Stuart, rather than
a heavenly, king. The rank and file were worried most about
the uncertainty of their pay. An army so divided had the power
but not the will. The vacuum was filled temporarily by the
return of some hundred and twenty members of the old Rump
Parliament, to whom Richard Cromwell handed in his resignation. He had his reward: after twenty years in obscure exile, he
was to be permitted to return to live out his days as a quiet
country gentleman until 1712. But this resurrected Parliament
could not control the army any more than Richard Cromwell
could. On the contrary, some army officers, among whom
John Lambert was the most active, were plainly determined
to establish 'sword government' – a prospect which other
officers found dismaying. Suddenly the Puritan movement,
which had seemed invincible while Oliver Cromwell lived,
was visibly disintegrating. The prophecy of the old Royalist,
Sir Jacob Astley, was coming true: 'You have now done your
work, and may go play, unless you will fall out amongst your-
selves.'

Once again, as divided MPs and confused soldiers struggled
for the government of England, both sides sought the support
of an army from Scotland – only this time the army was
commanded by George Monck, once a Royalist, latterly Oliver
Cromwell's trusted and very effective agent, a man who was
every inch a professional soldier and who included in his
professionalism convictions that soldiers ought to be paid well
but ought not to form governments. Monck commanded an

---

[2] See B. S. Capp, *The Fifth Monarchy Men* (London, 1972).

army that had done very well out of the Cromwellian conquest of Scotland, was paid regularly, and was loyal to him personally. He seemed just the man to rescue the conservative counter-revolution from the disorder into which it had been reduced by his master's death.

At the end of 1659 Monck's army crossed into England. On his arrival in London he made only one objective clear: the readmission of conservative MPs who had been excluded by Pride's Purge back in 1648. Then another aim emerged: the Long Parliament must vote for its own dissolution and for the election of a more representative 'convention'. This objective was achieved when the Parliament which had first met in 1640 dissolved itself on 16 March 1660. Before dispersing MPs showed their hopes of the future by also voting for the introduction of the full Presbyterian system in the Church. Such a prospect also appealed to many merchants in the City of London, who meanwhile were backing Monck against less constitutionally-minded soldiers such as Lambert. But Royalists were allowed to stand in the elections, and in his exile at Breda Charles strengthened their cause (although he angered hotheads) by issuing a vague but conciliatory declaration, drafted by Edward Hyde. If he was restored to his throne, the King promised a general pardon and religious toleration pending a permanent settlement by Parliament. Parliament was also to answer the key question of whose estates were to be restored. On the same day (1 May) that it formally received this declaration, the new House of Commons voted that 'the government is, and ought to be, by King, Lords and Commons'. By the end of that month Charles had been proclaimed king, had landed at Dover, and amid a rapturous welcome had entered London.

The Cromwellian counter-revolution had not, after all, outlasted Oliver Cromwell. Needing a monarchy and failing to find it in a Cromwellian dynasty, propertied men such as General Monck or the MPs turned back to the legitimate king. Only he could provide the stability they most wanted. Many hoped that much of the Cromwellian achievement would be preserved – that, for example, bishops (if there had to be bishops) would never again wield the powers of William Laud.

Presbyterian preachers were prominent in the welcome given
to Charles in May 1660 and heard with pleasure his praises of
the Bible. But stringent terms had not been imposed on the
new king, because no one, not even General Monck, had the
power or the will to impose them. With Oliver Cromwell dead,
there could be no guarantee of a political future for militant
Puritanism. The Lord of Hosts who had given them so many
victories, from Marston Moor to Worcester, in Ireland, in
Scotland and at sea, had not given the Puritans strength or
unity of purpose under the pressures released by the great
General's death. 'The Lord', said Major-General Fleetwood in
1658, 'has spit in our faces.'[3]

THE DEFEAT OF THE PURITANS

For about a year after the restoration of the king the outcome
for English religion was uncertain. It was a period when the
decisions were being made not by battles or riots but by
negotiations between a few men in London. The bulk of the
country seems simply to have waited, relieved that the threat of
anarchy was over, willing to accept any settlement to be
imposed, provided only that it was not Popery. Fortunately we
have the daily journal of Ralph Josselin, the vicar of the village
of Earl's Colne in Essex from 1641 to 1683, to remind us that all
through these crises what really mattered to the average man
was health or sickness or death affecting his family and neighbours, or sun or rain creating the harvest, with the hope of
heaven as the great consolation. Josselin was a devout Christian who brooded over the Bible's promises of the Kingdom of
God. And he was no fool. Having been the first clergyman in
Essex to swear loyalty to the Commonwealth, at this stage he
was noting that his fellow Englishmen were 'looking more to
Charles Stuart out of love to themselves, not him'. His awareness of current affairs must have been exceptional; he even
dreamed about politics. But the preoccupations of his diary

---

[3] Recent studies include *The Interregnum: The Quest for a Settlement*, edited by G.
E. Aylmer (London, 1972), and Ronald Hutton, *The Restoration* (Oxford, 1985).

were naturally and properly local, and often he would write in thanksgiving about his affairs: 'God was good to me.'[4]

No one in 1660 could be sure what the King's power would be in practice. Men had preferred him to Richard Cromwell because his hereditary right put him in an infinitely stronger position; so 1660 saw the restoration of a monarchy with a history of executive power stretching back through medieval to Anglo-Saxon days, and it was a restoration without conditions other than the imprecise promises in the royal exile's declaration 'given . . . at our court at Breda . . . in the twelfth year of our reign'. The King's own brother, James, was to show when he came to reign that he expected an unquestioning obedience to be given by his subjects as a religious duty. On the other hand, the Commons' agreement with the Lords on 1 May 1660, that 'according to the ancient and fundamental laws of this kingdom the Government is, and ought to be, by King, Lords and Commons' deserved to be analysed for its inclusion of Parliament as well as King in 'the Government'. In practice a body of MPs known to history as the Cavalier Parliament of 1661–79 was to have a mind of its own, although vociferously loyal to the monarchy in principle. It was to reject the leadership offered by the King's ministers and to secure their dismissal – and it was never to allow the King enough money with which to govern without Parliament. After 1660 there was no real intention of going back behind 1640, and Charles II recognized this even if his stupid brother James did not. He knew that the only way in which he could fight free of having to humour the Commons was the degradation involved in receiving subsidies from France. Although this was hidden from many eyes in 1660, the religious policy that was to prevail was the policy which commended itself to the House of Commons.

Equally uncertain was the motivation of the restored King in his new dialogue with the Commons. In public Charles II professed to be devoted to his father's Church – as did his brother and heir until he ceased to receive Holy Communion as an Anglican in 1672. During their exile their quarrels with

---

[4] Alan Macfarlane reconstructed *The Family Life of Ralph Josselin* (Cambridge, 1970) and edited *The Diary of Ralph Josselin* (Oxford, 1976).

their Roman Catholic mother had strengthened the impression of a sound English churchmanship. No doubt most Englishmen took it for granted that in religion Charles would be the royal martyr's son, at least formally. But those who knew him knew that the Church of England meant little to him religiously. He was a worldly womanizer (as was James at this stage). Unlike his father he had been willing to take the Presbyterians' Solemn League and Covenant and he owed his restoration to Presbyterian soldiers and merchants, not to any Cavalier uprising. It seemed perfectly possible that it would be his policy to conciliate the Presbyterians, either by including them in the National Church or by insisting on the 'liberty to tender consciences' promised in the Declaration of Breda. It also seemed likely that he would attempt to secure better terms for the Roman Catholics, many of whom had supported his father in the civil war. His decision to marry a Roman Catholic princess, as his father had done, caused no surprise; there were very few Protestant princesses available. There were, indeed, rumours in the early 1660s that in exile Charles had become a Roman Catholic himself, and a law had to be passed making it treason to repeat the story. The King's personal religion remained something of an enigma, until on his deathbed he was received into the Roman Catholic Church.

But in 1660 it was not even certain what would be the attitude of the leaders of the Church of England. During the Commonwealth Anglican leadership had been divided and, on the whole, ineffective.

'I secure myself the same way as the tortoise doth, by not going out of my shell' had been the confession of a comparatively brave bishop, Brian Duppa of Salisbury. He had been typical. The most respectable advocate of buying safety by judicious compromise had been Professor Robert Sanderson of Oxford. Although ejected from Oxford, he had advised his fellow Anglicans not to obtrude their loyalty to monarchy, episcopacy or the Book of Common Prayer to the extent of provoking retaliation. He had retained the respect of many, and at the Restoration was made Bishop of Lincoln although in his seventies. Indeed, Izaak Walton thought so highly of him that he added a *Life* to his studies of Anglican heroes such as

Hooker, Donne and Herbert. Even more caution had been displayed by the senior bishop, William Juxon, who had served Charles I as Bishop of London and Lord Treasurer, and had attended him on the scaffold. Under the Commonwealth he had retreated to his manor house in Gloucestershire and had devoted himself to prayer and hunting. He and his fellow bishops had not consecrated any successors after 1644, although loyally Anglican Royalists abroad were indignant at the risk being run. The result was that in the twenty-seven English and Welsh dioceses, by 1660 only ten bishops survived, mostly in their seventies. Bishop Skinner of Oxford was the only one of them who had openly expressed a willingness to ordain priests under the Commonwealth.

When Charles II exchanged pious remarks with Presbyterian ministers on his return to London, it therefore seemed possible that government of the Church by bishops would be forgotten. After all, the estates confiscated from the bishops and their cathedrals were now in lay hands. No one thought of restoring their formerly vast estates to the monasteries. Why revive the power and wealth of the bishops?

The theologian who had rallied Anglicans less willing to compromise with the Puritan rulers of England had been Henry Hammond, a learned scholar who before the war had been an exemplary parish priest. A man of outstanding holiness, he was extensively consulted in problems of conscience, and during the 1650s spread his views by writing more than twenty-five books. He always advised steadfast courage, although he was no fanatic in his attitude to non-Anglicans. There were others like him, who quietly did their duty and urged others to do the same – John Pearson, for example, who in 1659 completed an *Exposition of the Creed* based on lectures in a London church, a treatise which had great influence for two centuries; or Richard Allestree, an Oxford Scholar who almost certainly was the author of a very influential book for the laity on *The Whole Duty of Man*. Another scholar, Herbert Thorndike, wrote a book published in 1659 under the gloomy title *An Epilogue to the Tragedy of the Church of England*; it turned out to be a prologue to the triumph. But Henry Hammond was the spiritual leader in this circle, and it was a real tragedy for the

Church of England that he died prematurely, shortly before the Restoration.[5]

In the end the leadership went to those Anglicans who, like Hammond, had refused to compromise while their Church was under persecution (or at least under a cloud). This was partly because some of them had found refuge as chaplains to gentlemen whose sons became devoted to them and who were to sit in the Commons after the Restoration. But some of the most steadfast Anglicans went into exile and there did battle against Roman Catholic influences while also refusing to be classified as simply Protestant. One of the exiles was a Yorkshireman, Joseph Bramhall, who had become Archbishop of Armagh and who during the 1650s published massive defences of Anglican orthodoxy against the claims of Rome as well as against the scepticism of Thomas Hobbes. Another was John Cosin, so well-known as a defender of the faith while Anglican chaplain in the household of Queen Henrietta Maria in Paris that he was made Bishop of Durham in 1660, winning a further reputation as an energetic disciplinarian before his death in 1672. Cosin was, by Anglican standards, a High Churchman, who in the 1620s had been in trouble for ritualism offensive to Protestants and who in the 1630s had presided over the Cambridge college chapel where Richard Crashaw loved to worship; but when his own son became a Roman Catholic like Crashaw, Cosin disinherited him. While so many had compromised Cosin had been unyielding, and now had the reward which sometimes goes to the obstinate.

If the character of the leadership of the Church of England was uncertain in 1660, still less was it clear how many of the clergy and laity who had accepted the loosely organized National Church of the Commonwealth would now accept the bishops and the Prayer Book – or how much the bishops and the Prayer Book could be changed in order to accommodate the Puritan element. Not long after his return home the King was persuaded to appoint a dozen Puritan divines as his chaplains. Three of them – Richard Baxter, Edmund Calamy

---

[5] J. W. Packer studied Hammond's life and work in *The Transformation of Anglicanism, 1643–60* (Manchester, 1969).

and Edward Reynolds – were even offered diocesan bishoprics. Baxter and Calamy refused, because it was clear to them that the old Anglican system would be insufficiently changed; but Reynolds agreed to become Bishop of Norwich and wrote the General Thanksgiving added to the Prayer Book in 1662. And even after their refusals, Baxter and Calamy went on hoping that the authorities of the Church of England, who had compromised so often in the past, would now compromise with them.

The situation was clarified in the spring of 1661 by the elections to the Commons, which produced MPs thirsting for revenge on defeated rebels. The effects of the ecclesiastical appointments made by the King, advised by Edward Hyde now Earl of Clarendon, were decisive. About seven hundred ministers had been ejected in order to make way for Royalists who had been expelled under the Commonwealth, although there was as yet no insistence on ordination by a bishop. Appointments to bishoprics and cathedrals conveyed the message that the restored Crown would reward those who had been loyal to it through the Great Rebellion. The most effective of the new bishops were Gilbert Sheldon at London (from 1663 at Canterbury) and George Morley at Worcester (from 1662 at Winchester), and neither of them intended to go any distance to meet Puritan demands. Sheldon had been ejected from the Wardenship of All Souls College, Oxford, and after a brief imprisonment had lived quietly in the Midlands, collaborating with Hammond in giving advice and where possible relief to the ejected clergy. He celebrated the return of the King by giving the beautiful Sheldonian Theatre to his university. Morley, although he seems to have retained many of the Calvinist beliefs of an earlier Anglican age, had been a Wiltshire rector before the war and had done more than anyone else to keep the Anglican exiles in harmony and good heart. Both Sheldon and Morley were masterful men of business, pure in their own lives but in tune with the cocksure MPs of the Cavalier Parliament. Such men were eager to restore their Church, not to alter it.

A gathering of bishops and Puritans met in Sheldon's lodgings at the King's command. The motives of the Anglican authorities in this 'Savoy Conference' have been variously interpreted. It is quite possible that the King and Clarendon genuinely wanted an agreement along the lines of the declaration which they had issued from Worcester House (Clarendon's residence) the previous October: a declaration which had promised to make episcopacy more pastoral (by appointing suffragan or assistant bishops, for example) and the Prayer Book more acceptable to the Puritans. It can be argued that it was the royal policy to be more generously statesmanlike than the Royalists.[6] But it is also possible to conclude that the real initiative lay all the time with the strictly Anglican and fervently Royalist churchmen, since the King did not show enough interest in religion to risk unpopularity for its sake. The consistent loyalty to the Church of England which Clarendon liked to claim, as he looked back on his life as an old man in the 1670s, may have been sincere in the 1660s, so that any appearance of a willingness to compromise was then always insincere.[7]

Richard Baxter blamed the arrogance of the bishops in the Savoy Conference and their Cavalier backers in the Commons: 'We spoke to the deaf.' But the facts were far more complicated, including a genuine reluctance on the part of the King and the wise Clarendon to see Parliament passing an Act of Uniformity which they knew would cause great trouble if enforced. There is evidence that the government's pressure was exerted against the legislation which appealed to the vindictive Cavaliers, and it is certain that when that pressure failed the alternative policy was pursued of issuing an 'indulgence' on the royal authority until the King had to admit defeat. It seems probable that the bishops would have secured the King's favour had they been able to buy peace by a few acceptable concessions. But Baxter and his fellow Puritans did not help. Baxter was far too talkative; he did not concentrate on pressing home a few demands. And his fellow Puritans, although they reluctantly accepted him as their chief spokes-

---

[6] This was argued by George Abernathy, *The English Presbyterians and the Stuart Restoration* (Philadelphia, Pa., 1965).

[7] Robert S. Bosher interpreted *The Making of the Restoration Settlement* as 'the influence of the Laudians' (London, 1951).

man in the Savoy Conference, were too divided to agree on a
single, simple policy which might have been successful. Some
seem to have wanted places in a modified Church of England
(the policy of 'comprehension', although the word did not
become familiar before the end of the 1660s). They were not
really interested in a mere 'toleration', especially not in the
toleration of Papists. Others were far more radical, wanting
'toleration' for Protestant congregations gathered outside any
National Church and if need be even for the Roman Catholics.
The split had been obvious in Oliver Cromwell's day and it
was not going to be healed overnight.

Finally, the changes in the Church of England agreed to by
the bishops and by the clergy in a joint meeting of the
Convocations of Canterbury and York, and accepted by King
and Parliament, were modest. The most important changes
were negative. The courts of Star Chamber and High Commission, on which William Laud had depended, were suppressed.
This meant that the bishops once again had to rely on the
creaking machinery of the diocesan courts. The canons of 1640
were declared illegal. This meant that the only law of the
Church of England was now the out-of-date code of 1604. By
an unwritten agreement between Clarendon and Sheldon, the
claim of the Convocations to tax the clergy was abandoned.
The result was that the Convocations need not meet at all; they
were to be effectively suppressed from 1664 to 1689 and during
most of the next century and a half. Although the Prayer Book
of 1662 was the work of the Convocations, the Commons
agreed to accept this work, without debate, by a majority of
only six and insisted on its right to debate any future changes.
If Laudianism is to be understood as an attempt to reaffirm the
power of the clergy, we must say that the Restoration was by no
means a Laudian triumph. On the contrary, it can be better
understood as the climax of a process continuous since the
1530s: the triumph of the laity.[8]

But these changes were made in order to serve the worldly
interest of laymen prepared to accept the clergy's religious

---

[8] This was the sub-title of Claire Cross's study of *Church and People, 1450–1660*
(London, 1976).

ministrations, not in order to satisfy Puritan consciences. In the end Puritans were also disappointed by the changes in the Prayer Book, some six hundred in number but mostly minor. Some generally acceptable prayers were added and it was pointed out that a new service of 'Baptism of such as are of Riper Years' would be useful when dealing with 'Natives in our Plantations'. Forms of prayer for use at sea showed awareness of the newly revealed destiny of the Protestant island. The general tone of the revisions was cautious ('which' was retained in the Lord's Prayer although it was changed to 'who' elsewhere), and some churchmen who wanted a greater enrichment were almost as disappointed as the Puritans. But the Catholic tendency of the restored Church was apparent in touches such as the provisions for blessing the water at Baptism and for manual acts by the priests when consecrating the bread and the wine in the Holy Communion. A note that baptized children dying before committing a sin were 'undoubtedly saved' seemed to signify the rejection of the Calvinist doctrine of predestination.[9]

The Act of Uniformity incorporating this revised Prayer Book came into force on St Bartholomew's Day, 24 August 1662. Not all the parishes whose ministers had to accept it or depart had by then received copies of the new book, but the nature of the Restoration Settlement was clear to all: it was a crushing defeat for those who advocated the 'comprehension' of Puritans by allowing ministers much freedom (as Baxter, for example, urged) or at least by making optional the ceremonies such as signing with the cross at Baptism to which there had been Puritan objections since Elizabethan times. The critics of the new book were referred to in its preface as 'men of factious, peevish and perverse spirits' unlikely to be 'satisfied with any thing that can be done in this kind by any other than themselves'. More than four hundred of the ministers who objected to the Restoration settlement had been ordained by bishops, but all understood the intention behind the new book's insistence that only episcopally ordained priests should celebrate

---

[9] The long discussion leading to the revision was well summarized by G. J. Cuming, *A History of Anglican Liturgy*, pp. 149–67.

Holy Communion. Richard Baxter gave the lead by an early announcement that he could no longer preach in the Church of England. With impressive courage 936 ministers, with their families, left the security of their rectories or vicarages on or before St Bartholomew's Day – before the tithes for the year were collected at Michaelmas. They received no compensation. In all, some 1,760 ministers were expelled from their parishes for their Puritan convictions in 1660–62.[10]

There was still to be wide diversity over the country in local Anglican attitudes to those who would not conform. Some parish churches were still used for services not in the Prayer Book, and some ministers not acceptable to bishops stayed on as private chaplains to Puritan gentlemen and noblemen. In his Essex parish Ralph Josselin did not wear a white surplice until 1680. But nationally there was to be a cleavage between 'Church' and 'Dissent'. Although there were still to be schemes to bring the ejected ministers, their succesors and their followers back into the National Church, no such plan was to achieve success during the next three centuries.[11]

However, the greatest legacy of the Puritan movement was a spiritual achievement which was to be embodied in imperishable literature and to become the heritage of the whole English-speaking world.

RICHARD BAXTER

The legacy of English Puritanism to the nation and to the world, surviving the Restoration, is to be seen in the work of three authors of outstanding significance: Richard Baxter who

---

[10] A. G. Matthews, *Calamy Revised* (Oxford, 1934), is the standard study of the Great Ejection. It scrutinized the lists published by Edmund Calamy in 1702–27.

[11] The best studies of the results of the Restoration Settlement are by Anne Whiteman and E. C. Ratcliff in *From Uniformity to Unity*, ed. Geoffrey Nuttall and Owen Chadwick (London, 1962), and by I. M. Green in *The Re-establishment of the Church of England* (Oxford, 1977). Joan Thirsk edited a collection of documents and comments, *The Restoration* (London, 1976).

lived until 1691, John Milton who lived until 1674, and John Bunyan who lived until 1688.

Baxter, although he never held a post higher than the parish of Kidderminster, may be reckoned the most truly eminent English churchman of his century. He wrote almost a hundred and fifty books; one of them, his *Christian Directory*, contained over a million words. In them he dealt with almost all the problems in morality and church life. It was the heartache of his own life that the work he loved, the work of preacher and pastor in a parish, was closed to him in 1661 because he could not accept the 'new prelatical way', which meant the control of parish ministers by diocesan bishops, and uniformity of worship in every parish by the enforcement of the Book of Common Prayer. For the next thirty years his influence was mainly that of a writer, although he so ardently wished to preach that in order to do so despite the official prohibition he was ready to face spells of imprisonment. He was also ready to accept the forced sale of two libraries which he had collected.

By the example of his persistent courage as much as by his writing, Baxter became the first patriarch of the denominations emerging out of the disintegration of Puritanism. In 1672 he registered himself simply as 'a mere Nonconformist', for he refused to adopt the narrower position of a Presbyterian or Congregationalist or Baptist; and in 1689 he was able to look back over the whole struggle in his history of *The English Nonconformity as under King Charles II and King James II*. But he would have been delighted to become a Conformist, if only the Church of England would allow more power to its parish clergy to run their own parishes and to compose their own services, and meanwhile he thought of himself as a 'nonconforming churchman'. He attended many Prayer Book services devoutly and when he conducted Nonconformist worship did so at times which did not clash with the services in parish churches. He became a spiritually great man, speaking out of the Puritan tradition to the whole of the large Nonconformist element in later English life; speaking also to the coming Evangelicalism within the Church of England from which he never finally separated himself.

He faced many handicaps. Physically he was not strong; his autobiography refers to many ailments.[12] His daily pain seems to have made him irritable, but he had another handicap: because his parents had thought it unnecessary for him to go to a university, he always had the independence of the man who was self-taught and without the experience of arguing with equals while young. He had little tact; he did not know how to make friends among the great or how to use them to further his own schemes. When Oliver Cromwell had treated him to one of his long monologues about recent English history, Baxter simply asked what had been wrong with the ancient monarchy. When Richard Cromwell was plainly doomed, Baxter dedicated his *Holy Commonwealth* to him. When the ancient monarchy was restored, and the bishops were full of themselves, Baxter was no less full of his own experiences, opinions and demands. When Charles II tried to secure toleration for all, this perpetually awkward theologian resisted the attempt on the ground that it would benefit Papists and heretics. On the other hand, he refused to subscribe to the conventional view that the Pope was Antichrist. A man so unco-operative was, it is clear, not suited for the bishopric of Hereford, offered to him when Clarendon as the King's chief minister was still trying to rally all moderates. But for all his independence he was a consistent advocate of moderation, and although no diplomat he was superbly well-equipped to be the pastor of his own parish and the author of his own books.

The ideals which inspired his work at Kidderminster were immortalized in *The Reformed Pastor* (1656). It was a ministry over nineteen years from 1641, apart from five years away when he felt obliged to preach to the troops on the Parliamentary side. He tried to keep his parish isolated from the Presbyterian and Independent (or Congregational) movements; and he was always sure that the majority of the English shared this wish. On the one hand, he had no desire to see the full Presbyterian system established in accordance with the Solemn League and Covenant. The leading laymen in the

---

[12] Conveniently abridged in Everyman's Library (London, 1931), *Reliquae Baxterianae* was printed in full in 1696 and 1829.

Kidderminster church were called 'deacons' or 'seniors', not
Calvin's 'elders'; and he refused to accept Calvin's creed that
some people were predestined by God to damnation. On the
other hand, he was not a full Independent. He was highly
critical of the Savoy Declaration which John Owen and other
Independents published in 1659. He approved of the State
controlling the National Church. He thought that Richard
Hooker had made too many concessions to democracy, and
dismissed the work of the Levellers as an 'abundance of wild
pamphlets as changeable as the moon'. He saw society as a
large family under one father, and his insistence on social
stability was almost medieval.[13]

He believed strongly that congregations ought to be grouped
in a spiritual family. In the 1650s he took the lead in the
Worcestershire Association, a voluntary group of churches
where the most important power was the right to excommunicate any sinner. No church in the group would receive a person
thus punished. He was quite prepared to see a bishop presiding
over such an association, and it would not trouble him if this
bishop were to be appointed by the King. He had been
ordained by the Bishop of Worcester before the war (certainly
as a deacon, almost certainly also as a priest), and he always
allowed a place for bishops in the Church. He intensely
admired the moderate Archbishop Ussher, and would have
liked most the fulfilment of Ussher's dream of every minister in
pastoral charge of a market town becoming a bishop and
gathering for regular conferences the other parish ministers in
the neighbourhood.

What interested Baxter, we may conclude, was neither the
Presbyterian nor the Independent nor the 'prelatical' theory,
but what he regarded as the central working reality of church
life: the parish church as a family, strengthened by a family-
like local association. 'A particular church of Christ's institution by his apostles', he wrote, 'is a sacred society consisting of
one or more pastors and a capable number of Christian
neighbours consociate by Christ's appointment and their own

---

[13] His conservatism in relation to his contemporaries was brought out by R. L.
Schlatter, *Social Ideas of Religious Leaders, 1660–88* (Oxford, 1940).

consent for personal communion in God's public worship and holy living.'

His convictions about church order on the national level were less clear. 'It is better,' he wrote, 'that men should be disorderly saved than orderly damned; and that the Church be disorderly preserved than orderly destroyed.' It was only in the period 1676–84 that he despaired of seeing a national church order which he could accept, and towards the end of his life his optimism returned. But he leaves the impression of not being greatly bothered about details at the national level. The saying of Peter Meiderlin was one of his favourite quotations: 'Unity in things necessary, liberty in things unnecessary, and charity in all.' The key to the life of the 'sacred society' was the parish, and the key to the parish was discipline administered by the pastor.

In Kidderminster he refused to give Holy Communion to those who would not accept the church's discipline; according-ly the communicants were always a minority among the adult parishioners, some six hundred out of 1,800. Baxter did not hesitate to say that he must 'take my people for my children' – just as the magistrate must govern 'the rabble'. An example of his self-confidence came during the Savoy Conference with the bishops in 1661. Challenged to say what deviations from the Prayer Book should be permitted, Baxter went away and after a fortnight's work produced a whole alternative Prayer Book, his *Reformed Liturgy*. But in the parish, he insisted, the minister must give himself utterly to the welfare of his parishioners. Baxter saw families for an hour at a time in his house during seven hours each week, and his two assistant ministers visited other folk systematically in their own homes. The conversation was not light; it was about faith and morals. And while some of his parishioners resented their pastor's attentions, all must have known that he was zealous to defend their interests. For five or six years he acted as a doctor in Kidderminster. The last treatise that he wrote – in 1699, not long before his death – was *The Poor Husbandman's Advocate to Rich Racking Landlords*. And those around him at every stage of his life must have known that he was no hireling. At Kidderminster all through the 1650s he let the ineffective former vicar, George Dance, stay in the vicarage and draw part of the income. Later on he offered to work as Dance's honorary curate (in vain), and it was his boast that he never in his life accepted a fee for a sermon.

Through many years when Puritanism was under persecution, Baxter maintained these ideals. At the heart of his wordy – sometimes too wordy – testimony there always was a devotional ardour so genuine that many, including many Anglican churchmen, were outraged when in 1685 Judge Jeffreys abused him coarsely during one of his trials. The 'holy angels bright' of his most famous hymn did not seem far off. His hope that the Church of England might so relax its own plan of discipline as to find a place for him was doomed to disappointment, but when imprisoned in 1686 this astonishing old man occupied himself with a fresh study of the Revelation of St John the Divine, leading to a fresh conviction that it was right to have a National Church under a Christian King while they awaited the rule of the saints under King Jesus.

Before he died he seems to have sensed clearly enough that there would be room for his Nonconformist ideals – for the Bible at the centre of the local congregation – in the continuing life of England outside the established National Church. Looking back he was sure that it had been God's work to mock the ambition of Cromwell and to destroy the pride of militant Puritanism by the restoration of Charles II ('and without one bloody nose!') – although it had left 'the poor Church of Christ, the sober, sound, religious part', crucified. His conclusion was that 'Christians must imitate Christ, and suffer with him' – a conclusion confirmed by 'the observation of God's dealing with the Church in every age'; for everywhere in history could be seen 'his befooling them that have dreamed of glorious times'. With such words he could part with his own dreams at Kidderminster – dreams in which perhaps he, too, had been ambitious and proud. But Richard Baxter could also look forward with a sober hope. 'God will have other generations to succeed us,' he once wrote, 'let us thank him that we have had our time . . . The Gospel dieth not when I die: the Church dieth not: the praises of God die not: the world dieth not: and perhaps it shall grow better, and those prayers shall be answered which seemed lost: yea, and it may be that some of the seed that I have sown shall spring up to some benefit of the dark unpeaceable world when I am dead.'[14]

JOHN MILTON

Baxter's hope was to some extent fulfilled, but a greater immortality of reputation has surrounded John Milton, as a poet acknowledged by almost all to be second only to Shakespeare – whom he addressed in 1630 as 'the great heir of Fame'. Writing in 1940, at a time when it was fashionable to denigrate him in comparison with Donne, Lord David Cecil claimed that Milton 'did not live by faith, scorned hope, and was indisposed to charity'; but he admitted that Milton remained 'the greatest of English poets who have made religion their subject'.[15]

His education may be said to have been continuous from some time before his entry into St Paul's School in London, in or about 1605, right up to 1639, when he returned home from his Italian tour and moved back to London, to begin teaching his nephew and his nation. He was one of the best-educated Englishmen of his day, and one of his best prose writings was *Of Education* (1644), with its plea that some at least of his contemporaries might be instructed in part at least of the immense syllabus which he had covered ('as ever in my great Task-master's eye'). He owed this preparation to his father, a businessman of substance and an amateur musician of distinction. The father's wealth and encouragement enabled the son to set out to become a great poet, although a Latin poem *Ad Patrem* shows that the father grew impatient as year after year went by without the son earning his living.

A very strenuous course of reading occupied John Milton up

---

[14] The best biography is by Geoffrey Nuttall (London, 1965). R. L. Schlatter studied *Richard Baxter and Puritan Politics* (Brunswick, N.J., 1957), and A. H. Wood his ecclesiology in *Church Unity without Uniformity* (London, 1963). See also William Lamont, *Richard Baxter and the Millennium* (London, 1979).

[15] *Oxford Book of Christian Verse* (Oxford, 1940), p. xxi.

to his thirtieth year, with the result that his prose or poetry was
full, perhaps too full, of allusions to classical literature and to
the seventeenth century's culture in general. He was the
master of many languages, and wrote Latin as easily as English
(sometimes confusing the two languages, critics have complained). After the age of twelve he rarely went to bed before
midnight, so devoted was he to his candle-lit books; which was
why he went totally blind when little over forty. He was
nicknamed 'the Lady' while an undergraduate, being a prig as
well as a goodlooker. He grew out of much of his youthful faith;
for instance, although his favourite tutor, Thomas Young, was
to be the author of a book on Sabbath-keeping and a leading
Presbyterian, Milton became so convinced of the individual's
ability to worship God in solitude that Sabbaths were not
needed and presbyters not wanted. Once he had put aside all
thought of being ordained he dared to be independent in basic
theology, as Baxter did not. 'Custom without truth', he once
wrote, 'is but agedness of error.' He also dared to say that
ministers of the Gospel should be a few itinerant preachers,
dependent on people's alms, like the apostles in the New
Testament. But it was Puritanism – regarded always as the
release of religious liberty and virtue, never as the overthrow of
the traditional social order – that gave Milton the inspiration
for his life's task: 'To leave something so written to aftertimes,
as they should not willingly let die.'

   From the years of preparation came poems of rare promise.
An English paraphrase of Psalm 136, written when he was
fifteen, has become a familiar hymn: 'Let us with a gladsome
mind . . .' A Latin poem on the death of Bishop Lancelot
Andrewes, written two years later, concluded with the first of
his many literary visions of heaven. His first grand English
poem, *On the Morning of Christ's Nativity*, written at Christmas
1629, imagined the Bethlehem which had already inspired
countless English songs, and did so with a young exuberance
and with many quaintly charming touches, but it lacked the
passionate devotion to Christ of Richard Crashaw; the offering
brought by Milton was one of clever metres and abundant
'conceits', sometimes reminiscent of Donne although without
his impact. Before the next Easter he had attempted, and had

abandoned, a poem on Christ's crucifixion – a theme which, in fact, he never handled at any length. Far more successful was the pair of poems, *L'Allegro* and *Il Pensoroso*, celebrating the delights of innocent 'mirth' and studious 'melancholy' amid rural beauty and classical scholarship. The latter poem ended with all heaven brought before the poet's eyes by the combination of architecture and music in Anglican worship, presumably in the great chapel of King's College, Cambridge. It is an odd passage to find in John Milton, although his father had been a chorister at Christ Church, Oxford. A masque performed at Ludlow Castle in 1634, *Comus*, offered similarly exalted praises of piety and virginity. But among all these poems of the 1630s only *Lycidas* had the power which we think of as Miltonic; and it was powerful because it gave the poet an opportunity to tell the world about himself.

Lycidas was a lament for Edward King, a young graduate of Milton's Cambridge college (Christ's), drowned in a shipwreck in 1637. It seems that Milton had scarcely known King, but the death of a contemporary stirred him to ask whether all human ambition was futile. That was his own question, for

> Fame is the spur that the clear spirit doth raise
> (That last infirmity of noble mind)
> To scorn delights, and live laborious days . . .

And the fact that King had been a candidate for ordination in Laud's Church gave an excuse for the poet to curse the clergy:

> Blind mouths! that scarce themselves know how to hold
> A sheep-hook, or have learned aught else the least
> That to the faithful herdman's art belongs! . . .
> The hungry sheep look up, and are not fed,
> But swoln with wind, and the rank mist they draw,
> Rot inwardly, and foul contagion spread.

This assessment of the Church of England was put into the mouth of St Peter, who was also made to comment on the menace of Popery and on the promise of reform:

> Besides what the grim wolf with privy paw
> Daily devours apace, and nothing said;
> But that two-handed engine at the door
> Stands ready to smite once, and smite no more.

Exactly what the 'two-handed engine' would be, *Lycidas* did
not make clear. But Milton's next great outburst is to be found
in his five pamphlets against the bishops. As his own power
was about to be taken away Laud had commissioned one of his
more scholarly and saintly colleagues, Joseph Hall, to write a
book advocating the 'divine right' of the bishops to govern the
Church. Hall lived to see his own cathedral (at Norwich)
invaded by a mob which tore out more or less everything that
could be moved.[16] Scarcely less violent was the theological
controversy caused by his book, although he was a sound
Calvinist and therefore not a thorough Laudian. To the debate
Milton contributed with a pent-up energy rather like the
Norwich mob's.

He rejected all the compromising proposals of moderates
such as Archbishop Ussher and Richard Baxter, who pleaded
that episcopacy might be saved by being 'reduced'. He wrote
with bitter contempt, tearing down the false scholarship which
had found prelacy within the New Testament and demolishing
any claim on behalf of the religion which the prelates had
supervised. As he wrote, it began to seem that only this
prelatical system which the parliamentary engine could so
easily smite stood between England and the fulfilment of the
Reformation. Was not an age of glory beginning in the 1640s?
'Then', wrote Milton at the end of *Reformation in England*,
'amidst the hymns and hallelujahs of saints, some one may
perhaps be heard offering at high strains in new and lofty
measures to sing and celebrate thy divine mercies and marvellous judgements in this land thoughout all ages.' Milton meant
to be that 'one', the poet of what he called 'the jubilee and
resurrection of the state'. He saw why he had been prepared for
his task – for he saw Christ waiting to claim his Kingdom. In
another anti-episcopal pamphlet he prayed: 'Come forth out of
thy royal chambers, O Prince of all the kings of the earth! Put
on the visible robes of thy imperial majesty, take up that
unlimited sceptre which thy Almighty Father hath bequeathed
thee; for now the voice of thy bride calls thee, and all creatures
sigh to be renewed.'

---

[16] F. L. Huntley portrayed *Bishop Joseph Hall* (Cambridge, 1979).

Milton is next to be found using his great learning and powers of invective in pleading for a law to permit divorce on the ground of incompatibility. His own disastrous marriage to Mary Powell spurred him on. She was the young daughter of a Royalist squire who owed money to his father, and Milton – so complete in his literary education, so lacking in experience of life – seems to have married her within a month of their first meeting. The reason is plain in *Paradise Lost*, where the poet who had celebrated chastity in *Comus* now rejoiced that Eve did not refuse the 'rites mysterious of connubial love',

> Whatever hypocrites austerely talk
> Of purity and place and innocence,
> Defaming as impure what God declares
> Pure, and commands to some, leaves free to all.
> Our Maker bids increase; who bids abstain
> But our destroyer, foe to God and man?

Eve, of course, had no right to refuse – for in *Samson Agonistes* Milton made it plain:

> Therefore God's universal law
> Gave to the man despotic power
> Over his female in due awe,
> Not from that right to part an hour,
> Smile she or lour . . .

Milton's young bride, however, soon ran away – only to return with her family when the Royalist cause was finally ruined. There was some reconciliation; she gave Milton daughters. But the blow which the marriage inflicted on the poet's pride drove him into public controversy on the topic of divorce, then generally believed to be forbidden to Christians by Christ's own words.

The controversy is significant because it showed Milton exalting the individual's conscience. Milton pleaded that the permission of divorce in the law of Moses still stood. In public he hinted – and in private he argued – that the Old Testament's permission of many wives to the patriarchs was relevant to Christians. When a shocked Presbyterian preacher denounced one of his pamphlets in a sermon to the House of

Commons, demanding the suppression of such subversive
literature, Milton published his *Areopagitica*, pleading for the
abolition of licensing in advance of publication (although he
did not suggest that Popish or other authors of 'that which is
impious or evil absolutely, either against faith or manners'
should escape punishment). He was still on fire with optimism
about the capacity of the English to achieve virtue by their free
struggles for the truth. 'Lords and commons of England!
consider what nation it is whereof ye are, and whereof ye are
the governors: a nation not slow and dull, but of a quick
ingenious and piercing spirit; acute to invent, subtle and
sinewy to discourse, not beneath the reach of any point the
highest that human capacity could soar to.' In other words, he
trusted that the English (with the known exceptions of his wife
and her family) resembled Milton himself.

The refusal of the Commons to listen to him on this dangerous topic seems to have begun Milton's disillusionment with
parliaments, but it would of course be wrong to think that a
mind so strong could be swayed by personal grudges alone
(particularly since death brought Milton release from his first
wife and her tribe in 1652). Milton genuinely despised what
was left of the Long Parliament, thought it incapable of
governing, and believed that its policy of imposing Presbyterianism on the country was utterly wrong.

Still more did he despise the sentimentality which idolized a
living king and turned an executed one into a martyr. He
admired Cromwell, who (he maintained) had won victory over
his own passions before winning any battle in the war. He was
proud to be appointed Secretary for Foreign Tongues to the
Council of State, and doubly proud to be commissioned to
defend King Charles's execution. To the writing of his *Eikono-
klastes* (1649) he brought the full power of his harsh joy that
there was now no bishop and no king. To the writing of his
Defensio pro Populo Anglicano (1651) he sacrificed the remnants
of his eyesight. The fact that the majority of the English people
regretted regicide did not trouble him, any more than did the
fact that Cromwell did not dare to summon a freely elected
Parliament. The time seemed to have come for government by
the virtuous and for freedom of worship for all who accepted

that government. Only slowly did he acknowledge that what
he had written in his *Nativity* ode about the coming 'age of gold'
was still true:

> But wisest Fate says no,
> This must not yet be so.

After 1655 Milton drew a pension rather than a salary from the
government, and was again left free to work largely on his own.
At first the loss of his sight was a profound shock:

> When I consider how my light is spent,
> Ere half my days, in this dark world and wide,
> And that one talent which is death to hide
> Lodged with me useless . . .

And his loneliness became the more intense when his second
wife, Katherine, and the daughter born to them both died in
1658. In his grief he wrote his most moving poem:

> Methought I saw my late espoused saint . . .
> Came vested all in white, pure as her mind.
> Her face was veiled, yet to my fancied sight
> Love, sweetness, goodness, in her person shined . . .
> I waked, she fled, and day brought back my night.

When Cromwell (to whom he was never, it seems, personally
close) died in the next year, and when it turned out that the
political hopes of Puritanism had died with him, the blind poet
for a time feared the hideous execution inflicted on traitors,
before influential friends secured his safety. But he was spared;
presumably his blindness was an argument in persuading the
authorities not to hang the poet writing *Paradise Lost*, on the
ground that he had already written high treason against
Charles I. And that blindness, his bereavement and his political disillusionment all turned out to be indispensable factors in
the fulfilment of the ambition to stand alongside Chaucer,
Spenser and Shakespeare as a poet: the ambition which had
been laid aside in 1640. He used to lie in bed, particularly in the
winter months, until in the morning his daughters (with many
grumbles, we gather) and other assistants would come to 'milk'
him of the forty-odd lines he had composed in his mind.
Perhaps half of those lines would be allowed to remain when
the draft was read back to him. His third wife was a good cook

who controlled his daughters and any visitors. So the conditions for serious work were created. And the collapse of his political hopes made this always serious, always essentially solitary, genius ask with a new creative passion what were the values he thought eternal.

For a long time he had been fascinated by the early history of Britain. He had thought that it might be his vocation to write an epic poem on King Arthur, a deliverer only matched by Cromwell. He did some work, instead, on a *History of Britain* to the Norman Conquest; and in the 1660s he completed it – only now, a prominent theme was a lament that the British had not proved worthy of freedom when the Roman yoke was removed. For a long time his religion had been obstinately his own. Now he began to collect texts from the Bible with his own comments, in Latin, knowing that his heresies could not be published while either Puritans or Royalists held power. In fact, *De Doctrina Christiana*, which he seems to have gone on compiling until his death, was not discovered and prepared for the printer until 1823. For the time being, all that it could do was to clear his own mind. The long-delayed epic poem to which he gave himself could not be openly treacherous or heretical; but it could take a theme which was safe because scriptural. And it could tell an audience 'fit though few' what he had learned from the public and private achievements and tragedies which he had now experienced.

Paradise Lost (1667) and its sequel *Paradise Regained* (1671) were, of course, primarily narratives, expanded from the bare biblical text by the splendour of a poet's imaginative genius. The music of their words has been enjoyed by very many readers who have cared little for politics or theology; and being on the surface biblical, they got past the censors in the reign of Charles II. But like everything else of any real power that Milton ever wrote, they are also a very proud man's autobiography. Here, he knew, was his last, supreme chance of self-expression

> though fall'n on evil days,
> On evil days though fall'n, and evil tongues;
> In darkness, and with dangers compassed round,
> And solitude; yet not alone . . .

There is something of the excitement of the civil war in the account of the war in heaven in those books of *Paradise Lost* which were written while Cromwell was still alive. There is something of Milton's marriages in his portraiture of Adam and Eve and of Samson and Delila. The woman is subordinate (of course) and the first sinner (of course) – but the man loves her, in Adam's case enough to choose her rather than God. There is something of the poet's contempt for Stuart kings in his praise of Christ's rejection of the trappings of monarchy in *Paradise Regained*. There is also something of his contempt for Laudian prelates and priests in his description of the Philistines' religion in *Samson Agonistes* (a poem published in 1671 but written ten years or more earlier). The prayer of joy in nature which Adam and Eve offer ('unmeditated', the poet insists) in the middle of Book V of *Paradise Lost* seems to be Milton at his most positive and most impressive. And is there not a further self-revelation? Milton has such a reputation for cold arrogance that readers might expect him to appear in these poems as God. It was, however, one of the many curiosities of his religion that his God was not lovable and we must look elsewhere for the appearance of the poet, who certainly loved himself.

Some of Satan's speeches inciting the angels to rebellion against the divine tyrant, or defying God's revenging wrath, do sound rather like Milton. Plainly the poet enjoyed and admired Satan's 'courage never to submit or yield'. Indeed, William Blake suggested that 'the reason Milton wrote in fetters when he wrote of angels and God, and at liberty when of devils and hell, is because he was a true poet and of the Devil's party without knowing it.' But it is perverse to conclude that the mature Milton approved of Satan's rebellion when his whole theme was the calm acceptance of God's will. Most scholars are agreed that Milton identified himself mostly with the Son of God and with Samson (who was regarded as a precursor of Christ in the standard Puritan expositions of the Bible).

We readily understand how easy it was for Milton to speak through Samson, the blind hero who had once defended his people against the oppressor and who was now about to take vengeance on all his triumphant enemies as he died. It becomes easier for us to appreciate the personal link between the poet and the Son of God when we learn from *De Doctrina Christiana* that Milton believed that the Son of God was inferior to God.

In Milton's mature belief, God did not create the world 'out of nothing' as orthodoxy claimed. Instead, the primal chaos out of which the ordered world was created itself originated from God. The distinction may seem subtle, but it served to suggest that matter was in some sense divine. And God created not a fresh immortal soul for each new human being, but the one Adam, one body into which he breathed life or soul. Eve was made out of Adam, and all their descendants owed their souls as well as their bodies to sexual reproduction. God was therefore released from the 'servile' and risky work of soul-making. He was left free to uphold the ordinary course of nature or history, while men and women, made in the normal course of events, made their own destinies without any decisive initiative, interference or assistance from God. The advantage of this theology was that, although it made God out to be static, remote and remorseless, it freed him from the blame which is liable to attach to an Almighty Father who is believed to be willing to perform some miracles to rescue some people on some occasions. Only thus, Milton believed, could he 'justify the ways of God to man'.[17]

The Son of God did the work of creation in Milton's scheme, since God himself must not be involved. But Milton was an 'Arian' (after Arius, who died in c.336), in that he believed that the Son had been begotten by the Father within time, not as orthodoxy asserted 'before all worlds'. Although Milton accepted the orthodox anti-Arian statement that the Father and the Son were of one being (he translated the Greek *ousia* by the Latin *substantia*), he denied that they were of one essence (*essentia*). In the Father's address to the Son in Book III of *Paradise Lost*, the highest compliment which the former can pay to the latter is:

---

[17] A modern atheist can therefore commend Milton up to a point. See William Empson, *Milton's God* (London, 1961).

Both God and man, Son both of God and man.

And when the angels hymn Jesus at the end of *Paradise Regained*,
the praise is no higher:

> The Son of God, with God-like force endued.

These abstruse and obscure points of theology encouraged
the practical belief that men could imitate Christ and thus
become sons of God themselves. It was also important that
Milton was an Arminian, like the hated Laud. His rejection of
Calvin's teaching that some were predestined to damnation is
most famous because of his description of the fallen angels who

> reason high
> Of providence, foreknowledge, will and fate,
> Fixed fate, free will, foreknowledge absolute,
> And found no end, in wand'ring mazes lost.

But the point is that no true Calvinist could have been so
contemptuous of such talk, the normal reasoning expected
from the most trusted theologians. Milton's rejection of 'fixed
fate' meant that he could combine praise of the moral virtue of
the 'saints' with a moral condemnation of those who, exercising their own free wills, rejected God's call. Thus the Father
declares in *Paradise Lost*:

> Some I have chosen of peculiar grace
> Elect above the rest; so is my will.
> The rest shall hear me call, and oft be warned
> Their sinful state, and to appease betimes
> Th' incensèd Deity, while offered grace
> Invites . . .

For to Milton all men were free, 'sufficient to have stood,
though free to fall'.

After Adam's fall his heirs are still free to respond to the
promptings of conscience:

> And I will place within them as a guide
> My umpire, Conscience, whom if they will hear,
> Light after light well us'd they shall attain,
> And to the end persisting, safe arrive.

What was essential was that men, aided by God's grace, should cultivate the heroic virtues. That was why in Milton's poem Paradise, having being lost when Adam chose to love Eve rather than obey God, was regained when the Son of God heroically chose to obey God during his temptations in the wilderness. Milton, although he could sound orthodox enough about the Saviour's work and the Saviour's grace, never found occasion to write at any length about any atonement achieved by the crucifixion. He also made nothing important depend on Christ's resurrection. Indeed, he believed that even for the Christian saint after death 'the soul as well as the body sleeps until the day of resurrection'. This was 'Mortalism', leaving to the individual only the hope of resurrection at the end of the world. Heaven and hell, to say nothing of Dante's purgatory, thus receded from Milton's immediate concern. He still accepted the final judgement by God, but it seems probable that he thought of heaven and hell as being only states of mind, at least until that judgement – agreeing at this point with Satan:

> The mind is its own place, and in itself
> Can make a heav'n of hell, a hell of heav'n.

For practical purposes his mature religion austerely taught obedience to God in this life.

It was an attitude not essentially different from a Stoic or Muslim submission to fate; and it was an attitude perfectly possible for all the virtuous who were masters of themselves. Such a religion falls short of the love of the Father, of the Saviour and of the sinner as practised and advocated by the Christian saints. But not far short – as Adam shows when he concludes *Paradise Lost*:

> Henceforth I learn that to obey is best,
> And love with fear the only God, to walk
> As in his presence, ever to observe
> His providence, and on him sole depend. . . .

Moreover, Milton seems to have known, in some moods at any rate, what was lacking. In the poem the Angel congratulates

Adam on attaining the 'sum of wisdom' but warns him that in order to possess 'a paradise within thee' he must add

> Deeds to thy knowledge answerable, add faith,
> Add virtue, patience, temperance, add love,
> By name to come called charity, the soul
> Of all the rest . . .

What, then, of politics? Milton's final verdict on the Puritan Revolution resembled Richard Baxter's: the Commonwealth had been betrayed by the unheroic weakness of its own citizens. There had been a time when 'by the general instinct of holy and devout men, as they daily and solemnly express their thoughts, God is decreeing to begin some new and great period in his Church, even to the reforming of Reformation itself; what does he then but reveal himself to his servants, and as his manner is, first to his Englishmen?' So he had enthused in *Areopagitica*. But already in 1648 he showed his regret that the war had done such damage and had left such power in the army's hands. In his sonnet to General Fairfax he asked:

> For what can war but endless war still breed
> Till truth and right from violence be freed?

After the war Parliament had refused to rise to the central challenge of the 1640s, which was to give religious liberty to all, so that all might learn for themselves how to be heroic. The people had also been to blame – by refusing to achieve the heroism open to them, which was submission to the divinely decreed social order. And even Cromwell had been at fault in the 1650s, when unlike Christ he had unheroically yielded to the temptation to grab political power.

Amid the confusion of 1659 Milton published one of his last pamphlets, *The Ready and Easy Way to Establish a Free Commonwealth*. His way involved forgetting the very name of Parliament, all thought of popular direct elections, and all government by a 'single person'. Instead there was to be an assembly in each county guided by 'the nobility and chief gentry', if virtuous. There was also to be a General Council for the whole Commonwealth, elected for life by those with property; in a complicated scheme successive elections were envisaged in order to winnow out electors or candidates not possessed of sufficient virtue or sufficient property. And there was to be a Council of State, with no Lord Protector. The poet cannot have been entirely surprised when this 'ready and easy way' was disregarded by the politicians and the soldiers, so that the restoration of the king and the bishops became inevitable. He never again dictated thoughts directly about politics, so far as we know; his only publication in this field during his lifetime was in 1673, a pamphlet advocating the toleration of Protestants but emphatically not of Papists.

After 1660 the resurrection of the Puritan Revolution seemed to be as remote as the hope of heaven. But meanwhile it was open to men to reform and discipline themselves. If it was God's will, there might one day be a revolution ruled by saints, an England fit for heroes. And meanwhile the poet could find his rest, in a death accepted heroically. Samson says of himself:

> I was no private but a person raised
> With strength sufficient and command from heaven
> To free my country . . .

And after his death it is declared of him:

> Nothing is here for tears, nothing to wail
> Or knock the breast, no weakness, no contempt,
> Dispraise, or blame; nothing but well and fair,
> And what may quiet us in a death so noble.

As for the 'Good Old Cause' of the Puritan Revolution:

> All is best, though we oft doubt,
> What th' unsearchable dispose
> Of Highest Wisdom brings about,
> And ever best found in the close . . .
> His servants he, with new acquist
> Of true experience from this great event,
> With peace and consolation hath dismissed,
> And calm of mind, all passion spent.[18]

---

[18] Christopher Hill, *Milton and the Puritan Revolution* (London, 1977), puts the life against its background and lists many other studies. E. M. W. Tillyard, *Milton* (revised London, 1966), and Hugh Richmond, *The Christian Revolutionary: John Milton* (Berkeley, Cal., 1974), were usefully concise. C. S. Lewis assessed Milton as

JOHN BUNYAN

Two of John Bunyan's books will always be of supreme interest to anyone who would understand English religion. He was a preacher and pastor, born in 1628 and called to full-time service by his Bedford church in 1671. Tearing himself away from his wife and blind daughter (he compared that with 'the pulling of the flesh from my bones'), he accepted imprisonment for twelve years, with a second period to follow, rather than undertake not to preach. His imprisonment was not always severe; there is evidence that he was allowed to spend many nights at home and to go to London. He often preached to Nonconformist congregations while technically a prisoner. But he spent enough time in prison to suffer some privations – and to become a great writer. He came to believe that his imprisonment had been within God's providence because it had given him what his normal life would never have provided – the incentive and the time to write. And he wrote with a success which he naïvely celebrated. By the time of his death in 1688 (he had caught a chill on a journey undertaken in order to reconcile a father and a son) he was famous. His most outstanding gift was an extraordinary ability to recreate everyday English scenes and conversations, and to make them the symbols and dramas of the Puritans' spiritual world.

He was never a cool professional in religion. His autobiography, *Grace Abounding to the Chief of Sinners*, told of the tempests of self-accusation, religious doubt and existential despair which made year after year of his young life miserable. And he was never a literary gentleman. It was not only that he was innocent of Latin. Although he quoted the Bible so freely, his own prose was remarkably unlike the stately Authorized Version's. It captured on paper the colloquial speech of the day and was inspired by popular literature – fairy stories and cheap

---

'overwhelmingly Christian' in *A Preface to Paradise Lost* (Oxford, 1942), and C. A. Patrides presented him as a substantially orthodox Protestant in *Milton and the Christian Tradition* (Oxford, 1966), but see Arthur Sewell, *A Study in Milton's Christian Doctrine* (Oxford, 1939), and N. T. Burns, *Christian Moralism from Tyndale to Milton* (Cambridge, Mass., 1972). J. S. Hill, *John Milton: Poet, Priest and Prophet* (London, 1979), studied Milton's profound belief that he had been called by God – a vocation not ended by disaster.

novels. This often confused and barely educated man wrote for the people as he preached to the people, from the heart to the heart, with a mission which never separated him from them. English Nonconformity was to consist of millions like him.

Richard Baxter's wife was well-off, which was why he was able to spend his last thirty years as a writer. John Milton's rich father enabled the poet to spend his first thirty years as a student. But John Bunyan earned his living as a wandering tinker or odd-job-man, like his father. His idea of education was to thank God that he was able to read the two books which his first wife's father had left her when he died, *The Plain Man's Pathway to Heaven* and *The Practice of Piety*, 'though we came together as poor as poor might be (not having so much household stuff as a dish or a spoon betwixt us both)'. And he was never captured by middle-class conventions. He once wrote a book about a businessman whose acquisitiveness had the energy which some twentieth-century writers have suggested was given to the prospering bourgeoisie by Calvinism. Although it has been described as the first English novel, it is virtually unreadable because its central character was damned hopelessly from the start. It was called *Mr Badman*.

Two books of his have become classics. *Grace Abounding* (1666) is the direct story of how an ignorant but very introspective young man, psychologically (it would seem) sometimes depressive and sometimes manic, felt the threats and promises of the English Bible rolling over his soul like waves which almost drowned him. While playing tipcat on Elstow village green he heard a voice: 'Wilt thou leave thy sins and go to heaven, or have thy sins and go to hell?' 'One morning as I did lie in bed, I was, as at other times, most fiercely assaulted with this temptation, *To sell and part with Christ*; the wicked suggestion still running in my mind, *Sell him, sell him, sell him, sell him, sell him*, as fast as a man could speak.' 'The glory of the holiness of God did at this time break me to pieces.'

The Pilgrim's Progress (in two parts published in 1678–84) told basically the same story, but projected it into a journey such as would be taken by a tinker through the English countryside – with an anvil on his back which to the imagination became the burden of sin; sometimes admitted into the

'House Beautiful' and many humbler homes but spending far more time outdoors; falling in with many different companions on the road; finding that the road easily became a quagmire, the Slough of Despond; being rather frightened at Vanity Fair but needed to go there because he needed the work. The memory of the freedom of the road no doubt often came back to Bunyan while he slept in prison. That lies behind the famous opening: 'As I walked through the wilderness of this world, I lighted upon a certain place where there was a den, and laid me down in that place to sleep: and, as I slept, I dreamed a dream.'

The book was true to life in so many subtle ways. The action is somewhat repetitive and more than one of the sermons by which Christian is instructed hints that the preacher has fallen into an unexciting routine. But the adventure is provided by life itself, for it is impossible for Christian to tell what lies ahead. ' "Do you see yonder wicket-gate?" The man said, "No". Then said the other, "Do you see yonder shining light?" He said, "I think I do." ' It is also impossible for Christian to be secure until the end; even when Doubting Castle and the Valley of the Shadow of Death have been left behind, it is seen that there is 'a way to Hell even from the gates of Heaven, as well as from the City of Destruction'. And it is impossible for anyone who comes after to duplicate the same experiences exactly. For others the way may be harder; Christian's companion, Faithful, is put to death in Vanity Fair. But his own wife and four sons, who take Christian's road in the second part of the *Progress*, find the going much easier and have time for music and dancing during their pilgrimage (or, as Ronald Knox called it, their 'walking tour'). The only guidance which every pilgrim could and should follow is indicated by Mr Standfast when he looks back: 'I have loved to hear my Lord spoken of, and wherever I have seen the print of his shoe in the earth, there I have coveted to set my foot too.' But even for Mr Standfast, the heroic virtue of proud John Milton is impossible. Like the other pilgrims, Mr Standfast still needs a Saviour long after his conversion.

The church in Bedford to which Bunyan belonged was founded by eleven working men in 1650; it was one of the fruits of Cromwell's policy of toleration for Protestant 'separatists'.

It has usually been called a Baptist church, but it was described as Congregational when it applied for a licence under the King's Declaration of Indulgence in 1672. Certainly it was far removed from all the accusations of immorality and general rebelliousness which had brought scandal to the Continental Anabaptist movement in the sixteenth century. Respectable housewives such as Christiana felt at home there. It was possible to become a member of this congregation, a 'saint', without having been baptized as an adult – or at all. Baptism is not decisive in the *Progress*. Although Bunyan is known from his other books to have adhered much more closely to Calvin's scheme of salvation than did Milton, he was not rigid. The *Progress* is true to life in that it gives no sense that its characters lack the freedom to go forward or fall back. And the will of God is that they should go forward; 'the last words of Mr Honest were, *Grace reigns*'.

There was a future for the Puritan religion taught by John Bunyan: the Nonconformist future in England, the Evangelical movement among Anglicans, the missionary work around the world. Fanfares of fame have sounded for this imprisoned odd-job-man, as the trumpets sounded for Mr Valiant-for-truth when he had crossed the river of death, leaving his sword 'to him that shall succeed me in my pilgrimage.'[19]

---

[19] There is no really good biography, but see W. Y. Tindall, *John Bunyan: Mechanick Preacher* (New York, 1934); Monica Furlong, *Puritan's Progress* (London, 1975); *Bunyan: The Pilgrim's Progress*, ed. Roger Sharrock (London, 1976); N. H. Keeble, *John Bunyan: Conventicle and Parnassus* (Oxford, 1988).

Part Three

RELIGION IN
THE AGE OF REASON

CHAPTER TEN

THE QUAKERS

GEORGE FOX

George Fox began to preach in Nottinghamshire in 1647, the year when Charles I was defeated and the victorious army awaited the reconstruction of English society. A congregation was formed at Mansfield under his influence in the following year; and one incident, typical of many, helps to explain the magnetism of the man. Having interrupted a preacher in church, Fox was lynched by a mob and beaten with clubs until he fell unconscious. On regaining consciousness, 'I lay a little still, and the power of the Lord sprang through me, and the eternal refreshings refreshed me, that I stood up again in the eternal power of God and stretched out my arms amongst them all, and said again with a loud voice, "Strike again, here is my arms and my head and my cheeks".'

He was a lion among men, but his courage was not the most rare of his characteristics. 'He was of an innocent life,' wrote William Penn, 'no busy-body, nor self-seeker, neither touchy nor critical; what fell from him was very inoffensive, if not very edifying. So meek, contented, modest, easy, steady, tender, it was a pleasure to be in his company. He exercised no authority but over evil, and that everywhere and in all, but with love, compassion, and long-suffering, a most merciful man, as ready to forgive as unapt to take or give an offence.' And Fox himself pointed to the heart of his joy: 'I saw that there was an ocean of darkness and death, but an infinite ocean of light and love, which flowed over the ocean of darkness.' The ferment of radical religious ideas also produced groups such as the Seekers, who worshipped in silence rather than use words which had ceased to be authentic; the Ranters and Levellers, who rejected society's conventions rather than deny the Christ

in every man; or the Fifth Monarchy Men who pressed forward
impatiently into the reign of King Jesus. But the personality of
George Fox provides a large part of the answer to the question:
why did the Quakers survive when all these other groups were
forgotten?

Born in a Leicestershire village in 1624, he was the son of a
devout weaver nicknamed Righteous Christer. But the normal
pieties of family and village did not satisfy the boy. He left
home early and ceased to attend church. When 'towards
nineteen years of age' and working as a shoemaker, he became
convinced that he was called to be a pilgrim, literally – and
alone. As he lay sleepless one night after leaving a beer-party in
disgust, he saw 'young people go together into vanity and old
people into the earth; and thou must forsake all, both young
and old, and keep out of all, and be as a stranger unto all.'
Three years or more of wandering and seeking followed. He
consulted clergymen, and found that 'to be bred at Oxford or
Cambridge was not enough to make a man fit to be a minister
of Christ'. He consulted 'separatist' preachers and found that
they, too, could not satisfy him. But his search was rewarded.
'When all my hope in them and in all men were gone, so that I
had nothing outwardly to help me, nor could tell what to do,
then, Oh then, I heard a voice which said, "There is one, even
Christ Jesus, that can speak to thy condition", and when I
heard it my heart did leap for joy.'

Charismatic excitement marked the meetings which he
addressed. As he put it, 'now was I come up in the spirit
through the flaming sword into the paradise of God. All things
were new, and all the creation gave another smell unto me than
before . . .' He bade a Derby magistrate tremble at the word of
the Lord in 1650, and the magistrate's nickname for his
movement stuck: they were 'Quakers', although Fox wanted
them to be called 'Children of the Light'. Men and women
(whose equality was itself revolutionary) joyfully surrendered
themselves to ecstasies which sober churchmen had not expected to meet outside the pages of the Acts of the Apostles. Fox
claimed that there were many healing miracles, although most
of these claims were suppressed when his *Journal* was printed.
The Quakers met in each other's homes and often denounced

the priests of the steeple-houses. (Fox used the term 'priests' of all the clergymen, and called all churches 'steeple-houses'.) They saw no point in continuing the sacraments of Baptism and Holy Communion since the age of the spirit had arrived.

Not even the Bible retained its accustomed authority. With a thrill of excitement Margaret Fell heard George Fox exclaim in Ulverston parish church: 'You will say, "Christ saith this, and the apostles say this" – *but what canst thou say?*' That kind of question shocked not only the bishops but also Roger Williams, Richard Baxter and John Bunyan, all of whom were stirred to write against the Quakers. But many were glad to hear it asked and confident that they could answer it. John Lilburne, for instance, read Quaker books when he was imprisoned in Dover Castle in 1650, after his latest defiance of the political authorities. He was soon writing that he had 'really and substantially found that which my soul many years hath sought diligently after'. So he knew peace before he died, aged forty-two.

The customs of the Quakers outside their meetings drew further attention – sometimes fascinated, often hostile. They refused to use the pagan names of days or months; Sunday was the First Day, January the First Month. Fearing hypocrisy, they refused to wear any finery, to join most of the normal amusements, to use any titles, to remove their hats when addressing others, or to call anyone by the courtly 'you' instead of the plain, old-fashioned 'thou'. They were also convinced that the Sermon on the Mount forbade them to take any oaths, to participate in any violence, or to wear weapons. On several dramatic occasions they appeared in outlandish clothing, or in no clothing at all, as prophets in public places, 'for a sign'.

Their leaders were constantly on the move, often forced to sleep out of doors, often imprisoned, often surrounded by outbreaks of hysteria; and under such a strain they sometimes acted hysterically. George Fox walked barefoot up and down Lichfield crying 'Woe unto the bloody city!' To Fox's intense alarm, James Nayler allowed a little group of muddy women to chant 'Hosanna' and 'Holy, Holy, Holy' as he rode through Wells and Glastonbury and into Bristol in the rain one October day in 1656; he had just finished a long spell of fasting and

prayer in Exeter jail. But the main impression left by the early
Quaker leaders is not of hysteria.

Marmaduke Stephenson was not unique in his cold courage:
'In the beginning of the year 1655,' he recalled when he found
himself in Boston prison in Massachusetts not five years later,
'I was at the plough in the east parts of Yorkshire . . . and as I
walked after the plough I was filled with the love and presence
of the living God which did ravish my heart when I felt it . . .
And the word of the Lord came to me in a still small voice
which I did hear perfectly, saying to me in the secret of my
heart and conscience, *I have ordained thee a prophet unto the nations*.'
In 1658 he felt a call to go to the island of Barbados, leaving 'my
dear and loving wife and tender children', and while he was
there he heard that 'New England had made a law to put the
servants of the Living God to death'. This seemed to him an
excellent reason why he should proceed to Massachusetts and
refuse to leave it; and he was hanged.

Even James Nayler was not a mere hysteric. A ploughman
who had served in the New Model Army for nine years (mostly
as a quartermaster), he became an eloquent mystic whose
best-known book was called *The Lamb's War*. His fatal mistake,
the ride into Bristol, seems to have occurred because at that
time, after his imprisonment and its mystical raptures, he was
scarcely conscious of the everyday world. His body, like his
reputation, never fully recovered from his punishment for that
blasphemy; while he was walking home from London to
Yorkshire he was beaten up by robbers and soon died. But the
spirit in which he died showed that he was not unworthy to
speak of the spiritual war being led by the non-violent Lamb.
'There is a spirit which I feel,' he wrote, 'that delights to do no
evil nor to avenge any wrong, but delights to endure all things
in hope to enjoy its own in the end. Its hope is to outlive all
wrath and contention and to weary out all exultation and
cruelty and whatever is of a nature contrary to itself. It sees to
the end of all temptations. As it bears no evil in itself, so it con-
ceives none in thoughts to any other. If it be betrayed, it bears it,
for its ground and spring is the mercies and forgiveness of God.'[1]

---

[1] See Geoffrey Nuttall, *James Nayler: A Fresh Approach* (London, 1954).

George Fox, although like Nayler lacking in formal education, dictated a *Journal* recording his life to 1676. Published three years after his death in 1691, it took its place among the classics of English religion.[2] To call it literature would be inaccurate, but there is no denying its power to recreate physical and emotional dramas with words of strength and a simple dignity. More unusual still was Fox's organizing capacity. In the crisis caused by the indiscretion of the ride into Bristol, Fox had no hesitation in rejecting Nayler as a heretic. Nor did he hesitate to set up a system which would make sure that there would be no more Naylers. When Nayler offered him a kiss of reconciliation, Fox once felt guided to hold out his foot. He organized special meetings for counties or groups of counties, with a national meeting at Skipton in 1660. He was a cobbler, with leather breeches and a white (undyed) hat; but he somehow became the first Englishman to lead a nationwide denomination – meaning by 'denomination' a religious body not aspiring to be the National Church.

His vision crossed the seas. As early as 1652, as he looked down from Pendle Hill across Lancashire to the sea, 'the Lord let me see a top of the hill in what places he had a great people to be gathered'. Believing that Friends were called to 'walk cheerfully over the world, answering that of God in every one' (as he put it in 1656), he became the most internationally-minded man England had produced for many years. In 1671–73 he was in Barbados, Jamaica, Virginia and New England, declaring on his return: 'We can challenge all the world'. With his encouragement Quaker missionaries went not only to New England but also to the Netherlands, to Germany and to the East, announcing the 'Kingdom of Jesus' like the biblical apostles. George Robinson testified in Jerusalem. Mary Fisher lectured the Sultan. When he courteously asked what she thought of the Prophet of Islam, she replied that he had been a true prophet if what he spoke was from God: a verdict to which the Sultan could not take exception. In the East only the authorities in Rome violently resented this form of evangelism,

---

[2] *The Journal of George Fox* was edited by J. L. Nickalls (Cambridge, 1952), and *George Fox's Book of Miracles* by H. J. Cadbury (Cambridge, 1948).

and one Quaker, John Luffe, was hanged there. George Fox sent a letter to the Emperor of China 'from the People of God in England, in English called Quakers'. 'Friends,' he announced, 'there is a Power above all Powers, and this Power is making itself manifest.'

This explosion of religious energy created stirs in many places but had the most lasting consequences in Yorkshire, the Lake counties and other northern areas of England. There medieval Catholicism had at last died down but no Protestant minister had made much impact – often because the still medieval parish system left him with too big a district. In so far as Fox had a home and his movement a base, from 1652 onwards this was Swarthmoor Hall in Lancashire; in 1669 he married Margaret Fell, the widow of its owner. However, he was never a man to settle down to the life of a squire. Of their twenty-one years of married life – years of mutual devotion – he and his Margaret passed little more than five in each other's company. He was not a squire but an apostle, imprisoned nine times; and because of its uncluttered directness the movement which he led appealed to many countrymen in the backward southwest and to the working class in England's largest cities, London and Bristol. It is not surprising that after the rising of Fifth Monarchy Men in London in 1661 the Cavalier gentry assembled in Parliament rushed through a special Act to suppress the Quakers. Locally magistrates assumed that these eccentrics were revolutionaries and threw thousands of them into prison where hundreds of them died of gaol fever. But all the evidence confirms the Quakers' own claim that religious, rather than political, energy had been awakened. And there is no shortage of printed evidence about the motives of this movement founded by George Fox. It has been reckoned that a new Quaker book or pamphlet appeared every week from the first tracts of 1652 to the end of the seventeenth century.[3]

[3] W. C. Braithwaite studied *The Beginnings of Quakerism* (revised, Cambridge, 1955) and Hugh Barbour *The Quakers in Puritan England* (New Haven, Conn., 1964). *Early Quaker Writings* were edited by Hugh Barbour and A. O. Roberts (Grand Rapids, Mich., 1973). There is no good biography of George Fox, but the discussion by Michael Watts in *The Dissenters*, Vol. 1 (Oxford, 1978), pp. 179–212, is of special value.

FROM QUAKERS TO FRIENDS

In the great persecution of 1662–72 (which was less severe in
the period 1665–70), and under many further sufferings prolonged until the Toleration Act of 1689, the Quakers were
conspicuous for their courage. They deliberately left the doors
of the houses where they met for worship unlocked. If the
meeting was surrounded by an insulting mob, it carried on; if
its members were arrested, they resumed their worship in
prison. If the meeting house was pulled down, Quakers would
still be found on the spot the next First Day; and if no adult
Quakers were out of prison, it was not unknown for the
children to assemble. A Quaker meeting needed no preacher; it
did not even need a Bible; the 'inner light', it was claimed, was
the guide. The Spirit in their midst seemed to grow stronger as
the persecutors put themselves more and more in the wrong in
the eyes of ordinary Christians. Much evidence suggests that
although at the beginning of the persecution the movement
was regarded as ridiculous or as alarming, by the 1670s the
Quakers had won a respect which they have never forfeited in
England. 'They go like lambs without any resistance', wrote a
baffled Samuel Pepys in his diary. 'I would to God they would
either conform, or be more wise, and not be catched.'

The most difficult problem came to be not how to survive
persecution but how to survive prosperity.

One great strength of the Quakers under persecution was
their tight organization; in this, too, they resembled the early
Christians. They encouraged powerful leadership by treating
the leaders and other ministers (who were 'recorded', not
appointed or paid) as men or women inspired by God. They
'watched over' each other's moral progress. They were in each
other's company as often as possible, and recognized each
other by their strange customs even when they did not already
know each other by name. They founded schools to educate
each other's children. They supported each other very generously when in trouble. From 1667 onwards Fox systematically
organized Monthly Meetings which decided policy in matters
great or small. A national meeting held in London at Christmas 1668 became the London Yearly Meeting – at a time when

the Church of England itself possessed no comparable national
forum. The 'Meeting for Sufferings' was a committee which
from 1676 onwards kept a nationwide check on the English
Quakers' troubles. It retained its central role (and its name)
when the persecution had died down, and devoted much of its
time to the teething troubles of the Quaker settlements in
America. But with this organizational strength, problems
grew.

Even Fox did not escape fierce criticism from some Quakers
who resented the masterfulness of his personality. The mutual
care of Quakers could also be resented. It might seem to be
intolerable prying into each other's affairs, especially when
'elders' were appointed to lead the meetings (a custom made
nationwide in 1727). Their uniform could itself be criticized,
especially as people realized that the costume originally
adopted as plain everyday wear now seemed merely outdated
and queer. Quaker children thus garbed were tormented by
cries of 'Quack! Quack!' in the streets. Moreover, the well-to-
do adults' dress was often tailor-made and rather expensive.
The schools, founded on a large scale from 1750 onwards,
could be attacked because they kept young Quakers in a
hothouse atmosphere, with the inevitable rebellions. And the
growing moral pressure of the meetings to 'keep in the unity'
could be contrasted with the earlier days when the message
had appealed as an encouragement of the individual to 'keep
your feet upon the top of the mountains and sound deep to the
witness of God in every man' (as Fox wrote in 1660). It is the
judgement of more than one Quaker scholar that 'by 1800 the
Society of Friends had become a rigid institution, subject to the
very institutional faults against which the early Friends had
carried out their costly struggle.'[4]

Another great strength of the early Quakers lay in their
'convincement' that the Truth within was nothing less than the
Christ within. In the early days there seemed no need to be
theological about this. A man such as George Fox simply
assumed that what was true must be Christian. Although he
was a sturdy individualist and no great reader of other men's

---

[4] Harold Loukes, *The Quaker Contribution* (London, 1965), p. 66.

books, it was said that if the Bible had been lost it could have been recovered from his dictation. But inevitably many Quakers, particularly the more educated, became anxious to dissociate the movement from extremists, such as the Ranters who were frankly heretical. John Perrot refused to remove his hat when another Quaker was offering prayer to God in a meeting, and this 'hat heresy' had to be pursued when it was carried to the West Indies and New England. The problem was how to do battle against such heresies when there was no official creed, and when almost all the evangelists ('public Friends' was their title) had no theological training.

Robert Barclay, a Scot who became a Quaker in 1666, published a substantial *Apologia* in Latin ten years later. He remained enough of a Calvinist to teach very firmly that the 'inner light' was an 'inward and immediate revelation' of Christ, the saving Light of the World. In essence this was the old Puritan orthodoxy about the work of the Holy Spirit. Barclay was fascinated by a mystical sentence which he heard at the first Quaker meeting he attended: 'In stillness there is fullness; in fullness there is nothingness; in nothingness there are all things.' But he stressed that every Quaker meeting must end with only one 'sense of the meeting' – and that this sense must subordinate all things to Christ. Even during the seventeenth century this synthesis was under strain; George Keith, who had worked with Barclay, caused trouble among the Americans by organizing a movement known as the 'Christian Quakers' and ended up being ordained by the Bishop of London. The Quaker reliance on 'the Light of Christ within men without anything else' was, he kept on declaring on his return to America, insufficient; and he stirred up controversy until his death in 1716. Thereafter the controversy slumbered, but it caused serious divisions in the Quakers' ranks when it came out into the open in the 1820s and 1830s. The theological question, once raised after the strong simplicity of the first days, could not be suppressed.

The early Quakers were as untouched by wealth as they were by theology, But they were hard-working and honest. They came from social groups unaffected by aristocratic values, and it was from such groups that England's manufacturers and tradesmen were working their way into prosperity. By 'watching over' each other they to a large extent enforced the rigorous moral standards which Richard Baxter (for instance) demanded in his books. Quaker traders or bankers could be trusted; Quaker employers might even be loved. And honest toil was rewarded. Before the seventeenth century had ended there were rich Quakers, especially in London. Even the average Quaker was found to be reliable, and therefore eminently employable. Much was gained – but something was lost in comparison with the 1650s, when under George Fox's charismatic leadership poor men and women, the Children of Light, had challenged the 'world's people' to be spiritually rich.

PENN AND PENNSYLVANIA

The new respectability of the Quakers was associated with the personality of William Penn. The son of the admiral who had conquered Jamaica for Cromwell before becoming a distinguished servant of Charles II, he first heard Quaker preaching when a lad of twelve. As an undergraduate at Christ Church, Oxford, he was enough of a rebel against the Anglicans in control to prefer the teaching of John Owen, the ex-dean; and he was asked to leave. Not even travel as a young aristocrat in France and Italy, or residence as a young landowner in Ireland, could get the Quaker challenge out of his mind. He openly became a Quaker himself. Having publicly attacked the doctrines of the Church of England, he was imprisoned in the Tower of London, and there wrote a devotional classic: *No Cross, No Crown*. On his acquittal by a jury which refused to be intimidated, he was recognized as the best-educated and the most socially prominent Quaker. He often talked in that capacity with Charles II and James II.

Both kings admired him personally, in addition to their gratitude to his father. In 1681 Charles granted him extensive lands south of New England and New Jersey, and north of Maryland and Virginia. They had been won from the Dutch, who had never made much of 'New Netherland'. This tract was empty, apart from a few Dutchmen, Swedes and Finns together with Indian tribesmen who were declining in vigour; and, once cultivated, it would be fertile. The reason given for the grant (made when all efforts had failed to find a purchaser) was that the Crown was in debt to old Admiral Penn. It seems clear, however, the King hoped that William Penn would lead his fellow Quakers far away across the Atlantic, for he disliked having his peace troubled by their persecution as much as he disliked having his vices denounced by their prophecies. The idea of emigration had also occurred to Penn, who had already managed the purchase of lands on which to settle Quakers in New Jersey. The new 'province' was named Pennsylvania by the King; Penn had wanted to call it New Wales, and perhaps Charles was teasing him by insisting on the grandiloquent name, to be compared with the settlements of Carolina in the south. Penn spent only two periods there – periods of less than two years each, separated by fifteen years – but he made sure that his ideas were stamped on the growth of Pennsylvania.

From the first he insisted on liberty of conscience for all; on the promise that (in the words of the 1701 Charter of Privileges) no one should 'at any time be compelled to frequent or maintain any religious worship, place or ministry whatever, contrary to his, or her, mind.' He insisted, too, on friendly relations and fair bargains with the Indians. Benjamin West's painting of William Penn's treaty with the Indians under the great elm at Shackamaxon is familiar to many Americans (although there is no contemporary record of such a treaty). Penn welcomed George Fox's exhortation: 'Let your light shine among the Indians, and the Blacks and the Whites, that ye may answer the truth in them.'

Early Pennsylvania knew a remarkable measure of democracy. Penn drew up a *Frame of Government* which gave restricted power to himself as proprietor and governor, and much to an elected council of seventy-two. The council was to propose laws to an annual General Assembly of some two hundred, elected by all freemen with property. It was by no means a society of strict equality. Power lay with the council, the nucleus of Pennsylvania's future aristocracy. Penn owned a few Negro slaves, as did some other early settlers, and there were many 'bond servants' – immigrants who had bound themselves to their masters, usually for five years, in exchange for their transatlantic fares. But the Quakers practised a remarkable degree of brotherhood. There is truth in the claim made for Pennsylvania before about 1740 that 'this life was an artistic creation as beautiful in its simplicity and proportion as was the architecture of its meeting houses'.[5] In this strange colony, the proprietor himself had a book printed under the title *England's Liberties* (1682) which contained not only his patent from the Crown but also Magna Carta. And the brotherhood was not exclusively Quaker. The first Quakers arriving were given no privileges over the other Europeans already in the area. Philadelphia was planned with its streets like a chess-board; the houses varied in handsomeness and their owners varied in wealth, but all must fit into the ordered pattern of the City of Brotherly Love.

However, the establishment of Pennsylvania, promising as it was, involved William Penn in problems which had never burdened George Fox; and although he used others – including men who were not Quakers – as his deputies, he could not escape his responsibilities. Indeed, his correspondence often shows an irritated, even secular, tone as he insisted on his political and financial rights as proprietor. This 'Lord of the Soil' attempted to exercise over Pennsylvania a power which he denied to the kings in England. It is surprising neither that such claims were resisted nor that the opposition was led by two Welshmen, Thomas and David Lloyd. There were bitter disputes over land, rights and status among the settlers and between them and neighbouring colonies. There were crimes, and the criminals had to be punished – even hanged; in 1718 Pennsylvania adopted the same death penalties as England. There were threats from the French, and a promise that the Quakers would contribute to their own military defence was made a condition of the renewal of Penn's grant. For years the pacifism of the Pennsylvania Quakers was preserved by equivocations; in 1745, when they voted money for 'grain', the

---

[5] R. H. Bainton, *Friends for 300 Years* (New York, 1952), p. 184.

governor interpreted this as including gunpowder. There were quarrels with the Indians; although Penn in his lifetime could insist on the 'peaceable kingdom' and later Quakers obstinately clung to this vision, conflicts and massacres eventually led to the Indian war of 1756. Recognizing that military action was now inescapable, but being unwilling to participate in it, most of the Quakers then resigned from the General Assembly of Pennsylvania. This perfectionist withdrawal from government and war came fifty-five years after Penn's last visit to his province.

He lived to see the Quakers accepting some compromise in England. Although never willing to give evidence in criminal cases or to serve on juries, they solved the problem which they had created by being unwilling to take the Oath of Allegiance as well as lesser oaths, by now agreeing to the formula, 'I do declare in the presence of Almighty God, the Witness of the truth of what I say'. Penn was controversially involved in politics as a result of his friendship with James II; to the indignation of Anglicans, he accepted James's Declaration of Indulgence protecting the Roman Catholics. Although he also accepted that monarch's overthrow, he was more than once arrested on suspicion of treason after the revolution of 1688 – and it seems likely that he was aware of some of the plots of the Jacobites, even if only on the fringes. The unhappiness of his latter years was increased by a financial dispute with the heirs of the man on whom he had relied to handle his properties, by debts which caused his imprisonment for almost a year, and eventually by a stroke which deprived him of rationality. It seems clear that these miseries were caused chiefly by over-work, since he struggled to minister to the whole Quaker movement as George Fox's spiritual successor, while also being burdened by many more worldly responsibilities. He kept his mental powers long enough to write the movement's first history (*The Rise and Progress of the People Called Quakers*, 1694), and an eloquent defence of its principles (*Primitive Christianity*, 1696); but before his stroke in 1712 he must have sensed that there had been a decline in the spiritual power of the religious movement whose leadership he had inherited from George Fox. He died in 1718.

A factor in the Quakers' decline in England was the absorption of so many of them in the practical labours necessary to till the soil, to build the settlements, to expand the commerce and generally to run colonial America. Even at the time some English Quakers were worried about the psychological effects of the transatlantic migration – although the enthusiasm with which others corresponded with the new colonies, or crossed the Atlantic to visit them, was more pronounced. The American Quakers could not spare the energy needed to develop a new world of spiritual and intellectual life. Their schools were good and distinctive, and many individual Quakers who became leaders of commerce were well-educated; William Penn's secretary, James Logan, lived to become one of the most accomplished scholars, scientists and men of affairs in eighteenth-century America. But Rufus Jones, who wrote the first systematic account of the Quakers in the American colonies, lamented the lack of higher education on specifically Quaker foundations. It contributed, he believed, to the dearth of leaders of thought after Penn's death. 'The absence of constructive leaders, the later tendency to withdraw from civic tasks, the relaxing of the idea of reshaping the world, which this history reveals, were due, in the main, to the lack of expansive education.'[6]

Philadelphia, however, rapidly became the largest city in North America. It was the centre of a triangular commerce with England and the West Indies, but it was also a cultural centre lively enough to attract young Benjamin Franklin away from Boston and to respond to his many initiatives and inventions. One way in which it earned its wealth was that it was the first example of the ethnic mix which was to become one of the proudest achievements of the United States. Not

[6] Rufus M. Jones, *The Quakers in the American Colonies* (New York and London, 1911), p. xxvii. More recent studies include Frederic B. Tolles, *Meeting House and Counting House* (Chapel Hill, N.C., 1948), and *Quakers and the Atlantic Culture* (New York, 1960), and Geoffrey B. Nash, *Quakers and Politics: Pennsylvania 1681–1726* (Princeton, N.J., 1968). Catherine Peare, *William Penn* (Philadelphia, Pa., 1957), is the best biography, and Mary Maples Dunn, *William Penn: Politics and Conscience*, and Melvin B. Endy, *William Penn and Early Quakerism* (Princeton, N.J., 1967–73), are the best studies of his thought.

only Quakers found refuge in Pennsylvania. Strict Baptists came from far off Wales, with Protestant Huguenots as refugees from France, and persecuted Roman Catholics from nearby Maryland. Even Jews came, although they could not hold public office. Large numbers of Germans came from the Rhineland, importing 'Pennsylvania Dutch' (which remained a language in use for many years) and much jolly folk art. Most of these were either Lutheran or Reformed in religion, but the Mennonites and the Amish among them resembled the English Quakers. Many Scotch-Irish came from Ulster and pioneered in the wilderness inland. On this frontier they were able to find a reward for their energy, and a freedom for their Presbyterian faith, which had not been available in Ireland. With its satellite colonies, New Jersey and Delaware, Pennsylvania became a wonder; and the prosperity of its peacefully mixed population advertised the principles of democracy and religious liberty. Its success (despite many internal controversies) was the decisive model which inspired the shaping of republican independence. The Declaration of Independence read out to the cheering crowd in the yard of State House in Philadelphia on 8 July 1776, to the accompaniment of the ringing of the Liberty Bell, had been drafted by a Virginian – but Jefferson seems to have had his chance since Benjamin Franklin was too busy devising a new constitution for Pennsylvania itself. And certainly no eighteenth-century American, not even Franklin or Jefferson or Washington, left a sweeter memory behind him than the Quaker John Woolman, whose *Journal* shows that in his gentle way he was the friend of slaves, the friend of Indians and the friend of God.

It seems to be impossible to be accurate about the number of Quakers in eighteenth-century England. One Quaker historian guessed that numbers dropped from some sixty thousand in 1680 to only thirty-two thousand in 1800; another, that numbers remained steady at around fifty thousand. What we do know is that the records of local meetings often mention disappointment that there were few conversions or 'convincements' of outsiders. The majority of Quakers were brought into the society by their parents, although many brothers or sisters refused to join them. Quakerism, which had begun as a

world-wide movement, was becoming an hereditary sect, picturesque rather than explosive. Yet the same change won for
the sect an acceptance, even a popularity. A typical leader was
Penn's successor, George Whitehead. As the best historian of
the origins of the Society of Friends wrote, Whitehead 'was
now the leading survivor of the First Publishers of Truth, and
would guide the policy of the Society for the next quarter of a
century. He was the embodiment of worthy and drab respectability, devoid of genius, and of little humour, but industrious
and politic, one who had achieved so much for Quakerism that
he no longer sought fresh adventures or inspired new
enthusiasms.'[7]

Three verdicts may be considered as we try to assess the first
hundred years of this extraordinary society which George Fox
founded. A distinguished American historian has lamented
that 'their self-righteousness and their rigidity' made the
Quakers a sect in America, even in Pennsylvania itself. He
argues that their unconventional, energetic, practical religion
could have inspired the people of the emerging United States
far more widely – if only the Quakers had been more willing to
compromise on inessentials. To him 'this is the story of one of
the greatest lost opportunities in all American history'.[8] An
English historian might be tempted to use similar words about
the limited numbers of the English Quakers. But to Ronald
Knox, George Fox's enthusiastic perfectionism was so clearly
doomed from the start that even the dull survival of the small
Society of Friends was a marvel. 'What survived was', he
commented, 'a band of well-to-do reformers, distinguished by
their wide influence and active benevolence, but numbering
only a handful of adherents among the multitudes on whom
they had compassion. Among all the daydreams which flitted
through the mind of George Fox as he travelled about the roads

---

[7] W. C. Braithwaite, *The Second Period of Quakerism* (revised, Cambridge, 1961),
pp. 177–8. See also Arnold Lloyd, *Quaker Social History 1669–1738* (London, 1950),
and Richard T. Vann, *The Social Development of English Quakerism 1655–1755* (Cambridge, Mass., 1969).

[8] Daniel J. Boorstin, *The Americans: The Colonial Experience* (New York, 1958),
pp. 33–69.

of England, none, surely, was stranger than this.'⁹ And even that tribute did not do full justice to the astonishing facts; perhaps Knox, a firm and distinguished Roman Catholic, had to be too cautious.

'To maintain the Christian quality in the world of business and of domestic life, and to maintain it without pretensions or hypocrisy,' wrote G. M. Trevelyan, 'was the great achievement of these extraordinary people . . . The Puritan pot had boiled over, with much heat and fury; when it had cooled and been poured away, this precious sediment was left at the bottom.'¹⁰

---

⁹ R. A. Knox, *Enthusiasm*, p. 168.
¹⁰ G. M. Trevelyan, *English Social History* (London, 1942), p. 267.

CHAPTER ELEVEN

A CALMER CREED

WREN'S CHURCHES

The churches designed by Sir Christopher Wren after the Great Fire of London in 1666 were built at a time when the vice and squalor of much of the city continued to be obvious; and they were consecrated in an Anglican faith which was not yet completely secure, Protestant Dissent and Roman Catholicism being both still formidable challengers. But Wren's churches were the temples of a faith far less troubled than the religion of the English had been since the Middle Ages. The God to be worshipped in them was a God of order, of reason, of light; a God with whom well-behaved, reasonable, enlightened Englishmen felt at home. To understand their spirit is to understand much about the calmer creed of England, 1660–1760.

From the beginning Wren belonged to the governing class both by birth and by recognized ability. His father was Dean of Windsor under Charles I. His uncle was Bishop of Ely. In his youth he was entrusted with a personal message from Oliver Cromwell to his uncle: the old man could leave prison in the Tower of London. The invitation was rejected, because it would have involved accepting Cromwell's 'detestable tyranny'. Thus Christopher Wren inherited an impeccable position as a Royalist son of the Church of England. He also inherited a taste and talent for architecture (and for mathematics) from his highly cultivated father. At Oxford he caught the infection of science as an intellectual passion. His first posts were professorships of astronomy in Gresham's College, London, and at Oxford; and he was for many years active in the work of the Royal Society. While still in his twenties he was entrusted with the design of the Sheldonian Theatre at Oxford and the chapel of Pembroke College, Cambridge, and promised appointment as Surveyor General of the Royal Works when a vacancy occurred. Although his architecture was inspired by the Palladian buildings which were the last, lovely flowering of the Renaissance in Italy, he did not think it necessary to go to Italy. He spent half a year in France, but the rest he got from books. He was an English gentleman.

He was dismissed from his office under the Crown in 1717 after accusations that his assistants were fraudulent and incompetent. But by then he was in his eighties – and had done as much as anyone in history to glorify the English monarchy by noble extensions to the palaces at Kensington and Hampton Court, and by the great Royal Hospitals built for soldiers in Chelsea and for sailors at Greenwich. Had there been money available, yet more majestic buildings would have arisen: he prepared designs for a vast mausoleum for Charles I as part of a remodelling of Windsor Castle, for a palace and parliament house arising where fire had destroyed Whitehall Palace in 1696. Had the citizens of London been willing to accept his radical plan after the Great Fire of 1666, the huddled, stinking city of medieval and Tudor days would have been rebuilt on magnificently rational lines, with an embankment lining up great houses by the Thames and with splendid public buildings and paved squares giving drama to the long, straight streets.

As it was, support was not forthcoming for this imaginative scheme, or for any other of Wren's boldest ideas in the secular sphere. It was as a church architect that he won his enduring triumphs – because his style perfectly matched the feeling of London merchants that they, too, were becoming triumphant and should give thanks.

He built more than fifty churches for London after the Great Fire, and above their very cleverly varied steeples and towers rose one of the greatest buildings of the European Renaissance: St Paul's Cathedral. And he left his mark on other churches. He built a church dedicated to St James (under James II) in the newly developed area of Piccadilly, for instance, and, still working in his old age, rescued from decay the fabric of Westminster Abbey, adding for Westminster School a handsome dormitory block in the nearby garden. He had been a schoolboy at Westminster. Surviving plans show that if Wren had had his way, the abbey would have been crowned by a steeple or even a dome.

When he became London's leading architect 'Old St Paul's' was still standing, as the world's biggest church apart from St Peter's, Rome. Wren admired the gigantic classical portico added by Inigo Jones to the west end, and urged the replacement of the remnants of the spire on the decayed tower by a new dome, surmounted by a pineapple some seventy feet high. That problem was solved by the Great Fire in September 1666, although even then it took some time for the authorities to realize that the great black ruin of the medieval cathedral must be demolished totally.

Apart from the consummate mastery of the final design executed in Portland stone and marble, and the superb quality of the craftsmanship of most of the furnishings, what is most striking about the rebuilding of St Paul's is the determination of Parliament, and of the nation as a whole, to have a cathedral which would dominate London, whatever the expense. Within Wren's lifetime the work seems to have cost about £850,000, some two-thirds of the annual sum allowed by Parliament for the upkeep of the monarchy and government when Charles II was at the height of his power. While part of the cost was met by nationwide appeals for gifts, more than £800,000 came from a tax on coal entering London voted in 1670. Wren's city churches were financed from the same source, although there was no willingness to finance his visions of a royal palace. No one leader seems to have been decisive in securing the adoption of this boldly expensive plan. Gilbert Sheldon was then Archbishop of Canterbury, and William Sancroft, who was to follow him at Canterbury, was Dean of St Paul's; and both were able and active men. But the decision seems to have been more or less spontaneous. No alternative was really thinkable, although the obscure Bishop of London (Henchman) wrote a gloomy paper entitled 'Nine considerations against building a new cathedral'.

Wren deployed both genius and great patience in devising architecture which would respond to this unique challenge: the

creation of a cathedral when it had been assumed that the age
of cathedrals was over. The preliminary plans already broke
away from any idea of rebuilding in the 'Gothic' style (the word
was already in general use to refer vaguely to the architecture
of the Middle Ages after the Normans). But at the beginning of
his active involvement in the project for a cathedral – an
involvement which covered more than thirty-five years – Wren
had modest dimensions in mind. His first plan has been called
'box-like'. Then his imagination blazed and he produced the
far bolder plan known as the 'great model' because it was taken
seriously enough to be translated into a wooden model. That
plan still envisaged the cathedral as a larger parish church.
The whole point about Wren's churches was that they were
Protestant: the sermon mattered more than any sacrament,
and the aim was to seat the congregation within fifty feet of the
preacher. Wren imagined a larger congregation assembled
around the pulpit in the cathedral but seized the opportunity to
place over them a dome described as 'coloss and beautiful'.
The only concession which he made to conservatism was to
propose a large Corinthian portico, replacing the one by Inigo
Jones and joined to the symmetrical hall under the great dome
by a narthex including a lesser dome. The plan was in the end
abandoned because the clergy insisted on a long choir where
the daily services of Morning and Evening Prayer could be
sung. They also wanted most of the congregation to be able to
see the altar, which would have been tucked away in one of the
short arms of the 'Greek cross' plan in Wren's model. And they
wanted aisles as in the Middle Ages, although there were at
this time no processions to move round them.

Wren wept when his plan was rejected, but he went on to
produce a feeble plan in order to get the work started by a royal
warrant in 1675. As the work proceeded this plan was somehow transmuted into magnificence. Although less original
than the earlier 'great model', in the end this substitute
managed to satisfy both those who used the cathedral for
religious activities and the larger number who looked on it as
the massive centre-piece in London's skyline, assisted by the
fact that the portico on top of Ludgate Hill remained as one of
the concessions to conservatism. Through many years Wren's

close supervision continued; it was his practice to visit the site each Saturday. There were complaints about the delay and in 1697 Parliament decreed that half his salary should be kept until the work was complete; he had to petition for the arrears in 1711. But the main reason for the delay which cost him dear was his insistence on perfection. For his idea of what a cathedral, or a parish church, ought to be was very clear.

In Wren's churches the element of religious mystery was lacking. In medieval churches coloured glass illustrating the stories of the Bible and the saints kept out any sight of the surroundings, but Wren wanted clear glass, to unite the church with the world. The altar was not magnified to suggest separation from sinners. There were no candle-lit chapels or embroidered banners or painted statues to add tenderness and consolation, as in a medieval church. There were no dramatic paintings or carvings of the agonized Saviour, the blissful Mother or the swooning saint, as in the Baroque churches of Rome. For Wren, a church was not a refuge into which a mother could slip quietly in order to pour out prayers about a child. It was a meeting place for solid citizens who were growing accustomed to comfort in their own homes and who wanted to thank their divine benefactor. They met in order to recite the beautiful, legally authorized, words of the Book of Common Prayer and in order to hear a preacher who would remind them of the reasons why they should be grateful and in other ways dutiful.

While in church they were to be impressed by the sober beauty above them, but even in the cathedral Wren's architecture had its domestic elements. It showed off the carpentry of Grinling Gibbons or the ironwork of Jean Tijou – work which would have been admired in any drawing room or garden. Its restraint can be compared with the more dramatic work at Blenheim Palace and elsewhere of Wren's successors at the head of the architectural profession, Nicholas Hawksmoor (his pupil and assistant) and Sir John Vanbrugh (who came to architecture through soldiering, play-writing and scene-painting). And Wren's philosophy was not only domestic; it was very cautiously democratic. When commissioners were appointed in 1711 to build fifty new churches for London and

Westminster, and he was one of them, he advocated building churches near the homes of 'the better sort', even though the sites would be more expensive. But he added: 'a church should not be so fill'd with pews, but that the poor may have room enough to stand and sit in the alleys, for to them equally is the Gospel preach'd.'[1]

TWO GENTLE SPIRITS: TAYLOR AND BROWNE

Two of the most attractive Anglicans in the middle of the seventeenth century, Jeremy Taylor and Thomas Browne, wrote very beautiful prose – but they showed by the ambiguity of their arguments how necessary it was becoming for thinking Englishmen to find a new intellectual basis for religious belief.

Taylor became one of the most learned scholars and most distinguished writers in a great literary age; Coleridge later ranked him near Shakespeare and Milton. His father was a barber in Cambridge, and in that city he received his education. While an undergraduate he was sufficiently influenced by High Church clergymen for him to become one himself, attracting the patronage of Archbishop Laud. He was made a chaplain both to the Archbishop and to the King. His first book was *Of the Sacred Order and Offices of Episcopacy, by Divine Institution, Apostolic Tradition and Catholic Practice* (1642). He bravely dedicated another book, an attack on the work of the Westminster Assembly, to Charles I shortly after the King's execution. At the Restoration he was made a bishop in Northern Ireland and as such enforced the Act of Uniformity, expelling Presbyterian ministers from their parishes. His last books were treatises of which Laud and Charles I would have approved. He asserted the Catholic character of the Church he served in *The Worthy Communicant* and *A Discourse on Confirmation*,

---

[1] Wren's 'Thoughts on Churches' are in Martin S. Briggs, *Wren the Incomparable* (London, 1953), pp. 135–8. The second centenary of his death encouraged the publication of twenty volumes by the Wren Society. On that basis there are good biographies by Bryan Little and Harold F. Hutchinson (London, 1975–76). Additional material of interest is to be found in *A History of St Paul's Cathedral*, ed. W. R. Matthews and W. M. Atkins (London, 1957).

and defended it with vigour in *A Dissuasive from Popery to the People of Ireland*. His largest work, *Ductor Dubitantum*, was a conservative discussion of Christian ethics. Strongly Royalist, it was completed just in time to be dedicated to the restored king in 1660, when 'worthily to accept of our prosperity is all our business'.

Yet Taylor was not trusted by the conservative Archbishop Sheldon, who frustrated his hopes of an English bishopric and who described him when he heard of his death in 1667 as 'a man of dangerous temper, apt to break into extravagances'. The two men had begun their uneasy relationship when Gilbert Sheldon had been Warden of All Souls College, Oxford, and Taylor a poor young man from Cambridge who had been appointed to a fellowship against the college statutes which insisted on an Oxford education. But basically the problem was psychological. Taylor incurred suspicion not because he was deliberately heretical but because of the delicacy of his generously humane and cultured mind, reflected in a style which set out to commend faith and prayer by the beauty of holiness. It was reported that while he was a bishop he bought up all the unsold copies of his *Liberty of Prophesying* and burned them – but that plea for toleration, published in 1647, could not be forgotten. The civil war which he had witnessed had appalled him. 'If persons be Christians in their lives and . . . if they acknowledge the eternal Son of God for their Master and their Lord', he had asked, in 1647, 'why then should I hate such persons whom God loves and who love God?' He had urged Englishmen to bury their quarrels – 'to cling to the creed of the Apostles; and in all other things an honest endeavour to find out what truth we can.' Charles I had let his displeasure be known.

After this unpopular plea for liberty, Taylor turned to the writing of devotional literature. It was his real contribution to a troubled age. He was sheltered after the war by the hospitality of the Earl of Carbery in the great house of Golden Grove in Wales; and he was heartened by the encouragement of the young countess, on whose premature death he preached the most beautiful of a very lovely series of sermons. He wrote *The Rules and Exercises of Holy Living* for her, with *Holy Dying* as a sequel printed just in time for her funeral. For a wider public he wrote *The Great Exemplar*, the first life of Christ in English. It was not in any way a critical work, but it quietly glowed like a Nativity by an old master.

In these books he broke right away from the old monastic tradition. Some of the most wonderful passages were on marriage (which, 'like the useful bee, builds a house and gathers sweetness from every flower . . . and is that state of good things to which God hath designed the present constitution of the world') and on children ('their stammering, their little angers, their innocence, their imperfections, their necessities, are so many little emanations of joy and comfort to him that delights in their persons and society'). When such teaching was scrutinized by the orthodox, Taylor's God resembled a loving father to an extent that alarmed. Presumably this God would never willingly doom any of his children to the everlasting torments of hell, or condemn them for any offence except their own conduct. He would never decide one of his children's eternal destiny by seeing whether or not that child repeated a theological formula on his deathbed. Not only was Taylor an Arminian; he seemed to be reducing the Gospel to morality. So critics asked: was Christ *only* the 'great exemplar' and not the Saviour and the perfect sacrifice for sin? Some three centuries later the criticism was still being offered that 'Christianity is, for Jeremy Taylor, an enterprise only for those capable of helping themselves'.[2] The unorthodoxy alleged to poison the wine of Jeremy Taylor's devotional prose is said to have contributed to a disastrous emphasis in later Anglicanism on works, not faith. In the 1650s Gilbert Sheldon was one of the clergy who wrote to beg Taylor to withdraw or to keep silent. He received an unrepentant reply. 'You are a happy person, private and unharmed; my folly and forwardness hath wrought my trouble; but yet there was zeal in it, and I thought there was much reason, and I am sure I intended piously, and there are very many that do still think so.'

Taylor, who wrote exquisitely about the dawning sun or the falling rose, or the marks of the tide on the beach, or the shining

---

[2] C. F. Allison, *The Rise of Moralism* (London, 1966), p. 80.

of light on water, could never conceive how in such a beautiful world anyone could be an atheist. 'To see rare effects and no cause; an excellent government and no prince; a motion without an immovable; a circle without a centre; a time without eternity; a second without a first . . . these things are so against philosophy and natural reason, that he must be a beast in his understanding. This is the atheist: *the fool hath said in his heart, there is no God.*' So Taylor preached – but he never dealt with the religious problems suggested by those aspects of nature which do not make pleasant illustrations for sermons. If he had done so, he might have expressed some sympathy with the atheist; and he might have run into more trouble for doing so.[3]

In this age of many controversies another author with a magic style, Sir Thomas Browne, shared Jeremy Taylor's unwillingness to reduce the richness of life to any single system of dogmas.

In the mid-1630s he wrote down some of his musings about the 'religion of a physician' and what he had written was printed in 1642 without his permission as *Religio Medici*. Denounced by both Catholic and Protestant stalwarts, Browne replied that 'I have no genius to disputes in religion'. He then issued an authorized version of the book, and went on musing as he practised medicine in Norwich. He had no desire to overturn the old order, social or spiritual, which gave security to simple folk. Indeed, he shared many of the popular beliefs. The world of spirits seemed very real to him, as to his patients. 'I have ever believed, and do now know, that there are witches; they that doubt of these, do not only deny them, but spirits.' It was always his conviction that time mattered less than eternity, that the created world was a mere 'parenthesis in eternity'. But his study of medicine had taught him the beginnings of a scientific approach. He was insatiable in his desire to probe popular superstitions, to collect curiosities, to conduct

---

[3] See C. J. Stranks, *The Life and Writings of Jeremy Taylor* (London, 1952); H. Trevor Hughes, *The Piety of Jeremy Taylor* (London, 1960); F. L. Huntley, *Jeremy Taylor and the Great Rebellion* (Ann Arbor, Mich., 1970). H. R. McAdoo studied *The Structure of Caroline Moral Theology* (London, 1949).

experiments. 'The world was made to be inhabited by beasts', he wrote, 'but studied and contemplated by man; 'tis the debt of our reason we owe to God, and the homage we pay for not being beasts.'

This devout doctor reconciled the two worlds of religion and science by urging modesty on one and all. To him human life was perpetually surrounded by the mystery of death – a mystery which was impenetrable. When a collection of ancient funeral urns was discovered in a field, he felt inspired to assemble all that he could discover about burial customs. His thought (or feeling) was a tissue of many languages and civilizations, united only by the charm of his personality as he moved so gently among his grateful patients and among the dead who interested him equally. But he did not apologize for any confusion. He believed that the world of religion was as important as the world of science; that, however, there were two worlds, to be reconciled only in eternity; that before he dies man is 'that great and true Amphibium whose nature is disposed to live not only like other creatures in divers elements but in divided and distinguished worlds.'[4]

A RATIONAL THEOLOGY

To some, the time seemed to have arrived for a simpler religion. The doctrines which Jeremy Taylor could preach with an enchanting beauty seemed to others merely old and dangerous battle-cries. The ghosts of the Middle Ages who still haunted Sir Thomas Browne's mind looked to others thoroughly dead. It seemed far better to go straight to the Bible, interpreted in the light of the individual's reason and conscience. What was advocated has been called 'rational theology' but here was no shallow rationalism; the new, deeply

---

[4] See Joan Bennett, *Sir Thomas Browne* (Cambridge, 1962), and *Sir Thomas Browne: The Major Works*, ed. C. A. Patrides (Harmondsworth, Middx, 1977). Another whimsical writer whose prose was an enchanting contrast with the violence around him was the historian, Thomas Fuller. Sir William Addison studied *Worthy Dr Fuller* (London, 1951).

spiritual, creed was a kind of Quakerism for sober and educated Church of England people. The work of the theologians
who pioneered in this way deserves to be remembered, for it
was courageous work. In the whole history of Christianity,
there had been no exact precedent for its attempt to reconcile
religion and reason.

The danger which many Christians sensed was, of course,
that the educated individual might when interpreting the Bible
destroy all the power of the Gospel. Lord Herbert of Cherbury,
in his book *De Veritate* issued discreetly in Latin and in Paris in
1624, had listed five religious ideas common to all men in all
places. He had claimed that, in comparison with these, the
revelations claimed by priests were at best uncertain. The five
ideas were: (1) that God exists, (2) that he ought to be
worshipped, (3) that virtue is the chief part of worship, (4) that
there should be repentance for vices and crimes, and (5) that
there are rewards and punishments after this life. These were
not offensive ideas but it had been left to Lord Herbert's
brother, George, to make poetry out of a more heartfelt and
popular religion.[5]

Two other pioneers of this tradition had found rest in a
religion less cold than Lord Herbert's.

In 1628 William Chillingworth, a newly elected Fellow of
Trinity College, Oxford, and a godson of Archbishop Laud,
was temporarily persuaded by the arguments of Jesuits. He
abandoned Oxford and went to be trained as a Recusant priest
at Douai. 'I reconciled myself to the Church of Rome', he later
explained, 'because I thought myself to have sufficient reason
to believe that there was, and must be always in the world,
some Church that could not err; and consequently, seeing all
other Churches disclaimed this privilege of not being subject to
error, the Church of Rome must be that Church which cannot
err.' But he did not stay long in Douai. Laud claimed that 'my
letters brought him back'. Actually, he was influenced by his
own disillusionment and took some time to recover any conviction on any religious topic. His integrity was shown when he

[5] S. R. D. Beford, *The Defence of Truth: Herbert of Cherbury and the Seventeenth Century*
(Manchester, 1979).

refused to take up the offer of an income in the Church of England. He found a refuge in the library of the manor house at Great Tew near Oxford, the home of the liberal Lucius Carey, Viscount Falkland. There he wrote *The Religion of Protestants, a Safe Way to Salvation*, published in 1637.

The book is best remembered for its affirmation that 'the Bible, the Bible only' was the religion of Protestants. If that had been all its argument, it would have been one of many Puritan treatises. But it made a point of rejecting Calvinism, defending instead a few 'fundamental truths' to be found in Scripture's 'plain places'. Chillingworth had not reached the conclusion that Calvin could not err. Instead, he now viewed Roman Catholicism as a possible way to salvation – if a less safe one, because of the arrogance of its claim to infallibility. All divisions between Christians were regretted, because they were divisions within the Church; but schismatics, heretics, even heathen Turks, could all find that their good lives led them to salvation. This strange book condemned all persecution.

When the civil war broke out Chillingworth was very distressed: 'war is not the way of Jesus Christ'. But he joined the Royalist army as a chaplain. His friend Lord Falkland exposed himself to the musket-fire and was killed early in the war, not unwillingly; the hopes of the Great Tew circle seemed to be already dead. Chillingworth was taken prisoner in January 1644 and soon fell mortally sick. He was nursed by a fellow clergyman, Francis Cheynell, who being an ardent Calvinist hoped that he would live to repent of his heresies. When the patient had disappointed his nurse, his body was buried in the cloister of Chichester Cathedral. Cheynell threw a copy of *The Religion of Protestants* on top of it, 'that thou mayest rot with thy author'.[6]

A number of other able young men, searching for a way of peace, had shared the liberal hospitality and hopes of Lord Falkland at Great Tew. The only middle-aged theologian among them was John Hales. Born in 1584, he lived until 1656.

---

[6] See Robert Orr, *Reason and Authority: The Thought of William Chillingworth* (Oxford, 1967).

He, too, suffered. As a promising Oxford scholar he took part
in the Calvinist Synod of Dort in 1618 and because of what he
saw there – the mixture of tough politics with useless speculation and theological hatred – 'bade John Calvin goodnight'.
Back in England he happily resumed the obscurity of a Fellow
of Eton College, visiting Oxford to discharge his duties as
Professor of Greek. He told Edward Hyde that he was glad to
have few duties as a preacher, since he preferred to keep his
opinions to himself. The pamphlets that he did write pleaded
for Christian modesty and reunion, arguing that 'it hath been
the common disease of Christians from the beginning, not to
content ourselves with that measure of faith, which God and
the Scriptures have expressly afforded us'. Hales amassed a
great library and spent most of his days using it, but had to sell
it, apart from a few devotional books, when he was ejected from
his post in 1649. He forbade any bell-ringing when he was
buried in Eton churchyard, 'as in my life I have done the
Church no service'. But he had, in fact, done a service which he
thus described: 'the pursuit of truth hath been my only care
ever since I first understood the meaning of the word'. And
when in 1659 *The Golden Remains of Ever-memorable Mr John Hales
of Eton College* was published, the book showed that he was able
to teach a simple but fervent religion, close to Chillingworth's.[7]

Both Chillingworth and Hales were rumoured to be 'Soci-
nians'. The word, derived from an Italian named Sozzini who
died in Poland in 1604, suggested the denial of the divinity of
Christ and the Holy Spirit. In fact, neither Chillingworth nor
Hales advocated that heresy, and even Sozzini had been
cautious. He had approved of the adoration of Christ, who
possessed a *divinitas* of function although not the *deitas* of the
divine nature. It was only when the followers of Sozzini had
finally been expelled from Poland in the 1650s, as the Counter-
Reformation revived Catholicism, that a defiantly heretical
minority movement, Unitarianism, emerged into the open. In
England the first Unitarian theology was published in a
pamphlet of 1647 giving twelve arguments against the divinity
of the Holy Spirit. Its author was a Gloucester schoolmaster,

[7] J. H. Elson studied *John Hales of Eton* (New York, 1948).

John Biddle, who followed it up with some even more provocative statements about Christ. Banished to the Scilly Isles, on his release he insisted on returning to London and continuing his propaganda. He was thrown into jail and died of fever there in 1662. At the time his attacks on the doctrine of the Trinity seemed outrageous. The tendency of almost all those who wanted to simplify and rationalize Christianity was much less controversial: it was the insistence on 'the Bible only', interpreted reasonably.[8]

A considerable group of reasonable theologians, the 'Cambridge Platonists', rejected the harshness of Calvinism without involving themselves in Lord Herbert's aristocratic contempt for popular religion or in any denial of basic Christian doctrines such as the Trinity.

Their approach was epitomized when the most public figure among them, Benjamin Whichcote, replied to a warning from the strong Calvinist who had taught him as an undergraduate. The warning was that in his preaching there was too much emphasis on reason. Whichcote replied: 'I oppose not rational to spiritual, for spiritual is most rational.' His favourite text was one of the proverbs in the Old Testament (20:27): 'the spirit of a man is the candle of the Lord.' He was convinced that no unreasonable theology could be true; 'to go against reason is to go against God'. Reasoning about faith was a necessary discipline; 'we should doubt and deliberate, before we resolve and determine.' No previous theologian had possessed a name big enough to silence debate; 'believe things rather than men.' But others could share his own reasoned certainty about the essentials of Christianity, especially since 'the moral part of religion lies in a good mind and a good life; all else is about religion.' The greatest essential was love; 'universal charity is a thing final in religion.' His own life was infectiously happy. 'In the use of reason and the exercise of virtue,' he said, 'we enjoy God.'

He had no wish to quarrel with anyone. Appointed Provost of King's College, Cambridge, by Parliament in 1644, he

---

[8] H. J. MacLachlan surveyed *Socinianism in Seventeenth Century England* (Oxford, 1951).

remained on good terms with his ejected predecessor by allowing him half the income. Ejected in his turn at the Restoration, he found a happy outlet as a London preacher. His message was about a reality where Church and Dissent, beauty and goodness, happiness and holiness, could all combine in a calm assurance; and it was spread by his example, not by a fully developed theological system. He was a Platonist in the sense that he belonged to the great tradition which had derived from the Greek philosopher encouragement to believe that the reasoning soul of man could apprehend eternal truth. Every glimpse of goodness or beauty was a glimpse of that truth; 'the judgement of right is the reason of our minds perceiving the Reason of things.'

His ablest disciple in Cambridge, John Smith, died in 1652 while still in his thirties, leaving behind him ten 'discourses' preached in his college chapel. Smith spoke of man's soul as 'something really distinct from his body, of an indivisible nature'; and of Christ 'not only as a particular person, but as a Divine principle in holy souls.' The work was taken up by another of Whichcote's Cambridge friends, in whose house he died: Ralph Cudworth, Master of Christ's College, 1654–88. But Cudworth's two shapelessly vast books, on *The True Intellectual System of the Universe* and *Eternal and Immutable Morality*, were, and have remained, virtually unreadable. They tried to deal with everything: and it was too much. So cool was the reception given to *The True Intellectual System* that Cudworth never wrote the second volume which he had planned and was discouraged from completing his treatise on morality, which remained in manuscript for almost half a century after his death.

Cudworth's importance in the history of English religion is that he took the trouble to assemble his over-large intellectual system because he was the first theologian to take the challenge of atheism seriously. His example encouraged others, especially when his work was abridged and updated by Thomas Wise in 1706. Cudworth attempted to answer fourteen possible grounds of atheism, including these: 'No man can have an idea of conception of God . . . Everything that is must have been from eternity . . . God is not visibly extended, therefore he is not . . . To suppose an Incorporeal Mind to be the original of all things is nothing else but to make the abstract notion of a mere accident to be the First Cause . . . Mind stemmed from the chance arrangement of atoms . . . Reason is only human, and related to flesh and bones: therefore there can be no divine intelligence presiding overall. All living beings are concretions of atoms liable to death and dissolution . . . The world is so ill made that God could not be responsible for it in all its imperfections. All in human affairs is chaos and confusion: Providence is defective.'[9]

Henry More was the best-known author of this group which saw that the real challenge to Christianity was now sheer unbelief, not any of the issues being debated and fought over by the leaders of England's churches during and after the civil war. 'The age we live in', he wrote, 'is a searching, inquisitive, rational and philosophical age.' His father, a strong Calvinist, read Spenser to him as a boy; he shared the same tutor as Milton; he plunged deep into the received learning of his time; but in his introduction to his collected works he recalled how all his studies had 'ended in nothing . . . in mere scepticism'. What he needed more than learning was 'simplicity of mind'. From 1639 to 1687 he lived quietly and happily in Cambridge, expounding the Gospel of simplicity in many volumes.

He wrote poetry and much prose, including an *Explanation of the Grand Mystery of Godliness* as big as Cudworth's tomes. He was the first Englishman to consider at any length the philosophy of René Descartes, although he lost his first enthusiasm for the Frenchman when he came to realize the danger of Cartesianism's stress on the material and the mechanical to the religious view of the world as held in the Platonic tradition. He could not be expected to agree with the unmystical teaching of Descartes, who called the soul a 'thinking substance'.

He said of his arguments against atheism: 'I borrowed them not from books but fetch'd them from . . . indelible ideas of the soul of man.' He wrote about the pure vision of God in childhood. And he thought that all learning ought to be dedicated to the recovery of that vision. 'Ethics are defined to

---

[9] See J. A. Passmore, *Ralph Cudworth: An Interpretation* (Cambridge, 1951).

be the art of living well and happily' and 'happiness is that pleasure which the mind takes in from a sense of virtue.' The greatest happiness is taken in the supreme virtue, the soul's love of God. ' 'Tis by this the soul relisheth what is simply the best; thither it tends, and in that alone it hath joy and triumph. Hence we are instructed how to set God before our eyes; to love him above all; to adhere to him as the supremest good; to consider him as the perfection of all reason, of all beauty, of all love; how all was made by his power, and that all is upheld by his providence. Hence also the soul is taught how to affect and admire the creation, and all the parcels of it . . .'[10]

THOMAS TRAHERNE

Cudworth and More were thoroughly academic, and they overloaded their arguments with quotations from other writers ancient or modern. Cambridge libraries were their downfall. But it is clear that many of their less intellectual contemporaries were feeling their way towards a simpler religion and a rational theology.

That tendency accounts for the vast influence of John Tillotson, who went on from his curate's place in Benjamin Whichcote's church to become Dean of St Paul's in 1689 and Archbishop of Canterbury two years later. He wished for a generous latitude in the interpretation of the Church of England's requirements. Such a position was known abusively as 'Latitudinarianism'. One of its exponents, Edward Stillingfleet, Tillotson's predecessor as Dean of St Paul's, was Bishop of Worcester for ten years from 1689. Another, Simon Patrick,

---

[10] See Aharon Lichtenstein, *Henry More: The Rational Theology of a Cambridge Platonist* (London, 1962). The movement has been studied by F. J. Powicke, *The Cambridge Platonists* (London, 1926); W. C. de Pauley, *The Candle of the Lord* (London, 1937); Ernst Cassirer, *The Platonic Renaissance in England* (London, 1953); R. L. Colie, *Light and Enlightenment* (Cambridge, 1957). Two anthologies of *The Cambridge Platonists* have been edited by C. A. Patrides (London, 1969) and G. A. Cragg (New York, 1980). For links with earlier thinkers, see H. R. McAdoo, *The Spirit of Anglicanism* (London, 1965).

was Bishop of Chichester and of Ely. All three scholarly moderates had been at Cambridge under the Commonwealth.

Tillotson had accompanied Richard Baxter to the Savoy Conference as a Presbyterian, and to the end of his days he sought to include Presbyterians in the National Church. More successfully, he wanted to include all who would respond to his plain, rational style of preaching. It was a style totally different from the 'conceits' of Andrewes, Donne and Taylor. Another liberal bishop, Gilbert Burnet of Salisbury, wrote of Tillotson: 'he was not only the best preacher of the age but seemed to have brought preaching to perfection; his sermons were so well heard and liked that all the nation proposed him as a pattern.' A modern historian of preaching warns us, however, that 'it is frankly impossible to convey a true idea of Tillotson's achievement by the quotation of occasional passages, for his manner at its best is only gauged by the perusal of a complete sermon, such as the great sermon against atheism preached in 1664, entitled *The Wisdom of being Religious*. Only so can his architectonic ability in designing a sermon, the propriety of his examples, and the uniform dignity yet simplicity of his diction be fully appreciated.'[11]

Tillotson's sermons, so greatly admired by his age, would strike almost all twentieth-century readers as intolerably moralizing and platitudinous. That, however, is itself an explanation of their appeal to hearers bored or disgusted with theological controversy. And we can study the new search for a simpler religion in the work of a man who, although obscure in his own time and only thirty-seven when he died, possessed genius.

Thomas Traherne, after graduating at Oxford, returned there for some years of intense research. Unfortunately his field was controversy against Roman Catholicism, the resultant book being *Roman Forgeries* (1673). His next major project was *Christian Ethics*. He quoted St Thomas Aquinas at length and seems to have planned to be almost as comprehensive as Jeremy Taylor and Richard Baxter were in their tomes, but he

---

[11] W. Fraser Mitchell, *English Pulpit Oratory from Andrewes to Tillotson* (London, 1932), p. 337. A more recent study is L. G. Locke, *Tillotson* (Copenhagen, 1954).

was trying to make the key idea 'felicity', like Henry More. When he died in 1674 this project was incomplete. And that was substantially all that was known about him when in 1895 two notebooks were bought for a few pence from a barrow in a London street. One combined extracts from other authors with some original poems; the other contained more than five hundred short prose passages. Eventually it was noticed that the poetry was similar to that in *A Serious and Pathetical Contemplation of the Mercies of God*, a little work by an anonymous author who had been 'private chaplain to Sir Orlando Bridgman'. The chaplain's name was identified; his *Christian Ethics* was resurrected; and a printed passage of verse by him was found to be identical with one in the manuscripts. Thomas Traherne's two notebooks were then published, in 1903–08. It was instantly agreed that the volume of short prose passages, entitled in seventeenth-century handwriting *Centuries of Meditation*, was gold.

The life now revealed was a life spent in seeking to recapture 'felicity'. Traherne was the son of a Hereford cobbler who died when the boy was young, leaving him to be brought up by his uncle, a prosperous but very worldly innkeeper. Glimpses of glory in childhood were never forgotten. 'I was a little stranger which at my entrance into the world was saluted and surrounded with innumerable joys . . . The corn was orient and immortal wheat, which never should be reaped, nor was ever sown. I thought it had stood from everlasting to everlasting. The dust and stones of the street were as precious as gold. The gates were at first the end of the world. The green trees when I saw them first through one of the gates transported and ravished me, their sweetness and unusual beauty made my heart to leap and almost mad with ecstasy . . . The men! O what venerable and reverend creatures did the aged seem! Immortal Cherubims! And young men glittering and sparkling angels, and maids strange Seraphic pieces of life and beauty! Boys and girls tumbling in the street, and playing, were moving jewels. I knew not that they were born or should die. But all things abided eternally as they were in their proper places. Eternity was manifest in the light of the day, and some thing infinite behind everything appeared: which talked with my expectation and moved my desire. The city seemed to stand in Eden, or to be built in heaven. The streets were mine, the temple was mine, the people were mine, their clothes and gold and silver were mine, as much as their sparkling eyes, fair skins and ruddy faces. The skies were mine and so were the sun and moon and stars, and all the world was mine, and I the only spectator and enjoyer of it.'

Traherne was reflecting on childhood after the experience of adolescence and adulthood – on the raw material which reason, later on, had to make into religion. 'My knowledge was divine. I knew by intuition those things which since my apostasy I collected again by the highest reason. My very ignorance was advantageous. I seemed as one brought into the estate of innocence. All things were spotless and pure and glorious: yet and infinitely mine, and joyful and precious. I knew not that there were any sins, or complaints, or laws. I dreamed not of poverties, contentions or vices. All tears and quarrels were hidden from mine eyes. Everything was at rest, free and immortal . . .'

He knew what had destroyed childhood's glory. 'Once I remember (I think I was about four years old, when) I thus reasoned with myself, sitting in a little obscure room in my father's poor house. If there be a God certainly he must be infinite in goodness . . . He must do most glorious things and give us infinite riches. How comes it to pass therefore that I am so poor?'

He had fought his way out of poverty to Oxford and to life – only to find that all life conspired to destroy 'the first light which shined in my infancy'. In the Hereford inn he experienced 'rude, vulgar and worthless things that like so many loads of earth and dung did overhelm and bury it.' At the university he was impressed by the treasures of knowledge: 'I saw that logic, ethics, physics, metaphysics, geometry, astronomy, poesy, medicine, grammar, music, rhetoric, all kinds of arts, trades and mechanisms that adorned the world pertained to felicity.' But even Oxford disappointed: 'there was never a tutor that did professly teach felicity.'

He recovered 'felicity' when he returned to the Herefordshire countryside. He was made rector of the little village of

Credenhill, four miles from the cathedral city, in 1657. After a spell back in Oxford for further study, he gave himself to what the country had to give him. 'When I came unto the country, and being seated among silent trees and meads and hills had all my time in mine own hands, I resolved to spend it all, whatever it cost me, in search of happiness, and to satiate that burning thirst which nature had enkindled in me from my youth.' But he did not identify nature with God. He knew too well that nature's moods varied like his own – and left behind a classic description of the mood to be familiar to the twentieth century as anxiety, *angst*. 'Another time, in a lowering and sad evening, being alone in the field, when all things were dead and quiet, a certain want and horror fell upon me, beyond imagination. The unprofitableness and silence of the place dissatisfied me, its wideness terrified me, from the utmost ends of the earth fears surrounded me . . . I was a weak and little child, and had forgotten that there was a man alive in the earth.'

He knew that he needed both his Creator and the people who were his fellow creatures. The experience of utter loneliness that sad evening 'taught me that I was concerned in all the world: and that in the remotest borders the causes of peace delight me, and the beauties of the earth when seen were made to entertain me: that I was made to hold a communion with the secrets of divine providence in all the world . . .: that the presence of cities, temples and kingdoms ought to sustain me, and that to be alone in the world was to be desolate and miserable. The comfort of houses and friends, and the clear assurance of treasures everywhere, God's care and love, his goodness, wisdom and power, his presence and watchfulness in all the ends of the earth, were my strength and assurance for ever . . .'

In 1667 he accepted an invitation to join the household of Sir Orlando Bridgman, then Lord Keeper. As things turned out, the move was not so useful to a career as it must have seemed from the invitation. Sir Orlando was dismissed when he refused to affix the great seal of the realm to Charles II's Declaration of Indulgence in 1672; he protested that it would benefit the Papists. But Traherne had clearly been willing to live amid the physical and moral squalor of Restoration London in order that he might enjoy and serve his age to the full. In 1660 he had hastened to obtain ordination by a bishop, although previously he had been equally happy to obtain certificates of reliability from noted Puritan preachers in order that he might accept the offer of the rectory at Credenhill. It seems that he began writing his meditations while at Credenhill as a gift to a devout neighbour, Mrs Susanna Hopton, but continued adding to them while he was Sir Orlando's chaplain and left them uncompleted when he died, soon after his fallen patron.

His purpose was to encourage Susanna Hopton to be a joyful Christian. 'Remember always that thou art about a magnificent work', he urged her. His particular theme was that she would find felicity, as he had done, by loving all nature and all people because God had given everything and everyone to her to be enjoyed through love. 'You will never enjoy the world aright, till you see how a sand exhibiteth the wisdom and power of God: and prize in every thing the service which they do you, by manifesting his glory and goodness to your soul. . . . Your enjoyment of the world is never right, till every morning you awake in heaven: see yourself in your Father's palace: and look upon the skies and the earth and the air as celestial joys. . . . You will never enjoy the world aright, till the sea itself floweth in your veins, till you are clothed with the heavens, and crowned with the stars: and perceive yourself to be the sole heir of the whole world: and more then so, because men are in it who are every one sole heirs as well as you. . . . Till your spirit filleth the whole world, and the stars are your jewels, till you are as familiar with the ways of God in all ages as with your walk and table: till you are intimately acquainted with that shady nothing out of which the world was made: till you love all men so as to desire their happiness with a thirst equal to the zeal of your own: till you delight in God for being good to all: you will never enjoy the world.'

The criticism has been made that he never seems to have undergone the dark night of the soul, to have been purged so painfully that the death of the old self made possible a new life of union with God. Certainly he does not record such experience in the material which we now possess. It would, however, be unfair to condemn him as a thoughtless optimist or naïve nature-worshipper. He experienced many evils during his short life. He did not choose to tell Susanna Hopton about them; he was her pastor. But it is clear that when a fully mature man he was full of wondering gratitude that the glory of his childhood had been so largely restored to him. He marvelled, but not arrogantly, that 'all ages are present in my soul, and all kingdoms, and God blessed for ever. And thus Jesus Christ is seen in me and dwelleth in me, when I believe upon him. And thus all saints are in me, and I in them. And thus all angels and the eternity and infinity of God are in me evermore.'[12]

RELIGION, MAGIC AND SCIENCE

In Elizabethan England the triangular relationship of religion, magic and science had been different: there had been only a thin partition between magic and science. The Church was officially the enemy of magic, and scientists were afraid that this would make it their enemy too. To reassure a Christian society, Elizabethans interested in science emphasized that the new discoveries – the astronomy of Copernicus, for example – had only increased their awe as men surrounded by the marvels of creation. They also stressed the practical utility: more knowledge of the stars assisted navigation. But the problem remained that science seemed essentially dangerous, foolish and irreligious because, like magic, it seemed out of the ordinary. The leading scientist of Elizabethan England, Dr John Dee, was an alchemist trying to transmute baser metals into gold – and the Queen's favourite astrologer. His library and laboratory were wrecked by a mob in 1583. After the death of his royal patron he was left to die in poverty and to be satirized in Ben Jonson's play of 1610, *The Alchemist*.[13]

---

[12] Traherne's *Centuries, Poems and Thanksgivings* were edited by H. M. Margiliouth (2 vols, Oxford, 1958). See also Gladys Wade, *Thomas Traherne* (Princeton, N.J., 1944), and K. W. Salter, *Thomas Traherne: Mystic and Poet* (London, 1964).

[13] Recent studies include Paul H. Hocher, *Science and Religion in Elizabethan England* (New York, 1969), and Frances Yates, *The Occult Philosophy in the Elizabethan Age* (London, 1979).

Modern students are of course inclined to take Dee's side because of his courageous curiosity about nature and the possibility of gaining power to change it, if only into gold. If Dee is called a magician, we think of the benevolent Prospero in *The Tempest*. However, the fact seems to be that science was regarded by many Elizabethans and their successors as one vast trick, like magic. Magic was a very widespread cult, encouraged by the general unsettlement of the times but also by the end of the authority of the medieval Church. Medieval archdeacons had been stern in punishing 'sorcery', but medieval parish priests had been obligingly ready to exorcize evil spirits by their own incantations and to secure divine blessings by their intercessions – and medieval religion in general had offered plenty of officially authorized scope to the miracle-seekers and to the hysterical. In many ways, therefore, the Church had controlled the always vigorous market for magic in the Middle Ages. Now, in an England deprived of the supernatural powers which had been generally believed to be at the disposal of the medieval Church, any disaster could be blamed on magic, although many people were ready enough to use 'white' magic for their own convenience; and any woman who seemed mentally ill or merely eccentric to her neighbours could be gossiped about as a witch and perhaps eventually terrified or tortured into a confession. Popular fears were whipped up by the spread of the late medieval belief that witches had made a pact with the Devil – a belief to which Christopher Marlowe's play, *Dr Faustus*, was a witness at the end of 1580s. Despite protests against this popular nonsense by educated men such as Reginald Scot (whose *Discovery of Witchcraft* in 1584 discovered that it did not exist), Parliament pandered to the people by the fierce anti-witchcraft statute of 1604. It seems that about a thousand 'witches', mostly women, suffered death in England in the disgraceful century and a half which ended with the execution of Alice Molland at Exeter in 1685. In New England the belief was powerful for a rather longer period; a score of men and women suffered execution after the witchcraft scare in the Massachusetts village of Salem in 1692.

One reason for the progress of science in Restoration

England was that magic was then rapidly ceasing to be taken seriously by the public. Of course the belief lingered on. In the 1640s a professional witch-hunter, Matthew Hopkins, conducted a campaign which brought about two hundred women to their deaths, and such a memory was not easily forgotten. In a less harmful ritual of ancient tradition, Charles II 'touched' many thousands of his grateful subjects who were the victims of 'the king's evil', scrofula, caused by infected milk. Even the great Sir Isaac Newton, who became virtually the dictator of the new intellectual world of science, secretly dabbled in experiments in alchemy. But an historian who has investigated the very long story of battles between the Church and the 'cunning' men or 'wise' women who wielded a rival power in the villages concludes that 'the real change in attitude seems to have come with the Restoration of the Anglican Church after 1660. The inquiries after charmers and sorcerers which had been so prominent a feature of visitation articles before the civil war now silently disappeared from the list of matters on which the bishops and archdeacons normally sought information from their flock.'[14]

It might be expected that religion would decline rapidly along with magic. The two activities have not been unconnected. A large part of the hold of the Church on the mind of the Middle Ages had been due to credulity about the supernatural powers possessed by the Church's officials and sacraments, and a large part of the attack on ceremonies left over from the Middle Ages in the Book of Common Prayer had been inspired by the Puritans' conviction that Popery was merely superstitious; so that after 1600 a spread of disbelief in the Puritans' gospel itself, or in the godly preachers of the established Church of England, might be expected to be as fast as the spread of disbelief in magic. And in the long run this may have been the pattern in the profound secularization of modern England, still proceeding in the twentieth century and still beyond an objective historian's complete understanding. But

---

[14] Keith Thomas, *Religion and the Decline of Magic* (revised, Harmondsworth, Middx, 1971), p. 309. Alan Macfarlane studied *Witchcraft in Tudor and Stuart England* with special reference to Essex (London, 1970).

what actually happened in the seventeenth century was that the pioneers of science were almost unanimously anxious to make it clear that they had no quarrel with the Bible. Their attitude was that the medieval Church, in so far as it had been magical, had been less than Christian. Christianity was the true religion, revealed by the God who had long ago created nature and who had recently guided the scientists to discover their kind of truth about nature. It was the duty of intelligent men to accept both the Gospel and the natural laws confirmed or discovered by science, for both were the gifts of the one Creator.

There were many causes for the slow move of educated opinion out of the world of magic and into the world of science seen as contrary to magic. But it was the special work of two Englishmen to advocate the 'new philosophy' by reassuring Christians: Francis Bacon, Lord Chancellor under James I, and John Wilkins, Bishop of Chester under Charles II. Neither man was a major scientist in his own right. William Harvey, the great medical researcher, told John Aubrey that Bacon wrote philosophy 'like a Lord Chancellor', and it could have been said that Wilkins was as scientific as a bishop could be. But Wilkins, who was twelve years old when Bacon died in 1625, did more than any other Englishman of the seventeenth century to organize and popularize science along the lines for which Bacon had pleaded.

Born in 1561, Bacon saw that the many technical advances made in his lifetime could be assembled and developed in such a way as to create a far more rational and a far richer society. To this end he was prepared to sacrifice the medieval world-view with its strange combination of Aristotle, the Platonists, the Bible and popular mythology, but so far from thinking it necessary to sacrifice the Christian religion to science he claimed that religion and science could flourish in two compartments. The only condition was that the 'book of God's words' should be separated from nature, which was the 'book of God's works'; so that both theologians and scientists should be warned 'that they do not unwisely mingle or confound these learnings together'. To Bacon, religious truth was revealed by God and therefore not a fit subject for investigation. It was like the rules of games such as chess, to be 'received as they are and not disputed; but how to play a skilful and winning game is scientific and rational.' Everything except religion could and should be examined afresh, for the finding out of the true nature of all things 'whereby God might have the more glory in the workmanship of them, and men the more fruit in the use of them'. There should be no respect for the *idola* of conventional belief about the world; the Latin word, although usually translated 'idols', meant 'phantoms'. Noting how many were the causes of irrationality, Bacon distinguished between the *idola* of the tribe, the market place, the cave and the theatre. His whole call was to men to move out of this world of illusions into reality, but he never denied that the Christian religion had revealed God as the supreme reality. 'When the mind of man works upon nature, the creatures of God, it is limited thereby, but if it works upon itself or upon too small a part of material things, it spins out laborious webs of learning.' By limiting its material to the separate self-revelations of God in nature and the Bible, the human mind could achieve understanding of what was real.

That was the programme – but there was always something unreal about the idea of Francis Bacon as a scientist.

James I – who was a shrewd observer of his fellow men when not too drunk or too conceited to notice – appointed him Lord Chancellor for a time, but thought him capable of 'great volumes' rather than great deeds. Queen Elizabeth had given much the same reason when refusing him the political office for which he craved. William Cecil had encouraged his ambition to be a statesman in succession to his father, Sir Nicholas Bacon, since Cecil and old Sir Nicholas had married sisters; but it had not been auspicious when the young man, petitioning for a post in the civil service, had assured Elizabeth's chief minister that his real interest was in acquiring an income in order to be able to study, since he had taken 'all knowledge' as his province. Francis Bacon was not cut out to be a statesman – and, for all his genius as a visionary and as a writer, never had the time or aptitude to excel in the two arts which were vitally necessary before his hopes of a science-based society could be fulfilled. He never mastered either the art of making practical experiments like any workman, or the art of persuading practical men to collaborate so that by their experiments they helped each other. During the last journey of his life he made an experiment which caused a fatal chill. He had the coach stopped in order that a dead chicken might be stuffed with snow; he was pondering the effects of refrigeration. But he had founded no experimental, co-operative school of Baconians before he died.[15]

John Wilkins gained much by being born far more humbly than Francis Bacon. He was the son of an Oxford goldsmith, and throughout his life not only enjoyed discussing other men's technical experiments but also experimented himself. While he was a bishop he dissected a dolphin, and when he lay dying in 1672 he announced that he was 'prepared for the great experiment'. He was equally enthusiastic in his writing about recent discoveries and in his personal relations with other scientists, professional or amateur. Perhaps he inherited his mastery of these arts of popularity from his grandfather, the moderate Puritan preacher and saint, John Dod.

Before he began a literary clergyman's career as chaplain to successive noblemen, he made his mark with a book about the moon, written in his spare hours as an Oxford tutor. He was sure that the moon was inhabited and hopeful that it would one day be reached by a 'flying chariot'. The publication of another work of popular science, *Mathematical Magic* (which prophesied submarines), coincided with his appointment as Warden of Wadham College, Oxford, in 1648. At no stage of his life does he seem to have held strong doctrinal or political views, so that he was now as ready to accept Cromwell's ascendancy as he was to be to accept Charles II in 1660. Indeed, he was willing to marry the Lord Protector's sister Robina, although under Charles II he ungraciously claimed that the marriage had been forced on him. In a Puritan-dominated Oxford he persuaded his colleagues to make the college noted for its food, its music and its garden. In the garden was a hollow statue. Hiding in it,

---

[15] See Benjamin Farrington, *The Philosophy of Francis Bacon* (Liverpool, 1964), and for the background Richard Westfall, *Religion and Science in Seventeenth Century England* (New Haven, Conn., 1958).

he spoke, with what he hoped was an angelic voice, to a colleague who was walking about wrapped in meditation: 'Ashwell, go preach the Gospel in Virginia.' But he could speak more seriously; his time at Oxford was also remarkable for his ability to attract and encourage young scientists, including Christopher Wren. He did not introduce science into Oxford. The university had recently made distinguished contributions to medicine and to mathematics (then specially prized because of its use in the art of navigation). But he was able to get scientists to work happily together; a set of agreed rules survives for the Oxford Experimental Science Club in 1651. The contribution made by his personal magnetism was seen when this Oxford group disintegrated on his brief move to Cambridge as Master of Trinity College.

His position as Oliver Cromwell's brother-in-law was a definite embarrassment in the next reign, and he lost his Cambridge post. But he made no difficulties about accepting king or bishops, wanting to enlist the king as a patron of science and wanting to be a bishop himself in order to promote the causes dear to him. At Oxford members of the science club had been forbidden to mention religion, and Wilkins now still struggled both to protect science from rival dogmas and to enlarge the Established Church so as to 'comprehend' Protestant dissenters. He negotiated both with Cromwell's old chaplain, John Owen, and with Cromwell's old critic, Richard Baxter, in the hope of agreeing on a scheme full of compromises, but in the end failed to reach agreement and only made himself unpopular with the victorious Cavalier MPs and with stiff churchmen such as Archbishop Sheldon. He was financed by a variety of ecclesiastical posts, but his main life was in London before he was made Bishop of Chester in 1668. As chairman or secretary he played the key role in the formation of the Royal Society for the encouragement of science.

The society's first meetings in 1660 were held in Gresham's College, which had been founded by a legacy left by the financier Sir Thomas Gresham in 1579. It had always been a centre for some scientific activity, and under the Commonwealth there had been other encouragement given to technical experiments in London, for the Puritans in their time of power showed something of a Baconian interest in 'utility' for the benefit of commerce. Another influence favourable to the birth of the Royal Society had been the whole Puritan rejection of the medieval world-view with its cult of miracles and its blessing on superstitions. A theologian such as John Preston may have inadvertently assisted science by his declaration that outside the pages of the Bible 'God alters no law of nature'. But clearly a very strong motive was a simple interest in the experiments themselves, as they opened up the possibility of rewriting the whole of science with many profitable spinoffs. This delight was increased by the contrast between the rational peace of the charmed circle of experimental science and the bitter conflicts in religion and politics. It was a time when many felt 'the vanity of dogmatizing': that was the title of a book of 1661 by Joseph Glanvill, openly attacking the Ancient Greek philosophy still being taught in English universities and refraining from any long defence of the importance of dogmatic theology (although Glanvill defended belief in witchcraft).[16] And another factor was contact with the genial enthusiasm of John Wilkins, whose Oxford friends, now meeting in London, formed the core of the working Fellows of the Royal Society.

Wilkins had by this stage become chiefly an administrator, but he did have an intellectual passion for the simplification and rationalization of language, so that men could communicate without bewildering, insulting or excommunicating each other. He tried to work out the principles of a new universal language and (more usefully) himself gave an example of using plain English when speaking in or out of the pulpit. This example was picked up by his son-in-law Archbishop Tillotson, who edited for the press after his death his book on *The Principles and Duties of Natural Religion*. For the time being John Wilkins was defeated in ecclesiastical politics; the passions of intolerance were too powerful in an age when a more typical churchman was Bishop Seth Ward, once professor of astronomy in Oxford, now a fierce persecutor of the Dissenters. But the contribution which he made to the rise of science in England placed him not far from Lord Chancellor Bacon. And

---

[16] See J. I. Cope, *Joseph Glanvill, Anglican Apologist* (St Louis, Mo., 1956).

Bacon was – as Thomas Sprat, later Bishop of Rochester, declared in his *History of the Royal Society* (1667) – the 'one great man who had the imagination of the whole enterprise'.[17]

THE FAITH OF ISAAC NEWTON

Alexander Pope's famous epitaph shows his reputation:

> Nature and Nature's laws lay hid in night,
> God said, *Let Newton be!*, and all was Light.

Pope exaggerated, because science had made many advances before the publication of Isaac Newton's *Philosophiae Naturalis Principia Mathematica* in 1687. But Newton's mathematical genius has seldom if ever been equalled. Essentially what he did was to offer a convincing mathematical explanation of gravity, the force which kept the planets in their courses around the sun and which determined many natural movements on this planet; and he explained the composition of white light. After all the talk of semi-scientists such as the Elizabethan Dee about the mysteries of the stars and their effects on the earth, after all the half-light of medieval and Renaissance learning, that was the decisive burst of the light of science, although it could be followed up in many ways – as in the researches of other Fellows of the Royal Society, of which Newton was elected President each year from 1703 until his death aged eighty-five in 1727. Whilst an undergraduate William Wordsworth had rooms only a few yards away from the chapel of Trinity College, Cambridge:

---

[17] See Barbara Shapiro, *John Wilkins* (Berkeley, Cal., 1969). There has been controversy about the contributions made by different religious groups to science. Christopher Hill, *The Intellectual Origins of the English Revolution* (Oxford, 1965), stressed the Puritan contribution, but see Margery Purver, *The Royal Society: Concept and Creation* (London, 1967), and the further debate in *The Intellectual Revolution of the Seventeenth Century*, ed. Charles Webster (London, 1974). Charles Webster has provided a masterly account of 'science, medicine and reform, 1626–60' in *The Great Instauration* (London, 1975), and Michael Hunter a judicious survey of *Science and Society in Restoration England* (Cambridge, 1981).

> The antechapel where the statue stood
> Of Newton with his prism and silent face,
> The marble index of a mind for ever
> Voyaging through strange seas of thought alone.

Newton cared nothing for poetry's claim to illuminate the mysteries of the human heart, and almost as little for technology as improving the material lot of man; and because of these defects his influence was to be subjected to famous onslaughts by William Blake during the 'Romantic' revival. But he would not have been greatly disturbed by Blake, an avowed enemy of the Established Church. Newton was far more concerned to stay out of trouble with the Church and to demonstrate that his science supported true religion. He learned more than mathematics from his predecessor in the Cambridge professorship, Isaac Barrow, a distinguished theologian. He himself wrote a great deal of theology, but left almost all of it unpublished (although, it seems, prepared for the press) because the theology moved far beyond Barrow's safe position. His successor as professor of mathematics, William Whiston, and his scientific assistant, Samuel Clarke, both got themselves involved in bitter controversies with the orthodox clergy. Whiston founded a Society for the Restoration of Primitive Christianity. The more cautious Newton kept his reputation as a churchman well enough to be knighted by Queen Anne, made Master of the Mint, lionized by intellectual London and buried in Westminster Abbey. He was not going to expose himself as a heretic; it was enough for him that, watching the apple fall in the garden of Woolsthorpe in Lincolnshire, he had suddenly seen the force which kept God and man, earth and sun, moon and star in a beautiful order. And he understood the gravitational force which was to keep Church and State stable during the eighteenth century.

The noble vision of the Creator which he reached is summed up in a short passage in the *Principia* which Whiston translated. 'This Being governs all things, not as a Soul of the World, but as Lord of the Universe; and upon account of his dominion he is stiled Lord God, supreme over all. . . . The supreme God is an eternal, infinite, absolutely perfect Being, but a Being how perfect soever without dominion is not Lord God. For we say my God . . . but we do not say my Eternal . . . my Infinite . . . my Perfect . . . for these terms have no relation to servants.' Beyond doubt Newton, although often either fiercely quarrelsome or coldly arrogant in his dealings with other men, regarded himself as a servant of God. His private papers clearly record his profound humility as he contemplated the work of the Lord God who created matter and life (which were sharply distinguished) and who kept them in order. It was only to be expected that when according to his system the courses of the planets needed occasional adjustments he relied on God to do the adjusting. Leibniz said that this made God a bungling watchmaker, but Newton never understood the criticism.

Equally humble was his approach to the Bible. There he found God's own promises about the future, for history was to be brought fully under the 'dominion' of the orderly Creator. He was fascinated by the biblical prophecies and happily spent many months working out their chronology. His passionate intellectual curiosity was applied to many problems in these biblical studies, but never did he deviate from his belief that the Bible was, from cover to cover, the Word of God. He accepted the miracle stories of the Bible as the records of God's past interferences in history; after all, God also adjusted the courses of the planets from time to time. God's interferences had ceased, however, apart from those repairs to the planetary system. He told John Locke that 'miracles of good credit continued in the Church for about two or three hundred years.' He accepted Christ's death as a sacrifice to the Father, and also his resurrection, although most of the teaching of Christ seemed to be no more than the confirmation of the natural religion already known to all rational men. The biblical prophecies commanded his attention because they seemed to be predictions that in the future God would resume his widespread interventions in the course of nature and in the world's history.

Newton's theological beliefs seem to have been close to those developed in public by later Christian heretics but he was content to leave further explorations in religion, as in science, to the future. This proud genius wrote to his nephew: 'To

myself I seem to have been only a boy playing on the seashore,
and diverting myself in now and then finding a smoother
pebble or a prettier shell than ordinary, while the great ocean
of truth lay all undiscovered before me.'[18]

Around Newton many lesser lights were thrown on nature
by scientists, and were believed to reveal 'the wisdom of God
manifested in the works of the creation'. This phrase was used
as the title of a book by John Ray in 1691. It epitomized the
attitude of a considerable movement. Robert Boyle, the father
of chemistry in England, was the author of *The Christian Virtuoso*
(1690); and he endowed annual lectures to be delivered in a
London church, confuting atheism by science. He regarded the
human eye as a wonder which was particularly useful in
proving the creation by a benevolent God, but the Boyle
lecturers ranged far and wide over nature in the same cause.
This was the approach of John Ray, who is honoured as
the father of scientific botany in England. He retired from
Cambridge in order to pursue detailed scientific studies and
to write a series of 'physico-theological discourses' tackling
problems such as the relationship between the opening
chapters of the Bible and seventeenth-century knowledge.
The existence of fossils which seemed older than the time
allowed by the Bible for the world's history was one of
the few features of nature which gave him some temporary
difficulty.

Writers such as these cheerfully disregarded Bacon's warning not to mingle theology with science – and their punishment
came when, in later generations, they were laughed at both by
scientists and by religious believers. But their assurance shows
how little tension was thought to exist between the new science
and the Christian faith, in the age which would come to be
remembered as the age of Newton. The light of knowledge had
shone into the darkness of magic. It was appropriate that one of
the three Members of Parliament who sponsored the repeal of

---

[18] Recent studies include Frank E. Manuel, *The Religion of Isaac Newton* (Oxford,
1974) and *A Portrait of Isaac Newton* (London, 1980); Margaret C. Jacob, *The
Newtonians and the English Revolution, 1689–1720* (Hassocks, Sussex, 1976); Richard
Westfall, *Never at Rest: A Biography of Isaac Newton* (Cambridge, 1981).

the Witchcraft Act in 1736 was John Conduitt. He greatly
admired Sir Isaac Newton, whose niece he had married.[19]

TWO QUESTIONERS:
HOBBES AND LOCKE

In 1679 Thomas Hobbes died. He had been born in a Gloucestershire vicarage – prematurely, when his mother heard of the
approach of the Spanish Armada. He had lived to see the sharp
decline, if not the total fall, of the world of magic in which his
father's parishioners had believed; and his own writings were
part of the propaganda against belief in witches, fairies and
ghosts. He had often talked with Francis Bacon in the early
1620s, had been intoxicated by his discoveries of geometry and
mathematics, and had tried to get elected to the Royal Society
in the 1660s, but was repeatedly refused, it seems more because
of his reputation as an atheist than because of his limitations as
a scientist. He had learned how to write well by his deep studies
of the Greek classics and had formed the ambition to clear up
the mysteries of politics and religion by writing English with a
geometric or mathematical precision. All the superstitions
which Shakespeare, for example, put into people's mouths
without any evident disapproval were condemned by Hobbes.
Reality was substituted, reality being thus defined: 'external
objects cause conceptions, and conceptions appetite or fear,
which are the first unperceived beginnings of our actions.'
Using this approach to England, his *Leviathan* (1651) provoked
thought and argument long after he was dead. Charles II said
that the Church trained young clergymen by putting them on
to answer Hobbes as dogs were exercised by being encouraged
to bait a bear. For much of the eighteenth century clergymen
thought that all English infidels able to read were at heart
Hobbists. This genius asked questions which could not be
answered merely by making Christianity a simpler religion, or
by showing that the Fellows of the Royal Society managed to
be Christians even if somewhat unorthodox.

---

[19] See Mitchell Fisher, *Robert Boyle, Devout Naturalist* (Philadelphia, Pa., 1945),
and Charles Raven, *John Ray, Naturalist* (Cambridge, 1942).

Before the civil wars Hobbes earned his living as a secretary to rich gentlemen, mainly two Earls of Devonshire. *Leviathan* was written in exile in Paris when its author's mind was preoccupied by the need to end the miseries inflicted on England by the wars. Its great plea was for obedience to the sovereign, but it totally abandoned the Cavalier talk about the divine right of kings. God entrusted complete authority to whichever government had power – and the people consented because owing to their selfishness the only alternative was anarchy. When in their shared exile Clarendon asked him why he had written a book which justified any government in power Hobbes, half-joking, blurted out: 'The truth is, I have a mind to go home'; and not long after completing *Leviathan* he went to live in London under the Commonwealth. But we have no need to doubt the intellectual integrity of the main argument: the necessity of sovereignty. Nor need we doubt the horror with which Hobbes viewed Roman Catholicism as an enemy of the English state ('the ghost of the deceased Roman empire, sitting crowned upon the grave thereof'). Nor need we question his hatred of Protestant enthusiasm as an enemy of the social order. This basically political reaction to the harm done by religion inspired his denunciation of the 'kingdom of darkness' ruled by priests and preachers. It is, however, far more difficult to tell what Hobbes did actually believe in religiously. Friends such as John Aubrey presented him to the public as a kind, humorous churchgoer, and Hobbes often said that he was no atheist. His advice was that 'it is with the mysteries of our religion as with wholesome pills for the sick; which swallowed whole, have the virtue to cure; but chewed up, are for the most part cast up again without effect.' More than half of *Leviathan* dealt with the religious topics and showed a mastery of the Bible.

He did not let the Bible master him. He speculated about the origins of religion. Did it arise out of a foolish belief in ghosts? He noted the contemporary English Christian use of the phrase 'God the Holy Ghost'. Did it arise out of the absence of science, out of 'ignorance of causes'? He noted that 'this perpetual fear, always accompanying mankind in the ignorance of causes, as it were in the dark, must needs have for object something.' Did it arise out of 'devotion to what men fear'? Or out of the human inability to take 'things casual' for what they were? Hobbes concluded that religion was 'fear of power invisible, feigned by the mind, or imagined from tales publicly allowed.' He hastily added that 'when the power imagined is truly such as we imagine', the seventeenth century had 'true religion'. He added, too, that the 'wise and learned interpretation' of the Scriptures could guide men without running the risks of 'enthusiasm or supernatural inspiration'. But for practical purposes what was decisive in religion – as in law, or in life in general – was not the Scriptures but what the sovereign willed. The individual certainly had no right to force his views on others. If a man told others that God spoke to him in a dream, this 'is no more than to say he dreamed that God spoke to him'. Prophecy, like miracles, had long ago ceased.

About the Church as an institution, Hobbes could be more cheerfully and openly destructive. He defined a church as 'a company of men professing Christian religion, united in the person of one sovereign, at whose command they ought to assemble, and without whose authority they ought not to assemble.' Faith in the heavenly Christ and 'obedience to laws' were all that was necessary to salvation, and it was right to have faith in Christ because of who he was. Faith, Hobbes explained, is the kind of assent to a proposition which derives its reasons 'not from the proposition itself but from the person propounding'; it is assent which 'grows not from any confidence of our own, but from another man's knowledge'. But the sole concern of Christ was with heaven, and the sole message of the first Christians was 'that Jesus was the Christ, that is to say the King that was to save them and reign over them eternally in the world to come.' Such a Gospel could never give trouble to a sovereign.[20]

For many years English authors competed with each other to produce angry and contemptuous reasons for rejecting

---

[20] The best introductions are Richard Peters, *Hobbes* (Harmondsworth, Middx, 1956), and F. C. Hood, *The Divine Politics of Thomas Hobbes* (Oxford, 1964). For the debate about him see S. I. Mintz, *The Hunting of Leviathan* (Cambridge, 1962), and John Bowle, *Hobbes and His Critics* (London, 1969).

Hobbes. But there came a time when a new generation took up his questions more calmly. Belief in the divine right of kings was still powerful, but in politics the most influential viewpoint in the long run was that which John Locke expressed classically: because all the people who mattered had agreed only to a limited contract with the government, the power of the sovereign – the monarchy or the executive – must be subject to Parliament and to the laws made by Parliament. And in religion also, the questions which Hobbes asked were debated more freely when the censorship of printing was relaxed in the 1690s. Adventurous theologians were then no longer afraid to publish books which they had not previously submitted to the Archbishop of Canterbury or the Bishop of London, although it remained possible to prosecute them for seditious or blasphemous libel. The result was a flood of publications probing the character and status of the Christian religion. Francis Bacon had taught, probably with his tongue in his cheek, that 'we are obliged to believe the word of God, though our reason be shocked by it'; that, indeed, 'the more absurd and incredible any divine mystery is, the greater honour we do to God in believing it.' Such a caution still prevailed largely among the clergy – but not among laymen who followed the current debate.

Much of that debate was a commentary on the thought of John Locke, for 'it was Locke's appointed task to work up into a system all the assumptions about God, Nature and Man which, as the seventeenth-century storm clouds blew off, seemed to most men to stand firm and unquestionable in the light of common day'.[21]

John Locke was a widely accomplished layman, from 1667 until he fled to Holland in 1683 the secretary of an active politician, the Earl of Shaftesbury. He was himself no trouble-maker. He published his writings on religion anonymously and always denied that their intention was Socinian or in any other way heretical. He was so anxious to dissociate himself from Hobbes that he took to pretending that he had never read him properly. Although after his return from exile he found himself

---

[21] Basil Willey, *The Seventeenth-century Background* (London, 1934), p. 267.

highly honoured, the chief interest of his last years became writing a book on St Paul. He died in an armchair in 1704, having spent that day listening to psalms being read to him by his closest friend, Ralph Cudworth's daughter Damaris. But clergymen wrote against him. The two most prominent were Edward Stillingfleet, the Latitudinarian bishop, who thought that here latitude had been extended too far, and John Edwards, almost the sole surviving representative of the once dominant school of Cambridge Calvinism. And they were right to see in Locke's thought a challenge to every old orthodoxy.

In *An Essay concerning Human Understanding*, finished on the last day of 1686 and published just before Christmas 1689, he made a proposal. Its effect would be to banish many theological propositions from the intellectual world, as decisively as James II was exiled from England on account of his Roman Catholicism, between the writing of the book and its publication. For Locke confined the category of 'propositions according to reason' with a strictness which began the English emphasis on empiricism. Such propositions, he wrote, are those 'whose truth we can discover by examining and tracing those ideas we have from sensation and reflection, and by natural deduction find to be true or probable'. Among such truths was the existence of God. 'We more certainly know that there is a God, than that there is anything else without us.' But '*contrary to reason* are such propositions as are inconsistent with, or irreconcilable to, our clear and distinct ideas'; an example he gave was the polytheist's belief that there is more than one god. Locke's own claim for his work was modest. He was, he wrote, not one of the 'master builders' such as 'the incomparable Mr Newton'. It was for him 'ambition enough to be employed as an under-labourer in clearing the ground a little and removing some of the rubbish that lies in the way to knowledge.' But to theologians Locke seemed a remarkable 'under-labourer', in that he condemned ideas not derived from the sense, or from rational reflection on the evidence of the senses, as 'rubbish'.

At first Locke's views on theology seemed significant chiefly because, by showing how difficult it was to reach an understanding of religious matters that could be reckoned true knowledge, he helped to show how nonsensical it was to try to compel men by force into holding religious beliefs. Thoughts in favour of religious liberty which had been maturing in his mind through the troubled 1680s were conveniently ready to be published in defence of the Toleration Act of 1689. *A Letter concerning Toleration* was written during his exile in the Netherlands and published, anonymously and at first in Latin, in 1689. It was followed by two more *Letters* replying to its argument that civil government ought to be confined to securing men's lives, liberty, health and possessions, leaving the salvation of souls to religious bodies whose only sanction should be excommunication. Locke was cautious when drawing conclusions for England from this grand principle. He never welcomed liberty for Roman Catholics because he regarded them as the agents of a foreign power. He also refused to draw the conclusion that atheists should be given liberty as equal citizens. In the constitution which he helped to draft for the American 'province' of Carolina (in which his employer, the Earl of Shaftesbury, had the largest financial interest), the matter was made plain: 'No man shall be permitted to be a freeman of Carolina, or have any estate or habitation in it, who does not acknowledge a God and that God is publicly to be worshipped.' One reason was that only those who believed in rewards and punishments after death were thought fit to be trusted to make oaths and agreements. But with these important qualifications, Locke argued impressively for religious toleration as a consequence of the very nature of true religion. And he did so at a time when most English Christians wanted to be persuaded about such a solution to the nation's conflicts but had been taught to abhor the idea of toleration as an insult to Christianity.

In the new atmosphere of tolerance which he lived to see, there was a free debate about the hallowed doctrine of the ancient faith, both in conversation among those who frequented taverns or the new coffee-shops, and in print as the intellectuals or the ambitious hastened to persuade or insult each other in pamphlets and books.

Locke, somewhat like Hobbes, allowed room for doctrines which were 'above reason' rather than contrary to it; an example he gave was the doctrine of the resurrection of the dead. Faith in such doctrines was a 'firm assent of the mind . . . regulated . . . upon good reason'. Faith was distinguished from reason because it was not deduced from ideas got by the use of the senses or of reflection; but it was legitimate if it was assent made 'upon the credit of the proposer, as coming from God in some extraordinary way of communication. This way of discovering truths to men we call *revelation*.' When Jesus Christ proposed his doctrines, he was credit-worthy because of the 'outward signs': predictions of his coming were fulfilled, and miracles, supremely his own resurrection, were performed. On this basis it was reasonable to believe him. On any basis less reasonable, the acceptance of the teaching of Jesus would be wrong. 'Whatever God hath revealed is certainly true; no doubt can be made of it . . . but whether it be a divine revelation or no, reason must judge.'

Locke's own reason, and the reason of his age, refused to approve of the Calvinist interpretation of the New Testament; that was dismissed without much argument. But a more liberal interpretation could also be dismissed as not genuine revelation. Locke grew to be critical of the Cambridge Platonists. They had taught that every child was born with some ideas already innate before any education could be made from the evidence of the senses; and they had been confident of the ability of the mind to understand eternal substances. To Henry More, man's reason could become a 'divine sagacity'. Now Platonism, and other forms of metaphysics, seemed to be doomed if the only appeal allowed was to 'the ideas we have from sensation and reflection' supplemented by the plain teaching of Jesus.

What, then, was Christianity?

An essay on *The Reasonableness of Christianity as Delivered in the Scriptures*, which Locke published anonymously in 1695, reduced the religion in order to make it reasonable but claimed that this reduction was no more than a return to the New Testament. The essential faith was to believe that Jesus of Nazareth was the Messiah because of the prophecies and miracles. To those who so believed, God 'proposed' the forgiveness of sins 'for his Son's sake, because they gave themselves up to him, to be his subjects'; but men still needed sincerely to obey the laws of the kingdom which they had entered, for otherwise 'they were but the greater rebels'. The laws of this kingdom of the Messiah were old laws, arising from God's eternal nature, but it made all the difference that the Messiah commanded them. 'There is not, I think, any of the duties of morality which he has not, somewhere or other, by himself and his apostles, inculcated over and over again to his followers in express terms.' This 'morality' was superior to 'the attempts of philosophers before Our Saviour's time' because their systems fell short of 'the perfection of a true and complete morality'; but the main difference was now that Christians had a Legislator who taught morality with an authority and a simplicity which 'the bulk of mankind' could understand. 'The writers and wranglers in religion fill it with niceties, and dress it up with notions' – but 'the greatest part of mankind have no leisure for learning and logic, and superfine distinctions of the schools. Where the hand is used to the plough and spade, the head is seldom elevated to sublime motions, or exercised in mysterious reasonings. 'Tis well if men of that rank (to say nothing of the other sex) can comprehend plain propositions.'

Plain propositions, made reasonable because they had first been proposed by the Messiah who fulfilled the prophecies and performed the miracles, constituted the Christianity which John Locke recommended to his fellow Englishmen. It was a creed different from the creed of the Catholic centuries and from the religion held by his father, a Puritan lawyer in Somerset; but in Locke's own eyes, it was more truly biblical than Popery or Calvinism had ever been. Determined to die in peace, he left it to others to quarrel with the Church.[22]

---

[22] The best biography is Maurice Cranston, *John Locke* (London, 1957). See also *John Locke: Problems and Perspectives*, ed. J. W. Yolton (Cambridge, 1969). Paul Hazard's classic study of the intellectual crisis in which Locke figured prominently was translated as *The European Mind, 1680–1715* (London, 1953).

THE FAITH OF JOHN DRYDEN

But John Locke did not provide the only answer available to thinking Englishmen. The greatest poet of the age, John Dryden, became a Roman Catholic sometime in 1685 or 1686. In keeping with his conviction that literature should be only distantly related to the emotions, he left behind no account of his conversion and the psychology of it remains something of an enigma. He was said to have changed his religious beliefs in order to keep his appointments at court now that the King was a Roman Catholic, but it does not seem that James II was then insisting on such changes. There is this evidence of the convert's sincerity: he did not alter his beliefs again. Rather than take the oath to the Protestant William and Mary when James II had fled, he resigned as Poet Laureate and Historiographer Royal and accepted some real disabilities and humiliations as a Papist. We need not doubt that he was always a man of honour, a man who chose Roman Catholicism because he had come to believe that it was true.

Dryden wrote two long religious poems, one before and one after his conversion. *Religio Laici or a Layman's Faith* came in 1682 when he was at the height of his powers as a Tory satirist, and he acknowledged that from him 'the handling of so serious a subject wou'd not be expected'. The poem showed a close attention to current theology, but also a sturdily lay approach. Despite advice to be more cautious, he retained a criticism of St Athanasius for teaching that the heathen must be damned. He also criticized the Church of England's own clergy for neglect of their duties. The theology expounded was the standard Anglicanism of the time. A preface attacked the Papists 'because they have kept the Scripture from us, what they cou'd; and have reserv'd to themselves the right of interpreting what they have deliver'd under the pretence of infallibility.' In particular they were rebuked for their defence of 'king-killing'. The Puritans and their Dissenting heirs, now called 'the Fanatics', were dismissed with a more complete contempt. Perhaps Dryden was here reacting against being much preached at in his boyhood: his father was a Puritan and a justice of the peace in Cromwellian England. He wrote: 'If spiritual pride, venom, violence, contempt of superiors and slander had been made the marks of orthodox belief, the presbytery and the rest of our schismatics which are their spawn were always the most visible Church in the Christian world.'

Proudly distancing himself from such enthusiasts, Dryden declared that he was one 'naturally inclined to scepticism in philosophy'. Much has been read into this admission by some modern commentators. But he advocated a religion which partly accepted the obvious truths of Christianity and partly conformed to the laws of the State:

> Faith is not built on disquisitions vain;
> The things we *must* believe, are few and plain:
> But since men *will* believe more than they need,
> And every man will make himself a creed,
> In doubtful questions 'tis the safest way
> To learn what unsuspected ancients say:
> For 'tis not likely we shou'd higher soar
> In search of heaven, than all the Church before . . .
> And after hearing what our Church can say,
> If still our reason runs another way
> That private reason 'tis more just to curb
> Than by disputes the public peace disturb.
> For points obscure are of small use to learn:
> But common quiet is mankind's concern.

Five years after this defence of the Church of England in *Religio Laici*, he published *The Hind and the Panther*. It was a longer poem and far more interesting. Although still confined within the golden cage of the 'heroic couplet' and still addressed to a mainly Anglican readership which would understand scholarly references, it showed that his conversion to Roman Catholicism had brought John Dryden more maturity, calm, charitableness and sense of devotion. (How wrong was Macaulay, with his Victorian superiority, to say that 'Dryden knew little and cared little about religion'!) His argument was that the Church of Rome had the best claim to have preserved the revelation entrusted by the Saviour to the ancient, undivided Church. The Church of England taught 'nonsense' because of too many compromises, but the two Churches still

had much in common, in particular a common cause against
ignorant and intolerant Protestant fanatics:

> O happy regions, Italy and Spain,
> Which never did those monsters entertain!
> The Wolf, the Bear, the Boar can there advance
> No native claim of just inheritance.

And this poem of 1687, although written by a convert who
might have been expected to praise all attempts to convert
England, hinted broadly at a continuing dislike of Jesuit
influence and of any kind of provocative extremism; Dryden
combined his loyalty to the papacy, as he had combined his
loyalty to the Church of England, with a noticeable amount of
anticlericalism.

The preface commended the poem to the reader as a plea for
toleration, and the very first line presented the Roman Catholic Church not as an aggressor but as 'a milk white hind,
immortal and unchang'd'. The Church of England was depicted as a panther, but even in this image, which might have
been deeply offensive, there was some tact:

> The Panther sure the noblest, next the Hind,
> And fairest creature of the spotted kind;
> Oh, could her in-born stains be wash'd away
> She were too good to be a beast of prey! . . .
> Her wild belief in ev'ry wave is tossed,
> But sure no church can better morals boast.
> True to her king her principles are found;
> Oh that her practice were but half so sound! . . .
> Thus is the Panther neither lov'd nor fear'd,
> A mere mock queen of a divided herd.

A year before his death in 1700, Dryden wrote *The Good Parson* –
about an Anglican, an astonishing tribute from one who had
been so definitely anticlerical. Already in 1687 his poem ended
with the Church of England still open to persuasion, although
not exactly alert to it:

> Thus did the gentle Hind her fable end,
> Nor would the Panther blame it, nor commend;
> But with affected yawnings at the close,
> Seem'd to require her natural repose.

Concluding *The Hind and the Panther*, the poet was grateful for his own knowledge that God had provided an 'unerring guide', a Church with authority. Here was a conviction that only the old religion, the unchanged faith of Catholic Christendom, could give a man peace of soul amid all the debates and conflicts of the age. Here was a layman's confidence, a calm faith, in God, which would survive King James's or the Jesuits' antics:

> Thy throne is darkness in th' abyss of light,
> A blaze of glory that forbids the sight;
> O teach me to believe thee thus conceal'd,
> And search no further than thy self reveal'd;
> But her alone for my director take
> Whom thou hast promis'd never to forsake![23]

THE ATTACK ON ORTHODOXY

In the eighteenth century John Dryden's fears that Protestantism would result in an intolerable chaos of opinions seemed to be justified. One of the vocal 'Free Thinkers' was Anthony Collins, a well-to-do squire who as a young man won the aged Locke's friendship; his *Discourse of Freethinking* (1713) popularized the word. In *A Discourse of the Grounds and Reasons of the Christian Religion* (1724) Collins examined the Old Testament in order to show that its prophecies had not been literal predictions of the coming of Jesus; and he outlined further criticism of traditional Christian apologetics.

Three years later a Cambridge don who was so eccentric as perhaps to be of unsound mind began publishing *Discourses on the Miracles of Our Saviour*. In these discourses Thomas Woolston treated the story of the resurrection of Jesus as 'the most notorious and monstrous imposture, that ever was put on

---

[23] Philip Harth, *Contexts of Dryden's Thought* (Chicago, Ill., 1968), answered the charge that the poet was either a deep sceptic or a time-server. The best treatment is to be found in C. Douglas Atkins, *The Faith of John Dryden* (Lexington, Ken., 1980). For the intellectual life of the community which Dryden joined, see T. H. Clancy, *English Catholic Books, 1641–1700* (Chicago, Ill., 1974).

mankind'. He was imprisoned, but when a London preacher, Thomas Sherlock, defended the apostles' credibility he did so by imagining a trial where the most persuasive arguments were used by the counsel for the Apostles. His *Trial of the Witnesses of the Resurrection of Jesus* (1729) attracted and convinced many readers. But this clever book showed the Church being obliged to defend its teaching on territory which had hitherto been regarded as very much its own possession. And even when the resurrection of Jesus was still granted to be true and miraculous, other writers arose to affirm that the age of miracles in the Church had ceased with the deaths of the apostles – and to hint that its existence before that date was by no means as certain as the Church's tradition maintained.

If prophecies and miracles as proofs of the Messiahship of Jesus were open to such criticisms, what of the plain message which Locke had presented as the teaching of the Messiah? Here the attack on orthodoxy, so far from being silenced, came to a climax.

In 1690 a book by the Rector of Exeter College, Oxford, on *The Naked Gospel*, was burned and its author driven out by a furious Bishop of Exeter because the Gospel had been interpreted (or so it seemed) as a denial of the Church's creeds. Six years later John Toland, an Irishman in reaction against a Roman Catholic upbringing, published anonymously a book based on the independent reading and reflection which he had managed while studying at Edinburgh and Oxford. It was called *Christianity not Mysterious* and flatly denied that there could be any religious truths 'above reason'.

Jesus, Toland claimed, had taught nothing so absurd as 'the Gibberish of your Divinity Schools'. On the contrary, he had made the truth 'easy and obvious to the meanest capacities'. The complications had been introduced by 'priestcraft' from 'pagan mystic rites' and similar sources. This early publication did not suggest very clearly what was the truth about God, but Toland did not cease to develop and to write. He invented the term 'pantheist' in 1705 in order to equate God with the universe, and later published a Prayer Book based on this creed. He also wrote controversially in defence of Milton and in criticism of the New Testament narratives. His patrons included the third Earl of Shaftesbury (who had once been Locke's pupil and was now a philosopher in his own right). They did not include Locke, who was embarrassed by the Irishman's crudity while indignant at the storm with which the orthodox responded.

During Toland's lifetime a much more serious theologian questioned the orthodox doctrine of the Trinity. Hitherto this had been unthinkable for a priest of the Church of England. Indeed, whether inclining more to Catholicism or to Calvinism the Church had gloried in its claim to be impeccably orthodox, teaching the same faith as the Bible and an undivided Church. It was assumed that there was one continuous orthodoxy despite various heretical corruptions, and a characteristic Anglican contribution had been the work of George Bull, a learned parish priest who ended up as Bishop of St David's. In one major work Bull attempted to show that the teaching of the New Testament on the relationship between faith and works was a harmonious whole; in another, that the Fathers of the Church before the Council of Nicaea already held the same Trinitarian beliefs that the Council was to proclaim. But in 1712 Samuel Clarke, Rector of St James, Piccadilly, caused a sensation by his *Scripture-Doctrine of the Trinity*, examining 1,251 texts and concluding that there was in the Bible no single doctrine, let alone one which was orthodox as Nicaea was to define orthodoxy. While the author refrained from any clearly heretical conclusion, he suggested independence and indicated sympathy with some Unitarian objections to the Nicene definition. That tendency was what Anthony Collins had in mind when he observed that no one had doubted the existence of God until Dr Clarke had undertaken to demonstrate it.

This courageous book mattered because it was written by the leading philosophical theologian of the day – a brilliant man who was Isaac Newton's favourite pupil and was offered the Mastership of the Mint on Newton's death. While in his twenties Clarke had published Boyle Lectures, *A Discourse Concerning the Being and Attributes of God, the Obligations of Natural Religion, and the Truth and Certainty of the Christian Revelation*. That book had made his reputation, and it had been an orthodox reputation. Clarke had attacked Hobbes and the Dutch pantheist Spinoza, and although he had shown an understanding of Deist objections to orthodox Christianity he had not surrendered to them. Such a thinker might well have become a famous leader of the Church of England. Instead in the 1720s he let it be known that he could not subscribe to the Thirty-Nine Articles and when Sir Robert Walpole tried to make him a bishop even that all-powerful minister had to withdraw.[24]

The severity of the new challenges was made plain by Matthew Tindal – who, however, managed to retain his fellowship at All Souls College, Oxford, from 1678 to his death in 1733. He first appeared before a large public with a book of 1706, *The Rights of the Christian Church asserted against the Romish and all Other Priests who claim an Independent Power over it*. The title would have delighted the old Puritans, but Tindal left few of the Church's doctrines standing by the time he had finished asserting its rights. What was allowed to survive was no more than reason could demonstrate and the State could approve as being good for morality. In 1730 Tindal made his rejection of the Church's tradition still clearer by issuing *Christianity as Old as the Creation, or the Gospel a Republication of the Religion of Nature*. His argument was that 'the religion of nature is absolutely perfect; revelation can neither add to, nor take away from, its perfection.' It was then not possible for a Fellow of All Souls to say outright that Christianity was false; but it could be said that every reasonable man agreed with what it really was, and that Jesus had had a happy knack of telling memorable stories to illustrate the world's philosophical commonplaces.[25]

Tindal was a 'Deist' (although he called himself a 'Christian Deist'). That is: it seemed obvious to him that mankind as a whole believed in one orderly, benevolent God, or would have believed in him had priests not corrupted the original innocence. It seemed obvious, too, that what had always been

---

[24] James Ferguson studied *The Philosophy of Dr Samuel Clarke and its Critics* (New York, 1974), and Robert Sullivan, *John Toland and the Deist Controversy* (Cambridge, 1982).

[25] Extracts from this whole debate, and comments on it, were provided in *Religious Thought of the Eighteenth Century*, ed. J. M. Creed and J. S. Boys Smith (Cambridge, 1934). See also R. N. Stranberg, *Religious Liberalism in Eighteenth-century England* (Oxford, 1954), and John Redwood, *Reason, Ridicule and Religion: The Age of Enlightenment in England 1660–1750*, quoting many pamphlets (London, 1976).

presented as the distinctively Christian doctrines about God deserved to be forgotten now that the nature of religion was at last understood in an enlightened age. Surely the old picture of man as a sinner in danger of hell should be abandoned. It was no more credible than the old Christian insistence that, for men to be saved, the true God needed to be revealed by Christ. Not all Deists stopped there. Some dared to ask openly: in the new age of enlightenment, although all sensible men agreed with morality in theory, were they not right to sacrifice it to the higher laws of profit and pleasure? And although all sensible men believed in God, was it not true that God did not matter much, being powerless to influence either the individual or the march of history.

In 1714 a London doctor, Bernard de Manderville, published *The Fable of the Bees*, complacent about 'private vices' since the expenditure which these stimulated caused 'public benefits'. In the second edition he attacked churchmen for educating the children of the poor in the new charity schools; it was not a public benefit to put ideas into such heads. Later he issued a plea for the approval and licensing of brothels. Such books were only the tips of an iceberg of talk, for in many taverns and private dining rooms Restoration and eighteenth-century men tended to admire and debauch each other, now that the restraints of Puritan discipline had been removed. It remained only to remove the Puritan theory of man.

We have no need to trace the long process by which the dark picture of man bequeathed by Augustine of Hippo and developed by Calvin of Geneva was ridiculed and widely forgotten, but can note as a sign of the times that the philosophy of the third Earl of Shaftesbury affirmed the importance of man's moral and aesthetic senses apart from religion. In a widely influential book of 1738 on *The Scripture-Doctrine of Original Sin*, a Presbyterian minister, John Taylor, expounded the view that Augustine and Calvin had not even done justice to the men who wrote the Bible. The Bible itself, as Taylor read it, did not teach that Adam's guilt had been transmitted to all his descendants. If men were naturally corrupt, Taylor concluded, they were not morally responsible. He totally rejected the Calvinist belief that amid a general corruption a few had been predestined to salvation. It was his conviction that the Law in the Old Testament attached its penalties to individual's actual sins – for which Christ made Atonement, thus saving from eternal extinction all those sinners who repented and desired to partake of the 'grace' offered universally. 'Pray consider seriously,' he wrote, 'what a God he must be who can be displeased with and can curse his innocent creatures even before they have a being. Is this thy God, O Christian?'

As G. R. Cragg has said about the decline of Calvinism among Englishmen after 1600, 'seldom has a reversal of fortune been so complete. Within fifty years Calvinism in England fell from a position of immense authority to obscurity and insignificance . . . Calvinism had a magnificent opportunity, and for a brief period wielded wider powers than its popular support would probably have warranted. It prepared its own undoing; it failed to use its great advantages so as to win the sympathies of ordinary Englishmen.' And with the decline of belief in Calvinist gloom about the moral and spiritual condition of the average Englishman went a decline of belief in hell, so far as we can judge from what we know about sermons and popular reactions to them. A densely populated hell now seemed not terrifying but ridiculously unreasonable. For not only John Taylor rejected Calvinism with its claim that God had decreed in advance of any human actions the everlasting punishment of the majority of the human race. The most influential Anglican preacher of the age, Archbishop John Tillotson, made a quiet comment. 'That,' he said, 'is that which no good man could do.'[26]

TWO VOYAGERS: DEFOE AND SWIFT

While he was Queen Anne's chief minister from 1710 to 1714, Robert Harley employed two journalists of genius: Daniel Defoe and Jonathan Swift.[27] Defoe, who was able to commend

---

[26] G. R. Cragg, *From Puritanism to the Age of Reason* (Cambridge, 1950), pp. 30, 34. D. P. Walker has studied *The Decline of Hell* (London, 1964).

[27] See J. A. Downie, *Robert Harley and the Press* (Cambridge, 1979).

himself to almost any circle because he was so full of unaffected
admiration for his fellow men's lives and achievements, was
sent all over the country to make propaganda by conversation
as well as by writing. For all this work he was paid. Swift, in
contrast, remained a writer and in what he wrote did not
conceal his contempt for most of his fellow men (although to
the few whom he admitted into friendship, he was wonderfully
loyal: he was to be loyal after Harley's fall and imprisonment).
He was too proud to accept any ordinary fee for his journalism
although he hoped for a bishopric. And in the contrasting
personalities of the two great journalists, Defoe and Swift, lay
the origins of two very different convictions about English
Christianity in the eighteenth century.

Born in or about 1660, Daniel Defoe was the son of a Puritan
and was sent to one of the new 'academies' of the Dissenters in
the hope that he would become a preacher. No one has ever
been able to unravel all his often unsuccessful business enterprises, or to count up his literary output, but always he was a
preacher – in a sense. Although many of his fellow Dissenters
thought him insufficiently sober and honest, he risked and
incurred severe punishment for his savagely ironical pamphlet
in their defence, *The Shortest Way with Dissenters* (the shortest
way being to hang the preachers and exile the congregations).
Swift, in contrast, was born in 1667 in an impoverished
Cavalier family. He was proud to be an Anglican clergyman;
'gentlemen' was one of his favourite words. He despised
tradesmen and Dissenters. He particularly despised Defoe.

Both men wrote famous fiction which took advantage of the
popularity of books about voyages. Defoe's *Robinson Crusoe*
(1719) was based partly on the experiences of a sailor, Alexander Selkirk, who was shipwrecked on an uninhabited island in
1704 and came back to tell the tale five years later. But even
this novel was a vehicle for a Dissenter's message, spelled out in
a sequel consisting of moral essays, *The Serious Reflections of
Robinson Crusoe*. It seems that the hero's name was suggested by
the author's admiration for Timothy Cruso, a Dissenting
preacher; but mainly the message was implicit in the matter-
of-fact story itself, an eighteenth-century version of the Puritan
spiritual diary. The hero helped himself – and assessed every-

thing and everyone in economic terms. He preserved his morality through almost thirty years on his island, instructed the basically noble savage, Friday, in the Christian religion, and was assisted in his self-help by an approving God. In the world now opening up to the industrious middle classes of England, nothing seemed impossible to the determined individual. Defoe's *Tour*, published in 1724, showed Crusoe-like enterprise transforming Great Britain and, as he almost always thought, improving it – and he rejoiced to see men and women improving themselves in the process. As a lively novel of 1722 made clear, in this new society even respectability was not an impossible goal for a whore, if she was Moll Flanders. Over the seas lay many lands presenting still greater opportunities for profit and for mission. Defoe's God-fearing but self-helping Englishman was voyaging into the world, both to exploit it and to instruct it.[28]

Swift had a vastly more complicated purpose in mind when he published *Gulliver's Travels* in 1726. He attacked the prominence given by Defoe to commercial enterprise. When he realized the consequences for Ireland of economic exploitation by the English, he did not hesitate to say so – with a wrath which made Defoe's Dissent seem like a tea party. But he was not really interested in any isolated individual such as a shipwrecked sailor. To him the essential problem was man in society. The individual had to relate to others, and in order to do so had to come to terms with, and to control, the brutal power of the irrational passions of his animal nature. And while Defoe liked stories to have happy endings, Swift found no answer to his problem.

Lemuel Gulliver is sent on voyages to contrasting lands – Lilliput, where the inhabitants are six inches high, and correspondingly ridiculous, and Brobdingnag, where the gigantic inhabitants feel themselves in a position to assess the English as 'the most pernicious race of little odious vermin that nature ever suffered to crawl upon the surface of the earth'. He visits Laputa, a land where the men are mad about science and the

---

[28] See G. A. Starr, *Defoe and Spiritual Autobiography* (Princeton, N.J., 1965), and Peter Earle, *The World of Defoe* (London, 1976).

women are mad about visitors more interesting and more useful than the scientists. Finally he finds himself in a land ruled by the Houyhnhnms, horses whose 'grand maxim is to cultivate reason and to be wholly governed by it', but also peopled by the ugly, irrational, totally undignified, man-like Yahoos. The energy and brilliance of the imagination which conceived these various fantastic beings, and the half-convincing straightforwardness of the narratives about them, provide the explanation why *Gulliver's Travels* was instantly placed near the top of English prose and has retained much of its popularity ever since. As a children's book the first half has even rivalled *Crusoe*. But in writing the book Swift's 'chief end' was, as he put it, 'to vex the world rather than divert it' – for just beneath the surface were the great questions. What is man, so great or so small depending on circumstances and on the ambiguities of his own flawed nature? Do your disputes matter more than the dwarfs' squabbles? Are the beauties which arouse your greed or lust really more attractive than the colossal bodies, with their blemishes and stinks, which terrified and horrified Gulliver in the land of the giants? How helpful in the real challenges confronting man is your science? Are the people whom you profess to love really more admirable than the Yahoos?

Gulliver's Travels referred to the disputes between Catholics and Protestants: 'It is computed that eleven thousand persons have, at several times, suffered death, rather than to submit to break their eggs at the smaller end.' Wars costing many millions of lives have been fought over differences in opinion, 'for instance, whether *flesh* be *bread*, or *bread* be *flesh*; whether the juice of a certain berry be *blood* or *wine*; whether whistling be a *vice* or *virtue*; whether it is better to *kiss a post*, or *throw it in the fire*; what is the best colour for a *coat*, whether *black*, *white*, *red* or *grey* and whether it should be *long* or *short*, *narrow* or *wide*, *dirty* or *clean*, with many more.' And a similar tone marked the references to English politics in the age of Sir Robert Walpole. Among the Lilliputian dwarfs, Flimnap the Treasurer kept his high position by dancing on the tight-rope, and other ministers were awarded coloured silken threads for their lesser skills in acrobatics. Swift asked: are your much vaunted and well

rewarded religious and political activities really more than
that?

For half a century he took his place among his fellow men as
a priest. Those sermons which have survived are severely plain
and moral. His first major satire, *A Tale of a Tub*, was written
soon after he became a clergyman in 1694 and was based on the
theological reading which he had had to undertake in order to
be ordained. Its mockery of 'Peter' was the old Anglican attack
on the Papal claims; the doctrine of transubstantiation is
reduced to Peter serving up a brown penny loaf as mutton. Its
fiercer contempt for the coarser 'Jack' was the new Anglican
hatred of the Presbyterian followers of Jean Calvin and their
even more fanatical allies. Its hero was 'Martin', so named
because Anglicanism seemed to stand close to Martin Luther,
although in the mind of Swift its appeal was far more rational
than Evangelical.

Swift's *Argument against Abolishing Christianity*, written in
1708, was his first minor masterpiece of prose irony. Its serious
message was that 'real Christianity' had been 'for some time
wholly laid aside by general consent, as utterly inconsistent
with all our present schemes of wealth or power.' For men who
pursued wealth, power or wit after a rejection of rational
Christianity as defined by 'Martin', Swift had only contempt.
Had the current attacks on Christianity not given them a
suitable subject, he wrote, the 'Free-Thinkers' of the time
would have had nothing to 'divert their spleen from falling on
each other, or on themselves'. It is therefore possible to present
Swift as in religion and politics the perpetual Cavalier, who
'loved authority more dearly than anything else'.[29]

Much evidence has survived about his life as Dean of St
Patrick's in Dublin, between his arrival to take up residence in
the mood of an exile in 1714 until he was deprived of speech
and reason by a stroke in 1742. Most of his activities were
examples of the conduct hoped for from an eighteenth-century
clergyman. As he devoutly attended daily services, officiated at

---

[29] Nigel Dennis, *Jonathan Swift: A Short Character* (New York, 1964), p. 30. A study
of the religious background of *A Tale of a Tub* was made by Philip Harth in *Swift and
Anglican Rationalism* (Chicago, Ill., 1961).

a weekly Communion (the only such service in Dublin), preached once a month and administered the cathedral's affairs, he showed a rare devotion to duty. He allocated a third of his income to charities; he left almost all of what he saved to found a lunatic asylum. He wrote with such passion in defence of the Irish poor against exploitation that he became a popular hero, cheered in the streets. He also keenly defended the interests of fellow clergymen less privileged than he became. He first made himself known to the London politicians when the Irish clergy sent him over to argue for a reduction of their taxes; in the end he was successful by persuading Harley. Dean Swift, in the end undeniably the cleverest and most famous man in his Ireland, was in many ways an advertisement for 'real Christianity'.[30]

But he never wrote a theological or devotional masterpiece, or found much time in his later years to read other men's efforts in the religious field. His *Letter to a Young Gentleman lately entered into Holy Orders* (1721) was almost entirely taken up with warnings against preachers' affectations. He gave advice as a stylist; his own style is summed up by his advice that 'when a man's thoughts are clear, the properest words will generally offer themselves first, and his own judgement will direct him in what order to place them, so as they may be best understood.' He warned the young gentleman against attempting 'to explain the mysteries of the Christian religion'. 'If you explain them, they are mysteries no longer; if you fail, you have laboured to no purpose.' It was not that Swift was at heart an atheist or an agnostic: 'no gentleman of a liberal education, and regular in his morals, did ever profess himself a Free-Thinker.' But it seemed 'most reasonable and safe . . . upon solemn days to deliver the doctrine as the Church holds it, and confirm it by Scripture.' That did not suggest that his own thoughts on theology were clear.

Thoughts on Religion, published after his death, pointed dis-

---

[30] Louis A. Landa studied *Swift and the Church of Ireland* (Oxford, 1954). Ricardo Quintana, *The Mind and Art of Jonathan Swift* (Gloucester, Mass., 1965), decisively showed that Swift's motivation was Christian. See also Peter Steele, *Jonathan Swift: Preacher and Jester* (Oxford, 1978).

creetly to some uncertainty as to what would happen were the mysteries of Christianity to be explained. On the one hand, it was Swift's maxim that 'I am in all opinions to believe according to my own impartial reason'. On the other hand, reason might not always confirm conventional beliefs and 'the want of belief is a defect that ought to be concealed when it cannot be overcome'. The latter thought was worked out with evident sincerity. 'I am not answerable to God for the doubts that arise in my own breast, since they are the consequences of that reason which he hath planted in me, if I take care to conceal those doubts from others, if I use my best endeavours to subdue them, and if they have no influence on the conduct of my life.'

Swift's variety of rationalism was compatible with this conservatism, and he explained why. 'Liberty of conscience, properly speaking, is no more than the liberty of possessing our own thoughts and opinions, which every man enjoys without fear of the magistrate; but how far he shall publicly act in pursuance of those opinions, is to be regulated by the laws of the country.' That was where he parted from Defoe. He said of his profession: 'I look upon myself, in the capacity of a clergyman, to be one appointed by Providence for defending a post assigned me, and for gaining over as many enemies as I can.' But he never fully explained whether or not he was prepared to defend all the usual Christian doctrines – a remarkable silence in a clergyman so eloquent. About 'Christ's divinity' he wrote this: 'in a country already Christian, to bring so fundamental a point of faith into debate, can have no consequences that are not pernicious to morals and public peace.'

As a boy Swift longed to be 'used like a lord'. As a man, for many years he hoped for promotion in the Church and was dissatisfied with his Dublin Deanery because it was so far from the royal corridors and the coffee-houses of London. The main reason why he was never made a bishop or an English dean was, no doubt, that the politicians – even those whom he served as a journalist – were afraid of his independence, which he often flaunted. It cannot have helped that he was the author of a violent lampoon on the Duchess of Somerset, Queen Anne's friend. But the rumour may well have been true that the Queen was scandalized by *A Tale of a Tub* because it seemed to mock all religion (or at least so seemed when interpreted to her by her favourite archbishop, Sharp). It was Swift's fate that neither his brand of intellectual high spirits nor his insistence on asking questions could fit comfortably into the Church he had chosen to serve.

There is often in his writing the sense that human nature ought to be rational but cannot bear to be, and therefore needs to control its passions by religion. For Swift acknowledged the passions: they were life-giving. Men were not rational horses. He wrote: 'In two points of the greatest moment to the being and continuance of the world, God hath intended our passions to prevail over reason. The first is, the propagation of the species, since no wise man ever married from the dictates of reason. The other is, the love of life, which, from the dictates of reason, every man would despise, and wish it at an end, or that it never had a beginning.' Yet individuals and societies must discipline this pulsing life of the instincts by the acceptance (at least in public) of the religion and morality reckoned orthodox. The passions must be censored. The central Swiftian argument about religion can be presented simply: 'We need religion as we need our dinner, wickedness makes Christianity indispensable, and there's an end of it.'[31]

The trouble about Dean Swift was, however, that he could never bring himself to believe with his whole heart that the public religion of his society, the orthodoxy of the Church of England, was entirely reasonable. In *A Tale of a Tub* Martin may be right, but he is the tale's dullest character. Swift's own religion was deliberately dull. He despised 'the art of wetting the handkerchiefs of a whole congregation' or 'drivelling to a multitude'. Partly this was due to a fear of what he and others would have found, had he bared his heart to the public. His essay on *The Mechanical Operation of the Spirit* probed the emotional (including sexual) pressures which made men get excited about religion. It was not reassuring. As John Traugott has observed, Swift 'wanted to rebuild the churches in the

---

[31] Patrick Reilly, *Jonathan Swift the Brave Desponder* (Manchester, 1982), p. 215.

decayed parishes of London, to establish bishops in the New
World, to make the Church a reality in the daily lives of his own
parishioners, and yet his obsessive probing of psychological
realities which bring assumptions of the glory of the rational
faculty into question, his hatred of man's pretensions to
spirituality, make of his religion more of an anxiety than a
faith.'[32]

What he wanted to be his innermost religion is hinted at by
odd phrases: 'God's mercy is over all his works, but divines of
all sorts lessen that mercy too much.' 'We have just enough
religion to make us hate, but not enough to make us love one
another.' But actually the religion of love was not the heart of
Swift's religion. He himself hated more successfully than he
loved. He sometimes claimed that while he hated mobs he
could love individuals, and it is true that he attracted many
friends and was kind to many sufferers. There was, however,
some blockage in him which prevented the full joy of love either
for God or for any human being. He suddenly remarked: 'Most
kinds of diversion, in men, children and other animals, are an
imitation of fighting.' He was often coarse in his writing. He
wrote perhaps the cruellest poem ever written about a woman.

We simply do not know what this ultimately isolating
blockage was, since he burned almost all his private papers.
Many biographers have attempted to trace the consequences
of an obscure birth, of the humiliation of being, in his most
formative years, a mere secretary to Sir William Temple, of the
unwillingness to marry either of the two women, Stella and
Vanessa, who came to live near him in Ireland, to whom he
wrote immortal letters, and who both adored him. Was he the
illegitimate son of Sir William Temple's father? Was Stella the
illegitimate daughter of Sir William, whom Swift could neither
marry formally nor abandon? These are improbable suggestions, but they have been made. Their possibility is a reminder
of how deep the mystery of his personality remains. All that we
know is that he was afflicted with a disease of the ears which
often made him sick, dizzy and unable to relate to the stable,
everyday world. He was afflicted, too, with a lifelong sense of

---

[32] *Focus: Swift*, ed. C. J. Rawson (London, 1971), pp. 116–17.

frustration – as well he might be, for it has been said accurately about this Englishman exiled to Dublin: 'he towers head and shoulders above all his contemporaries both as a writer and as a man.'[33]

For some reason, what Swift felt in his heart tormented him. He found relief in preaching to others, but could not accept orthodoxy. He also found relief in defending the liberty of others, but could not accept democracy. W. B. Yeats translated the famous Latin epitaph, not mentioning Christ or penitence, which this unique dean wrote to go over his grave in his cathedral:

> Swift has sailed into his rest;
> Savage indignation there
> Cannot lacerate his breast.
> Imitate him, if you dare,
> World-besotted traveller; he
> Served human liberty.

BISHOP BUTLER'S TRIUMPH

It was the achievement of Bishop Joseph Butler to answer the most important of the intellectual attacks on Christianity made by his predecessors in the English debate. We do not belittle that achievement if we also notice that his arguments became less convincing in relation to the more radical attacks made after his death in 1752.

He wrote in the plain, conversational style of his age but his thought was both original and profound, and his mind was totally free of the coarseness which infected Swift. Although at home in the age of reason, he meditated, as did Swift, on the limits of reason's power in the real world. Walking one night in his garden (as was his curious habit), he suddenly stopped and asked his chaplain: 'What security is there against the insanity of individuals? The physicians know of none . . .' After another

---

[33] Bonamy Dobrée, *English Literature in the Early Eighteenth Century* (Oxford, 1959), p. 474. The standard biography is by Irvin Ehrenpreis (2 vols, London, 1962–67).

turn in the garden, he asked a still more searching question. 'Why might not whole communities and public bodies be seized with fits of insanity, as well as individuals? . . . Nothing but this principle, that they are liable to insanity equally at least with private persons, can account for the major part of those transactions of which we read in history.'

His life had a calm which contrasts with Swift's tempestuous voyage. His parents were Presbyterians. In 1713, when he was aged twenty-one, and still a pupil in a Dissenting academy, he wrote the first of a series of modest but acute letters to the great Samuel Clarke. 'I have made it, sir, my business, ever since I first thought myself capable of such sort of reasoning, to prove to myself the being and attributes of God.' Within a little over five years he had become an Anglican, an Oxford graduate, a priest and preacher at the Rolls Chapel in London. In 1726 he published *Fifteen Sermons* on ethical topics in that chapel. He had of course delivered many more, but he offered the public only the best.

In his will he was to order 'that all my sermons, letters and papers . . . be burnt without being read by anyone.' Ten years later, in 1736, he published *The Analogy of Religion, Natural and Revealed, to the Constitution and Course of Nature*, a book written in the very quiet but also very comfortable rectory at Stanhope in the diocese of Durham. Shortly before its publication Queen Caroline summoned him to be a member of the theological discussion group which met regularly in her private rooms. The favour of the monarchy and the applause of the educated public made him Bishop of Bristol; the Deanery of St Paul's was added to supplement the meagre income. Finally, in 1750, he became Bishop of Durham and lived long enough to deliver a 'charge' to his clergy in which he urged the fulfilment of pastoral duty with detail which showed that he was no recluse – and no optimist. The surviving evidence about his daily life is not much but indicates that he lived simply as a bachelor, gave much of his large income away, and spent much of what remained on the improvement of his official houses.

Butler's talk seems to have been like his writing: always serious, commonsensical and moral but never unaware of mysteries which he could neither express nor understand. It was the approach most likely to appeal to soberly and religiously minded readers in his age, and we can see the merit of it if we compare him with his fellow philosopher and fellow bishop, George Berkeley.

Berkeley was an Irishman of English descent, brilliantly gifted and most attractive. Dean Swift was among his many friends – and remained a friend even when his own Vanessa, who had hoped to marry him, left her fortune to Berkeley in her bitter disappointment. This paragon of the Irish virtues was a devout Christian and it was his ambition to answer current attacks on his religion by three responses: by the foundation of a college in Bermuda to train missionaries (including Red Indians) for the American colonies; by the writing of books which would be as learned and as witty as any adversary's; and by a new philosophy, better than Locke's, which would show God among the realities. He was confident. He announced that 'those difficulties which have hitherto amused philosophers, and blocked up the way to knowledge', were but 'dust'. Philosophers, having raised a dust, had complained that they could not see. However, his projects failed. The Bermuda college never received enough support from Sir Robert Walpole's government in far off London or from the Americans who were at least six hundred miles distant, although many private subscribers were fired by the idea. The learning and wit also foundered. Books in dialogue form such as *Alciphron* (published in 1732 on his return from America) allowed a philosophical atheist and an anticlerical rake to attack Christianity before being defeated. Although clever, the argument offended the godly without seriously impressing the sceptics; and rumours often surrounded Berkeley that, if not an atheist himself, he was a facetious fool.

The philosophy did not persuade. Its essential point was that to exist means either to be perceived or to perceive. Material objects are known to exist only in so far as they are perceived – either by us or by God. What most truly exists is what perceives: 'There is not any other substance than *spirit*, or that which perceives.' Yet the world could never be reliably perceived by human beings with their fallible senses of sight and touch, so that if the things of this world 'really exist, they are necessarily perceived by an infinite mind; therefore there is an infinite mind or God.' This argument Berkeley called 'a direct and immediate demonstration of God's existence – a short method of crushing scepticism.' The philosophy of immaterialism has continued to interest philosophers, but most Englishmen reckoned that they could refute it by much the same means as Samuel Johnson employed, when he kicked a stone. Berkeley did not defend himself against his critics at any length. He concentrated on work as Bishop of Cloyne in the extreme south of Ireland, and on writing about the medical 'virtues of tar-water'. Towards the end, his mind had ceased to perceive reality.[34]

Butler knew that the English who were likely to respond to a serious argument about religion were interested in goodness more than in Berkeley-type cleverness. The first great task of his life was therefore to answer cynicism about human nature. So he advocated right conduct by arguing that virtue corresponds with our nature and vice violates it; that we have a passion for 'benevolence' as well as a passion for 'self-love'; that we have a conscience which rightly demands absolute authority over all our passions and assures us that 'self-love', properly understood, perfectly coincides with 'benevolence' and thus with virtue. All the 'passions, affections and appetites' constituting human nature should, and could, be ordered in the performance of duty. 'Duty and interest', he wrote, 'are perfectly coincident: for the most part in this world, but entirely and in every instance if we take in the future and the whole.'

Up to this point, Bishop Butler's thought was similar to the moral philosophy propounded by the third Earl of Shaftesbury. Without recourse to any appeal to a revelation in religion, the conscience could assure any man that in the long run his true self-interest would coincide with his true duty to others. Meanwhile, 'self-affection' and 'benevolence' could be held in balance without much difficulty. This tension-free

---

[34] See A. A. Luce, *The Life of George Berkeley* (London, 1949), and, for the philosophy, G. J. Warnock, *Berkeley* (revised, Harmondsworth, Middx, 1969). Edwin Gaustad studied *George Berkeley in America* (New Haven, Conn., 1979).

moral sense was to Shaftesbury akin to the aesthetic sense by which men discerned the harmony in things; the conscience saw that life itself made an orderly system. And Butler agreed with Shaftesbury that the commands of the conscience would deserve to be obeyed, even if God did not offer heaven as a reward. He agreed, too, that the various affections made a neat system. But to him religion was essential, for the hope of heaven was a part of what it meant to be human. 'There is a capacity in the nature of man,' he wrote, 'which neither riches nor honours, nor sensual gratifications, nor anything in this world can perfectly fill up or satisfy.'

Butler's writing about God was a reply to the Deists' appeal to 'natural religion' as a reality far more reliable than Christianity's ridiculous claim to be the revealed religion.

Unlike Berkeley, Butler did not feel obliged to offer a direct consideration of atheism. In his *Analogy* he took 'it for proved, that there is an intelligent Author of nature and natural Governor of the world', but little apart from the sheer existence of God could be proved; instead of proof, 'probability is the very guide of life'. The *Analogy* began strangely with a discussion of the probable effect of death; but at least this beginning showed that the author had paid some attention to the possibility that we do not survive death to enjoy future rewards for morality – a possibility which the Deists disregarded, or pretended to disregard, in order to extoll the splendid certainty of 'natural religion'. The 'proper proofs' of natural religion were, Butler held, not intellectual certainties, demonstrable however immoral a sceptic might be. They were 'the proper motives to religion, from our moral nature, from our natural apprehension of God under the character of a righteous Governor and Judge'. It is the power of the conscience that leads us 'to consider this little scene of human life, in which we are so busily engaged, as having a reference, of some sort or other, to a much larger plan of things.' But that is as far as natural religion will take us. God's 'moral government', like the rest of his government of his creation, 'must be a scheme quite beyond our comprehension'. Natural religion was as uncertain as religion based on revelation.

Since his opponents protested that Christianity contained

'many things very different from what we should have expected,' he replied that this very unexpectedness was to be expected. He was therefore not ashamed to present Christianity in an orthodox way, with miracles and Christ's mediation between God and man, but he claimed that its total effect was to satisfy the conscience and thus the reason of mankind. 'The truth of our religion, like the truth of common matters, is to be judged of by all the evidence taken together.' Those who still persisted in rejecting it were sternly reminded that Christianity did not attempt to satisfy the immoral, although it was, 'in reason, sufficient to prove and discipline that virtue, which it presupposes'. The conclusion of the *Analogy* was a solemn warning that men should not 'vilify or disregard Christianity as if they had a demonstration of its falsehood'. Scepticism need not be the most rational attitude, and 'blasphemy and profaneness' were temptations arising from 'the wantonness of vanity or mirth'.

In that society there was sufficient weight in those arguments for the book to make a material difference to the situation described in the 'Advertisement' at the beginning. 'It is come, I know not how, to be taken for granted, by many persons, that Christianity is not so much as a subject of inquiry; but that it is, now at length, discovered to be fictitious. And accordingly they treat it, as if, in the present age, this were an agreed point among all people of discernment; and nothing remained, but to set it up as a principal subject of mirth and ridicule, as it were by way of reprisals, for its having so long interrupted the pleasures of the world.' In that 'Advertisement' Butler announced his aim: not to prove the truth of Christianity, but to show that 'there is strong evidence of its truth' – and no clear case that 'there is nothing in it'. He did not appeal to the authority of the ancient Church, as did more technically learned theologians who attempted to refute the new Deists – men such as the great conservative scholar, Daniel Waterland. He would go, as his opponents did, to the tribunal of reason. He did not name a single one of his opponents; and this calm silence was perhaps his most eloquent argument. Any reply to him would have to be made at his level of seriousness, integrity and rationality – and his contemporaries produced no such reply.

In the long run, however, Bishop Butler's intellectual triumph was far from complete. A Victorian sceptic who had formerly been a clergyman, Leslie Stephen, passed a fair judgement on the whole debate in three sentences full of wisdom. 'The Deists,' he wrote, 'had triumphed so far as they had insisted upon the impossibility of reconciling the historical conception of the Christian Deity with the conceptions of metaphysical optimism. The Christians, on the other hand, had shown as triumphantly that the attempt to transfer to the pale abstraction called Nature the emotions excited by the historical religion was futile in itself, and condemned by the broad facts of experience. The result was the decline of the pale shadow of Christianity which called itself Deism, and which had never excited enthusiastic or disinterested support; and, on the other hand, the practical admission that Christianity must seek for support elsewhere than in abstract philosophy.'[35]

HANDEL'S TRIUMPH

Henry Purcell created the vacancy which George Frederick Handel filled. Purcell's father and his uncle were leading musicians at the court of Charles II and he was appointed organist at Westminster Abbey in 1679, at the age of twenty. As fertile as his contemporary Christopher Wren, he produced new music to honour many royal occasions under the later Stuarts and William and Mary. He wrote the incidental music for over forty plays; he was the father of English opera, although the infant died when he died; his songs charmed the court and were sung in taverns. In church music his was the greatest name since Orlando Gibbons, who had died in 1625,

---

[35] Leslie Stephen, *History of English Thought in the Eighteenth Century*, Vol. 1 (London, 1876), p. 271. More recent studies include E. Mossner, *Bishop Butler and the Age of Reason* (New York, 1936), and Austin Duncan-Jones, *Butler's Moral Philosophy* (Harmondsworth, Middx, 1952). James Downey studied the surviving sermons of Butler, Berkeley and some contemporaries in *The Eighteenth Century Pulpit* (Oxford, 1969).

and some of his anthems are still in the repertoire wherever this choral tradition is kept alive. The tradition had been totally silenced by the civil wars, but some of Purcell's early anthems were in the Elizabethan style of polyphony with which he had grown familiar as a chorister in the Chapel Royal. He developed as a master of the new style, introduced from Italy and France under Charles II's patronage. The 'verse anthem' now combined some choral work with declamatory solos and long passages for the violins. The noblest music of this kind was composed for the funeral of Queen Mary. It was performed again at his own funeral, only eight months later.

This master musician has been greatly and rightly honoured, but his development was cut short by his death in 1695; his achievement was the work of a mere fifteen years. John Blow had taught him, and was both his predecessor and his successor at the organ of Westminster Abbey; but when Blow died in 1708 it was seen that there was no other successor of stature. Purcell's fame has also been limited by his failure to develop music which could support popular religion. He worked for the royal court, the royal churches and the London theatre. J. A. Westrup has written that his verse anthems are 'akin to the spirit of Renaissance architecture. It is impossible to feel that they are intended solely for the glory of God. They are also to be noted and approved by man; there is an element of ostentatious magnificence that is wholly absent from the church music of the Elizabethans.'[36]

Handel made his name among the English in 1713 by the *Te Deum* which he composed for the celebration in St Paul's of the peace of Utrecht; he was much indebted to Purcell. On various other grand occasions his music was the climax of the elevating theatricality which the Church of England could still produce in order to express a nation's faith in its own power and wealth and in God, its most reliable ally. The anthems which Handel wrote for performance by voices and orchestra in the chapel of the Duke of Chandos (who had done very well out of the war, as paymaster to Marlborough's armies) were also magnificent, but the most sumptuous of this inexhaustibly fluent com-

---

[36] J. A. Westrup, *Purcell* (revised, London, 1975), pp. 207–8.

poser's church music was heard at the coronation of George II in 1727. The ceremony in Westminster Abbey was conducted in considerable disorder due to slackness and the new king was well-known to be stupid, coarse and vicious. But Queen Caroline had shown her greater intelligence by becoming Handel's patron while he still lived in Germany; he was to repay her by a softly elegiac anthem for her funeral. Meanwhile the coronation anthems were admired by all. When the chorus first exploded in 'Zadok the priest', after the mounting excitement of the introduction by the strings, men knew that a high priest had arrived to consecrate the English Establishment.

Handel's music never voiced the self-surrender to the Saviour, the tender gratitude for salvation and the longing for death to be found in the Passion music or the cantatas of his German contemporary, J. S. Bach. Bach was content to remain within, and to perfect, the already great tradition of Lutheran church music. Handel had his opportunity as a young man to find security in that tradition; and he refused. His training to write *Messiah* was far more bizarre. He went to half-Catholic, half-pagan Italy, and dedicated himself to the opera – music with 'a spiritual climate as remote from Christianity as it is from Freud'.[37]

On his move to London in 1710, at the age of twenty-five, he began a campaign to persuade the richer inhabitants of the world's greatest city to support Italian operas, of which during his life he composed some forty. One reason why he turned to the 'sacred oratorio' in the 1740s was that not enough of the English shared his own devotion to these elegant trivialities. Samuel Johnson was to describe Italian operas as an 'exotic and irrational entertainment'. Handel's own contemporary, Dean Swift, denounced 'that unnatural taste for Italian music among us which is wholly unsuitable to our northern climate and the genius of the people, whereby we are over-run with Italian effeminacy and Italian nonsense.' What Swift preferred was shown by his active support of John Gay's *Beggar's Opera*, a musical comedy which extolled in English the merits of manly English vice; the girl who sang the leading part in that very

---

[37] Winton Dean, *Handel and the Opera Seria* (Berkeley, Cal., 1969), p. 11.

successful show found herself marrying a duke. It was noticed
with disgust that, in order to sing as adults, some Italian
choirboys agreed to be castrated. It did nothing to reconcile the
English that this practice had begun in the papal choir.

As a young man in Rome in 1708, Handel had turned to the
New Testament as a means of getting round the papal ban on
operas in the holy city. In one of the noblemen's palaces, before
a splendid audience of cardinals and other ornaments of a
music-loving aristocracy, he had presented *La Resurrezione*,
starring a *prima donna* as Mary Magdalene and adding a
dramatic appearance by Lucifer to the biblical text. There
were only two choruses. The sacred character of the libretto
did not conceal from anyone the true purpose of *La Resurrezione*,
which was to display a sumptuous union of counterpoint
composition derived from Handel's own Germany with the
Italian lyricism which he had acquired. The Pope rebuked
those who had taken part in this blasphemy, and Handel,
scenting danger, went on his way to Naples.

Messiah was an altogether more mature and serious work,
composed in London in the autumn of 1741 on the basis of
biblical texts selected by a rich patron of the arts, Charles
Jennens. The theme unlocked all the treasure-house of the
composer's genius and he wrote the music within three weeks.
But this speed was possible only because *Messiah* contained so
much music lifted from the secular operas; in a sense it would
be true to say that it had taken Handel more than thirty years
to write it. In his lifetime the work secured no great success. It
received its first performance at a charity concert in Dublin in
1742; Swift was still Dean of St Patrick's and had been very
reluctant to allow his cathedral's choristers to join Handel's
choir. When it was performed in London, no title was given; for
some years it was discreetly called 'a new sacred oratorio'. The
usual setting was a charity concert, in aid of the Foundling
Hospital. The score was not published until eleven years after
Handel's death. The basic difficulty was that the Church of
England agreed with the Pope that there must be no representation of Christ or of any other biblical personage on the
stage; and even this studiously non-dramatic oratorio, a *Messiah* without a Christ, was suspect for it echoed secular operas,

it was performed in theatres and it earned money for 'fiddlers' (as Swift called them). It is entirely understandable that after experiencing the Church's suspicion of *Messiah*, Handel left the New Testament alone. His only other handling of a Christian theme, *Theodora* (1750), was his own favourite among his oratorios but a commercial flop – as he complained, because rich Jews would not buy tickets for a piece which glorified a Christian martyr, and because rich ladies did not wish to see virtue praised.

His oratorios with Old Testament subjects varied in their popularity (and merits), but here was a world where the English felt at home. Handel heeded the warning given by the Bishop of London when the first of these oratorios was planned in 1732; although based on an Old Testament book which failed to mention God, *Esther* must on no account include any action on the stage. Within this limitation, the Hebrew scriptures provided many acceptable subjects. The English could recognize kings and high priests, war lords and matriarchs, and humbler heroes and lovers, who were agreeably energetic, combative and fond of food, drink and marriage. The victories and harvests which their tribal God had bestowed on the Ancient Israelites seemed to the English well-earned. The most popular of all these oratorios was *Judas Maccabeus*, composed in 1746 to celebrate the defeat of the Jacobite rebels at Culloden. The glory of the music helped the audience to forget that the event in Jewish history being celebrated was a successful rebellion.

Handel had arrived in London friendless and not knowing a word of the language. Many anecdotes were based on the fact that he never did master English – but about three thousand people insisted on attending his burial in Westminster Abbey in 1752. It is recorded that 'he would often speak of it as one of the great felicities of his life that he was settled in a country where no man suffers any molestation or inconvenience on account of his own religious principles.' That was a theologically enigmatic tribute; but the compliment was returned by the English. After a delay *Messiah* won its vast and enduring popularity. At the first London performance, George II began the practice of standing for the 'Hallelujah' chorus, and George

III continued the custom, as part of his passion for Handel's music. These Hanoverian kings did not, we may reckon, understand much; but they understood that a German composer of Italian operas had greatly helped the English to affirm their calmer creed and to celebrate the coronation of the King of kings and Lord of lords.[38]

---

[38] The best studies are Herbert Weinstook, *Handel* (revised, New York, 1959), and Paul Henry Lang, *George Frederic Handel* (London, 1967).

CHAPTER TWELVE

THIRTY YEARS OF CRISIS

THE RESTORED CHURCH
AND CHARLES II

We now turn from architecture, thought and music to church history. Here we find that the first thirty years after 1660 were a hectically active period, beginning with the restoration of Charles II, continuing with the turbulent reign of James II, and ending with the offer of the throne – or, rather, thrones – to William and Mary. These years saw the birth of the party system in English politics; the 'Tories' and the 'Whigs', although later sometimes honoured as the ancestors of the modern Conservatives and Liberals, were so named by their enemies from words used in Catholic Ireland and Presbyterian Scotland for despised outlaws. This fiercely quarrelsome time also saw the birth of the denominational system in English religion, and we shall look at the conflict from three points of view – Anglican, Protestant Dissenting and Roman Catholic.[1]

The Church of England became a denomination in sociological fact, if not yet in theological theory. The word 'denomination' was an eighteenth-century word and the word 'Anglican' did not come into general use until the nineteenth century, but in the period 1660–90 the Church of England effectively abandoned the attempt to be the Church of the whole English people. It became instead a church with its own fairly systematic teaching, exchanging the dream of national unity in religion for the possibility of becoming one day the mother of a

---

[1] The best political narrative is J. R. Jones, *Country and Court: England 1658–1714* (London, 1978). Norman Sykes surveyed ecclesiastical history, 1660–1768, in *From Sheldon to Secker* (Cambridge, 1959).

worldwide denomination, the Anglican Communion.[2]

The basis on which the Church of England contracted from its previous national comprehensiveness was the Act of Uniformity, to which the royal assent was given amid great ceremony on 19 May 1661. Under this act, 'every parson, vicar or other minister whatsoever' had to declare his 'unfeigned assent and consent to all and everything contained and prescribed' in the new edition of the Book of Common Prayer. He had also to declare that 'there lies no obligation upon me or on any other person, from the oath commonly called *The Solemn League and Covenant* to endeavour any change or alteration of government either in Church or State.' In particular, 'it is not lawful, upon any pretence whatsoever, to take arms against the king'. The Act, or the Prayer Book which it enforced, prescribed that it was not lawful for anyone to minister in the Church of England as a priest or a deacon without ordination by a bishop, or without the bishop's licence for a particular parish. It forbade anyone to teach in a school without the bishop's licence, or in a university without conforming to the Church of England. It also laid a new emphasis on confirmation by a bishop: 'there shall be none admitted to the Holy Communion, until such time as he be confirmed, or be ready and desirous to be confirmed'. The exceptive clause was necessary because while the layman might be willing to go to the bishop, the bishop might not be willing to hold a confirmation in the neighbourhood.

On the face of it the act applied to all Englishmen, but when it was passed everyone knew that there would be dissent from some who could plead either Protestant or Catholic scruples of conscience. This had been a deliberate decision not to include them. In effect the Act made the Church of England one religious body among others, a body united more firmly than ever before by a strict adherence to its Prayer Book, by an ardent obedience to its kings, and by the acceptance of a bishop's authority over his diocese. In Richard Hooker's time

---

[2] *Anglicanism*, ed. P. E. More and F. L. Cross (London, 1935), illustrated the thought and practice of the Church of England in the seventeenth century, but the word used in its title did not appear in any of the extracts in its 811 pages.

it had been an open question whether Queen Elizabeth's campaign against the Puritans would succeed. It had also been questionable whether episcopal ordination was necessary in order to minister in the Church of England. Some holders of distinguished offices – for example, Hadrian Saravia who ministered at Hooker's deathbed and wrote a defence of episcopal government – had never been made priests by bishops. Now the Church unambiguously adopted a church order which later generations would call 'Anglican' or (especially in the USA and in Scotland) 'Episcopal'. When Presbyterian ministers were consecrated as bishops for Scotland, they were carefully made deacons and priests first, as their predecessors had not been under James I. Only the willingness of many Anglicans to receive Holy Communion in Presbyterian or Lutheran churches when abroad remained from the old attitude.[3] When Izaak Walton, a London businessman who had retired to the bishop's palace in Winchester to pray and to fish, wrote gracious little biographies of leading Anglican divines of the previous period, he stressed their orthodoxy and if need be adjusted the facts a little.[4]

As Bishop of London and Archbishop of Canterbury, Gilbert Sheldon was the chief architect of the Church of the Restoration. He had not forgotten a vow made by Charles I that all the lands recently taken from the Church would be restored to it. He had kept this vow buried in the ground for the thirteen years of the Church's tribulations. Now the opportunity had come. Gilbert Burnet, a bishop of a later generation, deplored Sheldon's inflexibility towards the Dissenters and claimed that he did not have 'a deep sense of religion if any at all', religion being to him merely 'an engine of government and a matter of policy'. But the condemnation was unfair. Although certainly no preacher and incapable of appreciating the delicate Jeremy Taylor, Sheldon was a deeply convinced High Churchman. He was bold enough to rebuke both the King and the Lord Chancellor, Clarendon, for their indul-

---

[3] Norman Sykes, *Old Priest and New Presbyter* (Cambridge, 1956), probed the changing attitudes. See also Willem Nijenhuis, *Adrianus Saravia* (Leiden, 1980).

[4] David Novarr studied *The Making of Walton's Lives* (Ithaca, N.Y., 1950).

gence towards the Dissenters in defiance of Parliament – and to deliver this rebuke in no uncertain terms while the aged Juxon was still at Canterbury and it was still possible that the King and his chief minister might appoint a less outspoken church-man as Juxon's successor. His Anglican conservatism was sincere, had been tested in the fires of adversity, and was to inspire a strenuous, meticulous and effective feat of adminis-tration.

Moved to the archbishopric at the age of sixty-five, Sheldon achieved fourteen years of work. Although physically weak towards the end, his motto was 'Do well and be merry'. He interpreted his responsibility for the welfare of the whole Church as strenuously as William Laud had done. He insisted that his fellow bishops should work as hard as he did in their dioceses – and, to prove it, should send detailed reports to him. In practice this involved the supervision of a massive effort to restore the pre-war routine of cathedrals, colleges and parishes, although the buildings had been desecrated or neglected, service books and archives had been lost, and church life had become confused and demoralized in the strange half-persecution under the Commonwealth. To give a small instance: the tradition of boys singing in church choirs had to be started again from scratch. 'A cursory survey of Sheldon's immense correspondence', writes his modern biog-rapher, 'can only lead the reader to conclude that never was a church leader beset by a more stubborn, self-seeking, litigious, insubordinate corps of clergymen.'[5] Yet this old man and his assistants recreated a routine of church life which has not been interrupted since his day, for all its continuing imperfections.

Sheldon understood the laity better than Laud had done. Whereas Laud had relied on courts created by the prerogative of the Crown, Sheldon made do with the much less alarming diocesan courts. Whereas Laud had rejoiced to see the clergy treated as a separate and superior caste, Sheldon agreed that parsons should be taxed like other men and restricted to pastoral or intellectual work. And whereas Laud had alienated many of the richer laity (including the former spokesman of the

---

[5] V. D. Sutch, *Gilbert Sheldon* (The Hague, 1973), p. 152.

Commons who was now Earl of Clarendon and Lord Chancellor), Sheldon took infinite trouble to keep on good terms with MPs and with other gentlemen; his dinners for them were splendid and systematic. He criticized the King for not sticking closely to the wishes of the House of Commons, with the frankness which he also showed when criticizing him for his mistresses. And even the shifty and irresponsible Charles acknowledged Sheldon's invaluable strengths. Indeed, it has been suggested that the crucial decision-making event in the whole Restoration settlement was a private meeting in Canterbury on the evening of 25 May 1660 between Sheldon and the King, when Charles was making his triumphant return to his capital. Clarendon was the only other person present.

When Sheldon died in 1677, the King's chief minister was Thomas Osborne, Earl of Danby, a tough Yorkshireman. He lived to sign the invitation to William of Orange to intervene to stop the aggressive Roman Catholicism of James II. He had formed a working alliance with the old archbishop and had virtually promised the position to a close friend of his, who would carry on a policy acceptable to the Cavaliers in the House of Commons: Henry Compton, then in his mid-forties and Bishop of London.

The son of an earl killed in the civil war, Compton was one of the few clergymen of noble birth and had quickly been made a bishop and tutor to the King's two nieces, Mary and Anne, each a future queen. He was, however, much more than a careerist or a courtier. Although he had never properly functioned as a parish priest or theologian, he discharged energetically the duties of a bishop, still chiefly disciplinarian. He demanded high standards of care in the great diocese of London, holding regular conferences with his clergy; and, since the American colonies did not have their own bishop and were not likely to get one, he attempted to supervise their churches also, using previously rather vague rights as Bishop of London. He was equally self-confident when dealing with royalty and statesmen, and was a strong defender of Anglican against Roman Catholic claims. Like Danby, he signed the historic invitation to William in 1688. If he had been made Archbishop of Canterbury in 1677 he would have had at least thirty years in which to build on Gilbert Sheldon's achievement (he died in 1713).

However, he was passed over in 1677 and the leadership of the Church of England was offered to a Dean of St Paul's, William Sancroft. Compton had the same bitter experience in 1690, when he was again thought by many to be the inevitable choice for Canterbury. He had officiated at the coronation of William and Mary (introducing the ceremony of the presentation of the Bible) and had virtually taken over the duties of archbishop for more than a year. Yet once again a Dean of St Paul's was appointed – John Tillotson. Almost certainly Compton was frustrated in 1677 because King Charles was asked by his brother James not to promote a man so hostile to Roman Catholicism; and almost certainly he was frustrated in 1690 because King William was asked by his wife Mary not to appoint a man so worldly. During the excitements of 1688 he had escorted Princess Anne to safety at the head of a troop of cavalry. With reason King James had once told him that he talked like a colonel.[6]

Archbishop Sancroft was a man more delicately conscientious than Bishop Compton. By nature a scholar, he had already refused the bishopric of Chester. When Charles offered him Canterbury, he protested 'that he was very unfit for it thro' his solitary life which he had a long time led'. In saying that, he was too modest about his part in the rebuilding of St Paul's. Whilst archbishop he had the courage to take action against Bishop Wood of Lichfield, who had grossly neglected his duties and was now suspended from them for two years. But Sancroft's unhappiness in the political field became clear. He found great difficulty in dealing with the prolonged crisis created by James's conversion to the Church of Rome. While Compton was one of those who demanded James's exclusion from the succession ('the whole civil and religious constitution of the realm is in danger'), Sancroft defended the royal duke's hereditary right. When Compton refused to suspend one of his clergy for preaching against King James and was suspended himself by King James's Ecclesiastical Commission, Sancroft

[6] See Edward Carpenter, *The Protestant Bishop: Henry Compton* (London, 1956).

pleaded that he was too old to serve on that body. When the combative Compton leaked to the public the seven bishops' private petition against James's Declaration of Indulgence, Sancroft was uncomfortably surprised to find himself cheered by the mob and imprisoned in the Tower of London. He would not effectively defend King James against indignant Protestants such as Compton; yet he could not take the oath of allegiance to William and Mary. Suspended in 1689 and deprived of his archbishopric in 1690, he would not join in Jacobite plots to bring James back. He would have preferred William and Mary to be regents in James's absence, but put forward no workable alternative when they refused to fall in with this plan.

Activists such as Compton were insensitive when they despised this timid, good man for his agonies of conscience. No conscience as delicate as his could find it easy to know how the Church of England ought to interpret the 'divine right' of kings when the king was a Roman Catholic. Already under Charles II this had become a problem for those in the know.[7]

The year 1660 saw the restoration of a king; all else followed from that. And Charles II, a selfish sensualist, lacked any personal qualification to be Supreme Governor over a Church of England which during his reign was rich in pastors, in scholars and even in saints. The royal bedchamber was the place where he was most himself, with its unsynchronized clocks, yapping spaniels and feuding mistresses. It belonged to a universe utterly different from, say, Ralph Josselin's parsonage in Essex, where the earnest diary-keeping vicar worried endlessly over other people's problems – his wife's moods, his ten liveborn children's illnesses, his parishioners' sins and woes, his country's prosperity and its dealings with other nations – all in the faith that God could be prayed to and that he ruled over the world righteously, in small as in great matters. Charles has exercised a romantic appeal upon many generations, and in his lifetime he was often liked; he was amiable to all those who did not inconvenience him and was

---

[7] R. A. Beddard's work on the Church under Sancroft is awaited. W. G. Simon studied *The Restoration Episcopate* (New York, 1965).

admired by his people as a sportsman, wit and sexual athlete.
His court was preserved for posterity in the flattering portraits
by the Dutchman, Peter Lely, and the German, Godfrey
Kneller. But we know that Clarendon was dismayed by his
irresponsibility as a king, as was Archbishop Juxon. Those two
could be dismissed as boring and incompetent old men –
Clarendon went off into exile, to rewrite and complete his
History of the Rebellion and a sad autobiography, and to die – but
they should not be forgotten when we assess Charles II, for
they were churchmen and Royalists. In his *History*, Clarendon
pretended to have been more of a churchman and a Royalist in
the 1640s than he had been in reality.[8] Their disillusionment
was shared by every man of the age who cared seriously about
Church and State.

The 1650s had left scars on Charles's personality. Superficially the 'merry monarch', he was known by shrewd people
who watched him closely to be, at heart, very sad. He had
become a total cynic about human motives because he had
been for so long surrounded by fellow exiles at each other's
throats. For some deeply resented months he had been compelled to dissemble because he had been the guest of the
Presbyterian Scots. When he became king he did not know
what it meant to be loyal or honest. In exile he had been unable
to contract a marriage thought suitable, and had worked off his
sexuality with ladies of easy virtue and in brothels. The habit
persisted through his life, so that he acknowledged fourteen
bastards but never developed a deep relationship with any
human being apart from his sister, Henrietta-Anne, who died
in 1670. He also made a habit of being foul-mouthed. He seems
to have had no overriding policy, apart from survival in order
to take his pleasures as consolations for this unease at the heart.
If religious toleration was his policy at the beginning of his
reign, it was not at the end. If he had a patriotic wish to wrest
commerce and empire from the Dutch, he did not persist in it,
and the subsidies from France, which have sometimes been justified as part of an anti-Dutch policy, were surrounded by him

---

[8] See B. H. G. Wormald, *Clarendon* (Cambridge, 1951), and H. R. Trevor-Roper,
Edward Hyde, Earl of Clarendon (Oxford, 1975).

with secrecy: he knew how his people would react if told. If he was dynastically-minded and therefore resolved to leave his throne to his brother, he must have known that he was bequeathing a disaster to the nation and did nothing at all to avert it. His apparent acceptance of the suggestion that James's powers might be limited had been no more than a temporary trick.

What his religion was anyone could guess – and many did. When he knew that he was dying he was reconciled to the Church of Rome by a simple priest, Father Huddleston, who had helped him to escape after the battle of Worcester. Possibly he reckoned that this was a 'religion for gentlemen' (as he once declared Presbyterianism was not) – or at least a religion for a gentleman to die in, if by such a conversion he could get rid of a lifetime far from virtuous. Possibly Roman Catholicism was the only faith that had ever aroused any religious feelings in him, and he had postponed his conversion simply because, unlike his brother, he did not think the loss of his throne worth a Mass. But there remains the mystery of his professed willingness, in the secret treaty of 1670, to declare himself a Roman Catholic if the French would pay him to do so and send troops to put down any rebellion. Whether or not he meant this to be more than a diplomatic bargaining counter must remain uncertain. Probably not much weight should be attached to a promise to be reconciled with the Church of Rome when the 'welfare of his kingdom' would permit it.

It was not that he was hostile to the Church of England; he could sing its praises. From a distance he admired the holiness to be found in it. When a prebendary of Winchester Cathedral, Thomas Ken, refused to house Nell Gwynne, one of the King's mistresses, Charles did not hold it against him; not long afterwards he approved his appointment as Bishop of Bath and Wells, saying: 'God's fish! The little black fellow who would not give poor Nelly a night's lodging!' But when he lay dying and the moment of truth had come, Bishop Ken bent low over the Supreme Governor and asked him if he was a member of the Church of England. Charles stared at him silently.[9]

---

[9] For a more favourable portrait see, e.g., Antonia Fraser, *King Charles II* (London, 1979).

PURITANISM BECOMES DISSENT

In the fires of the Anglican persecution which Charles II had to
allow, Puritanism became 'Dissent' – a religious minority
which in the end was acknowledged because respected.

The development was possible because Puritanism, however aggressive, had always been essentially a religious
movement, not a programme to fulfil economic or political
ambitions. A twentieth-century scholar has provided this summary of his studies of the Puritans both in England and in the
new world: 'We have been told, with various degrees of crudity
and subtlety, that Puritanism was the ideology of the
bourgeoisie. On that subject there are two simple observations
to be made. First, Puritanism never offered itself as anything
but a doctrine of salvation, and it addressed itself neither
directly nor indirectly to social classes but to man as man.
Second, its attractions as a commitment were such that it
made converts in all classes – among aristocrats, country
gentry, businessmen, intellectuals, freeholders and small
tradesmen.'[10] Such observations appear to be valid; and this
scholar could easily have extended his list of the Puritans'
secular occupations lower down the social scale. Many men
without property, even 'masterless men' without regular employment, were Puritans no less than the earls so prominent in
the 1640s. They had all undergone the same process of conversion. They had found the same Saviour, and essentially the
same authority in some combination of the Scriptures and the
Spirit without any need of a priest as mediator or interpreter.

Because its religious energy was the lifeblood of Puritanism,
the movement was not destroyed when it met a political
catastrophe as sudden and as total as the Norman Conquest six
centuries before. It had been defeated largely because it had
not agreed on how to handle power, and now when persecuted
it was purified. A modern historian of the persecution has
written: 'Puritanism became, for a whole generation, more a
matter of life and less a subject of theological debate than it had
ever been before. With humble amazement, the greatest

---

[10] Alan Simpson, *Puritanism in Old and New England* (Chicago, Ill., 1955), p. 11.

spokesmen of the persecuted groups noted that their sufferings had led to fuller life and to incalculable spiritual benefits.'[11]

It was a real persecution, far more severe than the sufferings of the Anglicans under the Commonwealth. A censorship of printed books was created by the Licensing Act of 1663 and enforced by the 'surveyor', Sir Roger L'Estrange, who held office until 1688. At the Restoration ancient laws were revived under which Puritans could be punished as traitors. The Quakers, for instance, were made guilty of treason by the mere act of refusing to swear allegiance to the king. John Bunyan was imprisoned under the Elizabethan statute of 1593, 'for retaining the Queen's subjects in their due obedience'. But other laws were added inexorably. The Corporation Act of 1661 required all mayors, aldermen, councillors and borough officials to receive 'the sacrament of the Lord's Supper according to the rules of the Church of England'. The same initiation was demanded of all its members by the House of Commons in 1661. In 1664 the First Conventicle Act, replying to feeble disorders, forbade five or more people not of the same household to meet together for worship except in accordance with the liturgy, the penalties being fines or imprisonment or (on the third offence) transportation overseas for seven years. Next year the Five Mile Act forbade ejected ministers to come within five miles of any city, chartered town or Parliamentary borough or any other place where they had exercised their ministry, unless they would take an oath never to attempt 'any alteration of government either in Church or State'. Many ministers were now driven from their homes.

In 1670 the Second Conventicle Act imposed much heavier fines on preachers or hosts who defied the law. A third of the money was to be paid to any informer who brought them to justice. The seizure and sale of a Dissenter's goods was authorized. If he had been comfortable this could reduce him to poverty, and if he was already poor this often meant depriving

---

[11] G. R. Cragg, *Puritanism in the Period of the Great Persecution, 1660–88* (Cambridge, 1957), p. 87. See also C. E. Whiting, *Studies in English Puritanism, 1660–88* (London, 1931); A. C. Underwood, *A History of the English Baptists* (London, 1947), pp. 88–115; R. Tudor Jones, *Congregationalism in England, 1662–1962* (London, 1962), pp. 33–104.

him of the tools of his trade, or of his bed. The severity of imprisonment varied with the term of the sentence and with the prison; gaolers were very much left to their own devices, some being brutal and others indulgent, particularly if paid. But many prisons were so cramped and so foul that the risk of death, or at least of the permanet ruination of one's health, was high. Many a Dissenter needed Thomas Browning's consolation, written to his people from Northampton gaol: 'Come, the worst is death, and that is the best of all.'

The first period of persecution saw far fewer surrenders than was expected. Of the Puritan clergy ejected in 1660–62, only about 210 (about a tenth) conformed, and some fifty more were willing to take the oath required under the Five Mile Act. There could be no complete evidence about the numbers of laymen attending illegal worship (often having also attended their parish churches), but many reports of arrests in many parts of the country survive, alongside many complaints by bishops and others eager to see the law enforced. Obstinately ministers persisted in preaching, although many were reduced to abject poverty; Richard Baxter would recall that 'Mr Chadwick in Somerset for a long time had little but brown rye bread and water for himself, his wife and many children, and when his wife was ready to lie in was to be turned out of door, for not paying his house-rent.' The courage shown by Dissenting ministers who remained in plague-stricken London in 1665, when many of the Anglican parish priests fled, impressed contemporaries; it was to be recalled in a vivid novel by Daniel Defoe, a boy of four at the time (*A Journal of the Plague Year*, 1722). Congregations proved ingenious in providing means for a beloved pastor to escape from his pulpit at a moment's notice, or for women, preferably pregnant, to block the entry of constables. In order to escape detection they were willing to go to fields or woods, barns or caves; to meet very early in the morning or very late at night; or to pretend to be having a party when in fact they were holding a service. They were now bound together not by any belief that they could or should regulate their neighbours but by sheer courage in holding to their own convictions in a day of darkness.

Two great men paid tributes to the quality of the church life of the persecuted Dissenters. One was John Owen, and he paid it by what he did as much as by what he wrote (although he wrote many pamphlets). Appointed by Oliver Cromwell to be the leading figure at Oxford, he had remained active in national politics right up to the Restoration; the small congregation which he gathered in his London home, Wallingford House, had been the centre of opposition to Richard Cromwell and of support for General Lambert. After 1660 he could still have led a privileged life, for he married a rich lady and received an invitation to migrate to New England as the chief preacher in Boston. Yet he persisted in the dangerous course of ministering to a small Independent congregation in London, and added to the risk by doing all he could to keep in touch with the other Independents being persecuted. And the other tribute was paid by Richard Baxter, whose poem, 'written when I was silenced and cast out,' perfectly expressed the consolation to be found in these gatherings for worship under persecution:

> In the communion of saints
>   Is wisdom, safety and delight,
> And when my heart declines and faints
>   It's raised by their heat and light . . .
>
> Must I be driven from my books,
>   From house, and goods, and dearest friends?
> One of thy sweet and gracious looks
>   For more than this will make amends . . .
>
> The heavenly hosts world without end
>   Shall be my company above:
> And thou, my best and surest Friend,
>   Who shall divide me from thy love?

For there was a quality in the life of the small, 'gathered' congregation seldom found in the Established Church. The bishops' political and social duties in London took them away from the routine of their dioceses – and that mattered, because their pastoral duties could no longer be delegated to suffragan bishops. Despite promises, those invaluable assistants were not revived at the Restoration. The annual 'visitation' of the parishes by the archdeacons depended for its vigour on the archdeacon's personality, and in most dioceses the system by which the archdeacon was assisted by rural deans had fallen into disrepair. The conditions of the priests and the parishes seem to have varied widely. The minimum which bishops and archdeacons tried to enforce was Holy Communion at least three times a year, and Morning Prayer and Litany every Sunday. If possible other services were desirable on Sunday afternoons and on other holy days. Only in a few churches – and those mainly in London – were there daily services.

Many parish priests seem to have been quite well-off; in the 1680s Gregory King guessed that their average annual income was above £50, within the top fifth of the nation. We know that in Essex Ralph Josselin, the Puritan who had conformed, was making about £160 a year in the 1660s, £60 of this coming from his parish's tithes and the rest from land which he either leased out or farmed himself. But in 1670 John Eachard, a university don, published a widely noticed book lamenting the poverty and ignorance of the clergy in the parishes, and his charge that the clergy were held in contempt obviously did not lack all substance.

Attendance in the parish churches often fell off alarmingly as soon as Dissenters knew that they were legally free to worship elsewhere. A major cause must have been the average labourer's identification of the parson with the squire, whose local power was greatly increased by the Restoration. (It was now against the law for people to move to another parish seeking employment or better wages if they could be held likely to be charges on the rates, although the law could not be systematically enforced. Within a parish wages were supposed to be regulated by the justices of the peace, who were almost always squires and employers.) It seems a fair summary to say that the Church of England was not established in the hearts of the people as securely as it was established by the law.[12]

Being aware of the real situation in the parishes, many

---

[12] John H. Pruett, *The Parish Clergy under the Later Stuarts* (Urbana, Ill., 1978), was based on research in Leicestershire. Josselin's uniquely complete personal accounts were studied by Alan Macfarlane in *The Family Life of Ralph Josselin*.

Anglicans wanted to include at least some of the Dissenters in the National Church, despite the decisions of 1661. In 1668 Sir Orlando Bridgman led a substantial move in this direction but was defeated in the Commons. A considerable number of mayors, magistrates or juries refused to convict or punish Englishmen whose one offence seemed to be a determination to worship God in their own way. The King himself intervened to save Baptists from death in Aylesbury, to secure George Fox's release from Scarborough Castle, and on other occasions. It was clear even before the Act of Uniformity came into effect in 1662 that Charles wished to exercise his royal prerogative by allowing exemptions. Frustrated by Parliament's refusal to endorse his first Declaration of Indulgence in December 1662, he at last made the intervention he wanted by his second Declaration of Indulgence in March 1672. This allowed Protestant Dissenters to meet for worship if both the place and the preacher were licensed – and also allowing Roman Catholics to worship in private. The 'indulgence' not only confirmed widely held feelings of repugnance against the persecution, but also showed how limited its success had been. All the Quakers and some other Dissenters refused to apply for licences, but 1,610 were soon issued – 939 to Presbyterian congregations, 458 to Independents or Congregationalists, and 210 to Baptists. Almost five hundred prisoners were released. Parliament forced the King to withdraw his declaration a year after issuing it, but not before bishops had expressed alarm at the size of the Dissenting congregations – and not before the Presbyterians had seized their chance to hold fresh ordinations.

The King now abandoned the Dissenters, and under the Test Act of 1673 they (like the Roman Catholics) were excluded from office under the Crown unless they would first receive Holy Communion in the Church of England. But they could now be reasonably sure that the eventual outcome would be along the lines indicated by a bill which was passed by the Commons before being wrecked by the Lords. This allowed Protestants to meet for worship not in accordance with the Book of Common Prayer, if they took the oath of allegiance and subscribed to the doctrinal parts of the Thirty-Nine Articles. In the 1675 by-elections Dissenters began playing an active role in the Parliamentary struggle, supporting candidates thought to be sympathetic. They could not yet get to be elected themselves; of all peers and MPs in the Cavalier Parliament of 1661–79, only Lord Wharton publicly attended Dissenting worship, although a number maintained ejected ministers as their private chaplains. But Dissent was obviously going to survive, and its votes were going to count. When the Cavalier Parliament was eventually dissolved, the new House of Commons included more than twenty definite Dissenters, more than twenty close supporters; and the majority in it was commanded by the Earl of Shaftesbury. The movement he led was a definite party with a clear programme: the Whigs. Shaftesbury did not disdain help from Dissenters in his campaign to exclude the King's brother, James, from the succession to the throne as a confessed Papist. A Baptist printer, Francis Smith, was his most effective propagandist. During the struggle over 'exclusion' which ended with the dismissal of another parliament at Oxford in March 1681, Dissenters showed enough enthusiasm against James to alienate Charles permanently. They also angered the supporters of hereditary monarchy, now increasingly called 'Tories'.

The consequence was that during the period of triumph which lasted until his death, the King who had previously favoured toleration threw the Dissenters to the Anglican, Tory wolves. The renewed persecution included both the severe enforcement of the penal statutes and also some mob violence: the excitement of the 'exclusion' campaign had proved infectious. In despair an ejected Presbyterian minister and three Baptist ex-soldiers were involved in the Rye House plot to kill the King and his brother on the way back from the races in Newmarket, in 1683. Two years later many Dissenters in the south-west identified themselves with the rebellion led by the Duke of Monmouth against the new king, James II, who was at that stage still courting the Church of England; these rebels had the additional motive of despair about employment, due to the recession in the cloth trade. Both the plot and the rebellion were dismal failures, and the retribution was severe. Monmouth's defeat at the battle of Sedgemoor was followed by the 'Bloody Assize' under Judge Jeffreys, and hundreds of executions. But in March 1686 this, the severest period of the persecution of Dissent, came to an end. The King, seeing that the Church of England would never consent to the liberty he wanted for Roman Catholics, began courting the Dissenters. He issued a general pardon to those imprisoned for religious offences. Just over a year later he followed this up by his first Declaration of Indulgence, suspending both the penal laws and the Test Act.

The leading Dissenters refused to express gratitude to the King. They were well aware of the unpopularity both of James's policy to make his fellow Papists prominent in the country's government, and of his disregard of Parliament in his bid for the Protestant Dissenters' support. It needed no great political subtlety to calculate that the only assured protection for Dissent would come from the House of Commons. However, it also needed no great optimism to see that if the King's policy was to be frustrated his enemies, too, would have to bid for the Dissenters' support. The bishops, who astonished James by their petition against the reading of his second Declaration of Indulgence in church, took care to announce their 'tenderness' towards Dissent, and Lord Halifax spoke for most of the leading Anglican laity when he made handsome promises in his *Letter to a Dissenter*. From the Netherlands William made known his willingness to grant religious liberty. Plainly, a new day was coming.

In the Convention Parliament which assembled in February 1689, after James's flight to France, the leading High Anglican and High Tory statesman, the Earl of Nottingham, introduced the bill which three months later became law as the Toleration Act. Under this act Dissenters were still not allowed to enter public service; the Corporation Act and the Test Act remained on the statute book despite the new king's clumsy attempts to secure their repeal. Indeed, even the persecuting acts remained; their operation was only 'suspended' in that Dissenters could obtain licences to hold meetings for worship if they took the oaths of allegiance and left the doors unlocked, and their ministers who subscribed to the doctrinal articles (thirty-six of the thirty-nine) were exempt from the Five Mile Act. Quakers were allowed to make a declaration instead of taking an oath, but Roman Catholics were excluded from these concessions, as were Unitarians.

THE EFFECTS OF THE PERSECUTION

We do not know precisely how many Protestant Dissenters survived the great persecution with their religious loyalties intact. The general picture seems to be that many of the smaller sects which had proliferated under the Commonwealth were killed off, but that the main Dissenting denominations had kept enough members to be able to expand when the persecution ceased and public 'meeting houses' could be built. In 1676 an official census reported 108,676 Protestant Dissenters over sixteen, but the Dissenters' own counts in the 1690s showed that this was an underestimate, since the Anglicans wanted to belittle the problem. In 1715–18 a nationwide survey of Dissenting congregations was instigated by Dr John Evans on behalf of the committee of ministers of the 'three denominations' in London. At about the same time returns were made to their own central office by the Quakers. These surveys showed that in England (including Monmouthshire) there were then 638 Presbyterian, 203 Independent, 211 Particular or 'Seventh-day' Baptist, 122 General Baptist and 672 Quaker congregations. On this basis it has been calculated that those attending Dissenting places of worship then amounted to just over six per cent in the population of almost 5,500,000, nearly 180,000 of them being Presbyterians, nearly sixty thousand Independents, nearly sixty thousand Baptists and nearly forty thousand Quakers. Whether or not these figures are accurate, by 1715 Dissent was certainly a community of over a quarter of a million, mocking the Anglicans who had tried to exterminate it.[13]

The great persecution had, however, damaged Dissent in three important ways – by crippling its leadership, by narrow-

---

[13] See *Freedom after Ejection*, ed. Alexander Gordon (Manchester, 1917), and Michael Watts, *The Dissenters*, Vol. 1, pp. 267–89.

ing its appeal in society, and by destroying the Presbyterian system of synods.

Leadership was not given by martyrs of undying fame, although there were martyrs, and impressive ones. Of the Whigs who suffered after the Rye House Plot, Lord Russell, Algernon Sidney (executed because of his notes for a book he was writing) and Sir Thomas Armstrong (kidnapped back to England from Holland) had fine minds. And Abraham Annesley spoke for many when he said, before he was hanged after Monmouth's rebellion: 'As a true Englishman, I thought it my duty to venture my life in defence of the Protestant religion against Popery and arbitrary power . . . which I do not repent. For had I a thousand lives they should all have been engaged in the same cause.'[14] But such men could easily be reckoned traitors and did not make unambiguous heroes for the Dissenters to venerate. Most Dissenters would have nothing to do with rebellion.

No Dissenting minister who began his work after 1660 had the stature of Owen or Bunyan (they died in the 1680s), or Baxter or Fox (who died not long after greeting the Toleration Act). No doubt this was partly a quirk of history, but it must have been a factor that the difficulties of getting educated, encouraged, published and known were all so great. Dissent became a movement of quiet people, ministered to by steadily faithful pastors.

No Dissenter was politically prominent before John Bright, the Victorian Quaker. There were a few politicians willing to speak up loudly for Dissent, but none of them was very effective in that role in this period. The best known was the Earl of Shaftesbury, an immensely able man who had served Cromwell and Charles in his time and was always admired by his agent, the great John Locke. But Shaftesbury disliked clergymen, including Dissenting ministers, and he was called 'the greatest whoremaster in England' by Charles, an expert. His real interest came to be in limiting the powers of the monarchy. Determined to exclude James, he plunged recklessly into a

---

[14] See Iris Morley, *A Thousand Lives* (London, 1954), and Peter Earle, *Monmouth's Rebels* (London, 1977).

head-on confrontation when the predominant feeling in the country was against any risk of civil war; and he made the fatal error of backing the illegitimate and brainless Duke of Monmouth as the Protestant candidate for the throne. The reason seems to have been that Monmouth on the throne would have been under the Whigs' thumbs, whereas the more plausible candidate, James's own daughter Mary, was married to William of Orange, already a formidable ruler and to Shaftesbury an uncongenial one. This aristocrat of high ambition did not deserve the savagery of the satire heaped upon his head by John Dryden; but he also did not deserve much of the support which innocent Dissenters gave him. He gambled – and lost, dying in exile in 1683.[15]

In the House of Commons in the 1660s the totally altered position was shown when old William Prynne, who defied Laud and Cromwell alike, actually apologized for statements which were thought to encourage sedition. Later the leading Dissenter in social and political circles was William Penn, but his leadership, too, was handicapped; as we have seen, he was too involved in founding Pennsylvania and in guiding the Quakers, and then he became far too closely identified with James II. The leading MPs who represented Dissent in the 'exclusion' campaign and after were Richard and John Hampden, the son and grandson of the squire who had defied Charles I over Ship Money. The family remained very rich and could afford to pay a fine of £40,000 when the government was taking vengeance on people connected, however remotely, with the Rye House Plot. But the new John Hampden had a complex and tragic private life. During the 1680s he lost both his Christian faith and his adored wife (who died in childbirth), and was profoundly distressed; in the end his health gave way and he committed suicide, in 1696.[16]

The lack of leadership when the grand old Puritans had died off was connected with another development caused by the

[15] See K. H. D. Haley, *The First Earl of Shaftesbury* (Oxford, 1968), and J. R. Jones, *The First Whigs* (London, 1970).
[16] Douglas R. Lacey studied *Dissent and Parliamentary Politics in England, 1661–89* (New Brunswick, N.J., 1969).

persecution: the narrowing of Dissent's appeal in society. Although Puritanism had cut across the classes, that was not so true of the Dissent that emerged to enjoy toleration. There were many gentlemen still faithful to Dissent in 1700, but in the countryside the tenants or labourers of an Anglican squire often dared not offend him by forming their own chapel during the persecution, and when toleration came they did not have the energy. In the big houses or the towns everyone with social, political or intellectual ambitions was sorely tempted to forsake Dissent and many yielded to the temptation. Robert Harley, the son of a Puritan squire, would never have fulfilled his real vocation, which was to manage the House of Commons as Speaker or as Queen Anne's chief minister, if he had refused to worship with the Church of England. (Although always devious and often drunk, he seems to have remained a kind of Puritan.[17]) Bishop Joseph Butler was an example of a far more respectable man who had to abandon his parents' Presbyterian faith in order to enter his own kingdom of Oxford and philosophy. A boy who was at the same Dissenting academy as Butler, Thomas Secker, grew up to be Archbishop of Canterbury for ten years from 1758. Those left behind in Dissent were men and women whose ambitions, although still often eager, were more provincial and domestic. The backbone of Dissent came to be tradesmen in the towns, the men for whom Defoe wrote. They often prospered and the industrious thrift which they learned from parents and preachers helped mightily; but they were not going to risk spoiling good businesses.

The damage wrought by persecution also included the end of the Presbyterian system by which congregations had been linked in presbyteries and synods.

Such gatherings to discuss the problems of Church and State could not meet without arousing the fiercest wrath of the magistrates and central government; it was a time when it was officially argued that psalm-singing might conceal plotting for another civil war. Therefore they lapsed, even among those who still called themselves 'Presbyterians' – and they were not revived after 1689. The result was that the Presbyterians,

---

[17] Angus McInnes studied *Robert Harley, Puritan Politician* (London, 1970).

although they outnumbered the Independents and Baptists put together, ceased to possess their own system of church government and became virtually indistinguishable from their fellow Dissenters. The local 'meeting house' or 'chapel' was the be-all and end-all of church life – or, as it was put in the more theological terms which had been adopted by the Savoy Conference gathering representatives of more than a hundred congregations back in the still-hopeful days of autumn 1658, the Lord Jesus Christ called his followers out of the world 'to walk together in particular societies' and 'there are not instituted of Christ any stated synods in a fixed combination of churches'.[18] Of the ministers ejected from the Church of England in 1660–62, less than ten per cent are known to have accepted this Independent view of church order; yet twenty years later this view had prevailed in practice, thanks to the practical impossibility of the Presbyterian alternative. Indeed, among the Presbyterians control tended to be vested in a small group of elders or other trustees rather than in the congregation as a whole, and when the persecution was over those exercising this control tended to pride themselves on their progressiveness, success and respectability rather than on their theological orthodoxy.

The stage was now set for a theological development which would have seemed unbelievable in 1660. Presbyterian ministers were encouraged by the laymen closest to them to be progressive, and what progress meant to a minister was defined by what was taught at the best 'Dissenting Academies' where men were trained for this ministry now that the universities were closed to them. These academies often provided an education better, because wider and more modern, than the Oxford or Cambridge curriculum; it is said that some three hundred of their pupils were sufficiently distinguished to be included in the *Dictionary of National Biography*. But the academies, usually small and unstable, depended on the personalities of their staff. If the staff held unorthodox views, they could quickly and permanently influence their pupils. During

---

[18] See A. G. Matthews, *The Savoy Declaration of Faith and Order, 1658* (London, 1959).

the eighteenth century such pressures from the academies, reinforced by local trustees, inclined many, perhaps most, Presbyterian ministers towards an acceptance of current intellectual fashions, and therefore towards heresies which would have dismayed their Calvinist forefathers.[19]

THE END OF POPISH PLOTS

The third feature to be noticed in English church history 1660–90, is the end of the belief that Roman Catholics were about to impose their faith on the country by military, or at least political, action.

The end of Roman Catholicism as a political force did not mean the end of the Roman Catholic community. On the contrary, the community entered the eighteenth century as it had entered the seventeenth. On the ground it was a denomination drawing from the Mass a quiet strength which politics could neither give nor take away. Its size can be estimated with some confidence. In 1676 a census produced 11,867 names of Recusants over the age of sixteen in the Anglican province of Canterbury. In 1687 John Leyburn, the first Roman Catholic bishop to appear in the Midlands and the north for half a century, thought that he had confirmed about twenty thousand people. Although both figures were obviously rough, it seems reasonable to conclude that during the second half of the seventeenth century England included under fifty thousand Roman Catholics over sixteen. This community's priests were housed mainly in the homes of country gentlemen who had kept to the old religion, although some were in lodgings and tried to minister in towns. The papal agent,

---

[19] In *The English Presbyterians* (London, 1968), G. C. Bolam, Jeremy Goring, H. L. Short and Roger Thomas traced the evolution 'from Elizabethan Puritanism to modern Unitarianism'. Earlier studies included Olive M. Griffiths, *Religion and Learning* (Cambridge, 1935). In *English Education under the Test Acts* (London, 1931), H. J. MacLachlan studied the Dissenting academies. J. W. Ashley Smith, *The Birth of Modern Education* (London, 1954), put them in the context of the multiplication of private schools in the eighteenth century.

Agretti, estimated in 1669 that there were approximately 230 'secular' priests, 120 Jesuits, eighty Benedictine monks, fifty-five Franciscan friars and a few Dominicans and Carmelites. Other evidence suggests that this total of some five hundred clergy was about average for the period. In sum, the size of this community constituted no great threat to its fellow citizens, numbering over five millions.

Nor was there strong leadership. An old-fashioned community could be expected to look up to its aristocrats, but it so happened that at this time some leading peerages which had been identified with the old faith in the past were held by Protestants. Not a single Recusant peer or prominent gentleman of an 'old family' threw himself into supporting James II's schemes; the King had to use Anglicans, men such as Robert Spencer, Earl of Sunderland, whose conversion to the Church of Rome was manifestly political, or Irish and other strangers to London. The seventh Duke of Norfolk, who by historical precedent might have been expected to rally the old England around the old religion, announced that he was a Protestant and took himself off to Paris. Sunderland was therefore King James's closest confidant, and he was to show what he was made of by renouncing his conversion and serving King William. A compulsive gambler, he needed the money and, as has been said, 'it was a matter of indifference to him which master he cheated'.[20]

The clergy had no outstanding leader. Nominally their chief was the aristocratic Philip Howard, but he was a cardinal in Rome. Rome eventually, in January 1688, produced four bishops as 'vicars apostolic', but their powers over their four 'districts' – London, Midland, Northern and Western – were limited and none of them was of outstanding quality. The King was anxious that his favourite Jesuit, Edward Petre, should be made a bishop and a cardinal, but Innocent XI always refused. Locally the pastors were usually good priests operating in conditions which handicapped them; they could not wear cassocks in public or set up their own presbyteries. But they did

---

[20] David Ogg, *England in the Reigns of James II and William III* (Oxford, 1955), p. 193. J. P. Kenyon wrote a biography of Sunderland (London, 1958).

not include any hero of high spiritual stature. Saints such as
Henry More, who had ministered year after year among the
plague-stricken poor of London before being hanged in 1645,
were remembered but not replaced.[21]

Few laymen were in any mood for plots or aggression. What
they worried about was survival, and it was a financial worry.
Often they were on reasonably good terms with their neighbours and thus escaped the full rigour of the penal laws, but
Charles's grant of formal toleration to them in 1672 provoked
an ominous reaction. The Pope was burned in effigy on
bonfires.

The 'Popish plot' was announced in August 1678 by Titus
Oates, a disgraced naval chaplain who had fled to a Jesuit
college in Flanders and had been expelled from it. His patron
was Israel Tonge, a beneficed Anglican clergyman and a
maniac, already the author of virulent pamphlets against the
menace of Popery. It was plainly implausible to claim, as
Oates did, that the Jesuits were planning the murder of a king
who had already risked much to get his Roman Catholic
subjects tolerated. It was no more than an old wives' tale to
believe that the Jesuits would also arrange another great fire in
London. Even had their reports seemed more likely, it was not
to be expected that a jury would hang a dog, let alone the more
than thirty Englishmen who perished, on the testimony of such
self-evident rogues. But a story was told by Oates and others, of
sinister conversations overheard and treacherous correspondence which might still be intercepted. It stirred memories of
Guy Fawkes and of the Elizabethan plots, of the horrors
chronicled by John Foxe, of all the anti-papist folklore on
which the bulk of England had been half-educated. Perhaps
the Pope was after all Anti-Christ, although most English
theologians had become embarrassed by this tradition? And
the story was told at a time when the Earl of Danby was
nearing the end of five years as Lord Treasurer in an atmosphere of great suspicion. He had secured Parliamentary
finance for an army to intervene on the side of the Dutch

---

[21] Dom Basil Hemphill studied *The Early Vicars Apostolic of England, 1685–1750*
(London, 1954).

against the French; now the Dutch and the French had made peace, yet the army was still in being and at the King's disposal. What was that army for? Although Danby made much of being a defender of the Church of England, many people were prepared to believe that he was working to make Charles an absolute king on the model of Louis XIV – and that he was himself in the pay of the French. Above all, many people were alarmed by the prospect of the succession of a Papist to the throne, now that it was clear that Charles was not going to have legitimate children. In a pamphlet published in 1678, *An Account of the Growth of Popery and Arbitrary Government*, Andrew Marvell wrote: 'Popery is such a thing as cannot, but for the want of a word to express it, be called a religion; nor is it to be mentioned with that civility which is otherwise decent to be used in speaking of the differences of human opinion about divine matters.' This abuse showed how different 'Popery' seemed in London political circles from the peaceful lives of Recusant gentlemen in the countryside, who were undeniably religious and usually on terms of civility.

So the fantastic story of the 'Popish plot' got a hearing. Then the hearing became hysteria, because of two events which Oates and Tonge cannot have anticipated. Oates repeated his story on oath before a Westminster magistrate, Sir Edmund Berry Godfrey, who was friendly to Dissenters; and after a few days, in a mystery which has never been unravelled, Sir Edmund's body was found in a ditch with a sword through it. The story included allegations against a Jesuit priest, Edward Coleman, who belonged to the household of the Duke of York; and when Coleman was arrested for investigation correspondence between him and foreign Catholics, including the French king's Jesuit confessor, was seized. Coleman had discussed the dissolution of Parliament and toleration for Roman Catholics, although the Duke was not directly implicated.

It was now inevitable that Coleman should be hanged, followed by three other priests; and that everyone afraid of James, of the Jesuits or simply of Popery should join in the agitation. The Lord Chief Justice, Scroggs, made a name for himself by the brutal energy with which he hounded the alleged perpetrators of the Popish Plot. Those put to death included Lord Stafford, condemned by the House of Lords. The victims also included (in 1681) Oliver Plunkett, the saintly Roman Catholic Archbishop of Armagh, who was falsely said to have conspired to bring a French army over to Ireland. It was the judicial murder of a pastor who had always steered clear of politics.[22]

The fact that Coleman had distributed some French subsidies to Lord Shaftesbury and to other Whigs was forgotten when, contributing to the intense excitement, it became known that the Lord Treasurer had also asked for French money. That caused Danby's fall and his imprisonment in the Tower. The threat arose that he would be impeached and that under examination he would reveal Charles's own financial dealings with the French. The Cavalier Parliament was accordingly dissolved; and in the elections the Whigs were led to victory by their leader, Shaftesbury, who had already been made Lord President of the Council. James, who had been sent into exile, believed as did many others that his brother was about to abandon him as his heir – or at the very least agree that his powers as a future monarch should be strictly limited. All Roman Catholics except James were by the Second Test Act (1678) excluded from both Houses of Parliament, and for a time the whole community lived in acute fear. About four hundred gentry and their dependents were jailed for refusing to swear the oath of allegiance of which Rome still disapproved. About a hundred priests were also arrested; twenty-three died in prison and seventeen were executed.

In the end that crisis passed. The perjuries of Oates and his collaborators became too obvious to be ignored any further, and the hysteria which they had aroused spent itself. The King displayed a tactical skill and energy which were out of keeping with his previous, and subsequent, muddled indolence. But the basic fact was that Shaftesbury's Whigs had over-reached themselves in an England without any appetite for another civil war.[23]

---

[22] See Emmanuel Curtis, *Blessed Oliver Plunkett* (Dublin, 1964), and Thomas O'Fiaich, *St Oliver of Armagh* (Dublin, 1981).
[23] The best study is J. P. Kenyon, *The Popish Plot* (London, 1972).

It was realized that it would be very difficult to exclude James from the throne of Scotland, and that the Irish Catholics would probably fight in his defence. The English, too, now inclined to accept him. Led firmly by Archbishop Sancroft, the Church rallied round the principle of the divine right of the hereditary monarchy and on the whole believed James's repeated assurances that if he became king he would do no harm to the National Church. If Anglicans were anxious at the prospect of a Papist king, they reassured themselves by the thought that no child of his present wife, Mary of Modena, had survived infancy. Since 1681 she had not conceived, with the probable result that James's throne would be inherited by his daughter from his first marriage, Mary, who in 1677 was married to the Protestant champion, William of Orange – or by her sister Anne, who was even more staunchly attached to the Church of England. And to clinch the argument in favour of the hereditary principle, in the closing stages of his reign Charles found himself able to manage without recourse to Parliament since the French were willing to send adequate subsidies. He even found himself able to pay an army, always useful to deter rebellion at home.

James II therefore in 1685 inherited a position more secure than had been the lot of any previous Stuart. He often said as much – and took pride in the fact that he had thrown it all away in order to promote the Catholic religion. After the ruin of his plans and his flight into a dozen years of exile, he of course frequently asked himself why God had not granted success as a reward for his costly devotion to the true faith. Fortunately for his faith, an explanation could come pat: he had been punished for his notorious indulgence in the sins of fornication and adultery. But we must search for a fuller answer to the questions: why did the reign of James II, which began so auspiciously, develop into being the greatest and the last of the 'Popish plots' – and why did it end as disastrously as the reign of Mary I?

THE FALL OF JAMES II

James II was genuinely religious, even while unable to live chastely, but very arrogant and obstinate, sure that God had given him authority and that he had no need to concern himself much with lesser men's reactions. The one criticism he had of his father was that he had concealed his pride too often. He himself never took any trouble to do so. To the end of his days he seems to have been unaware why he was hated and feared. When seven Anglican bishops petitioned him to withdraw his Declaration of Indulgence, he was incoherently astonished at their impertinence. As they knelt before him he could only splutter: 'This is a standard of rebellion!'

Since his life would have been so much easier had he been able to satisfy his religious instincts in his father's church and place himself at the head of the Tories, historians have often asked why he became a Roman Catholic. He knew the price to be paid. On 29 January 1669 Charles and James met Lord Arundel of Wardour (a well-known Recusant) and two other courtiers, to announce their conversions to Rome and to seek advice about 'settling the Catholic religion' in England. The courtiers were sworn to secrecy, and James attempted in vain to get permission from Rome to regard himself as a Catholic while still attending the services of the Church of England. He did not cease to receive Holy Communion with the Anglicans until 1672, and he attended other Anglican services for another four years. He claimed that he incurred these sacrifices because he had been persuaded of the truth of Catholicism by reading Richard Hooker, but the rest of his life would not support any picture of him as a calm and scholarly theologian. He never wrote down any personal apologia, and was mentally incapable of doing so; but it is possible to reconstruct his psychology. As a proud soldier-prince James believed in religious authority; as a lustful sinner he needed it, to be sure that his sins could be forgiven. He knew that the Roman Catholic Church claimed a religious authority, and a power to forgive sins, far more imposing than the Church of England's. While he was king he caused scandal by kneeling before an archbishop on a mission from the Pope. If we ask why he did not allow his conversion to transform his sex life, we have to understand that for Catholic princes in that age a deathbed change was usually reckoned adequate. And if we ask why he paid no attention to the pleas for caution which came from his co-religionists, including the Pope, the answer seems to be that he was sure that he understood England. He was confident that, once Catholics were free to worship, to preach and to teach in public, and once those who listened could see that they would not be penalized for following their consciences, the converts would come in a flood. He brushed aside warnings because he was a great prince (he had defied the Pope by marrying Mary of Modena before the Vatican had approved the arrangements) – and because he was himself a convert (as his first wife, Clarendon's daughter Anne Hyde, had been). To his simple mind the spiritual authority of the Roman Catholic Church was a fact bigger than any pope's claim to advise princes about sex or politics; and it had only to be displayed in order to be believed.

On the basis of this psychology, the pattern of James's reign makes sense. His first aim was to persuade the Tory majority dominating the House of Commons to tolerate Roman Catholics. To him, it seemed not an impossible aim; after all, they were Royalists – and they were tolerating as their king one who openly attended Mass and who refused to include an Anglican communion in his coronation. When the Anglican Tories drew back, he changed his tactics completely. He allied himself instead with the Dissenters whom he had previously despised as 'republicans' (his worst term of abuse). He issued a Declaration of Indulgence on his own authority, suspending all restrictions on worship and all tests for office-holding. He thought it his duty to install teachers of the true faith in positions of influence; hence his determination to see Roman Catholics appointed as Dean of Christ Church and as President of Magdalen College at Oxford.

As opposition to this policy hardened, so his insistence on his authority hardened all the more. The moves which he took showed how much authority the Crown still possessed. Personally or through agents James brought pressure on his ministers to accept his religion; on MPs to support his programme; on electors to vote for loyal MPs and city councils. He dismissed his brother-in-law, Rochester, from his post as Lord Treasurer when he refused to be converted. Through the revived Ecclesiastical Commission under Judge Jeffreys he secured the suspension from office of the Bishop of London, who had refused to suspend a 'No Popery' preacher. He appointed fellow Catholics in considerable numbers to be Lord Lieutenants in the counties, justices of the peace and officers in the army. He placed Ireland under another Roman Catholic, the Earl of Tyrconnel. But he remained impervious to the popular clamour about 'Popery and arbitrary government', and it seems highly likely that one reason why he had this contempt for the clamour was that he knew that it was not his intention either to overthrow the Church of England or to abolish Parliament. He expected Anglicans soon to accept his right to govern according to his conscience and what he kept on calling 'the ancient constitution'. Surely their Tory Royalism would reassert itself? Eventually they would, he believed, accept their own moral obligation to be reconciled to the Catholic Church. He was certainly not the lackey of the French king, who offered him no help against either the Duke of Monmouth or William of Orange. Nor was he the lackey of the Pope, who at this stage was interested chiefly in his quarrel with the French king. It was very unfortunate for James that in 1685 Louis XIV began a successful police action to drive all the Protestants (the Huguenots) out of France, but there is no evidence that a similar intolerance was intended for England.

In September 1688 James began to retrace some of his steps in an effort to win back the support of the Anglican Tories. He was alarmed by the popular enthusiasm over the acquittal of the seven bishops who had petitioned him against the Declaration of Indulgence. They had been organized by Turner of Ely but had included Sancroft of Canterbury, the very embodiment of moderate Tory Royalism; and he had very foolishly put them in the Tower amid popular acclaim and had then brought them to a trial involving a jury – which had acquitted them.[24] But above all he was alarmed by evidence that Tories

---

[24] G. V. Bennett threw fresh light on this crucial incident in *Religious Motivation*, ed. Derek Baker (Oxford, 1978), pp. 267–87.

as well as Whigs had invited William of Orange to 'mediate' between him and the nation – and William was responding from the strength of his virtual kingship in the Netherlands.

With the advantage of hindsight we can think James idiotic because he had not forseen the power of the opposition to his policy, but a Stuart king was not a fool to discount the possibility of a rebellion under Anglican and Tory auspices. 'Rebellion is as the sin of witchcraft' (1 Samuel 15:23) was a favourite text with Anglican preachers; and in the battle which destroyed Monmouth's sad little rebellion, the Bishop of Winchester, Peter Mews, directed the royal artillery. Had there been more willingness to rebel effectively, there would still not have been the ability. It needs to be remembered that 'after 1680 England seemed to be moving inexorably towards absolutism and only the events of 1688 led to a change of direction, perhaps at the last possible moment . . . Opposition to the monarchy had been so completely crushed by 1688 that the English and Scots were no longer able, as they had been forty years before, to overthrow the king without foreign aid. A foreign prince with an army had to be called in.'[25]

We should also remember how unlikely it seemed that the very shrewd William would involve himself in such a risky rebellion. He was married to the English king's daughter, who always insisted that no harm should come to her father; and he had a major European war on his hands, so that he was unlikely to divert troops to a civil war in England. He had, indeed, given James vital military assistance against Monmouth. He knew that James controlled a strong fleet.

What altered the whole situation was once again the unexpected. On 10 June 1688 Mary of Modena gave birth to a son, and not even the baseless rumour that the lad had been smuggled into the royal bedchamber in a warming pan – the rumour that was the pretext of William's intervention – could undo the devastating political consequences. It now seemed certain that James's legitimate heir would be brought up a Roman Catholic, and very possible that in due course England would be allied with France against the alliance built up by

---

[25] J. R. Western, *Monarchy and Revolution* (London, 1972), p. 3.

William as his life's mission. The Anglican Tories had a new reason to feel desperate and William had a new reason to gamble.

The other unexpected event was that James vacated the throne. William (evading the English navy by luck or a 'Protestant wind') landed in Devon on an encouraging date for Protestants, 5 November. He received into his army many officers and gentlemen on whose loyalty James had been counting (such as John Churchill, the future Duke of Marlborough), and was even joined by the king's second daughter, Anne. And the King's nerve cracked. After that it did not matter that he had forty thousand troops while William had landed with twelve thousand. He did not stay to fight it out, as his father had done, or to argue it out, as his brother had done. He did not know how to deal with a large-scale rebellion which he had thought inconceivable. His dominant concern was, it seems, to save himself, his wife and his son from his father's fate. He fled to France – which was just what his enemies wanted, as was demonstrated when he was intercepted by fishermen and sent back to England, only to be allowed to escape again. His flight could be interpreted as an abdication; some of those with a conscience about the rights of his son could be persuaded by the tale that the infant was not his son; and those who felt that the succession ought in these circumstances to pass to Mary could be assured that as a dutiful wife Mary accepted her husband's refusal to be a mere consort. Events which could never have been anticipated led to the offer of the vacant throne by the Convention Parliament to William and Mary jointly – and to the Parliamentary provision, still unrepealed in the 1980s, that no monarch of England could be a Roman Catholic.

James reached a French port on Christmas Day 1688 and found much more happiness in exile than he or anyone else expected. His wife Mary, who previously had been forced to tolerate his attachment to his two Anglican mistresses, Arabella Churchill and Catherine Sedley, now became the dominant partner in the marriage. His sexual energies were exhausted as he grew older, while his appetite for devout practices proved insatiable. Just before he died in 1701, he said to his tearful wife: 'Consider, Madam, I am going to be happy for ever.'

What had he achieved in England for the Church in whose supposed interests he had lost his throne? It is tempting to answer: nothing. But it is better to agree with a modern historian that 'in the long run the reign perhaps did the Catholics some good. It added yet another episode to the anti-Catholic tradition but it killed, at last, the myth that there were innumerable secret Papists waiting to declare themselves. The Catholics had emerged to be counted and had been seen to be few. Their association with Jacobitism made them seem dangerous for some time more, but gradually the active animus against them died away'.[26]

ANGLICANS AS DISSENTERS

The Anglican 'nonjurors' refused to swear allegiance to William and Mary, and their story forms a touching epilogue to the story of 1660–90. In an age full of cynicism their integrity led them to renounce positions, homes and incomes rather than accept Parliament's right to dethrone James – although some of them had been foremost in the opposition to his politics. Of the seven bishops who had enraged James by their famous petition, five remained loyal to their oath to him: Sancroft of Canterbury, Ken of Bath and Wells, Lake of Chichester, Turner of Ely and White of Peterborough. Bishops Frampton of Gloucester, Lloyd of Norwich and Thomas of Worcester were also nonjurors. Bishop Cartwright of Chester had collaborated with James and now went into exile with him.

The size of this group of bishops remaining loyal to their king can be explained by the fact that almost all of them had been appointed in the 1680s specifically because they were known to

---

[26] John Miller, *Popery and Politics in England, 1660–88* (Cambridge, 1973), p. 268. Dr Miller has also written *James II: A Study in Kingship* (London, 1978), a more sympathetic portrait than F. C. Turner's *James II* (London, 1948). This was the first biography to use the exiled king's devotional papers.

be loyal; Turner, for example, had been a chaplain to James as Duke of York, then Dean of Windsor at the height of the Tory triumph under Charles. But it is still impressive that they did not desert James. Even more impressive is the fact that about four hundred clergymen in the parishes followed their example, being extolled by John Dryden:

> He join'd not in their choice; because he knew
> Worse might, and often did, from change ensue.
> Much to himself he thought; but little spoke:
> And, undepriv'd, his benefice forsook.

And distinguished clergymen who accepted William and Mary refused to fill the officially vacant sees. William Beveridge, exemplary as a parish priest and as a scholar, was unwilling to go to Bath and Wells, and John Scott the devotional writer refused Chichester. John Sharp, the Dean of Norwich who was to emerge as Archbishop of York and Queen Anne's ecclesiastical adviser, refused to take over the bishopric of Norwich from a friend. Robert South, the leading preacher of a conservative Anglicanism (who made congregations laugh), and William Wake, the future Archbishop of Canterbury then aged thirty-three, were others who refused promotion in these circumstances. No episode in the history of the Church of England does it more credit.

   Although most of the nonjurors would probably have supported Sancroft's proposal to acknowledge William as regent, they would not take oaths which to them would have meant renouncing the doctrine of non-resistance to the legitimate ruler. They recalled that Christ had not resisted Pilate. That was the 'doctrine of the cross' proclaimed in Thomas Ken's will: 'I die in the Holy, Catholic and Apostolic Faith, professed by the whole Church, before the disunion of East and West; more particularly I die in the communion of the Church of England, as it stands distinguished from all Papal and Puritan innovations and as it adheres to the doctrine of the cross.' In contrast with this heroic consistency the Anglicans who accepted the new regime were bound to seem morally inferior. Of the two men who succeeded Sancroft at Canterbury, Tillotson had impressed the doctrine of non-resistance on Lord

Russell before his execution under Charles II, and Tenison had repeated precisely the same standard Anglican teaching to Monmouth before his execution under James II. William Sherlock, who succeeded Tillotson as Dean of St Paul's, had ably upheld the divine right of kings in *The Case of Resistance* (1684) – and now had to publish an equally able defence of the Revolution in *The Case of Allegiance* (1691). When a wit saw him handing Mrs Sherlock into a carriage, he declared that the Dean now had his reasons for conforming to the new government at his finger tips.

But as time went on, the nonjurors had to face their own two moral dilemmas: should a schism be perpetuated in order to preserve the sacredness of the principle that the monarchy must be strictly hereditary, and was that principle really sacred in the circumstances of the eighteenth century?

Sancroft died in 1693. He had gone back to die in the Suffolk village where he had been born, refusing to worship in his parish church because William and Mary would be named there and urging a similar constancy on others. The old man was, although shattered by his recent experiences, venerated (as Swift's *Ode to Sancroft* shows). The more forceful Bishop Lloyd, to whom he had transferred the leadership, now decided to make sure that other bishops would carry on the true Church of England. George Hickes and Thomas Wagstaffe were accordingly consecrated. The legal problems were solved – at least in the eyes of those involved in this secret ceremony – by making them suffragan bishops. They took their titles from Thetford and Ipswich, in Lloyd's own diocese of Norwich, and as authority they quoted the disused statute of 1534. They also secured the consent of the exiled James. With his usual tact, James announced that he had obtained the Pope's permission.

Wagstaffe never functioned as a bishop; although he attended the dying Sancroft as a priest, he seems to have preferred to make himself useful as a medical doctor. But Hickes, the former Dean of Worcester, was a prodigiously learned scholar (his specialisms included Anglo-Saxon literature), a prolific and formidable writer of theology, and a determined 'primus' of the faithful remnant up to his death in 1715. Before dying he arranged for two Scottish bishops to join with him in consecrating Jeremy Collier and two others. Collier, who was already conspicuous for his writing against the immorality of the London stage and for his Jacobite sympathies, became an active leader in his turn, drawing up a 'Communion Office' richer than the Prayer Book of 1662 and negotiating for reunion with Eastern Orthodox bishops on the basis of a common faith and sacramentalism. His many publications included a large *Ecclesiastical History of Great Britain*. His liturgical revision has been valued by those Anglicans who have shared his own high regard for the usages which he restored (praying for the departed; mixing water with the wine in the chalice; asking for the Holy Spirit to descend on the bread and wine; offering the bread and wine as a sacrifice or 'oblation'; anointing the sick). Nor was his death in 1726 the end of the story. One nonjuring bishop consecrated another (with or without the two co-consecrators required by canon law), and the succession lasted until Charles Booth, who earned his living as a watch and clock maker and ministered to a congregation of about thirty in his own house in Manchester, died in 1805.

The trouble about this whole tradition was that it was either illegal or, at the best, remote from the mainstream of English life in the eighteenth century. In the next century the Whig historian, Macaulay, was to declare that the nonjurors suffered 'for the sake of a superstition as stupid and degrading as the Egyptian worship of cats and onions'. Undeniably there was something odd about a tradition which had ended up as this small underground movement but which had begun when some bishops had taken their stand on the precise letter of the law. The petition which they had presented to the enraged king on 18 May 1688 had made one point only: 'that Declaration is founded upon such a dispensing power, as hath often been declared illegal in Parliament, and particularly in the years 1662 and 1672.' When summoned on 8 June after the publication of this document (publication had never been intended when it had been signed), Sancroft had declined to tell the Privy Council whether or not the handwriting was his, on the legal ground that he should not be forced to incriminate himself. The seven bishops had been sent to the Tower solely because as peers they declined to offer bail or 'recognizances' to appear in court, and when they had appeared on 29 June their counsel had entered into intricate legal arguments before the jury acquitted them of seditious libel. Yet the very bishops who had then appealed to the letter of the law had now founded a movement which could be described as treasonable.

The nonjurors' reply was that the law still favoured James II and his heirs. But it was an uncertain reply. Before James fled the country he had done his utmost to create a legal vacuum, for example by dropping the Great Seal of England into the Thames; his had not been the conduct of a monarch who upheld the law. Such was the background to the resolution adopted by a majority of 62–47 in the Convention Parliament that the King, 'having withdrawn himself out of the kingdom, had abdicated the government, and that the throne had thereby become vacant'. King William was content to leave it at that so far as the bishops were concerned, exempting them from new oath-taking unless some fresh emergency should arise. His proposal to this effect was defeated in Parliament, but even then Bishop Ken is said to have assured a friend: 'I question not but that you and several others have taken the oaths with as good a conscience as I myself shall refuse them.'

What counted decisively with the average member of the Church of England was that providence seemed to be Williamite, for events or non-events gradually invited even the devout to accept the doom of Jacobite hopes. The perpetuation of the nonjurors' schism now seemed futile, and the biggest men among them gradually acknowledged this.[27]

Bishop Ken, for example, although personally fairly content to retire to read and write as a guest in splendid Longleat House for twenty years, was always conscious of the reality with which pastors had to deal. He avoided controversy as much as possible. He even refrained from publishing most of the literary output of his prolonged retirement, although morning and evening hymns which became famous were issued in

---

[27] Gerald Straka studied *The Anglican Reaction to the Revolution of 1688* (Madison, Wisc., 1962) and edited *The Revolution of 1688 and the Birth of the English Political Nation* (Lexington, Mass., 1963).

1700 for the use of the boys of his beloved Winchester, where he had been a scholar in the college and a prebendary in the cathedral. In 1703 Queen Anne readily agreed to a reconciliation with nonjurors. One part of the plan was that Ken should be invited to resume work as Bishop of Bath and Wells. He declared himself too old, but when his friend George Hooper was appointed he surrendered his claim to the diocese and accepted a royal pension. His heart was always with those who in the parishes of the Church of England would adhere to the pastoral ideal which he had always himself obeyed. In the midst of his long poem in praise of St Edmund, the king who long ago had been martyred by the invading Danes, came these lines, unconsciously his own self-portrait:

> Give me the priest these graces shall possess;
> Of an ambassador the just address,
> A father's tenderness, a shepherd's care,
> A leader's courage, which the cross can bear,
> A ruler's arm, a watchman's wakeful eye,
> A pilot's skill the helm in storms to ply,
> A fisher's patience and a lab'rer's toil,
> A guide's dexterity to disembroil,
> A prophet's inspiration from above,
> A teacher's knowledge, and a saviour's love.
> Give me the priest, a light upon the hill,
> Whose rays his whole circumference can fill;
> In God's own word and sacred learning vers'd,
> Deep in the study of the heart immers'd . . . [28]

With motives roughly similar to Ken's, the two leading laymen among the nonjurors conformed to the Church of England. One of these was Henry Dodwell, a learned theologian; he had remained a layman because, intending to write in praise of priests and bishops, he had thought it best not to lay himself open to the charge of self-seeking. In his *Epistolary Discourse* of 1706 he went so far in the praise of bishops as to attempt to prove, in the words of his subtitle, 'that the soul is a principle naturally mortal but immortalized actually for the pleasure of

---

[28] See Hugh A. L. Rice, *Thomas Ken* (London, 1958).

God. Wherein is proved, that none have the power of giving this divine immortalizing spirit, since the apostles, but only the bishops.' Like other nonjurors (and many conforming Anglicans), Dodwell denied the validity of baptism administered by Dissenters, but in this little book of 1706 he maintained two points yet more extreme: that those who rejected confirmation by a bishop sinned against the Holy Spirit and were damned eternally, and that baptism, even when administered by a priest, was only preliminary and 'purgative' – 'beneath the dignity of an apostle to perform in person'. Now Dodwell, without acknowledging that he had ever been in schism himself, seems to have allowed an element of Church of England commonsense to enter his mind. At about the same time, Robert Nelson, a rich philanthropist, identified himself with the Established Church and was now able to be a very generous supporter and encourager of all kinds of charitable and missionary work. He was universally respected.

Towards the end of Queen Anne's reign it seemed possible that she and enough other leading figures might recognize James II's son James (usually known as 'the Old Pretender') as her heir, rather than the remote and unattractive Hanoverians. In practical terms, however, his restoration to his father's throne depended on the Old Pretender becoming an Anglican, and in 1714 he made the great refusal. After that, however unpopular the Hanoverians might be, the turning-point had been passed. The Protestant monarchy was secure and the nonjurors who refused to recognize it were living in nostalgia. The Jacobite cause became an obviously spent force after the failure of the rebellion of 1745, and 'Bonnie Prince Charlie' seemed to be acknowledging one major cause of the fiasco when in 1750, during a secret visit to London, he was received into the Church of England. But soon it was clear that the fortunes of the house of Stuart had become inseparable from those of the Church of Rome. 'James III' was buried in St Peter's, Rome, in 1766. As 'Charles III' the Young Pretender went to live in Rome and accepted its faith again, together with the consolations of the bottle. When he died in 1788 he left his English claims to his brother, Henry, a splendid and sober man. 'Henry IX' kept up all the pretence of being a king but he

had been a cardinal since 1747 and when the French revolutionaries deprived him of his large income he was gracious
enough to accept a pension from George III. George IV
contributed to the cost of the monument to this last of the royal
Stuarts. It was erected in St Peter's, Rome, when Henry was
buried there in 1807.

Acknowledging reality, the Papacy had in effect recognized
George III, and with him the Protestant succession in
England, in 1765. By the 1790s even the Anglican bishops in
Scotland, who had been nonjurors to a man, had abandoned
the Jacobite cause. The few Englishmen who remained nonjurors were locked more and more into a private world. It was a
little world distinguished by some fine historical scholarship
(for example, by the learning of the Oxford scholar Thomas
Hearne, who was willing to be excluded from the Bodleian
Library rather than compromise his conscience). But the
nonjurors were also divided into factions accusing each other of
theological error now that it was possible to revise the Prayer
Book for their own use – as was done in 1718. The dispute led to
a schism between the 'Regulars' who clung to the Book of
Common Prayer, and the 'Usagers' who welcomed a richer
liturgical diet. And no extensive pastoral work could be
attempted.[29]

However, one of the nonjurors was William Law, whose
books, widely admired as elegant English prose, were also
valued as a reminder of the highest standards of Christian
holiness. He abandoned a Cambridge career because his
conscience forbade him to swear allegiance to George I. His
conscience always was active, perhaps over-active. While an
undergraduate he declared that 'no condition of this life is for
enjoyment, but for trial'. One of his books was on the 'absolute
unlawfulness' of the theatre, and when a gift from an admirer
enabled him to set up a semi-monastic establishment in his

---

[29] See L. M. Hawkins, *Allegiance in Church and State* (London, 1928); J. W. C.
Wand, *The High Church Schism* (London, 1951); Sir Charles Petrie, *The Jacobite
Movement* (London, 1959). More detail is in J. H. Overton, *The Nonjurors* (London,
1902), and Henry Broxap, *The Later Nonjurors* (Cambridge, 1924). There is material
about Hickes, Collier and Hearne in David C. Douglas, *English Scholars 1660–1730*
(revised, London, 1951).

native village (King's Cliffe in Northamptonshire) he annoyed
his neighbours by giving money without discrimination to all
beggars who presented themselves, deserving or undeserving.
Although he refused to become a bishop he did consent to be
ordained as a priest by the nonjurors (after a long delay) – and
there was always in his life something of the nonjuror's lack of
contact with the everyday world, even before his last phase
when he had been deeply influenced by the German mystic
Jacob Boehme. But he championed Christian orthodoxy
against the most heretical of the Whig bishops, Hoadly; he
championed God's love against the Calvinists ('God is love,
yea all love, and so all love that nothing but love can come from
him'); he wrote on *Christian Perfection* with a faith which stirred
John Wesley; and his *Serious Call to a Devout and Holy Life* (1728)
became a classic. Samuel Johnson reckoned it 'the finest piece
of hortatory theology in any language'. The book was written
in the Putney home of the Gibbons, to whom Law was acting as
a tutor. The great historian and sceptic Edward Gibbon, who
as a little boy had this contact with a saint, paid a guarded
tribute: 'the philosopher must allow that he exposes, with
equal severity and truth, the strange contradiction between the
faith and practice of the Christian world.'

Because Law did not wish to arouse controversy by presenting any of the specific doctrines of the nonjurors, he did not
include any substantial discussion of public worship in his
Serious Call. Its concern was with how an Englishman should
live when he got home from church. The omission might
suggest that Law was indifferent to the Anglican forms of piety,
but he made a point of attending every service in his parish
church. He even insisted that the girls in the school which he
ran should attend every funeral.[30]

Law's dislike of controversy was not unique at the end of the
thirty years of crisis, 1660–90. Through much suffering, those
years had drained away the poison of intolerance from many
parts of English religion.

---

[30] See A. W. Hopkinson, *About William Law* (London, 1948), and A. K. Walker,
William Law: His Life and Thought (London, 1973).

CHAPTER THIRTEEN

QUIETER CHURCHES

A FAILURE OF COMPREHENSION

The nonjurors were not alone in refusing to accept that the 'glorious revolution' had established a Protestant throne with an Anglican monopoly of political life but with toleration for Protestant Dissenters. There were both Presbyterian and High Anglican attempts to challenge the balanced decision.

In the crisis of 1688–89, at first it seemed likely that the Presbyterians would be able to insist on large changes in the Church of England before joining it. In Scotland the Established Church now finally threw out its bishops along with King James. The change, already probable in view of the rooted objection of the Scots to 'prelacy', was made inevitable when all but one of the bishops refused to accept King William. A Jacobite rising came to nothing and when Scotland was politically united with England in the next reign the Presbyterian character of the Church of Scotland was written into the treaty. In Ireland, too, Presbyterians gained from the defeat of James and his army. After the decisive battle of the Boyne in 1690, a Protestant ascendancy was imposed on the Catholic five-sixths of the population and it was not unreasonable to hope that this would be to the advantage of the Presbyterians. In England many wished to include the 'comprehension' of moderate Presbyterians in the Church of England. William of Orange, as he made his way to London and to the throne, showed that he expected it. He was himself a convinced Calvinist, who back in Holland had scandalized English visitors such as Thomas Ken by snubbing Anglican chaplains and never receiving communion with his Anglican wife, Mary. Mary had continued to live like a nun (that was her own phrase), but in every matter apart from her personal religion she obeyed her husband, as her religion taught her. In England William encouraged Dissenting ministers to be eloquent about the unity of the Reformed Churches, and himself addressed the Lords with this theme. To the alarmed clergy of the Church of England he often seemed to be as indifferent to their convictions as James II had been – and as late as 1775 Dr Johnson echoed the high Anglicans' prejudice when he called William 'one of the most worthless scoundrels that ever existed'.

Not only King William, who might be regarded as a latter-day conqueror of England, favoured the 'comprehension' of the moderate Presbyterians. So did William Sancroft while still functioning as Archbishop of Canterbury, together with other leading churchmen, including his two successors at Canterbury. In October 1689 a commission met to work out details such as the 'conditional' ordination of Presbyterian ministers to satisfy the bishops without claiming that Presbyterian ordination necessarily was invalid. A copy of the Book of Common Prayer survives, annotated with changes for which there would probably be agreement. At the very least, Dissenters would surely be welcome to sit in Parliament and on the towns' councils.

In the end nothing happened. The Prayer Book was not revised; the Test and Corporation Acts were not repealed; Dissent, although tolerated, was excluded as firmly from church life as it was from national and local politics. One reason was that William's speech from the throne in March 1689, about the need to admit 'all Protestants' to public offices, suggested alarmingly that many places would have to be found for other Dutchmen, whose presence in England was to be resented throughout the reign. Both Lords and Commons rejected the proposal by overwhelming majorities.

The main reason for the scheme's failure was, however, conservatism in the Church of England, voiced loudly by Bishop Compton and echoed in Parliament. Typical churchmen were in no mood to abandon their privileges, especially when they heard that some of the few clergy who supported their bishops in Scotland had been lynched or 'rabbled'. Many English parish priests were frightened that the whole Restoration settlement was about to be overthrown by another Cromwell, and many MPs prided themselves on being loyal sons of the National Church. Daniel Finch, Earl of Nottingham, made it his business to persuade William of the necessity of yielding to this Anglican conservatism if he was to have a quiet kingdom supplying money for his war against Louis XIV; and William gradually was persuaded.

His own psychology was a factor. The wishes of his wife, nominally the joint occupant of the throne until her death in 1694, do not seem to have been decisive. She remained a devout Anglican, inwardly distressed and driven to prayer by the curses of her father, James II. Mary, however, kept her distress to herself; in public she was simply the devoted wife. William – a cold man, asthmatic and it seems homosexual – never warmed to her when alive, although after her death he became devoted, and the couple's inability to have children had been established long before 1688. Essentially William had married not a wife but a cause. He was driven by the conviction that he had been predestined to save the Dutch nation from the French. He had no deep interest in England apart from the difference it could make to the nine years' war which he now conducted. His immediate problem was to hold the nation together through the military crisis of 1690. This was a serious crisis; on the day before the battle of the Boyne the Anglo-Dutch fleet was defeated off Beachy Head, and had the French army been prepared to cross the Channel it would have met with no effective resistance. Thus preoccupied, William had no energy left for English ecclesiastical problems. He permitted the Church of England to retain its exclusive privileges – just as in Ireland he permitted a system by which the well-to-do Presbyterians, no less than the miserably poor Catholics, paid tithes to the Anglican clergy, were excluded from sitting in Parliament, and until 1719 could not hold civil or military office under the Crown.[1]

---

[1] S. B. Baxter, *William III* (London, 1966), has been supplemented by Henry Harwitz, *Parliament, Policy and Politics in the Reign of William III* (Manchester, 1977). Pending the publication of his fuller study, the best guidance to the ecclesiastical history of the reign is provided by two articles by G. V. Bennett in *Essays in Modern English Church History*, ed. G. V. Bennett and J. D. Walsh (London, 1966), pp. 104–31, and *Britain after the Glorious Revolution*, ed. Geoffrey Holmes (London, 1969), pp. 155–76.

When John Tillotson became Archbishop of Canterbury in 1690 the idea of including Presbyterians in the Church over which he would be Primate was dead. And neither he nor Thomas Tenison, who followed him in 1694, was an ecclesiastical statesman. Tillotson was a preacher of everyday morality (and the first married man to occupy Lambeth Palace since Matthew Parker). Tenison was a pastor. From 1680 to 1692 he had made an admirable vicar in the crowded London parish of St Martin-in-the-Fields. A penitent Nell Gwynne had been among his grateful parishioners.[2]

A TORY FAILURE

It was now the turn of the Tories, who included the majority of the clergy, to attempt to overturn the settlement of 1688–89 by ending the toleration of Dissent.[3] To the resentment of the clergy at this toleration could now be added the resentment of the squires at the taxation of land to pay for a Dutch king's war and at the rise of 'monied' (rather than landed) men around the Bank of England as part of the stupendous effort needed to borrow money for the war on top of the taxes. Many signs pointed to a Tory reaction. One of them was the market for Clarendon's *History of the Rebellion*, brought out in the 1700s by the dead author's son, the Earl of Rochester, an active Tory politician.

At an earlier stage the Tories' natural leader would have been Henry Compton, but he was old and his disappointment at not being made Archbishop of Canterbury had bitten deep into his soul. He continued to make himself a nuisance to Archbishop Tenison when he could, but he concentrated on his work as Bishop of London and on the garden at Fulham Palace, where he collected plants from the colonies. He died in 1713, aged eighty-one. Another leading High Churchman was John Sharp, who consented to become Archbishop of York in

---

[2] See Edward Carpenter, *Thomas Tenison* (London, 1948).
[3] George Every studied *The High Church Party, 1688–1718* (London, 1956).

1694 and who under Queen Anne, when Tenison was pushed out into the cold, exercised many of the functions of an Archbishop of Canterbury. 'I hope we shall one day agree,' wrote the ever-mild Tenison to Sharp.[4]

The most highly placed leader of the High Anglicans was, however, Queen Anne herself, who had been Henry Compton's pupil. She was not a very intelligent woman, and was married to an even less intelligent man, Prince George of Denmark. From 1683 to 1700 she was pregnant every year. She had twelve miscarriages; of her six children, one was still-born and the other five died at an early age. She was sure that it was God's punishment for the treachery towards the legitimate king, although illogically she was not prepared to renounce her claim to the throne (in the fifteenth century Henry IV's attitude had been identical). When she became queen in 1702 she set herself to obliterate William's memory. She had thought it her right to succeed to the throne on her unhappy sister Mary's death. Now she would be an 'entirely English' queen, by which she meant an Anglican and a Tory sovereign. 'My own principles must always keep me entirely firm to the interests and religion of the Church of England, and will incline me to countenance those who have the truest zeal to support it.' So she said on her accession; and it was her practice. She renounced some of the taxes of the clergy ('annates' and 'tenths') which Henry VIII had secured for the Crown, and with the proceeds established Queen Anne's Bounty for the benefit of the poorer clergy. From that acorn planted in 1704 the wealth of the Church Commissioners would one day grow.[5]

The ablest spokesman of the extreme Tory attitude to the Church – so able and so extreme that he alarmed Queen Anne – was Francis Atterbury. He was also perhaps the most gifted English churchman of his generation, and one who had the additional strength of knowing that most of the parish clergy idolized him. His mind was formed by Oxford in the 1680s, the

---

[4] See A. Tindal Hart, *The Life and Times of John Sharp* (London, 1949).

[5] There are biographies of *Queen Anne* by David Green and by David Gregg (both London, 1980). See also Alan Savidge, *The Foundation and Early Years of Queen Anne's Bounty* (London, 1955).

Oxford which publicly burned the works of Thomas Hobbes and the Presbyterians' Solemn League and Covenant; the Oxford which resisted King James's attacks on the Anglican monopoly but which was very hesitant about King William and his broad-minded bishops.

Moving to London at Bishop Compton's invitation, Atterbury saw his chance: he would be a propagandist on behalf of the clergy as they were represented in the Convocation of Canterbury. That may not sound like an exciting role for a clergyman as ambitious as he was eloquent. The Convocation of Canterbury was revived in 1701 because King William had had to accept this as one of the policies of a Tory ministry, and it continued its stormy life under Anne. It usually met in Westminster Abbey. The bishops sat around the fire in the Jerusalem Chamber and the clergy in the cold chapel of Henry VII; and it was the theory of the bishops that the clergy were there to assist them when occasionally summoned into the warmth in order to answer questions. It was also the theory of the government that the meeting should confine itself strictly to the business for which the Crown had granted its licence. The reality in ecclesiastic politics was, however, that the bishops appointed by King William's government were alienated from the clergy. The quick-witted Atterbury saw that the bishops could be blamed for everything – for the withdrawal of parishioners to worship with the Dissenters, for the spread of immorality and heresy, even for the taxes. He saw, too, that it was possible to compare the House of Clergy with the House of Commons. In the 1680s the Commons had secured a settlement which prevented a king from governing without laws and taxes voted by Parliament; now in the 1700s the clergy could clip the wings of the bishops.

The higher and lower clergymen who met at the two ends of Westminster Abbey were as rude to each other as they dared to be. There was also a battle of pamphlets and books. Atterbury's writing (started by his *Letter to a Convocation Man* in 1697) was brilliantly controversial but not based on solid research into the history of the government of the Church of England. It was answered by salvoes from three big guns. Edmund Gibson, who had gone from the Lake District to become a poor but prodigiously learned scholar at Oxford, was Archbishop Tenison's librarian at Lambeth Palace and he defended his master against Atterbury, producing what became the standard account of the Convocation's procedures. Some laborious years later – years from which his health never recovered – he published the standard work on English canon law. William Wake, another Oxford scholar who was then rector of St James's, Piccadilly, accompanied Gibson's really unanswerable contributions by a magisterial history of the Convocations and other synods in England. White Kennett, almost their equal in learning and like Wake then a London parish priest, issued another reply to Atterbury, more readable because shorter.

In academic terms, therefore, victory went to those who defended the bishops. Wake and Gibson went on to the highest positions in the Church. Kennett, although not so well rewarded, became a hard-working Bishop of Peterborough and an influential writer; his influence so annoyed the Tories that in 1714 an altarpiece portraying him as Judas at the Last Supper was set up in church by the rector of Whitechapel in London.[6] Atterbury, in contrast, when he became a dean had to accept distant Carlisle. When at last he obtained a bishopric from the Tories in 1713, he got nothing better than poor Rochester, to which the Westminster Deanery was annexed.

The political question was, however, whether Tory policies which commanded the support of the Queen and the majority in the House of Commons could prevail. Could they be forced through the House of Lords, where the bishops' votes were often decisive? Three bills passed the Commons, to prohibit Dissenters from returning to their own meeting houses after receiving the Anglican sacrament in order to qualify for office ('occasional conformity'), but were thrown out by the Lords. Then from 1705 Whigs with little sympathy with the clergy took over the government; their chief interest lay in the Union Treaty with Scotland (which came into effect in 1707) and in supporting the armies led in the European war by the Duke of Marlborough. The Tories, who cared little for Scotland or the Continent, accordingly set up the cry: 'The Church in danger!'

---

[6] See G. V. Bennett, *White Kennett* (London, 1957).

This cry was worked into a very widely sold sermon, originally preached before the Lord Mayor of London in St Paul's in 1709 by Henry Sacheverell, a Fellow of Magdalen College, Oxford. The sermon was so full of half-concealed insults to the bishops and the Whig ministers ('false brethren') that when the preacher went on to deny that a subject had any right to resist a monarch, thus in effect denying the validity of the removal of James II, the government seized the opportunity to impeach him before the House of Lords for sedition. But Tory-inspired riots broke out in London, and when the Lords announced their verdict they showed where their feelings lay by a light sentence: Sacheverell was not imprisoned or fined but suspended from preaching for three years. He went in victorious procession through the applause of Oxford to a rich living.[7]

The incident was the signal for Robert Harley to begin engineering in the Commons the overthrow of the government led by the Duke of Marlborough's civilian ally and financier, the Earl of Godolphin; Harley had himself been forced out of that government in 1708. And one of the first fruits of the Tory victory was the passing of the fourth Occasional Conformity Bill into law.

Step by step the Tories, controlling the Commons, now advanced in a campaign which recalled their triumph in the 1680s. The Whig majority in the Lords was broken by the creation of fresh peerages. While priority was given to ending the war by the peace of Utrecht (1713), the demands of the Anglican clergy were not forgotten. The Schism Bill was passed with enthusiasm. It closed down all the Dissenters' schools and made it necessary for all future schoolmasters to procure a bishop's licence to teach. The next step was to be a bill ending the Dissenters' right to vote in Parliamentary elections. Bishop Gilbert Burnet, who had once been secretary to William of Orange, certainly thought that the 'glorious revolution' was being undone. In a new preface written in 1712 for his *Discourse of the Pastoral Care*, he told the clergy: 'I see imminent ruin hanging over this Church.'

But by now the Tories faced problems. One was that Harley

---

[7] See Geoffrey Holmes, *The Trial of Dr Sacheverell* (London, 1973).

(now Earl of Oxford) had become an incompetent Lord Treasurer; he was habitually the worse for drink. His junior colleague, Henry St John, Viscount Bolingbroke, was only too willing to replace him but faced great dangers. Already at this stage he would probably have preferred Anne's successor to be the Old Pretender, but he acknowledged that the English would prefer a Turk to a Papist as their king. The only real alternative had been provided for in the Act of Settlement of 1701, promising the throne to the Electress Sophia of Hanover, daughter of Charles I's sister Elizabeth, and to her descendants. Almost sixty people were more closely related to Anne than the Electress Sophia was, and in any case Sophia had recently died, leaving Hanover to her unattractive son George, who had never troubled to learn English. The sole merit of this extraordinary entanglement with a German state (which was never popular) was that it, and it alone, would make sure of the Protestant succession in England. Queen Anne had shown her feelings about the prospect by forbidding Sophia to visit England or to meddle in its politics, and it had fallen to Bolingbroke to communicate one rebuke which was alleged to have killed the Electress. Her son swore vengeance.

Bolingbroke needed time, but what he would have done with it must remain a matter for speculation. On 27 July 1714 he finally prevailed on Anne to dismiss his drink-sodden senior colleague. When the Queen consented to this, she was already very ill. Even now neither she nor her council would consent to make the erratic Bolingbroke Lord Treasurer; that honour went to a duke. On 1 August she died, and the proclamation of George I went off without incident. 'What a world this is,' Bolingbroke wrote to Swift, 'and how does fortune banter us.'

The triumph of the Whigs was assured by the death of Queen Anne. By the end of the year King George had made a clean sweep of the government, and one of his proclamations had stopped the clergy preaching political (by which was meant Tory) sermons. The Earl of Oxford was sent to the Tower for two years. Bolingbroke was in deep disgrace. In 1717 the Whig government, angered by the intention of the House of Clergy to proceed against Bishop Hoadly for heresy, suspended the Convocation of Canterbury by royal writ. For a century and a half the proceedings of the Convocation were formal, apart from a session in 1741 hurriedly dissolved when the old quarrels broke out. The clergy were not allowed to complete any business until 1852. In 1719 the Occasional Conformity and Schism Acts were repealed, although a plan to repeal the Test and Corporation Acts had to be abandoned because of Anglican opposition. An Indemnity Act gave Dissenters limited protection for a year (they could not be prosecuted for nonconformity if they had survived six months in a local office without being challenged). In 1727 and in many later years this Act was renewed, but what mattered more was that the Whigs gave the cue that Dissenters were not to be troubled too zealously.

The personal ruin of Bolingbroke and of Atterbury followed. The former, believing that 'the Tory party is gone', fled to the court of the Old Pretender. Later he returned to England and tried to rebuild Toryism by his pen, now making no secret of his contempt for the clergy whose champion he had pretended to be, and his life did not flicker out until 1751. He appealed to the idea of a 'patriot king' although one did not arrive on the scene before George III in 1760. As he went home through Calais in 1723, this disillusioned gambler passed a fellow Tory going into perpetual exile: Francis Atterbury. The bishop had written a violently anti-Whig and anti-Hanoverian pamphlet, *English Advice to the Freeholders of England*, and had become persuaded that the Tories' only remaining hope was in the Jacobite cause. He refused to be bought by the Whigs with an offer of the right to be the next Bishop of Winchester. But his Jacobite plotting was exposed by Sir Robert Walpole; despite his solemn denial of the charge, he was condemned by the House of Lords; and so for a time he took Bolingbroke's place at the court of the Old Pretender. He died, very sad, in 1732.[8]

Secure in power, the Whigs were now themselves tempted to alter the settlement of 1688–89 by altering the character of the Church of England.

---

[8] Recent studies include Sheila Biddle, *Bolingbroke and Harley* (London, 1975); H. T. Dickinson, *Bolingbroke* (London, 1970); G. V. Bennett, *The Tory Crisis in Church and State, 1688–1730: The Career of Francis Atterbury, Bishop of Rochester* (Oxford, 1975).

THE CHURCH UNDER THE WHIGS

Although George I and George II had to receive Holy Communion as a condition of being monarchs under the act of 1701, they cared nothing for the Church of England and little for anything else that was English. They usually left ecclesiastical appointments (together with much other business) to their Whig ministers. For the first time the cabinet began to meet regularly without the sovereign presiding.[9]

Although the politicians in power also had to conform to the Church since the Test Act had never been repealed, few of them had much personal religion. Benjamin Hoadly, whom they had been glad to make Bishop of Bangor, expressed their conception of the Church in a sermon of 1717 on the text 'My Kingdom is not of this world'. It was a sermon as notorious as Dr Sacheverell's had been at the other extreme of ecclesiastical politics; for Hoadly virtually dissolved the Church as a structured society. It contained 'no visible, human authority . . . no judges over the conscience.' The teaching on which the Church's members agreed was there in the Bible, or in those parts of the Bible which Hoadly thought sensible, and the Church was a voluntary society of those who accept Christ as 'lawgiver and judge in all matters truly relating to conscience or eternal salvation'. But God had no special favour towards the Church; 'the favour of God follows sincerity considered as such.' Here was the 'gathered' Church advocated by the Puritans, but the basis on which it was gathered was by Puritan standards the outright denial of Christianity. If Hoadly's view had prevailed, there can be little doubt that the Church of England would have formally abandoned the old standards of belief, as well as of behaviour, as many of the Presbyterians had already done.

William Wake and Edmund Gibson had by their scholarly labours helped to prevent the clergy from endorsing the ambitions of Atterbury, and it now fell to them to persuade the Whigs to abandon the radical policy recommended by Hoadly.

---

[9] The best introduction to English politics, 1714–60, is now W. A. Speck, *Stability and Strife* (London, 1977).

They achieved this by persuading the Whigs now in power, as William of Orange had been persuaded, that it was not politically realistic to encourage the Tories to keep up their cry of 'the Church in danger!' In their own interests the triumphant Whigs must swallow, or conceal, their general contempt for religious traditions.

Wake, the obvious man to promote to Canterbury in 1716, had already shown during eleven years as Bishop of Lincoln (the largest diocese) that he insisted on high standards in church life. While archbishop he was not willing to support any radical modernization of the Church of England's doctrine or any enlargement of the liberties of the Dissenters; he even opposed the repeal of the Occasional Conformity and Schism Acts. His real interest lay in negotiations with foreign churches, and for this purpose it was all the more necessary to be able to show the Church of England's orthodoxy.

It seemed a heaven-sent moment for Christian reunion. King William and the Duke of Marlborough had made England the centre of a great, and in the end victorious, alliance against the French – and as a reward, the British empire was beginning to be worldwide. Had not the hour struck for an alliance of the Christian churches against immorality and unbelief, and as a reward might not the Church of England gain an unprecedented prestige? On the continent, a number of Roman Catholics who resented interference by Rome took an interest in the Anglican claim to be Catholic without the Pope. A number of Protestants (for example, Frederick, the first King of Prussia) believed that the old divisions between Lutherans and Calvinists were outmoded; and they observed with admiration the spectacle of a Lutheran as Supreme Governor of the Church of England, whose Articles of Belief were moderately Calvinist.[10] And to match this hopeful hour, a scholar with broad sympathies was Archbishop of Canterbury.

William Wake corresponded industriously with anti-Roman Catholics in France ('Gallicans' whose base was the Sorbonne

---

[10] Norman Sykes studied *Daniel Ernst Jablonski and the Church of England* (London, 1950).

university in Paris), with Lutherans and with Calvinists. He acknowledged the validity of the sacraments of all the Reformed Churches; he accepted the current description of England under the Hanoverians as 'the head of the Protestant interest' and found no theological reason for disrupting this alliance. But he urged the continental Protestants to get together and to recover the time-honoured system of bishops and creeds, blessings which the wise Anglicans had never forsaken. At one stage there was a Lutheran suggestion that the apostolic succession of bishops might be transmitted across the Channel by letter. Wake also urged the Frenchmen to acknowledge that the bishops of the Church of England were validly Catholic and that its orthodox creeds were sincere. There was much explanation about the consecrations of the Elizabethan bishops. In the end all this correspondence fizzled out. The various groups on the continent had no serious intention of uniting with anyone, and no serious belief that the religious arrangements of the English provided a model to be copied outside that strange island. 'We all favour too much ourselves and our own opinions' was Wake's accurate analysis. But the correspondence had the effect of suggesting that, if it had to choose, the Church of England would prefer an agreement with fellow Christians abroad to an agreement with England's own sceptics.[11]

In the end the Whigs grew bored with this archbishop who seemed to be wrapped in dreams of Christian reunion while the vital matter was to defend the Protestant succession and the Whig supremacy against any threat of a Jacobite or Tory revival. The new Whig prime minister, Sir Robert Walpole, was ruthless in getting what he wanted throughout his twenty-one years in power, the 'Robinocracy'. It was he who got the crucial evidence which ruined Francis Atterbury, and in 1723 he also got rid of William Wake as the effective chief of ecclesiastical affairs. Wake remained Archbishop of Canterbury until 1737 but was ignored in matters such as the appointment of bishops. The power was transferred to

[11] Norman Sykes wrote a magisterial biography of *William Wake* (2 vols, Cambridge, 1957).

Edmund Gibson, who was made Bishop of London.

He was known to be ambitious. As Walpole, ever a cynic, wrote to the Duke of Newcastle: 'He must be pope and would as willingly be our pope as anybody's.' But Gibson was also a sincere believer in the importance of the Protestant succession on the throne to English religion, and the sincerity of his attachment to the Church of England had been demonstrated by the pains he had taken to codify its canon law; his nickname was 'Dr Codex'. He set himself to reconcile the Church to the Whigs.

On the Church's side this meant erecting a barrier to the promotion of Tories; the only Tory who got past this barrier to become a bishop was Thomas Sherlock, a man of outstanding ability who was favoured by George II's clever queen and who in the end succeeded Gibson as Bishop of London.[12] But on the side of the Whigs, the reconciliation as planned by Gibson involved considering the prejudices of clergymen and cultivating their loyalties. There must be no more open contempt for the traditional standards. Young dons from Oxford and Cambridge must be flattered by being summoned to preach in London with small stipends from the government, and professorships of modern history must be established in the universities so as to explain to them what had been happening in recent centuries.

Gibson's reconciliation of the Church and the Whigs was more successful than Wake's attempt to reconcile Catholics, Lutherans and Calvinists. But the Bishop's alliance with Sir Robert Walpole, on which everything depended, could not last. Walpole grew restive under Gibson's veto of any ecclesiastical appointments which he knew would provoke the clergy. The House of Commons, on which Walpole's own power depended, grew restive under a system which perpetuated so many privileges for the Anglican clergy, while (as we have already seen) the Dissenters kept lobbying MPs for further concessions in the spirit of toleration. In the 1730s bills began appearing which dismayed Gibson – to deprive incumbents of tithes unless there was proof that they had recently

---

[12] See E. F. Carpenter, *Thomas Sherlock* (London, 1936).

been paid; to deprive churchwardens of the right to levy rates for the repair of churches (but the magistrates were still to be authorized to do this); to deprive ecclesiastical courts of jurisdiction over moral offences; to deprive the bishops of any possibility that they might be translated to richer sees; to restrict gifts to charities including churches (the Mortmain Bill). Finally the Quaker Tithes Bill proposed to transfer financial disputes between the clergy and the Quakers from the expensive and usually hostile ecclesiastical court, or the national court of the exchequer, to local magistrates. Walpole's support of this proposal so angered Gibson that the Bishop announced that he would now concentrate on the care of his diocese to the exclusion of all public business.

When Canterbury fell vacant on Wake's death, it was given to John Potter, a good scholar but a colourless ecclesiastic. Gibson had to be persuaded out of his semi-retirement to give a lead against the Jacobite rebellion in 1745. Two years later, when Potter had expired, Gibson was finally offered the archbishopric. His quarrel with Walpole no longer mattered, since the Quakers had accepted defeat and Walpole himself had fallen from power. But he was now almost eighty years old and he refused the honour. So did his Tory rival, Thomas Sherlock, who pleaded that he was afflicted with gout. So another dull appointment was made to the Primacy, to be followed by others over which we need not linger. And 'no clergyman of anything like Gibson's force and influence spoke out in public for the clergy's claims until the 1830s.'[13]

The making of bishops and deans, and of many a canon or parish priest, fell into the willing hands of Thomas Pelham-Holles, Duke of Newcastle. This duke was a great landowner who became Prime Minister, having previously been a leading minister in the government led by his brother. Yet for some thirty years he personally conducted a voluminous correspondence with clergymen who applied for jobs great or small. Always an anxious man, he was as pious as he was practical; he

---

[13] G. F. A. Best, *Temporal Pillars* (Cambridge, 1964), p. 60. Norman Sykes provided a biography of *Edmund Gibson* (Oxford, 1926). Aldren Rowden did his best for *The Primates of the Four Georges* (London, 1916).

consulted some of the clergymen he promoted about the state of his soul. To him the labour involved in this exercise of patronage was as necessary as was all his attention to the details of electioneering in the parliamentary constituencies. He was glad to be asked to carry on the good work when in 1757 William Pitt took the rest of the world off his hands. Pitt's armies might conquer North America from Guadeloupe in the sunshine to Quebec next to the snow, but of what use was a transatlantic victory over the French if the Whig ascendancy over England was not secure?[14]

This cunning political manager could appeal not only to his correspondents' personal ambitions, but also to the fact that most Englishmen now had an incentive to keep the peace at home, since the nation was beginning to prosper in a modern way. The population growth slowed down, agricultural productivity rose and trade expanded. Capitalism had shown its power to win King William's war, to finance the beginnings of a great empire and to create industrial wealth. Those who benefitted from the system, particularly the aristocracy now building their Palladian stately homes, naturally looked indulgently on any defects; these seemed like the 'Gothic' ruins which were sometimes erected in a park. But the many hundreds of thousands of Englishmen always on the brink of starvation also usually accepted this society with all its injustice. The less privileged were encouraged to be quiet by harsh laws; death was the penalty for many offences, including participation in a crowd of twelve or more an hour after the reading of the Riot Act of 1715. And the poor were also kept quiet by the sense that the social order was secure, indeed inevitable. There was no efficient police force and there were no large-scale political upheavals. It is clear that 1688–89 was generally thought to have established a society which was at its worst tolerable.

Alexander Pope expressed the national mood of optimism which meant all the more since he was himself a dwarf, a lifelong invalid and, as a Roman Catholic, always in the last

---

[14] See Reed Browning, *The Duke of Newcastle* (London, 1975).

analysis an outsider. In the England of the Whigs he could profess to believe that

> All Nature is but Art, unknown to thee;
> All Chance, Direction, which thou canst not see;
> All Discord, Harmony, not understood;
> All partial Evil, universal Good.[15]

THE ALLIANCE OF CHURCH AND STATE

In his *Alliance of Church and State* (1736), William Warburton, then a country clergyman, sought to justify the establishment of the Church of England from 'the fundamental principles of the Law of Nature and of Nations'. At no point was Warburton less – or more – than complacent. He admitted that the Church had been disgraced by superstition in past ages but in a private letter he once pointed out that in Noah's ark there had been amid 'the unclean beasts and vermin that almost filled it . . . a little corner of rationality that was as much distressed by the stink within as by the tempest without'. He was sure that the Church now deserved in the main to be honoured because of this element of religious rationality; he was careful not to provoke his fellow churchmen. To him Church and State were two distinct bodies. That much he granted to the Protestant or Catholic Dissenters, abandoning Richard Hooker's attempt to reassert the total unity of England. On the other hand, it was inexpedient that an assembly of the clergy should transact any business, since no reforms were urgent; and it was wrong for the Church to excommunicate any citizen without gaining the State's approval. If there was more than one religious body within a nation, it was in accordance with 'civic utility' to choose the most numerous church and to reward it by establishment and endowment, since the welfare of society (for example, the keeping of oaths) depended on morality being

---

[15] Studies include D. H. Griffin, *Alexander Pope: The Poet in the Poems* (Princeton, N.J., 1978), and agree that religion was not decisive for him.

upheld by religion. It was also perfectly proper for the State to exclude from the government of nation or borough any member of a church it did not favour; the Acts which gave real or nominal Anglicans the monopoly of politics in England were among the arrangements which could be defended from the Law of Nature. On the other hand, the State was right to tolerate the worship of peaceable Dissenters – and to make sure that the Established Church's leaders were sensible, cooperative men by appointing such men to the leadership. Warburton was himself made Bishop of Gloucester, although he had never been to a university. As he once wrote with unusual candour, although miracles had been needed in the days of the martyrs 'now the profession of the Christian faith is attended with ease and honour; and the conviction which the weight of human testimony and the conclusions of human reason afford us of its truth is abundantly sufficient to support us in our religious perseverance.'[16]

Such a defence of the Revolution Settlement applied a coating of sweet theology to the sugar of political conservatism. In the circumstances of the time it was not a manifestly unreasonable argument. (The argument was at least more reasonable than that to be found in Warburton's later and much bigger book, *The Divine Legation of Moses*, to the effect that the Old Testament must have been inspired by God since if it had been merely human wisdom it would have taught more clearly about life after death.) The Established Church of England did seem to many to deserve its privileges because it was the largest Church in an England which was prospering. The literature of the period frequently showed the central position of the parish church. Thomas Gray's meditations amid the hallowed graves of Stoke Poges (*Elegy in a Country Churchyard*, 1750) became immensely popular, as did Oliver Goldsmith's novel about the fortunes of the blameless Dr Primrose and his more human family, *The Vicar of Wakefield*, completed in 1762. In *The Deserted Village* Goldsmith painted a little portrait of a parish priest without blemish (so far as he saw); it is thought to have been a portrait of his own father.

---

[16] A. W. Evans studied *Warburton and Warburtonians* (London, 1932).

Henry Fielding's Parson Thwackum would raise a smile but not total ridicule by his famous defence of the perfection of religion: 'When I mention Religion, I mean the Christian Religion; and not only the Christian Religion, but the Protestant Religion; and not only the Protestant Religion, but the Church of England.'[17]

But can the eighteenth-century bishops be defended?

Later generations have been horrified by the thought of the bishop who was in London whenever the House of Lords was sitting (usually from October or November to May or June); who voted in Parliament, and lobbied in local elections, at the bidding of his political patrons; who had little pastoral contact with ordinands, priests or people in his diocese; and whose teaching, such as it was, exuded satisfaction with the social order. These bishops, as they look out from their portraits, the faces florid under their wigs, often seem as if they have returned from a day's hunting in a vain attempt to shed the effects of the previous evening's drinking. However, in justice we ought to recall that bishops were then regarded as great officers of the State as well as of the Church, and that the prominence of twenty-six of them in the small House of Lords, holding their own with the secular aristocracy, was held to be a proof of how Christian the country was. As late as 1711 it was thought fitting for a bishop to be given high office in the government as Lord Privy Seal – John Robinson, a distinguished diplomat, who negotiated the peace of Utrecht but was less competent as Bishop first of Bristol and then of London.

Particularly in view of the veneration of this age for the rights of propertied individuals, it was not easy for an Archbishop of Canterbury or for anyone else to remove a bishop – or to rebuke him, as Archbishop Tenison found when he had to institute legal action against two exceptionally scandalous Welsh bishops. Even more difficult was it to rebuke Lancelot Blackburne, Archbishop of York 1724–43. A former naval chaplain,

---

[17] The standard modern studies are Norman Sykes, *Church and State in England in the Eighteenth Century* (Cambridge, 1934); S. C. Carpenter, *Eighteenth-century Church and People* (London, 1959); John Carswell, *From Revolution to Revolution: England 1688–1776* (London, 1973); E. G. Rupp, *Religion in England 1688–1791* (Oxford, 1986).

he was one of the worst bishops of the period, never holding a single confirmation. But the slackness of the average eighteenth-century bishop should not be exaggerated. His conception of his duty was probably not very different from the standard which had been normal in the Middle Ages and in most of the post-Reformation history of the Church of England. His essential functions in his diocese were believed to be jurisdiction (especially through the visitation which was supposed to be held every third year), ordaining and confirming – but no great damage was thought to be done if the routine of the jurisdiction had to be delegated to his subordinates (the chancellor, the registrar and the archdeacons); if young men seeking Holy Orders had to travel to where he was (perhaps in London); or if the laity seeking confirmation had to assemble in large numbers when he appeared. This was the system which many highly respected bishops had operated during and since the Middle Ages. While the spiritual level of the eighteenth-century bishops did not reach the best standards of the past, most of the new century's bishops were, it seems, on the whole faithful to their duties as they acknowledged them. Even the hated Benjamin Hoadly (who did not add to his attractiveness by being so crippled that he had to preach kneeling) appears to have been faithful in this limited sense as Bishop of Winchester.

One of the problems was the gross inequality in the incomes of the bishops (as in the Middle Ages). In the 1760s the richest bishoprics were worth many thousands – Canterbury 7, Durham 6, Winchester 5, York 4½, London 4 – at a time when Welsh bishops, or a Bishop of Bristol, Oxford or Rochester, got under £600. The poorer bishops were still expected to live in style and to maintain London houses, so that they had to be financed by being deans also. Inevitably the poorer bishops also had their eyes on succeeding their richer brethren. This could mean that they did not dedicate themselves to their present dioceses and that political patrons continued to have a hold over them. And whether or not they had been lucky in being transferred up the financial ladder, they would not resign. There was no system of pensions for bishops, and it seems never to have occurred to them that resignation in old age was a moral duty – any more than this has seemed the duty of twentieth-century popes or monarchs.

It was a morally indefensible system, but it is not necessary to blame all its defects on the eighteenth century; for the system was inherited. Nathaniel Crewe, for example, was said to have paid King Charles a large sum for the benefit of his mistress Nell Gwynne in exchange for the bishopric of Durham in 1674. If he did, it turned out to be a good investment. He enjoyed the revenues of the great bishopric until his death in 1721, although he accepted a seat on the Ecclesiastical Commission which King James instituted and retained some Jacobite sympathies. The Whig bishops cold-shouldered him. The ups and downs of politics in Westminster did not really disturb the Bishop of Durham, however. He maintained a nobleman's standard of living in Durham Castle, in Auckland Castle and in the great house in Northamptonshire which he inherited with the barony of Crewe from his brother. He was not a neglectful bishop by his own standards. When he examined the fitness of candidates for the priesthood, he bade them translate into Latin the English sentence from the Prayer Book, 'I have examined them and find them so qualified'. Lord Crewe left a benefaction which still enables his happy guests in the university of Oxford to consume champagne and strawberries in his memory each year.[18]

The eighteenth-century Church of England was, however, the home of at least one saint – and he was a bishop. Thomas Wilson, chaplain to the Earl of Derby and tutor to his son, was persuaded to agree to be consecrated bishop of the Isle of Man in 1698. The stipend was small; no seat in the Lords was attached; there had been a vacancy for five years; and Wilson was appointed because the Earl of Derby was also Lord of Man. He was the pastor of his diocese until he died in 1755 at the age of ninety-two. He gave much practical help to the poor and told the farmers about new agricultural methods; he fought the smugglers; he founded schools and a public library; he learned the Manx language in order to write the first books in it. Since the Act of Uniformity did not apply to the little

---

[18] See C. E. Whiting, *Nathaniel, Lord Crewe* (London, 1940).

island in the Irish Sea, he felt able both to add to the Book of
Common Prayer and to disregard any rule that communicants
must kneel. He conferred with his clergy (there were about
twenty-five of them) in an annual synod, and young men they
agreed would be suitable as future priests were taken to live in
his home for a year. He insisted on a strict discipline of sinners,
excommunicating a governor's wife for making slanderous
statements, suspending an archdeacon for giving communion
to her, and refusing to yield although imprisoned for two
months. He took an active interest in missionary work in
America, writing a little book which he hoped would be of help
while teaching Red Indians. He refused at least one invitation
to move to a more lucrative bishopric. On the Isle of Man he
had seen a vision rather like St John's on the island of
Patmos.[19]

Under bishops who might be a Lord Crewe or a Thomas
Wilson or something in between, the parochial clergy were a
mixed lot.

One problem was that many of the medieval parishes were
too small to support a full-time resident pastor at the standard
which he expected now that he was probably a graduate.
About half the parishes were worth less than £80 a year. Or
perhaps the parsonage was reckoned uninhabitable by a gentleman's family. Because there was no machinery for merging
parishes their incomes were merged, but this meant the scandal of a non-resident rector or vicar, often leaving the services
to be taken by an ill-paid curate. Rowlandson's cartoons of the
plump Dr Syntax with his starveling curate were fair comment.
Graduates were allowed to hold two livings if not more than
thirty miles apart. Non-residence was also allowed to those
who taught in the universities or schools, to chaplains to the
nobility, the army or the navy, to clergymen suffering from ill
health or where there was no suitable house. In the diocese of
Oxford in the 1780s about a hundred out of 165 incumbents

---

[19] The life and prayers of Bishop Wilson, first made widely known in a biography
of 1781, were studied by H. A. L. Rice, *The Bridge Builders* (London, 1961), pp. 66–8.
The Diaries of Thomas Wilson, the saintly bishop's far from saintly son, were edited by
C. L. S. Linnell (London, 1964).

were non-resident, mainly because they lived in the university. In the diocese of York the equivalent figure was 218 out of 836; in the diocese of Exeter, 159 out of 290. On the other hand, some of the medieval parishes into which England was still divided now contained a population far too large to be cared for adequately. Manchester, for example, possessed the one medieval parish church – for a population which was at least twenty thousand by 1750. Until 1818 an Act of Parliament was required to set up a new parish, and the trouble and expense seldom seemed worthwhile. The Church's pastoral work in the increasingly industrialized Midlands and North was crippled by the attitude summed up in a remark made by Archibishop Herring of York in 1758: 'I think philosophy, Christianity and polity are all against changes.'

In the Middle Ages the defects of the ecclesiastical system and of preaching had been compensated for by popular devotion to the Mass. It had been the ambition of both Calvin and Cranmer to retain the centrality of the 'Lord's Supper', week by week, in a reformed Church; but this ambition had never been shared by the English people. With the new emphasis on the importance of spiritual preparation for the sacrament had come a new reluctance on the part of the devout to attempt a worthy preparation frequently. The exceptionally pious Queen Anne communicated once a month, but in the diocese of York in 1743 only 72 out of the 836 churches had monthly celebrations of this service. And the undevout not unnaturally found Morning Prayer tedious, as many had done in a more generally religious period. Addison depicted his beloved squire, Sir Roger, nodding off but awakening to rebuke anyone else caught asleep – and as he passed through the bowing congregation after the service, asking after absentees. They were all his tenants.

However, it would be a mistake to think that the typical parish church in the eighteenth century was totally lifeless. Archdeacons were constantly pressing for Holy Communion to be held more frequently, and Morning Prayer every Sunday and Holy Days, with the Litany on Wednesdays and Fridays – and for the churches to be kept in good repair, for which a rate could be levied on all residents in the parish. Many churches were improved, and some new churches were built. The clergy, still paid mainly by tithes, were often busy in the duties as well as in the amusements of life in the countryside. Many of them were justices of the peace; all of them, and their church-wardens, were expected to report their parishioners' moral misdemeanours each year at the archdeacon's visitation. John Wesley was one of those who bore witness to the fact that few of the parish clergy were grossly immoral. An inquiry into church life in Devon led to a conclusion which surprised the scholar who made it. It revealed 'a Church intimately involved in the life of the people, providing a great deal of their justice, acting the unenviable role of moral policeman, settling their disputes over legacies, protecting their rights, educating their children, and even pioneering much that has come to be known as social security.'[20]

A fair assessment of church life in this period must also take the work of Thomas Bray into account. In 1693 this Warwick-shire rector with humble parents were chosen by Bishop Compton of London to be his representative or 'commissary' in the American colony of Maryland. Ten years earlier the Bishop had sent a tough Scotsman, James Blair, to begin a stormy but remarkably effective attempt to build up church life in a Virginia controlled by its increasingly prosperous tobacco planters. Blair's work as commissary lasted until his death in 1743, and included the foundation of William and Mary College at Williamsburg in 1693. Probably the Bishop envis-aged that Bray would make his home in Maryland, as Blair had done in Virginia. In the end, however, Bray spent only three months in America, in 1700. He could work better for the cause from an English base.

His first concern was to recruit clergy for the colony and his second was to arm them with books, since 'none but the poorer among the clergy here could be persuaded to leave their friends and native country and go so far'. He therefore opened a public

---

[20] Arthur Warne, *Church and Society in Eighteenth-century Devon* (Newton Abbot, Devon, 1969), p. 9. See also Basil Clarke, *Church Building in the Eighteenth Century* (London, 1963). Richard Gough wrote a vivid *History of Myddle* at the beginning of the century, recounting the secrets of the parishioners who would gather Sunday by Sunday (reprinted, Harmondsworth, Middx, 1981).

appeal for parochial libraries to encourage 'religion and learning in the foreign plantations'. It was not long before he realized that similar libraries needed to be provided to help clergy in England and Wales – and that the need was even greater for schools to give a rudimentary education to the children of the poor. As the needs impressed themselves on him, he looked with envy on the Sacred Congregation for the Propagation (*Propaganda*) of the Faith established in Rome in 1622. He dreamed of nationwide organizations to promote his schemes and talked to others about his hopes – with effects. Any close imitation of Rome in the Church of England was out of the question, but on 8 March 1699 four laymen met in London to found a Society for Promoting Christian Knowledge, the oldest missionary society in that church. It was to work in England as well as in the American colonies. Two years later a Society for Propagating the Gospel in Foreign Parts was founded with much the same support, its chief aim being the provision of 'a sufficient maintenance . . . for an orthodox clergy' in America. This SPG was more official as well as more specialized than the SPCK; it was granted a royal charter like the great trading companies, it had Archbishop Tenison as an active leader, and it was blessed by the clergy in their newly revived Convocation of Canterbury. For the time being India was closed to English missionaries, since the rapidly expanding East India Company had no wish to irritate the 'natives'. But the SPCK and the SPG were launched on work which would take them into all the continents. The SPCK was especially fortunate in that an American businessman, Henry Newman, found his life's work as the society's secretary, 1708–43 – and was extraordinarily effective. Thomas Bray also remained busy, in the creation of libraries and schools and in the support of the American clergy, until his death in 1730.[21]

One of the tasks undertaken by the SPCK was 'to promote and encourage the erection of charity schools in all parts of

[21] See H. P. Thompson, *Into all Lands: The History of the SPG* (London, 1951), and *Thomas Bray* (London, 1954); W. L. Cowie, *Henry Newman* (London, 1956); W. K. Lowther Clarke, *A History of the SPCK* (London, 1959).

England and Wales'. Hundreds of such schools were founded for the children of the poor by one means or another, in the century from 1690. It was a movement so notable that there was alarm in privileged circles. Were the Tory squires who were often patrons of these schools training up little Jacobites? Or were they educating the children above their station in life, giving them interests and skills which would make them discontented with their lot as servants and labourers? Bishop Gibson of London felt obliged to issue solemn instructions that in the charity schools there should be the strictest loyalty to the 'Protestant succession' on the throne and to the class system as ordained by God.[22]

Many voluntary societies for charitable work or evangelism, exhorted by preachers and strengthened by worship together in private or in church, flourished at the turn of the seventeenth and eighteenth centuries. In 1701 it was estimated that there were more than forty of them in London, where they originated (with young men as members) in the 1670s. They also existed in many provincial towns. Among them, from 1690 onwards, were 'Societies for the Reformation of Manners', in which Thomas Bray was heavily involved; *A Help to a National Reformation* (1700) was widely distributed by the SPCK. The Societies' chief aim was to prosecute offenders against the laws which still enforced morality. It is clear that with the destruction of the old Puritan censorship, drunkenness, prostitution, profanity, Sunday trading and similar behaviour flourished, and that no appeal to the law could by itself be effective in suppressing it. But it is also clear that there were many people in England who deplored the trend. After the death of Charles II a revulsion against the immorality which he had embodied was quite widespread. Even at his court there had been saints; John Evelyn wrote a biography of one of them, Mrs Godolphin, a lady-in-waiting to the Queen. The most dissolute of his courtiers, the Earl of Rochester, directed that a book should be published by Bishop Burnet recording his shame and penitence. And far away from London many people needed no persuading to criticize London's vice – men such as Sir Roger

---

[22] See Mary G. Jones, *The Charity School Movement* (Cambridge, 1938).

de Coverley, whom the devout Joseph Addison portrayed in his famous *Spectator* sketch, which was not entirely a work of the imagination. Even in the wicked city the righteous could be found. By 1720 the London societies were boasting in print that there had been 75,270 prosecutions since 1691. Within worldly London, preachers who exerted themselves could still gain a hearing. 'Orator' Henley, who offered popular journalism with an edifying tone, was so successful that admission to his congregation was by ticket only. In 1750 the Bishop of London issued a pamphlet warning his diocese that the recent earthquake had been caused by its flagrant immorality. The warning sold over a hundred thousand copies.[23]

Two very worldly earls may be cited as witnesses to the position of the Church of England in eighteenth-century society.

The Earl of Chesterfield's many letters of good advice to his illegitimate son were, immediately he was dead, sold to a publisher by the woman whom his son had married without his knowledge. In one of them mention was made of religion. The year was 1750. 'I have seldom or never written to you on the subject of Religion and Morality: your own reason, I am persuaded, has given you true notions of both; they best speak for themselves; but if they wanted assistance, you have Mr Harte at hand . . .' Chesterfield confined himself to 'the decency, the utility, and the necessity of preserving the appearances'. He hastened to assure the boy that 'I do not mean that you should talk or act like a missionary, or an enthusiast, nor that you should take up a controversial cudgel against whoever attacks the sect you are of.' He meant simply 'that you should by no means seem to approve, encourage or applaud, those libertine notions which strike at religions equally, and which are the poor threadbare topics of half wits, or minute philosophers.' 'Depend on this truth,' this earl who was an apostle of 'good-breeding' explained, 'that every man is the worse looked upon, and the less trusted, for being thought to have no religion . . . and a wise atheist (if such a thing there is) would, for his

---

[23] See D. W. R. Bahlman, *The Moral Revolution of 1688* (Princeton, N.J., 1957). Graham Midgley studied *The Life of Orator Henley* (Oxford, 1973).

own interest, and character in this world, pretend to some religion.'[24]

Frederick Hervey was a son of the first Earl of Bristol, which explains why he was made a priest in 1755, Bishop of Cloyne in 1767 and Bishop of Derry next year. His elder brother was for a year Lord Lieutenant of Ireland, although he never set foot there. Frederick Hervey's income as Bishop of Derry was at first around £7,000 a year but it rose to near £20,000 because he was a shrewd manager of the episcopal estates. He added another £20,000 a year when he succeeded to the earldom. He was sensitive to the fact that most of those who paid tithes to the clergy of his diocese were either Roman Catholics or Presbyterians, and he supported schemes to enable Roman Catholics to swear allegiance to the Crown and to change the hated tithes into the equivalent in land to be owned by the parson; although neither of these schemes came to anything. At one stage he made himself popular (although not with other Englishmen) by demanding that Irish Catholics should be given the vote. In the two very elegant palaces which he built for himself in his diocese he was hospitable. After dinner he liked to make his clergy run races. But his real interest lay in continental travel. His journeys were so extensive and so extravagant that it is said that all Bristol Hotels are named after him; innkeepers dreamed that he would turn up. One of Hervey's motives was to collect works of art to adorn his episcopal palaces, his London house or the great house at Ickworth in Suffolk, which he rebuilt very handsomely; but his main motive in his travels seems to have been an insatiable love of amusement and adventure. After 1782 he never saw his wife again; after 1791 he never saw his diocese again; after 1792 he never saw England again. As he wandered through Europe wearing a purple cap with a golden tassel he talked about the importance of political liberty, thus alarming some of his royal and aristocratic hosts; but when war came he also appointed himself a spy on behalf of the British government, and for this reason was for a time imprisoned by the French revolutionary

---

[24] Chesterfield's *Letters*, edited by Bonamy Dobrée in 6 volumes (London, 1932), have not yet been used in a good biography.

army in Milan. He died in 1803 while on the road to Rome.

Especially after 1791 the earl-bishop gave many people the impression that he was no Christian in belief or behaviour. George III refused to speak to this 'wicked prelate'. Nelson's mistress Emma Hamilton, who knew him well, was equally shocked by him. She reported that he 'was an avowed sceptic in religion, the doctrines and institutions of which he would not scruple to ridicule in the company of women, treating even the immortality of the soul as an article of indifference.' But he did not shock all his contemporaries. Jeremy Bentham, normally no friend to parsons, found him in 1782 'a most excellent companion, pleasant, intelligent, well read and well bred, liberal-minded to the last degree'. John Wesley, who met him twice during the 1770s, noted that a sermon by the Bishop on the Holy Spirit was 'useful', that he celebrated Holy Communion 'with admirable solemnity', and that he was 'plenteous in good works'. When he died an obelisk was erected to this 'friend and protector' of all Christians in his diocese, and the subscribers included the local Roman Catholic bishop and the leading Dissenting minister.[25]

The eighteenth-century Church of England was so richly established that it seemed natural for an Earl of Chesterfield to advise his bastard son to pretend to some religious belief even if he had none – and for an Earl of Bristol to include the duties of a bishop among the many projects which for a time took a very rich man's fancy. The two earls illustrate what Bishop Warburton meant by saying that 'the profession of the Christian faith is attended with ease and honour'.

PROTESTANT DISSENT IN DECLINE AND AT WORSHIP

One of the reasons why the Established Church was complacent in the eighteenth century was the numerical decline of its rivals.

---

[25] See Brian Fothergill, *The Mitred Earl* (London, 1974).

Among the Protestant Dissenters, the century witnessed a diminishment of the zeal for discipline which Richard Baxter had typified. Still in the 1680s it could be thought that a strict moral and theological discipline over its members, protesting against Anglican laxity, was the characteristic mark of a Dissenting congregation, just as the doctrine of the divine right of kings was characteristic of the Church of England; but during the eighteenth century it became plain that Dissenters, like Anglicans, had developed other interests.

One interest was now the basic discussion about the nature of God and the divinity of Christ. In the 1690s a fiery Welshman, Richard Davis, preached a Gospel which was enthusiastic but considerably simpler than Calvinism, and the controversy which he aroused, particularly among his fellow Congregationalists and among the Baptists, led to divisions. Almost thirty years later another dispute broke out in Exeter: a Presbyterian minister, James Pierce, was accused of not believing in the Trinity. Both sides now appealed to the Dissenting ministers in London, who argued the matter out during passionate meetings in Salters' Hall early in 1719. It was resolved by 57 votes to 53 that there was no need to insist on 'human compositions or interpretations of the doctrine of Trinity'. The defeated minority replied by subscribing publicly to a Trinitarian declaration. It did not follow that the 'non-subscribers' were all Unitarians (or even Arians), but gradually the trustees of a considerable number of Presbyterian chapels made it clear that they had no objections to up-to-date views in the pulpits. Any Calvinist in the congregation either kept quiet or walked out to the nearest Congregational chapel, and a number of Presbyterian congregations which wished to remain orthodox found it safer to become Congregational, since then the local church could be based on a covenant which all must accept.

Another interest growing among Dissenters in the eighteenth century was the feeling that there ought to be equality in all things with conforming members of the Church of England. Dissenters were tolerated, and in 1767 Lord Mansfield – the great judge who also declared that no slave could remain a slave on English soil – declared that the efforts of the corporation of the City of London to exclude occasional conformists were illegal because they amounted to 'persecution'; but there was no real equality. As late as 1770 the leading jurist of the day, Sir William Blackstone of Oxford, could assert that the laws against their worship were only 'suspended'. Dissenters were still required to take the Anglican sacrament ('occasional conformity') if they wished to hold public office; they were still unable to send their sons to Oxford, and young Dissenters could not take degrees at Cambridge; they must still be married in Anglican churches and buried in Anglican church-yards, sometimes in humiliating conditions; above all, they were still forced to pay tithes to support the Anglican clergy.

It might have been expected that the need to combine in order to exert pressure on Parliament would lead to a religious union among the Dissenters themselves, but in fact it was soon recognized that such a union was unobtainable and that what was needed was a combination for strictly practical purposes. Early in the 1690s a Common Fund to support poor ministers, and a 'Happy Union' of the ministers themselves, promised to unite Presbyterians and Congregationalists; but both joint efforts were dead by 1695 and no subsequent attempt to unite the two denominations was successful until 1972. Instead the London ministers of these denominations combined with Baptists to present various addresses to Queen Anne. The experience of being able to do this together slowly encouraged the formation of a body which would be the equivalent of the 'Meeting for Sufferings' which had organized the Quakers' approaches to the politicians ever since 1675. The Quakers were particularly active as a pressure group in the 1730s, when the other Dissenters knew that many of the Whigs would welcome their approaches; the Whigs had already set aside a thousand pounds of public money each year (the *regium donum*) to assist ministers' widows, as a token of good will. Many of the Dissenters set their heart on the complete repeal of the Test and Corporation Acts, to end the humiliation of having either to receive the Anglican sacrament or to abandon all hopes of public office; and in 1732 a committee of twenty-one laymen was established in London under the chairmanship of a wealthy banker, Samuel Holden. The Whigs were as polite to this committee as they could be without doing what was wanted. The only outcome was that a permanent and invaluable instrument of co-operation had been forged: the Protestant Dissenting Deputies.[26]

Thus the Dissenters found that the discussion of basic theology had become divisive – and that their congregations had little wish to unite as a great alternative church although it was possible to combine for the limited purpose of improving their political standing by patient lobbying. It was a situation which showed that the old fires of Puritan conviction were dying down. But just as it was inaccurate to think of the Church of England as being totally given over to worldliness, so it would be wrong to suppose that Dissent had entirely lost the Puritan heritage. Even when they prospered Dissenters could still be inspired by the Puritan spirit of self-discipline and self-sacrifice. Thus a Baptist layman who accumulated a vast fortune, Thomas Guy, used it all to build and endow Guy's Hospital in London. At a more academic level a minister, Daniel Neal, set himself the task of showing from history how it ought to have been possible to separate the Puritans' admirable piety and virtue from their less admirable intolerance. *A History of New England* (1720) was followed by *A History of the Puritans* in four volumes (1732–38). Gradually Neal's interpretation of the past won its way, constituting a fresh argument that the heirs of the English Puritans ought to be fully tolerated themselves. In 1730 a young man named Strictland Gough published *An Enquiry into the Causes of the Decay of the Dissenting Interest*, arguing that 'the spirit of the good old Puritans was nothing else but a spirit of liberty' and that the trouble was that not enough liberty had been allowed to modern theology. He was answered by a minister named Philip Doddridge. An orthodox believer although a 'non-subscriber', in Northampton he conducted the best small educational establishment in the country but was also an effective pastor of simple folk, as was shown by his book on *The Rise and Progress of Religion in the*

---

[26] See Bernard Lord Manning, *The Protestant Dissenting Deputies* (Cambridge, 1952), and N. Crowther-Hunt, *Two Early Political Associations* (Oxford, 1961). Duncan Coomer portrayed *English Dissent under the Early Hanoverians* (London, 1946).

Soul. 'Plain people of low education and vulgar taste,' he pointed out to the young modernist, 'constitute nine parts in ten of most of our congregations.' They needed a simple Gospel.[27]

This Gospel was given to Dissenters in an acceptable form by hymns. Doddridge wrote some which became much loved – by millions of Christians to come, as well as by these Dissenters – including 'O God of Jacob, by whose hand' and 'Hark the glad sound, the Saviour comes'. But the greatest work was done by Isaac Watts, who began writing hymns Sunday by Sunday for the little congregation in Southampton where his father was a deacon. He was well educated and called to be the minister of the Mark Lane congregation in London, to which the great John Owen had preached in the days of persecution, but after ten years of that he made his escape from pastoral routine, pleading that his health had broken down. He was a guest in the home of Sir Thomas Abney, a former Lord Mayor of London, for the rest of his life. The fact was that he had his own vocation, to write hymns and theology; to express the theology in the hymns. He inherited a tradition where worship was imprisoned by Calvin's insistence that only the words of Holy Scripture should be heard, apart from the exposition of Scripture in the preaching and the prayers. In practice that meant metrical psalms offensive to anyone who loved poetry and music and with little of the Gospel in them; 'of all our religious solemnities,' he wrote, 'psalmody is the most un-happily managed.' So he set himself the task of composing some seven hundred hymns, in the spirit of one of them: 'Come, let us join our cheerful songs.'

His output included *Divine Songs Attempted in Easy Language for the Use of Children* (1715). For adults or for children, his hymns all taught a theology which was orthodox but not rigid. In his prose works Watts suggested liberal compromises in the controversies over predestination and the Trinity, while his solution to the ecclesiastical problem was that there should be a National Church teaching a noncontroversial 'Natural Religion' and tolerating Dissenters and Anglicans alike. In the

[27] See Malcolm Deacon, *Philip Doddridge of Northampton* (Northampton, 1980).

hymns, however, his main aim was simplicity, although he acknowledged that it was 'difficult to work every line to the level of a whole congregation and yet to keep it above contempt.' Deliberately he strung plain Anglo-Saxon words together in a few well-known metres, with lines short enough to be announced before they were sung. His success was immense, preserving orthodoxy through a century when it was seldom heard so clearly from the pulpit. His *Hymns and Spiritual Songs* published in 1707 included 'When I survey the wond'rous cross'. A later collection consisted of *Psalms of David Imitated in the Language of the New Testament* (1719) and included two more hymns which became almost equally prominent features of English religion: 'O God, our help in ages past' and 'Jesus shall reign wher'er the sun'.

By the time Watts died in 1748, the use of these and other hymns had been accepted by all the Dissenters apart from Quakers and the Particular Baptists. Later in the century so stout an Anglican as Samuel Johnson admired the hymns for their purity of faith and of diction, and as the Church of England adopted the use of hymns the work of Watts became enduringly popular. There was an initial period of hesitation, when even hymns so orthodox seemed dangerous novelties to conservative Dissenters or Anglicans, who assumed that the limit of modernization had been reached with the metrical psalms. Slowly such hesitations yielded before the power of the hymns to make people love and voice a biblical faith. Watts, it has been said, 'sees the cross as Milton had seen it, planted on a globe hung in space, surrounded by the vast distances of the universe. He sees the drama in Palestine prepared before the beginning of time and still decisive when time has ceased to be.'[28] But even that tribute does not quite cover the theology which gave power to the hymns of Isaac Watts. He did not merely present the cosmic grandeur of the God revealed in Christ, as Milton had done. He expressed a warmly human

---

[28] Bernard Lord Manning, *The Hymns of Wesley and Watts* (London, 1942), p. 83. Horton Davies studied Dissenting as well as Anglican buildings and practices in *Worship and Theology in England from Watts and Wesley to Maurice* (Princeton, N.J., 1961). Other studies include Arthur P. Davis, *Isaac Watts* (London, 1948), and Harry Escott, *Isaac Watts, Hymnographer* (London, 1952).

love and gratitude towards the suffering Christ, as Milton had not done. Thus his work flowed into the hymns and into the spiritual revival led by Evangelicals such as the brothers John and Charles Wesley, who underwent their conversion experience ten years before his death. In Georgian England the religion of the Puritans seemed to be going through a depression, a winter. But here was a crocus, a herald of the Evangelical and Methodist spring, when Watts sang about the 'young prince of glory' on the cross:

> Love so amazing, so divine,
> Demands my soul, my life, my all.

CATHOLIC DISSENT IN OBSCURITY AND AT WORSHIP

Half the 'Papist' peers and hundreds of gentlemen went into exile with James II. Those remaining paid another price. In 1692 the vindictive strengthening of the penal laws included a long-lasting doubling of the land tax to pay for King William's army, and Papists were forbidden to go on any long journey without a special licence. The annual Mutiny Act claimed that the army was kept in being against militant Popery. In theory no Roman Catholic could inherit or sell land, although in practice Anglican trustees often got round the prohibition. Lower down the social scale a Roman Catholic faced prejudice and feared violence. It is not surprising that under this pressure there were many desertions from the 'old religion'. Although the general population seems to have started growing fast after about 1740 (due mainly to the conquest of smallpox and the disappearance of the rats which had carried 'the plague'), the Roman Catholic community was probably more or less static. A census of Papists conducted for Parliament in 1767 produced a figure just short of seventy thousand, and even if this was too low it seems probable that the community had grown in a hundred years by no more than twenty thousand.

The number of priests had to be reduced. Their own bishops counted fewer than four hundred of them at work in 1773, the year when the Pope suppressed the Jesuit order which had been growing increasingly unpopular. As the law stood, any Roman Catholic priest in the country could be imprisoned for life and any informer reporting the celebration of the Mass, which could be reckoned high treason, could earn £100. The last successful prosecution occurred in 1767, when John Baptist Maloney was sentenced to life imprisonment but soon released. However, the main reason why there were fewer priests was that there was less money to pay for them. In practice the authorities tolerated, although they also despised, what the priests did.

The steady pressure against Roman Catholicism was pushing its faithful adherents more and more to the margins of society. In America Maryland, which had previously been a refuge, was now made a royal colony, and the Church of England was formally established there in 1702. In England the church of James II and John Dryden was coming to seem, in John Henry Newman's words, 'no longer the Catholic Church in the country; nay, no longer, I may say, a Catholic community – but a few adherents of the Old Religion, moving silently and sorrowfully about as memorials of what had been . . . An old-fashioned house of gloomy appearance, closed in with high walls, with an iron gate and yews, and the report attaching to it that "Roman Catholics" lived there . . .' John Leyburn, who had been consecrated a bishop for the English back in 1685 when James II had been promising so much, was imprisoned after that foolish monarch's fall and, on his release, lived obscurely in London until his death in 1702. His successor, Bonaventure Giffard, led a life of equal obscurity (and, it seems, no great effectiveness) until his own death in 1734.

Yet that was not the whole picture. The political disaster of the 1680s, followed by the decline of the Roman Catholic aristocracy and gentry, ultimately liberated congregations. In the countryside and country towns, instead of being totally dependent on a patron the faithful sometimes now hired a room in an inn for Mass or built a public chapel with an unprovocative modesty; and they gradually became more prosperous themselves, as part of the general economic progress of the time. In London their numbers grew to about twenty thousand, mainly because desperately poor Irish immigrants moved there hoping to pick up a living. There was, however, a touch of Baroque splendour about some of the chapels attached to London embassies, with a considerable staff of priests and music that attracted large congregations. Other elegant chapels were to be seen in country houses. The eighteenth century also saw a modernization of medieval customs which had hitherto seemed obligatory. It was no longer thought shocking for a Roman Catholic to work on a saint's day or to take some food before working on a day which was a fast in the Church's calendar; and in 1777 Rome officially reduced the number of 'holidays of obligation' in England. Priests who had been forced to disguise themselves in public as laymen now felt more acceptable to society. It symbolized much that they tended to wear wigs and brown (not black) coats, like Dissenting ministers.

In 1715, and again in 1745, their peaceableness was tested. What had been feared since Elizabethan times came to pass: a Roman Catholic claimant to the throne aroused a rebellion. But the Jacobites were disappointed in the support they received from the priests. In 1715 some gentry in Northumberland, Durham and Lancashire joined the abortive rising but there was no widespread movement. Even less practical interest in the Jacobite cause was shown in 1745; the main reaction, it seems, was alarm about the barbarism of the Young Pretender's army of Highlanders. And another test of the new status of Roman Catholicism in the country came when in 1753 it was made a criminal offence for anyone who was not a clergyman of the Church of England to conduct a marriage, the motive being alarm at the number of clandestine marriages. In an earlier period great tension would have been created as Roman Catholic priests stopped their flocks from obeying a Protestant Parliament. Instead most of the priests behaved like the Protestant Dissenting ministers. They allowed Roman Catholics to be married in the Anglican parish churches, and blessed them afterwards.[29]

---

[29] Basil Hemphill told of 'Catholic life in the penal times' in his *The Early Vicars Apostolic of England*, up to 1750. John Bossy traced the change from 'the age of the gentry' to 'the birth of a denomination' in *The English Catholic Community, 1570–1850*. See also Hugh Aveling, *The Handle and the Axe*, pp. 238–321.

Thus in a quiet time when Roman Catholicism might seem to be dying out in England, in deepest reality it was being renewed by the transfer of its base from the houses of the rich to the hearts of the poor, from the hopes of a political conquest to the assurance of a spiritual appeal.

The new security was embodied in the self-effacing figure of Bishop Richard Challoner, who became vicar apostolic of the London district in 1741 and remained faithful to that calling as a pastor for forty years. He never compromised over faith or morals. Indeed, he did what he could to resist the 1753 Marriage Act, urging his flock to be married by one of their own priests and, if they did feel obliged to go to an Anglican church in compliance with the law, never to join in the prayers offered there. But after a time he had to admit defeat, especially when Rome refused to back him up, and he made no fuss about it. To him the incident merely illustrated the trend which he recorded in a private letter of 1769: 'Oh! 'tis a melancholy thing to see the great decay of piety and religion amongst a great part of our Catholics.' For many years he used an assumed name, 'Mr Fisher', and referred to the Pope in his letters as 'Mr Abraham'. And his pessimism about the results of any public activity by, or on behalf of, his community seemed to be justified when in 1780 there were 'No Popery' riots in London led by a lunatic peer (who later fled to France and became a Jew), Lord George Gordon.

But Richard Challoner commended his faith to the poor. The custom had been established of using aristocrats as bishops: his own predecessor in the London area was a Petre (who spent most of his time in country houses in Essex), and his most distinguished fellow bishop was Richard Stonor of Stonor Park, vicar apostolic of the Midland district (also for forty years). The theory was that such men would finance their dignity out of their own wealth and dine with the gentry on equal terms. Challoner, in contrast, lived in humble London lodgings off his own meagre stipend, and gave as much of that stipend as he could to the poor. His last word was 'charity', because he was carrying a small sum entrusted to him for the poor. Every day of his life he found time, if at all possible, to talk with the poor – the poor whose horrifying surroundings

were depicted in Hogarth's cartoons. This manner of life
helped him to ensure that the suppression of the Society of
Jesus did little to harm the English mission, In England the
Jesuits ceased to be Jesuits, because the Pope had so commanded; but many of them remained at work, for they did not
cease to be priests and pastors.

Challoner was the son of a Presbyterian trader, born in 1691
in the rabidly Protestant town of Lewes. His mother, when
widowed, entered domestic service and found employment in
the home of the daughter of Lord Strafford, the 'Papist' peer
executed at the instigation of Titus Oates. The boy was
converted to this lady's religion at the age of thirteen, following
his mother, and within a year had agreed to go for his
education to the college at Douai. Learning or teaching he
remained in Flanders until 1730, when he began half a century
of missionary labours in the London slums.

Most mornings, after long prayers, were devoted to writing,
and as an author he was both prolific and effective. His most
used work was *The Garden of the Soul*, a manual of devotion
issued anonymously in 1740. It was an unimaginative book,
and those brought up on it were to be called 'Garden-of-the-
Soul Catholics' in patronizing terms by later generations who
preferred more emotional and flamboyant devotions. It was a
book of its time, long before any liturgical movement had
spread a corporate picture of the Church. It advocated communion only eight times a year; it spoke about 'hearing Mass';
it encouraged private prayers during that service; it did not
translate the Latin canon (central prayer). But it was the book
of a holy man, written unpretentiously in order to help laymen
to be holy. Each communion was to be preceded by a week's
preparation; each day was to be prayed over in self-
examination; each important act was to be offered in prayer;
there must be a full confession of sins to a priest when possible.
It was a religion for Catholics who could not count on splendour or even regularity in their public worship. When no priest
was available, the faithful could still pray in quiet groups or
alone. And to show the standards at which the eighteenth
century must still aim in the cultivation of the soul, this saintly
bishop spent much time collecting for publication material

about four hundred Elizabethan or later missionary priests
(many of them martyrs) and about the medieval saints of
England (whose feasts he caused to be observed again after
neglect). In his controversial pamphlets he appealed to the
authority of the scriptures – and for his own flock he revised the
Douai Version of the Bible, producing an edition which remained standard until after the second world war.

Once, when he was reminded of the likelihood that increasing numbers of the gentry would desert a penalized religion, he
replied calmly: 'There will be a new people.' It was a prophecy
which began to come true even during his lifetime. An Act of
Parliament in 1778, prompted on the government's side by a
desire to recruit for the army among Roman Catholics in
Ireland and Scotland, was the beginning of this long-suffering
community's emancipation. It entitled Roman Catholic laymen to inherit or sell estates, and priests to function unharmed,
if they swore an oath of loyalty to the Hanoverian dynasty. It
had been negotiated by some of the remaining Roman Catholic
gentry with the government. Challoner seems to have been
informed, but to have agreed to leave the responsibility with
the government and his own laity. This enabled him to reassure the Vatican when an inquiry arrived about the compromise involved. 'They made it a point to take no notice of us
in this whole affair,' he replied to Rome on behalf of the Vicars
Apostolic, 'that they might not appear, as they said, to be any
ways governed in such affairs as these or influenced by their
priests.' And the Vatican accepted this explanation. The
contrast with the papal claim to depose Elizabeth I could
scarcely be greater. On the day after the royal assent to this Act
of 1778, Challoner formally required all the priests in his
district to pray in public for the Hanoverian Royal Family – a
touch which showed how far he was from resenting the gentry's
initiative. A reaction to this compromise came with the Gordon
Riots, aimed against well-to-do Roman Catholics in London;
but that reaction was hysterical and violent to an extent which
offended all decently-minded Englishmen. The persecution
which had begun under Elizabeth I was now effectively over.
By 1830 Roman Catholics would be allowed to vote in parliamentary elections. Because of further immigration from

famine-stricken Ireland, by 1850 there were to be half a million Roman Catholics in England, with complete freedom to worship and with no civic disabilities imposed on them because of their faith. Challoner's prophecy about a 'new people' had been fulfilled.

When this saintly pastor died in 1781, he was buried in a friend's family vault in the Berkshire village of Milton – until in 1946 his body was brought back to London, to lie in Westminster Cathedral. So in death he received the hospitality of an Anglican parish church, whose charitable rector wrote in his register: 'Buried the Reverend Richard Challoner, a Popish Priest and Titular Bishop of London and Salisbury, a very pious and good man, of great learning and extensive abilities.'[30]

---

[30] Edwin Burton compiled *The Life and Times of Bishop Challoner* (2 vols, London, 1909). Later research was presented in *Challoner and His Church*, ed. Eamon Duffy (London, 1981). The main background to Challoner's pastoral work was depicted by George Rudée, *Paris and London in the Eighteenth Century* (London, 1969).

Outline of Events

1687   *Principia Mathematica* by Isaac Newton
1688   James II flees after failure to protect Roman Catholics
1689   Act of Toleration; *Essay Concerning Human Understanding*
           by John Locke
1690   William III wins battle of Boyne
1693   Death of nonjuror ex-archbishop, William Sancroft
1702   Queen Anne begins reign, favours High Churchmen
1707   *Hymns and Spiritual Songs* by Isaac Watts
1714   Death of Queen Anne transfer power to Whigs
1719   Dissenting ministers' debate about Holy Trinity
1723   Archbishop William Wake deprived of power by Sir
           Robert Walpole
1726   *Gulliver's Travels* by Jonathan Swift
1728   *A Serious Call to a Devout and Holy Life* by William Law
1730   *Christianity as Old as the Creation* by Matthew Tindal
1736   *The Analogy of Religion* by Joseph Butler
1741   G. F. Handel composes *Messiah*; Richard Challoner
           becomes vicar apostolic of London district

INDEX

Volume Three

FROM THE EIGHTEENTH CENTURY TO THE FIRST WORLD WAR

Contents

Preface: Religion in Modern England

Secularization is the background to the story told in this volume. It is very much in the foreground of the minds of those commentators who are convinced that the process will end in the complete impotence of the churches (if not their total disappearance), any heartfelt 'religiosity' that may survive being confined to sects isolated on the margins of society. Sociologists and historians who have reached such conclusions tend to think that any emphasis on the vigour of Christianity is due to the desire to make propaganda. Thus Alan Gilbert at the end of his study of *The Making of Post-Christian Britain*(1980) complimented me on the 'breadth and understanding' of my earlier book *Religion and Change* (1969) but warned his readers that it was 'among the better examples of partisan discussion', presumably because I wrote about Christians as one of them while also trying to tell the truth about their problems. The damning adjective 'partisan' was not applied to the work of scholars who gloat over the churches' declining statistics.

This volume is more compressed than Volume Two because as I moved from the 1730s to the 1910s I felt in more danger of being overwhelmed by the mass of evidence about the strength of English religion. I tried to show how much of this strength was due to the very fact that English Christianity had to assert itself in evangelism, facing a rejection of its faith both by the educated and by the working class which had not been experienced since Anglo-Saxon days. Many of the leaders of religion were deeply troubled by the new situation, not only because they had become conscious of their urgent duty towards fellow-Englishmen to whom religion meant little or nothing but also because they had to articulate their own faith in response to at least some of the questions being asked. These leaders often seem to us to possess an assurance and consequent energy which most of their successors were to lack; I was struck by this when working on my *Leaders of the Church of England 1828–1924*(1971). But as I reconsidered these formidable men and women in preparation for this book I was struck also by the general absence of complacency. Theirs was an assurance under attack, an energy for great tasks. So the unifying theme which forced itself into my mind was the theme of revival (not understood narrowly). I now repeat without penitence a paragraph which I wrote in 1984.

This volume tells the story of how the Evangelical revival brought a new power to personal religion for many of the English including Methodists and other Nonconformists. It was followed by a Catholic revival both in the Church of England and in the enlarged Roman Catholic community, together with a new determination to respond to the needs of the larger population in the world's first industrial nation. Such revivals made Victorian England as religious as it was, with a faith which sustained poets from Wordsworth to Hopkins and much philanthropy – and which spread (like the connected British empire and commerce) into all the continents. Even this mere sketch of the Victorian age brings together many outstanding men and women. For all its faults it was an age full of courage and creativity, one of the peaks of Christian civilization; only people not fit to be compared with the Victorians will sneer at them.

That last phrase was of course a reference to the rebellious denigration of the Victorians which became fashionable in the 1920s, thanks to Lytton Strachey and the other wits grouped together as 'Bloomsbury'. Writing in the 1980s I could not help feeling that Strachey and his friends were now looking pathetic as the nation under Mrs Thatcher once again saw the point of 'Victorian values', meaning chiefly hard, determined work. However, responses to this volume and further reflections on its contents have helped me to emphasize that the revivals failed in two key areas. Both these failures became clear, even to enthusiastic clergymen, when the great war shot to pieces the long period which may be called pre-Victorian, Victorian and post-Victorian after a queen who had embodied many of its strengths and weaknesses. I thought that a recognition of the seriousness of these failures was sufficiently clear in the austerity of my concluding pages, but that was one of my own mistakes.

There was an intellectual failure, specially noticeable when one compares English with German theology. This volume, like its predecessors, refers to many Englishmen who strenuously applied great intellectual abilities to learning and expounding orthodox

Christianity as set forth in the Bible and interpreted in the traditions of the churches. It also shows that some who still identified themselves as Christians had a piercing insight into the religious searches and struggles of a new generation. The crisis of faith evoked some of the most moving poetry in the English language. But most of the intellectual energy of the professional teachers of religion went into controversies with each other: Anglican versus Nonconformist, Roman Catholic versus Protestant, High Church versus Evangelical, Arminian versus Calvinist, conservative versus liberal, fundamentalist versus modernist. These theological arguments were thought necessary if Christianity was to be faithfully represented to the people, but they consumed so much attention that it was impossible to agree on a syllabus for religious education in the State's new schools, and too little was done to restate Christian faith in harmony with the knowledge which grew as science expanded and in relation to the much more subtle modern understanding of human nature. Indeed, the restatement of basic beliefs for intelligent adults inclined to scepticism was no one's job. Almost all clergymen were expected to apply themselves to the pastoral care of their existing congregations or to the instruction of the young; thus theologians of the stature of Newman and Maurice were essentially preachers. Evangelists from Whitefield to Spurgeon felt driven to preach a 'simple' gospel, more or less involving fundamentalism. It was not for them to ask or encourage theological questions as they crusaded against spiritual destitution, any more than it was for philanthropists such as Wilberforce and Shaftesbury to raise awkward question about the structure of society as they attempted to relieve material poverty. And most of the Christian scholars produced by the universities, whether or not they could be called theologians, studied and taught religion only as it was expressed in ancient literature including the Scriptures. Those who wrestled with the new scepticism usually kept quiet about it; if they were clergymen they either resigned in order to take up other work or kept their public expressions of belief vague in order not to alarm the conventional ('not in front of the ladies'). Moreover, many lay people in the middle classes felt similarly inhibited when discussing religion for fear of disturbing the social order ('not in front of the servants'). On the other hand, the discussion of religion in the working class could concentrate on the alleged hypocrisy of churchgoers rather than on the content of the churches' teaching. For one reason or another the Christian faith was not restated on the scale required and a great Christian crusader against squalor and vice such as William Booth could reckon theology entirely irrelevant to his mission. In the end the teaching of Christianity seemed to be out of contact both with the bright promises of science in the world of H. G. Wells and with the apocalyptic realities of the great war.

There was also a failure in responding to industrialization, specially noticeable when one compares the English with the American churches. A radically new pattern of society was created as modern technology supplied the necessities of a population which multiplied as it grew healthier, without providing high wages or decent conditions for the majority. This volume, like its predecessors, refers to many Christian men and women who cared for the poor. They were missionaries to the rural poor and to the new England as it teemed and sprawled in towns and cities, just as some of their brothers and sisters were now missionaries to the heathen in other continents. But the churches were not quick to adjust either their organization or their styles to the growth in the population. The map of the parishes remained virtually unchanged between the thirteenth century and the nineteenth, and 'Old Dissent' was almost as aloof as was the Church of England. The rural poor were kept in their humble places, and for the proletariat there was no welcome and no room in the town churches. When conscience goaded Anglicans and Nonconformists into planting churches in the ugly new urban world – which was eventually done on a large scale – it was found that the world had already been formed. City life had acquired its pattern with no thought of what clergy and congregations might have contributed, and with only vague feelings about the God who seemed to belong to the very different, hierarchical, communities of the countryside and to the very different rural routine close to the creative mysteries of nature. There were exceptions to this alienation between church and people. Some branches of Methodism were spiritual homes for some of the poor; the previously gentry-dominated Roman Catholic Church was transformed by the post-famine influx of the Irish into England; the Church of England had its slum parishes; the Salvation Army and some other new movements were uninhibited in a 'vulgar' lifestyle which the poor could understand. The statistics of Victorian churchgoing proved that not only gentlefolk or professionals or managers went to church with their families. But the evidence leaves the general impression that most of those who went possessed, or aspired to possess, or were compulsorily attached to, some stake in society as then constituted (for example, they were shopkeepers or domestic servants). Even among those Christians who knew, or belonged to, the world of the really poor there was great caution in any protest against a social order which perpetuated glaring exploitation. So this volume ends with the churches seeming to be largely out of contact with the bulk of the working class.

As a Christian who accepts all historical truth I have to accept the very severe rebukes implied in these facts about Christian England in the first age of science and industry. But I do not find it necessary to think that the Christian religion was in principle incapable of meeting the intellectual and social challenges, so that all these failures were completely inevitable. On the contrary, I regret that the very impressive religious energy of the English during the revivals which I describe was not energetic enough, and I am not without hope for the responses of Christians in England now that both science and the economy have different characters. Any reader who finds the conclusion of this volume too enigmatic may be interested in the *History of English Christianity 1920–85* (1986) which I persuaded Professor Adrian Hastings to write when my energy was flagging, or even in my own book on *The Futures of Christianity* (1987), but here I can briefly make a suggestion. The statistical decline of the churches since the religious census of 1851, when about half the adult population was in church on a fairly normal Sunday, must sadden Christians. But it has not involved an equally catastrophic drop in the kind of religion that the New Testament advocates.

What has declined, it seems, is mainly what is called 'folk religion'. Such religion benefits Christianity, for it brings the bulk of the population within reach (however occasionally) of the Bible, and it encourages people to draw strength from prayer. It supplies the audience of a Wesley or a Booth. But 'folk religion' has also meant the use of religion to unite a nation in a way which suits its government; the use of a religious association to develop a social identity (such as middle class respectability or the aspirations behind sending working class children to Sunday School); the use of a religious label to assert an ethnic identity (the Irishness of Roman Catholicism was countered by anti-Catholic bitterness and some riots); the use of dignifying religious ceremonies as 'rites of passage' (at birth, marriage or death) or as entertainment on a Sunday otherwise empty; the use of religious sanctions (supremely the threat of hell) to commend common sense or a commonly accepted morality; the use of religious literature to answer questions which are best answered by scientists; the use of a religious institution to distribute charity for the relief of material distress; the use of a religious veneer to conceal a belief in magic or fate or miracles understood as the frequent intervention of supernatural power to suit one's convenience. At the end of his fair-minded chapter on religion in his *Modern Britain – A Social History 1750–1985*, Edward Royle wittily contrasted the Victorian secularist groups which often looked like churches with the twentieth-century churches, which in a very different climate of opinion have often looked like secular philanthropic movements. He commented: 'In the consumer society religious activities have suffered irreparably from secular competition.' That is true, but it may be the case that if activities using religion are not all Christian then England towards the end of the twentieth century is more Christian than is suggested by a superficial comparison with the thirteen centuries of Christian England.

D.L.E.

Part One

REVIVAL

CHAPTER ONE

CHALLENGES TO ORTHODOXY

THE NEW QUESTIONING

The England over which George III began to reign in 1760 was a great power for the first time in its history, thanks partly to its union with Scotland and its occupation of Ireland. Its manufacturing industry was the most advanced in the world. Its navy ruled the waves. Its army had conquered the heartland of Canada; the whole east coast of America down to Florida lay under its rule; and its merchants were extracting great wealth out of an India which was at the mercy of the East India Company's small forces. Its population was growing fast (more children were surviving and more adults were eating fresh meat during the winter) but was not yet dependent on imported food. Its roads were being improved and the network of canals – the greatest engineering feat in its history so far – was being constructed. Its aristocracy lived in splendour, and many landowners, financiers, manufacturers and merchants were probably more comfortable. The menace of the London mob was a reminder of the underworld of poverty to be found in the towns. It was also true that a bad harvest resulted in people starving, and that the low prices caused by a glut of corn were almost as disastrous for the countryside. But the poverty was worse in every other country in the world.

The new king, aged twenty-two and full of ideals, himself added to the official draft of his first speech to Parliament: 'I glory in the name of Britain.' His reign was to see many changes. Both he and his people in Britain and Ireland were to suffer much, while the Americans departed to fulfil their own manifest destiny. But before his death in 1820, the kingdom of George III had stood against the empire of Napoleon and had made the decisive naval, military and financial contributions to that empire's disappearance; and the colonies acquired during the course of that great war had been added to a second British empire.[1]

Much of English life remained stable and pleasant. The Church of England certainly looked well established in many rural parishes. To this day handsome Georgian rectories bear witness to the prosperity of many of the clergy, and there are books which show what some of them were doing. *The Natural History and Antiquities of Selborne*, published by its rector, Gilbert White, in 1789, the year of the French Revolution, was a beautifully written record of close observation of the Hampshire countryside. A diary for the years 1758–1803 preserved much of the life of James Woodforde – a conscientious man by the standards of his day, taking a service once a week, helping the poor with charity and elementary medicine, inviting neighbours to share the bounty of his table. No new idea ever disturbed the tranquillity of his days in Norfolk.[2] He was not unique.[3]

But it was also a time of new questions. The independence achieved by the Americans was matched by a radicalism in England. Some radicals continued to voice discontent although driven underground when all the conservative forces rallied to defend the old social order in responses to the major shocks of the French Revolution, the war against France and the post-war slump. New questions asked under the young George III and never forgotten probed the necessity of kings, the moral authority of a Parliament which did not represent the people, the whole alliance of Church and State. Some affluent Whigs now belonged to a society called 'the Friends of the People'. More alarmingly, radical agitators urged the people to be their own friends.

Essentially what happened in politics was that the stability

---

[1] Good introductions include Ian Christie, *Wars and Revolutions 1760–1815* (London, 1982), and Marilyn Butler, *Romantics, Rebels and Reactionaries* (Oxford, 1981), on the literature.

[2] James Woodforde's *Diary of a Country Parson*, edited by John Beresford, was first published in 5 vols. (Oxford, 1924–31). A one-volume selection appeared in 1935.

[3] A. Tindal Hart drew together many studies in *The Country Priest in English History* (London, 1959), *Clergy and Society 1600–1800* (London, 1968), and *The Curate's Lot* (London, 1970).

accepted after England's 'glorious revolution' of 1688–89 ceased to seem perfect even to those who had prospered. The social order could not satisfy all the new ambitions stirring the enlarged population. Change was becoming more revolutionary in the modern sense. In the arts, too, there was change. 'Sense' had been prized – often a trivial sense, or, when serious in intent, a satirical sense. Reason, decorum and elegance had been admired as the cultural equivalents of the political stability which had been such a relief after the turmoils of the seventeenth century. Now the sunny afternoon was over and the climate of opinion was stormy. A new restlessness and a new individualism emerged. Within the eighteenth century, 'sensibility' (what a later generation would call sensitiveness – but it could also mean an unhealthy selfishness) was usually kept well under control. What mattered most was still 'sense'; for self-discipline must be the stable framework of a rational, prosperous life. But gradually the new stirring became the nineteenth century's faith in intuition, emotion, energy and heroism. The day of the heroic ego, or at least of the sensitive self, had arrived. It became a cultural revolution, to be called Romanticism.

Even the clergy, whose lives often seemed so sheltered, could be vulnerable. In rural Norfolk Parson Woodforde, for all the stability of his public existence, was deeply troubled by anxieties in his heart, making him an unhappy recluse in his last years; and two short books by soul-searching country clergymen were minor landmarks in the wider movement of emotions. Edward Young's *Night Thoughts* was a poem about death reckoned by the Methodist hymn-writer Charles Wesley the most useful book ever published apart from the Bible. Laurence Sterne's *Sentimental Journey* (into France) recorded 'a quiet journey of the heart in pursuit of *Nature*, and those affections which rise out of her' – at a time when he, too, had night thoughts, for he knew that he was dying. And not all who questioned the old comfortable certainties remained within the Christian fold, as those literary clergymen did. Not everyone who observed the poverty in village or slum felt inclined to describe it in gentle poetry using heroic couplets, as another parson, George Crabbe, did. Some put their deep-probing

questions with a fierce contempt for all that the clergy represented.

William Hogarth, who died in 1764, engraved an immensely
popular series of prints which were hilarious or ferocious (or
both at the same time). In his vision of town life the pleasures of
the rich were empty, the consolations of the poor were coarse,
politics was a brawl, and selfishness reigned everywhere. One
level of society saw the harlot's progress to misery; another, the
rake's progress. The English prided themselves on their manly
freedom but used it to be cruel to each other and to animals.
Public executions were popular recreations and the Englishman's favourite sport was cock-fighting (to the death, with
heavy gambling). Hogarth felt no need to offer a cure for these
social diseases; he was a satirist. But in so far as he had a cure,
this seems to have been inspired by his patriotic trust in roast
beef, hard work and freedom. Some of his paintings – of his
servants, for example – show a real love of the people. With all
their vices the English were the world's best; and with more
roast beef, more industry and more freedom, they would be
better. Hogarth (who painted an amazingly frank portrait of
Bishop Benjamin Hoadly as a self-complacent criminal in his
splendid robes) certainly did not rely on religion for reformation or consolation. His print of a parish church in 1728, 'The
Sleeping Congregation', was contemptuous – but it was genial
in comparison with the coarsely savage prints which attacked
popular religion in the early 1760s: 'Enthusiasm Delineated'
and 'Credulity, Superstition and Fanaticism'.[4]

In 1761 Peter Annet, a schoolmaster, brought out the *Free
Inquirer*, the first journal openly to ridicule Christianity; and in
the 1790s there was a ready public for Tom Paine's two books
The Rights of Man and *The Age of Reason*, although every effort
was made by the authorities to suppress them. The first was so
favourable to the French Revolution that Paine had to flee to
France. The first part of *The Age of Reason*, written in Paris, was
a vigorous summary of Deism, the belief in an impersonal and

---

[4] See Derek Jarrett, *England in the Age of Hogarth* (London, 1974), and Ronald
Paulson (ed. Anne Wilde), *Hogarth: His Life, Art and Times* (New Haven, Conn.,
1974).

now inactive Creator which was probably all that was left of
the personal religion of the majority of Englishmen at the time
– so far from the truth was it that Deism had been 'defeated' by
the theology of Bishop Joseph Butler. Tom Paine compared the
Church's God with 'a passionate man who killed his son when
he could not revenge himself in any other way'. In Paris he
founded a society of Theophilanthropists, lovers of God and
man; it had its own temple. But the second part of *The Age of
Reason*, written in prison while Paine was awaiting execution at
the hands of the extreme revolutionaries, savagely attacked the
errors in the Bible and Christianity. In the end he openly
advocated that 'the churches be sold, and the money arising
therefrom be invested as a fund for the education of children of
poor parents of every profession'.

'The only idea man can affix to the name of God', wrote
Paine, 'is the first cause, the cause of all things. . . . The true
Deist has but one Deity; and his religion consists in contemplating the power, wisdom and benignity of the Deity in his
works, and in endeavouring to imitate him in everything
moral, scientific and mechanical. . . . The Almighty Lecturer,
by displaying the principles of science in the structure of the
universe, has invited man to study and to imitation. . . .
Religion, therefore, being the belief of a God and the practice of
moral truth, cannot have any connection with mystery. The
belief of God, so far from having anything of mystery in it, is of
all beliefs the most easy, because it arises to us, as it is observed,
out of necessity.' Or at least this kind of belief arose easily for
Tom Paine, the son of devout Quakers.[5]

Others found even Deism difficult. The earthquake which
devastated Lisbon on All Saints Day 1755 inspired Voltaire's
Candide and much other scepticism. David Hume, for one,
found no 'principles of science' or of morality taught by the
'Almighty Lecturer'. In his essay on miracles, published seven
years before the earthquake, he had scarcely troubled to
conceal his agnosticism beneath his irony. He concluded that
'the Christian Religion not only was at first attended with

---

[5] See Audrey Williamson, *Thomas Paine* (London, 1973), and James Boulton, *The
Language of Politics in the Age of Paine and Burke* (London, 1963).

miracles, but even at this day cannot be believed by any reasonable person without one. Mere reason is insufficient to convince us of its veracity: and whoever is moved by Faith to assent to it, is conscious of a continued miracle in his own person, which subverts all the principles of his understanding, and gives him a determination to believe what is most contrary to custom and experience.'

Hume was one of the Scots who reaped the advantages of the union with England. He found friends and patrons there, and when he was given charge of the lawyers' library in Edinburgh he used it to write the first systematic history of England, which in the end made him 'not only independent but opulent'. In his early twenties he had, like many intelligent young men, been the victim of introspective despair, and he had proceeded to question all external and conventional realities and moralities; but his mature and placidly comfortable policy was 'inattention' to the ultimate questions. It has been well described. 'He rightly judged that, if he pretended to instruct the world by a reason he had declared bankrupt, no one would notice the inconsistency. . . . What he would have approved of is the "carelessness and inattention" of generations of Anglo-Saxons who have pursued their business, or their studies, without regard to anything more than a vague utilitarianism. . . . That was his religion – a religion of sympathy, but not too much of it, and a great perseverance in caution.'[6]

Towards the end of the 1750s Edward Gibbon read Hume's philosophy and it confirmed his own rejection of dogmatic religion. He also began to see himself as an historian with Hume as his closest model. In his *History of the Decline and Fall of the Roman Empire* he never attacked the memory of that empire's victim and conqueror, Jesus of Nazareth. Instead, he patronized Jesus, whose 'progress from infancy to youth and manhood was marked by a regular increase in stature and wisdom; and after a painful agony of mind and body, he expired on the cross. He lived and died for the service of mankind. . . .' Gibbon could even bring himself to pay a few stately compli-

---

[6] C. H. Sisson, *David Hume* (Edinburgh, 1976), pp. 95–6. Antony Flew studied *Hume's Philosophy of Belief* (London, 1961).

ments to the Christian religion – particularly when the new religion of reason and revolution in France had dismayed him by its excesses. When himself middle-aged, he assured a pious aunt that 'I consider religion as the best guide to youth and the best support of old age'. But he had no real respect for Christianity; he had suffered too much from it while young. What Richard Porson wrote about him was accurate. 'He often makes, when he cannot readily find, an occasion to insult our religion; which he hates so cordially that he might seem to revenge some personal injury.'

The injury was this. During his second year at Magdalen College, Oxford, Gibbon came across a recently published *Free Enquiry* by Conyers Middleton into the miracles said to have occurred in the Christian Church in its first five centuries. The sceptical onslaught had the unintended effect of persuading this unhappy, lonely and bored student that if he was prepared to accept the ancient Church's miracles – as he then was – he might as well accept its dogmas. His conversion to Roman Catholicism meant that he could not return to Oxford. Instead he was packed off to Lausanne, to stay with a Protestant pastor – with good success. He acquired in Switzerland the command of French and the industrious love of history that were to be the foundations of his literary triumphs. He also acquired a hatred of the Catholicism which had been about to exclude him for ever from the cultured world.[7]

TWO TROUBLED CHRISTIANS

A conservative response to such challenges was possible, but it could look like a desperate clinging. Two examples were Samuel Johnson, the king of literary London, and King George III.

How near Samuel Johnson was to madness is not known. The most intimate documents which he left unburned were his

---

[7] The best biography is D. M. Low, *Edward Gibbon 1737–1794* (London, 1937). See also S. T. McCloy, *Gibbon's Antagonism to Christianity and the Discussions that it has Provoked* (London, 1933); J. W. Swain, *Edward Gibbon the Historian* (London, 1966); Sir Gavin de Beer, *Gibbon and his World* (London, 1968).

prayers, but the self-accusations in them revealed little that was exceptional. Probably the only person in whom he confided freely was Mrs Thrale. She left behind evidence that he thought he was close to insanity; but she had neither the medical nor the literary equipment to go into details. The men with whom he drank and talked, evening after evening, saw that he needed their company because he was unhappy; but most of them left only slight records behind. James Boswell never lacked either effrontery or the industry to record its achievements, but he could not extract from the cantankerous old sage the full story of his early years and of their psychological consequences.

Boswell did, however, find the solution to a puzzle which must otherwise perplex all who read his great *Life of Samuel Johnson*: why did people tolerate the Doctor's rudeness? It has never been enough to offer an explanation in terms of the wit and wisdom, since men so rude are usually left to be witty and wise by themselves. But Boswell propounded the solution: 'his loud explosions are guns of distress'. The unspoken fact in the famous conversations was that his shadowy companions, whose comments on questions seemed to be of value only in so far as they provoked the Doctor's genius, were more fortunate than he was – and they knew it.

Most of them knew also that Johnson's true nature was expressed in his constant kindness to those who were, as he was, miserable. Mrs Thrale reckoned that while she knew him he never spent more than £80 a year on himself or less than £200 a year on others. His home was a refuge for the destitute, and on his way to and from dinner he would empty his pockets for beggars or put pennies into the hands of children asleep on doorsteps. This tyrant of the dinner table would go out to buy oysters for his sick cat, Hodge. In his will he made his Negro servant his residuary legatee. Gruffly compassionate, disliking to be called 'Doctor' and seldom calling his friends 'Sir' (those were touches which Boswell added to make him sound more magisterial), Johnson was not joking when he told Sir Joshua Reynolds that the great business of his life was to escape from himself. He could not find sufficient relief in writing: he wrote surprisingly little which was deeply his own, although he

produced prolific journalism, most of which he did not trouble
to read through before it went to the printer. His distress drove
him to his fellow men in taverns. But fate, kinder than he
thought it was, sent him Boswell to preserve some glimpses of
his wounded personality and, with these, some echoes of the
English language's best talk.

Born in 1709, the son of an incompetent bookseller in
Lichfield, Johnson was marked for life by tuberculosis leading
to scrofula (the 'king's evil'). A visit to London to be touched
by Queen Anne failed to cure him. Surgery done clumsily on
him while a baby scarred his face; one ear was deaf and one eye
almost blind. And there were psychological scars. His involun-
tary tics and other compulsive movements became grotesque.
He usually looked unkempt and habitually lived in disorder.
Poverty wounded him also. It drove him from Oxford, where
he was laughed at because his toes showed through his shoes.

Having conquered a prolonged breakdown brought about
by that setback, he walked to London in 1737 and for nine
years earned his living as a hack journalist. Then he undertook
to compile the first comprehensive *Dictionary of the English
Language*, and after great toils its publication secured his fame.
He went on to edit Shakespeare and to make another major
contribution as a critic by his *Lives of the Poets*. But the wounds
of battle did not heal easily. His poem on *London*, a rather
conventional performance modelled on Juvenal's satire on the
corruption of Rome, might have been followed by creative
greatness. There were only magnificent fragments – a poem on
The Vanity of Human Wishes, also imitating Juvenal; *Rasselas*, a
story written in order to pay for his mother's funeral; some two
hundred essays written for the *Rambler* and amounting to an
exposition of morality as he understood it. For at least four
years he felt close to insanity, and his great *Preface to Shakespeare*
was written in the midst of that hell. Hating to be alone, he fell
into habits which, while not the 'sloth' he often called them,
were not conducive to the creation of great books. He would
dine in a tavern at four in the afternoon, drink tea and read on
his return home, get off to sleep at about four in the morning,
and rise for work at noon.

His pessimistic philosophy fed an austere religion. *Rasselas*,

published in the same year as Voltaire's *Candide*, attacked
shallow optimism as the savagely witty Frenchman did – but it
reached the conclusion that man's only perfect happiness lay in
heaven. It was not an easy conclusion to reach or retain; he
once said that 'he never had a moment when death was not
terrible to him'. He lived in constant horror of the possibility of
his own eternal damnation. His main argument for the immortality of the soul was that without it human life would make no
sense at all: 'the only thinking being of this globe is doomed to
think merely to be wretched, and to pass his time from youth to
age in fearing or suffering calamities.'

He respected clergymen, and wrote about forty solid, if dull,
sermons for some less eloquent friends to preach (just as he
wrote lectures on law to rescue a friend who had been made a
professor at Oxford). He was invited to accept ordination and a
parish, but could not face the 'assiduous and familiar instruction of the vulgar and the ignorant'. He had learning and piety
enough for a bishop, except that he reckoned that no one could
be made a bishop for learning and piety. In return for his
respect he wanted clergymen to be orthodox, hard-working
and decorous. 'I do not envy the clergyman's life as an easy
life,' he once declared, 'nor do I envy the clergyman who makes
it an easy life.' Once in a tavern he complained loudly about
some of the company; 'the merriment of parsons is mightily
offensive.' He refused to allow religion to be mocked, or vice to
be paraded, in his company. He was always chaste and,
although a greedy eater, for much of his life abstained from
alcohol. This was all the more remarkable because he preferred
laymen who would be merry.

He was by nature a sceptic; Mrs Thrale remarked on his
'fixed incredulity of everything he heard'. When a companion
confessed to 'shocking, impious thoughts', he replied: 'If I was
to divide my life into three parts, two of them would have been
filled with such thoughts.' Rightly he thought that for most
Christians doubt must always accompany faith; 'nothing is
granted in this world beyond rational hope.' But he was never
open about his doubts or precise about their theological solutions; he never wrote on religion at any length, and when he
spoke about it in company he tended to bluster. It was his

custom to receive Holy Communion at Easter only, having
fasted on Good Friday; but even then he was usually late in
church, unable to sit still in a pew, fearful of hearing nonsense
from the pulpit (or music which he detested almost as much).
He often accused himself of having neglected to 'take pleasure
in public worship' or to make a proper study of the Bible. He
had the habit of writing down beautifully expressed prayers – a
habit fairly common in his age, but one which did not suggest
intimacy with a heavenly Father.

It was only when he knew he was dying that he talked freely
to his friends about personal religion. 'Let me exhort you', he
said to a young Italian, 'always to think of my situation, which
must one day be yours; always remember that life is short and
eternity never ends.' When assured that David Hume had died
happily, he refused to believe it. Hume 'had a vanity in being
thought easy', he assured Boswell. His own deathbed creed
was addressed to the question which he had faced all his life:

> Must helpless Man, in Ignorance sedate,
> Roll darkling down the Torrent of his Fate?[8]

In the autumn of 1788 George III suffered a severe illness
which included delirium and nearly included death. He recovered but was similarly afflicted in 1801 and 1804. In 1811 his
mind finally gave way and he lived in a world of his own until
his death in 1820. Large sums were spent on the best medical
skill of the time, but diagnosis proved impossible, let alone
cure. Almost certainly this mental disease had a physical
origin, since no evidence suggests that the King's behaviour
was unbalanced during the first fifty years of his life. On the
contrary, he was the most popular monarch since Elizabeth I,
mixing freely and well with many people of all classes. He loved

---

[8] Among the many books on Johnson, the most useful for our present purpose are
Robert Voitle, *Samuel Johnson the Moralist* (Cambridge, Mass., 1961); Maurice
Quinlan, *Samuel Johnson: A Layman's Religion* (Madison, Wisc., 1963); Charles
Chapin, *The Religious Thought of Samuel Johnson* (Ann Arbor, Minn., 1968); James
Gray, *Johnson's Sermons* (Oxford, 1972); Charles Pierce, *The Religious Life of Samuel
Johnson* (London, 1983). W. Jackson Bate, *Samuel Johnson* (London, 1978), is the best
short life. James Clifford did not live to complete his standard modern life, but
achieved *Young Samuel Johnson* and *Dictionary Johnson* (London, 1955–80).

both hunting and music, and collected a large library. He was a faithful husband, the concerned father of a large family, a sober and self-disciplined man driven by a sense of his duty. He broke away entirely from the licentious habits of the first two Georges and would not live in Kensington Palace or Hampton Court, which he thought they had disgraced. Although he bought a house on the site of the later Buckingham Palace, he preferred to live quietly as a country gentleman at Windsor or Kew.

George III's character is relevant to our story because his respectability was based on his religion. He received the Holy Communion twelve times a year; it was symbolic that he took off his crown before communicating at his coronation. Thus inspired, he consistently opposed his age's vicious fashions. Soon after his accession the standard proclamation appeared 'for the encouragement of piety and virtue'. More surprisingly he reissued it in a strengthened version in 1784. He rebuked an aristocrat who occupied the Archbishopric of Canterbury from 1768 to 1783 (Frederick Cornwallis) for planning a ball in Lambeth Palace; he made no secret of his detestation of the morals of able politicians such as Charles James Fox; and his long quarrel with his own son and heir was inflamed by anger at the prince's sexual promiscuity, gambling losses and general irresponsibility (encouraged by Fox). He liked to believe that his relapse into mental illness in 1801 was caused by William Pitt's proposal to allow Roman Catholics the vote – as the King maintained, in defiance of his own coronation oath to preserve the Protestant religion – and Pitt had to promise never to mention the subject again. While insane the King was put under the brutal care of a clergyman, Francis Willis, who without being a qualified physician kept a private asylum and promised (as the qualified doctors did not) to effect a cure if given a free hand. At their first meeting the King rebuked Willis for changing from clerical to medical interests. According to the diarist Greville, he told him: 'You have quitted a profession I have always loved, and you have embraced one I most heartily detest.'

Samuel Johnson's pension which rescued him from poverty came from the secret service fund with the King's ready consent, and the two men approved of each other when they met. Johnson declared that it did a man good to be talked to by his sovereign. They had much in common. Their loyalty to the Church of England was defiantly old-fashioned. The Established Church seemed a precious part of the world of order and sanity; and they clung to its prayers because in their dark distresses they knew how it felt to be in hell.[9]

WILLIAM PALEY AND THE FAILURE OF COMPLACENT BELIEF

A more complacent defence of the Church could be offered, but in a time of questions and troubles its very complacency made it ultimately implausible.

William Paley happened to be born (in 1743) outside Yorkshire but his father was for forty-four years the schoolmaster in his native parish of Giggleswick. He spoke all through his life with a Yorkshire accent and never ceased to be blunt in his self-confident arguments. He spent seventeen years in Cambridge, first as a brilliant student, then as an effective college tutor, before holding a variety of ecclesiastical posts until his death in 1805. Three books of his were adopted as virtually the text books of the academic and ecclesiastical Establishment. The most important was *A View of the Evidences of Christianity* (1794); all Cambridge undergraduates were examined on their knowledge of this book from 1822 until 1920, unless they preferred the elementary logic or chemistry allowed as an alternative during the twentieth century. Paley also expounded the preliminaries to Christianity in his *Natural Theology* and its consequences in his *Principles of Moral and Political Philosophy*.

It may seem puzzling that such an influential champion of the Church of England's established role in society was not made a bishop; but the explanation is, like everything else about Paley, reasonable. He was happy to accumulate a large income from several humbler but less onerous positions which he held simultaneously. For their part, the bishop-makers

---

[9] The best biography is John Brooke, *George III* (London, 1974).

could not help noticing with alarm that he was no smooth courtier. He had retained his outspoken independence, especially in his talk, although the tendency of his writings was consistently conservative. Various private flippancies were repeated and did him no good. In a book he wrote that 'the divine right of kings is, like the divine right of constables . . . a right ratified, we humbly presume, by the divine approbation, so long as obedience to their authority appears to be necessary, or conducive to the common welfare.' The same book also referred to 'those futile arts and decorations which compose the business and recommendations of a court.' Obedience to rulers was usually expedient, Paley taught, even if the ruler were 'a child, a woman, a driveller or a lunatic'; and respect for property was usually also expedient, even if the property system resembled a flock all collecting grain to feed one superior pigeon. George III was said to have met William Pitt's recommendation of this philosopher for a bishopric with: 'What? Pigeon Paley? Not orthodox, not orthodox.'

Paley defended Christianity and the Church on the ground that they increased human happiness. Jesus was a man whose status as the Son of God was attested by the fact that although he 'had visited no polished cities' he was a surprisingly civilized teacher of religion and morality; 'there was no heat in his piety, or in the language in which he expressed it.' The religion taught by Jesus was, of course, the religion taught by William Paley. It had been temporarily commended by miracles but they had long ago ceased. It was successful and had led to the establishment of National Churches. Although the wealth of some clergymen put them in contrast with the Galilean fishermen, 'rich and splendid situations in the Church have been justly regarded as prizes held out to invite persons of good hopes and ingenuous attainments to enter into its service.'

The religious message which Jesus delivered with such elegance concerned the benevolence of God. Paley took it for granted that the order in the universe demonstrated its creation. Like a man finding a watch on the ground when crossing a heath, the student of nature could know that what lay before him had been designed by a maker. Paley dwelt on the

admirable design of the human body and on the many pleasures of human life, but also celebrated the happiness of God's
other creatures. 'It is a happy world after all. The air, the earth,
the water, teem with delighted existence. In a spring noon, or a
summer evening, on whichever side I turn, myriads of happy
beings crowd on my view. . . . If we look to what the waters
produce, shoals of the fry of fish frequent the margins of rivers,
of lakes, and of the sea itself. These are so happy that they do
not know what to do with themselves. Their attitudes, their
vivacity, their leaps out of the water, their frolics in it (which I
have noticed a thousand times with equal attention and
amusement), all conduce to show their excess of spirits. . . .'

The moral message of Jesus was the encouragement among
men of a benevolence similar to God's, with the promise of a
suitable reward. Paley defined virtue as 'the doing good to
mankind, in obedience to the will of God, and for the sake of
everlasting happiness.' An important part of happiness in
human life was to be busy, and Archdeacon Paley, observing
that many of his fellow clergymen were idle and therefore
bored, suggested suitable hobbies for them; for example, they
should fill in the time by gardening but add to their pleasure by
acquiring some knowledge of botany. He praised an interest in
politics; not only did this afford a harmless and intelligent topic
of conversation, but in politics men could do God's will 'as
collected from expediency'. The one test of political or private
morality for Paley was the increase of happiness. Sir Leslie
Stephen wrote that Paley had taught that 'Christ came into the
world to tell us that we should go to hell if our actions did not
tend to promote the greatest happiness of the greatest number.'
His modern biographer who has a liking for Paley comments
about this summary: 'it is not wholly unfair'.[10]

[10] M. L. Clarke, *Paley: Evidence for the Man* (London, 1974), p. 72.

JOSEPH PRIESTLEY AND
THE FAILURE OF RATIONAL DISSENT

It was possible to argue that Paley's mistake was to defend too much of the old orthodoxy and the old Establishment in Church and State; that Christianity could be shown to be a suitable religion for rationally happy men if only it could be rationalized more radically.

Another Yorkshireman, Joseph Priestley, was born to humble and pious parents in 1733. At the age of nineteen he entered the only higher education open to him since his parents had rejected the Church of England, and this was an 'academy' for the sons of such Dissenters. There he was taught by a minister who, although orthodox, encouraged young men both to debate theology freely and to develop many non-theological interests; and so Priestley entered the movement which came to be called 'Rational Dissent'.

After two ill-paid pastorates as a Dissenting minister he became a tutor in another Dissenting academy, and by publishing textbooks built up a national reputation. Later in his life he returned to preaching, in London and Birmingham. His religious views moved further and further away from the stern orthodoxy of Calvinism, with its doctrine that some were predestined to heaven and others (the majority) to hell – but his well-to-do congregations were far from dismayed. He came before them on Sundays to preach sermons which seemed eminently sensible, and he took trouble in explaining the Bible to their children. During the week he was at work in his library and his laboratory, and they took a pride in his wide-ranging intellectual distinction. This distinction was so marked that the Earl of Shelburne persuaded Priestley to spend seven years as his librarian and companion.

The scientific work was not all of the same quality. Priestley had received no proper training; in his early years he was so poor that the purchase of basic books and instruments was a major difficulty, and he always had many non-scientific interests to distract him. But he wrote on electricity, and made important contributions. He excelled as a chemist. He was the first to explain oxygen, chlorine, ammonia, hydrogen chloride and sulphur dioxide. His researches into the properties of iron, carbon and steam became of use to manufacturers and he was scientific adviser to Josiah Wedgwood, the brilliant developer and salesman of superior pottery – while his invention of soda water, originally intended to help sailors on long voyages, has given many millions a lighter kind of pleasure. He was acknowledged as the intellectual king of the expanding town of Birmingham, where James Watt had recently built a steam engine.

His deepest interests were, however, in religious and political thought. He fully shared Paley's conviction that the marvels of nature all pointed to the existence of the Creator. But 'have nothing to do with a parliamentary religion', he urged, 'or a parliamentary God.' Reading and reflection persuaded him that, just as some of the airs which he investigated had become noxious by the decay of vegetable matter, so orthodox Christianity had been corrupted; and he was determined to say that it smelt.

While a student he read David Hartley's *Observations on Man* (1749). That book acquired an astonishing prestige in the second half of the eighteenth century – astonishing because the nineteenth and twentieth centuries have agreed that its observations could be forgotten. Hartley seemed to Priestley to reveal the truth about the word 'soul', which was that it was a confusing way of talking. The reality was that the mind received impressions through the senses and associated several impressions to form ideas; but when the brain died, the mind died. It remained dead until resurrected at the end of time. And what was true about other men was true about Jesus.

After becoming a minister, Priestley read books about the divinity of Christ. They made him, by the end of the 1760s, a full-blooded Unitarian. Jesus, 'as much a creature of God as a loaf of bread', was now dead, but he had taught the truth about God's benevolence and man's duties and therefore had been the Messiah. Worshipping him had been nothing better than idolatry. There had been no need to make Atonement for the sins of the whole world, since God himself was responsible for the existence of evil, as of everything else, in a world where men necessarily behaved as instructed by their senses. In *The Doctrine of Philosophical Necessity*, Priestley wrote: 'A Necessarian cannot accuse himself of having done wrong in the ultimate sense of the word. He has, therefore, in the strict sense, nothing to do with repentance or confession or pardon, which are all adapted to a different, imperfect, fallacious view of things.' It was not that Priestley advocated vice, whatever his opponents might say. But he wished to set the improvement of human behaviour in its proper context, for he believed that 'the whole series of events from the beginning of the world to the consummation of all things makes one connected chain of events, originally established by the Deity.' The universe was as progressive as was Priestley himself.

He also experimented in political theory. He assured his well-to-do audiences that he was no violent radical, and certainly he had no wish to extend the powers of the State. His *Essay on the First Principles of Government* urged the State 'never to interfere, without the greatest caution, in things that do not immediately affect the lives, liberty or property of members of the community.' But he sought the admission of consistent Dissenters (such as those audiences) to the universities, to local government and to Parliament; and he sought electoral reform. He derided a corrupt system which meant that Birmingham's inhabitants (more than thirty thousand) had no representative in the Commons.

In the early 1780s it was possible to expect gradual progress for such rational radicalism. The Earl of Shelburne became prime minister in 1782 and negotiated the recognition of the Americans whose war for independence had been welcomed by Priestley and many other Dissenters. Many other political reforms were being talked about. Under such patronage the cause of Rational Dissent, corresponding with the educated opinion of the day, would surely prevail. Priestley was present when his friend Theophilus Lindsey, who had abandoned the Anglican priesthood, opened a Unitarian chapel in Essex Street, London, and was delighted when the chapel was filled with a distinguished congregation. In 1772 the House of Commons was petitioned by an ultra-liberal group of London clergy for more doctrinal freedom. Although this petition was rejected, the requirement (very rarely enforced) that Dissenting ministers should assent to the doctrinal articles was soon abolished. Within Dissent, the appeal of Unitarianism was so strong that members of the General Baptist denomination who objected to it split off to form a 'New Connexion' during the 1770s. The old word 'Presbyterian' was becoming more and more infrequent in every-day speech. Roman Catholicism seemed powerless to cause any trouble; in 1780 Priestley urged that it should be tolerated since 'it is cowardly to kick an old and dying lion'. The controversies of the previous century seemed to be so safely buried that in 1789 a motion for the total repeal of the legislation penalizing Dissent in the Test and Corporation Acts was defeated in the Commons by a mere twenty votes (122–102). Sermons and pamphlets poured out, mocking the idea that a modern government should be expected to enforce medieval doctrines.[11]

The popularity for a time of proposals for a radical and rational simplification of Christianity can be seen in the career of Richard Watson. In 1782 he was made Bishop of Llandaff by Lord Shelburne. The son of the schoolmaster at Hawkshurst (Wordsworth's school), he had won the highest honours in mathematics at Cambridge. Remaining in the university to teach, he had been appointed professor of chemistry. Although he made no secret of the fact that he had 'never read a syllable on the subject', Cambridge must not leave science to the Dissenters. Then he had been elected professor of divinity. He was no great heretic; he lived to write an *Apology for Christianity*, replying to Edward Gibbon, and an *Apology for the Bible*, replying to Tom Paine ('apology' meant 'defence'). Paine had announced that 'my belief in the perfection of the Deity will not permit me to believe that a book so manifestly obscure, disorderly and contradictory can be his work. I can write a better book myself.' But Watson was an admirer of the Bible, partly because it saved him from further theological work. 'I reduced the study of divinity into as narrow a compass as I could, for I determined to study nothing but my Bible, being

---

[11] This campaign was studied by R. B. Barlow in *Citizenship and Conscience* (Philadelphia, Pa., 1962).

unconcerned about the opinions of councils, fathers, churches, bishops and other men as little inspired as myself.'

However, any hopes that this uninspired bishop would be promoted to a leading position in the Established Church, and that Dissenters would be put on terms of political equality with its members, were wrecked. In 1789 Watson retired to a mansion on the banks of Windermere and there spent the rest of his life (he died in 1816). He visited his Welsh diocese, sometimes as often as once a year, and he kept in touch by letter with his deputy in Cambridge, where he remained a professor; and he also kept a benevolent, if remote, eye on the parishes which provided him with additional incomes. But he explained to inquirers that he felt an obligation to concentrate on the improvement of his estate for the benefit of his family since he could hope for no further advancement in the Church. Meanwhile radicalism went down to defeat. In the House of Commons, when the motion for the repeal of the Test and Corporation Acts came back in 1790, it was thrown out by 294 votes to 105. The Earl of Shelburne, already excluded from office since 1783, was driven into the political wilderness. The Tories entered what was to be almost exactly half a century of power.

Much of this swing to conservatism in Church and State was a reaction against the French Revolution. In 1789, only two months after the narrow defeat of the motion in favour of the Dissenters in Westminster, the Bastille was stormed in Paris. The overthrow of oppression which this symbolized was welcomed by Dissenters such as Richard Price, the minister of the congregation in London to which Priestley had preached. In a much-discussed sermon Price compared events in France with the English Revolution of 1688 and announced that all kings owed their crowns to the people. But a reaction far more typical among those of the English who enjoyed privileges came from Bishop Watson: he announced that the news from France had caused him to 'fly with terror and abhorrence from the altar of liberty'.

Price's radical challenge inspired Edmund Burke to write a classic of counter-revolutionary rhetoric. In *Reflections on the Revolution in France*, he declared that 'the glory of Europe is extinguished for ever' if the old alliance of the orthodox Church with the monarchical State was to be destroyed by mob violence and if the old religious emphasis on duty was to be replaced by an atheist philosophy extolling the rights of man.

Back in 1773 Burke, then fresh from a visit to the sceptical aristocrats of Paris, had poured out all his Irish eloquence in a warning to the House of Commons not to tolerate atheism. In the fifteen years since that warning his eloquence had grown richer, but so rich as to be a bore, the 'dinner-bell' of the Commons; and the causes which he had defended had not amounted to a simple righteousness. While he was advocating the freedom of the Americans, he was drawing pay from them. While he was urging the punishment of the 'plunderers' of India such as Warren Hastings, he was defending his brother who was a swindler. He had shown courage, and had taken pride, in being a 'friend of liberty'. He had sought a recognition of the religious rights of the Irish Catholics, for example. In 1773, while defending the Church of England against change, he had assured the Commons that he also wished to defend the rights of individuals to dissent from it; he would 'have toleration a part of establishment'. But he had always taken it for granted that such rights as he advocated would not destroy the fabric of society – or, to put it more bluntly, the class system – of the England where the Church was to remain established.

This vital qualification to his advocacy of freedom now came to the fore in his reaction to the French Revolution. The 'morality' of a community was more important than any individual's rights: 'men are qualified for civil liberty in exact proportion to their disposition to put moral chains upon their own appetites.' The class system was what the realities of human nature demanded; in comparison, talk about the natural rights of the individual was mere 'theory'. A society was made up of imperfect men, but 'he censures God who quarrels with the imperfections of men' and in order that imperfect, unruly men might be disciplined God had willed the State: 'he who gave our nature to be perfected by our virtue willed also the necessary means of its perfection.' The State was a sacred partnership, but that did not mean that it was a mere agreement between individuals for their private and temporary purposes. It was 'a partnership in all science, a partnership in all art, a partnership in every virtue and in all perfection . . . a partnership . . . between those who are living, those who are dead and those who are to be born.' And it was impious to change the terms of such a partnership to suit 'floating fancies or fashions' or the 'swinish multitude'. As Burke was to write in a sequel to these anti-revolutionary *Reflections*, 'the awful Author of our being is the Author of our place in the order of existence'.[12]

This passionate philosophy appealed to the religious, as well as to the other, convictions of those inclined to conservatism. George III said that every gentleman should read it, and the doomed Louis XVI translated it into French. It was a book which made or reflected a whole new mood. Among those many Englishmen who could not read the old Tory cry 'Church and King!' was heard more loudly than it had been for a century. William Pitt, who had at first seemed rather close to reformers such as Shelburne, found his destiny as a war minister, implacably resisting the aggressive French until he lived to see England secured by Nelson's victory at Trafalgar. In the England of Pitt and Nelson, bracing itself for the greatest war it had ever endured, Burke's creed of nation and class, of God and duty, was an inspiration. Rational Dissenters and any others who could be suspected of a Frenchified republicanism ('Jacobinism') were the inevitable targets of hostility at every level of a nation absorbed in what seemed to be a crusade.

But alarm about the French Revolution was not the only cause of the defeat of all that Joseph Priestley advocated. He was also unpopular because of his religious radicalism, which he expressed with an insensitive arrogance. He made almost no contact with the average clergyman or churchgoer, let alone with the poor, and his theology made almost no contact with the Christian tradition. It was attacked by Richard Price and other Dissenters as well as by a number of very angry Anglicans. These conservatives exaggerated the extent to which the

---

[12] Recent studies include Charles Parkin, *The Moral Basis of Burke's Political Thought* (Cambridge, 1956); Alfred Cobban, *Edmund Burke and the Revolt against the Eighteenth Century* (revised, London, 1960); B. T. Wilkins, *The Problem of Burke's Political Philosophy* (Oxford, 1967); Michael Freeman, *Edmund Burke and the Critique of Political Radicalism* (Oxford, 1981).

developed doctrine of the Trinity could be found in the New Testament and the early Church, but their replies could not be answered solely at the academic level. There, Priestley could score debating points. But the real strength of their replies was emotional. For many centuries Christians had prayed to the Father through the Son, and they had worshipped the Son as the divine Saviour. All the saints had encouraged them to do so. That had been the heartbeat of the Christian tradition. Priestley's comparison of God the Son with a loaf of bread seemed mightily offensive.

It is not surprising that this insensitive radical's Unitarian creed, contemptuous of Christian orthodoxy, was thought to be a new religion, hostile to all the institutions of England – without being friendly to England's poor. A modern biographer of Lord Shelburne has summed up Priestley's influence on that radical politician. 'According to the scale of values which he imparted to Shelburne, virtue was to be found in the middling station in life, liberty of conscience, private secular education, self-help, thrift and respect for property as the trust of the righteous and the test of political responsibility; vice was to be found in idleness, luxury, established religion, pauperism, and the life of the English poor generally'.[13] Such values could never inspire a popular religious movement in England; and when proclaimed in pamphlets and addresses sympathetic with revolution in France, they could seem aggressively unpatriotic and anti-social as well as anti-Christian. Edward Gibbon, for example, coldly rejected Priestley's attempt to form an alliance and in his memoirs called him a 'trumpet of sedition'. And Priestley's unpopularity now exploded into mob violence.

In Birmingham on the warm evening of 14 July 1791 a dinner inaugurating a 'Constitutional Society' was surrounded by a riotous crowd, inflamed by the appearance of the slogan 'This useless barn to be let or sold' chalked on Anglican church doors – and by the publication of a pamphlet recalling the fall of the Bastille on 14 July, and remarking on the venal, hypocritical, extravagant and oppressive British system of Church and State. These provocative acts were disowned by Priestley and

---

[13] John Norris, *Shelburne and Reform* (London, 1963), p. 84.

his friends, but the impression had been created that on that 14 July revolution was being planned in Birmingham. The diners escaped that evening but the mob moved off from the tavern to burn down the elegant chapel where Priestley preached and another meeting house occupied by Rational Dissenters. After that it proceeded to wreck the preacher's house, library and laboratory, together with almost twenty other homes belonging to leading Dissenters. All over Birmingham was scrawled the Tory slogan, 'Church and King for ever!' Those responsible for law and order – including the King – were acutely embarrassed by the riot, sent in troops to quell it, and hanged two of its ringleaders. But the principal victim must have known that King George, honestly declaring himself 'pleased that Priestley is the sufferer', voiced public opinion.

The preacher-scientist tried to resume his work in England, but could not. It was a time when Burke could assure the Commons that many thousands of daggers had been ordered for a revolution to begin in Birmingham. A bookseller received four years' imprisonment for selling Paine's *Rights of Man*. Priestley's position in England was not helped when he was made an honorary citizen of the First Republic in France, which a few days after guillotining Louis XVI declared war on England. In 1794 he decided to emigrate to tolerant Pennsylvania, where his sons settled as farmers. He spent the last ten years of his life in America. He was honoured by three Presidents; he took tea with George Washington, John Adams was polite, and Thomas Jefferson declared that he had read *The Corruptions of Christianity* with agreement 'over and over again'. In exile Joseph Priestley preached, he experimented, and he was correcting the proofs of a pamphlet an hour before his death. But he knew that in his own country his attempt to make religion 'rational' and radical was, for the time being, smashed along with his Birmingham home and laboratory.[14]

---

[14] F. W. Gibbs, *Joseph Priestley* (London, 1965), is mainly scientific and may be supplemented by Sir Anthony Lincoln, *Some Political and Social Ideas of English Dissent 1763–1800* (London, 1938).

CHAPTER TWO

THE EVANGELICAL REVIVAL

THE GREAT AWAKENING IN AMERICA

Had English Christianity remained entirely in hands such as Paley's or Priestley's, presumably it would have declined as Paine, Hume or Gibbon expected. It would have lacked emotional strength. When frightened people such as Burke turned to the Christian religion in reaction against the French Revolution, they would have found little remaining in it but the belief in benevolence and progress, a belief not very likely to flourish as the revolution plunged Europe into chaos and a long war, and as other political and emotional tempests raged. But in fact Christianity gained power among the English as it rose to the challenge. The nineteenth century was to be far more Christian than the eighteenth – both in England and in those large areas of North America which were still united with England culturally. Democracy was to grow; but the Christian Church in its many branches was to make strenuous efforts to grow with the people, to talk as the people talked and to form congregations where the people lived, fanning into flame the still glowing religious emotions or memories. Scientific knowledge was to expand, a science-based industrial revolution was to make life new and urban, and the popular mind was to become largely secular. The Christian religion, however, was to be redefined for those who remained faithful to it. It was to be made exciting. It was to be able to transform individuals and to inspire new groups of tightly knit friends. Among thoughtful believers, it was to be the surrender of self-sufficiency in exchange for an emotional assurance beyond the reach of the cold hand of science. It was to be the entry into a world beautified by the Creator, a world more glorious than any industrial city. A reborn faith was to be given authority in those mysterious depths of the heart which were to be explored in literature by the Romantic movement and its successors. A revitalized congregation was to be far more conscious that it believed in the revealed God and wished to worship him, while the surrounding society became increasingly godless. In the cities created by industry there were to be faithful congregations, even if not many members of the new working class belonged to them for profoundly religious reasons. This recovery was to enable Christian soldiers to march against secularization; to fight and sometimes to conquer.

There was a widespread reaction against the French Revolution's bloody chaos in the 1790s, and with that came a reaction against the revolutionaries' religion of reason. In many areas of Europe the reaction produced a positive intensity in belonging to the Catholic Church (even Napoleon had to come to terms with the Papacy in order to be an emperor) and in Germany the rebirth of nationalism in the struggle against the French was accompanied by a revival of Lutheranism. The psychological forces which rallied against the French Revolution had, however, begun to grow long before the 1800s or 1790s. Emotionally the strongest form of Lutheranism was 'Pietism', a movement which had been started as long ago as the 1660s. Pietism was always marked by a warmly personal devotion to Jesus as Saviour, by private Bible study, and by enthusiasm in hymn-singing and other forms of worship. The old faith had been given a new life. In the English-speaking world, when the reaction against the excesses of the French Revolution needed to be expressed in a powerful, conservative religion, the Evangelical movement already existed and reaped the benefit. It was a renewal of conservative religion in many ways parallel with the Pietism of the German Lutherans, but its first large successes were achieved when Calvinism burst into flame in colonial America.

In Pennsylvania and other American 'middle colonies' in the 1730s, Presbyterian preachers breathed life into a Calvinism which had become a dull orthodoxy, while in New England others revived the religion (without the politics) of the Puritans. But the greatest name was that of Jonathan Edwards. The son and grandson of Puritan preachers of the old school, his own power was fresh when at Northampton in western Massachusetts he proclaimed the revived faith in God's sovereignty. A widely distributed public lecture of 1731 was entitled 'God Glorified in the Work of Redemption by the Greatness of Man's Dependence upon him in the Whole of It'. By the summer of 1735, Edwards later recalled, 'the town seemed to be full of the presence of God'.

Although his style was not that of a popular preacher, he was willing to disturb the emotions in his offer of salvation. Indeed, his *Treatise concerning Religious Affections* argued with skill that true religion consisted of emotions, stirred by the Spirit of God. In a particularly famous sermon he spoke of what befell 'Sinners in the Hands of an Angry God' and since he believed that people who did not repent of their sins before death would be condemned to the endless tortures of hell ('the God that holds you over the pit of hell, much as one holds a spider, or some loathsome insect over the fire, abhors you . . .'), he could scarcely be expected to remain unemotional when preaching. But with this frank appeal to the heart went careful reasoning.

In a series of books published in the 1750s he expounded a Calvinist view of man by attempting to answer the claims of the rationalist enlightenment with its own weapons. Pondering the freedom of the will, or the nature of sin, or the character of 'benevolence' in the virtuous man, he deepened the discussion. He presented man as a whole person who had to choose between darkness and light; as a figure in a tragedy, in that he habitually chose darkness; but also as potentially a son of God, filled by God's grace with God's light. In many ways this ardent Calvinist was a civilized member of the eighteenth century, standing in the tradition of many of the English Puritans of the previous century but fully aware of more recent thought; his death in 1758 (soon after becoming president of the recently founded college at Princeton) was caused by his willingness to be inoculated against smallpox. And because his theology had this thoughtful quality, it had an enduring influence. It has been pointed out that 'in western Christendom, the Pietist movement did not generally produce a theological school. . . . Re-awakened piety in New England, however, thanks to the genius of Jonathan Edwards, was followed by and incorporated in a theological school; it thereby stands unique; it thereby survived.'[1]

For Jonathan Edwards life was far from serene. He had to leave his church at Northampton in 1750; most people in his congregation had become intolerably irritated by his habits – by his aloofness (he read or wrote for thirteen hours a day), by his refusal to admit new church members until they had first given an account of their faith which satisfied him, by his frequent absences as the spiritual leader of a revival which seemed questionable, and even by the salary he sought in order to maintain a handsome wife and family. He simply did not fit into a little community devoted to food, drink and gossip. So he moved to the frontier settlement of Stourbridge in the glorious Berkshire mountains. There he wrote his great books but also acted as a missionary to the Indians. More controversial still were some of those who assisted and followed Edwards. Lacking altogether his spiritual refinement and intellectual interests, these men became the founders of the notorious traditions of a debased revivalism or fundamentalism, exploiting the guilt and fear of simple people, welcoming hysteria and making a commercial profit. Such were some of the problems surrounding the Great Awakening which was called the 'new light'.[2]

The Calvinist awakening did not really touch the well-educated gentlemen who were the founding fathers of American independence – Washington and Jefferson the Virginian plantation owners, Franklin and Adams among the intellectuals. To them, as to many of the clergy, the new enthusiasm was irrational and its popularity was dangerous to the whole order of a respectable society. Nor should the popularity of Calvinism, or of any other kind of religion, be exaggerated. Harvard, Yale and other colleges adhered to the more peaceful 'old light' during and after the revivals. It is reckoned that by 1790 only about a tenth of the thirteen colonies' four million or

[1] E. S. Gausted, *The Great Awakening in New England* (New York, 1957), p. 138.

[2] See Perry Miller, *Jonathan Edwards* (New York, 1949), and *Jonathan Edwards: A Profile*, ed. David Levin (New York, 1969). The more human side was presented by Elisabeth Dodds, *Marriage to a Difficult Man: 'The Uncommon Union' of Jonathan and Sarah Edwards* (Philadelphia, Pa., 1975). I. H. Murray's biography of *Jonathan Edwards* (London, 1987) was full of admiration.

more inhabitants (three-quarters of whom were white) definitely belonged to a Christian congregation. But the orthodoxy of the new preaching did show that the coldly 'rational' religion was not going to have an unopposed victory; it did arouse the interest, however superficial, of hundreds of thousands; and it did convert thousands of individuals. In the southern colonies Baptist congregations began to multiply, providing a permanently popular alternative to an Anglicanism still aristocratic in its ethos. This warm-hearted version of Christianity provided a religion to which slaves could become converted, and it troubled the consciences of slave-owners sufficiently to prompt a few of them to encourage such conversions. More easily it appealed to the poor whites who had found themselves in virtual slavery as 'indentured servants', labouring to pay for their passages. In the middle colonies and in New England the revival led to the insistence of many congregations on taking responsibility for their own spiritual life, without control by the local group of ministers; since these independent congregations had now usually come to believe that baptism should be restricted to believing adults, they helped to make the Baptist denomination the largest in America.

This religious revival dramatically challenged the sheer materialism which, after the decay of Puritanism, had become the philosophy of free settlers rapidly getting richer. Americans had come to respect what was practical, what worked, what was self-evident; but now it seemed possible to demonstrate that Christian experience was in that category. A love of the Bible, an enthusiasm for personal improvement, a belief that the true Christian must be 'born again' – all these convictions began to be associated with the American character. They were to be transported into the wilderness as the Frontier moved west. Preachers also changed. They now depended far less on their status in society or on their theological scholarship, and far more on their down-to-earth appeal to the people.[3]

National unity was awakened. Because preachers travelled

---

[3] W. T. Youngs studied *God's Messengers: Religious Leadership in Colonial New England* (Baltimore, Md., 1976).

from church to church and from colony to colony, speaking in glowing terms about revivals in the places from which they had come, holding up a vision of Christian America, the lines of communication up and down the Atlantic coast were strengthened, challenging the inherent tendency of British imperialism to link each colony direct with 'home'. The awakening pushed the colonies towards a future in which the culture was to be still basically Christian, but proud of the new freedom enjoyed by many denominations; still indebted to the religious heritage of Europe, but newly confident in its own vigour. Although Calvinism was to become only one star on' the theological flag, the whole American idea owed much to this contribution. 'The Awakenings were not the sole source of the American sense of destiny,' a leading historian has written, 'but they made it convincing to masses of men and women, and they often intensified the feeling in the soul of a people.'[4]

The results were seen in the 1770s. The cutting of the political links with England might have been traumatic for all American religion – had the religion been as feeble, as dependent on initiatives from the old country, as it had been before the Calvinist awakening. As it was, the problems of independence seem to have been severe only for the 'Loyalists' who adhered to the Crown and the Church of England. Their churches and rectories now became obvious targets for some mob violence, and in the northern American colonies the situation was so tense that many thousands moved northwards. But American Anglicans had for long enjoyed a practical independence and were now determined to be faithful to the 'Episcopal' church order without remaining loyal to the English king or to the English bishops who had so long hindered Anglican expansion by their refusal to supply an American bishop. Most of the signatures on the Declaration of Independence (including Washington's) were of men who had been members of the Church of England in its days of privilege. A clergyman acceptable to these rebels, although he had denounced the rebellion, was sent over with strict instructions to

---

[4] Robert T. Handy, *A History of the Churches in the United States and Canada* (New York, 1976), p. 115.

return as a bishop. His name was Samuel Seabury. Having been
denied consecration in London (on the ground that he would
not swear allegiance to George III), he achieved it in 1784 at
the hands of Scottish bishops in Aberdeen. Three years later two
others were made bishops in London to shepherd the American
Episcopal Church, an Act of Parliament having recognized that
the step was inevitable – a century and a half too late.[5]

The other American denominations had fewer formal ties
with England, and in these there was far less confusion of
conscience about the rebellion. As the Declaration of Independence proclaimed, the truths on which it was based were
'self-evident' (in the original draft, 'sacred and undeniable').
The justification of England's own revolution of 1688–89 was
well known, particularly in the philosophy of John Locke. In
Locke was the key argument that a contract between the ruler
and the ruled could be broken. However, it is clear that
Calvinist theology also inspired men to rebel against a 'tyrant',
in America in the 1770s as in England in the 1640s. The only
clergyman to sign the Declaration of Independence was John
Witherspoon, a Calvinist who had succeeded Edwards in the
presidency of the Princeton college; but his signature did
represent a revived tradition that a people was divinely destined to freedom. Indeed, when the fires of the Calvinist revival
began to die down in the 1740s, some of the vision of the coming
reign of Christ on earth was still retained and translated into
American patriotic idealism. It has been observed that 'amid
the shifting intellectual currents of eighteenth-century New
England, one theme above all others maintained its hold on the
clergy. It was the solid conviction that their own community
had been chosen as a special people of God.'[6]

---

[5] See Carl Bridenbaugh, *Mitre and Sceptre: Transatlantic Faiths, Ideas, Personalities
and Politics 1689–1775* (New York, 1962), and for an English acknowledgement of
guilt H. G. G. Herklots, *The Church of England and the American Episcopal Church*
(London, 1966).
[6] Nathan O. Hatch, *The Sacred Cause of Liberty* (New Haven, Conn., 1977), p. 59.
Other recent studies include Alan Heimest, *Religion and the American Mind: From the
Great Awakening to the Revolution* (Cambridge, Mass., 1966); Bernard Bailyn, *The
Intellectual Origins of the American Revolution* (Cambridge, Mass., 1967); Robert
Middlekauff, *The Glorious Cause: The American Revolution 1763–1789* (New York,
1982).

After independence some efforts were made to preserve the legally established Churches with the plea that the alternative was atheism. In Virginia Patrick Henry defended the Anglican establishment against James Madison, but Thomas Jefferson's Bill for Establishing Religious Freedom was finally passed in 1786. The same period saw the end of the privileges of the Church of England in the other colonies, as the first written state constitutions in history were adopted. In Massachusetts, Connecticut and New Hampshire, however, the Congregationalist heirs of the Puritans delayed the change, merely offering other Protestant denominations a share in the taxes. The matter was settled by the First Amendment to the Constitution, which came into effect in 1791: 'Congress shall make no law respecting an establishment of religion, or prohibiting the free exercise thereof.' That was a bold new step; in Europe the Church had enjoyed privileges from the State ever since Constantine had established his own authority as the first Christian (or semi-Christian) emperor by the battle near the Milvian Bridge over the Tiber in 312. But in the infant United States the churches generally expressed confidence that they could flourish since they had a vital Gospel to preach.[7]

Surveying the deeply emotional appeal to individuals made by preachers such as Jonathan Edwards, H. Richard Niebuhr offered this assessment. 'The Awakening arose in the new world of emancipated individuals who had become their own political masters to an uncommon degree. It dealt with men and families who through the acquisition of free or cheap land had been made economically independent. It confronted men who were being intellectually emancipated from the dogmas of the past by the filtering down into common life of ideas developed by scientists and philosophers. It spoke to people who had been freed to no small extent from the bonds of customary morality. . . . It was no wholly new beginning, for the Christianity expressed in it was a more venerable thing

---

[7] The standard survey is A. P. Stokes and L. Pfeffer, *Church and State in the United States* (revised, New York, 1964).

than the American nation. Yet for Americans it was a new beginning; it was our national conversion.'[8]

With the achievement of American independence in politics and religion, a history of English Christianity must end its coverage of the United States. But an Englishman yet to be mentioned had been the greatest preacher of the Calvinist awakening in colonial America; and George Whitefield's work did much to suggest what would be the future of the Christian religion on both shores of the Atlantic.

GEORGE WHITEFIELD
AND THE SECOND BIRTH

George Whitefield crossed the Atlantic thirteen times. The feat was then very rare outside the ranks of professional sailors. Almost as rare were his American journeys between north and south. He made the greatest appeal to the public while still in his twenties, and the accounts of the hysterical adulation surrounding the 'boy preacher' in the 1740s have their closest parallels in the history of popular musicians. He was good-looking, although his eyes had a squint and he was satirized in a London play 'Dr Squintum', a nickname which stuck. And he was loud. People were fascinated by the extraordinary power of his voice without any artificial amplification; Benjamin Franklin, who became his friend but did not take seriously what he had to say, once calculated during a sermon that such a voice could reach thirty thousand people if the wind was favourable. Those who listened to the words found a delightful new style. 'He has', said that old cynic Lord Boling-broke, 'the most commanding eloquence I ever heard.'

Whitefield preached extempore in an age when the reading of sermons had become standard. He was a powerful story-teller; he once had Lord Chesterfield crying out in excitement during one of his many anecdotes. He was colloquial and controversial; in a pamphlet he wrote that Archbishop Tillot-

---

[8] H. Richard Niebuhr, *The Kingdom of God in America* (New York, 1935), pp. 99, 126.

son (still the idol of sensible Church of England men) knew as little about the all-important doctrine of justification by faith 'as Mahomet'. He expected emphatic approval or disapproval; a complaint was made to the Bishop of Gloucester who had just made him a deacon that his very first sermon 'drove fifteen mad'. Many, of course, disapproved of him; the gentle Isaac Watts rebuked his closest friend, Philip Doddridge, for 'sinking the character of a minister, and especially of a tutor among the Dissenters, so low as to collaborate with Whitefield.' But Whitefield was well received when he visited the dying Watts. David Garrick the actor said that such an orator could make people weep or cheer by the way he pronounced the word 'Mesopotamia'. But any entertainment provided by the sermon almost always ended up with a message which made the preacher weep as he delivered it. It was the message of the 'new birth', of a union with the Christ who had preached from the cross. That was what entitled Whitefield to be called 'the greatest evangelist of the British race'.[9]

Although a Calvinist, he seems never to have made any close study of John Calvin's works. His doctrine flowed out of his own experience. As a lad he had served beer in the inn kept by his widowed mother in Gloucester. At Oxford he had been a poor 'servitor' who waited on his fellow students, and away from the beery applause of the inn he had become socially insecure, lonely and morbidly introspective. His attempts to lead a rigidly pious and priggish life, his incessant self-examination and his very severe fasting had brought him to a collapse, like Martin Luther as a young monk in the 1510s. The turning point for George Whitefield had come when he had read a meditation by a seventeenth-century bishop, Joseph Hall, about Christ's words from the cross, 'I thirst'. He saw then that the helplessness of the sinner must be greater than the helplessness of the Saviour. All that could be essential was the prayer of naked faith, the total reliance on the merits of the Saviour who by the sacrifice of his death had satisfied the

---

[9] Albert D. Belden, *George Whitefield the Awakener* (revised, London, 1953), p. 3. For contrasting styles in the pulpit, see *The English Sermon, 1750–1850*, ed. Robert Nye (London, 1976).

justice of the angry God. And he saw this for himself without any living man's help, believing that his life had been changed solely by God's fully sovereign mercy, by the predestinating decree which saved some while damning others. The 'new birth' had redeemed this self-condemning, poor, isolated student when all his natural resources had broken down. The experience became the dominant, almost the only, theme of his preaching; and he began preaching less than a year after his crisis, which occurred soon after Easter 1735.

The pattern of his work was formed with an astonishing rapidity. He refused to be tied to any one parish, or to do general pastoral work. By talk and by letter he told individuals about the new birth and urgently invited them to share it; and if he was not allowed to preach in church he was ready to preach out of doors. This was not a completely novel action. George Fox, other Quakers and other radicals had preached out of doors in the previous century. A Welsh layman, Howell Harris, had begun such preaching soon after his conversion in 1735, and by 1739 there were nearly thirty little societies of converts, the origins of Welsh Calvinistic Methodism. But the Conventicle and Toleration Acts were still the law, forbidding preaching outside churches and licensed Dissenters' meeting houses; and at first a respectable clergyman such as John Wesley thought 'field-preaching' a 'mad action'. Within little more than three years of his own 'new birth' Whitefield had crossed the Atlantic and had caught the vision of all the American colonies 'ablaze for God'. He published a journal of this voyage – the first of much journalism about his mission. Returning home in order to be ordained priest, he had become an itinerant evangelist and as such had felt responsible for the souls of the notorious miners of Kingswood, near Bristol. On a Saturday afternoon in 1739, he advanced towards a little knot of them and called out: 'Blessed are the poor in spirit!' Before the end of his open-air sermon the miners' tears were making white rivers down their faces.

Inevitably such preaching was despised and rejected by many. David Hume (who held that Calvinism 'divinized cruelty, wrath, fury, vengeance and all the blackest vices') wrote to Gibbon: 'Among many marks of decline, the preva-

lence of superstition in England prognosticates the fall of
philosophy and the decay of taste.' The Duchess of Buckingham thought it 'monstrous to be told that you have a heart as
sinful as the common wretches that crawl on the earth.' Samuel
Johnson objected on other grounds: 'I believe he did good. But
when familiarity and noise claim the praise due to knowledge,
art and elegance, we must beat down such pretensions.' Many
popular satirists depicted him as 'a grotesque figure, a buffoon
– contemptible and ridiculous . . . lewdly squinting at this
congregation as he picks their pockets'.[10] But large audiences
trembled when reminded of the angry God or wept when told
of the Saviour's self-sacrifice.

Part of the impact of the message was due to the preacher's
own willingness to sacrifice everything to it. He defied the
authorities of his Church by being willing to preach in other
men's parishes uninvited – or in non-Anglican chapels. He
faced many journeys, perils and blows. And in part his success
was due to his ruthlessness. The southernmost English colony
of Georgia, with its little capital Savannah, had been founded
by General James Oglethorpe in 1732. The chief aim had been
to provide a refuge for Englishmen imprisoned for debt (a
subsidiary aim being the defence of the older English colonies
against the Spaniards in Florida). Oglethorpe had insisted that
no slaves – not even 'indentured' English servants – should be
used. The Georgians were to do their own work in clearing the
land for agriculture. Whitehead was soon appointed rector of
Savannah and might have been expected to have become the
idealistic colony's chief pastor. Instead he was seldom in his
own church, and his main contribution to the colony was to
insist that slaves were needed to develop the land around his
favourite project, an orphanage which was to train missionaries. But Whitefield could also be ruthless with his fellow whites.
When he proposed marriage by post to an English lady, his
letter to her was preoccupied by her future duties in the
orphanage. To her parents he wrote: 'I am free from the foolish
passion which the world calls *Love*. I write only because I
believe it is the will of God that I should alter my state; but your

---

[10] Albert M. Lyles, *Methodism Mocked* (London, 1960), p. 138.

denial will finally convince me that your daughter is not the person appointed for me.' It did.

At first he regarded the still more famous evangelist John Wesley as his spiritual father. When he had won fame as a preacher, he thought of Wesley as his successor first in Bristol and then in all England; he would concentrate on America. By 1740, however, the split between the two men had led to pamphlets issued on the two sides of the Atlantic and when they met again in the following year there was no deep reconciliation. On the surface the split was due to Whitefield's Calvinism. Wesley thought it monstrous to teach that God could predestine the majority of the human race to hell, and said so. He also thought it very dangerous to believe that one was among God's favourites, the 'elect', however one behaved; he had in mind his own brother-in-law Westley Hall, a fervent preacher who fled to the West Indies with one of his many mistresses. Whitefield, in his turn, warned Wesley about the dangers in his optimistic teaching that converted Christians could and should be 'perfect'; this preacher knew that he was not perfect himself and never expected others to be. However, it may be doubted whether a theological disagreement was the fundamental cause of the split. There was a clash of personalities.

Whitefield was not a rival organizer to Wesley; he knew that his talents did not lie in that field. He was delighted when a masterful woman appeared on the scene with strong Calvinist convictions and great wealth – Selina, Countess of Huntingdon. He accepted her money for two buildings, a 'tabernacle' for his preaching at Moorfields in London and a larger 'chapel' in Tottenham Court Road, and wrote to his patron: 'A *Leader* is wanting. This honour has been put upon your Ladyship by the Great Head of the Church.'[11] He never set himself up as a leader to whom a network of societies should be attached. He often said: 'Let the name of Whitefield perish!' He once catalogued his own faults: 'I have been too rash and hasty in giving characters, both of places and persons. . . . Being fond of Scripture language, I have often used a style too apostolical.

---

[11] See J. B. Figgis, *The Countess of Huntingdon and her Connexion* (London, 1982).

. . . I have been too bitter in my zeal. . . . I have published too soon and too explicitly what had been better kept in longer or told after my death. . . .' (The last confession rightly lamented the indiscretion of publishing his journals up to 1741 as a naïve autobiography – a gift to the wits.) But of one thing Whitefield was sure. He had been called by God to preach the new birth. Trying to conquer asthma in the bedroom of the Presbyterian minister's house in a little town in Massachusetts, he told a young assistant: 'A good pulpit sweat today may give me relief; I shall be better after preaching.' The young man expressed the friendly wish that he would conserve his energies and not preach so often. This evangelist who longed to be in the pulpit again had, after all, preached about a thousand times a year for some thirty years. He had probably spoken to more people than anyone else in the world's history. But he was obstinate when his young companion warned him against over-exertion. 'I had rather wear out than rust out', replied George Whitefield.[12]

THE CONVERSION OF THE WESLEYS

In his native England the only plainly visible results of all George Whitefield's preaching were the congregations of a few chapels registered as Dissenting meeting houses. The contrast is great with Methodism, led by John Wesley. When he died in 1791 the *Gentleman's Magazine* paid John Wesley a generous tribute, while implying that he had little to offer a gentleman. 'By the humane endeavours of him and his brother Charles a sense of decency in morals and religion was introduced into the lowest classes of mankind. . . . He was one of the few characters who outlived enmity and prejudice, and received in his later years every mark of esteem from every denomination. . . . His personal influence was greater than any private gentleman in the country. . . . Instead of being an ornament to literature he was a blessing to his fellows; instead of the genius of his age, he was the servant of God.'

---

[12] See Arnold Dallimore, *George Whitefield* (2 vols., London, 1970–80), and John Pollock, *George Whitefield and the Great Awakening* (London, 1973).

John Wesley's dominance over Methodism made it Arminian, not Calvinist; its journal, founded in 1778, was for many years called the *Arminian Magazine*. At first sight it is bewildering that the Arminian theology condemned by James I as a Dutch heresy, but adopted by Charles I and the Cavaliers, should now become the creed of a popular religious movement. But it is clear that for almost all the early Methodists what mattered about Arminianism was that it inspired much evangelism, and released many converts from nightmares, by its insistence that Christ had died in order to save *all*, not merely the predestined elect, from hell. The 'all' which had attracted the prosperous early disciples of the Dutch professor named Arminius, and which had then attracted the court of Charles I as a slogan to defend civilization against religious fanatics, was now a trumpet-blast to summon English sinners from all kinds of feckless living. Certainly the early Methodists, who responded to that 'all' with changed lives, were not absorbed in theological speculations. On the contrary, Methodism was a vibrant and often vulgar form of popular religion, thanks to two brothers. One was an organizer of religion, more effective than any other Englishman had been in that role since William the Conqueror's archbishop, Lanfranc; the other was a poet who wrote seven thousand hymns which the people could sing. When we study the origins of Methodism, we study an appeal to the people – in principle, to 'all' – made by John and Charles Wesley.

We also study the effects of the training which they had received in Epworth Rectory in Lincolnshire. John Wesley often repeated that he was a High Churchman and the son of a High Churchman. Charles Wesley wrote hymns which taught a more Catholic understanding of the Eucharist than could be heard from any Anglican bishop or professor in that age. Their father, Samuel Wesley, Rector of Epworth for thirty-eight years from 1697, was a convert to this high Anglicanism from Dissent. He was also rigid, dictatorial and hot-tempered, resolved to do his pastoral duty as he saw it although many of his parishioners responded with insults or physical violence. The remote and water-logged area where his parish lay had been drained in the reign of Charles I, and the parishioners had then lost many of their ancestors' rights. That seems to be one reason why the cause of Church and King was locally unpopular. But the rector's arrogance did not help. After his own ordination, John Wesley always insisted on managing the affairs of anyone who was at all willing to allow him to interfere. He gave people spiritual, moral, financial, political and medical instruction. Although he was supremely unqualified for this role, he even distributed marriage guidance. He could not help preaching, even when talking or writing to women who were hoping to hear from him some profession of love. When his mother died, he wrote to his brother: 'My heart does not, and I am absolutely sure God does not, condemn me for any want of duty towards her in any kind, except only that I have not reproved her so plainly and fully as I should have done.' And he was never willing to collaborate with anyone who might be an equal.

Yet in the final analysis, his power was spiritual – and his spiritual greatness was forged in the heat of his relationships with these parents. His father loved going to London as a member of the militantly Tory House of Clergy in the Convocation; and his patron was Queen Anne's favourite, Archbishop Sharp. When the Convocation was suspended and Queen Anne dead, he still clung to an orthodoxy imbibed in Oxford in the 1680s. When in 1724 John Wesley had graduated and was preparing for ordination, Samuel sent him a long list of standard theology to absorb; and he added: 'If you have any scruples about any point of Revelation or the scheme of the Church of England (which I think exactly agreeable to it) I can answer 'em.' Less amusing is the way in which Samuel Wesley treated the most beautiful and the cleverest of his daughters, Hetty, who became pregnant as a result of a night with a lawyer whom she wrongly believed was going to marry her the next morning. Her father never forgave her, drove her into a wretched and totally unsuitable marriage, and was unmoved when her first child and three others died. John tried to reconcile his father to his sister, but we can see how he formed his own early image of God as the unmerciful Judge.

Samuel Wesley married Susanna Annesley (and had to leave the parish which he held before moving to Epworth because he objected to the squire's mistress talking to his respectable wife). Susanna was the twenty-fifth child of a clergyman who possessed a private fortune and an independent mind, ending up as one of the leading Dissenting preachers. Defoe said that 'nothing in him was little or mean'. Although from the age of thirteen Susanna dissented from Dissent, her father's standards were passed on to her own nineteen children – or to those of them who survived infancy. She was as inflexible as her father or her husband. As a Jacobite she refused to say 'Amen' when Samuel Wesley prayed for William III, and did not yield even when Samuel left home for a prolonged period of sulks and threatened to enlist as a chaplain in the navy. John Wesley was born in 1703, nine months after their reconciliation.

Samuel mismanaged his affairs (he was once imprisoned for debt) and consoled himself by writing books which very few people wanted to read. He was a clumsy poet and his great work was a Latin treatise on the Book of Job. (This work, which he was sure would make his fame and fortune, was presented to the Queen after his death. She observed that it was 'bound prettily'.) His rectory was twice burned down, perhaps by hostile parishioners, and John Wesley was nearly left to perish in the flames in 1709 – which was why he thought of himself as a 'brand plucked out of the burning'. The much more practical Susanna rebuilt home and family after these disasters, although their furniture and clothing were never grand, and food and heat were often problems. She conducted family life with the routine to be expected in a very strict boarding school, and undertook the religious instruction of each of her children in private. As an adult John Wesley still recalled his Thursday evenings alone with her, and wrote to her for guidance. She also instructed the parishioners on a Sunday evening in her kitchen, while her husband was away and she disapproved of the curate. She was widely read. Her own missionary work in this fenland parish was inspired by reading about what Danish missionaries were doing in India, and her religion of the heart was fed by the *Pensées* of Blaise Pascal. It was characteristic of her that, while her husband urged John to study standard Anglican theology before ordina-

tion, she begged him to concentrate on 'practical divinity'. By
that she meant partly the writings of her father's fellow Puritans, but also a larger literature. Both she and her son grew to
be deeply interested in Pascal's fellow Catholics in seventeenth-century France. In the 1730s John Wesley, still encouraged by Susanna, was fast becoming an authority on the
literature of mysticism.[13]

Between them, therefore, Samuel and Susanna Wesley conveyed a complex heritage. Such a childhood produced three
priests of the Church of England who in many ways resembled
their parents – John, Charles and their elder brother Samuel (a
schoolmaster who disapproved of Methodism as a novelty). It
is impressive that these parents, although so often in debt,
managed to send their sons to public schools and to the
university for the best education then available in England,
and it should never be forgotten that one great advantage
possessed by the Wesleys was that they were the intellectual
equals or superiors of their critics. But a terrible price was paid.
The parents were not able to be of much help in the general
emotional development of their children. Of all of them, only
Charles made a happy marriage. And even the religion on
which all the family's efforts were concentrated was bound to
lead to an explosion.

In the eighteenth century comfortable and rational Anglicans often regretted that, with such parents, John and Charles
Wesley were bound to be enthusiasts or fanatics. In the years
1745–48, an eminent churchman (who called himself 'John
Smith' but almost certainly was Thomas Secker, later
Archbishop of Canterbury) wrote a series of six thoughtful
public letters to John Wesley about the dangers in the movement he had started. Typical was the warning: 'The son of a
Wesley and an Annesley is in no danger of *lukewarmness*, but
ought to take great care on the side of *impetuosity* and *zeal*.'

---

[13] John A. Newton has presented *Susanna Wesley and the Puritan Tradition in
Methodism* (London, 1968). Maximin Piette, S. J., *John Wesley and the Evolution of
Protestantism* (English translation, London 1937), stressed the interest in Catholic
spirituality which she also encouraged, while Elsie Harrison's highly readable *Son to
Susanna* (London, 1937) claimed that she had altogether too much influence
emotionally.

Actually, however, before the religion of Epworth Rectory could explode into nationwide Methodism, it had to implode inwards, into a very distressing psychological crisis produced by the understanding of religion as a life of strict obedience to a stern law.

Both John and Charles Wesley seem to have been fairly normal at school and as university freshmen. While at Oxford, however, they studied devotional books; John recalled Jeremy Taylor in 1725, Thomas à Kempis next year, and William Law 'a year or two after'. These books summoned them back to the strict standards which had been impressed on them as little boys. So they tried their utmost to be obedient to the law of holiness – but as they tried, their very successes seemed failures to their over-active consciences. They had to suffer much before love could liberate them from absorption in the question whether they were sufficiently obedient. Guilt accumulated – and the price to be paid for the removal of guilt seemed to be the total renunciation of the ordinary pleasures of life. Against this price they rebelled, being intelligent, energetic, strongly sexed and often attractive young men. They were plunged more miserably into themselves. A desperate longing for love and joy, rather than the stern logic of a law which all must in measure disobey, was the meaning of Charles Wesley's famous hymn:

> Love divine, all loves excelling,
> Joy of heaven, to earth come down. . . .

And the contrasting vision of Christ as Judge of the World has never been expressed better than in his Advent hymn, 'Lo, he comes with clouds descending'.

The brothers' self-absorbed religion seems to have made them incapable of ordinary friendships. In Oxford, for example, the 'Holy Club' was founded by Charles and directed by John from 1729. It did indeed cultivate personal holiness and did dispense charity with religious instruction to prisoners and other poor people. But the extravagance in fasting contributed to, or caused, George Whitefield's breakdown and the actual death of another member, William Morgan. No member of the club was of any real help to Whitefield in his spiritual torments, while the average undergraduate regarded the whole lot of them as exhibitionist prigs.

Soon after their father's death in 1735 both John and Charles accepted invitations to serve in the new colony of Georgia – the former as a missionary to the Red Indians, the latter (who was far more reluctant) as General Oglethorpe's secretary. John's motive was 'to save my soul' and 'to learn the true sense of the Gospel of Christ by preaching it to the heathen'. Finding that his main duties lay among the white settlers, he was so naïve as to believe that they would be willing to live like members of the Holy Club, while in his few contacts with the Indians he was surprised to find that they were not the innocent children of nature he had expected. Both the brothers were extraordinarily clumsy in their relationships with women. The feckless Charles sorely tried his employer, and despite a reconciliation, asked to be sent home. John had to make his escape having outraged the little colony by refusing to give Holy Communion to the girl who a few months previously had seemed about to become his wife, on the ground that her church attendance had lately been too infrequent. The whole of their missionary journey was a disaster.

After this humiliation in Georgia (where Whitefield became popular), it was evident to the brothers that they needed something. Worldly contemporaries thought that they needed common sense. They were, however, nothing if not religious, God-conscious, and they were sure that their need was to feel the forgiving love of God before they could preach that love effectively. They also knew that this assurance had to come from God alone; they could not earn it. They were ripe for the message that human morality or philosophy must be forgotten in the presence of the all-holy God; that forgiveness from this God must be accepted in penitence and joy, and could never be earned by keeping a law; that true holiness was not the cause of true faith in God, but the fruit of that faith; that everything depended on God being love, not wrath. The Wesleys already knew all this teaching as a theory. It was the Reformation doctrine of justification by faith alone, still proclaimed by the official documents of the Church of England although not much taught in this period. (John Wesley understood the great

Bishop Joseph Butler as saying of faith that it 'is a good work; it is a virtuous temper of mind'.) But the point was that the Wesleys had not felt the power of this doctrine for themselves.

In a state of physical and spiritual collapse, Charles Wesley went to lodge in a devout working-class home in London. He heard his hostess's sister say outside his door: 'In the name of Jesus of Nazareth, arise and believe, that thou mayest be healed of thy infirmities.' He then opened his Bible at random (a dangerous practice to which the brothers were always addicted) and fortunately found the words: 'He hath put a new song in my mouth, even a thanksgiving unto our God. Many shall see it, and fear, and shall put their trust in the Lord.' Before he slept Charles wrote in his journal: 'I now found myself at peace with God . . . I saw that by faith I stood. . . .' The day was Whitsunday 1738.

Within three days, on 24 May, John Wesley who was also in London, and also near to a complete breakdown, had a closely similar experience. That afternoon he attended Evensong in St Paul's Cathedral, where the anthem matched his mood: 'Out of the deep have I called unto thee, O Lord. . . .' That evening he went reluctantly to a meeting in Aldersgate Street of one of London's religious societies, and heard a visiting German preacher. The sermon was an exposition of a key document dating from the Reformation of the sixteenth century, Martin Luther's Preface to St Paul's letter to the Romans. And that night John Wesley was taken by friends in triumph to Charles's sickroom, exclaiming: 'I believe!' In the famous words of his journal: 'About a quarter before nine o'clock while he was describing the change which God works in the heart through faith in Christ, I felt my heart strangely warmed. I felt I did trust in Christ, Christ alone for salvation; and an assurance was given me that He had taken away *my* sins, even *mine*, and saved me from the law of sin and death.'

The experience which John and Charles Wesley underwent in 1738 was not totally transforming. Both brothers continued to know paralysing moods of depression and self-condemnation. 'I do not love God,' John wrote to Charles in 1766, 'I never did. I am only an honest heathen. . . . If I have any fear, it is not of falling into hell, but of falling into nothing.'

But in that same letter may be found words more typical of the
thoroughly converted, thoroughly dictatorial, preacher whom
England had come to know: 'O insist everywhere on full
redemption, receivable by *faith alone*; consequently to be looked
for *now*. . . . We must have a thorough *reform of the preachers*.' In
1738 John Wesley preached on 'Salvation by Faith' in the
university church at Oxford eighteen days after the warming of
his heart; and he preached at length and with power. And some
four years later, Charles put the brothers' experience into a
hymn which is a classic:

> Come O thou Traveller unknown,
> Whom still I hold, but cannot see,
> My company before is gone,
> And I am left alone with thee. . . .
>
> 'Tis Love, 'tis Love! Thou dieds't for me,
> I hear thy whisper in my heart!
> The morning breaks, the shadows flee;
> Pure Universal Love thou art. . . .[14]

JOHN WESLEY AND THE METHODISTS

John Wesley is said to have travelled about a quarter of a
million miles on horseback or, when old, in a simple coach; it is
the distance of the moon from the earth. He is also thought to
have preached about forty thousand times. A bibliography
published in 1896 listed 233 books or tracts by him, more than
a hundred others edited by him, and English, French, Latin,
Greek and Hebrew grammars which he compiled. The subjects which he handled included tea, electricity and the history

---

[14] The best introductory biographies are V. H. H. Green, *John Wesley* (London,
1964), and Stanley Ayling, *John Wesley* (London, 1979), both rather hostile. They
need to be supplemented by Martin Schmidt's 'theological biography', *John Wesley*
in 3 vols. (London, 1962–73), and by the background provided in *A History of the
Methodist Church in Great Britain*, edited by Rupert Davies and Gordon Rupp (vol. 1,
London, 1965). More details are in V. H. H. Green, *The Young Mr Wesley* (London,
1961); J. E. Rattenbury, *The Conversion of the Wesleys* (London, 1937); and J. S.
Simon, *John Wesley* (5 vols., London, 1921–34). Frederic C. Gill studied *Charles
Wesley the First Methodist* (London, 1964).

of Rome. He spent about three-quarters of the year on the road and was not deterred by the prohibitions of his fellow clergy, by the suspicions of the magistrates, by rioting mobs, by illness, by rain or by snow. He arose each morning at four, conducted a service at five on most days of his life, spent about ten hours a day riding (and usually reading or even writing at the same time), preached and dispensed pastoral guidance most evenings and was fast asleep soon after ten. He earned about £30,000 as an author but lived on under £30 a year, giving the rest away. In his old age the bitter unpopularity he had undergone was little more than material for his frequent reminiscences, and crowds flocked to see his snowy hair and his baby-like complexion. He had become a major celebrity, although many still scoffed at the irrationality of his message and at the low company he preferred. In 1791, the year of his death, there were 72,476 full members of 'societies' in the British Isles owing allegiance to him, with a much larger number of associates. Almost two centuries later there were in the world about eighteen million full Methodists, two-thirds of them in the United States.

When we come to assess John Wesley we are overwhelmed by the evidence. His *Journal* was published three or four years after the events being narrated, and a supplementary diary recorded his activities hour by hour. He wrote many letters in addition to all the material he put into print, and collected and polished up forty-four sermons which would provide an epitome of his theology. And the heart of Methodism beats still more audibly in *A Collection of Hymns for the Use of the People Called Methodists* which he edited in 1780; 480 of the 525 hymns were by his brother Charles. But the evidence still leaves a mystery. He never wrote a systematic treatise on theology or the Church, and it may be doubted if he was ever certain about his long-term aims.

What was the 'scriptural holiness' he wanted to 'spread throughout the land'? His experience in Aldersgate Street in 1738 was not often referred to in his lifetime, and the explanation may be that it suggested that a convert must simply be quiet and still. He was far too much of an activist to be still or quiet for very long, and when he had moved away from the

Moravians he said many harsh things about 'mysticism'. His understanding of faith was not Lutheran, although illumination had come to him through Luther. In his journal for 1741 he called Luther 'muddy and confused . . . deeply tinctured with mysticism'. He included none of Luther's works in the fifty-volume *Christian Library* which he edited between 1749 and 1755. And while the warming of his heart in 1738 brought assurance to him personally (in most moods), he came to reject the claim that a Christian could not be 'justified' if he or she had not been similarly assured. A conversion of his own type was, he came to see, only the 'common privilege'. It was not essential to salvation; the only essential was holiness, with love as its fruit. He welcomed dramatic evidences of conversion and when he preached a university sermon at Oxford in 1744, on the text 'And they were all filled with the Holy Ghost', he was so close to the New Testament that he was never asked to preach there again. But particularly after 1744 his main interest lay not in the eager beginnings of a Christian life but in growth in 'holiness' and 'knowledge'. It is one of the many paradoxes of his life that he who had braved so much hostility in order to preach salvation by faith alone lived to write (in his *Thoughts on Salvation by Faith*, 1779) that 'no man is finally saved without works'.

He was not entirely clear about the holiness he expected. He often spoke about 'the life of God in the soul of man', echoing the title of a book by a seventeenth-century Scotsman, Henry Scougal, that had meant much to him as a young man. He constantly taught converts to pray for 'Christian perfection' and seemed to his enemies to be reviving the folly of believing that converts did not need the conventional moral restraints. But he also taught that a strict and persevering self-discipline was absolutely necessary, and that without it a convert who had once been assured about his Saviour could still fall from 'grace' into hell. This teaching offended Calvinists, laying him open to further accusations that he still taught 'works-righteousness'. He defined sin in a limited way as the voluntary transgression of a known law, and it followed that his idea of 'perfection' was only freedom from sin so defined, a freedom which might prove temporary. On this basis he accepted claims made by some Methodists that they had achieved 'entire sanctification' and loved to record 'triumphant' death-beds. If he could, he would ask the dying: 'Do you see Jesus?' But he never claimed to be 'perfect' himself and what he meant about these Methodists was, it seems clear, the Catholic idea of the saint. Referring to the seventeenth-century Catholic saint, he once asked in a sermon: 'Who has spoken of sanctification in a stronger or more scriptural fashion than Francis of Sales?' But eighteenth-century England was not a place where it was easy to talk about the Catholic saints. Nor was Wesley willing to adopt the entire Catholic understanding of sanctity, since he did not believe that souls could be made holy in purgatory after death. Demanding of himself and others a real righteousness before death, rejoicing in the lives and holy deaths of the Methodists, he clung to this unsatisfactory term 'perfection'.[15]

About one thing he was absolutely clear. Holiness must be 'perfect love' – a transformed life with, and for, others. Therefore it must be 'social holiness', expressed by active membership of the visible Church and issuing in honest and loving behaviour in the world. In practical terms Methodism meant joining a Methodist 'society' – and for many years that meant, at least in John Wesley's eyes, fasting on Wednesday and Friday and attending two services every Sunday, before and after the two services to be attended in the parish church. It also meant being willing to be questioned and instructed about intimately personal matters of belief and behaviour. In effect the term 'Methodist', used in Oxford in the early 1730s to refer to men thought to be ridiculously methodical in their observance of the customs enjoined in the Book of Common Prayer, had come by the middle of the 1740s to mean people methodically Wesleyan. Preaching from a balcony in Philadelphia, Whitefield once cried out: 'Father Abraham, whom have you in heaven? Any Episcopalians? . . . Presbyterians? . . . Independents or Seceders? . . . Have you any Methodists?' And the answer from heaven came, according to Whitefield: 'We don't

---

[15] Methodist discussion includes R. N. Flew, *The Idea of Perfection in Christian Theology*, (London, 1934); W. E. Sangster, *The Path to Perfection* (London, 1941); C. W. Williams, *Wesley's Theology Today* (London, 1962).

know those names here.' It seems unlikely that John Wesley would have heard that answer.

It was his unique ability as an organizer and pastor that distinguished John Wesley from all his contemporaries – not only from Whitefield or the Welsh revivalists, but also from men such as Benjamin Ingham, who had been with him in the Holy Club and in Georgia and who returned to become an independent evangelist in the north of England. John Wesley's pastoral oversight was accepted by so many individuals after 1738 because it was accompanied by joy and love, as it had not been before 1738; and it endured after his death because while taking endless trouble over individuals he also created a system which would uphold them when he had gone. The central paradox of his life is that 'while he may have lacked a creative mind, he was a genius at adaptation' and therefore 'his religious conservatism harboured ecclesiastical radicalism'.[16]

His genius at adaptation may be seen in his dealings with the Moravians. The preacher whose exposition of Luther had warmed his heart in 1738, Peter Böhler, was a Moravian. Descended from some of the disciples of the fifteenth-century reformer of religion in Bohemia, John Huss, this group had retained its Protestant faith and had been revitalized by the Pietist movement.[17] In 1722 it had settled on one of the estates of Count Nikolaus von Zinzendorf, at Herrnhut in Saxony. Five years later it had undergone a corporate religious experience out of which had come a clear call to a worldwide mission – something without precedent in Christian history apart from the Jesuits. Zinzendorf had become a bishop and the dictatorial, but richly creative, leader in this mission. The Wesleys had already come across the movement; there had been Moravians on the ship bound for Georgia. The agitated brothers had been impressed by their calm courage during the voyage and by their wisdom during the missionary work. Soon after his Aldersgate Street experience John Wesley went to Germany to examine their organization more closely. He learned much: the

---

[16] V. H. H. Green, *John Wesley*, p. 155.

[17] See A. J. Lewis, *Zinzendorf the Ecumenical Pioneer* (London, 1962), and C. W. Towlson, *Moravian and Methodist* (London, 1957).

importance of hymn-singing, the practice of the almost month-ly 'love-feast' (where the fare was cake and water and the main nourishment came through testimonies of spiritual progress), the 'watch-night' service (on the Friday night nearest the full moon), the division of the larger congregations into 'bands' of four or five people (of the same sex and marital status) for the purpose of spiritual edification. All these Moravian customs were copied, to the enrichment of Methodism. But John Wesley was no mere imitator. A believer in fasting and res-traint, he rejected Moravian practices which he thought world-ly, unhealthy or over-ambitious: the indulgence in the delights of wealth (particularly on the part of Zinzendorf himself), the lushly sentimental details about the suffering of Christ, the physical contact involved in the 'kiss' of peace or in foot-washing, the ambition to build a worldwide movement within a generation. Indeed, he gradually came to regard the Mora-vians as 'German wolves'.

To the Moravian elements which he favoured, Wesley added his own practices, developed from old Puritan ideas. Many Puritans had stressed the spiritual fellowship to be enjoyed by a group of like-minded ministers, often called a *classis* from the learned Latin. Now Wesley developed 'classes' or groups of about a dozen lay men or women who would meet weekly in order to question and encourage each other about spiritual and material matters. The idea sprang out of the offer of one Captain Foy to collect a penny a week from poor Methodists towards the liquidation of the debt on the 'New Room' at Bristol in 1741, but by the time he had ridden back to London after the meeting where that offer had been made Wesley had seen that the idea could solve problems deeper than finance. Many Puritans had also believed in the covenant between members of a congregation. Now Wesley developed a 'covenant' service, when each Methodist bound himself or herself anew to the Lord Jesus on the first Sunday in the new year.[18]

As Methodism grew, Wesley relied on methods which Whitefield, the Welsh revivalists and the Moravians had

---

[18] Robert C. Monk studied *John Wesley: His Puritan Heritage* (London, 1966).

already introduced in a smaller way. In 1789 he defined the four essentials of the Methodist system, on which he would insist despite the disapproval of bishops and parish priests:

1. to preach in the open air
2. to pray extempore
3. to form societies
4. to accept the assistance of lay preachers.

Although he was nervous about following Whitefield's example in 'field-preaching' in Bristol in 1739, he soon saw that his exclusion from almost all the pulpits of the Church of England was not an unmitigated disaster. Preaching in the open air helped to recreate a New Testament atmosphere, and like the apostles of old John Wesley was not surprised if lives were changed dramatically, miraculous healings took place, and devils were expelled from shouting or writhing hearers. Nor was he dismayed if mobs assaulted him, as they had assaulted St Paul; it was his own way of doing battle against Satan. He believed that God controlled in detail not only the responses of his hearers but also the journey and the weather. He believed that good angels watched over the proceedings and their consequences. Although he loved to use the services of the Book of Common Prayer indoors (and was a frequent communicant), he also found that a blessing attended extempore prayer for the people in the open air. Indeed, the impression left by his *Journal* is that he was well aware that by being preached out of doors his sermons (which in themselves were not nearly so emotional as Whitefield's) attracted a publicity, and secured a response, which would not have come to him on anything like the same scale had he restricted himself to occasions when the parish priest invited him to preach during or after a Prayer Book service.

But John Wesley was not primarily a preacher. He was an organizer. In 1743 he determined not to preach where he could not organize – 'not to strike one stroke in any place where I cannot follow the blow'.

He formed societies – not everywhere, but wherever his preaching aroused a sufficient response or wherever someone else's preaching had led to the formation of a group willing to be taken over by him. His main bases were London and Bristol. He was also successful in other areas undergoing the beginnings of industrialization – in Newcastle and Sunderland where collieries had been developed, in Hull, Leeds and the West Riding of Yorkshire, in Cornwall among the tin-miners, in the still disorganized industrial towns in the middle of England such as Manchester, in the growing port of Liverpool. The rural south-east and south midlands were almost untouched by Methodism – while in East Anglia, although there was a popular welcome for a religion which would not be controlled by the rich squires and merchants, there was far more independence than John Wesley experienced elsewhere.

His speciality was to form societies of industrial workers and their families. Most of these had quite recently been uprooted from the countryside; the 'cake of custom' had been broken and they were ready for a new message. But industrialization had not yet created that anonymous mass, the proletariat. Nor had it bred atheism. These were men and women who could be recalled by a sermon to a sense of their own spiritual importance, to a sense of themselves as sinners accountable to God.

Of course the Wesleys often met with hostility or indifference, but it is striking how often these Oxford clergymen full of religious emotions, men for whom assurance of forgiveness by God was the chief need, found hearers who understood among these industrial workers. And the Wesleys did not withdraw their converts from these communities. Unlike the Quakers, the Methodists were not to be made conspicuous and ridiculous by unusual dress or other habits. But (again unlike the Quakers) they were given plenty of firm instructions about how to behave; decisions were not left to their agreement after silence. For example, they were instructed always to dress plainly; to 'gain all you can; save all you can; give all you can'. John Wesley insisted on honesty, writing *A Word to a Smuggler* and *A Word to a Freeholder* (against bribery in elections). He insisted on temperance (he forbade spirits although he enjoyed wine – and he was equally severe and self-denying about the expense of tea). He also insisted on the chastity of the single life or on faithfulness to vows (men and women always worshipped separately when under his control). He was equally emphatic about cleanliness and hygiene generally. And he gave these working men and women a new vision of what life could be. He lavished on them all the spiritual riches accumulated by his reading and experience. He taught them to believe that God had been so gracious to them that they could be perfect in love.

He encouraged them to read the Bible day by day – and much else, ordering his preachers to carry books and pamphlets around with them. For his people's benefit he supplied concise guides to the Bible, history, literature, philosophy, politics, economics, medicine and science, with a Dictionary. He encouraged them to educate their children. As early as 1739 he founded his own school for the children of the poor at Kingswood near Bristol, and opened another near it as a boarding school for the sons of his preachers: and in the 1780s he began being enthusiastic about Sunday schools for the children of the poor. He encouraged them to explore each other's hearts in their classes, so that they became psychologists and moralists; and to care for each other when physically ill, so that their 'stewards' collected and distributed considerable funds for the sick. He encouraged them to hope for heaven and meanwhile to work for heaven on earth, transfiguring their daily labours in the spirit of Charles Wesley's hymn 'Forth in thy name, O Lord, I go'. Those who were not willing to live and to labour in this spirit were told to go forth more rudely. There was a membership card renewable every quarter, and one of John Wesley's main tasks was expelling backsliders.

Joseph Priestley, although he deplored John Wesley's superstitions, wrote in his *Address to the Methodists* (1791): 'To you is the civilization, the industry and sobriety of great numbers of the labouring part of the community owing.' Had Priestley been interested in monasteries or sanctification, he could have added that somehow Wesley had created out of these working people a fellowship under semi-monastic discipline, a school for saints. Methodists had made the surrender which still echoes in the hymn by one of their preachers, Edward Perronet: 'All hail the power of Jesus' name'. George Lavington, Bishop of Exeter, included much which was abusive and much which was untrue in an attack on John Wesley's influence published in three volumes (1749–51), but the title of this onslaught implied a just estimate of John Wesley's spiritual influence as a leader fit to be compared with the great founders of the religious orders of the Catholic Church. The bishop's title was *The Enthusiasm of Methodists and Papists Compared*.

John Wesley's assistants were almost all laymen. The Church of England also used laymen, but only as churchwardens who were not expected to be spiritual men. Through sheer necessity Methodism had to use laymen to preach – and had to use men of lesser social status than the average churchwarden. Some were itinerant preachers, very modestly paid, the first being Thomas Maxfield in 1741; and for years John Wesley struggled to avoid allowing these preachers to receive any money at all since the gospels taught that food and clothing ought to be enough. Others conducted their neighbours' worship, or led a class of a dozen, without any material reward. This use of laymen aroused further ridicule; Laurence Sterne commented that Methodist preachers were 'much fitter to make a pulpit than to get into one'. But it released many talents hitherto buried. And in a Methodist congregation there were no gradations according to the worshippers' status in the world. In the eighteenth century both the parish churches and the Dissenters' meeting houses were often filled with pews, allocated according to rank (and the ability to pay rent for them). Seating parishioners in this style was a question which preoccupied churchwardens. But Methodist chapels had benches.

We should not, however, think that John Wesley was in any way a democrat. He accepted the class system outside the chapels, and within them he created a new one, arranged according to people's status in his eyes. His preachers, appointed and not infrequently dismissed by him, were divided into two classes; the more select and trusted 'Assistants' were superior to the 'Helpers'. He discouraged worldly ambition. One of his rules read: 'Do not affect the gentleman. You have no more to do with this character than with that of a dancing master.' He published his own sermons to guide theirs. He issued many other instructions to reshape their lives in the image he desired – and they accepted this supervision, far closer than any bishop's. They were his 'sons in the Gospel'.

In particular they accepted his exhortations because he lived like that himself. It was no prelate in the House of Lords who ordered them in 1745: 'You have nothing to do but to save souls. Therefore spend and be spent in this work. And go always, not only to those who want you, but to those who want you most.'

Among the souls to whom these preachers were to pay special attention were the class leaders, whose subordination was made clear: 'they are employed by the Assistant as long and as far as he pleases.' From 1744 (when ten of them gathered) onwards, Wesley summoned an annual national conference of his preachers. No one was entitled to attend without his invitation, and when in 1784 he decided that the legal powers of the conference should be limited to a hundred preachers (less than half the total), he simply selected those he wanted. The conference never included any representatives of the congregations. Under its control, local meetings of preachers, stewards and class leaders (the 'Circuit Meetings') took place every quarter from 1748 onwards. These meetings regulated the affairs of the 'societies'. Wesley completely rejected any notion that the laity of a particular congregation should have any such power.

It is indeed hard to see how the separation of this thoroughly Wesleyan organization from the Church of England could have been avoided. What postponed the formal recognition of the split until after John Wesley's death was the fact that, together with an obstinate refusal to be deterred or in any other way influenced by any bishop or parish priest, Methodism's dictator also frequently expressed an obstinate refusal to separate from the Church of which he was a priest. His mature attitude was defined (in so far as it could be defined) in his sermon preached in Newcastle in 1749 on 'The Catholic Spirit'. Catholicism he wanted; it spoke to him of the universal love of God, manifest in many times and places. But he advocated its generous spirit, not its traditional safeguards. His text was: 'Is thine heart right, as my heart is with thy heart? If it be, give me thine hand' (2 Kings 10:15). He had travelled far from Epworth and from Oxford, although he was very reluctant to admit it.

Clearly John Wesley, when he set out on his missionary

journeys, had no intention of founding a denomination. He took a pride in the blessing (however guarded) of the Archbishop of Canterbury, John Potter. In his interview with Bishop Gibson of London, one of the bishop's worries was about his practice of re-baptizing Dissenters, for at this stage John Wesley still believed that there was 'no salvation outside the Church'. In his historic interview with Bishop Joseph Butler on 16 August 1739 he seems to have tried to reassure the philosopher-bishop. The 'pretending to extraordinary gifts and revelations of the Holy Ghost' to which Butler objected – 'a horrid thing, a very horrid thing' – was not defended by Wesley, according to his own note of the meeting (we have no record of it from Butler). He replied that he claimed only 'what every Christian may receive and ought to expect and pray for'. Some of what the bishop objected to was blamed on Whitefield, some on hysterical women whom Wesley said he could control. When Butler said that he had been informed that Holy Communion was celebrated in Methodist meetings, Wesley simply said that the information was wrong. When he objected to Wesley preaching in the diocese of Bristol without a licence, the preacher claimed (incorrectly) that he was entitled to do this as a Fellow of Lincoln College, Oxford.

But one step was taken when in 1740 Wesley led his own followers out of the Fetter Lane Society (founded in 1738 and including Moravians too much inclined to 'mysticism'). This London group formed the nucleus of the congregation which now met in a previously disused building in Moorfields, the 'Foundery'. For many years almost all Methodist societies met in their members' cottages or barns, always avoiding the 'church hours' so as to show that they had no wish to be rivals with the parish churches. But gradually John Wesley had to acknowledge that many of the parish clergy insulted Methodists when they appeared in church – and that Methodists were willing to pay for their own simple buildings. He yielded, too, by permitting Holy Communion at Methodist meetings (first in 1743). However, he caused a legal problem by being unwilling before 1787 to see the buildings registered as Dissenting 'meeting houses' (except as a temporary measure in response to the riots of the 1740s). If the Methodists were not Dissenters, they were not entitled to the liberties specified in the Toleration Act of 1689. Even when he had yielded that point, Wesley still tried to retain the modest terms 'preaching house' and 'chapel'. There were about 470 such buildings when he died. In 1778 he led his London congregation out of the Foundery into the far more handsome New Chapel in City Road, complete with a burial ground.

Charles Wesley, although he preached there Sunday by Sunday before his death in 1788, refused to be buried in that ground. A parish churchyard must be his last resting place. For long he had struggled (in vain) to persuade his brother to restrict membership of Methodist societies to members of the Church of England. Many others warned John Wesley of the sin of schism, and he issued many assurances that he was not contemplating it. From time to time admirers would suggest that he ought to be made a bishop in the Church of England – either of a diocese or of the Methodists as a kind of religious order. But it was in practice inconceivable that he would accept the restrictions of a diocesan bishopric. It was equally inconceivable that the authorities would formally bless a situation where he exercised a detailed personal control over societies in many hundreds of parishes – even in the parishes of Evangelicals whose preaching he approved. His claim to take the world as his parish inevitably seemed alarming arrogance to the bishops (and to the politicians who appointed them). The Methodists could be compared with the medieval Franciscans who had also gone to the poor, but their disregard of ecclesiastical authority went far beyond anything permitted to any religious order under any Catholic system.

The crisis came through the need to make provision for the leadership of Methodism in America when the United States had secured their independence. Five years before the rebellion Francis Asbury – a gardener's son summoned to be a preacher from the life of an apprentice in a Birmingham ironworks – had been sent out, while still in his mid-twenties, to organize a movement which had sprung up spontaneously among lay people and had been only rather casually visited by itinerant Englishmen. He had won great success and the first American conference had been held in 1773.

John Wesley never suffered from inhibitions about his powers. Setting himself the task of compiling a version of the Book of Common Prayer for the American Methodists, he halved the original. But he knew that it was impossible for him to claim to exercise personal control any longer; not only was America a long way away, but during the war he had written four vehement pamphlets against the Americans' rebellion (while also pleading for more sympathy with their just claims before the war). Thomas Rankin, whom he had sent as special ambassador to impose discipline on the American Methodists (and on Asbury), had met with hostility. Wesley begged Robert Lowth, an able and friendly man who was Bishop of London 1777–87, to ordain Methodists as priests for the American movement, but the request was refused. John Wesley then, in Bristol in September 1784, 'set apart' two men as deacons and presbyters and also Thomas Coke as a 'superintendent'.

He was persuaded of his right to ordain priests or presbyters by his acceptance of the argument that in the New Testament the terms 'presbyter' and 'bishop' covered the same man (an argument which modern biblical scholars accept). He now drew the conclusion that he could in this pastoral emergency act as a bishop himself. What he, by status a priest, thought he was doing when he ordained Coke (already an Anglican priest) as a Methodist 'superintendent' he never fully explained. He presented Coke with a certificate saying simply: 'Know all men that I, John Wesley, think myself providentially called at this time to set apart some persons for the work of the ministry in America.' But when Coke on his arrival in America, together with Asbury, took to using the title 'bishop', John Wesley was indignant: 'How can you, how dare you, suffer yourself to be called Bishop? I shudder, I start at the very thought! Men may call me a knave or a fool, a rascal, a scoundrel, and I am content; but they shall never by my consent call me Bishop!' But Coke was not as willing as John Wesley was to act as a bishop (or archbishop) without being called one.[19]

---

[19] See *The History of American Methodism*, vol. 1, ed. E. S. Bucke (Nashville, Tenn., 1964).

Charles Wesley was 'thunderstruck' and angered by these ordinations, and attributed them to 'age'; John was already in his eighties. But it was not the act of a senile dodderer. John Wesley, undeterred by the protests, proceeded over the years to ordain more than twenty others to work overseas or in Scotland. At first he forbade those ordained for Scotland to appear as clergymen in England, but finally, in 1788, he ordained Alexander Mather to work in England – Mather subsequently claimed, as a bishop.

Another factor which brought about the separation from the Church of England was John Wesley's knowledge that he must die. In earlier days there had been an Anglican clergyman in mind to succeed him – his brother Charles or John Fletcher, by birth a Swiss, since 1760 the saintly vicar of the rough parish of Madeley in Shropshire. But neither man possessed John Wesley's single-mindedness or itch for organization; indeed, Charles settled down first in Bristol and then in London as the pastor of the local congregation and as the proud father of two musical prodigies. (Charles's son, the composer Samuel, was the father of the great Victorian cathedral musician, Samuel Sebastian Wesley.) John Wesley, in contrast, had such a clear vocation, and genius, as the leader of Methodism that he sacrificed marriage to his task. He did not press his suit with Grace Murray who would have made an excellent wife; then in 1751, on the rebound from that disappointment, he impulsively married an unsympathetic widow, Molly Vazeille. He refused to reduce his travels or his preacher's righteousness in letters to her during his many absences, and the marriage broke down completely amid much unpleasantness. Death released her in 1781; the event does not seem to have moved him greatly. It was not to be expected that a man who had sacrificed so much, including marriage, to his work would be content for that work to end with his death.

Eventually it became clear that only the Methodist Preachers' Conference could inherit his rights and responsibilities, and this he settled by a legally executed 'deed poll' in February 1784. It ought to have been clear to him that this arrangement ensured the·full emergence of Methodism as a denomination – although three years later he was still saying that when the Methodists left the Church of England God would leave them. The hundred preachers meeting as the legally constituted conference had not the slightest wish to dissolve their movement – or to be placed under bishops, either the Church of England's or their own. After John Wesley's death they pointedly did not elect as their first president either of the two men who nursed ambitions to succeed him as leader (Thomas Coke and Alexander Mather). But the preachers were men for whom it was unthinkable that Methodism, raised up by God through John Wesley, should cease with his earthly life. 'The best of all is, God is with us' – so said their master just before he died. They knew it, and they interpreted it as a mandate to leave the church which had treated their divinely inspired master with so little understanding.

When John Wesley died he left confusion behind him in Methodism's relationship with the Church of England, although he had been such a disciplinarian. Some of his preachers shared his own high doctrine of the Eucharist, celebrated solemnly on a Sunday morning; to others the central activity was the sermon on a Sunday evening, with hymns before and after. Some of his preachers used the Book of Common Prayer; others did not. Some refrained from baptizing, burying and preaching during 'church hours'; others did not. Some believed that only an episcopally ordained priest should celebrate the Eucharist or the Lord's Supper; others did not. Since it was tolerated, this confusion must have been implied in Wesley's own ambiguous position. He had founded a movement which must move. He knew that he had to spread 'scriptural holiness' and to 'save souls' from misery in this life and from hell in the next. But he did not know what would be the future of Methodism. It is a true verdict on his leadership of the people called Methodists that, like a vigorous rower, he looked back while he moved rapidly forward.[20]

---

[20] In addition to the books previously recommended, see Frank Baker, *John Wesley and the Church of England* (London, 1970); Bernard Semmel, *The Methodist Revolution* (London, 1974); and the more hostile E. P. Thompson, *The Making of the English Working Class* (London, 1963). There is valuable material in older books, for example the two by Leslie F. Church, *The Early Methodist People* (London, 1948), and *More about the Early Methodist People* (London, 1949).

EVANGELICALS IN THE PARISHES

The Evangelical awakening within the Church of England did not depend on the Wesleys. Its leaders could be called 'Methodists' – and for a long time they were so called by those who wished to insult them. But from the 1770s onwards the movement was increasingly referred to as 'Evangelical', and fairminded people recognized that it was resolved to remain loyal to the 'Evangel' or Gospel within the Established Church. When, beginning in 1779, the Countess of Huntingdon chose to register her chapels as Dissenting meeting houses rather than have any Anglican authority interfering with them, churchmen were shocked; and in 1782 the Evangelical clergymen who had been her chaplains resigned in a body. There was a similar, hardening, opposition to John Wesley's insistence on recruiting other priests' parishioners into Methodist societies where the orders were given by him and the hymns written by his brother. When in 1764 he sent out an invitation to some fifty clergymen inviting them to join an 'association', only three replied. Long before the Countess caused ministers trained for the work of her connexion to be ordained without any bishop in 1783, and before Wesley's own ordinations in the following year, Anglicans had shown a refusal to accept the claims of both dictatorial Founders.[21]

The vision of Christ as the believer's Saviour was at the heart of this Evangelical awakening because it retained much of the power which it had had in the days when Calvinism had been the Church of England's predominant theology. It was still available as the answer to many spiritual struggles. And Calvinist theology also retained something of its power as an interpretation of this vision. The sophisticated had long ago abandoned it, but there were still simple believers. The Devon clergyman Augustus Toplady spoke for them when he taught that if God was God, he must be free to choose whom he would save: 'I can discern no medium between absolute predestination and blank atheism.' Regarding Arminianism as 'the great religious evil of this age and country', he indulged in some very

---

[21] The standard study is L. Elliott-Binns, *The Early Evangelicals* (London, 1953).

bitter controversy against this element in Methodism. He was so angry because the Wesleys seemed to deny the towering, supernatural grandeur of the 'Rock of ages, cleft for me'. Approaching that rock, the sinner should not – could not – appeal to anything except God's decree of mercy; and Toplady knew very clearly that the mercy was for the predestined few. His poem entitled 'A Living and Dying Prayer for the Holiest Believer in the World' addressed Christ in 1776:

> Nothing in my hand I bring,
> Simply to thy Cross I cling,
> Naked, come to thee for dress;
> Helpless, look to thee for grace;
> Foul, I to the fountain fly;
> Wash me, Saviour, or I die!

In Rochdale, a quiet market town in Lancashire, William Grimshaw, then a curate, spent almost the whole of one Sunday in 1742 in ecstatic prayer. His rapture was caused by his sudden conviction about the truth of the book he had been reading, a treatise on faith by the old Puritan leader, John Owen. And his experience changed his life. Moved to the village of Haworth on the Yorkshire moors, he was able to transform a bleakly remote and largely pagan parish. He drove stray parishioners into church with a horsewhip, and appeared like an avenging angel when young people were indulging in horseplay rather than assembling for his instruction. His personality had not faded from his awed parishioners' memories when Patrick Brontë arrived to be rector in 1820, and some of the memories may have gone into Emily Brontë's *Wuthering Heights*.[22]

About Christmas in 1757 a similar experience changed the life and work of another clergyman, John Berridge. He had been a witty Cambridge scholar inclined to unconventional opinions. Then, moving to the village of Everton, he had been its devoted but not very convincing pastor. Now, 'as I was sitting in my house one morning, and musing upon a text of Scripture, the following words darted into my mind with a

---

[22] Frank Baker provided a biography of *William Grimshaw* (London, 1963).

wonderful power and seemed indeed like a voice from heaven, *Cease from thine own works.* . . . The tears flowed from my eyes like a torrent. The scales fell from my eyes immediately. . . .' He burned all his old sermons, for in the words carved on his tombstone, he 'fled to Jesus alone for refuge 1756'.

Thus the Evangelical revival first showed its power in quiet country parishes.[23] It was led by clergymen who made their own discoveries and preached to their own parishioners, and sometimes also elsewhere in their neighbourhoods. It took time for the movement to grow from these rural roots into the universities, the bishops' palaces, the homes of the rich and the pulpits of London. When in 1768 six students were expelled from St Edmund Hall, Oxford, for holding Evangelical views, Samuel Johnson commented: 'A cow is a very good animal in a field but we turn her out of a garden.'

No Evangelical was entrusted with a diocese until 1815 when Henry Ryder was made Bishop of Gloucester, perhaps largely because his brother was a prominent Tory peer. Only a few rich laymen were Evangelicals – although one of them was Robert Raikes, who among other business interests owned the local newspaper in Gloucester. In 1780 Raikes began paying four women to teach the children of the poor on a Sunday. On the other days of the week they would be at work. The main purpose was to teach them the Bible, but before they could learn that they had to learn to read and write. This was not the nation's first Sunday school but Raikes was able to secure publicity for it and the idea spread rapidly as a result.

John Thornton, another layman who showed what Evangelicals could do, had made an immense fortune in business, mainly through trade with Russia. His son Henry was equally rich and philanthropic; before his marriage he gave away six-sevenths of his income, and after marriage two-thirds. In 1792 Henry Thornton bought a house in Clapham, then a village at a distance of three pleasantly rural miles from London. Clapham gradually became a centre for Evangelicals of similar affluence and piety; the group was later (in 1844) called the Clapham Sect. They ate fine food and drank good

---

[23] Examples are in G. C. B. Davies, *The Early Cornish Evangelicals* (London, 1951).

wines at each other's tables, and their families struck up close friendships. In those days before the telephone the ease with which they could communicate as neighbours stimulated and assisted their labours for good causes, and a favourite meeting place was Henry Thornton's house, Battersea Rise, with its thirty-four bedrooms.[24]

E. M. Forster commented that Henry Thornton was, in most of his characteristics, typical of his family and wider circle but that 'what distinguishes him from the rest of them was his outstanding intellect. This appears not only in his public career but in his private letters. He never pens a sentence that is clumsy or feeble, and he knows exactly what he wants to say.' Henry Thornton's children grew up in a home which Forster well described as being full of 'affection, comfort, piety, integrity, intelligence, public activity, private benevolence; and transcending them all an unshaken belief in a future life where the members of the household would meet again and would recognize each other and be happy eternally.'[25]

For long the Evangelical movement had only one spokesman among all the preachers of London: the austere William Romaine. His message was so little appreciated by the gentry that his own churchwardens refused to provide light for his evening services; so he preached holding a candle. Then in 1779 the important church of St Mary Woolnoth in Lombard Street, at the very centre of the City of London's financial operations, was secured by John Thornton's influence for John Newton, the most interesting of all the first generation of the Evangelical clergy.

His Calvinism was implied in his famous hymns 'Amazing grace' and 'How sweet the name of Jesus sounds' – but it was accompanied by an equally firm adherence to the Church, expressed in 'Glorious things of thee are spoken'. Newton, although to the end a clumsy preacher, had a great gift for winning individuals to Christ and to the Church by private talk

---

[24] See E. M. House, *Saints in Politics: The Clapham Sect and the Growth of Freedom* (Toronto, 1952), and Michael Hennell, *John Venn and the Clapham Sect* (London, 1958).

[25] E. M. Forster, *Marianne Thornton* (London, 1956), pp. 23, 29. See also Standish Meacham, *Henry Thornton of Clapham* (Cambridge, Mass., 1964).

and by letter, because he was affectionate and because he could tell them his own story of spiritual rebirth. Ten years of his life had been spent in the slave trade, first as a sailor who became virtually a slave himself and then as the master of a ship. Through many sufferings and adventures he had hardened and coarsened but had not forgotten either his mother, who was a devout Dissenter, or the childhood sweetheart who eventually became his devout wife. At one stage he had picked up a copy of *The Imitation of Christ*, the only book available with which to pass the time, and had asked himself: 'What if these things should be true?' During a shipwreck on the coast of Newfoundland he had sworn to give his life to God if he survived. After his conversion came another spell in the slave trade; 'I never had the least scruple as to its lawfulness', he recalled later, when he became an opponent of it. But his vocation to help white fellow sinners had been insistent. After a shore job in Liverpool (a port growing rich through this infamous trade), he had persuaded a bishop to ordain him, at the age of thirty-nine.

Few clergymen have had a more sensational story to tell — and Newton told it, in *An Authentic Narrative* published soon after his ordination (in 1764). Twenty years later Coleridge was staying with Wordsworth, and Wordsworth was reading this book. It is almost certain that the *Authentic Narrative* was one of the books of travel that fed Coleridge's own *Tale of the Ancient Mariner*. In that poem, the mariner's blessing of the water-snakes lifted the curse off him; 'the self-same moment I could pray'. In the narrative of his life Newton told how he had once exclaimed 'almost without meaning': 'if this will not do, the Lord have mercy on us.' As he recalled, this was 'the first desire I had breathed for mercy for the space of many years'; and the little phrase halted his previously incessant flow of blasphemous oaths. He, too, found that he could pray.

This autobiography in its first draft had an immediate effect on an Evangelical peer, Lord Dartmouth. He invited its author to become the curate in charge of Olney, a tumbledown village in Buckinghamshire. Newton baffled most of his parishioners, but won some response as he went round the homes of the poor in his sailor's blue jacket and as he fumbled in the pulpit for words with which to tell others that they could be saved from slavery to sin as he had been. The centre of his work became the intimately informal Tuesday evening prayer meeting, for which he tried to provide a new hymn every week. Some of these were written by a poet who became his close friend and who rented a house in the village, William Cowper.[26]

Cowper was a minor poet reckoned major because his age was so unpoetical. Although he celebrated *The Ride of John Gilpin* and the delights of nature and of home life, like George III or Samuel Johnson he was the victim of a mental disease which cannot now be diagnosed with certainty. Because he was swept into the Evangelical revival it is possible to blame his madness on his religion. But it seems fair to say that Cowper's tormented fear that he had committed the unpardonable sin and was doomed to everlasting punishment was the symptom, not the cause, of the periods of mental illness which afflicted him long before his Evangelical conversion or his friendship with Newton. A just verdict has been passed by a fellow poet, Norman Nicholson. 'Without the Revival he would never have become a poet, for it gave him a deep emotional experience, a prolonged fervour which for many months lifted him like a love affair above the compromises and consequences of everyday life.'[27]

Some of Cowper's most moving poems are among the sixty-six which he contributed to *Olney Hymns*, a collection edited and largely composed by John Newton (and financed, like so many other projects, by John Thornton). 'Oh! for a closer walk with God' expressed his longing for a 'calm and serene' life and his knowledge that rural peace could not entirely satisfy that longing. 'God moves in a mysterious way' would serve as a commentary on the storms in Newton's life but seems to have been in fact a courageous acceptance of new

---

[26] Biographies include Bernard Martin, *John Newton* (London, 1950), and John Pollock, *Amazing Grace* (London, 1981). A modern selection of Newton's spiritual letters is available in *The Voice of the Heart*, ed. William Culbertson (Chicago, Ill., 1950).

[27] The best studies are Maurice Quinlan, *William Cowper: A Critical Life* (Minneapolis, Minn., 1953), and William Hutchings, *The Poetry of William Cowper* (London, 1983).

storms springing up in Cowper's own mind amid the rural
peace. And 'Jesus, where'er thy people meet' was written in
1769 for the opening of a room in Olney for weekly prayer
meetings. There, among his fellow villagers, this man of
sorrows found comfort.

CHARLES SIMEON
AND HIS DISCIPLES

The time was coming when Lord Melbourne would complain
to Queen Victoria: 'Nobody is gay now, they are so religious.'[28]
But when Charles Simeon became a 'serious' Christian in 1779
he did not know anyone to whom he could go for help. During
his first term at King's College, Cambridge, he was warned
that he would be required to receive Holy Communion on
Easter Day. His schooldays at Eton had left him in a moral
condition which he later recalled: 'Satan himself was as fit to
attend as I.' However, he had enough religion left in him to be
alarmed by the approach of the compulsory service and turned
to 'the only religious book that I had ever heard of', *The Whole
Duty of Man*. This anonymous exposition of morality as sustained by the customs of the Church of England had been
famous ever since the middle of the seventeenth century. It
made him more miserable. But the thought flashed into his
mind: 'I can transfer all my guilt to Another!' And by Easter
Day he was convinced that this Another 'is risen today' – so
that at the once dreaded Communion he found 'the sweetest
access to God through my blessed Saviour'.

Although the guilt had been replaced by assurance, Simeon's life remained in many ways a classic example of
eighteenth-century privilege. Without passing any examination he became a Fellow of King's College, almost his whole
duty being now not to marry. He was ordained – as were most

---

[28] See Muriel Jaeger, *Before Victoria: Changing Standards and Behaviour 1787–1837*
(London, 1956); Ford K. Brown, *Fathers of the Victorians: The Age of Wilberforce*
(Cambridge, 1961); Ian Bradley, *The Call to Seriousness: The Evangelical Impact on the
Victorians* (London, 1976).

of his colleagues, although it did not make their attendance at chapel much more regular. Because his father knew the Bishop of Ely, he was entrusted with the care of Holy Trinity church in Cambridge at the age of twenty-two. All through his life he remained very much the gentleman, fond of horses, well-dressed, elegant in his hospitality, anxious that his guests should wipe their shoes. Many thought him affected and vain, and this did not help him when he faced opposition. His colleagues in King's snubbed him during most of his life there; the churchwardens of Holy Trinity led a prolonged and bitter opposition to his ministry; worldly undergraduates said cruel things about the young 'Sims' he attracted; even fellow Evangelicals sometimes resented his clumsy attempts to win their devoted friendship and complete confidence. He recorded a moment which was typical of much of his life. 'When I was an object of much contempt and derision in the university, I strolled forth one day, buffeted and afflicted, with my little Testament in my hand. . . . The first text which caught my eye was this: *They found a man of Cyrene, Simon by name; him they compelled to bear his cross.*'

Yet his funeral in 1836 was the most impressive Cambridge had ever seen, town and gown uniting to honour 'the old Apostle'. He achieved this influence by staying at his strategic post for half a century. Primarily he was a preacher. On Sunday mornings and evenings he preached in his own church, usually for fifty minutes. During the afternoon it was his practice for many years to ride out to preach in one of the villages; then he changed his habit and taught preaching to ordinands in Cambridge. On Friday evenings he welcomed all undergraduates to 'conversation parties' in his college rooms; the conversation consisted of questions to him about religion and the drink was tea. He published 2,536 sermon outlines and always he tried to combine the Bible-based passion of the earlier Evangelicals with the clear reasonableness of the eighteenth century.

His base continued to be his handsome rooms in King's College, but from this base he made effective expeditions into his parish and into the nation. He did not hurry through the Prayer Book in church; he read it out like a man who relished

every word. He did not keep worship coldly formal; he delighted in hymns and formed prayer meetings and societies to
provide fellowship between the services. And he knew the
importance of visiting parishioners in their homes. In 1796 he
was at last able to appoint a full-time assistant curate who was
not a substitute during his absence (as curates were then
generally regarded) but a partner in the pastoral work which
previously he had undertaken single-handed. He needed such
a colleague because he had set himself a national task in a style
which was rare for any preacher or parish priest.

When the small and innocuously named Eclectic Society,
the first national organization for Evangelicals, had been
formed around John Newton in 1783, Simeon attended its
London meetings whenever he could. He went round to other
groups of like-minded clergymen, building up the confidence of
a nationwide progress. He bought up the right to present a
rector or vicar (the 'advowson') in a considerable number of
key parishes. As a biblicist he could not defend the method of
making appointments which made this spread of the Evangelical message possible in return for cash – but he cheerfully took
advantage of the system. He supported the emergence of great
national societies designed to stimulate the parishes and to do
on their behalf work which they could not tackle. These
societies solicited subscribers, employed itinerant agents and
published literature. Simeon was a great believer in the distribution of Bibles to the laity, and took the lead amid much
controversy in the foundation of a 'local auxiliary' to support
the British and Foreign Bible Society, which had been
launched in 1804 and which included Dissenters; his decisive
move in this Cambridge drama was to secure a royal duke as
chairman.

He was involved in missions overseas. In 1796 at a meeting
of the Eclectic Society, he raised the question: 'With what
propriety, and in what mode, can a Mission be attempted to
the heathen from the Established Church?' In 1799 – the year
of Napoleon's campaign in Egypt – a society was formed to
attempt just that, although all the bishops stood aloof. At first
called 'the Society for Missions to Africa and the East', this
bold little group was soon to be known far and wide as the

Church Missionary Society. One of Simeon's disciples, Henry Martyn, translated the New Testament into Urdu, revised the unsatisfactory versions in Arabic and Persian, and by a journal published after his death commended the mission to India.[29]

So the pattern of the Evangelical parish took shape. Its worship was lively, its preaching intense and systematic, its laity were regular readers of the Bible capable of conducting their own family prayers at home, and it supported missions to the heathen. Its loyalty to the Church of England was unquestionable; Simeon may even be said to have sacrificed his life to this, since he caught a fatal chill by insisting on going to Ely to pay his respects to the new bishop. Congratulating his former curate Thomas Thomason over his pastoral work in Calcutta – work which transformed the English community there – he wrote in 1824 that 'the whole world seems to have received somewhat of a new impulse: and glorious times are fast approaching. The sun and moon are scarcely more different from each other than Cambridge is from what it was when I was first Minister of Trinity Church: and the same change has taken place throughout the whole land'.[30]

WILLIAM WILBERFORCE AND THE SLAVES

William Wilberforce was determined to show that an Evangelical could still make a very agreeable member of the governing class and could even be the acceptable guest of the Prince Regent in Brighton. It was not that he was personally ambitious, at least not on the scale of others with his gifts in the House of Commons. What he wanted was support for his schemes. Many of these schemes concerned the 'reformation of manners' in England. To a considerable extent that meant the reformation of the lower orders by their social superiors. Aristocrats were sought as subscribers to good causes; thus the Prince Regent, a notorious debauchee, patronized the London

---

[29] See Constance Padwick, *Henry Martyn* (London, 1922).
[30] See Charles Smyth, *Simeon and Church Order* (Cambridge, 1940), and Hugh Evan Hopkins, *Charles Simeon of Cambridge* (London, 1977).

Female Penitentiary. However, the attention of the Evangelicals was also turned towards the moral improvement of the
upper class by personal evangelism. Wilberforce went to dinner parties with what he called 'launchers', carefully prepared
conversational gambits which would launch the talk into the
ocean of religion from which souls could be fished. He wanted
their support – but he also wanted them.

He had a winning personality. 'There never lived on earth, I
am sure, a man of sweeter temper than Mr Wilberforce', wrote
Dorothy Wordsworth. Sir James Mackintosh, in politics a
radical and in religion a sceptic, reckoned him 'the most
"amusable" man I ever met in my life. Instead of having to
think of what subjects will interest him, it is perfectly impossible to hit one that does not.' A small and slight man suffering
from much ill-health (he took opium every day), his head often
dropping forward in a manner which might have been thought
grotesque, he seemed to be a threat to no one and a delight to
everyone. As a young man he was very willing to sing and to
dance. His private conversation was always full of affection,
playfulness and cultured knowledge. He made it his business to
win friends by hospitality, and for this purpose kept open house
in his home a few yards away from the House of Commons. In
public debates he could be the equal of any man in his age, the
greatest age of English oratory. His melting power as an orator
as well as his wealth as the son of a Hull merchant made him
one of the Members of Parliament for Yorkshire, the most
numerous and most prestigious constituency in all England,
and kept him in that position for almost thirty years. But
perhaps what attracted them most was his real saintliness. It
was characteristic of him that he organized a pension for
Charles Wesley's widow (John Wesley did not), and that when
his eldest son lost vast sums in business he paid the debt
although it meant that for the last few years of his life he had no
home. Large numbers of friends flocked round him even when
he had married his beautiful and pious Barbara, who took no
interest in politics and very little in running his household.

His Evangelical conversion did not withdraw him from
Parliament or from popularity. Early in 1785 he read Philip
Doddridge's *Rise and Progress of Religion in the Soul* and through

that book recovered his boyhood's intellectual acceptance of the Bible's teachings. Later that year, during continental travels, he read the New Testament in Greek. He returned to England profoundly convinced of his sinfulness, but by Easter 1786 this despair had been replaced by a joyful acceptance of Christ. John Newton comforted and guided him in his emotional crisis – and had the sense to see how badly he was needed in public life. The moral standard of the Commons fell below its standard of eloquence. Not until 1812 was a definite Evangelical appointed to high political office (Nicholas Vansittart then became Chancellor of the Exchequer). The bishops of the age, while more moral, were scarcely prophetic, and the Archbishopric of Canterbury had been condemned to a further period of snobbish mediocrity in 1782, when it had been turned down by the two most able bishops, Robert Lowth of London and Richard Hurd of Worcester.

In intervals of this public life he wrote a book of almost five hundred pages, which was published in 1797 under the title *A Practical View of the Prevailing Religious System of Professed Christians in the Higher and Middle Classes in this Country Contrasted with Real Christianity*. It was a disorganized book, and theologically amateurish; but it criticized its readers from within their own world and it was totally free of theological bigotry. 'Real Christianity' was to Wilberforce a straightforwardly biblical religion, to be accepted as the guide and rule of all human life. God's love was for him the essence; and the morality he urged was always loving conduct. So this *Practical View* had an influence both wide and deep in the classes to which it was addressed. Edmund Burke spent the last two days of his life reading it.

Such a religion could easily be associated, as the old Puritanism had been, with repression of the people's vices – and also of the people's political views, for Wilberforce was the intimate friend of the Tory Prime Minister, William Pitt. He voted for all the harshly repressive legislation which Pitt and his successors enacted in order to suppress threats of an English revolution (without a proper police force). In the years 1817–20 civil war in England seemed closer than it had ever been since the 1640s; in those three years 427 people were executed and in their panic gentlemen such as Wilberforce, sorry as they might be, agreed that the severity was essential. What Wilberforce might have become can be seen from the example of Hannah More. An intellectual lady (the term 'blue stocking' was invented to describe her and a little group like her), after her conversion she was self-sacrificing enough to pour her energies into the foundation of schools for the children of her poorest neighbours in Somerset. It was a charity which Wilberforce, like Henry Thornton, helped to finance. Hannah More was not afraid to castigate upper-class vice, as in her booklet on *The Manners of the Great.* But in the eyes of posterity she has made herself ridiculous or odious by the tracts which she wrote for the instruction of the poor – vividly written tracts (three a month appeared in the series of 'Cheap Repository Tracts' launched in 1795), exhorting them to accept the ordering of society as well as the Christian Gospel.[31]

Wilberforce, too, might have been branded as a mere moralizing conservative. Indeed, many attempts have been made to place him as a reactionary by historians willing to forget that like others of the Clapham Sect he pressed for some control over working conditions in factories, the rescue of chimney boys, the abolition of press gangs to force sailors into the Royal Navy, civil rights for Roman Catholics, prison reform, Parliamentary reform, church schools for the poor and some other causes which the future would regard as progressive. However, for one achievement he has always been given credit. He was the chief spokesman in the long campaign against Britain's large share in the shipping of slaves out of Africa and against slavery itself in the sugar-growing islands of the British West Indies.

In 1787 his agreement to speak against the slave trade in the House of Commons was an indispensable encouragement to those who had begun to care less conspicuously – men such as the young Thomas Clarkson (who had been forced to brood over those horrors by being set slavery as the subject for an essay-prize in Cambridge) and Glanville Sharp (who had become involved by meeting in a London street one of the

---

[31] See M. G. Jones, *Hannah More* (Cambridge, 1952), and John McLeish, *Evangelical Religion and Popular Education* (London, 1969).

thousands of ex-slaves then roaming around England). Twenty years later 'Wilberforce' was the name praised amid emotional scenes as the slave trade was made illegal for British ships. He retired from Parliament in 1825, but just before he died in July 1833 he knew that he and his associates had won the emancipation of the West Indian slaves.

Of course he was not alone in the public struggle. The campaign would have found success even harder than it did had it not been for the almost incredible toils of a Scot, Zachary Macaulay, in amassing and analysing the facts, and of James Stephen in presenting them with all the skills of a first-class lawyer. The whole Clapham Sect had to be mobilized – and it was a group with as much talent as any cabinet and as much appetite for factual detail as any civil service. Other men of wealth and talent were enrolled; a brewer, Thomas Fowell Buxton, took over the leadership from Wilberforce for the last ten years of the struggle. Much was also due to the Quakers (the first religious body to forbid its members to have anything to do with the slave trade, in 1758) and Methodists. A Congregationalist missionary, John Smith, who died in prison in 1824 after being falsely accused of stirring up riots among the slaves on Demarara, was the movement's martyr. The Evangelicals even admitted an avowed Unitarian, William Smith, MP, into their counsels and their friendship because he, too, was a friend of the slaves. Nor did they avoid all collaboration with the Whig leader Charles James Fox, whose morals were notorious.

Especially in its later stages the campaign had to become something new in English history – a nationwide, popular agitation, reaching far beyond the religious world. It was in this English fight against slavery that modern propaganda techniques hitherto unknown were developed. Large public rallies were assembled and addressed; great petitions to Parliament were arranged (one contained a million signatures); notes were supplied to feed speakers and preachers on less spectacular occasions; speakers were sent out as paid agents of the Anti-Slavery Society; journals scholarly and popular were distributed; the art of lobbying influential men in private was perfected; and to supplement this barrage of words a Wedgwood cameo was manufactured which depicted an enchained

Negro kneeling in supplication and uttering the plea, 'Am I not
a man and a brother?' Thus a swelling chorus from many
quarters surrounded Wilberforce's speeches to the Commons.

So did changing economic conditions. The slave trade and
slavery itself became less important to Britain during the
philanthropists' long campaign against them. The trade in
slaves did not decline before it was made illegal, but other
industries developed rapidly to absorb capital and promise
profits, so that the slave-based sugar colonies no longer had the
significance in the British economy which they had possessed
twenty years before. The prohibition of the sale of British-
shipped slaves to Britain's actual or potential enemies came in
1806, and it ended two-thirds of the trade before the total
prohibition the following year. It was also realized that the loss
of seamen's lives through disease in the slave ships was larger
than the large loss of the lives of slaves; while another non-
ethical factor in the ending of slavery was the knowledge that
the heavy pioneering work of clearing the ground of the sugar
plantations in the British West Indies by slave labour was over.
It began to seem possible that 'free' labour could be hired at
low wages to do the remaining routine work. After 1807 such
labour was easier to handle than slave labour; for the slaves
now showed their discontent and in 1832 their impatience
boiled over into a rebellion on Jamaica. By the 1830s English
consumers knew that other sugar merchants had arisen to
break the West Indian monopoly. The East India Company
had ventured into production; sugar was being produced in
abundance in Cuba and Brazil; sugar beet was now being
grown in Europe. Indeed, these new sources were usually able
to supply sugar at a lower price than seemed possible in the
West Indian plantations, often run inefficiently for absentee
owners. In the period 1815–30, the price of sugar in the
London market fell from £70 a ton to £30.

Yet when all these other factors have been allowed for, the
glory of William Wilberforce's personal achievement remains.
For right up to the end the defence put up by the traders and
owners of slaves was very powerful in the only assembly which
ultimately counted, Parliament; and a fraction of the profits of
the slave and sugar trades was enough to finance counter-

propaganda on a very large scale. Ports such as Liverpool and
Bristol were reminded vigorously that they owed their prosperity to a trade which had probably by now shipped eleven
million human beings across the Atlantic (perhaps as many
slaves had died during the course of the journey). The profits
made out of the slave trade and its immediate consequences
had been an indispensable source of finance in the vital early
stages of Britain's industrialization. The strength of the economic arguments in favour of shipping slaves could be seen by
anyone who meditated on one fact: it had been more profitable
for the slave-owners to buy more labour from the slave-
shippers than for them to make the elementary arrangements
needed to ensure that their existing slaves had plenty of healthy
children who could grow up to be useful labourers. Nor were
subsidiary arguments lacking. It was argued (by Nelson, for
example) that during a great naval war it would be madness to
damage British shipping. It was feared – with good reason, as
events showed – that when the war against Napoleon was over
it would be a hard and thankless task for the Royal Navy to
suppress slave-running in the ships of other nations. It was
suggested that those who were opposed to slavery were probably in their hearts the enemies of all forms of private property
and commerce; and it was urged that a Britain passing through
hard times could not afford to compensate the West Indian
owners of slaves for this invasion of their sacred property
rights. It was also pointed out, with far more truth, that
Africans themselves supplied the slaves whom the British
shipped – and did not have equally desired products to exchange for the English goods which they coveted. The abolition of the slave-trade and of slavery might, or might not, be
desirable in principle; it might, or might not, be less disastrous
economically than had recently seemed certain. But of one
thing realists were still sure. Its speedy abolition seemed a
Utopian dream, as nuclear disarmament was to seem a century
and a half later.[32]

---

[32] The best short study is Basil Davidson, *Black Mother* (revised Harmondsworth, Middx., 1980). See also Roger Anstey, *The Atlantic Slave Trade and British
Abolition 1760–1810* (London, 1975), and D. B. Davis, *The Problem of Slavery in an Age
of Revolution* (Ithaca, N.Y., 1975).

With all these forces and arguments arrayed against them, Wilberforce and his fellow campaigners were often close to despair. Between 1799 and 1804 they had not the heart to introduce into the Commons their private bill for the slave trade's abolition. For many years they had to deny that they sought the end of slavery as well as the trade. Wilberforce was a Christian crusader, and that dimension was needed to end an evil which the more secular philosophy of the eighteenth century had often deplored – but tolerated. Had he not arisen so often from his seat in the House of Commons to plead for justice, and had he not been so systematically hospitable in winning friends to this cause, it is likely that the slaves of the West Indies would have had to wait longer. The difficulties had been enough to wring from John Wesley his prophecy to William Wilberforce, in the last letter he wrote: 'Unless God has raised you up for this very thing, you will be worn out by the opposition of men and devils. But if God be for you, who can be against you? Are all of them together stronger than God?'

In the end, the prestige acquired by these great moral victories helped Wilberforce and his Evangelical companions to open up Africa and India to Christian missionary work, understood as another kind of liberation. They had to concentrate first on Sierra Leone, which they founded in 1787 as a colony on the coast, to enable ex-slaves facing destitution or crime in England to settle in Africa as farmers and traders. The small colony around Freetown suffered many calamities and was virtually destroyed by a French squadron in 1794, to be rebuilt by Zachary Macaulay who was willing to spend five years there as governor. The Evangelicals remained inflexible in their support until at last in 1808 missionary work that proved permanent was established, using a mighty river, the Rio Pongas – and in the same year the colony was taken over by the Crown. Gradually the conviction spread that whites owed something to the 'dark continent' after all the horrors of the slave trade; and that the Christian Gospel was among the white man's blessings which he ought to share with Africans despite the violence often encountered, despite the degradation which the trade in human flesh had left behind, and despite the killer-diseases including malaria. And this mission was planted on African soil during the great war against Napoleon. For many reasons it was a mission which up to the 1840s was one of almost overwhelming difficulty.[33]

Still the eyes of the Evangelicals were on India. Until quite late in the eighteenth century it had been generally assumed that the English were in India simply in order to make money. The East India Company had taken to paying for its purchases in India out of the heavy taxes which it levied on the land – and had allowed many of its servants to make their own fortunes by private trade, by receiving bribes or by straightforward plunder. The English word 'loot' had come from India. But gradually official profits had dwindled until the company had got deep into debt, and private profits had been curbed; the turning point had been the impeachment of Warren Hastings for corruption while Governor General. And at a time when it was obviously incapable of supplying an efficient government, the company had clearly acquired a massive political responsibility.

The decline and fall of the Mogul empire had led to the disintegration of India, to gross corruption and inefficiency in the successor states, and to a growing feeling that the victories won by Englishmen such as Clive over 'native' princes and French rivals were clear signs that the political vacuum must be filled. The spectacle of a commercial company chartered by Queen Elizabeth on the last day of 1600 stumbling into the government of Bengal and most of India's west coast had been too much for the conscience to swallow even in the eighteenth century. The English Crown had been involved to some extent ever since Charles II's Portuguese queen had brought Bombay as a dowry, and in 1773 Parliament established a Governor General resident in India, with a supreme court in Calcutta to hand down English justice to any who appealed to it. Eleven years later the Governor General's powers were enlarged, a small Board of Control was set up in London, and the company's directors were forced to defer to it in all questions of political policy.

The belief that the English were in India to exercise a trusteeship mysteriously placed in their hands by Providence

---

[33] See John Peterson, *Province of Freedom: A History of Sierra Leone* (London, 1969).

now began to prevail. It was much encouraged by the Evangelicals who penetrated India's new government. The most
influential of these was Charles Grant, who had gone out to
India in 1767 and had undergone an Evangelical conversion in
the course of his grief over the deaths of two young daughters.
In his later life a leading resident of Clapham, he became
chairman of the company's directors. His well-trained son
Robert became Governor of Bombay, and the spirit in which
Sir Robert Grant governed Indians is shown by his authorship
of the hymn 'O worship the Lord all glorious above'. Among
Grant's collaborators was John Shore (Lord Teignmouth),
who on becoming Governor General in 1793 made no secret of
his religious inspiration. He declared: 'I consider every native
of India, whatever his situation may be, as having a claim upon
me.' A more flamboyantly ambitious Governor General, Lord
Wellesley, although without a personal religion, officially
attended church. He spoke about England's 'sacred trusteeship' in India – and acted on this principle, ruling, annexing
or 'protecting' the sub-continent to such an extent that the East
India Company, alarmed about the expense, recalled him in 1805.

Meanwhile horrified Englishmen read reports such as
Charles Grant's *Observations on the State of Society among the Asiatic
Subjects of Great Britain* (1792). They were told about the temple
prostitutes, about the enormous car called the Juggernaut
(from the place Jagannath) under which devotees of Krishna
allowed themselves to be crushed, about the thugs who strang-
led travellers as a sacrifice to Kali, about the murder of
unwanted daughters and the old or the sick, about widow-
burning (*sati*). Not only Evangelicals despised the Hinduism
which had produced such customs. Contempt for degrading
superstition also inspired a *History of India* published in 1817 by
the leading Utilitarian philosopher, James Mill. When the
East India Company refused to interfere in such customs, or
even to criticize them, on the ground that trade might suffer,
England's honour seemed to be diminished.[34]

---

[34] G. D. Bearce, *British Attitudes towards India 1784–1858* (Oxford, 1961), may be
compared with P. J. Marshall, *The British Discovery of Hinduism in the Eighteenth Century*
(Cambridge, 1970).

There had for long been a Roman Catholic presence in India. Indeed, the first Englishman known to have set foot on Indian soil had been a Jesuit, Thomas Stevens, who had sailed in 1579 after reading St Francis Xavier's description of the mission; and letters sent home by that Jesuit missionary to his father, a London merchant, had helped to arouse the interest leading to the East India Company's foundation. The company had of course done nothing to encourage Roman Catholic missionary work, but for many years, from 1714 onwards, it had given some assistance to Lutheran missionaries. These were supported by a Church of England society (the Society for Promoting Christian Knowledge) in the Danish colony at Tranqubar near the southern tip of India. The company had given them free passages to India and had often paid salaries for their work as chaplains. It had also turned a blind eye to missionary work by a few English enthusiasts. With such precedents, it was impossible to maintain for ever the official attitude that Englishmen in India must avoid spreading Christianity as if it were a disease.

The company's charter was due for renewal in 1813. Anticipating this, one of the company's own chaplains, Claudius Buchanan, devoted himself to propaganda in favour both of missionary work and of a much enlarged 'Indian Ecclesiastical Establishment' to convert the godless English; and when 1813 came, the Evangelicals seized the opportunity to secure the admission to India not only of merchants who were not members of the company but also of persons wishing to enter it 'for the purpose of enlightening and reforming Indians'. The new charter also instructed the company to devote £7,500 a year to education. To lead the chaplains still to be appointed by the East India Company, and to exercise an undefined influence over any missionaries, there was to be a Bishop of Calcutta on a noble stipend, £5,000 a year, assisted by three archdeacons. The preamble to the East India Company's new charter declared: 'It is the duty of this country to promote the interests and happiness of the native inhabitants of the British Dominions in India; and such means ought to be adopted as may intend to the introduction among them of useful knowledge and of religious and moral improvements.' The connection between the island and the sub-continent was no longer to be predominantly commercial.[35]

Wilberforce's personal following in the Commons should not be exaggerated; the group of MPs known as 'the saints' was seldom more than twenty-five. But the series of achievements associated with his honoured name were a remarkable development in a religious movement which had begun in a few obscure parishes, and were all the more remarkable because they brought benefits to African slaves or to Indians who were not Christians (although of course the Evangelicals hoped for their eventual conversion). 'Christianity', Wilberforce declared during a three-hour speech in the decisive debate of 1813, 'assumes her true character . . . when she takes under protection those poor degraded beings on whom philosophy looks down with disdain.' And he went on to assure the Commons that they need not fear that the missionaries would make Indians into Christians by force. 'Compulsion and Christianity! Why, the very terms are at variance with each other – the ideas are incompatible. In the language of Inspiration itself, Christianity has been called the "law of liberty".'[36]

---

[35] See P. J. Marshall, *Problems of Empire: Britain and India 1757–1813* (London, 1968). A. T. Embree, *Charles Grant and British Rule in India* (New York, 1962), showed the change from the eighteenth-century background well sketched by Percival Spear, *The Nabobs* (London, 1963). The biographical sketches in Philip Woodruff, *The Men who Ruled India: The Founders* (London, 1953), went from 1600 to 1858.

[36] Biographies include Lord Furneaux, *William Wilberforce* (London, 1974), and John Pollock, *Wilberforce* (London, 1977). The growth of the belief among Evangelicals that it might be the will of God to reform the working of the market has been studied by Boyd Hilton, *The Age of Atonement* (Oxford, 1988).

CHAPTER THREE

CHURCHES IN CHANGE

THE NEW POPULATION

The conventional idea of a country parish was expressed by Shelley. One morning early in the summer of 1815 the 'atheist poet' was walking in the country with his friend, Thomas Love Peacock. He was in a restless mood, having recently made final his separation from his wife, Harriet. The two men stood outside a vicarage. According to Peacock, Shelley mused aloud: 'I feel strongly inclined to enter the Church.' When his companion expressed astonishment, Shelley explained that an English clergyman's assent to the supernatural part of Christianity was 'merely technical'. He went on to expound how much good a good clergyman may do 'in his teaching as a scholar and a moralist; in his example as a gentleman and a man of regular life; in the consolation of his personal intercourse and of his charity among the poor. . . . It is an admirable institution that admits the possibility of diffusing such men over the surface of the land. And am I to deprive myself of the advantages of this admirable institution because there are certain technicalities . . . ?'

Although she belonged heart and soul to the 'admirable institution' on which Shelley looked from outside, Jane Austen viewed it more realistically. Born in a rectory, she meekly followed her clerical father to retirement in Bath. Two of her brothers were ordained and another, a naval officer, caused a mild stir by kneeling during church services. She was always pondering moral questions and she conducted her own life in a manner which made her burial in Winchester Cathedral in 1817 entirely appropriate. She acknowledged her need of a Redeemer (her well-lettered tombstone said so), but the lack of sensitivity and reserve with which the Evangelicals pressed the point was entirely against the values of her family and her class. She was suspicious of the Evangelicals' claim that God inspired their many utterances and arranged every detail of their lives to their spiritual advantage. With a sharp eye for humbug she admired not 'zeal' but modesty, tact and prudence; not 'seriousness' but liveliness, irony and wit; not the urge to distribute Bibles but the contentment which produces the wish to be agreeable to others; not the heights of holiness but reasonableness and elegance. She took her share in local good works but observed 'causes' from afar.

So far as we know, she never opened her heart about religion (although some evidence may have been lost because her sister Cassandra, a lady even more discreet than she was, destroyed some passages in her surviving letters). Her novels never seriously consider a religious topic – or a clergyman's soul. They are about how people behave in society, not about their philosophies or yearnings. The conversation in them is confined to the upper middle class in the rural south of England and a few fashionable towns, with only faint echoes of the great war being fought at the time. But occasionally in the remaining letters we are given a glimpse of a faith at once firm and cool. When she received the news that Sir John Moore had spoken of England before dying on the battlefield of Corunna, she wished that he 'had united something of the Christian with the Hero in his death'.

A letter of 1814 reminds us that her sensible tolerance could extend even to Evangelicals – who were, however, still kept at their distance. She had to act as Aunt Jane to motherless Fanny Knight who was having one of her many love problems. This time the young man, John Plumptre, was attractive in many ways; handsome, with good manners and (as Aunt Jane reminded her) 'the eldest son of a man of fortune'. But was he dull? Evidently he was, for he disappeared from Fanny's life – and Aunt Jane (who never married) warned her: 'Anything is to be preferred or endured rather than marrying without affection.' But this broad-minded aunt wrote: 'And as to there being any objection from his *goodness*, from the danger of his becoming even Evangelical, I cannot admit *that*. I am by no means convinced that we ought not all to be Evangelicals, and am at least persuaded that they who are so from reason and feeling, must be happiest and safest. – Do not be frightened from the connection by your brother having most wit. Wisdom is better than wit, and in the long run will certainly have the laugh on her side; and don't be frightened by the idea of his acting more strictly up to the precepts of the New Testament than others.'

Jane Austen did not paint with strong colours or on a broad canvas; she analysed her art as 'the little bit (two inches wide) of ivory on which I work with so fine a brush'. But her unsentimentally happy and quietly optimistic prose (achieved after many revisions) defended her world against internal and external enemies. In her world, the Church of England was unobtrusively dominant; and conduct was judged by a code which, although it fell short of the heights of 'the precepts of the New Testament', was intended to be humanely Christian.[1]

When Charlotte Brontë was urged to write like Jane Austen, she replied that *Pride and Prejudice* was 'a carefully-fenced, highly-cultivated garden, with neat borders and delicate flowers; but . . . no open country, no fresh air. . . .' Her own writing marked a general movement out of the garden into the storm. Her *Shirley* is for our purpose the most illuminating of the novels which she and her sisters wrote. Published in 1849 but set in Jane Austen's time, it begins with a picture of three bachelor curates having dinner together – abusing the dinner, its cook, their parishioners and each other. Jane Austen would have shuddered at their vulgarity. Their pastoral work lies in the industrial villages of a Yorkshire which is miserable because the new machines have reduced employment while the war is reducing exports; so they leave the dinner-table to become the allies of the owners who defend their mills, pistols in their hands. *Shirley* is, however, not an anticlerical novel. Its author was to marry, and later to fall in love with, one of the curates – a man who appears in the novel with the remark that

---

[1] See Mary Lascelles, *Jane Austen and Her Art* (Oxford, 1939), and Marilyn Butler, *Jane Austen and the War of Ideas* (Oxford, 1975). The materials on which any biography – for example, Lord David Cecil's *Portrait of Jane Austen* (London, 1978) – must be based are in *Jane Austen's Letters*, ed. R. W. Chapman (second edition, Oxford, 1952).

'the circumstance of finding himself invited to tea with a
Dissenter would unhinge him for a week'. *Shirley* is not even
anti-capitalist. Its main theme is the human condition, understood as a storm of suffering. Caroline is told by her mother: 'O
child, the human heart *can* suffer. It holds more tears than the
ocean holds waters. We never know how wide, how deep it is,
until misery begins to unbind her clouds, and fill it with
rushing blackness.' In the year before those words were
printed, the little-understood disease of tuberculosis had
claimed three victims in the author's family, two of them in the
very house where *Shirley* was written. Charlotte Brontë had
seen her tragic brother die, closely followed by her sisters,
Emily and Anne. Each of the sisters left behind an isolated
novel to disclose a major author, and each was a poet; Emily
was a major poet of the mystic's lonely encounter with God in
the midst of an evil world. The same disease that had taken
them was soon to kill Charlotte.

A redeeming influence in this world of suffering was compassionate love; and among those who showed such love was the
father, Patrick Brontë. An Irishman, he was a snob (he was
born in a tiny cottage and his surname was originally Brunty)
and a failure as a scholar and poet. In the eyes of many
admirers of his brilliantly gifted daughters, he was a half-mad
tyrant. But he loved them; in many ways he nurtured their
genius, he endured the degradation and death of their brother
in whom he had set high hopes – and with all his oddities he
was, it seems, appreciated by his parish. In 1861 the whole
village went into mourning for his funeral. Mrs Gaskell, whose
memoir of Charlotte Brontë first gave a wide circulation to the ·
gossip about him, knew little about his pastoral work in
Haworth over forty years. But she recorded that when Patrick
Brontë was nearly blind, very tired and lonely, and full of grief
after many storms of adversity and bereavement, 'he was out of
doors among his parishioners for a good part of each day'.[2]

The most serious moral question for the England of the

---

[2] The voluminous literature includes L. and F. M. Hanson, *The Four Brontës*
(Oxford, 1949), and John Lock and W. T. Dixon, *A Man of Sorrow: The Life, Letters
and Times of the Rev. Patrick Brontë* (London, 1965).

Brontës was whether the degrading conditions under which millions of men, women and children now suffered were, or were not, essential if the greatly increased population was to be supported. Was it essential that one in every two of the children born in the new industrial towns should die before the age of five, and that agricultural labourers in the Suffolk of John Constable's tranquilly glowing pictures should bring up a family on far less than a pound a week, supplemented by six shillings from the poor-rate?

Later generations have on the whole agreed that the answer is obvious: these conditions were caused by the wickedness of factory owners and landlords, and the Christian Church ought to have been foremost in demanding their abolition. And so it seemed to many radicals at the time. But most Anglicans – and most Dissenters – sincerely believed that the moral question must be answered by saying that the country could not afford higher wages or greater subsidies if the economy was to develop in the interests of all.

In his *Essay on Population* (1798) a Cambridge scholar, Thomas Malthus, first absorbed the fact of a rapidly expanding population into a major – although not large – treatise on economics and ethics. He noted that while the population grew, the means of subsistence did not grow equally. He recognized the absolute necessity to limit population growth and in this necessity he found consolation for the checks on breeding which distressed him as a clergyman – famine, disease, war and vice. He also advocated 'moral restraint': since artificial contraception was wrong, people should postpone marriage and be chaste before it. At first he was explicitly complacent in the belief that this whole set of stern limits to human wishes had been decreed by the divine Providence; but more maturely regretting and suppressing the brutality of some of those early statements, he announced that he relied mainly on moral restraint.

He had raised questions which were to be taken very seriously by all thoughtful people in the second half of the twentieth century – and they were recognized as real questions during the first half of the nineteenth. Apart from moral restraint, the main answer seemed to be the increase of the means of subsistence by the improvement of the techniques used in agriculture and in manufacturing. England was then a developing nation, the very first nation in all the world to have the opportunities presented by modern farming and industry. But at the time the extent of the prosperity ahead, to be helped by birth control, was inconceivable. This was the age of iron, not gold.[3]

In a two-volume work of 1816 a future Archbishop of Canterbury, John Bird Sumner, an Evangelical, based his hope for the country on the Bible. His work was entitled *A Treatise on the Records of the Creation*, but his most interesting argument was on the controverted frontier between economics and ethics in an age considerably later than the creation. He applauded Malthus for his realism about the danger of over-population, but drew from the best economists known to that age (particularly Adam Smith) the optimistic belief that the means of subsistence could be increased if the economy were left to grow by trusting to the incentives to private enterprise and to the disciplines of the free market. Later on Sumner lost much of his faith in the sweat of the brow as the panacea for worldly grievances and fell back on the Evangelical consolation that a heaven awaited those who behaved properly in this vale of tears; and few other churchmen displayed his talents either for economics or for ethics. But a less systematic acceptance of the iron laws taught by the economists did lie behind what was taught by almost all the leading churchmen. It was the conventional doctrine that men, women and children must work or starve, and in the conditions of the industrial revolution must endure poverty in order that one day there might be plenty. Meanwhile the low prices made possible by low wages afforded some consolation. And allied to this conviction about economic laws there was a sincere belief that God had arranged the order of society just as he had set the stars in their courses. To interfere with the rights of private property seemed to be not only against the law of England and the long-term interests of the poor, but also against the law of God. The rich had their duties – to use their talents to the full, to set good

---

[3] See Patricia James, *Population Malthus* (London, 1979).

examples, to avoid extravagance, to be just and to be charitable. To pay more than standard wages was not among their duties.

The violence of the French Revolution, and of the great war to which it led, deeply frightened the propertied classes and strengthened their belief that the society under their control must be defended as a divinely ordained hierarchy – particularly because the revolutionaries were, or were reckoned to be, atheists. Many English preachers regarded the revolutionaries (and later Napoleon) as Antichrist and turned to the Bible for the interpretation of the dramas of the age as signs of the end of the world. Samuel Horsley, onè of the ablest of the conservative bishops, declared that in 1800 mankind was facing the greatest crisis 'since the moment of our Lord's departure from the earth'. This apocalyptic mood continued in the post-war world when it was feared that English agitators might revive the revolution which Nelson and Wellington had crushed in their victories over the French. Amid such alarms reform of modest dimensions could easily be identified with revolution and revolution with the destruction of Christianity. Even Christians who avoided the extremes of reaction felt it a religious duty to preserve the constitution, the social order and the morality now under threat. In 1834 a fifth of the magistrates in the country were Church of England clergymen. They embodied the enormous investment by the Churches in social stability.

But many churchmen saw that the Church of England was not doing enough to influence – and, as it was usually hoped, to quieten – the new England. On Easter Day 1831 out of a total population of just over thirteen million, only about 605,000 received Holy Communion at its altars. All the irrationalities in its system which had been conspicuous in the eighteenth century were even more notable now. One example was the non-residence of their incumbents in thousands of the rural parishes. It was true that many of these parishes were deep in the countryside, with very small populations; but it was still scandalous that pastoral reorganization had not changed the pattern bequeathed by the Middle Ages.

Parliament was persuaded to legislate in 1803, but five years later was informed that some seven thousand priests were still not resident in parishes to which they had been appointed. By

1812 there were still over a thousand parishes where there was
no resident incumbent or curate. One result of this reform was
that a brilliant and deservedly popular talker and writer,
Sydney Smith, found himself exiled from the company of his
fellow wits and Whig patrons in London to his remote Yorkshire parish of Foston. He was miles from the nearest lemon, as
he complained, but he wrote to his friend Lady Holland that he
had given himself quietly up to 'horticulture and the annual
augmentation of my family'. He became in fact the pastor,
magistrate and amateur doctor of the village, for twenty years
from 1809, before his return to London as a canon of St Paul's.[4]
However, even after this tightening up the bishops and parish
priests had still not been redeployed to meet the movement of
population to the industrial towns and villages. Nor had they
been inspired to make a widespread appeal to those remaining
in the countryside. William Cobbett's *Rural Rides*, reporting
about the English people in the 1820s, concluded that 'the
labouring people have in a great measure ceased to go to
church'. It was a situation in which the Established Church
needed more than wit for its defence.

In 1820 a journalist, John Wade, published anonymously a
'Black Book' in which he argued that the Church's wealth was
so immense as to be the source of its immense vices. Three
years earlier Jeremy Bentham's *Church of Englandism*, of almost
seven hundred closely printed pages (although unfinished),
had poured scorn on the chaos of an institution so heavily
endowed. 'The Church of England system is ripe for dissolution', he concluded. 'The *service* provided by it is of a bad sort:
inefficient with respect to the ends or objects professed to be
aimed at by it: efficient with respect to divers effects which,
being pernicious, are too flagrantly so to be professed to be
aimed at.' Such books found a sympathetic readership, and, as
their message was passed on, an indignant audience; and the
criticism exploded when John Wade's polemic reappeared as
The Extraordinary Black Book of 1831. We cannot wonder that
when the reform of the electoral system in 1832 (against the
votes of most of the bishops) was believed to have destroyed the

---

[4] See Alan Bell, *Sydney Smith* (Oxford, 1980).

Church of England's chief support, intelligent men thought that its wealth was about to be confiscated. Three days after the Reform Bill became law, Thomas Arnold, Headmaster of Rugby, wrote: 'The Church as it now stands, no human power can save.'[5]

SAVING THE CHURCH

But was it necessary for the Church to remain unreformed – to fall because its sons left it to perish 'as it now stands'? It is scarcely too much to say that the Church of England was saved because laymen decided that it deserved to be equipped with the means to discharge its mission to the new population. An early leader among them was Joshua Watson. A wine merchant with wider commercial and financial interests, he was one of those who had done well out of the war; but he retired from business in 1814 to devote himself to good works. He had a house conveniently close to Parliament, but his home was in Hackney, still (like Clapham) a village; and there a group of High Churchmen gathered, to be called the Hackney Phalanx in deliberate contrast with the Evangelicals of the Clapham Sect. Their journal was the *British Critic*. They included pastors who represented the best of the Church's steady life in the parishes. However, Watson was influenced most by the example of William Stevens, who had died in 1807 but who for many years before that had been the treasurer of Queen Anne's Bounty (the nearest the Church of England got to a central administration) and the central pillar of many church societies. Watson set himself to do for a new generation what Stevens had done for his.

He succeeded in so many of his aims because, although he was determined to get what he wanted and prepared to work

---

[5] R. A. Soloway has researched into a period little covered in the standard histories, in *Prelates and People: Ecclesiastical Social Thought in England 1783–1852* (London, 1969). E. R. Norman, *Church and Society in England 1770–1970* (Oxford, 1976), was strong on this period. Two short studies have illuminated English popular religion or irreligion in a European context: A. D. Gilbert, *Religion and Society in Industrial England* (London, 1976), and Hugh McLeod, *Religion and the People of Western Europe 1789–1970* (Oxford, 1981).

for it (unlike the archbishops), what he wanted was acceptable to the Tory government. Spencer Perceval, the Prime Minister who was assassinated in 1812, had shared many of the feelings of the Evangelicals since Cambridge days and might have done much for church reform had death not come to him at the age of fifty. Lord Liverpool, his successor for fifteen years, actively encouraged Watson.[6] The central problem was that the Church of England had lacked its own national assembly; nothing could be done except by Parliament. To wait until Parliament was in the mood for radical reform meant waiting until the appointment in June 1832 of a Royal Commission to inquire into church revenues – by when Watson was a tired, backward-looking man, whose caution had become so great that he had advocated a commission composed entirely of clergy and with a very limited mandate. But when at the height of his powers he had done what he could, which was much. 'I remember so well, as a lad', wrote Bishop Selwyn, who heroically founded the Church in New Zealand, 'case-hardening myself against the name of Joshua Watson, which I was continually hearing as a final authority on all Church matters, and I pictured to myself a hard, dry, impenetrable man, who had no sympathies beyond a committee room.' Although there was truth in that picture, it is also revealing that in the 1810s Watson was trusted by the government and the public to administer two large half-public, half-private funds – one to relieve a war-ravaged Germany, the other to benefit the widows and orphans left by the battle of Waterloo.

Two other great charities in which Joshua Watson was prominent were directed to challenges within England.

One was the National Society for Promoting the Education of the Poor in the Principles of the Established Church, of which he was treasurer from its foundation in 1811. Its purpose was to encourage parishes to start their own schools, and the grants which it distributed were enough of a stimulus to ensure the education of a hundred thousand children by 1815 and of

---

[6] The best introduction to the politics is now Norman Gash, *Aristocracy and People: Britain 1815–65* (London, 1979). See also Denis Gray, *Spencer Perceval the Evangelical Prime Minister* (Manchester, 1963).

nearly a million twenty years later. The society was not supported by a government grant until 1833, but in the years before Watson's resignation in 1842 it bore the main burden of responsibility for the primary education of England's children. It also carried the main hope that these children would grow up to be supporters of their parish churches. At the time it seemed unnecessary that the State (or the tax-payer) should shoulder this burden.

State aid in education also seemed wrong, for it would deprive the Established Church of its duty to educate the new generation. The bishops in the House of Lords did not hesitate to wreck any proposal (beginning with the brewer Samuel Whitbread's bill of 1807) that there should be a national system supported out of rates or taxes, and as the years went by even those who had advocated such a system acknowledged that the National Society was achieving a considerable success by evoking private charity. As late as 1839 F. D. Maurice, one of the two most creative theologians of nineteenth-century England, was giving lectures which Joshua Watson welcomed in answer to the question: 'Has the Church or the State the power to educate the nation?' And the success of the National Society seemed so obvious that Watson was encouraged to play a leading part in the foundation in 1828 of a new Anglican institution of higher education, to supplement Oxford and Cambridge – King's College, London.[7]

The other great charitable effort which Watson led was the movement to build new churches. For the children now being educated by the Church must be given the opportunity to grow into regular churchgoers; and Watson and his associates were so optimistic as to suppose that if they were given the opportunity they would take it. Yet it was very difficult for private enterprise to solve the problem, even if the money could be found. To create a new parish required an Act of Parliament until 1818, and to build a new church within an existing parish required the consent of the patron and of the incumbent, either of whom might feel that his rights (including the rights to tithes

---

[7] See John Hurt, *Education in Evolution: Church, State, Society and Popular Education 1800–1870* (London, 1971).

and fees) were being infringed. The result of the neglect could be seen in the populated but unchurched towns – not only the new industrial towns in the north such as Sheffield (where there was seating in church for 6,280 out of 55,000) or Manchester, but also the fashionable towns in the south such as Bath or Brighton. Richard Yates, a London clergyman, wrote a pamphlet full of statistics and warnings. Its title was the old rallying-cry: *The Church in Danger*.

In 1818, however, substantial progress was made. An Incorporated Church Building Society was formed by Watson. This was widely regarded as an appropriate thanksgiving for the total victory over Napoleon – and as a sound investment in the country's own peace. In the same year the government under Lord Liverpool established an official commission with a grant of a million pounds. Another half a million was voted in 1824. It was the most solid recognition in English history that taxpayers had a duty towards the Established Church. The Parliamentary grants had been used up virtually by 1828 and were not renewed, but such was the stimulus given to private subscribers that the commission did not cease work until 1857, two years after Watson's death. By then it had built 612 new churches accommodating about 600,000 people.[8]

Side by side with Joshua Watson we may place Reginald Heber, who did much to rescue the name of the clergy. Well born, well educated and well endowed with literary talents, he might have become an English dean or bishop of distinction, remembered for his hymns, including 'Holy, Holy, Holy, Lord God Almighty', 'God that madest earth and heaven' and 'Brightest and best of the sons of the morning' – and among scholars, by his edition of the works of Jeremy Taylor. Instead, Heber left his delightful Shropshire rectory (designed by himself) and his prospects in England to sail out to India in 1823, to be the second Bishop of Calcutta at the age of forty. Three years later he was dead. Neither of his two successors survived in India for as long as two years.

---

[8] See A. B. Webster, *Joshua Watson* (London, 1954), and M. H. Port, *Six Hundred New Churches* (London, 1961). E. R. Wickham studied Sheffield in *Church and People in an Industrial City* (London, 1957).

Most members of the Church of England who supported the new mission in India were delighted when a man so gracious assumed the leadership, although some wondered how hard he would work. In his parish he had been a dedicated pastor – and that he now became to India, regarding himself as the 'Chief Missionary'. He was acceptable both to the Evangelicals of the Church Missionary Society and to the High Churchmen of the rejuvenated Society for the Propagation of the Gospel. He had, indeed, in his more innocent days drawn up a scheme to merge the two societies, and one of his hymns, written rapidly for Whit Sunday 1818, became a missionary classic, 'From Greenland's icy mountains'. He knew how to get on with the civil authorities, so that the Bishop of Calcutta's powers were clarified and enlarged for his benefit, but he did not cling to all the conventions; he shocked an archdeacon by wearing white trousers. He was not full of a sense of his own importance, as the first bishop (T. F. Middleton, formerly an archdeacon) had been. Nor did he believe that all Hindus and Muslims were going to hell; on the contrary, he had a Romantic enthusiasm for the people of the East. As a young man he had made an exciting journey through Russia ending up among the Cossacks. Without hesitation he now ordained a Tamil convert, Christian David, who had been refused the priesthood by Bishop Middleton; David became an evangelist in his native Ceylon. Reginald Heber went to India because he was an English gentleman with a chivalrous sense of duty. He had heard a call to work as a clergyman and to share the quiet joy of his Christian faith. The Church which could breed such a man was not doomed.[9]

THE BIRTH OF NONCONFORMITY

Although the *Nonconformist* was not founded as a weekly magazine until 1841, the great movement which the Victorians knew

---

[9] His vivid journal was edited with an introduction by M. A. Laird as *Bishop Heber in Northern India* (Cambridge, 1971). There has been no biography since George Smith's in 1895.

as Nonconformity had its origins earlier in the nineteenth century. Both Methodism and the 'Old Dissent' prospered during the years of war and industrialization, the 1790s and 1800s – so much so that many in the Established Church became alarmed. Lord Sidmouth, who had been Prime Minister as Henry Addington, instituted an inquiry and then introduced a proposal into the House of Lords in 1811. No one should be allowed to preach unless vouched for to the magistrates by six 'substantial and reputable householders'. Unless illiterate preachers ('cobblers, tailors, pig-drovers and chimney-sweepers') were suppressed, he warned, 'we should be in danger of having a sectarian people'. The snobbish intolerance of the proposal shocked even the Lords. The outcry against it first brought Methodism into common action with the Presbyterians, Baptists and Congregationalists (or Independents) of the 'Old Dissent'.[10]

The key factor was the same spiritual awakening that we have observed in the response to Whitefield, to the Wesleys and to the Evangelical clergy who remained in the Church of England. For the Evangelical revival transformed many Dissenting ministers and their congregations, turning them into the force which Lord Sidmouth feared. And among the Evangelical Dissenters the most famous was William Carey, the son of a village schoolmaster. Young William was apprenticed to a shoemaker and married to his master's illiterate sister-in-law. He was, however, bored by the parish church, and an act of petty dishonesty troubled his conscience. He joined a small Dissenting congregation, underwent adult baptism and early in 1785, at the age of twenty-three, was given a pittance to preach as a Baptist without any formal training. But this young worker was already reading any books he could get hold of, and so he absorbed Captain James Cook's narrative of voyages to Australia (1768–76). It was not long before he was asking a question at a meeting of Baptist ministers in Northampton. 'Was not the command given to the Apostles, to

[10] A good survey, concentrating on the birth of Nonconformity in the industrial areas, is W. R. Ward, *Religion and Society in England 1790–1850*, while David M. Thompson, *Nonconformity in the Nineteenth Century*, is an illuminating collection of documents with a commentary (both London, 1972).

teach all nations, obligatory on all succeeding ministers to the end of the world, seeing that the accompanying promise was of equal extent?'

The question was ruled out of order by the chairman; Carey was only an 'enthusiast' who must be told to 'sit down'. But in 1792 he published a pamphlet, *An Enquiry into the Obligation of Christians to use means for the Conversion of the Heathen.* The 'enquiry' was, in fact, a clear plan. Three weeks later he persuaded another meeting, also in Northampton, to form something unprecedented: the Baptist Missionary Society. He was fortunate in that Andrew Fuller, a neighbouring minister, was an ex-wrestler, eager for spiritual exertions, who was to toil as the Missionary Society's secretary until his death in 1815. Fuller also toiled at preaching and writing, his main theme being that 'it is the duty of every minister of Christ plainly and faithfully to preach the Gospel to all who will hear it'. That was no platitude among these Particular Baptists, who had often interpreted Calvin and the New Testament to mean that the elect were few and were converted already, so that preaching the Gospel to others was a waste of time. Now the urgency of the Gospel for the world could inspire a mission to England – and to India. With Fuller's encouragement, in 1793 Carey determined to go to India, thirty years before Reginald Heber.

His doggedness was extraordinary. He faced destitution until he obtained a position as manager of a small indigo factory; he endured great loneliness until colleagues joined him in 1800; he had to overcome countless difficulties as he struggled to come to terms with the local languages and customs; he had no satisfactory base for his work until he was invited to set up a mission in the Danish settlement of Serampore near Calcutta; his wife became insane; and seven years passed before he baptized an Indian. His faith was tested very severely – although before leaving England his motto had been: 'Expect great things from God; attempt great things for God.'

Carey and his colleagues laid foundations. He went on preaching in India. He married again and much more happily, he became an expert botanist, and he established a prolific printing press. He also turned out to be a brilliant linguist. He and his assistants translated the entire Bible into six Indian languages, and parts of it into many more. All this work was to need revision, but he had shown what could be done. He compiled dictionaries and grammars and translated Hindu classics into English. He founded schools and a college for Indians, and at Fort William College became a professor paid by the government to share his great store of 'oriental' knowledge with young Englishmen. He earned large sums – and kept only a fraction of them for his own needs.

Thus this 'consecrated cobbler' (it was Sydney Smith's gibe) did many of the great things which he had advocated in his *Enquiry* in 1792. And at the end of it all, in 1834, he was buried in Serampore. His grave bore simple words, adapted from a hymn by Isaac Watts, recalling the Evangelical experience of his youth in the far-off English village of Paulersbury: 'A wretched, poor and helpless worm on thy kind arms I fall.'[11]

Many other 'worms' were stirred into new life and action by the touch of the Evangelical revival. Carey's first letter home inspired a group of Congregational ministers in Bristol to work towards the foundation of the London Missionary Society in 1795. The new venture was not denominational; an Evangelical rector in the Church of England, Thomas Haweis, did more than any other man to get it off the ground. A 'fundamental principle' was adopted: 'Our design is not to send Presbyterianism, Independency, Episcopacy or any other form of Church Order and Government . . . but the Glorious Gospel of the blessed God to the Heathen.'

In this spirit they immediately decided to send a little band of missionaries to the Pacific island of Tahiti – a place very much in the imaginations of Englishmen because of Captain Cook's visit there some twenty-five years before. The place was reputed to be a paradise. But Tahiti's promiscuous women often murdered their babies; and since the arrival of the Europeans, the population had been halved by venereal disease. The ship *Duff* had on board four ordained ministers, while the rest of the missionary band of thirty 'understood the mechanic arts'. Not many of them persevered in a paradise full

---

[11] See E. D. Potts, *Baptist Missionaries in India* (Cambridge, 1967), and Mary Drewery, *William Carey* (London, 1978).

of carnal temptations. The mission as a whole yielded to the
temptation of using the power of the local king to enforce
Christianity – the very contradiction of Dissent. But when a
Russian explorer dropped anchor at Tahiti in 1820, he noticed
how strict was the observance of the Sabbath. He noticed, too,
that the young girls' lascivious dances which had delighted
Captain Cook's crew were all now prohibited, and that men
and women alike wore European clothes.[12]

Within England the Evangelical impetus quietly transformed Dissenting life in town and village. Under its challenge
those Dissenters who denied the divinity of Christ became
self-conscious and formed the Unitarian Society in 1791,
supplemented by the Unitarian Fund in 1800 and the aggressive British and Foreign Unitarian Association in 1825. Some
prominent Dissenters who were in practice Unitarians deplored the separate organization. Thomas Belsham, the most
influential preacher with the new message, was now minister of
the most distinguished of the Unitarian congregations, in
Essex Street in London; and he objected to any suggestion that
he was less than a respectable Dissenting minister. William
Smith, a rich and cultured gentleman who became a Unitarian
under Belsham's influence, was for many years (1805–32)
chairman of the Protestant Dissenting Deputies. A leading
Whig MP, he persuaded his Parliamentary colleagues to pass
the Unitarian Toleration Act in 1813. Although the laws
against blasphemy remained, the polite denial of Christ's
divinity was no longer to be a crime. Yet by the 1830s Smith
seemed a figure out of the past, the contemporary of his more
secular fellow Whig, Charles James Fox.[13]

The real progress in Unitarianism was being made by
ministers who built it up as one denomination among many,
not large but strong in its appeal. It appealed to the more
intelligent and benevolent type of employer in the great centres
of industry such as Liverpool, Manchester and Birmingham;

[12] Niel Gunson studied *Messengers of Grace: Evangelical Missionaries in the South Seas, 1797–1860* (Melbourne, 1978).
[13] See Richard W. Davis, *Dissent in Politics 1780–1830: The Political Life of William Smith, M.P.* (London, 1971).

and it appealed to some of the more intellectually ambitious members of the new industrial working class. Naturally the employers and the workers usually worshipped in separate congregations, but nineteenth-century Unitarianism was as a whole not now so indifferent to the problems of the poor as Joseph Priestley had been. Even the ministers of affluent congregations changed their style. 'Ministers no longer preached only on Sunday and spent the rest of the week in the conduct of a school in order to supplement an inadequate income; in any case, there was by 1850 less opportunity for schoolmastering, now that the great national voluntary societies were at work. Instead the minister was urged to take up a double task: on Sunday mornings to preach to his middle-class congregation and for the rest of Sunday and during the week to conduct a variety of philanthropic activities, centred in the Sunday School, for a quite different body of people, of the poorer classes.'[14]

Among Dissenters who remained Trinitarians, resistance gathered to this Unitarian missionary zeal. Successful legal efforts were made to force some chapels to return to the orthodox Presbyterian faith of their founders – until the Dissenters' Chapels Act of 1844 made such litigation far more difficult. More important was the spiritual revival of orthodox Dissent; and there was growth, on a scale to which the Unitarians never aspired.[15] The inspiration was to be seen in the *Evangelical Magazine* – for 'Ruin, Redemption, Regeneration' was the clear message. With older children teaching the younger, schools for the poor spread according to methods brilliantly advocated by a Quaker, Joseph Lancaster. Much energy was put into the Religious Tract Society (1799) and the British and Foreign Bible Society (1804), managed jointly by Dissenters and by churchmen who agreed on the Evangelical mission to spread the scriptures and to offer simple explanations. And perhaps most influential of all was the Sunday school movement. In its early years it was usually non-

---

[14] H. L. Short in *The English Presbyterians*. p. 263. R. V. Holt presented *The Unitarian Contribution to Social Progress in England* (London, 1938).

[15] A. D. Gilbert, *Religion and Society in Industrial England*, pp. 32–6, 52–68.

denominational, which made many of the clergy and ministers suspicious. It was the only education, indeed almost the only recreation, available to many of the children employed in the new factories – and the rich could wonder uneasily what was being taught. But by 1816 Henry Brougham, after a survey, could estimate that some 420,000 children attended Sunday schools in England and Wales.[16]

By the mid-1820s about a third of the adult population was identified with this movement which was to become Nonconformity. With such a harvest obtainable if mobs and magistrates let them alone, most preachers had no wish to add Revolution to 'Ruin, Redemption, Regeneration'. They did not, however, neglect the duty of charity to relieve individual distress. In 1828 came the reward for their political loyalty. They secured the repeal of the Test and Corporation Acts – an objective which had been just beyond the Dissenters' grasp in the 1780s and plainly impossible during the years of anti-revolutionary reaction. Now the royal Duke of Sussex presided over a celebratory dinner with a sumptuous menu and twenty-four enthusiastic toasts.[17]

Dissenters were convinced that many opportunities must come through the widening of the Parliamentary electorate in 1832 and through the act of 1835 which similarly reformed the government of 178 cities and towns. They objected to paying church rates to repair parish churches which they did not attend, to being excluded from university education, to being married and buried according to the rites of the Church of England, and to being unregistered at birth unless they were baptized in the Church of England.

A response to the last grievance came quickly. Registrars were also authorized to attend Nonconformist marriages, although until 1856 applications for this privilege had to be made to the Poor Law Guardians. In 1836 a royal charter was granted to the new university of London, where University

---

[16] Thomas W. Laquer studied *Religion and Respectability: Sunday Schools and Working Class Culture* (London, 1976).

[17] Studies of the transition include Raymond G. Cowherd, *The Politics of English Dissent 1815–1848* (London, 1959).

College (founded in 1828) was open to Dissenters. But an anticlimax followed when the Whigs failed to deliver further reforms. In 1837 only one Dissenter was elected to Parliament – Edward Baines, the campaigning editor of the *Leeds Mercury*. By now many disillusioned Dissenters or Nonconformists, having at last acquired a taste for politics, were turning away from their Whig patrons towards self-help and radicalism. Partly for this reason, 'that year marks the beginning of the process of substituting for the Whig party and its aristocratic leadership a Liberal party with a middle-class leadership.'[18] The story of Victorian Nonconformity was beginning. But the swing to radicalism was still resisted by many of the preachers, and battles between radicals and conservatives split Methodism, which by the 1830s accounted for two-thirds of the numerical strength of Nonconformity.

CONFLICTS IN METHODISM

Almost all historians are now agreed that Methodism was not an alternative to a revolution. To claim that Methodism stopped England going the way of France is to exaggerate both the popularity of Methodism and the likelihood of a violent upheaval.[19] But for Methodists the struggle to decide their own future was an exciting battle where principles could be invoked on both sides – principles which were basically political, Right against Left. The sixty years after John Wesley's death in 1791 witnessed conflicts in Methodism which would have distressed him greatly by their bitterness resulting in schisms, but part of the explanation is that these conflicts brought to the surface tensions between suppressed political energies.

On the one side were the conservative Wesleyan Methodists, convinced that they were being faithful to John Wesley's principles. Wesley's death left 'Church Methodism' still an option theoretically, and those who advocated it could rightly

---

[18] R. Tudur Jones, *Congregationalism in England*, p. 207. Clyde Binfield studied the Baines family in *So Down to Prayers* (London, 1977), pp. 54–100.

[19] The classic study was Emile Halévy, *The Birth of Methodism*, translated and introduced by Bernard Semmel (Chicago, Ill., 1971).

plead Wesley's refusal to separate himself from the Church of England. But soon that option melted away, and what replaced it was the determination to build a church more strongly organized than the Church of England – a shadow Establishment. The Methodist Conference (of preachers only) was to be the 'living Wesley', entitled to govern as the founding autocrat had governed but delegating its local powers to the superintendent ministers appointed by it. These superintendents were entitled to expel any unsatisfactory Methodist without anyone's consent. Together with this hierarchical conception of church government went a 'no politics' rule which in practice tended to mean no radical politics. The upshot for the Wesleyans, as for John Wesley himself, was the acceptance of a hierarchical society as the work of Providence; and for the poor the political consequence of the Gospel was obedience.

On the other side were rebels – who believed that they were being faithful to John Wesley's own impatience with man-made rules, loyal to his own appeal to the poor over the heads of the king, clergy and gentry. Laymen must be included in church government at every level, from the national conference to the local society. Ministers must be regarded as servants rather than masters, happy to serve at low pay for a limited period. The minister's one essential function was to evangelize, to make new recruits for a Christian family where all were equal. Implied (and sometimes stated) in this alternative vision of Methodism was a revolutionary vision of England.

When their founder or 'father' was taken from them, the Methodists all agreed to follow 'Mr Wesley's plan'. The difficulty lay in agreeing what that was. Four years after John Wesley's death it was already necessary for the Methodist Conference to appoint a committee to draw up a 'plan of pacification'. While insisting that Holy Communion should never be celebrated in a Methodist chapel at the same time as in the parish church, this plan allowed the celebration if the majority of the local leadership desired it, subject to a veto by the conference; and it allowed a certain right to the local leaders to alter the conference's 'stationing' of ministers. Locally the admission and expulsion of members were to be agreed on by ministers and lay officials. On this basis Wesleyan Methodism controlled 631 preachers by 1815, and after 1818 they could use the title 'Reverend'. But the 'new Connexion' did something to assert its slogan, 'liberty and equality', by forming a splinter group. In 1800 it possessed only twenty preachers. By 1815 it had about 275.

The next major split from the Wesleyan Methodists occurred with the formation of the Primitive Methodists around Hugh Bourne in 1811. Bourne was a carpenter erecting windmills and watermills to serve the new industries in Staffordshire. After experiencing an Evangelical conversion ('like Bunyan's pilgrim I had to make my way alone'), he became a wandering preacher, and when the emotionalism of his preaching so alarmed his fellow Methodists that the Burslem society expelled him he simply carried on, dedicated to evangelism in the open air and earning his living as a casual labourer. Under the influence of an American, Lorenzo Dow, Bourne imitated the revivalist 'camp meetings' which were at that time winning thousands of converts for Methodism on the American Frontier.

'Camp meetings' were condemned by the Methodist Conference but won a considerable response. To their fellow workers these evangelists offered not only the rich emotional experience of a religious conversion, and not only a new direction in daily life, but also the support of a hearty fellowship into which no employer would intrude. In sickness or unemployment or old age these Methodists would visit each other; in prosperity they would buy from each other. To protect their family life they would renounce alcohol and be 'sparing in smoking tobacco'. Chapels were to be built not by the gifts of one benefactor, or of a few close neighbours, but by the united efforts of the whole society; 'all the society is considered as one family, the burden is to be borne by the whole.' And the preachers were to stay close to the people. None of them was to earn more than £15 a year (at a time when an Anglican incumbent drawing under £150 a year was reckoned poor), and they were to be appointed or dismissed by a predominantly lay conference. 'O Lord,' ran a prayer, 'bless the work of our servant, thy minister!'

As a representative of many working people who found

fulfilment within Primitive Methodism, Hugh Bourne developed great skills as a leader. He continued to preach until well into his seventies; it was his habit to walk around the country, although he sometimes used the new railways. He visited America, edited a hymn book, conducted a magazine and published and wrote many booklets. He sometimes had disputes with collaborators as rough as himself, but when he died in 1851 large crowds of adults and children sang hymns as his coffin was carried in triumph.

A roughly similar breakaway movement, the Bible Christians, flourished in Devon and Cornwall, with revival meetings which lasted for several days and nights. But all this only added to the conservatism of the main Methodist movement. After a bloody confrontation between a crowd and over-excited soldiers in Manchester – the so-called 'Peterloo Massacre', in 1819 – the workers were urged to rely on Providence, not on 'tumultuous assemblies'. Even after the 1832 Reform Act the Methodist Conference issued another of its warnings against listening to political debates 'with too warm an interest'. 'No politics' remained throughout this stormy period the official policy both of Wesleyan Methodism and of the groups which broke away from it. Many individual Methodists, particularly in the splinter groups, continued to defy such discouraging guidance, however. Of the six Dorset agricultural labourers who were sentenced to transportation to Australia for seven years for attempting to form a trade union in 1834 (the famous 'Tolpuddle Martyrs'), five are known to have been active Methodists. What went on in 'class' meetings could never be controlled by any national conference or full-time preacher.[20]

It was perhaps partly as an alternative to political radicalism that the official leadership provided a fresh outlet for Methodist enthusiasm: foreign missions. But it is certain that the Methodists did catch the infection of a genuine missionary enthusiasm. Work among the slaves in the West Indies captured the restless mind of John Wesley's most able associate,

---

[20] The standard study is still R. F. Wearmouth, *Methodism and the Working-Class Movements of England 1800–50* (London, 1937). See also John T. Wilkinson's biography of *Hugh Bourne* (London, 1952). Thomas Shaw studied *The Bible Christians* (London, 1975), and Joyce Marlow *The Tolpuddle Martyrs* (London, 1971).

Thomas Coke. Then early in 1813, having been disappointed in his hope that the authorities of the Church of England would make him Bishop of Calcutta, Coke formed the plan of a Methodist mission to the east. Local missionary societies were formed in Yorkshire and elsewhere to support him. He died during the voyage out, at the age of seventy-six, but the mission went ahead.[21] And one of the Yorkshire ministers who built up support for Coke's scheme was Jabez Bunting. A man with extraordinary talents, energies and ambitions, Bunting had already been called in to straighten out the mission's accounts, since the visionary and elderly Coke paid little attention to such details.

Jabez Bunting was no doubt sincere in his own support of the Methodist mission at home and abroad, but he was also sincere in believing that he was indispensable to that mission's success. He was often called the 'Pope of Methodism'. John Wesley had been called the same, but it has been said truly that 'Wesley's was the ascendancy of a saint, Bunting's the ascendancy of a masterful ecclesiastic'.[22]

The formal basis of Bunting's power was not large. He was secretary of the Methodist Conference and of the missionary society which now emerged on a nationwide scale; in order to discharge these two posts, he was glad to move to London in 1833. During conference debates and in business between those annual sessions, he was head-and-shoulders above his fellow ministers in administrative and argumentative power, and was also quite unusual in his lack of scruple. He had no hesitation in insisting that others should obey the regulations ('it is no sin for a man to think our discipline wrong, provided that he quits us'). He also had no hesitation in breaking those rules himself. With these qualifications he was elected president of the conference for a second term in 1828, again in 1836 and yet again in 1844. He persuaded the Wesleyans to open a 'theological institution' with himself as the active president; his last surviving letter is a veto of the radical idea that young men intending to be Methodist ministers should learn German. His

---

[21] See John Vickers, *Thomas Coke: An Apostle of Methodism* (London, 1969).

[22] E. R. Taylor, *Methodism and Politics 1791–1851* (Cambridge, 1935), p. 129.

firm hand was also applied to editing the denomination's magazine.

The real secret of Bunting's hold on his colleagues who became his subordinates was that he was known to possess the decisive influence in 'stationing' ministers and to be ruthless in punishing any who dared to criticize him. This was effective since every preacher was frequently moved about the country and no layman was ever admitted to the decision-making conference until 1878. In 1836 he arranged that men should be ordained more solemnly, with the laying-on-of-hands at the Methodist Conference. He also arranged that the leadership should be housed more grandly: a large headquarters, the Mission House, was built for himself and the missionary society.

In any local disputes he upheld the rights of ministers to instruct and to discipline their flocks. In 1827, for example, he insisted that the Brunswick Chapel in Leeds should have an organ, although most of the Methodists there considered this instrument a symbol of clericalism, if not of Popery, and in protest formed their own denomination. In a speech of 'several hours' he warned the conference against the 'insurrection' of the organ's enemies. Using a voice almost as loud as the organ, he proclaimed that disobedience to those ministers of whom he approved was wickedly like disobedience to employers; that 'Methodism agrees as well with democracy as with sin'. His first controversy came in 1812 when he refused to conduct the funeral of a man who had taken part in the Luddite riots against the new machinery. Although in general 'we stand stock still' was his motto, he managed to combine this conservation of discipline with many pleas for support for those who were achieving the economic progress of the nation as well as for those who were making Methodism more efficient. The unifying factor in his philosophy was a belief that the people must obey those appointed to lead – even when the leadership moved forward.

Such a philosophy, backed by an ecclesiastical dictatorship, was at the time hard for Wesleyans to resist. In 1835 one of his opponents, Samuel Warren of Manchester, was expelled from the Methodist Conference – in effect, for being an opponent –

and it was ruled legally that Warren could not change his church into a Congregational church, with the result that another splinter group, the Wesleyan Methodist Association, had to be formed at considerable expense. For those who did not wish to be thrown out of Wesleyan Methodism, it seemed safest to let Bunting dominate and define Methodism. During the 1840s, however, his policy and his personality were attacked furiously in anonymous pamphlets or *Fly Sheets* and by an opposition newspaper, the *Wesleyan Times*. At a stormy conference in Manchester in 1849 James Everett, a disgruntled preacher and satirist, was accused of the authorship of the *Fly Sheets* (almost certainly with justice) and was expelled, along with two contributors to the *Wesleyan Times*. Public meetings of protest followed; a union was effected with those who had walked out after Dr Warren; and in 1857 the United Methodist Free Churches were formed, Liberal in politics and lay in ecclesiastical emphasis, with James Everett as the first president and almost forty thousand members. In all, Bunting's excessively masterful ascendancy is reckoned to have aroused reactions which meant the loss of about a hundred thousand members from Wesleyan Methodism, more than a quarter of the total. It also aroused many feelings of disillusionment and bitterness. One historian of Methodism writes of 'a spiritual earthquake that shook the very foundations, undermined the work of past generations, and threatened the whole structure with collapse'.[23]

These conflicts, accompanied by much bitterness, certainly diverted Methodism from evangelism among the unchurched, and contrasted strangely with the claims made among the heathen on behalf of Christianity as the Gospel of peace and love. Yet it is surely also fair to say that the very intensity of these quarrels within Methodism pointed to its vitality. They showed how much religion was coming to mean to many hundreds of thousands of ordinary English people. It is significant that the Methodist 'connexion' left behind by John Wesley was sufficient to attract and absorb the ambition of a

---

[23] R. F. Wearmouth, *Methodism and the Struggle of the Working Classes 1850–1900* (Leicester, 1954), p. 91.

man as talented as Jabez Bunting, the son of a radical tailor in Manchester. And when Wesleyan Methodism fell under the control of conservatives among whom Bunting was supreme, these leaders did not lack followers. On the contrary, more than a quarter of a million adult Wesleyan Methodists (full membership was some 260,000 in 1855, at the depth of the reaction against the Bunting regime) accepted his control of their national life, and the local rule of ministers acceptable to him. Basically they wanted the Gospel which they believed had been entrusted by God to these authoritarian pastors. After the impact of Jabez Bunting there was no more talk about returning to the Church of England, because in the Wesleyan Methodism which this man had refashioned many of the English found a spiritual home.

After his census of churchgoers in 1851 Horace Mann estimated that about two million people were in the habit of attending Methodist chapels of one sort or another. In Yorkshire the various brands of Methodism included about a sixth of the population, in Cornwall about a third. In England over twenty thousand laymen were Methodist local preachers.[24]

CATHOLIC EMANCIPATION

Alarmed by the Irish rebellion in 1789, in 1800 William Pitt had secured the union of Ireland with England, Scotland and Wales under one King, in Parliament, and this union still

---

[24] W. R. Ward edited *The Early Correspondence of Jabez Bunting* (London, 1972) and *Early Victorian Methodism: The Correspondence of Jabez Bunting 1830–58* (Oxford, 1976). The fullest account of the often unseemly conference debates remains Benjamin Gregory, *Side Lights on the Conflicts of Methodism 1827–52* (London, 1897). John Kent offered a defence of Bunting as 'the last Wesleyan' in *The Age of Disunity* (London, 1966) and Robert Currie a hostile view in *Methodism Divided* (1968). In *A History of the Methodist Church in Great Britain*, vol. 2 (London, 1978), essays by John Kent and John Wilkinson represented the Wesleyan and Primitive traditions. J. C. Bowmer, *Pastor and People: A Study of Church and People in Wesleyan Methodism* (London, 1975), admitted Bunting's arrogance but regarded him as essentially a defender of the 'classical Wesleyan' church order. Oliver Beckerlegge studied *The United Methodist Free Churches* (London, 1957) and D. A. Gowland *Methodist Secessions* in Manchester, Rochdale and Liverpool (Manchester, 1979).

seemed vital if Britain was to be Great. Yet the Irish peasants, and many in the middle classes, had emerged from the eighteenth-century persecution still loyal to their Catholic faith. Slowly this Irish majority was being allowed to compete with the ruling and exploiting Protestants; Catholics suitably qualified by property ownership had been given votes for the Irish Parliament in 1793. The conviction grew in the largely conservative mind of Pitt, and in the even more conservative minds of his Tory successors a quarter of a century later, that the stability of political union could not be secured unless Irish Catholics could vote for, and be elected to, the United Parliament. Without that, the oppression of the Irish was too naked. It became logical to make the same concession over town councils – and to extend it to the whole of the United Kingdom. Thus 'Catholic emancipation was carried because the Irish were prepared to fight for it, and the English government was not prepared to put down a rebellion'.[25] The main obstacle to be overcome was the prejudice which reigned at every level of English public opinion, from the monarch to the mob. What eventually quietened this prejudice sufficiently was the sheer absence of any evidence that the Roman Catholic community was either able or willing to deprive Protestant Englishmen of their liberties. 'It was an entirely secular settlement; tolerant conviction played no part in the government's purpose', it has been truly said. 'On the other hand, intolerant conviction was not strong enough to defeat this purpose.'[26]

In 1801 all William Pitt's services to his king and country were not sufficient to save him as Prime Minister once he had formed a conviction that Roman Catholics must be given the vote, and in 1807 the same fate befell the coalition government which had taken over after his recall and death. The prejudice against 'Popery' was so strong that the clerical leaders of the Catholic cause – the diocesan bishops in Ireland and the four

---

[25] Ursula Henriques, *Religious Toleration in England 1787–1833* (London, 1961), p. 260.

[26] G. I. T. Machin, *The Catholic Question in English Politics, 1820 to 1830* (Oxford, 1964), p. 178. See also R. B. McDowell, *Public Opinion and Government Policy in Ireland 1801–46* (London, 1952).

vicars apostolic in England – were for long ready to appease it. For instance, they were willing to allow the English government a veto in the appointment of their successors. They did not immediately reject a scheme originating among English Tories to pay the Irish Catholic clergy out of taxes – in other words, to buy their loyalty. Among the leading English gentry who had remained faithful to it, Catholicism was presented as a respectable religion and their private affair. They stressed that it was inconceivable that any pope should absolve them of the allegiance which they owed to the Crown, and in church affairs they were often 'Cisalpine': they did not question the Papal primacy but had no wish to see English affairs controlled from the other side of the Alps. Neither bishops nor laymen were ambitious for political power or for numerous conversions; they simply wanted to make sure that the long persecution of their faith really had ended. It was only in 1808 that the Irish peasants forced their bishops to abandon this fawning attitude to the English government, with the result that the most forceful of the vicars apostolic in England, John Milner, who was also the Irish bishops' agent, joined the refusal to give guarantees. As late as 1815 Pope Pius VII annoyed the Irish by being willing to compromise on this issue.

An Anglo-Irish 'Catholic Association', revived in 1823, began to demand emancipation as of right, without concessions – and began also to threaten, or at least to hint at, disorder. These shows of strength naturally provoked a Protestant reaction. 'Orange' and 'Brunswick' Clubs were formed in England, with the cry that the Hanoverian dynasty was once again in danger from Popish plots, and there were some large public meetings. Had the electoral system been more democratic at this stage, no Parliament meeting in Westminster would have offered any relief to the Papists. However, the system was such that if the King and the leading Tory politicians were ever to be persuaded to concede some relief in order to avoid further trouble, popular English prejudice would be powerless to prevent it.

That was what now happened. The leading members of the Tory government were the Duke of Wellington and Sir Robert Peel. Wellington had been born into one of the 'orange'

Protestant families ruling 'green' Ireland, and Peel's Protestantism had been so outspoken that his nickname was Orange Peel. But they were both at heart pragmatists, priding themselves on their truly patriotic superiority to popular clamours. They became persuaded that Catholic emancipation had to be granted, since the only alternative was the serious risk of civil war; and a tearful George IV found himself unable to think of any political alternative to allowing them to proceed. Many bitter words were still spoken against the betrayal of the 'Protestant' or 'Happy' Constitution, but they remained words and although many of them had been spoken by bishops of the Church of England, in the end ten bishops brought themselves to vote in the Lords with Wellington. In April 1829 Catholic emancipation became a fact.

It did not, however, result in any great increase in the influence of those Roman Catholic gentlemen who were now free to become MPs. In 1830 only five of them were elected by English constituencies. Internally, the Roman Catholic community was no longer deferential to the gentry. It had become a people's church, appealing to much the same class as Primitive Methodism; yet because of 'Catholic principles' lacking in Methodism, the church's leadership was able to be authoritarian in a manner which perhaps Jabez Bunting, stout Protestant as he was, secretly envied. So the decline of the gentry had been to the advantage of the priests, and above all of the bishops and the Pope.

A modern historian of Roman Catholicism in England sums up the period 1771–1830 as 'The Victory over the Laity'.[27] Certainly this period, and even more the period 1830–1860, saw a transformation. In its day a book such as *The State and Behaviour of the English Catholics to the Year 1780*, defending enlightened Catholic laymen and like-minded clergy, had caused a stir. Its author was Joseph Berington, a priest who survived many attacks by more conservative Catholics because he was taken into gentry households as a chaplain. 'I am no Papist', he wrote, explaining that the Pope was only 'the first magistrate in a well-regulated State.' He denounced the super-

---

[27] Hugh Aveling, *The Handle and the Axe* (London, 1976), pp. 322–45.

stition of foreign Catholics and was contemptuous of monks and Jesuits, but hailed the growth in England of a reasonable Catholicism, as simple as the primitive Church's. No other Catholicism, he was sure, would have a future. The Catholic equivalent of Joseph Priestley, he, too, found his voice drowned by the general conservatism which reacted to the French Revolution – but he consoled himself by writing a large *History of the Rise, Progress and Decline of the Papal Power*, never published. Even Bishop Milner, the author of *The Divine Right of Episcopacy* and one who attempted to assert that right in his work as vicar apostolic in the Midland district for twenty-three years from 1803, was no ardent Papist. He advocated worship in English not Latin and took care to keep on cordial terms with neighbouring Protestants. Before making his base in industrial Wolverhampton he had been for twenty-four peaceful years the priest in Winchester. John Lingard, who ministered in a village near Lancaster and whose work as an historian was respected by Protestants, had a similar mind, loyal to two heritages, Catholic and English.

What now happened was the transformation of the laity.[28] In the eighty years after 1770, when it numbered about eighty thousand, the Roman Catholic community in England seems to have increased to some seven hundred thousand. It was the most dramatic religious change seen in the country since the restoration of the Church of England with Charles II.

Some of the increase was due simply to the nation's growth in population, more than doubling between 1770 and 1850. The growth in churchgoing should not be exaggerated, since there were just under 253,000 at Mass on the Sunday in 1851 when a census was taken. But some evidence suggests that the Roman Catholic priests were rather more successful than their opposite numbers in the Church of England in persuading people to attend worship in the new industrial towns and villages. Back in the countryside these people or their parents had probably gone to Mass, if available, more often than

---

[28] The standard account was provided by Bernard Ward in seven volumes on *The Dawn of the Catholic Revival in England, The Eve of Catholic Emancipation* and *The Sequal to Catholic Emancipation* (London, 1909–15). For a more recent analysis see John Bossey, *The English Catholic Community 1570–1850* (London, 1975), pp. 295–363.

many a villager had supported his parish church – and when they moved to the new work the priest might be able to set up a chapel, often also a school, without facing the legal difficulties which encumbered the Established Church, and without feeling any need to make a building expensively handsome.

The main cause of the growth in the community was, however, not recruitment from the English. Just as Catholic Emancipation in 1829 had been due to Ireland, so the later, massive numerical growth was due to the immigration into England of the Irish.

Bishops in England complained that the Irish clergy would not come over to help, and parish priests complained that half the immigrants were scandalously irreligious. Many of these peasants whose faith and life-style had been little changed since the Middle Ages were thoroughly demoralized by life in an English factory, or roaming the countryside as casual labourers, or building the railways in the notorious gangs of 'navvies'. In his account of *The Condition of the Working Class in England* (1845), Friedrich Engels recorded of the Irish in Manchester that their standard of living was the 'lowest conceivable in a civilized country'. But the Irish immigration was bound to change the face of England's industrial cities. From its very beginning the Industrial Revolution in England had drawn labour from Ireland (whose economic development the English had wrecked), but the tide became a flood when the potato crop on which the Irish peasantry depended for survival was ruined by disease in the years 1845–47. During the 1840s about a quarter of a million of the Irish died because of the famine, and about a million fled overseas. By the census of 1851, almost 520,000 people born in Ireland were living in England, three per cent of the whole population, in addition to their children born in England; and ten years later there were eighty thousand more. The great majority of these incoming Irish were, at least nominally, Catholics; Irish Protestants tended to go to Scotland. By the 1820s the Irish Catholics in England seem to have outnumbered the English Catholics. By the end of the 1840s about three-quarters of the Roman Catholics in Liverpool, Manchester and London were of Irish extraction. In some other new industrial areas the proportion was similar.[29]

The leadership of this expanded community fell to men who could offer a faith strong enough to survive its ugly and harsh surroundings – strong enough to attract the Irish back to Mass, to recruit priests, to build churches and schools. The strength did not come from the old Catholic tradition in England, a tradition of inconspicuous reserve (priests were called 'Mr' and dressed as laymen), of a sober piety (churches contained no statues or side altars), of an emphatic English patriotism. The incoming Irish cared for none of these things. A style which had shielded the English Catholics' piety from inquisitive Protestant neighbours made no appeal at all to half a million destitute Irish who, if they were not to sink completely into an animal-like existence in their English exile, needed to be rescued by vigorous pastoral expeditions, hardhitting sermons and dramatically impressive services, preferably not in English. Only in that way could their Catholic religion, which had probably been rather slack in Ireland, become the foundation on which these refugees could rebuild their devastated lives.

Who, then, was to supply spiritual leadership and fill the vacuum? In 1840 there were only about five hundred priests at work in England. The Irish could, and gradually did, produce their own priests but in the emergency other priests came from the continent; the outstanding missionaries of the 1840s were two Italians, Aloysius Gentili and Dominici Barberi, both of whom, worn out, died young. Such men linked England with a wider Catholic revival.

When Napoleon had been compelled to conclude a concordat with the papacy, Christianity in its Catholic form had seemed necessary to provide emotional food for the French and some legitimacy for the new empire. When Napoleon had been toppled the Catholic religion had been patronized by the

---

[29] The chapters on 'The Increase in Population' and 'The Religion of the People' are among the valuable features of G. Kitson Clark, *The Making of Victorian England* (London, 1962). Cecil Woodham-Smith told the story of *The Great Hunger: Ireland 1845–59* (London, 1964).

victorious reactionaries, and the restored altar placed near the restored throne; the Pope's triumphant return to Rome in 1814 had seemed to symbolize all the return of the old days. When the time came for the recovery of a revolutionary (or at least liberal) spirit, many Catholics – for example, the brilliant group around the French paper *L'Avenir* – dreamed of a reconciliation between the Church and democracy under prophetic priests and popes. When the papacy itself reacted by condemning *L'Avenir* and the leader of that group wandered off heartbroken, many did not take his path into the wilderness, being prepared to accept even a Church which declared war on democracy and modern civilization. Not even the identification of the cause of the Church with the maintenance of the temporal power of the popes as the sovereigns of Rome and a considerable part of Italy could end this recovery of the Catholic faith to be seen in nineteenth-century Europe. When the slow rise of modern intellectual scepticism did disturb some believers, the surrender of the mind to the old Catholic faith in its mysterious beauty and supernatural authority could seem all the more of a relief. Many in Europe felt like that; and these thoughts or dreams were in the minds of some Englishmen who during the 1820s and 1830s were like actors, waiting in the wings before the serious drama of the Catholic revival could be performed on stage.[30]

The most important member of this hopeful group was Nicholas Wiseman. Of Irish descent although born in Spain, he was sent to the school and seminary established at Ushaw in County Durham in 1795. The spiritual climate at Ushaw was too dull to do much for him, but the very fact that he received this schooling in England was significant. Previous generations of Catholic gentlemen's sons had been compelled to go to the colleges abroad. Such colleges were now closed thanks to the French Revolution, but that was no disaster since there was now freedom to run Catholic schools in England. There was even some new sympathy with, and respect for, the Catholic

---

[30] See Alec R. Vidler, *Prophecy and Papacy* (London, 1954); W. G. Roe, *Lamennais and England* (Oxford, 1966); Owen Chadwick, *The Popes and European Revolution* (Oxford, 1981).

clergy; thousands of them had been temporarily exiled from the continent into England by the terror of the revolution.

In 1818, at the age of sixteen, Nicholas Wiseman was sent to Rome as one of the first six students to reopen the English College. It had been looted and closed by the revolutionaries twenty years before. He never forgot the first walk in silence through the empty college's halls, through the library with its unused and disordered books, through the chapel with the desecrated graves. Remaining in Rome as a priest, he became an accomplished scholar and ardent preacher.

In 1835 he returned to England. In a large mansion overlooking Bath, Bishop Baines, the vicar apostolic of the Western district, was establishing a school and seminary which he hoped would rival the colleges already in existence at Ushaw, at Oscott near Birmingham and at Ware in Hertfordshire. There was talk of a Catholic university, and of Nicholas Wiseman at its head. The trouble with the grandiose scheme was that so few people trusted Bishop Baines. He was a Benedictine monk, but the monks of Downside Abbey in his district had resisted an earlier scheme which would have made their abbey his headquarters. The monks of his own monastery, Ampleforth Abbey, had resented the fact that so many of their small community had been summoned away from Yorkshire to Bath, where the monk-bishop lived in excessive state. When they met, Baines and Wiseman soon discovered that, charming as they both could be, they did not charm each other. The breach was just as well for Wiseman's career, since the school-cum-palace from which Baines looked down on Bath was soon destroyed by fire, and the obstinately courageous Bishop had to spend the rest of his life trying to raise money to rebuild it. After delivering some highly successful lectures in London, Wiseman was better off back in Rome.

When he finally returned to England in 1840, it was to the Midland district where he assisted old Bishop Walsh. He also took charge of the school and college at Oscott. He still kept in touch with the world of ideas, editing the new *Dublin Review* which was financed by the Irish leader O'Connell but directed towards the literary end of the Catholic market. A lover of food, wine and wit, he moved easily among other gentlemen. He admired John Talbot, the fabulously rich sixteenth Earl of Shrewsbury who shared his own romantic illusion that the English were about to return in very large numbers to the old religion of the Catholic Church. The heir of the finest tradition in medieval chivalry, the earl's main interest lay in building churches for Catholic worship in the new industrial towns. His favourite architect was Augustus Welby Pugin, who from the design of fashionable Gothic chairs had moved on to construction of Gothic churches with a consistently Gothic style in the furnishings and vestments. To Pugin, such a revival of medievalism was itself an act of Christian worship and witness. This romanticism aroused Bishop Wiseman's appreciation. He was, however, willing to incur Pugin's wrath by resisting the introduction of a rood screen into St Chad's Cathedral, Birmingham. He opposed it because it would separate the priests from the people.[31]

---

[31] See Brian Fothergill, *Nicholas Wiseman* (London, 1963), and for the Romantic background Denis Gwynn, *The Second Spring 1815–52* (London, 1942), and *Lord Shrewsbury, Pugin and the Catholic Revival* (London 1946).

CHAPTER FOUR

THREE POETS

BLAKE AND MAN

During these richly formative years English Christianity was, however, not only a religious revival which could be organized into Methodism, Evangelicalism, the quieter High Church recovery, the birth of militant Nonconformity and the transformation of Roman Catholicism. It was also something much harder to pin down: a movement of thought about man and God. And it is the good fortune of the student of pre-Victorian religion that three great poets are available to act as guides to this spiritual movement – William Blake, William Wordsworth and Samuel Taylor Coleridge.

The more conventional Robert Southey failed to think out his religious position thoroughly, or at least failed to make honest and deep thoughts public, because after a radical youth he became a prolific Tory journalist. It is not necessary to condemn him as 'Mr Feathernest', who abandoned the revolutionary cause solely in order to make money out of royalist and patriotic effusions as Poet Laureate and best-sellers such as *The Book of the Church*. As late as 1812 Shelley got the impression from their only meeting that Southey 'tho' far from being a man of great reasoning powers is a great man'. During their talks the older poet apparently agreed with 'my idea of the Deity, a mass of infinite intelligence' – and recommended that Shelley should get in touch with the philosopher William Godwin, a recommendation with fateful consequences. All the evidence suggests that Southey was sincere in his hatred of the excesses of the French Revolution and in his fear that English civilization was about to be brought to an end by mob violence accompanied by economic collapse. He regarded the Church of England as one of the great institutions of the country, so

useful that it deserved to be defended from its enemies
although he could not accept all its theology. In 1814 he
confessed to a friend: 'I am neither enthusiast nor hypocrite,
but a man deeply and habitually religious in all my feelings,
according to my own views of religion, which views differ from
those of the Church which I defend. . . . *Not* believing in the
inspiration of the Bible, but believing in the faith which is
founded upon it, I hold its general circulation as one of the
greatest benefits which can be conferred on mankind. *Not*
believing that men are damned for not being Christians, I
believe that Christianity is a divine religion, and that it is our
duty to diffuse it.'[1]

At the other extreme, the unconventional Shelley failed to
exert much influence on English religion because he could so
easily be dismissed as an eccentric who was in rebellion for
rebellion's sake – or as a very wicked man who did not dare to
live in England. This great poet and wide-ranging and
courageous thinker, for all the passionate sincerity of his hatred
of the oppressors of the English poor, was too much the son of a
very rich baronet ever to feel at ease with the actual poor. In
much the same way, his lofty conception of a purified new
religion was accompanied by such provocative, often adolescent, attacks on Christian doctrines and morals that his notoriety meant that he could never gain a hearing among the
religious. Despite his 'simultaneous perception of Power and
Love in the absolute, and of Beauty and Good in the concrete'
(the tribute was to come from Robert Browning), the reputation with which Shelley went to Oxford – 'the Eton Atheist' –
dogged him. It was still his reputation when he died in his
twenty-ninth year; and he had done much to earn it.

The pamphlet which brought about his expulsion from
Oxford, while itself a perfectly reasonable demonstration that
the existence of God could not be proved, was entitled *The
Necessity of Atheism* and was mailed to all the bishops and all the
heads of colleges. Had he lived to the same age as his father he
would have died in 1882 and might have become a mature
philosopher. But in a letter dated to Shelley in 1820, Southey

---

[1] Geoffrey Carnall, *Robert Southey and His Age* (Oxford, 1960), pp. 216–17.

expressed respectable England's reaction to the life that had been lived. Shelley had driven his first wife to suicide: 'You robbed her of her moral and religious principles, you debauched her mind. ... You have reasoned yourself into a state of mind so pernicious that your character, with your "domestic arrangements" as you term it, might furnish the subject for the drama more instructive, and scarcely less painful, than the detestable story of the Cenci. ... It is the Atheist's Tragedy.'[2]

We shall study William Blake instead, for he rose above the conventions to glory. Born in 1757 in London, he lived mainly there until his death in 1827. His background was middle class; his father, a solid tradesman, was a member of a Dissenting congregation. In youth he read widely, in a number of languages; in old age he learned Italian in order to read and illustrate Dante. No other reading, however, had as much power for him as his delight in the imagery of the Bible. At the age of four he thought he saw God pressing his face against the window, and on another occasion his father almost beat him for claiming to have seen angels in a tree. He learned draughtsmanship by drawing the monuments in Westminster Abbey; he loved that great church (and the Gothic architecture which it represented), and had a vision of Christ and his apostles walking through it. His devotion to Jesus was so clear, and so eloquent, that countless orthodox Christians have loved to pray in his words. His poem 'On Another's Sorrow' may be judged the finest statement in English of the compassion of God expressed in the birth and death of Jesus. All through his life eternity seemed close to him and he claimed that he often talked with the dead. Among all the English poets he felt closest to Milton, about whom he wrote a major poem. There is a story that he and his wife Catherine were once discovered by a bewildered Thomas Butts sitting naked in the garden; they were Adam and Eve, reading *Paradise Lost* aloud. Asked what the poet did when his vision faded, his wife once replied factually: 'he prays.' In 1802 he wrote to Thomas Butts: 'I still and shall to all eternity embrace Christianity and adore him

---

[2] Richard Holmes, *Shelley: The Pursuit* (London, 1974), p. 608.

who is the express image of God; but I have travel'd thro' perils and darkness not unlike a champion.'

But like Shelley, Blake was in total rebellion against all authority in Church and State. His parents, who allowed his formal education to cease at the age of ten, at least had the insight not to try to make him conform. What he really inherited from his family was the Levellers' tradition, radicalism seeking a revolution, and it seems that he concealed the extent of this radicalism beneath a cloud of mythological writing and drawing in order to protect himself in an age when an Englishman flaunting 'anarchism' and 'atheism' would invite imprisonment and probably hanging. He had an argument with a private soldier during the invasion scare in the autumn of 1803, while he was living near the sea at Felpham; he was accused of sedition but no evidence about his connections with dangerous radicals was produced at his trial, and he was acquitted. When Bishop Watson published his *Apology for the Bible* against Tom Paine, Blake wrote on his copy: 'To defend the Bible in this year 1798 would cost a man his life.' But what was the Bible to him? We face a further difficulty as we try to get at his real opinions: in private conversation Blake liked to tease, making a point by exaggerating it with a shocking sense of humour. Henry Crabb Robinson met him in December 1825 and found this 'Artist or Genius – or Mystic or Madman' so fascinating that he recorded his private opinions. Blake 'eagerly concurred' in Robinson's suggestion that the soul existed before the body's birth and after his death. He had, indeed, often conversed with Socrates and with Jesus. But he added: 'we are all coexistent with God, partakers of the divine nature.' On being questioned about the divinity of Christ, 'he said *He is the only God*, but then he added – "And so I am and so are you".'

Many scholars hold that he really was an anarchist and an atheist. 'Blake's visionary universe', writes one commentator, 'began at every point from the experiment of assuming that the supreme reality in the universe was not, as the Jews, Christians and exponents of natural religion seemed to suppose, a distant, holy and affectionate God but man – man conceived in the fuller nature which was revealed to him by the workings of his energies and his imagination.'[3] But we cannot be certain that this is the correct assessment of Blake's basic position, for it is also possible to assemble passages which suggest another conclusion – that he was, as another scholar has said, 'a monotheist; God is the source of all being, the One "who only Is".'[4] Blake wrote that 'I see the face of my Heavenly Father, he lays his hand upon my head and gives a blessing to all my works'; and much else that was compatible with a devout orthodoxy. The truth seems to be that he was a mystic poet, not a philosopher, and that it was enough for him to record his intuition that God was to be adored in the creation, without troubling to be precise in his metaphysics. His working philosophy was summed up in *The Marriage of Heaven and Hell*: 'God only Acts and Is in existing beings or men.'

It is certain that his child's vision of God at the window never left him. But actually the face seen at the window was a man's face; and his vision of Jesus was of a man who was no conformist:

> He scorn'd Earth's parents, scorn'd Earth's God,
> And mock'd the one and the other's rod;
> He seventy disciples sent
> Against Religion and Government.

So Blake hated Protestants as well as priests, holding that they had all joined in the age-old conspiracy to invent a God who is distinct from man. They had attributed to that imaginary God either a cold rationality ('Urizen' was Blake's name for the Deity thus conceived) or else a fiery wrath in upholding the conventions (another name for God was 'Nobodaddy'). Blake's positive creed, the theme of all his attempts to replace the God of the evil imagination, was threefold: 'Man has no body distinct from his soul. . . . Energy is the only life, and is from the body. . . . Energy is eternal delight.' He adored 'the Eternal Great Humanity Divine'.

That sounds like the famous affirmation of Keats: 'I am certain of nothing but of the holiness of the heart's affections

---

[3] John Beer, *Blake's Visionary Universe* (Manchester, 1969), p. 1.
[4] J. G. Davies, *The Theology of William Blake* (Oxford, 1948), p. 85.

and the truth of Imagination. What the Imagination seizes as Beauty must be truth – whether it existed before or not. . . .' But Blake meant by 'eternal' that the spirit of man really was indestructible; when his brother Robert died, he saw his spirit rising through the ceiling, 'clapping its hands for joy'. He sang on his own deathbed. He meant by 'energy' (a great Romantic word) sexual energy but also many lesser forms of delight in the 'minute particulars' of the visible world. Although he advocated a man's right to enjoy many wives or mistresses, in practice he seems to have been satisfied with his patient wife, and his basic message was that the world was full of a glory which could be known as surely as a woman could be known in bed. Even the 'tyger burning bright' was glorious because sublimely energetic in his wrath. His vision was that

> The pride of the peacock is the glory of God.
> The lust of the goat is the bounty of God.
> The wrath of the lion is the wisdom of God.
> The nakedness of woman is the work of God.

He affirmed that 'everything that lives is holy'; that 'if the doors of perception were cleansed everything would appear to man as it is, infinite'; that the sun when it rises is not 'a round disk of fire somewhat like a guinea' but is 'an innumerable company of the heavenly host crying, "Holy, Holy, Holy is the Lord God Almighty"'.

This vision of glory endured despite the sufferings which he saw in the London streets as the symptoms of a desperately diseased age:

> I wander thro' each charter'd street,
> Near where the charter'd Thames does flow,
> And mark in every face I meet
> Marks of weakness, marks of woe . . .
>
> How the chimney-sweeper's cry
> Every black'ning church appalls;
> And the hapless soldier's sigh
> Runs in blood down palace walls.

He took no pride in England's industrialization and foresaw none of the advantages which it was to bring to the people. He was saddened by the wars against the Americans and French, and his paintings of the 'spiritual forms' of Pitt and Nelson, the war heroes, were ironic: he saw them as men of semi-angelic intelligence, guiding great monsters to destruction. He could not take pleasure in battles when

> Each outcry of the hunted hare
> A fibre from the brain does tear.

In the Evangelical revival he found nothing except the condemnation of the pleasures with which the people sought brief escapes from their miseries. In his response he had to be himself, not the convincing analyst but the haunting artist. 'I will not reason and compare', he wrote; 'my business is to create.' *Jerusalem* was the culminating statement of his understanding of the poet's task as being

> To open the eternal worlds, to open the immortal eyes
> Of man inwards into the worlds of thought; into eternity,
> Ever expanding in the bosom of God, the Human Imagination.[5]

WORDSWORTH AND GOD

If William Blake is not inconceivable as a professional preacher of Radical Dissent, William Wordsworth had periods in his life when he was very close to being a clergyman of the Church of England. When his uncles paid for him to proceed from Hawkshead grammar school to Cambridge, it was in the belief that he would obtain a fellowship of a college and then settle down in a parish. As late as 1793 his sister Dorothy, to whom he poured out all his secret thoughts, still dreamed of the time when she and William would be snug together in a 'little parsonage'. In the course of that year his uncles admitted to themselves that William, who had had an illegitimate daughter by a Roman Catholic Frenchwoman, and who even more

[5] There is a large literature on Blake, but the most useful books in this context are Bernard Blackstone, *English Blake* (Cambridge, 1949); David Erdman, *Blake: Prophet against Empire* (revised, Princeton, NJ, 1969); Morton D. Paley, *Energy and Imagination: A Study of the Development of Blake's Thought* (Oxford, 1970); Michael Davis, *William Blake: A New Kind of Man* (London, 1977).

scandalously had fallen in love with the French Republic, was not going to be ordained. Yet within twelve years he had become a fully convinced Christian believer and an upholder of the Church of England. When his long poem about the growth of his mind was eventually published after his death in 1850 and named *The Prelude*, almost all the passages written half a century or so before and hinting at heresy had been adjusted to the sincerely accepted demands of orthodoxy. When his official biography was written by his nephew Christopher (a future bishop), no reference was made to his illegitimate daughter and as little reference as possible to other indiscretions of his youth.

For the historian of English religion, however, the fascination of Wordsworth's life is seeing 'the river' (a favourite image of his) taking its own way to this sea.

His mother's death when he was aged eight left him with a father absorbed in sorrow and business (and the father also died, in 1783). He wrote so much about the happiness of childhood that it comes as a surprise to learn that his 'home' for many holidays was a place of rebellious misery, a flat above the shop owned by an uncongenial uncle in Penrith. His whole world might have been ruined by his parents' deaths had it not been for the joy he found in nature – and had an Elizabethan archbishop (Sandys) not founded an excellent grammar school at Hawkshead, which he attended as a boarder, living in the cottage of kind Ann Tyson. His closest friend was a humble 'packman' or tinker who recited folktales and ballads and took him on long walks.

After Cambridge, nature again had to heal a deep distress. Wordsworth had gone to France as a tourist, not as a womanizer or as a student of revolutionary politics. We are reminded of this by the facts that Annette Vallon, to whom he gave his heart, was a domestic soul four years older than he was – and an ardent Royalist. The liaison was an act of gross folly. He could not earn his living in France and she would be disapproved of in England; so he had to abandon her and their daughter, and it says much about her that she reproached him so little. That experience was so profoundly humiliating that he never wrote about it except obliquely. He was also reduced to despair when he saw his high hopes for the revolution, hopes which he celebrated in fine poems, guillotined by the Jacobins in their reign of terror.

Shattered, Wordsworth crept back to lodge with his brother in London. He later walked over the Salisbury Plain, having seen the fleet in the Solent preparing for battle with the French; and nature did not prevent him having many dreams about the violence of the early Britons who had lived on the same plain. He remained a political radical for some years, but he did not live in the revolutionary underworld of London which Blake inhabited. Instead he gave himself to nature, being enabled by a small legacy to rent very simple accommodation which he could share with his sister. And perhaps that itself became a problem. It is possible (although there is no certain evidence) that he was conscious that his relationship with his sister developed unhealthily, so that it was emotionally (although not physically) incest before his marriage to Mary Hutchinson in 1803.

He now offered to nature not a religious faith but a religious longing. He recalled in *The Excursion* how

> In such access of mind, in such high hour
> Of visitation from the living God,
> He did not feel the God: he felt his works . . .
> Such hour by prayer or praise was unprofaned,
> He neither prayed, nor offered thanks or praise,
> His mind was a thanksgiving to the power
> That made him: it was blessedness and love.

Of course such a spirit could not be satisfied by materialism:

> The world is too much with us; late and soon,
> Getting and spending we lay waste our powers:
> Little we see in Nature that is ours. . . .
> It moves us not. – Great God! I'd rather be
> A Pagan suckled in a creed outworn . . .

Richer than the 'wealth of nations' were the moments when

> we are laid asleep
> In body, and become a living soul;
> While with an eye made quiet by the power

> Of harmony, and the deep power of joy,
> We see into the life of things.

His first poem in which his genius was at full stretch was composed 'a few miles above Tintern Abbey' in 1798. The beauty of nature has been approached through questions

> in lonely rooms, and 'mid the din
> Of towns and cities. . . .

These are questions about human suffering,

> the heavy and the weary weight
> Of all this unintelligible world. . . .

He remembers a time when after 'the coarser pleasures of my boyhood days' he had reached the 'aching joys' and 'dizzy raptures' of a time when 'nature to me was all in all'. But even in that time he had not sought absorption into nature as the complete nature-mystic would. He had been too conscious of his unhappiness,

> more like a man
> Flying from something that he dreads than one
> Who sought the thing he loved.

Now 'that time is past'. But he does not mourn, since he has had an 'abundant recompense': he has deepened the questions which he brings to nature, because he has deepened his understanding of humanity's burdens and powers. He has heard

> The still, sad music of humanity,
> Nor harsh nor grating, though of ample power
> To chasten and subdue.

He has learned, too, that the understanding of nature comes from the creative imagination. He speaks

> of all the mighty world
> Of eye, and ear – both what they half create
> And what perceive.

This creative insight is what has equipped him to find in ambiguous nature

> The anchor of my purest thoughts, the nurse,
> The guide, the guardian of my heart, and soul
> Of all my moral being.

The vision of nature which consoled him in 1798 was not precisely defined in terms of theological or philosophical prose. In so far as it could be so defined, it probably should be classified as pantheism; it was what Coleridge was to call 'the misty rather than mystic confusion of God with nature'. The lack of precision was inevitable because, in the words of a modern critic, 'Wordsworth was not primarily a thinker but a feeler. The determining events of his career and the sources of all that is essential in his poetry were the personal tragedies, the anguished decisions, the half-conscious, half-animal, terrors and ecstasies, and *not* the discoveries of the intellect'.[6] But the unclear answer given by nature to his distress in 1798 was beyond dispute grand:

> I have felt
> A presence that disturbs me with the joy
> Of elevated thoughts; a sense sublime
> Of something far more deeply interfused,
> Whose dwelling is the light of setting suns,
> And the round ocean and living air,
> And the blue sky, and in the mind of man:
> A motion, and a spirit, that impels
> All thinking things, all objects of all thought,
> And rolls through all things.

The next major poem which is sublime is the ode, *Intimations of Immortality*. Most of it was written early in 1804. The first part had been abandoned in 1802, when Wordsworth had only got so far as to record the waning of his ecstasies in the presence of nature:

> Whither is fled the visionary gleam,
> Where is it now, the glory and the dream?

His answer at that stage was that the glory could be recaptured by remembering childhood's 'vision splendid' – and that

---

[6] F. W. Bateson, *Wordsworth: A Reinterpretation* (London, 1954), p. 40.

children had this vision of nature's glory because they were
closer to nature's God. The poet was here using the belief,
taught to the West by Plato, that the soul existed before birth.
The belief appealed to a number of literary-minded people in
that time; Blake held it, and Shelley once startled a mother
crossing Magdalen Bridge in Oxford by asking her what her
baby remembered of heaven. Within the next year, 1805,
however, Wordsworth was addressing questions to nature
which no half-serious belief could satisfy. For his brother John,
whom he regarded as a saint, was drowned at sea when in
command of one of the East India Company's great ships. And
William Wordsworth then asked with all the passion of his soul
whether darkness or light prevailed.

For some days he and Dorothy could do little but weep
together. Then he could put his question into words. 'Why
have we a choice and a will, with a notion of justice and
injustice, enabling us to be moral agents? Why have sympathies which make the best of us so afraid of inflicting pain
and sorrow, which yet we see dealt about so lavishly by the
Supreme Governor? Why should our notions of right towards
each other, and to all sentient beings within our influence,
differ so widely from what appears to be his notion and rule, if
everything were to end here? Would it not be blasphemy to say
that, upon the supposition of the thinking principle being
destroyed by death, however inferior we may be to the great
Cause and Ruler of things, we have *more of love* in our nature
than he has? The thought is monstrous; and yet how to get rid
of it, except on the supposition of *another* and a *better world*, I do
not see.'

In that tormented letter he did not say that John could not
perish utterly because he was a part of nature – although one of
the 'Lucy' poems had experimented with that solution,

> Rolled round in earth's diurnal course
> With rocks, and stones, and trees.

Nor did he say that he knew that John was alive because Christ
had risen. What he implied was that nature had revealed to
him that there was a 'great Cause and Ruler of things' but had
left him bewildered about the fate of individuals. Because life

was so unjust his own moral sense rebelled against God the 'Cause and Ruler' – unless there was a 'better world' of persons in eternal relationships, upheld by the immortal, personal and loving God. Was there such a world? He could not be a total rebel; the sense of being a creature was fundamental to his sense of being anyone at all. So in the end 'the supposition of *another* and a *better* world' was what he chose. 'Christianity', a modern scholar has concluded, 'reached Wordsworth neither through a sense of sin nor a sense of glory but through wanhope, a colourless despair. ... Wordsworth does not embrace Christianity: it is forced on him by the exclusion of alternatives. ... The most certain thing about Wordsworth's religion is its initial poverty.'[7]

His religion did not remain poor. 'Theologians may puzzle their heads about dogmas as they will,' he wrote to an intimate friend (Sir George Beaumont) in 1825, 'the religion of gratitude cannot mislead us. Of that we are sure, and gratitude is the handmaid to hope, and hope the harbinger of faith. I look upon Nature, I think of the best part of our species, I lean upon my friends, and I meditate upon the Scriptures, especially the Gospel of St John; and my creed rises up of itself with the ease of an exhalation yet a fabric of adamant.' He did not mention in that letter that he was a regular churchgoer; but so he was, after his brother's death.

He knew that his faith fell short of knowledge, but as he wrote to Lady Beaumont in 1815, he was undeterred by the scorn of 'London wits and witlings' because he did not regard them as superior thinkers; 'for we have no thought (save thoughts of pain) but as far as we have love and admiration.' By then he knew that he could never complete the major philosophical poem, *The Recluse*, 'containing views on Man, Nature and Society', which Coleridge had urged on him. But he had been entrusted with the power to write poems 'to console the afflicted, to add sunshine to daylight by making the happy happier, to teach the young and the gracious of every age to see, to think and feel, and therefore to become more actively and securely virtuous; this is their office, which I trust

---

[7] John Jones, *The Egotistical Sublime* (London, 1954), pp. 49, 52, 168.

they will faithfully perform long after we (that is, all that is mortal of us) are mouldered in our graves.'

As the years went by, the power of the poetry to 'console' and to make men 'securely virtuous' was subjected to the cruellest of tests. His own children died, and Dorothy became prematurely senile. An eye disease nearly blinded him, and he knew that he was often mocked by his former allies; it was a solid fact that he who had been an ardent radical in the 1790s lived to become an almost complete Tory (and a civil servant). The poetry survived all these tests with its 'healing power' (Matthew Arnold's phrase, which became the standard Victorian tribute). He grew strong as he repeated it with wonder to himself during his walks, or to the many visitors who came on pilgrimage. The recitals usually struck others as egotistical but innocent. It was as if the poet had been given gifts greater than his own personality, to preach and to worship, like a priest.

It was a painting by Sir George Beaumont (John Constable's most important patron) that inspired Wordsworth to record his conversion to Christian belief in a poem written in the decisive year, 1805. The painting was of Peele Castle in a storm. Wordsworth had known the castle during a summer's holiday, when the air around it was 'calm' and the sea near it was 'glassy'. He could then have painted it serenely

> To express what then I saw; and add the gleam,
> The light that never was, on sea or land,
> The consecration, and the Poet's dream.

But as it was, the storm in the picture now matched the storm of his grief for his brother – and the storm had driven him closer to the rest of suffering mankind, with its strange sense of God's control, its suffering which seemed utterly to contradict that control, and its hope.

> So once it would have been – 'tis so no more;
> I have submitted to a new control:
> A power is gone, which nothing can restore;
> A deep distress hath humanized my Soul. . . .
>
> But welcome fortitude, and patient cheer,
> And frequent sights of what is to be borne!

Such sights, or worse, as are before me here. –
Not without hope we suffer and we mourn.[8]

COLERIDGE AND THE VICTORIAN FUTURE

When Samuel Taylor Coleridge moved to the village of High-gate overlooking London in 1816, nothing would have appeared more improbable than his influence on the Victorian future – an influence so formative that in a famous essay John Stuart Mill declared him to be one of the two seminal minds of the nineteenth century, with his insistent question: 'What is the meaning of it?' (The other mind was Jeremy Bentham, with his question: 'Is it true?')[9]

In 1816 Coleridge seemed the opposite of a Victorian sage. He had moved into a home for drug addicts – and while there he continued to buy opium surreptitiously. As a counter-stimulant, he used brandy excessively. For ten years he had been separated from his wife, having endured a marriage in which the happiest moments were, he told a friend, those which he spent alone in his study, crying. He had also lost touch with Sara Hutchinson (the sister of Mary who married Wordsworth), the woman he had come to prefer to his wife. He had quarrelled with the two poets with whom he had formed alliances, collaborations and intimate friendships – Southey and, far more important, Wordsworth. He had seen his powers as a poet drying up while Wordsworth appeared to compose endlessly and effortlessly. He had turned to the metaphysical philosophy of Germany, but deep down he must have known that he was incapable of the highest flights in that realm. He formed the habit of incorporating considerable passages from

---

[8] The best biography is Mary Moorman, *William Wordsworth* in two volumes (Oxford, 1957–65). Among all the criticism, Geoffrey Hartman, *Wordsworth's Poetry 1787–1814* (New Haven, Conn., 1964), and John Beer's two volumes on *Wordsworth and the Human Heart* and *Wordsworth in Time* (London, 1978–79) are of special value. Michael Friedman studied *William Wordsworth: The Making of a Tory Humanist* with sympathy (New York, 1979).

[9] John Stuart Mill's *Bentham and Coleridge* was edited by F. R. Leavis (London, 1950).

German books without acknowledgement. Was he, after all, a journalist? He had done much journalism – partly for his own little radical papers, both of which had disappeared in debts, but mainly where he had written at the editor's command. The verdict is just: 'Coleridge straddled too many fences, was aware of too many contradictory trends, and lacked the profound power of integration necessary to launch a true theological movement.'[10]

He really had only two assets left in 1816 – and he kept them both until he died in 1834. One was the power of his talk.

He was a compulsive talker, probably compensating for a lonely childhood. (His father had been an impractical clergyman who died when the boy was only nine, and he had never got on with his aggressively practical mother.) His 'conversation' could be called 'one-versation', virtually always a pontifical monologue, taking up practically any subject but tending always to philosophy. Schoolfellows such as Charles Lamb remembered from their time at Christ's Hospital how he had been discoursing even then on metaphysics, with 'a hunger for eternity'. To less friendly hearers the monologue could seem like eternity. John Keats said that Coleridge, unlike Shakespeare, lacked *'Negative Capability*, that is, when a man is capable of being in uncertainties, mysteries, doubts, without any irritable reaching after facts and reasons.' Thomas Carlyle, who was himself not a bashful talker, included in his *Life of Sterling* an impression of Coleridge's Thursday evening parties, when he 'sat on the brow of Highgate Hill, in those years, looking down on London and its smoke-tumult, like a sage escaped from the inanity of life's battle. . . . To the rising spirits of the young generation he had this dusky sublime character; and sat there as a kind of *Magus*, girt in mystery and enigma.' The ruined poet held court in this way for eighteen years. Carlyle was among those influenced during the 1820s – although on the whole he was cynical, indignant when the 'Church of England cobwebs' seemed to be ensnaring clever young men.

---

[10] James D. Boulger, *Coleridge as Religious Thinker* (New Haven, N.H., 1961), p. 219.

Coleridge's second great asset remaining from the wreckage of his young manhood was the power of his Christian faith (which Carlyle rejected: he preferred the Infinite).

He dictated on his deathbed his conviction about 'the Absolute Good . . . the eternal reality in itself and the ground and source of all other reality.' And to this faith in God he added a Trinitarian faith in the divine Spirit proceeding from the Father through the Word or *Logos* ('the person of the *Logos* by whom that reality is communicated to all other beings'). But the Trinitarianism was not a lifeless orthodoxy. When he had begun to think for himself in Cambridge, he had become an admirer of Joseph Priestley's brand of Rational Dissent. He had nearly accepted an appointment as a Unitarian minister, until Priestley's friend Josiah Wedgwood had promised him a small annual pension so that he might become a great poet instead. He had reached the Trinitarian faith through much suffering. That was what made its reality communicable, although he spoke or wrote only in aphorisms or in mysterious fragments of the theological system which would never be complete. 'The truth is', Robert Southey once complained, 'that he plays with systems, and any nonsense will serve him for a text from which to deduce something new and surprising.' There was truth in that criticism. But it was not the whole truth about Coleridge's religion.

It was typical of the enthusiasm of his earlier years that the *Ancient Mariner*, first conceived as a popular ballad for a magazine in order to raise some cash for a trip to Germany, ended up as an affirmation of the sacredness of all life, the sin of man who thoughtlessly destroys life, and the redeeming power of the prayerful love of life. It was also typical of him that, when the trip to Germany came off, he used it to learn the language and to begin to study German metaphysical philosophy (whereas Wordsworth spent the winter writing poetry and would later 'thank Heaven' that he had never read a word of German metaphysics). For a time Coleridge, like the young Wordsworth, saw nature as animated by the God of the Unitarians – or was it the God of the pantheists? In the original draft of *The Eolian Harp* he asked:

> And what if All of animated Life
> Be but as Instruments diversely fram'd
> That tremble into thought, while thro' them breathes
> One infinite and intellectual Breeze? . . .
> Thus *God* would be the universal Soul,
> Mechaniz'd matter as th' organic harps
> And each one's Tunes be that, which each calls I.

This was not a self-centred vision; the ego was far less prominent than in the young Wordsworth. Anyone who reads the notebooks which tell the sad story of the young Coleridge's mismanagement of his life must be astonished that, so far from being as conceited as many thought he was, the poet had no ambition except to be a poet serving his vision; and that, so far from being full of self-pity, immediately after noting some personal calamity his mind would move into the observation of nature or into a philosophical speculation. When as an older and sadder man he looked back, he thought that his youthful opinions were 'in many and most important points erroneous' but he accurately recalled that 'in the expansion of my enthusiasms I did not think of *myself* at all'. And in that he had not been completely unique. It was a time when, as Basil Willey observes, 'not Coleridge alone but all speculative Europe was smitten with longing for the Great, the Whole and the Indivisible, hoping to find the One in the Many and the All, and feeling the presence of One Life within us and without'.[11]

What made Coleridge see more in 'the One' than the pantheists did was his exceptionally intense drive to see more because in his growing introspection he felt himself to be a sinner. He had rejected David Hartley's philosophy of the mind as a blank sheet on which sensations were imposed by nature, for the doctrine was contrary to his experience as a poet with a glorious power of imagination. Now he rejected also David Hartley's doctrine that progress to perfection was necessary, for the doctrine was contrary to his own experience of multiple miseries and to his self-condemnation. Rejecting William Paley, he once wrote: '*Evidences* of Christianity! I am

---

[11] Basil Willey, *Samuel Taylor Coleridge* (London, 1972), p. 86. See also T. B. McFarland, *Coleridge and the Pantheist Tradition* (Oxford, 1969).

weary of the word. Make a man feel the *want* of it; rouse him, if you can, to the self-knowledge of his *need* of it; and you may safely trust it to its own Evidence.' He did not believe that it was of any use doing theology in the detached mood of the eighteenth-century intellectuals. 'Christianity is not a Theory, or a Speculation, but a *Life*; – not a *Philosophy* of Life, but a Living Process. . . .TRY IT.' On the other hand, he could not be satisfied by a religion of the emotions alone; he once compared the 'Methodist stove' with the Unitarians' 'moonlight' and concluded that he needed sunshine – the mind's light as well as the heart's heat. 'He who begins by loving Christianity better than Truth', he wrote, 'will proceed by loving his own Sect or Church better than Christianity, and end by loving himself better than all.' Sinner as he was and knew himself to be, he remained a reasoner as he approached the mystery of the One. 'Faith', he observed out of his own experience, 'is a *total* act of the soul; it is the *whole* state of the mind, or it is not at all, and in this consists its power, as well as its exclusive worth.'

For Coleridge, there was a kind of 'reason' which was superior to the mere 'understanding'; and it was supremely this reason – the conscience – that judged one's existence and whispered the meaning of that existence. So Immanuel Kant was teaching at this time in Germany, and Kant's teaching took possession of Coleridge's mind 'as with a giant's hand'. Coleridge gladly echoed the German giant's conclusion that the 'practical reason' demanded the three highest truths: *God* as the source of this moral law, *freedom of the will* because the conscience said that righteousness was possible, and *immortality* because the conscience also said that righteousness must be rewarded. But Coleridge also went further than Kant, in that he believed that this kind of 'reason' actually enabled one to know God, to receive God's self-revelation, to use one's freedom to accept God's gifts and forgiveness leading to immortality. 'Reason' drove him to enter the world of religion which always remained closed to Kant; to do for England, in English, something of what was being done for the German Protestants by a far greater theologian, Schleiermacher, in answer to the challenge of Kant.

He found inspiration in 'the old England, the spiritual

Platonic old England'. By that he meant the England of
Shakespeare and Sydney, an England where a spiritual reality
was always present in nature and history and where this reality
challenged the poet and philosopher; not the England of John
Locke and David Hume. He read the seventeenth-century
Cambridge Platonists with delight. He admired the teaching of
Bishop Berkeley that nature was the 'visible language' of God.
He once mused on the Platonic tradition in these words. 'Every
man is born an Aristotelian or a Platonist. I do not think it
possible that any one born an Aristotelian can become a
Platonist; and I am sure no born Platonist can ever change into
an Aristotelian. . . . Aristotle was, and still is, the sovereign
lord of the understanding; the faculty judging by the senses. He
. . . never could raise himself into that higher state which was
natural to Plato.'[12] The Christian Platonism in which he came
to believe was to him the truth from eternity conveyed to the
mind of man by symbols, in much the same way as the symbols
in nature conveyed a message to the poet. But to say that
religious truth was symbolic was not to belittle it, for a symbol
'always partakes of the Reality which it renders intelligible'.
And to teach this truth with power, to spread sunlight, the
Christian had the Church and the Bible.

When he had finally abandoned the Unitarians he was
insistent that true Christianity was found only within the
visible Church, the 'sustaining, correcting, befriending Opposite of the World'. 'My fixed principle is: that a Christianity
without a Church exercising spiritual authority is vanity and
illusion.' He became proud of the Book of Common Prayer; its
imperfections were only 'spots on the sun'. He became proud of
the Church of England's comprehensiveness; he saw in 'the
Church-Establishment . . . the greatest, if not the sole, bulwark
of toleration.' He became proud of the parish system, rejoicing
'that to every parish throughout the kingdom there is trans-
planted a germ of civilization; that in the remotest villages
there is a nucleus round which the capabilities of the place may

---

[12] Recent studies include René Wellek, *Immanuel Kant in England, 1793–1838*
(Princeton, N.J., 1931), and David Newsome, *Two Classes of Man: Platonism and
English Romantic Thought* (London, 1974).

crystallize and brighten; a model sufficiently superior to excite, but sufficiently near to encourage and facilitate, imitation.' And the Church was more than a civilizing agency. Basically, its authority over the consciences of its members derived from the fact that the Gospel entrusted to it had been revealed by God. Indeed, 'all religion is revealed religion'.

To Christians, therefore, the Bible was indispensable. But Coleridge explicitly attacked 'the belief that every sentence found in a canonical book, rightly interpreted, contains the dictum of an infallible Mind.' Instead, the Christian must examine the purpose of the particular passage and relate it to the whole Bible, 'for it is the spirit of the Bible, and not detached words and sentences, that is infallible and absolute'. In his *Confessions of an Enquiring Spirit* (written 1825–27 although not published until 1840), Coleridge commended this approach which at that time in England, a country almost entirely innocent of biblical criticism, was boldly radical. He wrote as a lover of the Bible. 'Need I say that . . . I have found words for my inmost thoughts, songs for my joy, utterances for my hidden griefs, and pleadings for my shame and feebleness? In short whatever *finds* me bears witness for itself that it has proceeded from a Holy Spirit, even from the same Spirit "which . . . in all ages enters into holy souls and maketh them friends of God and prophets".' If any enemy of fundamentalism could disarm the Evangelicals, Coleridge could. He wrote: 'This I believe by my own dear experience – that the more tranquilly an inquirer takes up the Bible as he would any other body of ancient writings, the livelier and steadier will be his impressions of its superiority to all other books, till at length all other books and all other knowledge will be valuable in his eyes in proportion as they help him to a better understanding of his Bible.' In his notebooks he left behind many fragments of an attempt to write a commentary on the whole of the Bible.

It was supremely in his call to the Church to apply the principles of the Bible to the whole life of England that Coleridge was in the end influential. In the politics of his time (when, he thought, 'the principles are worse than the men'), he had little impact. But the principles which he expounded gradually won influence in the elite which he called the 'clerisy'

– widening that term to include not only the clergy but also doctors, lawyers, musicians, teachers and others in a 'permanent, nationalized learned order' responsible for the civilization of the country, somewhat like the guardians in Plato's *Republic*. It has been well said that 'the most valuable ideas that Coleridge had to communicate were not, in fact, such as would provide simple solutions to specific problems; they were ideas relating to a new kind of political and social consciousness, the development of which would slowly but inevitably lead to the solution of these problems'.[13] His was a gospel, disturbing and suggestive if not complete, for a nation – in an age when the message of the Methodists or the Evangelicals remained largely individualist and Wordsworth's conversion to Christianity was (like Southey's) accompanied by his conversion to a reactionary Toryism. He believed that 'religion, true or false, is and ever has been the centre of gravity in a realm, to which all other things must and will accommodate themselves.'[14]

---

[13] John Colmer, *Coleridge, Critic of Society* (Oxford, 1959), pp. 169–70.

[14] The best introduction is Walter Jackson Bate, *Coleridge* (London, 1969). John Cornwell, *Coleridge: Poet and Revolutionary 1772–1804* (London, 1973), is a critical biography, and *Coleridge's Variety*, ed. John Beer (London, 1974), a collection of scholarly essays. The best study of *Coleridge and Christian Doctrine* is by a Jesuit, J. Robert Barth (Cambridge, Mass., 1974). See also C. R. Sanders, *Coleridge and the Broad Church Movement* (Durham, N.C., 1942); D. P. Calleo, *Coleridge and the Idea of the Modern State* (New Haven, Conn., 1966); Ben Knights, *The Idea of the Clerisy in the Nineteenth Century* (Cambridge, 1978).

Part Two

THE VICTORIAN
CHRISTIANS

CHAPTER FIVE

THE VICTORIAN CHURCH

THE QUEEN'S RELIGION

The Victorian age was given its artificial unity by the fact that the Queen, born in 1819 and reigning from 1837, did not die before 1901. Had death come to her at an age then more normal, Victorianism would have ended in time for the last quarter of the nineteenth century to be associated with the name of her son Edward – and that sign that things had changed would have been illuminating. The last part of the age which we have to call Victorian saw the beginning of the rise to power of the working class, whose members mostly disbelieved that any religious institution had earned the right to influence their behaviour. This period saw, too, an expansion of scientific and technical education. The expansion was an inadequate response to the needs of an industrial nation now facing competitors, but it began to provide a positive alternative to traditional religion among the educated. In sophisticated circles it became the fashion to be openly bored with Puritanism. In the serious arts realism became the mood. With modernization, secularization was conquering in all these ways and in 1882 a Cambridge theologian (F. J. A. Hort) warned a new Archbishop of Canterbury (E. W. Benson) about the Church of England's 'calm and unobtrusive alienation in thought and spirit from the great silent multitude of Englishmen, and again of alienation from fact and love of fact.' The Queen scarcely lived in the same England as the workers, the scientists or the sophisticated. That is quite obvious in her published journals – and would no doubt have been even more obvious had her daughter Beatrice not destroyed many passages thought to be embarrassing. Her survival, however, did not mean that her values survived in the great multitude with their old authority.

Thus after about 1875 much of English life may be reckoned modern or Edwardian. Yet there are ways in which it is right to think of *Victorian* England as entering the twentieth century. Imperialism in India, in Africa and in the empty lands of Canada and Australia became a potent force after 1876, the year when the Queen eagerly assumed the title of Empress of India; and the imperial self-confidence which blazed like the fireworks around her Diamond Jubilee of 1897 still had some basis in the economic realities. Gross national income doubled between the 1840s and the 1880s, and the value of Britain's exports quadrupled. The real value of industrial wages within England rose by two thirds between the 1860s and the 1890s, and began to fall only in the new century – and only that fall brought back the widespread labour unrest of the 1840s. The decline of British agriculture became apparent during the 1870s, when the railways and steamships began to distribute the limitless harvests of North America and the mutton and beef of Australasia and the Argentine, but there was enough strength in the çoal, iron, steel and textile industries with their immense exports to postpone the great day of reckoning with industrial competitors. Able to sustain a population which almost doubled in the second half of the century, England was a very powerful nation – by many standards (supremely sea power), more powerful than any other in the world. Waited on by many servants, its governing class felt assured of an imperial destiny despite problems best left to the future. Queen Victoria's last Prime Minister, Lord Salisbury, was descended from the Cecil who had served Queen Elizabeth – and three of his sons were elected to the House of Commons. The Conservative cabinet under Salisbury consisted entirely of rich men.

The last ten years of the Queen's life were, indeed, the most successful in her relations with the public. She had emerged from her youthful indiscretions and tantrums, and from the unpopular seclusion of her bereaved middle years. This little old lady, less than five feet tall, had become the half-legendary mother of the largest empire the world had ever seen, and the grandmother of the emperors of Russia and Germany. And her unyielding resistance to the loose morals and careless religion of the circle around the Prince of Wales reflected the con-

tinuing power of Victorian values in the middle classes and
among the respectable workers. That part of Victorian England was never Edwardian – or at least was seldom openly so.
To widespread admiration, the Queen believed in a close but
ordered family life; in hard work including some inventiveness
but without the expression of any dangerously unconventional
thoughts; in doing one's duty without accepting that the
working class had any right to say what one's duty was; in the
sacredness of the class system tempered by some compassion
for the poor as individuals and a liking for servants who loyally
fitted into the system; in patriotism tempered by an eventual
willingness to overcome prejudices against the Jews, the Irish
and the Indians when such strange people could be useful to
England. Despite doubts she also believed in the non-dogmatic
kind of Christianity which had been taught to her as a girl.

The young Victoria was influenced by her Lutheran mother
and her tutor, George Davys, a mild Evangelical, but mainly
her mind was formed by her governess, Baroness Lehzen, a
woman of simple piety and morals. Nature meant Victoria
(called 'Drina' when young) to be a merry and mischievous girl
with an ear for music and languages. It was her misfortune to
spend her childhood with her domineering mother; a rogue
who in his turn dominated that widowed mother; no brothers
or sisters; and the uneasy sense that, although not rich now, she
would one day inherit the throne from her wicked uncles. What
she absorbed from her early training, and what sustained her
during her clashes with adults, was a simple Protestant ethic,
untroubled by theology. She expressed it on being told in 1830
how close to the throne she was (since her wicked uncles could
not produce legitimate, long-living children): 'I will be good.'
On succeeding to the throne she became spoiled and petulant,
and the advice which she eventually received from Lord
Melbourne, a cynic who sentimentally doted on her, was not so
sound as has usually been claimed. She became a partisan and
often indiscreet Whig. She was rescued from much of her
wilfulness by her marriage to the German prince who was not
only a handsome lover but also a very successful substitute for
a father. Earnest and efficient, tireless in his dedication to the
progress of his adopted country, Albert became (at least in her

eyes) a duplicate prime minister. Together, they were not particularly pious but decidely good.[1]

When in 1861 Albert fell a victim to typhus and left her a widow at the age of forty-two, her personality and religion became far more morbid. Her greatest comfort was to pray in his mausoleum at Frogmore, and to scatter many memorials to him around her dominions. Although she insisted on the deference of politicians she refused to play her proper role in public life now that she was 'alone'. Her relationship with her eldest son, whose immorality she illogically blamed for Albert's death, became notorious. She was rescued from this pathological grief by her growing love of the Highlands, to which Albert had taken her for holidays at Balmoral. She approved of the Protestantism which she found there. It was simple; she had a horror of ceremonial in church (and most unwisely persuaded Disraeli to persecute the Anglo-Catholic ritualists in the Church of England). But it was not a denial of the world; she had an almost equal horror of total abstinence from alcohol, preferred whisky to tea, and accepted drunkenness in her favourite servant, John Brown. She first took part in the sacrament of the Lord's Supper in the Church of Scotland (where no bishops had survived) in 1873. Her reply to protests about disloyalty to the Church of England's insistence on bishops was virtually to cease to be an Anglican communicant. Thus when she did reappear in the world, it was with the strength provided by a version of Christianity much the same as the religion she had learned as an innocent girl.

She never became a theologian. She called Oxford 'that monkish old place which I have a horror of'. She probably did not often touch on Calvinism in her talks with her favourite preacher in Scotland, Norman Macleod. In England her favourite clergyman was Dean Stanley of Westminster – and like him, she never achieved certainty about what she believed. When she was an old woman she sometimes exchanged confidences with Randall Davidson, the Dean of Windsor, whom she liked because he was a handsome and sensible young Scot.

---

[1] The best biography is Robert Rhodes James, *Albert Prince Consort* (London, 1983).

'She asked me,' he wrote, 'if there ever came over me (as over her) waves or *flashes* of doubtfulness whether, after all, it might all be untrue.' This confession showed her to be a typical Victorian. Doubt was in her private mind. It was almost as strong as the sense of decorum which prevailed in public. Essentially it was doubt whether goodness really would have its eternal reward. We have, however, no reason to question that she was a sincere Christian who as she lay dying (with her head propped up, hour after hour, by the German Kaiser) was 'earnestly trusting to be reunited to my beloved Husband', just as her will had declared would be the case. Beside her bed in the great house which she and Albert had built at Osborne on the Isle of White – the bed where she died – was a large picture of the dead body of Christ.[2]

REFORM AND THE CHURCH OF ENGLAND

The blind conservatism of the Church of England's leadership was shown in the struggle against Parliamentary reform. The votes of twenty-one bishops in the House of Lords helped to kill the second Reform Bill in October 1831. Infuriated mobs burned the bishop's palace in Bristol (four men were hanged for this) and raged against other bishops, nearly hitting the stately Archbishop Howley in Canterbury with a dead cat as late as August 1832. Even Englishmen who would never throw a cat at an archbishop were indignant that the bishops seemed determined to destroy the old political system altogether rather than adjust it to the demand that the constituencies should reflect the geographical distribution of the middle classes. The first Reform Bill had been introduced, as was said, in order to 'satisfy all reasonable demands, and remove at once, and for ever, all rational grounds for complaint from the minds of the intelligent and independent portion of the community.'

During the winter of 1831–32 civil war was feared, until it became clear that the Tories were unable to form a convincing

---

[2] The best biography is *Victoria RI* by Elizabeth Longford (London, 1964). The American title is *Queen Victoria, Born to Succeed*.

government. William IV was forced not only to summon back the reforming Whigs but also to threaten the Lords that their ranks would be swollen by the creation of new peerages unless reform was passed. So the peers, including most of the bishops, yielded – and found that, after all, reform did not spell revolution. As the result of the Reform Act of 1832 no more than a fifth of adult men in England and Wales, and no women at all, possessed the vote. The Tories usually collected the largest number of votes although they were generally outnumbered in the Commons by the Whigs in coalition with small groups such as the Irish and the radicals. In the unstable political situation thus created, moderate reform was both the minimum and the maximum that could be successful.

Moderate reform had to include church reform. The alternative was obvious in an atmosphere still thick with talk about disestablishing and disendowing the Church of England. In Ireland there was what seemed to many like a rehearsal for drastic action in England: the foundation in 1833 of Ecclesiastical Commissioners with about £150,000 a year derived largely from mergers of underpopulated dioceses and from an income tax on the richer incumbents. In a clause dropped in response to the hostility of the Lords, the authors of this Church Temporalities Act had originally provided that any surplus in the funds of the new commissioners was 'to be applied to such purposes as Parliament shall hereafter appoint and direct'. Philip Pusey, a brother of the more famous theologian Edward, translated a German hymn dating from the terrible period of the Thirty Years' War. It expressed what many sons and daughters of the United Church of England and Ireland were feeling in 1834:

> See round thine ark the hungry billows curling;
> See how they foes their banners are unfurling;
> Lord, while their darts envenomed they are hurling,
>   Thou canst preserve us.

Of crucial importance in re-establishing the Church of England's popular position was the need to meet financial grievances. Most Englishmen resented the collection in the parishes of compulsory tithes to support the parson, and of compulsory rates to repair the church. Until 1868 Parliament was unwilling to abolish compulsory church rates in England, and disputes continued; but this grievance declined in practical importance. Legal judgements made it clear that the rates could not be collected unless authorized by the churchwardens and the majority of the council known as the 'vestry'. Dissenters were entitled to vote in the election of both authorities, and thus church rates lapsed in many towns and cities – in Birmingham, for example. At least this was better for the Nonconformists than a scheme which the House of Commons accepted at one stage, to repair all the parish churches out of taxes.

Over tithes, Parliament did something. The Tithe Commutation Act of 1836 ended the quarrels between tithe-owners and the local farmers over the interpretation of the ancient law that a tenth of all the produce must be sacrificed to the Lord, to his priests or to the laymen who had over the centuries acquired this privilege. In future local bargains were to be struck – as they already had been in about a thousand parishes – commuting payment in kind for cash. The sum of money was to be based on the average of the prices of corn, oats and barley over seven years. Special arrangements were to be made for market-gardeners and for the growers of fruit and hops, and disputes were to be decided by Tithe Commissioners. In 1891 all responsibility for tithes was fixed on the shoulders of landlords not tenants. It was an additional easing of the relationship between a county parson and his less wealthy parishioners.

The disadvantages to the clergy were considerable, although largely unexpected. They could not profit, as they had previously done, from improvements in land values and, because agricultural prices fell disastrously during the last quarter of the nineteenth century, £100 worth of tithes in 1835 was to be worth less than £67 in 1901. It was 'the Church's worst financial crisis since the middle of the sixteenth century.'[3] In the 1880s and 1890s the incomes of many parish priests in the

---

[3] G. F. A. Best, *Temporal Pillars* (Cambridge, 1964), p. 471. This is the standard history of Queen Anne's Bounty and the Ecclesiastical Commissioners.

countryside fell by about a third. In 1893 a report to the Convocation of Canterbury observed 'that this clerical distress is not only very severe but also widespread, and that it has been borne with the noble spirit of patient endurance.' It was in response to this financial crisis that the custom began (and continued until the 1970s) of giving to the parson the collection on Easter Day. But the new custom showed how much the atmosphere had improved since the old days of quarrels over compulsory tithes. The clergy were both poorer and more popular.

In their financial problems they looked for help to a central authority. They did not now look in vain, for the Ecclesiastical Commissioners created by Sir Robert Peel brought about the overdue administrative reformation which had hitherto seemed impossible. Peel deserves to be remembered for the feat. A distinguished historian of the Victorian age remarked that 'it is an arguable proposition that if any one man saved the Church of England, it was Sir Robert Peel.'[4]

The son of a rich Lancashire cotton-spinner, Peel could seem to various eyes at various times a coldly efficient administrator, a coldly obstinate conservative, and a coldly cynical traitor to the Tory cause. But his letters show that he was a churchman no less devout than was his brother, a clergyman. He was eager to discuss the moral aspects of politics with his former tutor, Bishop Lloyd of Oxford, and warm feelings inspired those changes in his policies which brought him the hatred of more extreme conservatives. He grew to be convinced that some reforms were essential – Catholic emancipation, Parliamentary and ecclesiastical reform, the highly controversial grant out of taxes to the Roman Catholic seminary at Maynooth in Ireland in 1845, and eventually the repeal in 1846 of the corn laws which had kept the industrial workers' food dear by protecting the prices charged for grain by English farmers against foreign competition. With a rare courage Peel was perfectly ready to sacrifice his popularity with his own party, and his career, to his new convictions about his duty; and in the end, he was also prepared to sacrifice his party's prospects of

---

[4] George Kitson Clark, *The Making of Victorian England*, p. 156.

power. It has been said with justice that this unemotional man invented the Victorian idea of politics as morality.[5]

Commissioners appointed by Parliament to inquire into the Church of England's 'revenues and duties' met for the first time in Peel's home in February 1835. Next year they were converted into an executive by an Act of Parliament sponsored by Peel's Whig successors. The explanation of this procedure is that during the 1830s, and for a considerable period later, it was thought acceptable that the government, as it hesitantly extended its interests in the welfare of the public, should operate through boards or committees containing a strong voluntary element, rather than through a civil service still very small. The Ecclesiastical Commissioners were conceived in this context. They were expected to prepare 'orders' for endorsement by the Privy Council and where necessary bills for Parliament, and at first it was thought that a few bishops and a few lay nominees of the government would be adequate to supervise the secretary and his assistants in this limited programme. By 1850 it was apparent that all the diocesan bishops must be commissioners, at least in name, and that three Church Estates Commissioners must be appointed, two of them salaried, to take the lead in the business which grew more complicated year after year. The Earl of Chichester served (or domineered) as First Church Estates Commissioner 1850–78, and Lord Stanhope then filled this seat until 1905.

Because there was never any radical change after the withdrawal of Peel's innovating hand, the Ecclesiastical Commissioners never became a government department answerable to Parliament through a minister. They retained a degree of independence thought necessary in the 1830s if reform was ever to triumph over the opposition of vested interests in the House of Lords and in the Church at large. Inevitably, however, the initiative at the most vital points in the development of this powerful office had to come from the government, for the Church of England possessed no effective assembly of its own. Nor did it possess courts of its own with effective powers. The

---

[5] Norman Gash wrote the best biography of Peel (London, 1976) and W. J. Baker an account of Charles Lloyd, *Beyond Port and Prejudice* (Orono, Maine, 1981).

highest ecclesiastical court, the Court of Delegates established
in 1534, was quietly abolished in 1833; its functions were
vested in the Judicial Committee of the Privy Council. A more
comprehensive scheme to reform the church courts was abandoned, as being (as one exasperated reformer put it) 'of
second-rate importance and of first-rate difficulty'. This was
not a period when the Established Church seemed capable of
reforming itself.[6]

The respectable way for clergymen to resist the Ecclesiastical Commissioners was to complain not about the government's
initiative but about the Church's centralization.[7] There was
some substance in such complaints. The leading commissioners, whether bishops or laymen, always knew how to look after
themselves, and their staff were paid at civil service rates to
deal with clergymen often much poorer. The meetings had to
be in London – suggestions of decentralization were made, but
defeated easily – and in practice that meant that the control
was exercised by a small number of men, effectively controlled
by nothing except their consciences. Nor were the staff exempt
from human frailty. C. K. Murray, who shaped the work of the
office as the commissioners' secretary 1836–49, had to flee to
Australia having used some of their funds for his own speculations in railway shares. The suspicion which surrounded the
Ecclesiastical Commissioners resulted in an unwillingness to
insist that their work should be merged with that of a much
smaller but older-established office dealing with the clergy,
Queen Anne's Bounty. In 1830 when John Paterson could not
continue as Treasurer of Queen Anne's Bounty after applying
£30,000 of its funds to his own purposes, or in 1871 when his
successor was persuaded to retire at the age of eighty-seven, it
might have seemed that the case for reform and a merger was
overwhelming; but it did not overwhelm until 1948.

Fortunately one of the bishops, C. J. Blomfield of London,

[6] The background was studied by Olive Brose, *Church and Parliament: The
Reshaping of the Church of England 1828–1860* (Oxford, 1959), and Richard Brent,
Liberal Anglican Politics: Whiggery, Religion and Reform 1830–41 (Oxford, 1987).
[7] Kenneth A. Thompson explored *Bureaucracy and Church Reform: A Study of the
Church of England 1800–1965* (Oxford, 1970).

was both willing and able to be the mastermind among the commissioners when Peel had lost office. Blomfield was himself not entirely a reformed churchman; he had been a non-resident incumbent and a tutor to young aristocrats. He was unwilling to sacrifice any of the income which he had taken over on becoming Bishop of London in 1828, and when he retired in 1856 it was only after insisting on a very large pension. His cure for the poverty of so many other Englishmen was to take a lead in the movement which produced the Poor Law of 1834 and so created the hated workhouses which Dickens portrayed in *Oliver Twist*. All this made Blomfield the most unpopular of all the bishops. But he was a bold, tireless and very capable administrator both in his own diocese and on the new commission. The Archbishop of York confessed that 'till Blomfield comes, we all sit and mend our pens, and talk about the weather.'

For long many in the Church refused to believe that the commissioners would prove permanent or powerful. Church finance was a field where by tradition the diocesan bishops were theoretically supreme, although in practice almost powerless. But gradually it was seen that there was no alternative to extending and prolonging the commissioners' mandate; for the need was undeniable.

In 1832 Peel's Evangelical brother-in-law, Lord Henley, had issued a *Plan of Church Reform* which had fastened on two necessities: there must be more equality in the incomes of the bishops, and some of the endowments of the cathedrals must be used to sustain pastoral work in the parishes. Loud were the protests of bishops and cathedrals, but gradually action was taken – although not nearly such radical action as Henley had wanted. Most of the bishops were now paid £4,000 a year (but had to meet heavy expenses out of their own pockets), and the deans of the cathedrals £1,000. The money thus released was used to bring the stipends of parish priests looking after more than two thousand people to £200 (and proportionately for smaller numbers). Many new parishes were created; too many, for the number doubled between 1850 and 1900 and had to be reduced in the next century. In 1888 grants for curates in the poorest areas were added, although it was not until 1907 that some arrangements were made for the clergy's pensions, encouraging them to retire.

In all these reforms, the rights of the parishes' private patrons were safeguarded – but with the authority of Parliament, these commissioners had the will and the power to treat the wealth of the mightiest cathedral as belonging to the Church as a whole. It was the decisive move away from the medieval idea of the Church as a collection of corporations and office-holders with inviolable rights. In its own way it mattered as much as the suppression of the monasteries under Henry VIII.

THE EVANGELICALS

'Victorian England was religious.' So Professor Owen Chadwick's masterly two-volume study of *The Victorian Church*, published in 1966–70, began. A similar assessment was made in Sir Robert Ensor's volume in the *Oxford History of England*. 'No one will ever understand Victorian England', he wrote, 'who does not appreciate that among highly civilized, in contradistinction to more primitive, countries it was one of the most religious that the world has known. Moreover its particular type of Christianity laid a peculiarly direct emphasis upon conduct; for, though it recognized both grace and faith as essential to salvation, it was in practice also very largely a doctrine of salvation by works. This type, which had come to dominate churchmen and Nonconformists alike, may be called, using the term in its broad sense, Evangelicalism.'[8]

What, then, was Victorian Evangelicalism?

The attack on desolate Sabbaths in the third chapter of *Little Dorrit* was not the only occasion on which Dickens expressed contempt for the Evangelicals. In *Bleak House*, for example, we meet Mrs Jellyby, who cares so much for the natives of Borrioboola-Gha that she neglects her own children. Many

---

[8] R. K. A. Ensor, *England 1870–1914* (Oxford, 1936), p. 137. A similar verdict was reached in G. M. Young's *Victorian England: Portrait of an Age* (annotated by George Kitson Clark, Oxford, 1977).

other Victorian novels provide satirical or hostile portraits;
Anthony Trollope's sketch of Obadiah Slope the oily chaplain
in *Barchester Towers* was somewhat more benevolent than the
portraiture in his mother's novel, *The Vicar of Wexhill*.[9] And
some famous exposures of Evangelical homes were published
by writers outside the realm of fiction.

Two books, Samuel Butler's *The Way of All Flesh* and Sir
Edmund Gosse's *Father and Son*, have, indeed, often been taken
as accounts of typical childhoods stifled by Evangelicalism.
Published in 1903 and 1907, they were greeted as key documents in the reaction against Victorianism and they have
certainly deserved their status as modern classics about the
artist as a frustrated, misunderstood, cruelly ill-treated young
man. But it is improbable that the childhoods which they
described were typical of Evangelical homes. Samuel Butler
frankly disliked his parents. His portraits of Theobald and
Christina Pontifex corresponded with the reality of his actual
parents in patches, and other rectories contained parents like
them – the father without the power of independent thought or
the capacity to communicate at any deep level with the new
generation, exhorting his parishioners and chastising his children as a matter of duty; the mother frightened of the father
and of life in general. But there is no evidence that Canon and
Mrs Butler were as cruel to their son as he was to be to their
memories. Edmund Gosse was far more affectionate when
painting his portrait of his father. It may be taken as a largely
accurate account of that unhappy man and of the congregation
to which he was the unpaid preacher. But Philip Gosse and
that congregation belonged to a group of extreme Puritans
known as the Brethren. And he was a recluse even before he
became a widower, his main work being the writing of books on
marine zoology based on solitary study.

Both *The Way of All Flesh* and *Father and Son* were poisoned by
the bitterness of the debate aroused by Charles Darwin's
science. Samuel Butler while an undergraduate expected to be

---

[9] There was a chapter on 'The Low Church Contribution' in Margaret Maison,
Search Your Soul, Eustace: A Survey of the Religious Novel in the Victorian Age (London,
1961), but Elisabeth Jay, *The Religion of the Heart* (Oxford, 1979), was a more
thorough treatment of the Evangelicals in Victorian fiction.

ordained. When he had discovered that he was no longer a Christian, his central interests became those of an amateur scientist, arguing that evolution was not so purposeless as the Darwinians tended to believe. He despised men such as his father, whose faith seemed untroubled. Edmund Gosse knew that his father's most heartfelt book had been a religious response to the new science. Pathetically, old Philip Gosse had attempted to argue that God had made the world just as Genesis said – but with the fossils already in the rocks, as a test for the faith of the Victorians. This did not destroy all the value of Philip Gosse's research (indeed, Edmund Gosse wrote a conventional biography which praised him), but it was hard for a son to take such a father with intellectual seriousness.[10]

The group to which Philip Gosse belonged was part of a much wider stirring of interest in the idea of the perfect Christian, often coupled with the idea of the perfect world. Another such group was the Catholic Apostolic Church, the name taken by the followers of Edward Irving. As a young minister of the Church of Scotland Irving was equally effective among the poor in Glasgow and (from 1822) among the fashionable in London, but he became more and more fascinated by the traditional faith in the Second Coming of Christ to reign for a thousand years. *The Coming of Christ in Glory and Majesty* (the title of a book by a Spanish Jesuit, which he translated in 1827) now seemed to Irving to be the one hope of sinful mankind; and for the Church his main hope was that the tongue-speaking and charismatic excitements which broke out around his preaching in 1831 were signs that the end, the millennium, was near. He came to believe that the Lord's Supper must be restored to be the central act of Christian worship every Sunday, as part of a general restoration of practices recorded in the Acts of the Apostles. He also became fascinated by the theological question about Christ, arguing that God the Son had assumed human nature including its sinfulness. For these indiscretions and heresies he was deprived of his ministry by the Church of Scotland and he died in

---

[10] See Philip Henderson, *Samuel Butler: The Incarnate Bachelor* (London, 1953), and Edmund Gosse, *Father and Son*, ed. James Hepburn (Oxford, 1974).

1834 soon after the start of the Catholic Apostolic Church. His most effective ally, and virtual successor, was a rich banker, Henry Drummond, who inspired and subsidized the new Church until his own death in 1860. Under his influence the Catholic Apostolics developed a strong attachment to High Church ritual. Many of them worshipped in Anglican churches when they could not sustain a congregation of their own.[11]

In contrast, the 'Brethren' enjoyed neither the delights of ecclesiastical ritual (to them mere relics of paganism) nor the blessings of an undivided leadership. It was their misfortune to be led by more than one man with too strong a personality and too long a life. J. N. Darby was a young Irish clergyman, eccentric in appearance and theology but charismatic in his influence on a disciple and never afraid to tackle an enemy. Not for nothing was his middle name Nelson. His disputes with the Anglican authorities were inevitable; he was indignant when the 'Established Church Home Mission' was closed down as being too enthusiastic, and proceeded to write an article entitled 'Parochial arrangements destructive of order in the Church' and a pamphlet called *The notion of a clergyman the sin against the Holy Ghost*. But his enthusiasm attracted some remarkable brethren into a movement which, because it was launched in Plymouth in 1831, was called by the public 'the Plymouth Brethren'. It usually called a chapel 'the Room' and it did its best to be completely cut off from the vanities of the world. Several adherents were well-off and highly educated, but they gave away their wealth and accepted a thorough fundamentalism. The Brethren gathered every Sunday to 'break bread' together in the Lord's Supper, and any one was entitled to preside or to preach if he could persuade others that this was the will of the Lord. However, Darby's leadership did not always commend itself as being divinely inspired, so that this small perfectionist movement was split by bitter disputes.[12]

---

[11] A. L. Drummond studied *Edward Irving and His Circle* (London, 1938), and J. F. C. Harrison *Popular Millenarianism 1780–1850* (London, 1979).

[12] See Harold Rowdon, *The Origins of the Brethren* (London, 1967), and F. Roy Coad, *A History of the Brethren Movement* (London, 1968).

If we want to understand the Victorian Evangelicals, it is far more relevant to see how with their quiet and steady leadership they absorbed the fruits of powerful spiritual revivals.

The revival beginning in the USA in 1857, and reaching England two years later, has been called the 'Second Evangelical Awakening'. To some extent it deserves that grand title. Many of its gatherings on both sides of the Atlantic were as full of excitement as the congregations of Whitefield and the Wesleys, and its leaders could travel around and address evening meetings far more easily than the pioneers could, thanks to the steamship, the railway and gas light. Some striking characters became famous in this way – Richard Weaver the English miner who had previously been Undaunted Dick the boxer, converted to Christ when he saw blood streaming down the face of his opponent; Reginald Radcliffe, formerly a solicitor, who sent out assistants on to the streets of Liverpool urging men to come to the services conducted with shock tactics every half hour in the mission hall; and Mrs Phoebe Palmer as the pioneer of the women preachers, now at last beginning to be acceptable to male sinners. The hymn 'Stand up, stand up for Jesus' is a lingering echo of the enthusiasm, although it seems that in general the Evangelicals of the Church of England held aloof, worried by the emotionalism. They put their trust in quieter methods of evangelism leading to church membership and practical social work. And the churches where this sober Gospel was preached became the spiritual homes of many of those converted by revivalist preachers.

The most effective of all those who were converted was Dwight L. Moody. A rough but energetic businessman who was never ordained, he accepted the Evangelical Gospel in 1857, in Chicago. Three years later he felt called to full-time leadership in Christian work, particularly in the Young Men's Christian Association, and in 1875 the revival which he led reached London. Another event of 1875 was the holding of the first Keswick Convention, a rallying point for Evangelicals seeking commitment and inspiration in a definitely English version of American revivalism. Seven years later Moody made a great impact on the young men of Cambridge, transforming some privileged undergraduates into missionaries. The Cambridge Intercollegiate Christian Union, like the annual Keswick Convention, became a powerful spiritual force.[13]

Definitely Evangelical teaching was now legitimate in the Church of England. That was established in 1850, when an attempt by the Bishop of Exeter to resist the appointment of George Gorham to a parish in his diocese was ended by the Judicial Committee of the Privy Council.[14] In 1865 the Church Association was formed to assert the merits of such teaching more militantly, and under the editorship of Alexander Haldane the Evangelical and Tory *Record* was positively vituperative in its commentary on events and personalities. By and large, however, the Evangelicals were on the defensive theologically, first against the Oxford Movement in the Church with its revival of Catholicism, then against the Darwinian movement in science with its revival of unbelief; and they produced no very significant theologian. Their intellectual weapons were already outdated when they used them, for they assumed the validity of their interpretation of the authority of the Bible and of the Reformation (seldom of Calvinism in particular). That ought not to have been taken for granted. They had the post-Reformation tradition of the Church of England on their side, and proved it; but the nineteenth-century question could not be settled by any appeal to the past. It was about truth.[15]

More impressive than the Evangelical defences of an old theology were the practical activities of men such as J. C. Miller, vicar of St Martin's in the heart of Birmingham for twenty years from 1846 and the inventor of children's services. Hundreds of vicars or rectors were as dedicated to pastoral

---

[13] See J. E. Orr, *The Second Evangelical Awakening* (London, 1949), and for a more critical study John Kent, *Holding the Fort* (London, 1978). J. C. Pollock, *Moody without Sankey* and *The Keswick Story* (London, 1963–64), presented the facts simply and sympathetically.

[14] J. C. S. Nias studied *Gorham and the Bishop of Exeter* (London, 1951).

[15] The case to the contrary was argued by Peter Toon, *Evangelical Theology: The Response to Tractarianism* (London, 1979). But documents illustrating *Religious Controversies of the Nineteenth Century* were edited by A. O. J. Cockshut (London, 1966), and by their very silence about contributions from this school they provided one more proof of the sad intellectual isolation of the Evangelicals.

work as he was, and by the 1860s the Church Pastoral Aid Society, one of the Evangelicals' favourite charities, was supporting five hundred curates. The highest placed Evangelical (but not extreme) clergyman was John Bird Sumner, appointed Archbishop of Canterbury in 1848 after working for twenty years as bishop of the very large diocese of Chester. While archbishop he made his mark chiefly by his simplicity; in contrast with the previous prince-archbishops, he would pick up his umbrella and walk from Lambeth Palace to the House of Lords. His brother Charles was another moderately Evangelical bishop, appointed to the see of Winchester at the age of thirty-seven on the recommendation of Lady Conygham (one of George IV's mistresses), but thoroughly justifying the strange appointment by his charm and pastoral energy. More Evangelical appointments were made in the years when Lord Palmerston was Prime Minister (1855–65, with an interval of fifteen months). Palmerston was bored by clergymen, but he was advised by Lord Shaftesbury; Lady Shaftesbury was almost certainly his illegitimate daughter. And the Evangelical peer produced for him nineteen hard-working, if dull, pastors.[16]

Shaftesbury himself possessed a character more interesting than any Evangelical clergyman's – and far more complex. He often wrote in his egotistical journal, which foolishly he did not destroy, that people wanted him only for his title – together with many other uncomplimentary remarks about his contemporaries in Church and State. The truth was that he had become too hard a fighter to arouse love in those closest to him. Although as a young man he had shown a considerable interest in science, he developed into an intolerant fundamentalist who held that 'Satan reigns in the intellect, God in the heart of man'. As he moved from the chair of a committee to the chair of a public meeting, he tried to make up for his lack of fresh thought by being pompously garrulous. And he was quick to reply by coldness to what he thought to be a personal slight. Yet few suspected that he was quite so bitter and depressed as

---

[16] Michael Hennell introduced some leading Victorian Evangelicals in *Sons of the Prophets* (London, 1979).

he told his journal night after night, and what they knew was that his experience of human suffering had made him determined to relieve it. To know about the suffering of his childhood is to be ready to forgive him the sourness of his adult relationships – and to learn about his manhood is to admire him for the self-discipline which he maintained when not writing up his journal.

His father, who was chairman of the committee work of the House of Lords for forty years, presumably transmitted an appetite for public work. The fact that his father was a large landowner enabled him to borrow money – as he had to, until he was fifty – so that he could devote his life to public service; and the constituency which first elected him to the House of Commons was controlled by his mother's father, the Duke of Marlborough. But more deeply important for his character was the fact that his parents were loveless and grossly neglectful, so that his childhood would have been utterly miserable without his nurse. She introduced him to the Evangelical message, but he does not seem to have undergone any dramatic crisis of religious conversion. His conversion to the duty to care about the poor was not too profound to prevent his first years in Parliament taking the pattern normal for a young, handsome and ambitious Tory aristocrat. Probably he would never have become a great man had the misery of his own childhood not given him a motive to help the wretched – a motive which gradually become his predominant characteristic.

He agreed in 1833 to take over the Parliamentary sponsorship of the Ten Hours Bill from a Tory MP (Michael Sadler) who had lost his seat in the recent election. At that stage he had never visited a factory, and the approach from the factory reformers filled him with 'astonishment and doubt and terror'. His chief, Sir Robert Peel, who as we have observed was courageous in other directions, was convinced that the restriction of working hours by Parliament would so damage the economy that unemployment would increase disastrously. Even John Wesley had approved of the employment of children in factories. When the use of children was restricted to six and a half hours a day in 1833, the reform was accompanied by gloomy prophecies of economic disaster. The factory owners were able to embarrass the young MP by proving that his father's labourers in Dorset were much worse off than their own employees, and his discomfiture was completed when he lost his seat as part of Peel's defeat. When the Ten Hours Act was passed in 1847 he was therefore not able to sponsor it. And when the factory owners got round that legislation by working 'relays' or a shift system, he was denounced by the workers' leaders for suggesting as a compromise the change of the maximum of ten hours a day to the maximum of sixty hours a week.[17]

The destruction of Shaftesbury's career meant, however, that he concentrated entirely on religious and charitable work, earning his eventual reputation as the Working Man's Friend and his inappropriate commemoration by the statue of the Greek god of love in Piccadilly Circus. He became president of innumerable Evangelical societies (including the Bible Society and the Parker Society to reprint the works of the divines of the English Reformation). He became the architect of the humane Lunacy Act of 1845 and gave countless hours to his work as one of the commissioners supervising the new lunatic asylums. He was also a mainstay of the Public Health Commission formed in 1848 to force sanitation into one town after another – although until 1872 one death in three was still to be caused by infectious diseases. He did more than any other man to regulate the lodging houses where so many working-class people had to live. He befriended the blind, the cripples, the destitute incurables; the women and children wearing their bodies out in factories or underground in the mines or as 'gangs' at work on the farms; the exploited flower-girls and millinery workers; the boys made to climb chimneys as sweeps; the children beaten into being acrobats; the vagrant boys or adult thieves whose only hope of escape from a life of crime was the scarcely believable luxury of emigration or training; even the cabmen who needed cheap and respectable clubs. He insisted on denouncing the British profit from the opium trade imposed on China; he probed into the conditions of work in Indian factories; he defended the liberties of Italians and Poles;

---

[17] See J. T. Ward, *The Factory Movement 1830–55* (London, 1962).

he fought to restrict the vivisection of animals in laboratories. His chief pleasure became his visits to the 'ragged school' run by volunteers for very poor boys and girls, but much of his time was given to the personal inspection of scenes of work and poverty in London and the industrial towns, scenes that made him weep.[18]

When we seek to understand the strength of the Victorian Evangelicals, we ought to see Shaftesbury finding a ragged boy asleep in the roller used in Regent's Park. We ought to think of Elizabeth Gilbert, the blind daughter of a bishop, opening the first workshop for blind men in her home in 1853. We ought to remember the missions to workers in jobs which most of the country was happy to ignore. Evangelicals noticed the navvies who built the Crystal Palace which was the marvel of London; and Catherine Marsh made them seem marvellous in the book she wrote about her work among them, *English Hearts and English Hands*. They cared for the deepsea fishermen who found cheap alcohol the best way of forgetting the cruel conditions on their little boats in the North Sea. The Victorian Evangelicals did not merely condemn. Nor did they live only among the respectable. They followed their Master in seeking out the lost. And without intending to do this, they laid the foundations of the twentieth-century Welfare State by putting into practice their acknowledgement of a duty to interfere in the results of the working of the laws of capitalist economics.[19]

Such lives impressed Mary Anne Evans, who used the pen-name George Eliot and whose mind had travelled far from an Evangelical youth. Her first poem had been pious enough to merit publication in the *Christian Observer* in 1840. But she read Sir Walter Scott's novels and her imagination was stretched; she noticed that miners nearby, while Methodist, were certainly not moral; and she made unorthodox friends. Early in 1842 she told her father that she could no longer go to church.

---

[18] There are modern biographies by G. F. A. Best (London, 1964), Georgina Battiscombe (London, 1974), and Geoffrey Finlayson (London, 1981).

[19] See David Roberts, *Victorian Origins of the Welfare State* (New Haven, Conn., 1960); Kathleen Heasman, *Evangelicals in Action* (London, 1962); Ian Bradley, *The Call to Seriousness* (London, 1976).

Already a widower, he was heartbroken. As she wrote to him during this crisis: 'While I admire and cherish much of what I believe to have been the moral teaching of Jesus himself, I consider the system of doctrines built upon the facts of his life and drawn as to its notions from Jewish materials to be most dishonourable to God and most pernicious in its influence on individual and social happiness.' Yet she never forgot. 'What she brought from her Evangelical background,' the far from pious F. R. Leavis wrote, 'was a radically reverent attitude towards life, a profound seriousness of the kind that is a first condition of any real intelligence, and an interest in human nature that made her a great psychologist.'[20]

THE OXFORD MOVEMENT

The Oxford Movement arose in circumstances scarcely favouring its growth as a spiritual renewal which was in the end to transform the Church of England and to influence both the worldwide Anglican Communion and the Roman Catholic Church. For it was originally a protest against the reform of Anglicanism in Ireland – a protest made by clergymen in Oxford University and applauded by clergymen in English country parishes.

It could not be plausibly argued that the apparatus of Anglicanism in Ireland did not need reform. When he moved to hew it down in 1868, Gladstone compared it with 'some tall tree of noxious growth, lifting its head to heaven and poisoning the atmosphere of the land so far as its shadow can extend'. In the 1830s a government census showed that just over eighty per cent of the Irish population was Roman Catholic and about eight per cent Presbyterian. Yet the Church of Ireland, united with the Church of England by Act of Parliament in 1801, was more notorious than the Church of England itself for the combination of wealth and inefficiency in its leadership and for the non-residence of many of its parish clergy. A considerable

---

[20] F. R. Leavis, *The Great Tradition* (London, 1948), p. 24. The standard biography is Gordon Haight, *George Eliot* (Oxford, 1968).

number of its parishes did not even have churches in use. Particular reasons why it was hated included the restriction of government grants for education to the schools of this Established Church, and the obligation imposed on the peasants to pay tithes and church-rates to Protestant clergymen, often non-resident and usually regarded as heretical intruders. The extravagance of this colonial Church's finances was paraded in Dublin by the existence of two Anglican cathedrals (St Patrick's where Swift had been dean and Christ Church). The cynical attitude to Irish ecclesiastial affairs traditionally taken by English politicians was shown once again when in 1831 Earl Grey, the Whig Prime Minister, casually offered the archbishopric of Dublin first to the most faithfully Whig bishop in England, Henry Bathurst of Norwich, aged eighty-seven, and then to an Oxford tutor, Richard Whateley, of whom he had not previously heard but who was recommended as clever and liberal if eccentric. The Archbishop of Dublin had an income larger than all but six of the English bishops – although three Irish Anglican bishops were richer, the Archbishop of Armagh being almost twice as rich.

The Church Temporalities Act of 1833 provided that when vacancies occurred two of the four Irish archbishoprics should be demoted into bishoprics, and there should be ten mergers between dioceses. The estates previously managed or mismanaged by the agents of the bishops were to be reduced gradually, the bishops being increasingly paid by new Ecclesiastical Commissioners – and paid at levels more uniform and more adjusted to the levels on which lesser clergymen had to live. Underpopulated parishes were also to be merged (together with the two Deaneries in Dublin), and the richer incumbents were to be taxed for the benefit of the poorer. The Anglican parishes were no longer to have the power to levy rates for church repair or other purposes, but were for the first time to be supervised by archdeacons with power. Tithes remained a source of grievance, but in fairly recent years more than half the parishes had already commuted their tithes for cash payments, and the process was to continue until in 1838 a new system was enforced by Parliament, turning all tithes at three-quarters of their former value into a rent-charge payable by landlords not tenants, and granting a million pounds to the Anglican clergy in lieu of unpaid tithes.[21]

All this surely constituted the minimum of reform necessary to satisfy for the time being the grievances of Roman Catholics and the consciences of Anglicans. It certainly did not spell disaster to Irish Anglicanism; when the next religious census was taken, in 1861, the numerical relationship of Anglicans and Roman Catholics in the total population was virtually unchanged. Yet in the 1830s many Anglicans were outraged by these reforms, for they were enforced by a Parliament for which Roman Catholics and Protestant Dissenters had just been permitted to vote. The Irish Anglican bishops, whose views were confused, had not been consulted formally and the Irish clergy had no means of making their opinions known. It was the imminent likelihood that the Westminster Parliament would accept these reforms that caused John Keble to preach his sermon on 'National Apostasy'. John Henry Newman always remembered that date, Sunday, 14 July 1833 as 'the start of the religious movement' of which he became the greatest leader.

It was the 'Oxford Movement' and the sermon was preached in St Mary's, the university church; appropriately, for the university was a very rich institution monopolized by Anglicans, teeming with irrationalities and remote from most contemporary realities. All its members had been compelled to declare their acceptance of the Thirty-nine Articles. Many of its graduates became clergymen without any further training, yet no instruction in pastoral work was available. The wealth lay in the hands of the colleges and most of the power was exercised by the heads of these houses who were clergymen, as were all on the teaching staff above a certain seniority. To call most of the fellows of the colleges teachers would, however, be an exaggeration, since they were young men waiting for appointment to a parish (often a parish where the college was the appointing patron), largely in order to be able to marry. The 'tutors' among the fellows delivered lectures but under-

---

[21] D. H. Akenson studied *The Church of Ireland: Ecclesiastical Reform and Revolution 1800–1885* (New Haven, Conn., 1971).

graduates had to pay extra for any private tuition, and for most of them university life was neither intellectually nor morally challenging. A young man reading for a pass (not honours) degree could afford to drink considerably more than he read. Chapel attendance, although compulsory, was lethargic. The situation at Cambridge was roughly similar, except that Dissenters were allowed in as undergraduates (they were not permitted to take degrees), and the position given to mathematics had kept alive a tradition of harder thinking, at least in the intellectual elite of the undergraduate body.[22]

The lives of Pusey and Keble show the real but limited kind of sanctity that was possible for the leaders of a movement with these origins.

When Edward Bouverie Pusey, then a young Fellow of Oriel College, went to Germany to learn the language and the new biblical scholarship in 1825, he believed that only two men in Oxford already knew German. When he had heard a few lectures analysing the Bible, the thought struck him: 'This will all come upon us in England and how utterly unprepared for it we are!' On his return home he found that a Cambridge man, H. J. Rose, had issued some lectures claiming that German theology amounted to no more than rationalism; so he published a reply, admitting that there was some pernicious rationalism but blaming it on the dead orthodoxy of Lutheranism, not on the contemporary scholars.

On the strength of this unusually thorough preparation Pusey was appointed Regius Professor of Hebrew in 1828, when he was not yet thirty. Wrapped in his studies, he did not read Keble's sermon on 'National Apostasy' – and his studies were of a technical rather than philosophical kind, so that his own writing tended to be a string of quotations. But the three *Tracts for the Times* which he contributed to the series edited by Newman were, as Richard Church later reckoned, 'like the

---

[22] The hothouse atmosphere was caught in Sir Geoffrey Faber's *Oxford Apostles* (London, 1933). The story of reform was told by W. R. Ward, *Victorian Oxford* (London, 1965), by A. J. Engel, *From Clergyman to Don* (Oxford, 1983), and by Sheldon Rothblatt on Cambridge, *A Revolution of the Dons* (London, 1968). On the wider needs, see Michael Sanderson, *The Universities in the Nineteenth Century* (London, 1975).

advance of a battery of heavy artillery on a field when the battle has been hitherto carried on by skirmishing and artillery'; and soon afterwards he launched a *Library of the Fathers* in translation (to be completed in almost fifty volumes over almost fifty years) and made such a generous gift to building new churches in London that he had to reduce his standard of living. He seemed all set to become the learned and devout, but aware and relevant, leader that Oxford University and the Church of England needed.

Then in 1839 his deeply loved wife, Maria, died. Already his relationship with her had brought him severe emotional problems. Forbidden by his overbearing father to marry when he had fallen deeply in love as a student, he had absorbed himself in overwork and self-denial during the years of waiting. By the time that marriage proved possible he had become as inflexible as his father – inflexible in a regime of austerity which fatally damaged his wife's health. Now he was convinced that his previous self-discipline had not been severe enough to deflect the wrath of God which had thundered in the infliction of this overwhelming tragedy. The bereavement which lasted until his own death made him a recluse, refusing to dine with his colleagues or to enter his own drawing room. Often he worked all through the night as well as all through the day. To his surprise he was eventually able to smile again, but the smiles were to be very few. He also became a more extreme conservative, believing that God had punished him for his youthful liberalism, that an inflexible orthodoxy must now be part of a life of penitence. His isolation and general unpopularity increased when the Oxford Movement seemed to have become a nursery of converts to Rome.

He was revered as a holy man by those who knew him. The sermon for which he was condemned by the vice-chancellor of the university in 1843 was a devout exposition of the Holy Eucharist in line with the teachings of the Fathers, and at the time of Newman's sensational submission to Rome his own main preoccupation was the building of St Saviour's, a new church for the poor in Leeds, entirely at his own expense although anonymously. And he aroused holiness in others. He heard many private confessions and gave counsel. He it was who heard the vow of celibacy taken in 1841 by a young woman, Marian Hughes, who after further years of waiting because the superior of an Anglican religious order. He it was who guided the foundation of a small sisterhood in London in 1845, the first 'nunnery' to be set up in the Church of England since the Reformation. Three years later he was similarly the godfather at the birth of another sisterhood under the formidable Priscilla Lydia Sellon, an admiral's daughter. This second sisterhood became larger, and eventually popular, because of its work among the diseased poor of Plymouth and Devonport – work which Victorians could not deny was honourable work for Christian women, whatever they made of Pusey's appeals to precedents in ancient years. The first stable religious community for men was founded in Cowley, a suburb of Oxford, in 1866, by R. M. Benson, who had been deeply influenced by Pusey while an undergraduate. It was the Society of St John the Evangelist.[23]

He hated the word 'Puseyism', but his own answer to a correspondent's question, 'What is Puseyism?', was to define the holiness being sought in these six points:

1. High thoughts of the two sacraments.

2. High estimate of episcopacy as God's ordinance.

3. High estimate of the visible Church as the body where we are made and continue to be members of Christ.

4. Regard for ordinances, as directing our devotion and disciplining us, such as daily public prayers, fasts and feasts etc.

5. Regard for the visible part of devotion, such as the decoration of the house of God, which acts insensibly on the mind.

6. Reverence for and defence of the ancient Church, of which our own Church is looked upon as the representative to us, and by whose views and doctrines we interpret our own Church when her meaning is questioned or doubtful; in a word, reference to the ancient Church, instead of the Refor-

---

[23] Studies of this revival of the religious life include A. M. Allchin, *The Silent Rebellion* (London, 1958); T. J. Williams, *Priscilla Lydia Sellon* (revised, London, 1965); Michael Hill, *The Religious Order* (London, 1973). *Benson of Cowley* was edited by M. L. Smith (Oxford, 1980).

mers, as the ultimate expounder of the meaning of our Church.

Pusey never became a complete conservative. He granted that the universe had not been made in six days, and when he defended the accuracy of other passages of the Bible he did so with arguments which he genuinely reckoned to be scholarly. His advocacy of the Holy Communion as the central weekly act of worship in the parishes, and his decision to defend the 'ritualists' who revived medieval ceremonies dignifying this service, made him the enemy of those Conservatives such as Disraeli who linked ritualists with rationalists, 'rits' with 'rats', as disturbers of the peace. He was not sorry. Politically, as he wrote in a letter of 1865, 'I could not be a Conservative, i.e. I could not bind myself, nor risk the future of the Church, on the fidelity or wisdom of persons whose principle it is to keep what they think they can, and part with the rest. I believe that we are in the course of an inevitable revolution; that the days of Establishments are numbered, and that the Church has to look to her purity, liberty, faithfulness to Catholicism.'

But in his loyalty to the ancient Church he had abandoned the kind of intellectual development which could have been predicted before his wife's death and the isolation of the 1840s. In 1852, when a government commission was bent on making Oxford professorships more important and on opening college fellowships to life-long laymen, he wrote an hysterical pamphlet arguing that 'the aim of a university is not simply or mainly to cultivate the intellect'; a university existed to form minds 'which shall discharge aright whatever duties God, in his providence, shall appoint them' and because of this in a university 'all things must speak of God, refer to God, or they are atheistic.' When he was defeated, he wrote that 'Oxford is lost to the Church of England . . . there is nothing more to fight for.' But he fought on. He published a vast book completely rejecting other scholars' work on the Book of Daniel. In 1865 he assured a cheering Church Congress that 'faith lives above the clouds of human doubt, in the serene sunshine of the Eternal Light'; and he showed what that light had come to mean to him by opposing plans to revise the Authorized Version of the Bible

– perhaps forgetting that as a young man he had begun work on his own revision of the seventeenth-century English of the Old Testament. When for a time he was optimistic that the Vatican Council of 1870 might bring Anglicans and Roman Catholics nearer, the basis he recommended was one that left little room for development since 'the English Church preserves the entire faith, such as our Lord left it with the Apostles, to evangelize the world.' The decision of 1873 that the Athanasian Creed must still be recited in church at Christmas, Easter and other great festivals was due in no small measure to his insistence on the preservation of the ancient faith in its entirety. Here was a long, technical document full of curses against the unorthodox; but he had announced that he would resign his position in the Church of England were its use to be made optional.

His last substantial book appeared in his eightieth year: *What is of Faith as to Everlasting Punishment?* It showed the intelligence, grandeur and intense moral seriousness of the man. Hell fire need not be understood as material fire; God does not predestine anyone to it; 'none will be lost whom God can save without destroying in them his own gift of freewill'; after death there is a 'vestibule' for those who long for the Beatific Vision but are not yet ready for it. But the everlasting punishment of the obstinately wicked was to him a fact and he had a rule, on getting to bed, to confess every night that he was unworthy to lie down except in hell. In comparison, no other fact mattered. That was the context in which this holy man believed in the Holy Catholic Church and in the Holy Communion. However, after all Pusey was a professor until his death – and he deserves to be judged on intellectual grounds. There it must be said that his conservatism in responding to the challenges of the nineteenth century became tragically extreme during the last forty years or so of his influential life. He was intransigent at the many – too many – points where he thought Christianity was under threat. Because of his moral prestige, his failure at this point played no small part in holding up the reception of biblical scholarship in England and the necessary reinstatement of Christian theology. He set an example to the Victorians of a clergyman's duty to renounce independent thought on religious topics unless he was prepared to go through the agony of resigning his Holy Orders. The Germans complained that too much English theology was written within the sound of church bells.[24]

Until he won a scholarship to Oxford at the age of fourteen, John Keble's education was entirely in his home; and as his best-loved hymn, 'New every morning is the love', reminds us, his heart never left home. Home was a house in the small Gloucestershire town of Fairford. His father, born in that house in 1745, died there in 1834, and it was not until 1835 that John Keble felt free to become vicar of Hursley in Hampshire, a village almost entirely owned by a squire who had been an admiring pupil in Oxford. There he remained until his death in 1866. The squire would allow no Dissenter, let alone an atheist, among his tenants. The vicar would thwack boys slow to raise their caps to him, and would refuse to discuss 'infidelity', saying briefly to a young inquirer in 1851 that most of the men who had difficulties with Holy Scripture were 'too wicked to be reasoned with'. He denounced the State's provision of facilities for divorce in 1857. He was, however, powerless to make sure that brides entered his church as virgins; 'a village wedding is in general the most melancholy of all ceremonies to me'. Lamenting the lapse of the practice of confession of sins to a priest, he recorded 'how blindly I go about the parish, not knowing what men are really doing; and whenever I do make discoveries, they disclose a fearful state of things.'

Keble, although in the eyes of Oxford men a practical parish priest, lacked worldly wisdom and this accounted for three disastrous pieces of advice which he gave to Newman. He urged the publication of the journal (or *Remains*) left by a close friend of theirs, Hurrell Froude, who had died in his early thirties, a journal full of indiscreet remarks about the hatefully Protestant character of the Church of England.[25] His contribution to the series of *Tracts for the Times* drew from the mysticism of some of the Eastern Fathers the apparently dishonest doc-

---

[24] No modern study has replaced *The Life of E. B. Pusey* by his disciple, H. P. Liddon, and others in 4 volumes (London, 1893–97) and his *Spiritual Letters* (1898), but the essays in *Pusey Rediscovered*, ed. Perry Butler (London, 1983), are of high value.

[25] Piers Brendon studied *Hurrell Froude and the Oxford Movement* (London, 1974).

trine that some religious truth was so sacred that there must be 'reserve' when communicating it. And he urged the publication of Newman's Tract Ninety, which brought the series to a crashing end by arguing for a large measure of agreement between the Thirty-nine Articles and Roman Catholicism. Those three publications largely accounted for the reputation of the Oxford Movement (or 'Tractarians') as a movement where young men became morbidly self-absorbed or wrapped in mystic nonsense, and were deprived of any manly sense of the difference between truth and falsehood.

Why, then, was Keble College founded in Oxford as a national monument to this escapist country priest? And why did *The Christian Year*, Keble's book of poems published in 1827, run into almost a hundred printings in his lifetime, being more of a monument than the college, as Pusey declared at the college's opening? The explanation is that he gave an example of contentment by ministering to an obscure parish and by writing verses based on the Book of Common Prayer in an age when so many (including Newman) thought that, whether the Established Church was right or wrong, it could never be poetic. In country or town parishes many thousands of Anglicans, ordained or lay, whose religious opinions or sentiments might otherwise have led them towards Rome, felt a pride in belonging to and serving the Church of England because it was the Church to which John Keble had given his heart. Often they looked to such an example because their own bishop was too Protestant or too worldly; the first bishop to identify himself with the ideals of the Tractarians was W. K. Hamilton, who in 1854 took over the diocese of Salisbury. Gradually the heirs of the Tractarians became more confidently militant, organizing themselves into the English Church Union (1859) and enjoying the often vitriolic propaganda of the weekly *Church Times* (1863). But in his sermon of 1833 Keble had announced that the victory of the Church would be 'complete, universal, eternal' – and had implied that it would be not at all vulgar or loud. It showed his confidence in this victory that he was willing to take such trouble over daily services in his church, visiting the cottages, and preparing the young people for Confirmation. His poem 'Blest are the pure in heart' made

both a hymn and a self-portrait. He was the priest to whom
Pusey confessed. Thanks to the Oxford Movement, the Catholic religion as believed in, and practised by, Anglicans could
seem assured, beautiful and a school of saints.[26]

NEWMAN

It was supremely through the life of John Henry Newman that
the Oxford Movement first stirred the consciences of young
men and then moved and renewed more than one Church,
winning a greater influence in the twentieth century than in the
nineteenth. Partly because he had been an Evangelical while
young, Newman broke decisively away from the tradition that
those Anglicans who emphasized their Catholicism must be
'high and dry', formal in manner, legalist in argument, backward looking in theology, wedded to the social order of the old
England. The 'high and dry' tradition was embodied among
the Victorians by Henry Phillpotts, who was appointed Bishop
of Exeter by the Duke of Wellington's last act as Prime
Minister in 1830. He survived in that diocese until 1869,
having been engaged while bishop in more than fifty lawsuits
and in even more fierce attacks in the House of Lords on
proposals to change the old order in Church and State.[27]

The motto which Newman took as a cardinal was (in Latin)
'heart speaks to heart'. He fascinated many by his preaching
and writing as an Anglican priest, and when he had been
despised and rejected showed that he could revive that fascination by a classic among autobiographies, *Apologia pro Vita Sua*
(1864). The book was sparked off by two casual and mon-
strously unjust sentences in an article by the novelist, Charles

---

[26] See Georgina Battiscombe, *John Keble: A Study in Limitations* (London, 1963),
and Brian Martin, *John Keble: Priest, Professor, Poet* (London, 1976). Two useful
collections of documents are *The Mind of the Oxford Movement*, ed. Owen Chadwick
(London, 1960), and *The Oxford Movement*, ed. E. R. Fairweather (New York, 1964).
Geoffrey Rowell assessed the movement's influence in *The Vision Glorious* (Oxford,
1983).

[27] G. C. B. Davies provided a biography of *Henry Phillpotts, Bishop of Exeter*
(London, 1954).

Kingsley. 'Truth for its own sake has never been a virtue with
the Roman clergy. Father Newman informs us that it need not,
and on the whole ought not, to be; that cunning is the weapon
which heaven has given to the saints wherewith to withstand
the brute male force of the wicked world which marries and is
given in marriage.'[28] So Kingsley wrote. What he had in mind
in addition to Newman's failure to marry was his habit of
recommending 'reserve'. As an Anglican, that often meant in
practice a reticence in saying how Roman Catholic his restless-
ly changing convictions already were. There was a certain lack
of integrity in this position. But when Newman had became a
Roman Catholic the continuing 'reserve' in his conduct
amounted to no more than loyalty to his superiors in public. It
has rightly been suggested that 'Catholicism improved his
character'.[29] His private criticisms could not be kept secret,
and they wrecked his ambitions; for when he had made his
submission and therefore in theory had 'no further history of
my religious opinions to relate' (so he ended the *Apologia*), in
practice he distanced himself from the Roman Catholic authorities by retaining many Anglican attitudes. When he
defended papal infallibility on the ground that all Catholics
believed it, he did not wish to see it defined, and wrote that if he
had to give a religious toast after dinner 'I shall drink to the
Pope, if you please – still to Conscience first, and to the Pope
afterwards.' Illuminated by that very English remark, Newman's spiritually may be seen to rise above the controversies of
his time. It continued to appeal to Anglicans when they had
forgiven his desertion of their Church. He has also appealed
deeply to some Lutherans.[30] When the Second Vatican Council met a hundred years after the publication of his *Apologia*, the
growth of his influence on that time of brave renewal was such
that he could be called the Council's 'invisible father'.

---

[28] Newman's *Apologia* was edited by Martin Svaglic (Oxford, 1967). See also G.
Egner, *Apologia pro Charles Kingsley* (London, 1969).

[29] Robin Selby, *The Principle of Reserve in the Writings of John Henry, Cardinal Newman*
(Oxford, 1975), p. 42.

[30] The Swedish scholar, Yngve Brilioth, contributed what remains the most
profound theological study of *The Anglican Revival* (London, 1925), and gave *Three
Lectures on the Oxford Movement and Evangelicalism* (London, 1934).

In his *Apologia* he recalled how as a boy he had already formed the habit of resting his mind 'in the thought of two, and two only, absolute and self-evident beings, myself and my Creator'; and as an old man he would say that there had never been a period when he had not known God in his conscience ('I know that I know'). At every stage in his adult life he sought men friends who would be disciples, but the only women who meant much to him were his mother and sisters, particularly Mary, after whose premature death he wrote: 'What a veil and curtain this world of sense is.' The material world and its improvement he always reckoned unimportant; he recalled how in childhood 'I thought life might be a dream, or I an angel, and all this world a deception, my fellow angels by a playful device concealing themselves from me, and deceiving me with the semblance of a material world.'

His father was a banker who was ruined in 1816 and who subsequently failed in attempts to manage a brewery. That seemed to be the end of the world for the boy; and in that sad year of 1816, at the age of fifteen, when left behind at school in the holidays, he fell under the influence of an Evangelical schoolmaster. However, he never underwent a full Evangelical conversion producing an assurance about the Saviour greater than his childhood sense of God in the conscience – as readers of his *Apologia* pointed out to him. The Evangelical book that most impressed him was Joseph Milner's *History of the Church of Christ*, for it was the Church that seemed able to assure him when God seemed remote. Later he expounded the Evangelical doctrine of justification by faith with the emphasis on the Church's sacraments, since the human heart by itself was unstable, deceitful, and wicked, cut off from God by sin. His own brothers, who trusted in their hearts, showed the dangers. Francis – whom we met in connection with the Brethren – became a very unorthodox Christian and a very eccentric man, and Charles an atheist and a recluse. Of Hurrell Froude's brothers, Richard the historian wrote a novel about *The Nemesis of Faith* and a history of England celebrating Protestant anti-clericalism, and William the scientist became an agnostic. These Newman and Froude brothers were liberals in religion – and that in John Henry Newman's view was their fatal mistake. 'Now by liberalism', he explained in his *Apologia*, 'I mean false liberty of thought, or the exercise of thought upon matters, in which from the constitution of the human mind, thought cannot be brought to any successful issue, and therefore is out of place. Among such matters are first principles of whatever kind; and among these the most sacred and momentous are especially to be reckoned the truths of Revelation.'

He became a Fellow of Oriel College, the vicar of the university church, and the learned author of *The Arians of the Fourth Century*. He ceased to be a Calvinist but never abandoned the belief in God's predestinating care of him. During a holiday in Italy to recover from overwork he nearly died of a fever but pulled himself together with the conviction that he still had work to do in England. While convalescing on the voyage home, he wrote the poem that became the famous hymn 'Lead, kindly light'. He reached home five days before Keble's attack on 'National Apostasy' shone a closer light on his eager face. A born journalist, he enjoyed editing sixty-six short *Tracts for the Times* in two years. It was apostolic activity, for 'I am sure the apostles did not stay still'. More deeply he enjoyed preaching, although he was no actor; he read his sermons monotonously, leaving pauses between the long sentences. His most frequent theme to parochial congregations was the holiness of the Christ of the gospels, demanding the hearer's moral obedience. To a university audience he would expound the differences between reason and faith, rebuking his own past tendency 'to prefer intellectual excellence to moral'.[31]

He saw that his fellow clergy might soon cease to enjoy the 'secular advantages' of 'your birth, your education, your wealth, your connections', as he told them in Tract One, urging them to remember instead 'our apostolic descent' since priests were 'assistants, and in some sense representatives', of bishops. But the Bishop of Oxford was not in full agreement with him, so that Newman turned to dead bishops such as Andrewes and Laud, to the Fathers on whose works he was

---

[31] See *Newman's University Sermons*, ed. D. M. MacKinnon and J. D. Holmes (London, 1970), and Roderick Strange, *Newman and the Gospel of Christ* (Oxford, 1981).

already England's leading authority, to the English saints whose lives he caused to be rewritten in a new series of volumes. 'It still remains to be seen', as he wrote at this stage, 'whether what is called Anglo-Catholicism . . . is capable of being professed, acted on, and maintained on a large sphere of action and through a sufficient period, or whether it be a mere modification or transition-state either of Romanism or of popular Protestantism.' Or was it a mere 'paper religion', incapable of leading living men to the living God? In 1839 he felt that the Anglican appeal to 'Antiquity' was 'absolutely pulverized' by an article by a Roman Catholic (Wiseman), who presented the Papacy as the guardian of Catholicism against the Donatists, fifth-century schismatics in North Africa. In 1841, in Tract Ninety, he announced (or implied) that at the Reformation the Church of England had become a modification of Romanism. It is surprising not that his university and the bishops united to condemn that, but that Newman was 'quite unprepared for the outbreak'.

However, he did not become a Roman Catholic until 9 October 1845, when he was received into the Church by an Italian missionary, Fr Dominic Barberi. He spent the intervening years largely in the historical study which lay behind his book on *The Development of Christian Doctrine*, 'one of those works of genius in which a man's whole store of learning is mobilized under great existential pressure'.[32] He did not inquire into the contemporary reality of Roman Catholicism; he used to say that he had never met a Roman Catholic until he became one. His driving concern was to find and to show that there must be development, since the authority of the dead past would make only a 'paper religion'; yet the development must be legitimate, the 'notes' of legitimacy being listed – preservation of type, continuity of principle, power of assimilation, logical sequence, anticipation of its future, conservative action on its past, chronic vigour. The councils of the undivided Church could legitimately develop the doctrine to be found in the New

---

[32] Paul Misner, *Papacy and Development* (Leiden, 1976), p. 61. See also Owen Chadwick, *From Bossuet to Newman: The Idea of Doctrinal Development* (Cambridge, 1975), and Nicholas Lash, *Newman on Development* (London, 1975).

Testament and because development was necessary ('in a higher world it is otherwise, but here below to live is to be changed, and to be perfect is to have changed often'), uncertainty was possible. Consequently holiness was very difficult, unless there was an 'infallible expounder'. But was the Roman Catholic Church that infallible expounder of developing doctrine? All that Newman had thought so far could be regarded as no more than the working out of two proverbs he had learned as a schoolboy from the writings of Thomas Scott, the Evangelical whose works had taught him Trinitarianism. These proverbs were: 'Holiness rather than peace' and 'Growth the only evidence of life'. But he now saw that only the Papacy made universal claims about itself, claims which surely agreed with the universal nature of Catholicism. And the integrity in his character, more basic than any of the tactical devices he had employed as an Anglican, now came out as he followed his conscience and asked to be received into the Catholic Church.

When he reached Rome as a humble student in 1846, taking his theory of development with him, no theologian in the Eternal City could understand it. They were content with second-rate manuals of conventional doctrine. In fact Newman never found a sphere worthy of his gifts. Because the bishops were too suspicious of the liberalism remaining in him, he had to abandon the editorship of a magazine and schemes to found a great school in Birmingham, a chaplaincy in Oxford, a university in Dublin. He grew to love the 'Oratory' in Birmingham which he made his headquarters, but was not completely fulfilled. Usually he recognized that it was his vocation to be a solitary thinker, communicating by letter rather than conversation, at his best when at prayer; his greatest communication was to be *The Dream of Gerontius* (1865), a poem about the soul's approach to God through death. But at times he felt too solitary. He once wrote in his journal: 'I have no friend at Rome, I have laboured in England to be misrepresented, backbitten and scorned. . . . O my God, I seem to have wasted these years that I have been a Catholic.' He criticized or pitied his own failures like this while feeling that the religion he wished to advocate was in retreat. As he wrote in a letter of

1877: 'My apprehensions are not new, but above fifty years' standing. I have all this time thought that a time of widespread infidelity was coming, and through all those years the waters have in fact been rising as a deluge. I look for the time, after my life, when only the tops of the mountains will be seen like islands in the waste of waters.'[33]

Despite the intensity of his determination never to rebel against the Church to which he had so dramatically surrendered, his heart was with much that was said by the bolder critics of the prevailing trends. An article in which he urged that 'the faithful' – he meant chiefly educated Roman Catholic laity – should be consulted by the bishops was reported to Rome for heresy. Fiercer criticisms of the bishops' regime came from a few laymen such as the rich and learned Sir John Acton. Acton's mind possessed a true historian's penetration and it had been trained by another great historian, Professor Döllinger of Munich, who openly rebelled against the definition of papal infallibility in 1870 and was excommunicated. Acton had no wish to suffer Döllinger's fate – and escaped it.[34] Newman was usually still more submissive in public. But the publication of their private papers has shown how close in many of their questionings the two men were – and how isolated they often felt as reaction seemed triumphant.

Over twenty years he struggled to write a philosophical defence of religious belief, and his *Essay in Aid of a Grammar of Assent* appeared in 1870. It was a subtle analysis of 'real assent' to doctrines – an assent which was neither shallow nor yet a simple matter of logical inference. This assent resulted in 'certitude'. But the book made no great impact. On the one hand, Protestants and sceptics marvelled that a man so intelli-

---

[33] Studies of these sad episodes include Joseph Altholz, *The Liberal Catholic Movement in England: the 'Rambler' and its Contributors 1848–64* (London, 1962); Francis McGrath, *Newman's University: Idea and Reality* (London, 1951); Dwight Culler, *The Imperial Intellect: A Study of Cardinal Newman's Educational Ideal* (New Haven, Conn., 1955).

[34] See David Matthew, *Lord Acton and His Times* (London, 1968), supplemented by Hugh McDougall, *The Acton-Newman Relations* (London, 1962); D. McElrath, *Lord Acton: The Decisive Decade 1864–74* (London, 1970); Peter Gunn, *The Actons* (London, 1978).

gent had given his assent to dogmas and miracles which they regarded as nonsensical. It was often felt, and sometimes said, that he had sacrificed his intellect to his imagination in order to avoid the atheism to which he felt the argument was moving. On the other hand, most of Newman's fellow Catholics could make little of his 'illative sense' which yielded 'certitude' about doctrines which the book did not specify. To them, what they wanted was logic to prove the doctrines actually taught by the Holy Roman Church. Their attitude was expressed perfectly by Pope Pius IX, who in 1864 issued a *Syllabus of Errors*, one of the errors being the suggestion that the Roman Pontiff should accommodate himself to liberalism or to 'progress' in any other nineteenth-century form. Newman had submitted to an authoritarian Church and his remaining sympathy with theological liberalism, even with the age's scepticism, won no sympathy for him until the official atmosphere was somewhat changed under Leo XIII, an aristocratic pope more benevolent towards modern civilization. In 1879 he was made a cardinal and assured his friends that 'the cloud is lifted from me for ever'. He did not die until he was almost ninety, and during his last years he knew that he was honoured in the Church he had joined as well as in the Church he had left. But it was now far too late to achieve the work which had never been entrusted to him when he was at the height of his powers. The wide influence which was denied him during his lifetime (although he always had devoted disciples and was always admired for his style as a preacher) was to come during the twentieth century.

By 1964 Pope Paul VI could declare that Newman, 'guided solely by love of the truth and fidelity to Christ, traced an itinerary the most toilsome but also the greatest, the most meaningful, the most conclusive, that human thought ever travelled during the last century, indeed one might say during the modern era, to arrive at the fulness of wisdom and of peace.'[35] Gradually Christians in many countries and in many

---

[35] Christopher Hollis, *Newman and the Modern World* (London, 1967), p. 215. See also *The Rediscovery of Newman: An Oxford Symposium*, ed. John Coulson and A. M. Allchin (London, 1967), and John Coulson, *Newman and the Common Tradition* (Oxford, 1970).

Churches have appreciated Newman's direct intuition into the reality of God, and his courageous dismissal of the reality of this world; his power so to read the gospels that the holy Christ walked out of them to command discipleship; the patient determination of his search for fuller religious truth. They have come to share his understanding of faith as a movement by the whole person, not a mere assent to a doctrine, not a decision into which one could be either argued or tortured. The truth to be discerned by faith with 'certitude' must be much more than any 'paper religion' – a criticism of the Anglican appeal to history but also (at least potentially) of Roman dogmatism. Although he never worked out a modern theology, Newman left behind him a feeling that a modern theology was needed. He wrote in 1839: 'We cannot, if we would, move ourselves back into the times of the Fathers; we must, in spite of ourselves, be Churchmen of our own era, not of any other, were it only for this reason, that we are born in the nineteenth century, not the fourth.'[36]

MAURICE AND CHRISTIAN SOCIALISM

Chartism, the first great working-class political movement in the history of the world, was a movement born out of anger about the failure of more peaceful popular movements which had respected the Reform Act of 1832. All the protests against the harsh new Poor Law did not secure its repeal, and the 'Ten Hours' movement to reduce the exploitation of factory workers also seemed to be defeated. Most of the leaders of those movements were Tories and churchmen whose consciences

[36] There are many–too many–books on Newman. There is even a book about his political thought, by Terence Kenny (London, 1957). Meriol Trevor's *Newman's Journey* (London, 1974), was based on her biography in 2 vols. (London, 1962). The short studies by C. S. Dessain (3rd ed., London, 1980) and Owen Chadwick (Oxford, 1983) took account of Newman's *Letters and Diaries*, ed. C. S. Dessain and others in 31 vols. (London, 1961, onwards). His *Autobiographical Writings* were edited by Henry Tristram (New York, 1957). Studies of his theology include David Pailin, *The Way to Faith* (London, 1969), and Thomas Vargish, *Newman: The Contemplation of Mind* (Oxford, 1970). On his spirituality, see H. C. Graef, *God and Myself* (London, 1967).

had been stirred by conditions in the industrial north. There were laymen such as Michael Sadler, the MP who realized what was happening to the children when they fell asleep in his Sunday school; or Richard Oastler, who put his money as well as his mouth into the 'Ten Hours' agitation. There were parish priests such as George Bull, an Evangelical Tory who was moved by the helplessness of the poor in an industrial village near Bradford. The fact struck them that in Yorkshire, which William Wilberforce had represented in Parliament, there was slavery as bad as anything to be found in the West Indies. There had been poverty in England for many centuries, but the poor now crowded into factories and disease-ridden hovels, their misery apparent to each other and to sensitive people who saw them.[37]

The Chartists, however, no longer trusted either Tories or parsons to provide effective leadership. That must come from men who stood closer to the workers and who were not afraid of advocating violence if the workers' demands were not met. The demands were varied, but the theme of 'the People's Charter' for which signatures were collected was that every adult man in England should be entitled to vote in secret in the election of a new Parliament each year, with equal constituencies and salaried MPs.

At a meeting in 1848, when this agitation was at its height, Charles Kingsley stammered out sensationally that he was a 'Church of England parson – and a Chartist'. But he exaggerated. He drew up a placard after the failure of the largest Chartist demonstration: 'The Almighty God, and Jesus Christ the poor Man who died for poor men, will bring freedom for you. . . . Workers of England, be wise, and then you *must* be free, for you will be *fit* to be free.' It was not a demand for the vote now. From 1844 until he died there in 1875, his beloved home was the large and lovely, if damp, rectory of Eversley in Hampshire. Moved by the poverty of the agricultural labour-

---

[37] Cecil Driver wrote a biography of Oastler entitled *Tory Radical* (New York, 1946), and J. C. Gill one of *Parson Bull of Byerley* (London, 1963). See also *Popular Movements c. 1830–1850*, ed. J. T. Ward (London, 1970); J. T. Ward, *Chartism* (London, 1973); David Jones, *Chartism and the Chartists* (London, 1975).

ers he produced journalism under the name of 'Parson Lot' and
a novel, *Yeast*, in 1850 to stir up the heirs of landlords if not the
landlords themselves; and in that aim he was successful. The
novel had sequels – *Alton Locke* about the sweat shops in the
tailoring trade, *Two Years Ago* about the importance of sanitation, *The Water Babies* to popularize the cause of the chimney
sweeps. These novels were sufficiently radical to mean that he
was not offered promotion until Prince Albert made him tutor
to the Prince of Wales and persuaded Lord Palmerston to make
him a part-time professor. But social reform was not his only
interest. He wrote much else, partly for pleasure and partly for
the money – including his best books, *The Heroes* to re-tell the
myths of Ancient Greece to children, and the patriotic novel for
boys, *Westward Ho!* He was an amateur scientist, a devoted
fisherman, a preacher and practiser of 'muscular Christianity'
(in order to cure his own tendency to introspective melancholy). So many were his interests that Dean Stanley aptly called
him 'a layman in the guise or disguise of a clergyman'.[38]

In contrast, Frederick Denison Maurice used to insist that
his only vocation was theology. Men without sympathetic
patience would dismiss his thought as merely muddled; listening to him was, Aubrey de Vere thought, 'like eating pea soup
with a fork'. But he inspired colleagues and disciples, including
some who did not fully grasp his theology – men such as
Thomas Hughes who wrote *Tom Brown's Schooldays* and did
much else; John Ludlow, the intensely practical Christian who
became legal adviser to the first of the modern trade unions
(the Amalgamated Society of Engineers), and Chief Registrar
of Friendly Societies, and who lived to plead that 'Christianity
must be applied to the economic system' at the Pan-Anglican
Congress of 1908; or the more heretical Edward Vansittat
Neale, a rich barrister who sacrified his fortune and himself to a
philanthropic life as a founder and general secretary of the
British Co-operative Union. Because of the influence of his
principles on such disciples and on a wider public, Maurice
has, indeed, usually been reckoned the greatest moral and

---

[38] Two biographies marked the centenary of his death: Brenda Colloms, *Charles
Kingsley*, and Susan Chitty, *The Beast and the Monk* (London, 1975).

social prophet to arise within the Victorian Churches. The Working Men's College which he founded in London in 1854 has not been the only place to keep his memory green.[39]

In 1848 he nervously allowed Ludlow to edit a short-lived magazine called the *Christian Socialist*; but to him 'Socialism' was merely the opposite of individualism. He was certainly no Chartist; he deplored the extension of the electorate in 1867, as he deplored trade unionism. It is fair to say that he was, 'in plain language, a Tory paternalist with the unusual desire to theorize his acceptance of the traditional obligation to help the poor.'[40] None of these idealists had any sympathy with Karl Marx's demand that the State must own the means of production; Marx denounced Christian Socialism as 'holy water'. They saw much more glory in the application to economic life of the Christian idea of co-operation (preferring producers' co-operatives to the consumers' 'co-op' shop which eventually emerged as the substance of the Co-operative Movement). But the experiments came to very little. It was difficult to secure orders since the products were often clumsy and their distribution was another problem; and it was difficult to secure brotherhood since wages had to be paid at commercial rates. As conceived by these Christian Socialists, co-operation was a gallant gesture in defiance of the capitalist system, a gesture comparable with the utopian agricultural communities which were another doomed creation of nineteenth-century idealism. What remained was the haunting idea of a decentralized, power-free, humanly fulfilling 'Guild Socialism' which was to attract later generations of Christian social pioneers.[41] And for students of Christian thought, Maurice's theology also remained, its most powerful expression being in 'Letters to a Quaker' published as *The Kingdom of Christ* (1838), when he was a hospital chaplain amid the slums of Southwark.

---

[39] Recent studies include E. C. Mack and W. H. G. Armytage, *Thomas Hughes* (London, 1952); N. C. Masterman, *John Malcolm Ludlow* (Cambridge, 1963); P. N. Buckstrom, *Christian Socialism and Co-operation in Victorian England* (London, 1974); Edward Norman, *The Victorian Christian Socialists* (Cambridge, 1987).

[40] Edward Norman, *Church and Society in England 1770–1970*, pp. 171–2.

[41] W. H. G. Armytage studied utopian communities and their fates in *Heavens Below* (London, 1961).

This prophet's vision of God as the very foundation of all unity in the family of man resulted from his experiences as a boy. He was the son of a Unitarian minister and of a mother who became a Calvinist in the Church of England without believing that she was numbered among God's elect. One sister became a Baptist, the other an Anglican; and this theologically divided family made a practice of writing letters of religious exhortation to each other while living under the same roof. The boy was fond of them all and distressed by the divisiveness of their Christianity or Christianities. In 1831, at the age of twenty-six, he was baptized into the Church of England, but he was never willing to exclude from the communion of the Church anyone who claimed to be a Christian. He valued the Church not as an institution confronting the world but as the supreme sign of the 'Kingdom of Christ' already established in the world. And he went further than that. In lectures on *The Religions of the World* published in the 1840s he claimed that non-Christians were sincerely seeking God (then an original suggestion) and twenty years later he published a similar claim about the philosophers of the West. He was deprived of his professorship at King's College, London, for daring to hope for the 'salvation of all'. Christianity was to him not merely one religion; 'we have been dosing our people with religion, when what they want is not this but the living God.' It was not the rescue of the individual sinner, as in Evangelicalism. Nor was it the imposition on the individual of a discipline derived from the past, as in the Oxford Movement. It was not the encouragement of any 'sect' or 'party' or 'system' or 'notion' outside or inside the Church. It was a message about the unity of England and of all mankind under Christ as 'Head and King' and under the Father.

The key to Christianity was that 'God has claimed us all in Christ as his sons'. 'I tremble to think', he wrote, 'what a crushing of all systems, religious and political, there must be, before we really do feel our gathering together in Christ to be the hope of the universe.' Baptism was the sacrament which asserted the 'constant union' between God and his children; the Church's worship was 'the speech and music of humanity'; the Christian ministry was a sign of the universality of the

Church; church buildings were hints that 'the city and the men in it are holy'; the whole life of the Church was a sign of what the world could become and, deep down, already was. The Atonement did not change God's will, as the Evangelicals then usually asserted; it declared that will and thus declared also the true character of humanity – something far more important than any individual conversion. It showed that the Father is love, that we are most fully ourselves when loving, that sacrifice is 'the law of our being'.

This theology, accepting both the Church and the world, could be interpreted in a way that encouraged the worldly complacency which has often accompanied the privileges of the Church of England. John Stuart Mill complained with some justification about Maurice's belief 'that the Church of England had known everything from the first, and that all truths on the ground of which the Church and orthodoxy have been attacked (many of which he saw as clearly as anyone) are not only consistent with the Thirty-nine Articles, but are better understood and expressed in those articles than by anyone who rejects them.' In his own day Catholics and Evangelicals, believers and unbelievers, found his synthesis of their positions confused and unsatisfactory. They agreed in complaining about his muddled mind, and in 1971 an American scholar, Olive Brose, summed up the enigma of his personality in the title of her study, *Rebellious Conformist*. Such a man was bound to make all the conventional, including the conventional rebels, uneasy.

Certainly he wrote far too much and too rhetorically to be precisely authoritative; it was his custom to dictate his books, which read too much like sermons. A crucial weakness was that he never seems to have become calm enough to think out clearly what was the authority of the Bible and the creeds. He would leap to their defence without really listening to their critics. But in an age when religious vitality was usually expressed in a narrowminded and intolerant enthusiasm for some neat creed narrower than the Bible, for some small system of belief and church life, he was a reconciler. He bequeathed to thoughtful Anglicans a hunger for a more comprehensive Catholicism on a firmly scriptural basis, and a

Roman Catholic commentator has rightly observed that
among Anglicans the theological victory has been won by the
theory of a Catholic-Church-in-becoming, to the development
of which all who aspire to Catholicity may contribute.[42] This
turning to the future has largely replaced earlier Anglican
dependence on the claim to be at least a branch of the pure
Catholicism of the past. Such was the influence of Maurice's
vision of Christian unity. He also deserves to be remembered as
a man who did what he could to end the class war which Karl
Marx was sure would intensify. Before his death in 1872, he
talked much with his son Frederick about his failures, but he
added: 'The desire for unity and the search for unity both in the
nation and in the Church has haunted me all my days.'

THE CHURCH AT WORK

When Bishop George Selwyn returned from New Zealand, the
manly hero of the hour, to preach at Cambridge in 1854, he
declared that 'a great and visible change has taken place in the
thirteen years since I left England. It is now a very rare thing to
see a careless clergyman, a neglected parish or a desecrated
church.' That assessment may have been too rhetorical, but
the evidence of parish registers, newspapers and novels supports the impression of a revival. A modern student of the
transformation which overtook the Victorian Church selected
this quotation from the *Guardian* in 1857: 'True theology has
revived, pluralities have been abolished, residence enforced,
services multiplied, schools built; while the clergy as a body
have displayed a zeal, a diligence and a liberality which will
bear comparison with the brightest periods of ecclesiastical

---

[42] George H. Tavard, *The Quest for Catholicity* (London, 1963) p. 200. Other recent
studies include M. B. Reckitt, *Maurice to Temple: A Century of the Social Movement in the
Church of England* (London, 1947); A. M. Ramsey, *F. D. Maurice and the Conflicts of
Modern Theology* (Cambridge, 1951); Torben Christensen, *The Origin and History of
Christian Socialism, 1848–54* (Aarhus, 1962), and *The Divine Order: A Study of F. D.
Maurice's Theology* (Leiden, 1973); A. R. Vidler, *F. D. Maurice and Company* (London,
1966); F. M. McClain, *Maurice Man and Moralist* (London, 1972). In *The Integrity of
Anglicanism* (London, 1978), Stephen Sykes questioned the merits of Maurice's
influence.

history'.[43] In the fifty years 1830–80, the number of Easter communicants doubled.

Part of the reason for the greater efficiency was the increase in the number and morale of the clergy. In 1831 there were 10,718: twenty years later, 17,621. The priest was now expected to be devout, and a growing number of churches actually had Morning and Evening Prayer daily, as the Prayer Book directed. He was expected to consult with brother priests; from 1835 onwards the post of rural dean was revived in order to draw the clergy together. The clergyman was expected to be an educated man (in 1878, 16,297 of the 23,612 clergymen had been to Oxford or Cambridge), yet a father to the children and the poor; to be, as Archbishop Tait put it in 1873, 'the accredited minister of the National Church, resident in the midst of every community with incomparable advantages for gathering the people round him, and organizing them for any good purpose which may subserve the kingdom of Christ.' He was expected to show that he was on duty by dressing in black, although the cut of his coat could disclose whether he was an Evangelical or a Tractarian. He was usually not expected to hunt with the gentry, or to labour on his glebe land, or to drink in a public house. He was different from his neighbours – and, because he was sacred, different from much in his own profession's past.[44]

The clergyman's training also became more professional than it had been since the arrival of Christianity in England. In 1869 a board of theological professors at Oxford began to build up a faculty of theology capable of teaching and examining. At Cambridge, where the theologians had been less suspicious of each other, such a board already existed and the 'tripos' or examination in theology was begun in 1874. Durham University and King's College, London, also taught theology at the undergraduate level. Diocesan theological colleges hesitantly modelled on the Roman Catholic system provided extra training for graduates preparing to be priests; the earliest were at Chichester and Wells (1839–40). Other colleges still more

---

[43] Brian Heeney, *A Different Kind of Gentleman* (Hampden, Conn., 1976), p. 31.
[44] Anthony Russell traced the development of *The Clerical Profession* (London, 1980).

hesitantly catered for non-graduates. Although no central body to supervise this training for the ministry existed until 1912 (and then it was only a 'central advisory council'), the Victorian bishops became able to be far more thorough than their predecessors in examining candidates.[45]

These mid-Victorian clergy left a very large legacy behind them in the shape of new or restored churches. The new churches were almost always in the 'Gothic style' which put into stone the yearning to recover the Faith and the Christendom of the Middle Ages – although the partly mechanized nineteenth century contributed its rapid (sometimes too rapid) building methods. In 1876 Parliament was told that 7,144 churches had been restored in the parishes of the Church of England since 1840, and 1,727 new churches had been built. The achievement was a spectacular fulfilment of the dreams nursed by a small group of young churchmen in the Camden Society at Cambridge. Led by John Mason Neale they founded a national Ecclesiological Society in 1845, and up and down the country clergy and laity became enthusiastic for the new pattern – pews which were modest and free, unobtrusive heating, a stone font near the entrance, on opposite sides of the church a brass lectern for the Bible and a pulpit for biblical preaching, an organ replacing the little band of often clumsy instrumentalists, a long sanctuary with a robed and surpliced choir, the altar as the climax beneath the stained glass in the east window. 'Few undergraduate societies have exercised such an influence', it has been observed.[46]

John Mason Neale, the warden of a little community of nuns in Sussex and dead before he was fifty, revolutionized what went on in church by translating hymns. From a past hitherto unknown to Protestant England came majestic hymns such as 'Come thou Redeemer of the earth' or 'The royal banners

[45] F. W. B. Bullock provided *A History of Training for the Ministry, 1800–74* (St Leonards-on-Sea, Sussex, 1955).

[46] G. W. O. Addleshaw and Frederick Etchells, *The Architectural Setting of Anglican Worship* (London, 1959), p. 203. Basil Clarke studied *Church Builders of the Nineteenth Century* (London, 1938), and J. F. Whyte *The Cambridge Movement* (Cambridge, 1962). J. Stanley Leatherbarrow described the building of a fairly typical church in Lancashire in *Victorian Period Piece* (London, 1954).

forward go' or 'The strife is o'er' or 'The Day of Resurrection!'
or 'Come, thou holy Paraclete' or 'Of the glorious Body telling'
or 'O what their joy and their glory must be' or 'Jerusalem the
golden' – although he was on occasion not ashamed to be
popular, as in 'Good King Wenceslas'. When the *English
Hymnal* was compiled forty years after his death, seventy-two of
its 656 hymns were his. He was said to speak twenty languages,
but his great gift to the Church of England was to assure it that
hymns, previously composed mainly by Dissenters, Methodists or Evangelicals, were fit to be the language of a 'happy
band of pilgrims' (his best loved hymn other than his translations). The pilgrims sang – accompanied by the organ. During
Neale's lifetime (in 1864), the Royal College of Organists was
founded, marking the now widespread distribution of what
was becoming the Church's favourite musical instrument,
replacing the village band.[47]

John Ellerton, like Neale, made some Latin hymns famous
by translating them. These included 'Sing alleluia forth in
duteous praise' and 'O strength and stay upholding all creation'. But his best-known hymns were both of his own composition, and both about evening – 'Saviour, again to thy dear
name we raise' was meant to be the last hymn of the Sunday in
the gaslit parish church of Crewe, and 'The day thou gavest,
Lord, is ended' was to remind his parishioners that now the
Christian Church was worldwide, so that as Crewe went to bed
'our brethren 'neath the western sky' began their praise. When
Hymns Ancient and Modern, which had begun life as a small book
of 1861, entered one of its many new editions in 1889, it
contained twenty-six Ellerton hymns. Even better loved as an
evening hymn was Henry Lyte's 'Abide with me' (1847), the
prayer of a priest facing premature death. It was as simple in its
faith as Mrs Alexander's 'There is a green hill', written by the
bedside of a sick child; but it became the favourite both of
football crowds and of F. D. Maurice.[48]

---

[47] A. G. Lough studied *The Influence of John Mason Neale* (London, 1962), and *J. M.
Neale: Priest Extraordinary* (London, 1975).
[48] Ellerton was for a time rector of Barnes near London and appears in John
Whale's history of the parish, *One Church, One Lord* (London, 1979), pp. 130–49.
B. G. Skinner wrote about *Henry Lyte* (Exeter, 1974).

Other favourite Victorian hymns were more robustly cheerful. Henry Lyte's most enduring hymn turned out to be 'Praise,
my soul, the King of heaven', and the Christian life was
compared with a military march as often as with a lonely
pilgrimage. Sabine Baring-Gould, a handsome young Yorkshire curate who at about the same time insisted on marrying
an illiterate mill girl, wrote 'Onward Christian soldiers' for the
children of the Sunday school in 1864. Later he translated from
the Danish 'Through the night of doubt and sorrow', fathered
fifteen children and wrote 160 books.[49]

Victorian country parsons often took the lead which landowners ought to have taken in the relief of distress and
ignorance. Because only efficient farming thrived and it required capital, the class of 'yeoman' or independent small-
holder famous in English life and literature declined miserably,
and just over three-quarters of the land in Victorian England
came to be owned by only seven thousand families. The
farmers who were the tenants of these landlords could get as
much labour as they wanted with low wages and often poor
housing, since for most of the century the countryside remained overpopulated. When the decline of British agriculture
had begun in the 1870s, not even employment at this low level
was readily available. The charitable relief of the sick and poor
was needed – and it often came in daily visits from churchgoers when the parson and his wife led by exhortation and
example.

Many parishes ran savings banks with clothing, boot and
coal 'clubs' to encourage saving – and many distributed these
necessities free to those without the required pennies. Much of
the clergy's work was educational and was not confined to the
Sunday school or the private tutorial establishment. J. S.
Henslow, who had taught botany to Charles Darwin at Cambridge, built a school and paid for it out of his own pocket in his
remote parish. John Keble's parish had a school, where he
taught every day; Charles Kingsley's did not, but he could
spend six evenings a week during the winter supervising classes

---

[49] William Purcell's biography was called *Onward Christian Soldier* (London,
1957).

for adults. A lending library encouraged reading, and for the majority who still found reading difficult 'penny readings' were an entertainment. In the vast drawing room of the rectory in Old Alresford in Hampshire, in 1876, Mrs Mary Sumner founded the Mothers' Union which was to become worldwide. It gave advice both spiritual and practical to 'cottage mothers', and proved to be a vastly successful exercise in adult education. Nor were the husbands neglected. Many of the clergy included the improvement of agriculture in their amazingly wide range of studies, badgered the landlords into building better cottages, and provided allotments on their own 'glebe' land. Church halls were built to provide recreation, and involvement in church life became itself an education. Towards the end of the century voluntary church councils were replacing the old 'vestries' which had mixed secular with ecclesiastical business, and 'lay readers' – first recruited for London and other great towns in the 1860s – were beginning to take services in the country parson's absence. Such developments mostly heralded the twentieth century, where rural religion was going to depend increasingly on the laity.

Although there was much activity, it should not be exaggerated. A realistic portrait of the laity in a stagnant area of the mid-Victorian countryside has been provided by a modern examination of part of Lincolnshire. In 1851 it had 237 parishes served by 154 clergy, although half of these parishes contained under five hundred souls, and the standard of pastoral duty was higher than ever before. But church attendance was 'low to middling' and mainly female, and the numbers of communicants were usually small. Most of the young people confirmed seem to have made their communions once, if at all. The churches were usually locked on weekdays. The clergy's basic problem was, it seems, that their churches were not really regarded as the people's spiritual homes. Some of those who did attend probably did so in order to establish their respectability or in order to please the squire, who might well be also the employer and the landlord. The religion which really involved, and even excited, the people was Methodism, often charismatic and boisterous in its enthusiasm. At least the chapel was a scene of democracy and a source of entertainment in dull lives.[50]

Lives in early Victorian towns were often worse than dull. Many town parsons, knowing the problems because they visited the homes and also chaired the 'vestries' which were largely responsible for local government in its early stages, were acutely worried about the diseased slums which had been spewed out by industrialism. They became active in the whole mid-Victorian movement to make urban sanitation less barbaric, the movement which had as its banner the Public Health Act of 1848. With the removal of the filth came the decline of the two killer-epidemics, cholera and typhoid, and although other diseases continued to claim many victims because the towns were overcrowded and dirtied by coal, progress came. Hard work, together with the advantages possessed by industrial and colonial Britain in world trade, enabled a predominantly urban population which doubled in the second half of the century to pay for its food and for much else. Praised by his superiors for his self-discipline, the urban worker was awarded the parliamentary vote in 1867.

This was the background to the labours of town priests such as Walter Hook, vicar of Leeds 1837–59, who raised the money to build twenty-two churches, twenty-three vicarages and twenty-seven schools. His ecclesiastical position was conservative (so he clashed with Pusey) but his religious energy was new in the Church of England's urban mission, and he more than anyone else established the pattern of the devoted and inexhausible vicar, like an admiral commanding a squadron of curates in the battle for a city's souls. Later on the most admired pioneers were the 'slum priests' of the Anglo-Catholic movement – men who believed that the poor deserved not only

---

[50] James Obelkevich examined *Religion and Rural Society: South Lindsey 1825–75* (Oxford, 1976). Other studies include A. Tindal Hart and Edward Carpenter, *The Nineteenth Century Country Parson* (Shrewsbury, 1954); G. Kitson Clark, *Churchmen and the Condition of England 1832–85* (London, 1973); Brenda Colloms, *Victorian Country Parsons* (London, 1977); Peter Hammond, *The Parson and the Victorian Parish* (London, 1977). Joyce Coombes studied the origins of the Mothers' Union in *George and Mary Sumner* (London, 1965). For the background, see G. E. Mingay, *Rural Life in Victorian England* (London, 1977).

devoted love and the Evangelical call for definite conversions, but also all the drama, colour and consolation of 'advanced' religious ceremonies. Typical of them was Charles Lowder of St Peter's, London Docks. He won the love of the people by his heroism in the cholera epidemic of 1866, and his funeral in 1880 was a triumph. Such 'Anglo-Catholics' were the heirs of the Tractarians, but broke right away from academic privilege.'

In lectures published as *The Parish Priest of the Town* in 1880, John Gott talked to young men in Cambridge about his ideal of the priesthood as one of Hook's successors in pastoral work among the people of Leeds. 'The first day of my diaconate I was given charge over a district of eight thousand souls and that day was the true sample of my life till today.' He was intensely proud of his profession; 'every word spoken at present by a leading clergyman is a deed, and every deed is a force.' But his pride was based on the willing acceptance of very hard work. The town priest should systematically teach the children in church and school, should appoint district visitors to cover the whole parish, should visit people's homes every afternoon. 'The true pastor discovers sickness almost by instinct; through his visitors, Sunday or day teachers, and kind-hearted neighbours, his eye is everywhere, and he is often on the spot before the doctor.' Each Sunday evening he should mark on a list all the present and absent communicants, with a view to visiting during the week. There should be a personal interview with every communicant every Lent.

While so many hard-working pastors and churchgoers are forgotten, one man, Richard Church, can be remembered as a figurehead of the rural and urban mission of the Church of England in the Victorian age. Gladstone wrote in 1878 that 'there is no one whose ultimate judgement would carry more weight with one.' He wanted to make him a bishop, perhaps

---

[51] See C. J. Stranks, *Dean Hook* (London, 1954), and Lida Ellsworth, *Charles Lowder and the Ritualist Movement* (London, 1982). K. S. Inglis surveyed *The Churches and the Working Classes in Victorian England* (London, 1963), and the background was presented by J. F. C. Harrison, *Early Victorian Britain*, and G. F. A. Best, *Mid-Victorian Britain* (London, 1979). John Kent contributed a suggestive essay on 'Feelings and Festivals' to *Victorian City: Images and Realities*, ed. H. J. Dyos and Michael Wolff (London, 1973), vol. 2, pp. 855–71.

even Archbishop of Canterbury, and did succeed in dragging
him from eighteen years in a parish with two hundred inhabitants (Whatley in Somerset) to London as Dean of St
Paul's in 1871. Walter Hook had declined the post; he was too
old.

Richard Church was one of Newman's closest friends, but
when Newman ceased to be an Anglican, Church's reply was
to be found with other friends in the *Guardian*, a weekly paper
where a moderately High Church theology was to be combined with a sensitive commentary on social and cultural
events. His own writing was wide-ranging and of great distinction, and he was no enemy of scientists; he had a small
laboratory in his rectory. No man did more to reassure Anglicans that they belonged to a tradition Catholic both in the
sense of being loyal to ancient church order and also in the
sense of embracing the best in the contemporary world. At St
Paul's until his death in 1890 he remained literary and shy but
was deeply respected for his wisdom and saintliness. Fortunately the cathedral had H. P. Liddon as a canon. A professor
at Oxford and in London, a preacher of great eloquence and
force, Liddon was in effect the spokesman of his master, Pusey.
A similarly gifted, but rather more flowery and liberal
preacher, Henry Scott Holland, was appointed a canon in
1884. Sir John Stainer was a great church musician. There
were others, too, who worked to make St Paul's more beautiful,
and much more used as a church, than it had ever been. So
Dean Church lived to see new life all around him. In 1877 he
referred to 'the victories which the revived English Church
has achieved and which, in spite of disasters and menacing
troubles, make it the most glorious Church in Christendom'.[52]

---

[52] B. A. Smith studied *Dean Church: The Anglican Response to Newman* (London,
1958), and G. L. Prestige, *St Paul's in Its Glory* (London, 1955). Alan Haig analysed
The Victorian Clergy as a profession (London, 1984) and B. I. Coleman used the 1851
census to assess the effectiveness of their work in *The Church of England in the Mid-
Nineteenth Century* (London, 1980). He stressed that the Established Church had
fewer than 44 per cent of church attenders in Northumberland, County Durham,
Yorkshire, Lancashire, Lincolnshire, Staffordshire, Nottinghamshire, Derbyshire
and Cornwall.

BISHOPS IN THE CHURCH

Many of the Victorian bishops were decisive leaders. They were not elected by their dioceses and did not feel answerable to them: they belonged to the governing class. On the other hand, when they were nominated by the Prime Minister of the day for appointment by the Queen (subject to a formal election by the cathedral chapter), it was seldom for mainly political reasons. They were chosen on their records as outstanding parish priests or university scholars in order that they might lead the Church vigorously in the direction of which the Prime Minister approved. It was seldom an extremist direction. Opinionated as they were in their own territories, they often saw each other in London; they had to learn to work together; and their general tendency was to plead for loyalty to the Church.

Several of the bishops were highly effective organizers, but supreme among them was Samuel Wilberforce, Bishop of Oxford 1843–69 and of Winchester 1869–73. Had Gladstone become Prime Minister in October instead of December 1868, Wilberforce would have become Archbishop of Canterbury – although Gladstone had warned him that his reputation among politicians was 'that of a most able prelate, getting all you can for the Church, asking more, giving nothing'. Disraeli, who refused to promote him in 1868, referred to him in his novel *Lothair* (1870): 'He was fond of society, and justified his taste in this respect by the flattering belief that he was extending the power of the Church; certainly he was favouring an ambition which could not be described as moderate.'

His ambition had been encouraged by his father, William Wilberforce, and by Sir Robert Peel. Peel made him a bishop at the age of forty, only seven months after making him Dean of Westminster. Already he was widely known as a public speaker with his father's magic, and to the end of his life he held forth on platforms up and down the country, or in the House of Lords, on what he reckoned to be the good causes of the day. But it was unjust to think of him as being a climber like, say, Disraeli. He was truly convinced about certain High Church principles, and when he compiled his father's *Life and Letters* (in

seven volumes, with his brother Robert) he never made it quite
clear how much of an Evangelical his father had been. His
convictions, he reckoned, damaged his career. He burst out
privately in 1857: 'You do not suppose that I am so blind as not
to see perfectly that I might have headed the Evangelical party
and been seated by them at Lambeth.' But he was responding
to a new spirit in the Church, to be seen in the fact that his three
brothers, his daughter Ella, his sister-in-law Mary, and two
other Anglican clergymen who married the beautiful sisters of
his beautiful wife, Emily Sargent, all became Roman Catholics. He remained a convinced Anglican, and his convictions
became inflexible when he mourned his Emily's premature
death in 1841 – as he did all the rest of his life.

His remedy for grief was work; he was afraid to be alone or at
leisure, and one result was that his theology was frozen in the
1830s. His work was to be seen at its enduring best in his own
diocese, which included three counties in addition to the
university which was the flashpoint of theological controversy.
'It is the bishop who must be the main instrument in encouraging the zealous,' he wrote to Lord Shaftesbury, 'in stirring up
the faint-hearted, in animating the despondent.' He made
ordinations intensely devotional occasions; he used horses or
the railways to be all over his diocese for confirmations or for
inspections of the six hundred parishes; he consecrated more
than a hundred new churches and approved of more than
seventy new parsonages and more than 270 church restora-
tions; he received regular reports on the parish priests from the
rural deans, and wrote many letters of praise or blame in his
own hand; he addressed the clergy in spiritual retreats and the
laity in parochial missions; he founded a college to train priests
and another for schoolmasters. And from this diocesan
achievement went on to become, in Walter Hook's phrase, the
'Lord Bishop of England'. He was the leading advocate of the
revival of the Convocations of the clergy which in the period
1851–61 began to transact business as they had not done since
1717. In the 1860s Church Congresses began to gather the laity
more informally. It was not unreasonable for S. C. Carpenter,
in his history of *Church and People 1789–1889*, to see Bishop
Wilberforce's work as the turning point, saying about the

Oxford Movement: 'The Church accepted it in the same modified sense as that in which he accepted it.'[53]

Samuel Wilberforce's great rival, Archibald Campbell Tait, was the Queen's successful candidate for Canterbury in 1868. He was everything that she liked best in a clergyman – a Scot, a Protestant, earnest about the work of the Church without being fanatical about its rights, liberal in taking account of contemporary laymen's feelings without being controversially theological. But his preparation for becoming Bishop of London in 1856 on his way to Lambeth Palace was, as he noted in his journal after being offered the appointment, 'deep affliction'. As Dean of Carlisle he had faced bitter opposition to his new ideas from the canons of the cathedral – and had also seen five of his daughters die of scarlet fever within a month.

Tait (like Wilberforce) found the work of a diocese a consolation for grief, but his religion differed from his rival's. In childhood his soul had been fed by a beloved Evangelical nurse and her influence was never obliterated. While Bishop of London he preached in the open air, encouraged services in theatres, and persuaded Westminster Abbey and St Paul's to hold Sunday evening services for the poor. He also set his firmly Protestant face against Anglo-Catholic ritualism ('this childish mimicry of antiquated garments'). But Tait was never a straightforward Evangelical. Disraeli described his complexity to the Queen in 1868: 'an ecclesiastical statesman obscure in purpose, fitful and inconsistent in action, and evidently, though earnest and conscientious, a prey to constantly conflicting convictions.' Tait regretted that 'Broad Churchmen' sometimes treated sacred subjects with a lack of earnestness: that was why he signed the bishops' declaration reacting against the manifesto of liberal scholars in 1860, *Essays and Reviews*. But he also had a keen sense that most laymen were

---

[53] Standish Meacham supplied a modern biography: *Lord Bishop* (Cambridge, Mass., 1970). See also Owen Chadwick, *The Founding of Cuddesdon* (Oxford, 1954); Diana McClatchey, *Oxfordshire Clergy 1777–1869* (Oxford, 1960); David Newsome, *The Parting of Friends* (London, 1966). Dieter Voll, *Catholic Evangelicalism* (London, 1963), studied some of the Victorians who used the Wilberforce approach in urban churches.

now reluctant to see liberal scholars driven out of the Church; that was why he supported the Judicial Committee of the Privy Council when it decided that clergymen holding such views could also keep their appointments. He was undeterred when eleven thousand clergymen – the majority – signed a manifesto reaffirming the everlasting punishment of the wicked in hell and the divine inspiration of the Bible 'without reserve or qualification'.

As Archbishop of Canterbury he was far more decisive than his predecessor (C. T. Longley, a hard-working bishop for more than thirty years but scarcely a constructive ecclesiastical statesman). His supreme purpose was to preserve and strengthen the establishment of the Church of England, because the Church was to him the guardian of the simple Christian truths which the nation had adopted as its faith. He contrasted England with the continent, where 'either you have atheistical philosophers or you have superstitious devotees'. He urged the clergy to remember that England was still at heart Christian England; that sceptics would feel differently 'in hours of sickness and approaching death, and when friends are taken from them; then we may find their consciences awake and their hearts open, ready to return to the faith of their childhood and to believe in the great Redeemer.' In the year before he died, he claimed that 'on the faithfulness of the Church of England in the discharge of its highest duties rests the future welfare of this English nation and not of the English nation only, but I may also say, of the Christian Church throughout the world'.

Tait gave his reasons for devoting so much attention to the battle against ritualism. 'I have great sympathy with earnestness, and I have great sympathy with liberty, but I have no sympathy with persons who make the Church of England something quite different from that which it was made at the Reformation.' He feared 'lest the foolish conduct of a few might so shake the confidence of the people in their National Established Church, that they would consider it no longer worth preserving.' The explanation, entirely subordinating the alleged requirements of Christian worship to the alleged requirements of national life, was one more reminder that his values were those of a Protestant, patriotic layman. Such values led him into the blunder of supporting the Public Worship Regulation Act, under which parish priests who had revived medieval practices could be, and were, sent to prison. Accordingly, most of the Anglo-Catholic clergy hated him. Their organ, the *Church Times*, declared: 'What music is to a man with no ear, that religion is to Archbishop Tait.'[54]

Tait's two successors in the archbishopric of Canterbury repeated the contrast which had existed between him and Wilberforce. Edward White Benson held High Church and Conservative convictions, and had put them into practice as the first Bishop of Truro; but he was out of touch with lay thought, including the psychological oddities and religious doubts of his own wife and children. Frederick Temple, on the other hand, was cautiously liberal like Tait, in theology as in politics. His real work had been done as a headmaster and bishop before he went to Canterbury in his old age. Indeed, despite all his labours, probably his most lasting contribution to church history was to demonstrate that a headmaster who had contributed to the liberal volume of *Essays and Reviews* could become a bishop and archbishop. When Gladstone appointed him to the see of Exeter there was an outbreak of indignation, although his contribution had been no more than the reworking of a sermon comparing the progress of humanity with the maturing of an individual. The ablest of Temple's fellow contributors, Mark Pattison and Benjamin Jowett, were ruined as theologians by the reception of their essays; the orthodox never forgave them, and they became increasingly more embittered, sceptical and cynical in Oxford. But while he was a bishop Frederick Temple's clergy forgot that he had ever been branded as a heretic. Although they feared him because they found him gruffly authoritarian, he could set them on fire

---

[54] Randall Davidson and William Benham compiled Tait's *Life* in 2 vols. (London, 1890). Despite its unjustified title, P. T. Marsh's study of *The Victorian Church in Decline: Archbishop Tait and the Church of England, 1868–82* (London, 1968), was well researched. M. A. Crowther studied theological controversies in *The Church Embattled* (Newton Abbot, Devon, 1970), and James Bentley studied legal battles in *Ritualism and Politics in Victorian Britain* (Oxford, 1978).

when he preached about national righteousness and the English mission to the world.[55]

Other Victorian bishops had a national standing while being mainly absorbed in diocesan work. One became known as the saintly pastor of agricultural labourers – Edward King of Lincoln; another as the champion of working men – James Fraser of Manchester. A third was famous as a writer of Evangelical tracts – J. C. Ryle, the first Bishop of Liverpool (who rebuked Fraser for his support of an agricultural workers' strike: both men spent many years as country parsons before moving to great industrial cities). A modern biography of Ryle assesses him in terms which could be applied to many of these bishops. 'Respect is perhaps the key word in describing the mutual relations of Ryle, the father, presbyter and bishop, and his family and flock. His undoubted ability, his strong convictions, his commanding appearance, his faithfulness and his sincerity created respect.' Edward King, however, was loved.[56]

Several of the Victorian bishops possessed international reputations as scholars. There were two great historians: William Stubbs, Bishop of Chester and Oxford, and Mandell Creighton, Bishop of Peterborough and London. Like Fraser and Ryle, these two also had spent happy years as country parsons. It was the boast of Stubbs that 'I knew every toe of every baby in the parish'. While in that parish and while a professor at Oxford, he did more than any other man of his generation to put English history before the Reformation on a new basis – the study of original documents (even if, being a good Victorian, he did tend to interpret the politics of the past

---

[55] A. C. Benson compiled *The Life and Letters of E. W. Benson* (2 vols., London, 1899). More informal material is to be found in A. C. Benson, *The Trefoil* (London, 1923), and E. F. Benson, *As We Were* (London, 1932). Books about the family include Betty Askwith, *Two Victorian Families* (London, 1971), and David Williams, *Genesis and Exodus: A Portrait of the Benson Family* (London, 1979). Braving his prohibition of a biography, E. G. Sandford compiled *Memoirs of Archbishop Temple by Seven Friends* (2 vols., London, 1906). Geoffrey Faber wrote about *Jowett* (London, 1957) and Ieuan Ellis about *Seven against Christ: A Study of Essays and Reviews* (Leiden, 1980). See Peter Hinchcliff, *Benjamin Jowett and the Christian Religion* (Oxford, 1987).

[56] Peter Toon and Michael Smout, *John Charles Ryle* (Cambridge, 1976), p. 103. See also John Newton, *Search for a Saint: Edward King* (London, 1977).

in terms of statesmen defending or developing a parliamentary democracy associated with the Anglo-Saxons). Creighton dared to put the history of the Renaissance Papacy on a solid foundation in books which he wrote in a vicarage in Northumberland. Partly because of his tolerance towards the sins of the popes the Victorians often suspected Creighton of cynicism – but they were unjust. He believed in generosity towards the dead and the living as a part of his Anglican faith. 'Current morality, philanthropy, high aims in politics, ideas of progress, of liberty, of brotherhood – what you will – owe their position to Christianity', he once claimed.[57]

Two Cambridge theologians, J. B. Lightfoot and B. F. Westcott, were successively Bishops of Durham. They had both been schoolfellows with the future Archbishop Benson at King Edward's School, Birmingham, in the 1840s. Jointly they did much to justify Bishop Creighton's claim about Christianity's influence in Victorian England.

Lightfoot was a matter-of-fact man. Apart from a part-time canonry at St Paul's he lived in the academic peace of Cambridge until he went to Durham at the age of fifty-one, and he was immensely learned. 'Does it not sometimes happen to you', he once innocently asked a young clergyman, 'that when you have read a book you forget in what language it was written?' While a bishop he continued these scholarly labours, but gave his main energies to his diocese. He preached about the local saints; but he was also practical with an unexpected vigour. The over-large diocese was divided by the creation of the diocese of Newcastle, and in what remained, the administration and finances were reorganized. Forty-five new churches were built in ten years, and lay people were encouraged to assist the clergy in preaching and visiting. The Bishop had young men who wanted to be priests to live with him in Auckland Castle, and was often in the villages and towns – as a pastor, not a prince.[58]

---

[57] See W. H. Hutton, *William Stubbs* (London, 1906). His widow Louise compiled *The Life and Letters of Mandell Creighton* in 2 vols. (London, 1905), and W. G. Fallows considered *Mandell Creighton and the English Church* (Oxford, 1964).

[58] See *Lightfoot of Durham*, ed. G. R. Eden and F. C. Macdonald (Cambridge, 1932).

When Lightfoot had worn himself out by this work, he was succeeded by the slightly older Professor Westcott. The term 'mystic' was often applied to Westcott, a man who was unwordly but not vague. He worked with another Cambridge scholar, F. J. A. Hort, on a revised Greek text of the New Testament, using manuscript sources superior to those available to previous generations of scholars. This text was published in 1881, just before the Revised Version of the New Testament in English which it had assisted. He encouraged the beginnings of the Cambridge degree course in theology, of the 'university extension' movement for adult education, of the Cambridge Mission to Delhi – believing that 'no nation, no church . . . was ever called to fulfil a greater work than that to which the English nation and the English Church are now summoned'. And he wrote much, his constant theme being that all men had been taken by the humanity of Jesus the Consecrator into the life of God. The Resurrection and Ascension were to him pledges that the long process of evolution, so far from being merely a struggle for existence governed by accident, was progressing to the final unity and transfiguration of the universe which God had created in his love; so that Christ was 'Consummator' as well as Consecrator. And he plainly believed that the Victorian age had brought the consummation somewhat nearer. It was Westcott's belief that 'the Church educates and inspires society, which moulds the State'.

The Conservative Prime Minister scotched the Queen's suggestion in 1890 that Westcott should be made Archbishop of York, by drawing her attention to 'the Socialist tendencies of the speeches which he has made since becoming a bishop'. By 1892 he was sufficiently trusted by the (mostly Methodist) miners of County Durham to be asked to mediate between them and their employers during a strike by about 10,000 men which had reduced most of their families to destitution. Westcott negotiated a compromise which lessened the reduction in wages proposed by the employers. It was an achievement unusual in the history of mysticism.[59]

---

[59] His son Arthur compiled *The Life and Letters of Brooke Foss Westcott* in 2 vols. (London, 1903). See also A. C. Benson, *Leaves of the Tree* (London, 1911), and

The Christian Social Union of which he was president can be criticized as a middle-class, predominantly clerical, effort to form study groups which talked about brotherhood instead of joining the necessary revolution. It can also be said to have been too vague about questions such as how St John's gospel was related to miners' wages. A recent historian has commented about this and other manifestations of the revival of Christian Socialism towards the end of their century, that 'their "Socialism" was an intellectual ragbag, and most of them never faced up to the dominant question: "What is specifically Christian about Christian Socialism?" '[60] George Bernard Shaw presented the Christian Socialist as an over-confident orator in his play *Candida* (1898), and there was always an amateurish flavour to the movement. For example, Stuart Headlam who founded the Guild of St Matthew in 1877, and was its leading spirit until its dissolution in 1909, was an Etonian who had become a ritualist while serving as a curate in the East End of London. He had a sincere belief that the Eucharist was meant to be a rehearsal for a drama in which justice would be distributed far more evenly among the poor. And he had courage; he met Oscar Wilde, who had been imprisoned for homosexual practices amid great unpopularity, on the morning of his release from prison, and looked after him until he went into exile. But he always kept up the tastes of a gentleman. He loved cigars, he was a devotee of the ballet, he had little taste for economics.[61]

Even the more practical northerners of the Church Socialist League founded in 1909, or individualists such as Conrad Noel who was appointed vicar of the lovely Suffolk church at

---

Geoffrey Best, *Bishop Westcott and the Miners* (Cambridge, 1967). A Swedish scholar, Folke Olofsson, wrote a study of Westcott's theology: *Christus Redemptor et Consummator* (Uppsala, 1979).

[60] Peter d'A. Jones, *The Christian Socialist Revival 1877–1914* (Princeton, N.J., 1968), p. 449.

[61] Reginald Groves, *Conrad Noel and the Thaxted Movement* (London, 1967), may be compared with Walter Kendall, *The Revolutionary Movement in Great Britain 1900–21* (London, 1969). Late Victorian social idealism was studied by Melvin Richter, *The Politics of Conscience* (Cambridge, Mass., 1964). Studies of Headlam, Noel and other Christian Socialists were edited by M. B. Beckitt as *For Christ and the People* (London, 1968).

Thaxted in 1911, advocated a decentralized 'Guild Socialism' on a medieval pattern. They could be (and were) dismissed as sentimentalists by those who looked forward to the great take-over by the State or who simply demanded higher wages. G. K. Chesterton commented about the Christian Social Union:

> And so they sang a lot of hymns
> To help the Unemployed.

Yet Chesterton himself wrote a much used hymn about social righteousness ('O God of earth and altar'), while Scott Holland's hymn 'Judge eternal, throned in splendour' found echoes in many hearts with its plea for the cleansing of a great empire, in 1902. In 1909 William Cunningham, who in addition to being an archdeacon was an economist very critical of inexpert idealism, noted that 'in any gathering of clergy and ministers, there are sure to be many who take a pride in declaring that they are Christian Socialists. It may be doubted whether any such change in public opinion occurred even at the Reformation itself.'[62]

It was the natural tendency of the Church of England throughout the nineteenth century to be 'the Conservative party at prayer' (a much-repeated gibe of uncertain authorship). The appeal of Christian Socialism to some of the best of the Anglicans was therefore a remarkable tribute to the influence of intellectual leaders such as Maurice in the middle of the century and Westcott towards its end. Their teaching inspired idealism. Still more remarkable was the evolution of the conscience of the devout Anglican layman who was the century's most fascinating and creative force in English public life.

THE GREATEST VICTORIAN

It was Disraeli who made the most famous of the announcements that Victorian England was divided into two nations,

---

[62] George Kitson Clark, *Churchmen and the Condition of England*, p. 312.

the rich and the poor. This was in his novel *Sybil* (1848), where a Chartist's daughter was loved by an enlightened young aristocrat. And Disraeli did much for the working class. He secured votes in future elections for workers who occupied their own houses – in 1867, the year when the first volume of Karl Marx's *Das Capital* was published obscurely in London. When he had made sure of the leadership of the Conservative party by the skill of that feat, he proceeded to make the Conservatives popular by a programme of limited social reforms at home and unlimited imperialism abroad, asserting that others could rise as he had done. The man who emerged as his successor in the Conservative leadership after his death in 1881, Lord Salisbury, also wooed the people by social reforms and imperialism. However, being more of a philosopher than Disraeli, he was also more of a pessimist. The most that the Conservatives could do, in his honest conviction, was to postpone the day when his whole world would lie in ruins.[63]

But it was William Ewart Gladstone, the greatest of all the Victorians, who contributed most to the union of the rich and poor. In the final analysis he did not do it in order to win political victories for himself or his party; had his motivation been entirely selfish, he would probably have led the Conservatives not the Liberals, and would have retired from politics to bask in scholarly leisure and a prestige above controversy long before he got himself and his party bogged down in the insoluble problems of Ireland. When he died in 1892, he was assessed by Lord Salisbury in the House of Lords (an institution which had narrowly escaped from his wrath) in words which were more than funeral flattery. Salisbury declared that 'what he sought were the attainments of great ideals' which 'could have issued from nothing but the greatest and purest moral aspirations'. To Salisbury and to others who had recently been his embattled opponents Gladstone was an example,

---

[63] Recent studies include Robert Blake, *Disraeli* (London, 1966) and *The Conservative Party from Peel to Churchill* (London, 1970); Paul Smith, *Disraelian Conservatism and Social Reform* (London, 1967); A. L. Kennedy, *Salisbury 1830–1903* (London, 1953); M. Pinto-Duschinsky, *The Political Thought of Lord Salisbury 1854–68* (London, 1967); C. H. D. Howard, *Splendid Isolation* (London, 1967).

'to which history hardly furnishes a parallel, of a great Christian'.

This tribute to Gladstone was more accurate than the more famous verdict of Disraeli: 'a sophisticated rhetorician inebriated with the exuberance of his own verbosity, and gifted with an egotistical imagination that can at all times command an interminable and inconsistent series of arguments to malign an opponent and to glorify himself.' From adolescence to death, Christianity was his deepest interest and most powerful inspiration – which was also true of Salisbury.

Gladstone received this faith in an Evangelical shape, from an intensely religious mother. His father, a Liverpool merchant involved in many highly profitable projects including the ownership of slaves in the West Indies, for some time associated with the Whig Unitarians dominating his prosperous city but, when he grew rich himself, became an Anglican and a Tory.[64] He had social and political ambitions which he could only fulfil by handsomely subsidizing the early career of the most brilliant of his children. The son of such parents was, not surprisingly, a prig while at Oxford after Eton. When not yet twenty he wrote an immense document beginning: 'The state of religion in Oxford is the most painful spectacle it ever befell my lot to behold.' When his attraction to the 'sublime duty' of a clergyman had been discouraged by his father, he entered the House of Commons (in 1833) in a missionary frame of mind, improving his delivery as an orator by reading other men's sermons aloud to himself. As late as 1844 he still saw himself primarily as a member of the Church of England whose vocation happened to be political leadership. As he then wrote to his intimate friend, James Hope: 'The purpose of Parliamentary life resolves itself with me simply and wholly into one question, Will it ever afford the means under God of rectifying the relations between the Church and the State and give one an opportunity of setting forward such a work?'

His first speech in the House was a defence of his father as a slave-owner. His very heavy election expenses, which at a later date would have been considered corrupt, had been met partly

---

[64] S. E. Checkland studied *The Gladstones* (Cambridge, 1971).

by his father and partly by the reactionary duke who in effect dictated to the small electorate. He proceeded to delight the duke by opposing almost all social reforms under debate. His devout eloquence pleading for no change would probably have won for him a devoted congregation, a bishopric and an archbishopric had he become the priest he always was in half his heart; and in the political life which he had accepted as his destiny he now spoke and wrote copiously in defence of the Church.

His book on *The State in its Relations with the Church* (1838) expounded his political creed. Macaulay reviewed it as a nonsensical utterance from 'the rising hope of those stern and unbending Tories', and the Tory leader Peel, who was a realist, despaired of Gladstone's future when he distastefully dipped into it. The book did indeed seem naïve. Gladstone ardently supported the establishment of the Church of England, but not because Church and State were one people (as Hooker had argued in the sixteenth century) or because it was useful to ally them for the benefit of society (as Warburton had argued in the eighteenth). There was now a plurality of Churches, but the State was a corporate 'person' with a conscience, and its sacred duty was to support the Church which taught the truth. The alternative was a nightmare: 'social atheism'. The chapter which caused most surprise was one in which Gladstone surveyed the relations of Church and State in the colonies over which Victoria had begun to rule, everywhere urging the benefits of establishing the Church of England because of its true faith. The experience of the rebellious colonies which had become the United States was dismissed. It seemed to be implied that since Anglican endowments and other privileges in Ireland could be justified on this basis although it meant favouring a minority, a similar establishment would have to be erected in India were that sub-continent ever to be brought under the direct government of Westminster.[65]

Gladstone was, however, rescued from the fate of being

---

[65] Gladstone's teaching on Church and State was examined by A. R. Vidler, *The Orb and the Cross* (London, 1947). Perry Butler, *Gladstone: Church, State and Tractarianism* (Oxford, 1982), went from 1809 to 1859.

remembered in history as 'the last man on a sinking ship' (his own phrase in 1867). He developed a theology which upheld his real convictions about the Church better than any establishment and endowment by the State – and which could continue to give strength and power to the Church after the removal of the State's support.

In the year before he went up to Oxford, he had many talks about religion with his sister Anne, his godmother and 'a perfect saint', who was ill and dying. She persuaded him to enlarge his Evangelicalism, as she had enlarged hers, by accepting 'one Baptism for the remission of sins' and by studying Richard Hooker's theory of the Church as a visible society fed by sacraments and needing beauty and order. After his graduation at Oxford in 1831 (with high honours, but without coming under the influence of the men who were to become the Tractarians), he went on a long holiday to Italy. He was not impressed by the Italian Protestants, but in St Peter's, Rome, he had a vision of the unity of Christendom as the historic body of Christ. In Naples six weeks later he examined the Book of Common Prayer closely, having no other English books to read. The study brought home to him the truth in the Catholicism which his sister had propounded – and, with that, the fact that the Church of England maintained that truth. 'It presented to me Christianity under an aspect in which I had not yet known it: its ministry of symbols, its channels of grace, its unending line of teachers joining from the Head.' So he became sure that the Evangelical acceptance of Christ was likely to lead to the Catholic acceptance of the Church. Gladstone recalled with pride meeting Charles Simeon in 1815, but twenty years later recorded an unshakeable conviction that 'in substance the movement termed Evangelical and that falsely termed Popish are parts of one great and beneficent design of God, and that in their substance they will harmonize and co-operate.'

His book *Church Principles Considered in Their Results* (1840), worked out this belief in terms of the Anglican insistence on a sacramental system authorized by bishops in 'the Apostolical Succession' – and in terms of the Anglican denial of the claims of the nineteenth-century Papacy. And these convictions stayed with him through the 'terrible time' of the early 1850s, when to his anxiety about the future of the Church of England after the Gorham Judgement were added personal sorrows including the agonized death of a daughter and the conversion to Rome of James Hope and Henry Manning, his friends who had helped him revise his books for publication.

Another factor in Gladstone's rescue from the fate awaiting eccentric ultra-Tories was the extraordinary ability which he showed in mastering the problems accompanying high political office. This work was, in his eyes, his duty as a Christian. Here, as people observed, the 'Liverpool' in his heritage showed itself beneath the 'Oxford'. Peel believed in this practical ability despite his bafflement about the operations of the young man's religious conscience. (What could Peel or anyone else in politics make of a conscience which forced him to resign while he was greatly enjoying the Presidency of the Board of Trade, merely because Peel proposed to make a grant to the Roman Catholic seminary at Maynooth in Ireland – a grant which Gladstone thought wise, but which contradicted his book of 1838?) Until old age Gladstone was respected by all MPs, and feared by his political enemies, because on suitable occasions he could give such a superb performance as a statesman. He could discern a moral issue which would appeal to the people, as no other administrator could; he could draft a long bill and steer it to triumph as an Act of Parliament, as no other visionary could; and above all he could make speeches, in the House of Commons and far outside it – speeches which stunned by the authoritative assembly of a mass of details, and which elevated by the equally authoritative announcement of a crusade in the cause of righteousness. Nor did he shirk the drudgery. Sir James Graham said of the young Gladstone that he could do in four hours what it took anyone else sixteen to do – and he worked sixteen hours a day.

Such a statesman, however puzzling his religion might be, could not be dismissed as a naïve idealist. When Disraeli had unscrupulously destroyed Peel's leadership of the old Tories, there was an attempt to enlist Gladstone for a senior position among the new Conservatives. This attempt was renewed by Disraeli in 1858 despite his own intense dislike of the man.

When Gladstone chose instead to serve as Chancellor of the Exchequer under the Whig Lord Aberdeen, the Queen was one of the many who admired his work. When Lord Palmerston had emerged as the leader of the new Liberal Party, a coalition of Whigs and Radicals, he gave Gladstone much freedom as Chancellor of the Exchequer although he, too, disliked him. Ten years of success as Chancellor of the Exchequer, laying important foundations for the mid-Victorian prosperity, were what made him 'the People's William'. It also made his identification with the Liberals so complete that he went into opposition with them in 1866. His disciple and biographer, John Morley, truthfully remarked that 'in other matters he followed, as it was his business and necessity to follow, the governing forces of the public mind; in finance he was a strenuous leader.' The direction of his leadership was towards limited although efficient government, curbing public expenditure, keeping taxation light although just, and freeing trade from control or protection. All these policies he advocated as a moralist and executed as an administrator of genius.

This career was still going strong and making history half a century after the publication of *The State in its Relations with the Church*. His contemporaries – themselves no idlers – marvelled at the sheer energy which helped him to form fresh convictions and to push through fresh programmes when almost all men would have felt that they had contributed enough. The energy derived in part from his physical fitness and toughness; tree-felling really was one of his favourite relaxations in old age. It also derived in part from his confidence about his social position. He was a handsome young man known to be a millionaire's favourite son, and after frightening off two young women with whom he was in love, he married Caroline Glynne. She was related to many of the leading Whigs and brought with her the large estate around the castle at Hawarden in North Wales. Gladstone had to put much of his own time and money into the estate in order to rescue it from mismanagement, but it assured his status. Although too aristocratic to be conventional or competent, Caroline Glynne was in many ways an excellent wife for him. Certainly he liked to have aristocrats around him in public life, but there is no evidence that he felt inferior to any of them.

Probably the most important source of his energy was, however, a rare combination of religion and sex. His religion instructed him, and helped him, to sublimate his passions by putting them into charitable and political work; but when his diaries began to be published in 1968, readers were surprised to see how fierce were his temptations and self-reproaches. It is clear that he was highly sexed, although we have no reason to doubt the truth of his statement to his son Stephen (a priest) in 1896 that he had 'not been guilty of the act which is known as that of infidelity to the marriage bed'. Throughout his adult life until 1886 (when he at last yielded to entreaties from his political associates) he devoted countless evenings and a vast sum of his own money to rescuing prostitutes.

It was Christian charity, which his wife approved of and assisted; he maintained that this form of lay work had become his when a small group of Christian young men in Oxford cast lots in seeking divine guidance about their duties. But his diaries show repeatedly that he needed the stimulus of the company of these young women; that he greatly enjoyed discussing their lives with them; and that he never pretended to himself that his motives were wholly virtuous. He refused to give up this work, even when he was blackmailed, even when he was Prime Minister. He thought it possible that reports about it helped to poison the Queen's mind against him. And even when he ceased to accost prostitutes in the street (in his mid-seventies), he still kept up correspondence with women from this background and still held private conversations with society beauties and actresses whose morals were not 'Victorian'. Nothing could show more clearly how tireless was the drive resulting from a sexual energy which had been christened.

Thus superbly equipped as a Christian statesman, Gladstone felt driven into the leadership of radical causes. It was not a rapid or complete conversion. As early as 1848 he caused a sensation by voting for the admission of Jews to the Commons; but as late as 1862 he caused another by foolishly announcing that in the American civil war the slave-owners of the southern states had 'made a nation'. When he had at last succeeded Palmerston and Lord John Russell in the leadership of the Liberals, he was still so conscious of the remaining Whig element in Liberalism – and in his own mind – that he allowed Disraeli to outmanoeuvre him by introducing a more radical proposal, so that in the end it was the Conservative party that could claim the credit for the doubling of the electorate by the Reform Act of 1867. With his divided mind Gladstone so often was an enigma. In all his governments it was again and again difficult for his colleagues to tell in advance where he would be more radical than they were, and where more conservative, and where simply bored.

Above all, he remained conservative in his loyalty to the Church of England and its historic institutions. When he was defeated in his attempt to continue to represent Oxford University in Parliament (in 1865), he wrote in his diary: 'A dear dream is dispelled.' But it never was totally dispelled. When he lay dying in great pain from cancer, he dictated his thanks for one message. 'There is no expression of Christian sympathy which I value more than that of the ancient university of Oxford, the God-fearing and God-sustaining university of Oxford. I served her, perhaps mistakenly, but to the best of my ability. My most earnest prayers are hers to the uttermost and the last.' He remained sure that there was no electoral mandate for the disestablishment of the Church of England, although he expected that to come after his death and he wished the Church to be prepared for it. He admitted that the Anglican case was weaker in Wales, but he privately described his own party's proposals for disestablishment there as 'plunder'. As the squire of a village in North Wales he saw no need to supplement the education provided by the church school. Although in 1870 his own government had created the Board Schools where religious education according to a denominational document such as the Book of Common Prayer was forbidden, in 1894 he was still asserting to his son Stephen that 'an undenominational system of religion, framed by or under the authority of the State, is a moral monster. . . . Whether the Act of 1870 requires or permits anything of the kind, I cannot say; but if it did, its provisions would involve a gross error.'

Yet he came to see that almost all the causes which he had defended as a young man were wrong. Fundamental to his development was a broadening of his religion. He never ceased to be a devout Anglican; he attended morning and evening services every day while at Hawarden, and wrote many prayers for use at Holy Communion. He was always, as he wrote to a Unitarian friend in 1865, 'one altogether attached to Christian dogma, which I believe to be the skeleton that carries the flesh, the blood, the life of the blessed thing we call the Christian religion.' But he added: 'I do not believe that God's mercies are restricted to a small portion of the human family. . . . I was myself brought up . . . to believe that salvation depended absolutely upon the reception of a particular and very narrow creed. But long, long have I cast those weeds behind me.'

He now repudiated the notion that the State always had a duty to support a Church – or to support that religion on which all the Churches might agree. The letter of 1894 just quoted expressed his opinion that 'the State has no charter from heaven such as may belong to the Church or to the individual conscience. It would, as I think, be better for the State to limit itself to giving secular instruction (which of course is no complete education). . . .' And he believed that if refounded on the basis of the voluntary support of its own members, an Established Church which had served only a minority of the citizens would find that it was more effective in its spiritual mission because less open to the charge of worldliness. He gave 30,000 of his own books and an endowment to St Deiniol's Library which he built in Hawarden; there the clergy of the future would equip themselves for a mission which would continue and flourish when their present privileges had been withdrawn.

His boldest demonstration of his new beliefs about Church and State was the disestablishment and partial disendowment of the Irish dioceses in the United Church of England and Ireland. When he received the Queen's summons to power in 1868, he declared: 'My mission is to pacify Ireland.'

To those who later looked back, the step seemed inevitable. Of a population of about 5,800,000 in Ireland in the 1860s,

fewer than 700,000 were Anglicans. When the Irish National
Association was founded in 1864, it agreed to 'demand the
disendowment of the Established Church in Ireland as a
condition without which peace and stability, general respect
for laws, and unity of sentiment and action for national objects,
can never prevail in Ireland.' So in March 1868, before the
general election, Gladstone secured a majority of sixty-five in
the House of Commons for motions endorsing this policy. Yet
credit is due to him for his courage in seizing the initiative.
Many others reckoned that the problem was too explosive to
handle. That was why handling it had been postponed for so
long. One question among many which had deterred British
politicians was whether some of the Anglican endowments
should be given to the Roman Catholics and Presbyterians – a
suggestion which seemed equitable to many, but which was
denounced by Anglicans as theft and by Roman Catholics
and Presbyterians as a bribe. It was also very difficult to decide
how much of the endowments should be left with the Anglicans
(in the end the decision was: almost two-thirds the financial
assets and all the buildings, with nothing going to the Roman
Catholics or to the Presbyterians). The complicated and controversial Irish Church Bill needed all Gladstone's advocacy –
and thus made him eat many of his own previous words; the
publication of *A Chapter of Autobiography* was thought essential.
His desertion of what he called 'Church Principles' was deeply
resented by many of his fellow Anglicans.[66] When disestablishment came into effect on the first day of 1871, Mrs Alexander's
new hymn was sung in Londonderry Cathedral:

> Look down, O Lord of heaven, on our desolation!
>   Fallen, fallen is our Country's crown,
> Dimly dawns the New Year on a churchless nation. . . .

Gladstone's reforming government was defeated in the general
election of 1874 mainly because its treatment of education had
alienated the Nonconformists. At sixty-five Gladstone
announced hs withdrawal from the Liberal leadership; he later
claimed that he had 'deeply desired an interval between

[66] P. M. H. Bell studied *Disestablishment in Ireland and Wales* (London, 1969).

parliament and the grave'. In fact, however, he was active for another twenty years – believing, as he told a young audience, that 'life is a great and noble calling; not a mean and grovelling thing, which we are to shuffle through as we can, but an elevated and lofty destiny.' He wrote extensively on the poetry of Homer. But was he not himself born to be a hero? He edited the works of Bishop Joseph Butler. But was not life for moral action?

It was typical of his religion that his one departure from orthodoxy was to suggest that after death the wicked would simply cease to live. For him, life was righteous or it was nothing. It was also typical of his approach to ecclesiastical affairs that when he denounced 'Vaticanism' in long pamphlets after the First Vatican Council he made the mistake of concentrating his fire on the alleged Roman Catholic threat to civil obedience and political loyalty, when what happened in Rome in 1870 was the claim to a spiritual empire by the proclamation of papal infallibility at the very time when the papacy's temporal power was ended by the Italian national-ists' occupation of Rome. He thus laid himself open to devas-tating replies, but religion to him was politically involved or it was nothing. Examining himself in his diary during 1878, Gladstone noted: 'I am still under the painful sense that my public life is and has the best of me . . .'

His politics became the politics of liberty. 'I was brought up to distrust and dislike liberty', he told John Morley in 1891; 'I learned to believe in it. That is the key to all my changes.' And in 1876 liberty for the Bulgarians brought him back into political leadership. A revolt in Bulgaria, then a part of the Turkish empire, was brutally suppressed, and Disraeli ordered a British fleet to the Dardenelles as a warning to Russia not to interfere. In British upper-class circles these actions were generally accepted, and Disraeli had so little idea that a storm would break that he accepted an earldom from an admiring Queen and began to enjoy being Prime Minister in the tran-quillity of the House of Lords. But Gladstone published his pamphlet on *The Bulgarian Horrors and the Question of the East*; and impressed an initially hostile House of Commons by the greatest speech of his whole parliamentary career, pleading for

the Bulgarians as fellow Christians and fellow Europeans.
After a sensational victory in a rural, Conservative constituency (Midlothian), he was inescapable as the next Liberal Prime
Minister. Within his previous experience of government Britain had entered the Crimean War believing that it could
forcibly support a corrupt government in Muslim Turkey
without interrupting its own life as a Christian democracy
interested in manufacturing and commerce. But he had been
one of those who had absorbed that bitter experience of a war
that brought only shame. Always after that he was for peace.
He urged 'the pursuit of objects which are European by means
which are European, in concert with the mind of the rest of
Europe and supported by its authority.' He meant a moral
authority – for when he spoke about Europe he had in mind the
continent of the Christian conscience, the Europe of Dante.[67]

In domestic affairs, the Reform Act of 1884 which gave the
vote to the agricultural labourers was the climax of a mental
evolution which he had first made public twenty years previously, shocking Palmerston. In 1866 he had replied to the
Liberal anti-democrat, Robert Lowe, that the men whose
qualifications to become electors were being disparaged were
'our fellow subjects, our fellow Christians, our own flesh and
blood.' He then concluded: 'You cannot fight against the
future.' His failure to unite the Liberals sufficiently to obtain
the credit for the enlargement of the electorate in 1867 showed
that Palmerston and Lowe were by no means alone. But
Gladstone's conviction could not accept defeat. 'All the world
over,' he declared in 1886, 'I will back the masses against the
classes. . . . The heart, the root, the beginning and ending of
my trust, is in the wise and generous justice of the nation.'

The most courageous crusade of his life was his fight to win
more liberty for the Irish. He came to see his moral duty to curb
the profits of Ireland's landlords, most of whom lived in
England, so that by the Irish Land Act of 1881 he created

---

[67] Olive Anderson studied the psychological impact of the Crimean War in *A
Liberal State at War* (London, 1967). C. C. Eldridge, *England's Mission: the Imperial
Idea in the Age of Gladstone and Disraeli* (London, 1973), was a study in reluctant
imperialism.

tribunals to establish fair rents for tenants. He also became convinced that it was his duty to create a parliament in Dublin capable of dealing with almost all Ireland's internal affairs, and he introduced his first Home Rule Bill in 1886. It was not easy to work out a plan acceptable to the Irish, since there were two enormous problems – how to make rule from Dublin in the predominantly Roman Catholic south acceptable to the Protestants in Ulster, and how to retain an Irish element in the Westminster Parliament, where the Irish Nationalist MPs were often able to trade their votes in political deals since as a large minority they often held the balance of power between the Liberals and the Conservatives. And if such problems were difficult, the problem of how to make any plan acceptable to the majority of the British electorate seemed utterly insoluble. The 1880s and 1890s were the heyday of British imperialism – a cause promising both glory and profits, with an appeal so powerful that even Gladstone had to go along with it. Yet here was a proposal to dismember the British empire by abandoning the large island next door to Britain after an imperial connection dating back to the reign of Henry II. The emotional and economic investment of the British in Ireland was so great that by adopting Home Rule Gladstone in effect condemned his party to division (Joseph Chamberlain, his natural successor, was a Unionist) and to twenty years of paralysis.[68]

When in 1892 the Liberals were returned to power, he was still at their head, and still determined on Irish Home Rule despite bitter disagreements in his cabinet, violent storms in the Commons and rejection by the Lords. The setback only encouraged Gladstone to seek another general election with a programme of restricting the power of the Lords to block the people's path to justice and liberty. This time, however, the cabinet refused to follow him. His colleagues also refused to support him against demands for greater expenditure on the navy. Seeing that his magic was gone, he did at last retire – but even in his last few years he could not refrain from controversy. In June 1896 he sent a public letter to Rome about the

---

[68] J. L. Hammond's classic *Gladstone and the Irish Nation* was reissued with an introduction by M. R. D. Foot (London, 1964).

'ineffable emptiness' of the papal condemnation of Anglican orders. A few months later he spoke for an hour and a half at a great public meeting in Liverpool, passionately condemning the latest Turkish massacre of Armenian Christians.

He died on Ascension Day 1898. His son Stephen gave him the Church of England's last blessing just before his heart stopped beating.[69]

---

[69] Many biographies were published before Gladstone's *Diaries* began to be printed in 1968. *The Life of William Ewart Gladstone* was compiled by John, later Viscount, Morley (3 vols., 1903), and deserved its great popularity, but as an agnostic Morley was handicapped and D. C. Lathbury filled a gap by his *Correspondence on Church and Religion of William Ewart Gladstone* (2 vols., London, 1910). Of the later biographies, the best were by Sir Philip Magnus (London, 1954), E. J. Feuchtwanger (London, 1975), and Richard Shannon (vol. 1, London, 1982). D. A. Hamer was down-to-earth in *Liberal Politics in the Age of Gladstone and Rosebery* (Oxford, 1972). J. P. Parry explored *Democracy and Religion: Gladstone and the Liberal Party 1867–75* (London, 1986). H. C. G. Matthew summed up his editing of the diaries in a fresh study of *Gladstone* (Oxford, 1986).

CHAPTER SIX

NONCONFORMITY

A POLITICAL FAILURE

In various crises Victorian Nonconformity offered a real political threat to the Church of England. In 1847 the Protestant Dissenting Deputies sponsored committees all over the country to secure the return of MPs known to favour 'those ecclesiastical principles which constitute the sole basis of religious freedom and equality'. The Deputies' eagerness to influence general elections then dwindled, but the gap which they left was filled from 1853 onwards by the Liberation Society and its long struggle for the Church of England's disestablishment. That campaign had much to do with Palmerston's defeat in the Commons in 1857, with subsequent elections including the return of almost ninety Nonconformists in 1865, and with the triumph of the righteous Gladstone as the worldly Palmerston's successor at the head of the Liberal Party. The Liberation Society employed agents to influence the constituencies before either of the political parties did.

Nonconformity made its weight felt in the much wider pressure which led to the creation of state schools (or, to be more accurate, of locally-controlled, rate-supported 'Board Schools') under the Education Act of 1870. The State had given grants to church schools since 1833, but its direct intervention in education had been delayed partly because Nonconformity had previously been so negative. Many Nonconformists, over-optimistic about their own resources, had fought for the 'Voluntaryist' principle, campaigning against all state aid to schools. Later there had been an agitation to exclude all religious teaching from any school which was supported by public money. Still in 1870 there was intense resentment against church schools. Only slowly had Nonconformists admitted that they would never be able to match the Church of England's network, so that local School Boards were essential if education was to be made compulsory between the ages of five and thirteen. Even slower had been the agreement that the local board could arrange non-denominational religious education – so deep and embittering had been the suspicion of Anglican influence.[1]

Other pressures persuaded Parliament to allow Nonconformist ministers to conduct funerals in parish churchyards, and to create parish councils, elected by all, which would take over the responsibility for village administration which had been the monopoly of the Anglican incumbent, churchwardens and vestry. These two reforms were postponed until 1880 and 1894. The comment is fair that 'there was not a single issue on which the Anglican Church met them with generosity. It yielded its privileges only when it was compelled to do so.'[2] Almost three-quarters of the Anglican clergy signed protests against the admission of Nonconformist funerals.

Nothing, however, was done to remedy the Liberation Society's main grievance: the Church of England's establishment. Indeed, in this crusade even the Liberation Society lost heart – and lost subscribers. Queen Victoria's successor took exactly the same oath to defend the Established Church that Queen Anne had taken, and as the twentieth century dawned bishops maintained their medieval positions in the House of Lords. At this central point, all the Nonconformist pressures failed – and we must ask why.

Some of the explanation is to be found in the recovery of morale in the Church of England, giving some slight excuse for Anglican arrogance. In 1859 the Church Institution was founded 'for defensive and general purposes', and by the 1880s

---

[1] Recent studies include A. B. Bishop, *The Rise of a Central Authority for English Education* (Cambridge, 1971), and, for local battles, Derek Fraser, *Urban Politics in Victorian England* (Leicester, 1976).

[2] R. Tudor Jones, *Congregationalism in England*, p. 276. W. H. Mackintosh told the story of the Liberation Society in *Disestablishment and Liberation* (London, 1972), and G. I. T. Machin studied *Politics and the Churches in Great Britain 1832–68*. A particularly notorious case after the death of a child aged two was reconstructed by Ronald Fletcher, *The Akenham Burial Case* (London, 1974).

it was printing half a million tracts a year. But even before the Anglican recovery could make itself felt in politics, the Church of England was in a position stronger than appeared. The Whig statesmen on whom the Nonconformists had to rely before the 1860s simply assumed in their hearts that the Church always would remain established; it was part of the country they loved, part of the constitution which needed only improvement. Lord Melbourne despised the Nonconformists, as did Lord Palmerston. Lord John Russell owed more to them, but he was himself firmly a Protestant layman of the Church of England, and when denouncing the new Roman Catholic dioceses in 1850 he spoke with enthusiasm about the rights of the bishops whom the Queen nominated. As a modern authority on the period has written: 'The Whigs were at no time prepared to lead a central attack on the Church of England, and without Whig parliamentary leadership organized Dissent could do very little. They were formidable in agitation; they were effective in obstruction. . . . What they could not do was to formulate and impose a policy of their own. They lacked the unity, the positive organization and still more the human material for parliamentary strength.'[3]

Essentially the same problem remained when the Whig Party gradually became the Liberal Party, guided by a slightly more popular leadership and supported by a much more popular press. Naturally this party attracted many votes from Nonconformists since it was the only alternative to the Conservatives. Indeed, some wealthy, confident and well-known Nonconformists, mainly from Yorkshire and Lancashire, now sat as Liberals in Parliament and one of them, John Bright, joined the cabinet in 1868. But some equally prominent Liberals with more conservative instincts went against Nonconformity in two test-cases of public morality in the 1860s, supporting the more aristocratic south in the American civil war and applauding Governor Eyre when he returned from Jamaica accused of excessive cruelty to the negroes. Many Wesleyan Methodists in Yorkshire and Lancashire continued

---

[3] Norman Gash, *Reaction and Reconstruction in English Politics 1832–52* (Oxford, 1965), p. 108.

to vote Conservative, and the Liberation Society itself opposed unsatisfactory Liberal candidates in elections even when this meant letting in a Conservative.[4]

John Bright's own life illustrates the difficulty of applying Nonconformity to mid-Victorian politics. He was born (in 1811) and he died (in 1889) in the Lancashire town of Rochdale, and was brought up in a Quaker home. His powers as an orator were discovered through the agitation against the landowners' corn laws, and he was often ready to attack the Church of England; as late as 1883 he spoke on 'The National Church and National Righteousness', contrasting the two. Since he was also a man of independent means (his father was a successful mill-owner), he seemed the natural political leader of Nonconformity. Yet he was unhappy as an MP – and not only because his wife refused to join him so far south as London. A series of nervous breakdowns forced him to resign from office under Gladstone and to curtail his political activities during the rest of his life. The tension was probably due to his failure to reconcile his Quaker heritage with the facts of power as he experienced them. Although he advocated peace and resigned from Gladstone's government when it bombarded the Egyptians in Alexandria in 1882, he did not concentrate on the international vision as did his fellow crusader against the corn laws, Richard Cobden. Although he advocated the vote for all, he disapproved of the Public Health Act of 1848 (which launched the struggle to clean up England's cities); of Lord Shaftesbury's crusade to improve factory traditions; and of later trade unionism. He refused to join the anti-slavery agitation and the pressure to have alcohol prohibited locally; and he was no more than a 'looker-on' when the Nonconformists demanded popular education free of Anglican interference. As firmly as any Whig grandee in former times, John Bright declined a call to become the preachers' tame spokesman in Westminster.[5]

---

[4] See John Vincent, *The Formation of the British Liberal Party 1857–68* (London, 1966), and P. F. Clarke, *Lancashire and the New Liberalism* (Cambridge, 1971).

[5] Keith Robbins supplied a biography of *John Bright* (London, 1979). Donald Read explored an often uneasy partnership in *Cobden and Bright* (London, 1967).

It comes as no surprise that although the Liberal Party emerging in 1859 relied heavily on the votes of Nonconformists, its refusal to cut off all aid to the Church of England's schools and to disestablish the Church killed off the enthusiasm. In 1877 Gladstone cannot have felt able to take the future for granted when he declared that 'Nonconformity supplies the backbone of English Liberalism'. The alliance survived this coolness partly because Disraeli was even more suspect. Lloyd George was to recall from his childhood the Welsh minister's prayer: 'Kill him, O Lord, kill him. We cannot kill him without being hanged ourselves, but thou canst kill him.' It was, however, also a factor that Nonconformity itself, in its disillusionment, was becoming discouraged about the prospects of disestablishment in England. Although the Liberation Society resolved in 1874 that 'the now shattered Liberal Party' needed the cause of disestablishment for its own reconstruction, a number of Nonconformist leaders voiced doubts about the wisdom of aggression, and after 1874 the loudest spokesmen for the cause were John Morley, who as an agnostic wanted a secular state, and Joseph Chamberlain, who was a Unitarian but above all a modernizer. Chamberlain's 'Alternative Programme' of 1885 incorporated Morley's proposal that all churches and cathedrals built before 1818 should be shared between the denominations or turned over to secular uses – a proposal which further alarmed many Nonconformists as being needlessly provocative.

It is conceivable that Chamberlain's radicalism, had he persisted in it, might have gradually won over many of these Nonconformists who hesitated, since they or their successors accepted Gladstone's more cautious movement to 'trust the people'. It seems possible to speculate that had the Liberal Party backed by the Nonconformists championed working-class interests earlier, it might have been able to resist more successfully the argument that an Independent Labour Party was needed in the 1890s. There might have been many more Liberals such as Joseph Arch, the farm-worker and Primitive Methodist lay preacher in Warwickshire, who led the sensational strike of 1872; or the miner Thomas Burt (the first working man to enter the House of Commons, in 1874); or the

stonemason Henry Broadhurst, secretary of the Parliamentary
Committee of the Trades Union Congress for many years from
1875, and briefly a junior minister under Gladstone (the first
working man to serve in a British government); or the engineering apprentice John Burns, President of the Local Government Board in 1905 (the first working man to enter a British
cabinet). Even if one judges that the birth of the Labour Party
was inevitable, one can see that a stronger involvement of the
Nonconformist–Liberal alliance to encourage working-class
progress would have strengthened the 'Lib–Lab' element in
politics at the beginning of the new century and thus would
have grown a larger crop of Christian, and definitely non-
Marxist, Socialism. Later on there would have been more
Labour leaders like Arthur Henderson, Philip Snowden and
Ellen Wilkinson. All were among the chief architects of the
twentieth-century Labour Party and all were deeply convinced
Methodists. Blake's poem about Christ in England, 'And did
those feet . . . ?', was often sung at Labour Party meetings. It
might have meant more than it usually did.

However, most Nonconformists seem to have had little
interest in Socialism.[6] The decision of the Trades Union
Council in 1894 to support 'the nationalization of the land and
of the whole means of production, distribution and exchange'
aroused the scorn of the *Primitive Methodist Magazine*. Liberal
leaders left it to the Conservatives in 1875 to change the law
which had exposed strikers to prosecution and imprisonment
as conspirators to 'restrain trade'. Their lethargy in the matter
was ominous. Gladstone championed Home Rule for Ireland
rather than any of the causes dearer to the Nonconformists. His
successor was an immensely rich landlord, the Earl of Rosebery. The Liberal programme in the 1895 election was heavily
indebted to the Nonconformists, but Rosebery made a thoroughly incongruous champion of it and the electorate's verdict
reduced the number of Liberal MPs to the lowest point since
the 1860s. 'Down goes the middle-class Radicalism and the

---

[6] Robert F. Wearmouth rejoiced in *Methodism and the Struggle of the Working Classes
1850–1900* (Leicester, 1954) and *The Social and Political Influence of Methodism in the
Twentieth Century* (London, 1957). But Robert Moore, *Pit-Men, Preachers and Politics*
(Cambridge, 1974), corrected some exaggerated claims.

Nonconformist conscience', wrote Canon Scott Holland; but these old causes had already gone down in the minds of the Liberal leaders in the twilight of the age of Gladstone.[7]

Rosebery resigned as leader (although his sadly isolated life did not end until 1929), and was free to attack social radicalism openly when the Liberals next returned to power. But the Boer War then brought a fresh division. It was applauded by many Liberals but in 1901 just over half the Nonconformist ministers in England signed a protest against it. Agitated efforts were now made to bind Nonconformity more tightly to Liberalism; R. W. Perks, an MP who was a Wesleyan Methodist and a Liberal imperialist, formed the Nonconformist Parliamentary Committee for this purpose in 1898. But not many Nonconformists could stomach efficiency and imperialism as Liberalism's new creed, and it was only the increased support for church schools in the Conservatives' Education Act of 1902 that revived the old spirit of battle. Anger about education helped to ensure the election of about two hundred MPs from a Nonconformist background in 1906, in a landslide victory for the Liberals. A modern scholar reckons that this anger 'transformed – seemingly overnight – the Nonconformist commitment to Liberalism from a vague sentiment to an active electoral alliance.'[8]

All the hesitations and controversies over radicalism at home and imperialism abroad were forgotten in 1906. For a few years Liberalism and Nonconformity marched hand in hand as in the golden days of Gladstonian crusading, to rescue the ratepayer from captivity in that den of privileged Anglicanism or Roman Catholicism, the church school. But the fervour of the alliance did not last, as we shall see. In general the lesson of this story of ups and downs seems to be that Nonconformity was effective on religious or moral, not political, territory. Its political aim was usually negative, opposing the Established Church but having no clear vision of an alternative society. It never won the total allegiance of a major statesman, or formed

---

[7] See R. R. James, *Rosebery* (London, 1963), and H. C. G. Matthew, *The Liberal Imperialists* (Oxford, 1973). Ian Bradley provided a good overview of Victorian Liberalism in *The Optimists* (London, 1980).

[8] Stephen Koss, *Nonconformity in Modern British Politics* (London, 1975), p. 38.

a strongly coherent and inflexibly determined group in Parliament.

Part of the reason was that it never developed a sophisticated culture as soil in which effective political activity – about education, for example – might grow. Politics often seemed to the Nonconformists a dirty business, to be redeemed only for a time when some prophet arose to lead a moral crusade against a flagrant iniquity; and when the crusade ran out of energy, the previous feeling that saints ought not to be troubled about the world reasserted itself, coupled with the feeling that the saints would be rewarded for their virtuous private lives by financial prosperity. Victorian novels abound in conflicts between enlightened but isolated Nonconformists and the armies of their narrow-minded co-religionists who were in full retreat from the world, apart from the need and the duty to make money. The tradition was still going strong in 1901 when Arnold Bennett's *Anna of the Five Towns* portrayed the sensitive women surrounded by money-minded Methodists in Staffordshire. Mrs Oliphant's *Salem Chapel* (1865) is the story of a young minister who resigns, disgusted with the gossip and backbiting in his congregation; her own brother William had a similar experience. Mrs Gaskell's *Ruth* (1853) is the story of another minister who supports an unmarried mother against the Pharisaical condemnation of laymen in the chapel; the novel outraged the congregation to which her husband ministered in Manchester. Mrs Gaskell's *Cousin Phillis* (1864) is mainly an idyll of innocent rural Nonconformity, with hymns rising as the sun sets, but it does include a scene where the saintly minister is rebuked for his sins by his fellow ministers; he must be a sinner, because God has sent 'brain fever' to his child Phillis.[9]

The protest against Nonconformity's narrow-mindedness was made with a clumsy sincerity in the work of William Hale White, the most extensive treatment of chapel life in nineteenth-century fiction.

His forefathers had belonged to the chapel in Bedford named after John Bunyan, but he was disgusted when simple and sensible inquiries about the Bible which he made when in

---

[9] The best study is Angus Easson, *Elizabeth Gaskell* (London, 1979).

training to be a minister were silenced with anger by his ultra-orthodox teachers; his own father defended him on this occasion in a pamphlet entitled *To Think or not to Think*. He was even more disgusted by what he saw of everyday Nonconformist narrowness and humbug once his eyes were adult and open. So his pilgrimage led him from Bunyan's chapel into the wilderness of a civil service job and journalism in London, just as it led the hero of his most famous novels, Mark Rutherford, to seek deliverance from chapel life. The poems of Wordsworth, the books of Thomas Carlyle, his own cruelly honest thinking about himself and his contemporaries – all these made him radically dissatisfied with the debased Puritanism which he had encountered, although he was never able to find any alternative to make his brooding, self-torturing, soul happy. In vain did he tell himself and his readers that it was his duty to be happy. 'The highest form of martyrdom', he wrote, '. . . is not living for the sake of a cause, but living without one, merely because it is your duty to live.'[10]

In his *Culture and Anarchy* (1869), Matthew Arnold summed up the impression which this political and cultural failure left on many sensitive Victorians. 'Look at the life imaged in such a newspaper as the *Nonconformist* – a life of jealousy of the Establishment, disputes, tea meetings, openings of chapels, sermons; and then think of it as an ideal of human life completing itself on all sides, and aspiring with all its organs after sweetness, light and perfection!'

A RELIGIOUS STRENGTH

Victorian Nonconformity inherited a powerful position in English religion. The official census of churchgoing taken on Sunday 30 March 1851 suggested that there were about 4,500,000 attendances at the principal Nonconformist chapels, only some 800,000 fewer than attendances in all the Church of

---

[10] Wilfred Stone studied *The Religion and Art of W. Hale White* (Stanford, Cal., 1954), and Irvin Stock, *William Hale White: Mark Rutherford* (London, 1956). A comprehensive study of Nonconformity in the nineteenth-century novel by Valentine Cunningham was entitled *Everywhere Spoken Against* (Oxford, 1975).

England's churches. In Wales, where Anglicanism had been established since Tudor times, more than eighty per cent of worshippers were non-Anglicans. But this inherited position needed to be renewed by a constant supply of personal commitment, and particularly in the 1850s anxious Nonconformists asked whether the supply was still flowing. The scandal of the schisms in Methodism coincided with a national mood of militarism responding to the Crimean War and the Indian mutiny. In the towns there were cholera epidemics and in the countryside there was distress. In 1854 the Primitive Methodist Conference recorded that 'provisions have risen, to the humbler classes of society, to almost starving price. The result is that thousands who were cheerful supporters of the Connexional Funds, and creditable members of society, have fainted beneath the pressure of poverty, and withdrawn from Church fellowship'.[11] Declining zeal, it was observed, explained the malaise among Nonconformists able to contribute to funds and to play their parts in chapel life. In 1846 the *Baptist Record* had reckoned that the Evangelical revival was exhausted. 'There are many indubitable signs of spiritual depression, of diminished vitality and power. Nor is this state of things confined to ourselves; wherever the results of close observation have been made known, we are called to notice the same melancholy fact.'

However, Victorian Nonconformity's religious progress was soon resumed. The *Christian World*, founded in 1857 as an organ for Nonconformity, soon achieved the largest circulation of the serious religious weeklies (over a hundred thousand). The revivalist meetings at the end of the 1850s spread enthusiasm, and the celebration in 1862 of the departure of the Dissenters from the Church of England was no occasion either for nostalgia or for reconciliation with the Anglicans; it inspired a spurt of chapel-building. And the forty years after 1862 saw much continuous vitality. In 1897 a Methodist leader, Hugh Price Hughes, boasted that a council of the Free Churches would represent 'a majority of the Christian people of England'. Obviously this boast depended on not reckoning either the Roman

---

[11] H. B. Kendall compiled *A History of the Primitive Methodist Church* (London, 1919).

Catholics of the Church of England's occasional church-goers among the 'Christian people', but the statistics quoted by Hughes were undeniably impressive. The Free Churches had, it was claimed, 1,807,723 communicants, almost 30,000 more than the Church of England. They had 327,685 Sunday School teachers, about 173,000 more; and 3,103,285 pupils, about 774,000 more. They could seat just over 7,600,000 people in their churches, about 832,000 more. And other figures which Hughes did not quote were also to the credit of the Free Churches. They had under 9,000 full-time ministers as compared with over 21,000 clergy in the Church of England. Healthily, they relied on the support of their own lay members to lead the life of some 20,000 chapels. Of particular importance were some 48,000 lay preachers. More than 1,750,000 English people were full members of these congregations, only about a quarter of a million fewer than those who at Easter presented themselves at the altars of the Church of England. Since the population of England grew immensely in the second half of the nineteenth century, Nonconformity never escaped the haunting sense of the uncoverted masses; yet in each denomination the growth of full membership during that period gave encouragement. In round figures the Wesleyan Methodists grew to 435,000 from 240,000; the Primitive Methodists to 200,000 from 100,000; the Congregationalists to 258,000 from 165,000; the Baptists to 243,000 from 140,000.[12]

The 'temperance' campaign was an important example of mainly Nonconformist activity, for alcoholism was a major social problem. When the Victorian age opened alcohol had come to dominate daily life, to an extent which was disastrous for health, for thrift and for a rational expenditure on food, housing, clothing, culture and other goods. Spirits were the ruin of rich and poor alike, combined with too many bottles of

---

[12] Ian Sellers, *Nineteenth-Century Nonconformity*, and David Thompson, *Nonconformity in the Nineteenth Century*, are helpful about the Victorians as well as about their predecessors. John Briggs and Ian Sellers have collected documents illustrating *Victorian Nonconformity* (London, 1973). Kenneth Young collected more personal memories in his *Chapel* (London, 1972). *Chapels and Meeting Places* as architecture were studied by Kenneth Lindley (London, 1969). For the distribution of Nonconformity, see John D. Gay, *The Geography of Religion in England* (London, 1971).

port for rich men and too many gallons of beer for poor men
(and women and children). Heavy drinking seemed essential
because water and milk were both too dangerous, because
cooking was often primitive, because homes were often
squalid, and because social gatherings without this aid seemed
intolerably dull. Because there was no alternative accommodation, committees and societies tended to meet in public houses
– and to refresh themselves. And it was by no means easy to
find an answer appropriate to a free people. In order to reduce
the consumption of spirits, the trade in beer was freed from
almost all taxes and restrictions in 1830, but now that a pint of
beer was as cheap as a cup of tea naturally the consumption of
beer increased dramatically without harming the sale of spirits. A similar effect was achieved when the wine trade was
encouraged in 1860.

The result of these disappointments was the growth of the
self-denying 'total abstinence' movement, the United Kingdom Alliance for this purpose being founded by a Baptist and a
Quaker in 1853. At the end of the 1870s the 'blue ribbon' for
those who had taken 'the pledge' spread to England from
America, again with Nonconformist support. There was an
accompanying agitation to discipline those unable to take such
vows for themselves, leading to the re-imposition of firm
licensing restrictions on the drink trade as a whole. In 1876 no
fewer than 23,000 people were sent to prison for drunk and
disorderly behaviour. 'Bands of Hope' were formed for young
people who had taken the pledge against alcohol and were
urging their elders to be brave; by the end of the century there
were three million such children. 'Coffee palaces' and similar
establishments were opened to assist these elders. The People's
Café Company, directed by the great Congregationalist and
philanthropist Samuel Morley, began its work in 1874, using
the French name because that work was so strange to England.
The first non-alcoholic music hall, the Old Vic, was opened in
1880. But 'the trade' hit back in alliance with the Conservative
Party (heavily funded by brewers), and the enemies of alcohol
were divided on key questions – should the restrictions be
national or should local restrictions be merely permitted by
national legislation? And should the aim be total prohibition?

A bill to permit local prohibition was introduced by a Nonconformist MP, Sir Wilfrid Lawson, each year between 1864 and 1880. It was never passed, but during the 1880s the customs of using public houses to pay wages and to hold committee meetings at election time were prohibited, and during the 1890s Sir William Harcourt revived Lawson's campaign, contributing to the Liberal disaster in 1895. The battle continued until the 1920s, when it became clear that the 'pleasures of the poor' could now be varied and satisfactory enough to reduce the temptation of drunkenness, while the problems of the poor were clearly no longer attributable mainly to drink. It seems fair to conclude that although total abstinence arose as a working-class movement in the 1830s outside all the Churches, a fight so prolonged and so confused could never have been sustained without the religious determination put into it by the Nonconformists. They had as allies some Church of England people (usually Evangelicals) and a few Roman Catholics.[13]

The moral fervour which attempted to dry up this ocean of alcohol also encouraged many thousands of Nonconformists to take part in the campaign led by Cobden and Bright in the 1840s to get cheaper food for industrial workers by repealing the protectionist corn laws.[14] And they responded eagerly to some later calls such as Gladstone's denunciation of the massacres of the Bulgarians – when, as Gladstone wrote privately, 'there is now, the first time for a good many years, a virtuous passion'. Where the Nonconformists were united in such a passion they could make their strength felt decisively, and shrewd politicians made their calculations accordingly. At the end of Victoria's reign Joseph Chamberlain begged the Conservative party managers to remember this strength, and when to his horror he saw it massing against the Conservatives he produced 'tariff reform' in an effort to attract votes in the

---

[13] See Brian Harrison, *Drink and the Victorians* (London, 1971), with more details in Kathleen Heasman's chapter on 'Gospel Temperance' in her *Evangelicals in Action*. For a parallel movement, see John Wigley, *The Rise and Fall of the Victorian Sunday* (Manchester, 1980).

[14] Norman McCord studied *The Anti-Corn Law League 1838–46* (London, 1958).

Midlands and the north by the promise of protection against American and German industrial competition. Chamberlain's revival of protectionism did not, however, get many of those votes. Vote-getting crusades could not be manufactured to order. Gladstone himself discovered this when he failed to arouse Nonconformist enthusiasm for Home Rule in Ireland since it seemed too like Rome Rule.

The life of the mind was not entirely neglected, but no major theologian left behind a literary monument to Victorian Nonconformity. On the contrary, the concentration on preaching seemed to be so important and so satisfactory that there was little energy left for quiet and independent wrestling with the new questions posed by science or by historical research into the Bible. The great men were not professors but preachers – for example, R. F. Horton who fascinated the Hampstead intellectuals but also drew some working men because he was so clearly honest, or Alexander Maclaren, whose steady preaching from the Bible filled Union Chapel, Manchester, with businessmen for forty-five years from 1858.[15] And most of the preachers remained conservatively Evangelical until the 1870s or 1880s. A storm was aroused among Congregationalists by the publication of a liberal (and sentimental) collection of *Hymns for Heart and Voice* edited by T. T. Lynch in 1855. In 1857 Samuel Davidson was forced to resign as a professor at the Lancashire Independent College in Manchester because he had thrown doubt on the Mosaic authorship of the first books in the Bible. As late as 1884 the editor of a magazine for preachers, the *Expositor*, was dismissed by its publishers because he had shown too much willingness to expound the results of German biblical criticism. From the 1870s onwards there was widespread acceptance of the critical approach to the Bible among ministers, but even in 1888 a fairly mild presentation of this approach, R. F. Horton's *Inspiration and the Bible*, was still able to produce a shock. Up to the end of the century, Nonconformist preachers who wanted to be 'progressive' had to rely mainly on the stimulus of intellectual imports from Germany, from Scotland and even from the Church of Eng-

---

[15] See Albert Peel and J. A. R. Marriott, *Robert Forman Horton* (London, 1937).

land; and there was a tendency to reduce the suggestiveness of those imports before passing them on to the laity.[16]

The most effective reply to Matthew Arnold's strictures on Nonconformist culture eventually came in the shape of two adjacent colleges in Oxford – Mansfield College, a Congregational foundation, and Manchester College, sponsored by the Unitarians.

⸱ These colleges were in effect the creation of two notable theologians, Andrew Fairbairn and James Martineau. Fairbairn, a Scot with Evangelical convictions, fell under the influence of German theological liberalism without ceasing to be a devout believer in the unique saviourhood of Christ. A scholar whose reading was wider than theirs, he was well able to hold his own with the Anglicans when Mansfield College was established under him in 1886. He wrote a series of books on current religious problems without ceasing to be at the service of Congregational churches all over England.

The Unitarian leader James Martineau was even more distinguished. After a long preaching ministry to an intelligent and affluent congregation in Liverpool, he became a part-time professor and then principal at the Unitarian college first in Manchester and then in London, combining this with pastoral work. He, too, was a prolific author. He opposed the idea of a further move to Oxford, but when he had retired the foundation stone of Manchester College was laid (in 1891) and his own thought provided the new college's main inspiration. When he died at the age of ninety in 1900 it was said of him by an ex-Anglican, Stopford Brooke: 'The victory that the ideas of God and Immortality are now beginning to secure over their enemies is largely due to Martineau's stern and quiet leadership, under the banners of the intellect and the conscience, of the soldiers of religion.' It was always his contention that religion need not be either dogmatic or 'rational' (conceding almost everything to intellectual criticism) in order to be real. He discounted miracles; 'miraculous events cannot be regarded as adequately attested, in the presence of natural

---

[16] Willis B. Glover studied *Evangelical Nonconformists and Higher Criticism in the Nineteenth Century* (London, 1954).

causes accounting for belief in their occurrence.' His main
concern was to defend belief in God as the basis of ethics. In
Loss and Gain in Recent Theology (1881) he claimed that, in
relation to that supreme purpose, the loss of 'External Authority' in religious belief was sheer gain. In reply to Anglican
dogmatism, he wrote as early as 1839: 'We believe, no less than
you, in an infallible Revelation . . . you in a Revelation of an
unintelligible Creed to the understanding; we in a Revelation
of moral perfection, and the spirit of duty in the heart; you in a
Revelation of the metaphysics of Deity; we in a Revelation of
the character and providence of the infinite Father; you in a
Redemption which saves the few, and leaves with Hell the
triumph after all; we in a Redemption which shall restore to all
at the length and image and immortality of God.'

Fairbairn and Martineau held different views about Christ's
divinity, but the quality of their thought was a quietly devastating reply to Matthew Arnold's charge that Nonconformists
were uncultured 'Philistines'. Surely there would have been
more thinkers of this quality, had Nonconformists been
allowed more access to higher education.[17]

FORWARD INTO THE CITIES

'Almost every village of any size has two distinct sets of
apparatus for doing good', Edward Miall reminded the House
of Commons in 1871 '– the one worked by Churchmen, the
second by Dissenters. Every town has its exclusive circles of
social intercourse – the one appropriated to Churchmen, the
other to Dissenters.' And the strategic decision of Victorian
Nonconformity was to throw this strength to be seen in the
villages into the battle for souls in the new cities and their
suburbs. The measure of success achieved in this battle
perhaps explained why on the whole Nonconformity did not
display a consistent and implacable anger against the estab-

---

[17] W. B. Selbie provided *The Life of Andrew Martin Fairbairn* (London, 1915), and
James Drummond and C. B. Upton, *The Life and Letters of James Martineau* (2 vols.,
London, 1902), supplemented by J. E. Carpenter, *James Martineau* (London, 1905).

lishment of the Church of England. Joseph Chamberlain, who
believed that Gladstone had 'suddenly sprung his Irish policy
upon the country . . . to prevent one from placing the disestablishment of the Church of England in the forefront of the
Liberal programme', was impatient with Nonconformity's
political caution. He once burst out that because they had
refused to follow him against Gladstone 'you Nonconformists
have got nothing – nothing'. It was not true. In the cities and
towns of Victorian England, the Free Churches could win
many victories without Chamberlain's help. They were religious victories.

In 1843 a widely discussed book by a Congregational Minister, Robert Vaughan, announced the arrival of *The Age of the
Great Cities*. The importance of the new urban age became a
constant theme of the Nonconformists' publications and conferences, and thousands of ministers resolved either to draw
crowds into the existing inner-city chapels or to build new
'churches' (a more respectable word increasingly preferred) in
the suburbs to which the middle classes retreated. In the last
quarter of the nineteenth century the Congregationalists, for
instance, built some five hundred new churches. Success in
Birmingham or Manchester or the industrial towns of Yorkshire was encouraging, and London remained the Jerusalem of
the new crusade. 'Our watchword should now be "London and
the large towns!" ' declared the secretary of the Home Missionary Society of the Congregationalists in 1861. In 1885 the
Wesleyan Methodist Conference agreed that 'this great centre
of national, imperial world-life is the prize, the citadel, for
which the powers of light and darkness must contend.' There
was a special significance in this ambition to storm London, in
that the 1851 religious census had shown that Methodism was
fairly strong in England's cities and large towns – apart from
London.

This battle for the city was seen to be urgent since it was fully
appreciated that Nonconformity was suffering from the decline
of British agriculture towards the end of the century. The
Baptist Union Council commented in 1893: 'Many years ago
. . . the tenant farmers of this country were the backbone of
religious Nonconformity. That class of supporters may today

be looked for almost in vain among our village churches.' The
Primitive Methodists found in 1896 that three-quarters of their
chapels were in villages but that 516 'societies' had been closed
during the last twenty-five years and only 236 begun. Both the
Baptists and the Primitive Methodists might have yielded to
the temptation to accept decline; because the population in the
villages was decreasing, it could have been assumed that these
denominations must decrease. Instead, both bodies were active in the fight to plant Nonconformity in towns and cities.[18]

Considerable success rewarded the Nonconformist urban
mission, even in London. Although the Nonconformists failed
to draw either the rich or the really poor, a census of churchgoing in London published in 1904 showed that they had
slightly more success than any other religious body with the
lower middle and working classes. The numbers of working
people's children in their Sunday schools were very large,
although the common working-class attitude was that only
children needed to go to church or chapel Sunday by Sunday.
The Nonconformist share of the total population of London
had declined since a census organized by the *British Weekly* in
1886–7, but not so badly as the Church of England's share.[19]

Basically, what the Nonconformists were now providing for
a minority in the cities was what they had provided in many
villages (for Methodists, more in the north and the south and
for Congregationalists and Baptists more in the east and the
west than in either the north or the south). Studies of rural
Nonconformity have shown how difficult it is to make true
generalizations since the villages differed greatly, but one
constant factor was that the chapel flourished most easily in
villages where there was no resident landowner in league with
a resident parson. Like flowers growing on a wall wherever
they could find a little soil, in these villages Nonconformity
had offered intense fellowships where there was no rival
centre, and the exploration of the inner world of mind and
spirit where there was no rival teacher. And that was what

---

[18] Some useful studies were collected in *The Church in Town and Countryside*, ed.
Derek Baker (Oxford, 1979).
[19] Hugh McLeod analysed the social background in London in *Class and Religion
in the Late Victorian City* (London, 1974).

was offered to the inhabitants of the unchurched new cities.[20]

Naturally biblical language was used in the new urban mission, but as a rule the tone of Nonconformity was not hostile to the more respectable pleasures of mankind. 'Hell fire' preaching was less frequent than later generations have tended to suppose.

We can take the life of a small body, the Quakers, as an illustration of some wider tendencies in Nonconformity. At the beginning of the Victorian age the Quakers were strongly under the influence of the Evangelical revival. In 1835 a Manchester businessman, Isaac Crewdon, published *A Beacon to the Society of Friends*, in which he urged the supremacy of the Bible over the tradition which extolled the 'inner light' in every man. He also urged that worship should be Bible-based rather than a silence leading to individual testimonies. Later he advocated the use of the two sacraments, Baptism and Holy Communion. This Evangelical influence persisted. It meant that almost all the Victorian Quakers resisted suggestions that they should join the Unitarians, and it meant an emphasis on benevolent activity rather than on passive quiet. But the Evangelical influence was limited. In England the Quakers consistently refused to accept a paid preaching ministry (accepted by the American Quakers); they refused to adopt any creed or doctrinal declaration; and they refused to be guided by Isaac Crewdon's beacon, so that he left to found his own small sect.

The changes which did secure the approval of the Victorian Quakers were all designed to bridge the very gap which separated their heritage from the society around them. In 1860 it was agreed that they need no longer wear distinctive dress or face expulsion if they married outside the Society of Friends – two traditional features of Quaker life which had been the main causes of the society's numerical decline from about twenty thousand full members in 1800 to about fourteen thousand in 1860. A feature of the history of the Victorian Quakers is their outstanding leadership in business life; from this small society came household names such as the Lloyds and Barclays

---

[20] Alan Everitt studied *The Pattern of Rural Dissent: The Nineteenth Century* (Leicester, 1972).

in banking, the Rowntrees, Cadburys and Frys in cocoa and
other food, Clarks in shoes, Bryant and May in matches, Allen
and Hanbury in pharmacy, Reckitts in starch. But the record
in philanthropy was not quite so bold. Although the Quakers
continued to be active in many good works such as prison
reform, adult education, the defence of peace and the suppression of prostitution, they mostly failed to support the movement to improve the conditions of industrial workers while that
'factory movement' was battling; they were too closely identified with the vested interests of the manufacturers. Later in
the century, however, Joseph Rowntree of York and George
Cadbury of Birmingham thoroughly earned their national
reputations as model employers, and Rowntree closely studied
the workers' problems.[21]

The story of the Unitarians is somewhat similar. At the
beginning of the Victorian age the energy of the Evangelical
insistence on Christ's divinity provoked many Unitarians into
a more eager denial of that divinity. No longer fearing the
blasphemy laws, this aggressive Unitarianism remained a
force throughout the century, with its own training college for
ministers and its own denomination, the Unitarian Association. Unitarians of this sort could be found among the ranks of
secularists and the Socialists. But the congregations gathered
by this militant message were mainly working-class. Unitarians who were socially superior liked to think of themselves as
heirs of the English Presbyterian tradition, and opposed any
new denominational identity. They set themselves to be moderate and generous, keeping something of the old belief that
God was incarnate in Christ but adding that he was also
incarnate in every other member of the human race. Mrs
Adams, who wrote the universally acceptable hymn 'Nearer
my God to thee' for a Unitarian chapel in 1840, briefly
acknowledged the need to be raised by 'a cross' but also
implied a high estimate of the Victorian worshipper's own
ability to get nearer.

The Unitarian belief in the dignity of everyman did not

---

[21] Elizabeth Isichei, *Victorian Quakers* (Oxford, 1970), is the best study of any
denomination in this period.

remain mere rhetoric; it produced some memorable pioneers in uplifting humanity. William Rathbone and Charles Booth were rich Liverpool businessmen, distressed because good deeds were done so inefficiently; the one organized district and workhouse nursing and was the main founder of the Charity Organization Society, the other studied London's social problems with a thoroughness without precedent. Mary Carpenter created 'reformatories' to keep juvenile delinquents out of prisons; Henry Solly 'working men's clubs' to keep their fathers out of public houses; Mary Beard 'nursery schools' to give some help to their overburdened mothers. The 'domestic missions' run by Unitarian congregations in many towns were originally 'domestic' in that the poor were visited and advised in their own homes, but special Sunday evening services and other activities on church premises developed, inaugurating the 'institutional church' which many other Nonconformists copied. Much of all this activity was inspired by the example of philanthropic Unitarianism in New England, then at its height in energy and prestige.

The richer Unitarians delighted to build churches in a medieval or Gothic style; for, whatever a pope might say, they found no difficulty in thinking of their creed as liberal Catholicism. James Martineau wrote that 'for nearly fifty years I have been a most unwilling Nonconformist'. The magazine conducted by the moderates who shared Martineau's feeling of affinity with all other Christians (and with all other believers in God) was called the *Inquirer*, in contrast with the more militant section's *Christian Life*. In 1907 J. M. Lloyd Thomas, the minister of the historic Unitarian congregation in Birmingham, was to take this tendency to its extreme by advocating sacramentalism and even ritualism in *A Free Catholic Church* – and by practising what he preached, with a few others. It was not until 1928 that the militant and moderate traditions were brought together to form the General Assembly of the Unitarian and Free Christian Churches.[22]

---

[22] D. G. Wigmore-Beddoes, *Yesterday's Radicals* (Cambridge, 1971), explored the affinities of these Free Christians with the Anglican Broad Churchmen. See also H. L. Short in *The English Presbyterians*, pp. 252–86.

Generally speaking, Victorian Nonconformity as it moved
into the cities took the same path as these Quaker or Unitarian
moderates. It conformed to the spirit of the age, which included a strong streak of practical philanthropy. Before 1850
the tradition remained strong that Dissenters should live
rather like monks, returning to the chapel on many weekdays
for prayer meetings, Bible classes or other definitely religious
acts. But in the second half of the century a broader understanding of Nonconformity prevailed and many of the chapels
housed a great variety of semi-secular activities: education for
the young and the adults, youth organizations galore, a football team, a choral society, a literary society, a 'provident' or
'friendly' society as insurance, a savings bank, a maternity
club, and 'temperance' societies including the Band of Hope
for the children. Many were the laments that the new activities
did not lead to the commitment of the old-style membership –
that in Methodism the class meeting often went dead and
became optional, or that in Congregational churches there was
no pressure to experience a conversion which could be told to
the congregation.

H. W. Clark's second volume in a large *History of Nonconformity*, published in 1913, had the theme that Nonconformity
had lost its old Puritan ideals by its worldly eagerness to
provide entertainment and to flatter the people it wanted to
attract. Even a sympathetic historian of the nineteenth century
is liable to be even more severe on the compromises involved,
painting a portrait of the Free Churches at the end of the
century with these words: 'Free souls, having encapsulated
God within themselves, surveyed majestically a world ripe for
Utopian experiment.'[23] Whatever we make of such criticisms,
we must observe that in the next century much of the role of
Victorian Nonconformity in these social activities was taken
over by better-financed and definitely secular activities – the
improved school and public house, the cinema, radio, televi-
sion, the Bingo hall, with the bicycle or the motor car offering
yet another alternative for Sunday. Thus the churches' popu-

---

[23] Ian Sellers, *Nineteenth-Century Nonconformity*, p. 23. J. W. Grant, *Free Churchmanship in England, 1870–1940* (London, 1955), also denounced declericalized Congregationalism.

larity in the second half of the nineteenth century proved
ephemeral. Yet probably at the time no other course was open
to a religious movement aspiring to be popular. Entertainment
was what the people wanted, to counteract the drabness and
loneliness of life. And it is fair to remember that with the
entertainment went a great deal of care for often desperate
needs. It would not be right to forget ventures such as England's first school for mentally defective children, opened by a
Congregational minister, Andrew Reed, in London in 1848. In
1849 Edward Miall, himself the son of a poor man, argued in
The British Churches in Relation to the British People that Nonconformity had become too much the religion of manufacturers
and traders. 'I have endeavoured to put myself in the position
of the humbler classes, and have asked myself, "What is there
here to interest them?" I have been at a loss for a reply.' That
could not be said half a century later.

'We are living in the midst of a great reaction from Puritanism', the Wesleyan Methodist Conference declared in 1890. An
anonymous but semi-official book, *Methodism in 1879*, had taken
a pride in measuring the advance of the denomination by
worldly standards – the educated eloquence of its preachers,
the wealth of its leading laymen, the money collected, the
churches built. This mid-Victorian period in Methodist history became known as the 'mahogany age', referring not only
to the wood used for many pulpits but also to the dining tables
of many laymen. The *Methodist Recorder* had voiced the younger
element's impatience when founded in 1861, but gradually it
became the organ of a sedately established denomination. In
local Wesleyan churches pews were rented by the well-to-do,
although the custom would have horrified John Wesley. In
their national conference, the Wesleyan Methodists admitted
laymen for the first time in 1878, and eleven years later also
admitted that it was not necessary for a Methodist to belong to
a 'class'. These concessions, too, would have dismayed the
Founder, and they led up to the replacement in the 1890s of the
title 'Wesleyan Methodist Society' by 'Wesleyan Methodist
Church'.[24]

---

[24] *A History of the Methodist Church in Great Britain*, vol. 3 (London, 1983), included
valuable essays pointing to the need for a thorough history.

Even the Primitive Methodist Conference noted in 1892 that 'intelligence, wealth and respectability are becoming increasingly characteristic of us as a community.'

The Congregationalists also took the attitude that successful laymen were to be admired and consulted deferentially; in the words of Thomas Binney, 'it is not wrong to be rich'. Binney's book of advice to young men had the title *How to Make the Best of Both Worlds*. In 1894 the chairman of the Congregational Union delivered an address on 'The Secularization of the Church', remarking that 'Christian parents no longer forbid their children to read novels or to learn dancing; some of them accompany their sons and daughters to the theatre and the concert; in many Christian homes billiards and cards are allowed, and both in occupation and amusement the line that once divided the world from the Church is tending to disappear.'

Victorian Nonconformity eventually came to believe that the first step in its approach to the urban working class was to offer some of these pleasures which the middle classes were now taking for granted. The most sustained effort in this direction, the Pleasant Sunday Afternoon, was invented in West Bromwich in 1875. Its motto was 'Brief, Bright and Brotherly'. This meant a meeting with short addresses (not all of them religious) broken up by non-dogmatic hymns and solos; a hymnal, *Worship Song*, was edited for this purpose in 1907. The PSA was organized with a definite membership by an elected committee and took a pride in being non-sectarian. The motive of many of its backers was the hope that working people would return to the normal evening services, and the PSA did produce many thousands of new faces on church premises, particularly in the Midlands; but that hope was not fulfilled on any larger scale, and one disadvantage to the long-term prospects of Nonconformity was that almost all the ministers failed to attach enough importance to the meetings of working people in the trade unions now becoming a major force in non-ecclesiastical surroundings.

The success in the cities was, however, enough to inspire some optimistic dreams. John Wilson, in his Presidential address to the Baptist Union in 1904, asserted that a hundred years previously the Nonconformists had been only one in thirty in the population. Now they were one in two, and in fifty years' time they would, he trusted, be two to one. To give substance to such hopes John Shakespeare, who took over as the Union's secretary in 1898, raised a Twentieth Century Fund. The Baptists soon had an elaborate headquarters, a publications department, a new hymnal, a good newspaper (the *Baptist Times*) and a stronger agreed statement about their beliefs. Another appeal was successful in raising the stipends of ministers to a decent level, and a similar fund was raised for local purposes within the Congregational Union. There, the old tradition that each congregation was independent had already been eroded by the need to subsidise weaker churches if they employed 'authorized' ministers. In the 1870s and 1880s an able secretary, Alexander Hannay, had begun to build what had once seemed inconceivable: Congregationalism as a national organization.[25]

PREACHERS TO LONDON

Among the Nonconformists who preached to Victorian London, two were similar in a remarkable number of ways. Both the Baptist, Charles Haddon Spurgeon, and the Congregationalist, Joseph Parker, came from working-class homes and never went to any university or college. Both accepted a conservative theology. Both attracted such crowds that new churches had to be built around their pulpits, and both taught by the printed as well as the spoken word; yet both failed to impose their views on their denominations. This failure is a reminder that Victorian Nonconformity contained many ministers who were almost as sure as Spurgeon or Parker about what they believed – and almost as much admired by their own people in their own pulpits. It is worth studying the personal history of Spurgeon and Parker because through that history we can explore how it felt to be a Nonconformist – in an age

---

[25] The official histories, well documented, are E. A. Payne, *The Baptist Union* (London, 1959), and Albert Peel, *These Hundred Years: A History of the Congregational Union of England and Wales 1831–1931* (London, 1931).

whose historians have too often been stunned by the biographies of bishops.

Spurgeon's father was a clerk in a coal yard who was also a
part-time Congregational pastor. The home in Essex was so
poor that until he was seven the boy was brought up by his
grandfather, a full-time minister. Through the books which
were still kept by such Dissenters the boy became acquainted
with John Bunyan and other Puritans of the sixteenth and
seventeenth centuries. He was to collect some seven thousand
of their books in his own library, and was often called the last of
the Puritans. But he had to undergo his personal conversion
(on a snowy Sunday morning in January 1850, when in a
little chapel he heard a Primitive Methodist lay preacher
expound the text 'Look unto me and be ye saved'). This was
followed by baptism in a river. He had become convinced,
simply by reading the Bible, that baptism was for adult converts only.

When not yet twenty years old he was called to preach in a
famous but run-down Baptist church in London, and he soon
accepted an invitation to become its permanent minister,
although he always refused to be ordained formally. He later
recalled that on his first night in London he had been mocked
for his countryman's clothes, a huge black smock and a very
large blue handkerchief with white spots, before he crept off to
bed in a London boarding house. 'On the narrow bed I tossed
in solitary misery, and found no pity. Pitiless was the grind of
the cabs in the street . . . pitiless even the gas-lamps which
seemed to wink at me as they flickered amid the December
darkness. I had no friend in all that city full of human
beings. . . .' And next morning when he saw the small, gloomy
congregation in the big, gloomy chapel he was not much
comforted.[26]

That was in 1853. On a typical Sunday in October 1886 a
count of worshippers in London's churches organized by the
British Weekly recorded that about ten thousand people heard
Spurgeon preach. The country lad with the blue handkerchief
had established himself as the biggest crowd-puller in the

---

[26] C. H. Spurgeon, *The Early Years 1834–59* (new edition, London, 1962), p. 248.

history of English religion. Soon after his arrival the crowds coming had been so great that he had had to preach in public halls. Finally he had his own church built – the Metropolitan Tabernacle, opened in 1861, in South London in order to be accessible to the teeming population there. There were few really poor people in his congregation, and even fewer professional men or fashionable women, but Spurgeon addressed himself to thousands upon thousands in families struggling to be respectable.

Why did they come? At first he became known because he was a 'boy preacher', like his hero George Whitefield. Then further publicity came just because of the crowds. But he did not remain a boy wonder. Actually, he became overweight because he took no exercise, and chesty because he smoked heavily – and since he was afflicted by gout, he had to use a stick to walk. And the novelty wore off. He preached twice on almost every Sunday until his death in 1892, and most of his sermons were printed. A monthly magazine and many books, lectures and weekday sermons added to the output. Yet still the crowds came.

He was never 'popular' in the sense of entertaining his audience. There was no organ in the Metropolitan Tabernacle in his time, and the sermon usually occupied three-quarters of an hour. He preached a modified Calvinism; he was a kind man who could not believe that any baby who died went to hell, and he was an evangelist who could not believe that anyone who listened to him was doomed to reject his message. ('Lord,' he prayed, 'hasten to bring in all thy elect, and then elect some more.') But he always regarded himself as a Calvinist. When the Tabernacle was opened, he got visiting preachers to expound the five points of classical Calvinism – human depravity; the election by God of those to be saved; 'particular redemption'; 'effectual calling'; 'final perseverance'. Although he did some visiting of families in his early years (his courage when visiting the victims of cholera was not forgotten), before long he had to admit that he could not carry six thousand names in his head, so much pastoral work as was done for the congregation had to be delegated to elders, each in charge of a district. Yet still the people came, each feeling that the sermon was addressed personally – and when his coffin was brought to the Tabernacle, some sixty thousand filed past it. So personal was his people's loyalty that they called his son Thomas to be their minister after his death, although numbers declined.

Once when asked by an American for the secret of his success, he replied: 'My people pray for me.' It was not a sham modesty. He was loved. He founded an orphanage with funds provided by his admirers, an evening school free to all, and a college to train boys without educational advantages to be preachers; and he gave much of his time and income to these and other charities. Another way of showing his love for the people was to preach in a style they loved. 'The histrionics and sentimentalism of Spurgeon in the pulpit are hard to credit', in the view of a distinguished scholar.[27] But J. C. Carlile, a shrewd man who himself became a leading Baptist minister, maintained that Spurgeon's preaching 'revealed to me the magic of the human voice and the stupendous power of sincerity. . . . Spurgeon was to religion what Shakespeare was to drama.'[28] The power came in part from the preacher's confidence in the authority of the Bible, which he regarded as the Word of God from cover to cover.

The tragedy of this marvellous pastor and preacher was that, while his congregation never left him, he felt increasingly isolated from his fellow Baptists because they were infected by the liberal ideas in the air of the nineteenth century. In 1887 his impatience boiled over and he accused them of betraying fundamental doctrines: 'The Atonement is scouted, the inspiration of Scripture is derided, the Holy Spirit is degraded into a fiction, and the resurrection into a myth, and yet these enemies of our faith expect us to call them brethren and maintain a confederacy with them.' In particular he was indignant at the lack of belief in the eternal punishment of the wicked in hell. His resignation from the Baptist Union caused consternation for a time, but the council of the Union refused to be browbeaten and passed a resolution affirming that charges against 'men who love the truth as dearly as he does' without

[27] Donald Davie, *A Gathered Church*, p. 89.
[28] J. C. Carlile, *My Life's Little Day* (London, 1935), pp. 56–8.

giving names 'ought not to have been made'. To this it added a Declaratory Statement of the essentials of belief.

Spurgeon continued to complain, but not very effectively. There were four hundred churches where men trained in his Pastors' College were in the pulpit, but no new denomination was formed around him. As has been observed, 'he was one of the few men of his generation who really felt more certain of the truth of the Bible than of the truth of contemporary science.'[29]

Among other princes of the Victorian pulpit, the most princely was Joseph Parker who reigned for a quarter of a century in London, north of the Thames at the City Temple.

The son of a stonemason, he left school at the age of fourteen and never had any formal training for the ministry; yet such became his reputation that in 1869, he was invited to become the minister of the oldest Congregational church in the city of London. One reason why he accepted the call to London was that the congregation was about to sell its present chapel and to buy a larger and more central site. The new 'City Temple' was opened in 1874 – was opened, and was filled morning and evening every Sunday. On Thursdays a lunch-hour service attracted a thousand. In the 1902–03 survey of churchgoing in London it was found that the average Sunday attendance was just over seven thousand, three times the numbers in St Paul's Cathedral.

Until he died in 1902 they went to hear Joseph Parker. A style that may seem to us dictatorial was then magnetic. He prayed aloud as the spirit moved him, and he gradually changed his preaching style from the more formal, written sermon expounding a long text to a much more personal, rambling and extempore discourse based on a few words of Scripture. Although he always reckoned himself an Evangelical, he did not stress the old Puritan doctrines and morals as did Spurgeon. Indeed, he published an open letter to Spurgeon in 1890: 'I accuse you of a bluntness which can only be accounted for by the worst kind of spiritual ignorance. The universe is not

---

[29] W. B. Glover, *Evangelical Nonconformity and Higher Criticism in the Nineteenth Century*, pp. 163–83. Biographies include J. C. Carlile, *Spurgeon* (London, 1934), and E. W. Bacon, *Spurgeon, Heir of the Puritans* (London, 1967).

divided into plain black and white, as you suppose. . . . Believe
me you really are not infallible.' He tried to present what he
believed to be the modern message of the Bible to the young
men (many of them clerks in city offices) and women (many of
them maids in the West End houses of the rich) who sat under
him in large numbers. He kept them awake by explosions; his
'God damn the Sultan!' echoed throughout England in 1899, a
year of indignation against the Turks. Many other preachers
came to listen in the hope of learning the secret of his popularity, only to discover that what he did all the time was to
expound the Bible dramatically; at one stage he took seven
years to work his way through it, Sunday by Sunday. He
published a *People's Bible* including a commentary by him, in
twenty-five volumes.

Explaining why he would not accept an invitation to move to
New York, he declared: 'There is only one London, and it is to
all intents and purposes the centre of the commerce, the
literature and the religion of the world.' In that London, he was
Spurgeon's rival.[30]

PREACHERS AND POLITICIANS

Intellectually abler than Spurgeon or Parker, R. W. Dale
found his life's work in the pulpit of the Congregational chapel
in Carr's Lane, Birmingham, and in the politics of that boom-
ing industrial city. He had no ambition to be a popular
preacher; although the leaders of Birmingham's life came in
considerable numbers to hear his austerely theological sermons, it has been justly remarked that 'no man made fewer
concessions to his hearers'.[31] He did have an ambition to write
books that would last, and to a large extent that ambition was
fulfilled by his authorship of *The Atonement* (1875). There he
rejected both the Calvinist idea that Christ died in order to
save a limited number of the elect from hell and the liberal idea

---

[30] William Adamson compiled *The Life of the Rev. Joseph Parker* (Glasgow, 1902).
[31] Horton Davies, *Worship and Theology in England from Newman to Martineau*, p. 331.
The whole of Chapter X, on 'The Power of the Victorian Pulpit', is valuable.

that Christ died in order to make an appeal to every man's conscience. He affirmed that anyone who repented was saved from the punishment incurred by sin, while after death the souls of the impenitent were annihilated. Certainly Christ's death made a moral appeal, but it provided more than a mere example. It was something *done* for man; it was something objective, not depending for its effectiveness on man's response; it was what made man's penitent response to God possible. Christ, declared Dale, 'endured the penalties of sin, and so made an actual submission to the authority and righteousness of the principle which those penalties express. What we had no force to do, He has done; and through our union with Him, His submission renders our submission possible.'

Born in London in 1829, Dale found his work in Birmingham because after a spell as a schoolmaster he went there to be trained as a Congregational minister and was invited by the distinguished but elderly John Angell James to remain as his colleague at Carr's Lane. He was called in 1859 to be the sole pastor. In Birmingham he would provide models for Church and State – and from Birmingham he would move out to spread his vision over the nation. In order to serve these causes, he was ready to let the great theology of which he was capable remain unwritten.

For Dale, any idea of the priesthood as a separate caste providing the Church with sacraments was hateful because contrary to the Bible. He always dressed as a layman and announced that he had an invincible objection to the title 'Reverend'. He denounced the argument that the National Church needed to be supported and controlled by the State. To argue that was to deny the power and the rights of the living Christ over the congregation of the faithful. When he died he left incomplete a large *History of English Congregationalism* which was published in 1907 and which traced this ideal of the congregation of the faithful back 'through century after century of corruption, superstition and spiritual tyranny' to the 'religious societies to which the New Testament attributes an extraordinary dignity and sanctity'. Yet he taught a high doctrine about the whole gathered congregation as a microcosm of the Catholic Church. His *Manual of Congregational*

Principles (1884) seemed so High Church that it was attacked by Spurgeon, and an edition had to be printed without the section on the sacraments. A prominent theme of his preaching was that Christ was alive, reigning over the Church, and he chose an Easter hymn for most Sundays in the year. With this theme by justified the baptism of infants, baptism being the offer of salvation made by the living Christ before the baby could respond; and he argued for the central importance of Holy Communion. Both sacraments were, he insisted, primarily acts of God, creating and feeding the Church; they were not primarily acts of the minister or the congregation.[32]

He was too much of a theologian ever to think that a 'Municipal Gospel' was enough. Indeed, he constantly emphasized the difference between religion and politics, between Church and State. Pursuing the logic of this difference, he was prepared to shock men such as Spurgeon who supported everything that made England more Christian. Dale urged that no religious teaching should be given in the State's schools (although he conceded that the Bible might be read as a masterpiece of literature); that the House of Commons should be open to the atheist, Charles Bradlaugh; that the Town Hall should be open on a Sunday for lectures on secular subjects. In church preaching the Gospel always had for him the top priority – and his was a theology almost as conservative as Parker's, as may be seen by comparing it with the far less doctrinal message of two other Birmingham preachers influentially involved in radical politics, George Dawson of the independent 'Church of the Saviour' and H. W. Crosskey of the Unitarian 'Church of the Messiah'.

It was as a citizen who was also a Christian that he felt impelled to be active in the great reforms of his time. When the Reform Act of 1867 made Parliament more democratic he would have been ashamed had he not already campaigned for it; and he was delighted when his friend Joseph Chamberlain, then a Unitarian businessman who had made a fortune by mass-producing screws, became Mayor of Birmingham (1873

---

[32] Dale's teaching about the Church was studied by J. W. Grant, *Free Churchmanship in England*, pp. 1–123.

−78) and led the crusade to turn Birmingham into a fine modern city. Dale never doubted that it was his duty to speak at many Town Hall meetings and to spend evening after evening exhorting the wards of the Chamberlain-controlled Liberal Party. His son recalled that 'he threw himself into the struggle with exultant energy. . . . During those years a succession of serious questions came before the burgesses – the acquisition of the gas- and the water-supply by the community, the provision of public parks and public buildings, a more efficient system of sanitary measures, a costly sewage scheme, the establishment of free libraries and an art gallery, a plan for sweeping away the slums in the heart of the town – great measures conceived and advocated on broad lines of municipal statesmanship, but of a kind to provoke prejudice and to call forth a false cry of economy. In dealing with such questions, Dale spoke with full and exact knowledge. He, too, could see visions and dream dreams. . . . But he was ready to meet critics and opponents on the ground of solid fact. . . .' Above all he was an enthusiastic advocate of the building and maintenance of 'Board Schools' with high standards. He took endless trouble as the chairman of the committee responsible for Birmingham's schools under the Act of 1870, and in the 1880s was an active member of the Royal Commission on elementary education.[33]

Gradually, however, he became disillusioned with Gladstone, who failed to meet the Nonconformists' demands over education and disestablishment; and when in 1886 Joseph Chamberlain broke with Gladstone over Home Rule for Ireland, he followed Chamberlain although with many reservations. Consequently he found himself so unhappy in the atmosphere of the Congregational Union that he ceased to attend its meetings. In his private life he experienced bereavements which greatly saddened him; and although he was still in his fifties, his health broke down. He never regretted that he had been one of the leaders of progress in the city to which he had

---

[33] There is a fine chapter on 'Birmingham: the Making of a Civic Gospel' in Asa Briggs, *Victorian Cities* (London, 1963). See also E. P. Hennock, *Fit and Proper Persons* (London, 1973), pp. 61–176.

given his heart; in 1892 he recalled with pride that 'the men who took part in the great and successful movement for reforming our administration and ennobling it had learnt the principles on which they acted and caught the spirit by which they were inspired very largely in the Nonconformist churches of Birmingham.' But after his death in 1895 an unfinished sermon was found on his desk. It was on unworldliness. It spoke of the vision of God; of 'constant fellowship' with God; of a 'personal and vivid experience of the greatness of the Christian redemption'. The last, incomplete, sentence proclaimed the 'full assurance that, after our mortal years are spent, there is a larger, fuller, richer life in . . . .'

Towards the end of his life Dale encouraged a young admirer, Charles Silvester Horne. When the great man had died, Horne recalled how he had been a boy dreaming of becoming a preacher when he had first met him. 'My lad,' Dale said then, 'remember *our* temptation is not as a rule money.' Then he pointed through the open door of the vestry to the crowded church: '*That* is our temptation.'

In that warning Dale was a prophet, for Horne went on to become immensely popular – by means which Dale would have suspected. He was called to be a preacher in the most fashionable part of London, at Kensington Chapel. Well-informed on many topics, light and lively, very happy in his family life and with a host of friends, patently sincere as he talked in a non-dogmatic way about Jesus, he charmed laymen wherever he went. He was a spiritually minded man, but his most obvious enthusiasm was for the contribution which the Free Churches could make to the progress of the nation. He wrote popular histories of the Free Churches and encouraged the conviction that their greatest days were just beginning.

In 1903 he accepted a call to move from Kensington in order to put new life into a famous church, Whitefield's Tabernacle in Tottenham Court Road, because he was fascinated by the opportunities awaiting in a district full of shops, business houses, smart flats and slums with a cosmopolitan population. To the distressed he offered a tender sympathy; to the successful, a vibrant optimism. In addition to the normal services which became crowded he developed many varied activities, most notably the Sunday afternoon lecture on a topical subject. There was even a room for billiards. The church became an 'institutional' church, attracting thousands to the Whitefields Institute who might, or might not, stay on for the preaching service. Similar churches were associated in the 'Brotherhood movement', defined by the Labour leader Keir Hardie as 'an association for the promotion of fellowship among those who love Jesus' – a category which included other Labour leaders (Crooks, Henderson, Lansbury, Snowden). This movement was formally organized at a national conference in 1906 and soon spread overseas.[34] He returned from a very cheerful visit to Germany in 1909 full of hopes for peace and progress. While chairman of the Congregational Union next year he spoke eloquently about the value of the Free Church tradition which combined freedom and brotherhood and was now flourishing in many countries. Elected to Parliament for Ipswich in 1910, he claimed that 'there is no church meeting held in this country that is more constantly and practically concerned with living religious problems than the House of Commons'. In the spring of 1914 he went to America to lecture on *The Romance of Preaching*. He was received with enthusiasm, and went on to address a great Brotherhood meeting in Toronto. As the boat entered the harbour he was on deck with his wife, eagerly admiring the Canadian city – and suddenly fell down dead, fortunate to the last.[35]

FORWARD TOGETHER?

The most powerful movement to take the English Free Churches into the twentieth century emerged out of Wesleyan Methodism. It was associated with the controversial personality of a Welshman with a Jewish mother, Hugh Price Hughes. When in 1898 he was elected President of the Wesleyan Methodist Conference he declared in his first speech from the chair, 'I am not afraid of any one of you'. He went on to point

---

[34] See J. W. Tuffley, *Grain from Galilee* (London, 1935).
[35] W. B. Selbie compiled *The Life of Charles Silvester Horne* (London, 1920).

out that it was the first honour that his Church had ever paid to him.

Hughes knew that the old style of Wesleyan Methodism could sometimes be effective; his own father was a much loved preacher and pastor. He also knew that in practice the old style of preaching had usually meant conservatism in politics; when he began his own preaching, he was himself an ardent Tory. But gradually he found himself driven by experience to support radicalism, and always his support was active. While a student he became an active supporter of the Liberation Society; while a minister in Dover he became an active supporter of the temperance movement; while a minister in Oxford he became an active supporter of the enrichment of Methodist worship even if it partly meant copying the Church of England; and while a minister in London he became an active supporter of 'Christian imperialism', believing the British empire to be making a major contribution to the coming of the kingdom of God.

On all these issues he was in tension or conflict with the caution, the 'deadly respectability', which had prevailed in Wesleyan Methodism. He was not daunted, for he was sure that God was the greatest radical. In 1885 he founded his own weekly paper, the *Methodist Times*, to 'ventilate' new ideas. This it did very successfully, much to the annoyance of the supporters of the official *Methodist Recorder* – who spoke contemptuously about the 'Hughesful' new paper. Determined to outvote the conservatives, Hughes rallied his supporters in a pressure group which took the provocative name: the Forward Movement.

Experience convinced him that the traditional Methodist chapel would never move forward in a modern city. He advocated, and eventually secured, 'central halls' at strategic points – large buildings not looking like churches, the centres of many social activities in addition to worship. It was typical that those who built these halls (beginning in Manchester in 1887) preferred an orchestra to an organ, chairs to pews. The minister in charge was not to be moved every three years, as was the Methodist custom in all the normal 'circuits'; he was to have the chance to make an impact as a powerful local personality. The whole 'mission' was to be adequately

financed out of special funds, and was to be supervised by the
national conference not by the local chapels. The building of a
Central Hall in Westminster, close to the Abbey and to
Parliament, particularly delighted him. On these conditions he
was himself appointed to lead the West London Mission, from
1887 to his death. His assistants in the social work included
Methodist 'sisters' – and they survived the inevitable protests
that they looked suspiciously like nuns. The work had its
prominent centre in St James's Hall, Piccadilly, and into it
Hughes threw all his energy as an evangelist and pastor, all his
inventiveness (one Harvest Festival brought a live sheep to
bleat in a pen beneath his pulpit), all his facility as a lecturer on
current topics and personalities, and all his courage as a
prophet of social righteousness.

He claimed to be the spokesman of a body of opinion which
no politician could ignore. In particular he claimed to be able
to set the terms of Methodism's alliance with the Gladstonian
Liberals. When his children asked who Mr Gladstone was, he
replied: 'A man who says his prayers every morning.' But when
Gladstone died, he observed that 'on this side of the Tweed his
following was strong only where Methodism was strong: that
is, in the West, in the great Northern Counties and among the
peasants.' And no politician was too eminent to be subjected to
a moral scrutiny if he wanted Methodist votes. When the Irish
leader Parnell was cited as an adulterer in a divorce case, a
denunciation was delivered by Hughes on a Sunday afternoon
in 1890. 'We love Ireland. We passionately desire her well-
being; but our first obedience and our highest devotion must be
to God. We have sacrificed much for Ireland. She is entitled to
many sacrifices at our hands. But there is one thing we will
never sacrifice, and that is our religion. We stand immovably
on this eternal rock; what is morally wrong can never be
politically right.' That last sentence echoed all over England –
and Ireland. The Irish Catholic bishops joined in the denunciation, as did most of the Irish MPs. By the end of 1890 Parnell
was broken, and by the end of 1891 he was dead.[36]

---

[36] The tragedy was set in its context by F. S. L. Lyons, *Charles Stuart Parnell*
(London, 1977).

One result of this confident new style was to draw Methodism closer to other morally clear missionaries. This was a major development; in 1834 Jabez Bunting had declared openly that 'we cannot be friendly to Dissent. One of its first principles is – Every man shall choose his own minister. Can you be friendly to that?' Now the successors to Bunting were answering yes to that question. As part of that answer, they were abandoning the defence of wine and beer. In contrast with 1840, when two young candidates for the Wesleyan Methodist ministry had been compelled to promise to give up the heresy of teetotalism, forty years later it was proudly reported that eight hundred ministers had pledged total abstinence from alcohol. By 1908, when the House of Lords threw out the Liberal government's Licensing Bill, the whole of Methodism was united with the rest of Nonconformity against the brewers.

In November 1892 Hughes made the opening speech at the first Free Church Congress, in Manchester. When the National Council of Evangelical Free Churches met for the first time in 1896, he was elected President. Encouraged by generous financial backing by the Quaker, George Cadbury, he declared: 'Representing the majority of the Christian people at home, we represent an immense majority in the British empire, and an overwhelming majority in the English-speaking world. If the failures and humiliations of the past, as well as the bright hopes of the present, have at last taught us their Divinely-appointed lessons, the future of British Christianity and of the British Empire is in our hands.' For the true idea of the Church was to be found in the Free Churches and nowhere else. 'We are "High Churchmen" ', he claimed in 1897, 'so High that we can no more tolerate the interference of the secular power than could the Popes of the Middle Ages. . . . We are "Catholic High Churchmen", for we do not hold ourselves in schismatic separation from our fellow Christians. . . . We do not boycott or excommunicate. . . .'

The growing unity in the Free Churches was sufficient to support a new penny paper, the *British Weekly*, edited from the start in 1886 to 1923 by a brilliant journalist, William Robertson Nicoll, who had been a minister in the Free Church of

Scotland. The opening article began: 'The creed we shall seek to expound in this journal will be that of progress, and while independent of any sect or party we shall aim at the ends of what is known as Advanced Liberalism. We are believers in progress because we are believers in the advancing reign of Christ.' By 1906 it had a circulation over a hundred thousand, with such a status that Liberal politicians took care to win the approval of its editor.[37] Other activities included Free Church Missions in London and the other main cities.

In order to awaken some seven hundred local Free Church Councils into activity, Hughes now set himself a gruelling programme of visits and addresses in city, town and village, nationwide, disregarding warnings that his health had already suffered from overwork in London. As a result, he had a fatal heart attack in a London street in 1902. It was the crusader's death for which he would have wished. In his eyes the 'Nonconformist conscience' had ceased to be mere dissent from the Established Church. It had become the main carrier of the religion of a prospering nation and an expanding empire. So complete did the contrast seem between 1800 and 1900.[38] Yet questions remained which, in his enthusiasm and eloquence, he had neglected. Was Nonconformity really prepared to take over the leading role from the Church of England? Had it ever been willing to do so? The identification of 'Free Church' unity with the Liberal Party alarmed many, and in 1909 an influential although anonymous book on *Nonconformity and Politics* issued warnings about worldliness which were widely discussed. In the discussion many Free Churchmen clung to the militant alliance with Liberalism, but no great new campaign was launched when the education controversy had to be allowed to die down. Even in the 1890s, when the phrase 'the Nonconformist conscience' had come into general use, the emphasis had still been on preparing the moral ground for a better kind of politics – not on the business of day-to-day politics as experienced by Liberal politicians.

---

[37] T. H. Darlow gave some account of *William Robertson Nicoll* (London, 1925).
[38] His daughter Dorothy compiled *The Life of Hugh Price Hughes* (London, 1904), and E. K. H. Jordan told the story of *Free Church Unity* down to 1941 (London, 1951).

Looking back, an historian of the Victorian Nonconformist conscience found in it three essential features. He drew attention to 'a conviction that there is no complete boundary between religion and politics; an insistence that politicians should be men of the highest character; and a belief that the State should promote the moral welfare of its citizens.' That did not amount to a political programme – and indeed, at its deepest level Nonconformity always knew that it was not a political movement, that its origins lay in a spiritual hunger which the Church of England could not satisfy, as well as in the protests of social groups excluded by the privileges of the Establishment. This scholar has concluded that the euphoria of 1906 was shortlived, that the old distaste for politics soon returned, and that by 1910 'the period of the Nonconformist conscience had come to an end.' Such a verdict may be exaggerated, but it usefully stresses that the real strength of Victorian and post-Victorian Nonconformity was always not political or cultural but religious.[39]

---

[39] See D. W. Bebbington, *The Nonconformist Conscience* (London, 1982). G. I. T. Machin studied the rise and fall of the crusade for disestablishment in *Politics and the Churches in Great Britain 1869–1921* (Oxford, 1987). Kenneth Brown has studied the *Social History of the Nonconformist Ministry in England and Wales 1800–1930* (Oxford, 1988).

CHAPTER SEVEN

ROMAN CATHOLICISM

THE SECOND SPRING

Newman's most famous sermon was on 'the Second Spring'. It was preached in 1852, in the chapel designed by Pugin at Oscott near Birmingham, celebrating the restoration of twelve Roman Catholic dioceses in England two years previously. Cardinal Wiseman openly sobbed during it. It was a masterpiece of religious emotion in chastely beautiful English. But it showed that the preacher was out of touch with the realities.

It suited Newman's religion, both supernatural and nostalgic, to consider the centuries since the Reformation as a long decline fit to be compared with autumn and winter, so that the bishops could be welcomed like daffodils appearing by a miracle to herald the return of the Middle Ages. 'The past *has* returned,' he exulted, 'the dead live.' It also suited his purpose to prophesy greatness on the medieval scale for the bishops of the future; about the present, he was discreetly vague. 'Canterbury has gone its way, and York is gone, and Durham is gone, and Winchester is gone. . . . Westminster and Nottingham, Beverley, Hexham, Northampton and Shrewsbury, if the world lasts, shall be names as musical to the ear, as stirring to the heart, as the glories we have lost; and saints shall rise out of them, if God so will, and doctors once again shall give the law to Israel, and preachers call to penance and to justice, as at the beginning.' So Newman said.

In reality, however, the task confronting the bishops in the 1850s was to build churches and schools where the priests could teach the Irish and any others willing to be taught. There were never enough priests – only just over a thousand in 1860 (when the Church of England had 19,000 clergy), still under three thousand in 1900 (when the Church of England had almost 25,000 clergy). But these priests worked; some 440 new churches were built in the quarter-century, 1850–75, and many more arose before 1900. In the annual *Catholic Directory* lay numbers grew to one and a half million by the end of the century, although it was never claimed that all these were present at Mass every Sunday.

The ban on contraceptives contributed to growth not only in numbers but also in the sense that this community was separate, even holy. Celebrating the centenary of the political emancipation in 1829, Professor Denis Gwyn could take pride in the refusal of the community to be emancipated in sex. 'It is not only the moral discipline of Catholicism,' he wrote, 'but the whole Catholic outlook upon life that prevents modern birth control propaganda from making headway even among the poorest Catholics, upon whom the burden of large families falls most heavily. A different sense of values, which attaches more importance to the fundamental realities of life than to its material comforts, produces an attitude towards family life which remains steadfast'. In contrast, 'the more sophisticated and pleasure-loving drift inevitably towards race suicide'.[1]

The ban on contraceptives would not have been effective had there not been a strong religious faith within this community. This faith influenced the numerous children born to Roman Catholic parents – and also many converts.

Obviously it is impossible for any historian to write in full detail the story of Roman Catholic religion in the everyday life of Victorian England.[2] Much of the story never escaped from the strict secrecy of the confessional, where the penitent was expected to bare his life and thoughts regularly to the judgement of the parish priest; or from the privacy of the home, where any family known to be Catholic was liable to be visited by the priest if any of its members seemed to be either

---

[1] Denis Gwyn, *A Hundred Years of Catholic Emancipation* (London, 1929), p. xxvii.

[2] The impossibility was fully acknowledged in *The English Catholics 1850–1950*, ed. G. A. Beck (London, 1959), but that volume is indispensable. J. Derek Holmes, *More Roman than Rome: English Catholicism in the Nineteenth Century* (London, 1978), was more independent and Edward Norman, *The English Catholic Church in the Nineteenth Century* (Oxford, 1984), fuller in Maisie Ward's two volumes on *The Wilfred Wards and the Transition* (London, 1934–38) abounded in memories.

dangerously sick or dangerously sinful; or from the obscurity of the classroom, where the Faith was taught as a child's most precious inheritance. Such contacts not only kept the individual's piety going at some heat in a cold world, but also exercised a profound influence on the whole pattern of his life.

Despite their poverty and their well-known temptations to drink, rowdiness, crime and general fecklessness, the Irish often went from their weekly Mass to live as exemplary parents and workers; and the effect can be seen clearly in the history of their assimilation into English life.[3] In the 1840s and 1850s Irish immigrants were often regarded as disease-carriers, and there was great resentment about their open willingness to accept lower pay than the already low average of the English labourer. They militantly opposed Chartist activity, allowed themselves to be used as strike-breakers, and engaged in bitter and bloody battles with the native workmen in many parts of Britain. But by the 1910s prejudice against 'Paddy' had greatly diminished. Catholics of Irish descent were struggling alongside the English in the trade unions – and fighting alongside them in the British army. They and their fellow Catholics never formed a distinct group in English politics, for although the Liberals were applauded for their sympathy with Irish grievances the two leading Catholic weeklies, the *Universe* and the more sophisticated *Tablet*, were Conservative in their political tendency, one of the reasons being the Liberals' dislike of church schools. On the whole the community was, like Nonconformity, non-political. But in his history of *Catholicism in England* Archbishop David Mathew was surely right to emphasize the quiet impressiveness of 'the great mass of the Catholics of the working class. . . . As the families sat in the kitchen at the hot Sunday dinner, with the girls in their print dresses and the boys talking of the new League Football and the first boxing successes of Jim Driscoll, they would always have the money ready for the collector coming Sunday after Sunday for the school building. This generation among the workers had a

---

[3] L. P. Curtis, Jr., studied anti-Irish prejudice in Victorian England in *Anglo-Saxons and Celts* (Bridgeport, Conn., 1968) and *Apes and Angels* (Newton Abbot, Devon, 1979).

profound reverence for the Mass; broad constant humour;
vitality; a virile faith'.[4] And the rest of England noticed the
regular giving of the pennies of the poor, just as it noticed the
pious munificence of the Duke of Norfolk or the religious
courage of the Marquis of Ripon, who despite his conversion
became Viceroy of India in 1880.

The best loved teachers of Roman Catholicism were the
nuns, who brought grace to so many parishes and schools. It
would be tedious to compile a catalogue of all the Orders, old
or new, to which these sisters belonged. It is, however, the
opposite of tedious to notice the extraordinary talents of
women such as Cornelia Connelly, formerly an Anglican
clergyman's wife and now foundress of the Society of the Holy
Child Jesus, an order which has had to its credit a chain of
schools conducted on enlightened lines; of Margaret Hallahan,
who founded five convents for Dominican Tertiaries with an
extensive work of evangelism and education in the Midlands;
and of Laura Jerningham, a widow who expanded the work of
the Sisters of Notre Dame in many schools and in the great
Catholic Training College in Liverpool.[5]

Most of the members of the religious orders for men were
more highly educated than the average parish priest. The
Jesuits' school at Stonyhurst, tracing its ancestry back to the
college at St Omer for boys from Elizabethan England, had
flourished since its move to that great house in Lancashire in
1794. The Jesuits' chief church in London (in Farm Street) was
served by an eminent succession of preachers, and the quality
of the Jesuits' literary work was to be seen in their journal, the
Month. The Benedictines established famous schools at their
abbeys at Downside and Ampleforth. At a more popular level,
Roman Catholics in Victorian England were served magnificently by the energy of the English branches of the newer
Italian orders – Rosminians, Redemptorists, Passionists and
Oratorians. Before Westminster Cathedral was consecrated
the Brompton Oratory in Kensington, founded in 1853, was
Catholic London's grandest church, dominated by the ex-

    [4] David Mathew, *Catholicism in England* pp. 234–7.
    [5] See Julia Wadham, *The Case of Cornelia Connelly* (London, 1956).

travagantly sentimental personality of F. W. Faber, an ex-Anglican convert. Ordinary parish priests disliked its flamboyance, and the Baroque architecture and Italianate practices seemed calculated to outrage Victorian Protestants. Votive candles were kept shining before an image of Our Lady ('Mamma' to Faber); the reserved sacrament was talked about as if Our Lord were there as a man, waiting to be visited or to be moved about; unguarded invitations to confess to a priest indicated how to give 'all for Jesus' or 'all for Mary'. Yet Faber also had a totally genuine and lifelong sense of God; his best-known hymn began 'My God, how wonderful thou art'. This communion with the All-Holy communicated itself to men and women, and with that burning light at the centre Faber was able to make the spirituality of the Counter-Reformation a part of the public life of Victorian London.[6]

The parish priests were less glamorous but they thoroughly earned the title 'Father' which now became customary for the first time. The 'Roman collar' which they wore acquired such prestige as a uniform that it was gradually adopted in the Church of England and even in Nonconformity. Naturally their pastoral work became more effective as it became possible to establish in the relevant centres of population a network of small parishes with schools attached – as in Liverpool under the two very formidable bishops, O'Reilly and Whiteside, who devoted their energies to this steady expansion from 1872 to 1921.[7] However, these priests were managed by their bishops in many details of their work, the explanation being that when the dioceses were restored in 1850 the parishes were not restored. Until the revision of canon law was completed in 1918, parish priests in England had the status merely of rectors or assistants in 'missions' under the direct control of the diocesan bishop or his vicar general. The bishop owned the buildings, appointed the priests, authorized their payment according to his estimate of their value, and had detailed reports and accounts submitted to his office.

---

[6] See Ronald Chapman, *Father Faber* (London, 1961).
[7] Conor K. Ward studied the sociological results in *Priests and People* (Liverpool, 1961).

Three of the vicars apostolic who became diocesan bishops in the 1850s were stout northerners with long experience of pastoral work – Briggs at Beverley, Hogarth at Hexham, Brown at Liverpool – and only two of the rest were nonentities. Five new bishops were needed. Among them were two who had come from the same background as Wiseman: Thomas Grant, the young rector of the English College in Rome, and the older George Errington, who had served as Wiseman's assistant both there and at the Oscott seminary. But neither of these remained on good terms with Wiseman. Grant as Bishop of Southwark was a thorn in the flesh of successive Archbishops of Westminster. Errington, first made Bishop of Plymouth, was soon called to act as Wiseman's colleague with the right of succession at Westminster. A strict disciplinarian and a highly competent businessman, Errington angered Wiseman by criticizing his slackness. After much unpleasantness he was dismissed by the personal intervention of the Pope, but it says much for him that the leading parish priests of the diocese nominated him as successor to Wiseman on the Cardinal's death, braving the Pope's fury. It says even more for him that after his fall Errington lived quietly as a parish priest and professor.

Grant and Errington were among the bishops who publicly criticized the 1870 definition of the Pope's infallibility.[8] So was the formidable Yorkshireman, Bernard Ullathorne, Bishop of Birmingham 1850–88, although in the end he voted for it. After a brief spell at sea as a cabin boy, and another spell as a novice and monk with the Benedictines, he had gone to Australia in 1833 while still in his mid-twenties, the senior priest in a vast area; nominally he was vicar-general to a bishop in far-distant Mauritius. He had bravely ministered to the convicts and pioneer settlers – and with equal courage on his return home had spoken and written freely about the harsh conditions of their lives. This man who on the other side of the world had often ministered to convicts before execution was well able to

[8] Cuthbert Butler's account of *The Vatican Council* (London, 1930) has been supplemented by F. J. Cwiekowski, *The English Bishops and the First Vatican Council* (Louvain, 1971). See also *Lord Acton and the First Vatican Council*, ed. Edmund Campion (Sydney, 1975). The reasoning behind the opposition was illuminated by Damian McElrath, *The Syllabus of Pius IX: Some Reactions in England* (Louvain, 1964).

keep the over-subtle Newman's deepest respect, to comfort him when he tormented himself, and to rebuke Westminster's two cardinals, Wiseman and Manning, for arrogance in the one case and for duplicity in the other. Noting that his achievements included the opening of more than a hundred new schools, the historian Philip Hughes judged that Ullathorne, 'despite his subordinate rank, was to be the real centre of English Catholic activities . . . all in all, surely the greatest of the ninety bishops whose lives make up the first century of the restored hierarchy.'[9]

THREE CARDINALS IN WESTMINSTER

When Nicholas Wiseman arrived in Rome early in September 1850, it was in the belief that the Pope intended him to reside there permanently as a cardinal. To him, this was a bitter disappointment. During the previous ten years he, who formerly had taken such delight in Rome, had been in England, absorbed in the hope of restoring his nation to the Catholic Church. He had received many converts into the Church and had confirmed Newman in a service when ten former Anglican clergymen had been together in the chapel. He had seen churches, religious communities and schools springing up, and many thousands of the Irish returning to the sacraments. He had acted as vicar apostolic of the London district since 1847 and had frankly hoped to be archbishop – 'to stand at the helm in the capital of this empire', as he had written to a friend, 'while the Church is bearing all before it.' When he had taken leave of Bishop Ullathorne in Birmingham, he had been in tears.

But before the end of September Pius IX not only proclaimed the restoration of the English hierarchy but also

---

[9] *The English Catholics 1850–1950*, pp. 74–5. Ullathorne was honoured by a titular archbishopric on his retirement. In 1941 Sir Shane Leslie edited his autobiography as *From Cabin-boy to Archbishop*, based on the original draft completed in the last months of his life but not going beyond 1852. Cuthbert Butler compiled *The Life and Times of Bishop Ullathorne* (2 vols., London, 1926).

announced Cardinal Wiseman's appointment as the first
Archbishop of Westminster. The news and the consequent
ceremonies left Wiseman (who by temperament alternated
between depression and euphoria) elated, and in this almost
intoxicated condition he dashed off a pastoral letter to be read
in the churches of his new diocese, before beginning a triumphant journey home. Entitling this epistle 'From out of the
Flaminian Gate', he wrote: 'Till such time as the Holy See shall
think fit otherwise to provide, we govern, and shall continue to
govern, the counties of Middlesex, Hertford and Essex as
ordinary thereof, and those of Surrey, Sussex, Kent, Berkshire
and Hampshire, with the islands annexed, as administrator
with ordinary jurisdiction. . . . The great work, then, is complete; what you have long desired and prayed for is granted.
Your beloved country has received a place among the fair
Churches, which, normally constituted, form the splendid
aggregate of Catholic Communion; Catholic England has been
restored to its orbit in the ecclesiastical firmament, from which
its light had long vanished, and begins now anew its course of
regularly adjusted action round the centre of unity, the source
of jurisdiction, of light, and of vigour.'

It was in his carriage in Vienna, 'full of satisfaction at the
events of the past month and reading my *Times*', that the new
cardinal found that his appointment had been the subject of
the leading article in that newspaper. 'If this appointment be
not intended as a clumsy joke,' the editor had thundered, 'we
confess that we can only regard it as one of the grossest acts of
folly and impertinence which the Court of Rome has ventured
to commit since the Crown and people of England threw off its
yoke.' Before long the Prime Minister, Lord John Russell,
assured the Bishop of Durham that 'there is an assumption of
power in all the documents which have come from Rome . . .
which is inconsistent with the Queen's supremacy, with the
rights of our bishops and clergy, and with the spiritual independence of the nation.' And he translated his indignation into
the Ecclesiastical Titles Act.[10]

---

[10] Relevant documents were collected by E. R. Norman, *Anti-Catholicism in
Victorian England* (London, 1968).

The penalties announced in that act for any invasion of the rights of the Church of England were never imposed. Many soon felt ashamed of this outburst of intolerance, and within a week of his arrival in London Wiseman had a pamphlet ready for the printer, *An Appeal to the Reason and Good Feeling of the English People*. It was as clever as his letter from the Flaminian Gate had been foolish. First he appealed to 'that love of honourable dealing and fair play which, in joke or in earnest, is equally the instinct of an Englishman.' Next he pointed out that if Catholics did not recognize the spiritual authority of 'the bishops appointed by our gracious Queen' neither did the Church of Scotland or the Protestant Nonconformists of England. Then he assured the bishops of the Establishment that they would be deprived of none of their 'worldly advantages'. Finally he defended the use of Westminster in his new title. 'Close under the Abbey of Westminster there lie concealed labyrinths of lanes and courts, and alleys and slums, nests of ignorance, vice, depravity, and crime, as well as of squalor, wretchedness, and disease; whose atmosphere is typhus, whose ventilation is cholera; in which swarms of huge and almost countless population, in great measure, nominally at least, Catholic; haunts of filth, which no sewage committee can reach – dark corners which no lighting-board can brighten. This is the part of Westminster which alone I covet. . . .'

By the end of the year the cardinal was seen to be morally vindicated. He followed up his success with brilliant lectures and with a novel about fourth-century Rome, *Fabiola*. But the success did not last. He neglected routine business, alienated Newman and many others by a combination of grandeur with clumsiness and inefficiency, and relied in his dealings with Rome on a monsignor who went mad. He grew very fat and very depressed. His death in 1865 was a release not only for him but also for those who had tried to share the work with him. As he lay dying, he said with truth: 'I have never cared for anything but the Church. . . .' Newman wrote *The Dream of Gerontius* while Wiseman was on his deathbed, and his funeral was the largest in London since the Duke of Wellington's, showing that despite everything many Englishmen acknowledged the talents and ideals which had made this man the spokesman of a great tradition now revived.[11]

Under Wiseman the provost of the chapter of Westminster had been Henry Manning, the former Anglican Archdeacon of Chichester who had thrown away brilliant prospects in the Established Church and Gladstone's intimate friendship. He would never have been elected as Wiseman's successor, being far too unpopular, but the Pope appointed him – and his rule was, just as other priests had feared, uncomfortable.

Once enthroned, the new archbishop vetoed any political activity on behalf of the English Catholics unless it was under his control, and he even stopped the informal religious discussions of a London group known as the 'Academy of the Catholic Religion', brought together by Wiseman. By his self-confident ability and by his command of Pius IX's support, Manning was able to impose his policies on this large and growing community right up to his death in 1892, although his grip slackened somewhat when Pope Pius died in 1878.

The symbol of his supremacy was the prohibition of any Roman Catholic enrolment for higher education at Oxford and Cambridge. Some of the richer Roman Catholics defied the prohibition, but not many. Manning's own 'university college' in Kensington collapsed amid debts and scandals, but his policy was inflexible for Oxford and Cambridge represented the Anglicanism from which he had escaped. His loyalty to Pius IX was so extreme that the cardinals managed to delay his promotion to join their number until the Pope finally had his way in 1875. But when papal infallibility had been defined despite the hesitations of most of his fellow bishops in England, Manning had the satisfaction of seeing them all accept the decree, along with Newman. Out of his own experience as a convert he knew well that there was no coherent spiritual and

---

[11] Brian Fothergill's 1963 study of *Nicholas Wiseman* was more psychological than Wilfrid Ward's *Life and Times of Cardinal Wiseman* (2 vols., London, 1900). E. E. Reynolds portrayed Wiseman with Newman and Manning in *Three Cardinals* (London, 1958), and S. W. Jackman studied his writings in *Nicholas, Cardinal Wiseman* (Gerrards Cross, Bucks, 1977).

intellectual alternative to the confident dogmatism now centred on Rome. It seems a fair comment by an historian (admittedly an Anglican) that among Roman Catholics in England to the end of the century 'the atmosphere of simplicity was not of the credulous but of the childlike. And a sophisticated leader like Manning preferred to have it so. He saw the strength of simple faith . . . in order that the values inherited from the past could be preserved.'[12]

The last years of Cardinal Manning had their sadnesses. The new pope, Leo XIII, responded to the Duke of Norfolk's petition that Newman should be made a cardinal. It would be a sign of his policy of taking the arts and sciences under his patronage, bridging the gap which Pius IX had deliberately widened between the Church and modern civilization. Manning chose to interpret a private letter from Newman, who was suitably modest, as a refusal, and made this public – only to find that Newman made clear his determination to accept the honour. Bishop Ullathorne interpreted Manning's role in this incident in the worst possible light, probably rightly. Rebuffed in this and in other ways by the new regime in the Vatican, Manning never visited Rome during the last nine years of his life.

His true glory was his sympathy with the poor. He bravely championed the agricultural labourers; in the 1880s he issued two pastoral letters in defence of the urban poor; and in 1889 he had his biggest chance to befriend the low-paid in London, when he successfully mediated in the dockers' strike. So Manning was 'the lonely pioneer of Social Catholicism in England'.[13] His successor attributed it to senile decay, and his first biographer, E. S. Purcell, was more dismayed by this involvement in 'Socialism' than by any other aspect of his life. But many others respected him as a brave prophet – and he certainly had a prophet's face. In the words of a Nonconformist journalist, 'it was as if wrinkled parchment was stretched across a fleshless skull, out of which, however, blue eyes

---

[12] Owen Chadwick, *The Victorian Church*, vol. ii, p. 408.
[13] A. R. Vidler, *A Century of Social Catholicism 1820–1920* (London, 1964), p. 71.

gleamed brightly, while a pleasant smile gave life and human fervour to the features of an ascetic.'[14]

His successor in 1892, Herbert Vaughan, shared all his dedication to the triumph of the 'Roman spirit' and all his contempt for Anglicanism. Alarmed by Anglo-Catholic efforts led by the Earl of Halifax to secure some recognition of the Church of England in Rome, he was delighted when in 1896 Pope Leo issued the enclyclical *Apostolicae Curae*, making clear the invalidity of Anglican ordinations: they were 'absolutely null and utterly void'. Vaughan then wrote to Halifax, urging 'the necessity of submission to the Church – the Church of which the Pope is the legitimate Head.'[15] In a pastoral letter which he and other bishops issued in 1900, he expressed his own faith – the faith which his family had kept since the days of Elizabeth I, and which had made five of his brothers priests. 'When our Lord Jesus Christ was upon earth, God spoke through the lips of His Sacred Humanity', they declared. 'After He had ascended into Heaven the Divine Teacher spoke through the mouth of Peter and the Apostles, and He now teaches and will continue to teach through their legitimate successors, "until the consummation of the ages".'

But in other ways Vaughan was more smoothly businesslike than Manning. Not for nothing had he been liked by the businessmen of Manchester as the very active Bishop of Salford, concentrating on the multiplication of schools under his own firm control. He now obtained permission for Roman Catholics to study at Oxford and Cambridge, with careful arrangements for their spiritual care; and he allied himself with the Conservatives who championed church schools for the poor. From him there were no indiscretions about Christian Socialism.[16]

---

[14] E. S. Purcell, *Life of Cardinal Manning* (2 vols., London, 1896), has been supplemented by Sir Shane Leslie, *Henry Edward Manning: His Life and Labours* (London, 1921); *Manning: Anglican and Catholic*, ed. John Fitzsimons (London, 1951); and V. A. McClelland, *Cardinal Manning: His Public Life and Influence* (London, 1962).

[15] See J. J. Hughes, *Absolutely Null and Utterly Void* (London, 1968).

[16] See V. A. McClelland, *English Roman Catholics and Higher Education 1830–1903* (London, 1973).

He told a cousin who met him at the railway station on his arrival as archbishop-elect that his biggest project would be to build a cathedral; and so it was. Early in 1894 he was assured of the support of wealthy men such as the Duke of Norfolk. Next year the design by John Bentley – massive, brick and basically Byzantine, so as to avoid comparisons with Westminster Abbey – was accepted and the work was begun. By the middle of 1902 the domes and campanile were almost complete, although the exhausted architect was dead. Most of the decoration in mosaics had to be left to later generations, but a greater frustration was that the idea of bringing Benedictine monks back to Westminster for the daily singing of the Divine Office came to nothing. The abbeys consulted refused to release monks unless they could also do pastoral work in the area; and Vaughan refused to entrust them with this responsibility. But provision was made for a 'secular' establishment of priests and musicians who would be clearly under the archbishop's control. The whole bold and rapid construction expressed, in brick and in worship, what the word 'triumphalism' means.

On a June day in 1903 the cardinal's body was brought to Westminster Cathedral for a Requiem Mass. It was the first public service held in the great church. But he was buried in his own college for training missionaries at Mill Hill, where he had always remained the Superior General. Knowing that the triumph depended on the mission, he had chosen to die there.[17]

---

[17] Arthur McCormack, *Cardinal Vaughan* (London, 1966), supplemented J. G. Snead-Cox, *Cardinal Vaughan* (2 vols., London, 1911). See also *Letters of Herbert Cardinal Vaughan to Lady Herbert of Lea*, ed. Shane Leslie (London, 1942).

CHAPTER EIGHT

UNCONVENTIONAL
VICTORIANS

WOMEN AS CRUSADERS

It is quite wrong to think that all Victorian Christians were
smugly comfortable.

Three women astonished the public because as Christian
crusaders they dared to learn about, to enter and to transform
prisons, hospitals and the lives of prostitutes. After much
hesitation, their own nineteenth century applauded what they
did. The next century was to be no less interested in who they
were; for these were women of indomitable personality who
dared to carve out their own beliefs and lives in defiance of
long-established conventions. Thus they liberated not only the
victims of sordid evils, but also themselves. And by their
example they helped to liberate their sex.[1]

Elizabeth Fry is revealed in her journals (too indiscreet for
use in the early biographies) as a portly matron with many
anxieties, depressions and nervous illnesses, needing the
plentiful use of wine and opium. Her emotional problems arose
out of her position in society, enviable as that might seem to
almost all other women in her age. Herself one of twelve
children, she had eleven of her own. Her father was a wealthy
merchant and banker in Norwich, John Gurney, her husband a
dealer in tea, Joseph Fry. Her position was complicated by the
fact that both of them were Quakers. On the one hand, this
provided an outlet for her religious energies: she became a
'plain' Quaker, accepting the dress and speech of the little
Puritan community, and was recognized as a minister. On the

---

[1] E. K. Prochaska studied *Women and Philanthropy in Nineteenth-century England*
(Oxford, 1980).

other hand she was repelled by the emphasis now being given to quiet but steady money-making, and was indignant when the Quakers disowned and expelled her husband after the failure of a bank which he had started over-ambitiously. She was herself ambitious. She wanted to speak in public, to control others; and she wanted fame. She was ashamed of enjoying her work away from home, but she did enjoy it.

Thus mixed motives impelled her to lead a revolution within England's prisons. Prison reform had been frequently debated since the enquiries made by another Quaker, John Howard, in the 1770s; but remarkably little had been done. In January 1813, at the age of thirty-two, Elizabeth Fry was asked by a fellow Quaker to make some clothing for the babies of the women in a London prison, Newgate. The request led her to visit the prison, which was horrifying. Not only were the babies starving and disease-ridden, but the adult women were brutalized by subhuman conditions. She conducted services and a school there, and reorganized the whole of the women's side of the prison under a matron and monitors, with the co-operation or bemused assent of the men in charge. And the logic seemed inescapable – if women were to be cleaned up like that, why not men? And if Newgate was to be reformed, why not every other prison in the land? And if the fate of English prisoners was to be eased, what about the convicts being transported in their thousands to Australia? Elizabeth Fry had found her life's work. When she began this crusade, prisons were under no kind of national control. Everything depended on the local magistrates and on ill-paid and unsupervised gaol-keepers. In theory some two hundred crimes were to be punished by death, but in practice most criminals were imprisoned, in gaols which became more and more overcrowded. In 1823 Parliament intervened to establish some minimum standards of decency, but more was due to Elizabeth Fry. Tirelessly travelling and protesting, by the time of her death in 1843 she had made the Christian Gospel once more what it had been at the beginning: good news for prisoners.[2]

---

[2] The most candid biography is June Rose, *Elizabeth Fry* (London, 1980). Kathleen Heasman summarized the work of Victorian successors in her *Evangelicals in Action*, pp. 169–88.

Florence Nightingale's personality was in many ways similar. She, too, was born into a rich family, although her parents were dedicated entirely to the pursuit of pleasure; she owed her Christian name to the fact that she was born (in 1820) in Florence. She refused all the proposals of marriage made to her, with the result that the conventions of her class decreed that she should devote her life to these parents. It was only in 1851 that she was allowed to stay for a time in Kaiserswerth, a hospital with schools attached run by the Lutheran deaconesses in Germany; 'Now I know what it is to live and to love life.' It was only in 1853 that she finally broke away from her family to become the superintendent of a small Institution for the Care of Sick Gentlewomen in Distressed Circumstances.

There was then no training for nurses, the pay was very low, and most nurses were sluts who drank heavily. Not a few were, or had been, prostitutes. Even Miss Nightingale could never have done much to change such traditions had she not been commissioned by her friend Sidney Herbert, then in charge of the relevant department of the War Office, to lead a party of nurses out to the Crimean War in the autumn of 1854. She walked into two years of hell – and into fame as 'the lady with the lamp'. Her inflexible aims were now to secure a Royal Commission on hygiene and hospitals in the army, to feed it with facts, to make sure that it recommended the right reforms, and to see that its recommendations were carried out – all in the teeth of opposition. After the strain of the war she collapsed into invalidism, but always exploited her status as an invalid; she summoned eminent men to console her in her helplessness and when they arrived told them in detail what they must do for the army's hygiene. Nor was this the limit of her slow triumph. The standards forced on the army must also apply to the general public, and she founded Britain's first schools to train nurses and midwives. Her emphasis on character was, however, such that she resisted the registration of nurses who had merely passed an examination. And the same standards must apply to the far-off British army in India. From her invalid's room in London she corresponded on such a large scale that although she never saw the places she discussed she made herself the leading authority on all matters of hygiene in India. In 1870, during the war between Germany and France, she began directing the activities of the new society which later became the British Red Cross.

When asked for the secret of her success she would reply 'hard work' – that, and never denying God anything. She sometimes relaxed a little from her toils to write down thoughts on religion, some of which were published. They show that she had a burning sense of personal mission, fuelled by an intense experience of God the Father (not of Christ). That was her inspiration, although she wrote: 'I must remember God is not my private secretary.'[3]

Prostitution was a thriving trade – as was shown by the number of efforts to 'rescue' prostitutes. Men of the world accepted it as the necessary consequence of the facts – middle-class men did not marry until they were able to support a wife and family; they did not then expect their 'pure' wives to take any pleasure in sex; but, once married, they did not get divorced. At the same time sex between men and women in the working class was often free and easy, the 'age of consent' being twelve. Women with this experience behind them were easily tempted to offer sex to men who could pay for it. Few jobs were open to them apart from factory work (often in brutal conditions), and humiliating and ill-paid domestic service. There were 3,228,000 unmarried adult women in England in 1871. Everything seemed to conspire to make them sell their bodies – often for sixpence, of which they kept twopence. Many thousands of prostitutes roamed the streets of London and all the cities including Liverpool, then one of the largest ports in the world.[4]

There, in the late 1860s, Josephine Butler discovered the problem in human terms. Parliament had recently passed Contagious Diseases Acts intended to protect soldiers from venereal diseases. Prostitutes working in towns where there

---

[3] The best biography is Cecil Woodham-Smith, *Florence Nightingale* (revised, London, 1955).
[4] Recent studies include Judith Walkowitz, *Prostitution and Victorian Society* (Cambridge, 1980), and Paul McHugh, *Prostitution and Victorian Social Reform* (London, 1980).

were many soldiers had to register and to be inspected regularly. Women suspected of belonging to this profession could be apprehended by plain-clothes policemen, subjected to a medical examination, and ordered to report back regularly. Those who did not co-operate could be imprisoned. Roughly similar laws existed in most European countries, and before the spread of clinics to treat venereal diseases this control could be defended as protection. Most gentlemen preferred not to notice; the legislation had received very little comment in Parliament.

Josephine Butler, although the wife of the headmaster of Liverpool College, noticed. She noticed that the State tolerated and regulated vice. She noticed the indignities to which women were subjected, including innocent women, and she noticed the lofty or amused indifference shown by men. She noticed a departure from the English tradition of justice, which assumes a person to be innocent until proved guilty. And her crusading zeal would not be quenched until she had charmed, bullied, persuaded or simply exhausted men into seeing the need to extend English justice to women. First the compulsory medical examination without proof of prostitution was abolished. She went on campaigning when threatened by the brothel-keepers, when rebuked by people whose opinions she greatly valued, when supported by sensation-loving journalists, when moved to Winchester Cathedral Close where her husband was now a canon, and when widowed. Eventually in 1886 the Contagious Diseases Acts were repealed and her victory was complete, although prostitution remained a major phenomenon of English life into the 1910s. And the indefatigable Josephine Butler took 'the Cause' to stir Paris, Geneva and other centres of 'the Trade'.[5]

---

[5] Modern biographies are by E. Moberly Bell, *Josephine Butler: Flame of Fire* (London, 1962), and Glen Petrie, *A Singular Iniquity: The Campaigns of Josephine Butler* (London, 1971). A more personal *Portrait of Josephine Butler* was provided by her grandson, A. S. G. Butler (London, 1954).

SOLDIERS OF SALVATION

In 1883 a pamphlet issued by the London Congregational Union described a city which to the comfortable was still almost another continent. 'Whilst we have been building our churches and solacing ourselves with our religion and dreaming that the millennium was coming, the poor have been growing poorer, and the wretched more miserable, and the immoral more corrupt. The gulf has been daily widening which separates the lowest classes of the community from our churches and chapels, and from all decency and civilization. . . . *This terrible flood of sin and misery is growing upon us.*'

This pamphlet asked of the homes of many of London's poor, in 'rotten and reeking tenements': 'how can those places be called homes, compared with which the lair of a wild beast would be a comfortable and healthy spot?' It gave some shocking details about the unemployment, about the 'sweated' trades where work was little better than unemployment (a shilling for a seventeen-hour day sewing trousers), about the cruelly excessive rents, about the misery of children. 'Who can wonder that every evil flourishes in such hotbeds of vice and disease?' The pamphlet acknowledged the work of a 'noble army of men and women who penetrate the vilest haunts, carrying with them the blessings of the Gospel'. It praised 'Missions, Reformatories, Refuges, Temperance Societies . . . theatre services, midnight meetings and special missions.' It concluded as a result of 'long, patient and sober enquiry' that 'we are simply living in a fool's paradise if we suppose that all those agencies combined are doing a thousandth part of what needs to be done.'[6]

Movements which became internationally famous were included among these agencies battling with the social problems of Victorian London. At the more respectable end of the spectrum were the YMCA and YWCA, responding to the fact that London needed the ill-paid, unexciting but still 'respect-

---

[6] *The Bitter Cry of Outcast London* has been reprinted together with Octavia Hill's 1875 pamphlet on *Homes of the London Poor* (London, 1970). Recent research was summarized by Gareth Stedman Jones, *Outcast London* (Oxford, 1971).

able' work of tens of thousands of young men and women, clerks in offices or assistants in shops. Some had their accommodation provided by their employers, as had been the old custom with apprentices; but most were condemned to find cheap and cheerless lodgings. They could not marry since they aimed to be reckoned middle-class and the convention was strong that a man did not marry until he could support his wife and children. The innumerable prostitutes presented the most obvious temptation both to the young men to relieve their frustrations and to the young women to make more money. But probably most young men and women in this class went to church on a Sunday; there was little else to do. If the church was Evangelical, they would hear great promises and ideals proclaimed by the preacher – but after the thrills they would go their own ways back to shabbiness, isolation and boredom.

In 1844 about a dozen young men with such a background founded the Young Men's Christian Association in the bedroom of George Williams, then a young apprentice in a drapery business. The first international conference of YMCAs was held in Paris in 1855, and the YMCA held its first big meeting in London in 1878.[7]

A similar pattern, of Evangelical origins broadening out, may be seen in work for London's destitute children.

Dr Barnardo's Homes were only one of a number of similar efforts. For example, a civil servant, Edward Rudolf, the superintendent of the teachers in a Sunday school in Lambeth, was disturbed by the daily spectacle of tens of thousands of destitute children on the streets of central London. His own childhood had been poverty-stricken – but nothing like that. So in 1881 he founded the Waifs and Strays Society, later called the Church of England Children's Society, and administered it until retirement in 1919.

Thomas Barnardo's name has survived because he was a forceful, often controversial individualist. Born in 1845 to a German father and Irish mother and brought up in Dublin, he experienced an Evangelical conversion in 1862 and immediately threw himself into religious work among the Dublin

---

[7] See Clyde Binfield, *George Williams and the YMCA* (London, 1973).

poor; naturally he joined the YMCA. Moving to London in order to train as a medical missionary, in 1868 he converted two cottages as the first base of the East End Juvenile Mission. Later he raised funds to purchase a large public house, banning alcohol but welcoming large numbers to enjoy the Coffee Palace. A little lad called Jim Harvis showed him some of the places where he and hundreds of other boys slept in the open air of a winter's night. Barnardo became passionately determined to search for such boys (and girls) and to provide a home for them. And he encouraged others to come; 'No destitute child is ever refused admittance' became his motto. With a flair for publicity, he poured out pamphlets and articles; he habitually worked for seventeen hours a day; and with great self-confidence he personally obtained and administered large funds, scornful of many charges that his financial methods were so personal as to disregard the conventions. In one sense he did well for himself out of the great charity which was always to be linked with his name: he found fulfilment. Before his death in 1905 he had assumed the entire responsibility for rebuilding almost 60,000 young lives.[8]

William Booth was even more of an autocrat. Given a pound a week by a benefactor in order to turn from the hated work of a pawnbroker's assistant to revivalist preaching, he had rejected the Methodist splinter group ('the New Connexion') which had tried to sponsor and control him, and had founded his own 'Christian Mission' in London's East End in 1865. In 1878, when he was almost fifty, he renamed it the 'Salvation Army'. The name was a stroke of genius. The mission halls were now called 'barracks', prayer was called 'knee-drill', and the magazine was renamed the *War Cry*. Banners were paraded, with brass bands to enliven the marches, drown any opposition and accompany the 'songs' (usually very simple hymns, sung to tunes already popular in the music halls). Showmanship to attract audiences was encouraged, but the army did not have to rely on individual eccentrics; it created a stir by being itself in its military uniforms. And it developed practices which

---

[8] The best biography is Gillian Wagner, *Barnardo* (London, 1979). The story of the Waifs and Strays was told by John Stroud in *Thirteen Penny Stamps* (London, 1971).

distinguished it still more from the churches, for it abandoned
the sacraments of Baptism and Holy Communion and gave
equal status to men and women – all under General Booth,
who owned all the property.

The opposition was often violent; to break up meetings, a
'Skeleton Army' was hired by men who saw that the drink
trade was threatened. In one year alone, 1882, 669 Salvation
Army officers were knocked down or assaulted, about a third of
them being women, and some sixty of their buildings were
damaged. But 1882 was also the year when the Church of
England paid them the compliment of imitation, founding the
Church Army; for these soldiers without weapons seemed not
to heed their wounds. 'Blood and fire' was one of their mottoes.
William Booth's daughter Kate led the army into France; his
very able private secretary, George Railton, organized it in
America; a former civil servant, Frederick Tucker, outraged
the English rulers of India by leading a group which used
Indian names and which looked, lived, begged and preached in
the style of the Hindu holy men.

Gradually this evangelism was accompanied by more and
more social work. In Australia the Salvation Army opened a
home for discharged prisoners; in Sweden a home for the deaf
and dumb; in London a legal aid scheme for the poor, night
shelters for the homeless, 'farthing breakfasts' for hungry
children, the country's first labour exchange, and a missing
persons bureau. By the end of 1890, often working beside the
bed where his deeply loved wife and collaborator, Catherine,
lay dying of cancer, William Booth had collected material for
an explosive book about the social problems of London and
other English cities: *In Darkest England and the Way Out*. He
asked for an emergency fund and outlined great projects – a City
Colony of linked institutions to relieve distress, a Farm Colony
to make sober farmers out of the poor, and great emigration
schemes. He was disappointed in these unrealistic hopes, but
his vision had many practical results in England – and by now
the international army under his command was winning victories which were very widely reported and respected. In
Tokyo it fought prostitution, in New York alcoholism, with
dramatic public marches. It was heroic in bringing relief after

the great San Francisco earthquake, in founding a leper colony in Java, in many other tasks which no other body in all the world could tackle so well. Its social work commended it to rich and poor alike, although the novelty of its military-style revivalism had worn off.

In 1912 the General of this unique army was 'promoted to glory', as Salvationists phrased it; and the streets of central London were silent for four hours to honour his funeral procession.[9]

THE RELIGIOUS UNSETTLEMENT

Social problems were, however, not the only challenge to Victorian religion. It was also an age when the unsettlement of 'unbelief' spread – and could not be stopped by any religiously orthodox revivalism. The first man to use the word 'secular' in its modern meaning was George Jacob Holyoake, who in 1842 had been imprisoned for blasphemy. He was not committed to atheism, preferring the more ambiguous terms 'free thinking' and 'rationalism', but he lived to see the more loud-mouthed Charles Bradlaugh founding the National Secular Society in 1866 and taking his seat in Parliament. He himself founded the Rationalist Press Association in 1899 and continued to organize propaganda for secularism until his death seven years later.[10]

The greatest name in the more intellectual movement in secularization was that of Charles Darwin, whose disciple T. H. Huxley coined the word 'agnostic'. Darwin, too, never liked to be classified as an outright atheist, but during his voyage on HMS *Beagle* (1831–36) lost the complacent Christianity which he had imbibed from the *Evidences* of William Paley. It could

---

[9] The best biographies are Richard Collier, *The General Next to God* (London, 1965), and Catherine Bramwell-Booth, *Catherine Booth* (London, 1970). Robert Sandall wrote the official *History of the Salvation Army* in three volumes (London, 1947–55), followed by two volumes by Arch Wiggins (London, 1964–68).

[10] The best survey is Susan Budd, *Varieties of Unbelief* (London, 1977). More detail is in Edward Royle, *Victorian Infidels* and *Radicals, Secularists and Republicans* (Manchester, 1974–81).

not survive when he had glimpsed the real world with its many religions. He drew three lessons – first that the Old Testament 'was no more to be trusted than the sacred books of the Hindoos, or the beliefs of any barbarian', second that clearer evidence than was available 'would be requisite to make any sane man believe in the miracles by which Christianity is supported', and third that God had never given an authoritative revelation of himself. Then the amount of suffering inflicted by nature on animals in the interests of the 'survival of the fittest' gripped his imagination and his conscience, making it impossible – or, as in some moods he preferred to say, very difficult – for him to believe any longer that a good and loving Creator, revealed or unrevealed, could have ordained and foreseen the whole bloodbath.

His key idea of 'natural selection' by the 'struggle for existence' became plain to him when, two years after returning home from the *Beagle*, he read the *Essay on Population* by Thomas Malthus. His *Origin of Species* (1859) was sensational not because it propounded a complete explanation of the evolution of man from lower animals, but because men who had open eyes concluded that the Bible could not be literally true in its accounts of creation – and became inclined to suspect that the Bible was not true in any sense. Leslie Stephen, for example, was the son of a great Evangelical and a conspicuously clever and industrious clergyman; but in 1862 he resigned as a Cambridge college tutor because his mind could find 'no real stopping-place' in religion once he had abandoned belief in the infallibility of the Bible. It is curious that in England the main challenge to the old authority of 'revelation' came from the new science, whereas in Germany much more interest was taken in detailed historical criticism of the Old and New Testaments.[11]

'Nothing is more remarkable', Darwin recorded in his old age, 'than the spread of scepticism or rationalism during the latter part of my life.' Although conventional in his own domesticity, he thought that a morality independent of the discredited Christian religion was necessary. Sometimes

---

[11] L. E. Elliott-Binns made this a theme in *English Thought 1860–1900: The Theological Aspect* (London, 1956).

Christianity appeared to him to be actively immoral. 'I can indeed hardly see how anyone ought to wish Christianity to be true; for if so, the plain language of the text seems to show that men who do not believe, and this would include my father, brother, and almost all my best friends, will be everlastingly punished. And this is a damnable doctrine.' What a man needed was a rule of life 'only to follow those impulses and instincts which are strongest or which seem to him the best ones.'

These were disturbing thoughts. Disraeli put his finger on what people were feeling in his famous speech to the Oxford Diocesan Society in 1864. 'What is the question now placed before society with a glib assurance the most astounding? The question is this – Is man an ape or an angel? My Lord, I am on the side of the angels.' Four years previously at a meeting of the British Association for the Advancement of Science in Oxford Bishop Samuel Wilberforce had tried to ridicule Darwin's newly published *Origin*; he added his own wit and self-assurance to information or misinformation largely supplied by a leading anatomist, Sir Richard Owen. He teased T. H. Huxley, who was present and who had been reported as saying that it did not matter to him personally whether or not his grandfather was an ape. Would Huxley be content to trace his descent through an ape as his grandmother? Huxley, having muttered a biblical text to his neighbour ('The Lord hath delivered him into mine hands'), rose and with a deliberate coolness replied in words that burned. A later account of these words was that he would 'unhesitatingly affirm my preference for the ape' rather than have as grandfather 'a man highly endowed by nature and possessed of great means of influence and yet who employs these faculties and that influence for the mere purpose of introducing ridicule into a grave scientific discussion.'

Many of the clergymen and Christian ladies present applauded Huxley (then and afterwards) – and Bishop Wilberforce has been universally condemned for his folly although he tried to make light of the incident. But behind the flippancy of Disraeli and of the bishop who was his ally, we ought to see something more serious. It was a grave question for many

intelligent mid-Victorians whether the dignity of mankind
(especially the respect given to 'pure' women such as Bishop
Wilberforce's grandmothers) could be maintained after the
revelation of truth by Charles Darwin. As Professor Sedgwick
of Cambridge warned Darwin after the publication of his
Origin, if the 'moral or metaphysical part of nature' were to be
ignored 'humanity would suffer a damage which might brutal-
ize it, and sink the human race into a lower grade of degradation than any into which it has fallen since its written records
tell us of its history.' Darwin privately asked about belief in
God: 'Can the mind of man, which has, as I fully believe, been
developed from a mind as low as that possessed by the lowest
animal, be trusted when it draws such grand conclusions?'
Perhaps the power of the belief in God was caused solely by
children being taught it? His was a questioning position very
far removed from the centuries of trust in man's godlike reason
– and from the 'will to believe' of the Victorians. Whether or
not they were fundamentalists in their religion, many of the
great Victorian scientists – Michael Faraday, Lord Kelvin,
Joseph Lister, Clerk Maxwell, the leading medical men –
always remained devout Christians. And when T. H. Huxley
died in 1895 three lines from a poem by his wife were inscribed
on his tombstone by his wish:

> Be not afraid, ye waiting hearts that weep;
> For still He giveth His beloved sleep,
> And if an endless sleep He wills, so best.

It was not the last testament of a consistent secularist.[12]

The lives of many Victorian laymen illustrate this confusion
or conflict between opposed tendencies: the nostalgia for the
religious foundations of family life and other agreeable features
of the old England, and the awareness that a time had come for
which there might be no over-ruling God, no ever-living
Christ, no realistic morality other than self-interest.

---

[12] The *Autobiographies* of Charles Darwin and T. H. Huxley were edited by Gavin
de Beer (Oxford, 1974). Studies include William Irvine, *Apes, Angels and Victorians*
(London, 1955); David Lack, *Evolutionary Theory and Christian Belief: The Unresolved
Conflict* (London, 1957); Gertrude Himmelfarb, *Darwin and the Darwinian Revolution*
(London, 1959), and *Victorian Minds* (London, 1968); James R. Moore, *The Post-
Darwinian Controversies* (Cambridge, 1979).

Matthew Arnold's poetry is full of the tension. He was a son of the great Thomas Arnold whose headmastership of Rugby School did so much to make the public schools more earnestly Christian (and more humane and scholarly), and he was himself an educationist and a kind of lay preacher. He devoted many years to his work as an Inspector of Education and many essays to his battle for the enlightenment and enlargement of the Victorian mind. The two Arnolds, father and son, may be recalled when we read the verdict of a Canadian scholar: 'This was the great accomplishment of the Church in Victorian England. Through the writing, teaching and preaching of its creative minority, it gave to the powerful new middle classes an ethic of service, based upon Christian principles.'[13]

Matthew Arnold, however, had to strain language to its most ambiguous limits when he paid his loyal tributes to his father's faith. His own belief was that 'the peace of God' was 'the Christian phrase for civilization', and 'the kingdom of God' was 'the ideal society of the future'. 'Christian principles' now needed a non-dogmatic basis since truly religion was 'morality touched by emotion'. 'To one who knows what conduct is, it is a joy to be alive; the *not ourselves*, which by revealing to us righteousness makes our happiness, adds to the boon this glorious world to be righteous in. That is the notion at the bottom of the Hebrew's praise of the Creator.' Or at least, that was the creed at the bottom of Matthew Arnold's attempt in a number of books or essays to reconstruct Christianity after the virtual disappearance of God.

Intellectually, it was all that seemed possible if a mid-Victorian who was highly educated in the terms of his own day was to be honest. But emotionally, he knew it was not enough – and his poetry revealed his distress. In 'The Scholar-Gipsy' he addressed a wanderer:

[13] Desmond Bowen, *The Idea of the Victorian Church* (Toronto, 1968), p. 258. See T. W. Bamford, *Thomas Arnold* and *The Rise of the Public Schools* (London, 1960–67). Other studies include Frances Woodward, *The Doctor's Disciples* (London, 1954); David Newsome, *Godliness and Good Learning* (London, 1961); Meriol Trevor, *The Arnolds* (London, 1973); J. R. de S. Honey, *Tom Brown's Universe* (London, 1977). The best biography of Matthew Arnold is by Patrick Honan (London, 1981).

> Thou waitest for the spark from heaven! and we,
>   Light half-believers of our casual creeds,
>   Who never deeply felt, nor clearly will'd,
>   Whose insight never has borne fruit in deeds,
>   Whose vague resolves never have been fulfill'd. . . .
>   Ah! do not we, wanderer! await it too?

In 'Dover Beach' he addressed the conventionally minded wife he was marrying:

> Ah, love, let us be true
> To one another! for the world, which seems
> To lie before us like a land of dreams,
> So various, so beautiful, so new,
> Hath really neither joy, nor love, nor light,
> Nor certitude, nor peace, nor help for pain. . . .

For his father's world had been left empty by the retreat of religious confidence from the minds of honest thinkers:

> The Sea of Faith
> Was once, too, at the full, and round earth's shore
> Lay like the folds of a bright girdle furl'd.
> But now I only hear
> Its melancholy, long, withdrawing roar,
> Retreating, to the breath
> Of the night-wind, down the vast-edges drear
> And naked shingles of the world.

The result for Matthew Arnold's heart as shown in his poems was a scene of confusion and terror. It was a world very different from the 'glorious world to be righteous in' of his lay preacher's prose – and from the strongly moral discharge of duties in his daily life. This was his vision:

> And we are here as on a darkling plain
> Swept with confused alarm of struggle and flight,
> Where ignorant armies clash by night.

Thomas Hardy was a novelist and a poet who became an example of a secularization more decisive than the battle going on in Matthew Arnold's mind between belief and unbelief. As late as 1865, when he was twenty-five, Hardy was still considering the possibility of being ordained. His chief interest as an architect was in the restoration of churches, and his first wife distributed Evangelical tracts. But the clergyman who had given him his real education committed suicide, various love affairs came to desolation, faith died, and by 1912 he could make his mature position clear in a deeply melancholy poem on 'God's Funeral'. Although it became his habit to speak nostalgically or obliquely about religion, a critic of his work has observed that almost everywhere the driving force was a belief 'that the universe was non-sentient, a kind of machine; that consciousness was an accident and a misfortune as well. Most of the quirks, obsessions and insights for which Hardy is famous, the mechanical imagery, the peculiar home-made mythology, the trivial incidents, the fascination with the workings of "Chance", and much else besides, could be logically derived from this "core". . . .'[14]

A very public example of what the Victorian confusion of spiritual crosscurrents meant to a sensitive spirit is to be found in the novels and life of Charles Dickens.

Born in 1812, Dickens came from the lower middle class and his central achievement was to put the life of that class into print. He knew how to depict it as a good life. Indeed, it has been said that 'no novel could move further than *Pickwick Papers* toward asserting not only that the kingdom of God is within each man but that it is possible to establish something that resembles the kingdom of God on earth – and this, as much as anything, accounts for its enduring, universal popularity'.[15] But the central vision of Dickens was very different. It was a nightmare vision of English life being poisoned by the Victorian age – by its exploitation of those forced to labour in factories or offices, but also by the psychological damage which the dominant materialism inflicted on the successful.

No institutional form of religion played much of a part in his thought or life. He wrote to a friend in 1843 about his disgust with 'our Established Church, and its Puseyisms and daily

---

[14] Kenneth Marsden, *The Poems of Thomas Hardy* (London, 1969), p. 15. Robert Gittings, *Young Thomas Hardy* and *The Older Hardy* (London, 1975–76), and Michael Millgate, *Thomas Hardy* (Oxford, 1982), are the best biographies.

[15] Steven Marcus, *Dickens: From Pickwick to Dombey* (London, 1965), p. 51.

outrages on common sense and humanity'. This was not an
isolated outburst, but in his novels his hostility was directed
against Evangelicals, almost always portrayed as oily, canting
and fatuous. Only in his deathbed scenes, when Victorian
convention decreed that the angels must be on hand to take
away innocent girls, did he begin to write like an Evangelical
novelist. In his accounts of his travels he was as contemptuous
of Catholicism in Italy as of Protestantism in America; only in
his account of the Gordon Riots in *Barnaby Rudge* did he begin
to show sympathy with Roman Catholics. Many members of
the class from which he came were happily absorbed in the life
of English Nonconformity, but all that he noted about the
chapels in the 'Coketown' of *Hard Times* was that there were
eighteen denominations and it was puzzling to know where
their adherents all came from. The nearest he came to being
involved in church life seems to have been in 1842–43, when he
and his family became members of a Unitarian chapel in
London, and towards the end of his life he subscribed to his
parish church as a local squire. He was never more deeply
committed because he shared the assumption of (for example)
Hogarth that in comparison with the honest life of English
streets and homes any religious enthusiasm, in the pulpit or on
a layman's lips, must be humbug.

However, scholars have usually agreed that Dickens was
non-ecclesiastically and non-dogmatically religious. Angus
Wilson, indeed, claimed that 'he thought of himself as centrally
a Christian' and that he was right, for in profound ways the
Christian religion makes sense of his work.[16] The intensity of
his hatred of cruelty was totally sincere; and so was his belief
that love was blessed by the God who in the mysterious
background presided over human affairs. It seems clear that he
prayed twice a day and read the Bible regularly. He often
assured correspondents that his novels were intended to support the teaching of the Saviour. In his last will – no conventional document, for the first of his legacies was a comparatively small sum left to the young actress who was his mistress
– he wrote: 'I exhort my dear children humbly to try to guide

---

[16] *The English Novel*, ed. Angus Wilson and A. E. Dyson (London, 1976), p. 55.

themselves by the teaching of the New Testament in its broad
spirit, and to put no faith in any man's narrow construction of
its letter here and there.' He wrote a *Life of Christ* for these
children of his; it was not published until 1934. Many Christians loved and admired him. They believed that he had been
one of them when they buried him in Westminster Abbey, near
Handel.

His glimpse of hell came in the months of 1824 when he was
put to work in a London factory making blacking polish, while
his parents were imprisoned as debtors. The boy who introduced him to the work was named Fagin. The humiliation
made him inflexibly determined to succeed – and gave him the
raw material for his genius, since one of his assets was his
knowledge of the lights and shadows of London life at most
levels below the top. Despite his extraordinary vitality and his
supreme gift for comedy, the dominant theme of his work
became his hatred of the institutions which had, he believed,
ruined his class and his time; he began writing *Oliver Twist*
before he had finished *Pickwick Papers*. Thus Mr Pickwick,
although he benevolently shared with the twenty-four-year old
author a fame which became immortality as the years passed,
was not fully Dickensian. He was the man at the sunlit door
inviting the public to enter an exhibition hall showing the evils
of industrialism and commercialism. The hall grew darker as
the greatness of the literary achievement grew. In the last
novel, the unfinished *Edwin Drood*, Rochester, the enchanted
cathedral city of childhood and of *Pickwick*, had become a city
of night and death.

In his war against the institutions which had stunted the life
of his England, Dickens was more than a prophet. He was a
story-teller whose characters and dramas – at first melodrama-
tic, then far more subtle – fascinated a public which would
never have opened books full of coldly stated ethical propositions. The propositions can be listed, however. *Martin Chuzzle-
wit* added to its fun the exposure of a society of the selfish made
worse by Pecksniff's hypocrisy. *Nicholas Nickleby* attacked
schools and jobs which tormented or corrupted the young.
Bleak House denounced a legal system which was part of a social
system where, in a fog-like confusion of justice, parasites had

power. The story of *Oliver Twist*, so far from romanticizing the underworld as had become the convention, expounded the thesis that poverty, when treated as a crime, breeds criminals because it supplies pupils for the Fagins of this world; and the story of *Dombey and Son*, so far from romanticizing the captains of commerce, contained the thesis that the dominance of money-making destroys the true life of the heart even for those who prosper. *Hard Times* was a horrifying picture of a factory town, but *Our Mutual Friend* saw a horror in the very success of Victorian England, with a fortune founded on 'dust', a Victorian euphemism for garbage and dung. *Little Dorrit*, perhaps the greatest of his novels, was certainly the most profoundly Christian. It showed in how many ways adults could allow themselves to be imprisoned in situations which crippled their own humanity, and it contained one more not very convincing sketch of the good woman who was the liberator.

In his own life Dickens never found that woman (which helps to explain why in the novels the women are often too good to be true). *David Copperfield* and *Great Expectations* contained strong elements of autobiography and show how the ups and downs of his own life made him understand an age when greed prevailed over innocence, ambition over integrity, snobbery over compassion – and when marriage was often loveless. But this great revealer of the human heart never came to terms with his own tragedy, and this great communicator never told his own story. He gave *Great Expectations* a happy ending because he took the advice that a tragedy would not sell so well. He never told his own wife or children about the most significant event in his life (often returning in his dreams) – the fall from the paradise of his childhood into the blacking factory, total disaster when he had been a precociously bright and sensitive boy scarcely twelve years old. His lifelong pain was that fame and fortune could not convince him that he was loved or lovable. As his intimate friend and first biographer John Forster wrote with reticence, he 'believed himself to be entitled to a higher tribute than he was always in the habit of receiving.' In his own family he longed for a complete appreciation, obedience and devotion, with the result that he became separated bitterly from his wife – and did not find the understanding he had looked for from his mistress. In the end he was not close to most of his ten children, although he had been a merry enough father when they were little. He added to his follies by publishing a fatuous public statement about his domestic crisis. His favourite daughter, Katey, paid the tribute which is often regarded as the excuse: 'He was not a good man . . . he was wonderful.' But his public destruction of his marriage was a terrifying reminder of the failure of the kind of religion in which he sincerely believed to heal his own deep hurt. It has been well said that in the novels 'delight in the pleasures of home, in food and drink and children's games . . . is expressed with an intensity of feeling far beyond the normal. And yet, in spite of all, the marriage, the home, the children, the festivities, all after twenty years are flung violently away, as though the discrepancy between what he had and what he *meant* to have, the lack of that "one happiness I have missed in life, and one friend and companion I never made", had become finally unbearable.'[17]

His chosen form of death has raised very disturbing questions. For long he had been pathologically restless. In order to maintain lavish households and to entertain his friends, he needed to earn more and more of the money he attacked in his books; and although he could still have earned a great deal as a writer, he now chose to give public readings of passages from the novels, with a harrowing double climax in the murder of Nancy and the hanging of Sikes from *Oliver Twist*. He persisted in these readings even when he always ended them prostrated. The pleas of doctors and friends were rejected. For what he really needed, more than all the money, was a substitute for the lost home of his boyhood. And since even a living audience could not be sympathetic enough, what he finally needed most of all was the nearest approach to suicide which Victorian England could allow to a man who wished his reputation to survive. It was to be a reputation flawed by the centrality of his unresolved personal problems.

Essentially he was a dramatist. Had the Victorian theatre offered as much scope for genius as the Elizabethan theatre,

---

[17] Margaret Lane in *Dickens 1970*, ed. Michael Slater (London, 1970), p. 171.

presumably he would have written more, and more serious, plays. But since his novels were dramas personifying social evils, and since as a magazine editor and journalist he was responsible for much non-fictional comment on the problems of his time, he has not escaped assessment as a social thinker. In the cold light of analysis an element of confusion in his ideas is obvious, and it is also obvious that his enthusiasms for particular reforms changed. Angus Wilson has observed that 'the young Dickens aspired to a respectable middle-class radicalism attacking particular social evils and ended as a middle-aged revolutionary with a particular hostility to the middle classes.'[18] This undeniably compassionate man was too wounded in his own spirit, and too preoccupied by those wounds, to be quite the reformer believed in by many of his most fervent admirers. There was in him a pouting child and a sneering adolescent, a bitter cynic and even an isolated criminal, as well as the Dickens who was, as *The Times* said when he died, the world's 'unassailable and enduring favourite'.[19]

POETS OF PAIN AND FAITH

Such an age was for religious poetry the 'bleak midwinter'. But the fact that this phrase comes from the most famous poem of Christina Rosetti, who was a technically accomplished and often impressive poet, shows that it was possible to make something of the doubt with its mental pain: to make a faith which was not at all complacent. Christina Rosetti belonged to a family thoroughly unsettled in religion and life; and in her own life she knew failure, loneliness and very painful illnesses. Yet she could write much poetry of which this was the epitome:

---

[18] In *Charles Dickens: A Critical Anthology*, ed. Stephen Wall (Harmondsworth, Middx, 1970), p. 436.

[19] Denis Walder studied *Dickens and Religion* (London, 1981), Philip Collins *Dickens and Crime* and *Dickens and Education* (London, 1962–63), Norris Pope *Dickens and Charity* (London, 1978), and Michael Slater, *Dickens and Women* (London, 1983). On the fiction see F. R. and Q. R. Leavis, *Dickens the Novelist* (London, 1972), and other criticism mentioned there. The best biography is Edgar Johnson, *Charles Dickens: His Tragedy and Triumph* (London, 1977), supplemented by Norman and Jeanne Mackenzie, *Charles Dickens: A Life* (Oxford, 1979).

My faith burns low, my hope burns low,
  Only my heart's desire cries out in me
By the deep thunder of its want and woe,
  Cries out to thee.[20]

As a young man Alfred Tennyson was often profoundly miserable and close to suicide; very uncertain about his own future, even in the field of poetry to which his serious energies were confined from early years; and noted as a heavy smoker and drinker. He spoke about the 'black bloodedness' of his family. One of his brothers spent almost sixty years in a lunatic asylum, and another (who was ordained) was for a time separated from his wife who could not stand his addiction to opium. Other brothers were alcoholic or at least morbid. The shadow was cast by their father, a Lincolnshire parish priest without a vocation. But Alfred Tennyson lived to publish *In Memoriam* in May 1850, to marry next month a devout girl who had previously been alarmed by his irreligion, and to be appointed in November Poet Laureate in succession to Wordsworth. He himself summed up *In Memoriam* as 'my conviction that fear, doubts, and suffering will find answer and relief only through faith in a God of Love.' It was a 'conviction' not entirely convinced; and as eloquent as any confession of faith was the theme that there was no personal immortality in the hands of God, there was nothing left of the dignity of man in an unfeeling universe.

No, like a child in doubt and fear:
But that blind clamour made me wise;
Then I was as a child that cries,
But, crying, knows his father near . . .
And out of darkness came the hands
That reach through nature, moulding men.

He became famous, a peer, a sage – but one of his last poems was *Akbar's Dream*:

I can but lift the torch
Of reason in the dusky cave of Life,
And gaze on this great miracle, the World,
Adoring That who made, and makes, and is,

---

[20] The best biography is by Georgina Battiscombe (London, 1981).

> And is not, what I gaze on – all else Form,
> Ritual, varying with the tribes of men.

In conversation he once said with emphasis: 'There's a something that watches over us; and our individuality endures: that's my faith, and that's all my faith.'

T. S. Eliot called this faith a 'poor thing' and W. H. Auden once wrote about Tennyson: 'There was little about melancholia that he didn't know; there was little else that he did.' But this was a faith strong enough for Tennyson; and it had a massive appeal to the Victorian public in its religious unsettlement. An American critic has well said that 'from first to last his best poetry raised a psychological protest against the commonplace fact he knew with the intellect or acutely perceived with the senses. In the perspectives of evolutionary theory, he saw perpetual movement as the law of life; but with all his own passion of the past, he intuited a lasting order of values, a peace – both aesthetic and religious – untouched by the bewildering changefulness and relativity of the world.'[21] In his last years Tennyson's highest art went into poetry essentially religious and (what was much harder for him) peaceful. All the evidence of his private life corresponds with his public claim that as he drew towards death he found peace. While a boy he had flung himself sobbing on graves in his father's churchyard, envying the dead. Now he wanted 'no moaning',

> But such a tide as moving seems asleep,
> Too full for sound and foam,
> When that which drew from out the boundless deep
> Turns again home.

Despite his financial independence and the glory of his marriage with a fellow poet, Elizabeth Barrett Browning, Robert Browning spent many frustrated and unhappy years before he acquired his great fame. In his mid-fifties, in 1867, he wrote to a friend: 'The general impression of the past is as if it had been pain. I would not live it over again, not one day of it.' Thus the

---

[21] J. H. Buckley, *Tennyson: The Growth of a Poet* (Cambridge, Mass., 1960), p. 255. The most useful studies are Christopher Ricks, *Tennyson* (London, 1972); Philip Henderson, *Tennyson: Poet and Prophet* (London, 1978); R. B. Martin, *Tennyson: The Unquiet Heart* (London, 1980); Alistair Thomson, *The Poetry of Tennyson* (London, 1986).

poet was in his own person the despondent Saul, the cynical Karshish, the warped Caliban of some of his most famous poems. The years of his marriage (1841–65) were his most creative period – but part of the reason was that, stirred by the very intensity of his joy in that marriage, he entered so fully into the religious questioning of that time. When he was left a widower he became, at least outwardly, a literary lion who roared in favour of religion and morality, but even in this long, last period some of the most poignant lines in his unending output were moments of self-doubt, of an incurable sadness.

The 'optimism' to be found in so much of his poetry is the faith of an artist who cannot admit that a world so full of beauty can ultimately be pointless. In the early *Paracelsus*, which comes from a materialistic decade, the 1830s, when he was in rebellion against the stifling piety of his Nonconformist home, the beauty of the spring remains; and in that beauty 'God renews his ancient rapture'. Later, Abt Vogler at his organ, building invisible palaces to God, declares: ' 'Tis we musicians know.' And Fra Lippo Lippi finds the truth as a painter, although as a monk he is blatantly immoral:

> The beauty and the wonder, and the power,
> The shapes of things, the colours, lights and shades,
> Changes, surprises – and God made it all!
>   . . . This world's no blot for us,
> Nor blank; it means intensely, and means good;
> To find its meaning, is my meat and drink.

The 'optimism' of Browning is also the faith of a moral man who knows what is wrong with the world but cannot admit that self-purification and self-sacrifice (for example, the Grammarian's total dedication to precise scholarship) will go eternally unrewarded. The 'dread machinery of sin and sorrow' must be designed 'to evolve . . . the moral qualities of man' – in eternal life with God. As Rabbi Ben Ezra exclaims:

> All I could never be,
> All men ignored in me,
> This I was worth to God . . .

In his penetrating satires on religious leaders, something in religion itself is kept inviolate. The fraudulent medium, Mr

Sludge (a type known to him because his wife was a spiritualist), cannot discredit mankind's authentic glimpses of eternity. The worldly Renaissance bishop who begs his illegitimate sons to build a sumptuous tomb for him acknowledges something greater in the Mass to be muttered near that tomb 'through centuries'. The nineteenth-century bishop, Sylvester Blougram, boasting over the wine that his half-believed faith has done well for him, glimpses 'the grand Perhaps' although he holds that 'Creation's ... meant to hide him all it can'. Materialism obviously fascinated Browning; his prolonged delight in the art of the Italian Renaissance was part of the resurrection which was his marriage. But materialism could not be enough in the presence of death, that 'fog in the throat' where human futility had to be encountered finally along with beauty and love. The answer to the riddle had to be found beyond the calculations of reason. Bishop Blougram asks the journalist:

> 'What think ye of Christ', friend? when all's done and said,
> You like this Christianity or not?
> It may be false, but will you wish it true? . . .
> If you desire faith – then you've faith enough. . . .

This bishop's confession voices the mid-Victorian confusion or scepticism which accompanied the dissatisfaction with materialism. Here is the will to believe amid unbelief, the compulsion to doubt amid the clinging to belief:

> Just when we are safest, there's a sunset-touch,
> A fancy from a flower-bell, someone's death.
> A chorus-ending from Euripides –
> And that's enough for fifty hopes and fears
> As old and new at once as Nature's self,
> To rap and knock and enter in our soul,
> Take hands and dance there, a fantastic ring,
> Round the ancient idol, on his base again –
> The grand Perhaps! We look on helplessly –
> There the old misgivings, crooked questionings are –
> This good God – what he could do, if he would,
> Would, if he could – then must have done long since:
> If so, when, where, and how? some way must be –
> Once feel about, and soon or late you hit

> Some sense, in which it might be, after all.
> Why not, 'The Way, the Truth, the Life'?

In *Christmas Eve* Browning denounces the 'buffoonery' of papal Rome, and the 'loveless learning' of a German university – but finds himself back in his parents' Nonconformist chapel in South London, asking:

> What is left for us, save, in growth
> Of soul, to rise up . . .
> From the gift looking to the Giver,
> And from the cistern to the River,
> And from the finite to infinity,
> And from man's dust to God's divinity?

The accompanying, rather clumsy, poem *Easter Day*, written while he was in mourning for his mother, begins:

> How very hard it is to be
> A Christian! Hard for you and me . . .

And it ends with the difficulties not so much settled as put aside in a turning to the warmth of life as 'Easter Day breaks'. For it was, in the end, the religion of his parents that seemed to Robert Browning the best source of living warmth for mortals.[22] It was a religion which worshipped not Power but Love.

> The very God! think, Abib; dost thou think?
> So, the All-Great, were the All-Loving too –
> So, through the thunder comes a human voice,
> Saying, 'O heart I made, a heart beats here!
> Face, my hands fashioned, see it in myself . . .'

IMMORTAL DIAMOND

The name of Gerard Manley Hopkins was not known to the Victorian public, but he was one of the first to express frankly

---

[22] The best biographies are *The Book, the Ring and the Poet* by William Irvine and Park Honan and *Robert Browning* by R. B. Martin (London, 1974–82). Critical introductions to the major poetry include those by Philip Drew and Ian Jack (London, 1970–73).

the opinion, prevailing in the twentieth century, that Tennyson and Browning had been over-rated. He privately suggested that Tennyson's *Idylls of the King* should be renamed *Charades from the Middle Ages*. In another letter he wrote of 'Browning's way of talking (and making his people talk) with the air and spirit of a man bouncing up from table with his mouth full of bread and cheese and saying that he meant to stand no blasted nonsense.'

Hopkins has himself been taken seriously by many critics since his friend Robert Bridges edited a volume of his poems in 1918, almost thirty years after his death. He was a musician and an artist, absorbed in the struggle to make words which would be both music and colour, penetrating to the 'inscape' which was the secret of any scene in nature. And he was a Jesuit, made one in 1867 by his fascination with 'elected silence' and compelled by that vocation to keep his poems private when his superiors were alarmed by their strange sensuousness. The longest poem he ever wrote, 'The Wreck of the *Deutschland*', was accordingly suppressed despite its adoration:

> Thou mastering me
> God! giver of breath and bread;
> World's strand, sway of the sea;
> Lord of living and dead;
> Thou hast bound hones and veins in me, fastened me flesh,
> And after it almost unmade, what with dread,
> Thy doing: and dost thou touch me afresh?
> Over again I feel Thy finger and find Thee.

Many of the poems revive ecstasy, as Hopkins contemplates God's glory and Christ's presence in the flight of a falcon, in the gathering of the harvest, in the bugler boy at his first communion in Oxford, in the Liverpool workman anointed for death. But we know that in his isolation he also experienced 'that course of loathing and hopelessness which I have so often felt before, and which made me fear madness.' In his final exile, in Dublin, he wrote six sonnets of desolation and in 1889 – the sad last year of his own life – he mused in his journal about Christ's life: 'Without that, even outwardly the world could be so different that we cannot even guess it. And my life is deter-

mined by the Incarnation down to most of the details of the
day.' Many of his admirers have persisted in believing that he
ought never to have been a Jesuit, but he would never grant
that his double vocation had not been of God and at least it can
be agreed that for him the imitation of Christ was not a source
of sadness. In his most magnificent poem, in 1888, he explained why; and next year he could say that he was 'so happy'
to find himself dying. He saw all life within nature destroyed by
God's light, now become a fire. Then he saw a resurrection:

> Across my foundering deck shone
> A beacon, an eternal beam. Flesh fade, and mortal trash
> Fall to the residuary worm; world's wildfire, leave but ash:
> In a flash; at a trumpet crash,
> I am all at once what Christ is, since he was what I am, and
> This jack, joke, poor potsherd, patch, matchwood, immortal
>   diamond,
> Is immortal diamond.

Was that the answer to Charles Darwin or Charles Dickens –
the rescue of the spirit of man from the prison house of a brutish
materialism?[23]

---

[23] The best short biography summing up the evidence gradually made available
is by Paddy Kitchen (London, 1978). Other valuable studies include John Pick,
Gerard Manley Hopkins, Priest and Poet (Oxford, 1942); Alfred Thomas, *Hopkins the
Jesuit* (Oxford, 1969); Donald Walhout, *Send My Roots Rain* (Athens, Ohio, 1981).

CHAPTER NINE

A MISSION TO AN EMPIRE

THE MISSIONARIES

'God is working his purpose out' was a hymn affirming a quite widespread belief that the time was drawing 'nearer and nearer' when 'from utmost east to utmost west' the earth would be filled with a glory – 'the brotherhood of all mankind, the reign of the Prince of Peace.' The hymn was written by an Eton schoolmaster for a festival of the Church Missionary Society in 1894. Churchgoers found it easy to sing because for some twenty years their world mission had seemed a part of their destiny of world empire. All around them they saw peace, if not exactly brotherhood, imposed by the 'land of hope and glory' whose bounds, in an evolution which seemed providential, finally included a quarter of mankind.[1]

No history of English religion could be in any sense complete without some consideration of this movement; for the Victorian missionaries spread Christianity over the almost empty vastnesses of Canada and Australia, began to make Africa south of the Sahara a Christian continent, substituted the Gospel for cannibalism in New Zealand and other islands of the Pacific, powerfully challenged the grip of tradition on India, reached deep into a stagnant China, fought against the slave trade, helped to stop cruel practices such as infanticide and the execution of widows and slaves on the master's death, reduced hundreds of languages to writing, gave women a new sense of human dignity, and planted churches, schools, col-

---

[1] The best introduction to the political history is C. C. Eldridge, *Victorian Imperialism* (London, 1978), and a brilliant attempt to recapture the imperial atmosphere was made in the three volumes by James Morris, *Pax Britannica, Heaven's Command* and *Farewell the Trumpets* (London, 1968–78).

leges and hospitals in many areas where previously the main help expected from religion had been magical. The achievement was possible because a unique opportunity existed. The civilization which Victoria symbolized (Christianity could be introduced as 'the Queen of England's religion') had no equal competitor. Materially and spiritually there seemed to be a vacuum which 'Christian nations' must fill. In a book of 1910 one missionary, Thomas Moscrop, looked back on the growth of *The Kingdom without Frontiers*. He was proud that 'Christian nations' then possessed over eighty per cent of the earth's surface. 'It is very significant that during the nineteenth century the European peoples increased from 170 to 500 millions, and that this increase is likely to go on, whilst the rest of the world, as far as can be seen, is destined to remain stationary.' But it was also significant that his appeal for more missionaries was based mainly on this optimistic forecast of the future progress of the 'Christian nations' and their empires.

No longer was the main motivation a belief that non-Christians would all go to hell. No doubt there were many Christians who still held that belief in 1910, but the tendency in the main missionary societies was more liberal.[2] Non-Christian religions still seemed untrue; but what Thomas Moscrop wished chiefly to stress was that they were uncivilized. 'Indian pantheism does not result in social well-being', he declared. 'Buddhism seems to offer greater promise, but its root-teachings are wrong and so give no hope of social efficiency for the race. China is a large and painful illustration of the social effectiveness of Confucianism. As a social force Mohammedanism is hopeless. The lesser religions of Africa and of the isles of the seas show the same thing in a thousand examples.' For a more concise (if still historically inaccurate) expression of the same missionary imperialism, we may listen to a great empire-builder, Sir Harry Johnston, addressing the Basoga people deep in Africa in 1900: 'We were like you, going about naked . . . with our war paint on, but when we learned Christianity from the Romans we changed and became great.

---

[2] Geoffrey Rowell studied *The Victorians and Hell* (Oxford, 1974).

We want you to learn Christianity and follow our steps and you too will be great.'[3]

Eventually this proud alliance between the Christian mission and the British empire was to end, because the empire collapsed; and the alliance was to be denounced by most Christians. The word 'missionary' was to become almost as offensive as the word 'imperialism'. Mankind was to be amazed that Christians had ever thought it possible to spread a message of humble love from a position of economic, political and cultural strength often amounting to arrogance and exploitation. How, it was to be asked, could the Bible be treated as the Word of God if white men tried to sell that idea along with the trader's gin or opium? How could the Church – or the divided churches exported with all their disputes – grow out of the barrel of the rifle? It is, however, possible to suggest that in the future, when anti-colonial passions themselves belong to history, justice may be done to the Victorian missionaries. They accepted discomfort, loneliness, disease, the danger of violence and a heartbreaking failure to win converts. They sacrificed a normal family life, buried many wives and children in foreign graves, and often died at their posts. Their motives were very mixed but often included exceptional loves for God and neighbour. The results of their work were often unlike the dreams with which they had set out, but these men and women did more than any other group in all previous history or in their own age to make the Christian Church worldwide; and that made other men dream. Addressing the World Missionary Conference in Edinburgh in 1910, the Archbishop of Canterbury declared that 'the place of missions in the life of the Church must be the central place and none other'. And he added that 'if that come true, there may be some standing here tonight who shall not taste of death till they see the kingdom of God come with power.'

The role which the missionaries played in the unprecedented encounter of civilizations and cultures was even more ambiguous than their directly religious role; and it has even

---

[3] Roland Oliver, *Sir Harry Johnston and the Scramble for Africa* (London, 1957), p. 297.

more often been denounced. In the first half of the century they were often drawn from a working-class background, and the committees of the societies which sent them out hoped that their practical skills would not only impress and improve the 'natives' but would also render substantial salaries unnecessary. Some missionaries did indeed prosper on this basis, whether or not they made many converts, but in the process they sometimes became traders or farmers themselves. The alternative was destitution. In the course of the century a different danger to the missionary's spiritual integrity developed. Many middle-class men and women felt drawn to this idealistic and increasingly prestigious work, and although they were prepared for many adventures and sacrifices when they reached settled 'mission stations' they often attempted to reproduce the comfortable homes they had known in England, staffed by many servants; it seemed to be their natural right. They felt obliged to provide employment for converts who had been thrown out of their own families or villages, and thus they became the directors of sizable economic enterprises. In general they were the patrons of the 'native' Christians and this often meant that they were patronizing. 'Natives' could be assistants (the village catechist was in fact the backbone of the worldwide mission) but they could not be colleagues or friends. The missionaries regarded themselves as the allies and social equals of the leading commercial and colonial figures in the area. If they were in physical danger, either they or their supporters expected the colonial authorities to rescue or revenge them – an operation which might involve the extension of the empire. And all these things might compromise them as ambassadors of Christ.

The missionaries often did further damage to their spiritual mission by clumsy failures to understand the inner significance and importance of 'native' customs which seemed to them merely 'savage' or 'barbaric' – customs which for many centuries had regulated sexual relationships and had socialized families, villages and tribes. They were encouraged to admire instead certain customs selected from a British way of life which in other respects was often deplored by these keen Christians: the 'missionary position' in sexual intercourse, teetotalism, the wearing of European clothes, the singing of European hymn tunes, in the towns the building of Gothic stone churches. Converts were also expected to put away all wives except one. This was in accordance with the teaching of the New Testament, but many of the converts felt that the sudden attack on the age old custom of polygamy was not in accordance with local realities or with their own consciences. In a word, the missionaries were intruders.

But those who wish to do justice to them will recognize that it would have been impossible to recruit, or to pay for, an army whose only weapons were the spiritual weapons of the best saints. If there were to be missionaries in any number, then their attitudes had to be more or less the attitudes generally held in the societies from which they came. We should also recall two other facts. It was not rare for missionaries to defend the 'rights' of the 'natives' against traders and government officials, causing intense irritation and contempt. And many of the missionaries recorded observations of 'native' life which laid the foundations of the modern science of anthropology. They were far too clumsy in their attitudes to the traditional way of life which they were helping to destroy; but at least they had bothered to go to these places and to observe strange customs with motives which included love.

Certainly the whole meaning of the Church could be transformed by their activities. The power of the Gospel to convince people in all the continents brought great encouragement, and the need to evangelize rapidly gave the churches a new understanding of their own nature. The Church of England at work overseas could not permanently rely on powers and privileges deriving from the government. Bishops had to be prepared to rough it like other missionaries; the idea of the 'missionary bishops', unfamiliar since Anglo-Saxon days, was revived in America in the 1830s and soon inspired some sturdy evangelists who became heroes in England. By the 1890s there were more than ninety colonial or missionary bishops at work outside the USA. Laymen in the colonies could not depend on the government to pay for clergy, nor could the English system of compulsory tithes be acceptable. In these British colonies, as in the USA, laymen had to take over responsibility for the financial support of the clergy – and demanded in return that the clergy should consult them about the Church's policy. In these ways modern 'Anglicanism', as distinct from support for the Established Church of England, was born in nineteenth-century Canada, Australia and New Zealand. Non-Anglican Churches were also changed. It was not enough to be merely 'Dissent' or 'Nonconformity' when the purpose was to convert the heathen to Christianity and to win or retain the large numbers (more than ten millions) who migrated from the British Isles in the Victorian age. In the free competition for voluntary adherents the non-Anglican Protestants were often more successful than those still burdened with the memory or the image of a privileged Establishment. And Roman Catholics found a new confidence in their claim to universality because they were often the most courageous and most effective of all the Christian missionary forces – although not many of the English were to be found in the ranks of this international army, strictly disciplined under the direct authority of the office called *Propaganda* in Rome.[4]

ANGLICANISM DEFINED IN CANADA AND SOUTH AFRICA

We can begin a Victorian world tour in Jerusalem. This starting point is specially appropriate because the English confusion about the possibility of missionary work based on the Holy City illustrated both the legal problems facing Anglicanism outside the English Establishment and the evangelistic problems facing all the English who wished to address non-Christians. In 1841 a bishopric in Jerusalem was founded by the British and Prussian governments acting jointly. It was to be held by their nominees alternately, and the excuse given was that Protestants in the area needed pastoral supervision. In

---

[4] K. S. Latourette studied the nineteenth century in *Christianity in a Revolutionary Age* (5 vols., London, 1957–61). Max Warren provided a British perspective in *The Missionary Movement from Britain in Modern History* and *Social History and Christian Mission* (London, 1965–67), and Stephen Neill supplied a concise *History of Christian Missions* (Harmondsworth, Middx, 1964). Between them these books list the standard histories of the missionary societies.

fact there were very few Protestants and the aim was political:
the bishopric was to be a means of bringing pressure on the
Turks, to whose ramshackle empire Palestine belonged. The
chief result having been to scandalize those Church of England
men (such as Newman) who disliked being reckoned Protestants and those Prussians who opposed their king's liking for
bishops, the scheme had to be brought to an end in 1886. But
the Act of Parliament which made it possible also made
possible the consecration of other bishops for work outside the
British empire, and so had some important consequences – for
example, in Canada.

The story of Anglicanism in Canada had begun when Sir
Francis Drake used the Book of Common Prayer after landing
on the west coast in 1578, but the main story is to be dated from
the movement up the east coast during and after the Americans' successful rebellion some two hundred years later. Many
of the refugees were Anglicans, and many went to Nova Scotia.
Among them was Charles Inglis, who had seen Trinity church
in New York, where he had been the loudly Tory rector,
burned down. It was natural for the government in London to
seek to strengthen the existing branch of the Church of England in Nova Scotia, with Inglis as the first bishop in 1787. The
number of Anglican clergy in Nova Scotia was never large
enough to fulfil the bishop's plans; nor (it was complained) was
the annual parliamentary grant large enough. But there was a
sustained attempt to build up church life on the traditional
pattern. 'We love the place, O God', a hymn which breathes
love for altar, font and the rest of the model Anglican church,
was written by a lover of St Paul's church in Halifax, the naval
base which became the colony's chief town.[5]

Nova Scotia's daughter dioceses were the places where
Canadian Anglicanism gained a new self-understanding as a
Church not depending on government support. The diocese of
Quebec, founded in 1792, was first led by a bishop as conserva-
tive as Charles Inglis. This was Jacob Mountain, who re-
mained for thirty-three years; like Inglis he had a son who

---

[5] See William Nelson, *The American Tory* (Oxford, 1961), and Judith Fingard, *The
Anglican Design in Loyalist Nova Scotia* (London, 1972).

became bishop of the diocese. The small upper class of English settlers supported Mountain's efforts, and a cathedral was built for him by the Royal Engineers. But it was impossible to establish the Church of England as Mountain wished in 'Lower Canada', since Methodist and other preachers entering from the United States were active and the bulk of the population desired nothing else than that it should remain fervently Roman Catholic, as the old-fashioned 'New France'. The Anglican bishop who was most appropriate to the real, modest, mission in the area was Charles Stewart, who came between the two Mountains. He was an earl's son and a fine scholar who had embraced a life of apostolic poverty, humbly sharing all the hardships of the settlers as a missionary travelling up and down the St Lawrence river.[6]

Another of Nova Scotia's daughter dioceses was Newfoundland, founded in 1839 when it included both Bermuda and Labrador but only eight Anglican clergymen. The second Bishop of Newfoundland was the first bishop in the Church of England overseas to embody the American idea that a bishop could be a hard-living missionary. Sailing up and down the stormy coast, disregarding the cold, reaching his people who were scattered and mostly illiterate, Edward Field, who had once been snug in an Oxford fellowship, was so attractive that one of his many admirers gave him a handsome yacht and enrolled himself as its honorary skipper.

The greatest of the early champions of Canadian Anglicanism was John Strachan, a Scot who was the first Bishop of Toronto (1839–67). When epidemics of typhus broke out (caused by the arrival of destitute Irish immigrants in the 1840s) he never slackened in his pastoral work. When the modern church which served as his cathedral seemed inadequate, he built a stone one; when the stone church burned down, he built another; and when the third cathedral was also destroyed by fire, he built a fourth. When a university was needed, he founded King's College; and when that university was secularized, he led another group which built Trinity

---

[6] T. R. Millman provided biographies of *Jacob Mountain* (Toronto, 1947) and *Charles James Stewart* (London, Ont., 1953).

College. When the government's endowment of the clergy was
ended in 1854, he obtained compensation which eased the
change to a complete reliance on the generosity of parishioners.
His main problem was the leading Methodist preacher, Adol-
phus Ryerson, whose own character was as indomitable and
whose hostility to Anglican pretensions was implacable. Indeed, the Bishop's task was to win voluntary support by being
as ready to work among the people as the preacher was. Thus
Strachan and the Anglicans who followed him had to refound
their Church as a voluntary association alongside others in a
democracy – although it remained the 'Church of England in
Canada' until 1955.[7]

On this voluntary basis the Anglican and other Churches
could flourish as the Canadians multiplied, agreed to their
self-governing federation in 1867, and spread to the west. The
non-Anglican Churches were far more active in the west –
which largely explained the census figures of 1891 when the
Anglicans had only 13.5 per cent of the population, the Roman
Catholics forty-one per cent, and the Presbyterians and
Methodists mostly shared the rest. For the Churches as for the
Canadian people, there was plenty of room for expansion. A
leading historian of Christianity in Canada and the USA has
stressed that 'the religious tone of these two "Christian nations"
in the nineteenth century was quite different, for Canada was
more cautious, traditional and church-oriented than the United States.' In Canada most denominational schools received
some support out of public funds. Part of the explanation is
that Canadians fell back on their religious traditions as a
barrier against absorption into the USA. But another factor
was that the deep division of Canada into British and French
traditions meant that it was difficult to invest the nation as
such with the religious aura which surrounded 'the Union' in
the USA and which had Abraham Lincoln as its prophet.[8]

Canadian Anglicans had found that one of the keys to

[7] Philip Carrington wrote a history of *The Anglican Church in Canada* (London, 1963).
[8] Robert T. Hardy, *A History of the Churches in the United States and Canada*, p. 259. The basic book is John S. Moir, *The Church in the British Era: From the British Conquest to Confederation* (Toronto, 1972).

self-supporting strength in church life was the use of synods where bishops could meet their clergy (and their laity, unless one held very High Church views) – and where bishops could meet each other. Such synods had a special meaning in a land where the difficulties of travel were so great; and when in 1865 the Canadian Anglicans' Provincial Synod, covering the eastern half of the country, heard of the problems which had arisen for Anglicans in South Africa, they were sure of the remedy: the bishops of England's colonies around the world must meet.

The South African problems were causing concern because not all missionaries linked with Victorian England were as ready as the Canadians to sink their differences for the sake of their mission. On the contrary, in South Africa there was a clash between the two outstanding English missionaries, a clash about the basic definition of Anglicanism.

One of the rivals was Robert Gray, who sailed out to be Bishop of Cape Town in 1847. Formerly a parish priest in County Durham whose main distinction was that his father had been Bishop of Bristol, he was alarmed to be taking responsibility for a new diocese containing a quarter of a million square miles but very few regular supporters of the Church of England. The descendants of the original Dutch settlers, the Boers, adhered fervently to their Calvinist faith. Although many of them had made the Great Trek to the north in the 1830s and later (rather than accept the abolition of slavery), it was clear that the English would not be able to forget their existence. Among the English colonists such religious activity as took place tended to be Nonconformist. William Shaw, for more than thirty years the pioneer of Methodism in South Africa, managed to be equally active both as a pastor to the settlers whom he joined in 1820 and as a missionary to the tribesmen over the frontier.[9] Bishop Gray, however, turned out to be as hard-working, and as defiant, as any of the Canadians. He never became strong, physically or emotionally. The photographs show a face deeply lined; the

---

[9] *The Journal of William Shaw* was edited by W. D. Hammond-Tooke (Cape Town, 1972).

biographies cannot conceal exhaustions and breakdowns. But he travelled up and down South Africa, rejoicing in the flowers of the unspoiled country although at first rejoicing in little else. Everywhere he tried to plant the Anglican system as he understood it in a moderately High Church way. He called for more bishops.

One of these bishops was the other outstanding missionary of Anglicanism in South Africa, John William Colenso. And with him came trouble. The dean of his cathedral in Pietermaritzburg protested against his doctrine, and Gray felt obliged to adjudicate. Orthodoxy must be vindicated, despite his past friendship with the Bishop and his personal dislike of the Dean. Then this troublesome bishop's book on *St Paul's Epistle to the Romans* (1861) demonstrated that he did not believe that non-Christians such as the Zulus were in danger of everlasting punishment in hell. God did not need to be reconciled to them, for he already loved them abundantly. In order to be saved they did not need to accept personally that Christ had borne the punishment due for their sins. All men were already united with Christ. A later book on *The Pentateuch* demonstrated that Colenso did not believe that it was his duty to assure the Zulus that the Old Testament was entirely the Word of God, including its mathematical impossibilities. Instead, he agreed that the Bible contained some legends not altogether unlike the Zulus' own mythology. For such offences, he was deposed from his bishopric.

Gray took the responsibility for this expulsion of a heretic, and many people in many places applauded. The hymn 'The Church's one foundation' was written during the controversy by one clerical admirer, S. J. Stone. But when appealed to in 1865 the Judicial Committee of the Privy Council refused to uphold his authority, this time pleading that since the Cape Town colony now had its own legislature the Letters Patent from the Crown which had given Gray the right to discipline Colenso had been invalid. In response South African Anglicans drew up a new constitution and in 1870 prohibited any future appeal to the committee on any question of doctrine. But Colenso returned to work as a bishop among his beloved Zulus, defying the bishop whom Gray recognized, and on his tomb was inscribed the one word *Sobantu,* 'Father of the People'. By his stand he had helped to vindicate the right of missionaries to use a liberal generosity in their understanding of their task, and while the official Anglican 'Church of the Province of South Africa' remained doctrinally orthodox and predominantly High Church, its chief distinction came to be a struggle of which *Sobantu* would have approved: the fight to defend the dignity of the black man. This combination of Catholic devotion with broad interests was to be increasingly typical of Anglicanism.[10]

Another result of the Colenso controversy was the birth of the first of the worldwide denominational associations among the heirs of the Reformation.

Anglican Canadians were alarmed by the Judicial Committee's refusal to deal with the legal problems of the Church in South Africa, as well as by its refusal to condemn Colenso's theology. On their initiative seventy-six bishops met in the first Lambeth Conference, in 1867. They decided nothing but their successors met again in 1878 – and in 1888 another Lambeth Conference declared: 'We have realized, more fully than it was possible to realize before, the extent, the power, and the influence of the great Anglican Communion. We have felt its capacities, its opportunities, its privileges.' And Churches without bishops came to think that they, too, would benefit if representatives from the British empire and the United States, with any others who were suitable, met to feel their own capacities, opportunities and privileges. The Alliance of Reformed Churches first met in 1875, the Ecumenical Methodist Council in 1881, the International Congregational Council in 1891 and the Baptist World Alliance in 1905.[11]

---

[10] See Audrey Brooke, *Robert Gray* (Cape Town, 1947). Peter Hinchcliff wrote a history of *The Anglican Church in South Africa* and a biography of *John William Colenso* (London, 1964–65). Norman Etherington presented more detailed research in *Preachers, Peasants and Politics in South East Africa 1835–80* (London, 1978).

[11] Alan M. G. Stephenson studied *The First Lambeth Conference* (London, 1967), and *Anglicanism and the Lambeth Conferences* (London, 1978).

OPENING UP AFRICA

It would of course have been better had nineteenth-century Africa produced of its own Christian heroes abundantly, as twentieth-century Africa was certainly going to do. There were some efforts in this direction. In Sierra Leone Fourah Bay College was set up in 1847 as a training school for African evangelists, and among the tribes on the Gold Coast (now Ghana) Methodism spread almost entirely through African leadership.

In Nigeria a major Anglican experiment took place, thanks to the insistence of Henry Venn, the farsighted Secretary of the Church Missionary Society, on the policy of 'Africa for the Africans'. This policy was carried to the extent of securing the consecration of Samuel Crowther as Bishop on the Niger in Canterbury Cathedral in 1864. Twenty-two years earlier Crowther had been a terrified African boy recaptured from a Portuguese slaver and landed at Sierra Leone. Venn was determined that Bishop Crowther should now manage the mission to the interior, using the great river as a highway. He trusted his man completely and was confident that the experiment would prove the African's capacity for spiritual leadership. After Venn's death, however, the ageing Crowther was accused of financial malpractices and forced to resign.[12]

The hope that the decisive initiatives in the Christian mission to West Africa would be taken by Africans was probably unrealistic in the extraordinary circumstances of the time. The predominant fact was the destruction of traditional tribal patterns by European commerce. Africans were demoralized. The slave trade had already done untold damage (for example, by encouraging the little kingdoms to go to war with other Africans, using muskets supplied by the slavers, in order to secure more slaves). Now to that long-lasting dislocation was

---

[12] See *To Apply the Gospel: Selections from the Writings of Henry Venn*, ed. Max Warren (Grand Rapids, Mich., 1971), and T. E. Yates, *Venn and Victorian Bishops Abroad* (Uppsala, 1978). John Loiello summed up the evidence about Crowther in *Varieties of Christian Experience in Nigeria*, ed. E. Isichei (London, 1982).

added the lure of large profits for the chiefs from other forms of trade with Europe (for example, the export of palm-oil or cocoa beans). The white man appearing from the sea, who might be a missionary, was inevitably fascinating. When malaria had been understood medically (as its name suggests, it had been blamed on 'bad air'), and when steamships had shortened the voyage, there was no shortage of Englishmen eager to convert the kingdoms of West Africa. Thus Crowther was toppled by young Evangelicals fresh out of Cambridge. And when other confident Englishmen tried to 'conquer' the Muslim strongholds in Northern Nigeria and failed dismally, it was psychologically inevitable that they should call for the imposition of as much British rule as could be achieved – and, within this, for as much official encouragement of missionary work as could be extracted out of the nervous colonial administrators.[13]

In East and Central Africa Christianity was planted later than in the west. The chief differences were first that the export of slaves was still flourishing under Arab or Portuguese management, and second that it was possible for Europeans to settle in large numbers in the areas which eventually became Kenya and Zimbabwe. Both these differences increased the challenge to missionary work. The slave trade was, in David Livingstone's phrase, the 'open sore of the world'. The damage which it inflicted on African life intensified under the eyes of the explorers and pioneers, and neither naval patrols nor diplomatic treaties were able to stop it. The Africans seemed helpless, inviting the outsider's intervention by their powerlessness if not by their voices. Every chivalrous instinct in Victorian Englishmen was stirred, particularly since it seemed an opportunity to make amends for England's shameful role in the slave trade from the west coast. And to make

---

[13] African scholars have contributed four illuminating studies: J. B. Webster, *The African Churches among the Yoruba 1888–1922* (Oxford, 1964); F. K. Ekechi, *Missionary Enterprise and Rivalry in Igboland 1857–1914* (London, 1972); J. F. Ade Ajayi, *Christian Missions in Nigeria 1841–91: The Making of a New Elite* (London, 1965); and E. A. Ayandele, *The Missionary Impact on Modern Nigeria 1842–1914* (London, 1966). Shorter studies include those collected in *Christianity in Tropical Africa*, ed. C. G. Baeta (Oxford, 1968), and in vol. v of the *Cambridge History of Africa*, covering c. 1790 to 1870 (Cambridge, 1976).

intervention more attractive, it appeared to be quite easy to establish houses, farms and whole villages under the control of European missionaries, shining as lights in the 'dark continent'. In 1874 a settlement for freed slaves was founded near Mombasa in order to train evangelists for what is now Kenya, but the missionaries maintained such a discipline over the Africans, and treated them so contemptuously, that not even the limited experiment of consecrating another black bishop like Crowther was contemplated.[14] Instead the imaginations of English missionaries and of their supporters at home were seized by a wandering white man. He had a dream that Africa, East and Central, could rapidly be freed from the slavers, and brought into the Christian Church, once it was exposed to European 'commerce'. He was David Livingstone, who at the age of ten had been a lad in a factory in Scotland.

He went to South Africa in 1841 as a doctor-evangelist. He had first chosen China (but there was a war on) and had then been excited by the talk of Robert Moffat. Turned from a gardener into a missionary by Methodist preaching, Moffat claimed to have 'sometimes seen, in the morning sun, the smoke of a thousand villages where no missionary had ever been'. But when Livingstone reached Moffat's mission station at the northernmost outpost of South African Christianity, he found that there were not a thousand inhabitants within ten miles. He found, too, that Moffat (who was best as a translator) did not mind his own tortoise-like progress in making personal contact with Africans. So the impatient Livingstone married Moffat's daughter and found his own life by making great journeys across the Kalahari desert and into the tropical north. At first he told himself that he was looking for more profitable sites for missionary work, but he founded no church, school or hospital. He also discovered that he was happier and more effective when he travelled without any white companion. He sincerely believed that his life would be charmed until his work was done, and in that faith accepted hardships which would

---

[14] A. J. Temu studied *British Protestant Missions* (London, 1972) and Robert W. Strayer *The Making of Mission Communities in East Africa* (London, 1978). T. O. Beidelman, *Colonial Evangelism* (Bloomington, Ind., 1982), drew interesting general conclusions from a study of the work of the CMS in what is now Tanzania.

have broken almost anyone else. His work was simply to get to know and to love Africa and the Africans, recording his observations with meticulous care.

In 1856 he returned to England having crossed Central Africa from coast to coast, having discovered large lakes and dramatic falls hitherto unknown to Europe, and having accomplished the beginning of an understanding of two mighty rivers, the Zambesi and the Congo. Such marvels moved a man grown unfamiliar with English to eloquence as an author and orator. In particular the Zambesi inspired him. To him, it was a river along which legitimate traders could move. That would end the African chiefs' temptations to collaborate with the Arab slavers. With the traders would arrive European settlers who would find the interior highlands delightful. There it would be easy to find coal and to grow cotton and other highly profitable crops. In a very little time churches would be built and crowded by converts. The promise of the Zambesi was what Livingstone meant when he told the undergraduates of Cambridge on an afternoon of December 1857: 'I know that in a few years I shall be cut off in that country which is now open; do not let it be shut again! I go back to Africa to try to make an open path for commerce and Christianity; do you carry out the work which I have begun. I leave it with you.'

Cruel disappointments followed. It was found that the Portuguese who controlled the lower reaches of the Zambesi did not welcome Englishmen, who anyway could not smoothly steam up the river as Livingstone had promised. The mission later called the Universities' Mission to Central Africa was formed and a bishop sent out – who found his apostolic mission bogged down in tribal wars, in conflicts with the Arab slavers, in fevers. Had he not died of dysentery he would probably have been killed in a war, for he used his gun like the others.

Meanwhile Livingstone resumed his journeys – this time, as he maintained, seeking the sources of the Nile. No longer was he an agent of the London Missionary Society; first he was a British consul, then he was merely himself. Spectacularly 'found' by the journalist Henry Stanley in 1871, he deeply

impressed that strange man (who had been born John Row
lands, an orphan in North Wales – and who ended up as Si
Henry, a Liberal MP). Instead of returning to civilization
penniless and defeated, he wandered off into Africa with
Africans – to be found dead on 1 May 1873, kneeling in praye
by his bed in Chitambo's village. Then came the most impress
ive journey in his story, when his body was taken by his African
servants to the far-distant coast and to Westminster Abbey fo
burial.[15]

Four years after his death, Anglican missionaries arrived i
Uganda in response to a letter to the *Daily Telegraph* from
Stanley, who had penetrated to the court of a despotic ruler
the Kabaka of Buganda, and been assured that Christianity
would be welcome. Two years later White Fathers arrived a
Roman Catholic missionaries. The Kabaka, Mutesa I, turned
out to be more interested in hoped-for guns and gunpowde
than in the rival versions of Christianity, but the missionarie
were allowed to teach their faith to the sons of members of the
Kabaka's court while they also introduced the wheel, house
with windows and other marvels. The main explanation of thi
royal welcome – for which there are few parallels in the history
of African missions – appears to be that the Kabaka was wel
aware that his tyranny needed reinforcement against the Arab
coming south from the Sudan; but there is some evidence tha
the tyrant grew more merciful as the years went by. Unfortu
nately this king who might have become a Christian died and
was succeeded by the eighteen-year-old Mwanga. The new
king had learned vices from the Arabs but not much else. H
had three of the lads being instructed by the Christian mis
sionaries horribly mutilated and slowly burned alive, and late
in 1885 he ordered that Bishop James Hannington, who wa
arriving to take over the leadership of the mission, should b
murdered during his journey. Next year other African men an
boys who refused to renounce Christianity were burned; and

[15] The best biographies are Cecil Northcott, *Robert Moffat* (London, 1961)
Oliver Ransford, *David Livingstone* (London, 1978); Owen Chadwick, *Mackenzie
Grave* (London, 1959); Richard Hall, *Stanley: An Adventurer Explored* (London, 1974)

period of confusion followed until the British established a 'protectorate' in 1894.[16]

A story involving English Nonconformist missionaries hints at many of the themes running through much of the rest of African history.

The modern missionary presence on the great island of Madagascar began in 1818 with the arrival of agents of the London Missionary Society. They and their immediate successors were men like the pioneers who had broken into India and Tahiti – Evangelical in their religion, uncomprehending towards the local religion, but acceptable to at least some of the 'natives' because they included in their ranks craftsmen whose skills and products were coveted. In the end it was felt necessary to expel them and to persecute their converts because their influence seemed to threaten the ruler's own authority. In 1835 Queen Ranavalona promised highly unpleasant forms of death to all who would not abandon the missionaries' religion, and the persecution continued until her own death in 1861. Within eight years another ruling queen had been baptized as a Protestant. The religion taught by the London Missionary Society gradually became the official religion. Most of the people seem to have admitted that it was the superior religion of a superior people; converts to it were expected to wear European dress, to be attentive during sermons by preachers whom it was difficult to understand, and to accept subordinate positions in church life. Missionaries were often carried by 'natives' bearing litters, instead of walking: it seemed proper. But attacks on customs which had bound the people together were deeply resented, and in the background was the fear that the white man would soon take the land. This fear was justified. The French were allocated this part of Africa by the other European powers; in their turn they acknowledged the British rights on the mainland. In 1895 they occupied Madagascar – and the

---

[16] See John V. Taylor, *The Growth of the Church in Buganda* (London, 1958), and J. F. Faupel, *African Holocaust* (London, 1962). These events were put in the context of colonialism by Roland Oliver, *The Missionary Factor in East Africa* (London, 1952), and were seen through African eyes by Anne Luck, *African Saint* (London, 1963), and by M. Kiwanuka, *A History of Buganda* (London, 1971).

religion of the London Missionary Society became once again a minority creed.[17]

INTO THE PACIFIC

The spread of English-speaking people and of their Churches over the three million square miles of Australia was marked by much of the courageous energy which we have already observed in the history of Canada. In Canada, however, despite all the difficulties missionaries could appeal to many whose sentiments were already favourable to British (or French) Christianity. In Australia, the task facing the Churches was more deeply discouraging. The first clergyman, Richard Johnson, was a humiliated chaplain to transported convicts (in 1788). About 150,000 men and women, almost all from the labouring class and almost all being punished for theft, were transported before this system was ended in 1840 – and even after 1840 the colony of New South Wales and its offshoots remained rough places. In the second half of the nineteenth century Australia had its economic ups and downs, from the gold rush of the 1850s to the depression and drought of the 1890s, without ever experiencing any widespread religious revival like the Great Awakening which had changed American colonial life. By 1870 all state aid for the denominations had been effectively withdrawn throughout Australia, but no popular Protestantism really replaced it. The universities in particular became noted for their atmosphere of secular rationalism, most children having been educated in state schools, where there was no religious instruction as the Churches understood religion.

In such circumstances the Anglican authoritarianism of William Grant Broughton, who became the first Bishop of Australia in 1836, was destined to perish – like the courage of

---

[17] Bonar Gow studied *Madagascar and the Protestant Impact* (London, 1979). Other relevant studies by objective scholars include Robert Rotberg, *Christian Missionaries and the Creation of Northern Rhodesia* (Princeton, N.J., 1965), and T. O. Ranger and John Weller, *Themes in the Christian History of Central Africa* (Berkeley, Cal., 1975).

many of the explorers in the immeasurable desert which formed the interior.[18]

Another dream that perished was the idea that Roman Catholicism in Australia could be shaped by Benedictine monks who would become bishops, use monasteries as cathedrals and establish schools to spread an advanced Christian civilization. It was an idea held tenaciously by Australia's first vicar apostolic, Bishop Ullathorne, and by his successor, John Podling, who was active as Archbishop of Sydney (despite Broughton's fury) until 1877; both were monks. But Benedictine ideals could not survive in control when the bulk of support came from Irish immigrants and when to most Australians a monk was someone to be sent back to the Middle Ages. When the Commonwealth of Australia was formed in 1901 the leading Roman Catholic figure was Archbishop Patrick Moran, a champion of the Irish and of the trade unions.[19]

Nor were these conservative visions the only dreams to end in Australia. In 1836 the colony of South Australia was inaugurated. Instead of convicts, its founders were mainly English Nonconformists. They had ideas not totally unlike those which had driven the Pilgrim Fathers over the Atlantic, and they made some enduring impact; but much of the life of the colony was gradually assimilated into the secular ethos already prevailing in Australia.[20]

It proved very difficult to persuade the 'blackfellows' or aborigines to accept a religion which few of the white Australians seemed to take very seriously, particularly since it meant persuading them to abandon the habit of wandering over vast areas. The main impact of 'civilization' was to destroy them by disease and demoralization – and in Tasmania the aborigines were completely exterminated, many of them being shot down

---

[18] See G. P. Shaw, *Patriarch and Patriot: William Grant Broughton* (Melbourne, 1978), and Ross Border, *Church and State in Australia 1788–1872* (London, 1962). The background was illuminated by L. L. Robson, *The Convict Settlers of Australia* (Melbourne, 1975), and J. M. Ward, *Empire in the Antipodes* (London, 1966).

[19] See T. L. Suttor, *Hierarchy and Democracy in Australia* (Melbourne, 1965), and P. J. O'Farrell, *The Catholic Church in Australia: A Short History* (Melbourne, 1968).

[20] D. H. Pike studied *Paradise of Dissent: South Australia 1829–1857* (Melbourne, 1957). The religious and general development of the nation was presented authoritatively in *A New History of Australia*, ed. F. K. Crowley (Melbourne, 1974).

in a sporting spirit. But slowly missionary work was done, and from Australia Christianity spread to the evergreen islands of New Zealand.

First came a period when missionaries tried to win the friendship of the Maoris by introducing some of the 'arts of civilized life'; the Maoris, who were cannibals, had never before seen horses, cows, potatoes, corn, wheels or iron instruments. The inspirer of this phase was Samuel Marsden, a small, stout, ruddy and muscular Yorkshireman whose father had been the village blacksmith. Some Evangelicals discovered him in his twenties and sent him to a grammar school and a university, from which he was summoned by William Wilberforce to sail out in 1793 to assist poor Richard Johnson in pastoral work in the Australian penal colony. Unlike Johnson, Marsden stayed on and fought back. He became the first man to build a permanent church in Australia (at Parramatta), and in order to supplement his inadequate salary 'the best practical farmer in New South Wales' (as the hostile governor admitted). He was the first farmer to take Australian wool back to England. But all that did not absorb his energies. When he concluded the first church service ever held in New Zealand, on Christmas Day 1814 at Oiki on the Bay of Islands, his text was: 'Behold, I bring you good tidings of great joy.' But he was sure that it was premature to preach the full Gospel until the Maoris had been persuaded to forget the insults and illtreatment which their people had received at the hands of visiting English seamen, in those waters mainly in order to hunt whales. That was why, in the seven visits which he paid to New Zealand before his death in 1838, his whole emphasis was the peaceful and utilitarian instruction of the Maoris.[21]

A second period came in which the emphasis was on a more determined evangelism. Methodists crossed over from Australia, as did Roman Catholic priests, and more fervent Anglican missionaries were sent under the leadership of the ex-sailor

[21] See A. T. Yarwood, *Samuel Marsden the Great Survivor* (Melbourne, 1977). *Letters and Journals of Samuel Marsden* and *Marsden's Lieutenants* were edited by J. R. Elder (Dunedin, 1932–34), and Eric Ramsden studied *Marsden and the Missions* (Sydney, 1936).

Henry Williams, a strong man who in due course became an archdeacon. Inevitable but tragic steps were taken – the Maoris were persuaded to part with some of their land by 'agreement' with the English settlers, including Williams and other missionaries; and on other occasions they were 'punished' because, being themselves habitually men of war, they had hit back at the white men occupying their country. Pressure grew for larger schemes of English colonization and Edward Gibbon Wakefield, a man who had spent some time in a London prison and who had there composed *A Letter from Sydney*, proved an alluring propagandist. A body of Anglican colonists, the Canterbury Association, went out to found Christchurch; a similar body from Scotland, mainly rebels against the Established Church there, founded Dunedin. Disagreements between the settlers, the missionaries and the Maoris mounted, and in 1840 the Maori chiefs were persuaded to accept the British government's 'protection' in return for a promise that their lands would never be taken away against their will. Archdeacon Williams acted as interpreter during the treaty-making at Waitangi. During the subsequent wars and disasters of the Maoris, that treaty was remembered as the great betrayal. But there followed the full colonization of New Zealand including the building up of church life on the British pattern, the creative Victorian bishop being George Augustus Selwyn.

Selwyn's most attractive activity arose out of his concern for the Melanesian peoples on their many islands to the north. At first his strategy was to gather sons of the island chiefs to be educated in a school which he built next to his cathedral in Auckland. But the school was a failure and another had to be opened on Norfolk Island. Even then Selwyn acknowledged that before enough pupils could be recruited the confidence of their fathers must be won – and the Melanesians had been alienated, like the Maoris, by ruthless sailors. The most notorious culprits were the 'blackbirders' who were virtually slave-traders, but other sailors pursued an alternative policy: in order to clear the islands for settlement by white men they put ashore 'natives' infected with measles, a disease against which there was no resistance. Selwyn saw that the islands must be visited systematically, with courage but also in hope.[22]

To a man of Selwyn's convictions that must mean the recruitment of another bishop. Fortunately non-Anglicans had already shown what could be done. In many of the Polynesian islands to the west, Christian communities had grown in response to missionary work. One missionary, John Williams of the London Missionary Society, had won a special fame by building a boat to get from island to island and by being willing to meet a martyr's death. He had been clubbed to death and eaten on the island of Erromanga in 1839; the islanders had been enraged by the activities of the blackbirders. A Roman Catholic missionary bishop had been killed in similar circumstances in 1845. But in Fiji an astonishing number of conversions had rewarded Methodist missionaries, who had landed in 1835 and who had stayed despite persecutions and despite witnessing the horrors of cannibal feasts. In some Polynesian islands the opposite of martyrdom had awaited missionaries. In the kingdom of Tonga, for example, what was in effect a Methodist State Church was built up while the Christian king who in 1830 took the baptismal name of George reigned until 1893; two missionaries, John Thomas and Shirley Baker, succeeded in each other in almost dictatorial powers. So Bishop Selwyn had a reason to hope that eventually a reward would come. Meanwhile the best plan for the conversion of the Melanesians seemed clear.[23]

He picked a saint who, like him, was an English gentleman, an Etonian and an athlete – but who possessed a gentler character. John Coleridge Patteson was consecrated a bishop for this perilous mission in 1861. He learned the technique from Selwyn: to swim ashore alone and unarmed, pushing in front of him a top hat full of simple presents for the islanders. His great gift for friendship, allied with linguistic ability which had won him a fellowship at Oxford, worked like a charm –

---

[22] John H. Evans wrote a biography of Selwyn as *Churchman Militant* (London, 1964). B. J. Dalton studied the background in *War and Politics in New Zealand 1855–70* (Sydney, 1967), and W. P. Morrell in *Britain in the Pacific Islands* (Oxford, 1960).

[23] A. A. Koskinen studied *Missionary Influence as a Political Factor in the Pacific Islands* (Helsinki, 1953). Niel Gunson's later study of *Messengers of Grace* took the Protestant story to 1860.

until, like Williams before him, he visited an island which had been troubled by the blackbirders; five of its men had been kidnapped. His murder followed. His lifeless body was placed in a canoe and pushed back to his companions. On it was a palm branch, with five knots. In the words inscribed on a cross later built at the place of his death on a converted Nukapu island: 'His life was taken by men for whom he would gladly have given it.'

The mission continued, most of it the work of converts, and the next bishop was Bishop Selwyn's son John, a man as beloved as Patteson. It was too late to save the islands from depopulation, but the Melanesian Church so developed in its faith and its unity that by 1918, when it had a bishop who treated the 'natives' like children, it was able to compel him to resign and go back to England.[24]

TO INDIA

It would obviously be impossible to retrace every step taken by the Victorian missionaries in the east – and it is not necessary, since the patterns repeated themselves. For example, the story of Francis McDougall, who sailed out to Sarawak in 1847 and returned home in 1868 having laid the foundations of a strong Anglican Church amid head-hunting primitive tribesmen, hostile Muslims and Chinese pirates, is in its way as remarkable as the story of his patron James Brooke, the Englishman who was made Rajah of Sarawak; but in its essentials the story of Bishop McDougall is very like the story of Bishops Selwyn and Patteson. We must confine ourselves to an outline of the story of how Englishmen helped to break the dominance of traditional religion over India and China, often with a disastrous clumsiness.

Despite the hopes which surrounded the full admission of

---

[24] Sir John Gutch wrote biographies of Williams and Patteson as *Beyond the Reefs* and *Martyr of the Islands* (London, 1971–74). C. E. Fox wrote a history of the Anglican mission to Melanesia as *Lord of the Southern Islands* (London, 1958).

Christian missionaries into India in 1813, there was no large movement by Indians into Christianity. A modern historian who recorded with praise the decisive influence of Evangelical preachers and administrators on social reform was frank about the missionaries' disappointment as they counted their converts. 'Among the Indians generally, suspicion far outweighed the acquiescence – it can scarcely be described as anything more active – of some of the lower classes and the occasional support of a far smaller number among the higher castes. Sometimes, too, there was open hostility to individual missionaries. From the British government in India the missionaries might look in general for approval extending at times to active support, but an incautious step might produce immediate recriminations'.[25]

For the missionaries almost totally failed to appreciate the Indian point of view. Their pride in their alliance with the men who now ruled India blinded them to the difficulty of securing a hearing for a spiritual message on the basis of that alliance. Indians justly believed that on the whole they were far more religious than their new conquerors, and that their holy men knew far more about the life of the spirit than did the Europeans who tried to use an Indian language to preach from the Bible in a crowded bazaar, or who had to be listened to as the price of receiving a modern education. Indians prepared to see merits in innovations by their conquerors would grant the merit of some social reforms; but they still thought that English talk about morality was hypocritical, for the ending of the East India Company's commercial business in 1833 still left India open to exploitation on a very large scale. Indians observed that the missionaries when they destroyed the centuries-old fabric of custom had no idea about how to replace it from within the Indian tradition. Any convert willing to be baptized had to forfeit his place in his family and his caste, and the almost certain result was that he was economically dependent on the missionaries. In these circumstances the converts were almost certain to be unhappy individuals, people without any

---

[25] Kenneth Ingham, *Reformers in India*, p. 19.

real stake in the Indian society saturated by the religious tradition which Europeans called Hinduism.[26]

In 1857 sepoys in the Bengal Army mutinied. It was the signal for a revolt which included atrocities on both sides. In defending British rule the leading general was an austere Baptist, Henry Havelock, and, specially when he had died of dysentery at the end of this triumph, he became a hero; his last words were to his son – 'Come now, and see how a Christian can die.'[27] But what was needed was more tactful living by Christians, for the causes of the rebellion were clear to all with eyes to see. The British conquest of India had just been completed, and it had been made compulsory for Indian soldiers to serve the British in other imperial wars if so ordered. The threat of the new empire to Indian traditions had been shown by the issue of new cartridges for the troops' rifles; these needed to be bitten off, and so the soldier's mouth would come into contact with grease probably derived from cows (sacred to Hindus) and pigs (unclean to Muslims). The cartridges were withdrawn, but the impression of contempt for Indian religious feelings had been created – or, rather, confirmed.

Despite the smallness of the British army in India (only 45,000 in 1857), the revolt was suppressed because its leadership had no coherent plan and most of the Indians remained either loyal or indifferent.[28] The day of Indian nationalism had not yet come. But Anglo-Indian relations were never the same again. The replacement of company rule by direct government by the Crown did not make much practical difference. The difference was that the degree of innocence, of optimism about the transformation of India, to be seen in British attitudes at

---

[26] The classic modern Indian indictments of the intrusion of the missionaries and their imperial allies were Jawaharlal Nehru, *The Discovery of India* (London; 1946), and K. M. Panikkar, *Asia and Western Dominance* (London, 1953). There was an earlier and more balanced judgement by a leading Indian Christian: K. T. Paul, *The British Connection with India* (London, 1928). For a British scholar's summary, see M. E. Chamberlain, *Britain and India: The Interaction of Two Peoples* (Newton Abbot, Devon, 1974).

[27] See J. C. Pollock, *Way to Glory: The Life of Havelock of Lucknow* (London, 1957).

[28] The best British narrative of *The Great Mutiny* is that by Christopher Hibbert (London, 1978). The best Indian study is S. N. Sen, *Eighteen Fifty-Seven* (Calcutta, 1957).

the height of the Evangelicals' influence vanished. Government officials still talked, often sincerely, about the British having a responsibility for 'the happiness of millions'. But the British now found it harder to think that they could trust, or even understand, the Indians. It was their duty to rule them; but part of their duty was to keep the ruling race uncontaminated.

After the mutiny missionaries were able to take advantage of the policy of the government, introduced in 1854, to bear about two-thirds of the cost of education which it deemed satisfactory. Mission schools gradually made the Christian minority the most highly educated section of Indian society apart from the sections which derived a superior education from an older community's tradition (most notably the Parsees) or from wealth. Some converts from the higher castes were obtained through the chain of colleges established by the missionaries for higher education, but most of the baptisms were of outcasts of the bottom of society or of hill tribesmen. By 1890 there were about 600,000 Indians in churches served by Anglican or other Protestant missionaries, but significantly there were almost a quarter of a million more Roman Catholics, whose priests were seldom English. It is significant, too, that such 'mass movements' into Christianity as did occur did not come in the areas where English influence was felt most strongly. One explanation is to be found in the fact that not until 1912 was an Indian made a diocesan bishop by the Anglicans.[29]

Here was the paradox of the British mission to India. It became well-intentioned but always wounded. It accepted many sacrifices. When independence came in 1947, probably there were two million British graves in India, most of them filled by disease. It contributed much, as independent Indians have often acknowledged. Yet even when it was being self-sacrificial, acting as conscience dictated in justice and kindness, bringing to India Christianity and many other benefits,

---

[29] Relevant studies include Michael Hollis, *Paternalism and the Church* (London, 1962); Mildred Gibbs, *The Anglican Church in India* (New Delhi, 1972); Duncan Forrester, *Caste and Christianity* (London, 1980). An Indian scholar, Sarvepalli Gopal, examined *British Policy in India 1858–1905* (Cambridge, 1967). Stephen Neill recounted the *History of Christianity in India 1707–1858* (Cambridge, 1987).

the British presence in India was wounding because it was patronizing. The work of Rudyard Kipling shows all this very clearly – although Kipling was bitterly cynical about the work of most of the missionaries, and the vagueness of his own religious beliefs would have shocked his grandfathers, who were both Methodist ministers. He suffered because his parents had left England to earn a living in Bombay. Without any explanation he was deposited with strangers in England at the age of five, and felt an alien when he returned to India in 1881 at the age of sixteen. There were neurotic undertones in much of his work. He contributed much; he wrote about the life of the people of India and about the magic of the land as no one had written before. But in the last resort he could not regard India as his home. Hinduism he despised even more thoroughly than missionary Christianity, and Indians he thought would always need to be commanded while they were being served. Marriage to an American in 1892 meant that he left India except for one brief visit and his dreams.[30]

In 1899 Kipling urged Americans to follow the British example by colonizing the Philippine islands:

> Take up the White Man's Burden –
>   Send forth the best ye breed –
> Go bind your sons to exile
>   To serve your captives' need;
> To wait in heavy harness
>   On fluttered folk and wild –
> Your new-caught sullen peoples,
>   Half-devil and half-child.

TO CHINA

On a Sunday in June 1865 James Hudson Taylor walked by the sea at Brighton. With his agitated mind he saw not the English coast but the Chinese empire. For a missionary to go

---

[30] The best introduction is Angus Wilson, *The Strange Ride of Rudyard Kipling* (London, 1977), and fuller studies include Alan Sandisan, *Wheel of Empire* (London, 1967).

deep into China seemed as difficult as for a non-swimmer to go
far into the sea; and eleven years previously Taylor had begun
his first, disappointing, experience of the problem when he had
joined the missionaries making highly nervous expeditions into
the interior from the 'treaty port' of Shanghai. He had returned
to England for training as a medical doctor, but his health and
his spirits were broken.

To the Chinese, the 'Middle Kingdom' was the only civilization in the world and 'barbarians' must be kept out of it since
they only cheated, corrupted and made trouble. Robert Morri-
son went from Northumberland to China while in his early
twenties, in 1807, with the support of the London Missionary
Society, but at that time Canton was the only port open to
foreigners, who were severely limited to trade on the water-
front. In 1818 he founded the 'Anglo-Chinese College' at
Malacca, and the next year he completed a translation of the
Bible, but in a quarter of a century he and his few British
Protestant colleagues baptized only ten Chinese. Inside China
there were remnants of the fairly extensive Roman Catholic
missionary work of the previous two centuries, but these
remnants were small and persecuted.

In the period 1839–44 wars were fought in order to compel
the Chinese to accept the import of opium from India; for the
British, too, claimed what Chinese emperors had always
claimed – the 'Mandate of Heaven'. The weakness of the
imperial government invited a peasant revolt – and for the first
time in Chinese history the next revolt, the Taiping rebellion,
contained a Christian element, however confused its theology
may have been in the eyes of Evangelicals such as Major
Charles Gordon, enlisted to stiffen the imperial army.[31] With
the defeat of these rebels the missionaries had learned the fatal
lesson of dependence on this kind of foreign military intervention in Chinese affairs, but we cannot be surprised that James
Hudson Taylor, when he contemplated the Christian mission
to China from the Brighton beach in 1865, was depressed.

The son of a Methodist lay preacher who had run a little

---

[31] The best account of this life, which ended dramatically in Khartoum in 1885, is
Anthony Nutting, *Gordon: Martyr and Misfit* (London, 1966).

chemist's shop in Yorkshire, his own religious faith was simple. He believed that, without any opportunity to hear and believe the Gospel, the Chinese must die in their sins and be punished everlastingly; he reckoned that a million a month were going to hell. And on that Sunday in 1865 the essentials of a new plan for the evangelization of China suddenly became clear as he pondered and prayed. He would lead a mission which would take full advantage of the promised toleration even if the toleration amounted to little in practice. The missionaries would not live permanently in mission stations, supervising their dependants in the hope that a church would slowly grow. Their message was too urgent for that. Having proclaimed their Gospel, they would move on to other towns and villages. They would not receive regular salaries; God would provide. Meetings held to support them would take no collections, yet no debts would be incurred. They would not be confined to any denomination and they would not be controlled by any committee remaining in England. They would welcome fellow missionaries from any nation and any level of education, and women would be given a wide scope. To symbolize their break with their homes they would wear Chinese dress and speak the local language – but they would preach salvation, not ingratiate themselves by any technical aid.

Fifteen fellow missionaries who accepted Taylor's guidance sailed with him and his wife to China. Thirty years after his Brighton vision the China Inland Mission included 641 missionaries, about half the Protestant missionaries in China. Taylor's letters home breathed the spirit of a mystical union with Christ in prayer and total self-dedication; but he was also a brilliant organizer, able to hold a team together. His courage, shown repeatedly, could not fail to move the Chinese however bewildered they were by his flexible methods or by his uncompromising message. He died in China in 1905.[32]

Three years later the last formidable Manchu ruler of China, the Dowager Empress, died. The imperial dynasty had been fatally discredited by its failure to cope either with the in-

---

[32] The best biography remains that by his son Howard (abridged, London, 1965).

numerable penetrations by offensively over-privileged foreign
merchants or with the rebellion of the 'Boxers' in 1897–1900.
This rebellion, which murdered some 32,000 Christians, was a
great cry of protest against the humiliation of China at the
hands of foreigners. But, strangely, it turned out to be a prelude
to a time of hope for Christianity. Its violence warned the
European powers off the policy into which they had previously
been drifting – the policy of colonizing China; and its suppression by a European expedition gave an opportunity to Sun
Yat-sen, who had been baptized while a student, to found the
Republic of China in 1911. For a time a Republican modernism looking to Japan, America and Europe seemed to promise
the regeneration of China. After their long exclusion and their
long struggle for recognition, the Christian Churches felt
themselves to be on the crest of a wave. Schools, colleges and
hospitals proliferated and many students went abroad to
study. The Anglicans formed the 'Holy Catholic Church in
China' in 1912, uniting their dioceses with much hope for a
glorious future; but the chief gains were won by the Roman
Catholics and by the interdenominational Protestants of the
China Inland Mission. In 1913 the Temple of Heaven in
Peking, formerly the 'Forbidden City', was used for a series of
Christian evangelistic meetings. The Churches' statistics
claimed that the number of their adherents had doubled, to
about a million and a half, within ten years of the defeat of the
Boxers. It was an achievement to be seen in its context – a
population of some four hundred millions. But the progress in
China was the largest cause of the optimism reigning in the
missionary movement on the eve of the First World War.[33]

How are we to assess this complex story now outlined?

It was often true about the Victorians and post-Victorians
abroad, as it was often true about them at home, that 'they
pretended to be better than they were. They passed themselves

---

[33] K. S. Latourette, *A History of Christian Missions in China* (London, 1929),
remains standard. More recent accounts include the mainly Catholic Columba
Cary-Elwes, *China and the Cross* (London, 1957), and the entirely Protestant Pat
Barr, *To China with Love* (London, 1972). There is background material, revised in
the light of post-1948 studies, in Vincent Shih, *The Taiping Ideology* (Seattle, 1967),
and Victor Purcell, *The Boxer Uprising* (Cambridge, 1963).

off as being incredibly pious and moral; they talked noble
sentiments and lived – quite otherwise.'[34] But not all the
Victorian Christians were hypocrites; and about those who
included self-deception in their characters, this was not the
whole truth. Their energy and courage flowed from a self-
confidence which had its origins partly in Evangelicalism,
although also in more secular sources. They were so proud of
their technical superiority to other peoples that they came to
believe in themselves as the explorers of a world which was
somehow 'unknown' before their arrival, as the missionaries of
a civilization which was incomparably the best and which
included the various denominational interpretations of Christianity. They were slow to see how ready Canada, Africa, the
Pacific islands and Asia were to be exploited, governed and to
some extent converted – but they did see it and in the end they
seized their opportunity, changing the course of history. They
gave what they could to the world.

---

[34] Walter E. Houghton, *The Victorian Frame of Mind 1830–1870* (New Haven,
Conn., 1957), p. 395. This classic study avoided moral condemnation – unlike the
Victorians. The Victorians, especially the missionaries, were censured by John
Kent, *The Unacceptable Face* (London, 1987). A fresh survey of political and social
history has been provided by E. J. Feuchtwanger, *Democracy and Empire: Britain
1865–1914* (London, 1985).

CHAPTER TEN

THE END OF AN ENGLAND

DOMESTIC QUARRELS

There were many warnings to the English Churches. In *The Condition of England* (1909) an Anglican layman, C. F. C. Masterman, paid a tribute: 'The Churches are extraordinarily active, endeavouring in this way and that to influence the lives of the people. Their humanitarian and social efforts are widely appreciated.' But he added: 'Their definite dogmatic teaching seems to count for little at all. They labour steadily on amid a huge indifference.' In 1904 the *Daily Telegraph* printed a long correspondence under the title 'Do We Believe?' It showed much scepticism in the paper's middle-class readership. A book such as *Religion: A Criticism and a Forecast* by Galdsworthy Lowes Dickinson (1905) expressed the superior scepticism of a Cambridge don, the key sentence being the claim that 'religious truth, like all other truth, is attainable, if at all, only by the method of science'. Under such influences, many idealistic and intelligent young graduates who would have been ordained in Victorian times were now turning to the other professions which were being rapidly developed. In the Church of England, ordinations which had reached their peak with 814 new deacons in 1886 were below six hundred a year throughout the period 1901–14. And the autobiography of Eric Gill, a Nonconformist minister's son who was to become famous as a sculptor and as a Roman Catholic, records what he found in a place far removed from the atmosphere of the ancient universities. He was employed with other clerks by the Ecclesiastical Commissioners to serve the Church of England – and he was almost overwhelmed by the contempt for religion which he found among other young men in this office.

An examination of the religious life of Lambeth, the crowded

South London borough which surrounded the Archbishop of Canterbury's palace and Spurgeon's old pulpit, during the early years of the twentieth century has been made by an American scholar. He accepted a survey which suggested that about a tenth of the population could be found in church on a Sunday morning or evening. His broad conclusion agreed with Masterman's verdict: secularization was already strong, although there was still a lot of churchgoing and there was even more charitable activity by churchgoers. The Churches, he wrote, 'intended to persuade the entire nation to attend Sunday services, and there indoctrinate churchgoers with Anglican or Nonconformist values. Instead they persuaded only a portion of the upper and middle classes to attend church, and created a vast parochial and philanthropic network which provided the sacraments and social services to the working classes and the poor.'[1]

Did the remedy lie in more effective religious instruction in the schools? Possibly; but when the Conservatives' Education Act of 1902 subsidized church schools out of the local rates by the payment of teachers and the maintenance of buildings, the Baptist leader, John Clifford, led the 'passive resistance' to this as a holy war against clerical despotism, a war calling for martyrs who would refuse to pay rates. Up and down the country this conflict made relations between Nonconformists and Anglicans worse than they had been for a century and a half. 'Wake up, Oliver Cromwell, wake up the spirit of our Puritan ancestors,' cried Clifford to the Free Church Congress, 'and once more lead us to victories for freedom and for God!' In the end, however, all that happened was that the Anglican church schools survived with a diminishing proportion of the nation's children in them, the Roman Catholic schools survived with greater enthusiasm, and in the new 'council schools' the Bible was taught in a broad way of which most Anglicans and Roman Catholics disapproved. 'A boneless, fibreless, structureless, colourless, tasteless religion, absolutely wanting in every constituent needed to build up the Christian charac-

---

[1] Jeffrey Cox, *The English Churches in a Secular Society* (New York, 1982), p. 6. Hugh McLeod summed up recent studies in *Religion and the Working Class in Nineteenth Century Britain* (London, 1984).

ter' was how this education was described by a Jesuit, Bernard
Vaughan. But if such criticism of the council schools was partly
justified, the absorption of the denominations in their own
narrow concerns was partly to blame. A few of the wisest Free
Church leaders, such as the Methodist John Scott Lidgett (a
great man who combined a theology of the love of God with
leadership in London's social work and education), pleaded for
a settlement in the interests of the children. So did the
Archbishop of Canterbury, Randall Davidson, who was defeated in his efforts at a compromise. Agreement about the
syllabus to be used in religious education in the majority of the
nation's schools could not be recorded in an Act of Parliament
until 1944. And by then the mind of England was moving away
from all the Churches. It was partly because they were divided
that the Churches' statistics fell.[2]

Did the remedy lie in the drastic reduction of Anglican
privileges – the only point (it seemed) on which Nonconformists and Roman Catholics agreed? Possibly; but the easiest
point of attack seemed to be the disestablishment of the Church
in Wales, and even this measure was resisted bitterly by most
of the Anglicans, with their Conservative allies. The first
Welsh Disestablishment Bill to be given priority in the government's business was introduced in 1895. The fourth and last
was in its last stages when war broke out. With financial
provisions more generous than the original proposals, it came
into effect in 1920. A direct confrontation with the Church of
England was once again postponed, an important factor being
the diplomatic skill of Randall Davidson. For example, he led
most of the bishops to support the Parliament Act of 1911,
which ended the veto of the House of Lords over Liberal
legislation. As we have seen, many of the broader-minded
clergy and laity were in this period expressing sympathy with
the ideals of Christian Socialism. Thus the identification of the

---

[2] Benjamin Sacks studied *The Religious Issue in the State Schools of England and Wales
1902–14* (Albuquerque, N.M., 1961) and M. Cruickshank *Church and State in English
Education: 1870 to the Present Day* (London, 1963). Sir James Marchant's memoir of
John Clifford (London, 1924) may be supplemented by H. E. Bonsall and E. H.
Robertson, *The Dream of an Ideal City* (London, 1978). J. Scott Lidgett recalled *My
Guided Life* (London, 1936).

Established Church with the Conservative Party, although substantial, was not complete and the Gladstonian tradition of an Anglican presence within the Liberal Party was not obliterated.[3]

Did the remedy lie in more vigorous preaching? In 1904 a large survey of *The Religious Life of London* reached this conclusion although it also argued for a new kind of church around the pulpit – 'large, handsome central halls, well lit and well ventilated, furnished throughout with seats of one pattern' and sponsoring many clubs for 'active, aggressive social work' seeking the 'redemption and development of body, mind and soul'. But the question then arose – what was the preacher to say that was not being said by the politicians or the newspapers? And in each of the denominational traditions into which English religion was now divided, there were sharply conflicting answers.

In the Church of England the challenge was thrown down by the Anglo-Catholic movement, which had increased its attractiveness to churchgoers while the support of duller Evangelical preachers had declined from the 1880s onwards. In 1906 it acquired in the *English Hymnal* the richest collection of hymns yet brought together in the English language. It proclaimed firm doctrines and dramatized them by colourful ceremonies.

When a Royal Commission was appointed to inquire into ecclesiastical discipline in 1904 (by the Conservative Prime Minister, Balfour, in consultation with Archbishop Davidson), 'practices of special gravity and significance' were noted, as demanded by outraged Protestants. Showing how little had been achieved by Victorian discipline, these practices included the interpretation of prayers and ceremonies belonging to the Roman Canon of the Mass, 'the reservation of the sacrament under conditions which lead to its adoration', processions and 'benediction' with the sacrament, the invocation of the Virgin Mary and other saints in hymns and prayers, the observance of the festivals of the Assumption and the Sacred Heart and the

---

[3] See P. M. H. Bell, *Disestablishment in Ireland and Wales*, pp. 225–329, and K. O. Morgan, *Wales in British Politics 1865–1922* (Cardiff, 1963). G. K. A. Bell compiled a masterly biography of *Randall Davidson* (2 vols., Oxford, 1935).

veneration of 'images'. But 'the two main conclusions' of this commission gave the Protestant disciplinarians little hope. 'First, the law of public worship in the Church of England is too narrow for the religious life of the present generation. It needlessly condemns much which a great section of Church people, including many of her most devoted members, value; and modern thought and feeling are characterized by a care for ceremonial, a sense of dignity in worship, and an appreciation of the continuity of the Church, which were not similarly felt at the time when the law took its present shape.' 'Secondly, the machinery for discipline has broken down. The means of enforcing the law in the ecclesiastical courts, even in matters which touch the Church's faith and teaching, are defective and in some respects unsuitable.'

However, if the worship of the Church of England was to be revised in order to accommodate the new richness of Catholic devotion, difficult problems became inescapable. Not only was there the problem of how to persuade Parliament either to produce a Prayer Book acceptable to churchmen or to let the Church produce it for itself. (Between 1880 and 1913 there were 216 bills to regulate ecclesiastical matters introduced into the House of Commons; only thirty-three became law.) There was also the problem of how to secure a new basis of Anglican unity now that the Establishment was cracked wide open, at home and overseas. The Anglo-Catholics reacted touchily, even hysterically, to movements very different but equally Anglican. For example, in 1913 there was a discussion of a possible federation of the Protestant, including Anglican, Churches in Kenya: it aroused the wrath of Frank Weston, Bishop of Zanzibar, and of other Anglo-Catholics. Bishop Weston announced that he was no longer in communion with those who had taken part in the discussion in Africa, and was no less enraged when reports reached Africa of criticisms of their holy book by English Christians. Among some of the clergy as among many of the laity, questions were being asked – however tentatively – about the virgin birth, the miracles and the physical resurrection of Jesus, and about the whole historical basis of Christianity. A few preachers aired their doubts openly and bishops deplored such indiscretions. In 1909 a

theological journal published a much-discussed special number called *Jesus or Christ?*, contrasting Jesus of Nazareth with
the Christ of the Church's orthodoxy. A volume by Oxford
scholars of 1913, *Foundations*, showed that the doctrinal foundations were being shaken in the Church of England, although as
yet only gently.[4]

These winds of theological change blew more fiercely in the
minds of two preachers outside the Church of England – the
Congregationalist, R. J. Campbell, and the Roman Catholic,
George Tyrrell.

Campbell was the great Dr Parker's successor in the marble
pulpit of the crowded City Temple. Whether Parker knew how
much more liberal this young man's views were is a mystery.
The congregation, however, soon saw it; and the crowds
continued to pour in. Campbell's views developed rapidly.
Some words of his criticizing the workers' attitude to Sunday
were reported in newspapers – as many of his words were – and
led to a private meeting with Labour leaders, a novel experience which converted the preacher to a form of Socialism. In
contrast, when he repeated orthodox words about salvation
they seemed to fail to arouse much interest, while all around
him lay the capital of a great empire, full of inequalities but also
full of promises about the progress to come in the twentieth
century. In 1907 two books resulting from his pulpit work were
widely discussed. In *Christianity and the Social Order*, Campbell
maintained with much passion that 'the practical end which
alone could justify the existence of Churches is the realization
of the kingdom of God, which only means the reconstruction of
society on a basis of mutual helpfulness instead of strife and
competition'. This challenge to the Churches was urgent, since
while the contrast between wealth and poverty was shocking
(estimates were quoted that more than one half of the land was
owned by 2,500 people while the average annual income of
11,500 working-class families in York was £85), 'charities
demoralize the poor and gospel missions fail to touch them'.

---

[4] The most important literature is referred to in Roger Lloyd, *The Church of
England 1900–65* (London, 1966), and in Owen Chadwick's study of a controversially liberal preacher, *H. H. Henson* (Oxford, 1983).

The New Theology was even more provocative in its definition – or lack of definition – of the Gospel. Jesus, Campbell maintained, 'was God because his life was the expression of Divine Love'; but he bestowed almost similar praise on progressive humanity. 'Jesus was God, but so are we.' The Spirit of God dwelt in every man, to such an extent that there seemed no need for any clear distinction between the Creator and the creature, or between the Saviour and the saved. 'The *roué* you saw in Piccadilly last night,' he informed first his congregation and then his readers, 'who went out to corrupt innocence and wallow in filthiness of the flesh was engaged in his blundering quest for God'; and to see the Labour leader, Keir Hardie, pleading for justice in the House of Commons was to 'see the Atonement'.

There were many replies to Campbell. The most weighty came from a fellow Congregationalist, P. T. Forsyth. The son of a postman and a domestic servant, Forsyth was rather better informed than Campbell about the conditions of the poor – and more convinced that the poor needed the 'positive preaching' of the 'Holy Church' about the 'Holy Father'. He had begun as a liberal, but had come to see that liberty was not enough; 'now we want to know what makes and keeps us free, and what we are free for.' He had found the liberation, the salvation, required in the gracious God revealed and active through the divine Christ, and wrote a trenchant book on *The Person and Place of Jesus Christ* (1909): 'it is through the work of redemption that I know the person of the Redeemer'.[5]

However, the most immediately effective reply to *The New Theology* came from Charles Gore, Bishop of Birmingham, an Anglo-Catholic saint and scholar. The presentation of the timeless Catholic Faith as the corrective of Campbell's own hasty and muddled thinking shook him to the core. He became convinced that 'either Jesus was what the Catholic Church said he was, or he did not exist; either he was the Man from heaven, a complete break with the natural order of things, the representative of a transcendental order, supernatural, super-rational, super-everything, or he was nothing.' He was con-

---

[5] See W. L. Bradley, *P. T. Forsyth: The Man and His Work* (London, 1952).

firmed and ordained by Gore, and began a thoroughly orthodox, but dull, ministry in the Church of England. His story
sums up the central dilemma of the Free Churches in his day.
Were they to add a touch of down-to-earth Christianity to the
popular causes of the time? Or were they to be more supernatural in their message, and if so was their worship supernatural
enough to defy the current trends? This dilemma was eating
away at their success, although superficially it is true to say
that 'the years 1900 to 1914 seemed to fulfil the extravagant
hopes that the Free Churches had for their future'.[6]

Charles Gore had seemed the obvious man to appoint as the
first Principal of Pusey House, Oxford, when that centre of
Anglo-Catholicism was founded as a memorial to the theological patriarch. But in 1889, only seven years after Pusey's
death, the self-confidence of a new generation of Anglo-
Catholics had been shown by the publication of *Lux Mundi*, a
collection of essays edited by Gore. Throughout that volume
the tone had been optimistic. The mostly young and Oxford-
trained authors seemed to expect the light shining in Bethlehem – a light plainly visible to the wise men from Victorian
England – to be welcomed by the world. The beauty of nature
and the strictness of man's own conscience united to testify to
the reality of the Creator and Judge. Mankind's history and the
individual's own experience, although they might include
suffering, united to prepare for the coming of Christ. Christ
emptied himself of divine power in order to be close to men (the
'kenotic' theory of the Incarnation, which brought accusations
of heresy from the ultra-orthodox) – rather like a wealthy
young man from Oxford visiting the London slums. Christ the
incarnate Son taught that all men were sons of God, but called
Christians to an attainable holiness as the salt of the earth,
leaving behind a moral law to guide them, sacraments to feed
them, and the Church to be his continuing Body, 'an organization for the spiritual life'. Into this confidently clear picture of
Lux Mundi it had seemed possible to fit pretty well every fact
significant in the Victorian world, and the book had secured a

[6] Paul Sangster, *A History of the Free Churches* (London, 1983), p. 171. R. J.
Campbell retraced *A Spiritual Pilgrimage* (London, 1916).

wide influence as an Anglican intellectual manifesto. It is not
surprising that in the 1900s the confused Campbell seemed an
upstart to Bishop Gore – and Gore a 'Father-in-God' to him.

Gore was encouraged by Campbell's conversion to affirm
still more strongly the power of the everlasting Gospel entrusted to the Church. He rightly declared that no other Gospel
had ever been admitted into the foundation documents of the
Church of England. The Gospel, in his conviction, produced a
Catholicism which was always open to fresh insights (that was
why he called himself a 'liberal' Catholic) but which was
always fundamentally a coherent whole. He expounded that
Gospel by teaching and by a life which to many seemed the best
light in all the world. Yet he could not deny that questions
about the doctrines in the historic faith, and about the historical facts on which the faith rested, were being asked by men as
devoutly Christian as he was himself, as well as by a more
sceptical mass of men. If he never felt the full force of those
questions in his own mind, that did not prove their unreality or
unimportance. An undergraduate once shrewdly compared
Gore's mind with an 'awfully jolly' merry-go-round at a fair.
The young man's complaint was that the merry-go-round
never stopped so that he could make his own way on to it.[7]

Essentially similar cross-currents of thought were to be
found in the Roman Catholic community. The unchanging
faith was taught with a quiet conviction to growing numbers. It
was taught by, for example, Francis Bourne, appointed
Archbishop of Westminster in 1903. He was often called the
'quiet' cardinal and that meant 'dull'. Presumably his steady
reliability in Roman eyes was the reason why he was
appointed, although the youngest of the bishops. He was no
saint. His quarrel with Peter Amigo, his successor as Bishop of
Southwark, grew so embittered that his old diocese refused to

---

[7] Contrasting assessments were offered in H. D. A. Major, *English Modernism: Its
Origins, Methods, Aims* (Cambridge, Mass., 1927), and A. M. Ramsey, *From Gore to
Temple* (London, 1960). James Carpenter supplied *Gore: A Study in Liberal Catholic
Thought* (London, 1960), and Thomas Langford a survey of English theology,
1900–20, against its social background in *In Search of Foundations* (Nashville, Tenn.,
1969). G. L. Prestige wrote *The Life of Charles Gore* (London, 1935). See also Alan M.
G. Stephenson, *The Rise and Decline of English Modernism* (London, 1984).

congratulate him when he was made a cardinal and he refused to preach in it. When Liverpool and Birmingham were elevated as archbishoprics in 1911, he was unsuccessfully anxious to have the primacy of Westminster more sharply defined. This touchiness about his status came out again in the following year, when he was invited to Buckingham Palace. But before accepting this gesture of friendship he demanded the proper honours: 'Our position is that the Holy See has, even in the eyes of the Foreign Office, the rank of a Sovereign Power and that the Cardinals are Princes of that Power.' It was not a claim likely to persuade a straightforward ex-sailor such as George V that the Cardinal was as patriotic as he was. But Bourne embodied the religious orthodoxy of his own community, for most of whom the inherited or adopted road to truth was – to use the title of Hilaire Belloc's book of 1901 – *The Path to Rome*.

It was not to be expected that such an ecclesiastic would make any very profound response to the challenge of new thought. In contrast, the movement called 'Modernism' was a theological attempt, marked by a passionate integrity and courage, to come to terms with the questions which destroyed belief for (for example) Edward Elgar. In 1906 that great musician, who had made a master-work out of Newman's *Dream of Gerontius*, and had followed it up with the two oratorios *The Apostles* and *The Kingdom*, ceased to feel loyalty to his inherited Catholicism. And so he ceased to find inspiration in explicitly religious themes. Music continued to pour out of him, often with sincerely patriotic words, but his best music was nostalgic and haunted; and the riddle of a sad world now made his personal philosophy an enigma.[8]

In 1907 Pope Pius X issued an encyclical, *Pascendi Gregis*, in which 'Modernism' was defined and condemned by listing a series of propositions all said to be destructive of Catholicism and of Christianity. The propositions had in common a desire to see the Church adjusting itself to modern thought – for example, by accepting the critical, scholarly study of the Bible.

---

[8] Ernest Oldmeadow wrote a biography of *Francis, Cardinal Bourne* (2 vols., London, 1940–44), and Michael Kennedy a much better *Portrait of Elgar* (revised, Oxford, 1982).

The chief international organizer of Modernism was based on London and it might have been expected that this man, Baron Friedrich von Hügel, would be excluded from the sacraments as Loisy had been. But so far from being excommunicated, the Baron was accorded great honour among Christians of all shades in England, until he was buried in the Benedictine monastery at Downside in 1925. It helps us to understand his immunity if we notice that he was a lay aristocrat. Although a well-known writer of religious books and letters, much sought after as a guide to spiritual progress, he was without a priest's formal responsibility. It also helps to notice that he was a scholarly saint, massive in his sense of the holiness and omnipresence of God, massive in his love of the mystical tradition of the Church, often referred to as Newman's successor; the two men talked over several days in 1876. The motive behind his risky involvement in the Modernist controversy was expressed in a letter on the last day of 1900: 'May this New Year and New Century bring us all much good – much work, and some achievement, visible or invisible, in the direction of a synthesis of Sanctity and Science, in the Church and for the Church.'[9]

An official condemnation was more likely to fall on George Tyrrell, von Hügel's close friend. For Tyrrell was a Jesuit. In that lay both his strength and his trouble. Joining the Jesuit order must have had something to do with his transformation from an idle and feckless Irish schoolboy into an industrious writer with a powerful style, producing many passages of spiritual insight and brave integrity. The Jesuits trained him and then gave him leisure. But they never made him completely happy. Dismissed from the order in 1906, he was dismayed. Forbidden to do more than attend Mass, he ordered that the words 'Catholic priest' should be inscribed over the grave where he was buried in 1909, in unconsecrated ground.

In his posthumously published *Christianity at the Cross-roads* he paid many tributes to what he had called the 'faith of the

---

[9] Recent studies include L. V. Lester-Garland, *The Religious Philosophy of Baron F. von Hügel* (London, 1933); Michael de la Bedoyère, *The Life of Baron von Hügel* (London, 1951); Joseph P. Whelan, *The Spirituality of Friedrich von Hügel* (London, 1971); L. F. Barmann, *Baron Friedrich von Hügel and the Modernist Crisis in England* (Cambridge, 1972).

millions'. 'The Jesus of the first century would be more in
sympathy with just those elements of Catholicism that are least
congenial to the modern mind – not to say the mind of
Modernists – not only with the transcendental, but with the
literal, value of the Catholic presentment of the transcendental; with sacraments, priests, temples, priests and altars; with
miracles, diabolic possessions and exorcisms; with devils and
angels and all the supernaturalism of his own age and tradition. For all these things he had no word, no thought of
censure, but only for their abuse and exploitation. . . .' What
Tyrrell rebelled against was the Roman insistence that all
the historical assertions in the Catholic creeds must be
accepted as accurate history. Here his conscience as a modern
man overcame his loyalty to a deeply comforting system. To
him the virgin birth or the resurrection of Christ was as
symbolic as the claim that Christ was seated at the Father's
right hand. There was truth here, but it was the same kind of
truth as was conveyed by the statue in Prague of the Christ
child robed as a king. Artistic, poetic or mystic truth a modern
man could accept, if only the Church did not continue to teach
'medievalism'.

Prophetically, Tyrrell rested his hope on a development
which he thought might be slow or very rapid. As he moved
towards death he wrote: 'It is the spirit of Christ that has again
and again saved the Church from the hands of her worldly
oppressors within and without; for where that spirit is, there is
liberty. Deliverance comes from below, from those who are
bound, not from those who bind. It is easy to quench a
glimmering light caught by the eyes of a few; but not the light of
the noonday sun – of knowledge that has become objective and
valid for all. It is through knowledge of this kind that God has
inaugurated a new epoch in man's intellectual life and extended his lordship over nature. Shall he do less for man's
spiritual life when the times are ripe? and are they not ripening?
Are we not hastening to an *impasse* – to one of those extremities
which are God's opportunities?'[10]

---

[10] Recent studies include Alec Vidler, *A Variety of Catholic Modernists* (Cambridge,
1970), and David Schaltenover, *George Tyrrell: In Search of Catholicism* (Shepherds-
town, W.V., 1981).

THE GREAT WAR

The declaration of war by the British empire against the German empire on 4 August 1914 ended many things, including the post-Reformation phase of English Christianity. Slowly, very reluctantly and often silently, the more perceptive of the church leaders found themselves compelled to acknowledge that here was the end of an England – for here was a horror to which conventional piety and morality seemed largely irrelevant.[11]

The war was a catastrophe which very few expected. In the hot summer of 1914 the church press reflected the nation's absorption in the questions of whether the Unionists would use force in Ireland, whether the strikers would use their industrial muscle successfully, whether the peers would dig their defences against the people, whether the militant suffragettes would make the men surrender, whether the Nonconformists would conquer the church schools. None of these inflexibly determined agitators dreamed that before 1915 was out the war's most popular poem would be published in *Punch* –

> In Flanders fields the poppies blow
> Between the crosses, row on row . . .

On 1 August the Archbishop of Canterbury replied to an invitation to take part in the celebration of the four hundredth year of the Reformation in Germany, in 1917. He was anxious about the international situation, but took the opportunity to say that 'war between two great Christian nations of kindred race and sympathies is, or ought to be, unthinkable in the twentieth century of the Gospel of the Prince of Peace.' On 2 August what was to be called the 'World Alliance for Promoting International Friendship through the Churches' was founded at a conference in Constance. But the unexpected war was supported with an unexpected enthusiasm in the English Churches, including Nonconformity.

---

[11] The best studies are Arthur Marwick, *The Deluge: British Society and the First World War* (revised, London, 1973); Albert Marrin, *The Last Crusade: The Church of England in the First World War* (Durham, NC, 1974); Alan Wilkinson, *The Church of England and the First World War* (London, 1978).

On 7 August the editorial leader of the *British Weekly* was headed 'United We Stand'. Three months later a crowded meeting in the City Temple pledged Nonconformity to the goal of victory. The keynote speech was made by Lloyd George, previously best known as a radical champion of progress, whom the *British Weekly* soon began supporting as a determined war minister. The first Conscription Act of January 1916 created the term 'conscientious objectors' and most of these were Nonconformists or sectarians, but only about 16,500 such men had been registered by the tribunals by November 1918, including about 3,300 who accepted 'non-combatant service'. The total was about a third of one per cent of the men who volunteered or were conscripted during the war. About a third of the men of military age belonging to the pacifist Society of Friends enrolled to fight.[12] The patriotism of the Free Churches was universally acknowledged, and on Sunday 16 November 1918 the King and Queen attended a thanksgiving service in the Albert Hall, the first time that a British monarch had ever attended Nonconformist worship.

The Church of England's patriotism was conspicuously displayed during the recruiting campaigns which were necessary before conscription was thought acceptable; and it was put into practice when thousands of 'padres' (a new word in English) ministered to the fighting men. The Chaplain-General, Bishop Taylor-Smith, a hearty Evangelical stalwart, was so insensitive to the complications of the problems of a much more varied set of chaplains in a much enlarged army that a true saint, Bishop Llewellyn Gwynne of the Sudan, had to be put in charge of the cruelly testing spiritual work in France as Deputy Chaplain-General. Yet Gwynne was no less deeply patriotic than Taylor-Smith. On the eve of the murderous battle of Passchendaele he sat down by the roadside when the last of the troops had gone forward, and prayed with all his might. He thought he heard a voice from the crucifix behind him, saying: 'Only the best can give the best.'[13]

---

[12] See Martin Cleadal, *Pacifism in Britain* (Oxford, 1980).
[13] H. C. Jackson, *Pastor on the Nile* (London, 1960), p. 155. Michael Moynihan assessed the army padres in *God on Our Side* (London, 1983).

The Roman Catholic Church in England similarly identified itself with the sacrifices of the war effort, despite the neutrality of the papacy. It was only slowly that a much more tortured Christian reaction came to the surface in all the Churches and outside them.

In 1916 Henri Barbusse published in French a novel (translated as *Under Fire*) which described a low flight over the front lines one Sunday morning. Sounds from religious services being conducted by army chaplains on the two sides seemed to reach his plane. '*Gott mit uns!* and "God is with us" – and I flew away. . . . What must the good God think about it all?' And now an even harder question was whether there was a God who was both omnipotent and good. It was a question asked by – among many others – Oswin Creighton, a chaplain who was the son of Mandell Creighton, the former Bishop of London. On Easter Day 1918 Creighton wrote to his mother: 'God so hated the world that he gave several millions of English-begotten sons, that whosoever believeth in them should not perish, but have a comfortable life.' He was among the three quarters of a million Englishmen killed in the war.

Up to a point, the questioning can be studied in an impressive series of reports. In October 1916 a National Mission of Repentance and Hope was launched by the Archbishops of Canterbury and York. There was criticism that a 'national mission' was too grandiose, and in fact the mission chiefly influenced the missioners and their already committed supporters, whose thoughts about the ineffectiveness of the Church were stirred. There was also criticism that a nation conducting a crusade did not need to be called to 'repentance', and in fact this call to the nation was often muted at the parish level. But the official outline explained the thinking behind this ambitious venture. 'We have a righteous cause in the great war; but the civil war which seemed imminent in Ireland in the summer of 1914, and the great industrial war for which preparation was then being made, were evidence of something radically wrong among ourselves.' It was acknowledged that the Church had concentrated its message too heavily on the individual. The time had come to proclaim repentance and hope to a whole society in crisis, as the Old Testament prophets had done; and it was this task that made the Church's weakness so painfully obvious. Five 'Committees of Inquiry' were appointed by the archbishops to examine the Church's 'teaching office', worship, evangelism, administration and involvement in industry. When published in 1919, their reports all began with confessions of the Church of England's failure.

The Church's delivery of its message was 'out of touch with the thoughts and ideas of the time'. Its clergy needed to be trained and retrained more systematically, particularly in relation to science and moral and social questions. The clergy had got out of touch with ordinary people – as the chaplains had learned for themselves in the army, where three-quarters of the troops were classified as 'C. of E.' but only a handful would appear at voluntary acts of worship. The Prayer Book urgently needed reform. The laity needed to be involved more in worship and taught how to pray in private.

Evangelism suffered because the Church was regarded as 'the hereditary enemy of the working classes', although among wartime soldiers and peacetime workers there was much 'inarticulate religion' looking for a 'fellowship' often found in the Labour movement. 'The call to service is being found to have more arresting power than the old evangelistic appeal.'

The committee considering industrial problems showed that some notice had been taken of the Russian revolutions of 1917, of the strikes in British factories now expected to become more bitter, and of the unrest in Britain's own armed forces which at the turn of 1918–19 brought the Royal Navy to the edge of open mutiny and forced the government to demobilize the army far more quickly than it wanted. The committee observed that the war 'had a tremendous effect in awakening the social conscience of Christians' and the future would probably look back on 'some features of our industrial system' with the same feelings as they looked back on slavery. Wages, leisure, unemployment benefits, schooling (up to sixteen) and housing must all be improved drastically, and the 'mutual antagonism and suspicion between employer and employed' must be ended. Many more working-class clergy must be recruited.

A much stronger history of identification with the working class led to a warmer welcome to the Roman Catholic chaplains. In his Pastoral Letter for Lent 1918 Cardinal Bourne showed how in this setting even an innately conservative leader could be radical. He announced that 'Capitalism really began with the robbery of Church property' and that 'the army is not only fighting, it is also thinking. . . . They have learned to be suspicious of official utterances and bureaucratic ways. And the general effect of all this on the young men who are citizens of "after the war" is little short of revolutionary.' But it could not be claimed that either the Roman Catholic Church or Nonconformity possessed all the answers to the problems now seen to confront the Church of England. *The Army and Religion* was the title of a report published in 1919 after extensive investigations financed by the YMCA and beginning in 1917. The war had revealed that the results of all religious education were 'strangely small'. Only about twenty per cent seemed to be in touch with any of the Churches. Yet most soldiers were not godless, prayed before battle, showed compassion for each other, and were appropriately buried under a cross.

What did that cross mean? What did Christianity mean in the hearts of Englishmen, whether or not they survived the war?

In reality the problems of the Churches were far more difficult than any report fully acknowledged at the time; for the great war made it harder for millions to believe that the God worshipped in church truly was the sovereign Lord and Judge, punishing the wicked and protecting the faithful or the righteous. At first it was hoped that the war would be 'over by Christmas' with a resounding defeat of the aggressor; but during four appalling years the reliance on the speedy help of the God of battles in a crusade inevitably grew weaker. It was also believed that one purpose of war within the will of God was to punish both sides for evils which had flourished during peace, and in 1914 the vicar of All Saints, Margaret Street, in London announced that the 'angel of death' had appeared because 'hard, godless women were springing up in multitudes around us, increasing numbers of them refusing to bear children'. But the suffering of 1914–18 inevitably seemed far beyond anything which a just God could have intended as chastisement for the use of contraceptives by London women, for the use of brothels by soldiers, or for any other sin, even German sin. It seemed to be part of the Christian faith that the believer or the innocent man would be protected, especially if prayed for; but the working creed of the British army came to be fatalism, the belief that 'the bullet will get you if it has your name on it' whatever may be the victim's piety or morality.

Before the war the belief in hell had been losing much of its ancient grip on the Christian imagination, but the belief that an individual's eternal destiny was decided at the moment of his death, so that it was wrong to pray for him after death, had remained ingrained in many Protestants including Anglican Evangelicals. Much evidence suggests, however, that during the war two momentous religious developments occurred in the mind of the average English Christian. First, it became incredible that the good God would sentence many of his children to everlasting punishment when they had already suffered so much through no fault of their own; Flanders was hell enough. Second, all God's children were such a mixture of good and bad that if a Christian prayed for them at all it was right to continue to pray for them when they were dead.

Above every other religious change rose the question: who or what was God? The Christian tradition was that God was the Almighty Father, controlling history and unlimited in his power, dispensing justice unerringly and himself immune from suffering. On that William Paley and Joseph Priestley, George Whitefield and John Wesley, Charles Simeon and John Henry Newman would all agree. But that was now hard to believe. Men were wrestling with mysteries and despairs greater than anything that had afflicted the mind of Browning or Tennyson or Hopkins or George Tyrrell. Nine months before he was killed, Oswin Creighton wrote home: 'I sometimes feel inclined to wonder why God hides himself so inscrutably from our experience. Or is it that the Church has taught us for so long to look for him in the wrong places?' Before the war such a feeling might have produced a faith in a God who was immersed in human progress – R. J. Campbell's City Temple faith, for example. But now the reality of the trenches in France and Flanders overwhelmed any reminders of home and peace and progress, at least for the 800,000 Englishmen who were normally on duty in them; and the wet, slimy, rat-infested, corpse-stinking 'front' was all the more ghastly because it was so near (seventy miles away) that an officer could have breakfast there and dine in his London club that evening. The idea of human progress, presided over by a genial Father, was inevitably one of the casualties in the great war. In 1916 R. J. Campbell collected some recent articles under the title *War and the Soul*. He began with a recognition of 'a widespread feeling of the utter insufficiency of religion, as commonly understood, to interpret for us the terrible situation in which we find ourselves.' Later he asked: 'What ground is there for believing that human affairs must inevitably progress towards betterment?' And he answered: 'None whatever. History almost demonstrates the contrary.'

One answer was to stress the transcendence of God, his holiness in contrast with a world of sin. In 1916 P. T. Forsyth's *The Justification of God* presented this answer in terms of a theology within the limits of a still fairly liberal brand of Nonconformity. The old words sin, evil, forgiveness and grace were restored to the theological currency. Essential to Christian faith was the completed victory of Christ; despite its continuing sins, 'it is a vanquished world'. Here was the English equivalent of the 'neo-orthodox' movement among Protestant theologians on the Continent – a movement which Karl Barth saw to be necessary when in 1914 he read the names of the most honoured theologians of Germany at the foot of an 'appeal' in defence of the Kaiser and the war. And in the Roman Catholic Church, Hilaire Belloc was typical of a militant, defiant neo-orthodoxy responding to the horror unleashed in 1914. He had lost a son whose body was never recovered from the mud at the front. His biographer has explained that 'to proclaim, and where possible to prove, the truth of Catholicism; to show the Church as the salt and savour of such civilization as survived in Europe; to demonstrate the price paid by his own country for the loss of Catholic belief – these now became a single, urgent, public task to which he addressed himself with all the force of his will.'[14]

---

[14] Robert Speaight, *The Life of Hilaire Belloc* (London, 1957), p. 373.

But even Protestant or Catholic orthodoxy, to which significant numbers clung or returned in this time of troubles, now often included the idea of the suffering God. The idea was proclaimed in the powerful, if rough, 'rhymes' of the best-known of all the army chaplains, Geoffrey Studdert Kennedy. An ugly little man nicknamed 'Woodbine Willie' because he used to distribute Woodbine cigarettes to the troops in France, he was courageous whether in ministering to the wounded in battle or in speaking his mind to generals. He toured the whole army on behalf of the National Mission of Repentance and Hope. After the war he became the chief missioner of the new Industrial Christian Fellowship. His message was now that God had 'the hardest part'; that the crucified Christ was the revelation of the pain in the heart of God. 'How does God deal with sin? . . . He takes it upon himself, and he calls on us to share his burden, to partake of his suffering.'[15]

This God was not often found in the books of Christian theology; but he could be found among suffering men. In a letter written in July 1918, the poet Wilfred Owen described training new troops. 'For fourteen hours yesterday I was at work – teaching Christ to lift his cross by numbers, and how to adjust his crown; and not to imagine his thirst until after the last halt. I attended his Supper to see that there were no complaints; and inspected his feet that they should be worthy of the nails. I see to it that he is dumb, and stands at attention before his accusers. With a piece of silver I buy him every day, and with maps I make him familiar with the topography of Golgotha.'[16] Owen was to be killed a week before the end of the war, joining many of the men he had loved.

Was this idea of the suffering God merely a symptom of a whole civilization's sickness, of the degradation of everything noble, including the idea of the divine holiness? Should it be resisted in the name of the God who was entirely 'other' than sinful man – and in the name of man who needed, more than anything else, to be assured that he could enter the transcendent joy of heaven? So Friedrich von Hügel (for example) now

---

[15] See William Purcell, *Woodbine Willie* (London, 1983).
[16] *Collected Letters of Wilfred Owen* (London, 1967), p. 562.

maintained. Or was this image of humility at last the truly Christian Gospel of God, destined to replace the bogus orthodoxy of centuries where the thought as well as the life of the Churches had been too much absorbed in power and privilege? Or had the terrible truth to be faced in the twentieth century that God was indeed crucified by tragedies beyond his control? Was God dead, if he had ever existed? If so, would man rise to unprecedented heights of splendour now that he had shaken off the religious illusion? Some hoped so – for example, the Communists who had seized control of Russia. Yet man's demonic cruelty to his own species had been exhibited on a spectacular scale, making him less than the other beasts. If there was no God, was man merely the product of blind chance in an indifferent universe? If so, had he any hope of survival now that he had laid his habitually violent hands on modern technology? If God was dead, could man live?

When the Great War ended with the armistice on 11 November 1918, these were the basic religious questions confronting an England which was no longer Christian in any very substantial sense. The answers were held by the future.[17]

---

[17] Alan Wilkinson studied the effects of the two world wars on the morale of the English churches in *Dissent or Conform?* (London, 1986) and Adrian Hastings told the wider story magisterially in *A History of English Christianity 1920–85* (London, 1986).

Outline of Events

1836 Ecclesiastical Commissioners established; W. G. Broughton becomes Bishop of Australia

1837 Queen Victoria begins reign

1838 *The Kingdom of Christ* by F. D. Maurice

1839 John Williams, missionary to Polynesian islands, murdered

1840 New Zealand taken under British 'protection'

1841 Jerusalem bishopric founded by Anglicans and Lutherans

1844 YMCA founded by George Williams

1845 Irish potato famine causes migration to England; J. H. Newman received into Roman Catholic Church

1847 Ten Hours Act regulates factory work; consecration of Anglican colonial bishops including Robert Gray for Cape Town

1848 Chartist demonstrations in London

1850 Restoration of Roman Catholic hierarchy; Judicial Committee protects Evangelicals in Gorham Case; *In Memoriam* by Alfred Tennyson

1851 Horace Mann's census of churchgoing

1853 Liberation Society begins disestablishment campaign

1854 Florence Nightingale leads nurses to Crimean War

1856 David Livingstone returns to England from Africa

1857 Indian Mutiny

1859 Second Evangelical awakening begins; *The Origin of Species* by Charles Darwin

1860 *Essays and Reviews* arouses controversy over Church of England's doctrine

1861 *Commentary on the Epistle to the Romans* by J. W. Colenso; *Hymns Ancient and Modern*

1863 C. H. Spurgeon opens Metropolitan Tabernacle; *Selections* popularize Robert Browning's poetry

1864 *Apologia pro Vita Sua* by J. H. Newman; Samuel Crowther becomes Bishop on the Niger

1865 Henry Manning succeeds Nicholas Wiseman as Archbishop of Westminster; China Inland Mission founded by James Hudson Taylor

1867 First Lambeth Conference of Anglican bishops

1868 A. C. Tait becomes Archbishop of Canterbury instead

of Samuel Wilberforce; Thomas Barnardo begins
East London Juvenile Mission

1869 Irish Disestablishment enacted

1870 Papal infallibility defined by Vatican Council; Education Act establishes state schools; death of Charles Dickens

1871 J. C. Patteson, Bishop of Melanesia, murdered

1873 David Livingstone dies in central Africa

1874 Joseph Parker opens City Temple

1875 G. M. Hopkins writes 'The Wreck of the *Deutschland*'; *The Atonement* by R. W. Dale

1878 Salvation Army named by William Booth

1885 Five hundred societies represented at Lord Shaftesbury's funeral; Bishop James Hannington murdered in Uganda

1886 Josephine Butler secures repeal of Contagious Diseases Acts; Gladstone fails to secure Home Rule for Ireland

1889 London Dock Strike ended by Cardinal Manning; *Lux Mundi* edited by Charles Gore

1890 B. F. Westcott succeeds J. B. Lightfoot as Bishop of Durham

1895 Cardinal Vaughan begins building of Westminster Cathedral

1896 National Council of Evangelical Free Churches formed; Anglican ordinations declared void by Pope Leo XIII

1897 Diamond Jubilee invokes imperialism; Boxers' rebellion in China reacts against missionaries

1901 Death of Queen Victoria

1902 Education Act subsidizes church schools; John Clifford leads passive resistance of Nonconformists

1906 Liberal victory with Nonconformist support; *English Hymnal* enriches Anglican worship

1907 *The New Theology* by R. J. Campbell; Modernism condemned by Pope Pius X

1914 Sudden outbreak of First World War

Index

BIOGRAPHIES

Bonhoeffer
Eberhard Bethge

"Will surely stand as the definitive and authoritative work on the subject . . . more than just a fascinating exploration of a hero of our time. It is, as well, a spiritual experience."
Malcolm Muggeridge, The Observer

A Backdoor to Heaven
Lionel Blue

". . . an extraordinary man . . . an extraordinary auto-biography . . . not to be missed."
The Tablet

Audacity to Believe
Sheila Cassidy

A "humorous, warm, moving, terrifying and enormously readable . . . account of one woman's struggle to under-stand what Christian obedience demands . . ." in South America.
The Baptist Times

Thomas More
Richard Marius

"A biography as good as this one — uncluttered, brightly written, yet scrupulous in its use of sources — brings a complex man out of romantic legend and puts him square-ly in the clear light of history."
Times Educational Supplement

Also available in Fount Paperbacks

BOOKS BY C. S. LEWIS

The Abolition of Man

'It is the most perfectly reasoned defence of Natural Law (Morality) I have ever seen, or believe to exist.'

Walter Hooper

Mere Christianity

'He has a quite unique power for making theology an attractive, exciting and fascinating quest.'

Times Literary Supplement

God in the Dock

'This little book . . . consists of some brilliant pieces . . . This is just the kind of book to place into the hands of an intellectual doubter . . . It has been an unalloyed pleasure to read.'

Marcus Beverley, Christian Herald

The Great Divorce

'Mr Lewis has a rare talent for expressing spiritual truth in fresh and striking imagery and with uncanny acumen . . . it contains many flashes of deep insight and exposures of popular fallacies.'

Church Times

I Believe
Trevor Huddleston

A simple, prayerful series of reflections on the phrases of the Creed. This is a beautiful testament of the strong, quiet inner faith of a man best known for his active role in the Church – and in the world.

The Heart of the Christian Faith
Donald Coggan

The author ". . . presents the essential core of Christianity in a marvellously simple and readable form, quite uncluttered by any excess of theological technicality."

The Yorkshire Post

Be Still and Know
Michael Ramsey

The former Archbishop of Canterbury looks at prayer in the New Testament, at what the early mystics could teach us about it, and at some practical aspects of Christian praying.

Pilgrim's Progress
John Bunyan

"A masterpiece which generation after generation of ordinary men and women have taken to their hearts."

Hugh Ross Williamson

BOOKS BY WILLIAM JOHNSTON

Silent Music

A brilliant synthesis which joins traditional religious insights with the discoveries of modern science to provide a complete picture of mysticism – its techniques and stages, its mental and physical aspects, its dangers, and its consequences.

The Inner Eye of Love

"This is a lucid comparison and exposition of eastern and western mysticism, from Zen to the Cloud of Unknowing, which can do nothing but good all round."

Gerald Priestland, The Universe

The Mirror Mind

"William Johnston continues his first-hand studies of Zen meditation and Christian prayer . . . At his disposal he has had a twofold large and demanding literature. His use of it can be startlingly luminous."

Bernard Lonegan

The Wounded Stag

This book examines the Old and New Testaments, the Christian mystical tradition, the Eucharist and mystical prayer, and explains how these can lead to the resolution of the conflict within men's hearts. A book with a message for today.

Fount Paperbacks

Fount is one of the leading paperback publishers of religious books and below are some of its recent titles.

- ☐ THROUGH SEASONS OF THE HEART
  John Powell £4.95
- ☐ WORDS OF LIFE FROM JOHN THE BELOVED
  Frances Hogan £2.95
- ☐ MEISTER ECKHART Ursula Fleming £2.95
- ☐ CHASING THE WILD GOOSE Ron Ferguson £2.95
- ☐ A GOOD HARVEST Rita Snowden £2.50
- ☐ UNFINISHED ENCOUNTER Bob Whyte £5.95
- ☐ FIRST STEPS IN PRAYER Jean-Marie Lustiger £2.95
- ☐ IF THIS IS TREASON Allan Boesak £2.95
- ☐ RECLAIMING THE CHURCH Robin Greenwood £2.95
- ☐ GOD WITHIN US John Wijngaards £2.95
- ☐ GOD'S WORLD Trevor Huddleston £2.95
- ☐ A CALL TO WITNESS Oliver McTernan £2.95
- ☐ GOODNIGHT LORD Georgette Butcher £2.95
- ☐ FOR GOD'S SAKE Donald Reeves £3.50
- ☐ GROWING OLDER Una Kroll £2.95
- ☐ THROUGH THE YEAR WITH FRANCIS OF ASSISI
  Murray Bodo £2.95

All Fount Paperbacks are available at your bookshop or newsagent, or they can be ordered by post from Fount Paperbacks, Cash Sales Department, G.P.O. Box 29, Douglas, Isle of Man. Please send purchase price plus 22p per book, maximum postage £3. Customers outside the UK send purchase price, plus 22p per book. Cheque, postal order or money order. No currency.

NAME (Block letters) _____

ADDRESS_____

_____

_____